The BEAULIEU ENCYCLOPEDIA of the AUTOMOBILE

The BEAULIEU ENCYCLOPEDIA of the AUTOMOBILE

Volume 3
P-Z

Editor in Chief
NICK GEORGANO

Foreword by
LORD MONTAGU
of **BEAULIEU**

FITZROY DEARBORN PUBLISHERS
CHICAGO · LONDON

© The Stationery Office 2000

Published in the United Kingdom by
The Stationery Office Limited, St Crispins, Duke Street, Norwich NR3 1PD.

Published in the United States of America by
Fitzroy Dearborn Publishers, 919 North Michigan Avenue, Chicago, Illinois 60611.

A Cataloging-in-Publication record for this book is available from the Library of Congress.

ISBN 1-57958-293-1 Fitzroy Dearborn

First published 2000.

Reprinted with amendments 2001.

Produced and designed by The Stationery Office.

Design by Guy Myles Warren.

Reproductive services by Colourscript, Mildenhall, Suffolk.

Printed and bound by Butler & Tanner, Frome, Somerset.

Dedication

To the memory of George Ralph Doyle, John Pollitt, and Michael Sedgwick.

G.R.Doyle (1890–1961) was the first man to compile a worldwide address list of car manufacturers. *The World's Automobiles*, first published privately in 1932, stimulated the interest of countless enthusiasts. Without Doyle's pioneering work, the compilation of this encyclopedia would have been a near impossibility.

John Pollitt (1892–1958) was one of the most painstaking of researchers into motoring history. After his retirement from the Rover company in 1945, he devoted his entire time to investigations and correspondence on the subject, the fruits of which he wrote up in twenty eight files, running to several million words. These files, generously lent by the late Dennis C. Field) were among the most important cornerstones of the encyclopedia.

Michael Sedgwick (1926–1983) was the most tireless researcher into motoring history from the early 1960s to the day of his death in October 1983. He was Curator of the Montagu Motor Museum (today the National Motor Museum) from 1958 to 1966, and subsequently the Museum's Director of Research, Assistant Editor of *The Veteran & Vintage Magazine*, and a regular contributor to practically every old car magazine in the world. His enthusiasm and knowledge extended to any period and variety of road vehicle. He would have loved this book.

Contents

Alphabetical List of Biographies included in Volume 1

Alphabetical List of Biographies included in Volume 2

Alphabetical List of Biographies included in Volume 3

Alphabetical List of Colour Illustrations included in Volume 2

Alphabetical List of Original Manufacturers' Promotional Images included in Volume 1

Alphabetical List of Original Manufacturers' Promotional Images included in Volume 2

Alphabetical List of Original Manufacturers' Promotional Images included in Volume 3

Foreword
by Lord Montagu of Beaulieu

It has long been a dream of mine that the National Motor Museum at Beaulieu should be closely associated with a major international motoring work of reference. The opportunity came after a meeting at Beaulieu with Rupert Pennant-Rea shortly after he took over as Managing Director of Her Majesty's Stationery Office (HMSO), soon to be privatised and relaunched as The Stationery Office.

The *Beaulieu Encyclopedia of the Automobile* can trace its roots back to a slim volume, published privately in 1932 by George Ralph Doyle entitled *The World's Automobiles*. Keen-eyed readers will notice that this encyclopedia is dedicated to Ralph Doyle. 'Doyle', as this work of reference became known, was just a listing of manufacturers, dates, and addresses – the first ever to be published. Whilst studying at Oxford, Nick Georgano found a copy of Doyle and realised that with fuller facts that he had accumulated from his own researches, he could enlarge on that slim volume. The two enthusiasts met and became firm friends. When he died in 1961, Ralph Doyle left all his research notes to Nick Georgano, and the fourth and last edition of Doyle was put together by Nick for publication. Throughout this time, he had been developing ideas for a much more comprehensive book which would have biographical details of all manufacturers as well as photographs. A chance meeting in 1965 with British motoring historian Tim Nicholson resulted in Nick being introduced to the publishers George Rainbird Ltd, who had been thinking along similar lines. Thus was born the great *Complete Encyclopædia of Motor Cars*, published by Ebury Press in 1968, and this now famous work of reference has sold over 90,000 copies and been translated into five languages. There have been three editions, the last being in 1982, and to quote the words of Michael Lamm, Editor of *Special-Interest Autos* (and a contributor to this encyclopædia), in 1971:

'If an auto historian were sentenced to life in prison and allowed only one book in his cell, that book would have to be Georgano's *The Complete Encyclopædia of Motor Cars, 1885-1968*. I consider it the single most important work ever published in the field of automotive history – the one book about 20th century cars that 25th century historians will still keep handy. The dog-eared copy I bought in 1968 stands in the most accessible spot on my desk.

Even aside from the encyclopedia's reference value, I find myself picking it up constantly and reading it for pure pleasure – or just looking again and again at the 2000-odd photos. Anyone who has even glanced through this book has marvelled at the monumental job it must have been to compile.'

That splendid bible of motoring knowledge has long been out of print and second-hand copies change hands at inflated prices. We all knew that Nick Georgano was capable of great things and I persuaded him to put his name forward again as the editor for a brand new reference work which we were to propose to The Stationery Office. The result is a book of tremendous detail, produced from many years of research by many different people and three years of concentrated effort by Nick Georgano. So many people have helped over the years that it would be invidious of me to single out any one person but I would like to pay tribute to the late Michael Sedgwick, for so long my historical mentor at Beaulieu and the Museum's Director of Research. Sadly, Michael died in October 1983 but his memory lives on in many ways, including much of the background work in these volumes.

I am delighted that the National Motor Museum at Beaulieu was chosen by The Stationery Office to be its partner in this important work. Beaulieu has been connected with motoring from the earliest days. My father, who had a lifelong interest in all forms of transport, purchased his first car in 1898, followed a year later by the first 4-cylinder Daimler to be built in England, which is now owned by the Science Museum but is a prize exhibit on display at the National Motor Museum. Motoring is in the blood here at Beaulieu, in terms of both driving motor cars and recording their history. My father wrote a number of books about driving in the early days and in 1902 became founder editor of the weekly magazine *Car Illustrated*, which he continued to edit until the beginning of World War I. Many years later, in August 1956, I started *Veteran & Vintage* magazine, which ran through until August 1979 and is now incorporated with *Thoroughbred and Classic Cars*.

Palace House opened to the public in April 1952 with just a few old cars on show, and from this grew the Montagu Motor Museum and latterly the National Motor Museum. In 1960

I opened a Library of Motoring at Beaulieu based on my father's collection of books and in 1962 this was supplemented by a Photographic Library and later, in 1979, a Film and Video Archive. These Libraries are now renowned as important research establishments throughout the motoring world and much of the background research for that first encyclopædia was done by Nick Georgano at Beaulieu, whom I first met when he was trawling through the Montagu Motor Museum Library in Palace House for photographs to use in that first edition. I am pleased that the majority of the photographs in this book have come from our own files here at Beaulieu, supplemented from the private collection of Nick Baldwin, who is Chairman of the National Motor Museum's Advisory Council.

There are motoring historians in practically every country in the world, many of whom are members of the Society of Automotive Historians, and I know that much research in the future will start with a look into this encyclopedia. The study of motoring history is not adequately covered by Universities, one reason being because it is a new subject, but even so its impact on design, engineering and social history has been tremendous. The development of motoring has profoundly influenced the landscape around us and the way we live; the motor vehicle has carried goods to help keep the wheels of industry turning and has completely revolutionised personal mobility. We remember with affection not only our first car and those which have given us good service but also all the bad vehicles that stick in our minds.

Whilst there are nearly 1000 motor museums in the world, relatively few can claim to also be academic institutions, as we strive to do at Beaulieu. As competition increases for people's leisure time, motor museums find themselves struggling to stay afloat and have relatively few resources available for future research or publication. I hope we can reverse this trend in the next few years and I am confident that this great work of reference will be a catalyst for future research.

Montagu of Beaulieu

Acknowledgements

My thanks are due, first and foremost, to the contributors who not only delivered their material on time, but also answered the many queries that inevitably arose during preparation of the entries for the publishers.

I would like to thank Lord Montagu of Beaulieu and Michael Ware, former director of the National Motor Museum, for their tireless efforts to revive the encyclopedia over a number of years, culminating in the successful link with The Stationery Office.

Annice Collett, Marie Tieche, and Mike Budd of the National Motor Museum's Reference Library were always painstaking and prompt in replying to my abstruse queries, as was Jonathan Day of the Photographic Library in providing last-minute photos. Caroline Johnson, Library Secretary, was very helpful in rapid delivery of photocopies and information. The bulk of the illustrations have come from the collections of the National Motor Museum or Nick Baldwin, but others who have provided many excellent and rare photos include Mike Worthington-Williams, Bryan K. Goodman, John A. Conde, Keith Marvin, Halwart Schrader and Ernest Schmid, who lent a number of photos used in his excellent book on Swiss cars. Mike has also been very helpful with additional information and picture identification, as have Malcolm Jeal and Peter Heilbron. Gary Axon and Richard Heseltine gave valuable help with small postwar makes. Philip and Sue Hill toiled for many hours preparing a list of *Automobile Quarterly* entries for the further reading sections. Countless other people have provided help in many ways; to name some would be invidious but to name all would be impossible.

On the publishing side I am deeply grateful to Mick Spencer, Editorial Manager at The Stationery Office; always patient with last-minute changes and additions, he has enabled the encyclopedia to be up-to-date to within three months of publication. The layout has been the responsibility of Designer Guy Myles Warren, who has worked wonders fitting some 3500 photos of assorted shapes and sizes and a text of almost 1.5 million words into something under 2000 pages. The complete text was checked by Editor Sallie Moss, and the galley proofs were read by freelance proof reader Lynne Davies.

Finally, I should thank my wife Jenny without whom this book could never have been produced. She has been responsible for dealing with all correspondence, filing, packing and posting proofs, often at very short notice, as well as providing a steady flow of tea, coffee, and, sometimes, stronger beverages.

NICK GEORGANO
Guernsey, May 2000

Introduction

According to the Oxford English Dictionary, an encyclopedia is 'an elaborate and exhaustive reportory of information on all branches of some particular art or department of knowledge, especially one arranged in alphabetical order.'

This seems as good a definition as any for what we have set out to do in this encyclopedia, although some limitations have to be placed on the concept of exhaustiveness. For a name to qualify as a 'make of car', there must be some evidence of an intention to manufacture, even if it was not a success, and resulted in no more than a single prototype. This is clearly not a water-tight definition, for to establish 'intention to manufacture' one would have to read the minds of men long dead. In the early days many people built a car to prove to themsleves that they could do so, and to make some improvements on what had gone before. Their friends might say "That's nice, will you make one for me?" and some sort of production would follow. Louis Renault might never have become a manufacturer had friends not admired his first effort and asked for replicas. Many of his contemporaries took a stand at the Paris Salon on which to show their hastily-assembled prototype, and if no customers came forward they went no further, and never formed a company. These must, nevertheless, be considered as makes.

On the other hand there were countless backyard tinkerers who built a car or two purely for their own amusement, but through lack of capital or interest in business never planned to make cars for sale. They flourished chiefly in the years up to 1914, though some appeared up to World War II, such as Willard L. Morrison of Buchanan, Michigan, who built a Ford V8-powered streamlined sedan in 1935.

Also in this category are the 19th century steam car makers, with the honourable exception of Thomas Rickett, who not only buiilt two 3-wheelers to the order of British aristocrats, but placed an advertisement in *The Engineer* offering replicas for sale. This earns him a place in the encyclopædia, unlike his contemporaries Yarrow & Hilditch or on the Continent, Etienne Lenoir, Gustav Hammel, or Siegfried Markus, whose vehicles were purely experimental.

Other categories not included are the following;

1   Motorcycles are obviously ruled out, though some 2-wheelers with car-like bodywork, such as the Atlantic, Monotrace and Whitwood Monocar, are included. A more difficult problem is posed by the distinction between a tricycle and a 3-wheeled car. Early tricycles, such as the De Dion-Bouton, were no more than motorcycles with a third wheel, but from about 1903 a type of vehicle appeared which used the frame, saddle, engine and final drive of a motorcycle with two wheels in front, and a body, often of wickerwork, for a passenger. Known as tri-cars, they were still of motorcycle descent, but gradually the driver's saddle became a seat and the handlebars were replaced by a steering wheel, giving them the appearance of a tandem car on three wheels. With makes such as Riley it is almost impossible to decide at what point they became cars. The more car-like vehicles, such as the Bat or Rexette are included, while the many makes which never progressed beyond saddle, handlebars and wickerwork, are not.

2   Cars built purely for racing, and not usable on public roads, such as Formula One and Indy cars.

3   A number of makes listed in earlier encyclopedias are absent as research has placed them in the one-off experimental category. Sometimes evidence is lacking that they ever built even one car, despite advertising that they did. An exception is made for the Owen of Comeragh Road, which persisted on paper for 36 years, and is one of the great conundrums of motoring history.

No attempt has been made to describe every model made by any firm, large or small. In 1927 Daimler listed 27 models, and to mention them all would be tedious and wasteful of space. However, we have endeavoured to indicate the range of models, highlighting any unconventional or unexpected designs, and technical features which were unusual for the period. Up to about 1900, when there was great diversity, and engines might be at the front, centre or rear of the frame, vertical or horizontal and cooled by water or air, these features are generally mentioned. With the coming of a relatively standard layout of front-mounted vertical water-cooled engine, driving by a 3- or 4-speed sliding pinion gearbox and propeller shaft to a bevel rear axle, it is only the exceptions which are noted. Front wheel brakes were noteworthy in the early 1920s, but later were noteworthy only by their absence, as on the 1950 Bond Minicar or its contemporary, the Mochet.

The dating of cars, especially in the illustration captions, may cause confusion because of the discrepancy between the model and calendar year. Normally the date represents the year in which the car was made, a practice followed by the Dating Committee of the Veteran Car Club of Great Britain. An exception has to be made for American cars, which were generally announced in September or October of their model year. The Mercury was introduced in November 1938, (hence a starting date of 1938 in our entry) but even the first cars were always thought of as 1939 models. Similarly, Ford Thunderbird enthusiasts will not recognise that there was a 1954 Thunderbird, though quite a number were made in that calendar year.

The nationality of a make is indicated by the letter(s) used on touring plates, and refers to the country where the parent firm was located. An exceptions is EU which is not yet a nation state, but is used for Fords built in various European factories and which are quite international in design. The Fiesta is no more British than it is German, Belgian, or Spanish. Dual nationality may occur in two ways:

- Cars like the Pennington which had factories in two countries at the same time, are indicated by (US/GB).
- Cars whose nationality changed for political reasons, such as Bugatti and Mathis, which were German up to 1918 when the province of Alsace became French, are indicated by (D;F).

The makes are listed in alphabetical order, but the following points should be noted:

- Makes which consist of Christian and surnames are listed under the Christian name e.g., Georges Irat, not Irat, Georges.
- Makes beginning with Mc are listed between MCC and M.C.M., not at the beginning of the letter 'M'.

- Makes beginning with De are listed under the letter 'D'. Thus De Lavaud is found in 'D', not 'L'.
- Makes using initial letters joined by 'and', such as S & M Simplex are treated as if they were spelt S M.
- Chinese names are romanised using the Pinyin system.

We hope that this encyclopedia will be not only readable, but accurate. Some familiar stories have been corrected. For example, it was long held that Ned Jordan started his upward progress by marrying the daughter of his boss, Thomas Jeffery. Not so; recent research has revealed that his bride was Lotta Hanna whose father ran a furniture store in Kenosha, Wisconsin. History is being rewritten all the time, and it would be unrealistic to suppose that production figures and other statistics may not be revised in the future. More generally, one cannot do better than quote the words of the great historian and journalist Laurence Pomeroy Jr. 'It is manifestly desirable that any reference book should be wholly free from error, but this is an ideal which it seems impossible to realise. The author can only plead that he, like others, has found that "sudden fits of inadvertancy will surprise vigilance, slight avocations will seduce attention. and casual eclipses of the mind will darken learning"'.

NICK GEORGANO
Guernsey, May 2000

Further Reading

Readers seeking more detailed information are referred to marque histories or serious historical articles in magazines. For obvious reasons of space, we are not including contemporary magazine announcements or road tests. These can be found in the Reference Library at the National Motor Museum, which offers a photocopying service and is happy to answer queries by post, telephone, fax or e-mail.

The Reference Library, National Motor Museum, Beaulieu, Hampshire SO42 7ZN, tel. 01590 614652; fax. 01590 612655; e-mail motoring.library@beaulieu.co.uk

Photographic enquiries should be made to the Photographic Library at the same address, tel. 01590 614656; fax as above; email motoring.pictures@beaulieu.co.uk

Again, for space reasons we have not referred under each entry to the many excellent books devoted to the makes of one country or era. Among the more valuable of these are:

Great Britain

A to Z of Cars of the 1920s, Nick Baldwin, Bay View Books, 1994.

A to Z of Cars of the 1930s, Michael Sedgwick and Mark Gillies, Bay View Books, 1989.

A to Z of Cars, 1945-1970, Michael Sedgwick and Mark Gillies, (revised by Jon Pressnell), Bay View Books, 1993.

A to Z of Cars of the 1970s, Graham Robson, Bay View Books, 1990.

A to Z of Cars of the 1980s, Martin Lewis, Bay View Books, 1998.

The Complete Catalogue of British Cars, David Culshaw and Peter Horrobin, Veloce Publishing, 1997.

Germany

Autos in Deutschland 1885-1920, Hans-Heinrich von Fersen, Motorbuch-Verlag, Stuttgart, 1965.

Autos in Deutschland 1920-1945, Werner Oswald, Motorbuch-Verlag, Stuttgart, 1981.

Autos in Deutschland 1945-1975, Werner Oswald, Motorbuch-Verlag, Stuttgart, 1980.

France

In First Gear. The French Automobile Industry to 1914, James M. Laux, Liverpool University Press, 1976.

French Cars 1920–1925, Pierre Dumont, Frederick Warne, 1978.

Toutes les Voitures Francaise 1935, René Bellu, Herme-Vilo,1984.

Toutes les Voitures Francaise 1939, René Bellu, Edita Vilo, 1982.

Les Voitures Francaise des Annees 50 (actually covers 1945-1959), René Bellu, Editions Delville, 1983.

Switzerland

Automobiles Suisses des Origines à nos Jours, Ernest Schmid, Editions du Chateau de Grandson, 1967.

Schweizer Autos, (expanded version of above, in German) Ernest Schmid, Editions du Chateau de Grandson, 1978.

Netherlands

Autodesign in Nederland, Jan Lammerse, Waanders Uitgevers, Zwolle, 1993.

Belgium

Histoire de l'Automobile Belge, Yvette and Jacques Kupélian and Jacques Sirtaine, Editions Paul Legrain, c.1972.

Austria

Gesichte von Oesterreiche Kraftfahrt, Hans Seper, Oesterreiche Wirtschaft Verlag, 1968.

Spain

El Automovil en Espana, Pablo Gimenez Vallador, RACE, Madrid, 1998.

Historia de l'Automobilisme a Catalunya, Javier del Arco, Planita, 1990.

Italy

Marche Italiane Scomparse, Museo dell' Automobile Carlo Biscaretti di Ruffia, Turin, 1972.

Hungary

A Magyer Auto, Zsuppan Istvan, Zrini Kiado, 1994.

Canada

Cars of Canada, Hugh Durnford and Glenn Baechler, McLelland & Stewart, 1973.

United States

There are many titles, but none can rival the incomparable:

The Standard Catalog of American Cars 1805-1942, Beverly Rae Kimes and
   Henry Austin Clark Jr, Krause Publications, 1996.

For more recent cars, and in the same series:

The Standard Catalog of American Cars 1946-1975, edited by John A. Gunnell,
   Krause Publications, 1982.

Japan

Autos made in Japan, Jan P. Norbye, Heicher Verlag, 1991.

Terms and Abbreviations Used

Throughout the encyclopedia technical and other terms are generally described according to current English usage. For the convenience of American readers a short list of the more frequently-used terms whose meaning differs in American usage is given below.

English	American	English	American
bonnet	hood	paraffin	kerosene
boot	trunk	petrol	gasoline
capacity (of engine)	displacement	saloon	sedan
coupé de ville	town car	sedanca de ville	town car
dickey (seat)	rumble seat	shooting-brake	station wagon
engine	motor	silencer	muffler
epicyclic (gears)	planetary (gears)	track	tread
estate car	station wagon	two-stroke	two-cycle
gearbox	transmission	windscreen	windshield
hood	top	wing	fender
mudguard	fender		

The following have generally been used in the text for frequently-repeated terms.

bhp	brake horse power
cc	cubic centimetres
cr	compression ratio
CV	cheveaux-vapeur (French horsepower rating)
fwd	front-wheel drive
GP	Grand Prix
GT	GranTurismo
hp	horse power
ifs	independent front suspension
in	inch(es)
ioe	inlet over exhaust
km	kilometre(s)
km/h	kilometres per hour
kg	kilogram(s)
lb	pound(s)
LPG	liquid petroleum gas
lwb	long wheelbase
mm	millimetre(s)
mpg	miles per gallon
mph	miles per hour
ohc	overhead camshaft(s)
ohv	overhead valve(s)
PS	Pferdestärke (German horsepower rating)
psi	pounds per square inch
rpm	revolutions per minute
rwd	rear-wheel drive
sv	side valve(s)
swb	short wheelbase
TT	Tourist Trophy

PABIAN (US) c.1903

Bob Pabian, Prague, Nebraska.

This was a small car with single-cylinder engine mounted under the seat, 2-speed gearbox and single-chain drive. Probably only one was made, which still exists. Dated 1897, its appearance is clearly that of a car several years younger, with frontal bonnet and equal-sized wire wheels.

NG

PACE (US) c.1990

Pace Motors, Renton, Washington.

The Pace Countach was a replica of the Lamborghini of the same name, and was built on a space-frame chassis. General Motors running gear was used throughout, including a 5700cc Chevrolet engine driving through an Oldsmobile Toronado transaxle.

HP

P.A.C.E. (GB) 1990–1992

Performance Automobile Construction Engineers, Lancaster.

This company's first offering was a Ferrari 308GTB kit replica. It used a substantial box-section steel chassis, into which was bolted a complete Lancia Beta front subframe over the rear axle. You also used Beta brakes, instruments, pedal box and steering rack. Two one-piece self-coloured fibreglass body styles were offered: a straight coupé and GTS-style targa top. Apart from the Beta, engine options included Lancia Thema, MG Maestro, Rover 800 and other V6/V8 units with suitable transaxles. The car transmuted into the LE MANS, while P.A.C.E. also took on the MAELSTROM.

CR

PACHIAUDI (F) 1995 to date

1995–1997 Pachiaudi, Culoz.
1997 to date Sté Vibraction, Roanne.

Racing driver Yves Pachiaudi's Bugey-Bug was an unusually-styled 4 × 4 on/off-road vehicle with a hint of buggy about it. The doors and roof were both removable. Powered by a Renault 2.1-litre turbodiesel engine, it could be had with 2- or 4-wheel drive.

CR

PACIFIC (i) (US) 1914

Portland Cyclecar Co., Portland, Oregon.

The Pacific was a tandem 2-seater cyclecar, with a 1.1-litre 2-cylinder air-cooled engine. It is claimed that it was succeeded by a full-size car called the Portland.

NG

PACIFIC (ii) (US) c.1980

Pacific Automotive Designs Ltd, Mountain View, California.

This was an MG TD replica on a Volkswagen chassis with a water-cooled 4-cylinder Honda engine.

NG

PACIFIC COACHWORKS (US) c.1980–1983

Pacific Coachworks, Goleta, California.

The DiNapoli neo-classic was designed by Nick DiNapoli and built by Pacific Coachworks, a division of MINICARS, Inc. Minicars built safety cars for the government, so the DiNapoli crew had access to sophisticated equipment when designing their car. It used the cab section of a Buick Regal, and the Buick chassis was stretched 42in (1066mm) to give a 150in (3807mm) wheelbase. The body was then mounted in its normal location, and a long bonnet with a chrome radiator grill grafted on. They were only sold in fully assembled form for over $65,000. The DiNapoli was later carried by MARAUDER.

HP

PACIFIC COAST (US) c.1984–1986

Pacific Coast Cobra, Redlands, California.

This kit car company sold a line of three Cobra replicas. Their 289 F.I.A. kit replicated the 289 racing cars, while the 427 duplicated the 427 Cobra. Both were built on 91.5in (2322mm) space frame with live axle or irs. Their 460 model was the STALLION Cobra replica built on a stretched 95in (2411mm) wheelbase chassis.

HP

1901 Packard Model C runabout.
NICK GEORGANO

1909 Packard Model 30 landaulet.
NICK BALDWIN

PACIFIC SPECIAL (US) 1911–1913

1911–1912 California Car Co., Fruitville, California.
1913 Cole-California Car Co., Fruitville, California.

The Pacific Special was a tourer powered by a 4-cylinder Continental engine and priced at $1750. The prototype was running in late 1911, and 12 cars were said to be ready for delivery the following summer. Little more was heard until 1913 when Frederick Cole bought the company, renamed it after himself and announced the manufacture of a low-priced four and/or a higher-priced six. Probably none were made, because in early 1914 the company was found to be in default of lease payments on their factory and was closed down.

NG

PACKARD (US) 1899–1958

1899–1901 New York & Ohio Automobile Co., Warren, Ohio.
1900–1902 Ohio Automobile Co., Warren, Ohio.
1902–1903 Packard Motor Car Co., Warren, Ohio.
1903–1955 Packard Motor Car Co., Detroit, Michigan.
1955–1958 Studebaker-Packard Corp., Detroit, Michigan.

More than one great car has resulted from someone's dissatisfaction with another car. One example is Henry Royce and his Decauville, another is James Ward Packard (1863–1928) who bought a Winton in 1898, and when he took it back

1914 Packard Series 3-48 all-weather tourer.
NICK BALDWIN

c.1920 Packard Twin Six tourer.
NICK BALDWIN

1928 Packard Custom 443 town car by Rollston.
NICK BALDWIN

to the makers he was told that if he was so smart he had better build a car himself. At least that is the gist of the words he is supposed to have had with Alexander Winton, as recorded by journalist Hugh Dolnar in 1901, three years after the event.

James Packard and his brother William were manufacturers of electric bells, dynamos and lamps (another parallel with Henry Royce), and it was in their Warren, Ohio, factory that the first Packard car was built, being completed in November 1899. Ironically, the brothers were helped by two men they had lured away from Winton, George Weiss and William A. Hatcher. The Model A Packard had a large horizontal single-cylinder engine of 2337cc, 2-speed

epicyclic transmission, and single-chain drive. Four more cars were built in the remaining months of 1899, and the last was also the first Packard sale, to a Warren businessman, George D. Kirkham.

The Model B of 1900 was generally similar, but had an automatic spark advance, unusual for the time, and a foot accelerator. The same 2-seater body was offered, at $1200, with a *dos-à-dos* seat as an optional extra. Forty-nine cars were sold that year, and the B was continued for 1901, alongside the more powerful Model C. This had a 3012cc engine, still a single cylinder, and was offered with

MICHAEL LAMM

GUBITZ, WERNER (1899–1971)

Werner Hans August Gubitz was born in Hamburg, Germany on 29 July 1899. In 1905, he and his parents moved to the USA where his father took a job with the Venus Pencil Co. in Jersey City, New Jersey.

As a teenager, Gubitz loved automobiles and showed great flair as a graphic artist. In 1919, he approached Fleetwood's Ernst Schebera in New York and asked for a job. Schebera hired Gubitz as a delineator. According to Gubitz's longtime friend, designer and design historian W. Everett Miller, young Gubitz soon moved to LeBaron Carrossiers, where he worked for Ray Dietrich and Tom Hibbard. He left LeBaron in 1922 to join J. Frank deCausse. DeCausse had just lost his Locomobile account, hadn't yet picked up Franklin and was designing custom bodies for east-coast coachbuilders on the same basis as LeBaron. Gubitz also entered the Massachusetts Institute of Technology in 1924, but didn't graduate.

When Murray Corp. of America set up Dietrich Inc. in 1925, Ray Dietrich asked Gubitz to join him in Detroit as an illustrator/designer. Gubitz stayed with Dietrich for a short time, then moved to Cleveland to work first for Peerless and then for the Ohio Body & Blower Co. Among Ohio Body's customers were Moon, Jordan and Gardner.

Cleveland car makers were not doing at all well, so Gubitz left the design business to open a restaurant. He and his wife, Lillian, poured not only their hearts but their life savings into the venture, all to no avail. Everett Miller recalled Gubitz telling him that the only thing he and Lillian saved from the restaurant was a glass juice squeezer.

So it was with considerable relief that, in 1927, Werner Gubitz found a job back in Detroit with Packard. Packard had no real styling department at that time, but his new boss, Vincent D. Kaptur Sr, asked Gubitz to make scale side-view renderings of all of Packard's production bodies. Gubitz used that very tight, wonderfully detailed style that Roland Stickney had brought to LeBaron.

a forward-facing rear seat in addition to the *dos-à-dos* at $1500. A steering wheel replaced the tiller of the earlier cars.

81 cars were sold in 1901, followed by 179 in 1902 when the new model was the F. This used the same engine as the C but in a longer chassis and with a 3-speed sliding gearbox. Artillery wheels gave the Model F a much more substantial look, and it was a major step in the Packard's progress from light buggy to proper car. For 1903 the wheelbase was extended still further, to 88in (2233mm), and a short bonnet was fitted, although the engine was still under the seat. During the

1935 Packard Twelve 1208 sedan.
JOHN A. CONDE

1937 Packard Six 115 club sedan.
JAN P. NORBYE

At Packard, Gubitz shared a large office with two engineers, this on the fourth floor of the company's headquarters on East Grand Boulevard. According to Miller, Gubitz often worked far into the night, long after everyone else had gone home. And he soon developed a way of creating perhaps six to eight sketches at once by drawing in one component at a time. He would first outline the body in pencil, then start painting in the details in groups: all the tires at one sitting, then all the brightwork, followed perhaps by brilliant renderings of textured convertible canvas tops and highlighted sheet metal. He would do the reflections and shadows together, too. Undercarriages were done in muted colours, and then he would turn his attention to doing perfect lettering on the hubcaps and representing every nut and bolt exactly where it was in real life. His drawings would all be finished together, as a set.

Kaptur left for General Motors in August 1928, and from that time on Gubitz gradually took on more actual design responsibility. He transposed some of Ray Dietrich's custom design ideas into Packard's production bodies and, after Dietrich left Murray, Werner Gubitz effectively became Packard's chief stylist, although he didn't have that title. He at first shared some of his stylistic duties with airbrush artist F.W. Walker. Young W.E. Miller arrived at Packard as a designer in February 1929. Miller commented that for some time after he got there, he and Gubitz were Packard's sole in-house stylists. Gubitz now reported to chief body engineer Archer Knapp and would style all the production bodies. Miller designed 'custom' Packard bodies for the company's captive coach-building department under sales manager Horace Potter.

In 1932, Packard announced the establishment of a formal styling section, and company president Alvan Macauley named his son, Edward, to head it. Ed Macauley began hiring a few additional designers, among them Count Alexis de Sakhnoffsky, Howard F. Yeager, Harold J. Gottlieb and Lynn Mosher. Mosher had previous experience with Derham and Gottlieb with Fleetwood.

Ed Macauley was more a design manager than a designer, and Gubitz did most of Packard's actual styling throughout the classic period. Gubitz gave Packard not only the unmistakable grace of its 1930s designs but also the all-important styling continuity it enjoyed during those years. All factory-bodied senior Packards - particularly the large, classic, closed body styles - had an elegance and an awe-inspiring, cathedral-like aura that no other car builder began to match. Cadillac and Lincoln formal sedans and limousines seemed amateurish alongside Gubitz's wonderfully understated Packard Super Eights and V12s.

Throughout his life, Werner Gubitz was quiet and almost shy. He stood about 5ft 7in tall, had a medium build, was liked by everyone who worked with him, and it's not known why he left Packard at so early an age; he was only 48 when he retired.

Everett Miller and his wife remained close personal friends of the Gubitzes throughout their lives. When Gubitz left Packard, the Millers talked Werner and Lillian into moving to California. Werner Gubitz had long been a camera buff, an excellent movie and still photographer, and he also enjoyed carpentry, cabinet-making and model-building. When the Gubitzes moved to Palm Desert in 1947, Werner designed a number of houses for their property and modelled them all in scale. Local architects and house builders heard about his skill and asked Gubitz to make house models for them, too. He eventually constructed an entire miniature city in his home, complete with houses, factories, stores, streetcars, railroads and an oil refinery. Werner Gubitz died on 27 September 1971.

ML

summer of 1903 a Model F named Old Pacific achieved fame when it was driven across the continent from San Francisco to New York in 61 days by Tom Fetch and Marius Krarup, editor of *The Automobile*. This beat the previous record, set by a Winton, by two days.

Packard's famous slogan 'Ask the Man Who Owns One', was first used in an advertisement in October 1901; by then owners included New York millionaire William D. Rockefeller who had previously bought Wintons, another blow to the rival firm. The link between the conservative rich of the East Coast and the little firm from Ohio had begun. The next logical step in making a larger and more powerful car was to increase the number of cylinders, but James Packard was opposed to this. 'Two cylinders in a Packard would be like two tails on a cat, you just don't need it', he is reported to have said, but his 3-litre cylinder was large enough anyway, and anything larger would have been impossibly rough. Against his wishes a 2-cylinder Model G was announced in the late summer of 1902, which employed two of the Model F's cylinders in a flat-twin engine with a capacity of just over 6-litres. This was very large for a twin, and not really the solution at all, and it is not surprising that only four Model Gs were made. In November 1902 came the first 4-cylinder Packard, the 4116cc Model K. It was also the first to have a front-mounted engine, 4-speed gearbox and shaft-drive. It should have been a success, but it was very highly priced, at $7300, and only 34 were made. More popular was the Model L, which arrived in November 1903. This had a 3960cc 4-cylinder engine, 3-speed gearbox combined with the differential, and was the first Packard to use the famous radiator. The price was a realistic $3000, and 207 were sold.

An important event of 1902 was the arrival of Henry B. Joy, (1864–1936) a Detroiter who brought welcome investment from businessmen in his city. This resulted in a move of the factory to Detroit in October 1903. The Packard brothers remained in Warren, and had only a nominal connection with the company. James held the title of President until 1909, but Henry Joy was the man in charge.

With an increase in engine capacity to 4354cc, the Model L became the Model N for 1905, when a wider range of body styles was offered, three open cars and two closed. Unlike some luxury car makers, Packard had their own

1938 Packard Twelve convertible victoria.
NICK BALDWIN

1940 Packard Super 8 160 sedan.
NICK GEORGANO

1940 Packard Darrin Victoria 2-door convertible.
NICK GEORGANO

body shops, and built a high quality product, so that customers did not need to go to specialist coachbuilders, though chassis were supplied. The golden age of custom coachwork on Packard chassis did not come until the 1920s. T-head engines and magneto ignition arrived with the 1907 Model S, also known as the 24hp, though actual output was around 40–50bhp. Capacity was now 5734cc and the engine was increased still further, to 7077cc on the 1907 Model U, better known as the 30hp. This was made until 1912. Partial electric lighting was available from 1911, although headlamps were still acetylene up to the 1913 season. For 1909 a smaller companion model joined the Thirty, the 4354cc Model Eighteen, selling for around $1000 less. It did not sell as well as the makers hoped, only 802 finding buyers in the 1909 season, compared with 1501 Thirtys. The two models sold side by side until an all 6-cylinder range appeared for 1913.

The first 6-cylinder Packard had in fact appeared in April 1911, selling alongside the fours. The engine was a pair-cast T-head unit of 8603cc developing 74bhp. It was a very impressive car, riding on wheelbases of 133in (3376mm) or 139in (3528mm), with a top speed of up to 80mph (130km/h). Thirteen body styles were available, from $5000 to $6550. Originally called the Packard Six, it was

renamed the 48 for 1913, when it was joined by a smaller six, the 6800cc 38 which had an L-head engine. It was the first Packard to have an electric starter and lhd. The 38's pair-cast cylinders were replaced by two blocks of three for 1914, while the 48 acquired lhd and spiral bevel rear axle in the same year, and an L-head engine in 1915.

In May 1915 the sixes were joined by a brand-new model, the V12 Twin Six which was the work of two men who were to play an enormous part in Packard's history. One was Alvan Macauley (1872–1952), formerly general manager of the Burroughs Adding Machine Co., whom Henry Joy hired as Packard's general manager in 1911, the other was Jesse G. Vincent (1880–1962), another Burroughs man who was invited by Macauley to join Packard as chief engineer in 1912, and who remained with the company for nearly 40 years. The Twin Six was planned by Macauley and designed by Vincent. The world's first quantity-produced 12-cylinder car, it had an 88bhp 60 degrees L-head engine of 6950cc. The engine was very flexible, enabling the car to accelerate in top gear from 4mph (6.4km/h) to its maximum of around 70mph (112km/h). One might have expected the Twin Six to be very expensive, but in fact it was cheaper than the Model 48, prices running from $2600 to $4600. The first series had the unusual combination of lhd with lefthand gearchange, abandoned on later series which also had detachable cylinder heads.

The 6-cylinder cars were dropped after the 1915 season, and the Twin Six was the only Packard model up to 1921, when it was joined by the Single Six. It was made for a further two years, being discontinued in 1923. A total of 30,951 were built, making it the largest-selling American-built V12. Two wheelbases were offered, 125 and 135in (3172 and 3426mm). From these were derived the model names, the first series of 1915–6 being the 1-25 and 1-35, the second series of 1917 the 2-25 and 2-35, and the third series of 1918–19 the 3-25 and 3-35. The shorter wheelbase was phased out in 1919, one car being completed in 1920, and the 3-35 was then the only model, although in fact its wheelbase was lengthened to 136in (3452mm). Postwar inflation pushed prices up as high as $8000 for a 7-passenger duplex sedan, and it was clear that Packard would have to find a cheaper car. Henry Joy resigned the chairmanship in 1917, chiefly because he wanted to expand Packard's market through mergers, not a popular idea with the rest of the board. Packard would remain fiercely independent for another 38 years.

Jesse Vincent's second design was a new 6-cylinder car, logically if rather uninspiringly called the Single Six. It had a 3957cc L-head engine and a short wheelbase of only 116in (2944mm), which gave it a boxy look, especially in its closed models. Introduced in September 1920, the Single Six received considerably longer wheelbases of 126 (3198mm) and 133in (3376mm) in the 1922 models, which were correspondingly better looking. The 6-cylinder car was made up to 1928, being called simply the Six from the 1926 season onwards. As with the Twin Six, the various models were designated by their series and wheelbases, thus the first series of 1922–3 were the 126 and 133 (126 and 133in (3198 and 3376mm) wheelbases), the second series of 1924 the 226 and 233, and so on. Total production of the 6-cylinder Packards of the 1920s was 154,028.

The Straight Eight

In June 1923 came the company's first straight-8, the series 136 and 143 Single Eight. The nine-bearing L-head engine had a capacity of 5863cc giving 85bhp. 4-wheel brakes were fitted for the first time to a Packard, and there were two wheelbases, each 10in (254mm) longer than on the Six, as indicated by the designations 136 and 143. The 1924 models were known as the First Series, and this annual numbering of series continued up to the 26th series of 1953. It was also applied to the Sixes made up to 1928. The name Single Eight was dropped after the first season, later cars being known simply as Eights. They were excellent value at $3650–4950, and soon became one of America's most respected cars, both at home and abroad. Bijur chassis lubrication was introduced on the 1925 models, while from 1927 all Packards had hypoid rear axles. Also for 1927 there was a considerable increase in power, to 109bhp, resulting from a larger engine of 6306cc, aluminium pistons and improved cylinder head and manifolding.

The 1926 Packard Eights saw a move towards custom coachwork, with several designs by well-known firms being offered on the 143 chassis. Presented as 'Original Creations by Master Designers', they included a Sedan Cabriolet by Judkins, Stationary Town Cabriolets by Fleetwood and Derham, a Limousine Sedan by Holbrook, and several designs by Dietrich. Only one wheelbase, the 143, was listed for 1928, but there were two series, Standard and Custom, in addition to the true customs with outside coachwork. For 1929 there was a new Standard

Packard Six

1947 Packard Super Clipper club sedan.
NICK GEORGANO

Eight which replaced the Six. Its 5231cc engine was similar to that of the Custom Eight, but with a smaller bore. Prices were in some cases about $100 higher than the Six, but most body styles were priced the same.

The 626 and 734 Speedsters

A striking new model for the 1929 season was the 626 Speedster. Despite its name it was available with three different body styles, phaeton, roadster and sedan, and used a tuned version of the big eight engine in the Standard Eight chassis. The high compression engine with high-lift cams gave 130bhp, with a top speed of nearly 100mph (161km/h). Production was limited to just 70 cars, at a price of $5000. Only one is known to survive today. The 1930 version was not much commoner, with 113 built. Known as the 734 Speedster, it had a longer wheelbase of 134.5in (3414mm), and was available with different cylinder heads and gear ratios. The hottest combination, 8:1 cr (145bhp) and 3.3:1 differential, gave a top speed of more than 100mph (161km/h). Five body styles were listed, from $5200 to $6000. These limited production Packards are the most sought after of any model today.

Some of the engine improvements of the 734 were used on all Packards for 1931, giving the Standard Eight a boost from 90 to 100bhp, and the larger Eights from 105 to 120bhp. The 1931 models were characterised by vee-radiators, which were carried on, with styling changes, up to the war.

The New York Automobile Show held in January 1932 saw two new Packards, the Light Eight and the Twin Six. The former was an attempt to counter the Depression with a cheaper car, but it was not cheap enough, and although attractive to look at, sales were low at 6750. It was powered by a 110bhp version of the 5.2-litre engine in a 128in (3249mm) wheelbase, and came in four body styles priced from $1,750–1,795. The Light Eight did not survive the 1932 season, but the idea was revived in the 120 of 1935.

The Twin Six was a reply to the multi-cylinder cars made by rivals such as Cadillac, Lincoln and Pierce-Arrow. Two prototypes were built, one with a straight-12 engine, and the other with a V12 driving the front wheels, but the production model was more conventional, with a 7292cc L-head V12 developing 160bhp and driving the rear wheels. Two wheelbases were offered, 142.5in (3617mm) and 147.5in (3744mm), and a wide variety of standard and custom coachwork was listed, at prices from $3650 for a 2/4-seater coupé to $7950 for an all-weather 5/7-seater landaulet. A 3-speed synchromesh gearbox, new for all Packards in 1932, was featured, as were vacuum-assisted brakes. The first

year's production saw 549 Twin Sixes delivered, out of a total of 9010 for all Packards. This was a terrible drop from the 50,054 cars made in 1928, but worse was to follow, with only 6265 cars delivered in 1934.

The historic name Twin Six was used only for the 1932 models, later 12-cylinder Packards being called simply Twelves. They were made up to the 1939 season, with numerous changes which generally paralleled those of the smaller Packards. These included aluminium cylinder heads, slanting radiators and forward engine mounting for 1935, ifs and hydraulic brakes for 1937, and vee-windscreens for 1938. Engine size was increased to 7756cc (180bhp) in 1935. Annual production of the Twelve only reached four figures with 1300 delivered in 1937, and the total made was 5811. A small figure compared with other models, it still beat Cadillac's 4403 for their V16, and Pierce-Arrow's c.2100 V12s, let alone European V12s such as the Rolls-Royce Phantom III (710) and Hispano-Suiza 54 CV (114).

Scarcely less imposing than the Twelves were the larger Eights, made with 6306cc engines up to the end of the 1936 season, after which the largest engine was a 5244cc unit giving 135bhp. However, the demise of the Twelve in 1939 left a gap at the top of the market which Packard was reluctant to leave to its rivals, so for 1940 a new nine-bearing 5832cc engine was provided for the 160 and 180 series. These had similar styling to the smaller Packards, but higher quality coachwork including air-conditioning. As in the late 1920s, a series of custom bodies was available in the 160 and 180. The number of coachbuilders had shrunk, but there was still Rollson (formerly Rollston) to build cabriolets and town cars, while a striking new style was the Darrin convertible victoria, with European-style cutaway doors and no running boards.

A Move to the Popular Market

After the Depression Packard realised that they could not survive on their prestige cars alone, so for 1935 they brought out a new low-priced eight which was to prove the company's saviour. The 120 had a 3668cc engine developing 110bhp, and a 120in (3046mm) wheelbase which gave the car its name. It shared the suspension, brakes and hypoid drive of the larger Packards, but its prices extended ownership to thousands who had longed to drive a Packard but could never have afforded one. The business coupé cost less than $1000, and the other five styles ran from $1020 to $1095. Ten thousand orders were received before the 120 was ready for delivery, and production for the 1935 season was 24,995, compared with less than 7000 for all other Packard models.

The 1936 120 had a 4620cc engine giving 120bhp, so wheelbase and output were now reflected in the name. There were no great changes for this year or for 1937, when new body styles included a limousine and a station wagon. Total production of the 120 over three seasons was 130,137, a figure unheard of in earlier Packard history. For 1938 the 120 was replaced by the Eight which used the same engine but rode on a longer wheelbase of 127in (3223mm). There was also a massive 148in (3756mm) wheelbase for limousine bodies which was longer than that of the Super Eight or Twelve. The same wheelbases were available in 1939, when the 120 name was back, to remain through the 1941 season. Styling was gradually updated, with headlamps faired into the wings for 1941, but Packard were alone among American manufacturers in retaining their traditional vertical grill right up to the 1942 season. From 1937 a 3570cc 6-cylinder engine was offered in a range basically similar to the 120 on a shorter wheelbase. This was 115in (2919mm) so the 6-cylinder car was called the 115. For 1938 capacity was increased to 4020cc and wheelbase lengthened to 122in (3096mm), so the name 115 was no longer appropriate. The cars were called Sixes for 1938 and 1939, and 110 for 1940 and 1941.

Enter the Clipper

Sensing that the traditionally-styled Packards seemed old-fashioned among their rivals, the company brought out the striking new Clipper in April 1941 as a mid-season model. Designed by Packard's Werner Gubitz and freelance Howard Darrin who had styled the convertible victoria, the Clipper was lower than any Packard and most other 1941 American cars, with a wide, side-opening bonnet, full-faired headlamps and wings that merged into the front door. Only one body style was offered initially, a 4-door sedan at $1420, midway between the 120 and the 160. Unlike other mass-produced Packards, the Clipper's body was not built in-house, but by Briggs. This proved to be an unwise decision, as Packard experienced many problems with quality control on Briggs bodies immediately after the war, and when Briggs was acquired by Chrysler in 1953 they could no longer supply bodies to Packard, who had to start making their own bodies all over again. The Clipper's engine was the 4620cc unit used in the 120. It was well received, selling 16,600 in less than half a season, as the 1942 models came out in August 1941. For the new season, Clipper styling was extended to more models, downward to the 6-cylinder 110 and upward to the 160 and 180, although traditionally styled models were available as well. Additional Clipper styles were a 2-door coupé and a convertible. They were made up to January 1942, when the war halted all car production.

The Postwar Years

The Clipper's success encouraged Packard management to concentrate on medium-sized cars after the war. They were said to have sold the body dies for the handsome and traditionally-styled 1942 180 limousine to the Soviet Union, where it appeared in 1945 as the ZIS-110. There is some doubt about the truth of this, but whatever happened to the dies (a former employee said that they were rusting on a plot near the factory for some time), the big Packards were not revived after the war. It was not a wise decision, as Cadillac found they could sell all the expensive cars they made, and took Packard's place as America's leading luxury car.

The 1946 Packards were all in the Clipper style, with 4020cc six and 4622 or 5838cc eight engines. Closed models only were made, a 2-door club sedan, 4-door touring sedan, and a sedan and limousine on an extended wheelbase of 148in (3756mm). Production of the 1946 models was 29,293 cars, and of the generally similar 1947s, 49,296. These included a number of taxicabs in both years, a new market for Packard.

In August 1947 the first of the new 22nd Series cars appeared. They were considerably restyled, with a wider, lower grill derived from that of a prewar show car called the Phantom, and straight-through lines from front to rear wings. Two new engines were offered, a 4720cc in the Standard Eight, and a 5358cc in the Super Eight, with the Custom Eight retaining the old 5838cc unit. Sixes were no longer offered except for taxis and export cars. Convertibles were back in the higher-priced lines, and there was a curious Station Sedan on the Standard Eight chassis with birch wood panelling which was part of the structure only in the tailgate region.

The 22nd Series Packards were made from August 1947 through to May 1949, with a total of 146,441 cars built. They were followed by the generally similar 23rd Series 'Golden Anniversary' models which were built up to August 1950, with 102,926 cars delivered. An important development for 1950 was Ultramatic automatic transmission. The only automatic system developed by an independent manufacturer without help from a transmission manufacturer, Ultramatic was smoother than GM's Hydramatic, but gave more leisurely acceleration. New and lower styling marked the 24th Series cars for 1951, but engines were still side-valve straight-8s, whereas Packard's rivals were offering new ohv V8s by this time. Only two sizes of engine were made, the 4.7- and 5.4-litre giving 135 and 150/155bhp. Model names were 200, 250, 300 and 400 Patrician, the latter replacing the Custom Eight.

NATIONAL MOTOR MUSEUM

JOY, HENRY BOURNE (1864–1936)

Henry Bourne Joy put up most of the capital to start the Packard Motor Co. and served as its president from 1902 to 1916, and chairman from 1916 to 1933. Born in Detroit, the son of James F. Joy, president of the Chicago, Burlington and Quincy railroad company, he grew up in the milieu of Detroit's wealthiest families (such as the Algers, Newberrys and Booths). He was educated at the Phillips Andover Academy and Yale's Sheffield School, graduating in 1886. His first job was mining in Utah, where he stayed for three years, before returning to Detroit and going to work in the management of his father's various railroad and banking enterprises. He came in contact with Charles B. King who sparked his interest in automobiles. In 1896 he became president of the Fort Street Depot Co. and began discussing his ideas of making cars in Detroit with his brother-in-law, Truman H. Newberry. Their search for a worthy product took several years. They liked the quality of the Locomobile but rejected it because it was a steamer. In 1901 they met James W. Packard and saw the car he was building at Warren, Ohio. This led them to invest in the Ohio Automobile Co., moving it to Detroit and reorganising it as the Packard Motor Co., where Joy modestly claimed the title of factory manager. They hired Joseph Boyer to serve as General Manager, and engaged Charles Schmidt to design a 4-cylinder car to replace Packard's single-cylinder machines.

He saw no way to fight the Selden patent, and the company joined the A.L.A.M. where Joy made every effort to reduce the royalties paid by the members. Still, during the years 1903–1907, the Packard Motor Co. alone paid up $27,000 to the A.L.A.M.

He dominated Packard's affairs during his years as president, taking a back seat role when he was elected chairman, but intervened in matters of policy and financial planning. His health began failing when he turned 65, forcing him to retire in 1933.

JPN

1948 Packard Eight Station Sedan Wagon.
NATIONAL MOTOR MUSEUM

1951 Packard 200 De Luxe sedan.
NATIONAL MOTOR MUSEUM

By 1952 sales were seriously down, with only 76,075 cars delivered the previous year, and the factory was operating at only 50 per cent capacity. James J. Nance was brought in as president, and planned to take Packard back into the luxury market with a range of 8-seater limousines and the glamorous Caribbean convertible. This had a 180bhp engine, wire wheels and many extras, as well as coming in four special colours. A limited edition of 750 Caribbeans was made in 1953, selling at $5210. The price went up to $6100 in 1954, when 400 Caribbeans were sold. The 1955 figure was 500, including a few hard-tops.

Nance's other move was to revive the Clipper name for the base model, selling for around $600 below the next model up. This appeared in the 1953 range, being essentially the 200 renamed, and for 1954 the Clipper was marketed as a separate make in order to isolate it from the luxury Packards. The 4.7- and 5.4-litre engines were used, and production was 23,073, and of the larger Packards, 8098. A new 212bhp 5883cc engine was used in the Caribbean and Patrician models.

For 1955 Packard at last received a V8 engine, two in fact, both oversquare ohv units of 5244 and 5768cc, developing 225 and 245–275bhp. The 1955 Packards were all new, with fresh styling and Torsion Level suspension. This involved 108in (2741mm) torsion bars on either side of the chassis, which twisted anti-clockwise to the front and clockwise to the rear. The rear leveliser bars were linked to an electric motor. This system was featured on the more expensive Clippers (Clipper Custom) and on the regular Packards. The cheaper Clipper De Luxe had normal suspension and manual gearbox, while the others had Twin Ultramatic transmission.

The 1955 Packards sold well, 55,517 for the model year, but Packard was pulled down by its association with Studebaker. Spurred by the Hudson-Nash merger, Nance felt that independent manufacturers were too small to survive on their own, and chose Studebaker as a partner as it made cheaper cars which would complement Packard, and also offered a range of trucks. However, the Studebaker factory was operating far below its capacity, and below the economic break-even point. Its poor image did Packard no good at all, and another blow to the Detroit company was the loss of their body contract with Briggs. They set up a cramped body plant which was never large enough, and caused many problems with production and quality control. 1956 was the last year for the

independent Packard cars. A new model called the Executive filled the gap between the Clipper and the cheapest Packard, and the small V8 engine was dropped. The 5.8-litre unit was retained, and there was a larger 6129cc for the Patrician, 400 and Caribbean, giving 290 or, in the case of the Caribbean, 310bhp. Production slid to only 28,799 for the 1956 models, and the Detroit plant built its last car on 15 August 1956.

The Packard name survived through the 1958 season, but only on a badge-engineered Studebaker. The 1957 Packard Clipper was a Studebaker President with 4736cc V8 engine, made only as a 4-door sedan or station wagon, while the 1958 Hardtop and Hawk were 2-door models similar to Studebakers except for a different grill, which was a bolted-on fibreglass unit. The Hawk shared Studebaker's 275bhp supercharged engine, being the only supercharged car to bear the Packard name. Production of the 1957 models was 4809, and of the 1958s only 2622. The last Packard-badged car was made on 13 July 1958.

Unlike many manufacturers, Packard only had the one factory in the United States, at East Grand Boulevard, Detroit. Their only foreign branch was an assembly plant at Windsor, Ontario, which operated from October 1931 to 1939.
NG

Further Reading
Packard, a History of the Motorcar and the Company, edited by Beverly Rae Kimes, Automobile Quarterly Publications 1978.
'Packard Clipper, Lost Continuum of an American Instutution',
Richard M. Langworth, *Automobile Quarterly*, Vol. 34, No. 1.
The Coach built Packard, Hugo Pfau, Dalton Watson, 1973.
The Packard, 1942–1962, Nathaniel T. Dawes, A.S. Barnes, 1975.

PACKARD-BAYLIFF (US) c.1992–1993

Packard-Bayliff, Lima, Ohio.
C. Budd Bayliff started this company to build 'new' 1934 Packards. The fibreglass bodies were not exact replicas, but were based on the styling of LeBaron-bodied roadsters. The chassis were new Ford Crown Victorias, and production models used 4600cc Ford V8 engines. The prototype had an original Packard Super-8 Special engine. It had 149in (3782mm) wheelbase and 18in (457mm) wire wheels for an authentic appearance. They were only sold in fully assembled form for $130,000, and Packard-Bayliff had plans to add a hard-top coupé, a limousine and a hearse.
HP

PACKET *see* BRASIE

PACO (US) 1908–1909

Pietch Auto & Marine Co., Chicago, Illinois.
The Paco was a typical high-wheeler in specification, with 10/12hp flat-twin engine under the seat and chain drive, but it looked more car-like than some because of its frontal bonnet. It was offered as a runabout, surrey or light delivery van.
NG

PADUS (I) 1906–1908

Fabbrica Automobili Padus, Turin.
This company made a small number of light cars using either 6hp single-cylinder or 10hp 2-cylinder engines. Three were entered in a voiturette race at Turin in 1908, but none finished the course.
NG

PADWIN (GB) 1951

Samuel Elliot Ltd, Reading, Berkshire.
This company made some early INVACARS under contract, and in 1951 produced their own design of invalid car, powered by a rear-mounted 197cc engine with 3-speed gearbox, which they called the Padwin. It did not receive Ministry of Health approval, and was never produced in series.
NG

P.A.F. (GB) 1921

Plant & Foulkes, Moston, Manchester.
This was a cyclecar powered by an 8hp V-twin JAP engine, with Enfield 2-speed gearbox and final drive by shaft. With a 2-seater body it was priced at £220.
NG

P.A.G. (BR) 1988–c.1990
Projets d'Avant Garde Ltda, Santana do Parnaiba.
The P.A.G. Nick was a 2-seater coupé based on the VW Saviero pick-up, and powered by 1595cc (GL) or 1781cc (GLS) engines driving the front wheels. With the larger engine top speed was 112mph (180km/h).

NG

PAGANI (I) 1999 to date
Modena Design, Modena.
The Pagani Zonda C12 was a supercar with central carbon-fibre chassis with chrome-moly steel space frames at either end, and carbon-fibre body panels. It was powered by a mid-mounted 6-litre Mercedes-Benz V12 engine installed longitudinally and driving through a 6-speed gearbox. In 'normal' form the engine gave 394bhp but Pagani planned to offer the C12S with AMG-tuned 7-litre engine giving well over 450bhp. One C12 was shown at the 1999 Geneva Show, when Pagani had three other cars under construction, to sell at £250,000 each. The 2000 Geneva Show saw the restyled Zonda S, with the AMG-tuned 7-litre Mercedes Benz V12 giving 550bhp. Nine cars had been built by February 2000, and the makers hoped to turn out 25 during the year.

NG

PAGE (US) 1906–1908
Page Motor Vehicle Co., Providence, Rhode Island.
The first Page was a 2-seater runabout powered by a 10hp 2-cylinder ohv air-cooled engine, with 2-speed transmission and shaft drive. The company was organised in 1905, and reorganised in February 1906 when they announced that three runabouts had been made. The following year a 20hp 4-cylinder runabout on a longer wheelbase was announced, but only 25 cars were made of both types. The car was named after two of the partners, Arthur A. Page and Victor W. Page. The latter would appear again after World War I, with an accent added to his name, to make the VICTOR PAGÉ car.

NG

PAIGE-DETROIT, PAIGE (US) 1909–1928
Paige-Detroit Motor Car Co., Detroit, Michigan.
After selling its automobile business in 1907, the RELIANCE Automobile Manufacturing Co. concentrated on trucks for two years. Then General Motors bought the truck part of the firm, and former Reliance president Fred O. Paige decided to re-enter the automobile business. He was joined by coal merchant Harry M. Jewett, whose investment helped form the Paige-Detroit Motor Car Co.

The Paige-Detroit car used a 3-cylinder 2-stroke engine designed by E.O. Abbott and W.K. Ackerman, a relic of the Reliance car. Displacing 1632cc, it was rated at 25hp, and drove a selective gearbox through a leather-faced cone clutch. Some 300 cars were built in 1909–1910 before quality problems became manifest. While visiting the company's dealers, Jewett learned of a myriad of troubles with the car, such that on return to headquarters he pronounced it 'rotten. A piece of junk', and set about manoeuvring Fred Paige out of the company and reorganising.

A 'new' Paige-Detroit for 1911 used a 4-stroke 4-cylinder engine and better-engineered components, but its appearance was much the same as the 1909–10 cars. A Model E roadster sold for $800, and a canvas-hooded 'Physician's Car' on the same 90in (2284mm) wheelbase was listed at $875. A longer-wheelbase Model B was also available. Increased sales resulted in a boost to production. The 1912 line dropped 'Detroit' from the marque badge, although it was retained in the company's name. Paiges moved slightly upmarket and adopted posher model names: the Brooklands roadster, Pinehurst tourer, Rockland runabout and La Marquise coupé, for example. The higher price proved an impediment to sales, so prices were relaxed the next year, although the quaint names remained.

A 6-cylinder Paige, the Model 46, was added to the line in 1915. This was powered by a 4969cc Continental side-valve engine. Sales continued to improve, and the 4-cylinder cars were dropped the following year. The model replacing them, Model 6-38, used a 3772cc Rutenber engine. In a marketing campaign aimed subtly at women, its makers now called the Paige 'The Most Beautiful Car in America'. In conjunction with supplier C.R. Wilson Body Co., Paige pioneered the so-called 'convertible' sedan and coupé in 1917, a style which featured removable door and window posts, giving a fixed-roof open car. Many other manufacturers adopted the style within the year.

1988 P.A.G. Nick coupé.
NICK GEORGANO

1920 Paige Model 6-42 tourer.
JOHN A. CONDE

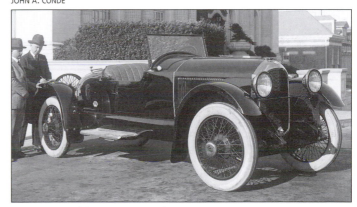
1922 Paige Model 66 Daytona roadster.
NATIONAL MOTOR MUSEUM

A new, slightly smaller Paige was introduced at the New York Auto Show in January 1921. The Model 6-44, it rode a 119in (3020mm) wheelbase and used an in-house 4080cc 6-cylinder engine. A larger Model 6-66 debuted that year, with a 5.4-litre Continental side-valve 8, on a long, 131in (3325mm) wheelbase. The icon of the 6-66 line was the Daytona, a speedster-like roadster with cycle wings and a pull-out jump seat on the side. Ralph Mulford set a number of records in the car, including a Class B speed record at its namesake Daytona Beach venue.

Taking note of HUDSON's success with the low-priced ESSEX badge, Paige managers started to plan their own 'companion car'. Named JEWETT, in honour of the company president, the car entered the marketplace in March 1922, selling for just over $1000 and was an immediate success. The smaller Paige was discontinued after the Jewett's introduction. The larger cars, now called 6-70, continued, largely unchanged from the 6-66 despite the difference in nomenclature.

1926 Paige 6-65 cabriolet.
NICK BALDWIN

1923 Palladium 11.9hp tourer.
NATIONAL MOTOR MUSEUM

But of the nearly 50,000 cars produced by the Paige-Detroit Motor Car Co. in 1923, only 4047 were Paiges. Despite loquacious advertising, sales stagnated; the Daytona speedster, its racy image notwithstanding, proved unpopular and was dropped.

The company remained healthy financially, buoyed principally on Jewett sales. A spate of industry rumours in 1925 linked Paige-Detroit to a possible merger with PIERCE-ARROW and HUPP, although this came to naught, as did a reported takeover bid from DODGE in 1925. A lower priced Paige was announced in 1925, with the company's own 4-litre engine, which was basically the unit used in the Jewett. Both Paige and Jewett orders rose in 1926, but both badges were hampered by slow deliveries of bodies from the Murray Corp. of America, their principal supplier. Murray was undergoing 'friendly' receivership, from which it emerged, but in the meantime MARMON and Hupp gained the upper hand as favoured Murray customers.

The Jewett line was folded into the Paige catalogue in early 1927. The New Day Jewett became a Paige 6-45. Newly designed bodies, now being delivered in reasonable quantities from Murray, gave the cars a new look, but mechanically they were essentially the same as the previous models. An 8-cylinder Straightaway Eight, had been added to the line in mid-1926. Powered by a Lycoming 4895cc 4H side-valve engine, it used a Warner Gear 4-speed Hy-Flex gearbox. Corporate sales were less than half those at the 1923 apex. Harry Jewett retired from the presidency in February 1927, his departure suggesting that other organisational changes might follow. They did. The Graham brothers purchased the Paige-Detroit Motor Car Co. on 11 June 1927, after which it became the GRAHAM-PAIGE Motors Corp. A transitional line of 1928 Paiges debuted in August; they would be the last cars so badged.

KF

Further Reading
The Graham Legacy: Graham-Paige to 1932, Michael E. Keller,
Turner Publishing Co., 1998.

PALLADIUM (GB) 1912–1925

1912 McMahon's Motor Exchange, London.
1913–1914 Palladium Autocars Ltd, Kensington, London.
1914–1925 Palladium Autocars Ltd, Putney, London.
Palladium vehicles were originally sold from premises in London's Euston Road, and it appears that commercial vehicles preceded passenger cars by two years. These were imported from France, being introduced in December 1910. Cars were announced in 1912, from the same address, though there is evidence that they were assembled in Twickenham. Three 4-cylinder models, of 10, 12 and 15hp were listed, with overhead-inlet valve engines. In 1913 they moved to Normand Road, Kensington, and in 1914 to Felsham Road, Putney. The 1914 range included 10/18, 12/22 and 18/30hp fours and a 15/26hp six. It is difficult to establish the amount of English input into these cars. Engines were probably still French, including some by Chapuis-Dornier, with English coachwork.

After the war Palladium cars were all-English, although the commercial chassis, which were popular for charabanc work, had Continental engines and Timken axles. A prototype cyclecar was built in 1919, with a 1.3-litre flat-twin air cooled engine, cooled by a fan blowing air into cowlings on the cylinders. It had friction transmission and chain final drive. Few were made, and it was only after the collapse of the truck market that Palladium returned to cars, in 1922. Their 12hp was a conventional light car powered by a 1496cc Dorman engine in unit with a 4-speed gearbox. They were made in Touring and Victory models and had front-wheel brakes from 1923. The Victory was a sports tourer for which 60mph (97km/h) was claimed. 280 12hp cars were made up to 1925, and there was also a 1794cc 15hp which probably never emerged from the prototype stage, though a chassis was shown at Olympia in 1922.

In 1925 Palladium moved to smaller premises in Putney where they assembled a few cars with British Anzani engines. These were called the New Victory and Empire models. There is a possible link between these and some models of SURREY which also had a factory in Premier Place, Putney.

NG

PALM (i) (AUS) 1918–1921

E.W. Brown Motors Pty Ltd, Melbourne, Victoria.
Edwin Walker Brown had spent several years marketing motorcycles, including his own EWB, before deciding that cars were the way forward, in his case with a rebadged Model T Ford. The Ford Motor Co. of Canada issued a writ alleging that Brown was offering its goods without due acknowledgement. However, it seems to have had little effect, as the Palm name continued until it was replaced by the RENOWN label in 1922.

MG

PALM (ii) see PALMERSTON

PALMER (i) (US) 1906

Palmer Automobile Manufacturing Co., Ashtabula, Ohio; Cleveland, Ohio.
Designed by Herbert R. Palmer, this was a 2-seater runabout powered by an 8hp single-cylinder engine without valves. The mixture was admitted and burnt gases expelled through ports in the cylinder wall, which were uncovered by the movement of the piston. The runabout was on a short wheelbase of 60in (1523mm), had a 4-speed epicyclic transmission and final drive by rope belt. Plans to build 300 cars in 1906 were never remotely achieved, despite the company having factories in Ashtabula and Cleveland. At the year's end Palmer gave up his own car, and later made the EUCLID (ii) in Cleveland.

NG

PALMER (ii) (US) 1914–1915

Palmer Brothers, Cos Cob, Connecticut.
The Palmer brothers, Frank and Ray, built an experimental car in 1899, but did not enter commercial production until 1914 when they joined the ranks of the cyclecar builders with a 4-cylinder machine made in two models, the Bear Cat Roadster at $325 and the Stream-line Roadster at $350. When they discontinued these in 1915 they were offering 30 models of marine engine, from 2 to 75hp, and the company continued to be active in this field until the early 1970s.

NG

1914 Palladium 18/30 landaulet.
NICK BALDWIN

PALMER-SINGER (US) 1908–1914

Palmer & Singer Manufacturing Co., Long Island City, New York.

This company was founded by Henry U. Palmer, a successful barrel maker, and Charles A. Singer of the famous sewing machine family. At first they dealt in other cars, especially high-quality expensive machines such as Isotta-Fraschini, Matheson and Simplex, which they sold from a showroom on Broadway. The first cars under their own name appeared in 1908 and were made for them by Matheson until their Long Island City factory was ready. They included the Skimabout, a roadster with 28hp 4-cylinder engine and Renault-type dashboard radiator, and the Model 6-60 with 60hp engine of 10-litres capacity on a 126in (3198mm) wheelbase. Whereas the Skimabout was quite reasonably priced at $1950, 6-60 prices ran from $3100 to $3500. The 6-60 had shaft drive from its introduction, quite unusual on such a powerful car in 1908.

In 1911 a Palmer-Singer covered 60 miles in 60 minutes at night during the 24 Hour Race at Brighton Beach, which led to 1913 and 1914 models being called the Brighton. The 1914 Brighton Six was a most attractive car, with vee-radiator in the Mercedes style, though not so pronounced, torpedo tourer body and wire wheels. Buyers were offered the option of electric or compressed-air starting. In addition, it was advertised as 'The Strongest-Built Car in the World'. However, sales were slow, and in a desperate attempt to gain publicity Palmer-Singer announced new cars in December 1913 which it called 1915 models. The only novelty was the Magic Six which used the slide-valve 6-cylinder engine designed by the Swiss Martin Fischer and used in his FISCHER cars, and also in the American-built MONDEX MAGIC. It was not a success, and contributed to Palmer-Singer's bankruptcy in March 1914. The company was sold to Willliam

1908 Palmer-Singer Skimabout roadster.
JOHN A. CONDE

Wooster who planned to build a $500 car, but changed his mind and sold it back to Charles Singer. He replaced the Magic engine by a conventional Herschell-Spillman six and sold the car under his own name. A plan to make Palmer-Singers in Canada under the name MARITIME SIX failed after perhaps half a dozen had been made.

NG

1910 Palmer-Singer 28/30hp landaulet.
NICK BALDWIN

1912 Palmer-Singer Model 46 toy tonneau.
NICK BALDWIN

PALMER SPECIAL (GB) c.1933–1934

Palmer-Reville & Co., Wimbledon, London.

This was a tuned version of the 9hp front-wheel drive B.S.A., said to be designed for dirt track work, although it was also suitable for general road use. It was advertised in November 1933 by Palmer-Reville & Co. as 'The new 9hp 70mph front-wheel drive hand-made Palmer Special'. The regular front-drive B.S.A. would not be capable of 70mph (113km/h) until 1938, when it had a larger engine, so Palmer-Reville's tuning was clearly to some effect.

NG

PALMERSTON; PALM (GB) 1920–1923

Palmerston Motor Co. Ltd, Boscombe, Bournemouth, Hampshire.

This company made two models of light car. The first to appear was the Palmerston, powered by a 5/7hp flat-twin Coventry-Victor engine. In 1922 it was joined by the Palm which had a larger engine of 9hp. Both had 3-speed gearboxes and shaft drive to a bevel axle. Wire or disc wheels were available. They had polished brass radiators and lighting was only by acetylene. In late 1921 the company was known as the Palmerston Lytcar Co. and then Palmcars Ltd.

NG

PAN (US) 1919–1921

Pan Motor Co., St Cloud, Minnesota.

The story of the Pan automobile is extraordinary and a prime example of swindling, double dealing and crooked stock manoeuvring which, for a time, appeared to be remarkably successful. Samuel Conner Pandolfo, a promoter and high-pressure salesman, had grandiose plans for the production of a car named after himself and centred operations for his endeavour at St Cloud, Minnesota where he constructed a factory and a residential community adjacent to it in which to house his employees and their families. He had several cars, projected as prototypes, built in Indianapolis and began production of the Pan automobile.

The car, in appearance, differed little from a host of other cars of its time. Powered by a 4076cc 6-cylinder F-head engine which was built in the Pan factory,

developing 50bhp at 3000rpm, it had a wheelbase of 108in (2741mm) and was built almost exclusively as a 5-seater touring car priced at $1190 to $1250, plus a few roadsters. To further promote his project, Pandolfo compiled a large, illustrated catalogue comprising every detail and aspect of the car and his company. This included not only the basic history of the enterprise, but its management as well and was undoubtedly the most elaborate and expensive brochure ever published by any automobile company. One ploy Pandolfo emphasised in his promotion was the arrangement of seats which folded down to form a bed and gave rise to the expression that 'no father would allow his daughter to go out with a boy who drove a Pan'.

Despite the initial success of manufacturing, Pan production ground to a halt when a Federal grand jury indicted Pandolfo for fraud involving the manipulation of nearly $10 million in the sale of stock. A total of 737 Pan cars had been completed but the Pan operation failed due to the publicity surrounding Pandolfo's crooked manoeuvring of stock. He was sentenced to 10 years in the Federal Penitentiary at Leavenworth, Kansas.

Released after serving 2$\frac{1}{2}$ years in prison, Pandolfo enjoyed a varied career in several fields involving a health food enterprise and a patented device for making doughnuts. He lived to his mid-80s.

KM

PANACHE (GB) 1983–1987

Panache Cars, Blackburn, Lancashire.

The Panache can rightly be said to have had absolutely none of the eponymous quality. It was an early attempt by Paul Lawrenson to produce a Countach 'lookalike', initially for a full-length VW Beetle floorpan. The body incorporated a Bond Bug-style flop-forward canopy, perhaps persuading its maker to claim that it was 'the most exotic and futuristic component car available'. A special chassis was developed for mid-mounted engines up to V8s and a more accurate Countach LP400 replica was also briefly offered.

CR

PANAM (US) 1902–1903

Pan-American Motor Co., Mamaroneck, New York.

Designed by William M. Power and backed by several prominent Wall Street financiers, the Panam began with an unusual engine in which the inlet valves were fitted inside the exhaust valves. Tests proving unsuccessful, the directors ordered a more conventional design which would follow the best current European practice. Two models were built, the 15hp Model C on a 84in (2132mm) wheelbase and the 25hp Model B on a 96in (2436mm) wheelbase. Both had 4-cylinder engines, 3-speed gearboxes and double-chain drive. Only 25 Panams were made.

NG

PAN-AMERICAN (US) 1917–1922

1917 Pan-American Motor Corp., Chicago, Illinois.
1917–1922 Pan-American Motor Corp., Decatur, Illinois.

The Pan-American initially, and before its move to Decatur, marketed its car as the Chicago Light Six, changing this to Pan-American later in 1917, a name which it would retain for its six years of production in Decatur. The car was a typical product of the smaller independent automobile manufacturer of its time with standard components throughout. Although the car had used both Rutenber and Continental engines during its first two years, by 1920 the 6-cylinder cars were equipped with the Continental 7R. A 4-cylinder, less-expensive companion model was introduced in 1919 but, proving unsuccessful in the marketplace, it was withdrawn within the year. For 1921 a Herschell Spillman 1100 six replaced the Continental 7R and would remain with all Pan-American cars throughout 1921 and for the relatively few completed the following year. A point of confusion to latter day automotive historians was Pan-American's 'American Beauty' series, the name of which conflicted with the more prolific line of Auburn cars built at the same time under the name of the 'Beauty Six'. A wheelbase of 121in (3071mm) was standard with the Pan-American. The cars were priced as low as $1285 in the earlier days of manufacture but, after 1920 the figure was increased to $2000 for the roadsters and touring cars which comprised most of Pan-American output. A seldom-seen 5-seater sedan was introduced for 1920, priced at $3000, but this was discontinued after that year. Few Pan-Americans were built in 1922 when the company went out of business.

KM

Panhards in 1892 (R to L) front-engined 2-seater, front engined 2-seater, 1890 mid-engined 4-seater *dos-à-dos*, front-engined 2-seater.
NICK BALDWIN

PANDA (US) c.1956
Small Cars Inc., Kansas City, Missouri.
The Panda was a small, sporty 2-seat economy car. The roadster bodywork had a rectangular grill and a tall windscreen. Two engines were offered, an air-cooled Kohler 2-cylinder with 1100cc or a water-cooled Aerojet with 15hp. The 70in (1777mm) wheelbase Panda sold for about $1000 in 1956.

HP

PANDARUS (AUS) 1983–1985
Pandarus Sports Cars, Seaford, Victoria.
Built by Austin-Healey specialists, this was a fibreglass replica mounted on a Toyota Crown chassis and powered by a Leyland Australia alloy V8 driving via a 5-speed gearbox. A lower cost 6-cylinder Holden engine could be fitted, as could large Chevrolet or Ford V8 engines for top performance. The body by Colin and Noel Simmonds was, apart from extended wheel arches, true to Austin-Healey lines, but it was found that most customers for replicas preferred the Cobra shape.

MG

PANEK (CS) 1921
Panek, Rakovnik.
Panek manufactured some light cars with 2-cylinder 12bhp water-cooled engines and with open 2-seater bodies and wire wheels on leaf springs. Although only a few were made, his vehicle won a prize in the cyclecar category at the International Spa Towns automobile races that year.

MSH

PANGRA (US) c.1972–1995
Pangra Enterprises, Inc., Philadelphia, Pennsylvania.
The Pangra was a fibreglass body kit that bolted onto a Ford Pinto sedan or station wagon. It consisted of a long, droop nose that improved the aerodynamics and looks as well. Retractable headlights were hidden when not in use. Pangra would install performance equipment to improve power and handling, and V8 engine swaps were offered as well.

HP

PANHARD-LEVASSOR (F) 1890–1967
1890–1967 Sté Panhard & Levassor, Paris.
1897–1965 Sté Anonyme des Anciens Établissements,
Panhard & Levassor, Paris.
1965–1967 Sté de Constructions Mécaniques Panhard & Levassor, Paris.
In 1891 Panhard & Levassor built a batch of four identical cars, followed by series after series of increasing numbers, which, chronologically, makes Panhard-Levassor the world's first make of car in continuous production. Although Benz and Daimler had built their first automobiles earlier, they were isolated examples and not part of any sustained programme.

1900 Panhard tonneau.
NICK BALDWIN

c.1906 Panhard limousine by Barker.
NATIONAL MOTOR MUSEUM

1910 Panhard 25hp tourer.
NATIONAL MOTOR MUSEUM

NATIONAL MOTOR MUSEUM

NATIONAL MOTOR MUSEUM

PANHARD, LOUIS FRANÇOIS RENÉ (1841–1908)
Son of Adrien Panhard, coachbuilder and rent-a-carriage entrepreneur in Paris. Born on 27 May 1841, René was educated in local schools and graduated from the Ecole Centrale des Arts et Manufactures in 1864. He became a partner of Jean-Louis Périn, inventor of a band saw, and manufacturer of wood-working machinery in the Rue du Faubourg Saint-Antoine, Paris.

In the early summer of 1908 he went to La Bourboule, a spa in the Massif Central for treatment of asthma, other respiratory diseases, and skin problems, where he died on 16 July 1908.

JPN

PANHARD, ADRIEN HIPPOLYTE FRANÇOIS (1870–1955)
Hippolyte was born at Hyëres (Var), the son of René Panhard on 5 October 1870. A pioneer motorist, he was only 23 when he drove a Panhard car from Paris to Nice and back in 1893. He served as a member of the Panhard-Levassor board from 1897 to 1915, when he became chairman, an office he held until 1946. For the rest of his life, he held the title of honorary president.

JPN

The roots of Panhard & Levassor have been traced back to 1830 when Adrien Panhard began making carriages and operating a livery service in the bastille district of Paris, trading under the name of Prieur. His son René went to work for Hippolyte de Longueil's wheel factory at Courbevoie, where he came into contact with all the suppliers, including a wood-working machine maker since 1845, Jean-Louis Périn of the Périn & Pauwels enterprise in 97 rue du Faubourg Saint-Antoine in Paris, heart of the fine-furniture trade. Pauwels died in 1866, and Périn began looking for a new partner.

After marrying Marie de Longueil, René Panhard left her father's business to go into partnership with Jean-Louis Périn and the Société des Machines Bois Périn was transformed into the Société Périn, Panhard & Cie in 1866. Périn had patented a band saw in 1853. They also made circular saws and machines for mortice and tenon joints. In the 1870–71 war, the company also bored cannons and assembled them.

In his student days at the École Centrale des Arts et Manufactures, René Panhard had befriended a fellow pupil, Émile Levassor. They met again after Levassor had gone to work for the Durenne company at Courbevoie in 1869. René Panhard introduced Émile Levassor to Jean-Louis Périn, and Levassor joined the company in 1872.

Their little factory was bursting at the seams, and they secured a spacious factory site at Ivry, where they began to move in in 1873. René Panhard kept his residence on the prestigious Place des Vosges, while Levassor rented rooms in the building behind the new factory.

René Panhard talked to Émile Levassor about a second product line, to stabilise the activity during downturns in the cyclical market for wood-working machinery, and their cannon-boring experience led them to think in terms of metal construction rather than wood. They knew about Lenoir's industrial engines and agreed that a market existed for something more modern and efficient. In 1875 Périn, Panhard & Cie began producing Deutz gas engines under Otto &

1912 Panhard 12hp coupé cabriolet.
NICK BALDWIN

Langen patents. The company prospered, and when Jean-Louis Périn died in 1886, the firm was renamed Société Panhard & Levassor, formally recognising Émile Levassor's equal status with René Panhard.

It was in 1887 that events began to occur that gently steered the company towards the making of automobiles. The primary factor in this connection was Édouard Sarazin, another graduate of the École Centrale des Arts et Manufactures, who had known Émile Levassor well at the time they were both working for Cockerill at Seraing near Liège, Levassor in the machine shop, and Sarazin in the sales department.

Sarazin's fateful contact with the motor industry was made on 27 July 1872, when N.A. Otto engaged him to prepare the case for suing Gabriel Dehaynin for patent infringement. That case came to nothing, but Sarazin later represented Deutz in a suit brought by the makers of the Lenoir gas engines and so impressed his clients in Cologne that they named Sarazin their French representative.

Thus, Sarazin was instrumental in selling manufacturing rights to the Deutz gas engines to the company Émile Levassor was working for. Sarazin was also acquainted with Gottlieb Daimler and Wilhelm Maybach, who left Deutz in 1872 and moved to Stuttgart, where they developed and patented the Daimler engine. Basic German patents for their 4-stroke internal combustion engine were issued in 1883 and 1885.

In 1879 Deutz set up its own subsidiary in France, Compagnie Parisienne d'Éclairage et de Chauffage par le Gaz, with both Édouard Sarazin and Gabriel Dehaynin as co-founders and board members. This office was no big burden for Sarazin, who intuitively saw a greater future for Daimler than for Deutz. In 1886 he travelled to Stuttgart and met with Gottlieb Daimler, who granted him exclusive rights for Daimler engines in France, and empowered him to apply for French patents corresponding to those issued to Daimler in Germany, and to exploit those patents in France by making licence agreements. When Sarazin wanted demonstration engines made in France, he spent a lot of time persuading Émile Levassor to build them. Levassor finally agreed, but Sarazin fell ill and died on 24 December 1887.

Sarazin had explained to his wife the immense earnings potential of the Daimler patents, and Louise (née Cayrol) Sarazin (1847–1917), a brunette from southern France, took immediate steps to secure in her own name the rights granted to her husband. She also wanted a licence agreement with Société Panhard & Levassor, as proof of her ability to make money for Daimler. During the winter of 1888, her business kept her in frequent contact with both Gottlieb Daimler and Émile Levassor. In 1889, Louise Sarazin and Émile made at least one visit together to Stuttgart. Finally, on 1 November 1889, the documents were signed as she wanted them.

Panhard & Levassor would pay a 20 per cent royalty to Madame Sarazin for every engine, of which more than half (60 per cent, equal to 12 per cent of the selling price) would be passed on to Daimler Motoren Gesellschaft.

Shrewdly, Émile Levassor had made it clear from the beginning that his company would not begin to produce Daimler engines without some guarantees of having

NATIONAL MOTOR MUSEUM

PANHARD, JOSEPH PAUL RENÈ (1881–1969)
Son of Léon Panhard, nephew of René Panhard, Paul was born at Versailles on 1 August 1881. He joined the family firm in 1906 and became its sales director in 1913. He led the company as president and managing director from 1916 to 1951, his management and outlook becoming increasingly conservative with advancing age. In 1945 he received the gold medal of the French Resistance for his wartime record of opposition to the occupation forces. He died in March 1969.
JPN

1925 Panhard 14/20hp tourer.
NATIONAL MOTOR MUSEUM

1929 Panhard 20CV sport coupé.
NICK BALDWIN

1929 Panhard 20/60hp saloon.
NICK BALDWIN

customers for them. For he had not yet, even at the end of 1889, any plan at all to make complete automobiles, motorboats, or other equipment powered by Daimler's engine.

Both Daimler and Levassor knew Armand Peugeot, who did want to make automobiles. In the spring of 1889, Daimler and Émile Levassor had travelled together to Valentigney to see Armand Peugeot, and proposed using Daimler engines, manufactured in Paris by Panhard-Levassor, in the cars Peugeot would build. Only on the strength of an agreement with Armand Peugeot would Émile Levassor commit himself to production of Daimler's engine.

The first two engines were shipped to Peugeot in March 1890. It was around that time, that Levassor decided to build a car himself, so he would at least have some basis for making a rational decision on whether or not to begin car production in the Panhard-Levassor factory. On 17 May 1890, Louise Sarazin and Émile Levassor were married. Later, Gottlieb Daimler signed a supplementary contract, extending her rights to include Daimler patents issued in Germany in 1889 and 1890.

Levassor was highly critical of Daimlers cars, yet his first design resembled a Daimler more than a Peugeot. It was built by Émile Mayade (1855–1899) the shop foreman who was to serve also as head of the test department and manager of automobile production, from June to October 1890, with four wheels (small in front, big on the rear axle) and a vertical, 921cc V-twin 1½hp (at 700rpm) engine with a separate gearbox and final drive by chain. The engine was mounted centrally in the chassis, between the *dos-à-dos* front and rear seats.

NATIONAL MOTOR MUSEUM

LEVASSOR, ÉMILE (1843–1897)

Émile Levassor was born on 21 January 1843, at Marolles in the Hurepoix agricultural plains southwest of Paris. After local elementary school he proved a brilliant student, and he attended the École des Mines at Saint-Étienne, but found the discipline hard and the curriculum not to his liking. He applied to the École Centrale des Arts et Manufactures and was admitted, graduating in 1864. Amongst his fellow students was René Panhard.

In 1864, he went to work in the machine shop of John Cockerill at Seraing, Liège, in Belgium, where he came to know Edouard Sarazin. Returning to Paris in 1869, he went to work for Établissements Durenne at Courbevoie.

After joining Périn, Panhard & Cie. in 1872, his entire career was with that enterprise. He designed the Panhard-Levassor cars and drove them in road races.

Levassor told his assistants, 'faites lourd, vous ferez solide' (make it heavy, and it will be strong). He also treated the imperfections of his gearboxes with humour: 'c'est brutal mais ça marche' ('it's brutal but it works').

He won a famous victory in the Paris–Bordeaux–Paris race of 1895, but did not live to see the statue erected in his honour at the Porte Maillot. He was injured in an accident during the Paris–Marseilles road race of 1896, caused by him swerving to avoid hitting a dog, and although his doctors warned him not to work too hard, he ignored their advice. He died on 14 April 1897, and is buried at Père Lachaise cemetary.

JPN

1937 Panhard Dynamic saloon.
BRYAN K. GOODMAN

The first successful test trip was a 20km run along the boulevards on the south side of Paris, in January 1891. A second car was under construction by that time, the main difference being the engine installation, moved closer to the rear axle, with the gearbox and chain-drive jackshaft in front of it. It was completed on 20 June 1891, with a 1025cc V-twin and successfully made the trip to Etretat on the channel coast and back to the factory.

In March 1891, Levassor decided to move the engine to the front end of the chassis, primarily in order to protect it against the effects of road shock and vibration. Four cars with 817cc V-twin front-mounted engines were built and sold before the end of the year. The second car sold was later bought by the Abbé Gavois, a parish priest from Rainnerville, near Amiens, who used it regularly until 1921, and occasionally for seven years more, after which it was bought back by its makers.

Over the next five years, Levassor maintained a very busy correspondence with Gottlieb Daimler, discussing at great length all the problems of clutches and gearing, ignition, steering, frame and suspension design.

The factory produced 15 cars in 1892, 37 in 1893 and 41 in 1894. In Germany, Daimler had begun production of the parallel-twin Phoenix engine in 1892, but Levassor stuck with the V-twin, built in sizes of 2hp 1025cc, 3hp 1184cc and 4hp 1290cc until 1895. Both chassis and body designs evolved, as the model range proliferated. The front-engine concept was used for all dog-cart, *dos-à-dos*, open 2-seater and rear-entrance tonneau bodies, but forward-control chauffeur-driven town cars and the so-called Omnibus, had their engines under the front seats. Panhard-Levassor did not make bodies, but contracted with coachbuilders, notably Védrine and Rothschild.

Émile Levassor first saw the Phoenix engine on a trip to Stuttgart in 1893, and was impressed. It weighed only 165lb (75kg), compared to 330lb (150kg) for a V-twin of similar power, and was fitted with Maybach's new spray-jet carburettor, the Ivry works were retooled for the new engine (spelled Phénix for the French market), going into production for the 1895-model cars, which also featured Levassor's new all-enclosed gearbox with sliding gears (for which he neglected to apply for a patent).

The first Phénix was a 1201cc 4CV, supplemented by a 2447cc 10CV twin, they were joined in 1906 by a 1648cc 6CV twin and a 4-cylinder unbalanced (because composed of two twins without adapted crankshafts) 8CV engine of 2402cc.

Levassor designed a light vehicle with a single-cylinder 600cc engine, the Voiturette de Parc which did not go into production. After building 74 vehicles in 1895, the factory put out 106 in 1896, 170 in 1897 and 341 in 1898.

Émile Levassor died on 14 April 1897, succumbing to injuries sustained in an accident during the Paris–Marseilles race of 1896. His last visit to Stuttgart had been for the occasion of Gottlieb Daimler's re-marriage. The same day that he died a daughter was born to Lina and Gottlieb Daimler. She was christened Émilie.

René Panhard duly reorganised the company as a joint stock corporation, attracting a number of investors, and announced a capital stock of FFr 5m. He named his son Hippolyte, and René de Knyff, the prominent racing driver, and Adolphe Clément, the bicycle manufacturer, to the board of directors.

The other board members were investors with names such as Ménard, Holtzer, Pierron, Prevost, Dorian and Lavertujon. Georges Pierron was named works manager, and Arthur Constantin Krebs, head of technical services.

At Avenue d'Ivry, Krebs's first priority was to develop balanced 4-cylinder engines, starting with the 8CV, then quickly adding the 3296cc 12CV and 4837cc 16CV 4-cylinder models to the range. For 1898 he also created a 5313cc 20CV 4-cylinder model.

Levassor had begun to modernise the chassis, for some of his 1896 models had steering wheels on vertical columns with worm-drive gear, and the 1897 models had a rear mounted gilled tube radiator instead of merely a water tank.

Krebs began tilting the steering column on the 1898 Paris-Amsterdam racing car, and then adapted it to all the production models. In 1899 he moved the radiator to the front of the chassis, starting with the Paris–Bordeaux racing car, and put the Krebs compensating diaphragm carburettor on the Panhard-Levassor engines. Two years later he discarded Daimler's hot-tube ignition for a coil-and-battery system, first seen on the 1901 30CV 6928cc 4-cylinder model.

In 1898 Krebs also designed a very low-priced small car with a single-cylinder 797cc engine for Adolphe Clément, who produced several hundreds of them in his Levallois-Perret factory up to 1901. Adolphe Clément resigned from the Panhard-Levassor board, in January 1903, because he was becoming too big a rival.

Panhard-Levassors production climbed steadily, from 461 units in 1899 to 510 in 1900 and 831 in 1901. The plant was no longer making Deutz gas-engines, but the wood-working machines were still an important part of the enterprise.

During 1901 Krebs designed and developed the Centaure family of 2- and 4-cylinder engines, with redesigned valve gears breaking with Daimler traditions, and throttle control on the inlet side, eliminating the governor on the exhaust side.

As the Centaure engine gradually replaced the Phénix units, René Panhard trimmed the royalty payments to Madame Levassor (and the Daimler Motoren Gesellschaft). Widowed with three children in 1897, she was associated in 1900 with J. de Boisse, who had designed a primitive and over-long 3-wheeled motor vehicle. They contracted with Panhard-Levassor for its production, but the sales never exceeded a level of mediocrity.

She promptly sued for royalties on the Centaure engines, and the case was tied up in litigation until 1914 when it was settled out of court. Panhard-Levassor paid her a compensatory amount, and put her son, Henri Sarazin, on its board of directors. Louise Levassor died in 1917 at the age of 70.

Beginning in 1902, Krebs redesigned the Centaure engines, abandoning cast-in-pairs cylinders in favour of individual barrels. The new 4-cylinder Centaure Leger had a 5-bearing crankshaft and 3 valves per cylinder. Between the vertical-twin 1206cc 5CV and the 10CV 2402cc 4-cylinder units, he inserted the P-series 1801cc and 2472cc 7CV 3-cylinder pioneering example on modular design. In 1903 he developed the Centaure S-series family, with Eisemann magneto ignition and T-head construction with mechanical inlet valve operation. The 4-cylinder S-series engines ran from a 2402cc 10CV unit to a 7360cc 35CV type, with three intermediate sizes (3296cc 15CV, 4072cc 18CV, and 5313cc 24CV). They were joined for 1905 by a giant 50CV 10,560cc model.

Krebs was also determined to get rid of the gilled tube radiator, and began fitting honeycomb radiators in 1905. He started the switch from chain drive to shaft drive in 1908, beginning with the lower-powered models. The last chain-driven model was the 28CV of 1913.

The Centaure twins were taken out of production at the end of 1905, but small series of vertical-twins were again produced in 1908–09. The P-series 3-cylinder engines were not used in passenger cars after 1904, but equipped the company's light commercial vehicles up to 1908–09.

Panhard-Levassor had 1500 workers and 40,000m^2 floor space in 1905. Motor vehicle production had reached 1059 units in 1902 but dipped to 959 in 1903 and 1052 in 1904.

Recovery came in 1905 with 1275 vehicles, followed by 1336 in 1906. That year the board of directors determined to diversify into truck and bus production, even if it meant an end to the company's motor racing effort.

That was an important policy change, and changes in top personnel were to follow. René Panhard died on 16 July 1908, and his son Hippolyte took over the management, while Paul Panhard, son of René's brother Léon, having joined the company in 1906, worked in various executive positions until he was promoted to sales director in January 1913. Sales took a downturn in 1907, when only 1043 cars were built, followed by 831 in 1908 and recovery – to 1142 cars – in 1909. A new record was set in 1910 with an output of 2024 cars.

Early in 1909, René de Knyff met with Hippolyte Panhard to tell him of his experience of driving the new Daimler with the Knight sleeve-valve engine. He was enchanted with the silence and smoothness, and urged the chairman to obtain a licence and start mounting sleeve-valve engines in Panhard-Levassor cars. René de Knyff arranged for the loan of a Daimler in Paris.

The head of the experimental department, Charles Schaeffer, was impressed and supported de Knyff. Paul Defly, who was head of the drawing office, did not take sides, but Charles de Fréminville, an engineer from the École Centrale des Arts et Manufactures who happened to be the brother-in-law of Arthur Krebs, and worked on plant organisation and production matters at Ivry, remained openly sceptical.

As a man of speed, de Knyff worked fast, got Hippolyte on his side, and soon Krebs agreed to go ahead with sleeve-valve engine design. The first one was a 20CV 4398cc 4-cylinder model that went into production late in 1910.

A 15CV 3603cc sleeve-valve engine replaced the poppet-valve 18CV in 1912. The X-17 appeared at the same time with a 15CV 2614cc sleeve-valve engine.

No official announcement was ever made that the Levassor name would be dropped from the trade mark. The big Plinacircle emblem, adopted in 1906, was never changed. And the company title never lost the Levassor part. But after 1912, the company's advertisements began calling their product Panhard, after which the shortened name was commonly used by the press, and glided into popular usage.

1953 Panhard Dyna 130 saloon in the 1954 Monte Carlo Rally.
NATIONAL MOTOR MUSEUM

1954 Panhard Dyna 54 saloon.
NICK BALDWIN

The first 6-cylinder sleeve-valve Panhard was a 30CV 6597cc unit with separately cast cylinders, fitted in the new X-18 model introduced in 1912. It was not the company's first six, however, for two poppet-valve sixes had gone into production in 1909, the 30CV 4950cc U 5 and the 65CV 12,020cc U 4.

However, Krebs did not intend to abandon poppet-valves entirely, particularly in the lowest-priced cars. The new 10CV of 1913 (type X-19) had a 2150cc 4-cylinder L-head engine with three main bearings, coupled to a dry, single-plate clutch and 4-speed gearbox.

Two additional models with sleeve-valve engines were displayed at the 1913 Salon in Paris, the X22 20CV Sport derived from the X-14 of 1911, with a 4850cc engine, and the X-24 35CV 7360cc 6-cylinder model which replaced the X-18 after a run of only two years.

The 1914 model range was composed of eight different chassis, with prices from FFr 7500 for the 10CV – to FFr 20,000 for the 35CV – not including the coachbuilders' prices.

During World War I, Panhard-Levassor produced cars, trucks, marine and aircraft engines, tractors, tools, machine guns, and ammunition, despite a large part of the work force being drafted for military service. Both Hippolyte and Paul Panhard spent part of the war years in uniform.

The first aircraft engines made at Ivry were in-line sixes for the propulsion of dirigibles in 1910, but in 1915 a 275hp water-cooled poppet-valve V12 aeroplane engine went into production, followed by a 350hp sleeve-valve V12 in 1917.

Some of the car chassis were fitted with ordnance or ambulance bodies, and the most notable truck was the 4 × 4 Chatillon-Panhard with its 6-cylinder poppet-valve engine.

Hippolyte Panhard was elected chairman of the board in February 1915. A year later, Arthur Krebs announced his retirement, effective from the end of the year. For several years, he remained in Paris as a consultant to Panhard-Levassor, then moved to Quimperlé in Brittany where he died in March 1935.

1954 Panhard Dyna Junior roadster, in the 1954 Monte Carlo Rally.
NATIONAL MOTOR MUSEUM

Louis Pestourie, an engineer with a diploma from the École des Arts et Métiers in Paris, was engaged to replace Krebs, but left in 1919. Paul Panhard, managing director since 1916, then hired Eugène Gorju, an experienced engineer whose strength lay in manufacturing rather than product engineering. He inherited a competent staff, with Paul Defly and Charles Schaeffer still in harness, Louis Dufresne who had joined Panhard-Levassor in 1913, immediately after graduation from the École Centrale des Arts et Manufactures, and Louis Rigoulot who left Peugeot and signed up with Panhard-Levassor in 1915.

Postwar production for the civilian market began in March 1919, with the prewar X-19 poppet-valve 2150cc car and a new X-28 model with a 3180cc 4-cylinder sleeve-valve engine.

In 1919–20 Paul Panhard modernised the factories, which had 80,000m² floor space and a work force of 6800. The wood-working machine department occupied a fair amount of space, and the aircraft-engine activity was continued with a view to expansion.

For 1920, two additional models joined the range. Type X-31 had a 12CV 2275cc poppet-valve engine in the same chassis as the X-19. The X-29 was a long-wheelbase version of the X-28, with a 4-cylinder 4850cc 20CV sleeve-valve engine. The 10CV X-19 was replaced at the end of 1921 by a new 1190cc sleeve-valve 10CV car named X-37. Its gestation had begun in 1917, only to be shelved and dusted off again in 1920. From then on, all new Panhard cars would have sleeve-valve engines.

Type X-38 was Panhard's first straight-8, conceived as two X-28 4-cylinder engines joined end to end. The twin-carburettor 6350cc engine delivered a true 100hp, and with a sports torpedo body, the 35CV model could reach 87–90mph (140–145km/h). With a standard wheelbase of 148.4in (3766mm), it became the basis for deluxe coachwork by Labourdette, Kellner, Belvallette, Binder, Proux, Janssen, and Driguet.

The model range was rationalised from eight different chassis in 1922 to just five in 1923. The X-35, X-36, X-37 and X-38 continued, with the addition of the X-39, a 2318cc 12CV 4-cylinder with a 3-bearing crankshaft, which replaced the X-31. The following year it evolved into the X-40, while the X-35 20CV was equipped with 4-wheel brakes and renamed X-41. The 35CV model was stretched to 150.4in (3817mm) wheelbase and renamed X-42.

Arriving as a 1925-model, type X-44 had a new chassis with reversed quarter-elliptic springs on the rear axle (under Bugatti licence) and a new 1390cc 4-cylinder engine with the SEV Dynastarter mounted on the front end of the crankshaft, which ran in two main bearings only. The X-44 chassis weighed 1760lb (800kg) and was priced at FRF 25,500. It was also built in X-44 sport and X-44 long versions.

Beginning in 1926, lightweight steel sleeve-valves replaced the old cast-iron type across the full engine range.

Paul Panhard decided to revive the 20CV Sport, using a high-compression 4850cc X-41 engine with a 2-barrel carburettor. It became a favourite with Labourdette and Million-Guiet who had both begun making lightweight fabric-covered bodies under Weymann licence in 1923.

In 1926 Panhard-Levassor took over Delaugère-Clayette, car and truck builders in Orléans, and converted the plant into body manufacturing shops. Most of the Panhard models made in 1927 came with factory-built standard coachwork.

In 1927 the sketches of Louis Bionier, a young engineer who had recently joined the company, came to Paul Panhard's attention, and overnight, he found himself chief body engineer. Bionier turned out to have great stylistic talent, and it was mainly due to his efforts that, beginning in 1930, Panhard traded its poor-relation reticence for up-to-date body design.

One thing the Orléans plant could not do was build cabriolets. Janssen became the preferred provider of soft-top bodywork, although Panhard also continued to collaborate with Vanvooren and Million-Guiet on convertibles.

By 1927 Paul Panhard saw that his cars were growing entirely out of the 4-cylinder market, yet he still wanted to offer a 10CV. Before the end of the year, Gorju and Defly provided him with a 6-cylinder 1830cc 10CV Sport engine that went into the X-59 chassis.

For 1928, the 20CV Sport engine grew in size to 5322cc and was renamed X-56. The X-47 was renamed X-60 but its 4-cylinder 1480cc could not compare with the X-59 for smoothness or performance, and was discontinued in 1929. The same year saw the end of the big 35CV. When the 1931-model line-up was announced, there were no 4-cylinder Panhards.

The new sixes were the work of the old team, but Defly and Schaeffer retired in 1930, followed by Gorju in 1931. Paul Panhard had several candidates who could take over. There was Godillot, a graduate of the École des Arts et Métiers, who had joined the company in 1927 as a project engineer for trucks and buses. Another was Pasquelin, who had done a great job of developing the 20CV engine for speed record runs back in 1925–26, and a third was Delagarde, who had been at Avenue d'Ivry since 1921 and designed trucks, Panhard's diesel engine, and military vehicles. Eventually it was Pasquelin who was named technical director, and held that office until replaced by Jean Panhard in 1937.

The 1931 models were offered with new short-stroke sixes in sizes of 2344cc and 2516cc, and a 5084cc straight-8 had been introduced in 1930. All the 1931 models had lower, lighter frames, and coachwork with the pleasantly rounded lines favoured by Louis Bionier.

The old-generation sixes, 2650cc X-63 and 3450cc X-57, were taken out of production at the end of 1931, leaving only four models in the 1932 line-up: the 3507cc 20CV six (X-66), the 8-cylinder X-67, the 2344cc 13CV X-68 and its 2616cc 14CV derivative, X-69.

Bionier invented a 2-piece windshield pillar with a piece of curved glass, aimed at curing pillar-obstruction of the driver's view. It became standard on the 1934 models, advertised as the Panoramique. The 14CV, 16CV, 23CV, and 27CV versions had the same chassis and body, differing only in the power train. Pasquelin adopted full pressure lubrication and put a harmonic crankshaft balancer on all engines. A free-wheel became optional. The 14CV Panhard was priced above Delahaye's 18CV model, but below Delage and Talbot cars of equivalent power.

Growing steadily bolder, Bionier and Pasquelin developed the Dynamic which made its debut as a 1937 model. Not only was it a radical streamliner with 3-abreast seating front and rear – with the driver in the middle – but it had a unit-construction body shell, with major portions of a conventional frame welded into the structure. Torsion-bar suspension was used front and rear, with ifs and an underslung-worm drive rear axle. It also had dual-circuit hydraulic brakes. The only traditional part of the design was the sleeve-valve engine, of 2516 and 2861cc. The smaller engine was dropped for 1939, and replaced by one of 3834cc.

With the Dynamic, Panhard set itself apart from all other French automakers, revealing itself as progressive as, for instance, Adler in Germany or Lancia in Italy.

French drivers, however they felt about sitting in the middle of the car, did not like having to slide across one of the passenger seats whenever getting in or out, and on the 1939-model Dynamic, the steering wheel was moved to the left, placing the driver next to the door again. Production ended when France mobilised its army in August 1939.

During World War II, the factory maintained truck production at a certain level for the German occupants, and supplied track elements for German tanks. Most of its capacity, however, was dedicated to making gas generators burning wood or charcoal to fuel France's (and in the latter stages of the war, also the Wehrmacht's) road transport fleets.

At all levels, the brains of Panhard-Levassor were oriented towards preparation of the postwar car models. With age, Paul Panhard settled into a mood of resisting change. He wanted to update the Dynamic and continue production of those

1961 Panhard PL17 saloon.
NICK BALDWIN

big cars as if the market would never change. His son Jean, on the other hand, realised that the economics of the car market would be fundamentally different, and felt that the postwar Panhard should be a small economy car with plenty of personality.

The passenger-car drawing office, with a staff including Delagarde and Bionier, was transferred to Tarbes in the Pyrenees in 1939. Here, Louis Delagarde designed a 350cc air-cooled flat-twin engine for a small front-wheel drive car in 1941–43, while Bionier laid down what he saw as the basic principles for a lightweight, streamlined body. Due to the pressure of other business, the project was shelved in 1943.

In 1945 the management of Panhard-Levassor discovered to its dismay that the company had been left out of the Pons Plan for the auto industry, and consequently without any allocation of raw materials.

Paul Panhard planned to get around that obstacle by creating a new car around a Hotchkiss body shell, with a choice of a Panhard-built 2500cc ohv 4-cylinder engine and a 3485cc 20CV Hotchkiss engine.

Jean Panhard had other ideas. He found out that the Aluminium Français prototype designed in 1942–43 by J.A. Grégoire had been offered to H.T. Pigozzi of Simca, but that Fiat (then in majority control of Simca) had vetoed it. He decided to buy the design, which brought the full support of Aluminium Français to bear on the Pons Plan, and secured the requisite supplies for Panhard-Levassor to continue motor vehicle production. The company was thrown together with truck builders Somua and Willème to form the U.F.A. Group (Union Française Automobile).

The AF-Gregoire prototype featured a cast aluminium frame with a 592cc air-cooled flat-twin carried in the front overhang, driving the front wheels via a 4-speed gearbox with fourth overdrive, all-independent suspension with a transverse leaf spring in front and trailing arms with progressive horizontal coil springs at the rear.

J.A. Grégoire was quick to blame Panhard-Levassor for making changes, such as the adoption of an irs with a triple set of torsion bars, and changing the valve gear on his engine from coil springs to torsion bars. He did not know then that the Panhard engineers did not change his design; they merely substituted some of their own, which predated his.

The 350cc Panhard test engine differed fundamentally from Grégoire's in having integral cylinder heads, a built-up roller-bearing crankshaft, and one-piece con-rods. These characteristics went into the production-model Dyna-Panhard.

The idea for the 4-speed gearbox with overdrive top may have been Grégoire's, but the Dyna-Panhard also had the refinement of a fixed-ratio down-gearing between the gearbox and the final drive. Louis Bionier also did not want to accept the risk of cracks, fissures and disintegration that comes with cast-aluminium structural members, and insisted on a pressed-steel platform. Jean Panhard was quick to agree, seeing that the use of steel would lower the cost without adding significantly to the weight. The body was made up of sheet aluminium castings, the stampings supplied by Montupet and the pressings by Facel-Métallion, who assembled the body shell at Colombes. The AF-Grégoire was a 2-door coach, but Bionier's Dyna-Panhard was a 4-door mini-limousine. The final pre-production model was shown at the Paris Salon in October 1946, with a 610cc air-cooled flat-twin which put out 24hp at 4000rpm. The complete car weighed 1210lbs (550kg) and could reach 62mph (100km/h). Production got under way in the spring of 1947, but at such a slow rate that less than 80 cars were completed that year. In 1948, the production total was a modest 1350 units.

Bionier wanted to demonstrate the possibilities of aerodynamics for cars, which had always been on his mind. Back in 1943 he had made a scale model shaped like an aeroplane fuselage. He adapted this shape to the Dyna chassis with the standard 24hp engine. The complete Dynavia prototype weighed 1865lbs (848kg), reached 87.8mph (141.27km/h) on the test track, and would cruise at 62mph (100km/h) with a fuel consumption of 5.6l/100 km.

It was on display at the Salon in 1948, but the public was not told that some of its design elements would become the basis for a future production car.

In 1949 Jean Panhard was named joint managing director, and he engaged André P. Tranié to replace him as technical director. Tranié was then 37 years old, a graduate of the École Polytechnique and a scientist rather than an engineer, with no previous automotive experience.

The 610cc Dyna engine was partly-redesigned in 1949, with the torsion-bar valve springs under cover (they were exposed on earlier engines) and ball-stud-mounted rocker arms. Compression was raised from 6.25:1 to 7.75:1, increasing the output to 28hp at 5000rpm. It went into production in January 1950, and only three months later, the cylinders were bored out from 72 to 79.5mm, raising displacement to 745cc, and the output to 33hp at 5000rpm.

A 2-door cabriolet and a 2-door station wagon were added as 1950 models, along with a 4-door cabrio-coach having a full-length canvas sunroof. Production numbers swelled to 4834 cars in 1949 and 10,014 in 1950.

A sprint model with 2-barrel carburettor, became optional in 1951, rated at 38hp at 5000rpm. A year later, the engine was bored out to 85mm and 851cc, with 38hp standard and 40–42hp in Sprint form. Paul Panhard retired in 1951, and Jean Panhard took over as chairman and managing director. Production peaked in 1951 with 14,219 cars, dropping to 9645 in 1952 and 5964 in 1953.

In 1950 Panhard sold a Dyna licence to Ernst Loof, who built 176 Dyna-Veritas cabriolets over a 3-year period, with bodies by Baur of Stuttgart. The Dyna engine and chassis were also used for the 1952–53 Scarlet made by the Société Industrielle de l'Ouest Parisien, who had introduced the Rosengart Ariette in 1951. The Scarlet shared the Ariette body, but only about 200 units were made.

Small-industry sports car manufacturers with names like Deutsch-Bonnet, Monopole-Poissy, Marathon, Arista and Callista, used the Dyna-Panhard engine and often the complete chassis, in the 1950–53 period.

Panhard-Levassor ended up producing its own roadster/cabriolet, the Dyna Junior, from 1952 to 1956. It came about because Fergus Motors of New York City wanted a low-priced European sports car, and turned to Panhard-Levassor. Jean Panhard discussed the project with the Di Rosa family, owners of the Société Industrielle Aéronautique et Automobile of La Garenne-Colombes, who maintained a regular business of making bus and truck bodies on Panhard chassis. Their designer, Albert Lemaitre, sketched a simple body which Fergus Motors turned down, sending back sketches of American-style ideas. Although Di Rosa built new prototypes, they could do nothing to please Fergus Motors, who withdrew from the project late in 1951.

Jean Panhard decided to bring it to fruition. Albert Lemaitre made new styling suggestions, which Panhard accepted, and placed an order for 500 bodies with Di Rosa. Their shops at La Garenne were fully occupied, so they rented factory space at Saint-Denis, but still failed to meet Panhard's delivery schedule. From early 1952 to late in 1953, 770 Dyna Junior roadsters were assembled. A face-lifted model was introduced in 1953, and 3937 cabriolet models were made up to 1956.

Early in 1952 Louis Bionier had briefed Jean Panhard and A.P. Tranié on his next project: a 6-seater family streamliner propelled by the latest Dyna flat-twin engine. The apparent incompatibility between the power unit and the type of vehicle was imaginary, explained Bionier, producing graphs and figures to prove his point. They told him to go ahead.

The Dyna-54 was announced in July 1953, and Panhard dealers began taking orders for it in October 1953. Production began early in 1954, with the car priced at FFr 699,000. Bionier's design had an evolution of the Dynavia front end, with bumpers, lights, etc to meet legal requirements, and the body was widened to seat three abreast, front and rear, on bench seats, with four doors. The tapered tail end was changed to a practical saloon shape with a spacious trunk styled to repeat the front-end theme. The aerodynamics were developed in collaboration with the Institut Aérotechnique de Saint-Cyr and the Laboratoire Eiffel. The unit-construction body shell was made entirely of Duralinox and weighed only 220lbs (100kg), and kept the weight of the complete car down to 1446.7lbs (657.6kg).

The platform was fabricated from two rectangular-section side members and two tubular cross-members, with a sheet-aluminium floor pan. Bionier wanted the body sides, i.e. the door frames with sills, made as a single stamping. He also specified doors with integral window frames, made as single stampings. The bonnet, integral with the front mudguards, roof, and boot lid were also single stampings. The front bulkhead was fabricated from two stampings, and the rear mudguards were spot-welded to the body sides and rear panel. A.P. Tranié felt that Facel-Métallon did not have the press capacity to make these big parts, and gave the body-construction contract to Chausson, who had.

Delagarde was now getting 42hp at 5000rpm from the 850cc flat-twin. The engine, clutch, gearbox, differential, drive shafts and universal joints had a combined weight of 570.7lbs (259.4 kg). A total of 13,585 cars were produced in 1954, followed by 19,289 in 1955.

All of Jean Panhard's plans came in for sudden annihilation in April 1955, when Citroën purchased a 45 per cent block of shares in Panhard-Levassor and imposed its executive will on every aspect of the activity at Avenue d'Ivry.

The Citroën management ordered a stop to Dyna Junior production, and re-engineered the Dyna-54 body for steel construction. The main structure was changed to steel in May 1956, followed by the bonnet, boot lid and doors in September 1956. Vehicle weight increased to 1826lbs (830kg), production cost was reduced by approximately 15 per cent, and the retail price was cut to FFr 659,000.

Citroën dealers also became Panhard dealers, and car production increased to 25,703 units in 1956, and grew to new proportions (37,991) in 1957. The 50hp (at 6300rpm) 850cc Tigre engine became optional in 1959, raising the car's top speed to 90mph (145km/h). Nevertheless, production was cut back to 24,427 cars in 1959, due to reduced demand.

After a face-lift revealed in July 1959, the car was renamed PL 17 for 1960, and the sales curve climbed again in 1962 to 33,698. A PL 17 station wagon was added for 1963, and the output of the Tigre engine was boosted to 60hp at 5750rpm. The Deutsch-Bonnet partnership had broken up, and a Panhard-CD Gran Turismo streamlined coupé designed by Charles Deutsch was added to the 1963 model line-up.

It was not built on the PL 17 platform, but had a steel-tube backbone frame from the bulkhead to the rear cross-member, with a fabricated aluminium front fork to support the engine and front suspension. The CD coupé bodywork was fibreglass-reinforced plastic. Mario Mordacci, director of Aeromare, installed in a former Aereo-Caproni factory at Trento, and head of Pan Auto s.p.a. planned to produce the CD coupé as well as the PL 17 saloon, cabriolet and station wagon, but the project fizzled out.

In July 1963, Panhard-Levassor announced the PL 24 coupé with a crisp-lined 2-plus-2 body designed by Louis Bionier. It had an all-steel Chausson-built body shell on the PL 17 p1atform, and a choice of the 42hp standard (24 C) and 60hp Tigre (24 CT) engines. The PL 17 was renamed 24 B or 24 BT (according to power unit). But production of the coupé started slowly, and production volume fell to 27,910 units in 1964.

In 1965 Citroën completed its merger with Panhard-Levassor, creating the Société de Construction Mécanique Panhard & Levassor primarily to continue the production of Panhard's range of military vehicles, secondarily to phase out the Panhard passenger cars.

A.P. Tranié resigned, Bionier and Delagarde went into retirement. Panhard car production fell to 11,631 units in 1965, and a catastrophic 3845 in 1966. Pierre Bercot, president of Citroën, ordered a halt to Panhard car production at mid-year, 1967, and the last one – a 24 BT saloon – came off the Ivry assembly line on 20 July 1967.

Chausson's executive engineer Gottmann and Clavrol, chief of the Chausson design studio, appealed to Citroën to make some use of their Panhard bodies. Jacques Né had the brilliant idea of creating a junior SM, putting a twin-ohc 4-cylinder Citroën engine (designed by Becchia) in the 24 CT platform-and-body with suspension elements from the DS. It got as far as a prototype, but no further.

This was not the end for Panhard vehicles, however, as Jean Panhard continued to make armoured cars, since 1973 at a new factory at Marelles en Hurepoix, 22 miles from Paris. By a strange coincidence, this small town was the birthplace of Émile Levassor, 132 years before.

JPN

Further Reading
Panhard. *Le Grand Livre*, Dominique Pagneux, EPA, Paris, 1996.
Toutes les Panhard, René Bellu, published privately.
Panhard, ses voitures d'après guerre, Bernard Vermeylen, ETAI, 1997.
Panhard. La doyenne d'avante garde, Benoit Perot, EPA, 1979.
Panhard, les Premieres Tours de Roue, Benoit Perot, CPC, 1991.
'Dyna Panhard, Evolution and Extinction', John Matras, *Automobile Quarterly*, Vol. 32, No. 1.

PANOZ (US) 1989 to date

Panoz Auto Development, Hoschton, Georgia.
Although perhaps best known for their successful line of endurance racing cars, Panoz also built street sports cars with Ford running gear. The Panoz roadster project was started when Danny Panoz bought the failing TMC Costin sports car project in Ireland. It was re-engineered to take the 5000cc Ford V8 engine and a new, more modern cycle-mudguard roadster body was designed. The first cars were sold in 1992. Ford running gear was used throughout, but at $37,000 sales were slow. The first roadsters had steel space frames with aluminium bodies, but the later Roadster AIV (aluminium intensive vehicle) used an aluminium frame as well. The 5000cc ohv Ford V8 was also replaced with the 4600cc all-aluminium double-ohc 32-valve engine. The Roadster was joined by the more conventional 2000 Panoz Esperante, which made extensive use of aluminium. It had an extruded aluminium chassis with a 2-seat full-mudguarded convertible body using the same running gear as the Roadster.

HP

PANTHER (i) (D) 1902–1904

Panther Fahrradwerke Oskar Vormbaum, Magdeburg.

Bicycle maker Oskar Vorbaum entered car manufacture with a 3-wheeler powered by a De Dion-Bouton engine driving the two rear wheels. He followed this with a 20hp 4-wheeler which also showed bicycle influence in its design. In 1904 Panther was taken over by DÜRKOPP and was integrated into their main factory at Bielefeld.

HON

PANTHER (ii) (GB) 1906–1908

F.M. Russell & Co. Ltd, Willesden, London.

This was an imported car, probably German, according to historian John Pollitt, with a 14hp 4-cylinder engine. Russell also handled another import, the WESTMINSTER.

NG

PANTHER (iii) (US) 1909

Panther Car Co. Inc., Boston, Massachusetts.

This was a very light car weighing only 300lb (136kg) and powered by a 7hp single-cylinder engine. It had no gearbox; drive was direct through a small multi-disc clutch to the differential. The makers promised a top speed of 40mph (64km/h) on the level, and 20mph (32km/h) on a 15 per cent gradient.

NG

PANTHER (iv) (I) 1954–1955

Panther Diesel SpA, Milan.

A surprisingly sophisticated microcar with an intriguing specification, the Panther was unique in several ways. It boasted a twin-cylinder diesel engine of 520cc, plastic bodywork (no other Italian car used plastic in its bodywork at that time) and front-wheel drive, all highly unusual for an Italian car. The first model of 1954 was bodied by Colli and was an attractive looking coupé claiming to offer 50mph (80km/h) and 90mpg. A petrol-engined version was also tried (using an 18bhp 480cc 4-stroke 2-cylinder unit and slightly longer full 4-seater bodywork). A rather prettier Zagato-bodied Panther was another variation in 1955. Licensed production was due to take place in France (by Salmson), Belgium and Argentina, and a company called Industria Sanmarinese Costruzione Automezzi (I.S.C.A.) was formed to manufacture the Panther in the principality of San Marino, but nothing came of any of these projects.

CR

PANTHER (v) (US) 1962–1963

Panther Automobile Co., Bedford Hills, New York.

The Panther was a DEVIN-bodied sports car with a Daimler V8 engine. The standard version had a mildly modified engine while the Model M had a more powerful version. They were built on a tube frame with a 94in (2386mm) wheelbase.

HP

PANTHER (vi) (GB/ROK) 1972–1996

1972–1979 Panther Westwinds Ltd, Walton-on-Thames, Surrey.
1980–1988 Panther Car Co., Weybridge, Surrey.
1988–1992 Panther Car Co., Harlow, Essex.
1992–1996 Panther Car Co., Seoul, Korea.

Run by ex-Superspeed founder Robert Jankel, Panther Westwinds started life with pastiches of bygone classics, but there were plenty of attempts to create something unusual and striking. Jankel consistently claimed that he never built a car unless he already had a buyer for it. His skill in producing what his wealthy customers wanted, and the speed at which he did it was unsurpassed in the industry.

The J72 was Britain's first nostalgia car. Inspired by the prewar SS100, it used a 3.8-litre Jaguar XK engine (later with XJ 4.2 and 5.3 V12 units). The V12 version was a ferocious beast, possibly the fastest-accelerating car then produced, and attracted the custom of the rich and famous (over 430 would eventually be built). The chassis was a traditional-style tubular frame carrying rigid beam front and rear axles (later ifs).

The second Panther was the equally extraordinary Ferrari FF of 1974, created at the request of the Swiss coachbuilder Willy Felber. It had a Ferrari 125S-style body based on, unbelievably, a Ferrari 330 GTC chassis. A square-tube frame

1974 Panther (vi) J72 sports car.
NICK BALDWIN

supported the unstressed aluminium bodywork. Also in 1974 came the Lazer, an extraordinary wedge-shaped 'buggy' which resembled a life-size version of one of the wildest imaginings of a Corgi Matchbox stylist. Ordered by a wealthy Canadian, the Lazer had a lavish specification and was based around Jaguar mechanicals; however, only one was built.

The De Ville is perhaps Panther's most notorious model. Its unrestrained opulence, vaguely Bugatti Royale styling and superb craftsmanship attracted an exclusive clientele, yet it was also widely judged as singularly vulgar. The 4-door saloon was based on a massive ladder chassis, upswept at both ends and cross-braced. The hand-formed aluminium body was supported on a spaceframe superstructure. Mechanically, the De Ville was all Jaguar XJ12 (later also XJ6). In 1976 came the 2-door De Ville Convertible, which then ranked as Britain's most expensive new car.

The concept behind the 1975 Panther Rio was quite sound: to create a small, economical car with the finish and luxury of a Rolls-Royce. Unfortunately, it suffered from comparisons with the car on which it was based, the Triumph Dolomite. Every body panel was reskinned in hand-beaten aluminium, an upright grill fitted and the interior completely retrimmed in leather and burr walnut. It was far too expensive to have much impact and only 32 were made.

Perhaps Panther's most significant model was the 1976 Lima. The recipe was simple: a 1930s-style 2-seater open body on a strengthened Vauxhall Magnum floorpan. In a bid to keep costs down, Panther departed from its normal practice and made the bodywork from non-stressed glassfibre. The Lima was sold through selected Vauxhall dealers, which proved a mixed blessing: sales were strong, but there were problems with dealers not used to selling sports cars. Variants included DTV tuned and 178bhp Turbo versions. Over 900 Limas were made in all.

Of all Jankel's creations, the Panther Six of 1977 was the most over-the-top, for this was a 6-wheeler with four steering front wheels, inspired by the Tyrrell Formula 1 car. The three-seater interior boasted such innovations as a dash-mounted TV, electronic instruments and a radio telephone. The engine was a twin-turbo Cadillac 8.2-litre V8 rated at 600bhp, sited in the middle of the car and Panther claimed a top speed of over 200mph (320km/h). Despite taking orders for 15 cars, only two were ever made.

Over-extended by a plethora of models, cash-flow problems forced Panther into liquidation in 1979, after which it was bought by a Korean financier called Young C. Kim. Jankel stayed on for a short time before departing to concentrate on his conversion business, Robert Jankel Design and the LE MARQUIS marque. J72 and De Ville production was kept going for a few years after the 1979 crash and a revised J72 model, the 2+2-seater Brooklands, was launched in 1981.

The Lima was then re-engineered to accept Ford parts and the resulting Kallista was the most popular Panther ever. All-Ford components were used, including Cortina double-wishbone front suspension and a Capri live rear axle. The revised bodywork was now in aluminium rather than glassfibre and was made in Korea alongside the chassis. Two Ford engines were offered initially: the 1.6-litre XR3 unit and the 2.8-litre V6.

In 1987, Kim sold 80 percent of Panther's assets to the Korean industrial giant SsangYong, which invested its energies into the Solo, a brave supercar attempt. Conceived as a low-priced mid-engined coupé, the first prototype Solo was shown at the 1984 London Motor Show with a 1.6-litre Ford Sierra engine.

1977 Panther (vi) Six convertible.
NICK BALDWIN

1986 Panther (vi) Kallista sports car.
NICK BALDWIN

1987 Panther (vi) Solo coupé.
NICK BALDWIN

Its attractive 2-seater bodywork was styled by Ken Greenley and John Heffernan, while the chassis was the work of Ford GT40 man Len Bailey. The Solo project was redirected up-market and after a six-year gestation period, the Solo 2 was launched, sporting heavily reworked and lengthened composite bodywork. The monocoque aluminium-and-carbon-fibre chassis, completely re-engineered by John Canvin, was fitted with the Ford Sierra Cosworth 2.0-litre turbo unit and Ferguson 4-wheel drive, making it the world's only mid-engined 4-wheel drive production car. There was also now nominal 2+2 seating. But it was uneconomic to make and, after one of the shortest production runs ever, the Solo was axed with just 12 cars sold.

UK production of the Kallista ceased in 1990 after a run of 1733 cars, but the Korean parent company restarted production in 1992 in South Korea with lightly revised models fitted with the latest 2.0-litre and 2.9-litre Ford engines. After a production run of 60 aluminium-bodied cars, a new glassfibre Kallista was launched in 1994, but vanished soon after. SsangYong itself was later taken over by DAEWOO.

CR

Further Reading
Panther, the Inside Story, Bruce Powell, Academy Books, 1995.

PANTHÈRE (F) 1922–1923
Automobiles Panthère, Paris.
Assembled in the Boulevard de Grenelle, the Panthère was a light car powered by a 904cc 4-cylinder Ruby engine, with 3-speed gearbox and shaft drive.
NG

PANTZ (F) 1900–1901
Charles Pantz, Pont-à-Mousson, Meurthe et Moselle.
Pantz introduced a 30cwt truck in 1899, and a year later a car on the same lines. The design incorporated a horizontal 2-cylinder engine of 6 or 9hp, tiller steering and transmission by fast-and-loose pulleys giving four forward and two reverse speeds. Pantz' commercial vehicles outlived the cars, being made up to 1907.
NG

PAQUOTTE (F) 1984 to date

Jean-Claude Paquotte, Marseilles.

Artist Jean-Claude Paquotte built a handful of very unusual fish-shaped Citroën-based sports cars, all inspired by the memory of actor James Dean. Paquotte's first car, the Syndrome Dean, was built around the engine and underpinnings of the Citroën DS, a car that was launched the same day James Dean died. Standing less than one metre high, the front-engined Syndrome Dean had four seats and gull-wing doors. Paquotte's next creation was the Luco Dean, an unusual 2-seat roadster using Citroën GS power. This was followed by the 1998 Jamyx prototype, a 2CV-based 2-seater using the small Citroën's rear wings as front wings, and front wings as rear panels.

CR

PARABUG (GB) 1971–1978

North East Fibreglass Ltd, Tullos, Aberdeen.

Made by a boat builder, the Parabug was a jeep-style kit car intended for a VW Beetle floorpan. The fibreglass body was rigidly square in design and featured stressed panels and a fold-flat windscreen which fixed by magnets.

CR

PARAGON (i) (US) 1906

Paragon Automobile Manufacturing Co., Detroit, Michigan.

This 2-seater runabout was almost identical to the LA PETITE, which J.P. La Vigne had designed for the Detroit company before his departure. The wheelbase was increased from 65 to 68in (1650 to 1726mm), but the same 5hp single-cylinder 2-stroke engine and epicyclic transmission were used, and the $375 price tag was unchanged. Later in the year a 2-cylinder engine was substituted, but the make was not continued into 1907.

NG

PARAGON (ii) (GB) 1913–1914

K. Portway & Co., Manningtree, Essex.

This was a typical cyclecar with JAP or Fafnir engines, air- or water-cooled, with belt drive. Few were made, but the company had a little more success with motorcycles after the war. At one time in 1920 they were making six per week, but were out of business by the end of the year.

NG

PARAGON (iii) (US) 1920–1921

Paragon Motor Car Co., Connellsville, Pennsylvania.

The Paragon was widely promoted toward 1920 and introduced at the Cleveland Automobile Show in February 1921, where a roadster and a touring car were exhibited, both priced at $3000. It was a 4-cylinder car featuring its own design which developed 60bhp at 3600rpm, a wheelbase of 122in (3096mm) and wire wheels which would be available optionally at no further cost. The Paragon also sported a radiator shaped like that of the Packard with the name 'Paragon' embossed on the shell plus a special patented prismatic windshield. An additional four prototypes were under construction when the car's expected backers in Connellsville unexpectedly backed out of the venture.

Shortly afterwards a group in Cumberland, Maryland, expressed interest in continuing the project and, toward this goal, an additional three pilot models were constructed. Unfortunately, the Cumberland group interested in projecting the car decided against continuing it and Paragon, without any financial backing, no factory, and most of its plans still on paper, went out of business.

KM

PARAMOUNT (i) (US) 1923–1924

Paramount Motors Corp., Azusa, California.

The Paramount automobile, although something of a novelty, was heralded as a car which could be either an open or closed model depending on the whim of the owner. With a chassis of 112in (2843mm) and a motorcycle-type air-cooled engine, the 'All Weather' model was priced at $750. Grandiose plans on the part of Paramount's backers came to little apart from a handful of prototype models and Paramount was out of business before the end of 1924.

KM

1913 Paragon (ii) belt-drive cyclecar.
NATIONAL MOTOR MUSEUM

PARAMOUNT (ii) (US) 1927–1931

Paramount Cab Manufacturing Co., New York, New York.

Although the Paramount was exclusively restricted to the manufacture of taxicabs, a few of them were conservatively painted and marketed for personal use as an adjunct line by at least two dealers whose franchises with other makes augmented them.

The Paramount Cab, despite its advertised 'Manufacturing Company' in New York City, was in fact one of the many cabs manufactured by the M.P. Möller Motor Car Co. of Hagerstown, Maryland, which was winding up its manufacture of the sporting Dagmar automobiles at the time of the Paramount's introduction. The first Paramount cabs were equipped with Buda 4-cylinder engines but these were supplanted by various 6-cylinder types from other makes after 1927.

Although Paramount offered both a sedan and town car styles, as far as can be determined only the sedan was sold privately at $2475. After Locomobile failed in March 1929, Paramount Cab rented space in one of its factories for servicing and repair.

KM

PARAMOUNT (iii) (GB) 1950–1956

1950–1952 Paramount Cars (Derbyshire) Ltd, Swadlincote, Melbourne, Derbyshire.
1952–1953 Meynell Motor Co. Ltd, Swadlincote, Melbourne, Derbyshire.
1953–1956 Paramount Cars (Leighton Buzzard) Ltd, Linslade, Buckinghamshire.

The Paramount, first shown in 1949, had a tubular steel underslung chassis and an aluminium convertible body on an ash frame. It was a bulbous car from the Austin A90 Atlantic school of design, but was spacious and well-detailed with reasonable luggage space and a particularly well-designed hood arrangement.

The prototype had Alvis running gear, which would have made the car prohibitively expensive so it was offered for sale with Ford Ten mechanicals instead. This meant that performance was mediocre but, on the other hand, new cars were scarce and the Paramount well-made, well-equipped and keenly priced.

Two- and 4-seater versions were offered, but it seems that only the latter was made. It was probably the best, and most practical, 4-seat convertible within its price band. Had it reached serious production in 1950, it would probably have been a success, but the original makers spent too long trying to perfect the design instead of modifying it on the run.

By the end of 1951 it had passed to a separate, but related, company which modified the body style in detail, but few were made. This second company

1956 Paramount (iii) 1½-litre tourer.
NICK GEORGANO/NATIONAL MOTOR MUSEUM

1900 Parisienne Victoria Combination voiturette.
NATIONAL MOTOR MUSEUM

1901 Parr 5hp tonneau.
NATIONAL MOTOR MUSEUM

essayed a very pretty 2-seat sports car, which looked like a Frazer Nash Targa Florio with a BMW grill, but this remained a prototype.

At the beginning of 1953 the original passed to a third company, Camden Cars Ltd, and production moved to Leighton Buzzard, but the price had risen and Paramount had to compete with more modern, and cheaper, cars at a time when restrictions on supply of new cars to the home market had been lifted. Some cars had Shorrock or Wade superchargers and in 1954 the 1.5-litre ohv Ford Consul unit was an option but, by then, Ford was marketing its own convertibles. The Paramount, with a Consul engine, cost £1009 while the Consul convertible cost £808; and out-performed it in every important area.

The company folded in 1956 and the stock passed to another firm which sold off the surplus of 26 cars at knock-down prices. A few chassis passed to another

company which fitted proprietary bodies, usually a Rochdale fibreglass shell. Total production of Paramounts was 72 cars.

MJL

PARANT (F) 1906–1907
Parant Frères, Neuilly, Seine.
Announced in December 1906, the Parant tourer had a 16/20hp 4-cylinder Ballot engine, a metal-to-metal clutch inside the flywheel, 3-speed gearbox and chain final drive.

NG

PARENT (F) 1913–1914
Paul Faitot (Automobiles Parent), Maisons-Alfort, Seine.
The Parent was made in two models, one with a large single-cylinder engine of 704cc, the other with a 905cc four. Both models were shaft-driven and had pointed radiators. The make was listed in *l'Annuaire Général de l'Automobile* for 1921, but nothing is known of the postwar cars, and they may never have existed.

NG

PARENTI (US) 1920–1922
Parenti Motors Corp., Buffalo, New York.
The Parenti was unique among its peers for several reasons. It featured a V8 air-cooled engine of its own design. It was designed without axles, transverse springing being used as a substitute – two springs located in the front and one in the rear. Haskelite plywood was used not only in the frame and body but in the car's disc wheels as well. And to attract the public, a handful of the earlier cars were painted in yellow, bright orange, and purple. The Parenti featured several body types, including a touring car, a sedan, and a limousine, the latter priced at $5000. The Parenti operation was plagued by continuous financial difficulties and in 1921 it sued Adria for a patent infringement (an interesting point: both Parenti and Adria would be out of business within weeks of each other). The air-cooled 8-cylinder engine was scrapped in favour of a Falls water-cooled six for 1922 which also saw the plywood design supplanted by a steel frame and aluminium body. The changes were to no avail. According to historian Beverly Rae Kimes, Parenti 'production' numbered 18 cars.

KM

PARENT-LACROIX (F) c.1901–c.1903
Parent et Lacroix, Villefranche, Rhône.
This company made voiturettes designed by Petrus Lacroix, but no details are known.

NG

PARISIA *see* OWEN (i)

PARISIENNE (F) 1899–1903
Sté Parisienne E. Couturier et Cie, Paris.
This company made bicycles and tricycles, as well as the very light front-wheel drive voiturette known as the Victoria Combination or Eureka. The engine, 2.75hp De Dion-Bouton or 3.5hp Aster, was mounted between the front wheels and drove the front axle. The whole power system, engine, transmission, axle and wheels turned with the steering, which was by tiller. The body was a very simple 2-seater without weather protection, although they were also sold with small box-van bodies. Some of the bodies were made by Belvalette who later did rather more substantial work on chassis such as Hispano-Suiza and Panhard. Despite a reputation for flimsiness, a Parisienne averaged 18mph (29km/h) over a 150-mile trial, with no involuntary stops. More than 400 were made. The manufacturers also made larger and more conventional cars with 5 or 6.5hp Aster engines and shaft drive. They were known as the Duc-Spider with two seats, and Duc-Tonneau in 4-seater form.

NG

PARIS-RHÔNE (F) 1942–1944
Éts Paris-Rhône, Lyons.
This was one of the smallest of the electric cars made in wartime France, a 3-wheeler powered by a 1.8kW (about 2hp) motor driving the rear wheels. The original model VPR, sometimes known as the Baby-Rhône, had a doorless

1990 Parradine V12 sports car.

PARRADINE

2-seater body with a single headlamp above the front wheel, and was also made as a light truck. The improved VPR-2 was an enclosed coupé with twin headlamps. The bodies were made by Faurax et Chaussende, well-known for buses and coaches, and whose premises were less than a mile from the Paris-Rhône works, whose main business was in electrical equipment. About 50–60 were made; although one was registered in 1946, it is not thought that they were still being built then.

NG

PARIS SINGER (GB) 1900
Paris Singer Ltd, Clapham, London.
Paris Singer was one of the sons of the sewing machine pioneer, Isaac Merritt Singer, who named his children after the cities of their birth. His car was a 2-seater powered by a 4½hp 2-cylinder engine placed horizontally under the seat, and driving by chains. It was described as being 'as noiseless as many electric vehicles', but it did not go into production.

NG

PARKER (i) (GB) 1901–1902
Thomas H. Parker, Wearwell Motor Co., Wolverhampton, Staffordshire.
Thomas Parker was a versatile inventor who designed the Bushbury Electric Cart, a 3-wheeler steered by reins which used components made by the Star Cycle Co. of Wolverhampton, which later made STARLING and STUART light cars. The Bushbury was built in 1897, and four years later Parker built a steam car with a flash boiler under the bonnet, a 10hp compound 2-cylinder engine and shaft drive. Resembling a contemporary DAIMLER, it was built in the Wearwell factory, where WEARWELL cars and Wolf motorcycles were made.

NG

PARKER (ii) (CDN) 1922–1923
Parker Motor Car Co. Ltd, Montreal, Québec.
Built in the former FORSTER plant, the Parker was based on the American BIRMINGHAM. Originally it was to have used the Birmingham's Wright-Fisher suspension, but when Birmingham set up a Canadian factory the Parker directors were forced to think again. The Parker which appeared in the Spring of 1922 had conventional semi-elliptic suspension, but it did share the American car's Haskelite body. This consisted of quarter-inch plywood sheets on a hardwood frame, glued and screwed together and covered with Fabrikoid.

The engine was a Continental six, and the car sold for a hefty $3675. Fewer than 10 Parkers were made, mostly with sedan bodies.

NG

PARKIN (US) 1908
Parkin & Son, Philiidelphia, Pennsylvania.
This was a 6-cylinder, 60hp car that cost more than £3000. One source claims it was made as early as 1903, but there is little evidence of this.

NG

PARNACOTT (GB) 1912–1913;1920
A.E. Parnacott, Penge, London.
Mr Parnacott was unlucky with his cars, building two prototypes, one just before World War I and the other shortly after it, but did not succeed in getting either into production. His 1913 car had a 3½hp 4-cylinder air-cooled F.N. motorcycle engine mounted transversely, and all-round independent suspension by transverse leaf springs which took the place of axles. He priced his chain-driven Cycar at £95, and invited financial interest in his enterprise. Apparently none was forthcoming. His postwar design was more powerful, with a 1478cc flat-twin engine, all-independent suspension and shaft drive. A price of £300 was quoted.

NG

PARR (GB) 1901–1902
J. Parr & Co. Ltd, Leicester.
The Parr light car used a 5hp single-cylinder engine of the company's own manufacture, with double-chain drive. It had a comfortable front seat for two passengers, and a rather cramped rear-entrance tonneau for a further two. Though they were not made for long, it was said that a number of them were still about in Leicester in 1912.

NG

PARRADINE (GB) 1987–1991; 1998 to date
1987–1991 Parradine Motor Co. plc, Appleby, South Humberside.
1998 to date J.J.R. Automotive Ltd, Thealby, Scunthorpe, Yorkshire.
Having produced the DELTAYN Proteus for a number of years, John Parradine approached stylist Richard Oakes to design a new open sports car to be called the Pegasus V12. This was billed as a modern re-interpretation of the A.C. Cobra and

1912 (New) Parry Model 51 roadster.
NICK BALDWIN

boasted extremely strong performance. A space frame chassis accepted Jaguar running gear and V12 power. After discussions with Jaguar to supply new parts, a lightly restyled Pegasus was launched at the 1990 Geneva Salon, offered in fully-built form at prices from £90,000. The company was due to relocate to France with the guarantee of government finance but that did not materialise and a total of only 25 examples of the Pegasus were built. In 1998 the project was set for relaunch under the name Parradine V8S, this time with a Ford 4.6-litre Quad Cam supercharged V8 engine. The production run was to be limited to 50 cars. A price of £110,000 was quoted at the end of 1999. In 1999 details of an all-new model were released, the 525S. This was a very highly-specified 2-seater roadster powered by a 525bhp 4.6-litre V8 engine and 6-speed gearbox. Composite bodywork clothed the spaceframe chassis, while the interior featured race instrumentation and LCD screens for rear-view cameras, which were mounted in the doors.

CR

PARR-EAGLE (GB) 1919

The Parr-Eagle was a cyclecar powered by an unconventional 500cc V4 2-stroke engine with sleeve-valves. Transmission was by friction discs, it had an Austin Seven-like A-frame and front-wheel brakes, the latter unknown on such a small car in 1919. It all sounds too good to be true, and perhaps it was, for after a glowing description in *The Motor Cycle* in May 1919, in which the reporter looked forward to trying one of the experimental chassis which were to be produced during the summer, no more was heard of the Parr-Eagle.

NG

PARRY; NEW PARRY (US) 1910–1912

1910 Parry Auto Co., Indianapolis, Indiana.
1911–1912 Motor Car Manufacturing Co., Indianapolis, Indiana.
The Parry Manufacturing company were large-scale makers of horse-drawn carriages in the 1890s, when David Parry built his first experimental car. It was not a success, and he had no further involvement with motor vehicles until July 1909 when he set up the Parry Auto Co. with a workforce of 389 men. The first cars were ready for the 1910 season, when he hoped to make 5000, although actual output was very much less, about 900. They were conventional cars, a 4-seater runabout with 35hp 4-cylinder engine, and a 40hp 5-seater tourer. For 1911 and 1912 they were called New Parry, although there was very little difference apart from a wider range of bodies and slightly higher prices. There was a short-lived smaller model, the 25hp Bulldog Gentleman's Roadster which sold for $900 in 1911, while other New Parrys were in the $1350–1750 range. Lack of working capital put David Parry into receivership in 1910, and new management came in who changed the name to the Motor Car Manufacturing Co. In 1912 they introduced a new car, the PATHFINDER, though the New Parry was made alongside it for a year.

NG

PARSONS (US) 1906

Parsons Electric Motor Carriage Co., Cleveland, Ohio.
John G. Parsons' first electric vehicle was a 5½ cwt panel delivery van introduced in January 1906. A month later came a 2-seater stanhope with 8hp Elwell-Parker engine, a 4-speed transmission and double-chain drive. The frame was a combined wood and steel structure. The $1600 stanhope did not survive the year of its introduction.

NG

PARTIN; PARTIN-PALMER (US) 1913–1917

1913–1915 Partin-Palmer Manufacturing Co., Chicago, Illinois.
1915–1917 Commonwealth Motors Co., Chicago; Rochelle, Illinois.
This company was formed from the merger of the Partin Manufacturing Co., a sales organisation, despite having 'manufacturing' in its name, and the Palmer Motor Car Co. which had built a prototype 4-cylinder car. They planned to build a three-car range, a cyclecar to be called the PIONEER (iii), a 45hp tourer to be called the Partin, and a 38hp tourer called the Partin-Palmer. The Pioneer lasted only a year and the Partin became part of the Partin-Palmer range during 1913 and was dropped for 1914. The 38, which used a Mason engine, was continued into 1915, with only one body style, a 6-seater tourer. It was joined in 1915 by a smaller car powered by a 20hp Lycoming engine, and in 1916 they added the Model 8-45 with 45hp V8 engine. This model did not survive a move to Rochelle, where two fours, of 20 and 32hp, were made up to the summer of 1917. The name was then changed to COMMONWEALTH.

NG

PARVILLE (F) 1927–c.1929

Édouard Parville, Paris.
This was a light electric car with 5hp motor, five forward speeds and front-wheel drive.

NG

PASCAL (F) 1902–1903

Automobiles Pascal, Paris.
The Pascal was a large car powered by a 24hp 4-cylinder engine, with chain drive and 4-seater tonneau body. It was built in the BARDON factory for Baron Henri de Rothschild, a doctor who gave his services free of charge to Paris hospitals under the pseudonym Dr Pascal. It was offered on the British market for £860, and there was a rumour that the name would be changed to *Le Roi Soleil* after a famous race horse owned by the Baron. However, it was still called the Pascal at the 1903 Paris Salon, after which it faded from view.

NG

PASHLEY (GB) 1953–1957

W.R. Pashley, Birmingham.
The first Pashleys, produced from 1950, were light 3-wheeled delivery trucks and ice cream 'stop-me-and-buy-ones'. In 1953, the company turned its attention to the Pelican, a commercial vehicle that was also available as a rickshaw-type passenger vehicle. This was another 3-wheeler but this time with the motorcycle-style single wheel at the front. The driver sat astride the vehicle, just as in a motorcycle, with doorless rickshaw-type bodywork to the rear (made of transparent fibreglass!) carrying two rows of conventionally seated passengers. A 600cc JAP 4-stroke engine was used. More significant was a conventional 3-wheeler along the lines of the Bond Minicar, also launched in 1953. This had a welded steel chassis and a light alloy open, doorless body. The 197cc Villers 2-stroke engine and transmission were mounted, Bond-style, with the front wheel. Light vehicle production ceased in 1957 but the company continued to produce bicycles and tricycles.

CR

PASING (D) 1902–1904

Automobilwerk Pasing Albert Regensteiner, Pasing.
This light car bore some resemblance to the AAG or KLINGENBERG, having a single-cylinder combined engine and gearbox integral with the rear axle.

HON

PASQUALI (I) 1998 to date

Pasquali Macchine Agricole srl, Calenzano, Florence.
From the makers of agricultural machinery came the Risciò (Rickshaw), a very small electrically powered 3-wheeled city vehicle. It used four 6V batteries, had a top speed of 25mph (40km/h) and was claimed to have a range of 50km. It had a single rear wheel and single front headlamp and was available in two versions: a single-seater requiring no driving licence and a 2-seater for which a licence was needed.

CR

PASQUINI (I) 1976–1980

Studio Paolo Pasquini, Bologna.

This was very small 2-seater economy car, sold under the name Pasquini Valentine. A 251cc 12bhp 2-cylinder engine was standard, with a 246cc for export and 48cc and 125cc versions for 16-year olds without a driving licence. In all cases the engine drove the front wheels via a single-speed transmission. A steel tube roll-cage-cum-chassis was fitted with a removable front subframe carrying the engine, steering and MacPherson strut front suspension. The enclosed 2-seater bodywork was made of plastic. For Italy a 3-wheeled version was built, though a 4-wheeled model was made for export.

CR

PASSE PARTOUT see REYROL

PASSONI (I) 1905

Maurizio Passoni showed a voiturette with tubular frame and cycle-type wire wheels at the 1905 Turin Show, but it remained a prototype.

NG

PASSY-THELLIER (F) 1903–1907

Sté Passy-Thellier, Levallois-Perret, Seine.

This company launched a range of conventional cars in 1903, powered by 2-cylinder Aster engines of 8/10 and 10/12hp, and fours by Abeille (12/14hp) and Aster (16/20hp). All were shaft-driven. Later in the year a 24hp 4-cylinder Buchet-engine chassis was added. This range was continued throughout the company's life, with the addition of a 6/8hp single-cylinder voiturette in 1906. The cars sometimes went under the name Mendelssohn, after one of the directors, E.G. Mendelssohn-Bartholdy, of the same family as the composer Felix Mendelssohn-Bartholdy.

NG

PASTICHE see NG and MIDAS

PATERSON (US) 1909–1923

W.A. Paterson Co., Flint, Michigan.

This company was formed by Canadian-born William A. Paterson. He began making carriages and buggies in 1869 and built a prototype car in 1907. His first production car was a typical 2-cylinder motor buggy, but in 1910 he brought out a conventional 30hp 4-cylinder tourer, and buggy production ended. The Model 30 was continued through 1912, joined by a 45hp that year, and from 1913 larger engines were used, of 40 and 45hp. The 1911 range consisted of six body styles, all open (Paterson did not list a sedan until 1918), but two years later this had shrunk to one or two styles on each chassis. Continental 6-cylinder engines were added in 1915, and for the rest of the make's life were standard. There was nothing remarkable about the Paterson, but it had a good reputation for quality. They had at least one dealer in each of the 48 states, and also enjoyed some export sales. A Dutch catalogue issued in 1919 described the Paterson as 'The Rolls-Royce of American cars'; this was the only sentence in English in the catalogue.

Annual production rose steadily to reach a peak of just over 2000 in 1920, then fell back to 1483 in 1921, 906 in 1922 and 562 in 1923. Competition from the mass producers was just too much for the Paterson, as it was for so many comparable makes.

NG

PATHFINDER (US) 1912–1917

1912–1916 Motor Car Manufacturing Co., Indianapolis, Indiana.
1916–1917 The Pathfinder Co., Indianapolis, Indiana.

The Pathfinder was a successor to the NEW PARRY, a one-year re-christening of the PARRY; the Motor Car Manufacturing Co. was a reorganisation of the Parry Automobile Co. after its 1910 receivership. The new model Pathfinder, a $1750 car competing against Hudson and Cadillac, was introduced in 1912. High style and colour were the principal concerns of the company, although its slogan said the car was 'known for reliability'. Its selection for highway survey work by the US Office of Public Roads and the American Automobile Association was apropos its name, although adverts boasting it to be the 'official car of the US Government' were somewhat over the top.

1999 Pasquali Riscio electric coupé.
NICK GEORGANO

1910 Paterson Model 30 tourer.
NICK BALDWIN

1913 Paterson 40hp tourer.
JOHN A. CONDE

The initial Pathfinder was the Series XII, a 40hp 4-cylinder car on a 118in (2995mm) wheelbase. Power was supplied by a 4607cc side-valve Continental Red Seal engine, driving through a leather-faced cone clutch, Brown-Lipe 3-speed gearbox and torque tube. Offerings included a Model A tourer, Model B phaeton,

1919 Paterson Model 6-45 tourer.
MICHAEL WORTHINGTON-WILLIAMS

1912 Pathfinder Cruiser roadster.
NICK BALDWIN

1916 Pathfinder Twin Six V12 tourer.
MICHAEL WORTHINGTON-WILLIAMS

Model C 'armoured roadster' and the stately Model D Martha Washington coach. The next year's Series XIII added a Model E cruiser and a delivery wagon. A 6-cylinder car, the Leather Stocking tourer on a 134in (3401mm) wheelbase, was introduced in 1914. With a massive 6910cc Continental side-valve engine, it sold for $2750, a decidedly upmarket move. The veed radiators of the sixes added to the cachet of the already stylish cars. Two sizes of sixes became available for 1915, and the 4 was dropped; that year's imaginative name was the Daniel Boone tourer, in the 5705cc 34hp 6-cylinder line, built on a 124in (3147mm) wheelbase.

Pathfinder's pinnacle was the 12-cylinder Pathfinder the Great, King of Twelves, which bowed in 1916. The Weidely-built engine, a 60-degree ohv unit of 6393cc, developed 60hp; models included a LaSalle tourer and a Cloverleaf roadster. For 1917, the 6-cylinder cars were discontinued and a pair of touring roadsters replaced the LaSalle and Cloverleaf. These cars had a novel 'bustle' rear, which

provided storage for the hood when lowered and an ingenious locker underneath for two spare tyres. The company was renamed Pathfinder that year, after the car, but materials shortages brought on by World War I soon curtailed production. A rumoured merger with EMPIRE (iii) did not come about, and the assets of the company were sold in December 1917.

KF

Further Reading
'The Pathfinder, Indiana's Aspiring Aristocrat', John Katz,
Automobile Quarterly, Vol. 25, No. 3.

PATIN (F) 1899–1900
Compagnie Électrique O. Patin, Paris.
Although short-lived, this company made a variety of electric vehicles, from a light tandem 2-seater to a heavy-looking 5-seater victoria with artillery wheels. There was also a 3-wheeler with a motor driving the single front wheel, called the Patin et Réquillard. The company was dissolved in December 1900.

NG

PATRI (F) 1923–1925
Éts Patri, Paris.
This company made a 5hp 2-cylinder cyclecar called La Forinette, and a larger car powered by a 1095cc 4-cylinder ohv Chapuis-Dornier engine.

NG

PATRIA (i) (D) 1899–1901
Weyersburg, Kirchner & Co., AG. Solingen.
This manufacturer of bicycles, tricycles and quadricycles turned to cars with a voiturette powered by a single-cylinder proprietary engine. Very few were made.

HON

PATRIA (ii) (E) 1920–1921
Fábrica Nacional de Motocicletas, Sidecares y Bicicletas Patria, Badalona.
Specialist in motorcycles and bikes Patria decided to enter the passenger car market with a magnificent 4-cylinder 1500cc sports car called the Grand Sport. It had ohc, aluminium pistons, and a 4-speed gearbox; together with French Perrot brakes. Speed was about 70mph (113km/h). The company wanted to offer a 2000cc engine good for 85mph (137km/h) and a new 6HP with different car bodies, but only a few of the Grand Sport were definitely built.

VCM

PATTERSON-GREENFIELD (US) 1916–1919
C.R. Patterson & Sons, Greenfield, Ohio.
C.R. Patterson was born into slavery in Virginia in 1833, and as a free man moved to Ohio in 1865 where he became a blacksmith and later set up a carriage works which was flourishing by the turn of the century. His son Fred may have built a car in 1902, but the family did not go into production until 1916, when they launched a conventional tourer and roadster powered by a 30hp 4-cylinder Continental engine. It was the first car to be built in Highland County, and the only known make to be run by an African-American family. Fred's son Postell estimated production over three years to have been about 150 cars, though other sources quote as few as 30. The company abandoned cars in favour of commercial vehicle bodywork in 1919, and continued in this field making buses, hearses, bakery and milk delivery vans up to 1939.

NG

PAUL BANHAM (GB) 1994 to date
Paul Banham Conversions, Rochester, Kent.
Paul Banham was a prodigious producer of budget kit-form replicas. His first offering was the 130 Spyder, a body conversion for the Skoda Estelle that was made to look like a Porsche 550 Spyder. Also on offer was the Sprint (a Mini-based replica of the Austin-Healey 'Frogeye' Sprite), the XJSS (a Jaguar XJS rebodying exercise), the Redina (an open-topped body conversion for the Skoda Rapide), the PB200 (Ford RS200 replica) and the X99 (an Audi TT lookalike based on Rover Metro mechanicals).

CR

PAULET *see* LÉON PAULET

PAWI (D) 1921

Paul Victor Wilkem, Berlin-Reinickendorf.

The Pawi was a light car powered by a 1598cc 6/18PS 4-cylinder engine, with a 4-seater tourer body. The company was better-known for light vans for urban deliveries. They also made motorcycles between 1923 and 1925.

HON

PAWTUCKET (US) 1901–1902

Pawtucket Steamboat Co., Pawtucket, Rhode Island.

As its name implies, this company was primarily involved in marine work, but they announced a heavy steam carriage powered by a 7hp double-acting engine with vertical tubular boiler and solid tyres. It was designed by James A. Moncrief, and is sometimes listed under his name. The first, built by Moncrief privately with components supplied by Pawtucket before he joined the firm, weighed 1700lb (773kg), but subsequent models were lighter at 800 and 1100lb (364 and 500kg).

NG

PAX (F) 1907–1909

Automobiles Pax, Suresnes, Seine.

The Pax was offered in two models, both with 4-cylinder engines of 10/15 or 16/20hp, with 3-speed gearboxes and shaft drive. Body styles included tourer, limousine, landaulet and delivery van, but probably more were used as taxicabs than as any other type. About 200 were in service in Paris in the summer of 1908. The engine castings were made by Piat et Cie, who had made a cumbersome steam wagon at the turn of the century.

NG

PAXTON (i) (US) 1951–1954

Paxton, div. McCulloch Motors, Los Angeles, California.

Robert Paxton McCulloch started the Paxton division of his chainsaw company to develop new products for the automotive industry. Although it would later gain fame as a manufacturer of superchargers, in 1951 Paxton began development of a luxury coupé with radical power packages that was intended to sell in the $10,000 range. The unusually sculpted body was designed by renowned stylist Brooks Stevens, and steam car pioneer Abner Doble was hired to develop a steam power plant. It was a 4-cylinder, 8-piston compound engine with a steam generator. Paxton also considered a 2-cycle, horizontally opposed, 3-cylinder engine with 6 opposed firing pistons. It was lightweight, air cooled and supercharged with a power output of 150 to 200hp. The prototype body was a convertible with a retractable hard-top that lay on top of the boot area. It was powered by a Porsche 1500 engine while the Paxton engines were being developed. The project was shelved in 1954 due to high development costs and time constraints.

HP

PAXTON (ii) (US) c.1995

Paxton Products, Camarillo, California.

The Granatelli Signature Series Z-28 was a supercharged Camaro with upgraded brakes, suspension and custom body panels. The prototype had a 6-speed transmission with 435hp with a top speed of 185mph (298km/h). They were sold fully assembled on a new Z-28 for $26,995 in 1995, or a kit was sold for $10,000.

HP

PAYDELL (GB) 1924

Paydell Engineering Co., Hendon, London.

Countless small firms launched light cars and cyclecars in the 1920s, but the Paydell was rather more substantial with a 2120cc 4-cylinder ohv Meadows engine in unit with a 4-speed gearbox, also by Meadows. The chassis price was £450 and a complete car cost £575 so they were seriously undercut by firms like Morris. Probably no more than prototypes were made.

NG

PAYNE & BATES (GB) 1898–1902

Payne & Bates, Coventry.

1899 Patria (i) voiturette.
HANS-OTTO NEUBAUER

1900 Payne & Bates 6-seater *dos-à-dos*.
NATIONAL MOTOR MUSEUM

This company was an offshoot of the Godiva Engineering Co. of Coventry, which had been founded in about 1890 to make gas engines and, from 1893, Payne's Oil Engine. In 1897 Walter Samuel Payne was joined by George Bates who invested additional capital, and a new company was formed, Payne & Bates, Steam and Oil Engineers. The following year they made a car closely based on the single-cylinder BENZ Velo. A few of these were built, with bodies by Hawkins & Peake of Coventry or Arthur Mulliner of Northampton, followed by a more individual design with 2-cylinder engine of Payne and Bates' own manufacture. These were rear-engined, but in 1900 they brought out a car with a front-mounted vertical-twin engine, double-chain drive and a 4-seater tonneau or *dos-à-dos* body. They were now making their own bodies.

Some cars were sold under the name Godiva, but Payne and Bates also sold cars to R.M. Wright of Lincoln who marketed them under the name Stonebow, and to the International Motor Co. of London who sold them as the Royal. In 1901 Payne & Bates advertised that they were making cars of 7, 9, 14 and 25hp, with 2- or 4-cylinder engines, but the larger cars were never built. The company was wound up in March 1902, though Walter Payne re-opened his small workshop and made engines. This continued until his death in 1934, his customers including Dan Albone, maker of the Ivel tractor.

NG

Further Reading
'Fragments on Forgotten Makes, the Payne & Bates', Bill Boddy, *Motor Sport*, February 1982.

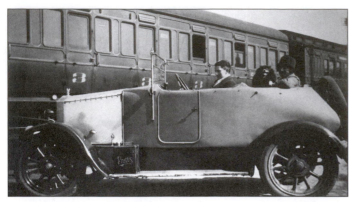

1921 Payze 10hp cloverleaf 3-seater.
MICHAEL WORTHINGTON-WILLIAMS

1912 P.D.A. cyclecar.
MICHAEL WORTHINGTON-WILLIAMS

PAYNE-MODERN (US) 1907–1908

Modern Tool Co., Erie, Pennsylvania.
Sometimes known simply as the Modern, this car lived up to its name, with air-cooled V4 and V6 engines of 24 and 36hp respectively, a 4-speed gearbox with lever on the steering column, and shaft drive. The semi-elliptic springs were inclined at an angle of 15 degrees, with the outboard ends above the frame and the inboard ones below. The make did not have a very long life; perhaps it was too advanced, and the 36hp car was pretty expensive, at $4000 for a runabout or tourer.

NG

PAYZE (GB) 1920–1921

Payze Light Car Co. Ltd, Cookham, Berkshire.
Although it was announced in late 1919, it does not seem that even a prototype Payze was running before the spring of 1920. Designed by Captain A. Payze, it was a conventional light car powered by a 1490cc 4-cylinder Coventry-Simplex engine, with Moss gearbox and a 3/4-seater cloverleaf body. It had a Rolls-Royce-type radiator and was advertised as 'the light car with the comfort of a limousine and the simplicity of a scooter'. They also went in for punning advertising, telling potential customers 'It Payze you to run this car'. Few people took this advice, though, and total production has been estimated at between 15 and 20 cars.

NG

Further Reading
'Advertising Payze', M. Worthington-Williams, *The Automobile*, May 1998.

P.B. (F) 1955–1956

Appearing at the 1955 Paris Salon, the P.B. was one of innumerable microcars of the period. It was a very small 3-wheeler with dumpy open doorless bodywork and a single headlamp. Its Ydral 175cc engine powered the ultra-light 187lb (85kg) P.B. to a top speed of 50mph (80km/h).

CR

P.D.A. (GB) 1912–1913

Pickering, Darby & Allday Ltd, Birmingham.
This was a cyclecar which was offered with a choice of V-twin engines by Blumfield, JAP or Precision, with 2-speed gearbox incorporated in the rear axle and shaft drive. One of the partners was G.J. Allday who later became a prominent early member of the Veteran Car Club of Great Britain. Only about 12–15 cars were made.

NG

PEARSALL-WARNE see WARNE

PEARSON-COX (GB) 1909–1916

Pearson & Cox Ltd, Shortlands, Kent.
The Pearson-Cox was the last new make of steam car to appear in Britain, where nearly all steamers were imported. Henry Pearson and Percy Cox opened a garage at Shortlands, near Bromley, in the summer of 1908, and the following year they announced their car. It had a 3-cylinder compound engine, semi-flash boiler and shaft drive. With a bonnet which contained the boiler, and a 2-seater body, it looked just like a petrol car. The first model was rated at 12hp, but later both 8 and 15hp models were advertised, the larger with a 5-seater body. In 1910 they formed a private company with capital of £2500, and even appointed a North of England distributor at Gateshead, but production was only on a made-to-order basis, and probably no more than 20 cars were made.

In 1913 they built a petrol-engined cyclecar powered by an 8hp JAP engine, and with belt drive to a gearbox over the rear axle, and from 1914 to 1917 they offered the ultimate eccentricity, a steam-driven motorcycle.

NG

PECK (CDN) 1913

Peck Electric Ltd, Toronto, Ontario.
Compared with the industry in the United States, electric cars were pretty rare north of the border. The short-lived Peck was a high-quality coupé which incorporated a number of special features, including a control lever that applied power to the Diehl motor and also operated the brakes, and a steering column that could be locked to prevent theft. The Peck coupé could be had with wheel or tiller steering and chain or shaft drive. There was also a roadster with wheel steering and chain drive only. The company slogan was 'Keeps Pecking', but it pecked no longer after 1913. Its demise was attributed to the arrival of the electric starter, but a high price of up to $4000 probably did not help sales.

NG

PEDELUX (GB) c.1928–1930

This was a pedal-powered single-seater with 3-speed transmission, hand and foot brakes, electric lighting, hood and sidescreens. A speed of 30mph (48km/h) could be achieved on the level. There were two models, that of 1928 having upright lines, while for 1929 it was more streamlined. Though of British manufacture, it was announced in an American journal, where prices of $100 were quoted for 1928, and $155 for 1929. These were equivalent to £21 and £32.25.

NG

PEDERSEN (US) 1922

L.C. Pedersen Motor Car Co., Chicago, Illinois.
This was a late example of a cyclecar, powered by a 2-cylinder air-cooled De Luxe engine, with 2-speed gearbox and shaft drive. It was priced at a very modest $295, and was said to be available by mail order.

NG

PEEL (GBM) 1955–1966

Peel Engineering Co., Peel, Isle of Man.
As a fibreglass pioneer, this Manx company was encouraged by the appearance of several plastic-bodied cars to launch its own car. Its first project was the Manxman, a small 3-wheeler with a steel tube chassis and an enclosed fibreglass body. Initially a rear-mounted 350cc Anzani 2-stroke twin drove the single rear wheel by chain, but later a 250cc Anzani unit was fitted. Entry was gained via a most unusual system: the semi-circular door pivoted at its rear base, swinging upwards and back, flush with the bodywork. The plan was to sell the Manxman

1909 Pearson-Cox Model F 12hp steam car.
NATIONAL MOTOR MUSEUM

in kit form for £299 10s, but it is very unlikely that any were made. However, Peel did make several examples of its larger fibreglass bodyshell for Ford Ten chassis, called the P1000.

Peel's most remarkable product was the P50 of 1962, almost certainly the world's smallest ever passenger car. The prototype measured just 50in (1270mm) long, 33in (840mm) wide, and 46in (1170mm) tall, with production cars 53in (1350mm) long and 39ins (990mm) wide, and weighing a mere 132lbs (60kg). This was essentially a single seat surrounded by a one-piece fibreglass shell incorporating a single front headlamp. A DKW 49cc fan-cooled engine sat underneath the driver, driving the single rear by chain via a 3-speed gearbox.

Peel's next model was the Trident 3-wheeler of 1965, which was larger than the P50, but only just (measuring 72in (1827mm) long). The Trident's fibreglass body consisted almost entirely of a forward-hinging section which had a transparent Perspex dome as a roof and a flat glass windscreen. The umbrella handle-shaped steering column was also hinged and rose with the canopy. The Trident could seat two side by side or some were supplied as single-seaters with a shopping basket beside. The engine was the same 49cc unit as the P50 and the car was advertised as being 'almost cheaper than walking', having a consumption of about 100mpg. A 4-wheeled electric version also appeared in 1966, offering an unusually good range and brisk acceleration. Other projects included the Viking Sport, a Mini based fibreglass coupé body (subsequently made by VIKING), a jeep-type vehicle measuring only 87in (2208mm) long and an all-fibreglass Mini replica shell.

CR

PEER GYNT (D) 1925

Dickmann AG, Berlin.

This was a cyclecar powered by a single-cylinder 2-stroke engine, with plywood body, presumably named after the Ibsen character immortalised in Grieg's *Peer Gynt Suite*.

HON

1962 Peel P50 49cc coupé.
NICK GEORGANO

PEERLESS (i) (US) 1901–1931

1901–1905 Peerless Manufacturing Co., Cleveland, Ohio.
1905–1931 Peerless Motor Car Co., Cleveland, Ohio.

For many years Peerless was one of the 'Three Ps', aristocrats of American motordom, the other two being Packard and Pierce-Arrow. In its beginnings, Peerless had quite a lot in common with the latter. They began by making

1905 Peerless (i) Model 10 30hp tourer, Barney Oldfield at the wheel.
NATIONAL MOTOR MUSEUM

1924 Peerless (i) Model 66 sedan.
JOHN A. CONDE

1927 Peerless (i) Model 6-80 sedan.
NATIONAL MOTOR MUSEUM

clothes wringers (Pierce-Arrow made birdcages), then both companies turned to bicycles in the 1890s, and their first cars were both light runabouts powered by single-cylinder De Dion-Bouton engines. Launched in June 1901, the Peerless Motorette was made in two models, the two-seater 2¾hp B and the 4-seater 3½hp C. They were licence-built De Dion-Boutons, and although admirable for European conditions, they were not ideal for America's rough roads. Peerless' chief engineer, Louis P. Mooers had already built a car of his own in 1897, while working for the New Haven Bicycle Co, and he set about designing a new Peerless more suitable for local conditions. His first car still had only one cylinder, but it was mounted vertically at the front, and drove via a propeller shaft. Completed in the summer of 1901, it was soon superseded by a 12/16hp vertical twin, which was the first of Mooers' designs to go on sale, priced at $1750.

About 90 cars were built in 1902, and in August 1903 three 4-cylinder models were introduced. These had engines of 24, 35 and 60hp, known respectively as the Types 8, 7 and 12. They all had channel-section steel frames dropped in the centre to give a lower centre of gravity. An invention of Mooers later adopted by many other manufacturers was the jointed steering column, which could be folded back to allow stout drivers to slip behind the wheel without too much squeezing and puffing. Prices were now as high as any in America, from $4000 for the Type 8 tourer to $6250 for the Type 12 Victoria tonneau. For the 1905 season the 16hp twin was dropped, and there were four 4-cylinder models, from 24 to 60hp.

Mooers left Peerless in 1905, joining the Moon company, and his place was taken by Charles Schmidt from Packard. The 1905 Peerlesses had pushrod ohvs, but Schmidt reverted to side-valves in a T-head for 1906 when 30 and 45hp models were listed. Peerless built 1176 cars in 1906, about 500 less than rivals Packard or Pierce-Arrow, but still a creditable figure for a luxury car maker whose products sold from $3750 to $6000. Schmidt's first 6-cylinder car appeared for 1908, a 60hp of more than 10-litres capacity. It was made in two wheelbases, a limousine costing the very high figure of $7000. Peerless's slogan at this time was 'All That the Name Implies', and they were indeed highly regarded cars, equal to Pierce-Arrow and on a higher level than Packard who would not bring out a six until 1911.

The range of 4- and 6-cylinder cars was made with little change until 1912, when the sixes were increased to three models, 38, 48 and 60hp, together with fours of 24 and 40hp. Electric lighting was adopted in 1910, and starting in 1913. For 1915 Peerless introduced a less complex range; the old 48hp six was continued, and there were only two other models, both monobloc engines, a 3621cc four and a 4736cc six. They were more modestly priced than earlier Peerlesses, ranging from $2000 to $3350. However, the profit margin was very small, and within a year Peerless were looking in a different direction.

They had noticed the success of the newly-introduced Cadillac V8, and decided to follow the Detroit firm with a one-model policy, also a V8. The 5457cc 78bhp unit was generally listed as Peerless' own, but in fact it was made for them by Herschell-Spillman. The carburettor was made by Peerless, and was an unusual design with a small low speed venturi and a secondary high speed venturi. The secondary throttle was interconnected with the primary throttle linkage and cut in at 2000rpm, about 40 to 45mph (65 to 72km/h). The result was an engine flexible enough to work at walking speed in top gear, yet with good, if somewhat noisy, breathing at high speeds. The engine was advertised as the 'Two Power Range V8'. The Peerless V8 was very similar to the Cadillac, in size, weight and price, the latter being slightly lower at $1890–3060, compared with Cadillac's $2080–3600. The one-model policy paid off in production terms, for 1916 saw 4210 cars delivered from the Cleveland factory, 600 up on the previous best year, 1915.

The V8 was made without major change until 1928 but there were many changes in company personnel. In October 1921 Peerless was bought by Richard H. Collins, formerly president and general manager of Cadillac, and he brought with him a number of Cadillac men, including Benjamin H. Anibal as chief engineer. William Strickland, Peerless' chief engineer went over to Cadillac. Anibal was responsible for the 1923 Peerlesses, which had longer wheelbases, underslung rear springs and more modern bodies. Production for 1923 was 5775 cars, slightly less than the record 6213 made in 1920. Collins, Anibal and his team left Peerless in December 1923, Collins selling the company a new design for a medium-priced 6-cylinder car which he had developed with Anibal in the period between leaving Cadillac and joining Peerless. Using a Continental-based engine, one prototype Collins Six was made in 1921, and the design went into production as the Peerless 6-70 for 1925. Like the V8s that year it had hydraulic 4-wheel brakes, and sold for $2285–3470. For the 1927 season another six joined the Peerless range; known as the 6-90 it had a 4727cc Peerless-built engine, and was joined the next year by the smallest six yet, the 3262cc 6-60 which used an engine bought in from Continental. This sold for only $1295–1345. Peerless now had four 6-cylinder models and the V8, but the latter was an ageing design, and for 1929 it was replaced by a 5277cc straight-8 made by Continental 'specially for Peerless'. For 1930 Peerless offered an all-straight-8 programme, the 4040cc Standard Eight and the Master and Custom Eights powered by the larger unit. They were good looking cars styled by Alexis de Sakhnoffsky, and not overpriced at $1495 for a Standard Eight sedan to $3345 for a Custom Eight limousine. However, the

Depression was biting into the disposable incomes of the typical upper-middle class customer who bought Peerlesses, and only 3642 were sold in America in 1930, compared with 8318 in 1929, and a peak of 10,437 in 1926. Peerless had slipped from 25th in the American production league in 1928 to 28th in 1929 and 30th in 1930. Although 1932 models were announced, the last Peerless left the factory in June 1931, production that year being only 1249 cars.

There was, however, a remarkable swan song in the shape of the aluminium VI6 made in conjunction with Alcoa (Aluminium Co. of America), another Cleveland firm. This had an all-aluminium block with a capacity of 7603cc developing 170bhp. The sedan body by Murphy was also of light alloy construction, and it was intended that the chassis should be as well, but it had to be strengthened with steel, which added to the weight. Three VI6 engines and one VI2 derivative were made, but there was only one complete car, and so far as is known, no price was ever fixed for it. James Bohannon, president of Peerless at the time, kept the car until 1946, when he handed it over to the Thompson Products Museum (now Frederick C. Crawford Auto-Aviation Museum) where it still is today.

Car production was over, but the factory had a new lease of life as a brewery. Bohannon had long admired the Canadian Carling beers, and when Prohibition (of alcoholic drinks) ended in the USA in 1933 he acquired the licence to brew Carling products in Cleveland. By the time he died in the 1960s the organisation was among the top ten breweries in the USA.

NG

Further Reading
'All That the Name Implies, the Peerless Story', Maurice Hendry, *Automobile Quarterly*, Vol. 11, No. 1.

PEERLESS (ii) (GB) 1957–1960
Peerless Cars Ltd, Slough, Buckinghamshire.
When it was announced in 1957, the Peerless was among the first of a new style of low-cost British GT car. It was designed by Bernie Rodger, a racing mechanic, and was commissioned by two former racers, John Gordon (later of the Gordon Keeble) and James Byrnes. The prototype was called the Warwick, but production cars were named Peerless after John Gordon's business, Peerless Motors. Peerless GTs featured a space frame with a De Dion rear axle suspended on semi-elliptical springs and Triumph TR3 running gear and front suspension. Overdrive was fitted to the top three gears so it had, in effect, a 7-speed gear box.

It cost £1500 in Britain, including all taxes and had room for a family and its luggage. Top speed was 112mph (180km/h) with 0–62mph (0–100km/h) in 10 seconds. Initial reaction was favourable, and predicted sales of 2000–3000 a year seemed feasible, but the company was under-financed, build quality was indifferent, and you could buy a Jaguar 2.4 for the same money. The project was finished by 1960 when 325 cars had been made.

After Peerless folded, Bernie Rodger modified the design and revived it as the WARWICK (ii), which was a short-lived venture. John Gordon used the Peerless chassis as the basis of the Gordon Keeble.

MJL

PEGASO (i) (E) 1951–1958
Empresa Nacional de Autocamiones SA, Barcelona.
Named after the winged horse, Pegasus, the Pegaso was one of the most exotic jewels of the postwar motoring scene, made by a company whose previous experience was confined to diesel-engined trucks and buses. It had an automobile ancestry in that the state-owned E.N.A.S.A. (Empresa Nacional de Autocamiones SA) had acquired the Barcelona factories of Hispano-Suiza in 1946, and it was from their training works that the remarkable Pegaso emerged in 1951.

It was designed by Wilfredo Ricart (1897–1974) who had been responsible for some twin-ohc racing cars in the 1920s, the Ricart-Espana tourer of 1928–29, and the rear-engined Alfa Romeo Tipo 512 GP car of 1940. Shown at the 1951 Paris Salon, the Pegaso Z.102 was a very complex design, with a 2473cc V8 engine with two ohcs to each block. This was the world's first 4-camshaft V8 road car, previous examples being confined to racing cars such as the Mercedes-Benz W154 GP car and the American Miller and Novi. Ferrari did not make a 4-cam road car until the GTB4 Daytona of 1968.

The camshafts were driven by triple roller chains, but this was soon abandoned in favour of a train of gears. Other features of the engine were dry sump lubrication and sodium-cooled exhaust valves. Output was 165bhp at 6500rpm,

1929 Peerless (i) Model Six-61 sedan.
JOHN A. CONDE

1958 Peerless (ii) GT coupé.
NICK BALDWIN

1952 Pegaso Z-102 coupé.
NICK BALDWIN

though the engine was said to run up to 9000rpm. Transmission was by a 5-speed non-synchromesh gearbox mounted at the rear in unit with a ZF limited slip differential. Early cars had coupé or convertible bodies built by the factory, but later the chassis were shipped to Milan to be bodied by Touring, while there were some very flamboyant specials by Saoutchik. The Touring-bodied cars were very expensive, and to reduce costs the final Pegasos were bodied in Spain to Touring design, or styled by Serra.

After a few cars had been made with the 2473cc engine it was enlarged to 2816cc (Z.102B) and offered with a Marshall-Nordec supercharger. This and the larger capacity increased power from 165 to 220bhp. In 1954 a 3178cc (Z.102SS) engine was offered, developing 190bhp unblown and 225bhp with supercharger. Top speed was not as high as one might have imagined, about

1954 Pegaso Z-102SS Spyder.
NICK BALDWIN

120mph (193km/h) with the 2.8-litre engine. This was not as fast as the much cheaper Jaguar XK120, and by 1955 Pegaso had the Mercedes-Benz 300SL to compete with, as well as Ferraris and Aston Martins. Pegaso prices seem to have been a matter of rumour rather than hard fact, but on the US market they were quoted between $15,000 and $30,000, while £7800 was mentioned for one at the 1952 London Motor Show, when an Aston Martin DB2 could be had for £2724. It is hardly surprising that few Pegasos were sold, and those mainly on the Spanish market, where there was a small number of rich customers who found it very difficult to import foreign cars, due to their country's currency restrictions. Exact figures are not known, but between 100 and 125 cars have been quoted by various sources. The last four Z.103s were somewhat different, having larger engines with pushrods replacing the complex 4-camshaft layout. Capacities were 4-, 4.25- and 4.7-litres, the latter giving 300bhp and a claimed 150mph (240km/h) top speed.

Pegaso commercial vehicles are still made today, the company now being owned by the international group Iveco. For a more recent car, see PEGASO (ii).

NG

Further Reading
'Pegaso, El Caballo Volador de Espana', Nicolas Franco Jr,
Automobile Quarterly, Vol. 6, No. 2.
'Pegaso Thrill', Winston Goodfellow, *Automobile Quarterly*, Vol. 39, No. 3.
Ricart-Pegaso: La pasion del automovil, Carlos Mosquera
and Enrique Coma-Cros, Arcris, 1990.

PEGASO (ii) **(E/GB)** 1992–1993
International Automotive Design (UK) Ltd, Worthing, Sussex.
Revivals of great names were a fad of the 1990s, and the famous Spanish Pegaso marque was recreated in a joint Spanish–British endeavour. The 1953 Serra-bodied Z103 was reproduced with painstaking accuracy, but the mechanical side was very much updated. A 191bhp Rover 3.9-litre V8 engine and 5-speed gearbox with limited slip differential were used, as well as four ventilated disc brakes,

wishbone front suspension, and a De Dion rear axle. I.A.D. built no more than 12 cars at its Worthing base, and the I.A.D. operation was bought in 1993 by Daewoo.

CR

PEGASSE (F) 1924–1925
M. Arboval, Boisguilbert.
The Pegasse was a chain-driven cyclecar powered by a 2-cylinder engine.

NG

PEGASUS (US) c.1975–1977
The March Hare was a kit that fitted on a shortened Volkswagen chassis. It was a wildly stylised sports coupé with a 'Kamm' back and plunging side lines. VW, Corvair, Porsche or Ford engines could be adapted.

HP

PEILLON (F) 1899–1900
This voiturette with 2½hp engine was shown at the 1899 Paris Salon, but may never have made it into production. It was built at Boulogne-sur-Seine.

NG

PEKA (D) 1924
Pe-Ka Fahrzeugwerk, Dresden.
This was one of many firms which tried to market 3-wheelers in Germany in the 1920s. It was more modest than most in being only a single-seater. It had a single front wheel and a 1.5PS DKW engine drove the rear wheels.

HON

PEKING *see* BEIJING

PELHAM *see* BAILEY & LAMBERT

PELL (GB) 1996 to date

Pell Automotive, Bradford, Yorkshire.

The Pell Genesis was an interesting open sports car designed around motorcycle componentry. The mid-mounted 1100cc 145bhp engine came from the Kawasaki ZZR, while the drive to the rear wheels was by chain. A later alternative was a Peugeot 205GTI engine driving through an Audi transaxle. The chassis was an aluminium-panelled space frame and incorporated fully-adjustable suspension. The fibreglass bodywork lacked any doors.

CR

PELLAND (GB) 1978–1981/1989–1992

1978–1980 Pelland Engineering, King's Lynn, Norfolk.
1980–1981 Pelland Engineering, East Dereham, Norfolk.
1989–1992 Pelland Engineering, Harleston, Norfolk.

Peter Pellandine was one of the men behind the ASHLEY and FALCON before he emigrated to Australia, where he produced the PELLANDINI in the 1970s. On his return to Britain in 1978 he recommenced manufacture of his low-slung Sports model, using a rear subframe to accept a centrally-mounted VW Beetle or Ford engine, plus special rear suspension. An optional targa/gullwing hard-top was offered. The Sports was sold on in 1981 to become the Ryder Rembrandt (see ROYALE entry). Meanwhile Pellandine set to work on a prototype in which he attempted several times to break the world land speed record for steam-powered cars. In 1989 he adapted the bodywork of this prototype to become a new roadgoing Sports model. Into the fixed coupé or full convertible fibreglass monocoque went double wishbone independent suspension and a mid-mounted Alfa Romeo Alfasud engine. This model became the KUDOS when it was sold on in 1992.

CR

PELLANDINI (AUS) 1970–1979

Pellandini Cars Pty Ltd, Cherry Gardens, South Australia.

Peter Pellandine founded Ashley Laminates and Falcon Shells, producers of fibreglass bodies, in England before he moved to Australia. In 1970 he showed a coupé with gull-wing doors powered by a mid-mounted Mini-Cooper power pack. A roadster, with conventional doors, was offered in 1974. By the late 1970s he had state funding for experimental work with a steam-powered roadster but in 1979 he returned to England where this was sold as a VW-based kit under the Pelland name.

MG

PEMBLETON (GB) 1999 to date

Pembleton Motor Co., Leamington Spa, Warwickshire.

The Pembleton Grasshopper Super Sport was a 3-wheeled roadster in the spirit of the Morgans of the 1920s. Sold only in kit form, the Grasshopper was powered by a 602cc Citroën 2CV engine, and retained the 2CV's suspension. With aluminium bodywork, mounted on a rigid chassis, the two-seater tipped the scales at a featherweight 350 kg.

CR

PENDLETON (US) 1899–1905

Trumbull Manufacturing Co., Warren, Ohio.

The Trumbull company traced its ancestry back to the Warren Machine Works which had been founded in 1850. One of the partners, William C. Pendleton, built a car in 1899 with a single-cylinder engine mounted under the seat, but it was not a success. He followed this with a steam car in 1901, and a petrol-engined car in 1902. Two tourers were made in 1905, one with a 28/42hp 4-cylinder engine. Only seven cars were made in all, which were called either Pendleton or Trumbull. A brochure was issued, but cars were only a sideline to tool manufacture and other engineering work. The company still survives, as the Warren Tool Corp.

Warren, Ohio's other car was built by James Ward Packard, and became rather more famous, although production was soon moved to Detroit.

NG

PENELLE (F) 1900–1901

C. Penelle, Melun, Seine-et-Marne.

In appearance the Penelle owed much to the contemporary Benz, though the horizontal 6hp engine mounted under the seat was by Buchet. Drive was taken

1897 Pennington Autocar 3-wheeler.
NICK BALDWIN

by belt to a countershaft on which a train of spur gear wheels meshed with pinions on a differential shaft, from which final drive was by chain.

NG

PENN (i) (US) 1911–1912

Penn Motor Car Co., Pittsburgh, Pennsylvania.

The Penn Thirty was a conventional car powered by a 3.7-litre 30hp 4-cylinder engine, and made in two open models, a 2-seater roadster and a 5-seater tourer. For 1912 they added a Comet roadster, which was presumably more sporting, and a 45hp chassis. In 1912 they moved into a new factory at New Castle, Pennsylvania, but no cars were made there as their backers pulled out and bankruptcy followed. The Canadian McKAY was based on the Penn Thirty.

NG

PENN (ii) (GB) 1995–1997

The Penn Motor Co., High Wycombe, Buckinghamshire.

A used car dealer by trade, Penn produced its own accurate, but short-lived, replica of the Ford GT40. Using Ford V8 running gear, the Penn GT40 was sold only in fully built turn-key form.

CR

PENNINE (GB) 1914

Built near Halifax, Yorkshire, the Pennine was a cyclecar powered by an 8hp V-twin JAP engine.

NG

PENNINGTON (US/GB) 1894–1902

1894–1895 E.J. Pennington, Cleveland, Ohio.
1895–1896 Racine Motor Vehicle Co., Racine, Wisconsin.
1896–1897 Great Horseless Carriage Co. Ltd, Coventry.
1898–1899 Pennington & Baines, London.
1899 Pennington Motor Co. Ltd, London.
1899–1902 Anglo-American Rapid Vehicle Co., New York, New York; Philadelphia, Pennsylvania.

These addresses cover the main locations where Edward Joel Pennington (1858–1911) planned or claimed to build cars, though not all saw actual manufacture. Described by the eminent historian Michael Sedgwick as 'the company promoter and charlatan *par excellence* of the horseless-carriage era' and even by his own patent agent Eric Walford as a mechanical charlatan, Pennington claimed to have built an electric 3-wheeler in 1887 and an airship in 1890. His first attested road vehicle was a motorcycle with large balloon tyres, said to be 'unpuncturable'. He published a well-known drawing showing one of these flying through the air for 65 feet. Though he applied for a patent in Cleveland, he probably did not make anything there, instead he persuaded a wealthy Racine businessman, Thomas Kane, to build 2- and 4-wheelers under the name Kane-Pennington. The 4-wheelers, called the Victoria, consisted of two lady's bicycles coupled together by a platform frame and powered by two small engines mounted at the rear. He announced that six of these machines would run in the 1895 Chicago *Times-Herald* Race, but they did not reach the starting line. Probably two or three were made at Racine, but none went very well.

Having exhausted the possibilities of exploitation in America, Pennington crossed the Atlantic (had he lived today he would undoubtedly have flown everywhere on Concorde) and met a man of his own kind, the company promoter Harry J. Lawson. It is a tribute to Pennington's powers of persuasion that he induced Lawson to part with £100,000 for his patents, and to assign him one floor of the Motor Mills in Coventry for his experiments. From here emerged what was probably the best-known Pennington vehicle, the 3-wheeled New Patent Autocar. This had a tubular frame made by Humber and a parallel-twin engine of very long stroke, 62.5 × 305mm, giving a capacity of 1840cc, with chain drive to the single rear wheel. It could be steered from a seat at the front or a saddle at the rear, and had four transverse saddles in between for additional passengers. Photographs were published showing it laden with no fewer than nine passengers, though it can hardly have run with such a load. To be fair, even Pennington's flamboyant advertising did not claim it to be more than a 4-seater. He did claim that it was the lightest and strongest machine to carry four people, also that 'it will *not* blow up, and passengers do not run the risk of being set on fire'.

A New Patent Autocar was entered in the London–Brighton Emancipation Run in November 1896, but withdrew when one of its 'unpuncturable' tyres burst. At most five were made, of which one survives in the National Motor Museum at Beaulieu, the only known Pennington in existence today. His London agent for the Autocar was William Baines, and his next venture was in conjunction with Mr Baines. This was the so-called Raft Victoria, with 3½hp engine, front-wheel drive and rear-wheel steering and rope final drive (later changed to belt). He offered this car at under £100, and claimed to have 400 orders. However, the public were not encouraged by Hubert Egerton's attempt to drive one from Manchester to London; he gave up at Nuneaton after using up 72 sparking plugs! Two Lancashire firms, the Eclipse Machine Co. of Oldham and the Protector Lamp & Lighting Co. of Eccles, later to make the ROTHWELL and BIJOU cars respectively, were commissioned to make components for Raft-Victorias, but no more than three cars were completed. One had a body by Stirling of Granton, and was known as the Stirling-Pennington. A number of deposits had been paid on these cars, and when they failed to appear the frustrated customers pressed for their money. Pennington's response was to dissolve Pennington & Baines, and form a new company, the Pennington Motor Co. Ltd. This was very short-lived, and in October 1899 he returned to America.

There he formed the Anglo-American Rapid Vehicle Co., said to be the largest motor vehicle company in the world, which made a few 4-wheeled versions of the Torpedo, for which 72mph (116km/h) was claimed, and the British Government were supposed to have ordered 1000 for use in the Boer War. He was back in England in 1901 where he demonstrated a 'war motor' which was no more than a tricar with a light shield over the forecarriage. All his later adventures took place in America. These included the TRACTOBILE avant-train for attachment to buggies (1901), the Continental sparking plug with self-contained combustion chamber (1905), and attempts to make cars at both ends of the scale, from a $300 16hp to super-luxury cars of 160hp selling for $20,000–30,000 each. While entertaining lavishly he left at least three hotels in various parts of the country without paying the bill. In 1910 he was in Springfield, Massachusetts, promoting an airship and running a flying school. He collapsed while walking in the street in Springfield in March 1911, and died three days later. At a generous estimate, he had made no more than 20 cars.

NG

Further Reading
'The Elusive Mr. Pennington', Robert F. Scott,
Automobile Quarterly, Vol. 5, No. 4.

PENNSY (US) 1916–1919

Pennsy Motors Co., Pittsburgh, Pennsylvania.

Elmore Gregg, who had tried to make the PENN Thirty in New Castle, Pennsylvania, returned to Pittsburgh to make another car called the Pennsy. It was on much the same lines as the Penn, though larger, and the fours were joined by the Six-48 using a 6-cylinder Continental engine. Pennsy Motors absorbed the truck-building Kosmath Co. of Detroit but this closed down in 1916, as did Pennsy three years later.

NG

PENNSYLVANIA (US) 1907–1911

Pennsylvania Auto-Motor Co., Bryn Mawr, Pennsylvania.

The first Pennsylvania was a touring car powered by a 35hp 4-cylinder Rutenber engine, but later cars used engines of the company's own make. These ranged from a 29hp four to a massive 75hp six with a capacity of 9.1 litres and a 137in (3477mm) wheelbase. It was a high-quality car with bodies from the distinguished coachbuilders, Quinby & Co., and prices were up to $4700. The association with Quinby proved the Pennsylvania's downfall, for they failed to pay the coachbuilders, and were put into bankruptcy in October 1911.

NG

PENSARE (US) c.1987

Pensare Automotive Manufacturing, San Jacinto, California.

The Feroce GTB/4 was a Ferrari Daytona replica based on the Datsun 280ZX. Coupé and convertible versions were offered and they were sold in kit and completed form. The coupé version had a lift-off roof panel.

HP

PENTE see WEISS MANFRED

PEOPLE'S (US) 1900–1902

People's Automobile Co., Cleveland, Ohio.

In 1900 there was a prolonged strike by Cleveland's tramcar operators, and in response a group of businessmen decided to build motor buses to replace the trams. Designed by Paul Gaeth, they were unrealistic to say the least, having 3hp single-cylinder engines to power a bus 22 feet long and with seating for 26 passengers. Another problem was that the striking tram men refused to allow the buses onto the streets. The promoters therefore removed the engines from the buses and put them into small 2-seater runabouts for which they were much more suitable. These they marketed under the name People's. The venture did not last long (about six were made) and in 1902 GAETH began to make a car under his own name.

NG

PEREDY FROG (H) 1998

Peredy Studio, Budapest 1998.

Zoltán Peredy exhibited his Fiat 126p-based fun-car at the 1998 Budapest International Autoshow. With a suitable investor, the car could be produced in bigger quantities.

PN

PEREGRINE (GB) 1961

Falcon Shells Ltd, Epping, Essex.

Peregrine operated from the same workshop as Falcon Shells and was really a Falcon. It was based on the spaceframe originally designed by Len Terry for his Terrier Mk II clubman's car, although that design had undergone modifications to its detriment and it did not benefit by being fitted with a larger and heavier Falcon fibreglass body. Ford Anglia running gear was used and the Peregrine was available as an open car or with a hard-top. Very few were made during the car's one production year, 1961.

ML

PERENTTI (AUS) 1983–1988

Revolution Fibreglass Pty Ltd, Bayswater, Victoria.

The producers of the CONDOR introduced a Chevrolet Corvette replica and named it after Australia's largest lizard. It was mounted on a Holden commercial chassis and engines were Holden 6-cylinder and Chevrolet or Holden V8s to choice.

When Bill Kain decided to concentrate on boat building, the car projects were sold in 1988. Fred Martin of Bendigo then offered the Perentti Mk 2 as a coupé and convertible but only as kits.

MG

PERFECTA (I) 1899–1903
Bender e Martiny, Turin.
This company offered a wide range of vehicles, including electric cars with Gaillardet motors, a belt-driven single-cylinder car based on the ORIENT EXPRESS, and motor quadricycles. Perfecta was the name used by DARRACQ for their factory (Usines Perfecta) and for their quads, and it could well be that all the vehicles offered under this name in Italy were imports.

NG

PERFECTION (US) 1907–1908
Perfection Automobile Works, South Bend, Indiana.
This company planned originally to build the C.F. car for the Chicago firm of Cornish-Friedberg, but when they decided to make their own cars, the Perfection was launched. It was made as a 42hp four or a 70hp six, the latter with a capacity of 7.8 litres, both made only with tourer bodies. Few were made.

NG

PERFECT PLASTICS (US) c.1985
Perfect Plastics Industries, New Kensington, Pennsylvania.
The Tuff tub and Boss Bug were kit cars based on Volkswagen running gear.

HP

PERFEKT (A) 1909–1914
1906–1909 Frantisek Petrasek, Strojirna a tovarna automobilu, Trutnov.
1910–1914 Frantisek Petrasek, Kralovehradecka tovarna automobilu 'Perfekt', Kukleny.
F. Petrasek (1877–1932) built his first light car with single-cylinder 5bhp motorcycle engine in about 1906–1908, the second one had a water-cooled single-cylinder 8bhp power unit, and was called 'Perfekt'. In 1910 he employed 30 workers who assembled about ten 2-seater voiturettes. The new type B with 2-cylinder 1114cc 10bhp SV engine was manufactured until World War I, after which production continued under the name START.

MSH

PERFETTI (I) 1922–1923
Perfetti Automobili, Milan.
The Perfetti used a 1491cc 4-cylinder proprietary engine but was highly unconventional in other ways. The body was on a separate frame from the chassis. The driver sat in the centre of the body with a passenger on each side of him, and a fourth passenger behind. The steering column was nearly horizontal. The car probably did not emerge from the prototype stage.

NG

PERFEX (i) (US) 1912–1913
The Perfex Co., Los Angeles, California.
The Perfex was a 2-seater roadster with a tall, narrow radiator and a narrow bonnet which housed a 3260cc 4-cylinder T-head G.B. & S. engine. It was priced at $1050. A truck using the same engine was launched in July 1913, and before the end of the year it was announced that trucks would be the only product of the Perfex company. Roadster production may have been as high as 125, and most were sold in Southern California.

NG

PERFEX (ii) (GB) 1920–1921
Perfex Manufacturing Co., Bournemouth, Hampshire.
Despite the similarity of name and use of the same G.B.& S. engine, there was probably no connection between this car and the Los Angeles make which had been discontinued seven years earlier. The British Perfex was not in any way sporting, being offered with tourer, 2-seater and saloon bodies at prices too high (£700–975) to make it a commercial success. Two of the directors were S.H. and A.T. Arnott, later famous for their superchargers.and, in postwar years, for the sports cars made by Daphne Arnott.

NG

1921 Perfex (ii) 2-seater.
NATIONAL MOTOR MUSEUM

1998 Perodua Nippa 850GX hatchback.
NICK GEORGANO

PERKINS (US) c.1994
Perkins Engineering, Austin, Texas.
The Perkins M2 was a high-performance mid-engined exotic sports car with a Ford SHO V6 engine. It used a composite monocoque chassis with fabricated suspension using Ford Thunderbird components. The engine was modified to produce 300hp in normally aspirated form, or up to 500hp with turbocharging. Styling of the body and interior were overseen by company president Michael Perkins, who had originally intended to produce a street version of the BMW M-1. When this proved to be financially impossible, he built the M-2, which had a combination of BMW M-1 and Ferrari Testarossa lines. They were sold in kit form for $45,000, or fully assembled for $125,000.

HP

PERL (A) 1921–1926; 1951–1952
1921–1926 Automobilfabrik Perl, AG, Vienna.
1951–1952 Automobil Bestandteile- und Karrosserie-Fabrik Perl-Auhof GmbH, Vienna.
Perl began to make commercial vehicles in 1907, and built their first passenger car in 1921. It was a light car with an 800cc 3/10PS 4-cylinder engine, had a typical Germanic vee-radiator and 2- or 3-seater bodies, including an angular coupé. In 1924 an improved model appeared with the same capacity but increased output. Now with a flat radiator it was made as the Norma and was followed in 1925 by the slightly larger 4/17PS Suprema. Car production was suspended in favour of commercial vehicles in 1926, but after World War II another attempt was made in the car field. The Perl-Champion was closely based on the German CHAMPION (iv), but only a few were built.

HON

PERODUA (PTM) 1994 to date
Perodua Motors, Serendah.
Malaysia's second car maker after PROTON, the Perodua Kancil (a small Malaysian deer) was based on the former 844cc 3-cylinder DAIHATSU Cuore (Mira), and was made as a 5-door hatchback. The first exports went to Brunei,

1915 Perry 11.9hp 2-seater.
NICK BALDWIN

1914 Perry 8hp 2-cylinder 2-seater.
NATIONAL MOTOR MUSEUM

followed by Cyprus and Malta, and, in 1997, Great Britain where it was known as the Nippa. 1999 models were available in two versions, standard EX and higher specification GX. At just under £5000 the EX was the cheapest car on the UK market.

NG

PERREAU (F) 1923–1925
Automobiles Perreau, Epinay, Seine.
The Perreau was a light car powered by a 1088cc Ruby engine with shaft drive. It may never have passed the prototype stage.

NG

PERRY (GB) 1913–1916
Perry Motor Co. Ltd, Tyseley, Birmingham.

The history of the Perry company dated back to 1824 when James and Stephen Perry started to make pens in London. By the 1890s the company was in Birmingham and engaged in the bicycle business. They were on the point of collapse when they were bought by James William Bayliss of Bayliss-Thomas whose son Cecil (1892–1969) was to be instrumental in the first Perry car. A motor tricycle was built in 1899 and a forecar in 1903, and in 1911 Cecil Bayliss, aged 19, designed a cyclecar powered by an 800cc Fafnir engine, with 2-speed epicyclic gearbox and overhead worm drive. It proved under-powered, and his next design, which became the first production Perry car, had an 875cc vertical-twin engine made in the factory, with pistons that rose and fell together rather than alternately, in unit with a 3-speed gearbox, and overhead worm drive as on the prototype. The standard body was a 2-seater on an 84in (2132mm) wheelbase, although a 90in (2284mm) chassis was later available which enabled a dickey seat to be fitted. A doctor's coupé followed for 1914, and there was also a sports model with tuned engine, higher axle ratio and raked steering but this never saw production. About 800 twins were made, including one chassis assembled in 1919.

In 1914 a larger Perry with 1794cc 4-cylinder engine joined the twin. It had a separate gearbox and straight bevel rear axle, as did the later twins. The bodies were 2- or 4-seater tourers, mostly made by Mulliners of Birmingham. About 300 were made up to 1916, and a further three assembled from parts in 1919. By then the design had been sold to BEAN, who introduced it as the 11.9hp Bean.

NG

Further Reading
'Cecil Bayliss and the Perry', Jonathan Wood, *The Automobile*, 1998.

PERRY DESIGN (US) c.1997 to date
Perry Design, Corona, California.
The Perry Spyder was a Porsche 550 Spyder replica that fitted on a standard-length Volkswagen Beetle chassis. By lengthening the body, Perry added more interior room for taller drivers. They also sold trim and interior options including vintage upholstered bucket seats. They were sold in kit or fully assembled form.

HP

PERSONA (US) c.1980

Economy Vehicles Inc., Fort Myers, Florida.

Resembling a CHEVROLET Vega in appearance, this was a glassfibre coupé fitted to a standard VW Beetle floorpan. V8 and diesel options were possible.

NG

PESCATORE *see* AUTO MIXTE

PESTOURIE ET PLANCHON (F) 1922

Cyclecars Pestourie & Planchon, Paris.

Like the early M.B. and postwar ISETTA, this was one of that breed of 4-wheeled car which bore a superficial resemblance to a 3-wheeler as the rear wheels were set close together. Only 33cm separated the rear wheels, so there was no need for a differential. It was powered by a 904cc 4-cylinder Ruby engine, had a wooden body and chassis, and disc wheels.

NG

P.E.T. (US) 1914

P.E. Teats, Detroit, Michigan.

Philip Teats was assistant accountant to the city of Detroit, and announced a 4-cylinder cyclecar at $340 to be built with the aid of Canadian capital. It is thought that no more than a single prototype was made.

NG

PETER-MORITZ (D) 1921–1925

Automobilwerke Peter & Moritz, Zeitz, Naumburg.

This was a light car with 1325cc air-cooled flat-twin engine closely based on the ROVER Eight. A 2-seater body was standard. Later, a water-cooled version was made.

HON

PETER PAN (US) 1914–1915

The Randall Co., Quincy, Massachusetts.

Though described as a cyclecar, this was really a light car with 4-cylinder ohv engine made by the Wollaston Foundry Co., in whose factory the Randall Co. was located. It had a 3-speed gearbox and shaft drive and was offered as a 2-seater roadster and 4-seater tourer at $400 and $450 respectively. Its appearance was enhanced by a vee-radiator.

NG

PETERS (US) 1921–1922

1921 Peters Automobile Co., Pleasantville, New Jersey.
1921 Peters Automobile Co., Trenton, New Jersey.
1922 Peters Autocar Co., Bethlehem, Pennsylvania.
1922 Peters Division, Romer Motors Corp., Danvers and Taunton, Massachusetts.

The Peters car was a sort of 'much-ado-about-little' proposition despite its myriad wanderings as a centre of manufacturing which was little more than badge engineering of the Brook and, like the Brook, nearly all of its production was by the Spacke Machine & Tool Co. of Indianapolis, Indiana. Like the Brook – which had been built under the Spacke badge in 1920 – the Peters was a midget car with a 90in (2284mm) wheelbase and a 2-cylinder 9hp air-cooled engine. The Peters was available only as a 2-seater roadster at $385. In 1922, the Peters was purchased by Romer Motors Corp. of Danvers, Massachusetts – with a factory in Taunton – erstwhile manufacturer of the Romer car a year earlier. It is unlikely that production of the Peters under Romer aegis actually began.

KM

PETERS-WALTON (US) 1915

Ludlow Auto Engineering Co., Philadelphia, Pennsylvania.

This was an unusual 3-wheeler powered by a 9hp 2-cylinder engine mounted over, and driving, the single front wheel, in the style of the PHÄNOMEN. Two passengers were seated in tandem. In 1916 the name was changed to Peters Tricar, but it seems that these were all made with delivery van bodies.

NG

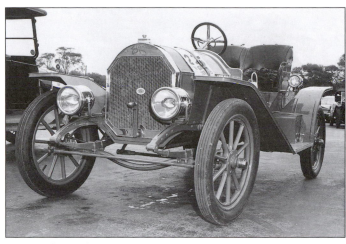

1909 Petrel 30 roadster.
NATIONAL MOTOR MUSEUM

PETIT (F) 1909

Little is known about the Petit which was made at Tarare, Rhône, except that it was a friction-driven voiturette powered by a single-cylinder Aster engine.

NG

PETREL (US) 1909–1912

1909 Petrel Motor Co., Kenosha, Wisconsin.
1909–1912 Petrel Motor Car Co., Milwaukee, Wisconsin.

This car saw the light of day in the former EARL (i) factory in Kenosha, but before the end of the year they moved to Milwaukee, into a factory owned by the furniture makers W.S. Seaman. The presence of a car manufacturer in their midst persuaded Seaman to build car bodies, initially for Petrel, but later for a wide variety of other makes, becoming a leader in the field, before becoming the captive bodybuilder for NASH. The Petrel was made with 4- and 6-cylinder engines of 30 and 50hp, and was generally conventional apart from using friction transmission, unusual on so powerful a car. Final drive was by chains until 1910, when shaft drive was adopted. The six was dropped after 1909, and for the next three years Petrel made 4-cylinder cars in several sizes, 22, 30 and 40/45hp, all with open body styles. In 1911 Petrel was sold to Filer & Stowell, makers of the Corliss steam engine, who moved production to a new factory, continued the Petrel and introduced another car, the F.S. By the end of 1912 both makes had been discontinued. Total production of Petrel and F.S. cars is thought to be under 1000.

NG

PETTENELLA (I) 1975–1976

Automobili Pettenelli snc, San Leo, Pesaro.

Reprising the role played by Zagato's 1750 Gran Sport of 1965, the Leontina was an evocative recreation of the 1929 Alfa Romeo 1750 Gran Sport. Into its ladder frame went authentic-style suspension consisting of rigid axles, leaf springs and friction dampers, and even the disc brakes were hidden by fake drum covers to complete the illusion. The engine was a modern Alfetta 2-litre unit, plus the same car's 5-speed manual transaxle placed at the rear.

CR

PETTER (GB) 1895–1898

1895–1896 Jas. B. Petter & Sons, Yeovil, Somerset.
1897–1898 Hill & Boll, Yeovil, Somerset.

Petters were already well known as engine manufacturers when their first vehicle was made, powered by one of their 3bhp motors with hot-tube ignition and automatic gear ratios for the chain drives to either rear wheel. It was found to be insufficiently powerful for practical use, even on the mild hills around Yeovil, and subsequent models were fitted with a larger 2-cylinder unit, also horizontally mounted under the seat. The prime mover behind this venture had been Percival Petter, but the wisdom of more cautious members of the family firm prevailed and the rights were transferred to the local coachbuilding firm of Hill and Boll. The cars were rugged but primitive, and attracted limited local interest

1896 Petter 3hp dog-cart.
NATIONAL MOTOR MUSEUM

1891 Peugeot Type 2 'Valentigney- Brest' *vis-à-vis*.
PEUGEOT

only. Hill and Boll also marketed an electric version. It is believed that about 12 cars in all were sold. Petters flourished subsequently as makers of stationary engines and a later attempt at car manufacture (the SEATON-PETTER of 1926) was also quite hastily abandoned. The first Petter ran in the Emancipation Run of 1896, but is believed not to have completed the course.

DF

PEUGEOT (i) (F) 1890 to date

1890–1896 Les Fils des Peugeot Frères, Valentigney.
1897–1900 S.A. des Automobiles Peugeot, Audincourt.
1900–1910 S.A. des Automobiles Peugeot, Paris.
1910–1926 S.A. des Automobiles et Cycles Peugeot, Paris.
1926–1965 S.A. des Automobiles Peugeot, Paris.
1965 to date Peugeot S.A., Automobiles Peugeot, Paris.
Alongside Panhard & Levassor, Peugeot ranks as the oldest make of car in the world. Benz and Daimler may have invented the car, but they did not produce cars as part of their core business, nor in a continuous fashion, as early as the French companies.

Peugeot was a prosperous and old established enterprise before making its first cars. Armand Peugeot (1849–1915) had started bicycle production and was eager to make cars. In 1888–89 he built three (or four) high-wheeled chassis destined for Serpollet steam engines. That was the cue for Gottlieb Daimler and Émile Levassor to persuade Peugeot to produce cars based on a Daimler concept with engines made by Panhard & Levassor under Daimler licence. The first

three-way contact was made in 1888. Daimler's wire-wheeled car was shown at the Universal Exposition in Paris in the summer of 1889, and a Peugeot engineer was taken for a 50km demonstration ride on it. Directly after the closure of the Exposition, Levassor and Daimler travelled to Valentigney for a meeting with Armand Peugeot, and an agreement was made.

The task of developing the wire-wheeled car into a real automobile fell to Louis Rigoulot, who had joined Peugeot in 1872 and was in charge of bicycle production. He had an engineering diploma from the École des Arts et Métiers at Angers, and had the first Peugeot prototype (with a vertical single-cylinder engine)) ready in April 1890. Auguste Doriot and André Rubichon were instrumental in its construction. Adopting the V-twin engine, they completed another prototype in June 1890, and a third in August 1890.

Production began tentatively at Valentigney with five cars in 1891, each one a new type, although basic similarities were kept. All had rear-mounted V-twin engines and chain drive, tubular steel frames, and tiller steering. The first elements of series production appeared in 1892, when Peugeot made 29 cars, followed by 24 in 1893 and 40 in 1894. As Rigoulot gained confidence in his own theories, he designed the 1895 Type 12 with its 1645cc V-twin engine located under the front seat. Only two Type 12s were built out of the 72-car total for 1895. By that time, Armand Peugeot had decided to make his own engines. The contract with Daimler blocked Peugeot from selling cars in Alsace and Switzerland without using Daimler as a middleman, and Peugeot wanted a free hand.

A horizontal parallel-twin was designed and patented by Gratien Michaux, and phased in, starting in 1896, as new models replaced older ones. It first appeared on Type 14, a commercial vehicle, next in Types 15, 16, 17, 18 and 19 passenger cars, and a small bus, Type 20. The last Panhard-Daimler powered models were Types 7, 9 and 11. Peugeot built 92 cars in 1896, but it was not enough for Armand. Fed up with the inertia of the family firm, he broke away and independently founded S.A. des Automobiles Peugeot in 1897, taking with him some of the best engineers (Rigoulot, Michaux, Doriot) and erected a new factory, specifically laid out for automobile production, at Audincourt. Peugeot's first series-produced model was Type 15, as the Audincourt plant turned out 276 phaetons from 1897 to 1902. A total of 87 *vis-à-vis* cars, Type 17, were also built there from 1897 to 1900.

At Armand's insistence, the Valentigney plant of Les Fils de Peugeot Frères was not to produce any more cars, but Eugène Peugeot made some quadricycles there between 1898 and 1901, and took up motorcycle production in 1899.

In 1899 Armand Peugeot set up a second auto plant, choosing a site in the Fives district of Lille, and a year later, he moved the head office to 83 boulevard Gouvion St Cyr, Paris XVII, near the Porte des Ternes. Peugeot's presence in the capital was reinforced in 1902 when Armand opened an experimental shop and drawing offices at Levallois and hired Louis Delage to run them.

In 1905 Delage left to set up his own company, and Armand Peugeot also lost the services of two other top-rank engineers, Michaux and Kuntz, to his brother Eugène, who – by offering a cash payment of one million Francs a year – persuaded Armand that building economy cars (Lion-Peugeot) at Valentigney would not hurt Armand's business. Armand then hired Ernest Mattern and Alfred Giauque who went on to long careers with S.A. des Automobiles Peugeot and S.A. des Automobiles et Cycles Peugeot.

Peugeot produced 323 cars at Audincourt in 1899 and 500 in 1900. The light cars, Types 24, 25, 26, 30 and 31 had rear-mounted engines, while the heavier ones, Types 27, 28 and 29 carried their engines under the front seat. All were behind the times, but modernisation began in 1901 with the arrival of Type 36, the first Peugeot with a steering wheel (on a raked column), powered by a vertical single-cylinder engine mounted under the driver's seat. Available as a spider or rear-entrance tonneau, it was built at Audincourt for an 18-month period, to a total of 111 cars.

In 1902 Peugeot adopted front-mounted engines for all new models, beginning with the single-cylinder Type 48 and the make's first 4-cylinder car, Type 39, which was also the first model made at the Lille factory. Chain drive was retained for the 2042cc 10hp Type 39, but the 6½hp 833cc Type 48 and 5hp 562cc Type 37 featured shaft drive, which was then phased in, starting from the low-powered end, with Types 54, 56, 58 and 63. The last chain-driven passenger cars were Types 112 and 113 in 1909. Type 39 was built at Audincourt as well as Lille, to a total of 100 cars. The same engine was used for Types 43 and 44 in 1903, to a total of 132 cars, all from the Lille plant.

1900 Peugeot Type 16 1000-Mile Trial 2-seater.
NICK BALDWIN

The most popular Peugeot was Type 54 from Audincourt, a 652cc 5hp single-cylinder car, with 250 units produced in 1903. Audincourt also turned out 100 Type 37 in 1902, 149 Type 57 in 1903, and 131 Type 48 in 1902. The biggest Peugeot yet was the 18hp 3635cc Type 42, built at Lille in 1903 in a quantity of 79 cars.

As Lion-Peugeot grew in importance and Armand's personal fortune diminished, he reached a new agreement with Eugène in 1910 whereby they combined all their automobile activities, but left Les Fils des Peugeot Frères as sole owners of the bicycles, motorcycles, steel and tool branches. The general idea, which probably came from Ernest Mattern who had successfully reorganised the Lille plant, reducing the time taken to complete a chassis from 10 days to three, was to consolidate all car production in one factory – but which? The choice fell on Sochaux, close to Beaulieu, Montébliard, Valentigney and Audincourt, where S.A. des Automobiles et Cycles Peugeot took over the ROSSEL plant in 1910. A friend of Armand's, Frédéric Rossel had been producing a small car there since 1903. Armand had originally backed him in setting up a coil-ignition factory as early as 1898, and a year later the École Centrale graduate, whose career began with the Société du Téléphone in Paris, became a vice-director of Automobiles Peugeot. But Armand was no longer in control. His nephew Robert Peugeot took charge of the Audincourt, Valentigney, Beaulieu and Lille factories in 1910.

It was a long-term plan, however, for in 1912 Ernest Mattern began to modernise the Audincourt factory, and a year later, Armand Peugeot persuaded the coachbuilder Henri Gauthier of Villeurbanne near Lyon to set up a body plant at Mandeure near Beaulieu to fill Peugeot's orders more efficiently. The Beaulieu plant was completely retooled in 1912 to produce a small car based on a Bugatti prototype from 1911. The 6CV Type BP-1, popularly known as the Bébé Peugeot was produced from 1913 to 1916 to a total of 3095 cars.

Car production ended at Lille, however, in 1914, its last models being the 150 and 150 S, elegant high-performance touring cars with a 40hp 7478cc long-stroke 4-cylinder engine. It was converted to make parts for the other assembly points, and produce rear axles for trucks, Peugeot became heavily engaged in the transport side of war production, and began assembling trucks at Sochaux, in 1913. During World War I, Peugeot acquired factories in the Paris suburbs of La Garenne, Clichy, and Issy-les-Moulineaux, and produced 6000 trucks, 3000 cars and ambulances, 10,000 motorcycles and 60,000 bicycles.

The technical management had begun to change in 1905 with the arrival of Giauque and Mattern. Doriot left in 1906 to build his own cars in partnership with Ludovic Flandrin, and the faithful Rigoulot withdrew in 1915 to join Panhard & Levassor. Twice Robert Peugeot sent Alfred Giauque on study-tours of the American auto industry (1915 and 1917) and after his second return to Levallois, Giauque was placed in charge of preparing all new models. Giauque had

PEUGEOT

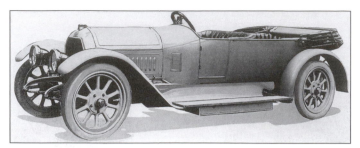

1912 Peugeot 22/30hp tourer.
NICK BALDWIN

1914 Peugeot Bébé 6hp 2-seater.
NICK BALDWIN

1912 Peugeot Type 135 tourer.
BRYAN K. GOODMAN

been a member of the original design team for Type 153 in 1912–13, and supervised its revival in 1920 as the 153 B with the same engine bored out to 2746 cc and uprated to 14hp. No less than 1325 units were produced at Audincourt from 1920 to 1922. The 153 BR, BRA, BRS and 153 C from 1921 to 1925, to the tune of 1831 units, had a 2951cc version of the same engine.

Robert Peugeot felt that competition from Panhard forced him to offer silent engines, at least in the high-priced models, so Giauque's staff developed a 5954cc 6-cylinder sleeve-valve engine for the 1921 Type 156. It was the first car produced at Sochaux, a luxury car on a 145in (3670mm) wheelbase, available in five body styles from torpedo to limousine. But Giauque's greatest success was the Type 163 which he began preparing in 1917 and went into production at Audincourt in 1919. It was a 10hp all-purpose car which enjoyed such success, that demand could only be met by drawing also on Beaulieu's capacity, and 9349 were built over a 5-year span.

The 1919–20 Type 159 was a brand-new model meant to replace the Lion-Peugeot, with a 4-cylinder 1452cc engine. It was assembled at Beaulieu alongside the Type 161 Quadrilette which replaced the Bébé Peugeot.

Most of the capacity at Beaulieu was also used for production of the Type 161 Quadrilette, a narrow economy car with two seats in tandem, powered by a 667cc 4-cylinder L-head engine, with cast-iron block and integral head, with the crankshaft running in two (main) roller bearings. The gearbox was combined with the worm drive rear axle. Over two years, 3500 Quadrilettes were made. The Quadrilette was redesigned as Type 172 in 1922, with staggered seats, and 8705 of them were produced at Beaulieu in less than two years. In 1924, production was transferred to Sochaux, and later the engine size was increased to 720 cc. Type 172 M was produced up to August 1928, to be replaced two months later by the 5CV Type 190 S which inherited the 695cc engine from the 172 M and was produced up to April 1931 in a run of 33,677 units.

Peugeot was still a long way from rational car production, for the Audincourt factory remained active; car production began at Issy-les Moulineaux in 1922, with Type 174 which had a 75hp 3828cc 4-cylinder sleeve-valve engine, and even the Levallois shop produced nine cars, Type 164, with a 4-cylinder 2951cc engine in 1920.

Peugeot's finances suffered in 1921–22, and Ernest Mattern recommended changing to a one-model programme, which would permit closure of the most inefficient plants. But he came into conflict with the managing director, Alexandre Lemoine, who wanted to maintain a full range of cars. In protest, Mattern resigned in November 1923, and was immediately snapped up by Citroën. Realising the seriousness of the situation, Robert Peugeot turned to Lucien Rosengart, well-known in financial circles for his rescue operation at Citroën. To open a new credit line for Peugeot, Rosengart founded Société d'Extension de l'Industrie Automobile, with a capital of FFr 20 million. With a director's title at Peugeot, he began a frenzied run of sales promotions and publicity stunts, and established Peugeot Maritime to make motorboats with engines taken from the car programmes. In 1926 he went to the Bourse, offering a new Peugeot stock issue at FFr 550 a share. At he same time, the bicycle/motorcycle branch was spun off as a separate firm, Société des Cycles Peugeot.

The Audincourt plant turned out 12,636 Type 183 12-Six L-head 1991cc cars from 1927 to 1931, a sensible family car competing against lower-priced Citroën models. Three models (14CV Type 176, 18CV Type 174 S and 22CV Type 184) with sleeve-valve engines were still being produced at Issy-les-Moulineaux in 1929. They were up-market cars, and production totals were 1512 Type 176, 208 Type 174 S, and a mere 31 Type 184.

In 1927 Peugeot purchased a licence to manufacture Junkers 2-stroke diesel engines, and began retooling the Lille plant, which was incorporated in 1928 as the Compagnie Lilloise des Moteurs.

In January 1928, Robert Peugeot dismissed Rosengart (with a handsome cheque) and sought out Mattern, offering him the title of technical director. He rejoined Peugeot in February 1928 and within 18 months had brought the average number of man-hours per car down from 1000 to 500. Ernest Mattern (1879–1952) had an engineering diploma from the École des Arts et Métiers, and now he was in command of new-product planning and development as well as production. He set about making reality of his old idea of a one-model programme. Alfred Giauque was still running the drawing office, but Mattern gave him an assistant in the person of Louis Dufresne (1890–1958) from Bourg-en-Bresse who had an engineering degree from the École Centrale and worked for Panhard & Levassor from 1913 to 1917, then with Citroën until 1922, and Voisin until 1927, when he joined Peugeot to work in advanced design and take charge of competition cars, from economy runs to endurance racing. Together they led the design team for the Peugeot 201, under Mattern's orders.

It was almost a new car from the ground up. The 6CV SE-series engine was a 1122cc L-head design with aluminium pistons and a 2-bearing crankshaft which put out 23hp at 3500rpm. The 3-speed gearbox and worm drive rear axle were newly developed. The new pressed-steel frame had straight channel-section side members, spaced wider at the back, with four cross-members but no X-bracing. The rear suspension was made under Bugatti licence, with reversed quarter-elliptics, and the original front suspension, strictly a stop-gap solution, was lifted from the 190 S.

Assembled at Sochaux and introduced in October 1929, it did not immediately replace anything but the 172 S. The 190 S and 190 Z were phased out during

1931, and the 1991cc 6-cylinder Type 183 was also produced throughout the 1931 model year.

Long-planned factory closures were finally made. The Issy-les-Moulineaux plant was shut down in 1929, at the end of the Type 184 production run, and the Audincourt plant closed in 1931 and was sold to Les Fils des Peugeot Frères in 1933. Les Fils des Peugeot Frères was reorganised as Aciers et Outillage Peugeot on 15 December 1941. By 1932 Peugeot had also disposed of the Clichy and Levallois facilities, concentrating Paris-area activities at La Garenne. Sochaux produced 43,303 Type 201 cars in 1930 and 33,322 in 1931. At the end of 1931, the 201 was in fact the sole model in production, and Sochaux was the only production centre, with a work force of 8000.

The one-model policy, however, burst at the seams. To preserve its clientele, Peugeot needed a bigger car, and the 301 was cleverly created as a stretched 201 with a slightly bigger (1465cc) version of the same engine. It appeared in June 1932. The 201 C, launched in October 1931, featured ifs, which was also adopted for the 301. The basic 201 was kept in production for another year. Total 201 production sank to 28,317 cars in 1932, while the 301 was off to a fast start with 20,371 cars made in its initial nine months on the market. During 1933 both models were restyled by Henri Thomas, an artist who had designed a number of bodies for Binder and often worked directly for individual customers, and went to work full-time for Peugeot in 1932. Peugeot also had a contract with Jean Andreau for advice on aerodynamics.

The 201 D of 1934 had a redesigned engine, 1307cc with a 3-bearing crankshaft, which put out 35hp at 4000rpm. The 301 engine was not enlarged but was also given three main bearings. But from October 1933 to August 1936, Peugeot built no more than 13,174 Type 201 D while in the same period the 301 reached a total of 17,417 units. For 1937 the old 301 was renamed 201 M and 16,66 cars were made from August 1936 to September 1937, when the line was halted to make room for the 202.

Earlier, Alfred Giauque had retired, and Louis Dufresne was named chief engineer. Soon he hired Lucien Godard, whose engineering degree came from the École des Arts et Métiers, and Guy de Sèze, with a degree from the École Centrale des Arts et Manufactures, as members of the technical staff.

The model line-up spread with the addition of the 401 in September 1934, scaled up from the 301, although common parts were few. The 4-cylinder 1720cc engine was basically an old 12-Six with two cylinders chopped off, shorter stroke and bigger bore, tuned to deliver 44hp at 4000 rpm. The Sochaux plant turned out 13,545 of them before it was replaced by the 402 in October 1935. A six cylinder 2148cc version went into the 601, launched in May 1934 and discontinued in July 1935, after a production run of 3999 cars.

Jean Andreau had designed some streamlined bodies for Peugeot chassis, but they were advanced to the point of non-realism. The task of turning their shapes into practical car bodies fell to Henri Thomas and the chief body engineer, Schumacher. The 402 came first, in October 1935, standing on a 124in (3150mm) wheelbase and weighing 1195kg. The engine was a new 55hp 4-cylinder ohv design by Victor Dornier, 1991cc until July 1938, when it was enlarged to 2148cc and output climbed to 63hp. They had fastback 4-door saloon bodies without running boards, and were instantly recognisable by their headlamps mounted behind the radiator grill.

The same shape, somewhat shortened, was used for the body of the 302, which went into production in September 1936, with a 1658cc version of the 402 engine, followed in February 1938, by the 202. It was powered by an ohv 4-cylinder 1133cc engine which delivered 30hp at 4000rpm. The 402 became 402 B in July 1938, and the 402 B Légère was created by putting the 202 body (from the cowl back) on a shortened 402 chassis.

Now Peugeot had a coherent model programme, a logical extension of Mattern's old monoculture principle. When civilian car production was suspended in the summer of 1940, the 402 had reached a total of 67,840 units, the 302 reached 25,080, and the 202 (remaining in production until June 1942), 52,774 units. The planned 802, shown in October 1936, never progressed beyond the prototype stage.

Like the rest of France's auto industry, Peugeot was forced to turn its plants over to war production for the Nazi occupants. But Mattern and Godard gave the Germans such a hard time that, in 1943, they were deported to Germany!

The drawing office hummed with secret projects, the chief one being the postwar car. Guy de Sèze persuaded his colleagues to adopt unit body construction and created a new coil-spring rear suspension. Victor Dornier designed a new

1921 Peugeot Type 156 coupé de ville.
NICK BALDWIN

1930 Peugeot 201 saloon.
NATIONAL MOTOR MUSEUM

1932 Peugeot 301C roadster.
NICK BALDWIN

engine with hemispherical combustion chambers. But they could not yet build test cars. However, they did make 377 light electric cars called VLV (Voitures Légères de Ville), with four 12-volt batteries under the bonnet, giving a speed of 20mph (32km/h) and a range of 50 miles (80km).

The Peugeot plants in the Doubs were liberated on 17–18 November 1944. But during the occupation, the Germans had taken 1545 machines out of Sochaux alone to replace machines in bombed-out German plants. Only a few were retrieved. Peugeot's wartime losses were estimated at FFr 1.2 billion.

Production resumed in 1945 with the 202, and that year Sochaux turned out 2965 of them. It was kept in production until May 1949, with a total crop of 41,445 units built from 1946 to the end.

Robert Peugeot had died in 1944 at the age of 71 and his three sons took over the business: Jean-Pierre in Automobiles, Eugène in bicycles, and Rodolphe in

1935 Peugeot 601 cabriolet with electric hood.
NICK BALDWIN

1938 Peugeot 202 saloon.
NATIONAL MOTOR MUSEUM

c.1958 Peugeot 203 saloon.
NICK BALDWIN

tools and appliances. Jean-Pierre Peugeot was a graduate of the École Centrale des Arts et Manufactures who had been given his first responsibilities with the firm in 1921 and held executive office since 1934.

Jean Nicolas (1891–1984) was the Peugeot executive who was given the task of rebuilding the Sochaux plant in 1945. He was a civil engineer, graduate of the École des Mines de Paris, who had experience from Pechiney and Michelin before he joined Peugeot in the sales department in 1928.

The postwar car was given the number 203 and the first prototype was road-tested on 15 July 1946. It made its debut at the Paris Salon in October 1948, and a year later, Sochaux was building approximately 200 of them every day. Peugeot was once more back with a one-model programme. Thomas's new styling was American-inspired, making a complete break with the prewar models. The engine was a 1290cc four with splayed ohv actuated from a single camshaft in the side of the block, delivering 42hp at 4500rpm. It had a 4-speed gearbox with column shift and a worm drive rear axle. During its 12-year production life, very few modifications were made, and at the end, on 26 February 1960, Sochaux had built 685,828 units (not including the commercial versions – van and pick-up truck) with sedan, station wagon, coupé, and convertible (2- and 4-door) bodies.

Louis Dufresne was named Technical Director in 1950, with Lucien Godard as chief engineer. Maurice Jordan became a vice president in 1947, and François Gautier, a mining engineer who had joined Peugeot at the age of 24 in 1930, became assistant managing director in 1949. Another leader was Francis Rougé, graduate of the École Polytechnique, who came to Peugeot at the age of 32 in 1953.

Georges Boschetti succeeded Henri Thomas as head of body design in 1948, having joined Peugeot in 1943 at the age of 24, but Jean-Pierre Peugeot was worried about falling behind the styling trend and established contact with Pinin Farina in 1951. The engine design department passed from Victor Dornier to François Gastine.

Peugeot's one-model programme came to an end in April 1955, with the arrival of the 403, which was essentially an upscaled 203 chassis with a Pinin Farina body, retouched by Boschetti and produced at Sochaux. Lucien Godard served as project manager, with Marcel Dangauthier at his side. The 403 also had a 12-year production life, with a total of 894,638 cars (saloon, cabriolet, station wagon) not counting some 320,000 commercial versions, ending in October 1966.

Lucien Godard was also the project manager for the 404, which was launched in May 1960. It had a more modern Pinin Farina body design, and MacPherson type front suspension replaced the traditional transverse leaf spring. The initial engine was a 1618cc unit derived from the 203/403, tilted 45 degrees to the

1955 Peugeot 403 saloon.
NICK BALDWIN

1962 Peugeot 404 saloon.
NICK BALDWIN

1965 Peugeot 204 saloon.
NICK BALDWIN

right for a lower bonnet line. It was produced with an increasing number of body styles (station wagon at Sochaux, coupé and cabriolet by Pininfarina) and options (diesel engine, petrol injection, automatic transmission) up to 1975 in a quantity of 2,800,000.

Not having a small car in the range was seen as hindering the company's growth as early as 1951. The RV-54 pre-project from 1953 began with a 500cc V-twin model, soon discarded. By 1958 top management decided in favour of a car with the same interior space as the 203, but costing 20 per cent less. The DX project was defined as a front-wheel drive car with the engine mounted transversely, suitable for a number of body styles. It was formalised as the D-12 in 1959, under Dangauthier's overall command, with Paget as project manager. Paul Bouvot directed the styling in consultation with Pinin Farina, and Claude Chillon was responsible for the structure. Claude de Forcrand and Xavier Karcher drew up the suspension and steering. Soubise created a single-ohc 1130cc engine which put out 53hp at 5800rpm, and Michel Forichon designed the gearbox and final drive unit for the Peugeot 204.

This car broke new ground for Peugeot, and within 25 years of its April 1965 launch date, its general layout had been adopted for all Peugeot cars, from the smallest to the largest. The 204 estate car went into production late in 1965, the coupé and cabriolet following in 1966. When the 204 was taken out of production in 1976, over 1,600,000 had been made.

Jean-Pierre Peugeot retired in 1964 and Maurice Jordan inherited the presidency. In 1965, he established Automobiles Peugeot as a fully owned subsidiary of Peugeot, S.A. and François Gautier became the first president of Automobiles Peugeot.

A chance meeting in Canada between Maurice Jordan and Pierre Dreyfus of Renault in 1966 led to an agreement on a joint venture for engine production, which became reality in 1969 with the opening of the Française de Mécanique at Douvrin. Peugeot and Renault also agreed on further co-operation schemes. In March 1970 Peugeot and Renault signed a joint project for a transmission plant near Bruay-en-Artois, to come on stream in late 1971.

The marketing staff wanted a car to fill the gap between the 204 and 404. Appearing in September 1969, the 304 shared the wheelbase and platform of the 204, but was 150mm longer, and had a 58.5hp 1288cc version of the XL engine with a 1357cc diesel option. The 69hp 304 S of October 1972, was built with saloon, coupé and cabriolet body styles. Assembly of the sports models (which replaced the 204 coupé and cabriolet in April 1970) was subcontracted to Chausson, who also supplied the bodies. This arrangement ended in August 1975. The 304 saloon was discontinued in the summer of 1979.

Major changes had occurred in the executive suite. Francis Rougé became president of Automobiles Peugeot in 1973, but after his untimely death in 1976, Jean Baratte held that office for three years. The Peugeot family still held the reins, and in 1972 Roland Peugeot assumed the chair of the Peugeot SA supervisory board while continuing as a director of Automobiles Peugeot's management board.

François Gautier retired in 1976, and the next PSA president was Jean-Paul Parayre, a graduate of the École Polytechnique who had worked for state enterprises and ministries for 11 years before joining Peugeot in 1974. Jean Boillot, Peugeot's sales director, was promoted president of Automobiles Peugeot on 1 January 1980. Michel Forichon had succeeded Dangauthier in 1976, and in 1980 Jean Moulin replaced François Gastinne as head of engine design.

The 305, launched in November 1977, was only partly a replacement for the 304. It also replaced the low end of the 404 family. The wheelbase was increased to 103in (2620mm) and X-series engines of 65 and 74hp were offered. The 305 project manager was Yvan Plazanet, who had come to Peugeot in 1967 as a methods engineer at Sochaux. The body structure came from the 'synthesis safety vehicle' research project. A 305 estate car appeared in March 1980, and the 86hp (1472cc) 305 S arrived in October 1980. In September 1981, assembly of the 305 was transferred from Sochaux to Mulhouse.

A second-generation 305 went into production in September 1982, with aerodynamic modifications developed on the VERA research car, lowering the drag coefficient from 0.44 to 0.38. At the same time, the 305 received new XU-series engines and a wider front track. The one-millionth 305 was made in December 1982. The 84hp (1580cc) 305 GT came on the market in February 1983. The 305 was taken out of production in 1988.

Peugeot still took an orthodox approach to the big cars from Sochaux. The 504, introduced in September 1968, was aimed at the upper strata of the 404 market segment, and had rear wheel drive. The big change in the chassis was the adoption of irs, with trailing arms and coil springs, and the use of a torque tube for the propeller shaft. Built on a 108in (2740mm) wheelbase, the base model had a dry weight of 2640lb (1200kg). The standard 1796cc XM-series engine was tilted 45 degrees to the right. Coupé and cabriolet versions with a 103hp engine, on a shorter 100in (2538mm) wheelbase went into production in Pininfarina's Grugliasco plant at a rate of 20 units a day in March 1969.

From 1971 to 1975 a 110hp fuel-injection engine was offered in the sports models to be replaced by the 136hp V6. The 4-cylinder injection engine returned in 1978, when the V6 went to fuel injection and was restricted to the 504 coupé. The 504 estate car, with a heavy-duty rear axle in place of the delicate independent suspension, became available in April 1971. When 504 production ended in May 1983, Peugeot had produced 2,607,123 saloons, 645,208 estate cars, 16,746 coupé and 7211 cabriolets.

The 604 was meant as a luxury car, and the original design called for a V8 engine which was designed by François Gastinne. But its launch, in July 1975, followed two serious rises in the price of motor fuel, so the engine was hurriedly redesigned as a V6 (at the same 90 degree angle and with irregular firing intervals). The 604 SRD had the 73hp diesel engine from the Lille plant. Drive lines used PSA 4-speed gearboxes or ZF 3-speed automatic transmissions. Sales of the 604 never came up to expected level, but it was kept in production until 1988.

Peugeot was simultaneously expanding its range up-market with the 604 and down-market with the 104. The tiny 4-door 104 saloon was built on a 95in (2420mm) wheelbase and weighed 1672lb (760kg). The XV3 engine was mounted transversely. and almost horizontally (721 from vertical), driving the front wheels. It was the first car to be assembled at the new Mulhouse plant, beginning in October 1972. Peugeot began operations at Mulhouse in November 1962, making gearbox parts for the 403 and 404, and in 1968 a stamping plant and body-welding shops were added. The 104 ZS coupé was added in September 1975, and the ZS hatchback in July 1976. The 104 S appeared in September 1979, with a more powerful engine and (since July 1981) a 5-speed gearbox. The 104 was facelifted in February 1982 and got a 50hp XW-7 engine and faster gearing. The lively 104 ZL came on the market in September 1982. Peugeot produced 1,624,000 cars of 104 specification up to July 1988 when it was discontinued.

Jean-Paul Parayre came to Peugeot with ideas of new ways of expansion. He had his eye on Citroën, whose 1968 merger plan with Fiat had failed, and was doomed as an independent business, with huge debts and operational losses. Michelin had minority control of Citroën and was eager to sell. The government was ready to pay subsidies to save the jobs of Citroën's work force. Jean-Paul Parayre opened formal talks with François Michelin on 24 June 1974, and on 6 December 1974 Peugeot took a 38.2 per cent stake in Citroën, paying two Peugeot shares and one Michelin share per 30 Citroën shares. The government granted PSA a $68million low-interest loan to keep Citroën afloat. On 8 April 1976, Peugeot formalised the ownership by raising its shareholding to 90 per cent.

The following year a new engine subsidiary was set up, Société Mécanique Automobile de l'Est, with a big factory (and room to expand) at Tréméry in Lorraine, to produce the coming XU and XUD engines.

Dominique Savey was named director of planning and products, with the main task of co-ordinating the future model ranges of both makes in a rational production system. Born in 1932, he had a diploma from the IEP in Paris and two years' banking experience when he came to Peugeot in 1959 as a specialist in economics, finance, and pricing. Ten years later he was head of a new PSA office for economic forecasting and planning.

Citroën's former director of methods, Michel Durin, was moved up to group level in 1979 and spent two years as director of research. On 1 October 1981, he was named technical director for the group, with responsibility for putting Savey's plans to work – or change them.

The Citroën purchase doubled the production capacity and turnover of Peugeot SA, but Jean-Paul Parayre was still building his empire. For three days in August 1978, he sat at a table in London, facing John J. Riccardo and Eugene C. Cafiero, negotiating the purchase of Chrysler Corp.'s subsidiaries in Europe. Peugeot gave Chrysler $230 million and a $100 million loan plus 1.8 million PSA shares with a buy-back option.

This gave Peugeot three new production centres: the ex-Simca base at Poissy, the ex-Rootes factory at Ryton-on-Dunsmore and the ex-Barreiro's installations at Villaverde near Madrid, a number of new (and old) models, plus some useful engines. It took Peugeot until June 1986, to repurchase all its shares.

Integration of the ex-Chrysler operations with the PSA organisation proved to be a slow and costly process, and Peugeot SA ran into a period of heavy deficits. Jean-Paul Parayre got the blame, and was forced to resign in September 1983. He was replaced by Jacques Calvet, former president of the Banque Nationale de Paris, who had left the bank in 1982 to join Peugeot as a member of the management board.

The project that led to the 505 began in 1974, before the launch of the 604, and a full-size mock-up by Paul Bouvot was presented to management in February 1976. Tooling-up began in November 1976, at Sochaux; production started in April 1979. It did not so much replace the 504 as fill the gap between the 504 and the 604, but damaged the sales of both.

The 505 estate car, with a sturdy rear axle and dual-coil springs, came out in February 1982, along with a 505 Turbodiesel. The 505 TI appeared late in 1982

1975 Peugeot 605 saloon.
NICK BALDWIN

1977 Peugeot 504TI saloon.
NICK BALDWIN

with an ex-Chrysler engine renamed N9TE and the 170hp V6 ZN3J with its even-firing crankshaft became available in July 1986. The 505 was discontinued in May 1992, after a production run of 1,337,700 cars.

Work on Project M-24 began in 1979. It was a small hatchback aimed against the VW Golf. Forichon pinned down the definition and handed it over to Robert Marazzato, head of small-car projects. Yvan Plazanet was named project manager. Georges Oberlé (architecture), Armand Froumajou (chassis) and Jean Moulin (engines) were the principal engineers. Bruno de Guibert was in the drawing office at La Garenne and Michel Provent at Sochaux.

It was named 205, and 3- and 5-door hatchbacks went into production: in November 1982, at Mulhouse; in October 1983 at Poissy; in January 1984 at Villaverde, and in May 1984 at Sochaux. A Pininfarina-built cabriolet followed in March 1986.

Built on the same 95in (2420mm) wheelbase as the 104, the 205 incorporated lessons in lightweight construction from the VERA research car. The rear suspension was new, now using torsion bars instead of coil springs.

The 205 Turbo 16 4×4 rally car appeared in February 1983, and the 105hp 205 GTI sprang on the market in March 1984. The 205 TurboDiesel went on sale in June 1985. The one-millionth 205 was made in December 1985. The GTI went to 115hp in March 1986, and the 205 Automatic was also added. Production of the 205 passed the 5-million mark in February 1995, including 1,212,000 diesel cars and 56,000 cabriolets. It was discontinued in August 1998.

Chrysler had been working for some time on a project called C-28 which Peugeot took over and altered so it could use a maximum of 205 parts. It went into production at Poissy in September 1985 as the Peugeot 309 and was also made at the former Chrysler (originally Rootes Group) factory at Ryton-on-Dunsmore, Coventry.

What became the 405 began as Project D 60 in October 1982, under the overall direction of Michel Durin. It shared the platform with the Citroën BX, using coil springs instead of air springs, and had its own body, designed by Gérard Welter in consultation with Pininfarina. The 405 saloon went into production at Sochaux in June 1987, and Ryton in October 1987, followed by

1985 Peugeot 205 Turbo 16 hatchback.
NICK BALDWIN

1991 Peugeot 605 saloon.
PEUGEOT

the 405 estate car in January 1988. It was not a direct replacement for the 404, but a combined replacement for the 404 and 305.

The 405 Turbo 16 became available in June 1988, with a 220hp XU 10 V4 engine, and the 405 4 × 4 with ViscoDrive appeared in the spring of 1989. The final 405 from the Sochaux plant rolled off the line on 20 November 1996.

Next, PSA's management wanted a car to replace both the 604 and the 505. The project was given code name Z 6 and got the green light in September 1984. At the outset, the 605 was to share the Citroën XM platform, but converted to the rear-wheel-drive of the 505. Oberlé and Durin explained to management that such a plan would preclude optimisation of either product, and cause Citroën and Peugeot to develop two completely different cars, which would be too costly. They prevailed, and the Z 6 had to follow the basic layout of the 204. Georges Oberlé laid out the 605, Forichon directed the engineering, and Pierre Vuillaume was project manager at Sochaux. It went into production in November 1989, with 4-cylinder and V6 power trains. The 145hp 60 degree SRti came on the market in April 1993 and the new 600 V6 engine became available at mid-year 1997.

Project S 10 began in 1996 with Bruno de Guibert holding responsibility for synthesis, styling and engineering, and Pierre Béguin as project manager. Based

on the Citroën AX platform, it became the Peugeot 106 hatchback and went into production at Mulhouse in February 1991, and Sochaux in April 1997. The one-millionth 106 was built on 31 January 1995, and the 2-millionth 106 on 12 December 1997.

The 306 replaced the 309 on the Poissy assembly line in January 1993. The 4m long hatchback was a sister model to Citroën's ZX. Production of the 306 also began at Villaverde in March 1993, and at Ryton in June 1993. The 155hp 306 S 16 and the 123hp 306 XSI were added in October 1993, followed by the 306 cabriolet in March 1994.

Launched in May 1996, the 306 Maxi was a limited-production car with 275 hp and a 6-speed gearbox. A street version, the 306 GTI 6, appeared in January 1997, with a 163hp version of the same XU 10 engine, and a 6-speed gearbox. By April 1998, total production of the 306 was 1,867,528.

The project which became the 406 was started in January 1993, with Yvan Plazanet as project manager. It replaced the 405 on the Sochaux assembly line in June 1995. In a break with tradition, the styling was done entirely in the Peugeot studio by Gunat Murak who had been lured away from Mercedes-Benz to work under Gérard Welter. The turbocharged 406 SV 2 made its debut in July 1996, and the new ES 9 60 degree V6 became optional in October 1996. Late in 1996 Peugeot also showed the 406 Supertourisme, with a 300hp XU 9 engine and 6-speed gearbox.

The 406 coupé, designed and produced by Pininfarina, arrived in May 1997, followed by the 406 estate car in July 1997. By mid-year, 1998, total 406 production stood above 600,000 units.

The 206 project began in January 1995 and the new model replaced the 205 in September 1998. The 2- and 4-door hatchbacks were 150.5in (3220mm) in overall length and powered by TU-series petrol engines or DW-series diesel engines. The styling was another Gunat Murak creation, but his last for Peugeot, since he returned to Mercedes-Benz when production started.

The 206 is assembled at Mulhouse, its capacity needs forcing the transfer of 106 assembly to the Citroën plant at Aulnay. By its first birthday in September 1999 more than half a million 206s had been built, making it the fastest selling Peugeot model ever. In April 1999 Peugeot launched the 206 GT, as a limited-edition (4000 units) model, powered by a 137hp 1997cc engine in combination with the chassis elements of the 206 S.16.

Pascal Henault was named director of planning and products in January 1992, and has been vice president in charge of long-range planning since 1994. Born in 1946, he joined Peugeot in 1970 with degrees in mathematics and physics from the École Centrale de Lyon and a business-administration diploma from INSEAD.

Michel Durin retired in May 1993, and his place was filled by Henri Saintigny, born in 1944, and a graduate of the École Centrale in Paris. He joined Peugeot at Sochaux in 1968 and became head of the drawing office in 1988. Roland Julien took over the engine design office in 1993, with Jean Perez as head of advanced engine projects.

Dominique Savey and Jean-Yves Helmer became joint presidents of Automobiles Peugeot in 1992, replacing Jean Boillot on his retirement. Helmer had joined Peugeot in 1978 after holding a series of government posts and became director of the Poissy plant in January 1987. Five years later, he thought he was first-in-line to succeed Jacques Calvet, but when Calvet brought in a rival candidate, Jean-Martin Folz early in 1996, Helmer went back into government work. Folz, born in Strasbourg in 1948, was a mining engineer from the École Polytechnique who made his career with Rhône-Poulenc, Jeumont-Schneider, Péchiney and Eridania-Beghin-Say. He succeeded Calvet at the end of September 1997.

The 605 was dropped at the end of 1998 and replaced in September 1999, by the 607. (There was no 606.) It was 191.8in (4868mm) overall length, on a 110.2in (2797mm) wheelbase, made only as a 4-door saloon with styling at once simple and bold, extrapolating from the themes used on the 406 and 206. It was powered by new versions of engines from the 605 range, including a 160hp version of the 2230cc EW-12 4-cylinder, a 210hp version of the 2946cc ES-9 V6, and a 136hp turbo-diesel of 2179cc known as the DW-12. All had four valves per cylinder, and the petrol engines feature variable valve timing, electric accelerator, and sequential injection. The 4-cylinder DW-12 and EW-12 carry balance shafts, and the DW-12 has direct fuel injection (common rail), variable-geometry turbocharger, and a double flywheel. They were offered in combination with 5-speed manual and 4-speed ZF automatic transmissions.

JPN

Further Reading
Peugeot, sous le signe du lion, Pierre Dumont, EPA, 1976.
Armand Peugeot, Piere Casucci, Automobiles, Milano, 1988.
Les Sorciers du Lion, Christophe Dolteb and Alain Dusart, Calman-Levy, Paris, 1990.

PEUGEOT (ii) (RA) 1960 to date
1960–1963 Industriales Argentinos Fabricantes de Automotores S.A. (IAFA), Buenos Aires.
1964 to date Sociedad Anonima Franco Argentina de Automotores (SAFRAR), Buenos Aires.
IAFA SA started production of the Peugeot 403 under licence from Peugeot of France in 1960. This model was discontinued in 1965, after 22,120 had been made. The 404 was produced alongside the 403, but lasted until the 1970s. The 504 was introduced in 1969. Interestingly, some versions of the 504 were still being produced in 1999, particularly aimed at the taxi market. In 1999, Peugeot (ii) was producing the 306, which was introduced in 1995, the 405, and the 504 SL and 504 SLD.

ACT

PEUGEOT-CROIZAT (I) 1905–1907
1905–1906 SA Brevetti Automobili Peugeot, Turin.
1906–1907 Peugeot-Croizat SA, Turin.
Two models of Peugeot were built under licence in Italy, the single-cylinder Baby with capacity enlarged to 695cc and a honeycomb radiator in place of the original gilled-tube, and the 2.2-litre Type 71 four with T-head engine and chain drive. Few were made, and by 1908 the unsold stock of single-cylinder cars was being sold off in London.

NG

PEYKAN (IR) 1967 to date
Iran Khodro Vehicle Manufacturing Co., Teheran.
This national Iranian company began to make the 1725cc HILLMAN Hunter under licence; also a pick-up version which was sold in South Africa as the Dodge

1999 Peugeot 206 Gti hatchback.
PEUGEOT

2000 Peugeot 607 saloon.
PEUGEOT

Huskie. Production was halted during the Iranian Revolution, but was restarted in 1981 using a smaller engine of 1601cc from the TALBOT Avenger. This was still made, with little change, in 1999, alongside the PEUGEOT 405.

NG

PFLÜGER (D) 1900
Vereinigte Accumulatoren- und Elektrizitätswerke Dr Pflüger & Co., Berlin.
This battery manufacturing company tried to market electric cars, but very few were made.

HON

P & G see PRITCHETT & GOLD

P.G.E. (I) 1976–c.1982
Progetti Gestione Ecologiche, Milan.
This company developed a range of electric and hybrid vehicles for private and commercial use. Passenger vehicles included the 3P, a boxy looking 2/3-seater coupé and the 6P, an open 4-seater that closely resembled the Fissore Scout. All had light alloy bodies welded to tubular frames. A 72-volt motor drove the front wheels and the manufacturer claimed a top speed of 37mph (60km/h) and a range of up to 62 miles (100km). A hybrid internal combustion/electric option was also listed. P.G.E. instigated a computerised hiring system and a network of charging stations in Padua but the system did not spread nationally.

CR

P.G.O. (F) 1986 to date
1986–1990 P.G.O. Ingenierie, Pessac.
1990–1997 P.G.O. Automobiles SA, Nantes.
1997 to date Premium Greatest Oldmobiles, Étang sur Arroux.
This French company specialised in replicas. The C427 was an A.C. Cobra copy with a tubular chassis and all-independent suspension using either Ford V6 or Rover V8 engines, which was based on the SHELDONHURST kit. It subsequently launched a Porsche 356 Speedster replica on a shortened VW Beetle platform, assumed from a company called ROADSTER CAR. Both models had fibreglass bodywork and could be bought fully-built or in kit form. A further model was an electric microcar called the 204, which was a version of the PULI.

CR

1912 Phänomen Phänomobil Model 4 14/18hp tourer.
BRYAN K. GOODMAN

1925 Phänomen 12/50PS tourer.
NICK BALDWIN

1900 Phébus-Aster voiturette.
NATIONAL MOTOR MUSEUM

PHÄNOMEN (D) 1907–1927

1907–1910 Phänomen-Fahrradwerke Gustav Hiller, Zittau.
1910–1927 Phänomen-Werke Gustav Hiller AG, Zittau.

Karl Gustav Hiller (1863–1913) was an old-established bicycle maker who added motorcycles to his range in 1901 and 3-wheeled cars and vans in 1907. These had a single front wheel chain-driven by the engine which was mounted above it. At first a single-cylinder engine of 880cc was used, followed by a V-twin and from 1912 a 1536cc in-line four mounted transversely. Steering was by a long tiller, and some quite substantial vehicles were produced, with 101in (2563mm) wheelbase and 4-seater bodies, including landaulet and taxicabs. At least one 4-seater tourer was converted for snow travel, with skis replacing the rear wheels. The 3-wheelers, which were known as Phänomobils, were made up to 1927, though latterly most were delivery vans.

In 1911 Hiller introduced a conventional 4-wheeled car with 2590cc 10/12PS and 3968cc 16/45PS 4-cylinder engines. After World War I they were superseded by the Typ 412, a new design with shaft-driven single-ohc 4-cylinder engine of 3128cc and 50bhp. It was a promising high-quality car, and was made in short-wheelbase sports form with a 65bhp engine. However, in 1927 the company decided to concentrate on commercial vehicles with compressed-air cooling. After World War II the factory was nationalised, and vehicles were marketed under the name Robur. This continued until the early 1990s. Meanwhile Phänomen motorcycles were made by a new company in Bielefeld up to 1958.
HON

PHANTOM (i) (US) c.1981

Phantom Vehicle Co., Newport Beach, California.

The Turbo Phantom was a futuristic 3-wheeler that was powered by a turbo-charged Honda Gold Wing 1000cc motorcycle engine. Volkswagen front suspension was used with MG steering. The motorcycle rear suspension was heavily modified and disc brakes were used on all wheels. The body was a radical, fully-enclosed coupé with a wing-shaped forward section and a lift-up cockpit top. It was only sold in completed form. The Phantom Jet Fighter was their 3-wheeled kit car based on a motorcycle chassis and running gear mounted at the back. The two front wheels were enclosed by streamlined fairings that were attached to the main body shell by short wings. Phantom claimed 50 to 100mpg when their kit was built with a mid-sized motorcycle engine.
HP

PHANTOM (ii) *see* ADAYER

PHANTOM (iii) (GB) 1997 to date

Phantom Automotive, Kenilworth, Warwickshire.

The Phantom GTR was the first roadgoing project of a company that previously built only racing cars. It attracted immediate praise for the maturity of its design and conception. It was a 2-seater sports coupé with bespoke, race-derived suspension including push-rods at the front end. The mid-mounted powerplant was a Rover/Honda V6, although other possibilities were mooted. First seen publicly in 1997, it took a further two years to productionise the GTR.
CR

PHANTOM CORSAIR (US) 1937–1938

Rust Heinz, Pasadena, California.

This was a dream car built by Rust Heinz, second son of millionaire H.J. Heinz of 57 Varieties fame. It was powered by a Lycoming V8 engine as used in the CORD 810 mounted in a special chassis with an ultra-streamlined body designed by Heinz and built for him by Maurice Schwartz of the coachbuilders Bohman & Schwartz. The bench-type front seat could accommodate four passengers, with two almost uninhabitable seats behind it. Door opening was by electrically-operated push buttons. Heinz planned to market the car at about $14,000, but his death in a car crash (not in the Phantom Corsair) in 1939 put an end to the project. The car featured in the 1938 film *Young at Heart,* where it was called the Flying Wombat, and survives today.
NG

PHÉBUS (i) (F) 1899–1903

Noé Boyer et Cie, Suresnes, Seine.

Phébus-Aster tricycles had been made for some time when the Phébus-Aster car appeared. It was a 2-seater voiturette powered by a 3½hp single-cylinder Aster engine, with 2-speed transmission and spur gear drive. The first cars imported into Britain were called Automobilettes; they had 2¾hp engines and no bonnets, whereas the later cars had small bonnets. Noé Boyer, who also made BOYER cars, was the commercial director of the Phébus branch of Clement-Gladiator & Humber Ltd, who made the tricycles.
NG

1938 Phantom Corsair coupé.
NATIONAL MOTOR MUSEUM

PHÉBUS (ii) **(F)** 1921

Cyclecars Phébus, Lyons.

Probably no more than a prototype was made of the Phébus cyclecar which had a 2-cylinder engine.

NG

PHELPS (US) 1903–1905

Phelps Motor Car Co., Stoneham, Massachusetts.

The Phelps was an unusual car with 15hp vertical 3-cylinder engine which, with the transmission, was supported on the axles, avoiding the use of a traditional frame, and substituting a tube through which the drive shaft ran. A 5-seater rear-entrance tonneau was the only body style. Although the 3-cylinder engine was continued through the Phelps' life, it was steadily enlarged, to 20hp for 1904 and 24hp for 1905. The wheelbase was also extended each year, from 78 (1980mm) to 84in (2132mm), and finally to 106in (2690mm). The makers did little advertising as they said the cars were sold from the factory 'without noise or bombast'. For 1905 production was planned to be 125 cars, but L.J. Phelps retired in September, and this spelt the end for the Phelps car. A 4-cylinder car costing $4000 was said to have been available to custom order during 1905, and a new company, Courier Motor Co. was going to make this in 1906, but apparently they never did. Instead the SHAWMUT Motor Co. moved into the factory.

NG

PHÉNIX (F) 1912–1914

Automobiles Phénix, Puteaux, Seine.

This car was made by Prunel Frères, Dumas et Cie who had made the J.P, PRUNEL and PRUNELLO cars, and was the last product of this complex firm. Three models were shown at the 1912 Paris Salon of 10, 12 and 15hp, all with 4-cylinder engines and shaft drive.

NG

PHIANNA (US) 1916–1922

1916–1918 Phianna Motors Co., Newark, New Jersey.

1919–1922 M.H. Carpenter, Long Island City, New York.

The Phianna was the lineal successor to the S. G. V. which had been built in Reading, Pennsylvania from 1911 to 1915, its purchasers having bought its factory and related material, thereupon moving operations to Newark, New Jersey. Named after the twin daughters of one of the organisers – Phyllis and Anna – the concept of the Phianna was to continue the production of a car similar to the S. G. V., a 4-cylinder car of the highest quality and with custom coachwork when specified. The first Phiannas carried a distinctive and patented oval-shaped radiator, similar to the Brewster and the French Delaunay-Belleville

cars. These Phiannas were highly priced and production was limited, although the cars, with their in-house 4-cylinder engines, became relatively well known as one of the country's finest luxury automobiles. With the country's entrance into World War I, the Phianna company was taken over by the Wright-Martin Aircraft Corp. and, following the Armistice, Phianna did not resume automobile production and was offered for sale. It was bought by Miles Harold Carpenter, an automobile enthusiast who had purchased a Phianna and had some ideas of his own regarding automobile design. Carpenter moved the Phianna operations to Long Island City, New York and redesigned the car throughout, including a Rolls-Royce-shaped radiator. The new Phianna was enthusiastically received upon its introduction at the New York Auto Show in the Autumn of 1919 and subsequent sales, although not large, were consistent with a price bracket ranging from $6000 to $11,500, depending on the coachwork, which included several of the nation's top quality coachbuilders. The 4-cylinder Phianna engine was improved and the chassis was standardised to 125in (3172mm). Wire wheels were standard on all Phianna models and, although the car was domestically built, its slogan was 'The Foreign Car Made in America', a concession, probably, to a widely held view that European cars held a superiority in motordom. The well-deserved reputation of Phianna's excellence became widespread and a galaxy of prominent people became owners, notably the King of Spain, the President of Brazil, and Bainbridge Colby, the latter Secretary of State in the Woodrow Wilson Administration.

In addition to the manufacture of cars, Miles Carpenter continued to supply S. G. V. parts to S. G. V. owners, a policy initiated by the original Phianna company. By 1921 Carpenter was also building a handful of cars, powered by the converted Curtiss OX-5 aircraft engine, for Glenn Curtiss and, at the same time, working on a new design for a larger, more powerful Phianna.

The new, projected Phianna never proceeded beyond the drawing board, a victim of the depression that ended numerous automobile companies including the operations of Miles Harold Carpenter.

A handful of cars were built from remaining parts and sold as 1922 cars, some of them equipped with the Curtiss OX-5 engine which had also been featured in the contemporary Prado and Wharton cars.

Phianna production has been estimated at between 50 and 100 cars.

KM

PHILIPSON (S) 1946

Gunnar Philipson, Augustendal.

Philipson's intention was to make a modernised D.K.W. at a factory previously used to assemble Dodge and Chrysler vehicles. The familiar D.K.W. engine was retained but hydraulic brakes were added and the bodywork was improved. Scarce supplies of prewar D.K.W.s caused the early demise of this project.

CR

1981 Phillips Berlina coupé.
ELLIOT KAHN

1913 Philos 8CV 2-seater.
NATIONAL MOTOR MUSEUM

PHILLIPS (US) c.1979–1985

Phillips Motor Car Corp., Pompano Beach, Florida.
The Phillips Berlina was a neoclassic kit car with styling borrowed from 1930s vintage Mercedes sedans. They were built on Chevrolet Corvette chassis that were stretched 22ins (558mm). The Corvette cockpit area, along with the dashboard, seats and T-tops of the 1968 to 1982 models, were used. The standard model had side-mounted spare tyres, while the SE model had side exhausts in the same locations.

HP

PHILOS (F) 1912–1923

SA Nouvelle des Automobiles Philos, Lyons.
The Philos was a neat-looking 2-seater with vee-radiator, powered by a 1131cc 4-cylinder Ballot engine, and generally made in 2-seater form. Postwar models used a variety of engines, including a 1088cc pushrod ohv Ruby, 1328cc side-valve Altos, 1590cc side-valve Ballot and 1614cc S.C.A.P., which could be had with side- or overhead valves. In 1923 the Philos factory was acquired by the makers of the JEAN GRAS.

NG

PHIPPS-GRINNELL; PHIPPS ELECTRIC (US) 1911–1912

1911 Phipps-Grinnell Automobile Co., Detroit, Michigan.
1912 Phipps Electric Co., Detroit, Michigan.
Joel G. Phipps was an electrical engineer who obtained some backing from the Grinnell brothers who were music dealers. However, all that came out of the partnership were two 2-seater electric cars and one truck. In 1912 the Grinnells ended the partnership to make electric cars under their own name, while

Phipps made a longer wheelbase car which he called the Phipps Electric. How many were made is not known but there cannot have been many, for the Phipps Electric Co. was out of business by the beginning of 1913.

NG

PHIZACKERLEY (AUS) 1902

Isaac Phizackerley's Cycle Works, Sydney, New South Wales.
Established during the 1890s cycle boom, Phizackerley's shop made cycles and tyres. His motorcar was constructed on a tubular frame, in which was fitted a 6hp De Dion-Bouton engine coupled to a 3-speed gearbox. Apart from the engine, clutch and dash-mounted oiler, it was wholly built on-site. It was exhibited at the Sydney Show and was claimed to be the first car to travel the notorious Bulli Pass. A buyer was found but no further examples were noted.

MG

PHOENIX (i) (US) 1900–1901

Phoenix Motor Vehicle & Engine Co., Cleveland, Ohio.
This was the first automotive venture of the Owen brothers, Raymond M. and Ralph R., who were later concerned with the OWEN (ii) and OWEN MAGNETIC. The cars, which were known as Owens as well as Phoenix, had flat-twin engines with two forward speeds, 4-seater bodies and a top speed of 16mph (25km/h). They also made a 1000lb (455kg) delivery wagon. In the summer of 1900 they renamed their company the Owen Motor Carriage Co. but the following year they gave up car manufacture to become Oldsmobile dealers. Raymond M. Owen moved to New York where he sold Oldsmobile and then Reo cars.

NG

PHOENIX (ii) (GB) 1902–1904

Phoenix Motor Works, Southport, Lancashire.
The Phoenix was an interim make between the HUDLASS and the BARCAR. It was built in the same factory, after Felix Hudlass had left the firm, and the design was similar to that of the 12hp 2-cylinder Hudlass. In 1903 a new design of 3-cylinder car was made, and in 1904 this became the Barcar. The middle cylinder had a larger bore than the other two, and worked off the exhaust gases of its smaller neighbours, as in the American COMPOUND.

NG

PHOENIX (iii) (GB) 1903–1926

1903–1911 Phoenix Motor Co. Ltd, London.
1911–1926 Phoenix Motors Ltd, Letchworth, Hertfordshire.
The original Phoenixes were motor tricycles made by Belgian-born J. van Hooydonk who started his working life in England as a marzipan maker for the well-known confectioners, Pascalls. Belonging to the Phoenix Cycle Club, when he began to make motorcycles in 1900, he named them after the club. He formed the Phoenix Motor Co. with £10,000 capital in 1903, and began to make tricycles called Phoenix Trimo, powered by Minerva engines imported from his native Belgium. The Quadcar of 1905 had four wheels and a 6/7hp 2-cylinder Fafnir horizontal transverse engine. It had wheel steering and developed into a more car-like design, with side by side seating and a dummy bonnet.

The first proper car arrived in 1908; still with a transverse engine, an 8hp vertical twin Minerva or Imperia, it had chain drive to a 3-speed gearbox and also chain final drive. It was designed by Albert Bowyer-Lowe who was also responsible for the 1496cc 11.9hp 4-cylinder car which was made from late 1911. This was made in Phoenix's new factory at Letchworth, where there were facilities for making their own engines as well as most other components. The 4-cylinder Phoenix had a 3-speed gearbox and worm drive, and was distinguished by a Renault-type dashboard radiator and coal-scuttle bonnet. About seven cars a week were made by a workforce of 150. A 2-cylinder car was listed up to 1913, but most of Phoenix's production was concentrated on the four. It was revived in 1919, still with the dashboard radiator, whereas other British followers of this fashion went over to frontal radiators. Phoenix joined them in 1921, and a larger model was an ohc 18hp based on the ARROL-JOHNSTON Victory, but only prototypes of this were made.

In 1922 the 11.9hp was replaced by the 12/25 which used a 1795cc ohv Meadows engine in unit with a 4-speed gearbox, also by Meadows, and with spiral bevel drive in place of the worm gear of Bowyer-Lowe's design. It was made only as a tourer, but this had very good weather protection, with glass windows that folded down. In 1924 Phoenix went into liquidation after about 400 11.9s and 168 12/25s had been made. They made nine cars with 2692cc 18/45hp 6-cylinder Meadows engines in 1925 and one more 12/25 in 1926. The factory was later used for manufacture of the ASCOT (ii) and ARAB cars.

NG

PHOENIX (iv) (GB) 1905

Phoenix Carriage Co. Ltd, Birmingham.

This company made an electric hansom cab called the Alexandra. Ahead of the cab part were two seats in the open, with a vertical steering column, but a sliding roof was provided so that it could be converted into a closed car for four people. A feature, described as 'exceedingly ingenious', was that the doors and windows were designed to fall outwards in the event of an accident. The motor drove a differential countershaft from which drive was taken by chains to the rear wheels.

NG

PHOENIX (v) (ET) 1954–1956

Cairo Motor Co. Ltd, Cairo; Alexandria.

An English businessman called Captain Raymond Flower was behind the Phoenix, a rare example of an Egyptian-built car. The Phoenix was conceived as a high-powered sports car to compete at Le Mans. Based on a multi-tubular chassis, it was planned to use a 1960cc Turner 4-cylinder twin-cam engine with fuel injection and 145bhp, but it is believed that a Triumph engine was used instead. The Phoenix became the only car ever to wear the racing colours of Egypt (purple) but at the 1956 Reims 12-Hour race it failed to run. Phoenix also marketed the Flamebird, a sports car based on Fiat 1100 parts, around 30 of which were sold. Flower also built a microcar prototype powered by 197cc or 250cc 2-stroke Villiers single-cylinder engines, whose appearance was accentuated by a single up-and-over door for entry. Deteriorating relations between Britain and Egypt during the Suez crisis forced Flower to bring his microcar prototype back to Britain, where he intended to productionise the car at £345. Instead he collaborated with Henry Meadows Ltd, who made a much-modified version as the FRISKY.

CR

PHOENIX (vi) (GB) 1983–1986

Phoenix Automotive, Moreton-in-Marsh, Gloucestershire.

One of the main members of the CLAN company was Paul Haussauer, a fibreglass expert. He returned to kit cars in 1983 with the Phoenix, which was an attempt to make a completely rust-free and practical car. It used Mini subframes, reskinned doors and interior parts in a painted fibreglass monocoque body which was deliberately reminiscent of a Mini Clubman estate, albeit with a single tailgate.

CR

PHOENIX (vii) (GB) 1998 to date

Phoenix Automotive Ltd, Dilton Marsh, Westbury, Wiltshire.

This company – associated with LE MANS SPORTSCARS – produced the Avon Sprint, one of dozens of Lotus Seven lookalikes available in Britain. It used all-independent suspension and Rover K-series, Ford crossflow or Ford Zetec power.

CR

PHÖNIX (H) 1904–1912

Budapesti Malomépítészet és Gépgyár, Podvinecz & Heisler, Budapest.

Dániel Podvinecz and Vilmos Heisler opened a shop back in 1884 where they offered various agricultural machines. Soon they set up a workshop where they started to manufacture accessories for these machines. As business boomed they sought new ways to expand and moved to bigger premises. Here they were able to manufacture complete machines and also stationary engines.

Meanwhile, as automobile fever caught Hungary, the Podvinecz-Heisler pair decided to try their hand at cars. Without any experience, developing a horseless carriage would have been a daring adventure, so they looked for foreign help. The German Cudell company was in trouble, as its factory had burnt down, so when the Hungarians approached them they were happy to provide tools, drawings – everything to help establish the automobile arm of the Podvinecz-

1908 Phoenix (iii) 8hp 2-seater.
NATIONAL MOTOR MUSEUM

1910 Phoenix (iii) 8/10hp 2-seater.
NICK BALDWIN

1921 Phoenix (iii) 11.9hp 2-seater.
NICK GEORGANO/NATIONAL MOTOR MUSEUM

Heisler factory, which started operation in 1904. This was one of the first Hungarian companies entering into this business.

The Cudell-Phönix range consisted of 2- and 4-cylinder cars, with models ranging from 10/12PS (the first was the taxable power, the latter the real power) to 35/40PS. The latter was the top of the range, and also the world's first ohv engine.

Unfortunately, the Phönix-Cudell cars were hardly promoted at all, and only a handful were sold within three years. Established foreign makes, like Benz, Fiat or Peugeot gained more popularity.

In 1907 Podvinecz and Heisler decided that involving a bank would provide the necessary funds to market and develop new models. Leaders of the Pest

1907 Piccolo 7PS 2-seater.
NICK GEORGANO

1901 Pick 2¾hp voiturette.
NATIONAL MOTOR MUSEUM

Hungarian Commerce Bank were keen to become involved, but during the negotiations Podvinecz died.

In the early 1910s Phönix models were updated. Their brochure listed three models, powered by a 4-cylinder water-cooled engine. In addition to the usual touring body styles, closed limousines, buses, and trucks were also made.

In 1912 the company was renamed MÁG (Hungarian General Machine Factory) reflecting new company philosophy.

PN

PHOOLTAS *see* TRISHUL

PHRIXUS *see* O.P.

PICCARD-PICTET *see* PIC PIC

PICCHIO (I) 1991

This was one of several projects that flowered in an era when speculative prices encouraged such cars, but when the bubble burst this project, like so many others, foundered. The Picchio was designed by two ex-Ferrari employees, Ernesto Vita and Franco Rocchi. Its ambitious mid-mounted engine had no less than eighteen cylinders but no production run ensued.

CR

PICCOLO (D) 1904–1912
1904–1908 A. Ruppe & Sohn, Apolda.
1908–1910 A. Ruppe & Sohn AG, Apolda.
1910–1912 Apollo-Werke Apolda.
This agricultural machinery firm, founded in 1854, began to make cars with the appropriately named Piccolo light car. It had a 704cc air-cooled V-twin engine, with 2- or 4-seater bodies. It was a reasonably priced and popular car and sold well until 1907. On the first models the engine was un-enclosed at the front of the car, but a small bonnet was employed from 1906. In that year an in-line 4-cylinder 12PS engine was offered, but gave way in 1907 to a V4, also of 12PS. A simplified single-cylinder car of only 624cc was announced in 1910 and sold under the name Mobbel. In the same year the company name was changed to Apollo-Werke, and a new range of cars sold under the name APOLLO. The air-cooled cars were sold as Piccolos until 1912, thereafter as Piccolo-Apollos.

HON

PICK; NEW PICK (GB) 1898–1925
1898–1900 J.H. Pick & C. Gray, Stamford, Lincolnshire.
1900–1904 Pick Motor Co. Ltd, Stamford, Lincolnshire.
1908–1915 New Pick Motor Co. Ltd, Stamford, Lincolnshire.
1923–1925 Pick Motor Co. Ltd, Stamford, Lincolnshire.
The Pick is an interesting example of a small regional make that lasted for more than 25 years. It was the work of John Henry Pick (1867–1954), known as Jack, who began dealing in bicycles in 1896 and also making hoes and needles. In 1898 he launched his own make of cycle, the Pick of All, and in the same year completed his first car. This used an engine 'of French design' possibly a De Dion-Bouton, installed in a body of dog-cart style. Pick sold it to a local doctor for £85 and promptly started work on another, which he sold to the Marquess of Exeter. A group of local gentry, with the Marquess as Chairman, financed the Pick Motor Co. Ltd which was formed in March 1900. In December Pick exhibited his bicycles and two cars at the Stanley Cycle Show in London. These were the first 'production' Picks, a voiturette with 2¾hp single-cylinder engine, and a dog-cart with 4¼hp single-cylinder engine. Both were by De Dion-Bouton, and drove the rear axle directly through two friction clutches. The voiturette had an unusual front suspension by laminated springs extending from the front of the tubular frame.

During 1901 the engine was moved to the front and the dog-cart received a 6hp 2-cylinder power unit. Picks grew again in 1902, the range consisting of a 4hp single-cylinder, 6hp and 10hp 2-cylinder models, all with horizontally-opposed units mounted in front under a bonnet, with transmission by fast and loose pulleys on a countershaft behind the rear axle. The larger cars could carry 4-seater tonneau bodies. 1903 models had chain drive to the gearbox and single-chain drive to the rear axle. All were now twins, of 6, 10 and 12hp. However, in 1904 the Pick Motor Co. closed down, probably because of disagreements between Jack Pick and his directors. He moved into smaller premises, opposite the George Hotel in Stamford High Street and engaged in general engineering work.

In 1906 Pick completed a new car with 1998cc 12/14hp 4-cylinder engine with separately-cast cylinders, and two years later formed the New Pick Motor Co. to manufacture it. The production car had a larger engine of 2543cc and 14/16hp, and bodies were by the local firm of Hayes & Son. In 1911 the stroke was lengthened from 100 to 127mm, giving a capacity of 3230cc, and the cylinders were now of monobloc casting. 2- and 4-seater bodies were offered, as well as a 'semi-racer, well capable of 50mph (80km/h)'. The Torpedo models had rounded bonnets and radiators in the Hotchkiss mould. Car production lasted well into 1915, the later engines having a larger bore which gave a capacity of 3600cc.

Jack Pick did not return to car production straightaway after the war, though he did offer to make engines for William Morris. Instead he tried to enter the market for agricultural tractors with two machines, a highly unusual 3-wheeler in 1919 and a more conventional 4-wheeler in 1920. Neither was a success. In 1923 he announced another car. The engine was the same slow-revving 3600cc four of the prewar New Pick, but the bodies were new, made of aluminium on an ash frame. Four styles were offered, a 4-seater sports or touring car, 2-seater sporting model, coupé and saloon, the latter two with vee-windscreens. They had large disc wheels and stood high off the ground. This, combined with high gearing, enabled them to lope along, the engine turning at only 1000rpm at 40mph (64km/h), but must have made for very sluggish acceleration. Very few were

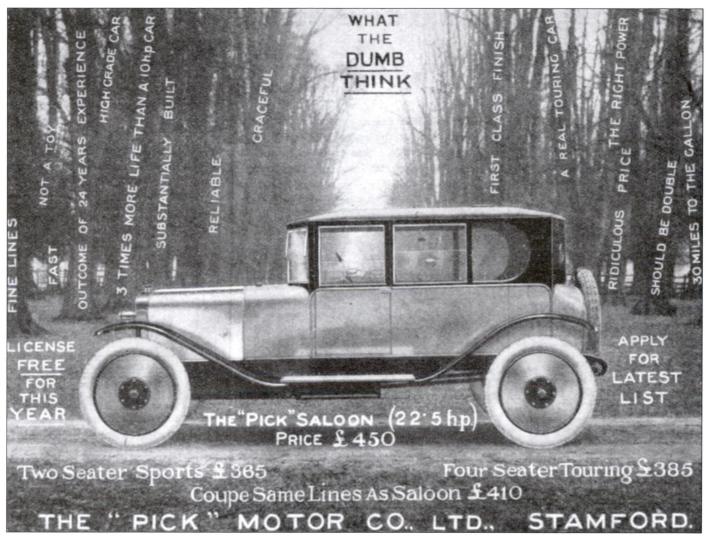

1924 Pick 22.5hp saloon.
NICK BALDWIN

made, although a sports model was tested by *The Motor*, and two coupés were sold off after the firm closed down. Jack Pick retired from car manufacture in January 1925 when he put his company into voluntary liquidation. He opened a greengrocer's shop on the site of his second motor car works, which he ran until his death in January 1954, at the age of 87.

NG

Further Reading
Pick of Stamford, Michael Key, Paul Watkins, Stamford, 1994.

PICKARD (US) 1909–1912

Pickard Bros, Brockton, Massachusetts.

The Pickard brothers, Emil, Benjamin and Alfred, built a car powered by a 5hp single-cylinder engine in 1903, but did not have anything ready for production until late 1908. This was a 25hp 4-cylinder car with 3-speed gearbox and shaft drive. Very conventional, in fact, apart from the use of air-cooling. The brake bands were lined with camel hair. Their slogan was 'A Lot of Car for the Money', and the money they asked for dropped over the years, from $850–1400 to $800–950 in their last season. However, shortage of capital brought the business to an end in mid–1912.

NG

PICKER-MOCCAND *see* LUCIA

PIC PIC (CH) 1906–1923

1906–1910 SAG Sté d'Automobiles, Geneva.
1906–1920 SA Piccard, Pictet & Cie, Geneva.
1921–1922 Ateliers des Charmilles SA, Geneva.
1922–1923 Sté des Moteurs Gnome-Rhône, Paris.

Paul Piccard (1844–1929), was a mechanical engineer and was later appointed as a professor at the Technical University of Lausanne, Switzerland. Together with Jules Faesch, he formed Faesch & Piccard in 1886, producing mechanical devices, machinery and turbines in their workshop in Geneva. When Faesch died in 1895, his place was taken by Lucien Pictet (1864–1928), who had already been with the company for five years and who was the brother of a banker of considerable means. The company was renamed Piccard, Pictet & Cie.

The first connection with automobiles was in 1904, when the DUFAUX brothers, Charles and Frédéric, ordered from Piccard, Pictet & Cie their 8-cylinder in-line engine for a racing car to take part in the Gordon Bennett event. They also were responsible for casting and machining the engine of the land speed record 4-cylinder monster of 1905. The enterprise was re-formed into a shareholders' company and Léon Dufour was hired as chief engineer and technical manager. Lucien Pictet, who strongly advocated the production of passenger cars on their own account, formed a separate marketing company, SAG Société d'Automobiles, Geneva. He contacted the young Swiss engineer, Marc Birkigt, director of the HISPANO-SUIZA company in Barcelona and signed an agreement for licence production in Geneva. An annual production of 120 chassis was planned and the licence fee was fixed at SFr300 per car.

At the second National Automobile Show in Geneva in April 1906, SAG proudly displayed a 20/24hp chassis which had been manufactured by SA Piccard, Pictet & Cie according to the drawings supplied by Hispano-Suiza. The T-head

1907 SAG (Pic Pic) 18/24hp landaulet.
ERNEST SCHMID

1908 Pic Pic 28/40hp 4-seater roadster.
NATIONAL MOTOR MUSEUM

1919 Pic Pic tourer by Carrosserie Eugéne Boulogne.
BRYAN K. GOODMAN

4-cylinder cast in pairs engine of 3770cc was mounted in a shaft-driven chassis of 114in (2900mm) wheelbase. A stronger 35/40hp model was announced and commercial vehicles were said to be under study, but never materialised. In 1907 a new 12/16hp model with an early monobloc 4-cylinder engine of 2540cc was launched. The 3-speed gearbox was bolted to the engine. The range was supplemented by a 28/50hp model with a big 4-cylinder engine of 6902cc capacity. At the Paris show later in the year, the first 6-cylinder cast in pairs of 5652cc, model 28/40hp, was clearly indicating the upper-class ambitions of the young marque. It cost SFr17,500 for the chassis and was slightly more expensive than the big four. With other famous makes, such as Delauney-Belleville, Hispano-Suiza, Hotchkiss and Rolls-Royce, also offering 6-cylinder models, Pic Pic was in good company. Castings in steel, aluminum and bronze as well

as mechanical work were done in-house. The open and closed bodies were made by coachbuilders, most prominent being Gangloff, of Geneva.

The licence agreement with Hispano-Suiza was soon giving the Spanish company headaches, as SAG was very active in export markets, thus providing rather unwanted competition. Even if the new models of 1907–09 did not exactly match the Hispano-Suiza versions, the general layout leaned heavily on their design. The contract was formally terminated in 1909. Despite several applauded sporting successes, high quality and a good range of models, sales were slow and neither Piccard, Pictet & Cie nor SAG could pay any dividends to shareholders.

In 1910 SAG was taken over by the mother company and from then onward the cars were marketed under the name of Pic Pic. Three 4-cylinder models, 14/18hp monobloc of 2412cc, 18/24hp of 3770cc and 35/45hp of 7960cc were available. The 6-cylinder, of which only a few were made, was dropped. All engines were pressure lubricated, and wet multiple-disc clutch and 4-speed gearboxes with direct top were fitted. Petrol was fed by means of a small air pump. A polished 14/18hp chassis and phaeton as well as a nice new 22/30hp of 4396cc, both with L-head 4-cylinder engines were displayed at the London and Paris shows. The two most powerful models were available either with normal chassis for formal or touring coachwork, or with shorter and lower sports chassis. With light 2-seater bodies these cars were among the fastest in the country and good for over 60mph (97km/h). They had a mechanical tyre pump driven from the gearbox. Total production for 1911 was estimated at 220 chassis; 22 taxis were ordered from Rio de Janeiro; the Swiss Army and the International Red Cross became customers for Pic Pics.

For some time already the design department was studying the possibilities of sleeve-valve engines which were in vogue throughout Europe. Instead of the double sleeves as promoted by Knight, Pic Pic chose a single sleeve, which in addition to its vertical movement was twisting, thus opening and closing the inlet and exhaust ports. When applying for the patent in August 1910 they found to their amazement, that the same principle had been protected a few months before by Burt McCollum. Fully convinced of the quality and advantages of the new engine design, they signed a licence agreement with a European partner, the Scottish automobile makers Argyll. The very first Pic Pic with the new 30/40hp sleeve-valve 4-cylinder engine of 4710cc capacity was hastily prepared for the official visit of the German Emperor Wilhelm II in 1912. It obtained a very luxurious landaulet body and Léon Dufour himself drove the Emperor to attend the manoeuvres of the Swiss Army. Afterwards it was sold for an uncommonly large SFr30,000 to a lady customer in Zürich. At the Paris Show the new model and one of 20/30hp with conventional poppet-valve 4-cylinder of 3815cc, were exhibited to the public. By 1914 Pic Pic was well established as number two in Switzerland behind Martini and had a good share of export sales in Europe and overseas.

Pic Pic cars were hailed in the press for elegance, high quality workmanship and excellent performance. They merited to be called the 'Rolls-Royce of Switzerland'. The programme comprised four 4-cylinder models: the 16/20hp of 2813cc and the 20/30hp now enlarged to 4324cc with poppet-valves; the 16/20hp of 2949cc and the big 30/40hp with sleeve-valves. Prices ranged from SFr10,500 to SFr17,500 for the chassis, making them more expensive than the Martini. At extra cost double-ignition (magneto/coil), special vee-shaped sports radiators, spare wheels and most important, electrical equipment, were available. With two specially built and prepared racing cars, Pic Pic took part in the 1914 French Grand Prix in Lyon. They were notable for their sleeve-valve 4-cylinder engines (97 × 150mm, 4432cc) supplying about 150bhp and their advanced 4-wheel brakes. Their drivers, Paul Tournier, works driver and Theo Clark were not successful though. They were both eliminated owing to a fire leading to mechanical trouble and by a bad accident respectively.

With the outbreak of World War I, some Pic Pic cars were ordered by the Swiss Army but otherwise car production came nearly to a standstill. A small 12/14hp model with a normal 4-cylinder engine of 2154cc was introduced in 1916, and this does not seem to have been built in substantial numbers. The company, however, produced igniters for artillery shells in huge quantities for the Allied Forces and this brought about a profit of nearly 4 million Swiss Francs in 1916–17. Total staff numbered about 7500 during the war years. International connections and interests led to a participation of British Electric Holding with a 40 per cent increase in capital and co-operation with the French Société des Moteurs Gnome-Rhône, famous for their rotary aero engines, was sought.

With the armistice of 1918, SA Piccard, Pictet & Cie suffered a downfall of large dimensions. For 1918–19 it made a loss of 1.5 million Swiss Francs. The reasons apparently were, apart from the lack of military orders, a wild diversification in other directions by buying various companies, and substantial profits were dwindling. A restart of automobile production and a considerable increase of the output to 1000 cars annually was envisaged, and the most up-to-date tool machines were ordered from the USA. For the coachwork by Gangloff, a new three-storey building was projected. But the downhill slide picked up speed.

In 1919 a new luxury car, 'Franco-Suisse', which was to be produced by Piccard, Pictet & Cie and Gnome-Rhône, was announced in the French motoring press. At the London Motor Show, the 30hp Pic Pic tourer with vee-shaped radiator and 4-wheel brakes was considered both advanced and pleasing. It had the new V8 sleeve-valve engine (85 × 130mm, 5881cc) which had been developed in Geneva and built in France.

With debts of a staggering 24 million Swiss Francs, the company went bankrupt in early 1920. This however was not quite the end of Pic Pic. A new, more modest company, Ateliers des Charmilles SA, Geneva, was formed in 1921 to produce turbines and automobiles. Prospective buyers were informed that Société des Moteurs Gnome-Rhône, Paris had secured the rights to produce the splendid Pic Pic chassis and that 1000 cars were under construction. Obviously this was a figure dictated by wishful thinking. The latest model R2 of 16/45hp was an improved 16/20hp of prewar days, the 3-litre sleeve-valve engine having dry-sump lubrication and Scintilla magneto. It was last shown at the Geneva Show of 1924 and advertised as 'the queen of mountain climbing'. Only a few were completed and sold. Finally the factory at Geneva was sold to a consortium for 6 million Swiss Francs. There were rumours of Lancia intending to set up an assembly plant in the buildings, but nothing came of it. By 1925 Charmilles was offering spare parts only for Pic Pic cars. They were durable cars and in 1929 there were still 399 Pic Pics registered on the roads of Switzerland. Many served their owners well up to the late 1930s.

Misjudgement of future possibilities, management mistakes, the importation of inexpensive cars starting after World War I and the protective import duty in many countries, made exporting difficult, and these factors were responsible for the rapid downfall of this highly respected marque. Very few Pic Pic cars survive in museums and private collections.

FH

Further Reading
Pic Pic mon amour, Alexis Couturier, published privately, 1994.
'Pic Pic', F. Hediger, *Automobil und Motorrad Chronik*, April 1980.
Le Hispano-Suiza, Emilio Polo, Wings & Flags, Madrid, 1994.

PIEDMONT (US) 1917–1922

Piedmont Motor Car Co., Lynchburg, Virginia.

The Piedmont, together with its stablemate, the Norwalk, owed its existence to a policy of manufacturing cars for other automobile companies bereft of their own factories. This policy also shared by other companies such as Crow-Elkhart, Huffman, Pullman, and Sphinx, to name a few, operated with a modicum of success at a time when virtually any and all brands of cars could be sold without much promotion to a clientele that did not care about basic design or the make of power plant provided. Piedmonts, and others like it, concentrated on providing their generic-appearing cars to other concerns with badges, hubcaps and related nomenclature fitted to order, otherwise being basically similar in design and basic specifications, the final promotion and determination of prices being up to the wholesale purchasers. The Piedmont offered 4- and 6-cylinder models, using Lycoming K and Continental 7R engines respectively, production targeted primarily to touring cars and roadsters. Technically, the Piedmont existed as its own make to all intents and purposes but, in a sense, the car failed to attract potential buyers. Due to orders from other companies, Piedmont dealers were not always able to have their orders filled and the public were not attracted to the cars as a result. This was further complicated by Piedmont's mail order business in selling its cars and an unsuccessful attempt to create an export market. Among the firms operating as independent makes by selling badge-engineered Piedmonts were Bush, Lone Star and Alsace, the latter being Piedmont's export car. Following the stabilisation of the country's automobile market following the postwar recession, cars such as Piedmont failed.In Piedmont's case, the company was reorganised as Virginia Motors and the last cars may have been marketed with that badge. Reorganisation was unsuccessful and the company failed early in 1923.

KM

c.1920 Piedmont Model 6-40 tourer.
KEITH MARVIN

1900 Pieper 3¹/₂hp voiturette.
NICK GEORGANO

PIEPER (B) 1899–1903

Sté des Établissements Pieper, Nessonvaux, Liège.

Henri Pieper founded an armaments factory in 1866, and added an electrical department in 1883, followed by bicycle manufacture in the 1890s under the name Pieper et Bayard. He built a prototype electric quadricycle in 1897, and two years later a petrol-electric 2-seater, one of the first vehicles of this type in Europe. This was the work of Henry Pieper junior and his brother Nicolas, who took over after their father died. Power came from a 3hp De Dion-Bouton engine. They also made pure electrics of very similar appearance to the petrol-electric, and a pure petrol car, again De Dion-Bouton-powered, with belt drive. All three types were offered in 1899.

By 1901 they were making 6CV single-cylinder and 8CV 2-cylinder models with a variety of bodies, 2-seater Duc, 4-seater *vis-à-vis*, tonneau and delivery van. In 1902 4-cylinder cars of 12 and 20CV were made, also a single-cylinder motorcycle, but production did not survive beyond 1903.

NG

PIERCE (i) (US) 1900–1904

1900–1901 Dr Pierce Auto Manufacturing Co., Newark, New Jersey.
1901–1904 Pierce Electric Co., Bound Brook, New Jersey.

A rare example of a car made by a medical man, the Pierce Electric was built in several styles including runabout, phaeton and delivery wagon.

NG

1901 Pierce (ii) Motorette 2-seater.
NATIONAL MOTOR MUSEUM

1907 Pierce Great Arrow tourer.
NATIONAL MOTOR MUSEUM

1919 Pierce-Arrow Model 48 tourer.
NATIONAL MOTOR MUSEUM

PIERCE (ii); PIERCE-ARROW (US) 1901–1938

1901–1908 The George N. Pierce Co., Buffalo, New York.
1909–1938 Pierce-Arrow Motor Car Co., Buffalo, New York.
A leading American quality marque, the Pierce-Arrow was ranked with Packard and Peerless as one of The Three Ps. The early products had much in common with those of Peerless, both firms making bicycles in the 1890s, followed by light cars powered by De Dion-Bouton engines and both called Motorettes. George Norman Pierce (1846–1910) was a prosperous Buffalo businessman who had made birdcages, iceboxes and refrigerators before he turned to bicycles.

These were so successful that he soon dropped the other products. It was his treasurer, Colonel Charles Clifton (1853–1928) who suggested the De Dion engine as a suitable motive power, though George's son Percy had built one or two experimental steam cars in 1900.

The first Pierce Motorettes had 2¾hp single-cylinder engines, two-speed planetary gearboxes without reverse, and spur-gear final drive. Priced at $650, they went on sale towards the end of 1901, and 25 were made in their first season. The designer was English-born David Fergusson (1869–1951) who came from the E.C. Stearns Co. and remained with Pierce until 1921. The first Motorette went by the curious name of Knockabout, and was joined by the Runabout which became the standard model for the 1902/03 season. This had a larger De Dion engine of 3½hp and a reverse gear. Top speed was 25mph (40km/h) and price $850. About 125 were made through 1902 and into early 1903, after which the De Dion engine was replaced by a 5hp unit listed as Pierce-built, though it was cast by Leland & Faulconer of Detroit. About 40 were made before the original Motorette was replaced by a new and larger model.

The Stanhope Motorette had a larger engine of 6½hp and a folding front seat so that four passengers could be carried. Apart from a further increase in engine size to 8hp at the end of 1903, and the replacement of the steering tiller by a wheel at about the same time, the Stanhope was little changed for the rest of its life, which lasted until 1906. About 420 were made.

The Pierce-Arrow

In late 1902 David Fergusson designed his first front-engined car, which was named the Arrow. It was powered by a 15hp 2-cylinder De Dion engine, and employed a 3-speed gearbox and shaft drive. The body was a rear-entrance tonneau, and the bonnet of Renault pattern. Fifty of these 1903-pattern Arrows were made, and were followed by 75 of the 1904 model, which had a larger Pierce-built 2-cylinder engine and a square, full-height radiator.

Also in 1904 came the company's first 4-cylinder car, which was called the Great Arrow. This had a 24/28hp pair-cast T-head engine of 3770cc, 3-speed gearbox with change-speed lever on the steering wheel, and shaft drive. It was the first Pierce to have a cast-aluminium body, in which sections 3.175mm thick were rivetted together, and finished so that the joints were imperceptible. This unusual process was used by the Pierce body department until 1921, when they changed to the more common pressed sheet aluminium. The Pierce Great Arrow cost $4000, compared with $2500 for the 2-cylinder Arrow, so the company was gradually moving up-market, a process continued when they brought out their first six as a 1907 model. This developed 60bhp, and had a capacity of 10,608cc. It was made alongside two 4-cylinder cars, the 4414cc 30hp and the 7075cc 40/45hp. Prices were $4000 to $6250 for the 4-cylinder cars, and $6500 to $7750 for the Big Six. During the 1907/08 season 400 30hp, 500 45hp and 166 60hp models were made.

Late in 1908 the company name was changed from the George N. Pierce Co. to the Pierce-Arrow Motor Car Co., and the Pierce Great Arrow became the Pierce-Arrow. In 1909 motor vehicles replaced horse-drawn carriages at the White House, and the first motor fleet included two Pierce-Arrows, as well as a Baker Electric and a White Steamer. The range was expanded in 1909, with two fours and four sixes, from the 30U, of which only three were made, up to the massive 60QQ of which 83 were made. The most popular model was a 48hp six, production being 359. Total production for 1909 was 956 cars, and Pierce-Arrow had little trouble in selling them. The anticipated output was often sold before the year began, a fortunate situation which lasted up to 1918. Pierce-Arrows were almost never raced, but they had many successes in long-distance reliability trials, especially the Glidden Tour, which they won every year from 1905 to 1909.

For 1910 the range was trimmed to just three models, all sixes. These were the 5866cc 36-UU, the 7424cc 48-SS and the 11,700cc 66-QQ. For 1912 the latter was enlarged to 13,514cc which was the largest engine ever used in a production passenger car. The 1917 Fageol, sometimes claimed to be the world's biggest-engined car, had exactly the same dimensions (5 × 7 inches, or 127 × 177.8mm), but no more than three were made, while the 'production' Bugatti Royale displaced only 12,763cc. The massive 66 had wheelbases of 140 or 147.5in (3556 or 3746mm), and prices ran from $5850 to $7300. In 1910 a tyre pump operated from the transmission became available, and a compressed air starter was briefly offered at the beginning of the 1913 season, before being replaced by a complete electrical system, including operation of the headlamps and klaxon horn.

1919 Pierce-Arrow Model 48 vestibule suburban.
JOHN A. CONDE

May 1913 saw the introduction of wing mounting for the headlamps, which was a distinctive feature of all Pierce-Arrows up to the end, although conventionally located lamps could be had to special order up to the early 1930s. These lamps, being wider and higher than ordinary drum lamps, gave better illumination of the road. They were the design of Herbert M. Dawley (1880–1970) who was trained in mechanical engineering, but whose contribution to Pierce-Arrow was mainly in the field of styling and interior decoration. He worked for the Buffalo company from 1906 to 1917, after which he became a major in the US Army, and then a noted theatrical director.

The years 1910 to 1918 were the best that the company were to know, with annual sales around 1500 to 2000. The Pierce-Arrow was probably the most popular car among the conservative rich families of the East Coast, being more expensive and exclusive than Packard. The make continued in favour with the White House during the terms of Presidents Wilson, Harding and Coolidge (1913–1929), the cars being leased from the company rather than bought outright by the government. Truck production for the US, British and French armies boosted profits to more than $4 million in 1915 and 1916. Expensive factory extensions in 1917 resulted in lower profits, and the drop in demand for trucks once World War I was over was a severe blow for Pierce-Arrow.

The three 6-cylinder models were continued up to 1918, though production of the enormous 66 declined. In the two and a half years from mid–1916 to the end of 1918, only 505 were made, compared with 4400 of the smaller sixes. The 48 had almost as good a performance, and its fuel consumption was better than the 66 which consumed around 70 litres per 100km. It also went through a set of tyres in about 6000 miles (9700kms). The 66 was dropped at the end of 1918, and the 48 at the end of 1920, leaving the 6792cc 38 as the sole model. The Series 5 models, introduced in July 1918, had four valves per cylinder, being known as the Dual Valve engines. They were still pair-cast T-heads, which were becoming distinctly old-fashioned by then. Officially the Dual Valve 66 engine was only experimental, but a few reached the public, and one survived in the Harrah Automobile Collection.

Monobloc engines arrived in 1921, when the last rhd Pierce-Arrows were made. They had clung to this feature longer than any other American car maker, it is said because the majority were chauffeur-driven, and rhd enabled the chauffeur to jump out smartly onto the pavement to open the door for his employer.

1923 Pierce-Arrow Model 33 roadster.
NATIONAL MOTOR MUSEUM

In 1916 Pierce-Arrow became a public company, and as so often happens, control passed increasingly to representatives of the bank which had floated the shares, in this case Seligman & Co. of New York. Over the next four years nearly all the senior staff left, George Birge at the end of 1916, Herbert Dawley in 1917, David Fergusson and Colonel Clifton in 1921. A recession hit the American automobile market in 1921, and Pierce-Arrow suffered a drop of more than 50 per cent in sales, from 2250 to around 1000. The Pierce-Arrow was competing in a new and brasher world, and more modernisation was needed than a monobloc engine and lhd. Ideally they should have gone for a straight-8 engine in order to keep up with rivals such as Packard and Cadillac, which were a more serious threat than they had been a few years earlier, but the new president Myron Forbes (1880–1966) continued with the six for another eight

1929 Pierce-Arrow Model 125 coupé.
NATIONAL MOTOR MUSEUM

1930 Pierce-Arrow Model B sedan.
NICK GEORGANO

1935 Pierce-Arrow Model 845 club sedan.
NATIONAL MOTOR MUSEUM

years. In August 1924 there appeared the smallest Pierce-Arrow for many years, the 80 powered by a 4727cc L-head monobloc engine. The wheelbase was only 130in (3302mm), and standard models sold for $2500–4000. It was the first Pierce-Arrow to have 4-wheel brakes. Although Pierce-Arrow still had their bodybuilding plant, various custom styles were available on the 80 chassis, by Brunn, LeBaron and Judkins. Seven styles of factory body were available in the 80's first year, a figure increased to 17 later.

First year sales of the 80 were encouraging, at about 4250, and rose to 7500 in 1926. However competition in this section of the market was very fierce, and 1927 sales were only 4500. For the following year the 80 was replaced by the 81, which had more aluminium in the engine, increasing speed from 2800 to 3200rpm, and power from 70 to 75bhp. The body lines of the 80 were modernised, and at prices from $3100–3500, Pierce-Arrow sold about 5000 in the one year they were marketed, 1928. They were also offering a much more expensive car, the 36, which was descended from the old 38, and still had a T-head engine. They had vacuum-assisted 4-wheel brakes. About 1500 of these were sold in 1927 and 1928, at prices from $5875–8000.

Studebaker Takes Over

In 1928 Pierce-Arrow merged with the Studebaker Corp. which gave the Buffalo firm a much needed injection of capital, enabling them to bring out a new range of straight-8 cars for 1929. Albert Erskine (1891–1933) president of Studebaker, became chairman of the board at Pierce-Arrow, while Forbes remained president until the end of 1929. The new cars were called the 133 and 143, from their wheelbases in inches (3378 and 3632mm). Both had a 5988cc 9-main bearing straight-8 engine with side-valves in an L-head, developing 125bhp. With not too heavy a body, a top speed of 84mph (135km/h) was obtainable. The blocks for the straight-8 were cast by Studebaker at South Bend, Indiana, but they were not re-worked Studebaker President blocks, as has been suggested. The rest of the car was made entirely at Buffalo. Prices were quite reasonable, running from $2875 to $3350 for the 133, and from $3750 to $5750 for the 143. 1929 sales were the best that Pierce-Arrow had ever enjoyed, at 9840. They were still quite encouraging in 1930, with 6916 cars delivered, but then the effects of the Depression began to be felt at Buffalo, and sales declined each year up to the end of production in 1938.

The range of eights was widened for 1930, with 4-wheelbases and three engine sizes, the 5568cc Series C, 5988cc Series B and 6318cc Series A. Power outputs were 115, 125, and 132bhp, respectively. The larger engine remained in production up to 1938, when it developed 150bhp, although it was not listed in 1932–33. In November 1931 Pierce-Arrow belatedly brought out a 12-cylinder car. Designed by new chief engineer Karl Wise, this came in two sizes, 6522cc (140bhp) and 7030cc (150bhp). The engine was still a side-valve, and the cylinders were included at the unusual angle of 80 degrees. Like the 8-cylinder cars, the 12s had 3-speed gearboxes with freewheels, and synchromesh on the two upper ratios. They came in three wheelbases, 125, 142 and 147in (3180, 3607 and 3734mm), and prices ran from $3435 for a convertible roadster on the short chassis to $7300 for a long-chassis all-weather town cabriolet. In an uncharacteristic burst of record-breaking, a VI2 roadster driven by Ab Jenkins averaged 112mph (180km/h) for 24-hours in 1932, 116mph (187km/h) for 25½ hours in 1933, and 127mph (204km/h) for 24 hours in 1934. These figures were achieved with tuned engines in stripped roadsters; a production roadster had a top speed of around 90mph (145km/h).

The New York Automobile Show which opened on 1 January 1933 saw a car which was probably the most famous Pierce-Arrow ever made. This was the Silver Arrow, a streamlined 4-door sedan on a 139in (3530mm) wheelbase powered by a 175bhp VI2 engine. Its advanced features included recessed door handles, an all-enveloping body covering the side-mounted spare wheels and running boards, and a luggage boot integral with the fastback body. The first Silver Arrow was completed in three months, built, like its four sisters, at the Studebaker factory. They were priced at $10,000 but were more of a publicity exercise than a serious commercial proposition. Three of the five made survive today. A modified form of Silver Arrow was sold in small numbers in 1934, but the styling was less radical, without the pontoon wings and all-enveloping body.

In the spring of 1933 the Studebaker Corp. went bankrupt, and the receivers sold off Pierce-Arrow to a group of Buffalo businessmen for $1 million, half what they had paid for the company five years before. The new owners, led by former Studebaker employee and P-A vice-president since 1928, Arthur J. Chanter, estimated that they could break even on 3000 cars per year, but they never reached this figure. 1934 sales were 1740, in 1935, 875, in 1936, 787, and in 1937, the last full year of production, only 167 cars were made. Although there were several changes in styling during these final years, Pierce-Arrows were largely the same mechanically as there was no money available for new models. The last innovations were Bendix vacuum-assisted brakes and an automatic choke on the 1936 models. From 1934 only the 6.3-litre straight-8 and a VI2 enlarged to 7568cc were made, with three wheelbases still offered. 1937 prices ran from $3195 for the cheapest coupé to $7270 for a Metropolitan Town Car on the long-wheelbase VI2 chassis. Only 17 1938 models were made, all hand-built from 1937 components. The very last was a VI2 sedan built in the summer of 1938 for Karl Wise, who went on to become chief engineer of the Bendix Aviation Corp. Total production of the straight-8s was 27,600 and of the VI2s about 2100.

In 1937 there were plans to make a medium-priced car to sell at $1200, using a Hayes pressed steel body, but tooling-up would have cost over $10 million, far more than Pierce-Arrow's total resources. In their 37-year history Pierce-Arrow made about 85,000 cars, of which an estimated 2000 survive today. The company assets were sold off during 1938, and rights to the VI2 engine were bought by the Seagrave Corp. for their fire engines. The Pierce-based VI2 was made by Seagrave up to 1970. Another fire engine connection is that the Pierce Manufacturing Co. of Appleton, Wisconsin, currently make appliances called Pierce Arrow.

NG

Further Reading
There's no mistaking a Pierce-Arrow, Brooks Brierley, Garnett & Stringer, 1986.
Pierce-Arrow, Marc Ralston, A.S. Barnes, 1982.
Issue devoted exclusively to Pierce-Arrow,
Automobile Quarterly, Vol. 28, No. 4.

PIERCE-RACINE (US) 1904–1911

Pierce Engine Co., Racine, Wisconsin.
The Pierce Engine Co. was established in 1893 by Andrew Pierce to make marine engines and launches. He built an experimental car in 1895, another in 1899, and a third in 1901. Two years later he built the first cars which were sold under the name MITCHELL, and in 1904 launched a car of his own which he called, logically, the Pierce-Racine. It was a light runabout with an 8hp single-cylinder engine, epicyclic transmission and single-chain drive. He made 25 cars in his first year, and 50 the second, when the runabout was joined by a 16hp 2-cylinder car, with 2-seater or 4-seater tonneau bodies, both rear entrance and side entrance. For 1906 the single was dropped and two fours of 18 and 24/28hp were added, but for 1907 Pierce decided on a single model policy, and chose to concentrate on a large 40hp 4-cylinder car with conventional gearbox and shaft drive, costing double the price of any of his previous cars. This policy paid off, sales reaching about 200 in 1907 and 300 in 1908 and 1909. In that year the company was reorganised, with additional finance coming from stockholders in the J.I. Case Threshing Machine Co. This paved the way for absorption of Pierce-Racine into Case. The last Pierce-Racines, smaller cars of 30hp, were made alongside the new CASE.

NG

PIERRE FAURE (F) 1941–1947

Pierre Faure, Paris.
This was one of many electric cars which were built in France during World War II to combat the almost complete absence of petrol for civilian use. It was a 4-wheeled coupé with narrow track rear wheels, seating two or three passengers, and also available as a delivery van. The 3-seater was said to be designed for owners who employed a chauffeur, who was seated at the front, with his passengers behind. Whether such a vehicle was built is not known; no photographs survive. The luxury 2-seater's body was built by Million-Guiet. The range was about 50 miles and top speed 25mph (40km/h). Prices ran from FFr29,800 to 36,000; by comparison the last prewar Renault Juvaquatre cost FFr20,900. The Pierre Faure made an appearance at the first postwar Paris Salon, in 1946, but like others of its kind, it could not compete once petrol cars became available again.

NG

PIERRE ROY (F) 1902–c.1908

Pierre Roy, Grand Montrouge, Seine.
The first Pierre Roy had a 10/12hp 2-cylinder engine and shaft drive. Later models, from 1905, had 14/20 and 24/30hp 4-cylinder engines, also with shaft drive. Although few were made, one survived into preservation in the 1950s and hopefully is still around.

NG

PIERRON *see* MASS

PIGGINS (US) 1908–1910

Piggins Bros, Racine, Wisconsin.
The brothers Charles R. and Frederick H. Piggins built a steam car in 1883, an electric in 1897 and a petrol car in 1902. All were experimental and there was no intention to manufacture cars at those stages. However, they began making 2-, 4-, and 6-cylinder engines for cars and also 2-stroke marine engines, and in 1908 they launched their own car, the Piggins Six. It was made in two models, of 36 and 50hp. The latter was a large and expensive car, with a 7.8-litre engine and a 135in (3426mm) wheelbase which carried a 7-seater tourer body. It cost

1907 Pilain (i) limousine.
NICK BALDWIN

$4700, and the smaller Piggins, $3500. In 1909 the brothers merged their business with the Racine Machinery Co., and a few cars may have been made into 1910. They then turned to truck manufacture, making the 'Practical Piggins' truck into 1916, when the name was changed to Reliance. These trucks were made up to about 1927.

NG

PIKE (GB) 1986–1988

Pike Automotive, Melton Mowbray, Leicestershire.
Ex-nuclear reactor engineers Arnold Pearce and Tony Brown were responsible for this near clone of the Merlin kit car. It was originally launched as the Pike Invader, but the name was quickly changed to Predator. The running gear came from the Ford Cortina, while there was independent suspension all round (the rear end courtesy of the Sierra). Engines came from Ford too, up to the 2.8-litre V6.

CR

PILAIN (i) (F) 1896–1920

1896–1897 Sté François Pilain, Lyons.
1897–1898 Sté des Voitures Automobiles et Moteurs (F. Pilain et Cie), Lyons.
1901–1920 Sté des Automobiles Pilain, Lyons.
François Pilain (1859–1924) worked for SERPOLLET and then LA BUIRE before setting up his own small engineering business in 1893. He built a prototype car with 1908cc 2-cylinder engine using hot-tube ignition, and final drive by belts. Two years later he had a staff of fifty, and issued a catalogue, probably the first in Lyons, for a similar car though now with electric ignition. His son remembered that the unwanted platinum burners were dumped in the garden where he retrieved them and had them melted down to make toy soldiers. Transmission was taken by half shafts carrying pinions that meshed with ring gears on the insides of the wheel rims, a system later taken up by CHENARD-WALCKER. Very few of these early cars were made and in 1897 Pilain left Lyons to work for VERMOREL, where he made a similar type of car which became the first Vermorel.

In 1901 Pilain returned to Lyons and set up a new company, the Société des Automobiles Pilain, sometimes called SAP for short. Few cars were made until 1904, though he experimented with 2- and 4-cylinder designs. He finally settled on the Type 4A, with 6124cc pair-cast 4-cylinder engine, 4-speed transaxle and the same rim drive as before. It was joined for 1905 by the 8621cc 40/60hp Type B with separately-cast cylinders and 3-speed conventional gearbox. There were also smaller models, the 16/24, 20/28 and 24/35hp. In 1906–07 about one chassis per day was being made. Coachwork was by various Lyons firms including Chaussende, later to become well-known bus and coach builders Faurax et Chaussende. They had round radiators in the Hotchkiss/ Delaunay-Belleville style, which were worn by all Pilains until 1913 when a vee-radiator was adopted, though some cars were still made with the old style.

1907 Pilgrim (i) 32hp landaulet.
NATIONAL MOTOR MUSEUM

1986 Pilgrim (iv) Bulldog sports car.
NICK GEORGANO/NATIONAL MOTOR MUSEUM

The recession in the French motor industry in 1907–08 hit Pilain hard, and they went into receivership. By 1909 they had emerged from this, but at the price of François Pilain's departure, for he had little financial acumen, and frittered money away on experiments. On his own he designed a car with 2-stroke engine and front wheel drive which he hoped to put into production had not World War I intervened. The new directors made a range of smaller cars, including an excellent 1944cc monobloc 10/12hp and a 3054cc 16/20hp available with two chassis lengths. Production doubled to 100 cars in 1911 and doubled again in 1912. Several new models were added in 1912 and 1913, including a 1085cc 8hp Type 4U and a small six, the 2389cc Type 6R. The 4197cc 18/24hp Type 4T had a very long stroke (85 × 185mm).

The Pilain factory was commandeered for manufacture of Hotchkiss trucks during the war, and in 1918 it was decided to liquidate the SAP. This was not quite the end of the Pilain name, as they merged their assets with a new company, the Société Lyonnaise d'Industrie Mécanique (S.L.I.M.) who made a new car called the S.L.I.M.-PILAIN.

NG

Further Reading
'Pilain – Pride of Lyons', David Burgess-Wise,
Automobile Quarterly, Vol. 31, No.1.

PILAIN (ii) *see* EMILE PILAIN

PILCAR *see* SBARRO

PILGRIM (i) (GB) 1906–1914

Pilgrims' Way Motor Co. Ltd, Farnham, Surrey.
This company took its name from the pilgrims' way from Winchester to Canterbury, which passed close to the factory site. The company was founded by Edward Armitage in 1905, and the first cars were ready a year later. Designed by F. Leigh Martineau, formerly with JAMES & BROWNE, they were unusual machines, with a 5585cc 25/30hp 4-cylinder engine mounted horizontally across the frame with the cylinder heads forward. Drive was by a 2-speed epicyclic gearbox and final drive by central chain. It was unusual to rely on a single-chain for such a large car. Because the engine lay under the floorboards, a substantial landaulet-body could be provided though the wheelbase was only 102in (2589mm). The short bonnet was fronted by a rounded gilled-tube radiator, similar to that of a Wolseley of a few years earlier.

After 18 of the 25/30 had been made the company went into receivership in March 1908, but was reorganised and brought out another unusual design in 1911. This was a 2-seater of Renault appearance, but the 1538cc flat-twin engine lived under the floor and drove forward to the front wheels via an epicyclic gearbox. It was designed by C.T. Hulme who had worked for Straker-Squire and Swift, and was also made as a forward-control 1-ton delivery van which was started by a handle at the rear of the chassis. Few were made, perhaps six vans and the same number of cars. The company earned their bread-and-butter from sub-contract work for other firms, making a large number of Wall Auto Wheel attachments for bicycles, and also making parts for Vauxhall. Although no cars were made after 1914, the company survived for many years as the Pilgrims' Way Engineering Co. They made precision tools and chassis lubrication systems between the wars, and small aircraft components for Vickers during World War II. Their last products were thief-proof messenger bags with built-in alarm systems, made from 1959 to 1962 when they closed down.

NG

Further Reading
'Fragments on Forgotten Makes, the Pilgrim', Bill Boddy,
Motor Sport, February 1962.

PILGRIM (ii) (US) 1913–1914

Ohio Falls Motor Car Co., New Albany, Indiana.
This was a conventional touring car powered by a 44/50hp 4-cylinder Continental engine, selling for $1800. It was built in the former JONZ factory and used bodies which had been made for the Jonz. Not more than 12 were built, although the company was reorganised as the Hercules Motor Car Co. which made the CROWN (iv) and HERCULES (iii) cars.

NG

PILGRIM (iii) (US) 1915–1918

Pilgrim Motor Car Co., Detroit, Michigan.
This was a light car made by William Radford who had previously been involved with the OXFORD (ii) and FOSTORIA cars. It had a 17hp 4-cylinder engine and 3-speed gearbox, and was offered in three models, tourer, roadster and cabriolet. Few were made because of charges of fraud against company chairman Clarence Leete. The car was redesigned with a slightly larger engine (22.5hp) and longer wheelbase for 1917, but again production seems to have been minimal.

NG

PILGRIM (iv) (GB) 1985 to date

Pilgrim Fibreglass, Brighton, Sussex.
From very humble origins, Den Tanner and Bill Harling's Pilgrim enterprise became one of the biggest kit car companies in the world. Their first model, the traditionally-styled Bulldog 2+2 roadster, may not have been particularly pretty, and its Morris Marina basis not very exotic, but its price was lower than any rival. It used a simple ladder frame chassis, which was developed in 1987 for Ford Cortina donor mechanicals. More significant was the Family Tourer (FT) model, a larger full 4-seater sister of the Bulldog launched in 1989. This was exclusively Cortina-based on a steel backbone chassis, with engines up to a 2.3-litre V6. Pilgrim also essayed the Hawthorn in 1986, a 1960s-style sports roadster, but this found few buyers. The same could not be said of the Sumo, a Cobra replica that cleaned up in the marketplace thanks to its low kit price (under £2000) and simple Ford Cortina running gear. A V6 power option and a sheet steel backbone chassis followed, while a more expensive and conventional Jaguar-based Mk III

arrived in 1993, using unmodified Jaguar XJ suspension and V8 power. Another model was the Martini, an unlikely Aston Martin V8 Volante lookalike based on the Ford Capri. It also developed a Lancia Stratos replica for mid-mounted Ford Escort CVH power, offered briefly in 1989. Pilgrim also took over the EAGLE RV in 1998.

CR

PILLE (H) 1931
Károly Zsolt, Budapest.

Home-made one-off creations are not the subject of this book, but Zsolt fabricated a handful of them. There was one which, according to his own words and a contemporary press report, was destined for the broader public. It was a 3-wheeler with a DKW motorcycle engine and a kick-starter. The body was made out of plywood. There was a second similar model, this one with a 350cc Villiers engine, but no-one was interested in this humble machine so it vanished into obscurity.

PN

PILLIOD (US) 1915–1916
Pilliod Motor Co., Toledo, Ohio.

Designed and promoted by Charles J. Pilliod, this car was announced with a sleeve-valve V8 engine which would have been a real novelty. However, when it was ready for production it had a 4-cylinder engine, though still using sleeve-valves. The only body style was a 5-seater tourer priced at $1485. Few can have been made as the company was bankrupt by June 1916.

NG

PILOT (i) (GB) 1909–1914
1909–1911 Motor Schools Ltd, London.
1911–1914 Pilot Works & Friction Cars Ltd, London.

Like the ACADEMY, this company specialised in driving and maintenance instruction, and showed a car at the 1909 Olympia Show. It had a 16hp 4-cylinder White & Poppe engine, 3-speed gearbox and shaft drive. The following year they showed another car with 19.6hp 4-cylinder Hillman engine, this time with belt and cone-pulley drive. These cars were probably one-offs. In 1911, when a new company had been formed called Pilot Works and Friction Cars, a smaller car was announced, with 7hp single-cylinder Coventry-Simplex engine and friction drive. Finally, for 1912 to 1914 they continued with the friction drive but used a 10hp 4-cylinder Chapuis-Dornier engine. In March 1914 a new company was formed to acquire the businesses of Motor Schools and Friction Cars, called Pilot Cars and Motor Schools Ltd.

NG

PILOT (ii) (US) 1909–1924
Pilot Motor Car Co., Richmond, Indiana.

The Pilot Motor Car Co. was headed by George Seidel, whose Seidel Buggy Co. had been operating in Richmond for some years. First built in the buggy factory, and then in a purpose-built plant in another part of town, Pilot cars were solid, assembled vehicles and not particularly exciting. Reportedly, Seidel named his car Pilot because of his aspiration to become a river boat pilot. The slogan he chose for his new vehicle was 'The Car Ahead'.

Pilot cars were medium priced ($1500 to $1800) machines, initially with 4-cylinder Teetor-Hartley engines. The Model Thirty-Five, built in 1909–10, was joined in 1911 by a Model Fifty with a larger 4-cylinder engine. All were built on 118in (2995mm) wheelbases. The Fifty was not repeated in 1912, but reappeared in 1913 on a 126in (3198mm) wheelbase, by which time a 6-cylinder Model 60 had appeared. The price for this car, a tourer on a 132in (3350mm) wheelbase, was up to $2500.

A 4.9-litre V8-engined Pilot, the Model 8-55, made a brief appearance in 1916, after which the cars were, without exception, sixes. An enclosed sedan was added to the line in 1919, and a coupé the following year. In 1920, a larger, 4080cc Herschell-Spillman engine was placed in the line.

A sleek sportster, introduced in 1922, dispensed with running boards, but the industry depression of the postwar period took its toll. After taking over the foundering LORRAINE Car Co. and producing a few hearses under that label, the Pilot Motor Car Co. went into receivership in 1923. Production of Pilots had never exceeded 500 cars per year. The last units were assembled early in 1924.

KF

1909 Pilot (i) 16hp landaulet.
NICK BALDWIN

1911 Pilot (ii) Model D 35hp roadster.
NICK BALDWIN

1918 Pilot (ii) Model 6-45 sedan.
JOHN A. CONDE

PILOT (iii) (D) 1923–1925
Pilotwagen AG, Bannewitz; Werdau.

This was a light car powered by a 6/30PS 4-cylinder engine. Soon after it was launched the company was acquired by the Sächsische Waggonfabrik, maker of railway carriages, and manufacture of the Pilot's bodywork was transferred to their plant at Werdau. Open and closed car bodies as well as delivery vans were made, but economic conditions were against small car firms, and in 1925 the wagon company concentrated again on rolling stock.

HON

PINART (B) 1901
Ernest Pinart, Brussels.

Ernest Pinart made a few voiturettes and light cars with 6 and 9hp 2-cylinder and 12hp 4-cylinder engines of his own manufacture. They had 3-speed

c.1907 Pipe tourer.
NATIONAL MOTOR MUSEUM

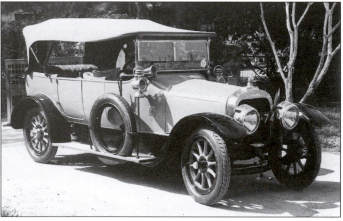

1913 Pipe 16/20hp tourer.
NATIONAL MOTOR MUSEUM

gearboxes and a vertical steering column. Six body styles were catalogued, with seating for two, three or four passengers. In February 1902 Pinart exhibited several engines at the Crystal Palace Show in London, of 6 and 8hp for cars, and 1¹/₂hp for motorcycles. It is not known if car production continued into 1902.

NG

PINGLE see HINDUSTAN

PINGUIN (D) 1953–1955
Pinguin Fahrzeugbau, Herne.
This company built a prototype 4-wheeled light car called the Passat in 1953. In September 1954 production began of an attractive-looking 3-wheeled coupé powered by a 200cc air-cooled Ilo engine driving the single rear wheel. Not more than 12 were made. The Pinguin name was also used for the Hungarian PULI microcar sold on the Swiss market.

HON

PINNACE see NORMA

PIONEER (i) **(AUS)** 1897
Australian Horseless Carriage Syndicate, Melbourne, Victoria.
An early but ill-considered publicity-driven effort, the Pioneer consisted merely of a 5hp stationary engine installed in a dog-cart. Although much trumpeting accompanied its debut and runs made, the smell, smoke and noise could not be ignored. The cycle trade press was critical of being excluded from its promotion while a 1900 report labelled it a fiasco and stated that it had sat in a Fitzroy shop window for three years.

MG

PIONEER (ii) **(US)** 1907–1912
1907–1909 W.R.C. Auto Works, El Reno, Oklahoma.
1909–1910 Pioneer Car Co., El Reno, Oklahoma.
1910–1912 Pioneer Car Co., Oklahoma City, Oklahoma.
Built by Edward Wright and Roy Roberts, who gave their initials to the company, the Pioneer was a high-wheeler, though more car-like than most, with a bonnet covering the 20hp 2-cylinder engine, epicyclic transmission and shaft drive. The wood-spoked wheels had solid tyres. By the spring of 1909, when they renamed their company, they had sold 22 cars. A 30hp 4-cylinder model was added for 1910 and was the only model for the remaining two years of the Pioneer's life.

NG

PIONEER (iii) **(US)** 1914
American Manufacturing Co., Chicago, Illinois.
This was a typical cyclecar powered by a 9hp air-cooled V-twin engine, with friction transmission and belt drive. The two seats were staggered, the passenger sitting about 12in (305mm) behind the driver as the body was only 40in (1015mm) wide. An associated company made the PARTIN-PALMER.

NG

PIONEER (iv) **(US)** 1959
Nic-L-Silver Battery Co., Santa Ana, California.
This fibreglass-bodied electric car was available in roadster, hard-top and station wagon body styles. Each rear wheel had its own electric motor and it was built on a 95in (2411mm) wheelbase.

HP

PIONIER (PL) 1953
In the early 1950s the Ministry of Road and Air Transportation decided to investigate the possibility of manufacturing a light car. Three prototypes were prepared, but the only one to run successfully was the Pionier built by Mieczyslaw Lukawski and Aleksander Wieckowski. It was a versatile vehicle with estate car body and folding seats. A 496cc 2-cylinder 2-stroke GAD 500 engine designed by Stefan Gajecki was used. The body was to have been made of scrap wood, but there were insufficient supplies of good quality wood, and the project was abandoned.

RP

PIONTEK (US) c.1990–1993
Piontek Engineering, Inc, Canton, Michigan.
Piontek built several versions of a motorcycle-powered 2-seat sports car. The first version was the Sports Tek, which sold for a pricey $15,000 and had a low, race car-like body. It was a high-tech design with a Suzuki GSX1000 motorcycle engine and fabricated suspension. The engine was enlarged to 1325cc and equipped with nitrous-oxide system that boosted horsepower to 150. With a weight of 1200lb (545kg) it was very quick. It was replaced by the Sport-tech, which was visually identical but had revised suspension, more foot room and round instead of square tubes in the frame. The Suzuki engine was now up to 180hp. By 1993 the Sport-tech had been renamed the Sportech and was being sold by Sportech International in Ewa Beach, Hawaii.

HP

PIPE (B) 1898–1922
1898–1903 Compagnie Belge de Construction Automobile, Brussels.
1903–1922 SA Usines Pipe, Brussels.
This company was founded by Albert and Victor Goldschmitt and the car was named after the metal pipes which the parent company made. The first car was built for them by the Usines des Moteurs à Grande Vitesse in Liège. Little is known about it but at the 1900 Brussels Salon Pipe showed a car made in their own new factory. It had a 6CV 2-cylinder engine and was designed by Vignal on Panhard lines. Lucien Hautvast drove one of these cars into third place in the Spa-Bastogne-Spa race, while the first 4-cylinder Pipe was driven in the 1901 Paris-Berlin race by Jean de Crawhez.

In 1902 there was a 15CV 4-cylinder production car, and that year a new and larger factory was acquired in the Brussels suburb of Anderlecht. At the Brussels Salon in December 1902 a 90CV Pipe was the most powerful car at the show. This was evidently not a production car, but the 15 and 20CV models sold well;

65 cars were made in 1903, 100 in 1904 and 180 in 1905. There were now four 4-cylinder models of 12, 15, 20 and 30CV, all with 4-speed gearboxes, chain drive and armoured wood frames. Side-valves were replaced by pushrod ohv in 1905. Hautvast finished sixth in the 1904 Gordon Bennett race, in a 13.5-litre 4-cylinder car with streamlined bonnet. A 1905 Pipe was the basis for the first cars built by NSU. Production rose to 300 cars in 1907, when the range consisted of 28, 50 and 80CV cars, as well as trucks and buses. The make's best sporting result came in 1907 when Hautvast finished second to Nazzaro's Fiat in the Kaiserpreis. Unfortunately the designer Otto Pfander was killed in trials for the Kaiserpreis, robbing the company of its most brilliant engineer. Because of this Pipe virtually gave up car manufacture for two years, concentrating on aero-engines.

A smaller car appeared in 1909, the 2670cc Type P4K, still with chain drive. Only in 1911 did one model, the 1766cc 12CV have shaft drive, and even then, only as an option. The others, the 18CV P4K, the 5341 and 6490cc sixes, and the massive 11,078cc 80CV four, were all chain-driven. An 80CV was shown at the 1910 Paris Salon with a striking saloon body by Kellner, with large vee-windscreen. In 1912 the advanced ohv engines designed by Pfander were dropped in favour of side-valve units, and shaft drive took over. The 1913 models were a 12, 12/16, 16/20, 24/30, and at the top of the range the 80CV was still available, though doubtless made in very small numbers.

Serious production never started after the war, although two prototypes were shown at the 1921 Brussels Salon, of 3- and 9-litres capacity. The latter was probably derived from the 80CV. Commercial vehicles were continued, however, up to 1932 when Pipe was taken over by Brossel. They merged Pipe's truck making activities with those of Bovy; Bovy-Pipe trucks were made up to 1950.

NG

PIPER (i) (GB) 1967–1974

1967–1968 Campbell Garages, Hayes, Kent.
1968–1971 Piper Cars Ltd, Wokingham, Berkshire.
1971–1973 Emmbrook Engineering Ltd, Wokingham, Berkshire.
1973–1974 Emmbrook Engineering Ltd, South Willingham, Lincolnshire.
George Henrotte, a garage owner and former racing driver who had dabbled in racing car construction, commissioned Tony Hilder to design a GT car and it was favourably received at the 1967 London Racing Car Show. The fibreglass body was moulded on a tubular backbone chassis which used Triumph Herald front suspension and a Ford live rear axle. A separate firm, under Brian Sherwood, took charge of production the following year and the design was developed although it was still essentially an unrefined kit car. Brian Sherwood died in 1970 and the company went into liquidation in 1971. It was revived in the same year, however, and an improved version, the P2, was offered. These cars had a fairly high specification and most were sold complete.

Piper was one of the marques which, in 1973, fell foul of the introduction of VAT to Britain and the economic uncertainty which followed the OPEC oil crisis. Production ceased early in 1975 after about 150 cars had been made. The parent company, now called Piper RS Ltd, still makes special camshafts and exhaust systems.

MJL

PIPER (ii) see MOTORCAR CLASSICS

PIRANHA (US) 1995 to date

Piranha Motor Car, Costa Mesa, California.
The Piranha was a kit that transformed the VW Beetle convertible into a custom hot rod. It included reworked front and rear wheel well panels, side rollpans, a rear spoiler and a dock that covered the rear seat that could be removed for carrying extra passengers. Open wheel and mudguarded kits were available, as were kits to extend the length of the chassis.

HP

PIRAT (PL) 1994 to date

1994–1996 Pro-Car Engineering, Katowice.
1996 to date J.A.K., Katowice.
In 1993 Ryszard Barnert and Jerzy Kwiatowski decided to make a kit car using FSO Polonez components. Kwiatowski designed the welded frame, suspension

1969 Piper (i) GTT coupé.
NICK GEORGANO/NATIONAL MOTOR MUSEUM

1998 Pirat sports car.
ROBERT PRZYBYLSKI

and 2-seater composite and aluminium body in 1930s style. In early 1995 the founders parted and a new company, J.A.K., was set up by Kwiatowski. The Pirat, renamed NESTOR, was put into production again in 1997, and in the same year a stretched Nestor with 4-door 5-seater body, called the Majestic, was added. About 30 cars had been made by the summer of 1999.

RP

PISA (US) c.1994 to date

Phoenix International Sports Automobile Corp., Phoenix, Arizona.
The Pontiac Fiero gathered quite a following for a sports/commuter car that was only sold for a short time. It was loved more for what it could be than for what it was. PISA sold parts to transform the Fiero into a high-performance sports car with bodywork to match. In addition to selling engine conversion kits and performance suspension upgrades, they sold several kit car bodies. The Artero was a handsome kit with European lines, a sloping bonnet and side scoops. It was not a replica of any specific car. The ZR-2 was another original design, but one that retained a distinctive Fiero feel despite a lower nose, scoops and spoilers. The SCORPION, XTC/gt and Finale were kits built by other companies and marketed by PISA. The Finale was built by Candy Apple Cars in England.

HP

PITCAIRN (US) 1934–1939

Pitcairn Autogiro Co., Philadelphia, Pennsylvania.
Although Pitcairn was famous for autogiro development, they also experimented with roadable aircraft. The A-35 was an autogiro that could take to the street after having its wing blades folded. A shaft ran forward from the engine to a front-mounted propeller. Harold Pitcairn flew the prototype in 1936, but it did not make it into production.

HP

PITT (GB) 1902

Pitt Yorkshire Machine Tool Co., Liversedge, Yorkshire.
This company announced a 4-seater rear-entrance tonneau powered by a 9hp engine, with Renault-type bonnet. It probably remained a prototype, as there are no references after its announcement in December 1902.

NG

1924 Pluto 4/20PS sports car.
HANS-OTTO NEUBAUER

PITTEVIL (B) 1899–1900
Metaalwerken van Antwerpen, Antwerp.
Founded by Alois Pittevil and Alphonse Dillen, this company was formed to make bicycles, sewing machines, tools and two types of car. One was of Austrian LEESDORFER design, which was based on the AMÉDÉE BOLLÉE, and the other was a belt-driven voiturette powered by a 2-cylinder Aster engine, known as the Pittevil or Phebe. Cars did not last long, and the company was soon renamed Ateliers du Canal, only to close in 1907.
NG

PITTLER see HYDROMOBIL

PITTSBURGH (i) see AUTOCAR

PITTSBURGH (ii) **(US)** 1908–1911
1908–1910 Fort Pitt Motor Manufacturing Co., New Kensington, Pennsylvania.
1910 Pittsburgh Motor Car Co., Pittsburgh, Pennsylvania.
German-born B.G. von Rottweiler planned to build the world's most powerful racing car, to be powered by an engine of nearly 34-litres capacity. Apparently he completed the engine but not the car, and for his production model chose something a little more modest, though still large. The Pittsburgh Six had a capacity of 9192cc and was mounted in a 121in (3071mm) wheelbase chassis. The engine was made in the factory but many other components came from well-known suppliers, such as Warner for the 3-speed gearbox, Hele-Shaw for the clutch and A.O. Smith for the rear axle. Roadster and tourer bodies were offered, and the prices were a relatively modest $2000-2500. They were probably too modest, for they were steadily increased thereafter. Sales were slow, and a change of company and location to Pittsburgh did not help. Von Rottweiler had left in 1908 to build a more powerful car for which he chose the name Vanderbilt. No more than one prototype was ever made, and it was probably a Pittsburgh reject.
NG

PIVCO (N) 1996 to date
1996–1998 Personal Intelligent Vehicle Co. AS, Oslo.
1998 to date Pivco Industries AS, Oslo.
This ambitious Norwegian electric car was one of the more well-developed and successful recent examples of zero-emissions vehicles. The CityBee was a very compact 2-seater with a smart thermoplastic body mounted over an aluminium space frame (both recyclable). A combination of nickel-cadmium and lead-acid batteries sat under the seats, powering a 40hp Brusa AC electric motor with a single-geared transaxle. Lotus assisted in the production engineering of this vehicle, which was a good performer, having a top speed of 65mph (105km/h). A development of the CityBee was the Th!nk (pronounced 'Think'). It again used an aluminium chassis and an updated plastic body for two passengers. The electric asynchronous electric motor was 27kW (36bhp) in power, fed by no less than 20 nickel-cadmium batteries. The company was liquidated in late 1998

but by the end of the year 51 per cent of a newly revitalised company had been purchased by Ford. They planned to launch it on the market as the Think City, together with an open-sided 4-seater for golf courses and resorts, called the Think Neighbour, and two models of electric bicycle.
CR

PIVOT (F) 1904–c.1907
Automobiles Pivot, Puteaux, Seine.
This company made conventional cars with 1-, 2- and 4-cylinder engines. The 2-cylinder models were of 6/7 and 9/11hp, both with 4-speed gearboxes and shaft drive. In 1905 the range consisted of three 4-cylinder shaft-driven cars, of 16, 24 and 30hp, and in 1906 singles were listed again, of 6 and 8hp, together with 8/10 and 10/12hp twins. Advertisements listed cars as powerful as 50hp, but these were probably 'to order only' and never built.
NG

P.K.A. see E.G.

PLANET (i) **(GB)** 1904–1905
Automobile Engineering Co. Ltd, Clapham, London.
This short-lived make offered four models, the smallest being a 2-seater with 6hp De Dion-Bouton engine, also a 12hp 2-cylinder and fours of 24 and 30hp with rear-entrance tonneau bodies. The 30hp was chain-driven, all the others had shaft drive. Prices ran from £152 for the 6hp to £499 for the 30hp.
NG

PLANET (ii) **(D)** 1907
Planetwerke Max Bohm, Berlin-Charlottenburg.
This car was named after the planetary (epicyclic) transmission which it featured. It was available with two engines, a 7PS 2-cylinder and a 10PS 4-cylinder. Lack of distribution and service facilities prevented its success.
HON

PLASTICAR (US) c.1954
Plasticar, Doylestown, Pennsylvania.
The Marquis was a special-bodied Renault sports coupé. The prototype was supposedly bodied in aluminium, although fibreglass was to take over for the production version. Price was to be $3100. It was an attractive, rounded shape with twin rear cooling vents similar to the Porsche 356, and appears to have been a version of the Alpine A-106 that was probably to be built under licence.
HP

PLAYBOY (US) 1947–1949
Playboy Motors, Buffalo, New York.
The Playboy was the result of an ambitious plan to sell a high-quality small car immediately after World War II. The brainchild of Louis Horwitz, the Playboy was originally intended to have a rear-mounted Continental engine. However, after the prototype was built they changed to a more conventional front-mounted engine. The prototypes were well received and a closed Chevrolet assembly plant was purchased in Buffalo. A pilot run of cars was made, including retractable hard-top convertibles and three station wagons. Engines used included Continental and Hercules 4-cylinder engines with 48hp. Playboy built 94 pilot models while the design was fine-tuned for production. Unfortunately, only three more cars were built before an unsuccessful stock offering and legal problems caused Playboy to declare bankruptcy in 1949. The assets were sold to the Lytemobile Co. of New York, who attempted to sell a lengthened and face-lifted version of the Playboy. This venture was unsuccessful as well.
HP
Further Reading
'Somewhere East of Laramie: The Unlikely Playboy', John A. Heilig, *Automobile Quarterly*, Vol. 31, No. 2.

P.L.M. (B) 1954–1955
Poelmans Merksen, Antwerp.
Under the name P.L.M., KELLER (ii) 3-door station wagons with Continental engines were manufactured and sold in Belgium.
CR

PLUTO (D) 1924–1927

1924–1927 Automobilfabrik Zella-Mehlis GmbH, Zella St Blasii.
1927 Pluto Automobilfabrik AG, Zella St Blasii.
When production of EHRHARDT cars ended, a new company was founded under Ehrhardt influence to continue production in the well-equipped factory. In contrast to the large and powerful Ehrhardts, the new product was a licence-built French AMILCAR sports car, in 1004cc 4/20PS and 1074cc 5/30PS models. These were equivalent to the French C4 and CGS respectively. The larger model was available with Roots supercharger when it was known as the 5/30/65PS. It had some success in competitions.

HON

PLUTON (F) 1901

Sté Industrielle d'Automobile Pluton, Levallois-Perret, Seine.
This was a light car powered by a front-mounted water-cooled 5hp De Dion-Bouton engine, with chain final drive. Bodies were a 3-seater spider or 4- seater tonneau.

NG

PLYMOUTH (i) (US) 1910

Plymouth Motor Truck Co., Plymouth, Ohio.
As its name implies, this company specialised in commercial vehicles, and in fact made only one passenger car. This was a 5-seater tourer with 40hp Wisconsin 4-cylinder engine and double-chain drive. It was distinguished by a large dome on the bonnet which housed a gravity-feed petrol tank. The filler cap was 8in in diameter, to enable filling from an ordinary bucket. The company decided to concentrate on trucks, of which they made between 150 and 200 between 1909 and 1914.

NG

PLYMOUTH (ii) (US) 1928–2001

Chrysler Corp., Detroit, Michigan.
The Plymouth was a late arrival among American mass-produced cars, but it had the backing of the Chrysler Corp. which had enjoyed a meteoric rise to fame since its foundation in 1924. The first Plymouth was in fact very similar to the 4-cylinder Chrysler 52, and replaced that model in the Chrysler line-up. Indeed, at its launch in July 1928, it was known as the Chrysler Plymouth, although it soon became recognised as a separate marque. Like the Chrysler 52, it had a 2790cc side-valve 4-cylinder engine, 3-speed gearbox and internal expanding hydraulic brakes. Priced between $670 and $725, it was over $100 more expensive than a contemporary Chevrolet or Ford, but the Plymouth was thought of as a slightly higher quality product, and its hydraulic brakes gave it the edge on both its rivals. 66,097 of the original Model Q were made, up to February 1929, when it was replaced by the Model U. This carried Plymouth rather than Chrysler Plymouth badging, but was generally similar in appearance otherwise. Under the bonnet, the engine had been enlarged to 2874cc, and was now Chrysler-designed rather than the Maxwell unit used in the Chrysler 52 and the first Plymouth. During the winter of 1929/30 a new factory was built for Plymouth manufacture, which had previously taken place in the Chrysler assembly plant at Highland Park, Michigan. The new factory was in Detroit, and the workers were busy assembling cars before the building was complete.

The Model U was made up to April 1930, with a production of 108,345. The calendar year 1929 saw Plymouth in 10th place among American manufacturers, but they rose to 8th in 1930 and to 3rd in 1931, a position they held almost every year until 1954. Walter Chrysler's low-priced baby was definitely one of America's 'Big Three', and has remained so ever since. There were no major changes until the arrival of the Model PA in mid–1931 as a 1932 model. The engine was now of 3213cc capacity, developing 56bhp. It was rubber-mounted in the chassis and suspended along its own centre of gravity, which greatly reduced the vibration suffered by passengers and, according to Plymouth advertising, gave the 4-cylinder engine the smoothness of an eight. The system was known as 'Floating Power', and was the beginning of the modern science of mounting engines. Other features of the PA were free wheeling and an 'Easy Shift' constant-mesh transmission. Its successor, the 65bhp PB appeared in April 1932, and was the last of the Plymouth fours. Probably the most famous owner of an early Plymouth was President Franklin D. Roosevelt. Crippled by polio, he drove a PA phaeton converted to all hand controls.

1931 Plymouth (ii) PA sedan.
NATIONAL MOTOR MUSEUM

1935 Plymouth (ii) PJ sedan
NICKGEORGANO

The 1933 Plymouths had 3110cc 6-cylinder engines and 70 or 76bhp according to compression ratios. The first models, introduced in November 1932, were the PC series, which had a 107in (2729mm) wheelbase, shorter than the 4-cylinder PB. This gave them a dumpy appearance which belied the 6-cylinder engine, and they were not well received. To improve matters Plymouth hastily brought out a mid-season model called the PD, which had 5in (127mm) extra wheelbase, modified wings and a painted instead of chromed radiator shell. This went into production in April 1933, and sold well, giving Plymouth a model year figure of 195,154, and 3rd place in the sales league. The shorter wheelbase was retained for the budget-priced PCXX, which sold for $445-510, compared with $545-595 for the PD. This two-level range was continued for 1934, the top model being the PE on a 114in (2895mm) wheelbase, the budget models being the PF, PFXX and PG on a 108in (2743mm) wheelbase. The same 3299cc engine was used in all models, but the PE, PF and PFXX had coil-spring ifs, while the PG retained the beam front axle. A new body style for Plymouth in 1934 was a station wagon called the Westchester Suburban. Only 35 were sold that year, but they were the forerunners of countless Plymouth station wagons in the years to come. The one-millionth Plymouth was built in August 1934, and was sold to a California lady who had bought the first-ever Plymouth in 1928. The independent suspension was not a success, so 1935 Plymouths reverted to a beam axle. The PJ series all had the same 3.3-litre engine, now giving 82bhp, and the same 113in (2870mm) wheelbase. Calendar year production for 1935 was 442,281, as America climbed out of the Depression. Between 1935 and the interruption of production by the war, Plymouth's changes were mainly in styling. Only one size of engine was offered each year, and this remained at 3299cc until 1942, when it was increased to 3517cc (95bhp). Hypoid rear axles came on the 1937 models, and 1939 Plymouths were considerably restyled, with 3-piece radiator grills, recessed headlamps and split windscreens. They also had steering column gearchange and a new ifs. A rare body style, not made since 1932 and revived just for 1939, was the 4-door convertible sedan. Only 387 were made. There was also a long-wheelbase (134in/ 3404mm) 7-seater sedan, which had been offered since 1936, and would continue through 1941. Plymouth built its four-millionth car in 1941, when

1939 Plymouth (ii) P8 De Luxe convertible sedan.
JOHN A. CONDE

1941 Plymouth (ii) P12 convertible.
NICK GEORGANO

429,869 cars were sold. By this time station wagons were a well-established part of the range, with 5811 being sold.

The entry of America into the war halted production of the 1942 models on 31 January 1942, after 27,645 had been sold. Apart from the enlarged engine and heavier frontal styling, they were not greatly changed from the 1941 cars. Plymouths sold abroad showed a number of differences from the home-market models, and even changes of name. In Australia Holden built 4-door tourer bodies on Plymouths later than the American factory, while in Great Britain, after 1932, the Plymouth was sold as a Chrysler Kew or Wimbledon, as it was felt that the Plymouth name was unfamiliar to British drivers. UK-market cars were sourced from Chrysler's Canadian factory, and could be had with a 2792cc engine as well as the regular 3299cc unit. The Scandinavian market was supplied from a Belgian assembly plant; Plymouths were sold in Sweden under their own name, but in Norway they carried Dodge badges.

Chrysler factories restarted production later than their rivals. Plymouth built only 770 cars in 1945, putting them in 12th place, way below their accustomed position. Although their catalogue claimed 50 improvements over the 1942 models, most were fairly small. Externally there was a new grill and fuller rear wings which slightly covered the wheels, while the engine had a higher cr, of 6.6:1, although power remained the same at 95bhp.

Because of the pent-up demand for new cars in the early postwar years, there was no need to change designs immediately, and the 1946 Plymouths were little altered until the first true postwar models appeared in the spring of 1949. These had fresh styling with notch-back 4-light sedan bodies in place of the fastback 6-light design which dated back to prewar days. They were still conservative in appearance compared with Ford and General Motors rivals, as radical styling was not favoured by Chrysler's president, K.T. Keller. Engines were also unchanged, and indeed the 6-cylinder side-valve engine was Plymouth's only power unit up to 1955, although enlarged to 3769cc on 1954 models.

Apart from annual styling changes there were few innovations on Plymouths in the early 1950s, and although sales held up well at first, in 1954 they lost their traditional 3rd place, falling to 5th behind Oldsmobile and Buick.

The 1955 Plymouths were all-new, with 'Forward Look' styling and new ohv V8 engines of 3949 and 4247cc developing 157 and 167bhp. They came in three series, the Plaza which was available with the old six or V8 engines, the Savoy mid-priced line with V8s only, and the Belvedere which was the expensive model, with better finish and equipment. Somewhat surprisingly, this could also be had with a choice of six or V8 engines. Automatic transmission (introduced in 1954) was an alternative to a manual gearbox on all models, though the latter remained the standard transmission on most Plymouth models up to the 1970s. Push-button selection of the automatic transmission was introduced in 1956.

The adoption of the V8 engine, which had reached other divisions of the Chrysler Corp. earlier, enabled Plymouth to enter the horsepower race, and to offer high-performance cars for the first time in its history. 1956 saw the Fury, a special hard-top with a 4965cc 240bhp V8 engine. Power increased to 290bhp from 5204cc in 1957, though later Fury engines were less highly stressed, and gave around 230/250bhp. Torsion-bar front suspension was introduced on all Chrysler Corp. cars in 1957.

1960 was the year when the Big Three launched their compact cars, following the success of American Motors' Rambler. Chrysler's contribution was the Valiant which was originally promoted as an independent marque, 'Nobody's kid brother, this one stands on its own four tyres', but it was sold by Plymouth dealers, and became a model of Plymouth in 1961. Made in Dodge factories, the Valiant had an all-new unitary construction body, and a 2800cc ohv slant-six engine which developed 101bhp. Sedan and station wagon bodies were made, and the Valiant rode on a 106.5in (2705mm) wheelbase, compared with 118in (2997mm) for the full-sized Plymouths. Valiant prices, at $2110–2546, were

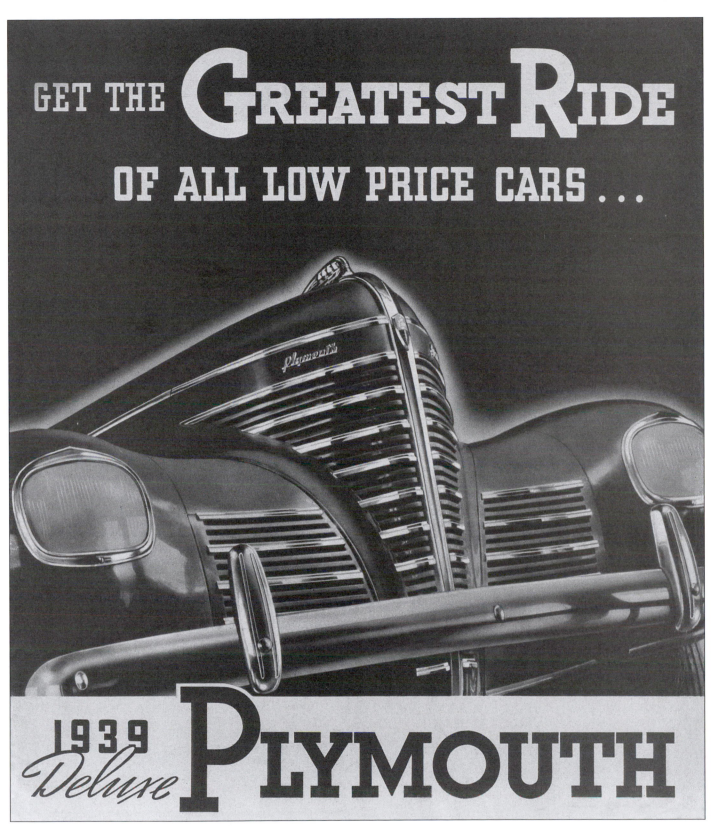

GET THE **GREATEST RIDE** OF ALL LOW PRICE CARS . . .

1939 *Deluxe* PLYMOUTH

1956 Plymouth (ii) Belvedere sedan.
NATIONAL MOTOR MUSEUM

1957 Plymouth (ii) Plaza sedan.
NICK BALDWIN

1965 Plymouth (ii) Barracuda coupé.
NATIONAL MOTOR MUSEUM

1969 Plymouth (ii) GTX coupé.
NATIONAL MOTOR MUSEUM

not all that much lower than the cheaper full-sized Plymouths, but the cars became popular because of their size, and first year production was an encouraging 127,558. A 2-door hard-top was added to the Valiant range for 1961, and two years later the car was restyled to become less distinctive, with a conventional horizontal grill and less elaborate body sculpture. A larger 6-cylinder engine of 3695cc and 145bhp was an alternative power unit from 1962. By 1963 the larger Plymouths could be had with a variety of engines. The stock unit was still the 230bhp 5204cc V8, but options included the 3695cc six used in the Valiant and several V8s up to the 6980cc Super Stock II 4-barrel Wedge engine which developed 425bhp. This was only available in the Fury, now made as a 4-door sedan or 2-door convertible, as well as the original 2-door hard-top.

When the restyled 1963 Valiant was being designed, a sports version was considered, and this saw the light of day in April 1964 as the Barracuda. A 5-seater 2-door hardtop coupé, the Barracuda had a large wrap-around rear window, the biggest fitted to any car, with an area of 172sq in (1115sq cm). Engine options were the Valiant's 2800 or 3695cc sixes, or 4474cc V8. In fact, about 90 per cent of the 23,443 Barracudas built in the first season used the V8 engine, hardly surprising as the car was promoted with a sporting image. For 1965 the Barracuda was no longer called a variant of Valiant but became a model in its own right. A 235bhp Commando version of the V8 was the most powerful engine option, and a Barracuda Formula S competition package was offered, with special chassis components and distinctive trim and badging, in addition to the Commando 273 (273cu in = 4474cc) engine. This was the beginning of the Barracuda's entry into the muscle car field, in which it followed the same path as Ford's Mustang and Chevrolet's Camaro from relatively tame personal car to a really high-performance machine. The second-generation Barracudas of 1967–69 came in three body styles, a convertible, a hard-top coupé and the original fastback coupé. Engine options were the 3695cc slant six, 4474cc V8 and a 6276cc V8 which gave a disappointing 280bhp, 45bhp less than the same engine in other Chrysler Corp. cars. The problem was that the engine compartment restricted the size of the exhaust manifolds. Indeed it was so crowded that there was no room for popular options such as power-assisted steering and brakes or air conditioning. Nevertheless, Plymouth engineers managed to extract 20bhp more from the engine in 1968, by using larger exhaust valves.

For 1969 power went up still further, to 330bhp, thanks to a high-performance camshaft, while the 1970 season saw a still larger engine of 7210cc and 375bhp. Also in 1970 the Barracuda received a new body with similar styling to the Dodge Challenger, although there were no common panels between the two. Convertible and notchback hard-tops were made, but the fastback with the enormous rear window, which had characterised the original Barracuda, was no longer available. There were nine engine options on the 1970 Barracudas, from the familiar slant six up to the 7.2-litre V8. The most powerful was the 426 Hemi, a 6980cc V8 with hemispherical combustion chambers and twin Carter 4-barrel carburettors, which developed 425bhp. Only 666 Barracudas were delivered in 1970 with this fabulous engine, although it was also available in the Plymouth Road Runner and GTX as well as in several models of Dodge. The same models were continued for 1971, but after that the Barracuda range was drastically pruned, losing the 383, 440 and Hemi engines as well as many of the performance and styling options. To add insult to injury the 1972 Barracudas were relegated to two pages at the back of a catalogue which also covered Valiants and Dusters. The Barracuda was listed up to the beginning of 1974, but was discontinued on 1 April that year, exactly ten years after it had been introduced. Production totalled 392,587.

Race-Bred Plymouths
For a long time the average Plymouth had something of a 'Granny' image, yet even in the days when design was at its staidest, in the early 1950s, the make was beginning to earn victories in NASCAR stock car racing. The V8 engine of 1955 enabled more powerful cars to be made, and between 1963 and 1972 cars equipped with the Hemi engine scored countless wins in USAC and NASCAR events, and also in drag racing. Output was as high as 600bhp. Plymouth won the 1965 and 1966 SCCA Manufacturers Rally Championships. Plymouth's most successful drivers were father and son Lee and Richard Petty, the team being managed by another son, Maurice.

Plymouth's racing programme had several spin-offs in the production car field. Most striking were the Road Runner Superbirds, of which 1920 were made between October 1969 and January 1970. They were based on the Road Runner, a high-performance coupé introduced in 1968, powered by a 335bhp 6276cc engine. It was named after a Warner Brothers cartoon bird, whose 'beep-beep' sound was imitated by the car's horn. For 1969 it was available with the 426 Hemi engine, and a convertible was added. Plymouth's 1970 NASCAR entries were based on the Road Runner, and to enable them to be homologated, something close to them had to be offered to the public, hence the Superbird. The regulations stated that Plymouth had to make at least half as many Superbirds as they had dealers across the US. They had streamlined nose extensions and large spoilers mounted at the rear above roof level. Priced at $4298 compared with $3034 for a regular Road Runner coupé, the Superbird was said to reach over 218mph (350km/h) in racing trim.

A companion to the Road Runner was the GTX, a mid-sized performance car in the Belvedere/Satellite series. Introduced in 1967, it had a 7210cc engine as standard, with the option of the 6980cc 426 Hemi. The GTX lasted until the end of the 1971 season.

Compacts and Sub-compacts

The Valiant range was continued up to the end of 1976, and was joined by two sub-series, the Duster coupé for 1970 and the Scamp hard-top for 1971. All three were available with the 3244 or 3695cc sixes, or a 5211cc V8. The Duster was also available with a 5571cc 265bhp V8 in the Duster 340. For 1977 the Valiant/Scamp/Duster series were dropped, being replaced by a new mid-sized range, the Volare, while below them were the imported sub-compact cars. The first of these to bear the Plymouth name was the Hillman Avenger, sold as the Cricket from 1971 to 1973. This was followed by the Arrow, a Mitsubishi-built coupé with 1.6 or 2-litre 4-cylinder engine, which arrived in 1976, and the Sapporo, also a Mitsubishi product, which went on sale for the 1978 season. The first sub-compact to be built by Chrysler's US factories was the Plymouth Horizon, also sold as the Dodge Omni. This was similar to the European Chrysler Horizon, built in Britain and France, having a 1.7-litre transverse 4-cylinder engine driving the front wheels, and a 5-door hatchback body. In 1980 there was a sports coupé derivative of the Horizon, not seen in Europe, called the TC3, and Horizons came with either the 1.7-litre European engine or a Chrysler-built 2.2-litre. The Horizons were still made in 1988, several years after the model was dropped in Europe.

The full-size Plymouth of the 1960s and 1970s was the Fury. The name was first used for a sub-series of the 1956 Belvedere line, and became a model in its own right in 1959. It was soon available in sedan, convertible and station wagon form, with a choice of 3695cc six or 5211cc V8 engines. The big 6276cc, 7210cc V8s were optional in the late 1960s, but the 426 Hemi was not available in the Fury. Special Fury sedans were made for taxicab and police work, for which they were widely used. 1972 saw the Gran Fury sedan and coupé, top of the market models with Chrysler-like styling. For 1974 the Fury name was given to intermediate-sized Plymouths, the full-size models being exclusively Gran Furys. The biggest engine option was still the 440 (7210cc) but it gave only 215bhp, due to emission controls. By 1983 only two engines were available in a down-sized Gran Fury, a 3687cc six and a 5211cc V8. These, and body shells, were shared with the Chrysler Fifth Avenue and Dodge Diplomat. The Gran Fury was continued to 1990, though since 1985, only with the V8 engine.

Plymouth's intermediate Volare, similar to the Dodge Aspen, was made from 1976 to 1980 with the same 6- and 8-cylinder engines as the Fury, though without the option of the 440. For 1981 it was replaced by a new front-drive design, the K-car sold as a Dodge Aries or Plymouth Reliant. This had transverse 4-cylinder engines, a 2212cc Chrysler or 2556cc Mitsubishi. For 1985 it was joined by the Caravelle, a slightly longer and more luxurious version which was made in Chrysler's Canadian factory. Also for 1985 some more Mitsubishi models were offered under the Plymouth label, the Colt 3- and 5-door hatchbacks, the Conquest Turbo (Mitsubishi Starion) and Vista (Mitsubishi Space Wagon). Autumn 1986 saw another new model in the compact class, the Sundance, powered by a transverse 2212cc engine developing 97bhp, or 148bhp with fuel injection and turbocharger. Made in 2- or 4-door sedan versions, the Sundance had a parallel model in the Dodge range, the Shadow. For 1989 the Reliant gave way to the Acclaim (Dodge Spirit), a slightly larger car with 2212cc or 2507cc fours, or a 2966cc V6 engine, available only as a 4-door sedan. A new model for 1989 was the Laser, a coupé built by the joint Chrysler/Mitsubishi Diamond Star company and also sold as a Mitsubishi Eclipse. In Plymouth form it had a single-cam 1755cc or twin-cam 1999cc engine, the latter available with

1977 Plymouth (ii) Gran Fury Brougham.
NICK BALDWIN

1980 Plymouth (ii) TC3 coupé.
NICK GEORGANO

2000 Plymouth (ii) Neon 2.0LX sedan.
CHRYSLER JEEP IMPORTS UK

turbocharging and intercooling to give 195bhp. The Horizon and its sports coupé derivative the Turismo, was made up to 1990 while Plymouth had a semi-forward control MPV called the Voyager (Dodge Caravan) since 1983.

For 1994 the Sundance and its V6 version, the Duster, were dropped, but a new model was the Mitsubishi-based Colt, the 2-door coupé derived from the Mitsubishi Colt and the 4-door sedan from the Mitsubishi Mirage. This model was also made as the Dodge Colt and Eagle Summit. New in 1993 was the Neon, a 4-door sedan or 2-door coupé with front drive from a 1996cc transverse 4-cylinder engine in single-cam 133bhp or twin-cam 152bhp forms, both with 16 valves. From 1994 the Neon was sold with both Dodge and Plymouth badging, while in 1996 Chrysler's Stratus was sold as the Plymouth Breeze, though only with a 2-litre 4-cylinder engine. Neon, Breeze and Voyager were continued for 1999, together with the striking Prowler, a two-seater sports car with hot rod styling, separate cycle-type front wings which turned with the wheels, and massive rear wheels larger than those at the front. Derived from a 1993

2000 Plymouth (ii) Prowler roadster.

PLYMOUTH

concept car which few expected to reach the showrooms, the Prowler was powered by a 3518cc 24-valve V6 engine, and was available in one colour only, purple. Production began in January 1997 at the same Detroit plant that built the Dodge Viper. Other colours were available in 1998, including yellow, red and black. A new colour for 2000 was silver. 3921 Prowlers had been made by September 1999. In October Chrysler announced that they would discontinue the Plymouth name at the end of the 2001 model year.

NG

Further Reading
The Plymouth and De Soto Story, Don Butler, Crestline, 1978.
'Barracuda: Braving Turbulent Waters', Jeffrey I. Godshall,
Automobile Quarterly, Vol. 25, No. 4.
'Form, Function, and Fantasy: Seventy Years of Chrysler Design',
Jeffrey I. Godshall, *Automobile Quarterly*, Vol. 32, No. 4.

PLYMOUTH (iii) (AUS) 1946–1957

Chrysler Australia Ltd, Keswick, South Australia.

Chrysler's increasing involvement in Australia's motor industry resulted in the selection of the P15 as the basis for a programme of increasing local content. Versions with DeSoto and Dodge grills and badges also appeared. This system was also followed with the new 1949 body until 1953 when the P24 Cranbrook was adopted for manufacture to 92 per cent local content. Desoto and Dodge editions accompanied it while manual, overdrive and automatic transmissions were available. A major 1957 restyle, with full-width grill and tail fins, was produced only as the Chrysler Royal, so bringing the era of badge engineering to an end.

MG

P.M. (B) 1921–1926

Sté Auto Mécanique P.M., Sclessin, Liège.

Making its appearance at the 1921 Brussels Salon, the P.M. was a fairly substantial light car powered by an 1820cc side-valve 4-cylinder Peters engine, with 3-speed gearbox. The initials may have come from the founder Pierre Mullejans or the administrator Pierre Malherbe, while they also corresponded to the chief engineer P. Mauconduit. Body styles included 2- and 4-seater tourer, cabriolet and saloon, and production ran at about 50 cars per year. The company was represented in the Congo, and there were plans to export to Australia. There were strong similarities between this Type D P.M. and the CARROW in which company the P.M. directors held a large number of shares.

The Type D was made up to the end of 1924, and was replaced by the Type F. This had a 1494cc single-ohc engine, probably by C.I.M.E., a 4-speed gearbox and a flat radiator in place of the rounded shape of the Type D. At this time P.M. also made road tractors and trailers for loads of up to 10 tons.

Car production ended in 1926 or 1927, and the company closed down in 1929.

NG

P.M.C. (i) (US) 1908

C.S. Peets Manufacturing Co., New York, New York.

The P.M.C. (Peets Manufacturing Co.) was a typical high-wheeler with 12hp 2-cylinder engine, epciyclic transmission and chain drive. What was untypical was its factory location at 60 West 43rd Street, in the heart of New York City, whose inhabitants showed little interest in this essentially country vehicle.

NG

P.M.C. (ii) see PREMIER (ii)

PNEUMOBILE (US) 1914–1915

Cowles-McDowell Pneumobile Co., Chicago, Illinois.

This car was so called because it used air springs in place of the usual leaf or coil system. Air-filled cylinders were mounted close to each wheel and contained plungers rigidly supported by the axle. There was no metallic connection between the wheels and the axles. For equalising purposes each cylinder was connected to a central piping system, on the lines of the Citroën DS19 of forty years later. The engine was a 4.8-litre 6-cylinder Buda, and the car was listed with two tourer bodies, for four and six passengers, and a roadster.

NG

POBIEDA see GAZ

PODEUS (D) 1910–1914

Automobilfabrik Paul Heinrich Podeus, Wismar.

This was one of the very rare ventures into car production in Northern Germany, Wismar being on the Baltic. Paul Podeus (1853–1924) was active in various fields, including a shipping company, and he started vehicle production with trucks in 1902. Passenger cars were made for a short time only. They included the 2248cc 9/24PS and the 2536cc 10/30PS, both with 4-cylinder engines and shaft drive. Most went for export to Russia, as did the trucks which were made up to 1918.

HON

PODVIN (F) 1983–c.1989

1983–1985 A.C.A. Podvin, Joigny.

1985–1986 Sté Le Sphinx, Looze.

1986–c.1989 A.C.A.P. Le Sphinx, Mortagne.

Fabrice Podvin, who also produced the Swiss SBARRO BMW 328 replica under licence in France, commercialised a fabulous replica under the name Le Sphinx. This was a close copy of the 1937 Peugeot 402 Darl'Mat and was developed with help from Peugeot engineers. In a strong tubular chassis were front wishbones and Peugeot rear suspension. It used a Peugeot 505 engine, optionally in GTi, V6 or Turbo form. The 2-seater roadster bodywork was in double-skinned polyester.

CR

POHLMANN (D) 1981–1988

Pohlmann KG, Kulmbach.

This company specialised in electric vehicles including an advanced 2-seater with monobox fibreglass 2-seater body with gull wings and two motors, one for each rear wheel. It was known as the Pohlmann EL, and was sponsored by the electrical company RWE. About 30 Pohlmanns were made, but it was found that they would cost too much to make to be a practical commercial proposition.

HON

POINARD (F) 1951–1952

This motorcycle sidecar manufacturer attempted production of a microcar. Its 3-wheeler retained motorcycle handlebar steering to the single front wheel and a saddle for the driver, although there was space for two passengers on a bench behind. Its 4bhp Ydral 125cc single-cylinder engine was hardly suitable for the job of transporting three passengers.

CR

POIRIER (F) 1928–1958

Éts G. Poirier, Fondettes, Indre-et-Loire.

Some models advertised as suited for general use were marketed by this firm, although their primary interest was invalid carriages, hand-, pedal- or motor-driven. Some early versions, with 175cc Train engines, had full bodywork, but with the introduction of the Monoto series after World War II, bodies were always rudimentary and doorless. The XW5 tandem 2-seater, available in beige or green, had a 4-speed gearbox with Cardaflex shaft transmission. The rear-mounted engine was standardised as a 125cc Ydral 2-stroke, vehicles up to this size needing no driving licence, although monocars and back-to-back 2-seaters had been built with Peugeot, Sachs and Gnome-et-Rhône engines before the war. Postwar invalid carriages utilised Sachs or VAP engines. Maximum speed of the XW5 was restricted to 28mph (45km/h), deemed adequate for commercial travellers and parish priests, as well as commuters, in the advertising literature. Always built to order only, demand for the voiturettes dwindled as the design was not updated and the tiny Usines des Roches, situated on the banks of the Loire near Tours, reverted to the manufacture of invalid carriages, stretcher trolleys, etc.

DF

POKORNEY *see* TRICOLET

POLI-FORM (US) 1984 to date

Poli-Form Industries, Santa Cruz, California and LaSelva Beach, California.

Poli-form had been building fibreglass car parts for 16 years when they built their first kit cars in the mid–1980s. They made two kits for Porsches, one that converted the lowly 924 into a 944 look-alike; the other updated the 911 into a pseudo-930. However, their main business was in hot rod kits. They made models based on the 1915 Ford Roadster, 1919 Ford Speedster, 1927 Ford Roadster, 1927 Ford Touring 4-door, 1929 Ford Roadster and the 1934 Ford 3-Window Coupé. They were designed to be built in hot rod form with V8 engines and with a Ford live axle or Corvette or Jaguar rear suspension. They were sold in kit or assembled form.

HP

POLONEZ *see* FSO

c.1913 Podeus 10/30PS tourer (left), with a c.1913 Singer Ten 2-seater.
NATIONAL MOTOR MUSEUM

1936 Polski-Fiat LS 3.6-litre V8 saloon .
ROBERT PRZYBYLSKI

POLONIA (PL) 1924

M. Karpowski, Warsaw.

Major Mikolaj Karpowski presented to the public the prototype of large car called the Polonia in June 1924. It had a 4769cc 6-cylinder engine developing 45bhp, with two Zenith carburettors. Brakes were on the rear wheels only. It was designed for easy maintenance, with three hatches on the cylinder block to ease inspection. One person could change the gear wheels in the gearbox in 15 minutes. Rear axle half shafts were easily changeable too. The prototype was made in the Army Workshops, and as Karpowski could not find any industrial firm to make his car it was sold as a prize in a raffle.

RP

POLSKI-FIAT (PL) 1932–1939

Panstwowe Zaklady Inzynierii, Warsaw.

The State Engineering Works (PZInz) was created in 1927 when the government took over the works which had made Ursus light trucks. Looking for fresh work, the government signed an agreement with FIAT in 1931 for licence production of the 621 truck and 508 Balilla small car. The trucks were given priority, but the cars came a year later. The standard 508 and later 508C were made, and from 1937 the larger 518 was added. The cars were sold through the Fiat dealer network under the name Polski-Fiat.

In 1936 it was decided to investigate production of a luxury car. Named PZInz 403, and commonly known as the L-S (Lux-Spor) it had a 3888cc side-valve V8 engine developing 96bhp, backbone frame, all-round independent suspension with wishbones and longitudinal torsion bars, and an aerodynamic body that was later copied by HANOMAG in their 1.3-litre saloon. Unfortunately, because of small-scale production, it would have been twice as expensive as a Buick, which was assembled at that time in Poland by Lilpop, Rau & Loewenstein.

1937 Polski-Fiat 508 saloon.
ROBERT PRZYBYLSKI

1924 Pomeroy (ii) sedan.
JOHN A. CONDE

The licence agreement with Fiat was terminated in 1941, although the association was revived in 1968 when FSO began to make the Fiat 125, sold under the Polski-Fiat name on some markets. Production of the prewar Polski-Fiats was about 6000 508s and 1000 518s.

RP

POLY'CARS *see* BUGANTIC

POLYCARTERS (F) 1970–1972

Polycarters sarl, Sorigny.

Two models were built by this company, run by G. de Tayrac. There was a *sans permis* microcar with a 50cc Sachs engine and a curious leisure vehicle with an open top and sides. The latter was sold in kit form and was based on Renault 4 parts.

CR

POLYMOBIL; POLYPHON (D) 1904–1909

Polyphon Musikwerke AG, Wahren, Leipzig.

This firm specialised in machine tools and automatic music machines. In 1904 they took out a licence to make the Curved Dash OLDSMOBILE. It differed from the American version only in having a *vis-à-vis* seat for two children facing the driver, and wheel steering in place of tiller. It was marketed under the name Gazelle. The public soon asked for something larger, which led to a model with longer wheelbase and frontal bonnet, though the engine was still under the seat. For this and subsequent models, the name Polyphon was used. In 1907 two more conventional models were introduced, the 2-cylinder 8/10PS and 4-cylinder 16/20PS. A new name was chosen in 1909, the cars being henceforth known as DUX.

HON

POMEROY (i) (US) 1902

Pomeroy Motor Vehicle Co., Brooklyn, New York.

B.H. Pomeroy's car was a light runabout powered by an 8hp 2-cylinder 2-stroke engine that ran on paraffin fuel, hence its original name of Keromobile, kerosene being American for paraffin. The body was mounted high above the ground, with the engine and transmission well separated from it. He also listed a 6-seater surrey, delivery wagon and Family Combination, which somehow combined the functions of runabout, surrey and delivery wagon. He said that his vehicles could be adapted to electric propulsion, which has led to some claims that the Pomeroy was an electric car, but it seems that he never made one.

NG

POMEROY (ii) (US) 1920–1924

1920–1922 Aluminium Co. of America,
(American Body Co., Buffalo, New York).
1922–1924 Pierce-Arrow Motor Car Co., Buffalo, New York.

The Pomeroy was not, as has sometimes been claimed, an 'all-aluminium car' but it did contain about 85 per cent of aluminium parts, notable exceptions being the gears and semi-elliptic springs. The engine blocks were of aluminium with cast-iron sleeves. It was designed by Laurence H. Pomeroy (1883–1941) famous for his work on the Vauxhall Prince Henry and 30/98. He was hired by the Aluminium Co. of America (Alcoa) to design their car, in which he was helped by Forrest Cameron, formerly of the CAMERON car. The car was built at the factory of the American Body Co., which had been bought by Alcoa, and had a 2718cc 4-cylinder engine, later enlarged to 3723cc. Bodies, designed by John S. Burdick, were a sedan, tourer and coupé. Four were made in all. Alcoa could not find a firm to put it into production, probably because no manufacturer wanted to commit themselves to a material of which one company (Alcoa) had a near monopoly of supplies. However, three further cars were made in the PIERCE-ARROW factory in 1923 and 1924. These had 4078cc 6-cylinder engines similar to the Pierce-Arrow 80, apart from a smaller bore, and 4- or 6-light sedan bodies styled on the lines of the 80.

NG

PONÇIN (F) 1981–1993

Véhicules Ponçin SA, Tournes.

Ponçin specialised in amphibious all-terrain vehicles such as the VP2000, as well as tracked multi-wheelers, but it also produced more conventional cars. The 1984 GP was a plastic-bodied utility car offered with a 602cc Citroën 2CV, 652cc Visa or 1299cc GSA engine. There was also an exceptionally versatile 4 × 4 open vehicle styled rather like a Suzuki SJ. It was powered by Renault 2.2-litre petrol or 2.1-litre turbodiesel engines and featured all-independent coil suspension, differential lock and 2/4-wheel drive. A 6-wheeled 6 × 6 model with more squared-off bodywork was also presented in 1990, and there was another model powered by a Ford 2.3-litre 4-cylinder engine.

CR

PONDER (US) 1923

Ponder Motor Manufacturing Co., Shreveport, Louisiana.

The Ponder was little more than the former BOUR-DAVIS car after the company changed hands in 1923. At least one Ponder car is known to have been built, presumably a prototype of the things to come, which never came. In all probability, the Ponder was a Bour-Davis which remained in stock and which was rebadged. A Continental 6-cylinder 6-N engine was used.

KM

PONTIAC (i) (US) 1907–1908

Pontiac Spring & Wagon Works, Pontiac, Michigan.

This company was formed in 1899, and in 1905 they took over production of the Rapid truck. Two years later they decided to enter the passenger car business with a high-wheeler. It was quite typical of its kind, with 12hp 2-cylinder engine, friction transmission and double-chain drive. Two models were offered, the runabout and a Model D No.8 Sales Car, presumably with accommodation for commercial travellers' samples. About 30–40 were made.

NG

PONTIAC (ii) **(US)** 1915

Pontiac Chassis Co., Pontiac, Michigan.

This company supplied chassis only, powered by a 25hp 4-cylinder Perkins engine with a 3-speed gearbox. The wheelbase was 106in, and tyres were not provided. In 1916 one of the directors, R.A. Palmer, started the OLYMPIAN Motors Co., which absorbed the Pontiac Chassis Co. It is reported that Pontiac built the chassis for the DURYEA GEM.

NG

PONTIAC (iii) **(US)** 1926 to date

1926–1932 Oakland Motor Car Co., Pontiac, Michigan.

1933 to date Pontiac Motor Co., Pontiac, Michigan.

The Pontiac was the brainchild of General Motors' president Alfred P. Sloan, aided at first by engineer Henry Middlebrook Crane (1875–1956) and later by a team led by Benjamin Anibal (1887–1977). When Sloan took over GM in 1923 he adopted the slogan, 'A Car for Every Purse', meaning that the company should cater for the whole market from the low price Chevrolet to the Cadillac at the upper end of the range. He was aware of a gap between the $525 Chevrolet and the Oldsmobile, whose prices began at $975.

The car he chose to fill this gap was to use a number of Chevrolet components, including many body pressings, but to have an all-new 6-cylinder engine. For this Sloan turned to his friend Henry Crane, who had built the luxurious Crane-Simplex cars. Crane favoured the short-stroke principle, and had built several engines with square dimensions. The design he finally adopted had a bore/stroke ratio of 1:1.15 (82.55×95.25mm), compared with 1:1.6 for many contemporary American cars. The engine was generously lubricated, with a full-pressure feed system to all main and conrod bearings. Apart from the engine, the design was not especially advanced, with 2-wheel mechanical brakes and wooden wheels.

Sloan decided that the new car should be a companion make to the Oakland, which was selling slowly, and whose factory therefore had spare capacity. At first it was built alongside the Oakland, but in 1927 a new factory was completed in the same town, Pontiac, Michigan. It seemed logical to name the car after its home town, which had itself been named for a famous Indian chief. The radiator badge showed two faces of a coin, one side bearing a picture of the chief with the words 'Pontiac-chief of the sixes', and the other, 'Product of General Motors' surrounded by a laurel wreath.

Ben Anibal joined Oakland in March 1925, and was responsible for all the final work on the Pontiac, Crane being more of a consultant by this time. The Pontiac was announced on 25 January 1926, with only two body styles, both closed, a 2-door sedan and a coupé, and both priced at $825. It was an immediate success, selling 76,783 units in its first season. Additional models in the form of a 4-door landau sedan and a delivery van came in August 1926, and it was soon obvious that the Pontiac was a much better seller than its parent, the Oakland. This was hardly surprising as it was cheaper by more than $200, and had an engine of about the same size. The only positive advantage offered by Oakland was its 4-wheel brakes, and when Pontiac received these for 1928 the scales were weighted still further in favour of the new make. An open roadster and cabriolet joined the Pontiac range in 1927, and the marque now offered six body styles from $775 to $975. Sales rapidly outstripped those of Oakland, so that by the end of 1929 Pontiac ranked 5th out of America's 33 car makers, and Oakland 21st.

Oaklands and Pontiacs were restyled for 1929 with a vertical bar down the centre of the radiator, but the next important development was the 4113cc 85bhp V8 engine introduced on 1930 Oaklands. This engine weighed only 16.8kg per horsepower and gave the car a top speed well in excess of 70mph (113km/h). When the Oakland name was dropped in January 1932 the V8 was given Pontiac badging, being additional to the 6-cylinder range which was still being made. These now had 3277cc 65bhp engines, with prices from $635 to $795. The seven models in the V8 line ranged from $845 to $1025. Pontiac were again 5th in the sales league in 1932. This was the bottom of the Depression, and sales of 46,594 were quite creditable.

The V8 engine was expensive to manufacture, and Pontiac lost money on each unit they made. Also it did not run very smoothly with the 5½ or 6:1 compression ratios demanded by the public. For 1933 Anibal and his team came up with a brand-new 77bhp 3660cc straight-8. To keep production costs down it had cast-iron pistons and five instead of seven main bearings, but it was a fine engine whose short-stroke design (80.96×88.9mm) lent itself to higher

1928 Pontiac (iii) Six coupé.
NATIONAL MOTOR MUSEUM

1933 Pontiac (iii) Eight coupé.
NICK GEORGANO

1938 Pontiac (iii) Eight convertible.
NATIONAL MOTOR MUSEUM

1941 Pontiac (iii) Torpedo sedan.
NICK GEORGANO

1951 Pontiac (iii) De Luxe Eight coupé sedan.
NICK GEORGANO

compression ratios, and which was made with only small changes up to 1955. The bodies of the 1933 Pontiacs were also new, designed by Franklin Quick Hershey who came from the famous Pasadena coachbuilders Walter Murphy. Skirted wings were novelties on most American cars, though pioneered by Graham on their 1932 Blue Streak. The radiator grill was in vee form and slightly sloping. For 1933 and 1934, the straight-8 was the only engine used by Pontiac, but from 1935 onwards two series were made each year, the eight and a six of initially 3.4-litres and 80bhp, gradually enlarged over the years, like the eights. Sales jumped nearly 100 per cent in 1933, to 90,198. 1934 Pontiacs had coil spring ifs advertised as 'Knee Action', and 'Turret Top' all-steel bodies came in 1935.

The dual line of sixes and eights were continued up to the war, by which time they were of 3919 and 4078cc respectively. Waterfall grills were featured on 1935 and 1936 models, which were called Silver Streaks, a name which was continued for a number of years. All-synchromesh 3-speed gearboxes were featured from 1935, although the cheapest Standard Six had synchro on the two upper ratios only, and non-independent front suspension. Steering column gearchange was optional ($10 extra) on 1938 Pontiacs, and standard from

KNUDSEN, SEMON EMIL (1912–1998)

Semon Emil Knudsen's nickname 'Bunkie' stemmed from camping trips with his father. He had his glory days with Pontiac but in later years ruined his career and reputation by strategic errors.

Only son of 'Big Bill' Knudsen, he was born in Buffalo, New York, on 2 October 1912, and grew up in Detroit. He attended Dartmouth College in 1931–32 and graduated from the Massachusetts Institute of Technology with a BS engineering degree in 1936. He spent the next three years working in independent machine shops in the Detroit area, and joined Pontiac Motor Division in 1939 as an inspector. He inherited some of his father's talent for efficient production, and became involved in parts processing and laying out assembly lines. Around 1943 he served as assistant chief inspector of Pontiac's gun manufacturing operations, and was made master mechanic in 1947.

In 1949 he was transferred to the GM Process Development Section, ending up as its director, and in 1953 he went to Allison Division as

NATIONAL MOTOR MUSEUM

manufacturing manager for aircraft engines. Two years later he was picked as general manager of Detroit Diesel Engine Division.

Just a year later, Robert Critchfield retired, leaving an opening for a new general manager of Pontiac. 'Bunkie' moved to Pontiac in July 1956, simultaneously gaining a GM vice president's title. He turned Pontiac upside down, gave it a new image, and sent a Pontiac team into stock-car racing. At the age of 44, he was GM's youngest car-division boss, and by 1960, Pontiac had overtaken Buick, Oldsmobile and Plymouth in sales volume. He created the 'wide-track' Pontiac in 1958 and his lucky star gave him the top job at Chevrolet in November 1961. He quickly toned down the Chevrolet Technical Centre. He brought out the Chevelle, fixed the road-behaviour defects of the Corvair and gave it new styling, and kept the Impala at the top of the sales chart.

He saw himself in the fast lane for promotion to the GM presidency which his father held for over three years, but that is not the way it worked out. He imagined he was being allowed to round out his experience, with his appointment as vice president for the Canadian and Overseas subsidiaries in July 1965, when in fact he was being sidelined. He was still optimistic in February 1966, when the board of directors placed him in charge of the Dayton, household appliance, engine, overseas, and Canadian groups. But in October 1967, when James M. Roche was made chairman, his former office as GM President went to Edward N. Cole (1909–1977). Knudsen was so angry about being passed over that he resigned from GM on 1 February 1968, and signed on as president of the Ford Motor Co. a week later. He was never totally accepted by other Ford executives and his relationship with Henry Ford II faded fast. He was never able to accomplish anything at Ford, and at the end of 1969 he was ousted in a boardroom struggle that brought Lee A. Iacocca to the Ford presidency.

In an alliance with trusted ex-Pontiac and ex-Chevrolet men, he then founded Rectrans to produce motor homes, but it failed. In April 1971, he managed to sell his 60 per cent holding of Rectrans shares to White Motor Corp. for a new issue of 400,000 shares of common stock in White. That made him the biggest White shareholder, and he moved to Cleveland, Ohio, as chairman and chief executive of White Motor Corp. on 1 May 1971.

He talked a banking consortium into granting White a $290m credit line, which he spent on improving the truck and farm-tractor plants. He sold off Diamond Reo in July 1971, put the Canton, Ohio, engine plant into a joint venture with Massey-Ferguson, and sold Superior Coach and Euclid earth-moving vehicles. By 1975, however, truck sales had plunged and White ran up heavy losses again. Knudsen was never able to effect any durable recovery, and resigned in April 1980. The White truck assets were sold to AB Volvo in 1982.

Semon E. Knudsen died on 6 July 1998 of heart failure.

He married Florence Anne McConnell in 1938. They had three daughters and a son.

JPN

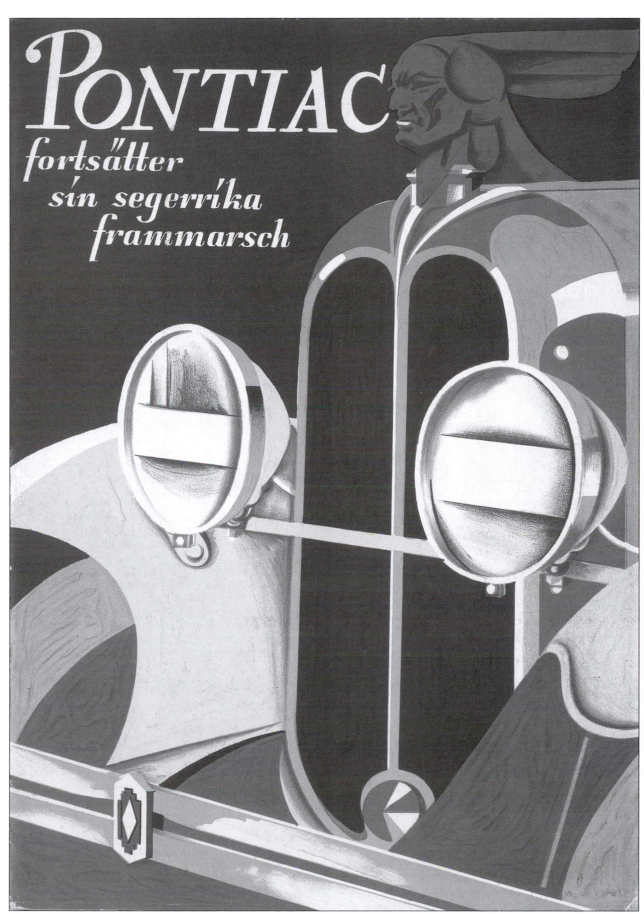

1961 Pontiac (iii) Tempest sedan.
NATIONAL MOTOR MUSEUM

1970 Pontiac (iii) GTO coupé.
NATIONAL MOTOR MUSEUM

1975 Pontiac (iii) Le Mans coupé.
NICK GEORGANO

1978 Pontiac (iii) Firebird Trans Am coupé.
NICK BALDWIN

1939, when styling was very close to that of Chevrolet. A 4-door convertible was a relatively rare and expensive body style offered in 1937 and 1938 only, but a more lasting new style was a 4-door station wagon, which was also new for 1937. It cost $992, being second only to the convertible sedan in price, and few were made.

A new model for 1940 was the Torpedo Eight, a 4-door 4-light sedan or 2-door coupé styled after the Cadillac 60 Special. The body pressings were those of the General Motors 'C-body', also used on the Oldsmobile 90 and the bigger Buicks, as well as Cadillac. This gave Pontiac an up-market line selling for $1016–1072 in addition to the cheaper Chevrolet-like sedans in the 6- and 8-cylinder lines, priced from $835 to $970. The Torpedo Eights accounted for 31,224 sales out of a total of 217,001 1940 model Pontiacs.

As with many American companies, the last year of peace saw record sales for Pontiac, with 330,061 cars delivered in the 1941 model year. The chief styling change for 1941 was the introduction of fastback 2-door coupés and 4-door sedans, known as Streamliner Torpedos and available in both 6- and 8-cylinder lines. Corporately these were known as the 'B-bodies', and were shared with Cadillac, Buick and Oldsmobile. The 'C-bodied' Custom Torpedo Eights were still made, as were convertibles and the lower-priced sedans which shared body pressings with Chevrolet and the cheaper Oldsmobiles. The C-bodies were dropped for 1942, when the rest of the range was generally similar to 1941 apart from a change of grill. Pontiac offered nine different body shells, with a total of 26 different models. Production ended on 10 February 1942, after 85,555 of the 1942 models had been made.

The Pontiacs of the immediate postwar years were little altered from the 1942 models, and apart from small changes in grill design, and the option of Hydramatic transmission for 1948, they remained the same until the 1949 season. They then received all-new full-width styling shared with Cadillac and Oldsmobile and the work of GM styling chief Harley Earl. A hard-top called the Catalina Coupé arrived for 1950, and 1953 Pontiacs sported small humps on the rear wings which somewhat resembled Cadillac's nascent fins. However, in general Pontiacs of the early 1950s had an old-fashioned middle-aged image, not helped by the continued use of the side-valve 6- and 8-cylinder engines which dated back to the early 1930s. Sales were dropping, and the immediate answer was a new V8 engine for 1955, backed up by new and lower styling.

Greater Power from V8 Engines

Pontiac was the last of the GM Divisions to adopt a V8 engine, and in its original form it was not very large or powerful, at 4706cc and 180bhp. All US-built Pontiacs had this engine, although the side-valve six was continued in some Canadian-built models. Others used a smaller Chevrolet V8 of 4342cc. The Pontiac V8 was initially available in two forms, 173bhp with a manual gearbox, and 180bhp with Hydramatic which absorbed more power. In March 1955 a 200bhp version with 4-barrel Carter carburettor was an option, for only $35 extra.

In 1956 Pontiac Division acquired a new general manager, Semon E. Knudsen, always known by the nickname Bunkie. At 43 he was the youngest general manager the Division had ever had, and over the next ten years he was to change completely Pontiac's staid image. Knudsen remained with Pontiac until 1961, when he became general manager of Chevrolet, being replaced by Pete Estes. At the same time the post of Pontiac chief engineer was taken by the controversial John de Lorean, who in turn became general manager from 1964 to 1969. Engine capacity went up to 5188cc in 1956, and the most powerful version delivered 227bhp. In mid-season an optional performance engine built for racing but available on all cars gave 285bhp. Over the next few years, capacity and output rose steadily, to 5686cc and 317bhp (maximum) in 1957, 6063cc and 330bhp (maximum) in 1958 and 6374cc and 345bhp in 1959. The maximum horsepower figures were obtained with optional performance packs costing up to $100 extra. Even the regular engines were pretty powerful, with 260–300bhp in 1959, according to whether manual or automatic transmission was used.

The 1959 Pontiacs were the first to be influenced by Bunkie Knudsen's thinking, and featured very wide bodies with two-piece grills which were also seen on Pontiac's entry in the compact car stakes. Named the Tempest, it had a 4-cylinder engine which was essentially half of a V8, with a capacity of 3187cc. In standard form, with a manual gearbox it gave 110bhp, but more powerful versions for use with Tempestorque automatic transmission gave 120, 130, 140 or 155bhp. Also available, although only 2 per cent of 1961 Tempest buyers chose it, was Buick's 3523cc 155bhp aluminium V8. The Tempest's transmission was unusual, with a flexible drive shaft to a transaxle gearbox. Suspension was independent all-round, by coils and wishbones at the front and swing axles at the rear. Made as a 4-door sedan, 2-door coupé and station wagon, the Tempest sold 100,783 units in its first year. For 1962 a convertible was added to the Tempest range, and the most powerful engine was the 185bhp Buick V8, though even fewer of these were sold than in 1961, just 1658 out of 143,193.

The Tempest helped Pontiac to total sales of 547,350 in 1962, to take 3rd place. They held this position for the next seven years. The Le Mans coupé and convertible versions of the Tempest had always had a sporting image, but from 1963 the Tempest acquired real power. The aluminium V8 was replaced by a 260bhp 5342cc cast-iron unit. By 1964 the V8 was a more popular power unit than the four, accounting for 58 per cent of Tempest sales. It was now a larger car, 5in (127mm) longer than the 1961 model, and called a 'senior compact'. The 326 engine (5342cc) gave 150 or 280bhp, and in October 1963 came the GTO version of the Tempest Le Mans. Named after the Ferrari GTO (Gran

Turismo Omologato), it had a 6374cc engine giving 325bhp. The GTO package cost $295 and included a 4-barrel carburettor, special shock absorbers, high-rate springs, low-profile tyres and bucket seats. If the customer wanted still more features, options included a Hurst-Campbell 4-speed gearbox, custom exhaust splitters and special wheel covers. The Tempest GTO was a real fireball, with 0–62mph (0–100km/h) in 7.7 seconds, and a top speed of 115mph (185km/h). For 1966 the GTO became a separate series with distinctive trim on the Tempest sheetmetal. The most powerful engine was the Tri-power 389 (6.4-litres) which now gave 360bhp. Although the Tempest name survived until the end of the 1970 season, it was used on less powerful cars, mainly with 6-cylinder engines.

Meanwhile, the full-sized Pontiacs also received the more powerful engines. From 1961 the 389 V8 was available with ten outputs from 215 to 363bhp. Late in 1961 a few cars were made with 6899cc 421 engines developing 373bhp. These were used in Pontiac's successful stock car racers of the period. Full-sized

NICK BALDWIN

SLOAN, ALFRED PRITCHARD, Jr (1875–1966)

Alfred Pritchard Sloan became known throughout the world as the supreme master of business management for his accomplishments as president of General Motors from 1923 to 1946.

Born in New Haven, Connecticut, on 23 May 1875, he was the son of a tea-and-coffee importer and distributor, and his wife, the daughter of a Methodist minister. The family moved to Brooklyn, New York, when he was a small boy, and that is where he grew up and received his elementary schooling.

He received his higher education at the Massachusetts Institute of Technology, graduating with a Bachelor of Science degree in electrical engineering in 1895, and joined Hyatt Roller Bearing Co. of Newark, New Jersey, as a draftsman.

Within four years, he was managing director of the company, and held a block of shares in it. Hyatt became a major supplier to the auto industry, and in 1916, W.C. Durant bought it and combined it with New Departure Manufacturing Co. of Bristol, Connecticut, Remy Electric Co. of Anderson, Indiana, Dayton Engineering Laboratories Co. of Dayton, Ohio, and the Perlman Rim Corp. of Jackson, Michigan, into a group registered as United Motors.

Sloan was named president and chief operating officer of United Motors, soon taking the initiative himself to take over Harrison Radiator Corp. and the Klaxon Co. In 1918 the assets of United Motors were acquired by General Motors, which remained under Sloan's management.

That made him a GM executive and gave him a lot of GM stock. He sat on the Executive Committee and the Finance Committee under Durant's rule. After W.C. Durant left in 1920, Sloan wrote an Organisational Study for GM, which was adopted as basic policy. Until then, all the companies owned by General Motors had been operating independently, without any co-ordination from above or at any level. Sloan imposed clear lines of command and areas of responsibility.

In 1921, when Pierre S. du Pont was president, Sloan acted as an executive vice president (without the title). When he became president, he formed the General Technical Committee, the General Purchasing Committee, and the General Sales Committee, cutting right across the lines of the organisation so as to make sure the entire operations staff was pulling in the same direction. The committees were vital to his style of management; 'I never give orders', he said. He ruled by consensus, and proved himself a master at getting men of opposing viewpoints to come to agreement.

He gave each of the GM car companies a well-defined price range in which to compete, with enough overlap to ensure in-house competition, Buick vs Cadillac, and Pontiac vs both Chevrolet and Oldsmobile.

Sloan created GM Art & Colour and took over Fisher Body, formed the GM Research Staff, and the GM Engineering Staff. He encouraged GM Investment in non-automotive industries (Electro-Motive), Allison, Bendix, North American Aviation, Eastern Air lines, Frigidaire). To expand GM's presence in Europe, he arranged the purchase of Vauxhall in 1925 and Opel in 1929. Responding to the economic depression in 1932, he turned the car companies into 'divisions' and the former presidents were given the title of general managers, with the bonus of upgrading to vice presidents of General Motors.

In 1934 he made over a good part of his personal fortune to the newly founded Alfred P. Sloan Foundation, which sponsored scientific education projects.

He left the presidency of GM in 1937 in favour of William S. Knudsen, only to resume the office in 1940 because Knudsen joined the government as head of the National Defense Advisory Committee. In World War II, the GM factories made trucks, armoured vehicles, aircraft engines and landing gear, and guns and ammunition.

In 1945 he was co-sponsor of the Sloan-Kettering Institute for cancer research at the M.I.T.

Sloan became chairman of the GM board in 1946 when leaving the presidency for the second time; finally retiring at the age of 81, though the directors insisted on having him around as honorary chairman. It is a mark of his dedication and discipline that he still kept an office in Manhattan's Rockefeller Centre, and a mark of his modesty and frugality that he went there carrying a homemade sandwich for his lunch.

He died from a heart attack on 17 February 1966.

JPN

1975 Pontiac (iii) Sunbird coupé.
NICK GEORGANO

1980 Pontiac (iii) Phoenix SJ sedan.
NICK BALDWIN

1981 Pontiac (iii) Grand Le Mans sedan.
NICK BALDWIN

1989 Pontiac (iii) 20th Anniversary Trans Am coupé.
PONTIAC

Pontiacs came in three series, Catalina, Ventura and Bonneville, in ascending order of trim and price, with the usual range of bodies in all series. From 1962 the Grand Prix replaced the Ventura. The 1967 Grand Prix had concealed headlamps, and the standard engine displaced 6555cc.

Firebird and GTO

In February 1967 Pontiac released their entry into the pony car market which had been started by the Ford Mustang. The Firebird came as a hard-top coupé or convertible on a 108in (2746mm) wheelbase, with the same engine options as in the Tempest and GTO ranges, from a 3769cc single-ohc six of 165bhp to a 6555cc V8 of 325bhp. Firebirds were made at the Chevrolet plant at Lordstown, Ohio, and were similar to Chevrolet's Camaro. The first season's production was 82,560, an encouraging figure since they were all made between February and September 1967. The first full season saw 107,112 Firebirds delivered, of which only 16,960 were convertibles.

The Firebird was not greatly changed in appearance until 1970, but an important new model which appeared in March 1969 was the Trans Am, a high-performance car named after the Trans Am stock car races. Standard equipment included the Ram Air 111 335bhp V8 engine, heavy duty 3-speed manual gearbox with floor change, heavy duty shock absorbers and springs, disc brakes on the front-wheels, white paint and full-length blue stripes from the bonnet over the roof to the boot. The Trans Am package cost $724 over the price of the base coupé or convertible. Only eight convertibles were ever sold as Trans Ams, and first year production of the coupé was 689.

The Firebird was restyled in 1970, the new models appearing at the end of February, so that they are familiarly known as 1970 1/2 models. They had Endura plastic nosepieces which added 3/4in (20mm) to the overall length, though the wheelbase remained unchanged at 108in (2746mm). There were now four series of Firebird, the base model, Firebird Espirit, Firebird 400 and Trans Am. The 400 had a 400 cubic inch (6555cc) 330bhp engine and 3-speed gearbox with Hurst floor shift while the Trans Am had the 400 engine in 330 or 345bhp forms and a 4-speed Hurst shift gearbox. 0–62mph (0–100km/h) took 5.5 seconds, while top speed was 135mph (217km/h). Only 88 Trans Ams were made with the more powerful engine in the 1970 1/2 series. Total production of the 1970 1/2 Trans Am was 3196, and they are generally regarded as the high point of the Firebird range. Later Firebirds and Camaros, though dramatic in appearance, were less powerful due to emission control regulations. 1973 engines used in the Trans Am were larger, at 7456cc but gave only 250 or 310bhp.

The 1973 Firebirds were the first to sport on their bonnet tops the bird with flames springing from its wings. Nicknamed 'The Chicken', this was the work of stylist John Schinella, and was available only on the Trans Am. In the later 1970s Trans Ams sold much better than before. In 1976 46,704 found buyers, making it the best-selling model of Firebird, instead of a limited-production specialist machine, but power and performance were sadly down. Even the big 7456cc engine gave only 200bhp. In 1978 a total of 187,285 Firebirds were made, of which 49.34 per cent were Trans Ams, 19.71 per cent Espirits, 17.45 per cent the base version, and 13 per cent Formulas, the replacement for the 400. 3- and 4-speed manual gearboxes were still available, also Hydramatic which was compulsory on cars sold in California. In 1979 Pontiac built 117,108 Trans Ams, making it the second most popular model of the make, after the base Grand Prix. A turbocharged Firebird was available in 1980, but even so the 4932cc engine gave only 205bhp. The Firebird has continued in production up to the present, receiving major restyling in 1982. The wheelbase was reduced to 101in (2565mm), and engines ranged from a 2.5-litre 92bhp four to a 5-litre 175bhp V8. It was restyled again for 1993, and in 1999 was available as a coupé or convertible, with 3791cc V6 or 5665cc V8 engines. With the latter 0–60mph (97km/h) took six seconds and top speed was 155mph (249km/h). Though generally tamed, the occasional high-performance Firebird was still made. At the 1988 Los Angeles Show there was a twin-turbocharged Trans Am billed as the world's fastest passenger car, with a top speed of 277mph (446km/h).

Pontiac's other high-performance car was the GTO, which was separated from the Tempest range in 1966. It was available as a hard-top or convertible, but the latter were comparatively rare. A high-performance model introduced in December 1968 bore the curious name, 'The Judge', from a line in a TV comedy programme, 'Here come da Judge'. It was the equivalent in the GTO range of the Firebird Trans Am, with a 365 or 370bhp Ram Air engine, front disc brakes and 4-speed floor change gearbox. In addition The Judge had a rear-mounted aerofoil. The full Judge package cost $332, and in 1969 they accounted for 6833

1999 Pontiac (iii) Trans Am convertible.
PONTIAC

sales, out of a total of 72,287 GTOs The Judge was continued to the end of the 1971 season, but the climate was becoming unfavourable for muscle cars, with emission controls and a move away from aggressive power.

In 1972 the GTO was no longer a separate series, but a model in the Le Mans range, and after 1973 the GTO name was shifted to the compact Ventura range. It did not last into 1975.

Pontiac in Competition
In order to counter Pontiac's staid image, Bunkie Knudsen entered teams in both NASCAR stock car racing and in the SCCA Trans-American Sedan championship. Between 1957 and 1963 Pontiac sedans captured a total of 69 NASCAR Grand Nationals, winning 30 stock car races in 1961 and 22 in 1962. Firebirds raced in both NASCAR and SCCA events, the veteran Buck Baker winning in NASCAR once in 1969 and twice in 1970. In 1969 the Firebird of Jerry Titus and Jon Ward finished 3rd overall and first in the GT class of the Daytona 24-hour Race.

Moves to Smaller Cars
The Tempest had begun life as a compact car in 1961, but ten years later it had grown in size and performance, leading to the Le Mans and GTO series. In order to re-enter the budget-priced compact field, Pontiac brought out the Ventura in mid–1970. Made by Chevrolet, this was no more than a Chevy II Nova with a Pontiac grill. The base engine was a 145bhp 4096cc six, though a 5030cc V8 was optional. The next season saw the Ventura SD, a bucket-seat sedan with floor change for the 3-speed manual gearbox. Probably 500 were made, exclusively in Chevrolet's Van Nuys, California, factory. A 3-door hatchback was a new Ventura model for 1973, and the name was continued until the end of the 1977 season, when it was replaced by the Phoenix. This was basically are-vamped Ventura on the same wheelbase but slightly longer overall. Initially made with a 3785cc V6 engine, the Phoenix could be had with a 2474cc four and 4932 or 5735cc V8 engines. It was made until 1980, when the name was given to Pontiac's version of the front-drive X-car.

In 1973 Pontiac's Canadian factory began production of a sub-compact car called the Astre. This was simply a Chevrolet Vega with Pontiac grill, and came in three body styles, hatchback coupé, station wagon and delivery van. It was powered by a 2294cc 4-cylinder engine, and for 1974, was available with a GT option package. Late in 1974 the Astre went into production at Chevrolet's Lordstown, Ohio, plant. The same three bodies were built, although the delivery

van was made only for export to Canada. In mid–1975 a notchback coupé was added to the Astre range.

The Astre was replaced in 1977 by the Sunbird, which had entered production the year before. This had a more sporty image than the Astre, though the base engine and wheelbase were the same. An Oldsmobile-built 3785cc V6 engine was an option. Only one body was initially made with the Sunbird name, a notchback coupé, but a hatchback was added for 1977 and a station wagon for 1978; this was in fact the old Astre station wagon renamed the Sunbird Safari. The notchback remained the most popular model, and in 1980 was the best selling car in the whole Pontiac range. Sunbirds were dropped at the end of 1981. Pontiac sales were higher than ever at this time, reaching 907,412 in the 1979 model year.

The largest engine used in full-sized Pontiacs was a 7456cc V8 which developed 370bhp when it was introduced in 1970. Increasingly strict emission controls reduced output to 310bhp in 1973 and only 200bhp in 1975. The cars were still large, though, the Gran Safari station wagon having a wheelbase of 127in (3226mm) and overall length of 231in (5875mm). The 1976 Bonnevilles, Catalinas and Safaris were completely restyled, and somewhat smaller, at 116in (2946mm) wheelbase and 215in (5456mm) the biggest overall length. By 1978 the largest engine used in any Pontiac was a 5735cc V8, but more popular were smaller V8s or the 3785cc V6. A 5735cc Oldsmobile-built V8 diesel engine was available from 1980. The Grand Am was dropped after 1980, and the Bonneville sedan after 1981, this name being used for a smaller car on a 108in (2743mm) wheelbase in 1982.

The last full-sized convertible was made in 1975, although custom body builders made open versions of the Phoenix and Firebird in the late 1970s, and in 1984 Pontiac once again offered a convertible, on the Sunbird.

Rationalisation
The 1980s saw growing rationalisation within the GM divisions, and, with one exception, Pontiacs became variants on the familar corporate models. The first to appear was the front-drive X-car, of which the Pontiac version was the Phoenix. This was made as a notchback 2-door coupé or hatchback 5-door sedan, and was powered by a 2474cc four, or 2835cc V6 engine. It was joined in 1981 by the smaller front-drive J-car, the J2000 and the even smaller rear-drive T1000 which was the same as the Chevrolet Chevette and Opel Kadett. The J-car, which shared components with the Buick Skyhawk, Cadillac Cimarron,

1934 Pope 900cc coupé.
NICK BALDWIN

1911 Pope-Hartford Model T 40hp tourer.
NATIONAL MOTOR MUSEUM

Chevrolet Cavalier and Oldsmobile Firenza, as well as the Opel Ascona and Vauxhall Cavalier, was made as a notchback coupé and sedan, hatchback coupé and station wagon. 1982 saw the larger A-car, Pontiac's version being called the 6000. This was a 2-door coupé or 4-door sedan, powered by the 2474cc four, 2835cc V6 or a 4293cc V6 diesel. Next up in size was the Grand Prix, part of the GM W-car range. By 1988 the only rear-drive Pontiacs were the Safari station wagon, cousin to the Chevrolet Caprice and Oldsmobile Cutlass Cruiser, and powered by a 4998cc V8 engine. A new low-priced model introduced in 1987 was the Le Mans, cousin to the Opel Kadett/Vauxhall Astra and made for Pontiac by the Daewoo Group in Korea. It survived until 1994. In mid–1988 a small number of 6000STE (A-cars) were made with 4-wheel drive, and a more powerful 135bhp V6 engine. The 6000 was dropped in 1992.

The Fiero

The one Pontiac which had no equivalent in other GM ranges was the Fiero, a mid-engined fibreglass sports coupé made from 1983 to 1988. Styled by John Schinella with some resemblance to the Fiat X1/9, the Fiero was powered by the 92bhp 2474cc 4-cylinder engine known as the Iron Duke, transversely mounted behind the driver. Transmission was a 4-speed all-synchromesh manual, or a 3-speed automatic. Top speed was 97mph (156km/h), or 115mph (185km/h) when the 2835cc V6 engine was added to the range in 1985. The Fiero sold well initially, because traditional British sports cars such as the Triumph TR7 and MGB were no longer available, and a Fiero Owners' Club was formed as early as 1984. Sales that year were 99,720, but by the 1987 model year they had dropped to 47,156. Bad publicity resulting from the 1987 recall of 136,000 cars was blamed, and also escalating insurance premiums for sports cars.

The rear-drive Safari Wagon was dropped in 1990, its place taken by the Trans Sport, a front-drive MPV which was Pontiac's version of the Chevrolet Lumina and Oldsmobile Silhouette. Other innovations of the 1990s were a completely restyled Grand Prix for 1992, in the same family as the Buick Regal and Oldsmobile Cutlass Six, with 2261cc 16-valve four or V6s of 3129 and 3392cc litres.

A new model for 1996 was the Sunfire, a 4-door sedan or 2-door coupé (convertible for 1997) in the BMW 3 Series-size bracket, powered by the old

120bhp 2180cc four or a new 155bhp 2392cc 16-valve four. The Grand Prix was revamped for 1997 with a new body and a choice of three V6 engines, a 3135cc and two 3791cc, one of them supercharged to give 243bhp. Its equivalents in other ranges were the Buick Century, Chevrolet Malibu and Oldsmobile Intrigue. The Grand Prix was continued for 1999, along with the Sunfire, Trans Am, Grand Am, Bonneville, Trans Sport and the evergreen Firebird. A new model for 2000 was the Aztec, a 4 × 4 Sport Recreational Vehicle powered by a 3.4-litre V6, with a 4-speed automatic transmission.

NG

Further Reading
75 Years of Pontiac Oakland, John Gunnell, Crestline, 1982.
The Fabulous Firebird, Michael Lamm, Lamm-Morada Press, 1979.
Pontiac, the postwar years Jan P. Norbye and Jim Dunne, Motorbooks International, 1979.
Pontiac, They Built Excitement, Thomas E. Bonsall, Stony Run Press, 1991.
'P stands for Possibilities: Pontiac's 1984 Fiero', Lowell Paddock, *Automobile Quarterly*, Vol. 21, No. 4.
'Firebird Trans Am: A Story of Detroit', Stan Grayson, *Automobile Quarterly*, Vol. 15, No. 3.
Firebird! America's premier performance car, Gary L. Witzenburg, Automobile Quarterly Publications.

PONTICELLI (F) 1985–1986
Ponticelli Frères SA, Gretz-Armainvilliers.
This major engineering company produced eight prototypes of the Vux 600, a basic open vehicle in the spirit of the Citroën Méhari, built in two wheelbase lengths. Indeed it was based on Citroën parts and had a BX 1.6-litre petrol or 1.9-litre diesel engine. Despite appearances at motor shows and the interest of several coachbuilders in creating bodywork for it, a production run never ensued.
CR

PONY RICHARD *see* BRASIER

POPE (F) 1933–1934
L.A. Pope, Paris.
This car was designed by an American resident in Paris. According to *The Motor*, L.A. Pope's Midland-Pope cars were well-known in the United States before the war. This is puzzling, because the only Pope connected with the Midland Motor Car Co. was C.H. Pope, and his link was an inglorious one, involving the disappearance of company books and papers, and even complete cars. Perhaps L.A. Pope was his son. His car was certainly unusual, having a 900cc ohv narrow-angle (28 degrees) V4 engine driving the front wheels via a 4-speed gearbox, ifs by a transverse spring, and a central backbone frame. The complete engine, gearbox and drive unit, including the wheels, could be easily detached. The body was a low-slung 2-seater coupé. Mr Pope was said to be looking for a British firm to take up manufacture, but no one did.
NG

POPE-HARTFORD (US) 1904–1914
Pope Manufacturing Co., Hartford, Connecticut.
The Pope-Hartford was the longest-lived of the five makes of car to bear the name of Col Albert Augustus Pope, and the only one made in the Pope Manufacturing Co.'s headquarter town of Hartford. A prototype single-cylinder car was built in the summer of 1903, and went into production the following year. It was of 10hp and offered in two body styles, the Model A 2-seater runabout and Model B 4-seater tonneau, both on a 78in (1980mm) wheelbase. The single was continued through the 1905 season, but other larger models appeared quickly. A 16hp twin came in 1905 and a 20/25hp four in 1906, while by 1908, when 393 cars were made, only 4-cylinder cars were listed, the 25hp Model R and 30hp Model M. A 7.7-litre 60hp 6-cylinder car on a 134in (3401mm) wheelbase was made from 1910 to 1913, in the price range $4000–5550. It was the most expensive of the Pope group of cars, apart from some models of the POPE-TOLEDO which was discontinued in 1909. A brief association with another make resulted in the Fiat-Portola, a chain-driven Fiat chassis with a Pope-Hartford engine. It was built in 1911, the name chosen to celebrate the 300th anniversary of the discovery of San Francisco in 1609 by Gaspar de Portola.

1908 Pope-Toledo Type XVII cape top landaulet.
JOHN A. CONDE

1912 was Pope-Hartford's best year, with 712 cars made, but they were in receivership the following year, probably brought about by offering too many models, 18 in a three-chassis range, which could not be justified by the volume of sales. The Pope-Hartford had a good reputation for quality, but was one of many similar expensive cars. The 60hp six was dropped for 1914, when the only offering was the 40hp four, and the receivers sold off the Hartford property before the end of the year. It was bought by aero-engine makers Pratt & Whitney.

NG

Further Reading
'Pope-Hartford, Too Good to Fail', Thomas F. Saal,
Automobile Quarterly, Vol. 36, No. 1.

POPE-ROBINSON *see* ROBINSON

POPE-TOLEDO (US) 1904–1909
Pope Motor Car Co. Toledo, Ohio.
The Pope-Toledo was the successor to the TOLEDO (i), made in steam and petrol forms by the International Bicycle Co., another of Colonel Pope's enterprises. Two models, both petrol-powered, were offered for the 1904 season, a 14hp twin and a 24hp four. The latter won several races on the West Coast in November 1903, earning itself the name 'The Mile a Minute Car'. A Pope-Toledo finished third in the 1904 Vanderbilt Cup, America's most important race at the time. The twin was dropped for 1905 and thereafter the Pope-Toledo

1906 Pope-Toledo Type XII 35/40hp tourer.
NICK BALDWIN

grew in size, price and prestige, reaching a peak with the 50hp limousine of 1907 which sold for $6000. Chain drive was retained up to 1908, which was the last full year of production. The last cars were made under receivership, and in January 1909 Richard D. Apperson, vice-president of the American National Bank of Lynchburg, Virginia, and no relation to the car-making Appersons of Kokomo, Indiana, said that he would take over manufacture and sell cars under the name Toledo. This never happened, and the factory was sold to OVERLAND for the production of a very different kind of car from the lordly Pope-Toledo.

NG

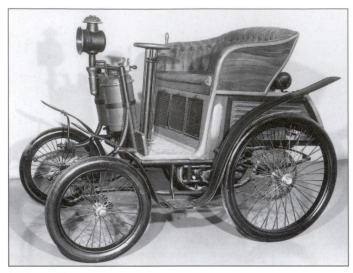

1898 Popp 7hp 2-seater.
NATIONAL MOTOR MUSEUM

POPE-TRIBUNE (US) 1904–1908

Pope Manufacturing Co., Hagerstown, Maryland.

This company made smaller and cheaper cars than the others in the Pope empire. It was headed by Harold E. Pope, son of the Colonel, and began as a runabout with a 6hp single-cylinder engine, selling for $650. It was designed by Gilbert J. LOOMIS who had made cars of his own at Westfield, Massachusetts. The price was reduced to $500 for 1905, when there was also a 12hp 2-cylinder model with 4-seater tonneau body. The size and price of Pope-Tribunes rose steadily after that, which meant that they lost whatever market they might have had with a simple $500 runabout. The 1908 models were a 16/20hp four at $1750 and a 30hp four at $2750. The factory had never made a profit, and was closed down in November 1908. Although assembled at Hagerstown, it is believed that some components for the Pope-Tribune came from the Pope-Hartford factory.

NG

POPE-WAVERLEY see WAVERLEY

POPP (CH) 1898

1898 Lorenz Popp, Basle.

The Swiss importer of Carl Benz vehicles asked Lorenz Popp in 1898 to build two cars which had similar engines and specifications; one was a phaeton, the other a heavier 4-seater victoria. It therefore is not surprising that the Popp phaeton looked quite similar to the Benz Velo. Both bodies were carefully coach-built by Otto Heimburger of Basle. The rear-mounted horizontal twin-cylinder engine had a capacity of 1590cc and delivered 7bhp. It possessed automatic inlet valves but a chain-driven ohc and rockers for the exhaust valves. Ignition was by hot-tube and belt transmission with chain final drive was chosen. In 1900 Lorenz Popp drove one of his cars to the World Fair in Paris and later to Leipzig where he was runner-up in his category in the race to Dresden. There does not seem to have been a regular production but the Popp phaeton is one of the cherished early automobiles of the Swiss Transport Museum in Lucerne. Lorenz Popp became the Swiss importer of the STOEWER and FIAT automobiles by about 1910.

FH

POPPY (US) 1917

Eisenhuth Motor Car Co., Los Angeles, California.

John W. Eisenhuth (1861–1918) was something of a minor league Edward Joel Pennington. He had got into several scrapes while making the COMPOUND in Connecticut, and found it advisable to change the name of his company from Eisenhuth to Eagle as his own name was something of a liability. In 1913, in San Francisco, he promoted a 'noiseless engine' that was anything but, and was arrested again. but four years later he was promoting another car to be called the Poppy. It had a 5-cylinder engine, said to be self-starting, 'conventional

transmission done away with, and a secret reverse system', to sell for the very modest price of $650. It is unlikely that it was ever built, and the secrets of its design died with Eisenhuth in May 1918.

NG

POPULAR MECHANICS (US) 1957

Popular Mechanics, Chicago, Illinois.

This home handyman magazine ran a series of articles on how to build an incredibly ugly plywood-bodied roadster on a variety of chassis. The prototype was built on a Crosley sedan and set new standards for crude construction and uninspired styling, with huge rear fins and a complete lack of compound curves.

HP

PORSCHE (D) 1948 to date

1948–1950 Porsche Konstruktions-GmbH, Gmünd (Austria).
1950 to date Dr Ing h.c. Porsche KG, Stuttgart-Zuffenhausen.

In 1945, surviving members of the Porsche design studio were operating from a timber mill in Gmünd, Austria, unable to return to their headquarters in Stuttgart. They made and repaired agricultural implements, and renovated cars. Prof. Ferdinand Porsche and some of his key personnel were invited by the French to advise on the Renault 4CV, and were then imprisoned on trumped-up war crime charges. His colleagues were released, but Porsche himself spent two years in prison, which broke his health. Eventually he was ransomed and the studio paid for his release with money earned designing an advanced GP car for Cisitalia.

In the meantime, Porsche's son, also Dr Ferdinand Porsche, but known as 'Ferry', built a Volkswagen special (his father had designed the VW) which was sold to a Swiss who arranged for a magazine to road test it. As a result of an enthusiastic review, a further batch was made. The first production car was the 356, Job 356 in the studio's portfolio. It was light and aerodynamic, and early cars had the Beetle's air-cooled 1131cc flat-four tuned to give 40bhp. Although top speed was a mere 84mph (135km/h), and brakes were cable operated until 1951, it had outstanding road holding for its day. It was rear-engined (the gearbox was in front of the rear axle line, the engine behind them) with a steel platform chassis and torsion bar springing: trailing links at the front, swing axles at the rear.

In 1950 the Porsche studio was able to return to Germany and, at first, cars were made in a part of Reutter's, the company which made bodies for Porsche.

Despite this unpromising start, the company grew and prospered, aided by an enviable record in sports car racing. Porsche also benefited from a royalty on every VW Beetle made and by licensing the Porsche synchromesh system which the studio had developed for the Cisitalia GP car. In 1950 Porsche established another company, Allgaier, which made a range of farm tractors powered by diesel engines with between one and four cylinders.

The 356's engine was soon reduced to 1086cc, so it could qualify for the 1100cc class and, in 1951, Porsche won the class on its first appearance at Le Mans. Also in 1951, a cabriolet version was offered and the following year the original split windscreen was replaced by a one-piece screen.

Ferdinand Porsche died following a stroke in 1952.

The engine grew to 1287cc, 1290cc (in 1954), and eventually two 1488cc versions were offered: the 55bhp 1500 and the 70bhp 1500 Super. A batch of twenty lightweight roadsters went to America and established Porsche's name in competition and these led to the 1954 Speedster with its low windscreen and stripped cockpit.

In 1953, Porsche made the 550 Spyder, a mid-engined sports racer, originally with a push-rod engine. In 1954 it received new double-ohc air-cooled flat-4 and the following year was sold to privateers. De-tuned versions of the engine would be used in the 1955 1500 GS Carrera.

The 365A of 1955 had softer suspension, a steering damper and smaller wheels. The 1290cc models (1300, 44bhp, dropped in 1957; 1300 Super, 60bhp) tended to stay in Germany. Elsewhere took the 1600 (60bhp), 1600 Super (75bhp) and the Speedster.

By 1959, 30,000 Porsches had been made and the 365B and Carrera 2 would more than double that figure by 1963. The new range had sharper styling with raised headlights, revised bonnet, larger rear window, and new bumpers and wheel trims. It was sold only with 1.6-litre engines and all models had drum brakes, VW steering gear, and a 4-speed gearbox.

1949 Porsche 356 coupé.
NATIONAL MOTOR MUSEUM

Porsche had gained an enviable reputation in sports car racing, dominating the 1500cc class and sometimes taking outright wins against cars with much larger engines. In 1959 came a single-seat version of its RSK sports racer which was successful in the 1.5-litre Formula Two. It qualified for F1 in 1961, and struggled while a bespoke F1 car, with a flat-8 engine, was disappointing. It gained two fortunate wins (one a non-championship race) and Porsche withdrew.

Porsche Research would design the TAG engine with which McLaren won three World Championships in the mid–1980s, but while Porsche supplied a sound basis, the real credit should go to Bosch, who developed the engine management system, and KKK which supplied the turbochargers. So poor was the V12 engine that Porsche supplied to Arrows in 1991 that it was dropped by mid-season. An engine developed for Indycar showed promise in 1989, but Porsche withdrew with just one win.

The 356C of 1963 was improved by a ZF steering system and a compensating transverse spring calmed the swing axle rear suspension. It was standard on the Super and Carrera, optional on the 1600. Disc brakes were available for the first time, and every model had them on all four wheels. Also in 1963, came the 904 GTS, a road/race car which was sold in two versions. A mid-engined 2-litre coupé, the 904 won the 1964 Targa Florio and was also second in the 1965 Monte Carlo Rally, run in heavy snow.

Porsche's most important new model was the 911 of 1964, which remained in production for more than 30 years, constantly modified and uprated. The 911 had a broadly similar layout to the 356, and springing was by torsion bars. MacPherson struts were fitted to the front and the rear had a trailing arm system. It has a steel platform chassis and though 911 was 2.4 in (61mm) narrower then the 356, interior space was improved. It had a new 130bhp, 1991cc, flat-6 air-cooled engine and drove through the 5-speed transmission first seen on the 904. Since the 911 was more expensive than the 356C, they were first produced in tandem. Variants of both the pushrod and 911 engines would be used to power light aircraft and even an airship.

A 'Targa-top' model was an option. Porsche claims to have invented the Targa top, but it was originated by Triumph (as the 'Surrey' top) on the TR4. While the 911 moved Porsche up-market, the 912 was a cheaper alternative.

1959 Porsche 356B coupé.
NICK BALDWIN

It was a 911 with a push-rod 90bhp 1582cc flat-4 which drove through the old 4-speed 'box, although the 5-speed transmission was an option. It was dropped in 1969, but was revived in 1976 for America as the fuel injected 912E.

There was also the 911T with a de-tuned 110bhp carburetted double-ohc engine, made from 1967 to 1973.

Ventilated brake discs were fitted from late 1968 and a 2.2-litre engine arrived the same year.

The 911E, made from 1968 to 1973, was the touring spec car, with fuel injection and 155bhp. Front suspension was by Boge self-levelling hydropneumatic struts, but these were dropped on all models in late 1969. A 5-speed transmission was standard, but Sportomatic was an option.

From 1969, Targa-topped models had a fixed wrap-round glass rear window, this replaced the former 'zip-out' plastic section, which often leaked and amplified engine noise. Power increased to 165bhp with the 2.4-litre engine of 1971 to 1973.

1963 Porsche 901 coupé.
NICK BALDWIN

1973 Porsche Carrera RS coupé.
NICK BALDWIN

The 917 appeared in 1969, a 4.5-litre flat-12 sports racer which allowed Porsche to compete for outright victory in endurance races. After a troubled beginning, the chassis flexed, it proved an outstanding car taking numerous wins, including two at Le Mans. Turbocharged versions, delivering a reputed 1300bhp, were successful in Can-Am racing.

Also in 1969 Porsche collaborated with VW to market the VW-Porsche 914, an angular mid-engined sports car available with either a VW engine or the 110bhp unit from the Porsche 911T. It was not a great success.

In 1971 the company was restructured to give a broader management base than the Porsche and Piëch families who held most of the stock. The restructuring would lead to the establishment of Porsche Design which made clothing and life-style accessories. Another division, Porsche Research, would undertake design and development for the motor industry, while other projects included fork-lift trucks and the cockpit of the Airbus.

The 911 continued to undergo steady development and, by 1971 had a 190bhp 2.4-litre engine and a 5-speed gearbox was standard. Major revisions appeared in 1972: wider wheels, and wheel arches, more controllable handling, and, from 1973, new bumpers. There was also the Carrera RS 2.7 and RSR 2.8, both were competition versions of the 911 made in limited numbers. 3-litre engines were introduced in 1973.

In 1974, Porsche added the 3-litre 911 Turbo to its range. Turbocharging had been around for some time, but the automotive world had been slow to exploit it save in competition. Although its 260bhp was not exceptional, torque was phenomenal and Porsche decided that a special 4-speed 'box was preferable to the usual 5-speed transmission. 0–62mph (0–100km/h) in 5.2 seconds was even more impressive than the top speed of 155mph (249km/h). It formed the basis for some competition models, notably the 935, which delivered up to 850bhp.

The single-ohc flat-6, which began as a 1991cc unit, reached 3.3-litres with the 911 Turbo of 1977. The increase in size was to maintain performance in US-spec cars which faced increasingly severe emission laws.

In European trim, however, this meant 300bhp and 161+mph (259+km/h) top speed. Brakes came from the 917 sports-racer, a Targa version was offered in 1987, and a 5-speed gearbox appeared in 1989.

Front Engines

In the early 1970s, Volkswagen commissioned Porsche to design a front-engined sports car. Late in its development, it was decided to market it as a Porsche and the 924 was hailed as the first front-engined, water-cooled, car from the marque, even though it was built by Audi. A 2-litre single-ohc fuel injected Audi van engine gave 125bhp and was fitted in a 2+2 coupé with VW MacPherson strut front suspension and rear trailing arms sprung by transverse torsion bars.

The 924 was good for 124mph (200km/h) (0–62mph (0–100km/h) in 9.5 seconds.) Early cars usually had a four-speed transaxle (five speeds from 1978) but some had a 3-speed automatic. It gave a welcome boost to Porsche's sales which had fallen following the OPEC Oil Crisis.

NATIONAL MOTOR MUSEUM

PORSCHE, FERDINAND ANTON ERNST 'FERRY' (1909–1998)

The son of 'Professor' Ferdinand Porsche, 'Ferry' was born on 19 September 1909, in Wiener-Neustadt, and showed a gift for mathematics even in elementary school. The family moved to Stuttgart in 1923, and he attended the Gottlieb Daimler Gymnasium in Bad Cannstatt. He was accepted as an engineering student at the Vienna Technical University, practically at the same time as his father moved to Steyr, late in 1928. After graduation, he worked briefly for Robert Bosch AG in Stuttgart before joining his father's engineering consultant office. He assisted in the design of many projects, from the P-Wagen V16 engine to the economy car prototypes (Zündapp, NSU, KDF). In 1937 he accompanied his father on a tour of America's industry, visiting Fisher Body Division of GM, the Budd Co., and Cincinnati Milling Machine Co. He also met Edsel Ford and was shown the Ford research centre. It was long after his return to Stuttgart that he began making sketches for a future Porsche sports car. Those plans were shelved when he became involved with the military versions of the Volkswagen. He was living on his farm near Zell am See, Austria, when the US army arrived, and he was put under arrest on 30 July 1945, but released in the first week of November. The French occupation authorities then held him under house arrest at Bad Rippoldsau for a period during 1946.

In 1947 he began working on a 4-wheel drive racing car, based on a prewar Auto Union project, for Piero Dusio, which became the Cisitalia.

The front-engined, 4-seat, 928 of 1977 was intended to replace the 911. It offered build quality and reliability practicality, which none of its rivals could match, and is the only sports car to be voted Car Of The Year. The 928 had a fuel injected single-ohc V8 engine of 4.5-litres which delivered its 240bhp through either a 5-speed manual transaxle or a 3-speed automatic. Coil springs all round were allied to double wishbones at the front, trailing arms at the rear. For those for whom 141mph (227km/h) and 0–62mph (0–100km/h) in 7.5 seconds were not enough, there was the 300bhp 4.7-litre 'S' version of 1979.

The Series 2 model of 1984 had a 4-speed automatic gearbox, derived from Mercedes-Benz, as standard (a 5-speed manual 'box was a no-cost option). Anti-lock brakes were standard, power increased to 310bhp which meant 149mph (240km/h) (0–62mph (0–100km/h) in 6.5 seconds).

1983 Porsche 944 Lux coupé.
PORSCHE CARS GREAT BRITAIN

1989 Porsche 928 S4 coupé.
PORSCHE CARS GREAT BRITAIN

Concurrently, he revived the Porsche sports car plan, revised in the face of economic and political realities, and drew up the Type 356, with a VW engine turned back to front, with the gearbox behind it, VW swing-axle rear suspension, and VW front suspension and steering, while the frame was a new tubular-steel structure. For the production model, however, the engine was moved into the rear overhang.

Fifty cars were completed in the former sawmill at Gmünd in 1948-49. In the spring of 1949 he went to Wolfsburg for a meeting with Dr Nordhoff, securing a steady supply of VW engines and other components, and signing a contract as consulting engineers to Volkswagen, netting Porsche a royalty on every Volkswagen car produced.

In 1950 he arranged the return to Stuttgart and secured new premises at Zuffenhausen. In 1952 he made another visit to America, returning with a contract to design a car for Studebaker, but it was never put in production. He decided that Porsche should make its own engines, since the cars needed more power than could be taken out of a VW flat-four, and built an engine plant at Zuffenhausen.

He led the Porsche company not only in its pursuit of technical progress, but also in terms of policy-making on all fronts. He was awarded the Bundesverdienstkreuz (federal cross of merit) in 1959, and in 1965 he was given the honorary title of Doctor of Engineering by the Vienna technical university. The 100,000th Porsche car was built in 1966.

With advancing age, he wanted to distance himself from the day-to-day running of the company, and took the title of Chairman on 1 April 1971. His grasp of engineering trends showed signs of frailty, for when Volkswagen began producing the Scirocco and the Golf in 1974, he went on record as saying that front-wheel drive was just a 'passing fad'. In any case, Porsche was no longer under contract to VW, all its proposals for a successor to the Beetle having been rejected. He also gave only reluctant approval to Porsche projects for cars with water-cooled front-mounted engines (924, 928, and 944) but backed the evolution of the 911 to the hilt.

It was in January 1993, that he announced his retirement and named Helmut Sihler, a former board member of Adam Opel AG and chairman of Heinkel since 1981, to take over as chairman of Porsche.

He died at Zell am See on 17 March 1998.

He married Dorothea Reitz on 10 January 1935, and they had four sons. Ferdinand Alexander–'Butzi'–was born on 11 December 1935, and worked in several departments of the Porsche factory. As chief of the styling studio, he created the 911 body. He left the car company to start his own business as an industrial designer, styling watches and other non-automotive products. Gerhard Anton–'Gerd'–was born on 5 June 1938. He never took an interest in cars and became a farmer.

Hans-Peter was born on 29 October 1940. He joined the Porsche car company in August 1963, and was trained in all aspects of its activity, becoming head of the production department in December 1965. He resigned, however, in April 1971.

Wolfgang Heinz–'Wolfi'–was born on 10 May 1945. He never worked in the Porsche organisation but went into business for himself, running a company jointly owned with his older brother, 'Butzi', importing Yamaha motorcycles and machinery to Austria.

For Ferdinand Porsche's biography, see VOLKSWAGEN
JPN

The Series 3 was a USA-only car with a double-ohc '4-valve' 5-litre engine. Europe received this unit in the Series 4 of 1986. Power increased to 320bhp and, with the manual gearbox, Porsche claimed a top speed of 167mph (269km/h).

In 1989 a GT version was offered with 326bhp, stiffer suspension, wider wheels, a broader rear track and a claimed top speed of 170mph (274km/h). Not long after it was launched, the 924 was challenged by the new breed of hot hatchbacks led by the Volkswagen Golf GTI which were close in performance and cheaper yet, with enormous chic. A turbo version (1978 to 1983) with 170bhp, and improved torque, tried to redress matters – 141mph (227km/h) and 0–62mph (0–100km/h) in 6.9 seconds were impressive figures for the time. Rear disc brakes replaced the 924's drums, but the bland styling told against it. It ceased production in 1985.

There was also a Carrera GT version in 1980, a turbocharged car homologated for racing and rallying which could be tweaked to deliver up to 400bhp.

Introduced in 1982, the front-engined 944 had more presence that the 924, thanks to a new nose treatment and wide wheel arches. It had a new in-line water-cooled four designed by Porsche, which was basically one bank of the 928's V8 although few parts were interchangeable. This 160bhp single-ohc 2.5-litre unit had twin counterweighted balance shafts to overcome the vibration inherent in large capacity 'fours'. In 1985 it was joined by the 944 Turbo which first gave it 217bhp but, by 1988, power had increased to 247bhp which gave a top speed of 152mph (245km/h) (0– 62mph (0–100km/h) in 5.7 seconds). In Britain it was marketed as the 944 Turbo SE, but designations varied from country to country, as did local specification. A cabriolet version was offered as a limited edition in 1991.

Sports car racing entered a new era in 1982 with the introduction of Group C, which attracted both specialist builders and major manufacturers. Porsche steamrollered the opposition for several years. 1986 saw the 924S which had a 160bhp engine from the 944 and the following year came the 944S with wider wheels, a double-ohc '4-valve' head, and 188bhp. A Cabriolet was offered from mid–1988 and the same year saw the base 944 receive a 2.7-litre 162bhp engine, while the 'S' was replaced by the 'S2' which had a 3-litre engine and 208bhp.

1994 Porsche 911 Carrera cabriolet.
NICK BALDWIN

2000 Porsche Boxster S roadster.
PORSCHE CARS GREAT BRITAIN

The Evergreen 911

With its burgeoning model range, and the need to build a 'world car' to meet different governments' requirements, in 1978 Porsche reduced the 911 series to the Turbo and the SC. Only a vigorous debate in the boardroom prevented the 911 from being phased out.

The normally aspirated 3-litre engine was good for 140mph (225km/h) (0–62mph (0–100km/h) in 6.5 seconds in European spec). Servo-assisted brakes were standard from 1979 and the list of luxury options grew. 1982 saw the first genuine cabriolet since the 356 series. In 1984, the single-ohc flat-6 engine was enlarged to 3.2-litres, and the SC became known as the Carrera.

1985 saw the SE (Sports Equipment) model which might be described as 'a Turbo without the turbocharger'. With 231bhp it was good for 143mph (230km/h) (0–62mph (0–100km/h) in 6.1 seconds), but was considerably more expensive than the Carrera and was not a success.

The Porsche 959 was designed for Group B, but that category had been dropped by the time it went on sale in 1987. The engine was a 2.9-litre flat-6, with water-cooled double-ohc '4-valve' heads and twin turbochargers. It delivered its 405bhp through a 6-speed transaxle allied to a permanent 4-wheel drive system with sensors to vary the torque split.

Performance was extraordinary: 189+mph (304+km/h) and 0–62mph (0–100km/h) in 3.7 seconds. To cope with that there were anti-lock brakes, competition style suspension (coil springs and double wishbones all round) with computer-adjusted ride height and, even, electronic monitoring for tyre pressures. The 'comfort' model had rear seats, additional sound insulation and air conditioning. Just 200 examples were made and while it was obsolete on arrival in competition terms, it served as a showcase for Porsche's technical expertise.

In 1988 came the 911 Carrera and although the style was identical to the 911, most of the body panels were new. The specification of the platform was similar to the earlier 911 but, again, it was all new and it finally tamed the rear-engine layout of the line. That same year, the 924 ceased production having played an important part in Porsche's growth.

In 1989, a heavily revised 911 was launched in the guise of the Carrera 4 which had permanent 4-wheel drive (31/69 split) and a 3.6-litre version of the flat-6 engine. Power increased to 247bhp which meant a top speed of 155mph (249km/h) (0–62mph (0–100km/h) in 5.2 seconds). A 2-wheel drive version, the Carrera 2 arrived in late 1989 and was fractionally quicker than the 4-wheel drive car.

In 1990, a version of the Turbo appeared on the Carrera 2 platform and shared most of its revised body panels, but was available only in fixed head form. It had even more power (320bhp) despite the fitting of a 3-way catalytic convertor, which meant 168mph (270km/h) (0–62mph (0–100km/h) in 5.0 seconds).

Both 2- and 4-wheel drive ranges offered fixed head, cabriolet, and Targa-top versions. Available as an option on the Carrera 2 was the ZF Tiptronic gearbox (automatic transmission with additional manual shift).

From 1990, world economic recession, allied to the collapse of the classic car market, were serious blows to Porsche's business. In 1991 came the last expression of the 928 which was given a 330bhp 5.4-litre engine and a new name, the 928 GTS. In the summer of that year, the 944 was replaced by the 968 which was a 944 with a revised body. The 968 failed to live up to expectations, and Porsche was in serious trouble. It delayed its programme of new models but, in late 1992, it launched a 360bhp 3.6-litre version of the 911 Turbo with a top speed of 174mph (280km/h).

A third generation of 911s was shown in 1993. The bodywork was revised, while retaining the flavour of the original, the floorpan was new and it had new multi-link, coil spring and double wishbone rear suspension. The engine was uprated to 270bhp and drove through either a 6-speed manual or 4-speed Tiptronic automatic gearbox. Also in 1993, Porsche offered the troubled 968 as a Turbo and also as a 'Club Sport' model with a skimpy interior and race-tuned suspension. It did no better than softer versions of the model.

Porsche added a 4-wheel drive 911 to its range in 1994 and tried to keep the 968 alive with a Sport model which was a standard car with the Club Sport's suspension and 17in wheels. The 928 ended its production life in 1995, as did the 968, and, the same year, a new 911 Turbo was released with 408bhp, a 6-speed gearbox, permanent 4-wheel drive and a top speed of 180mph (290km/h). Then came the 911 GT2, a limited-edition Turbo with 430bhp and rear-wheel drive. The 911 RS had a 300bhp 3.75-litre engine while a new Targa-top model had a roll-back glass roof.

Porsche made a major leap in 1995 when it introduced the Boxster, a practical 2-seat, mid-engined, sports car with a 204bhp 2.5-litre flat-6 engine. While redolent of the 550 Spyder, it was much cheaper than the 911 range and, unlike the 968, was perceived to be a 'real' Porsche. With a top speed of 149mph (240km/h) (0–62mph (0–100km/h) in 6.9 seconds) it was criticised for being under-powered, which was a back-handed compliment to the competence of its chassis.

In 1997 Porsche introduced an entirely new 911. It retained a family likeness to its predecessor which, in 4-wheel drive and Turbo forms, remained in production, but the 300bhp 3.4-litre flat-6 engine was water-cooled. More refined and supple than previous 911s, top speed was 161mph (259km/h) (0–62mph (0–100km/h) in 5.4 seconds. In 1998 it was joined by the even faster Cabrio (174mph (280km/h), 0–62mph (0–100km/h) in 5.2 seconds) and a 420bhp twin-turbocharged cabriolet was planned for a 2001 launch.

A competition version, the 360bhp, lightened GT3, was offered as a road car in early 1999. Very rich customers could also buy a road version of the Le Mans winning, mid-engined GT1, created by the factory using 911 components. In 1999 Porsche announced a new departure in the form of a Range Rover rivalling 4 × 4 powered by V6 or V8 engines. It was expected to be launched in 2001 under the name Cayenne.

In 1998 the company celebrated its 50th anniversary but, by a cruel irony, Ferry Porsche died in March 1998, aged 88. From a VW special, he had created an innovative and successful company whose products achieved the rare trick of being both objects of desire and examples of engineering integrity.

By the end of 1998, Porsche had won more than 23,000 races including 16 wins at Le Mans, four wins in the Monte Carlo Rally and nine World Championships for sports cars. Leaving aside single-seater formulae, Porsche can claim to be the most successful company ever to participate in international motor sport.

MJL

2000 Porsche 911 Turbo coupé.

Further Reading
Porsche, Excellence was Expected, Karl Ludvigsen,
Automobile Quarterly Publications, 1977.
The Porsche Book, Lothar Boschen and Jürgen Barth, Patrick Stephens, 1983.
Porsche, Double World Champions, Richard von Frankenberg
and Michael Cotton, Haynes, 1977.
Porsche 356, Dirk-Michael Conradt, Beeman-Jorgesen, 1989.
Porsche 911, Tobias Aichele, Beeman-Jorgesen, 1995.
Porsche 911 Turbo, Michael Cotton, Osprey, 1982.
Porsche 924 and 944, a Collector's Guide, Michael Cotton,
Motor Racing Publications, 1990.
Porsche 924, 928, 944 and 989, David Vivian, Crowood AutoClassics, 1993.
Ferry Porsche – Cars are my Life, Ferry Porsche and Günther Molter,
Patrick Stephens, 1989.

PORTER (i) **(US)** 1900–1901
Porter Motor Co., Allston, Massachusetts.
Designed by Major D. Porter, this was a light steam car made just outside
Boston. It had a 2-cylinder single-acting engine which could run on petrol or
paraffin. The body was unusual in being made entirely of aluminium, and being
more curvaceous than most, with compartments for fuel and water integral
within the body. Steering was by tiller which, when the driver's hand was
removed, cut off the power. Despite these attractions the Porter failed to last for
more than two seasons.

NG

PORTER (ii) **(US)** 1919–1922
American & British Manufacturing Co., Bridgeport, Connecticut.
The Porter was Finley Robertson Porter's third and final period of prominence
in the automotive world and it would be short-lived. Porter had been the
designer and engineer of the T-head Mercer, resigning that post in 1914 when
Mercer opted to market an L-head design, and forming the Finley-Robertson-
Porter Company at Port Jefferson, Long Island, New York for the production
of a high-powered luxury car carrying his initials. The F. R. P. car, with a 170hp
engine and a chassis priced at $5000 carried a pointed radiator and custom-built

1920 Porter (ii) tourer.

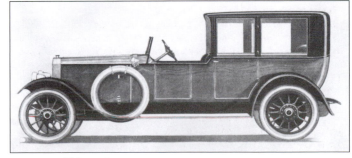

1920 Porter (ii) limousine.

bodies by well-known coachbuilders. As a sideline, Porter built two sleeve-valve-
engined racing cars under the Porter-Knight badge. The hand-built F. R. P.
automobile production ended in 1916 when the factory was taken over by the US
government shortly before World War I, total production of the cars estimated

1907 Porthos 24/30hp tourer.
NATIONAL MOTOR MUSEUM

at 10 to 19. Following the Armistice, a decision was made to continue automobile manufacture of cars which would carry the name Porter, and at a new location, the American & British Manufacturing Co. at Bridgeport, Connecticut, noted for the manufacture of early fire apparatus. Production of the Porter began in 1919 with a line of powerful, highly expensive cars, powered by a 5817cc 4-cylinder ohv engine of Porter's own design, developing 140bhp at 2600rpm. With a wheelbase of 142in (3604mm), the chassis price was $6750 which, with both open and closed body styles, increased the cost to upwards of $10,000. Custom coachwork was provided by Brewster, Demarest, Fleetwood, Jephson, and Porter's in-house Blue Ribbon company. The Porter radiator was similar to the Rolls-Royce and the cars featured rhd, by 1919 an anachronism in the US traffic pattern. A total of 35 Porters were completed, of which four were exported to Japan and one to Argentina (both of them with traffic patterns favourable to Porter's right-hand control). Most of the cars had been completed by early 1921. The recession of 1920–1921, combined with the archaic steering position and exceedingly high price of the cars, spelled the end for the Porter and as of 19 July 1921, 20 cars remained unsold. Porter, as a living entity, was last listed in the automobile trade journals in April 1922, and the Porter concern formally ended its existence shortly thereafter. A month later, Robert Porter, who had served as manager of the operation, went to New York City to help market the remaining cars, buyers for which had to be found. Finally, a United States auctioneer took over and sold the rest. To quote one who was present at that auction, 'These cars brought, as I recall, brand new, just under $4000, and with the possibility of no parts, I did not think it was a good buy' and concluded, 'But they were well thought of cars'.

KM

PORTHOS (F) 1906–1914
Sté Générale des Automobiles Porthos, Billancourt, Seine.
For most of its life the Porthos (presumably named after one of Dumas' Three Musketeers) was a large car, beginning with a 4560cc 24/30hp 4-cylinder T-head engine which was joined in 1907 by two large sixes, the 6838cc 50hp and 8138cc 60hp. They built a 10,857cc straight-8 for the 1907 French Grand Prix, but it retired on the fourth lap. The original company was wound up in 1909, and no cars were built until a new company was formed in 1912. They offered two fours, a 3183cc 16/20 and a 4560cc 24/30, and two sixes, a 4775cc 20/25 and a 6838cc 30/40. For 1913 they made a smaller model, the 3306cc 14hp, and for 1914 the even smaller 2-litre 10hp. Porthos did not survive the war.

NG

PORTLAND (i) see PACIFIC

PORTLAND (ii) (F) 1913–1914
Portland Light Car Co., London.
This make took its name from London's Great Portland Street, location of countless motor showrooms and offices, but not a single factory. Several models were listed, including a single-cylinder 6/8hp with 2-speed gearbox and shaft drive in 1913–14, and two fours, of 7 and 12/16hp in 1914. It must have been

another make, or makes, renamed, but their identity is not known. The dimensions of the single-cylinder engine correspond to those of Ruby as used in the ELBURN-RUBY and TWEENIE cyclecars. These were sold in France as the RUBY, so perhaps there lies the origin of the single-cylinder Portland.

NG

PORTUGAL (US) 1990 to date
Peter Portugal, Eureka, California.
The Portugal Dolphin was a neoclassic sports car design built by architect and artist Peter Portugal. Its most obvious feature was the body, made from strips of redwood glued together and formed with planes. The interior featured leather seats with a burr-walnut dashboard. It was finished with clear urethane. The chassis was a Datsun 280Z and similar cars were offered for sale at $65,000.

HP

POSTAL (US) 1906–1908
Postal Auto & Engine Co., Bedford, Indiana.
Designed by Fred Postal, this was a high-wheeler powered by a 12½hp 2-cylinder engine mounted under the seat, with final drive by steel cable. It was made in the works of the former ANDERSON (i), also a high-wheeler. To tie in with his name, Postal advertised his car as being specially suitable for rural mail delivery. With wings on the rear wheels only it sold for $475.

NG

POTTERAT (F) 1944
Julien Potterat was the man who built Russia's passenger car, the 1908 Russo-Baltique. Towards the end of World War II in France he conceived a revolutionary car design in his machine factory. It was to be a 4-seater saloon with a forward-control driving position and central doors on each side, but was never realised.

CR

POUPÉE (F) 1913
Automobiles Poupée, Douzies, Nord.
The Poupée (doll) was listed for 1913 as a 2-seater roadster powered by a 1130cc 4-cylinder engine.

NG

POWELL (US) 1955–1956
Powell Sport Wagon, Compton, California.
The Powell Sport Wagon was a postwar attempt to provide a pick-up truck for under $1000. Channing and Hayward Powell set up a company that bought used 1941 Plymouth sedans and rebodied them with slab-sided pick-up bodies. They wanted to build a pick-up that drove like a sedan and was priced far lower than Detroit products. The Powell sold well, and a station wagon was added to the line. A pop-up camper top for the pick-up was optional. By 1956 the supply of 1941 Plymouths donor cars had been used up and production ceased. Powell also built three motor homes in the early 1950s based on Cadillac chassis. Between 1000 and 1300 vehicles of all types are estimated to have been built.

HP

POWERCAR (US) 1909–1911
Powercar Auto Co., Cincinnati, Ohio.
The Powercar was made for the 1909 season as a conventional tourer with a 30hp 4-cylinder engine, 3-speed gearbox and shaft drive. For 1910 two further body styles were added, a 4-seater tourabout and a 2-seater roadster, and for 1911, when the wheelbase was extended from 108 (2741mm) to 115in (2919mm), there were just two styles, a tourer and a torpedo roadster. The company was out of business by the end of 1911, and from 1914 to 1916 the factory was used for the manufacture of the Alter truck.

NG

POWERDRIVE (GB) 1955–1958
Powerdrive Ltd, London.
One contemporary magazine described the Powerdrive as a '3-wheeler with an Austin-Healey air' and certainly this was a cut above the average economy trike. It boasted a larger-than-average open aluminium body designed by David Gottlieb and could seat three abreast. The engine (a British Anzani 322cc 2-stroke

was mounted just ahead of the single rear wheel and drove through a 3-speed Albion gearbox. Its high price of £412 consigned it to the margins.

CR

PRADO (US) 1921–1922

Prado Motors Corp., New York, New York.

The Prado was a short-lived, powerful and expensive car which surfaced on the American automobile scene in 1921 and which was out of business shortly after a one year existence and with a total production of less than ten units completed. The Prado was interesting in its choice of its power plant, a Curtiss OX-5 V8 aircraft engine, suitably converted for automotive use. The car was available in chassis form at $9000 or as a Deluxe Speedster at $11,800, although the meagre published material on the car at the time cited both 'Open Types' and 'Closed Types', and the one piece of known factory literature dated 25 April 1921 was illustrated with a sketch of a touring car. The engine boasted a bore and stroke of 4 × 5in (8226cc) and a maximum bhp of 100. The Prado, with offices at 25 Church Street in New York City, featured a wheelbase of 142in (3604mm) and weighed 3900lbs (1772kg), this being reduced by more than 700lbs (318kg) for 1922 when aluminium was substituted for steel in much of the chassis construction. Disc wheels were standard with two side-mounted spares and aluminium door steps were used in place of running-boards. Chassis serial numbers for 1921 were reportedly 211 to 215 with 221 and up listed for the Prado's final year.

KM

PRAGA (A/CS) 1907–1948

1907–1910 Prazska automobilni tovarna - Prager Automobil-Fabrik, Praha-Smichov.
1910–1927 Automobilni oddeleni První Ceskomoravske tovarny na stroje, Praha-Liben.
1927–1948 Auto Praga, Ceskomoravska Kolben-Danek, akc. spol., Praha-Vysocany.

One of the most important Czech makes, Praga, began in 1907 when První Ceskomoravska tovarna na stroje (the First Czech-Moravian Machine Factory) in Prague, and Fr. Ringhoffer Co. of Prague-Smichov founded the Prazska automobilni tovarna – Prager Automobil-Fabrik (Prague Automobile Factory Ltd), with trademark PAT-PAF. The company's management decided to purchase a licence to build the Isotta-Fraschini cars first: one was a 8044cc 60bhp 4-cylinder type with chain drive, the other a smaller 3052cc engined car with shaft drive. Later a 2-cylinder 1206cc Charron came, but very few of both marques were sold. More successful was PAT-PAF with truck production under the Dykomen licence. Nevertheless, in 1909, 58 workers produced only 33 vehicles of 9 different types, and automobiles were only a small portion of the factory's total output. From March 1910, all cars carried the name 'Praga', but the total for that period was only 15 cars, with many unsold cars filling the free spaces of the company.

A new era began when, in 1911, Frantisek Kec joined Praga. He designed and oversaw the production of 'cartrains' (now they could be called double semi-trailers) type V (vojensky – military) which established the fame of the firm and its commercial success. Kec created, as new constructor-in-chief, a whole scale of classic cars with main layout: 4-cylinder water-cooled side-valve engines, rigid axles in front and rear, semi-elliptic springs, and 4-speed gearbox. One of Kec's unwritten rules was that every new model should receive at least half its parts from a predecessor. All Praga cars should be conservatively designed and solidly built, the 'cars which lasted for hundreds of thousands of kilometres', as their slogan said.

The first passenger cars to fulfil this philosophy were the Mignon (1911, 1846cc 22bhp, 25 cars were produced in the first series) and the large Grand (1912, 3824cc 45bhp, 25 cars until 1919). Praga Grand started the tradition of its cars' participation at road rallies, being first in the 1912 Alpine Raid. That year, the Hungarian automobile manufacturer Raba negotiated a licence to produce Pragas.

In 1913, Praga introduced a 'people's car', the Alfa, powered by a 1130cc 15bhp engine, and this type was an attraction at the Prague Autosalon that year which Praga entered for the first time. Both the Grand and Alfa played key roles in the company's success for 25 years. In 1914, Mignon received an enlarged 2296cc 30bhp engine.

1956 Powerdrive 3-wheeler.
NATIONAL MOTOR MUSEUM

1913 Praga Alfa 15hp tourer.
NATIONAL MOTOR MUSEUM

1923 Praga Grand limousine.
NATIONAL MOTOR MUSEUM

Praga's passenger car production was shut down during World War I. The company produced a hydrostatic transmission at that time as well as the N model truck. Also, due to the high cost of petrol, Praga invested in a distillate fuel 'Pragolin' that was half the cost. Passenger car as well as truck production resumed after the war, when the independent Czechoslovakia was established on 28 October 1918. In 1921, 1922 and 1923 Praga entered the first 'Race of Reliability' 5-day 2000km contest around Czechoslovakia, in which they took prizes for the best reliability. Celebrating these (and another sports successes) the Praga radiator mascot of a bronze snail was replaced by the 'Genius of Motoring', an athlete running with a laurel wreath in hand.

The Alfa obtained a larger 1240cc 19bhp engine, and an open model cost 49,000 Kc. The Mignon was now powered by a 2296cc 30bhp engine. Praga produced 520 cars until the end of 1923.

At the 1924 Prague Autosalon Praga introduced the Piccolo, a small model with 707cc 10bhp engine, priced 34,500 Kc. This car grew over the years: in

1929 Praga Grand 8 limousine.
NICK BALDWIN

1933 Praga Piccolo 995cc sedan.
NATIONAL MOTOR MUSEUM

1939 Praga Piccolo 1.1-litre saloon.
NICK BALDWIN

1925–1926 it had a 824cc 12bhp engine, in 1927–1928 a 856cc 13bhp engine, and the eighth to twentieth series, built from 1928 to 1934, were powered by a 995cc 18bhp engine.

In 1924 200 Piccolos and 841 other Praga types were built. In 1925, Praga became the largest vehicle factory in Czechoslovakia, employing 1200 workers and 150 clerks, and producing 2050 vehicles.

In 1927, the Ceskomoravska-Kolben factory merged with the Breitfeld-Danek factory creating Ceskomoravska Kolben-Danek, known as CKD. Praga, as one division of this industrial giant, began to produce agricultural tractors and motorcycles. One year later, Frantisek Kec was promoted to general director,

and 5800 cars left the Praga factory. New designs appeared for the 6-cylinder types Alfa (1928–1930, 13th–16th series, 1496cc, 25bhp; 1930–1933, 17th–21st series, 1795cc 38bhp), Mignon (1927, 16th–17th series, 2498cc 45bhp; 1928, 18th series, 2636cc 50bhp), and 8-cylinder in-line type Grand (1927, 2nd–11th series, 3384cc 60bhp; 1928–1929, 12th–16th series, 3582cc 64bhp; 1930, 17th–18th series, 4429cc 87bhp engine).

By 1928 a contract was agreed between Praga and an agricultural factory in Oswiencim, Poland, called Potega in order to produce vehicles under the name Oswiencim-Praga. A factory was opened in December 1929. The idea was to bring in complete Praga chassis from the factory in Czechoslovakia, and the bodies would be built in Oswiencim. In 1930, 60 bodies were built and sold, including an 8-cylinder Grand passenger car. Trucks and some 12- to 50-seat buses were assembled, and tractors and motorcycles were also offered. By 1934 only about 250 vehicles had been built in Oswiencim. This was also the year the 8-cylinder engines were entirely discontinued for passenger cars. Under the name Oswiencim-Praga the Piccolo and Alfa continued to be offered in Poland as late as 1937.

In 1929, production peaked at 7500 vehicles, and the Piccolo was delivered also as a taxi. Thanks to simplified production, car prices could be reduced. In autumn 1930, the 4-seater Piccolo cost between 35,000 to 45,000 Kc, the 5-6-seater limousine Alfa between 65,000 and 69,000 Kc, the 6-7-seater limousine Mignon 95,000 Kc and the 6-7-seater limousine Grand with a radio cost 115,000 Kc.

In 1931, with 4700 workers employed in the factory, the 3316 car sales confirmed that the world economic crisis had arrived in Czechoslovakia. General directors of three largest car producers – Praga, Skoda and Tatra – formed the joint-stock company called MOTOR on 1 January 1932, in order to increase revenues and cut costs. Frantisek Kec was promoted to General Director, but very soon the bank of Zivnobanka, a major shareholder of CKD, cancelled the merger agreement. Praga sales fell to 3555 vehicles in 1932, and to 2222 the next year. Frantisek Kec had to leave the factory when his conservative approach to car construction could not respond rapidly enough to the new types of small car introduced by Skoda, Aero, Tatra and Z. With him went also Praga's sales director Frantisek Maly.

In 1934, Rudolf Vykoukal (later known for his advanced designs at Jawa Works) introduced the Baby, with a 996cc 21bhp engine – its 3-speed transmission was the first fully synchronised gearbox in Czechoslovakia. Another unusual feature for Pragas was the backbone frame and 4-wheel independent suspension. The Baby cost 22,500 Kc, and that year 2250 new vehicles were sold.

The Piccolo was produced in two engine volumes: as the Super Piccolo from 1934 to 1936, with 1660cc 35bhp engine, priced 43,000 Kc, or as Piccolo (31st–36th series) from 1937 to 1941, with 1128cc 28bhp engine, sold for 28,800 Kc. A streamlined Piccolo was specially built for the 1934 'Thousand Miles of Czechoslovakia' race.

In 1935, two brand new cars appeared. The Lady (1935–1941) was fitted with the same engine as the Super Piccolo, and with 4-door closed body cost 39,100 Kc. The Uhlik-bodied Lady cabriolet won first place for elegance at the 1936 Paris Auto Salon. A luxury 6-seater, the Golden (1935–38) was powered by a 6-cylinder 3912cc 78bhp engine, capable of 81mph (130km/h), and priced 95,000 Kc. The Lady and the Golden were given an innovative electromagnetic Cotal transmission.

A new Alfa with a 2492cc 6-cylinder 60bhp engine and a 4-speed fully-synchronised gearbox, was introduced in 1937, and after the production of the Golden was stopped in 1941, the Alfa was the largest passenger Praga car, being priced 69,000 Kc for the 4-door limousine. By the end of 1938, 2834 vehicles were sold.

On 15 March 1939 Germany occupied Czechoslovakia, and all production in the Protectorate of Bohemia and Moravia was attuned to the Wehrmacht's needs – 4849 vehicles were manufactured. During the war only military vehicles were produced, totalling about 4600 until 1945.

The Praga factory in Prague was 90 per cent destroyed by allied bombing on 25 March 1945. That year, on 28 October, all important industrial works were nationalised. It was decided to produce trucks and buses only.

The last Praga passenger cars appeared in 1946–1948, when 150 Piccolos and 150 Ladies were assembled from the surviving parts. On 2 September 1948 the company's name was changed to Auto-Praga, narodni podnik and two types of trucks, the petrol-engined RN and diesel RND, were put into production.

1938 Praga Lady 1.7-litre roadster.
NATIONAL MOTOR MUSEUM

Today, Praga manufactures many types of automatic and hydromechanic gears for commercial vehicles as well as the Unimog-like UV 80 4 × 4 light truck.

MSH

Further Reading
'Praga: The Hundred Year Saga', A.E. King and J. Krali,
Automobile Quarterly, Vol. 35, No. 2.

PRATT (i) (US) 1907

Pratt Chuck Works, Franfort, New York.

It is doubtful that the Pratt 6-Wheeler was intended for actual production, although two or three cars were probably built, their claim to originality being in a 6-wheeled principle. This design, consisting of two wheels in front and four in the rear was curious in concept with the wheels in front and the intermediate pair at the rear both being steerable, the latter turning in a lesser angle than the front pair. Power was transmitted to the leading rear pair of wheels by a transmission gear and two-part rear axle shaft. The Pratt was a touring car comprising three sets of seats and an overall length of 168in (4264mm). Power was by a 75hp 6-cylinder engine.

KM

PRATT-ELKHART; PRATT (ii) (US) 1909–1915

1909–1915 Elkhart Carriage & Harness Manufacturing Co., Elkhart, Indiana.
1915 Pratt Motor Car Co., Elkhart, Indiana.

The Pratt brothers, William and George, had run a successful carriage and harness making company since before the turn of the century, doing a lot of their business by mail order. Wanting to enter the motor business they built

1940 Praga Alfa 2½-litre saloon.
NATIONAL MOTOR MUSEUM

a high-wheeler in 1906, but were not happy with it and in 1909 they began to manufacture a conventional car powered by a 30/35hp 4-cylinder engine and offered for the first two years only as a 5-seater tourer. In 1911 they added a roadster and a limousine to the range, as well as an open tourer, in addition to a four-door tourer. Presumably the open tourer did not have doors to the front seats. For 1912 they added a more powerful engine, rated at 40hp and for 1913 and 1914 there was a 50hp. Production peaked at 203 cars in 1914, far short of what the brothers had hoped for, because selling cars by mail order was much more difficult than selling carriages and buggies. Manufacturers who had a dealer in every large town were at a distinct advantage over the Pratts. In fact

1914 Premier (i) Model 6-48 tourer.
NATIONAL MOTOR MUSEUM

1924 Premier (i) Model 6-D roadster.
JOHN A. CONDE

they turned to dealer-selling for the 1912 model year, but their network was not large. For 1915 they changed the name of their company and car to Pratt and launched their first six, of 34hp, in addition to a 27hp four. They only sold 191 cars that year, and before it was over they changed the name of their product again, this time to ELCAR.

NG

Further Reading
'Pratt Fall: The story of two brothers and one daisy of a car that deserved better than it got', Beverly Rae Kimes, *Automobile Quarterly*, Vol. 14, No. 4.

P.R.B. (AUS) 1979 to date

P.R.B. Motors, Drummoyne, New South Wales.
A Lotus 7-inspired clubman type built by Peter Bladwell, the PRB originally relied on the Ford Escort 1600 for its components. Built on a space frame, the body was aluminium with fibreglass mudguards. The increasing demands of emissions regulations were beyond that engine and progress was impeded until Toyota's twin-camshaft Corolla engine was released in 1986. Compliance with design rules, having a roll-over bar and side intrusion protection, brought about an increase in weight to 550kg. In 1998 the previous multi-tubular frame was superseded by a honeycomb structure.

MG

P.R.D. (CDN) 1981 to date

Prototype Research & Design Ltd, Campbellford, Ontario.
A number of replica vehicles was produced by P.R.D., all of them based on General Motors chassis. Replicas of the Mercedes 500K, Auburn Speedster and MG TD were hardly original, but the Chevrolet Bel Air 1955 replica certainly

was. The Bel Air had a fibreglass body and could be mounted on an original '55 Chevrolet chassis or a 1978-and-on Chevrolet. Cars were available completed or in kit form.

CR

PRÉCICAR (F) 1983

Préciculture SA, Fere Champenoise.
Heavy-handed frontal styling marred the Précicar PC49 microcar. Two engines were offered: a 49cc petrol and a Faryman 290cc diesel. There were also two body styles, a convertible and a mini-estate.

CR

PRECICO (CDN) 1975

Precico, Québec.
Little more than a golf cart released on to the road, Precico's Funcar was an extremely compact doorless 2-seater microcar. It was powered by a Kohler 340cc 2-stroke engine developing 24bhp.

CR

PRECISION DESIGN AND ENGINEERING (US) 1995 to date

Precision Design and Engineering, Escondido, California.
The GT250 was a replica of the Ferrari 250GT California spyder based on Ford running gear. This kit had formerly been built by MODENA. A steel backbone chassis was used, with Ford suspension and steering components. Fiat 124 seats and windshield frame were fitted.

HP

PRECISION MOTORSPORTS (US) c.1998 to date

Precision Motorsports, Dillon, Montana.
This Cobra replica had a very advanced chassis with rocker-arm suspension and cockpit-adjustable sway bars. It was purchased from SMC, who had developed the advanced design with the aid of race car driver and engineer Richard Hudgins. The body's unusual looks were due to the lack of side vents and a reshaped nose. They were sold in kit and turn-key form.

HP

PREDATOR (US) c.1993 to date

Predator Performance, Largo, Florida.
Jaguar replicas were the products of this kit car company. Their D-Type clone used a tubular steel chassis with XJ-6 suspension and Jaguar or Chevrolet engines. Their bodywork was pretty believable but their choice of wheels and trim often gave them away. Kit prices started at $15,000, with completed cars running about $45,000. Racing versions were also available. Their F-Type was a replica of the Jaguar XJ-13 prototype. It used a XJ-S donor car for the suspension with V12 Jaguar or Chevrolet V8 power. The transmission was a Z-F unit as used in the DeTomaso Pantera. It also used a steel tube chassis with fibreglass body panels. The F-Type was over twice as expensive as their D-Type replica.

HP

PREMIER (i) (US) 1903–1926

1903–1915 Premier Motor Manufacturing Co., Indianapolis, Indiana.
1915–1923 Premier Motor Car Co., Indianapolis, Indiana.
1923–1926 Premier Motors Inc., Indianapolis, Indiana.
George B. Weidely, who would later become renowned as a proprietary engine manufacturer, organised the Premier Motor Manufacturing Co. with partner Harold O. Smith. Weidely had built his first car in 1902, a water-cooled motor buggy, but felt that air-cooling would be more satisfactory for the Premier, whose name had been suggested by Sam Miles, publisher of *The Motor Age*. The firm adopted an oak leaf for its radiator badge, and later claimed this as the first use of an emblem as an automotive trademark.

The Premier had four cylinders, ohvs, and a sliding gear transmission. The 4-cylinder Models A and F were joined by a 2-cylinder model in 1904, the twin being interestingly larger and, at $2500, twice the price of the 4-cylinder Model A. Both air- and water-cooled models were offered by 1907, and the following year air-cooling was abandoned for good. Also in 1908, a 6-cylinder car was added to the line. Prices now topped $3700. Premiers completed three Glidden

1916 Premier (i) Model 6-56 tourer.
JOHN A. CONDE

Tours with perfect scores. Three Premier cars were constructed for the 1916 Indianapolis 500 race, but the best they could manage was a seventh-place finish. The other two cars did not complete the race, one experiencing a crash and the other succumbing to lubrication failure. George Weidely and Harold Smith had left the company following a 1914 receivership; the next year the firm's debts were settled by a syndicate headed by F.W. Woodruff, an Illinois banker. The firm was reorganised as Premier Motor Car Co.

'The Aluminum Six with Magnetic Gear Shift', the firm boasted in 1918. Premier engines were aluminium castings using aluminium pistons and crankcases. The 'Magnetic Gear Shift' was a novel and forward-looking product of the Cutler-Hammer Corp., which featured a set of gear-change controls mounted on the steering wheel.

L.S. Skelton, a physician who also promoted the SKELTON car of St Louis, Missouri, took control of the firm by 1920. Skelton's death in the following year resulted in yet another receivership, resolved by the intervention of Frederick L. Barrows and reorganisation as Premier Motors Inc. in 1923. Barrows also bought the MONROE car from Frank Strattan, who had purchased the moribund Indianapolis manfacturer. Barrows incorporated the Monroe into the Premier line as the Model B 4-cylinder car, which was produced alongside the 6-cylinder Model 6-D in 1924 and 1925. An order for 1000 taxicabs was taken in 1923, and shortly afterwards Barrows announced that Premier Motors would concentrate on taxi production. The firm sold out to National Cab and Truck Co. in October 1926, which dissolved soon thereafter.

KF

PREMIER (ii) (GB) 1906–1907; 1912–1913

Premier Motor Co. Ltd, Birmingham.

This Birmingham firm was an agent for the Italian MARCHAND, and the first cars sold under the Premier name were, in fact, Marchands, two 4-cylinder models, and a 20hp six. At the 1906 Olympia Show they exhibited a car of their own design, with a 10/12hp 2-cylinder Aster engine, but it did not last long. No more cars were made until 1912 when they announced the P.M.C. Motorette, a 3-wheeler powered by a 723cc 6hp single-cylinder engine, with chain drive to an epicyclic 2-speed gear in the rear wheel. The frame was tubular, the standard brake was on the rear wheel, but front-wheel brakes could be fitted for an extra 3 guineas (£3.15).

NG

1914 Premier (iv) 4/12PS 2-seater.
NATIONAL MOTOR MUSEUM

PREMIER (iii) (GB) 1912–1914

Premier Cycle Co. Ltd, Coventry.

Premier began making motorcycles in 1908, and in 1912 entered the cyclecar market with a neat-looking car powered by a transversely-mounted 998cc 7/9hp air-cooled V-twin engine, with chain drive to a 2-speed gearbox and to the rear axle. For 1914 they brought out a 1592cc 4-cylinder light car with 3-speed gearbox and shaft drive. In November 1914 the name was changed to COVENTRY PREMIER, these cars being made until 1923.

NG

PREMIER (iv) (D) 1913–1914

Justus Christian Braun Premier-Werke AG, Nuremburg.

This old-established firm making trucks and fire-fighting equipment entered car production with the KAISER (i) in 1911. They then merged with the German branch of the British Premier Cycle Co. to make a light car powered by a 1033cc 4/12PS engine, which they sold under the Premier name. The same car was built in the Premier factory at Eger in Bohemia, then part of the Austro-Hungarian empire, and sold under the name Omega or Premier.

HON

1265

1979 Premier (vi) Padmini 1100 saloon.
NATIONAL MOTOR MUSEUM

1902 Prescott steam surrey.
NATIONAL MOTOR MUSEUM

PREMIER (v) (A) 1913

Premier-Werke AG – Tovarna jizdnich kol a motocyklu 'Premier', Cheb.
In 1911, the British 'Premier Cycle Co. Ltd' and German 'Maschinenfabrik Justus Christian Braun AG' created a common cycle factory. In 1913 this factory also built 4-cylinder water-cooled 1033cc 4-12hp engined open 2-seaters, with many features used at that time by bigger cars: pressed steel frame; differential; high tension magneto ignition; semi-elliptic leaf springs all round. These light cars weighed 1067lb (485kg) and were capable of 37mph (60km/h). They were painted in blue or grey colours only, other shades on request.

MSH

PREMIER (vi) (IND) 1955 to date

Premier Automobiles Ltd, Bombay.
This company has made Fiat-based cars for many years. The longest-lived was the Padmini (formerly Fiat Delight) which was a badge-engineered Fiat 1100-103 4-door saloon, still offered on the Indian domestic market in 1999. It was joined in 1985 by the 118 NE which combined the body shell of the Fiat 124 with a 1171cc Nissan Cherry engine and 4-speed gearbox. 1997 production was over 13,000, but the ageing Premier models faced severe competition from the Indian market leader, MARUTI. A licence-built Uno was planned for 1999.

NG

PREMIER MARKETING (US) c.1993

Premier Marketing, Lake Oswego, Oregon.
The humble Porsche 914 attracted the attention of this kit car company. They made a rebody kit that added large side vents and a squarish revised nose to the 914. Premier also offered engine kits to adapt V6 and V8 engines.

HP

PREMOCAR (US) 1921–1923

Preston Motor Corp., Birmingham, Alabama.
The Premocar was launched in August 1920 in conjunction with the formal opening of its Birmingham factory, plans calling for the production of both 6- and 4-cylinder cars. The Six, powered by a 40hp Falls ohv engine, was available as a touring car and a roadster, both priced at $1295 and a 'Sporting Model', similar to the six but with a Rochester-Duesenberg 4-cylinder G-1 engine developing 81bhp at 2600rpm and replete with such niceties as optional wire or wood wheels, aluminium step plates, front and rear bumpers as standard equipment, and bevelled glass wind wings. Available in both roadsters and touring cars at $3865, few of them, designated as Model 4-8 found buyer and the four was dropped by the end of the year, their production, as with the lower-priced four, having begun in January 1921. The six was continued, the line theoretically augmented by a pick-up truck which, though announced, was probably never built. Perhaps the high point in the history of this rather undistinguished car was an especially built touring car, painted white and with a different engine, the Fischer Magic Six to escort President Warren G. Harding on a formal visit to Birmingham. According to Beverly Rae Kimes, the car was subsequently used in honour of bandmaster John Philip Sousa the following year. In May 1923, the company went into receivership. An estimated 500 to 600 Premocars were built during the company's three years in business.

KM

PRESCOTT (US) 1901–1905

Prescott Automobile Manufacturing Co., Passaic, New Jersey.
The Prescott was a steam car powered by a 7½hp 2-cylinder engine with single-chain final drive. An unusual feature was a steam-operated air pump for inflating the tyres. The first model was a 2-seater runabout, but from 1903 there was a folding front model giving two additional seats. The Prescott survived later than many of the small steam firms, and might have gone on longer still had not a trusted aide of A.L. Prescott disappeared with a large sum of money intended for setting up a European agency.

NG

PRESTIGE (GB) 1994–1995

Prestige Sports Cars, Ringwood, Hampshire.
Alan Milford bought an A.B.S. Monaco (an open-topped Countach kit) but found it hard to complete, since A.B.S. had gone bust. He re-engineered the package and tooled up to make the car in series as the Prestige Monaco, or with a fixed head as the Denaro. The engineering was basically the same set-up of a space frame chassis, Ford Granada-based front suspension, Ford steering and V8 power/Renault transaxle (though 4-cylinder and V6 options were listed). Only two were made for British customers before the project was sold to a Malaysian company.

CR

PRESTIGE CLASSICS (US) c.1982

Prestige Classics, Wayzata, Minnesota.
This kit car company made a number of replicas of classic sports cars. The Jaguar XK-120, MG-TD and 1957 Thunderbird were duplicated, more or less. They also sold a neoclassic kit called the Barrington that resembled the CMC Gazelle. All were based on VW Beetle chassis, except for the Barrington, which could also be built on Ford Pinto running gear.

HP

PRESTO (D) 1901–1927

1901–1907 Presto-Werke Gunther & Co., Chemnitz.
1907–1927 Presto-Werke AG, Chemnitz.
The Leipzig Motor Show of 1901 was the venue for the first appearance of the Presto car. With 3½, 4½ and 5½hp single-cylinder engines the early cars owed much to bicycle engineering, hardly surprising as Presto was one of the leading exponents of 2-wheelers, whether motorised or not. There was no significant output of cars until 1907 when they began to make various models of DELAHAYE under licence. From 1910 they began to make cars of their own design, the 2340cc 8/22PS 4-cylinder which was made only to 1912 and the 2078cc 8/25PS which was carried on into the postwar years and was the basis for the one-model policy starting in 1921. This was the 9/30PS Typ D with 30bhp 2350cc

4-cylinder engine, later increased to 40bhp as the Typ E. In 1926 the DUX works were acquired, together with their 6-cylinder Typs F (2613cc) and G (3119cc). When Presto was taken over by NAG in 1927 the 6-cylinder models were carried on under the name NAG-Presto, although most of these were fitted with delivery van bodies.

In 1936 the Presto name was revived for light motorcycles which were made in the NAG-Presto factory until 1941.

HON

PRIAMUS (D) 1901–1923

1901–1903 Kölner Motorwagenfabrik GmbH, vorm. Heinrich Brunthaler, Cologne.
1903–1909 Motorfahrzeugfabrik 'Köln' Uren Kotthuas & Co., Cologne.
1909–1921 Priamus Automobil-Werk GmbH, Cologne-Sulz.
1921–1923 Priamus-Werke für Fahrzeugbau, Cologne-Sulz.

The first product of this firm had a single-cylinder 5PS engine with 2-speed belt drive and a tubular chassis. It was designed by Wilhelm Uren who took over the firm in 1903, when the name Priamus was used for the first time. Pressed steel replaced the tubular frame, and larger models, 10/12 and 16/18PS twins and an 18/20PS 4-cylinder followed. The single- and 2-cylinder cars were dropped in 1905, but the 18/20 and 24/30PS fours were continued to be made in small numbers up to 1908. Priamus cars took part in the Herkomer Trials of 1905, 1906 and 1907, though without great success.

In 1908 Uren, Kotthaus & Co. went bankrupt as a result of over-production of expensive cars, and the firm was reorganised by new owners who concentrated on smaller cars. These included the 1592cc 6/16PS and 2262cc 9/22PS, both with 4-cylinder monobloc side-valve engines. The last prewar model, the 8/24PS of 1913, was continued after the war, joined by a 9/30PS. However, in 1921 Priamus was taken over by the coachbuilding firm Möllenkamp of Düsseldorf who launched a new 10/50 PS 6-cylinder car under the name MÖLKAMP.

HON

PRIDEMORE (US) 1914

Pridemore Machine Works, Northfield, Minnesota.

W.A. Pridemore designed a cyclecar more racy-looking than most, with an underslung frame, powered by a 12/14hp air-cooled 2-cylinder engine, with friction transmission and chain drive. He planned to make both side by side and tandem 2-seaters, and also a delivery van, but it is not certain that he made any more than the one car exhibited at a show in February 1914.

NG

PRIMA (F) 1906–1909

Sté des Automobiles Prima, Levallois-Perret, Seine.

These cars were made by Léon Lefèbvre who had previously been responsible for the BOLIDE. In 1906/07 two models were listed, a 9hp single-cylinder and 10/12hp 4-cylinder, and for 1908 the single was joined by larger fours of 12/15 and 20hp. Each type was available on three wheelbases, and a wide range of bodies was offered, tourers, doctor's coupés, limousines, landaulets, delivery vans and light trucks. They had unit construction of engine and gearbox, which was very advanced for the time. Two cars were entered in the 1907 Coupe des Voiturettes, but did not distinguish themselves.

NG

Further Reading
'Made on the Seine – the Prima', M. Worthington-Williams,
The Automobile, November 1994.

PRIMO (US) 1910–1912

Primo Motor Co., Atlanta, Georgia.

Launched as 'The Southern Automobile', the Primo had a 25hp 4-cylinder engine and was available in four body styles: a tourer, toy tonneau and 3-seater roadster on a 110in (2792mm) wheelbase, and a 2-seater roadster on a 100in (2538mm) wheelbase.

NG

PRIMUS (D) 1899–1903

Pfälzische Nähmaschinen und Fahrradfabrik vorm. Gebr. Kayser, Kaiserslautern.

1918 Presto 9/25PS tourer.
NICK GEORGANO/NATIONAL MOTOR MUSEUM

Manufacture of sewing machines was a useful apprenticeship for car making, and the Primus company launched a light car powered by a 5PS single-cylinder engine in 1899. 2- and 4-cylinder models followed, but production never amounted to much.

HON

PRINCE (i) (I) 1922–1923

Automobili Costruzioni di V. Carena e Mazza, Turin.

This short-lived light car had a Fiat-like radiator, and was about the same size as the Fiat 501, with 1460cc 4-cylinder side-valve engine and 3-speed gearbox. Industrial problems in Italy at the time dashed any hope of the car's success.

NG

PRINCE (ii) (J) 1955–1967

1955–1961 Fuji Precision Machinery Co., Tokyo.
1961–1966 Prince Motors Ltd, Tokyo.
1966–1967 Prince Motors Ltd (Division of Nissan Motor Co.), Tokyo.

The Prince was made initially by Tama Motors, a former aircraft company which had built the Datsun-based Tama electric cars in the early postwar years. In 1952 the electrics were dropped, and three years later a conventional 4-door saloon with a 1484cc 4-cylinder engine was introduced. It was called the Prince with the permission of Japan's Crown Prince Akihito, and in 1956 was given the model name Skyline, with styling similar to the contemporary American Ford Fairlane. It had a 4-speed all-synchromesh gearbox, De Dion rear axle and coil ifs. It was exhibited at the 1957 Paris Salon, being the first Japanese car to be promoted in Europe, a year ahead of Daihatsu who achieved the first serious sales.

In 1961 the Skyline was joined by the 1861cc Gloria, which received a 1988cc single-ohc 6-cylinder engine in 1962. The Skyline and Gloria cars, together with vans and minibuses, were made in two factories in Tokyo until 1966, when owners Fuji sold out to NISSAN. The two models were continued under the Nissan or Datsun names, according to overseas markets, for several years.

NG

PRINCEPS (i) (GB) 1902–1903

Princeps Autocar Co., Northampton.

The Princeps light car was powered by a 4hp Aster engine mounted under the seat, with a 2-speed gearbox. It had a 2-seater body and a tubular frame. In October 1902 they announced a larger car powered by a front-mounted 9hp engine, with shaft drive and a 4-seater tonneau body. The company's motorcycles were longer lived, being made until about 1910.

NG

1960 Prince Skyline saloon.
NICK BALDWIN

1976 Princess (iii) 2200HL saloon.
NATIONAL MOTOR MUSEUM

1923 Princeton sedan.
KEITH MARVIN

PRINCEPS (ii) (GB) 1920

This obscure light car, whose maker's name and address are unknown, had a 10.5hp Coventry-Simplex 4-cylinder engine, with friction transmission and chain drive. Body styles included 2-seater, 4-seater and delivery van.

NG

PRINCESS (i) (US) 1914–1918

1912 Princess Cyclecar Co., Detroit, Michigan.
1914–1918 Princess Motor Car Corp., Detroit, Michigan.

This car began as a cyclecar with 12hp 4-cylinder Farmer engine and a Renault-style bonnet, though the radiator was mounted at the front. It was called the Little Princess, but did not last out the year. A new group of investors took over and launched a larger car for 1915, although the smaller was continued for a season. Both were now called simply Princess. The larger car had a 23hp G. B. & S. engine and was made as a tourer, roadster and speedster. It was in production for three seasons, but in January 1919 the Princess Motor Car Corp. was said to be 'permanently out of business'.

NG

PRINCESS (ii) (GB) 1923

Princess Engineering Co. Ltd, Streatham, London.

This company's main business was the manufacture of shock absorbers, but for one year they marketed a light car powered by an 8.9hp air-cooled V-twin engine. It had a 3-speed gearbox and shaft drive to a worm gear rear axle. The price for a close-coupled 4-seater was £175.

NG

PRINCESS (iii) (GB) 1975–1982

1975–1978 British Leyland UK Ltd, Longbridge, Birmingham.
1978–1982 BL Cars Ltd, Longbridge, Birmingham.

The Princess name was first used by AUSTIN for the top model of their 4-litre postwar car, then for the 6-cylinder Rolls-Royce-engined VANDEN PLAS from 1964 to 1968. It became a marque in its own right in 1975, when it was used for the wedge-shaped 4-door saloon with transverse engine, formerly badged as an Austin, Morris or Wolseley 18-22. It was offered with choice of 1798cc ohv four or 2227cc single-ohc six engines, the latter with power steering, and all cars had Hydragas suspension. From mid–1978 the smaller engine gave way to the 4-cylinder single ohc 'O' series in 1698 or 1993cc forms. A small number of 7-seater long wheelbase versions were made by Woodall Nicholson. In March 1982 the Princess was replaced by the Austin Ambassador. Total production was 129,210.

NG

PRINCETON (US) 1923–1924

Durant Motors, Inc., Muncie, Indiana.

The Princeton was William C. Durant's car destined to bridge the gap in price between the Flint and his recently-acquired Locomobile and was launched at the New York Automobile Show in January 1923. A handsome car which was to be available in a series of closed and open body styles at $2485 to $3675, the Princeton was powered by an Ansted 6-cylinder ohv engine developing 75hp at 3000rpm and a choice of wood, wire, or disc wheels. Several pilot models were completed and plans were drawn up to go into production at Muncie when a last minute decision was made to switch operations to the Locomobile plant in Bridgeport, Connecticut. Hard on the heels of this decision, Durant changed his mind announcing that the Princeton would not be marketed under that name but would be, in fact, the luxury model of Flint. It has been speculated that the original plan for the Princeton was halted because even with its top price of $3675, a price gap of $3925 would remain between that figure and the $7400 for the least expensive Locomobile. There is some credence to this speculation as the price gap was subsequently filled by Durant's introduction of the Locomobile Model 90 which, with prices of $5500 to $7500 bridged it nicely.

KM

PRINETTI & STUCCHI (I) 1898–1902

Prinetti & Stucchi, Milan.

This company was a well-known maker of motor cycles and tricycles, but they also offered a light car powered by two front-mounted vertical single-cylinder engines, with belt final drive. They had tubular frames, as befitted their cycle ancestry, but were unusual in their suspension; at the rear of the body there were large C-springs which suspended the body on the chassis. In 1902 the name of the motorcycles was changed to Stucchi, manufacture continuing until 1926, but so far as is known, no cars bore this name.

NG

PRITCHETT & GOLD (GB) 1903–1904

Pritchett & Gold Ltd, Feltham, Middlesex.

This company was well-known for their batteries, but they also briefly offered two types of car. The petrol-engined design was the METEOR (iii) and the electric was known as the Pritchett & Gold or P & G. It was a 2-seater with a Renault-style bonnet.

NG

1899 Prinetti & Stucchi voiturette.

PRO AM (US) c.1994

Pro Am Parts & Accessories, Houston, Texas.
The CTX was a Cobra replica that was sold in kit or assembled form. It used a ford V8 mounted in a ladder style frame with Corvette-based suspension.

HP

PROBE (GB) 1969–1972

1969–1970 Adams Probe Motor Co., Bradford-on-Avon, Wiltshire.
1970–1971 W.T. Nugent Ltd, Bradford-on-Avon, Wiltshire.
1971–1972 Caledonian Probe Motor Co., Irvine, Ayrshire.
1972 Probe Ltd, Edinburgh.
An absolute storm of interest was created when Marcos stylist Dennis Adams created an extreme design study in 1969. The Design Probe Number 15 (quickly dubbed simply Probe 15 by the press) was a mere 29 in (736mm) tall, achieved by inclining the passengers almost horizontally, making the roof slide back for access and fitting a compact 875cc Hillman Imp engine in the tail. Demand led Adams to contemplate a production run but it was simply too impractical a car. *The Daily Telegraph* sponsored a revised design, the Probe 16, for its stand at the

1903 Pritchett & Gold electric car.

1970 Probe 16 coupé.
NICK GEORGANO/NATIONAL MOTOR MUSEUM

c.1900 Progress (i) 4½hp voiturette.
NATIONAL MOTOR MUSEUM

1969 London Motor Show. It was 5in (127mm) taller, had an electric sliding roof and a mid-mounted Austin 1800 engine. Only three or four such cars were made before the Probe 2001 of 1970. Still very low (37in (939mm) high), it retained the mid-mounted BMC 1800 engine but had a redesigned body, now featuring a rear aerofoil for roll-over protection. Four production 2001 cars had been built by 1971 but it is believed that a number of further bodyshells were made, so that perhaps 20 Probes of all types were made in all. A Probe 15 shell was later modified to become the CONCEPT Centaur.

CR

PROCTOR (AUS) 1957

Ted Proctor, Arncliffe, New South Wales.

The Proctor was an early fibreglass coupé for fitting to the VW base which rode 5in (125mm) lower, was 275lb (125kg) lighter and had less frontal area than the Beetle. The cost was contained by retaining all possible standard parts, such as windows and headlamps. The door handles were set into recesses which led cooling air to the engine. Although the performance and economy envelope was enhanced, the response by the market was disappointing. One car was completed to suit it for competitive use, this leading Ted Proctor into a long involvement with motor sports.

MG

PRODAL (US) 1909–1911

Motor Car Repair Co., New York, New York.

The Prodal was a handbuilt automobile which, in fact, was a sideline of a garage operated by P.A. Prodal and E.M. Dailey, which specialised in both the repair of expensive foreign cars for a well-to-do Manhattan clientele and affording garage space. The Prodal was powered by a 4-cylinder engine and constructed of standard components with coachwork by local craftsmen. Cars were built to order in both open and closed designs and mounted on a chassis designed by Messrs Prodal and Dailey which sported a slanted bonnet in the style of the Renault. 'Production' may have reached ten cars in all, most of them ordered by and sold to prominent New Yorkers, one of them to the Auchinloss family

KM

PROD'HOMME (F) 1907–1908

Éts Prod'homme, Ivry-Port, Seine.

This company offered cars with opposed-piston engines on the lines of the GOBRON-BRILLIÉ. They were of 2- and 4-cylinder layout.

NG

PROFESSIONAL PROTOTYPES (US) c.1985

Professional Prototypes, Clearwater, Florida.

The Dussen was a pseudo-Duesenberg replica that fitted on a steel ladder frame with a 125in (3173mm) wheelbase. It could be powered by VW Beetle engines in the rear or Ford Pinto 4-cylinders up front. It was virtually identical to kits sold by LINDBERG in California.

HP

PROGRESS (i) (GB) 1898–1903

Progress Cycle Co. Ltd, Coventry.

This cycle company was founded by Enoch J. West in 1891. His first car, called the Progress, was announced in 1899. It had a 2½hp De Dion-Bouton engine mounted under the seat at the rear of a tubular frame with single-chain final drive. It was a 2-seater but later Progress cars, with 4½hp De Dion or M.M.C. engines, had 4-seater *vis-à-vis* bodies and looked very like the contemporary De Dion.

In 1902 a new model appeared with pressed steel frame and front-mounted engines by Aster or De Dion. An 8hp Daimler engine was also available and bodies were by Mulliner. The Progress company was in liquidation by the end of 1903, but the Aster-engined car re-appeared in 1904 basically unchanged and sold under the name WEST-ASTER. About 150 of the *vis-à-vis* and 350–450 of the front-engined cars were made.

NG

Further Reading
E.J. West. *The Progress Cycle Co. and their Cars,* John Spicer, published by the author, 1991.

PROGRESS (ii) (GB) c.1928–1934

c.1928–1933 Seal Motors Ltd, Manchester.
1933–1934 Haynes Economy Motors Ltd, Manchester.

This 3-wheeled economy car was derived from the unconventional SEAL which was similar to a motorcycle and sidecar combination except that it was wheel-steered from the sidecar. The Progress was made as a light van of similar layout but instead of being controlled from the sidecar the driver sat alongside the load-carrying platform in a bucket seat. Three sizes of engine were offered: a 343cc Villiers, and 680 or 980cc JAP. It seems likely that the cars were on similar lines, but in 1932 a more conventional-looking van appeared with single front wheel driven by chain from a 680cc V-twin JAP engine mounted directly above it, Steering was by handlebars, but the 1934 model had wheel steering. Single- and 2-cylinder engines were offered. A passenger car version with a 980cc V-twin engine was listed in 1934, but probably most Progresses were goods vehicles. In 1936 Haynes Economy Motors offered a miniature 4-wheeler for fun fair or seaside promenade work, powered by a 196cc Villiers engine geared to give a top speed of 10mph (16km/h), and looking very similar to a RYTECRAFT. It is not clear if this also bore the name Progress.

NG

PROJECTA (GB) 1914

Percival White Engineering Works, Highbury, London.

The Projecta was a typical cyclecar in its engine and transmission, a V-twin JAP, 2-speed gearbox and belt final drive. Where it differed from the norm was in its very low canoe-like integral construction 2-seater body and frame.

NG

P.R.O.S.C.A (US) c.1996

P.R.O.S.C.A., Santa Clarita, California.

The P.R.O.S.C.A. Porsche 940 was a radically modified Porsche 914 with handsome, race-styled body panels and a lower profile due to the removal of the original roof. Suspension was based on Porsche 911 pieces, and a number of engines were offered, including Mazda rotary, Ford or Chevrolet V6 and V8 and modified Porsche. They were sold in kit form, or as assembled cars.

HP

PROSPER-LAMBERT (F) 1901–1906

Sté Prosper-Lambert, Nanterre, Seine.

The first Prosper-Lambert was a light car with 7hp single-cylinder De Dion-Bouton engine, and shaft drive. For the 1902–03 season a 12hp 2-cylinder car was added, the engines being now of the company's own design and manufacture, according to the catalogue. By 1905 there was a 16hp 4-cylinder model, and in 1906 there was a range of five cars, from a 9hp single, through 10 and 12hp twins, to 16 and 30hp fours, all with shaft drive. The cars were sold under the name JEAN BART in 1907, after which they disappeared altogether.

NG

PROSSER (GB) 1922

Prosser Automobile Co. Ltd, Birmingham.

This car was announced in July 1922 and seems to have had a very short life. It was a conventional light car, powered by a 10.5hp 4-cylinder Coventry-Simplex engine, with Wrigley gearbox and shaft drive. It had disc wheels and was available with 2- or 4-seater open bodies.

NG

PROTEA (ZA) 1957–c.1958

G.R.P. Engineering (Pty) Ltd, Crown Mines, Johannesburg.

Named after a flower of South African origin, this was a small sports car with fibreglass body by Collins & Myers of Johannesburg, powered by a 1172cc Ford 100E engine. The prototype was shown at Johannesburg's Spring Motor Show in 1957, with production expected to start in April. A slightly revised model was made for 1958, when the cars could be supplied engineless, the power unit being chosen by the customer. These included Fiat 1100, MG and Ford Zephyr.

1906 Prosper Lambert 16hp 2-seater.
NATIONAL MOTOR MUSEUM

1957 Protea sports car.
M. PURCHASE

1989 Proton 1.5SE Aeroback hatchback.
R.M.COMMUNICATIONS

They were raced with some success in 1957 and 1958. About 20 were made, of which one survives.

NG

PROTON (PTM) 1985 to date

Perusahaan Otomobil Nacional Sdn Bhd, Selangor.

The first car to be built in Malaysia, the Proton Saga was based on the MITSUBISHI Lancer and was made in 4-door saloon and 5-door hatchback forms, with 1.3- or 1.5-litre 4-cylinder engines. Production began on a small scale in the autumn of 1985, and exports to Europe started towards the end of 1988. In 1989 Great Britain was the largest export market, taking 77 per cent, with Ireland second and New Zealand third. Production rose from 24,200 in 1987 to about 80,000 two years later, and in 1998 it had reached 180,000.

Bodies were styled and built in Selangor, and local content accounted initially for 42 per cent of the ex-factory value of the car, a proportion which rose in succeeding years. Protons were well-equipped for their price, top-of-the-range models having power steering, central locking and electric windows as standard.

1998 Proton Persona 2.0TDi hatchback.
R.M.COMMUNICATIONS

1905 Protos landaulet.
HANS-OTTO NEUBAUER

1912 Protos 6-cylinder tourer.
HANS-OTTO NEUBAUER

1921 Protos Typ C 10/30PS tourer by Königstadt.
HANS-OTTO NEUBAUER

Protons have continued to be Mitsubishi-derived, though with considerable individuality in styling. The Persona, introduced in 1993, was derived from the Colt, and came in saloon, Compact 3-door hatchback and coupé form with four petrol engine options, 1299, 1468, 1597 and 1834cc, the latter with 16-valve engine developing 116bhp, as well as a 1998cc turbo-diesel. An all-new Persona was planned for 2000, developed entirely in-house, though still using Mitsubishi-derived engines in the same sizes as before. One size up from the Persona was the Perdana, introduced in 1996, with 126bhp 1997cc engine, available in 4-door saloon form only.

In 2000 the Compact and Persona were renamed Sabria and Wira, respectively.
NG

PROTOS (D) 1900–1926

1900–1904 Motorenfabrik Protos Dr Alfred Sternberg, Berlin.
1904–1908 Motorenfabrik Protos GmbH, Berlin.
1908–1926 Siemens-Schuckert Werke GmbH, Automobilwerk Nonnendam, Berlin.
Alfred Sternberg made small petrol engines for stationary purposes for several years before he began to make cars. His first was a light voiturette with single-cylinder engine, followed by one using his Kompens-Motor; this consisted of two working cylinders and a third one set at 180 degrees to the others and containing a freely operating piston to prevent uneven running. It was made from 1903 to 1905, when it was replaced by a conventional 4-cylinder T-head engine, the 4560cc 17/35PS. Also in 1905 Protos built a remarkable 100bhp 6-cylinder engine, although this did not go into production, it was followed by a line of sixes which earned the firm a very good reputation. The German Crown Prince Wilhelm was a satisfied customer of Protos. The company gained international fame when a 17/35PS was driven into second place in the New York-Paris race of 1908. In that year Protos was taken over by the large electrical concern Siemens-Schuckert. Production was concentrated on the 4560cc 18/42PS, developed from the 17/35PS, and the 6-cylinder 6840cc 26/50PS, although smaller models were made as well. These included the 1570cc 6/18PS and 2190cc 8/21PS (1910–1914). These 4-cylinder L-head cars were designed by Dr Ernest Valentin, who came from the Belgian NAGANT company.

After the war Protos concentrated on a single model, the 30bhp 2614cc Typ C. This was similar to prewar Valentin designs, but had the vee-radiator seen on all German cars in the early 1920s. It was developed into the more powerful 45bhp Typ C1 in 1924. These were not only used as private cars, but as the basis for high-speed delivery vans. A number of them serviced the Baltic seaside resorts with the latest newspapers from Berlin during the summer months. In 1926 Siemens sold Protos to another big electrical concern, AEG, who already had a car marque, the NAG. The Protos C1 was continued for a year as the NAG-Protos, and other models carried this title up to 1933.
HON

Further Reading
Autos aus Berlin-Protos und NAG, Hans-Otto Neubauer,
Verlag W. Kohlhammer GmbH, 1983.

PROTOTEC (US) c.1991

Prototec Industries, West Palm Beach, Florida.
The Ferrosa was a Pontiac Fiero-based kit car that resembled a shrunken Ferrari Testarossa. They were sold in kit and fully assembled form.
HP

PROTOTYPE RESEARCH *see* PRD

PROVA (GB) 1986 to date

Prova Designs Ltd, Darwen, Lancashire.
The first truly convincing Lamborghini Countach replica in the world, the Prova was created by Paul Lawrenson on a modified Ultima chassis. The bodywork was based on the VENOM shell (itself taken from a genuine Countach). This was also the first Countach copy to gain proper replica interior panels. Renault V6 power was used with a Renault transaxle, but later options included Rover V8 and Ford small block V8 power. On the same chassis Prova also built the ZL from 1989, a replica of the Lamborghini Miura. Prova emerged as probably the world's leading Countach replica firm.
CR

PROVINCIAL (GB) 1904–c.1905

Provincial Electric Construction Co. Ltd, Liverpool.

1913 Protos limousine with General Huerta, President of Mexico.
HANS-OTTO NEUBAUER

This company offered conventional assembled cars, possibly of LACOSTE ET BATTMANN origin, a 2-seater with 6½hp single-cylinder engine, and a 4-seater tonneau with 12hp 2-cylinder engine. They were shown at the 1904 Liverpool Show, but there is little evidence of them after that.

NG

PRUNEL (F) 1900–1907

Sté des Usines Prunel, Puteaux, Seine.

J. Prunel set up his business early in 1900, making a voiturette with 3½hp De Dion-Bouton engine and chain drive. Initially this was not sold as a Prunel but as an Atlas, by E.J. Brierre who also sold cars under his own name. By 1902 the name Prunel was being used, and at the 1902 Paris Salon he was exhibiting a 6hp car called the Indispensible, with Aster or De Dion engines, as well as a 9hp 1ton van. From 1903 onwards a variety of proprietary engines was offered, by Aster, De Dion, Herald, Pieper and Mutel, in sizes from a 9hp single to a 24hp four, although the company claimed to make every component except for the engine themselves. The Mutel-engined 24hp had a capacity of 3.8 litres, automatic inlet valves and chain drive. In 1905 the largest engine was a 4942cc 24/30hp, and in 1906 a 40/50hp.

From around 1905 cars were offered under a number of different names, though probably all came from the same factory. They were marketed in England under the names Gnome, Gracile, and J.P., the latter made by Automobiles J. Prunello, Prunello Frères, Dumas et Cie. Their address was in the same street in Puteaux as that of Prunel, so it was clearly the same concern, though why an Italian form of the name should suddenly appear is not known. In 1905 they offered cars from 10 to 40hp with shaft or chain drive. No cars seem to have been made after 1907, although the PHENIX was built in the Prunel factory from 1912 to 1914.

NG

1902 Prunel 2-cylinder runabout.
NATIONAL MOTOR MUSEUM

P.T.V. (E) 1955–1963

Automoviles Utilitarios SA, Manresa, Barcelona.

The P.T.V. microcar was a little more sophisticated than the Biscuter with which it competed, notably boasting independent suspension all round and hydraulic brakes. The fibreglass bodywork was almost sports car-like, with two seats and a convertible roof, and early cars had no doors. The engine was mounted in the tail and early examples had a 10bhp A.U.S.A. single-cylinder 247cc alloy-head

1958 P.T.V. 250cc 2-seater.
NICK GEORGANO/NATIONAL MOTOR MUSEUM

c.1912 Puch Typ V 17/42PS roadster.
NATIONAL MOTOR MUSEUM

2-stroke engine – maximum speed 43mph (69km/h) – but gradually engines increased in size: 350cc single-cylinder and 396cc twin-cylinder units were later available, the latter offered with a Rotativo supercharger. Around 1250 cars were built in all, and the company went on to produce fork-lift and dumper trucks.

CR

PUBLI-RÉTRO (F) 1983–c.1984
Publi-Rétro, Aix-en-Provence.
M. Cassoulet offered a kit replica of the Citroën 11 Traction Avant Cabriolet using original Traction mechanicals, wings and bonnet. The rest of the bodywork was in fibreglass.

CR

PUBLIX (US/CDN) 19847–1948
Publix Motor Car Co., Buffalo, New York; Fort Erie, Ontario.
This 3-wheeled convertible coupé had an aluminium body and chassis. Only 72in (1827mm) long, it was powered by an air-cooled 1.75hp Cauffel engine driving the rear wheels. The steering wheel could be moved from the left-hand side to the right-hand side.

NG

PUCH (A) 1906–1925
1906–1914 Johann Puch Erste Steiermärkische Fahrradfabriks-AG, Graz.
1914–1925 Puchwerke AG, Graz.
Johann Puch (1862–1914) was a successful manufacturer of bicycles (from 1891 to 1897 when he sold his business to the German firm which would later make DÜRKOPP cars) and motorcycles (from 1900). He built a prototype car in 1900, and another in 1903 after studying several French designs, but neither of these went into production as he was too busy making motorcycles. The first production Puch car came in 1906; it was a 2-seater with a 904cc 8/9PS V-twin engine, and was followed by the slightly larger 1135cc 9/10PS in 1908, also made in sports form. After 1908 4-cylinder models were made, and in 1912 Puch acquired a licence for the Knight sleeve-valve engine. This was used in the 4082cc 16/40 and 6898cc 27/60PS cars. They were not made for long, and in 1913 Puch brought out his most successful model, the 1560cc side-valve Alpenwagen. This was revived after the war and made until 1923. A smaller Alpenwagen with 1588cc engine was made from 1919 to 1920 only.

Car production was given up in 1925 in favour of motorcycles; in 1928 Puch merged with AUSTRO-DAIMLER and in 1934 with STEYR to form Steyr-

Daimler-Puch AG. Motorcycles were made in the Puch factory for many years, and from 1979 they made the G Series 4×4 vehicles for MERCEDES-BENZ, which were sold on some markets under the Puch name.

HON

PUCKETT AUTO WORKS (US) c.1995

Puckett Auto Works, Lakeside, California.

The P-250-GTO was a replica of the Series I Ferrari 250 GTO. They were sold in assembled form starting at $34,900 advertised with up to 600hp.

HP

PUCKRIDGE (AUS) 1904

F.B. Puckridge Cycle Works, Port Lincoln, South Australia.

Previously shown on some lists as KINMONT, the name of its owner, this little vehicle used a 2.75hp M.M.C. engine previously fitted to a motor-tricycle. A Longuemare carburettor superseded the previous surface system and a clutch and 2-speed transmission was fitted. Final drive was by belts and the steering was by a tiller. It could have been known as the Pride as that was the brand-name Fred Puckridge applied to the cycles and Minerva-engined motor-bicycles he made.

MG

PULCINO (I) 1948

Antonio Artesi, Palermo.

The first car to be built in Sicily following World War II, the Pulcino was a mature-looking microcar. Based on a cross-braced tubular chassis, the steel doorless open body had an American feel to it. It was powered by a rear-mounted 125cc 2-stroke single-cylinder engine driving via chain. The 2-seater project found no financial backing, however.

CR

PULGA (E) 1952

Onteniente, Alicante.

This was a very small 3-wheeler.

VCM

PULI (H) 1990–c.1997

1987–1991 Hódgép, Hódmez vásárhely.

1991–c.1997 Puli Járm és Gépgyártó Kft, Hódmez vásárhely.

Hódgép made agricultural machines but by the mid–1980s they were in deep crisis: outdated products combined with a slowly vanishing market both in Hungary and in all the COMECON countries. They noticed (not for the first time in Hungarian automotive history) the lack of a locally-made, cheap automobile, and they realized that in France, microcars, mainly used for shopping, were increasingly popular and that if they could make a good-quality microcar they would have an ace in their hands! It never happened. The first prototypes were powered by noisy Yanmar diesel engines. Soon these were replaced by Lombardini petrol units which were more efficient and produced less emission. But the quality of the Pulis (named after a popular Hungarian sheep dog) were still not up to expectations. Possible German and Swiss dealers asked for electric versions, and that was when the car-making arm became independent; the new company updated the car, with their own 9.9bhp (7.4kW) electric engines, and sent them abroad. But they arrived too late, and French models looked more stylish, and they were cheaper. Only a fraction of the export quantity was materialized. Making electric versions of the outdated Ukranian ZAZ Tavrija was not a succesful move at all. The company struggled for years, but the Hungarian government denied tax advantages for Pulis so they were insanely expensive. The Budapest Electric Co. and the Mayor's Office bought some, probably to demonstrate their helpfulness. The company finally went into receivership in 1997.

PN

PULLCAR (GB) 1906–1908

Pullcar Motor Co. Ltd, Preston, Lancashire.

Designed by J.S. Critchley who was also responsible for the first CROSSLEY, this was an unconventional design using originally a 12/14hp Fafnir and later a 15.9hp White & Poppe engine transversely-mounted under the seat and driving the front wheels through a 3-speed epicyclic gearbox. The first examples

c.1990 Puli microcar (sold in Switzerland as the Pinguin).
NICK GEORGANO

1908 Pullcar 15.9HP victoria.
NATIONAL MOTOR MUSEUM

had pneumatic tyres at the front and solids at the rear. These were taxicabs and more Pullcars were built for this work than as private cars. They were licensed by the Metropolitan Police for use in London, though few ran there.

NG

PULLMAN (US) 1903–1917

1903 Broomell, Schmidt & Steacy, York, Pennsylvania.

1905–1909 York Motor Car Co., York, Pennsylvania.

1909–1917 Pullman Motor Car Co., York, Pennsylvania.

The first car to bear the Pullman name was quite different from any of the others. Designed by A.P. Broomell, it was a 6-wheeler powered by a 2-cylinder engine which drove the centre pair of wheels. The front and rear pair turned in opposite directions for steering. It was built in the workshops of the Harding company, and is sometimes known as the Harding. It was not a success, and two years later Broomell added two cylinders, deleted two wheels and made a conventional car which was initially called the YORK (i). However, production models were all Pullmans.

The first to be offered to the public was an 18/20hp 4-seater surrey, of which just 13 were sold in 1905. Larger engines of 24/28 and 30/35hp were used in 1906 when production reached 273. The president was Broomell's friend Sam Baily and the designer was James Kline until he and Baily left in 1908 to make the KLINE KAR. A 40hp four was made in 1907 and a 30hp six in 1908, but the company was in difficulties and was rescued by financiers from New York, who changed the name to Pullman Motor Car Co. They dropped the 30hp six, although a larger six of 60hp and 8½-litres came in 1912 and was made up to 1914. Pullman cars were sold far afield and in 1911 one won three gold medals at an Exposition at Rostov on Don in Russia. Production reached a peak of 4136 in 1915, when the Cutler-Hammer push-button magnetic gear change was offered, but at the cost of quality, and the Pullman's reputation suffered. A line

1910 Pullman 35hp tourer.
NICK GEORGANO

of smaller and cheaper cars called Pullman Junior, with 22.4hp 4-cylinder G.B. & S. engines was introduced in 1916, but it could not save the firm. Pullman was bankrupt in December 1916, and the 1213 cars sold in 1917 were assembled from parts on hand. Some parts must have been sold to England, as from 1922 to 1925 a car called the London-Pullman, with the same G. B.& S. engine and British bodies, was sold by a firm in Hampstead.

NG

Further Reading
History of the York Pullman, William H. Shank,
The Historical Society of York County, 1970.

PULLMAN FLYER (US) 1907–1908
Pullman Motor Car Co., Chicago, Illinois.
This company was a well-known dealer and the cars they offered under the name Pullman Flyer were made for them by the MODEL Automobile Co. of Peru, Indiana. They were large cars with 7-litre 4-cylinder engines rated at 45/50hp, and made in tourer, limousine and 'speed car' models. A six was also available.

NG

PULSAR (i) (GB) 1978–1982
1978–1980 Mirage Developments, Biggin Hill, Kent.
1980–1982 M.R. Developments, Trowbridge, Wiltshire.
The CONCEPT Centaur Mk II passed on to new owners to become the Pulsar 2. Based on the Hillman Imp, it had 2+2 seating, or there was a lower 2-seater version called the Pulsar 3. Ford and Mini engine conversion kits were offered from 1981.

CR

PULSAR (ii) (GB) 1984–1987
1984–1985 Amplas, Chalgrove, Oxfordshire.
1985–1987 Lemazone, Leigh, Lancashire.
This was a not terribly convincing Porsche 911 lookalike based on VW Beetle parts. The fibreglass full convertible body sat on a box section steel chassis with subframes front and rear. Optional Carrera and Turbo bodykits were listed. The Pulsar was developed by Amplas but was soon assumed by Lemazone, which also offered the ex-SN1 in modified form as the Pulsar Comet.

CR

PUMA (i) (BR) 1967–1984
Puma Veiculos e Motores Ltda, São Paulo.
The success of the GT Malzoni, built in 1965 and 1966 round the mechanical elements of the 3-cylinder front-wheel drive D.K.W. made under licence by Vemag in Brazil, prompted Rino Malzoni, Milton Masteguin, Jorge Lettry and Anisio Campos, to create the Puma GT.

Like the GT Malzoni, the Puma, designed by Anisio Campos, was built round D.K.W. mechanical components. But in 1967, after only 135 cars had been made, Volkswagen do Brasil acquired Vemag. Then the group turned their attention to the 1500cc rear-engined Brazilian Volkswagen platform on which a sport coupé body, made in fibreglass was fashioned for the Puma GT. The Puma 4R was a limited production design, more radically styled, of which only three units were made in 1968. By 1969 all the cars had acquired disc front brakes and the option of the 68bhp, 1600cc engine of the Puma 4R. During 1971 the 1600 went on sale in Switzerland. For 1973 a new range of front-engined Pumas was added, with 4-cylinder 2.5-litre or 6-cylinder 4.1-litre Chevrolet engines.

1979 Puma (i) GTE sports car.
NICK BALDWIN

In 1975 Puma announced a city car, with a total length of 105in (2665mm), styled by Milton Masteguin, and powered by a 760cc ohv air-cooled flat-twin engine driving the front wheel. By 1979 the GTB was offered only as a six. The GTB and the 1.6-litre VW-based coupés and cabriolets made up the range in the 1980s. Production stopped in 1984 after about 50,000 vehicles had been made.

ACT

Further Reading
'Brazil's Puma GT: Bossa Nova on Wheels', Karl E. Ludvigsen,
Automobile Quarterly, Vol. 7, No. 4.

PUMA (ii) **(I)** 1979–c.1996
Puma SNC, Bagni di Tivoli, Roma.
Puma began making beach buggies as early as 1968 but it became a more serious car manufacturer when it agreed licensed production of the British NOVA. The Puma GTV was a lightly modified version, keeping the rear-engined VW Beetle basis, although it did develop a separate tubular chassis designed for Fiat power. The revised 1984 GTV-033 version, with conventional doors instead of the usual canopy, had the option of rear-mounted Alfasud power, while another version called the ETV had a Volkswagen 1.4-litre engine. Eventually the Puma could also be fitted with front-mounted engines. By 1991 a new version called the Boxer 90 was in production with a rear-mounted 105bhp 1.5-litre Alfa 33 engine. It was again revised with updated styling in 1994 and renamed the 248. Less successful was a further model, the short-lived Ranch of 1981, a jeep lookalike based on the VW Beetle chassis.

CR

PUMA (iii) **(F)** 1981–1982
M.D.P. Transmission, Neaufles St Martin.
This firm acquired the rights to the 50cc microcars made by VITREX, but the only model it revived was the Garbo, which was sold with a new name, Puma.

CR

PUMA (iv) **(US)** c.1982
Puma Motor Corp. of North America, San Jose, California.
The Project Puma was an off-road vehicle with a stylish aluminium body. It looked like a cleaner and lower version of the Jeep, but featured 4-wheel drive and Porsche or VW powertrains. They were sold in kit or fully assembled form.

HP

PUNGS-FINCH (US) 1904–1910
Pungs-Finch Auto & Gas Engine Co., Detroit, Michigan.
This car was made by W.A. Pungs and his son-in-law E.B. Finch who was the designer. They bought out the Sintz Gas Engine Co. and built the first few Pungs-Finches in the Sintz factory. They had 14hp 2-cylinder engines and shaft drive. 20 and 24hp 4-cylinder models followed for 1905 and 1906, but the latter year saw an enormous car with 8652cc 4-cylinder engine which featured hemispherical combustion chambers and a gear-driven single-ohc. It was called the Finch Limited and was offered in roadster or tourer form at $3000 and $3500 respectively. Only the roadster was made, and fortunately it still survives.

Pungs and his son-in-law parted company in 1908; Finch went to work for CHALMERS, later becoming a Chalmers dealer in Cleveland. Pungs carried on, making 4-cylinder cars from 22 to 50hp, but gave up in 1910.

NG

Further Reading
'Pungs-Finch Indeed!', Beverly Rae Kimes,
Automobile Quarterly, Vol. 8, No. 1.

PUP (US) 1948–1949
Pup Motor Car Co., Spencer, Wisconsin.
The Pup was a tiny economy car with no doors and a single-cylinder air-cooled engine. With 7.5hp it was not very quick but mileage per gallon was excellent. In 1949 a canvas top and side curtains were offered. The body was made of wood and a rubber bumper surrounded the entire car. Also in 1949, a 2-cylinder engine with 10hp replaced the original single.

HP

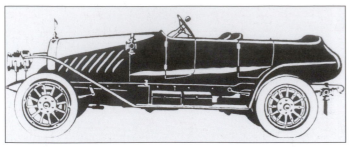

1912 Puzyrev 20/40 tourer.

PURITAN (i) **(US)** 1902–1905

Puritan Motor Car Co., Salem, Massachusetts.

Albert N. Locke ran the Locke Regulator Co. but formed a separate organisation to make the steam car he had designed, although it was made in the Locke Regulator factory. It was powered by a 6hp vertical 2-cylinder engine, with single-chain drive. Two advanced features for 1902 were a foot throttle and a steering wheel in place of the usual tiller. Moreover, the column could be folded forward to allow easy entry. Locke considered making petrol cars in 1904 but thought better of it and imported the WADDINGTON from England instead.

NG

PURITAN (ii) **(US)** 1913–1914

Puritan Motor Co., Chicago, Illinois.

This was a typical cyclecar, although the use of epicyclic rather than friction-disc transmission was somewhat unusual. The engine was a 10hp V-twin De Luxe, and final drive was by belt. The body was a streamlined side by side 2-seater.

NG

PUTOL (GB) c.1922

Tolputt & Co., Sheffield, Yorkshire.

This company claimed to make cars, engines and aeroplanes, but the only evidence for the car is a listing in *The Motor Car Red Book* for 1922 for a 1742cc 10/18hp 4-cylinder car priced at £575.

NG

PUZYREV (RUS) 1909–1914

Russkji Avtomobilnji Zavod I.P. Puzyrev, St Petersburg.

The first car by the Russian Automobile Works was built in 1911, the model 28/35 with a 5.13-litre engine and a 4-speed gearbox. Puzyrevs were mechanically sound and reliable, the overall quantity of cars with different bodywork is believed to surpass 30. A major factory fire of 1914 destroyed a number of semi-completed cars and numerous components ready for assembly. It was the end of the financially troubled make. Ivan Puzyrev died in September, 1914.

MHK

P. VALLÉE (F) 1952–1957

1952–1954 P. Vallée, Blois, Loir-et-Cher.

1954–1957 Sté Colas, Blois, Loir-et-Cher.

These shapely and lavishly equipped minicars generally used the 125cc Ydral motorcycle engine and gearbox, falling into the classification of light vehicles then requiring no driving licence. Suspension was by rubber in compression. Tiny wheels and 'dodgem car' lines did not encourage buyers to consider them as practical everyday transport and production was spasmodic. A revised version named the Chantecler, with the option of a 175cc motor, met with no better success.

DF

PYRAMID (US) 1914

Payne's Engineering Co., Chiswick, London.

This was a typical cyclecar powered by an 8hp V-twin JAP engine, with friction transmission and belt final drive. Its price was £125.

NG

PYTHON (i) **(AUS)** 1981 to date

G.V. Automotive, South Melbourne, Victoria.

In 1980 George Vidovick obtained moulds for a replica fibreglass Cobra body from Arntz in the United States, and has made the twin-skin bodies since. It was built on a box-section ladder frame of 2311mm wheelbase with Jaguar rear suspension, and Ford V8 engines of 4.7- to 7-litres were fitted. In 1997 his R 302 race car, with 378bhp, was admitted to the marque racing category.

MG

PYTHON (ii) **(GB)** 1981–1993

Unique Autocraft, Harlow, Essex.

Born out of Pete & Mart's Rod & Custom, Unique Autocraft took a different tack to Cobra replication with the Python. The chassis was not a Cobra clone but a very sturdy box section steel chassis that allowed the cockpit to be two inches longer than standard. Suspension was all-independent by Jaguar XJ, and engines ranged from Ford V6 to big block V8.

CR

Q.C.E. (US) c.1996 to date

Quality Construction & Engineering, Jay, Oklahoma.
Although they also sold Cobra and Ferrari F-40 replicas, Q.C.E. was best known for its advanced VW-based kit, initially called the McLela. It was quickly renamed the Blaze and went on to become one of the most popular VW-based kits. Designed by Australian Ray Lambard, it had styling elements from the Acura NSX and the McLaren F-1, but was scaled to work on the shorter VW platform. It was a simple kit to assemble. A similar kit, the Q.C.E. Spyder, was introduced that used a tubular frame with a mid-mounted General Motors V6 engine and Ford Mustang front suspension. They were sold in kit and turn-key form.
HP

QIGUAN (CHI) 1995

Kunshan Small Auto Works, Kunshan City, Jiangsu Province.
The Qiguan ('Wonder') JTZ 6420 sedan was a fibreglass-reinforced plastic-bodied small motor car. At least two different versions were made.
EVIS

1995 Qiguan JT 26420 saloon.
ERIK VAN INGEN SCHENAU

QILIN (CHI) 1999 to date

Pan Asia Technical Automotive Center, Shanghai Municipality.
In 1997 the Shanghai Automotive Industry Corp. and General Motors of America jointly invested in an automotive technology centre. Its first concept car was named Qilin, which stands for a mythological unicorn in Chinese legends. With a comparatively high chassis, the car was ideal for the road conditions in the countryside. The 5-door Qilin had front-wheel drive and allowed seating for up to five people. GM started assembly in Shanghai in 1999 with the Shanghai GM Buick series, which featured a 2.98-litre V6 engine coupled with an electronically controlled automatic transmission. A 7-seat W-Wagon mini-van was the second product rolled out by Shanghai GM.
EVIS

QINCHUAN (CHI) 1987 to date

State Operated Qinchuan Machinery Works, Xi'an City, Shaanxi Province.
This Army factory belongs to the Beifan (China North) Corp. Its first automotive product was the Qinchuan SX 720, later named QCJ 7050. This was a very small Daihatsu-powered mini-car (547cc/27.6bhp). It delivered a maximum speed of 56mph (90km/h). A total of approximately 500 were made.

In 1992 the factory introduced their licence-produced Suzuki Alto, the Qinchuan QCJ 7080, also sold as Beifan Alto and Xi'an Alto. Other motor cars made in 1997–98 were the QCJ 7081 hatchback and the QCJ 7082 saloon. The ZHONGHUA QCJ 7090 was registered as made by this factory, but production took place in the Zhonghua factory in Beijing. The FUXING QCJ 7085, designed under the authorisation of the Beifan Vehicle Research Institute was trial-produced in the Qinchuan factory in 1998.
EVIS

QINXING (CHI) 1996

Jinyang Qinxing Auto Works, Jingyang County, Shaanxi Province.
The Qinxing QX 6401 bore a strong resemblance to a mini-Shanghai Volkswagen Santana.
EVIS

QUADRANT (GB) 1906–1907

Quadrant Cycle Co. Ltd, Birmingham.
Quadrant was a pioneer British motorcycle manufacturer, making their first 2-wheeler in 1900. They were best-known for these and for tricars, but made a few 4-wheeled cars with 14/16 or 20/22hp 4-cylinder White & Poppe engines. Motorcycles were made until 1927.
NG

QUAGLIOTTI (I) 1904

Auto Garage Quagliotti, Turin.
Carlo Quagliotti built motorcycles, mainly Peugeot-powered, from 1902 to 1907, and also assembled a few cars using single-cylinder De Dion-Bouton or Aster engines, A larger car with 16hp 4-cylinder Aster engine was planned, but may never have been built.
NG

1996 Qinxing QX6401 saloon.
ERIK VAN INGEN SCHENAU

QUAIFE (GB) 1998 to date

Quaife Transmissions Ltd, Wokingham, Berkshire.
Quaife, well known for producing specialist transmissions for competition vehicles, unveiled the exotic GT-R at the January 1998 Autosport Show to announce its intent to race in the British GT Championship series. To qualify to compete in the Championship, Quaife also opened the order book for road-going versions of the GT-R, with an introductory price tag of £65,000. The GT-R used a mid-mounted Peugeot V6 engine, mated to one of the company's own transmissions.
CR

QUANTUM (i) (US) 1962–1963

Quantum Corp., Rockland, Massachusetts.
The fibreglass-bodied sports car was based on SAAB running gear. This preceded the first production Saab Sonnet by 5 years. Power was by the 3-cylinder 850GT engine and the Saab sedan chassis was shortened by 12in. They were sold in fully assembled form by Saab dealers. Quantum also built a line of successful Saab-based racing cars.
HP

QUANTUM (ii) (GB) 1988 to date

Quantum Sports Cars, Stourbridge, West Midlands.
The Quantum was a very thoroughly designed product using a fibreglass monocoque chassis, designed to use Ford Fiesta Mk I/II components and any Fiesta engine, up to the RS Turbo. There was modified Fiesta front suspension and four seats. A 2+2 Convertible arrived in 1992 (using a steel front subframe) and a revised front end was added in 1993. The H4 was an all-new design launched in 1997, a targa-topped sports car using a full chassis sandwiched into the fibreglass bodyshell, based on Fiesta Mk III mechanicals. The Quantum was

1990 Quantum Series 2 coupé.
QUANTUM SPORTS CARS

1968 Quasar-Unipower city car.
NICK GEORGANO

a sales success in kit car terms, as over 700 had been made by 1998. A further model was added when the Lotus 7-style SAVANT was assumed in 1998, and renamed the Xtreme.

CR

QUASAR-UNIPOWER (GB) 1968
Universal Power Drives Ltd, Perivale, Middlesex.
This extraordinary machine was made by the makers of the UNIPOWER GT but could hardly have been more different. Designed by a Vietnamese-born Paris-based fashion designer called N'Guyen Manh 'Quasar' Khan'h, it was essentially a glass cube on wheels. A metal tube frame held sliding toughened glass panels (on at least one version also sliding at the front), while the roof was made of heat-absorbing tinted glass. There were even transparent seats on one model. Into the steel tube chassis were fitted widened Mini subframes, a B.M.C. 1100 engine at the rear, automatic transmission and Mini wheels. It measured 64in (1624mm) long by 66in (1675mm) wide by 74in (1878mm) tall.

CR

QUATEX see E3D

QUDOS (GB) 1980s
This was an A.C. Cobra 427 replica made in Scotland during the late 1980s.

CR

QUEEN (i) (CDN) 1901–1903
Queen City Cycle & Motor Works, Toronto, Ontario.
This company was a well-known producer of bicycles, their products including a tandem that could be steered by either rider. Their car was a folding-front 4- seater powered by an 823cc single-cylinder engine mounted under the seat. Apparently it performed badly, with a throttle that was controlled only by the spark and a clutch so fierce that passengers were sometimes thrown out of the car. In 1903 the company president Cornelius Ryerson gave up on the Queen and bought a Cadillac. Possibly no more than one Queen was built, although enough parts had been made for several.

NG

QUEEN (ii) (US) 1904–1906
C.H. Blomstrom Co., Detroit, Michigan.
Blomstrom built 25 small cars under his own name before changing the name of the product to Queen. It was a runabout powered by a single or 2-cylinder engine, also offered as a detachable tonneau model. For 1905 the single-cylinder was dropped and a 24hp four added, other models being 12 and 16hp 2-cylinder cars. These had their flat-twin engines under the front seat, with 2-speed epicyclic transmission and single-chain drive, while the 24hp engine was mounted at the front under a bonnet with 3-speed gearbox and shaft drive. For 1906 the single was discontinued, but the others were continued, the 4-cylinder engine now being quoted as a 26/28hp, and on a wheelbase 4in longer at 100in (2538mm). The 1906s were the last Queens, for in August that year C.H. Blomstrom merged his

1905 Queen (ii) 16hp tonneau.
NATIONAL MOTOR MUSEUM

company with CAR DE LUXE, and set up the Blomstrom Manufacturing Co. elsewhere in Detroit to make cars under his own name again. He would later be involved with several other makes, the GYROSCOPE, REX and FRONTMOBILE. Production of the Queen was about 1500 cars.

NG

QUENTIN (F) 1908–1912
Quentin et Cie, Levallois-Perret, Seine.
This motorcycle maker built a few cars with single-cylinder engines and shaft drive to a rear axle without differential.

NG

QUEST (GB) 1969–1970
The Explorer Motor Co., London.
Few cars can have as unlikely a background as the Quest. The creator of the *Thunderbirds* TV series, Gerry Anderson, produced a film in 1968 called *Doppelgänger* and asked Alan Mann Racing to make three Derek Meddings-designed cars for the set. Under these space-age gullwing door 4-seater cars lurked nothing more futuristic than a Ford Zephyr chassis powered by a Cortina GT engine. Ford was interested enough in the project to bring Graham Hill to be photographed alongside one car. The design was subsequently purchased by David Lowes, who intended to make fibreglass-bodied replicas on Zephyr chassis under the name Quest with such gimmicks as fibre-optic warning lights and a radioactive illuminated dash. The plan foundered and the prototypes re-emerged in the *UFO* TV series.

CR

QUICK (US) 1899–1900
1899–1900 H.M. Quick, Paterson, New Jersey.
1900 Quick Manufacturing Co., Newark, New Jersey.
The Quick was a light 2-seater runabout with 4hp horizontal 2-cylinder engine and chain drive, with suspension by transverse full-elliptic springs. Production

1900 Quick 4hp runabout.
NATIONAL MOTOR MUSEUM

of one car per day was announced in December 1899, but it is not known if this figure was maintained for long.

NG

QUINBY (US) 1899–1900
J.M. Quinby & Co., Newark, New Jersey.
This was a leading nineteenth century American coachbuilder, having been founded in 1834. For two years they built electric carriages to order, then turned to coachwork on cars, though horse-drawn carriages were continued for a while. Quinby closed down as coachbuilders in 1917.

NG

QUINCY-LYNN (US) 1975 to date

Quincy-Lynn Enterprises, Inc., Phoenix, Arizona.
Robert Q. Riley Enterprises, Scottsdale, Arizona.
Although they did not build cars or kits themselves, this company sold a very popular line of plan sets to build a wide assortment of vehicles. Partners Robert Q. Riley and David L. Carey designed cars that could be built from scratch with bodies sculpted from foam and fibreglass. A variety of chassis and running gear were possible, including tiny, fuel-efficient diesels to electric/hybrid powerplants. One of their most popular plan sets was the Centurion, a front-engined sports-economy car built on a Triumph Spitfire chassis with a 17hp Kubota diesel engine. The Tri-Magnum was a high-performance 3-wheeler, and the Trimuter was a smoothly aerodynamic trike with electric or petrol power. The Town Car was a 4-wheeled 2-seat economy car with a hybrid electric/petrol power plant. The Urba Car was an angular petrol-powered sedan that achieved 50mpg. The Urba Electric was an electric car with a lift-up cockpit section, and the Urba Trike was a motorcycle-based electric vehicle with open bodywork and motorcycle-style steering. Quincy-Lynn also sold a series of van and camper plans including the Phoenix, which was a small van that expanded like a tent trailer into a large camper with room to sleep four. The Boonie Bug was based on a VW chassis and had lots of room inside its box-style body. The MiniHome was a camper back that attached to a cut-down VW Beetle. Plan sets for these vehicles were also frequently available from *Mechanix Illustrated* magazine. Quincy-Lynn also sold plans for boats, bicycles and mini-submarines. Robert Q. Riley took over the plan business and continued selling them through an internet website featuring alternative vehicles.

HP

QUINSLER (US) 1904

Quinsler & Co., Boston, Massachusetts.
Quinsler were carriage builders who made some hansom cabs for the Electric Vehicle Co., makers of the COLUMBIA (i). For 1904 only, they made a light car powered by a front-mounted 7hp single-cylinder De Dion-Bouton engine. It had a 2-seater body with a rather precarious-looking dickey seat for a third passenger. The price was $950, rather high for such a small car.

NG

QUINT (US) 1986–1989

Quint Industries, San Diego, California.
This kit car company bought two projects from ELITE Enterprises. They were the Laser 917, a pseudo-Porsche 917 replica based on a VW floorpan, and an Allard J2X replica. The Quint Laser 917 was also sold with a simple tubular frame that mounted Porsche, Mazda rotary or V8 engines. Their Allard replica used a steel frame with V8 engines and VW front suspension, which for once was better than the suspension the original came with. Naturally, they also had a Cobra replica called the Laser Cobra built along familiar lines with Mustang suspension and V8 power. In 1989 Quint sold their kits to HARDY Motors, who dropped the Laser 917 but continued to sell the Allard for some time.

HP

QUO VADIS (i) (F) 1900–c.1902

Laurent et Touzet, Lyons.
This was a light car powered by a 2-cylinder Aster engine driving the front wheels. It was an *avant train* design with centre-pivot steering, a primitive and largely outmoded system even in 1900.

NG

QUO VADIS (ii) (F) 1921–1923

Automobiles Quo Vadis, Courbevoie, Seine.
The second French car to bear the name Quo Vadis was described as 'une voiture légère de grande luxe' but was probably no more than the usual cyclecar of the period.

NG

QVALE (I) 2000 to date

Qvale Modena, Modena.
This company was formed by Americans Bruce and Jeff Qvale, sons of Kjell Qvale who was behind the Jensen-Healey and owned Jensen for a while in the 1970s. They acquired the rights to make the 4.6-litre Ford V8-powered De Tomaso Mangusta in their own new factory. It was marketed as a Qvale Mangusta and initial sales were to be to the US, with the European market being tackled in 2001.

NG

c.1922 Rabag-Bugatti 6/30PS sports car.
HALWART SCHRADER

RABA (H) 1904–1925

Magyar Waggon- és Gépgyár Rt, Györ.

The Hungarian Wagon and Machine Factory was established in 1896 by Austrian investors to manufacture railway carriages. Györ was close to the Austrian border, and it offered cheap land and workers.

It was a successful business. In 1903 they built electric trams for Amsterdam and later for Antwerp. Soon a bridge-making arm was added, and car-making was a natural evolution. Their first experience with steam cars was unsuccessful, but Austrian contacts secured them a contract with the Hieronimus company in Vienna to assemble chassis. Also, the Austrian Ministry of Defence asked them to build a 4-wheel drive lorry to Ludvig von Tlaskal's design. Another Austrian company, Austro-Daimler also supplied drawings and samples to enable a few 12/16 and 16/24 bhp small cars and trucks to be built. Orders from the Hungarian Post to manufacture postal vans to János CSONKA's plans were the biggest step towards larger-scale car-making; within three years they completed 60 of them.

Before World War I the company bought the licence of the Czech PRAGA cars and built the Alfa and Grand models under licence and marketed them under the brand name Rába. The name was chosen after the river running through Györ. One Grand was given as a present to the last King of Austria-Hungary, Charles IV. After the war, a few Grand models were made but more emphasis was put on trucks and buses. It is their main activity even today.

PN

RABAG-BUGATTI (D) 1922–1926

Rheinische Automobilbau AG, Düsseldorf; Mannheim.

The Bugatti was a German car up to 1918, but when Molsheim became part of French territory Ettore looked for a German factory and set up an agreement whereby the Brescia model would be made by the Union Werke of Mannheim, who also made their own BRAVO cars. Two models were made, the 1453cc 6/25PS and the 1495cc 6/30PS, corresponding to the Brescia and Brescia Modifié. The engines and chassis were made at Mannheim, while bodies came from Bendikt Rock in Düsseldorf, although some Rabags were bodied by custom coachbuilders such as Gastell of Mainz. Bodies ranged from stark open sports cars to a heavy-looking 6-light saloon. Most Rabags could be distinguished

1913 Raba 35/46hp tourer.
NATIONAL MOTOR MUSEUM

from the French product by their lipped radiators, but a few wore standard Brescia radiators. Rabag was part of the Stinnes concern (to which AGA and DINOS also belonged), and when that collapsed in 1926 the Rabag venture came to an end.

HON

RABOEUF (F) 1914

M. Raboeuf, Amiens.

This was a light car powered by a 10hp 4-cylinder Chapuis-Dornier engine, with 3-speed gearbox having direct drive on top and shaft final drive. It had a

1911 R.A.F. (i) 35hp landaulet.
NATIONAL MOTOR MUSEUM

1996 R.A.F. (ii) Mk1 sports car.
JAN P. NORBYE

2-seater body with dickey, and top speed of 45mph (72km/h). Being introduced in 1914, it had little chance of success before the war broke out, particularly as the Amiens district was quickly engulfed in the fighting.

NG

R.A.C. *see* DIAMOND (i) and RICKETTS

RACECORP (GB) 1990 to date
1990–1993 Racecorp Ltd, Chinnor, Oxfordshire.
1993 to date Eldon Autokits, Tonbridge, Kent.
Racecorp was involved in composite component manufacture for Formula 1 cars, and building the LA Roadster was essentially a spare time project. The car's main attraction was its square tube space frame chassis, though the Lotus 7-esque bodywork was familiar enough. There was a choice of a 5-link live rear axle or irs. Engine options encompassed various Fords, Mazda rotary and Fiat twin cam. Ownership of the project changed in 1993 and thereafter it was known as the Eldon Roadster. Rover V8 power became optional from 1994.

CR

RADAR (B) 1957–1960
This was an unusual-looking 2-door open sports plastic body designed for the Citroën 2CV chassis and produced by a company called C.E.C. It had an oval grill and very swoopy lines. Approximately 25 cars were built.

CR

RAD DESIGNS (US) 1997 to date
Rad Designs, Asuza, California.
Pontiac Fiero-based replicas were the stock and trade of this kit car company. Their line-up included clones of the Ferrari 512, F-50, F355 and Lamborghini Diablo. They were sold in kit and turn-key form.

HP

RADIA *see* L'AUTOMOTRICE

RADIOR (F) 1921
J. Chapolard, Automobiles Radior, Bourg, Ain.
This was one of a number of regional makes which never made it into serious production. It was powered by a 10hp 4-cylinder Ballot engine.

NG

RADWAN (PL) 1931–1932; 1937
Stefan Praglowski built a prototype light car which was started in 1931 and completed in 1932. It was powered by a 986cc BSA V-twin engine driving the front wheels, and had an advanced suspension system with interlinked coil springs *à la* Citroën 2CV. This small car, with a 106in (2690mm) wheelbase, was called the Galkar, after Galicyjskie Karpackie Naftowy Towarzystow, a Polish oil company, which was to have sponsored it but withdrew its support. In 1937 Praglowski tried again, with another small car called the Radwan. This had an 876cc 3-cylinder 2-stroke engine developing 25bhp, which was made by the Steinhagen I Stransky factory in Warsaw. Late in 1937 Suchedniowska Huta Ludwikow of Kielce planned to build the Radwan in series, but the World War II put an end to their plans.

RP

R.A.F. (i) (A/CS) 1907–1913
Reichenberger Automobil-Fabrik, Reichenberg (now Liberec).
At the beginning of the 20th century, a surprisingly large number of automobile factories offered their products to customers in Imperial Austria-Hungary. Only Laurin & Klement produced respectable quantities, all the others were more or less unprofitable.

In 1907, another marque joined the band, R.A.F. in Rosenthal near Reichenberg in Northern Bohemia (now Liberec, Czech Republic). The company was founded by the famous racing driver and owner of two textile manufacturing companies Theodor Freiherr von Liebieg, and his two partners, Alfred Ginzkey and Oscar von Klinger. Liebieg was born on 15 June 1872, and at the age of 21, he had become the only heir to his father's textile works. That year, 1893, he had bought a Benz Victoria and made trips through most of Europe. He participated as a driver in races and competitions in Vienna, Leipzig, Berlin and Nice. In 1894, Liebieg drove his Benz from Reichenberg to Rheims and back, making him probably the world's first long-distance automobile driver.

R.A.F. was founded by Czech Germans (Reichenberg/Liberec lay in the Südetenland of later fame), perhaps, with an eye to rival the Czech firm of Laurin & Klement. The first R.A.F. cars were unveiled at the March 1908 Prague Automobile Salon in two versions. The first already had 4-wheel brakes. This was equipped with an engine of 4 cylinders cast in pairs with valves on both sides (T-head), 4508cc displacement, generating 30hp. The car had a 4-speed gearbox, shaft drive, and a cooling fan driven by a bevel shaft. The second car was a smaller version with a twin-cylinder engine of 10hp. Both were available with the finest and most expensive bodies to attract a discriminating clientele.

Model T was soon followed by another heavy passenger car, the Model H 10. This car also had a 4-cylinder engine, but displacement and horsepower had been increased to 5336cc and 45hp. Ignition was by Bosch magneto and the crankshaft turned on roller bearings. The new model boasted no less than four brakes: two foot brakes (one on the gear box, the other on the rear wheels), a normal hand brake, and finally the emergency brake in the form of a sprag. The top speed was 56mph (90km/h).

The R.A.F. H 10 was available from 1909 to 1912. During this time, the Model FW 25 was developed. This was a smaller 4-cylinder of 3053cc, often fitted also with a wooden delivery truck body.

By 1910 another new model, the 14/18hp, was launched. Its engine, clutch and gearbox were mounted on an auxiliary frame – the whole unit could be lifted from the chassis within minutes for maintenance and repair work. The four cylinders were cast in one block and all valves were on the same side; this L-head engine was a novelty at the time.

Then a new period in the history of R.A.F. began. Paul Henze, already a well known designer and engineer, took up work at Reichenberg. Under his direction, the Model C 25 with an engine of 5699cc, and the 32hp Model 28 with a 3560cc engine were developed. Again, both were sophisticated and expensive automobiles. However, production dwindled and it became apparent that R.A.F. would have think of manufacturing a more popular smaller model. Based

1967 Rago 325cc coupé.
ALVARO CASAL TATLOCK

on existing business relations with the Hansa works in Varel, Oldenburg, Germany, R.A.F.'s management decided to produce under licence the Hansa 6/14PS and 10/22PS models. These small R.A.F. cars were practically identical to the Northern German originals. Hansa, for its part, produced a small numbers of the big R.A.F. cars but to order only.

In the meantime, R.A.F. had been seeking yet another European partner. The result was an exclusive licence from the Daimler Company of Coventry, England, to build Knight engines. This indicates that R.A.F. was in the forefront of the technology of its day. The LK1 was developed in 1912 and had a 4-cylinder sleeve-valve engine of 3053cc capacity and 25hp output. However, the production of the LK1 would be profitable only if another manufacturer provided the engine. R.A.F. granted a sub-licence to Puch (Austria) which built Knight engines both for R.A.F. and for itself.

R.A.F. had undertaken too much, and it was necessary to make some kind of arrangement with its competitors. Rather quickly, the company discovered a willing suitor in Laurin & Klement, which took over R.A.F. in 1912. R.A.F. continued to exist as a marque, and there were even two new Knight-engined cars added to the range, a 13/40hp and 18/50hp with 4710cc and 5699cc engines. Many of the later Laurin & Klement cars with sleeve-valve engines were based on the earlier R.A.F. designs. By this time, Paul Henze had left the company and moved to Belgium.

The name R.A.F. was kept until the outbreak of the World War I. After the war, Laurin & Klement itself was taken over by Skoda. The founder of R.A.F., T. von Liebieg, died in 1939. He was 67.

MSH

Further Reading
'R.A.F. – Automobile aus Reichenberg', Marian Suman-Hreblay, *AutomobilChronik*, No. 2, 1978.
'The R.A.F., Austria-Hungary's Knight-engined car', Marian Suman-Hreblay, *Automotive History Review, 1997*, No. 31.

R.A.F. (ii) (CZ) 1996 to date
The R.A.F. name was revived by a small firm in Plzen for a 1930s style 2-seater sports car with a welded-up one-piece aluminium platform and fibreglass body. Power options were 1.8- or 2-litre Ford Cosworth engines. The makers purchased the name from Skoda who owned it as a result of their predecessor Laurin & Klement's merger with R.A.F. (i) in 1912.

NG

RAFALE (F) 1952
Sté Dijon-Tourisme, Dijon.
The Rafele sports coupé was based on the mechanicals of the Dyna-Panhard but used a Renault 4CV Sprint engine, allowing it a claimed top speed of 87mph (140km/h). This was in part due to the extremely lightweight aluminium bodywork. It competed in a number of rallies.

CR

RAFFO (GB) 1985 to date
Raffo Cars, Southport, Merseyside.
An Italian-born Formula Vee builder, John Raffo built the Tipo 11 as his first effort at a road car and his first at a kit car. It might have looked odd but it was a real driver's car, and one intended equally for the race track as for the road. It had a space frame chassis, fibreglass body (the prototype had a Bond Bug-style canopy), an Alfasud power train mounted centrally, right-hand gear lever, Vauxhall Viva based front suspension and a wishbone rear. Later ones had wishbone front suspension, more enveloping bodywork and the option of V6 power, although these tended to be geared more towards pure racing use. The Belva was a new model in 1996, featuring attractive curved bodywork, gullwing doors and mid-mounted Ford Zetec 1.8/2-litre power.

CR

RAGLAN (GB) 1899
Raglan Cycle Co., Coventry.
This well-known cycle company made a modified version of the International BENZ. An initial run of 12 cars was announced, but it is not known if as many as that were completed.

NG

RAGO (U) 1967
Rago Hermanos, Montevideo.
Carlos and Waldemar Rago made 12 of these microcars. They were powered by a rear-mounted Hispano-Villiers 325cc 2-stroke engine with clutch and gearbox by the same maker. The fibreglass 2-seater coupé body, designed by De la Maria, could accommodate two adults and two children. The Rago brothers lost money on all the cars they sold, so they stopped production and turned to making fibreglass components for other firms. Some examples have survived. A Rago is a current exhibit at the museum of the Uruguayan Automobile Club, in Montevideo. Carlos Rago died in an accident, but Waldemar

1936 Railton (i) Cobham saloon.
NICK BALDWIN

Rago moved to the USA where he has a garage in New Jersey. The old Rago Hermanos concern in Montevideo is tended by one of Waldemar's sons. All the tooling and dies to make Rago cars still exist in Montevideo and are kept by the Rago family.

ACT

RAILSBACH (US) 1914

L.M. Railsbach, Saginaw, Michigan.
With a track of only 36in (914mm) this was really a cyclecar. It was a 2-seater with a 1.2-litre 4-cylinder engine, and it sold for $350.

NG

RAILTON (i) (GB) 1933–1950

1933–1940 Railton Cars, Cobham, Surrey.
1940–1950 Hudson Motors Ltd, London.
Although the Railton was named for speed merchant Reid Railton (1895–1977), it was principally the brainchild of Noel Macklin (1886–1946). Macklin had been building the INVICTA at Fairmile, his Cobham estate, but sold the enterprise to the Earl Fitzwilliam in the summer of 1933. Desiring to stay in the motor business, he cast about for another venture. The TERRAPLANE, a new model of the American HUDSON Motor Car Co.'s companion ESSEX marque, had been introduced to the British market in September 1932. Its lively performance had attracted considerable notice in the motoring press, and an even more powerful 8-cylinder version in 1933 drew Macklin's interest. A prototype sports tourer, with aluminium body probably by Ranalah grafted to a near-standard Terraplane chassis, was introduced in July 1933.

The actual contribution of Reid Railton to the endeavour is a matter of some conjecture. Probably he consulted on the design; certainly he collected a royalty on each car produced. Railton later served as consultant to Hudson in the USA, and lived out the remainder of his life in California.

The Railton-Terraplane, as the early cars were badged, had an English appearance, very much in the Invicta idiom. A stylish radiator shell, designed by artist F. Gordon Crosby, fronted a razor-edge bonnet; the earliest cars were tourers, although saloons and drophead coupés were soon advertised. The principal chassis modification was the addition of Andre Hartford Telecontrol shock absorbers, contemporary press reports to the contrary. The completed cars weighed only 2260 lbs (1027kg), so the performance from the 4010cc, 94bhp side-valve in-line eight was even better than the parent Terraplane. S.C.H. Davis, writing in *The Autocar*, said 'the performance of this car has to be experienced to be believed… This kind of car seems to be exactly what the average experienced motorist requires'. The price of £499, for saloon or tourer, was quite remarkable compared with other performance cars.

The following year the body offerings broadened, as other coachbuilders, among them Motor Bodies, Coachcraft and Carbodies, were enlisted as suppliers. Hudson had dropped the 8-cylinder Terraplane, so the Hudson eight chassis, which by this time mimicked the lightweight Terraplane design, was adopted. This meant a 4168cc, 113bhp engine, and a wheelbase of 116in (2944mm), three more than the original.

Railton production peaked in 1935, with 377 cars delivered. In this year, two specials, the Light Sports Tourers with doorless bodies by E.J. Newnes and

cycle wings, made their appearance. Their engines had been moved rearwards, for better balance, and this, plus the even lighter weight, made them faster still. 0–60mph (0-97km/h) times of under ten seconds in road-going dress and 8.8 seconds when stripped provided grist for legends, made memorable by photos of one of them, registered DPA231, airborne at the top of the Brooklands test hill. These cars had such a following that a number of latter-day collectors have constructed reproductions, usually from underloved Railton saloons.

Hudson offered 8-cylinder cars on two wheelbases for 1936, 120in (3046mm) and 127in (3223mm), so Railton followed suit. Hudson's duo-automatic hydraulic brakes, new that year, also appeared on Railton, as did a remote control gearchange and 12-volt electrics. A much wider range of bodies became available, including a smart drophead with dickey seat and two saloons and a limo by Coachcraft on the long-wheelbase chassis. For 1937, vertical bars replaced the mesh covering of the radiator grill, and wheelbases grew another two inches, to 122in (3096mm) and 129in (3274mm), as Hudson stretched the standard chassis. This added weight and cost, and performance suffered accordingly, although Railtons were always lighter, and hence faster, than the standard Hudson.

Two new models of Railton were added in 1938, a 6-cylinder model on the Hudson 117in (2970mm) chassis, using the small-bore, tax-dodging 2723cc (16.9hp rating) engine, and a 'baby' Railton on a Standard 10hp chassis. Drophead and saloon bodies, 37 of the former and only 14 of the latter, were built on the 10hp chassis. Both styles were by Coachcraft and appeared as miniature versions of the larger cars.

By 1939, Noel Macklin had begun to build torpedo boats, and car manufacture took a back seat. A Railton with the 3455cc Hudson 6-cylinder engine (21.6hp rating) was the only new model. Macklin sold the Railton enterprise to Hudson Motors Ltd, who continued to assemble cars at their London works in the Great West Road at Chiswick.

All such work was interrupted by hostilities; when the war clouds had cleared, Hudson Motors assembled a dozen cars on prewar chassis, bodied by Martin Walter and Whittingham and Mitchel, in addition to Carbodies. A 'real' postwar Railton, on modern ifs chassis (the configuration used by Hudson since 1940) appeared at the 1949 motor show, with drophead body by University Motors, heir to Coachcraft. The price was an incredible £4750, which made it an uneconomic proposition. A final car, with sleeker Airflow Streamline drophead body made its appearance in 1950. Even had there been a market for a £5000 'multicultural' car, the endeavour could not have continued. Hudsons from 1948 utilised semi-unit construction, inimical for coachbuilding, and regular imports of USA chassis were proscribed by postwar economic regulations.

But with nearly 1500 cars produced, Railton must be the most successful of the Anglo-American hybrids. Not only that, during the Fairmile years, the venture returned a net profit.

KF

Further Reading
'It's Quickest by Railton', Michael Sedgwick, *Automobile Quarterly*, Vol. 7, No. 4.

RAILTON (ii) (GB) 1989–c.1994

Railton Motor Co. Ltd, Wixford, Alcester, Warwickshire.
Willam Towns was the designer behind this revival of a famous 1930s marque. The new Railton was a conversion of the Jaguar XJS convertible, using an all-new aluminium body and reskinned Jaguar opening panels. The mechanical and interior components were left largely untouched, although unique trim commissions were offered. Two models were offered: the F28 Fairmile (a more sporting choice with wider wheels and tyres) and the F29 Claremont (a more touring choice with spats over the narrower rear wheels). A planned Lister V12-engined version never materialised.

CR

RAIMONDI (I) 1898

Fabbrica Biciclette e Automobili Ippolito Raimondi, Parma.
Raimondi was a bicycle maker who signalled his intention to make cars by a change of company name, but it appears that only one was made, a belt-driven light car with single-cylinder engine, probably De Dion-Bouton.

NG

1937 Railton (i) Fairmile drophead coupé.
NICK BALDWIN

RAINIER (US) 1905–1911

1905–1907 Rainier Co., Flushing, New York.
1907–1911 Rainier Motor Car Co., Saginaw, Michigan.

John T. Rainier (1861–1940) organised the Vehicle Equipment Co. of Brooklyn, makers of electric trucks and sightseeing buses, and of a few cars under the name V.E.C. In 1905 he brought out his own car, which was assembled at Flushing but used a 22/28hp 4-cylinder engine and 98in (2487mm) chassis made by Garford at Elyria, Ohio. The 1906 season saw a larger engine, of 30/35hp on a longer wheelbase of 104in (2640mm). This was priced at $4000 for a town car, and Rainier prices would rise further, to $5850 by 1910, making them among the more expensive American cars. They were well-thought of, with a good sporting reputation and advertised as the 'Pullman of Motor Cars'.

In 1907 Garford's contract with STUDEBAKER prevented them from supplying any more chassis to Rainier, so he moved to Saginaw and engaged a former Garford engineer, James G. Haeslet, to design a new range of cars with still larger engines of 45/50 and from 1910, 50hp, on a 119in (3020mm) wheelbase. They planned to make 300 cars in the 1908/09 season, but bankruptcy struck after 180 had been completed. The company operated for a while under receivership, and in March 1909 was bought by William C. Durant who made it part of his new General Motors Corp. The Rainier name was continued until 1911, but then was marketed by Durant as the MARQUETTE (i), a smaller and cheaper car. John T. Rainier returned to Flushing where he made trucks from 1916 to 1927.

NG

R.A.L. (B) 1908–1914

Automobiles Raskin, Liège.

The RAL was one of several Belgian makes which made extensive use of French components, including Decolange engines of 1590 and 1750cc. Three body styles were offered, open 2- and 4-seaters and a 2-seater closed coupé. Production was halted by the war and did not start again after the Armistice.

NG

1939 Railton (i) Ten drophead coupé.
NICK BALDWIN

1908 Rainier 40/50hp tourer.
JOHN A. CONDE

1932 Raleigh (i) 3-wheeler.
NICK BALDWIN

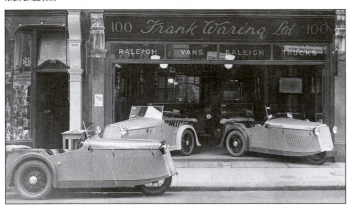

1934 Raleigh (i) Safety Seven 3-wheelers.
NICK BALDWIN

1927 Ralf Stetyz saloon.
ROBERT PRZYBYLSKI

RALEIGH (i) **(GB)** 1905;1916; 1933–1936

Raleigh Cycle Co. Ltd, Nottingham.

One of Britain's best-known bicycle makers, the Raleigh Cycle Co. was founded in the late 1870s by Frank Bowden who took over a small back street firm in Nottingham making penny farthings, and by 1896 was making 30,000 bicycles a year. Motorcycle production began in 1899, followed in 1903 by the Raleighette tricar. The company made a prototype car in 1905 with a 16hp 4-cylinder Fafnir engine, and several more during the cyclecar boom. After experimenting with 2-cylinder engines they chose a 1340cc 4-cylinder Alpha for their light car. This was listed for 1916, at a price of £220, but few, if any, reached the public.

Raleigh then concentrated on 2-wheelers until the 1930s. In September 1932 they announced a passenger car based on their 3-wheeled light van powered by a 598cc single-cylinder engine. It seated two passengers behind the driver who sat on a saddle and steered the single front wheels by handlebars. Tourer and saloon models were offered, at £89 for the saloon and slightly less for the tourer, and it was said that both models would be available through the usual Raleigh agents. Few reached the public, and in 1933 Raleigh launched the only model which became a production car. This was the Safety Seven, also a 3-wheeler with single front wheel, but built on proper car lines, with 742cc V-twin engine, 3-speed gearbox and shaft drive. It was a full 4-seater, and was made in saloon and tourer models. The price was £110.25 About 3000 were made. It was designed by T.L. Williams who bought the manufacturing rights to the van from Raleigh and launched it in 1935 as the Reliant, paving the way for the first RELIANT car in 1952.

NG

RALEIGH (ii) **(US)** 1921–1922

1921 Raleigh Motors Corp., Bridgeton, New Jersey.
1921–1922 Raleigh Motors Inc, Reading, Pennsylvania.

The Raleigh was the typical 'assembled car' of its brief two years of existence and, like many of its contemporaries, plans had been outlined for both 4- and 6-cylinder series. The four never came. Plans called for a 2-seater runabout, 5-seater touring car, a coupé, and a sedan, although it is unlikely that anything but touring cars were actually produced. The Special touring car, which included such extra equipment as dual spare tyres, was later designated the Princess Pat after the famed Canadian Army unit of that name, and the 1915 Victor Herbert operetta, *Princess Pat*. The first few cars were completed at the Bridgeton factory before Raleigh moved its operations to Reading, Pennsylvania. Plans for expansion and further production in Buffalo, New York, failed to materialise and the company went out of business in 1922. Approximately 40 Raleigh cars were completed and sold by the Philadelphia distributor. All Raleighs used Herschell-Spillman 6-cylinder engines.

KM

RALF STETYZ **(PL)** 1926–1928

Tow. Akc. Konstrucji Mostowych 'Rudski' (Rudski & Ska), Warsaw.

Designed by Stefan Tyszkiewicz, the two models of the Ralf Stetyz were built at the Rudski works in Warsaw. There was a 1.5-litre four and a 2.7-litre six, which used a Polish built Continental engine. The factory was destroyed by fire in 1928.

RP

RALLY **(F)** 1921–1933

Automobiles Rally, Colombes, Seine.

For much of its life the Rally was a typical French light sports car in the Amilcar/Salmson mould. Its origins were more unusual, in that the first models of 1921 were powered by American motorcycle engines, a 989cc V-twin Harley-Davidson with overhead inlet and side exhaust valves. The clutch and gearbox were also by Harley-Davidson. As well as offering complete cars, Rally offered three other solutions; they would convert a customer's motorcycle into a car, or deliver a complete chassis for the customer to fit his own engine, or supply a set of components, chassis, rear axle, steering gear, springs etc. Construction was no doubt helped by the large numbers of ex-US Army motorcycles available at relatively low prices. Rally offered the option of V-twin Indian or in-line 4-cylinder units by Harley-Davidson or F.N. On the complete cars the bodies were made by Carrosserie B.G. Rally was owned by a Monsieur Rotschild, no connection with the Rothschild bankers or coachbuilders.

In 1922 an 898cc 4-cylinder Chapuis-Dorner engine was offered, and it seems that the motorcycle units did not last for more than 12 months. An 1100cc C.I.M.E. engine was listed for 1923, when four models were available, Tourisme, Sport, Grand Sport (with 30bhp C.I.M.E. engine) and light van. By 1924 they were covering a wide range of light cars on two wheelbases, 86.6in (2198mm) and 90in (2284mm), 2- and 3-seater sports models, 3-seater tourers, commercial travellers' cars and the delivery van, For 1925 a larger touring model appeared on a 110in (2792mm) wheelbase, suitable for 4-seater, 4-door saloon or touring bodies. This was the PPR, powered by a 1202cc C.I.M.E. engine. There were also two sports models with either staggered or side by side seating. About 100 cars were made in 1925, when the marque had many sporting successes, mostly in hill climbs.

The 1926 catalogue included five models, the Grand Sport Spéciale with 1100cc ohv engine and a top speed of 78mph (125km/h), the twin-cam Grand Sport 1½-litre with 87mph (140km/h), the touring PPR and two new models with hemispherical combustion chambers and twin ohc, the 1100cc 4-cylinder Type R4 7CV Course, and the 1½-litre straight-8 Type R8 10CV Spéciale. The engines were to be made by Brault, who also supplied LOMBARD, but they did not have the capacity to provide Rally with enough power units, and these models never reached production. In 1928 came the Type ABC, the most attractive-looking Rally, with low-slung 2-seater bodywork, either open sports or closed coupé. The engine was a 1095cc Chapuis-Dornier, replaced in 1929 by 1100 or 1170cc SCAP units. A racing model had three valves per cylinder and the option of a supercharger. In this form its top speed was 105mph (169km/h).

SCAP and Chapuis-Dornier ceased making engines in 1930 so Rotschild turned to Salmson as a supplier. A few years earlier they would never have considered supplying engines to a rival sports car maker, but their competition days were over, and they were happy to see their engines still in sporting events. The Salmson unit was a twin-cam, like the Rallys, of 1300cc. It was offered in two chassis, the 95in (2411mm)) NC (N Court) and the 106in (2690mm) N. With tuned engines, these were the NCP and NP (P=Poussée). The short wheelbase cars were 2-seater sports, while the long chassis carried some very handsome coupés and a 4-door saloon. At the 1932 Paris Salon (the last for Rally) they showed the R15 which used Salmson's new 1465cc S4C engine. A very small number were supercharged (R15C). The same types of body were offered as for the N and NC, but there were three wheelbases, the longest being of 114in (2893mm). Rally closed their doors in the summer of 1933.

NG

Further Reading
'Les Automobiles Rally', Serge Pozzoli,
l'Album du Fanatique, December 1976–March 1977.
'Rally Alexis', *La Vie de l'Auto*, 24 April and 7 August 1997.

RAM (i) (GB) 1984–1998

1984–1986 L.R. Roadsters, Chingford, London.
1986–1993 L.R. Roadsters, Newmarket, Suffolk.
1994 Ram Automotive, Cardiff, Wales.
1994–1998 Ram Automotive, Witham, Essex.

Adrian Cocking, ex of D.J. Sportscars, set up on his own to make sports replicas. The first was a Cobra replica called the SC, whose main distinguishing feature was a round-tube backbone space frame chassis designed by Adrian Reynard. Suspension was Jaguar and engines were usually small block V8. The bodywork was fibreglass or, from 1991, alternatively aluminium. An interesting 4-wheel drive Cosworth version was launched in 1993, while the SEC was a cheaper Ford-based kit. Carroll Shelby's 1994 grant of official approval for the Ram SC was a real coup. A second replica from 1985 was the LM, a Jaguar D-Type copy. It shared the Reynard chassis developed for the Cobra replica, with the distinction that it could be fitted with any of the Jaguar range of straight-6 engines. Fibreglass bodywork was available in a variety of styles: long and short nose, fixed and detachable rear fins, and an XKSS bodystyle (dubbed the SS). Less popular was the RT, one of the first ever Ferrari Daytona replicas (launched in 1987). The chassis was a tubular backbone with stressed sheet steel structures at either end. The fibreglass body was also stressed and incorporated an integral steel tube support frame. True to the original, a V12 engine was shoehorned in the form of a Jaguar XJ12 unit. A Daytona coupé replica was also developed.

CR

RAM (ii) (US) c.1985

Russell Auto Motive Eng., Tustin, California.

This company built replicas of the Bugatti T-35. They were basic VW-powered kits available in any stage of construction.

HP

RAMAPAUGH *see* BALL

RAMBLER (i) *see* ROCKAWAY

1928 Rally 1100 sports car.
NATIONAL MOTOR MUSEUM

1905 Rambler (ii) Type 1 18hp tourer.
JOHN A. CONDE

1911 Rambler (ii) Model 64 landaulet.
NICK BALDWIN

RAMBLER (ii) (US) 1902–1913

Thomas B. Jeffery Co., Kenosha, Wisconsin.

The Rambler name dates back to the 1890s, when two Englishmen, Thomas B. Jeffery and R. Philip Gormully made Rambler bicycles in Chicago, also having an English branch factory at Coventry. In 1897 Thomas Jeffery and his son Charles built a light car powered by a rear-mounted single-cylinder engine. This was succeeded a year later by a more advanced machine, with front-mounted 2-cylinder engine. The Jefferys did not decide to go in for car manufacture straightaway, but in 1900, after the death of Philip Gormully, they sold their company to Colonel Albert Pope, who was already America's biggest bicycle maker, and bought a large factory at Kenosha, Wisconsin, for the manufacture of cars. The second design of Rambler was made in Chicago under the name Hydro-Car by Colonel Pope's American Bicycle Co. from 1901–1902 only.

Two more prototypes were made at Kenosha. Designed by Charles Jeffery, they were advanced machines with front-mounted engines and steering by a left-mounted wheel. Thomas Jeffery had doubts about the acceptance of such an unusual car, particularly by a conservative Middle Western market, and had the car redesigned with a single-cylinder engine under the seat, and right-hand tiller steering. With its bicycle wheels and single-chain drive, the Model C Rambler was now typical of the light motor buggy of the period, and it sold well at $750. The net profit on each car was $372, and with sales of 1500 in 1902, the new Thomas B. Jeffery Co. was set for success. In fact, the total was second only to Oldsmobile.

The single-cylinder Rambler was continued through 1905, with an increase in engine size and wheelbase, and the adoption of artillery wheels and wheel steering. 1904 saw new 2-cylinder Ramblers, and all models had frontal bonnets, though the engines still lived under the seat. Production in 1904 was 3242 cars. The first 4-cylinder Ramblers were offered for the 1906 season, with two sizes of front-mounted engine, 25 and 35/40hp. A limousine cost $3000, although a 2-cylinder two-seater runabout could still be had for $800. Rambler advertising took on a new, lyrical tone at this time, with such phrases as 'June Time is Rambler Time', thanks to Ned Jordan, who became Thomas Jeffery's secretary and general manager. This anticipated his even more lyrical prose when he made his own cars in the 1920s.

NICK BALDWIN

ROMNEY, GEORGE (1907–1995)

Well described as the father of the compact American car, George Wilcken Romney was born in Mexico, of English descent, his ancestors including William Romney, a 16th Century Lord Mayor of London, and the 18th Century portrait painter George Romney. His more immediate family were carpenters and members of the Mormon Church, which led to their expulsion from Mexico when George was five years old. They settled in Salt Lake City. Utah, where George attended The Latter Day Saints University High School and met Lenore Lafount, who would become his wife in 1931.

After an obligatory stint as a missionary for the Mormons in London and Scotland, he became a Senator's researcher in Washington, which gave him a taste for, and an insight into, politics, which served him well later on. He joined ALCOA (Aluminum Co. of America) as their lobbyist in Washington, where he stayed until September 1939, when he became manager of the Detroit office of the AMA (Automobile Manufacturers Association). This led to a senior position on the Automotive Council for War Production which was coordinated by the AMA. After World War II Romney helped to organise the 50th Anniversary of the auto industry celebrations in Detroit, including the 1000-vehicle parade, which gave many people their first sight of antique cars, and encouraged some to collect and restore them. The year 1946 also brought Romney a new boss, George Mason, head of Nash-Kelvinator and president of the AMA. He had been impressed by Romney's ability on the Council for War Production, and in April 1948 recruited him as his assistant at Nash. Among his important assignments was the contact with Pinin Farina and signing of the Italian as a styling consultant for Nash.

Within two years Romney had become a vice-president and on Mason's death in 1954 he assumed the presidency of the newly-formed American Motors Corp. Some members of the board were not happy and suggested splitting Mason's titles and offering Romney one of them, for the time being anyway. With characteristic forthrightness he rejected this idea; it was all or nothing for him, and he got his way. Even as a merger of two major companies, Nash and Hudson, it was a tough time for an independent firm struggling against the Big Three who were gaining a growing section of the market. Romney decided quickly that competing head on with the Big Three was a hopeless task, and he decided to concentrate on the compact Rambler. 'I became convinced that the Rambler was the car of the future,' he said, 'And that led, ultimately, to my dropping the other two lines and risking our future on the Rambler.' His faith in small cars was rewarded within three years. In 1958 American Motors posted its first profit, and in 1959 they beat the record for sales by an independent manufacturer, held by Willys since 1929. In 1960 and 1961 American Motors beat Plymouth into third place behind Chevrolet and Ford.

These achievements, though short-lived, made Romney the best-known businessman in the world. He was featured on the covers of *Time, Newsweek, Business Week, Forbes,* and other magazines. He had already become involved in local politics when he formed the non-party Citizens for Michigan to campaign on a variety of issues, especially reform of schools. When the incumbent governor John Swainson showed himself hostile to many of these reforms, Romney was persuaded to stand against him for Governor of Michigan. He was elected by a very small margin in 1962, and re-elected with much larger majorities in 1964 and 1966. In 1968 he decided to stand for the Republican nomination for President, against Richard Nixon and Ronald Reagan. Though a Republican, his religious beliefs inclined him towards support for civil rights and doubts about the war in Vietnam. In a speech he said that he had been brainwashed (by the generals and diplomatic corps) while visiting Vietnam, and this ended his chances of the nomination, which went to Nixon.

Politics had taken over from the car industry, and although American Motors kept the presidential seat warm for him for a few years, this did not last out his three terms as Governor. He never returned to the company, but joined the Nixon administration as Secretary for Housing and Urban Development, following this by promoting many volunteer activities. He was active and healthy up to the day of his death, which occurred 18 days after his 88th birthday. He left his wife of 64 years, 23 grandchildren and 33 great grandchildren.

NG

Further Reading
'George Romney, the Paths of Persistence', Patrick R. Foster
Automobile Quarterly, Vol. 35, No.4.

The last 2-cylinder Rambler was made in 1909, when the fours ran to 45hp and a 123in (3124mm) wheelbase. Production was running at about 2500 per year in 1910, and Thomas Jeffery did not want to see it rise much above this figure, to ensure maximum quality. However, he died suddenly in April 1910, and son Charles increased production to around 3500 in 1911. The best year was also the last; 1913 saw 4435 Ramblers sold, but at the year's end the car's name was changed to JEFFERY, 'To the end that his name may remain in the memories of men', said Charles. In fact, the name lasted only four years, being then replaced by NASH. The last Ramblers were big 4-cylinder cars, with 7-litre engines and side lights faired into the scuttle.

NG

RAMBLER (iii) (US) 1950–1970

1950–1954 Nash Motor Co., Kenosha, Wisconsin.
1955–1970 American Motors Corp., Kenosha, Wisconsin.

The Rambler name was revived by Nash for the compact car which they introduced in 1950. This remained a model of Nash until 1958, when the recently formed American Motors Corp. renamed all their range Ramblers. This became the marque name until it was replaced by American Motors in 1968. Company

1955 Rambler (iii) Country Club hard-top.
NATIONAL MOTOR MUSEUM

NICK GEORGANO

TEAGUE, DICK (1923–1991)

Richard A. Teague was born in Los Angeles the day after Christmas in 1923 and became a child movie actor. Dick's stage name was Dixie Duval. His mother found him jobs in four movies that Dick always stressed were not 'Our Gang' comedies. They were similar one-reelers by a producer named Stan De Lay.

At the age of six Dick and his mother were driving when she collided with another car. The accident left her an invalid, and Dick lost an eye, several teeth, and suffered a broken jaw, which ended his movie career. His father was killed a year later in another car accident.

Despite these unhappy experiences with cars, Dick developed an early interest in hot rods and went to school with Ed Iskendarian and other early Southern California speed merchants. His first car was a powder-blue 1932 Ford three-window coupé with 16-inch wire wheels and a chromed instrument panel. He was 16 and paid $125 for the car in Beverly Hills. He later owned several other Ford hot rods, including a four-port Riley Model A

and a V8-engined Model A, both of which he ran at Muroc, the dry lake north east of Los Angeles.

Teague drew cars a lot as a child. Because of his eye, he couldn't get into the military, so in 1942, aged 19, he took a job as an illustrator with Northrop Aircraft, where he worked under Paul Browne, a former GM auto designer who had been in Bill Mitchell's studio during the 1938 Cadillac 60-Special's creation. 'Both Browne and I were drawing cars when we should have been drawing aircraft', confessed Teague many years later. Browne encouraged Dick to get into car design and recommended he attend Art Center, which Teague did during World War II.

After the war, Dick worked briefly for Henry Kaiser in Oakland, designing a small, pre-Henry J economy car. He also did magazine illustrations, including an early cover for *Road & Track*. He attended an interview for General Motors in Los Angeles where the interviewer turned out to be Frank Hershey, who was also a friend of Paul Browne's; Teague got the job. He started at General Motors on 15 March 1948.

'All of us neophytes' recalled Teague, 'were put into Hershey's experimental studio over at 'Planet 8,' which we called boot camp. General Motors had two sections. Hershey got all the greenest kids, and then if we stayed, we graduated to Ed Anderson's area. Ed had a more advanced experimental studio.' Like all entering designers, Teague worked on details: lights, trim, bonnet ornaments – that sort of thing.

Teague remained a designer in advanced Cadillac and then left General Motors in early 1951, marrying and returning to California. Later that year he was offered, and accepted, the job of chief stylist at Packard. In early 1952 he became Packard's styling director under Ed Macauley, which was when he hired Richard C. Macadam, who later became Chrysler's design vice president.

By 1956 Packard was as good as finished, so Teague went to Chrysler along with Bill Schmidt. In September 1959 he took a job at American Motors Corp., under his old GM boot-camp mentor, Ed Anderson. 'It's funny', commented Teague, 'how you go around in a circle. A friend of mine says that if you stay in styling long enough, you'll eventually be working for your mother-in-law.'

Anderson left AMC in late 1961, and Teague took over as the corporation's styling director. He was named design vice president on 6 February 1964 and remained with AMC for a total of 24 years – until his retirement in 1983.

Dick Teague had a long and very passionate love affair with classic and antique cars. He haunted swap meets and did nearly all his own restoration work, often labouring long into the night to unwind from the stresses of his AMC routine. He amassed a wonderful collection of cars, which he loved to drive and occasionally showed at concours d'elegance. Few designers could match Teague's genuine devotion to automobiles and his broad knowledge of automotive history. He died in California in May 1991.

ML

1966 Rambler (iii) Marlin coupé.
NATIONAL MOTOR MUSEUM

president George Romney championed the Rambler, and it certainly paid off in sales.

For 1958 the former Nash Rambler with 3205cc 6-cylinder or 4097cc V8 engines was continued, the V8-powered cars being known as Rambler Rebels. The former Nash Ambassador with a 5358cc V8 was continued as the Rambler Ambassador in sedan, hard-top or station wagon form. A new model was the simple and low-priced Rambler American, which was a reversion to the original compact car theme. Powered by the 3205cc six, the American had a 100in (2540mm) wheelbase and the styling of a 1955 Nash Rambler. It was priced from $1775–1874, compared with $2047-2636 for the larger Ramblers. A station wagon was added to the American range for 1959, and a convertible for 1961. At $2369 this was the lowest-priced American-built convertible, and the only one with unitary construction.

1961 also saw new styling for the Ambassador, and a new aluminium ohv six which eventually replaced the old side-valve six. Capacity was the same at 3205cc but power was increased from 90 to 127bhp. The mid-sized Ramblers which used this engine were now called Classics, and the three series, American, Classic and Ambassador, were continued up to the 1966 season. In late 1961 Dick Teague took over as styling director, and in 1964 was made a vice-president of the Corporation. 1965 saw a new model with distinctive fastback styling called the Marlin. This was essentially a Classic with a lower, fastback roofline, and was American Motors' answer to the Ford Mustang. The standard engine in the Marlin was the 3802cc six, but V8s of 4703 or 5358cc 198 or 270bhp) were also available. Sports car features such as optional 4-speed manual transmission, rev counter and bucket seats were offered in the Marlin, but it lacked the precise handling and small size of a sports car, and did not sell well. First year sales were the best, at 10,327, the figures for 1966 and 1967 being only 4527 and 2545.

The Marlin was dropped for 1968, being replaced by the Javelin. This did not carry the Rambler name, and is described under the entry on American Motors. The Rambler American was continued into the 1969 season, when there was a muscle car version called the Hurst SC/Rambler. Tuned by Hurst Performance, it had a 315bhp 6390cc V8 and a 4-speed manual transmission, with beefed-up clutch and springs. 1512 were made. For 1970 the Rambler was no more than a model in the AMC range, in the same way as the Javelin or Ambassador were. The Rambler name disappeared in 1970, except for export models of the Hornet.

NG

RAMBLER (iv) (RA) 1962–1972
IKA Renault SA, Cordoba.
The first Argentinian Ramblers were produced in January l962. The Classic and the Ambassador were 4-door saloons. There was also a 4-door station wagon called Rural Classic. All of them were powered by the same 6-cylinder 3707cc 119bhp engine. Design changes came in 1963, following those being made by Rambler in the USA. When the Torino was born in 1966, this IKA Renault make, inspired by the Rambler but with Pininfarina elegance and higher performance, started to overshadow the bulky Ramblers. However, these continued to be available, even though sales kept falling. In 1966, 1533 Classics, 546 Ambassadors and 1077 station wagons were made, while in 1970 sales for these models dropped, respectively, to 307, 264 and 429. 1972 was the last year of production.

ACT

RAMSES (ET) 1958–1973
Egyptian Automotive Co., Cairo.
With President Nasser's blessing, the Ramses of George Hawi and Essam Abu became Egypt's first national car, sited at a factory in the shadow of the pyramids. This was a simple 4-seater based on the mechanicals of the NSU Prinz III, including its 583cc 2-cylinder engine mounted in the rear, 4-speed gearbox and all-independent suspension. However the bodywork was unique, ensuring the car had a 55 per cent local content. Three models were presented, a doorless open utility vehicle with rigidly straight lines, and two models designed by Vignale: the Gamila 2-door saloon and 2-door convertible. However in 1962 Ramses asked NSU to provide Prinz IV bodyshells, which the Egyptian company simply modified at the front – at least for the saloon model. The front end treatment was radically altered on an annual basis, while the all-purpose open car had gained doors by 1963, the cabriolet was dropped in 1965 and a 4-door saloon was added in 1971. In the company's best year (1964) over 400 cars were produced.

CR

RAMUS (F) 1900
Ateliers de Constructions Mécaniques Ramus Frères, Chambéry, Savoie.
The mountain resort of Chambéry was an unusual location for a car factory. Probably the Ramus brothers' business was no more than a garage. Their car

was powered by a front-mounted 4hp horizontal single-cylinder engine, with transmission by fast-and-loose pulleys.

NG

RANDALL (US) 1903–1905

J.V. & C. Randall, Newtown, Pennsylvania.

Clarence Randall was a leading carriage builder who made a small number of 3-wheeled cars. They were quite substantial machines, with four seats and a fringed top. The single wheel was at the front, and the 12hp air-cooled 2-cylinder engine located under the body drove the rear wheels via a friction disc transmission, and chain final drive. For 1905 a sliding gearbox was substituted. The price of the Randall was $800. Carriage building continued for some time after cars were discontinued.

NG

RAND & HARVEY (US) 1899–1900

Rand & Harvey, Lewiston, Maine.

Clarence Rand built a light steam car on his own in 1899, and two more in association with George E. Harvey. Though series production was planned, it never happened. The partners later sold Stanley steamers.

NG

RANDS (US) 1906–1907

Rands Manufacturing Co., Detroit, Michigan.

W.H. Rands built himself a touring car powered by a 30hp 4-cylinder air-cooled engine. It was mainly for his own use, but a few more were made into 1907.

NG

RANGER (i) (US) 1907–1910

1907–1909 Ranger Motor Works, Chicago, Illinois.

1909–1910 Ranger Automobile Co., Chicago, Illinois.

This company began by making a 2-seater buggy with under-seat 2-cylinder air-cooled engine, epicyclic transmission and double-chain drive. Tiller steering was an archaic feature for 1907. When the company was reorganised in the summer of 1909 the high-wheeler was replaced by a light runabout with pneumatic tyres and single-chain drive. It sold for $395.

NG

RANGER (ii) (GB) 1913–1914

Ranger Cyclecar Co. Ltd, Coventry.

Another product of Enoch J. West, (see PROGRESS (i), ACADEMY and WEST-ASTER), this was the WEST cyclecar renamed. Appearing in April 1913, it was generally similar to the West, but had a 964cc 8hp V-twin Precision engine in place of its predecessor's Chater-Lea, and a reverse gear was provided. Two body styles were offered, a 2-seater and a carrier body with load capacity up to 4cwt (450lbs). It drove through a 2-speed gearbox and single-chain final drive. By September 1913 the air-cooled Precision engine had been replaced by a water-cooled one, and in 1914 a Blumfield twin and 8/10hp Alpha four were also used. Advertising ceased in September 1914 and production must have ended at about the same time.

NG

RANGER (iii) (US) 1920–1923

Southern Motor Manufacturing Association, Houston, Texas.

Whether the Ranger was technically produced as late as 1923 is doubtful although claims were made to that effect at the time. It appears that the Ranger was produced only as a 4-cylinder car although a six had been announced and was ostensibly also on the production line. However, despite its advertising claims, the Southern Motor Manufacturing Association was little more than a stock swindle and such cars actually exhibited comprised those built to promote the operation. The Ranger Four touring car was priced between $1485 and $1850 and powered by an in-house L-head engine. Its larger 6-cylinder companion touring car which may never been built was priced at $3550. Final Ranger promotion for a 1923 model listed the substitution of a Supreme 4-cylinder engine, although it is doubtful that this ever reached the prototype stage. Such Ranger cars which remained after several officers had been indicted for fraud were sold at cost as 1923 cars.

KM

1962 Ramses convertible.
NATIONAL MOTOR MUSEUM

1913 Ranger (ii) 8hp cyclecar.
JOHN SPICER

1920 Ranger (iii) Four tourer.
MICHAEL WORTHINGTON-WILLIAMS

RANGER (iv) (ZA) 1968–1973

General Motors South Africa (Pty) Ltd, Port Elizabeth.

Although promoted as 'South Africa's Own Car' this was a cocktail of General Motors products, having a body shell from the Opel Rekord, Vauxhall Victor front suspension and a choice of 2120cc or 2570cc South African-built 4-cylinder Chevrolet engines. Holden automatic transmission was optional. In 1972 appeared the SS2500 hard-top coupé with vinyl roof, dual-choke Weber carburettor and 4-speed manual gearbox. The 1973 models used the Opel Rekord Mk II body shell, but from 1974 all South African-built GM cars carried the Chevrolet name.

NG

1973 Ranger (vi) 1100 utility.
NICK GEORGANO/NATIONAL MOTOR MUSEUM

1974 Ranger (vi) Cub 3-wheeler.
NICK GEORGANO/NATIONAL MOTOR MUSEUM

1906 Rapid (ii) tourer.
NATIONAL MOTOR MUSEUM

RANGER (v) (B) 1970–1976
General Motors Continental SA, Antwerp.
The Belgian Ranger was a short-lived attempt to market a domestically-built car which nevertheless owed all its components to Opel. Body shells were Opel

Rekord saloons or Commodore saloons and coupés, and engines were the Rekord's 1897cc single-ohc four or the 2784cc six as used in the Commodore. Disc front brakes and 4-speed gearboxes were standard, with automatic transmission an option, initially only on the saloons. A 1698cc engine was available from 1972. After 1976 lower tariffs between EEC countries made the separate Ranger marque a pointless exercise.
NG

RANGER (vi) (GB) 1971–1976; 1984–1985
1971–1972 E.J.S. Products, Romford, Essex.
1972–1976 Ranger Automotive, Leigh-on-Sea, Essex.
1984–1985 Ranger Ltd, Llangefni, Anglesey.
Operating from a disused cinema, Ranger offered a Moke-style utility type kit car. Unusually it used BMC 1100/1300 parts, including both subframes, the dash, seats, windscreen and lights, in a treated space frame chassis. The pre-coloured fibreglass body had a bonded-in plywood floor and options of an estate hard-top, soft-top or pickup cab. Around 1400 Rangers were made, making it probably Britain's most popular kit car in the early 1970s. From 1974 there was also the Cub, a Mini-based open 3-wheeler with a space frame chassis. Kits cost £199. An electric prototype Cub was built, as well as a handful of 4-wheeled versions. In 1976, Ranger Automotive was wound up but a modified revival in Wales occurred in 1984.
CR

RANGE ROVER *see* LAND ROVER

RAOUVAL (F) 1899–1902
Sté Mécanique Industrielle d'Anzin, Anzin, Nord.
The Raouval was a 4-seater tonneau powered by a 2-cylinder Pygmée engine, with final drive by chains.
NG

RAPID (i) (CH) 1899–1900
1899–1900 Zürcher Patent-Motorwagen-Fabrik Rapid, Zürich.
The newly founded Rapid company continued manufacturing the EGG & EGLI 3-wheelers, which it improved in various details and obtained a water-cooled single-cylinder engine of Swiss manufacture to the De Dion design, delivering slightly more than 3bhp. The belt drive was better protected and the cooling water tank formed the mudguard of the single rear wheel. The engine could be started with a pedal. The Rapid was better equipped and heavier than the EGG & EGLI. Hood and leg protection as well as the trailer were available at extra cost. Production was over 100 vehicles and Rudolf Egg, its designer, drove a Rapid tricycle to Paris for the World Fair in 1900. After one year only manufacturing came to an end. Other licence holders of the Egg & Egli 3-wheeler were BÄCHTOLD, Steckborn and WEBER, Uster but these did not attain the production figures of Rapid.
FH

RAPID (ii) (I) 1905–1921
Società Torinese Automobili Rapid, Turin.
This company was founded by Giovanni Batista Ceirano, who had set up Fratelli CEIRANO with his brother Matteo. On Matteo's departure to start another company, ITALA, Giovanni Batista brought in another brother, confusingly called simply Giovanni, who left in turn in 1904 to make the JUNIOR. Undaunted by this apparent lack of fraternal loyalty Giovanni Batista formed another company, the Società Torinese Automobili Rapid, whose initials conveniently abbreviated to STAR. This is sometimes listed as a make, but the cars were better known as Rapids.
The first Rapid had a 9½hp single-cylinder engine, and was followed by a 2.3-litre twin, but the typical Rapid was a T-head four with separately-cast cylinders, 4-speed gearbox and shaft drive, with an ingenious arrangement of three torque and radius rods mounted above and below, and parallel to, the propeller shaft. A variety of engines were made, including the 4.6-litre 16/24, 7.4-litre 24/40, and the 10.6-litre 50/70. Even as early as 1906 this enormous car had shaft drive, which was unusual for its size at that time. Rapids featured round radiators until 1908. A more modern design was the 2.7-litre 12/16 of 1907, with inlet-over-exhaust valves and pair-cast cylinders. The 3.1-litre 16/20

1946 Rapid (iii) 350cc 2-seaters.
ERNEST SCHMID

of 1908 also had pair-cast cylinders, but the valves were still of T-head layout, and this was the case on a number of Rapids up to 1912.

In 1910 some much more up-to-date designs appeared with L-head monobloc 4-cylinder engines in 1570 and 2614cc sizes, with optional compressed-air starters. In 1915 a one-model policy was adopted, with the 1.6-litre 10/12hp. This had a monobloc engine, 3-speed gearbox, detachable steel wheels and all brakes on the rear wheels, rather than on the transmission. Electric lighting and starting were available from 1916. This model was revived after the war, but Rapid closed in 1921, their assets being acquired by S.P.A. and C.I.P.

NG

RAPID (iii) (CH) 1946–1951

1946–1951 Rapid Motormäher AG, Dietikon, Zürich.

The miniature roadster Rapid was based on a prewar design and had certain similarities with the German STANDARD SUPERIOR of 1933, which was also the work of the gifted engineer Josef Ganz. A prototype named 'Erfiag' had been completed in 1938 and an improved second one in 1944. After World War II the market looked very promising for small cars and Rapid, the leading lawn mower producer of Switzerland, decided to take up production of the 2-seater. The Rapid had a central-tube frame and independently suspended wheels. Its 350cc MAG single-cylinder opposed piston engine was rear-mounted and air-cooled. It delivered about 7bhp, which were transmitted via a multiple-plate clutch and 3-speed gearbox to the rear axle. The smart little roadster with a canvas hood cost SFr 3600 but sales were slow and after a total of 36 cars were completed, Rapid ceased production in 1951. The only survivor is in the Swiss Transport Museum in Lucerne.

FH

RAPIER (GB) 1933–1937

1933–1935 Lagonda Ltd, Staines, Middlesex.
1935–1937 Rapier Cars Ltd, Hammersmith, London.

The Rapier was a move by LAGONDA into the market for high-quality small cars, and for the first two years of its life it was a model of Lagonda and made in the same factory as the larger cars. Designed by Timothy Ashcroft, it had a completely new 1104cc 4-cylinder engine with chain-driven twin-ohcs and hemispherical combustion chambers, twin SU carburettors, 4-speed ENV pre-selector gearbox and a top speed of 75mph (121km/h) with a 4-seater body. The 2in (51mm) main bearings were the same as those used in the 4½-litre engine. The engine could rev safely up to 6000rpm. The early engines were made

1935 (Lagonda) Rapier tourer by Abbott.
NICK GEORGANO/NATIONAL MOTOR MUSEUM

by Lagonda, but later ones were built by Coventry Climax to Ashcrofts's design. Coachwork came from a number of specialist firms, including Abbott who made the standard 4-seater tourer and also drophead and fixed-head coupés, and Newns who supplied a 2-seater sports car. Other firms who clothed the Rapier included Corinthian, Ranalagh, Maltby, Whittingham & Mitchel and Silent Touring. A semi-racing version with bored-out engine was offered by Lord de Clifford, and badged as the De Clifford Special. In 1935 Lagonda went into receivership and was bought by Alan Good who formed a new company, Lagonda Motors (Staines) Ltd. He discontinued the Rapier, but Ashcroft, aided by Bill Oates who had raced Lagondas before World War I, and financier Neville Brocklebank, bought the stock of Rapier parts and set up Rapier Cars Ltd in the old Lagonda sales depot at 196 Hammersmith Road. They restarted manufacture, or rather assembly, in August 1935, the only difference from the Lagonda Rapier lying in the badge. All Lagonda guarantees were honoured. Most bodies came from the coachbuilders Wylders of Kew, where final assembly took place. The Rapier was offered with a supercharger in 1936, and was made up to the end of 1937. The company was wound up in 1938 and finally dissolved in 1943, though Ashcroft had hopes of reviving it after the war. A few Rapiers were built up by enthusiasts from prewar parts up to about 1950. Lagonda had ordered 500 sets of components when they launched the Rapier; 470 had been used up by 1939.

NG

1980 Rapport Ritz saloon.
NATIONAL MOTOR MUSEUM

1980 Rapport Forte convertible.
NATIONAL MOTOR MUSEUM

1927 Ratier 750cc sports car.
NICK GEORGANO

RAPPORT (GB) 1980–1982
Rapport Engineering Ltd, Woking, Surrey.
Formed by Chris Humberstone, this company's main business was the conversion of Range Rovers into convertibles and 6-wheelers. As an alternative, the Ritz was a conversion of the Honda Accord, with luxury trim and a curious electrically-operated bar over the headlamps. The more ambitious Forte of 1980 used Jaguar XJ running gear and 6-cylinder or V12 engines mated to a GM automatic gearbox; turbocharging was optional. The solid roof could be folded hydraulically, although at least one fixed-top estate version was made.

CR

RASKIN see R.A.L.

RATIER (F) 1926–1929
Éts Ratier, Montrouge, Seine.

This company was a well-known maker of aircraft propellers, and in 1923 they built a car with frontal propeller driven by a 3215cc T-head 4-cylinder engine made by Janvier, who were neighbours of Ratier in the Paris suburb of Montrouge. It was purely experimental, but three years later they marketed a small sports car powered by a 748cc 4-cylinder engine with shaft-driven single-ohc and non-detachable cylinder head. This engine developed 34bhp, more than 1100s from firms like Chapuis-Dornier and Ruby. The rear of the chassis was under slung, giving the car a very low appearance. Three bodies were offered, a touring 2-seater, a sports 2-seater with pointed tail and a fixed-head coupé. For 1927 a Cozette supercharger gave 46bhp on commercial petrol, and with a benzol mixture, 61bhp at 6000rpm.

Ratiers competed with some success in the Bol d'Or and other events for small cars in 1926 and also at Brooklands, but not more than 30 were made. A development with streamlined single-seater body was called the Grazide. In 1929 they catalogued a six with the same cylinder dimensions as the four, giving 1122cc, but it was probably never built.

NG

Further Reading
'La 750 Ratier', Serge Pozzoli, *Le Fanauto*, March 1988.

RATIONAL (i) (GB) 1901–1906
1901–1903 Bassingbourn Iron Works, Bassingbourn, Cambridgeshire.
1903–1906 Heatly-Gresham Engineering Co. Ltd, Bassingbourn, Cambridgeshire.
In 1901 Harry Heatly and Frank Gresham took over the Bassingbourn Iron Works, which dated from the 1860s, and built a car of their own design, powered by a 10hp horizontal 2-cylinder engine, with 2-speed epicyclic transmission and chain drive. The chassis had a transverse front spring, and full-elliptic rear springs and further suspension was provided for the body which had semi-elliptic springs between it and the chassis. This gave the car a very high and old-fashioned appearance, even for 1901. Production cars, made from 1902 mostly had conventional suspension, and 10hp horizontal 2-cylinder engines, still with epicyclic gearboxes and chain drive.

All the parts for the Rational were made in the small Bassingbourn works, which employed 20 men. The first two bodies were also made there, but most came from Wilson of Royston, although a 4-door limousine of 1905 was made by Sanders of Hitchin. In 1904 Heatly and Gresham leased a factory at the newly-built Letchworth Garden City, being the first business to set up there. Though they never made cars there, they flourished at Letchworth for many years making air compressors and other components. Their last work at Bassingbourn was to make 13 taxicabs with underfloor engines and central driving position for the London Motor Cab Co. Like some of the cars they had solid tyres, although these were replaced by pneumatics in 1906.

NG

Further Reading
Seventeen Taxis, David Hamdorff, Ellis Editions, 1984.

RATIONAL (ii) (GB) 1910–1911
K.J. McMullen, Brimpton, Berkshire.
Thought to be unconnected with the Bassingbourn-based enterprise, this Rational was built in the stables of the private house of the proprietor, one Kenrie James McMullen of Irish origin, and the work-force consisted solely of his butler and his gardener-handyman. Few parts were made in the stables – the cylinder barrels were surplus air-cooled Fafnir motorcycle units, the carburettor a Longuemare, and the overhead worm drive was modified from Tasker traction engine steering gear. Crankcases and crankshafts were fabricated in Reading. The vaunted but troublesome 'torsion spring', fitted between clutch and gearbox, was intended to ensure a smooth drive take-up.

Two models were available, a 14hp V4-cylinder and a 20hp V6-cylinder. A letter in *Motor Sport* in November 1960 disclosed that one of the larger models found its way to North Devon, but the performance was disappointing and reliability unsatisfactory. McMullen also built an aeroplane using a similar engine but there is no record of its having flown, which cannot be said of McMullen himself, of whom there is no subsequent trace. In the mid–1960s Fafnir cylinder barrels were still being dug from the garden, and batches of brochures were found in the attics.

DF

RAUCH & LANG; RAULANG (US) 1905–1928

1905–1915 Rauch & Lang Carriage Co., Cleveland, Ohio.
1915–1920 Baker, Rauch & Lang Co., Cleveland, Ohio.
1920–1928 Rauch & Lang Electric Car Manufacturing Co., Chicopee Falls, Massachusetts.

German-born Jacob Rauch set up a business as blacksmith and wagon repairer in 1853, started making wagons in 1860, and merged with property developer Charles E.J. Lang in 1884. Within a few years they were the most important carriage and wagon builders in Cleveland. In 1903 they took on the Cleveland agency for the BUFFALO electric, and this led them to make electric cars of their own two years later. They made 50 cars in 1905, 2-seater stanhopes, coupés and depot wagons, the latter being a fairly substantial closed car with an open-drive section for the chauffeur. The motors were made by the Hertner Electric Co., and in 1907 they bought up their supplier, making John Hertner chief engineer. They were now making the whole car, and in 1908 delivered 500, with unfulfilled orders for 300 more. They had sales agencies in 20 cities. Most Rauch & Langs were the traditional closed coupé, which they called a coach, but they also made some open 4-seater tourers with short bonnets, and a 2-seater runabout with a longer bonnet, aping a petrol car in the same way that BAKER and DETROIT did.

By 1915 the popularity of the electric car was waning, and R & L merged with Baker, another Cleveland maker of electrics. The new firm was called Baker Rauch & Lang, but the Baker name was dropped on vehicles after 1916. R & L cars were made in quite large numbers, 700 being delivered in 1919, but thereafter production declined. From 1916 to 1919 the OWEN MAGNETIC was made in the Baker R & L factory. In January 1920 Ray S. Deering, president of STEVENS-DURYEA, bought the passenger car business of Baker R & L, and transferred production to a plant in Chicopee Falls next door to the Stevens-Duryea factory. The cars were called Raulang and the taxicabs, which were introduced in 1922 and became the most important product, went under the name R & L. Both petrol and electric cabs were made, the former being the most popular. Passenger car output declined from 143 in 1920 to 103 in 1921, less than 40 in 1922 and undisclosed figures thereafter. In 1924 only one model, the B-58 brougham was listed alongside the cabs, joined from 1925 to 1928 by the Model S-68 4-door sedan. After that the only products were petrol-electric cabs and delivery vans with Willys-Knight engines and General Electric transmission, which were theoretically available up to 1931. Three petrol-electric cars, based on the 1929 Stearns-Knight, were built for Colonel E.H.R. Green, son of the multi-millionaire and noted miser Hetty Green. He had invested in R & L and was attracted to the petrol-electric as a handicap prevented him from changing gear, but he found a pure electric car too slow. As a result of the 1929 Wall Street Crash he withdrew his support and R & L was doomed. His third car survives today.

NG

Further Reading
'Owen and Entz, an Electrifying Combination', Part 3, Karl S. Zahm, *Bulb Horn*, July–September 1991.

RAVA (US/IND) 1997 to date

Amerigon Inc., Monrovia, California.
The Rava was a very compact electric city car saloon with seating for 2+2. Its DC motor was fed by lead-acid batteries, giving it a range of up to 50 miles at speeds up to 40mph (64km/h). Around 50 pre-production prototypes were produced in America prior to a production line being set up in India.

CR

RAVASI (I) 1947

Giulio Ravasi, Milan.
This was an economy car project with front-wheel drive and torsion springing. The specially-conceived engine was especially noteworthy, a 3-cylinder 4-stroke unit with slanting valves and hemispherical combustion chambers. It had a capacity of 750cc and an output of 22bhp.

CR

1901 Rational (i) tonneau.
NATIONAL MOTOR MUSEUM

1903 Rational (i) tonneau.
NATIONAL MOTOR MUSEUM

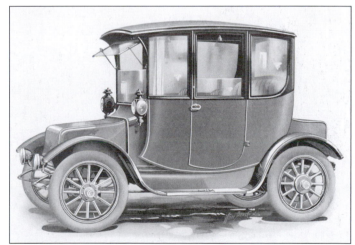
1915 Rauch & Lang J-5 coach.
NICK BALDWIN

RAVEL (i) (F) 1900–1902

SA des Automobiles Louis Ravel, Neuilly, Seine.
There seem to have been two unconnected Ravel cars made at Neuilly at about the same time. The one made by Louis was a voiturette with 5hp V-twin engine under the seat and spur gear drive to the rear axle. There was also a larger car, which may have been only a prototype, with 15hp 2-cylinder 2-stroke engine made in 1902 by Joseph and Édouard Ravel. The former, father of the composer Maurice Ravel, had made a light liquid-fuelled 3-wheeled steam car as early as 1868.

NG

1926 Ravel (ii) at Le Mans, followed by a Rolland-Pilain.
NATIONAL MOTOR MUSEUM

1912 Rayfield Six tourer.
JOHN A. CONDE

RAVEL (ii) (F) 1923–1929
SA des Automobiles Ravel, Besançon, Doubs.

This company was founded by Louis Ravel, maker of the Ravel (i), who left Paris in 1906 and joined Émile Amstoutz in the manufacture of engines at Besançon. In 1910 he helped Théophile Schneider to form Automobiles TH. SCHNEIDER, also in Besançon. In 1923 he began to make cars of his own, a conventional 2296cc 12CV 4-cylinder design, unusual only in that the engine was mounted on a full-width aluminium tray that could be slid out of the chassis. 4-wheel brakes were fitted from the start. In 1926 he introduced a 1460cc 9/11CV and a 13CV, as well as a 2½-litre 6-cylinder engine used in his Le Mans cars in 1927. They did not distinguish themselves in the race, and Ravel not only withdrew from competitions but also abandoned the six. Bodies were built locally, particularly by Langutt and Monjardet. Most were tourers, some of sporting appearance with pointed tails, but there were also some 4- and 6-light saloons. Between 150 and 200 Ravels were made.

NG

Further Reading

Franche-Comté, Berceau de l'Automobile, Raymond Dornier, Éditions l'Est Republicain, 1987.

'Ravel, an Early Name in Automobilism', Marc Douezy, *The Automobile*, June 1995.

RAWLSON (GB) 1982–1992
1982–1987 Rawlson Racing, Dover, Kent.
1987 Classic Replicars, Ashford, Kent.
1987–1988 Western Classics, Bradford-on-Avon, Wiltshire.
1988–1989 Western Classics, Trowbridge, Wiltshire.
1991–1992 Tiger Cars Ltd, London.

Although it was marketed by REPLICAR, this 250LM Ferrari replica was conceived and made by Rawlson, the well-known race car and fibreglass experts. Rawlson had previously dabbled with one road car project, the 1972 CR8, a joint effort with the Belgian specialist maker LIBERTA for a Renault or Simca based coupé. However, the first 250LM prototype was made as early as 1976. The production version arrived in 1982, initially with the ignominy of VW Beetle basis, but a Jago chassis for Ford CVH power was made in 1983. Various other companies marketed Rawlson's 250LM and one significant variation was the 1987 Classic Replicars 164LM, with a very similar body but a tubular steel chassis intended for mid-mounted Alfasud engines; it was taken over by Western Classics. The final owners TIGER offered the 250LM with VW Golf power; some cars even had Rover V8 or Porsche engines.

CR

RAYCO (US) 1998 to date
Rayco Inc., St Louis, Missouri.

The 986 Boxter styling package was a fibreglass kit that transformed the Porsche 914 into a more rounded and aggressive shape. The shovel nose was much lower and a full-width grill ran across the bottom. Engine choices included Porsche 914, Porsche 911, GM V6, GM V8 and Mazda rotaries. These were sold in kit and fully assembled form.

HP

RAYFIELD (US) 1911–1915
1911–1912 Rayfield Motor Car Co., Springfield, Illinois.
1912–1915 Chrisman, Illinois.

Rayfield was a well-known name in the carburettor field, made by Charles, while the cars were the work of his sons Bill and John. They began with a 14/16hp 4-cylinder Junior roadster which was soon joined by a 22/25hp six made in 4-seater toy tonneau and 6-seater tourer forms. In 1912 and 1913 it was quoted as a 30hp. Its distinguishing feature was a dashboard radiator and bonnet very similar to that of a Renault. 218 cars were made in 1913, and for 1914 the brothers launched a light car with 14hp 4-cylinder engine and 2-seater body. Production was 527 cars in 1914, which included some 30hp sixes as well as the light car, and in 1915, when only the light car was produced, 613 were made. Then the Rayfields made the big mistake of contracting production out to the GREAT WESTERN Automobile Co. of Peru, Indiana. Great Western failed to meet the contract, and this marked the end of the Rayfield company.

NG

Further Reading

'The Cars That Didn't Make Chrisman Famous', Mike Mueller, *Automobile Quarterly*, Vol. 32, No. 1.

RAYMOND (i) (US) 1912–1913
Raymond Engineering Co., Hudson, Massachusetts.

Arthur B. Raymond's roadster had a 22hp 4-cylinder engine and sold for $445, the low price reflecting the fact that, according to its designer, it had no clutch, change-speed gear or differential. What it used in place of these components was not explained but it was possibly a friction transmission and chain final drive.

NG

RAYMOND (ii) (F) c.1923–1925
This was one of a number of French cars which used Ford Model T engine and transmission, and doubtless other components. It was advertised from an address in the rue du Faubourg St Honoré in Paris, but the factory location is unknown.

NG

RAYMOND MAYS (GB) 1938–1939
Shelsley Motors Ltd, Bourne, Lincolnshire.

Raymond Mays was one of the best-known British racing drivers of the inter-war years, and was famous also for his sponsorship (with Humphrey Cook) of the ERA racing car which was built behind his house in Bourne. The Raymond Mays car was a separate venture from the ERA, though also made on his property. He named this company after the Shelsley Walsh hill climb, venue of some of his greatest exploits. The car used a 2868cc side-valve Standard V8 engine in a chassis with transverse leaf ifs. Sporting 4-seater tourer and drophead coupé bodies were made, but the car project ended after only five cars had been completed. Drawings exist of a 2-door saloon, but this was never built.

NG

1939 Raymond Mays V8 drophead coupé.
NATIONAL MOTOR MUSEUM

RAYTON FISSORE (I) 1984–1992; 1998 to date

1984–1988 Rayton Fissore, Savigliano, Cuneo.

1988–1992 Rayton Fissore, Chevasco, Cuneo; Laforza Automobiles Inc., Escondido, California.

1998 to date Magnum Industriale srl, Chevasco, Cuneo.

Founded as a coachbuilder in 1976 by the son of Bernardo Fissore, the well-established carroziera, Rayton Fissore's first production hope was the Gold Shadow, first seen in 1978. Based on the Autobianchi A112, it was a pretty 2+2 coupé that was scheduled for small-scale manufacture. Rayton Fissore sold the project to a Spanish company which hoped to produce it as the Guapa. Meanwhile in Italy Rayton Fissore did become a manufacturer with the Magnum in 1984, sometimes described as the 'Rolls-Royce of off-roaders'. It was a Range Rover style 4x4 vehicle, initially fitted with Alfa Romeo engines, but from 1988 with BMW 6-cylinder units and later VM turbodiesels. Its 5-door estate bodywork was a mixture of steel and fibreglass. Drive was normally to the rear wheels but 4x4 drive could be switched on. The Magnum found much favour with Italian police departments, and also in the American market, where the car was modified and assembled in California as the Laforza, equipped with a 4.9-litre Ford V8 engine. After a gap in production, the Magnum made a reappearance in 1998 with a restyled front and a wide range of bodystyles. Various engines, including 4- and 5-cylinder turbodiesels and three petrol engines (4-, V6- and V8-cylinder), were offered and there was a choice of 5-speed manual or 4-speed automatic transmissions.

CR

R.B.M. (GB) 1993–1996

1993 R.B.M. Motorsport, Finedon, Northamptonshire.

1993–1996 Midas Racing Services, Little Staughton, Bedfordshire.

The R.B.M. Pulsar was a Can-Am style road/racer on an alloy-panelled spaceframe chassis, using a Ford Escort rear axle and a wide range of engines (a Vauxhall 2-litre unit was fitted to the prototype). The very low, open bodywork was in fibreglass and was available in two versions: the 931 for racing and 942 for road use.

CR

1985 Rayton Fissore Magnum 4x4 estate car.
NICK BALDWIN

R.C.H. (US) 1912–1915

The Hupp Corp., Detroit, Michigan.

In 1911 Robert C. Hupp left the Hupp Motor Car Co. which he had founded in 1909 to make the HUPMOBILE because of the plans of his fellow directors to make a more expensive car. He then set up his own company to produce the kind of reasonably-priced car he had intended the Hupmobile to be. Named for his initials, the R.C.H. had a 22hp 4-cylinder engine, rode on a 86in (2183mm) wheelbase and cost, in its cheapest model, only $700. Demand was surprisingly strong; 7000 cars were sold in 1912 and Hupp had orders for more than 15,000 of his 1913 models. He lacked the capital to cope with this and stepped down as president in favour of Charles P. Seider. The 1913 models were larger, with 25hp engines and a 110in (2792mm) wheelbase which allowed for a full 5-seater tourer body as well as a coupé and a roadster. However, the R.C.H.'s reputation had suffered from hasty manufacture to meet the initial demand. Rather than try expensive publicity to rectify this Seider decided to close the business, and the last R.C.H. cars were made in the summer of 1915.

NG

1913 R.C.H. 22hp tourer.
NATIONAL MOTOR MUSEUM

1911 Reading (ii) 40 roadster.
JOHN A. CONDE

R&D (US) c.1997 to date
R&D Design Concepts, Omaha, Nebraska.
Bob Schumacher built and sold limited numbers of his Cobra Daytona Coupé replica kit. It had a simple tubular chassis with Ford-based suspension and V8 engines. They were only sold in kit form.
HP

R.D.1 (GB) 1998 to date
Hand Crafted Cars, Thornton Heath, Surrey.
Britain's first Lamborghini Diablo replica was the R.D.1. It followed kit 'supercar' practice in having a spaceframe chassis with fabricated suspension including 4-coil rear suspension, Ford Granada brakes and a choice of mid-mounted engines (typically Rover V8). The replica bodywork was in fibreglass.
CR

R.E.A.C. (F) 1953–1955
Recherches et Études Automobiles Chérifiennes, Champigny.
The rakish R.E.A.C. roadster was the brainchild of a young Moroccan engineer. Using an air-cooled Panhard Dyna engine, the R.E.A.C. debuted at the 1953 Paris Salon, where it was heralded as the first-ever French fibreglass-bodied car. It went on to sell 15 examples (including three with extraordinary turret-shaped hard-tops) before production stopped in 1955.
CR

READ (US) 1913–1914
Read Motor Car Co., Detroit, Michigan.
This company was founded in the middle of 1913 to make a very ordinary car with 20hp 4-cylinder engine. The only body style was a 5-seater tourer, and the most unusual thing about the car was its designation of 'Model X'. Read was out of business by early 1914, so few cars can have been made.
NG

READING (i) (US) 1901–1902
Steam Vehicle Co. of America, Reading, Pennsylvania.
This company was founded by Irvin D. Lendel to make a light steam car. The 2-cylinder model was typical of its kind, the four less so, although as this was an option one does not known how many 4-cylinder Reading Steamers were sold. It its layout the Reading was quite typical, with engine under the seat driving the rear axle by single-chain, tiller steering and wire wheels. Only two models were offered in 1901, but the 1902 catalogue listed seven body styles, which was probably too many for a small firm. Some had artillery wheels and small bonnets which gave them some distinction from the usual run of steam cars. In 1902 creditors moved in and a new company was formed, the Meteor Engineering Co. which made another steamer called the METEOR (ii). This lasted less than one year, and Lendel kept clear of the automobile business for 12 years, then formed the DILE Motor Car Co.
NG

READING (ii) (US) 1910–1913
Middleby Automobile Co., Reading, Pennsylvania.
This was a larger and more expensive companion make to the MIDDLEBY, having a 40hp 4-cylinder engine, 120in (3046mm) wheelbase and was made in two models, tourer and roadster. In 1911 the Reading tourer cost $475 more than the Middleby tourer, though both had 40hp engines and a 122in (3096mm) wheelbase. Surprisingly, the two makes were continued side by side until October 1913, when both were discontinued.
NG

REAL (US) 1914–1915
1914 Real Cyclecar Co., Anderson, Indiana.
1914–1915 Real Light Car Co., Converse, Indiana.
These two companies were founded by the splendidly named H. Paul Prigg, and the cars they made were both typical of their kind. The cyclecar had the unusual layout of a rear-mounted engine, a 2-cylinder air-cooled Wizard driving the rear wheels by belts, and tandem seating for two, though the rear seat could, 'if necessary, accommodate two'. The buyer was offered the choice of a 36in (914mm) or standard 56in (1421mm) track on the cyclecar, but the light car could be had only with the standard. It was otherwise totally different, with a front-mounted engine, 2- or 4-cylinder, and bucket seat ahead of a bolster tank, like a miniature MERCER 35. The company was bankrupt in December 1915, and Prigg moved to Florida to build boats.
NG

REBER (US) 1902–1903
Reber Manufacturing Co., Reading, Pennsylvania.
James C. Reber was a bicycle maker who was looking for new business when the cycle craze began to wane at the turn of the century. He built a car in 1900 but was dissatisfied with it, and hired James Heaslet from AUTOCAR to design a new car with 12hp 2-cylinder engine, double-chain drive and a rear-entrance tonneau body. It was marketed in 1902 and 1903, but Reber then brought in another designer, Viktor Jakob from DAIMLER (i) in Germany. The new car was called the ACME, and would be made until 1911.
NG

REBOUR (F) 1905–1908
Automobiles Rebour, Puteaux, Seine.
Although there are no references to cars earlier than 1905, this company is said to have made chassis for other firms. The 1906 range included four chassis, of 10/12, 18/22, 20/25 and 40/50hp, all with 4-cylinder engines, pair-cast cylinders, 4-speed gearboxes and double-chain drive. The radiators, and indeed the whole design, were very much on Mercedes lines. Rebour were said to have exported cars to Germany, which seems rather unlikely in view of the prevalence of Mercedes there, and also to Spain, where they were sold under the name Catalonia.
NG

RED ARROW (US) 1914

Red Arrow Automobile Co., Orange, Massachusetts.
The makers of this 12hp 2-cylinder cyclecar leased the factory that had formerly been used for the manufacture of GROUT steam and petrol cars. Only prototypes were built.

NG

RED BUG (US) 1924–1930

Automotive Electric Service Corp., North Bergen, New Jersey.
This was a very simple buckboard formerly known as the BRIGGS & STRATTON, from the makers of its engines, and before that as the SMITH FLYER. When it moved to New Jersey it was christened the Red Bug, or sometimes Auto Red Bug, but it retained the same layout of a slatted unsprung frame, two bucket seats and a 5hp single-cylinder motor wheel which was lowered to the road when the driver wished to move off. There was also an electric version which had only four wheels, and was powered by a 12-volt Northeast motor which was the same as Dodge used for their starters. It drove the nearside rear wheel, and a brake acted on the offside wheel. Both petrol and electric Red Bugs cost $150. They were used at holiday resorts and amusement parks; some were exported to Europe and were seen at fashionable French resorts like Deauville and Le Touquet.

NG

REDHEAD ROADSTERS (US) c.1994

Redhead Roadsters, Waitsburg, Washington.
This company bought a number of existing car projects and put them back into production. The Dauphin 2+2 was the old AURIGA kit, while the Vokaro had been built by VOPARD. They also re-introduced the STERLING. The Machette Speedster was a VW-based kit car that resembled a stylised dune buggy but with open wheels. The Coffin Nose was a neoclassic kit loosely based on the Cord 812. All RR kits were based on the Volkswagen Beetle floorpan, and were sold in kit or turn-key form with VW, V6, Mazda rotary or electric power.

HP

RED JACKET (US) 1904–1905

O.K. Machine Works, Buffalo, New York.
This was a conventional-looking rear-entrance tonneau powered by a front-mounted 10hp 2-cylinder engine, with 3-speed gearbox and double-chain final drive. It had a single acetylene headlamp and two oil side lamps.

NG

REDPATH (CDN) 1903–1907

1903–1905 Redpath Motor Vehicle Co., Berlin (later Kitchener), Ontario.
1905–1907 A.H. Robinson & Co., Toronto, Ontario.
Made by William Redpath and Andrew Reid, this was a light car powered by an 1172cc single-cylinder engine, with 2-speed gearbox and shaft drive. It had an angle-iron frame and the bodies came from Alfred Robinson of Toronto, who took up manufacture of the cars in 1905, calling them Redpath Messengers. Very few were made at either location; only three in Toronto, one of which still exists today.

NG

REES (US) 1921

Rees Motor Co., Columbus, Ohio.
The Rees was stillborn, one of many cars introduced during 1921 which failed to get beyond working prototypes. The company, with headquarters in Cleveland, acquired the plant used by Halladay before its move to nearby Newark, Ohio, and advertised the car with verbal accolades. 'A Light-Weight High Grade Car', ran the promotion, 'designed by J. Howard Rees, one of the foremost Automotive Engineers of today'. 'Associated with Mr Rees' it went on 'is a corps of American, French and British Engineers, direct from one of the largest and most successful automobile factories in the United States.' The copy did not identify the factory. The Rees was a small car with a 108in (2741mm) wheelbase, its own 4-cylinder engine developing 20bhp at 2200rpm, and its touring car – the only planned body type – priced at $1850. At least six prototypes were completed.

KM

c.1926 Red Bug electric runabout.
NATIONAL MOTOR MUSEUM

1911 Reeves (i) Octo-Auto tourer.
NICK BALDWIN

REEVES (i) (US) 1896–1898; 1905–1912

1896–1898; 1905–1910 The Reeves Pulley Co., Columbus, Indiana.
1911–1912 Milton O. Reeves, the Reeves Sexto-Octo Co., Columbus, Indiana.
Milton Reeves ran a successful company making pulleys for industrial use, and built his first car, which he called a Motocycle, to demonstrate the use of variable-speed belt pulleys in transmitting power. It was a substantial car with a 2-cylinder Sintz marine engine and, because neighbours complained of its noise, he fitted one of the first silencers. He made at least five vehicles up to 1898, with 6 or 12hp engines either by Sintz or of his own design. One was a 20-seater bus with rear wheels nearly six feet in diameter. After 1898 Reeves concentrated on making the VST (Variable Speed Transmission), though his air-cooled engines became more popular, and were sold to a number of car makers including AEROCAR, CHATHAM, MAPLEBAY and MARION. It was the failure of Aerocar to take their full order of 500 engines that led Reeves into car manufacture again. He made 4-cylinder shaft drive and 6-cylinder chain-drive cars and, in 1907, a high-wheeler called the Go-Buggy with 2-cylinder engine. However, by 1910 the demands of the pulley company were such that car manufacture was given up for the second time.

Milton Reeves was not through with cars, though, and in 1911 he built an enormous machine with four axles, which he called the Octo-Auto. With a wheelbase of 180in (4569mm) and overall length of 248in (6294mm), it was derived from a 1910 OVERLAND. Although it attracted a lot of attention it was too cumbersome to be a serious sales proposition, though Reeves quoted a price of $3200. He removed one front axle and called the result a Sexto-Auto, and followed this with another 6-wheeler based on a STUTZ. This was priced at $5000, doubtless reflecting the higher price of the Stutz. It remained a one-off. Though he had formed at least a nominal company for his multi-wheelers, Reeves made no more.

NG

REEVES (ii) (GB) 1985 to date

The Matrix, a dodgem-like 3-wheeler prototype, was exhibited at the Stoneleigh Kit Car Show in 1985. Three years later, a sports coupé 4-wheeler was presented

1903 Régal (i) 9hp 2-seater.
NICK BALDWIN

1910 Regal (ii) 30hp tourer.
JOHN A. CONDE

in 1988 but again no more was heard for several years. The production-ready Reeves Revera used the engine of the Austin Princess/Ambassador mounted centrally, which certainly limited its already scant appeal.

CR

REFLEX (GB) 1987–1993
1987–1992 Reflex Sportscars, Cardigan, Dyfed.
1992–1993 Reflex Sportscars, Preston, Lancashire.
Davrian was Wales' only car maker in the late 1970s and early 1980s. When it liquidated in 1983, ex-chief designer Gareth Atkinson attempted to go it alone with his own mid-engined sports car. The first example had a fibreglass monocoque designed to accept Fiat or Lancia Beta engines and running gear but a more practical option was a spaceframe backbone chassis, also available for Ford CVH power. The rear suspension employed Ford Escort XR3 struts while a modified Fiesta set-up was used at the front.

CR

REFORM *see* THEIN & GOLDBERGER

RÉGAL (i) (F) 1903–c.1905
O.C. Selbach, Paris.
Régal was one of the names under which LACOSTE ET BATTMANN cars were sold. The first was a 2-seater, powered by a 6hp De Dion-Bouton engine, but later Régals were larger cars with Aster and Mutel engines with 2- or 4-cylinders.

NG

REGAL (ii) (US) 1908–1918
Regal Motor Car Co., Detroit, Michigan.
The first Regals were conventional touring cars powered by 30 or 35hp 4-cylinder engines. In late 1910 they introduced the car that was to make them famous, the Twenty roadster with underslung frame. This was made alongside larger cars of 30 and 40hp with conventional frames. They were imported into England by

Seabrook of Great Eastern Street, London, and sold under the names R.M.C. (Regal Motor Co.) or Seabrook-R.M.C. In 1912 they introduced a Colonial Coupé on the 20hp underslung chassis, and in 1913, when power was increased to 25hp, the Model T tourer. For 1915 a 2.1-litre 20hp Light Four and a 40hp V8 were introduced, both made by the Port Huron Construction Co. Regals were made in quite substantial numbers, 8136 in 1914 and 8227 in 1915, but supply problems arose once America had entered World War I. Output dwindled to 823 in 1918, after which Regal Motor Co. closed down.

Seabrook showed a 3.8-litre 6-cylinder car they called an R.M.C. at the 1919 Olympia Show, but its origin is a mystery as Regal never made a six, or certainly never advertised or listed one.

NG

REGAL (iii) (CDN) 1910
Regal Motor Car Co. of Canada, Walkerville, Ontario.
This was a short-lived attempt to make the American Regal in Canada, in a plant just across the river from the American factory. A 30hp tourer was advertised, but very few were made.

NG

REGAL (iv) (CDN) 1914–1917
Canadian Regal Motors Ltd, Berlin (later Kitchener), Ontario.
The second Canadian Regal venture was more successful than the first, perhaps because it was run by the dynamic Henry Nyberg who had made cars under his own name, and was also involved in the MADISON. A 30hp four and the V8 were made in the Canadian factory, with local bodywork which had more attractive lines than the cars from Detroit. The factory was the first in Canada to have a proper test track and hill, and also boasted a club building with dining rooms (one for factory workers, one for white collar staff), reading room and pool room. Between 200 and 400 cars were sold up to the end of 1916 when supply problems arose with the Detroit factory. Doubtless they wanted to keep the dwindling number of components for themselves. Nyberg closed and sold the factory, then built another next door where he planned to make the SAXON. When this plan did not materialise he made the Dominion unit which converted cars into light trucks.

NG

REGAL ROADSTERS (US) c.1986 to date
Regal Roadsters, Madison, Wisconsin.
The Regal 1955 Ford Thunderbird replica was much more accurate than most T-Bird kit cars. The body was identical to the original, and it had a ladder frame that mounted Ford V8 running gear. President Chuck Siewert had started this company as a restoration shop, so he was concerned with making the kits look correct. In 1998 Regal added another version with customised bodywork and a bonnet scoop. It was designed to take 7000cc engines with heavier-duty suspension.

HP

REGAS (US) 1903–1905
Regas Automobile Co., Rochester, New York.
This car was made by Frederick Sager who named it from the reverse spelling of his surname. The first Regas had a 7hp single-cylinder engine, while for 1904 Sager branched out with a 12hp V-twin and a 20hp V-4, which carried 4-seater tourer as well as 2-seater runabout bodies. He used a Marble-Swift friction transmission and shaft drive. Sager exhibited five cars at New York's National Automobile Show in January 1904, but he was soon in financial trouble and sold out to new owners who planned a new 4-cylinder car with conventional 3-speed gearbox. This barely passed the prototype stage, and the Regas name died before the end of 1905.

NG

REGENT (D) 1903–1904
Machinenfabrik W. Stutznacker, Dortmund.
This was a well-established ironworks which turned out a few cars, but had little success on the market.

HON

REGINA (i) (F) 1903–1908
Sté l'Électrique, Paris.

1912 Regal (ii) 25hp tourer.
NICK BALDWIN

This company offered petrol and electric cars. The petrol cars were DIXIs, while the electrics generally went under the trade name Gallia. They were made with the usual styles of electric cars of the time, landaulets and closed coupés for town work, and there was also the Galliette, a light 2-seater runabout with the motor in the centre of the chassis, driving the rear axle by shaft. The larger Gallias had their motors, with 6-speed controllers, acting directly on the rear axle. Some Gallias were sold in America, surprising in view of the large number of native makers of electric vehicles.

NG

REGINA (ii) (F) c.1922–1925
Automobiles Regina, Paris.
This was a 3-wheeler with single front wheel, powered by a 4-cylinder engine mounted transversely at the rear and driving the rear axle. It had a starter which could be operated from the seat. To quote John Bolster (*French Vintage Cars*) 'This tricycle could be bought as a cyclecar 2-seater, which was reasonable, or as a 4-seater saloon, which was surely flying in the face of providence. Like most of these quaint conceits, the Regina was seen no more after 1925'.

NG

REGINETTE (F) c.1922
Built in Paris, the Reginette was a very light cyclecar made in single- or 2-seater form, both of which were powered by a rear-mounted 247cc 2½hp 2-stroke engine. Like the BRIGGS & STRATTON and RED BUG the Reginette had a wooden-slatted floor with no other springing, as the slats were said to be '*d'une souplesse extraordinaire*'. Like its American equivalents, it was popular on the seafront, and the Type Plage was a bodyless 2-seater. For an extra 300 francs there was the Type Sport, which had a light metal cowling over the driver's feet.

NG

REGIS (GB) 1989–1992
Regis Automotive, Bognor Regis, West Sussex.
The first product of Bruce Dixon's was the Ram 4S, a copy of the 1974 Lotus Elite based on Ford Cortina parts. A redesign produced an alternative hatchback coupé style called the Mohawk, which was launched in 1989. The Cortina basis was kept, though the suspension was modified. There was a space frame chassis and an unstressed fibreglass body. Any Cortina engine could be used, or a Rover V8 if desired.

CR

REGNER (F) 1905–1906
Daniel Regner, Paris.
This was a light car with 6hp single-cylinder engine and belt drive.

NG

REID (i) (NZ) 1902–1905
A.W. Reid, Stratford, North Island.
Reid's first steam car, with a paraffin-burning boiler, a 2-cylinder engine and chain drive, was made in 1902 and a batch of improved examples was constructed during 1905.

MG

1960 Reliant Regal VI 3-wheeler.
NICK GEORGANO

REID (ii) *see* WOLVERINE (i)

REINE *see* BRANDT

REINERTSEN *see* REX BUCKBOARD

REINHARD (F) 1911–1914
Sté de Construction des Moteurs Reinhard, Lyons.
Valentin Reinhard designed a sleeve-valve engine which he hoped to sell to DELAUGÈRE-CLAYETTE and MINERVA. Failing to succeed with either firm, he made a few cars using his own engines. The first had 2-litre 4-cylinder engines, chain drive and tourer bodies. A later model was known as Melanie and had a 3-litre engine and shaft drive. Reinhard did not make more than 20 cars.
NG

REISACHER-JULIEN (F) 1900
Éts Reisacher-Julien, Marseilles.
This company made a small number of cars with Reisacher engines and Julien bodies.
NG

REISSIG (D) 1912–1914
Automobilwerk 'Siegfried' Arno Kohl-Krugel, Reissig, nr. Plauen.
This small company made only a few cars with 9/26PS 4-cylinder engines. They were of solid construction and reliable, but production was not resumed after the war. They also went under the names Siegfried and RAW (Reissig Automobile Werke).
HON

REIVER *see* CHALLENGER

REKORD (D) 1905–1908
Internationale Automobilcentrale Dr Mengers & Bellmann, Berlin.
Rekord cars were assembled largely from French components, using engines from 8 to 80hp. The closest they came to fame was participation in the Herkomer Trials in 1905 and 1906, but they did not have much success.
HON

RELAY (US) 1903–1904
Relay Motor Car Co., Reading, Pennsylvania.
The Relay was powered by a 24hp in-line 3-cylinder engine with ohvs, made by the little-known Wyoma company. It had a 3-speed gearbox and shaft drive. Only one body style was offered, a 5-seater tourer, and the price was $2000. The company announced at the New York Automobile Show in January 1904 that they would make 25 cars that year, but it is not known whether they did.
NG

RELIABLE DAYTON (US) 1906–1909
Reliable Dayton Motor Car Co., Chicago, Illinois.
This was a high-wheeler powered by a 15hp 2-cylinder 2-stroke engine with final drive by rope. The open models had the typical high-wheeler appearance,

but the company also offered an enclosed coupé. This was continued on the 1908 model which had a little dummy bonnet, though the engine remained under the seat. The car's name came from William O. Dayton who also ran the Dayton & Mashey Automobile works which made the engines. Later models had 4-stroke engines. During 1909 the factory was taken over by the Fal Motor Co. for manufacture of the F.A.L. car.
NG

RELIANCE (US) 1904–1906
1903–1904 Reliance Automobile Manufacturing Co., Detroit, Michigan.
1904–1906 Reliance Motor Car Co., Detroit, Michigan.
This company was founded in late 1903, although no cars were built until the early months of 1904. They had 2-cylinder engines, originally of 15hp, enlarged to 18/22hp in 1905 and 28hp in 1906. Although even the first model had a 5-seater body, the wheelbase was increased from 86 (2183mm) to 109in (2766mm) during the make's short lifespan. They claimed that the 1904 model had America's first side-entrance tonneau body, but at least two other makes, ORLO and PEERLESS, had this feature in the same year. In 1906 they added a truck to their range and a year later discontinued passenger cars. In 1909 they were bought by General Motors, and two years later the Reliance truck became the GMC.
NG

RELIANT (GB) 1952 to date
1952–1963 Reliant Engineering Co. (Tamworth) Ltd, Tamworth, Staffordshire.
1963–1995 Reliant Motor Co. Ltd, Tamworth, Staffordshire.
1995–1998 Reliant Motors, Tamworth, Staffordshire.
1998 to date Reliant Cars Ltd, Burntwood, Staffordshire.
Reliant Engineering Ltd was established in 1935 to make 3-wheeled delivery vans powered by 747cc Austin Seven engines. Reliant later made these themselves, and in 1952 brought out their first passenger car. This was the Regal, a 4-seater convertible 3-wheeler with aluminium body on a box-section chassis. With only 16bhp it was hard put to reach 60mph (97km/h), but it was economical, and more roomy and car-like than rivals such as the single-cylinder Bond Minicar. In 1956 came the Regal Mk III with a fibreglass body of more rounded lines, available as a saloon and tourer. It was a significant development, as all subsequent Reliant vehicles, 3- and 4-wheelers, have had fibreglass bodies. In 1962 the 747cc engine was replaced by a Reliant-designed all-aluminium unit, initially of 598cc, enlarged to 701cc in 1967. 1962 also saw re-styled bodies now made of fully integrated fibreglass instead of the previous fibreglass panels on an ash framework. Known as the 3/25 and 3/30, these 3-wheelers were made, in closed form only, until 1973, when they were replaced by the Robin. This had an Ogle-designed body and engine enlarged to 750cc (850cc from 1976). This in turn gave way in 1981 to the Rialto with the same engine and updated styling, which was still in production in 1999, again under the Robin name. The Bond Bug 3-wheelers were also made by Reliant, as Reliant bought up the Bond company in 1969.
Reliant's first 4-wheeler appeared in 1958, though it was not sold under the Reliant name. The Sussita estate car was developed for manufacture in Israel by Autocars of Haifa. The bodyshells were moulded locally from moulds supplied by Reliant, and the power unit was from the Ford Anglia (see SABRA). This was the beginning of Reliant's business of providing a 'packaged motor industry' to countries which had little industry of their own. Subsequent examples of this were the Anadol saloon for Otosan Industries of Turkey, the Mebea pick-up for Greece and the Sipani Dolphin for India. There was also the Anziel Nova, an Anadol-like saloon which was to have been built in New Zealand, but this never went into production.
In 1964 Reliant brought out a small 4-wheeled saloon and estate car called the Rebel. This was powered by the 598cc engine from the 3/25 3-wheeler, and was intended to sell to owners who wanted to graduate from three wheels. However, it was expensive for what it offered, and most 3-wheeler graduates preferred a Mini or Ford Anglia. Only 700 Rebels were made in eight years, later examples having 701cc, then 748cc engines. 1975 saw the Kitten, a 4-wheeled version of the Robin, with 848cc engine and improved styling. This fared somewhat better than the Rebel, selling 4074 units up to 1982, after which Reliant gave up competing in the popular saloon market.

1963 Reliant Sabre sports car.
NICK BALDWIN

The car for which Reliant became best known originated in another Israeli product. The managing director of Autocars, Mr Shubinsky, wanted to get into the American market, clearly an impossible task with the utilitarian Sabra Sussita. He was impressed by the independently sprung chassis produced by Leslie Ballamy for the EB Debonair sports car, and also by the Ashley fibreglass bodies which were offered for Austin and Ford chassis. He suggested to Reliant's deputy managing director Ray Wiggin that the British company combine the two designs in a sports car which would be called the Sabra, after an Israeli cactus, also the name given to an Israeli-born citizen, as opposed to an immigrant.

When it appeared at the 1961 New York Show, the Sabra was somewhat different from Shubinsky's original concept; the LMB suspension needed considerable modification, and coils were substituted for the transverse leaves, while the Ashley body was not suitable as it stood. Reliant had to make a floorpan of marine plywood encased in fibreglass, which was bonded to the fibreglass outer shell. For power they chose the 1703cc Ford Consul engine, mated to a ZF all-synchromesh 4-speed gearbox. The first 100 Sabras were fully constructed at Tamworth, and two of them were retained by Reliant, built in rhd form and exhibited at the 1961 Earls Court Show under the slightly modified name Sabre.

A total of 208 Sabre 4s were made between 1961 and 1963, of which 55 were sold on the British market, and the rest exported. In addition, about 50 kits were sent to Israel for local assembly, but this never took place, as Autocars of Haifa went into liquidation. Despite a twin carburettor conversion which increased power to 90bhp, the Sabre 4 was thought to be underpowered, so the logical answer was to use a bigger Ford engine, the 2.6-litre six from the Zephyr/Zodiac range. With a restyled front end (also seen on the last eight Sabre 4s) and improved suspension, the Sabre 6 was a much better car, with a top speed of 108mph (174km/h). Several rally successes were achieved, of which the best were 1st and 2nd in class in the 1963 Alpine. A total of 77 Sabre 6s were made, all but two being GT coupés. This was in contrast to the Sabre 4, of which the majority were open cars.

At the 1962 Earls Court Show Ray Wiggin was attracted by the Ogle-designed 2+2-seater coupé on the Daimler SP250 chassis. Negotiations with David Ogle Design led to this being made by Reliant for mounting on the Sabre chassis, which needed to be lengthened by only 2in to make it acceptable for the Ogle

1965 Reliant Regal 3-wheeler.
NICK BALDWIN

body. This was a much more attractive design than the Sabre, and warranted a new name, Scimitar. The SE4A, as the original model was called, was made up to 1966, 296 being delivered. It was then replaced by the SE4B with Ford's 3-litre V6 engine, followed by an economy version, the 2.5-litre SE4C.

In 1965 Reliant built an interesting one-off, the result of a commission given to Ogle by Triplex Safety Glass. Known as the GTS (Glazing Test Special), it had an estate car type of body with a glass roof over driver and passenger, and curved glass panels at the rear. All these panels were of Sundym heat absorbent glass. After it had done the rounds of European motor shows, the GTS was bought by HRH the Duke of Edinburgh, who used it for about 18 months before selling it back to Triplex. It started a connection between Reliant and the British Royal Family, for in 1970 his daughter HRH the Princess Anne took delivery of a Scimitar GTE, the first of eight she subsequently owned.

The GT estate concept of the Triplex Special was put into production for 1969 as the Scimitar GTE. The wheelbase was extended by 6.5in (165mm) and the overall length by 3in (76mm). The low and yet roomy 2-door estate body set a fashion for the sporting estate car, later taken up in the Volvo 1800ES, Lancia Beta HPE and Honda Aerodeck. The engine was the 3-litre Ford V6, and there

1974 Reliant Robin 3-wheeler.
NICK GEORGANO

1976 Reliant Kitten estate car.
NICK BALDWIN

1988 Reliant Rialto hatchback.
RELIANT

1986 Reliant Scimitar SS 1800TI sports car.
RELIANT

was a choice of transmissions, manual 4-speed, manual 4-speed with overdrive, and automatic, the latter two available from 1971 and 1970 respectively. Top speed with a manual box was nearly 125mph (201km/h). The combination of speed and carrying capacity caught on with the public, and the GTE achieved better sales than any of its predecessors. Whereas the Scimitar coupé had sold only 1003 between 1964 and 1970, the GTE found 9416 buyers for the first version (1969–75), and a further 4857 of the improved SE6 which was made up to the end of 1986.

Reliant was booming in the mid-70s, with production of 350 3-wheelers and 50 Scimitars a week. The main changes in the SE6 were an extra 4in (102mm) in wheelbase and 1.25in (32mm) in width, giving additional carrying capacity, and in 1980, on the SE6B the German Ford 2.8-litre V6 engine was used. In the same year a convertible called the SE8B was launched, but only 442 of these were made before all Scimitar production was halted in November 1986. Production had dropped drastically, from a peak of 1600 in 1977, to a mere three cars per week in 1982. After an initial run of 300 GTC convertibles in 1980, only about 20 were made per year. As sales fell, due to the increasing sophistication of rivals, so unit costs of production rose, and Reliant had no alternative but to discontinue the Scimitar. Production rights were acquired in June 1987 by MIDDLEBRIDGE Engineering of Milton Keynes.

The next car to bear the Scimitar name was the SS1 (Small Sportscar 1), designed to fill the gap left by the demise of the MG Midget. This appeared in October 1984 with a choice of Ford engines, 1300 (69bhp) and 4-speed gearbox, and 1600 (96bhp) and 5-speed gearbox. It had a fabricated steel chassis made in Germany, with all-round independent suspension, and a Michelotti-styled fibreglass 2-seater body. This was initially made only in open form, but a hard-top was available from late 1985. Sales of the SS1 did not reach the anticipated 3000 per year, only 550 being sold between March 1985, when it went on the market, and the end of the year. The figures for 1986 and 1987 were only 277 and 183, despite the introduction of a higher-performance model powered by a turbocharged Nissan 1800 engine. This had a top speed of over 125mph (201km/h), compared with 110mph (180km/h) for the Ford 1600-engined car. There were rumours that the whole SS1 project would be sold, possibly to an American buyer. The body was restyled by William Towns in 1988, (SS2) and again in 1990 (SST) but these did not find many buyers. In March 1988 the factory at Two Gates, Tamworth, where SS1s were made was sold. Limited production continued at the Kettlebrook works where the 3-wheelers were made. The SST 1800 was renamed Sabre in 1992, the Ford-engined model still being called SST. A Rover K series engine replaced the Ford. Reliant went into receivership in December 1995, and in April 1996 it was taken over by Jonathan Heynes of Jaguar, son of William Heynes. His confidence in Reliant's future was shown by using his own money to pay the purchase price (just over £1m) rather than borrowing from a bank. The Robin went back into production in May 1996, starting with 14 partially completed cars left over from the previous regime. By November 1996 production was up to 20 cars per week, and a new sports car was planned for 1998. However, Heynes left in September 1998 and the sports car was abandoned. Instead Reliant's new owners, Glen UK, planned to import the Indian-made SAN Storm and Streak light cars, the LIGIER microcar and Piaggio Ape 3-wheeled truck. The only native product to be continued was the Robin, now made in a new factory shared with Fletcher International Sportsboats.

In 1985–86 Reliant built the 200 Ford RS200 Group B rally cars, whose career was cut short by the banning of such cars from European rallies. In 1989 they took over production of the Metrocab London taxi, and these continued to be made at the Kettlebrook factory.

NG

Further Reading
Reliant – the Scimitar and its Forebears, Don Pither, Court Publishing, 1987.

RELYANTE (F) c.1903
Relyante Motor Works, Walthamstow, London.
Although listed as British cars, most models sold by the Relyante company were imported from France. These included a 6½hp single-cylinder 2-seater from LACOSTE ET BATTMANN, a 12hp twin from DELAHAYE and a 10hp steamer from SERPOLLET. There was one model which cannot be linked with any import, and may have been home-grown. This was a shaft-driven 4-cylinder car with pressed steel frame and semi-elliptic springs which at the rear were

1977 Reliant Scimitar GTE.
NICK BALDWIN

mounted outside the frame. A step at the rear of the chassis indicated that a rear-entrance tonneau body would be fitted.

NG

REMAG (D) 1924
Richter & Maak, Chemnitz.
This was a light sports car powered by a 1-litre engine developing 24bhp, with a light metal 2-seater body. Production must have been minimal.

HON

REMAL-VINCENT (US) 1923
Steam Automotive Corp., Oakland, California.
This was a steam car powered by a V-4 engine designed by Ernest Vincent, and backed by a consortium of businessmen whose surnames made up the acronym R-E-M-A-L. A start-up time of two minutes from cold was promised, as was a price of $1500. Three demonstrators were built, but disagreements between Vincent and his backers put an end to the project.

NG

REMARQUE (CDN) 1984 to date
ReMarque Handcrafted Roadsters Inc, Stayner, Ontario.
This A.C. Cobra replica used a square-steel ladder chassis fitted with a steel floor, bulkhead and transmission tunnel. In other respects it was entirely conventional, and was marketed in the USA as a cheaper route to Cobra replica ownership.

CR

REMI-DANVIGNES (F) 1935–1939
Remi Danvignes et Cie, Paris.
A great motorcycle enthusiast, Remi Danvignes ran the Moto Bastille shop in Paris specialising in 2-wheeler equipment of all kinds. In 1935 he decided to enter the car market with a small sports car very similar to the 6CV GEORGES IRAT, though to start with Danvignes favoured 2-cylinder engines, which Irat never used. The prototype had an air-cooled Dresch motorcycle unit, but for production cars Danvignes made his own, a water-cooled 750cc vertical twin

with ohvs, in conjunction with a 4-speed gearbox also designed by Danvignes. The simple open 2-seater body was of aluminium, and rested on a tubular frame with all-round independent suspension. The price was 11,900 francs. Production ran at about two cars per week up to the summer of 1938 when Danvignes announced a new model powered by a 1078cc 4-cylinder Ruby engine. He now had a car very similar to the 6CV Georges Irat, just as the latter was moving on to a larger car powered by a Citroën engine. The gearbox, chassis and suspension were much as before, but the body was restyled and built by Pourtout. This model was made up to the outbreak of war.

NG

REMINGTON (i) (US) 1900–1904
1900–1901 Remington Automobile & Motor Co., Illion, New York.
1901–1903 Remington Automobile & Motor Co., Utica, New York.
1903–1904 Remington Motor Vehicle Co., Utica, New York.
Backed by Philo E. Remington, of the famous firearms and typewriter makers, the first Remington car was an unusual one, with a 4-cylinder engine using a mixture of hydrogen and acetylene gas for fuel. 4 or 6hp models were offered, with bodies for two or four passengers. Machinery was bought from the recently defunct QUICK Automobile Co. of Newark, New Jersey. Before long manufacture moved to Utica and the four was replaced by a more conventional 4/6hp single-cylinder car, followed by a 10hp twin in 1902. The company was re-organised in 1903, when ten cars were said to be under construction. The new owners offered the 10hp twin in 2- and 4-seater forms, but they were not a success, and in 1904 the factory was sold to the Black Diamond Automobile Co. who proceeded to make the BUCKMOBILE there. That venture lasted only 12 months.

NG

REMINGTON (ii) (US) 1914–1916
1914–1915 Remington Motor Co., Rahway, New Jersey.
1915–1916 Remington Motor Co., Kingston, New York.
After an abortive attempt to make a car in Charleston, West Virginia, which resulted in a single prototype, Philo Remington returned north to form a new company making a light car powered by a 1750cc 12hp 4-cylinder engine. An advanced aspect of the design was the clutch-actuated pre-selector transmission

1900 Renault 3½hp coupé.
NICK BALDWIN

c.1912 Renault Type AX coupé.
NICK BALDWIN

designed by Clarence Hollister, a system successfully used by HUDSON 20 years later. Also ahead of its time for a light car was electric starting. For 1915 it was joined by a larger four called the Narragansett Touring, and the Greyhound powered by a V8 Massnick-Phipps engine, which could be had in 2-, 4- or 6-seater versions.

In November 1915 production was moved to the former VAUGHAN factory at Kingston, and only the Narragansett was listed.

NG

RENAULT (i) (F) 1899 to date

1899–1908 Renault Frères, Billancourt, Seine.
1908–1922 Automobiles Renault, Billancourt, Seine.
1922–1945 SA des Usines Renault, Billancourt, Seine.
1945 to date Régie Nationale des Usines Renault, Billancourt, Seine.

One of the greatest automotive names in France originated because a young man found button making boring. Louis Renault (1877–1944) was the youngest of five children of Alfred Renault, who moved from Angers to Paris in the 1850s, where he added fabrics to his original trade of button manufacture. Louis was expected to join his brothers Fernand and Marcel in the family business, but he was always more interested in machinery, and in 1897 he joined the boiler makers, Delaunay-Belleville. His time there was interrupted by a year of military service, and when he was demobilised he decided not to return to his employers, but to build a small car of which he had long dreamed.

He set up a small workshop in the garden of the family home at Billancourt, on the south-western outskirts of Paris, and using a De Dion engine from a quadricycle, he built a very small car with tubular frame and a wheelbase of only 43in (1100mm). There is some uncertainty about the size of engine used; some sources claim it was of 198cc, others 270cc as were the first production cars of 1899. It is also possible that the size of the production engine was enlarged during 1899, from 240 to 326 and then to 402cc. The front-mounted engine and wheel steering were advanced for the period, but the point that distinguished the Renault from all other cars was its final drive which was by shaft to a bevel gear on the rear axle. Louis Renault never made a car with chain or belt drive, the standard solution of his contemporaries. What is more, the 3-speed gearbox had direct drive on top gear. Louis demonstrated this car to some friends on Christmas Eve 1898, and although he may not have intended at that time to become a manufacturer, he soon received requests from friends to build replicas. In March 1899, helped with capital provided by his brothers, he set up Renault Frères with a capital of 40,000 francs. They took a stand at the Paris Salon in June 1899, and were rewarded with orders for 60 cars. To build these necessitated larger premises, and the brothers bought a disused boathouse which they moved to the Renault garden. By the end of 1899 they had 60 workers, and had made 71 cars, all basically similar to the original prototype. Steering was by a semi-circular wheel with vertical handles at either end, on a vertical column. Two important milestones of 1899 were the first entries of Renault cars in competitions, when Louis and Marcel finished 1st and 2nd in the amateur drivers section of the Paris-Trouville Race in August, and the appearance of the first Renault advertisement in *La Nature* on 9 September. Louis Renault had called his 1899 car the Type A, so it was logical that his new model for 1900 should be the Type B. This was similar in appearance, but had a larger engine, still by De Dion, of 450cc and 2¾hp. Most were still open 2-seaters, but at least one very tall closed coupé was made, the body being by Labourdette. During 1900 the Type C appeared. This was a considerable step forward, with a 700cc De Dion engine, or a 450cc Aster, and a longer wheelbase which permitted 3- or 4-seater coachwork. The bonnet shape was changed from the little semi-circular cover of the Types A and B to a larger, squarer design. As the engines were now water-cooled, there were radiators on either side of the bonnet. This was continued until 1904 when the famous coal-scuttle bonnet with rear-mounted radiator was adopted. Production in 1900, of both B and C, was 179 cars. Sporting successes continued, with Louis winning his class in the Paris-Toulouse-Paris Race, and Schrader and Oury completing a 3100 mile (5000km) trouble-free journey around France.

The 1901 Types C and D were offered with wire or artillery wheels, and had inclined steering columns with proper wheels replacing the semi-circular types. The engines were the same De Dion or Aster units as before, but there was also a Type E intended for competitions, with a 1234cc De Dion engine. Few of these were made, but with their 28mph (45km/h) top speed, they were effective racing cars, taking the first four places in the voiturette class of Paris-Bordeaux, and Louis winning the class in the 686 mile (1105km) Paris-Berlin.

Own Engines and New Designs

1902 saw the first Renaults using engines of the company's own design and manufacture, although the small De Dion engines were used until the end of 1903. The new engines were designed by M. Viet, who came to Renault from De Dion, and were made in several sizes, twins from 1728 to 2650cc, and fours from 3143 to 4942cc. It is not certain how many touring models of the 4-cylinder Type K were made, but a 3.8-litre racing model gave Marcel Renault outright victory in the Paris-Vienna Race, defeating the 70hp Panhards with 13.7-litre engines. The first dashboard radiator Renaults appeared in 1904, though lateral radiators were still seen on some models. The dashboard radiator and coal-scuttle bonnet were copied by a number of firms, including Clément Bayard, Darracq, Hurtu and Th. Schneider, though none persisted with the layout as Renault did, up to 1928.

The 1904 engines were the first to have mechanically-operated inlet valves; they also featured pair-cast cylinders, L-heads, high-tension magneto ignition and thermo-syphon cooling. The direct drive top gear of the 1898 prototype was continued, as was the bevel rear axle. Four sizes of engine were offered in 1905, together with several wheelbases making a total of 15 models. They ranged from the 1060cc 2-cylinder Type AG, which became one of the most famous Renaults, through the 1885cc 2-cylinder Types Y and Z, the 3054cc 4-cylinder Type X-A, and 4398cc Type V-A. 1905 saw a change from tubular chassis to ones of channel section pressed steel.

'Airsport'

RENAULT

1919 Renault 18/22CV Type GR saloon.
JOHN A. CONDE

1921 Renault 10CV Type IG-1 2-seater
NICK BALDWIN

1925 Renault 40CV tourer.
NICK BALDWIN

Renault expanded greatly between 1902 and 1905, with factory area increasing from 7455sq.m to 27,730sq.m, and production from 600 to 2100. By 1913 Renault was the largest motor vehicle producer in France, with an output of over 10,000 cars and commercial vehicles. While a variety of models was made, including a 7.4-litre four and a 9.4-litre six, the bulk of Renault production was given over to the little 2-cylinder cars, the 1060cc AG (1905–08) and 1260cc AX (1908–1914). Five wheelbases were offered, from 77in (1950mm) to 100in (2550mm). They were intended for 2-seater coachwork, but many were fitted with 4-seater closed bodies, and it was particularly popular as a taxicab. By 1909 the Compagnie Françaises de Fiacres Automobiles had 3000 Renault taxis on the streets of Paris, and in London 1100 went into service in 1907 alone.

They won fame in 1914 when General Gallieni commandeered 600 Parisian cabs to transport troops to the Battle of the Marne, which saved Paris from the advancing German armies. Since then they have been familiarly known as the 'Taxis de la Marne'. Some of the London Renaults were still in use in the late 1920s.

Having found a successful formula, Louis Renault made few changes to his cars in the years up to 1914, apart from pressure lubrication in 1911. A smaller six of 3617cc was introduced in 1910, but by 1914 the two sixes were larger, of 5089 and 7541cc. The latter was known as the 40CV, and this designation was retained when the engine was enlarged to 9120cc after the war.

Racing, 1902–1908

Louis Renault entered his cars in competitions from the very first year. The first model aimed specifically at racing was the Type E of 1901, while the Viet-designed 3758cc 4-cylinder car with which Marcel Renault won the 1902 Paris-Vienna race outright was definitely a purpose-built racing car. The major event for 1903 was the infamous Paris-Madrid Race, for which Renault prepared six cars for the voitures légères class and four for the voiturette class. The larger cars had engines of 5304 and 6280cc, the four most powerful ones being driven by the Renaults, Louis and Marcel, Grus and Tart. Louis led the race for part of the time, and was second overall at Bordeaux when he learnt of the fatal accident to his brother. The race was stopped at Bordeaux anyway, but

Louis was so distressed that he never raced again, and his company did not support racing in 1904. They did build one car for the American driver Gould Brokaw, with a 4-cylinder oversquare engine of 12,300cc. Driven by Maurice Bernin, it failed in the Vanderbilt Cup, but took the record for the hill climb at Eagle Rock, N.Y. Louis lifted his ban on company racing in 1905, when three cars were sent to the Eliminating Trials for the Gordon Bennett Race. These had 12,920cc 4-cylinder engines derived from that of the Gould Brokaw car, but mounted in underslung frames. Unfortunately Renault made the mistake of forsaking his thermo-syphon cooling for a pump, which led to overheating, and the best position was 5th (Ferenc Szisz). This was not good enough to secure a place in the actual race. However Szisz finished 5th in the Vanderbilt Cup.

For the first Grand Prix, held in 1906, Renault built three cars, having the same size engines as in 1905, but with thermo-syphon cooling and conventional frames. Szisz won at an average of 66.5mph (107.5km/h), his teammate Richez being 6th. Szisz was 2nd in the 1907 Grand Prix, with a basically similar car, but the 1908 entries, with new undersquare engines of 12,076cc and detachable wheels, were less successful, Szisz retiring, and the other team cars finishing 8th and 15th.

When the Grand Prix was revived in 1912 there were no Renaults present, and indeed it was not until 1977 that the cars from Billancourt were again seen on the Grand Prix circuits. Two of the 1908 cars ran in the American Grand Prize, Strang finishing 6th, and stripped 35CV touring cars won the 24-hour races at Morris Park in 1907 and Brighton Beach in 1909.

La Belle Époque – Renault in the 1920s

Production in the early 1920s was divided into two types, the designs inherited from the prewar range, and new models, of which there were two, the 10CV

Louis Renault (*left*) at the wheel of his 1899 car.
NICK BALDWIN

RENAULT, LOUIS (1877–1944)

Louis Renault was born in Paris on 12 November 1877, the son of Alfred Renault, drapery maker with a shop at Place des Victoires in Paris. He was only 11 when he rigged up electric lighting in his bedroom, using battery power. A few years later he stowed away in the tender of a steam locomotive, to see how it worked. His initiation into automobiles came when Léon Serpollet gave him a ride on one of his steam cars.

At the age of 20, he was experimenting with an old De Dion-Bouton internal-combustion engine rather than pursue his studies to qualify for the École Centrale des Arts et Manufactures. In 1898 he began the construction of a small car with a single-cylinder De Dion-Bouton engine, 3-speed gearbox with direct drive on top (which he patented) and shaft drive. He persuaded his brothers Marcel (1874–1903) and Fernand (1864–1909) to join him in starting car production, and the Société Renault Frères was established on 21 March 1899, with a capital of FFr60,000. Marcel ran the office, and hired Paul Hugé as his assistant. Fernand sold cars and helped out where he could. By November 1899, they had built and sold 60 cars.

Louis was in charge of making the cars, with his assistant, Charles Édmond Serre. Neither had an engineering diploma. Serre had studied engineering at the École Colbert before going to work as a draughtsman for Durand, a gear-maker in rue Oberkampf, Paris, where Renault found him in 1899, a mere lad of 16.

When Renault decided to make his own engines, he hired Georges Bouton's brother-in-law, Viet, who designed the first 2- and 4-cylinder engines for Renault. He also hired Georges de Ram in 1903 and Alexander Rothmüller as chief engineer. Over the years, this team produced a number of inventions for improvements in all the systems on a car, but it was Louis Renault's name that was written on the patents.

The Renault brothers had approximately equal shares in the company (and their mother a token 2 per cent). When Marcel was killed in the Paris–Madrid race on 24 May 1903, it turned out that he had willed everything he owned to his mistress, Suzanne Daveney. Louis feared that she would marry and have children who would become important Renault shareholders. He talked to her about the high risk of failure in the automobile industry, implying that her shares could lose their value at any moment, and offered to buy them in return for an annuity for life, plus a new car every year. She accepted, and Renault and his successors kept the promise until her death in 1953.

Fernand had a liver complaint, and Louis feared that his days were numbered. Fernand was married and had two daughters, raising the spectre of widespread dilution of the shares. Fernand held out for a higher and higher share price, but sold to Louis in 1907. He now held 98 per cent of the company, which was reorganised in 1908 as Automobiles Renault, L. Renault, Constructeur. His brother-in-law, Richardière, took charge of the finances and the legal department, and Edouard Richet, an army buddy of Louis Renault's, became production manager.

The company became SA des Usines Renault on 17 March 1922. Alphonse Grillot, who had been manufacturing manager at Billancourt since 1916, found an ally in E. Tordet. They wanted to slim down the range of 4-cylinder models and mass-produce one basic low-priced car. By 1931 they had won the ear of Renault's nephew, François Lehideux, Fernand's son-in-law, but the factory had grown to such dimensions that any change took more time. It was not until 1937 that the Juvaquatre was ready, but the Primaquatre, Novaquatre, and Vivaquatre were still in production in 1939.

Auguste Riolfo (1894–1985) left Delage in 1932 to become director of testing for Renault. Newcomers to the drawing office in this period included Robert Quatresous, Jean Hourcade, Jean Cordier, Berthelon, Wagner and Fromentin.

Under the German occupation, Louis Renault made it his priority to keep the factory open and maintain the jobs, even if it meant working for the enemy. His son Jean-Louis served as finance director during the war years. After the liberation of Paris in August 1944, Louis Renault was arrested as a 'collaborator' and incarcerated at Fresnes prison. Old and in ill health, he was transferred from a cell to the prison hospital, where he died on 24 October 1944, as a direct result of vicious beatings by communist 'patriots' in the preceding weeks.

Renault married, in 1918, Christiane Boullaire, daughter of a Paris notary. They had one son, Jean-Louis, born in 1920. When the Usines Renault was nationalised in 1945, Jean-Louis Renault left to become president of Babcock & Wilcox. His mother lived until 1978.

JPN

Further Reading
Renault de Billancourt, Saint Loup, Amiot Dumont, 1955.

1930 Renault Vivastella coupé de ville.
NICK BALDWIN

1930 Renault Vivasix saloon.
NICK BALDWIN

introduced in 1919 and the 6CV which followed in 1922. A few 2-cylinder chassis were made, but it is believed that they were all bodied as taxicabs.

The traditional fours were the 2815cc JM (3123cc LS and KR from 1923) and 4534cc GR, while the sixes were the 4220cc JS (4866cc JY from 1922) and the 9120cc HF, which became the 40CV in 1923. They were little changed from prewar, though the fours had monobloc engines, and the entire range had full electrical equipment. A new model for 1919 was the 2120cc 10CV GS, a monobloc four smaller than any previous 4-cylinder Renault, with which Louis planned to tap the growing market for small cars. In design it was not very different from the larger models, although it could be distinguished easily by its disc wheels (larger Renaults used artilleries). The GS was the first lhd Renault, though for 1921 both left and right hand drive were offered in its successors, the IG and IC. For 1924 the 10CV became the KZ, characterized by front-wheel brakes and a bonnet which flowed into the scuttle. Although the radiator was still behind the engine, it no longer stood out from the bonnet, as it had since 1904. For 1930 the radiator was moved to the front, on the KZ-4.

1922 saw a still smaller Renault, the 950cc KJ, rated at 6CV. This was an obvious competitor for the 5CV Citroën and Peugeot Quadrilette. The first models had the traditional radiator, but from the KJ-1 of 1923 the flowing bonnet of the KZ was adopted. In 1925 it received front-wheel brakes, becoming the MT and from 1926 to 1929 it had a longer wheelbase and was known as the NN or NN2. These were normally fitted with 4-seater bodies, both open and closed, whereas the KJ and MT were mostly bodied as 2- or 3-seaters. The NN2 had a transverse rear spring which allowed for a lower chassis, and was

a feature of Renaults up to 1940. At the other end of the scale was the 40CV, descended from the big six of 1914. An increase in bore from 100 to 110mm increased capacity from 7540 to 9120cc, this engine being first seen on the HF, a new model for 1921. Several prototypes, or chassis made in very small numbers, followed in 1921 and 1922, including the HJ with transverse rear spring, and the HU with ohvs. The definitive 40CV appeared at the end of 1923 as the JP. This had cantilever rear springs, and front-wheel brakes had been optional in 1921 and standard from 1922. Other features of this massive, old-fashioned car were a fixed cylinder head and wooden wheels. The estimated power was 120bhp, giving a top speed of 75 to 80mph (121 to 129km/h) according to coachwork. The sporting KO had a 140bhp engine and higher rear axle ratio, giving a speed of 90mph (145km/h). Two wheelbases were offered, 150 and 157in (3807 and 3984mm), and a wide variety of bodies were seen. Many were formal limousines and coupés de ville, but there were also the *scaphandriers* by Kellner, sporting torpedos with tiny convertible compartments at the rear. The 40CV (45hp in England) was made up to 1928 with few changes. The 1925 NM was available with shorter wheelbases and had a front-mounted oil radiator. From 1924 to 1928 608 40CVs were made.

The 40CV was virtually the only Renault to make a mark in sport between the wars. A saloon driven by Repusseau won the 1925 Monte Carlo Rally and several records were taken at Montlhéry with both open and closed models.

Renault expanded tremendously in the 1920s; the demands of wartime production had led to the extension of the Billancourt works, while in 1919 they acquired a large steel foundry in Alsace as part of war reparations. They also bought the Ile de Seguin in the Seine opposite the Billancourt works. By 1931 this once rural island had been completely covered by the factory. 1922 saw 9500 cars made, bringing the total since 1899 to over 100,000. In 1924 the output was 46,000. These were cars only, and did not include important numbers of trucks, buses, agricultural tractors and railcars.

Sixes and Eights, the Stella Range

By the mid–1920s there was an urgent need to modernise the mid-range Renaults, which dated back to prewar days in their general conception. As the fashion was towards smaller sixes, the 4766cc PZ, which was being made in very small numbers anyway, was replaced by a smaller car, the 3180cc 15CV Luxe. This was made in two models, the RA with cantilever rear springs, artillery wheels, disc clutch, right hand gearchange and 4-speed gearbox, and the PG with transverse rear spring, disc wheels, cone clutch, central gearchange and 3-speed gearbox. The latter was, in effect, a larger KZ with two extra cylinders. At the 1927 Salon it became the Vivasix, the first of a long line of Renaults with the prefix Viva. The more old fashioned RA was dropped after the 1927 season, but a new, even smaller six appeared in the shape of the 1474cc Monasix, with detachable cylinder head (like the KZ and Vivasix), coil ignition and a range of bodies similar to those of the NN-2. For 1929, alongside the Monasix and Vivasix, Renault presented two new models with better equipment and dual colour schemes which were named the Monastella and Vivastella.

Also new for 1929 was the replacement for the 40CV. Named the Reinastella, it had a 130bhp straight-8 engine of 7125cc with nine main bearings and a vibration damper at the front of the crankshaft. For the first time, the radiator was at the front, behind a sloping, slatted grill. The Reinastella was a worthy replacement for the 40CV, and although perhaps with less character it was more comfortable, and its servo brakes gave it better stopping power. A range of open and closed bodies was made by Renault, and there was also some handsome coachwork by Hibbard & Darrin and Kellner, the latter making some *scaphandriers* as they had on the 40CV. The Reinastella was made up to 1934, joined by a 4-speed sporting version called the Reinasport. It was good value at 80,000 francs in 1934, compared with 95,000 for the smaller straight-8 Panhard. Total production of the Reinastella and Reinasport was 386 cars.

For 1930 all Renaults had frontal radiators, though only the Reinastella had thermostatically-operated slats. The smaller models, KZ-4, Monasix, Monastella, Vivasix and Vivastella, had a simpler grill though sloping at the same angle. This was replaced for 1932 by a more conventional grill closer to the vertical. A new model for 1930 was a smaller eight of 4240cc called the Nervastella; one of these won the 1930 Moroccan Rally. In 1934 the engine was enlarged to 4827 and 5448cc, becoming the prestige Renault after the demise of the Reinastella. A Nervasport coupé gave Renault their second Monte Carlo Rally win in 1935. The larger Renaults acquired synchromesh gearboxes in 1933, these reaching the whole range a year later.

1932 Renault Nervasport coach.
NICK BALDWIN

The 1934 Salon saw two Renaults with full-width aerodynamic bodies, headlamps faired into the wings which were themselves faired into the doors. Known as the Viva Grand Sport and Nerva Grand Sport, they used the engines and transmissions from the 6-cylinder Vivastella and 8-cylinder Nervastella. When they went into production the following year they were somewhat modified, with one-piece windscreens and the wings no longer faired into the doors. These wide aerodynamic Renaults were made up to 1939, the range being enlarged from the original 4-light saloons and cabriolets to include 6-light saloons/limousines and fixed-head coupés. Engines were enlarged to 4086cc in the Viva Grand Sport, and to 5448cc in the Nerva Grand Sport. The long wheelbase 8-seater models were called Nervastella for 1938 and Suprastrella for 1939; when the cabriolets also bore the name Suprastella. These big Renaults were the traditional transport for French Presidents, just as the 40CV had been in the previous decade. During the years of the Vichy government its head, Marshal Pétain, used a Suprastella with 4-door cabriolet body by Franay, while Général de Gaulle rode in triumph down the Champs Elysées in the same car after Paris was liberated. Ordinary customers for the big Renaults were limited in number. In 1936/37, 3189 sixes and 225 eights were sold, compared with 36,000 4-cylinder cars in the same period.

Popular Renaults in the 1930s

In 1930 Renault offered only one 4-cylinder car, the venerable KZ, in its final version known as the KZ-5. For 1931 they used the KZ's 2120cc engine in a Monasix chassis with bodies of Monasix type to make the Primaquatre. This proved a very successful car, with a top speed of 60mph (97km/h), although when fitted with a 7-seater body on a long wheelbase it was hard put to it to exceed 50mph (80km/h). Capacity was increased to 2383cc for 1936, and the Primaquatre was made up to 1939 with several updates of styling, though it was never streamlined in the manner of the Grand Sport models. The KZ was renamed the Vivaquatre for 1932, and was made in two wheelbase lengths, 114in (2893mm) for 5-seater and 123.5in (3134mm) for 7-seater and commercial models. Like the Primaquatre the Vivaquatre received the enlarged engine in 1936, but its bodies were considerably larger than those of the Primaquatre. Often seen as a taxicab, the Primaquatre was the most utilitarian

1938 Renault Celtaquatre saloon.
NICK BALDWIN

1959 Renault 750 saloon.
NICK BALDWIN

of the Renault range, and was made only as a 6-light saloon. The best-known taxi version was the KZ-11, familiarly known as the G7 because it was used in large numbers by the Compagnie des Automobiles de Place, whose number among the Paris taxi companies was G7. First made in 1932, many of these remained in service up to the late 1950s. From 1936 to 1939 the Vivaquatres had the same 4- and 6-light saloon bodies as the Viva Grand Sport.

For 1932 Renault brought out a new, smaller 4-cylinder car, the Monaquatre which was similar to the Primaquatre but had a 1300cc 7CV engine. It appealed to the economy minded, so long as they did not mind a top speed of under 55mph (89km/h). Originally made only as a saloon and coupé, the Monaquatre was also made in Airline saloon and cabriolet forms from 1934, when the engine was enlarged to 1453cc. In the same year it was joined by the Celtaquatre which was essentially similar, but with a shorter wheelbase. Intended to rival the advanced front-wheel drive 7CV Citroën, which it clearly did not, the original Celtaquatre was withdrawn at the end of the 1935 season, though the name was continued for a variant of the Monaquatre on the same wheelbase.

The 4-cylinder range was quite complicated in the late 1930s, with three models sharing the 2383cc engine, and four similar bodies. The 1463cc Celtaquatre was made up to 1938, and the Primaquatre to the end of 1939, and from 1938 there were also the Novaquatre and Primaquatre Sport. The Novaquatre was the basic model, popular as a taxi and with a 48bhp engine. Next in power and price was the 53bhp Primaquatre, and then the 56bhp Primaquatre Sport with a wider range of bodies. The cheaper cars were made only as 4-door saloons, but the Sport could be had as a 5-seater cabriolet, 2/3-seater cabriolet and 2/3-seater coupé. A special version of the Sport made in small numbers was the SAPRAR; this was Louis Renault's answer to the Peugeot Darl'mat, and like that car it was bodied by Pourtout. Made by a Renault subsidiary called SAPRAR, there were three versions, 2-door saloon, cabriolet and roadster.

The 1938 Salon saw a completely new small Renault, the 1003cc Juvaquatre. Although the engine was still a side-valve unit developing only 25bhp, it was advanced in other ways, with full unitary construction and ifs, though the familiar transverse leaf was still used at the rear. It was made as 2- or 4-door saloon, 2-door roll-top saloon and 2-door coupé. Prewar production was 27,714 and several thousand were made after the war, before the 4CV came into full production.

World War II and After
Production of the larger Renaults was suspended at the outbreak of war in September 1939, but the Juvaquatre, Novaquatre and Primaquatre remained in production until the fall of France in June 1940. Louis Renault's second in command, his nephew François Lehideaux urged him to make military vehicles for the French Army, but thinking that the war would be over soon he wanted no interruption to car production. This was an unwise decision, for when the Germans took control of the factories he was forced to make trucks and other materials for them, so stood accused of helping the enemy, while refusing to contribute to the French war effort. This contributed to his very harsh treatment when France was liberated (see biography).

From June 1940 the Renault factories were under the control of Prince von Urach, formerly of the press department of Daimler-Benz. Under his regime a new truck was developed, but all work on passenger cars was forbidden. Nevertheless several prototypes were built, including three of a Primaquatre development, and two of a completely new small car with a rear-mounted 760cc ohv engine. It is said that Louis Renault was not particularly keen on such a car, preferring the Primaquatre size, but he certainly knew about the project, contrary to some sources, and drove a prototype in September 1943.

Renault was soon back into production after the Liberation of Paris, with trucks being turned out from September 1944. The factories were nationalised in February 1945, becoming the Régie Nationale des Usines Renault. The new boss was former Resistance member Pierre Lefaucheux (1898–1955) who ordered that the rear-engined car should be developed with all speed, although the Juvaquatre was to remain in production until the new car was ready. The postwar Juvaquatre was made only as a saloon, estate car (from 1951) or delivery van, but improvements included an external access luggage boot and hydraulic brakes. The saloon was dropped in 1950, but the commercial versions soldiered on until March 1960, receiving the 4CV engine in August 1953 and the 845cc Dauphine engine in February 1956, these models being known as the Dauphinoise.

The first two prototypes of the 4CV had only two doors, but the third, ordered by Lefaucheux, had four, and was very similar to the production cars. It was running in early 1945, and several pre-series cars were tested in 1945/46 before the car was officially launched in September 1946. It was a remarkable design,

one of the smallest 4-door saloons ever made, with a wheelbase of only 82.5in (2094mm). The 760cc engine gave 19bhp, sufficient for a top speed of 57mph (92km/h). The engine was mounted at the very back, driving forward through a 3-speed gearbox with synchromesh on second and top. Other features included hydraulic brakes, rack-and-pinion steering and full unitary construction.

The 4CV did not go on sale until July 1947, but production quickly built up, so that in 1949 Renault delivered 83,107 cars, mostly 4CVs, beating Citroën's figure of about 65,000. This was a contrast to the 1930s, when Citroën consistently outsold Renault. By the time the 4CV was phased out in 1961, production had reached 1,105,543. Like many good designs the 4CV did not undergo many changes during its lifetime, and these mostly concerned the engine. For 1951 capacity was reduced to 747cc to bring the car into the 750cc competition class. Output was 21bhp, but for 1953 came the R1063 high performance engine, with special crankshaft, con rods, flywheel, exhaust ports and valve springs. This gave 42bhp and a top speed of 72mph (116km/h). The improvement in acceleration was more dramatic; the original 4CV took 38 seconds to reach 50mph (80km/h), but the R1063 could do it in 15 seconds. For 1956 an even hotter 4CV was available, with 4- or 5-speed gearbox and up to 80mph (129km/h). A Ferlec automatic clutch was an option from 1956. Although many specialist coachbuilders used 4CV running gear, the only factory alternative to the saloon was a roll-top version made by SAPRAR from 1948 to 1957. Among the 4CV-derived cars the best-known was the Alpine, but others included the Autobleu, Brissoneau, Ferry, Rosier (the work of racing driver Louis Rosier) and V.P.

The Ferry and V.P. were competition cars which ran at Le Mans, where Alpines and ordinary 4CV saloons were also seen. At Le Mans they were up against the Dyna Panhard and its derivatives, and did not do so well but they won the Bol d'Or in 1951 and 1952, and had a run of class wins in the Mille Miglia from 1952 to 1957. They were even more successful in rallying, with class victories in the Monte Carlo from 1949 to 1951, 1953 and 1956. In 1952 Mme Simon won the Paris-San Raphael *rallye feminin* outright.

In 1948 Lefaucheux sanctioned the development of a larger car, which emerged two years later as the Frégate. This was a 6-seater saloon in the same class as the Standard Vanguard or Fiat 1400, with a 1997cc 4-cylinder ohv engine developing 58bhp. Although the layout was conventional, with front engine and rear drive, the Frégate had a number of features in common with the 4CV including all-independent suspension and unitary construction. The 4-speed all-indirect gearbox had a difficult-to-operate column lever. The Frégate never attracted the praise given to the 4CV, but it was well-suited to French roads, straight but not always well-surfaced, and a total of 163,383 were sold between 1951 and 1960. Engine capacity was enlarged to 2141cc (77bhp) in 1956 when an estate car called the Domaine joined the saloon. The gearbox gained direct-drive top and all-synchromesh in 1956, and a Transfluide automatic option was available in 1958 when a more luxurious estate, the Manoir, was added to the range. No other bodies were offered by the factory, but Pichon-Parat made a few Frégate convertibles. Another Renault of the 1950s was more of a commercial vehicle. The Colorale (COLOniale et RuRALE) was a bulky machine powered by the prewar 2383cc engine and made in estate car, taxi or delivery van form.

In 1956 Renault announced the Dauphine, a 4CV development powered by an 845cc engine. The mechanics were similar to those of the 4CV, but the body was a 3-box type, a welded stress-carrying centre section to which were bolted the front and rear assemblies. The new engine gave an additional 9bhp over the standard 4CV, yet the Dauphine weighed only 350lbs (16kgs) more. The extra performance (top speed of 65mph/105km/h) made it rather dangerous in the hands of the inexperienced, and of course its wide sales brought it into the hands of many inexperienced drivers. Its problems, serious oversteer and a tendency to become airborne in a strong cross wind, had been present on the 4CV but, as Michael Sedgwick wrote, 'the latter's modest output discouraged speeds at which these became dangerous'. Nevertheless the Dauphine quickly became Renault's leading model; out of nearly 170,000 cars made in 1957, more than two thirds were Dauphines. It was the first Renault to sell in large numbers in the USA, which took more than 200,000 up to 1960. It was made under licence in Italy by Alfa Romeo and in Brazil by Willys Overland.

1957 saw the first high-performance Dauphine, with tuning by Amédée Gordini who had given up his own racing and sports cars to work as a consultant for the Régie Renault. With a redesigned cylinder head incorporating inclined valves, the Dauphine Gordini had a 38bhp engine, 4-speed gearbox and a top speed of 75mph (121km/h). In 1962 it was joined by the Rallye version, with a 1093cc engine, 55bhp and 102mph (164km/h). From the Dauphine Gordini was derived a 4-seater coupé called the Floride. This had fresh styling, lower and wider than that of the saloons, but its handling prevented it from being a true sports car. It was replaced in 1962 by the Caravelle, a name already used for Florides in the USA. It was similar in appearance, but had a 51bhp 956cc engine and disc brakes all round. From September 1963 the Caravelle had the 1108cc engine from the 8-1100, giving a top speed of 90mph (145km/h).

Though the Dauphine remained in production until 1968, it was joined five years before by a roomier rear-engine car called simply the 8. This had a 956cc engine, all-disc brakes and a more angular body. It was supplemented in 1964 by the 8-1100 with 1108cc engine and synchromesh on all speeds; 1965 saw the Gordini version with lowered suspension, servo brakes and 95bhp, giving a top speed of 108mph (174km/h). Later cars with 1255cc engine and 5-speed gearboxes were even faster. The final development in this series was the 10 with 1389cc engine and a longer nose, which had also been seen on the 8-1100 from 1965. All long-nose cars were called 10s in France from 1966, though not in export markets until the 1289cc engine appeared in 1969. In 1971 the rear-engined line was discontinued, giving way to the new front-drive 12, which had been introduced in 1969.

Once Amédée Gordini got his hands on it, the Dauphine became a successful rally car. They won the 1958 Monte Carlo and Tour de Corse outright, and were 2nd and 3rd in the 1959 Monte. The R8 continued the make's success, winning the Tour de Corse in 1964 and 1965. The last major wins for the little Renaults came in 1967, in the Rallye dei Fiori and Three Cities. By then Renault were relying increasingly on the Alpine sports coupés for their rallying programme.

Front-wheel Drive

Towards the end of the 1950s Renault were planning a replacement for the 4CV. Instead of continuing the rear-engined theme they took a leaf out of Citroën's book and turned to front-wheel drive. The Renault 4 which appeared in 1962 was in the same class as Citroën's rustic 2CV, though it had a 4-cylinder engine of 747cc (a 603cc R3 was made for the French market only). It had a sealed cooling system later used on all Renaults, all-independent suspension by torsion bars, and a curious push-pull gearchange on the dashboard. The body was a roomy 5-door estate; a cheaper version sold on the French market was a 4-light, but most 4s had 6-light bodies. An 845cc engine was available from 1963, and from 1960 a higher-geared 1108cc version called the 4GTL was added to the range.

The Renault 4 was one of those evergreen designs to which the French are addicted and, like its rival the Citroën 2CV, was made up to the 1990s. It was subsequently made in Renault's Yugoslav factory up to 1992, by which time 8½ million had been made. From 1968 to 1980 Renault also made the 6, a larger and better-appointed 4 with more stylish body and 845cc engine (1108cc from 1971). Front disc brakes also featured from 1971. Though not the enormous seller that the 4 was, the 6 did manage a creditable 1,773,304 sales in its 12-year life.

The next front-drive Renault was another classic that sold in seven figure numbers. The 16 was introduced in January 1965, being built in a new factory at Sandouville, near Le Havre. It had a 5-door hatchback body, one of the first of its kind, and was powered by an all-new light alloy 1470cc 63bhp pushrod ohv engine. 1968 saw the high-performance 16TS, with 1565cc and 88bhp, which was good for 100mph (162km/h). The larger engine was available in the standard 16 from 1970, and standardised the following year, automatic transmission being also available. The most powerful model was the 16TX (1973–79) with 1647cc and 93bhp, 5-speed gearbox and top speed of 105mph (169km/h). 16 production ended in 1979, when 1,846,000 had been made. Its place was taken by the 20 which had appeared in 1975 and used the same 1647cc engine in a new bodyshell, still a 5-door hatchback but with new, blander styling. This was shared with the 30, Renault's biggest engined postwar car, powered by the 2664cc PRV (Peugeot-Renault-Volvo) engine. This V6 ohc unit was made at a new factory at Douvrin by a joint company, the Compagnie Franco-Suédoise de Mécanique, and was also used in the Peugeot 604, Volvo 264 and, later, in the De Lorean coupé. The 20/30 series had all-coil suspension and floor gearchange in place of the 16's less satisfactory column change. Brakes were disc front/drum rear on the 20, and discs all round on the 30. The PRV engine was the only petrol unit used in the 30, though a 2068c turbo-diesel was introduced later and the 20 could be had with 1995 or 2165cc engines shared

1961 Renault Floride coupé.
NICK BALDWIN

1963 Renault 8 De Luxe saloon.
NICK BALDWIN

1971 Renault 16 saloon.
NICK BALDWIN

1971 Renault 4 saloon
NICK BALDWIN

1972 Renault 5 hatchback.
RENAULT

1984 Renault 25GTS saloon.
RENAULT

with the Peugeot 505, as well as the 2068cc diesel in 64 or 85bhp forms. They had a shorter life and much lower production than the 16, being replaced by the 25 in 1984, after 622,314 20s had been made, and 160,265 30s.

In 1972 Renault brought out their 3-door hatchback in the 'super mini' class, called the 5. By the time the original 5 was replaced by the Supercinq in 1984, 5,471,709 had been made. The 5 was designed by Michel Boué, who sadly did not live to see it go into production, and featured a front-mounted engine driving the front wheels, though this was mounted in line with the chassis rather than transversely as in rivals such as the Fiat 127 and VW Golf. Originally the capacities were 782cc (sold in France only), 845 and 956cc, but a 1289cc model was added in 1974 and an Alpine-tuned 1397cc version in 1976. This had 93bhp and a speed of 109mph (175km/h) with a 5-speed gearbox. It was a good example of the 'hot hatchback', and a series of one-model races was organised for it. Early 5s had a dashboard gearchange, but floor change was soon an option, and later standardised. There were front disc brakes on the most powerful models. The 3-door hatchback was the only body style until 1979 when a 5-door version appeared, although the Spanish factory built the Siete (7), a 4-door notchback saloon from 1974.

In 1978 a remarkable version of the 5 was announced under the name 5 Turbo. This was really a completely new car, though it retained some of the sheet metal of the ordinary 5. The 1397cc engine was turbocharged and tuned to give 160bhp, and was mounted behind the driver to drive the rear wheels. It was strictly a 2-seater, for the engine and 5-speed gearbox took up all the space between the seat backs and the rear hatch. The body was made of light alloy rather than steel, and the bonnet was of fibreglass. The Turbo was clearly recognisable by the large flared arches over the fat rear tyres, with air intakes in the front of the arches. The Turbo was very noisy, with the engine only a few inches behind the driver and passenger's ears, but it had a remarkable performance for a car derived from a family hatchback. Top speed was 125mph (201km/h) when the rev counter was held below the 6000rpm 'danger line', but if the driver ventured into the red zone, a speed of 130mph (209km/h) was possible.

The 5 Turbo was intended as a rally car, and 400 were built for Group Four homologation during 1979, before any were sold to the general public. Rally successes included the 1981 Monte Carlo (Ragnotti/Andrie) and 1985 Tour de Corse (Ragnotti/Thimonnier). It was still available commercially in 1985, at a price of 110,000 francs, compared with 61,500 for the front-engined Turbo 1400, and 36,400 for the basic 956cc 3-door hatchback. With the introduction of the Supercinq for 1985 the Turbo 2 was phased out, and was never made with the new sheet metal.

The Supercinq was announced in September 1984. It bore a close resemblance to its predecessor, too close many people thought, for the public did not perceive it as the new car that it was. It borrowed much technology from the 9, and its chief difference from the earlier 5 was the transverse location of the engine. These had the familar sizes of 956, 1108 and 1397cc, with outputs from 42bhp (Super 5C 950) to 72bhp (Super 5TS 1400). The most powerful model was announced a few months later; this was the Super 5 GT Turbo, with 115bhp and a speed of 125mph (201km/h). April 1985 saw 5-door versions of the Supercinq, and the 1988 range was a wide one, with four petrol engines from 1108 to 1721cc, and a 1595cc diesel. All except the basic 1108cc model had 5-speed gearboxes.

In 1990 the Supercinq was joined by the Clio, which eventually replaced it, though not until 1996, when it was made only in Slovenia and Morocco. The final Supercinq model was called, appropriately, the Bye Bye. The Clio was the same size of car, but with a completely restyled body and a wide range of engines from 1108 to 1764cc petrol and a 1870cc diesel. In 1993/4 the high-performance model was the Williams, named after the Formula 1 team, with a 150bhp 1998cc engine and 134mph (216km/h) top speed. A limited series of 6500 was made after which it gave way to the Clio Sport with 1998cc 16-valve Mégane engine. In 1998 came the restyled Clio II, which was remarkable for being priced around 15 per cent below the Clio I, which was continued. 1999 saw the hottest small Renault ever, the V6 Clio with mid-mounted 250bhp 3-litre V6 engine, to be built in limited numbers by TWR's plant at Uddevalla, Sweden.

Since 1992 the bottom of the Renault range has been represented by the Twingo, a 3-door hatchback with very short bonnet, powered by a 1149cc engine. An automatic clutch was available from 1994.

Medium and Larger Cars

The market for small/medium family saloons has been catered for by a variety of models over the past 30 years. First to follow the 16 was the 12, made from 1969 to 1980. This was also front-drive, but unlike the 16, the 12's engine was ahead of the gearbox. It was originally made in one size only, a 1289cc ohv unit developing 60bhp, but there was also a 110bhp 1547cc Gordini unit and a 1647cc unit for the 12 America, made only for the US market. Despite its size, this developed only 63bhp. There was no hatchback, but an alternative to the 4-door saloon was a 5-door estate. Though not a memorable or exciting car, the 12 sold 2,865,079 units. It was the basis for two sporting coupés, the 15 and 17. These used a variety of engines, 1289 and 1565cc in the 15, 1565, 1605 and 1647cc in the 17. The 1565cc unit was a fuel-injected version of that used in the 16TS, and the 1647cc was that of the 16TX. By the time these coupés went out of production in 1979, they had been made in quite substantial numbers, 202,854 15s and 92,589 17s. They were replaced by the Fuego coupé, restyled and with 1397, 1647 or 1995cc engines, the latter a 110bhp single-ohc unit.

A model not directly related to any other Renaults was the 14, a 5-door hatchback made from 1976 to 1982. This was powered by a transverse-mounted, almost horizontal single-ohc engine as fitted to the Citroën Visa and Peugeot 104, of 1218 or 1360cc. An unremarkable car, the 14 nevertheless sold just under one million units in its seven-year lifetime. The 12's successor was the 18, a 4-door saloon/5-door estate which was the first Renault of this size to use MacPherson strut suspension. A variety of engines were used in the 18 over the years, 1397, 1647, 1565 turbo (from 1980), 1995 ohc and a 2068cc diesel. More than two million 18s were made up to 1986, when the 18 was replaced by the 21. This was a 4-door notchback saloon with three sizes of engine, 1721 and 1995cc petrol and 2088cc diesel. An unusual aspect of the 21 design was

1990 Renault Espace Quadra 4 × 4.
RENAULT

that the smaller engine was mounted transversely and the two larger ones longitudinally. The wheelbase differed slightly, 104.7in (2657.3mm) for the transverse-engined cars and 102.3in (2596.4mm) for the longitudinal versions. An estate car called the Nevada was added in October 1986 and the summer of 1987 saw a 175bhp turbocharged version of the 1995cc engine, with a top speed of 140mph (225km/h). In February 1988 a 4 × 4 estate was added.

The American Connection

Renault's first serious penetration of the American market began in the 1950s, when the Dauphine sold more than 200,000 in four years. A connection with American Motors Corp. (AMC) began in 1963, when the Rambler was made under licence by Renault, this arrangement lasting until 1968. After some quiet years in the early 1970s, Renault launched a new American sales drive in January 1979 when they signed an agreement with American Motors under which the latter would market the 5 under the name 'Le Car'. This proved successful, but the feedback was that a larger car would sell even better. In October 1979 Renault invested $150 million in AMC, following this with a further $200 million a year later, to give them a 46.9 per cent stake in the American company. A new model was developed with the American market very much in mind. It was launched in September 1981 as the Renault 9, with an American version called the Alliance coming in 1983. It was a 4-door saloon powered by transverse 4-cylinder single-ohc engines in two sizes, 1108 and 1397cc. A 4-speed box was standard with the smaller engine, 5-speed or automatic with the larger. Later 9s had larger engines, including a 1595cc diesel and a 1721cc petrol, as well as a turbocharged 1397cc which was the most powerful in the range at 105bhp. In February 1983 came the 11, which was a hatchback version of the 9 made in 3- and 5-door models. The American-made versions of the 9 and 11 were known as the Alliance and Encore respectively; they were basically similar to the French, but had larger bumpers and different trim, while there were 2-door saloon and convertible versions of the Alliance, not seen in the French-built range. For 1988 they were dropped in favour of two larger cars, the Medaillon based on the Renault 21, and the Premier. This used the floorpan of the 25, with a new Giugiaro-styled saloon body. Launched in February 1987, the Premier went into production at a new factory at Brampton, Ontario, Canada. Power options were a 2.4-litre AMC 4-cylinder engine or a 3-litre version of the PRV V-6. The Premier was originally to have been much closer to the 25, but American dislike of hatchbacks prompted the new design with a prominent

1990 Renault 19TSE hatchback.
RENAULT

boot. American Motors was bought by Chrysler in 1987, and the Premier or Medallion were marketed under the EAGLE (x) brand.

For 1989 the 9 and 11 were replaced by the 19, a hatchback made in 7 different models, with five engine variants from 1237cc (55bhp) to 1763cc (140bhp), also an 1870cc 65bhp diesel. This was made until 1996, though a cabriolet introduced in 1991 survived for one season longer. Its place was taken by the Mégane, made in fastback and hatchback versions, and also as a 2-door coupé, a convertible, and as the Scenic, a small MPV. Engine options ran from a 1390 to 1998cc petrol and 1870cc diesel. Built at Renault's Douai plant, and also at Valencia in Spain, the Mégane was still current for 2000, when a 4 × 4 version was also offered.

Larger Models, 1980s to date

Although the 20 and 30 models were continued for a while for certain overseas markets such as Central Africa, they were replaced for European countries by a single new model in December 1983. This was the 25, a 5-door hatchback of low drag form with a choice of three petrol engines, 1995 or 2165cc four, or the 2664cc V6, and a 2068cc diesel. By 1985 there were 12 models in the 25 range, five petrol and four diesel saloons, two petrol and one diesel limousine. The latter were on a longer wheelbase, and were converted by the specialist coachbuilder, Heuliez. They were dropped in August 1986, after 800 had been made. The

1991 Renault Clio 1.7RT hatchback.
RENAULT

1995 Renault Twingo hatchback.
RENAULT

1998 Renault Mégane Scénic RXE.
RENAULT

most powerful car in the 25 range was the V6 Turbo, with 2458cc and 182bhp. In March 1992 the 25 gave way to the Safrane, a saloon in the same class with 1995 and 2165cc fours, and a 2975cc V6 engine, also a 2068cc diesel. The V6 was dropped in 1998, to be replaced in 1999 by a new 190bhp 2946cc V6. A Safrane replacement, the radically-styled Vel Satis saloon with 3½-litre Nissan engine was planned to reach the market in 2001.

The other model in the current Renault range is the Espace, a high-roof MPV of the type popularised by Japanese manufacturers. Introduced in the spring of 1984, the Espace was powered by a 1995cc engine driving the front wheels via a 5-speed gearbox, and had a fibreglass body capable of seating five or seven passengers. The front seats could be pivoted through 180°, turning the interior into a sitting room. The Espace was developed by Matra and built in their factory at Romorantin. An alternative engine was a 2068cc turbo-diesel, while in 1988 came the Quadra version of the Espace, with permanent 4-wheel-drive. The Espace was extensively revised for 1997, with transverse engines and two wheelbases, 106in (2690mm) for the Espace, and 113in (2868mm) for the 7-seater Grand Espace. By the summer of 1998 580,000 Espaces had been built,

with production running at 350 per day at two factories, Romorantin and Dieppe. 1999 saw a new type of car based on the Espace platform, the Avantime 5-seater Grand Tourer with 2946cc V6 engine.

A completely different car outside the rest of the Renault range was the Spider, a stark open 2-seater in the Lotus Elise mould, powered by a 1998cc 16-valve 4-cylinder engine mounted transversely behind the driver. It had a top speed of 135mph (217km/h). Originally made without a windscreen, one was available from 1998, but the Spider was dropped for the 1999 season. It was made, appropriately, in the former Alpine factory at Dieppe.

In 1999 Renault acquired a 36.8 per cent stake in Nissan for £3.3 billion.

NG

Further Reading
Dossiers Chronologique Renault, 1899–1933 (5 volumes),
Gilbert Hatry and Claude Le Maitre, Éditions Lafourçade, 1977–1982.
Les Renaults de Louis Renault, Pierre Dumont, Édifrée, 1982.
Renault, the Cars and the Charisma, J. Dewar McLintock,
Patrick Stephens, 1983.
Renault, l'Empire de Billancourt, Jacques Borge and Nicholas Viasnoff,
EPA, 1977.
Renault, the Challenge, Edouard Seidler, Edita, 1981.
Renault 5, 'Le Car', David Sparrow, Osprey, 1992.
Renault, Cent Ans d'Histoire, Jean-Louis Loubet, E.T.A.I., 1999.

RENAULT (ii) (BR) 1959–1968

Willys-Overland do Brasil SA, São Paulo.
On 2 November 1959, the first Renault Dauphine rolled out of the Willys-Overland do Brasil factory in Sao Bernardo do Campo, in São Paulo. The more powerful (and a bit more luxurious) Gordini was introduced in 1962. The Interlagos sports car which was based on the French Alpine, was introduced at the first Brazilian Automobile Salon in 1960. In 1967 the factory which made these cars was purchased by Ford and production ceased. Soon thereafter Ford announced that where the Renaults had been made, Project M would be started. In fact this was how the Ford Corcel was known before it was formally announced. Very few Dauphines and Gordinis survive now in Brazil. They were not well suited to Brazil's climate and road conditions, and in their day they were considered rather fragile.

ACT

RENAULT (iii) (RA) 1960 to date

1960–1968 Industrias Kaiser Argentina SAIC, Cordoba.
1968–1975 IKA Renault S.A., Cordoba.
1975 to date Renault Argentina SA, Cordoba.
In July 1960, the first Argentine Renault Dauphine was completed. In September, 1962, the Gordini was added to the line, and in 1964, the 4L. In 1967 production of the Renaults 6 and 12 started. Production of the Dauphine and Gordini stopped in 1970 after 53,643 and 34,566, respectively, had been made. In 1970 the 4L was dropped, after 60,221 had been produced. Only the R6 and the immensely popular Renault 12 entered the 1970s, and not until 1981 was a new model announced; it was the Renault 18. In 1982 came the Renault Fuego, in 1986 the Renault 11, in 1987 the Renault 9, and in 1989 the Renault 21. In 1992 the Renault Fuego was discontinued and the following year so was the 18. That same year the 19 was introduced. In 1994 the last Renault 12 came off the production line. Having been introduced 27 years earlier, it became the Renault with the longest production span in Argentina, and earned itself a reputation as a rugged vehicle, either in its 4-door saloon or station wagon versions. In 1996 the last Renault 9s and 21s were manufactured. In 1999, the Renault 19, the Clio – introduced in 1996, the Mégane – introduced in 1998 and the new-for-1999 Kangoo, were being made.

ACT

RENAULT (iv) (IVORY COAST) 1978–1981

Automobiles Régie Renault S.A., Abidjan.
Safar was the Renault representative in the Ivory Coast, and as well as assembling various Renault models from the R4 to the R16, it produced the self-designed Bandama from 1978. It was a rustic jeep lookalike based on the commercial version of the locally-assembled Renault 4. Annual production amounted to as high as 150 units.

CR

RENAUX (F) 1901–1902

Sté l'Énergie, Paris.

Mainly known as makers of tricycles, this company offered a shaft-driven light car powered by an 8hp Buchet engine.

NG

RENÉ BONNET (F) 1961–1964

La Sté des Automobiles René Bonnet, Champigny-sur-Marne.

From the mid–1930s to the mid–1960s, pilot, engineer and racing car constructor René Bonnet was at the forefront of French motor racing. An accomplished driver, Bonnet founded the D.B. sports car marque in 1938 with partner Charles Deutsch, finding fame in the 1950s with his diminutive Panhard-powered Monomille single-seaters and streamlined racing coupés. After numerous records and 'Index' victories at Le Mans, the Deutsch-Bonnet partnership was dissolved in 1961. Bonnet wasted little time in launching his own branded range of road and competition cars, all using Renault engines (while Deutsch retained Panhard). The René Bonnet marque made a promising competition debut at the Nürburgring in May 1962 with a class win in a small, advanced mid-engined tubular prototype. For the 1962 Le Mans, Bonnet entered a team of three prototypes; a barquette and two Djet coupés. Although none of the cars completed that race, Bonnet later gained numerous trophies with his prototypes and Formula 2 racers. To support his competition exploits, Bonnet unveiled a trio of road cars at the 1962 Paris Salon. The least expensive of these was the Missile; an ex-D.B. 4-seater cabriolet based on the platform and running gear of a Renault 4. The dearer 1.1-litre Le Mans model shared the Missile's GRP convertible body, but was distinguishable by its different front with stacked Facel Vega double headlamps. The range-topper was the pioneering Djet (derived from the racing prototypes) with the distinction of being the world's first mid-engined production sports car. Bonnet's racing spoils failed to endow his production cars with commercial success, and in late 1964 the René Bonnet marque was absorbed by French missile manufacturer MATRA. René Bonnet worked with the renamed Matra-Bonnet until 1965, overseeing production modifications to the Djet, and then left to run his own garage at Champigny (Val-de-Marne).

CR

RENÉ FONCK (F) 1920–c.1924

Sté des Automobiles René Fonck, Fraisse-Unieux, Loire.

René Fonck was the leading French fighter pilot of World War I, with 75 downed enemy aircraft to his credit, which was approaching a half of the total for the French Air Force. Like the FARMAN brothers and Gabriel VOISIN, Fonck turned to cars after the war, and showed his first chassis at the Brussels Salon held in December 1920. It had a 2615cc single-ohc 4-cylinder engine with unit construction of engine and 3-speed gearbox. The camshaft was driven by a vertical shaft placed on the left-hand side of the engine between the second and third cylinders. Also at Brussels was a straight-8 engine with the same dimensions as the four, giving a capacity of 5230cc. This was seen in a chassis at the 1921 Paris Salon. The engines were made for Fonck by C.I.M.E.; it is said that the four was designed by Grillot and the eight by Gadoux, but this is curious in view of the close similarity of the designs. The eight had front-wheel brakes, as did the 3923cc six which appeared in 1922, again with the same cylinder dimensions as the other cars. Like the Hispano-Suiza, the Fonck cars sported a stork mascot. Production was very limited; the best estimates, by Serge Pozzoli, are three or four 4-cylinder cars, one or two eights and at most six of the 6-cylinder model. The cars were bodied as tourers, and at least one limousine by Gaborit and coupés de ville by Gaborit and Van den Plas. The chassis were built by a steel works which supplied many French manufacturers. It has been suggested that they abandoned cars because they preferred to keep their clients than to be their rivals, but it is more likely that there was just not room in the market for another expensive car.

NG

Further Reading

'Fonck', Serge Pozzoli, *l'Album du Fanatique*, Aug/Sept 1969.

RENFERT (D) 1924–1925

Josef Renfert Motorfahrzeugfabrik, Beckum.

This light car was powered by a 780cc 3/12PS 2-cylinder 2-stroke engine, and had a 2-seater body.

HON

1964 René Bonnet Djet coupé.
NATIONAL MOTOR MUSEUM

1923 René Fonck limousine by Kremiansky.
NICK BALDWIN

RENFREW (GB) 1904

Scottish Motor Carriage Co. Ltd, Glasgow.

This was a conventional car made only as a 5-seater tourer, powered by a 3400cc 16/20hp 4-cylinder engine. It lasted no more than one year, but examples were entered in hill-climbs and Scottish Automobile Club trials.

NG

RENNIE (GB) 1907

Rennie Motor Manufacturing Co., Brighton, Sussex.

Few cars were made in South Coast resorts, though Eastbourne had the car of that name, and Shoreham was home to the DOLPHIN. The Rennie was short-lived, but was offered in three 4-cylinder models, a 10/12hp 2-seater, 12/15 and 25/30hp tourers, and a 30hp 6-cylinder tourer. They were guaranteed for a year, longer than the company lasted.

NG

RENOWN (i) (AUS) 1922

E.W. Brown & McLelland Pty Ltd, Melbourne, Victoria.

A rebadged FORD T fitted with after-market components, the Renown followed the similar PALM. The name is thought to have been derived from the warship in which members of the Royal family visited Australia. Its body was lowered, with a more raked steering column, and the fuel tank was located at the rear. A.E. Walker promoted it in Sydney where it was replaced by the SPARK.

MG

RENOWN (ii) (GB) 1922

Renown Motors, London.

The Renown was unusual among cyclecars in having a 4-seater body, and also in having a fuselage-type of integral construction, the main chassis members and the hoop-shaped body members being of ash wood. Body panelling was of steel. The engine was a transversely-mounted 8hp V-twin JAP driving through a 3-speed Wrigley gearbox, with chain final drive.

NG

REO (US) 1904–1936

1904 R.E. Olds Co., Lansing, Michigan.

1904–1936 Reo Motor Car Co., Lansing, Michigan.

The Reo Motor Car Co. was founded by Ransom Eli Olds (1864–1950) after he parted company with the Olds Motor Works for which he had designed the

1906 Reo 8hp runabout.
NICK BALDWIN

1907 Reo 16/20hp tourer.
NICK BALDWIN

1909 Reo 20/22hp tourer.
NATIONAL MOTOR MUSEUM

famous Curved Dash Oldsmobile, the world's first mass-production car. In August 1904 Olds set up the R.E. Olds Co., with financial backing from Reuben Shettler, who had earlier helped to finance the Olds Motor Works. The owners of Olds' original company objected to the use of his name in his new venture, so he quickly changed it to the Reo Motor Car Co., using his initials.

By October 1904 the first Reo car was ready for testing. It was larger and more expensive than the Curved Dash, having a 16hp 2-cylinder engine, although the planetary transmission and single-chain drive were familiar, as indeed they were in countless American cars of the period. The 16hp was priced at $1250, and was soon joined by a cheaper single-cylinder runabout at $685, just $35 more than the Curved Dash Oldsmobile. The little single-cylinder runabout remained in production until 1910, by which time the price was down to $500. A 24hp four joined the smaller cars in 1906. The twin had a capacity of 3.4-litres, and a carburettor for each cylinder.

The Reo company prospered, and in 1907 moved into 3rd place in the American production league, behind Ford and Buick, with 3967 cars delivered. They never held such a high place again, but they were in 6th to 8th position for a number of years, and it was not until 1918 that Oldsmobile managed to beat Reo's sales. An important new model for 1910 was a 35hp four with shaft drive and left hand steering, the first Reo four to be made in large numbers. In 1912 Olds brought out the car he named Reo the Fifth, 'The Car That Marks My Limit'. He claimed that he could not produce a better car, that this was his Farewell Car. It was in fact only a refinement of the previous four with a central gear lever its chief innovation. Ransom Olds played a less direct part in the company from 1913 onwards, having other business interests, but he still vetoed ideas he considered too modern. He would not sanction a 6-cylinder car until 1916, for example. This was the 45hp Model M with inlet-over-exhaust valves, a layout also seen on the 4-cylinder Reos. It had up-to-date styling known as Sheer-Line, and offered Reo's first fully-enclosed sedan bodies. Prices ran from $1225 to $1750, but there was still Reo the Fifth at $875. The 4-cylinder car remained in production until 1919 when it was the only model. The M had been dropped, and it was not until the 1920 season that its successor appeared, the 50hp T-6. Reo built no more 4-cylinder cars after 1919.

Sales and profits had been very good during the war years, thanks in part to truck production. In 1917 Reo made 25,577 vehicles, of which about one third were commercials. 1919 production was 9185 trucks and only 7303 passenger cars. During the 1920s cars and commercials were fairly evenly balanced, but in the next decade trucks and buses assumed greater importance, and ultimately outlived the cars by many years.

The T-6 was made up to 1926; among its features was a parking brake which was applied by depressing the clutch to its fullest extent, there being no handbrake, and a back-to-front gear change. There were no important changes to the T-6 in its seven-year run, and rear-wheel brakes were featured to the end. 1927 saw its replacement, the more modern Flying Cloud, named after one of America's most famous Clipper ships. This had a 4085cc 65bhp L-head 6-cylinder engine and hydraulic 4-wheel brakes. It was styled by Fabio Segardi who had been responsible for the Hudson Super Six. Five attractive body styles were offered, between $1500 and $1800.

Five months after the launch of the Flying Cloud, Reo brought out a cheaper car christened the Wolverine, and sometimes regarded as a separate make. As the Reo factories were fully occupied with the Flying Cloud, the Wolverine was assembled from outside components, a 3261cc Continental Six engine, Borg & Beck clutch, Warner gearbox and Salisbury axles. It shared the bigger car's Lockheed hydraulic brakes, and though it had a distinctive radiator and bonnet, from the cowl back it was typical Reo. Only one body style was offered, at first a 2-door brougham at $1195. Later a coupé and a 4-door sedan were added. The Wolverine did not sell too well, perhaps because Reo customers did not like the idea of an assembled car. Estimated production was 14,000 for the Wolverine and its companion truck model the Junior Speedwagon. For 1929 Reo replaced it with a smaller Flying Cloud, also with a Continental engine, called the Flying Cloud Mate. 1928 was Reo's best year, with 29,000 vehicles sold, but the Depression hit the firm hard; car production in 1930 was only 12,563 and in 1931, 6026.

However, Reo's last years saw the most exciting and glamorous cars ever to come from the Lansing factory. The Flying Cloud engine was enlarged to 4323cc for 1930, and in the following year came the Royale, a straight-8 with the same cylinder dimensions as the Cloud, to give 5886cc and 125bhp. One-shot chassis lubrication and thermostatic radiator shutters were featured. The wheelbase was 135in (3430mm), and enabled some very striking bodies to be built. These were designed by Amos Northup, chief stylist of the Murray Body Corp. who made them. The Royale was not over-priced at $2485, and the 8-cylinder engine could also be had in a Flying Cloud with 130in (3302mm) wheelbase and a price range from $1995 to $2080 For 1932 there was a long-wheelbase version of the Royale at 152in (3860mm), the longest in the American industry. 1933 Reos were restyled with mudguard skirts and sloping radiators, while a new feature was the Self Shifter, a two-speed 'automatic gearbox' with a two-speed supplementary gear operated by a dashboard-mounted handle. However it was not truly automatic, a clutch being employed and double de-clutching required for really rapid changes. Although it cost only $80 extra, the Self Shifter was not popular with customers.

1931 Reo Flying Cloud 8 coupé.
JOHN A. CONDE

1933 production was 4889 cars and 5398 trucks, and the company lost $2.5 million. The last of about 5800 Royales were made in 1934, and for 1935 Reo came up with a new Flying Cloud which used a Hayes-built body shared with Graham, and an 85bhp 6-cylinder engine. Only 3894 cars were made in 1935, and 3146 of a restyled model with 3734cc aluminium-head engine in 1936. Production ended in September 1936, and there were no 1937 models.

Truck and bus manufacture flourished though, aided by large orders during World War II. In 1957 Reo was taken over by White, who later acquired Diamond T and from 1967 to 1975 made a line of heavy trucks under the name Diamond-Reo. This company went bankrupt in 1975, but the name was revived by a dealer who continued to make Diamond-Reo trucks for about 20 years.

NG

REPETTI & MONTIGLIO (I) 1987
Repetti e Montiglio, Casale Monferrato.
Founded in 1960, this coachbuilder made military vehicles based on the Fiat Campagnola and briefly offered a leisure car based on the Fiat Panda 4×4. It used a tubular chassis and a 2-door jeep-style open body.

CR

REPLICAR (i) (GB) 1981–1996
1981–1993 Replicar Ltd, Faversham, Kent.
Alan Hatswell began importing kits from the USA but quickly adopted American practice by making a fibreglass Bugatti Type 35 lookalike body on a cut-down VW Beetle floorpan. The model was supplemented by the Type 35c (with foldable windscreen, hood and side screens) and Type 43 (a 4-seater version). The project was marketed by various other operations such as Chiltern Motors of Clavering, Essex, P.B.M. Motors of Carshalton, Surrey, and Lurastore Ltd of London. Another famous Bugatti roadster, the Type 55, was then replicated. Bizarrely, this classic was recreated on a BL Sherpa van basis. At least the engine was in the right place and the cart leaf spring suspension looked right. There was plenty of space in the engine bay to fit alternative engines, including straight sixes. Sherpa parts included both axles and running gear, all in Replicar's ladder frame chassis.

CR

REPLICAR (ii) (DK) 1980s
E.B. Replicar, Vedbaek.
Erik Koux produced, in very small quantities, a superb recreation of the Bugatti Atlantic coupé. Its bodywork, although in fibreglass, incorporated a riveted effect, giving it an air of authenticity. It was powered by a Jaguar XK 6-cylinder engine.

CR

1928 Reo Flying Cloud sedan.
NATIONAL MOTOR MUSEUM

1934 Reo Royale 8 sedan.
NICK BALDWIN

RÉPLICAR (iii) (P) 1992–c.1995
Réplicar, Lisbon.
This was an exacting replica of the Porsche 356 Speedster that used only brand new mechanical components from the Brazilian-built Volkswagen Beetle. That meant, for example, a fuel-injected 1.6-litre engine sat under the fibreglass bodywork. Réplicar's products were internationally distributed by Comauto SA in Valencia, Spain.

CR

1904 Repton 4hp 3-wheeler.
NATIONAL MOTOR MUSEUM

1920 ReVere Model A tourer.
KEITH MARVIN

REPLICARS (US) 1975–1980s
Replicars Inc., West Palm Beach, Florida.
These were replica Model-A Ford roadsters and phætons, using modern Ford running gear. The 1981specification included a 5-litre V8 engine, automatic transmission, and power steering.

NG

REPLI-CLASSICS (US) c.1985
Repli-Classics Inc., Clearwater, Florida.
The RC Auburn Speedster was a replica based on modified Ford or Chevrolet chassis. They were sold in several stages of assembly. The bodies were fibreglass and the trim was available separately.

HP

REPTON (GB) 1904
Repton Engineering Works, Repton, Derbyshire.
This was a very small 3-wheeler with a single-seater body and a 4hp water-cooled single-cylinder engine. It had a 2-speed epicyclic transmission and front-wheel brakes, which were very unusual for the time and hardly necessary to curb the top speed of 25mph (40km/h).

NG

REPUBLIC (US) 1910–1916
Republic Motor Car Co., Hamilton, Ohio.

The Republic started life as a large car with 35/40hp 4-cylinder T-head engine on a 116in (2944mm) wheelbase, made in 5-seater tourer or 2-seater roadster forms. It had an offset crankshaft. For 1913 the wheelbase was increased to 120in (3046mm), and there was a companion 6-cylinder model with 43hp engine on a 133in (3376mm) wheelbase. This became the only model from 1914 onwards. Manufacture ended in January 1917, probably because of shortage of materials brought about by the war. The company's slogan was 'The Classiest of All'.

NG

RESTELLI (I) 1920–1923
SA Officine Meccaniche Isola Bella, Milan.
The Restelli sports car was made in very small numbers. Its construction was unusual with no conventional chassis. Instead, the engine, gearbox and rear axle were rigidly connected, and attached to trunnions on which the springs were mounted. Two types of engine were offered, a 1490cc single-ohc four and a 1459cc twin-ohc unit, both built in-house. Antony Lago of Lago-Talbot fame drove a Restelli early in his career.

NG

REUMECH (ZA) 1990s
This operation made a range of ground-up 4-wheel drive vehicles, including the V8 Chevrolet powered A-Wagon with four doors, 4-speed automatic transmission and hard-top bodywork. There was also a Mercedes 5.7-litre straight-6 powered model called the Mamba.

CR

REVERE (US) 1918–1926
1918–1923 ReVere Motor Car Corp., Logansport, Indiana.
1923–1926 ReVere Motor Co., Logansport, Indiana.
The ReVere car is a pristine example of an automobile which would be built to the highest standard and targeted to the market comprised of sporting car buyers, but which failed throughout its ten year life by a series of poor financial backing, in-house fighting and other chicanery resulting in an approximate annual output of 25 cars.

The ReVere was widely touted in its time and exhibited in a number of automobile shows throughout the United States as the true idea of what a sporting car really was. Production, such as it was, did not get underway until early 1918.

The ReVere was fitted with a Rochester-Duesenberg 4-cylinder engine, modified by Adolph Monsen and which, depending on the source, was listed as both that of Rochester-Duesenberg or in-house which was essentially what it was. This horizontal-valve power plant developed 85bhp at 2600rpm, later being revised to develop 85bhp at 2600rpm, and subsequently 100bhp. Wheelbase was 131in (3325mm) and wire wheels standard equipment. Open models only were available until 1921 with a standard price of $3850. In 1921 these were increased to $4650 to $4850 with a sedan at $6500. Prices would be subsequently reduced in 1922 at $3850 to $4250 for open cars and $4500 for the sedan. The ReVere was heavily advertised in automotive journals of the time and was frequently the subject of feature articles, this promotion enhanced somewhat by the delivery of an open victoria to King Alfonso XIII of Spain. Among other outstanding features of the ReVere was its tall, 'cathedral' type radiator reminiscent of the Fiat or contemporary Kissel.

For 1925, ReVere introduced its Model 25 series, a less expensive model with a Continental 6J 6-cylinder L-head engine, available exclusively as a 5-seater touring car for $2750.

The year 1925 also saw cars equipped with balloon tyres and 4-wheel brakes, the larger tyres giving the cars a more solid appearance enhanced by a three-pronged radiator cap, its design reminiscent of a fairy swan's crown.

Although wire wheels remained as standard equipment, the ReVere buyer was given the option of two other wheel types, one of these an 11-spoked design of polished aluminium; the other, the Smith Wheel, a patented but short-lived option also used by a few other cars, including the larger models of Auburn and Lexington.

The one feature introduced for the 1925 cars was the dual-steering wheel which was a 'prehistoric' form of power-steering. This constituted a double wheel, one above the other. The upper wheel, larger in diameter, was set at a 7:1 ratio and used for steering after the car was underway from a standing position.

The lower wheel had a ratio of 14:1 which allowed easier turning and claimed as an advantage when parking in tight spaces. ReVere's powerful Model M series was continued into 1926 with a roadster and touring car priced at $3200 and a sedan at $4500. The 25 continued as a touring car at $2750. Few cars were sold this year which would be ReVere's final one.

KM

Further Reading
'ReVere's short ride', L. Spencer Riggs, *Automobile Quarterly*, Vol. 33, No. 2.

REVILLE (AUS) 1950
Reville Motor Co., Brisbane, Queensland.
Jean Reville had raced midget cars in England before World War II and had built the Palmer-Reville car at Wimbledon, all with the form of front-drive and independent suspension seen earlier on ALVIS and B.S.A. vehicles. In Queensland he represented several makes, including Daimler. His Ranger was a bare vehicle with 4-wheel drive, using the system of four quarter-elliptic springs per wheel, to be offered in low cost form with a Ford Ten engine or, more expensively, with a Lanchester Ten engine and its fluid flywheel and pre-selector gearbox, both in conjunction with his 'multi-variable' gearing. Daimler, however, stated that it would not supply the Lanchester engine and nothing more was heard.

MG

REVOL (F) 1923–1925
J.F. Revol, Fontenay-aux-Roses, Seine.
Two sizes of 2-cylinder engine were offered in the Revol cyclecar, a 990cc Train and a 1100cc Anzani.

NG

REWELL (AUS) 1938
Rewell Motors, Kensington, Victoria.
The D.K.W. was a seminal design which inspired many economy car projects. With the object of demonstrating that the type was within Australian manufacturing capability, A. Rewell built one car, with only the speedometer imported, and had another near completion when World War II broke out. After the war a group in Ballarat unsuccessfully attempted production.

M

REX (i); REX-SIMPLEX (D) 1901–1923
1901–1904 Deutsche Automobil-Industrie Friedrich Hering, Ronneburg.
1904–1908 Deutsche Automobil-Industrie Hering & Richard, Ronneburg.
1908–1921 Automobilewerk Richard & Hering, Ronneburg.
1921–1923 Elitewagen AG, Ronneburg.
Founded in 1888, Friedrich Hering's company made bicycle components and, from the late 1890s, proprietary parts for cars including chassis, wheels and axles. In 1900 they announced their first complete car. It used a 6hp single-cylinder De Dion-Bouton engine made under licence in Germany by Max CUDELL, in Hering's own chassis. Initially sold as the Rex, it soon took the name Rex-Simplex to stress the simplicity of the design. By 1903 a choice of De Dion or Fafnir engines was available and up to 1907 these makes supplied engines in single, 2- and 4-cylinder models. Rex-Simplex began to make their own engines in 1907. They became larger, the best-known being the 2120cc 9/16PS, 2680cc 10/28PS, and the very successful 4500cc 17/38PS. The largest model was the 7440cc 25/50PS of 1910–1912. Dr Ernst Valentin was the chief designer from 1911, later going to Russia to work for RUSSO-BALTIC which showed quite a lot of influence from his designs for Rex-Simplex.

After the war two updated versions of prewar designs, the 10/28 and 13/40PS were made, and in 1921 the company was taken over by the ELITE Motorenwerke AG. They continued one model only, the 3176cc 13/40PS, for two years.

HON

REX (ii) (GB) 1901–1914
1901–1902 Birmingham Motor Manufacture & Supply Co. Ltd, Birmingham.
1902–1914 Rex Motor Manufacturing Co. Ltd, Coventry.
The Rex name was better-known in connection with motorcycles than for cars, though the latter were made in a variety of names, Ast-Rex, Airex, Rexette, Rex-Remo and even Rex-Simplex which had no connection with the German make. The first Birmingham-built cars had 900cc single-cylinder engines, 2-speed

1905 Rex (ii) Rexette 3-wheeler.
NATIONAL MOTOR MUSEUM

1903 Rex (ii) 13hp tonneau.
NATIONAL MOTOR MUSEUM

1905 Rex (ii) Rexette 5hp tricar.
NATIONAL MOTOR MUSEUM

gearboxes and shaft drive. They had curious cylindrical radiators, at first mounted low down at the front of the frame, later moved to the rear.

In June 1902 they moved to Coventry, merged with the ALLARD (i) company and brought out a wider range of cars. The 900cc single was continued but there was also a 2.4-litre 12hp vertical twin with square cylinder dimensions, and 4-seater rear-entrance tonneau bodies. These were called Rex or, in 1904 and 1905, Rex-Simplex. In 1903 a motorcycle-based tricar was made, becoming more car-like in 1904 when it was called the Rexette. This had a seat for the driver instead of a saddle, a water-cooled single-cylinder engine and a 2-speed

1908 Rex-Simplex Prince Henry Tour tourer.
NATIONAL MOTOR MUSEUM

1996 Rex (iv) sports car.
MARGUS H. KUUSE

1907 Reyrol Coupe des Voiturettes roadster.
NATIONAL MOTOR MUSEUM

gearbox. In 1905 it became even more car-like, with a steering wheel and brakes on all three wheels. 1906 was the last year for the Rexette, which now had a transverse V-twin engine and was available with a 2-seater forecarriage. A smaller, cheaper and more motorcycle-like tricar was the Litette of 1907, with 726cc single-cylinder engine and selling for only £78.75. A wheel-steered model was made in 1908 and 1909, which saw the end of the Rex 3-wheelers.

A larger car introduced in 1906 was the Ast-Rex with 3.7-litre 4-cylinder Aster engine, followed by the 1.3-litre air-cooled V-twin Airex. All these cars had shaft drive, as did the Rex-Remo made from 1908 to 1911. This was made in two sizes, 2554 and 3029cc (16 and 20hp), and had 4-cylinder T-head engines and

3-speed gearboxes. They had gilled tube radiators, which were pretty old fashioned by then, and were concealed behind a honeycomb grill.

Motorcycles predominated from then onwards, although Rex nodded towards the cyclecar movement with a water-cooled V-twin machine with friction transmission and underslung frame in 1913, and the following year announced a light car powered by a 1100cc 4-cylinder Dorman engine. The war prevented it from going into production, and no more Rex 4-wheelers were made. The company merged with the Coventry Acme Motor Co. Ltd in 1922 and made Rex-Acme motorcycles until 1928, with an attempted revival in 1932.
NG

REX (iii) (US) 1914
Rex Motor Co., Detroit, Michigan.
This was a rare example of a front-wheel drive cyclecar with friction transmission. The engine was a conventional 14/18hp 4-cylinder unit designed, like the rest of the car, by C.H. Blomstrom, who had previously been involved with the QUEEN, BLOMSTROM and GYROSCOPE among other cars. The body was a 2-seater and the price a reasonable $395, but the Rex never got off the ground. The backers were said to be looking for a large factory, but the Rex never got further than the small workshop where the prototype was built. Blomstrom's next venture was the FRONTMOBILE.
NG

REX (iv) (EST) 1996 to date
Rexer Ltd, Tallinn.
Only a year after Estonia became independent of the former USSR in 1991, their first kit manufacturer was born. Mati Kits designed a lightweight fibreglass model called Vilgas. Its mechanicals came straight from Lada. Assembled at the Kavor works which had had a hand in building racing cars since 1960, it had a space frame, and the body panels were gradually improved. A 2-litre Ford engine was used in one of the first cars to be sold, and in 1996 Kits installed a 2.9-litre Ford V8 in his personal car which had a removable hard-top. The modernised vehicle was renamed Rex, and received Estonian Type Approval. Seven more cars were made in 1997–8, two of which were sold as far afield as Portugal. Kits saw no future merely updating the existing design, and prepared a completely new model for introduction in the summer of 2000. Called the Panthera, it had a unique-looking coupé body, and could take a Ford V6 or BMW straight-6 engine, with other components such as gearboxes also coming from these donor vehicles.
MHK

REX BUCKBOARD (US) 1903
Rex Reinertson, Pennsylvania Electrical & Railway Supply Co.,
Pittsburgh, Pennsylvania.
Reinertson had built a runabout in his native Wisconsin before he moved east to New York State and then Pittsburgh where he became superintendent of the Pennsylvania Electrical & Railway Supply Co. In his spare time, but in the company's workshops, he built a number of very light cars on the lines of the Orient Buckboard with single-cylinder 4½hp engines. They sold locally for $550 and were said to have a top speed of 30mph (48km/h).
NG

REXER see WEYHER ET RICHEMOND

REYMOND (F) c.1901
Automobiles Reymond et Cie, Chalons-sur-Saône, Saône-et-Loire.
The only evidence for this car comes from a surviving example, a 2-seater with 12hp V-twin engine and double-chain drive. No references have been found in any contemporary journals.
NG

REYNARD (GB) 1931
Reynard Car & Engineering Co. Ltd, Highgate, London.
The Reynard was a low-built 2-seater sports car powered by a 1496cc ohv Meadows engine with twin Zenith carburettors which developed 45bhp. This drove through a close-ratio 4-speed gearbox and Moss rear axle. Front suspension was by quarter-elliptics and at the rear there were full cantilever springs. It was

said that detail modifications could be made to the customer's wishes; for example the gear change could be central or, for traditionalists, right-hand. It did not pass beyond the prototype stage.

NG

REYNOLDS (GB) 1921
Reynolds Brothers, Barnsley, Yorkshire.
This was a 3-wheeler with 10hp V-twin Blackburne engine, 2-speed epicyclic gearbox and shaft drive to the single rear wheel. This was of the Sankey steel-spoked type, while the front wheels had cycle-type wire spokes. Probably only a prototype was made for *The Light Car & Cyclecar* reported 'The concern responsible for its inception have not decided finally on its manufacture, and we understand that they are desirous of getting in touch with anyone interested'.

NG

REYONNAH (F) 1950–1954
Robert Hannoyer, Paris.
A solution to parking problems has rarely been so radical as the Reyonnah's. Launched at the 1950 Paris Salon, the Reyonnah was the brainchild of Robert Hannoyer (whose name provided the anagrammatical basis for the car's name). It was a narrow-bodied tandem 2-seater powered by an Ydral 175cc or AMC 250cc engine placed in the rear, driving twin rear wheels which were placed only 20½in (520mm) apart. In normal circumstances the front wheels sat proud of the main body on parallelogram sponsons but could fold up underneath the bodywork for parking in narrow places (such as through doorways). Thus the car's width shrank from 52in (1320mm) to just 29½in (749mm). There were no doors on the Reyonnah, the passengers having to climb over the sides. Either a soft-top or a sideways-swinging Plexiglass dome protected the occupants from the elements.

CR

REYROL (PASSE-PARTOUT) (F) 1901–1930
Sté des Automobiles Reyrol, Neuilly, Seine (1901–1906);
Levallois-Perret, Seine (1907–1930).
These cars were known mostly as Reyrols, though Passe-Partout was used for some of the cars sold in France. The name, meaning 'Goes Everywhere', was also used by Dr Lehwess for a vast Panhard touring bus with which he attempted to cross Russia in 1902. The first Reyrols were light voiturettes powered by 5hp Aster or De Dion-Bouton engines, with belt and spur gear transmission and a vertical steering column. There were plans for it to be made by the Yorkshire Engineering Co., but bankruptcy ensued before any cars were made.

Single-cylinder engines were still being used in 1906, made by Buchet and of 785 and 942cc capacity. Armoured wood frames gave way to pressed steel in 1907, when a small monobloc 4-cylinder engine was offered. They had low-slung frontal radiators, though the cars which ran in the 1907 and 1908 Coupe des Voiturettes sported Renault-style dashboard radiators. The larger of two 4-cylinder models was called the 12/14 Passe-Partout or 12/16 Reyrol. The singles were not made after 1908, and Reyrol settled down to make conventional fours with 3-speed gearboxes. In 1913 there were five models, of 1.5, 1.7, 2.1, 2.3 and 2.7-litres.

Reyrol used mostly Chapuis-Dornier engines in the 1920s, side-valve units of 1243 and 2292cc, and from 1924 an ohv version of the latter and a smaller ohv 1494cc. Many of these cars carried saloon bodies. In 1927 the Passe-Partout name was revived for a front-drive car powered by a 1494cc ohc C.I.M.E., with three speeds and worm drive to the front axle. Its appearance was somewhat similar to that of a BALLOT 2LTS, making for a handsome little car, but few were made. Reyrol continued with rather pedestrian-looking saloons and tourers up to 1930. The company survived as a garage and repair works into the early 1950s.

NG

R.G. (i) (GB) 1913–1914
R.G. Motor Co. Ltd, Islington, London.
The R.G. company, whose initials stood for Richard Gartman, made a 10cwt delivery van with 10/12hp 4-cylinder engine mounted transversely behind the driver's seat. Drive was via a 3-speed epicyclic gearbox and single chain to the rear axle. The catalogue also described, and illustrated with a drawing, a 2-seater light car on the same chassis. Both car and van were priced at £195.

NG

1992 R.G. (ii) barchetta sports car.
ALVARO CASAL TATLOCK

R.G. (ii) (RA) 1992–1997
Automoviles R.G., Buenos Aires.
Named after its founder Ruben F. Garcia, this company made a 2-seater sports car with multi-tubular space frame clad in aluminium panels. Cabriolet, coupé or barchetta bodies were offered, and engine options included 1491, 1581, 1756 or 1995cc Fiat, or the 1995cc turbocharged unit as used in the Lancia HF Integrale. These were transversely mounted driving the front wheels. Garcia planned to make a twin-engined model with a second transverse engine driving the rear wheels, but it is not certain that this was ever built.

NG

R.H. (F) 1927–1928
Éts Raymond Hebert, Levallois-Perret, Seine.
Raymond Hebert built his attractive little sports car in the works of the family chassis-making company, Hebert et Nicolas. It was powered by a 1100cc 4-cylinder ohv C.I.M.E. engine but Hebert said that other engines could be fitted as well. The frame was hand-formed from sheet steel and constituted the lower part of the very low, doorless, body. Like some models of Chénard-Walcker, there were no brakes on the rear wheels, only on the front ones and the transmission.

NG

RHÉDA (F) 1898–1899
Sté des Automobiles Rhéda, Paris.
Two models of Rhéda were built, a 3-wheeler powered by a 2½hp horizontal single-cylinder engine, and in 1899 a 4-wheeler. They were probably both prototypes.

NG

RHENAG (D) 1924–1926
Rhenania Motorenfabrik AG, Berlin; Mannheim.
This company made a light car powered by a 1065cc ohv 4-cylinder engine developing 24bhp. Light metal bodies were fitted, a saloon and a sports car with curious horizontal front wings and headlamps faired between these and the bonnet sides.

HON

RHODE (GB) 1921–1931
Rhode Motor Co., Birmingham.
This company was a subsidiary of Mead & Deakin Ltd who made bicycle and motorcycle components, Canoelet sidecars and in 1912 had built two prototype cyclecars called MEDEA. In 1921 the Rhode Motor Co. was formed as a subsidiary of Mead & Deakin, to make a light car powered by their own design of 1087cc 4-cylinder engine. The use of a single-ohc was unusual on a light car at that time, though the rear axle was less up-to-date, having no differential. Apart from the Wrigley gearbox all the Rhode's mechanical components were made in the factory. The first model, known as the 9.5hp, had an Occasional Four body, but this gave way to a full 4-seater in 1924, with a 1232cc engine, and the added luxuries of a differential and a self starter. Another model in the 1924 range was the sports car with high-lift cams, lightened con rods and an outside copper exhaust pipe, said to be capable of 90mph (145km/h).

The Rhode became less sporting in 1926, when the single-ohc engine gave way to a pushrod ohv unit of the same capacity, though the ohc returned on the

1923 Rhode Occasional Four tourer.
NICK BALDWIN

1904 Ribble 8hp tricar.
NATIONAL MOTOR MUSEUM

1906 Ribble 12/16hp tourer.
NICK BALDWIN

Hawk made from 1928 onwards. In 1926 Rhodes were leaving the factory at the rate of about 50 cars per week, and it is thought that about 1000 9.5s and 1500 10.8s were made between 1921 and 1928. In that year it was taken over by McKenzie and Denley. Thomas McKenzie had made cars under his own name from 1913 to 1926, and H.B.Denley had been in charge of sales and testing at Rhode. Production was moved to a smaller factory at Hall Green, Birmingham. There appears to have been no engine-making facilities there, and the 1928–1931 Rhodes were presumably assembled from existing stock. When these ran out six 1496cc Meadows engines were ordered. There was a new body, though, the Hawk saloon on a 124in (3147mm) wheelbase. It was unusual, with normal-sized windows and two little oval quarter lights. Probably no more than 50 Rhodes were made at Hall Green, and the last was delivered no later than 1930 or possibly 1931, though the make lingered on in some lists until 1935.

NG

Further Reading
Lost Causes of Motoring, Lord Montagu of Beaulieu, Cassell, 1960.
'Fragments on Forgotten Makes. The Rhode', Bill Boddy,
Motor Sport, November 1989.

RHODIA (GB) c.1914–c.1922

This is one of those makes for which, like the CELER and the REYMOND, the only evidence lies in a surviving example, as no contemporary references have so far been found. The existing chassis was found in Scotland and has a 16hp pair-cast 4-cylinder side-valve engine, with central change 3-speed gearbox and shaft drive to a bevel rear axle.

NG

RIBBLE (GB) 1904–c.1908

Jackson & Kennings, Southport, Lancashire.
The first Ribbles were very simple 3-wheelers with single rear wheel. Two models were made, a single-seater with an 8hp engine, giving it a top speed of 50mph (80km/h), and a 2-seater whose engine only gave 4½hp, so performance was considerably lower. In 1907 they turned to conventional cars with 4-cylinder engines of 10/12 and 12/16hp, and tourer bodies, priced at £250 and £295 respectively.

NG

RIBOUD *see* VITREX

RICART (E) 1926–1928

SA de Motores y Automóviles Ricart, Barcelona.
After his separation from RICART-PÉREZ in 1926, Ricart continued, developing the 226, a 6-cylinder 1468cc engine, with two valves per cylinder and double-ohc. With a supercharger this was good for 85mph (137km/h). The car was shown at the Paris Salon in 1926, driven to the exposition by Ricart from Barcelona to Paris in 18 hours. It was equipped with a nice coupé body designed by Spanish coachbuilder Capella. The young engineer built several versions on the same chassis but with a shorter wheelbase, and a racing monoposto, the 266, with volumex turbocharger, achieved 100mph (162km/h). Ricart also developed the 166, with a special 4-cylinder 1600cc-engine, as an economical tourer. From this model he also developed a sport version. Ricart gave a three-year warranty for his engines.

VCM

RICART-ESPAÑA (E) 1928–1930

Sociedad Industrial Nacional Metalurgica (Fábricas Ricart-España Reunidos), Barcelona.
In 1928 Ricart joined forces with Francisco Battlo, founder of ESPAÑA. The new company continued with the 166 and 266, but also introduced high quality cars equipped with the 6-cylinder ohv 2.4-litre engine with twin carburettors. This car had very elegant open and closed bodies, and was one of the most luxurious cars built in Spain. Some of them were sold under the name of Alta to the Spanish Government. The company also prepared a 1.5-litre ohc racing-car, but the lack of money and a change of government brought production to an end. Ricart worked later as a consultant for several companies, specialising in diesel engines. He joined Alfa-Romeo from 1936–45, where he engineered the V16 Tipo 162 and the mid-engined V12-512 GP cars, and after World War II organised the whole Spanish car industry. He also created PEGASO (i).

VCM

RICART-PÉREZ (E) 1922–1926

Compañía de Motores Ricart & Pérez, Barcelona.
Together with the rich industrialist Pérez de Olaguer, Wifredo Ricart built small industrial engines with 1.5bhp to 90bhp, sold under the brand name Rex, with such success that the company survived until 1965. But in 1922 the restless Ricart prepared a sports car with a 4-cylinder 1498cc engine, double-ohc, 4 valves-per-cylinder and hemispherical combustion chambers, producing 58bhp at 5600rpm. This car had an excellent competition platform. Two cars were built and entered in several races, but Ricart's partner Pérez did not agreed with the production of cars, and the men separated.

VCM

RICCHIARDI (AUS) 1989–1991

Australian Technology Pty Ltd, Adelaide, South Australia.

Rick Hardy formed the notion of fitting Alfa-Romeo mechanicals into a fibreglass 2-seater styled on Ferrari Monza 750 lines. Doug Potts of Australian Technology adopted the idea and designed a space frame of 25mm square tube to accept the 4-cylinder 1.6- to 2-litre engines and components. Its wheelbase was 88in (2234mm), weight 1496lbs (680kg).

MG

RICHARD (US) 1914–1919

Richard Automobile Co., Cleveland, Ohio.

French-born François Richard was certainly a believer in the long-stroke engine. After making the ONLY and METROPOL cars at Port Jefferson, New York, he moved to Cleveland and launched the Richard which had a 200mm stroke, increased to 228mm in 1917, giving a capacity of 5768cc. This was mounted in a chassis of 137in (3477mm) wheelbase, on which four body styles were offered, 7- and 9-seater tourers, a 2-seater roadster and a 7-seater limousine, although it is not certain that even one example of all these styles was built. In 1916 he changed his name and that of his company to RiChard, insisting that it be pronounced Ree-char to stress his French origins. He planned a car with magnetic transmission on the lines of the OWEN MAGNETIC, but it never appeared. His last car was no less eccentric than the others, a V8 with dimensions of 95.25 × 171.45mm, giving a capacity of 9768cc, This was offered in the same 137in (3477mm) chassis, but clothed in a 9-seater boat-tailed body and priced at $8000. Finding few, if any, buyers for his enormous cars, he changed tack and for 1921 offered the straight-8 LA MARNE for a more modest $1485. Having no more success with this than with the Richard he became a freelance consulting engineer, and continued to live in Cleveland until his death in 1960.

NG

RICHARDSON (i) (GB) 1903–1907

J.R. Richardson & Co. Ltd, Saxilby, Lincolnshire.

Based in the small market town of Saxilby, Richardson offered three cars, with 6½hp single, 12/14hp twin and 18/20hp 4-cylinder engines. The two smaller engines were Asters. The 6½hp had a 3-speed gearbox, the others 4-speeds with direct drive on top, and all had shaft drive. In 1907 J.R. Richardson was the manager of the MASS factory at Courbevoie, as well as selling Masses on the British market. It is possible that some, if not all Richardsons were in fact Masses. Certainly the smallest Richardson of 1905 had the same Aster engine as the equivalent Mass.

NG

RICHARDSON (ii) (GB) 1919–1921

C.E. Richardson & Co. Ltd, Sheffield, Yorkshire.

Ebenezer Richardson made children's scooters and toys, including some of the first model aircraft. After World War I, when shell nose caps and other munitions were made, his sons Charles Ebenezer and Ernest decided to build cars for adults, settling on a cyclecar designed by Charles' brother-in-law Albert Clarke. It was powered by a 980cc JAP or 1090cc Precision, both air-cooled V-twins, with friction transmission and belt drive to the rear axle. The body and frame were of unitary construction, and apart from the engines it seems that the whole car was made at the works. The belt drive soon gave way to a chain, and in 1921 the ugly sloping dummy radiator of the original Richardson was replaced by a better-looking vertical one. Richardsons were made in larger numbers than many cyclecars, the 'production line' being in the tunnel of an old brick kiln. About five cars a week left the factory, and Charles Ebenezer estimated that 500 had been made by late 1921 when production ended, due to the slump following the prolonged moulders' strike. Charles Ebenezer became a successful property developer, but Ernest sold ice cream before spending the rest of his working life as a lathe operator.

NG

Further Reading

Cars from Sheffield, Stephen Myers, Sheffield City Libraries, 1986.
'Toys and Toy Cars', M. Worthington-Williams,
The Automobile, October 1999.

1919 Richardson (ii) 8hp cyclecar.
NICK BALDWIN

1922 Richelieu Model T-85 tourer.
KEITH MARVIN

RICHELIEU (US) 1922–1923

Richelieu Motor Car Corp., Asbury Park, New Jersey.

The Richelieu was one of the more handsome sporting type cars of its time but its existence was short-lived. Introduced at the end of 1921 at New York City's Automobile Show, the Richelieu appeared in touring car guise, its only available model, and with a price of $3950. It was a powerful car with a 4-cylinder Rochester-Duesenberg G-1 engine, a body by Fleetwood, wire wheels including two sidemounted spares and a wheelbase of 131in (3325mm). For 1922, two additional models were added – a roadster at $4200 and a 7-seater sedan at $6000. Attractive as Richelieus may have been, buyers were few, the company's finances low and the national economy weak. The company failed in 1923 after a production estimated at under 100 units.

KM

RICHMOND (i) (US) 1902–1903

Richmond Automobile Co., Richmond, Indiana.

The Richmond was a typical light steam car with a 6hp engine which weighed only 46lb, and was described as 'the most compact steam vehicle engine on the market'. The car had single-chain drive and a 4-seater *dos-à-dos* body. Only six were made.

NG

RICHMOND (ii) (US) 1904–1917

Wayne Works, Richmond, Indiana.

One or two Richmond cars had been made from 1901 onwards, but it was not until 1904 that production began. Air-cooled fours of 20, 26 and 30hp were made up to 1910 when water-cooling took over. The cars were then conventional fours made in several sizes from 22.5 to 40hp, all with open bodies. A 45hp six joined the range in 1914.

NG

1926 Rickenbacker Super Sport sedan.
NICK BALDWIN

1923 Rickenbacker Six tourer, the pace car for the 1923 Indianapolis 500 mile race.
NATIONAL MOTOR MUSEUM

RICHMOND (iii) (GB) 1913

Cumming & Co., London.

This was probably a foreign car sold with a typical English name from premises in London's Cromwell Road which were quite unsuitable for car manufacture. It had a 1460cc monobloc 4-cylinder engine, whose dimensions corresponded to a Ballot unit, 4-speed gearbox and shaft drive. It was advertised with London-made 2-seater bodywork at £225.

NG

RICKENBACKER (US) 1922–1927

Rickenbacker Motor Co., Detroit, Michigan.

Captain Eddie Rickenbacker (1891–1973) was the leading American air ace of World War I, with an official bag of 26 German aircraft and four balloons to his credit. When he returned to America in 1919 his was already a household name, and this undoubtedly helped to reap publicity for the brand new car which he launched in December 1921. He was backed by Barney Everitt, formerly of E.M.F., and who was running a large body-building plant in Detroit. This became the Rickenbacker factory.

Neither Everitt nor Rickenbacker was an engineer, so they hired Harry L. Cunningham and E.R. Evans to design the car which made its debut at the New York Automobile Show in January 1922. It had a 3482cc side-valve engine developing 58bhp, which ran very smoothly thanks to two flywheels, one at each end of the crankshaft. Three body styles were offered, tourer, sedan and coupé, at prices from $1485 to $1985. It was to have been called the American Ace, but it was a wise decision to rename it Rickenbacker. The slogan was 'A Car Worthy of the Name', and the trademark was a top hat coloured with the Stars and Stripes in a ring, signifying that the Captain had thrown his hat in the ring of automobile manufacture.

The Rickenbacker got off to a good start, with production running at 10 cars per day in March 1922, rising to 50 per day three months later. Little change was made in the 1923 models, apart from a new single-plate clutch and a $150 price increase, but in June came the announcement that all Rickenbackers would henceforth have 4-wheel brakes. This was a pioneering feature on a medium-priced car; Buick followed suit in August, and many other makes had four-wheel brakes on their 1924 models. Rickenbackers carried a warning on the spare-wheel cover 'Four Wheel Brakes', and continued to do so until the system was no longer a novelty.

The six was increased to 4180cc and 60bhp in 1925, and there was also a 4401cc straight-8 developing 80bhp. This was offered in ten body styles in 1926. The most striking model was the Super Sports boat-tail 2-door sedan which, with tuned engine giving 107bhp, was said to be America's fastest stock car with a speed of 90mph (145km/h). However, the cars were not selling as well as in the previous year, and sales of Rickenbacker stock were suspended in January 1926. The Captain resigned in September and Barney Everitt struggled on in receivership. The 1927 models were announced, but only 517 were made before the company closed down in January 1927. About 27,500 Rickenbackers had been made.

NG

Further Reading

'Hat in the Ring – the Rickenbacker', Beverly Rae Kimes, *Automobile Quarterly*, Vol. 13, No. 4 and Vol. 14, No. 3.

RICKETT (GB) 1858–1860

Thomas Rickett, Buckingham.

There were many builders of steam carriages in England in the middle of the nineteenth century, but Thomas Rickett can claim the status of a manufacturer in that he made vehicles not only for his own use, but offered replicas for sale. He was the manager and chief engineer of the Castle Foundry at Buckingham, which made ploughs and seed drills, and added steam engines in 1857. The next year Rickett made a steam plough which attracted the attention of the Marquess of Stafford. He ordered a 3-wheeled steam carriage powered by a 2-cylinder engine which drove the offside rear wheel by chain. The boiler pressure was

110psi. There was a bench seat at the front for three passengers, one of whom held the steering tiller and had under his control the regulator, reversing lever and brake lever. At the rear of the carriage sat, or rather crouched, the stoker, next to the coal bunker.

In 1860 the Earl of Caithness ordered a similar carriage, though with a slightly smaller engine and spur-gear drive in place of the chain. In August the Earl made a memorable 146 mile journey from Inverness to Barrogill Castle, accompanied by his wife and with Thomas Rickett as stoker. Encouraged by the Earl's enthusiasm, Rickett placed an advertisement in *The Engineer* in November 1860, quoting a price of £180–200 for his carriages. This was not expensive, and was less than the price of a carriage from a leading London coachbuilder, but there was no market at that time for self-propelled vehicles and it seems that there were no takers.

NG

RICKETTS (US) c.1907–1911

1907–1910 Ricketts Automobile Co., South Bend, Indiana.
1910–1911 Diamond Automobile Co., South Bend, Indiana.
This company began to advertise in 1907, but the first cars for which specifications exist were introduced for the 1909 model year. They were a 30/35hp four on a 115in (2919mm) wheelbase and a 50hp six on a 121in (3071mm) wheelbase. The engines were made by Brownell and the cars were of conventional design, with 3-speed gearboxes and shaft drive. In January 1910 the company name was changed to Diamond, a name sometimes borne by the cars as well. A fire in October 1910 destroyed 32 partially completed cars.

NG

RICKMAN (GB) 1987 to date

1987–1992 Rickman Bros (Engineering) Ltd, New Milton, Hampshire.
1992 to date Rickman Vehicles, Halesowen, West Midlands.
1995 to date Métisse Cars Ltd, Bridgend, Mid Glamorgan.
Produced by the famous ex-motorbike manufacturer and fibreglass moulder, the Ranger was a kit-built utility vehicle in the style of the Suzuki SJ. Based on Escort Mk I/II mechanicals, it had a very strong steel chassis with full roll-over protection and a boxy fibreglass body in estate or soft-top styles (and a stretched 7-seater called the Space Ranger). With the Métisse, Rickman moved bravely into the sports coupé market, although the styling never had the balance to do its engineering justice. The Ford Sierra supplied most of the mechanical side of the equation, as well as the doors, glass, rear lights, wiring and most of the interior trim. Cosworth 4×4 and Rover V8 powered versions were offered and there was even a steam-powered record-breaker! When Rickman went bankrupt it was taken over by LOMAX in 1992. The Métisse eventually passed on to a new Welsh company in 1995.

CR

RICO (GB) c.1997

Rico, Brighton, Sussex.
This Citroën 2CV specialist briefly took on the MANX project and also developed its own Citroën Méhari replica, as well as a fibreglass conversion to turn a 2CV saloon into a van.

CR

RICORDI & MOLINARI (I) 1905–1906

Società Italiana Costruzioni Automobili Ricordi-Molinari, Milan.
This company made an 8hp single-cylinder car with 3-speed gearbox, shaft drive, tonneau body and a round radiator. Giuseppe Ricordi, father of Max who made these cars, was said to have imported the first car into Italy in 1890 and to have marketed a Ricordi-Benz in 1900.

NG

RIDDLE (US) 1916–1926

Riddle Manufacturing Co., Ravenna, Ohio.
Riddle was a highly respected manufacturer of funeral cars and ambulances which, having started business in 1831, was one of the oldest builder of hearses in the United States. In 1916 Riddle expanded its operations to include limousines and large sedans for the use of pallbearers in funeral processions and, in addition, offered an invalid car sedan. This was to all intents and purposes

1860 Rickett steam carriage.
NATIONAL MOTOR MUSEUM

1990 Rickman Space Ranger estate car.
RICKMAN BROS

1921 Riddle Double Side Door Convertible 7-seater sedan.
KEITH MARVIN

a run-of-the-mill sedan, but, with the centre pillar missing on the right-hand side, allowed both doors to open simultaneously and, with a ramp, affording easy access and egress for wheelchairs which, once locked in place, provided an excellent car for a clientele who needed it. The Riddle cars closely resembled contemporary Cadillacs in appearance. All were built with Continental 6-cylinder engines with production ending in 1926.

KM

RIDER-LEWIS (US) 1908–1911

1908–1909 Rider-Lewis Motor Car Co., Muncie, Indiana.
1909–1911 Anderson, Indiana.
Like so many makes, this was the product of a financier and an engineer, in this case designer Ralph Lewis and promoter George D. Rider. The 40/45hp 6-cylinder engine had a single-ohc, quite advanced for the time, and was made as a tourer,

1901 Ridley (i) 2-seater.
NATIONAL MOTOR MUSEUM

1897 Riker electric victoria.
JOHN A. CONDE

roadster, limousine and a 4-seater 'tonneauette' which was a sporting tourer with no weather protection. All the body styles were priced at $2500, and in 1910 were joined by a smaller 4-cylinder car at $1050, which was the sole model for 1911. 250 cars had been made by December 1910, and a few more fours were made up to March 1911.

NG

RIDLEY (i) (GB) 1901–1907

1901–1904 John Ridley (later, Ridley Autocar Co.), Coventry.
1906–1907 Ridley Motor Car Co. Ltd, Paisley, Renfrewshire.
John Ridley built a light 2-seater car powered by a 3½hp De Dion-Bouton or 5hp Buchet engine, using a gearbox combined with the rear axle. It had vertical tiller steering and a tubular frame. The Ridley Autocar company failed after only a handful of cars had been made. However, John Ridley bought some semi-finished chassis from Horsfall & Bickham of Manchester, makers of the HORBICK car, to which he fitted his own design of single-cylinder water-cooled engine. He assembled these cars at his home address in Paisley.

NG

RIDLEY (ii) (GB) 1914

Thorofare Motors Ltd, Woodbridge, Suffolk.
The Ridley Carette was a neat-looking little cyclecar powered by a 2-cylinder Blumfield engine, with friction transmission and belt final drive. It sported a radiator of Rolls-Royce type. They were made in the factory where the LINDSAY had been built.

NG

RIEGEL (F) 1902

Transformations Automobiles Riegel, Paris.
As its name indicates, this company made *avant-train* units for the motorisation of horse-drawn vehicles. The unit consisted of a 10hp flat-twin engine with gearbox and drive to the axle, which could be transferred without difficulty from one vehicle to another.

NG

RIEJU (E) 1955

Riera & Juanola SA, Figueras, Gerona.
This well-known motorcycle manufacturer presented at the 1955 Barcelona Motor Show, a car with a body which resembled that of an Isetta, but which used normal side doors and a motorcycle engine from the company's range.

VCM

RIESS-ROYAL see BELL (ii)

RIGAL (GB) 1902–1903

English Motor Co., London.
This car was originally exhibited by the British Germain company but showed no resemblance to any Germain. Its general appearance and single-cylinder De Dion-Bouton engine suggest that it owed its origin to LACOSTE ET BATTMANN.

NG

RIKAS (D) 1922–1923

Rikas Automobil-Werke, Berlin.
Another of the many small makes of German car in the 1920s, the Rikas had a 6/14PS 4-cylinder engine.

HON

RIKER (US) 1897–1902

1897–1899 Riker Electric Motor Co., Brooklyn, New York.
1899–1900 Riker Electric Vehicle Co., Elizabethport, New Jersey.
1901–1902 Riker Motor Vehicle Co., Elizabethport, New Jersey.
Andrew Lawrence Riker formed his Electric Motor Co. in 1888, having fitted an electric motor to a Coventry Tricycle the previous year. He built his first 'car' in 1894, though it was no more than a pair of bicycles joined together and equipped with battery and motor. Two years later his electric racing car defeated a petrol car at the Narragansett Races, and in 1900 he covered a mile in 63 seconds, a record for the American continent, though not as fast as Jenatzy's kilometre in 34 seconds the previous year. He built his first proper car in 1895 and made his first sale in 1897. From then on a variety of electric vehicles bore the Riker name; light runabouts with three or four wheels, 4-seater victorias, 5-seater surreys, hansom cabs and heavy trucks. In December 1900 he merged his activities with the Electric Vehicle Co., makers of the COLUMBIA, and thereafter only trucks were made under the Riker name.

In 1901 he designed a petrol car which he offered to Electric Vehicle, but they were not interested. He formed the Riker Motor Vehicle Co. to make petrol cars and built two designs, an 8hp 2-cylinder and 16hp 4-cylinder. These were developed by the OVERMAN Co. of Chicopee Falls who merged with LOCOMOBILE in October 1902; they went into production in 1903 as the first petrol-engined Locomobiles.

NG

RILEY (i) (GB) 1898–1969

1898–1912 Riley Cycle Co. Ltd, Coventry.
1912–1914 Riley Motor Manufacturing Co. Ltd, Coventry.
1914–1948 Riley (Coventry) Ltd, Coventry.
1948–1969 Riley Motors Ltd, Abingdon, Berkshire.

One of the most respected British sporting marques, Riley, like so many other Coventry firms, entered the motor industry via the bicycle.

The Riley family were originally weavers who turned to cycles in the 1880s, William Riley founded the Riley Cycle Co. in 1896, and two years later one of his sons, Percy, built a light 2-seater car powered by a single-cylinder engine with the advanced feature of mechanical-operated inlet valves. This did not go into production, and the first Rileys made for sale were tricycles and quadricycles of 1900. Three years later came a tricar with 517cc engine, handlebar steering and a basketwork seat for the passenger ahead of the driver. These were made up to 1908, and gradually became more car-like, with a seat replacing the saddle, a wheel instead of handlebars and water-cooled 2-cylinder engines. Up to 1903 Riley tricars had used proprietary engines, mostly by De Dion-Bouton or MMC, but in that year Percy and his brothers Victor and William set up the Riley Engine Co. to make power units for the tricars, which were made by the Riley Cycle Co. 1907 saw the first 4-wheeled production car, which used a 1034cc V-twin tricar engine mounted amidships, with the 3-speed gearbox alongside it, and final drive by chain. One of these 9hp Rileys was W.O. Bentley's first car. Larger cars with front-mounted V-twin engines of 1390 or 2075cc were made from 1908 to 1914, these having round radiators, constant-mesh 3-speed gearboxes, shaft drive, and Riley-made wire wheels. There was a great demand for Riley detachable wire wheels which were supplied to many other car manufacturers at home and abroad. Among the better-known clients were Hispano-Suiza, Mercedes, Napier, Panhard, Renault and Rolls-Royce.

Around 1912 the Riley Cycle Co. was so busy making wheels that car manufacture was seriously threatened, so the brothers formed a new company solely for car manufacture, named the Riley Motor Manufacturing Co. Ltd. The Cycle Co. concentrated on wheels, and since they had abandoned bicycles in 1911, they changed the name to Riley (Coventry) Ltd. In 1914 the V-twins were joined by a 2949cc 4-cylinder car known as the 17/30. Few of these were made, either before or after World War I. Another brother, Stanley, took over the Nero Engine Co. to make a new 10hp 4-cylinder car of his own design, but only a prototype was made before the war intervened. However, the Nero Engine Co. acquired land at Coventry which became the main Riley car works after the war.

Redwingers and Nines

In 1920 Riley was one of many British car makers, well thought of by a small clientele, but not outstanding in any way. By the end of the decade it was a household name in Britain and was beginning to acquire fame abroad. This was due to two models, Harry Rush's 10.8hp and Stanley and Percy Riley's Nine. The 10.8 was the first Riley to be designed by someone outside the family. It had a 1495cc monobloc side-valve engine with alloy pistons, developing 35bhp. It was made by Riley (Coventry) Ltd who had abandoned wheel manufacture, and were henceforth the only Riley company making cars. The Riley Engine Co. assembled about six of their prewar 17/30 models, but after 1922 they concentrated on electric lighting and marine equipment.

The 10.8 was made mainly in open 2-seater or tourer models with disc wheels, but in 1923 came the Redwinger sports model with polished aluminium bodies, 2- or 4-seaters, and wire wheels. Most of them were supplied with red painted front and rear wings, hence the name, which was always unofficial. Top speed was 70mph (112km/h) and many sporting successes were earned, especially in trials. Victor Gillow and Frank Ashby raced stripped versions at Brooklands for several years, Ashby's car lapping at 103mph (166km/h). At the 1926 Motor Show there was an ohv version of the 10.8 with Riley-designed supercharger, said to be capable of 80mph (130km/h), but the ohv gear was said to have infringed a patent, and the car never went into production. The last of the side-valve Rileys was the 1645cc Twelve which was made up to 1928.

The 1926 Motor Show also saw another Riley, which was to become one of the most famous models the company ever produced. Designed by Percy Riley, aided by his brother Stanley, the Nine had a 1087cc 4-cylinder engine with ohvs operated by short pushrods from twin camshafts mounted high in the block, but not overhead. This gave the advantages of light reciprocating parts associated with ohcs with the easier maintenance of the pushrod layout. The cylinder head featured hemispherical combustion chambers, and was known

1901 Riker electric hansom cab.
NATIONAL MOTOR MUSEUM

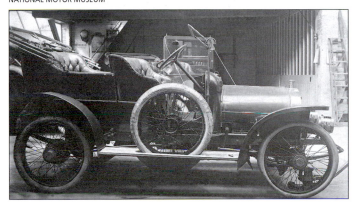

1907 Riley (i) 9hp tourer.
NICK BALDWIN

1922 Riley (i) 11hp all-weather tourer.
NICK BALDWIN

as the PR head, after Percy Riley. The basic layout was used by Riley until they ceased to have their own engines, in 1957. The Nine engine developed 32bhp in its original form, and was installed in a conventional chassis with fabric saloon and tourer bodies. Initially these had artillery wheels, but from 1929 wire wheels were used, which gave the cars a much better appearance. Before the end of 1926 the racing driver and record breaker J.G. Parry Thomas had started to develop a very low sports car derived from the touring Nine. The frame was dropped behind the front axle and underslung at the rear making a car so low that the driver could easily place his hand on the ground while seated at the wheel. The steering column was so raked that it was almost horizontal. The engine received a lot of attention too, with high compression pistons, special cams, twin carburettors, a 4-branch exhaust manifold and special oil pump.

1928 Riley (i) Nine tourer.
NATIONAL MOTOR MUSEUM

1931 Riley (i) Gamecock 2-seater.
NICK GEORGANO

1931 Riley (i) Stelvio II saloon.
NICK GEORGANO

Power was increased from 32 to 50bhp, giving a top speed in road trim of 80mph (130km/h). Stripped versions for racing were considerably faster. After Thomas' death in March 1927, development of the Brooklands Nine was taken over by Reid Railton. The early cars were assembled by Thomson & Taylor Ltd at Brooklands track, but later production was taken up at Coventry. About 100 to 110 Brooklands Nines were made, from 1928 to 1932, out of a total production for the Nine of around 10,000 (1926–1938).

The Nine was progressively developed though the 1930s, with a dropped frame in 1932, coil ignition in 1933 and an optional ENV pre-selector gearbox in 1934. A year later the Wilson pre-selector, made for Riley by Armstrong-Siddeley, was offered on the Nine, as on the larger Rileys. An all-synchromesh gearbox was catalogued for 1938, but never went into production. The range of bodies grew in the 1930s, to include the Merlin and Kestrel saloons, Lynx tourer, Ascot drophead coupé and Lincock fixed head coupé. Several of these styles could be had on the larger Rileys as well, and indeed almost any combination of engine, chassis and body could be had on request. A 1936 advertisement read, rather naively 'We make far too many models, of course. But then we have a pretty fertile design department, and we like making nice, interesting cars'.

The 1928 London Show saw Riley's first six, the 1633cc 14/6. This was very much an enlarged Nine, with similar valve gear, and pre-selector boxes available from 1934. An exceptionally wide range of bodies was made for the 14/6, 15 catalogued models, of which several were shared with the Nine, but there were also some exclusive to the 14/6, such as the Edinburgh and Winchester, both 6-light saloons or limousines. A smaller six, the 1458cc 12/6 was made from 1933 to 1935, and in 1935 the 14/6 was replaced by the 1726cc 15/6. This shared many features with the new 12/4, including a box-section frame and standardised Wilson gearbox. This was made up to 1938.

The 1496cc 12/4 was a new model for 1935, being Riley's biggest four since the 1920s. The engine was redesigned by Hugh Rose, with three main bearings, although the basic camshaft layout was retained. It was made in six different saloon styles, as well as the Lynx tourer and Sprite 2-seater sports. The Sprite engine, which had hotter cams, magneto ignition, a bigger capacity sump, and a new water pump, could also be had in the touring models, particularly the Kestrel saloon and Lynx tourer, but without the racing sump and using a standard 12/4 water pump. A Lynx-Sprite was capable of around 80mph (130km/h). Fewer than 8000 12/4s were made, yet a surprising number survive today.

Three sports Rileys were made in the 1930s, apart from the Brooklands Nine which went out of production in 1932. The first to appear was the Imp, which used the Nine engine in a new frame which was upswept over the front axle and underslung at the rear. They had stubby 2-seater bodies on a 90in (2286mm) wheelbase, and the cockpit was so small that anyone over 5ft 8in tall found it difficult to get behind the wheel. An ENV pre-selector or close-ratio manual gearbox could be had, and top speed was about 75mph (120km/h), not a high speed for a 1930s sports car, but the Imp gained friends by its beautifully taut handling. Only 75 were made, in 1934–5. Even rarer was the MPH-Six, generally similar in appearance to the Imp but with a slightly longer wheelbase and a choice of three 6-cylinder engines: 1458, 1633, and 1726cc. Like the Imp, the MPH was offered with a choice of gearbox, and the company claimed speeds of 90mph (145km/h) in top gear. The chassis was based on that of the 1933 TT racer underslung at the rear and passing above the front axle. The MPH was expensive, at £550 compared with £325 for the Imp, and only 15 were made, in 1934–5.

For 1936 both Imp and MPH were replaced by the Sprite which used a tuned version of the 1496cc 12/4 engine in a chassis similar to that of the MPH. The prototype had a typical Riley radiator, but most production Sprites wore narrow fencers' mask grills which some people think spoils their appearance.

Later versions had cross-flow cooling of the cylinder head, to enable higher compression ratios to be used with 80 octane pump fuel, as required by the regulations for the 1936 Tourist Trophy. This was carried over to the road cars, which were good for 84mph (135km/h). Estimates of road-going Sprite production vary between 47 and 50. So far, 47 have definitely been traced.

Riley's last years as an independent company saw two new larger models, a big four of 2443cc and a V8 of 2178cc. The latter appeared first, in 1936, and used a crankcase based on two Nine blocks, each with its separate inlet manifold and downdraught carburettor. Adelphi and Kestrel saloon bodywork was offered, but so far as is known only the Adelphi was actually built on the V8 chassis. The model was not a success, and only 37 were made, though an enlarged version of the engine was used in the AUTOVIA, a separate make of which Victor Riley was a director. By contrast the four was an excellent engine, and powered several successful Rileys before and after the war. At 2443cc it was the largest British-built 4-cylinder engine since the demise of the 4½-litre Bentley, and developed 85bhp in single-carburettor form. In Donald Healey's hands after the war, output went up to 106bhp. The big four had a new and stronger chassis, and other features included a hydraulic jack, Luvax hydraulic shock absorbers and 380mm Girling brakes. Four styles of saloon were offered, and the Lynx tourer, though only one of these was actually built.

"AVERAGE" CONFIDENCE

You can reach 30 m.p.h. with amazing rapidity and hold it effortlessly on all gradients. A flick of the Pre-selectagear lever, a touch on the accelerator, and you are cruising at fifty— having saved the seconds that make the minutes. With a Riley 1½ Litre the greater the distance and the more difficult the road the higher becomes your comparable average. And it is your AVERAGE that matters—going out to a bridge party or travelling across a continent.

The Riley is the easiest car in the world to drive. Pre-selectagear (a combination of an AUTOMATIC clutch and a pre-selective four-speed epicyclic gearbox) makes gear-crashing impossible. No other form of transmission offers so many advantages or is so acceptable to both novice and expert.

OWN A

RILEY 1½ LITRE

AND DRIVE WITH CONFIDENCE

1½ Litre Falcon Saloon, £335. 1½ Litre Kestrel Aeroline Saloon, £345. Dunlop Tyres and Triplex Glass. Annual Tax £9. Riley (Coventry) Limited, Coventry.

AS OLD AS THE INDUSTRY
Riley
AS MODERN AS THE HOUR

BUY A CAR made in the UNITED KINGDOM

1935 Riley (i) 12/4 Kestrel saloon.
NICK BALDWIN

1935 Riley (i) Imp sports car.
NICK GEORGANO

1948 Riley (i) RMD 1½-litre drophead coupé.
NICK BALDWIN

The Racing Rileys, 1927–1938

Although the Redwinger had been raced at Brooklands, Rileys only became famous in racing after the arrival of the Brooklands Nine. This won its very first race at Brooklands in late 1927, with Reid Railton at the wheel. Peacock won the 1100cc class in the 1928 Six Hours Race and in the 1928 and 1929 TTs. In the early 1930s there were two versions of the Brooklands Nine, one with little more than twin carburettors and a raised cr, and the Plus Series or Ulster Brooklands, with counterbalanced crankshaft, special rods and, if required, four carburettors. Victor Ashby drove a special Nine with two carburettors on each side of the head, which gave 71bhp and had a top speed of 130mph (210km/h).

Among many successes was a class victory in the 1931 Brooklands Double Twelve Hour Race.

In 1932 the best-known of Riley exponents appeared on the scene, Freddie Dixon. With his rebuilt Nine he led the TT before disappearing over a hedge at high speed, leaving the works Nines to finish 1st and 2nd overall. He took class records at Brooklands with a single seater, and in 1933 he won the Mannin Beg

race in the Isle of Man. In 1934 he produced the famous aluminium Rileys with single-seater bodies and long tails. With one he won the Brooklands 500 Mile Race, and in 1935 and 1936 won the TT outright, as well as the 1935 British Empire Trophy and 1936 500 Mile Race. Only the arrival of the ERAs, themselves Riley-derived, ended Dixon's run of successes in voiturette racing.

Many other successes came to Riley in the 1930s, including 4th overall at Le Mans in 1933 (Peacock and von der Becke), while 1932 saw the first 6-cylinder racing Riley, with 14/6 engine reduced to 1486cc. A development of this won the 1500cc class in the 1933 TT (C.R. Whitcroft), this model being the prototype of the MPH-Six. Also in 1933 Raymond Mays drove a Six with supercharger designed by Peter Berthon, which became known as the White Riley. This car, which was particularly successful in hill climbs, being second only to Whitney Straight's Maserati at Shelsley Walsh in 1933 and 1934, was the basis of the first ERA. Another successful racing Riley was the 2-litre 6-cylinder car; with Sprite chassis driven by Dobbs, which finished 3rd behind two ERAs in the 1936 International Trophy. Also in 1936 1½-litre TT Sprites finished 1-2-3-4 in the 2-litre class of the French GP, which was for sports cars that year. Riley's racing department was closed down after the Nuffield takeover in September 1938, but private owners continued to campaign the cars successfully until after the war. In 1951 a young Mike Hawthorn won the *Motor Sport* Trophy in a works 1935 TT Sprite, used in the 1935 TT and 1936 French GP. Several racing Rileys, works cars and others, still compete in VSCC events today.

The Nuffield Takeover

Up to 1936 Riley had been very profitable, and able to pay dividends of 20 per cent as well as to carry forward enough money for plant improvement and the development of new models. It was probably the latter which led to the company's downfall for, as we have seen, there was an enormous variety of permutations of body, chassis and engine. Low-production runs like those of the MPH-Six and V8 cannot possibly have covered their development costs, while a lack of direction from management was also a factor, as was competition from the new SS Jaguar. A new inlet manifold for the Nine, designed by Lewis Ord, who was a works study consultant rather than an engineer, was a disaster, and damaged Riley's image at a critical point. After two years of serious losses, a receiver was called in in January 1938, and in September Riley was acquired by Lord Nuffield for resale to Morris Motors. A new company, Riley (Successors) Ltd, was formed with Victor Riley as managing director. Two new models were announced for 1939, the 12hp with updated 12/4 engine and the 16hp with 2443cc engine. They carried identical coachwork, a saloon and drophead coupé in rather bland styling, and had ordinary synchromesh gearboxes and disc wheels. Riley enthusiasts were most disappointed, although there was the option of the Sprite engine with magneto ignition in the 12hp chassis. Surprisingly, in July 1939 the old-style Kestrel 6-light saloon was revived, using the big four engine only, but few were made because of World War II.

The postwar Rileys were a pleasant surprise. While other Nuffield products such as Morris and Wolseley were almost identical to the 1939 models, Riley brought out the very attractive RMA saloon with torsion-bar ifs and hydro-mechanical brakes. The 1496cc high-camshaft engine was little changed, but then it was the best part of the first Nuffield Rileys, so enthusiasts could have no complaints on that score. Before the end of 1946 the 2443cc big four engine had been revived, being installed in a lengthened RMA chassis of identical styling to make the RMB. Power was raised from 90 to 100bhp in 1948, giving the RMB a top speed of 94mph (152km/h), and comfortable cruising at over 80mph (130km/h). Apart from one or two drophead coupés made in 1946, the RMA was made only in saloon form, but there were two open models with the larger engine, the RMC 3-seater roadster, of which 507 were made from 1948-50, and the RMD 4-seater drophead coupé, of which 502 were made from 1948 to 1951. Saloon production was 10,504 RMAs, and 6900 RMBs. Both were made up to 1952, when they were replaced by the generally similar RME and RMF. These had hypoid rear axles and full hydraulic brakes, and the RME was distinguished externally by rear wheel spats and the absence of running boards. Fewer of these were produced as their runs were shorter, 3446 RMEs and 1050 RMFs. There were no open versions of these later RM series.

In 1953 the RMF was replaced by the Pathfinder, a slab sided saloon whose body was shared with the Wolseley 6/90, though the engine was the same big four, and the torsion bar ifs was another inheritance from the traditional Riley. Later Pathfinders had overdrive, and automatic transmission was available from 1956. 5152 Pathfinders were made up to 1957.

1938 Riley (i) Sprite sports car.
NATIONAL MOTOR MUSEUM

Subsequent Rileys were summarised by Michael Sedgwick as 'Wolseleys with an extra carburettor hung on', and this is not far short of the truth. The Pathfinder was replaced in 1957 by the 2.6, which not only shared a body with the Wolseley 6/90, but its 2639cc pushrod 6-cylinder engine as well. The Riley's individuality was limited to wider-section front tyres, bucket seats and a rev counter. The RMF was dropped in 1955, and its replacement, which came two years later, was the 1.5, Riley's version of the Wolseley 1500 which was really an extended Morris Minor with the B-series 1489cc engine. Its Morris suspension and steering gave it excellent handling, and with 68bhp and a speed of 84mph (135km/h) the 1.5 had some success in saloon car racing.

The last three Riley models were pure badge engineering; the 4/68 and 4/72 (1959–69) were 4-door saloons with the Farina-styled bodyshells of the Austin Cambridge/Morris Oxford/MG Magnette/Wolseley 15/60, the Elf (1961–69) was a Mini with small extended boot and wood veneer interior, and the Kestrel (1965–69) an Austin/Morris/MG 1100 or 1300 with the usual twin SU carburettors and wood veneer. The 1300s had all-synchromesh boxes as standard, and optional automatic transmission.

The Riley name was killed off by British Leyland in the autumn of 1969.
NG

Further Reading
Riley, the Production and Competition History of the pre–1939 Riley Motor Cars,
A.T. Birmingham, G.T. Foulis, 1965.
As Old as the Industry, David G. Styles, Dalton Watson, 1982.
Riley Sports Cars 1926–1938, Graham Robson, Oxford Illustrated Press, 1986.
The Golden Age of the Riley Motor Car, 1928–1938, Mark Gillies,
Altera (USA), 1998.

RILEY (ii) (RA) 1966–1967

Compania Industrial de Automotores SA, Monte Chingolo, Buenos Aires.
Compania Industrial de Automotores SA, took over the operations of SIAM Di Tella Automotores, in Monte Chingolo. They continued production of basically the same BMC line of motor vehicles. The Riley 1500 was a badge-engineered Morris 55bhp 1.5-litre saloon. There was also a pick-up version of the Riley. 2537 Riley saloons and 1053 pick-ups were made before the Monte Chingolo plant closed for good in April 1967, when production of the Morris 1500 and the MG 1650 also ceased.
ACT

1962 Riley (i) 4/72 saloon.
NICK BALDWIN

1965 Riley (i) Kestrel saloon.
NICK BALDWIN

1999 Rinspeed X-Dream.
RINSPEED

1914 Ritz 10/12hp cyclecar.
NICK BALDWIN

RINGSPED *see* ECO

RINSPEED (CH) 1995 to date

Rinspeed AG, Zumikon ZH.
Frank M. Rinderknecht, owner of a small specialist design company, had tuned and personalised cars for a few years, and launched his first creation, the Rinspeed Roadster, in 1995. The smart little 2-seater was based on the Ford Mustang and was as the model R with the standard V8 engine of 4942cc and 218bhp or model SC-R with supercharger and 305bhp propelling the car weighing 2310lbs (1050kg) to a speed of 165mph (265km/h).

In 1996 Rinspeed exhibited a neo-classic, the Yellow Talbo, at the Geneva Show. It was reminiscent of the prewar Talbot-Lago 150SS with the famous Figoni & Falaschi coupé body. The fibreglass body was made by TLC Carosserie Inc of West Palm Beach, Florida and the supercharged Ford V8 engine, now yielding 320bhp at 4250rpm was again used. One year later Rinspeed had another eye-catcher for the Geneva Show, the Mono-Ego, a truly unlikely single-seater for road use. The Ford Cobra V8 engine of 4601cc with two double-ohc and fitted with a supercharger offering 409bhp was mounted in front of the spaceframe. It looked like a GP racer of the 1950s except that the wider tyres had cycle-type wings. For the 1998 Geneva Show, Rinspeed prepared a more modern single-seater and called it the E-Go Rocket. It again hit the news. The beautiful girl ready for the photographers was helpful, but the car itself was spectacular indeed. The same tuned Ford Cobra engine was used but now placed midships and the composite body, again made in Florida, was much more streamlined. Top speed was indicated to be 160mph (257km/h), with 4.8 seconds for 0–62mph (0–100km/h). Production of the various Rinspeed models was very small and to order only.

At the 1999 Geneva Show, Rinspeed once again presented a most futuristic design. The X-Dream was a multipurpose vehicle with all-wheel drive, and Mercedes-Benz M-type V8 engine of 5.5-litres and 347bhp. The car had an integrated small hovercraft for travel on water, swamps, sand or snow.

FH

RIP (F) 1908–1912

SA des Voitures Automobiles Rip, Rive-de-Gier, Loire.
These cars were made with 5hp single-cylinder or 2120cc 10/12hp monobloc 4-cylinder engines. They had Renault-style dashboard radiators, but their most unusual feature was the suspension by transverse horizontal coil springs at front and rear.

NG

RIPERT (F) 1899–1902

Automobiles Ripert, Marseilles.
Two models of Ripert were offered, a 6hp and a 12hp, both with front-mounted 2-cylinder horizontal engines, 4-speed gearboxes and belt drive. They were made in a very small workshop in Marseilles.

NG

RIPPER (US) 1903

Ripper Motor Carriage Co., Buffalo, New York.
This was a light 2-seater runabout powered by a 5hp single-cylinder engine, with single-chain drive. Production must have been minimal as six months after the car was announced the man behind it, Victor E. Ripper, disappeared owing large sums, not only to his company but also to other businesses and two local banks.

NG

RISING HOUSE (US) c.1994 to date

Rising House Motors, Cambridge, Kansas.
The Rising House Replica Birdcage was a copy of the magnificent Maserati Birdcage but, incredibly, it was mounted on a tube frame with Volkswagen running gear. The body moulds were pulled off a real Maserati and they were sold in turn-key form for $20,000.

HP

RITTER (i) (US) 1912

Ritter Automobile Co., Madison, Wisconsin.
C.H. Ritter bought the assets of the DEMOT for which he had been agent and tried to build a 15hp 4-cylinder car made only in 2-seater roadster form. It had a very short life.

NG

RITTER (ii) (B) 1972–1973

Although this company specialised in beach buggies, it also presented the Slooghy sports coupé in 1972. Designed by Henri Rimbaud, it used a VW Beetle chassis with a 1.6-litre or specially-prepared 100bhp 1.7-litre engine. Production was scheduled for spring 1973 but it is believed that it never began.

CR

RITZ (US) 1914–1915

Ritz Cyclecar Co., New York, New York.
Despite the company name this was really a light car, with 10/12hp 2-cylinder engine (15hp 4-cylinder for 1915) and shaft drive. The cars were built for the Ritz Cyclecar Co. by the Drigg-Seabury Co. of Sharon, Pennsylvania, who also made the DRIGGS and VULCAN (ii) cars. The two companies fell out over deliveries and payments, and by the time the case was settled in November 1916 the fashion for such light cars had passed. Nevertheless, 205 Ritzes were made, of which some were exported to England.

NG

RIVAT ET BOUCHARD (F) c.1900

Rivat et Bouchard, Lyons.
This company made a small number of motorcycles, and at least one voiturettte, but proper production never started.

NG

RIVIERA (US) 1907

Lebanon Motor Works, Lebanon, Pennsylvania.
Designed by Milton H. Schnader, the Riviera was a touring car powered by a 20hp 2-cylinder engine with epicyclic gearbox and shaft drive, selling for $1850. Schnader was also involved with the UPTON (ii), made in the same factory.

NG

RJD *see* LE MARQUIS

R.L.C. (GB) 1920–1921
Argyll (London) Motor & Engineering Co. Ltd, Hornsey, London.
This was an unconventional light car powered by a 1230cc 10.8hp 3-cylinder radial engine, with 3-speed gearbox and shaft drive. It was the work of J.M. Rubury of 4-wheel brake fame and A.H. Lindsay, manager of Argyll's London service depot, where the R.L.C. was built. The 2-seater shown at the 1920 Olympia Show and priced at £315 was probably the only R.L.C. made. It is possible that the whole project was sold to France, to reappear as the LAFITTE in 1923, though that car had a considerably smaller engine.
NG

R. LÉONARD (F) 1994
The Marysa was a conventional microcar manufactured in small scale in two versions, one with a Lombardini 325cc single-cylinder engine, the other with a 505cc Perkins twin.
CR

R.M.B. *see* GENTRY

R.M.C. (i) *see* REGAL (ii)

R.M.C. (ii) (AUS) 1986–1996
Replica Motor Co., Kellerberrin, Western Australia.
This Cobra replica by Mike Moylan, operating in a town 125 miles from Perth, was given the model name Snake. Built on a space frame, it used Jaguar-pattern front and rear suspension and installed a 5-litre Ford Windsor V8 engine coupled to a 5-speed gearbox. In 1990 fuel injection was adopted for unleaded fuel use. While being emphatic about size and style conforming to the original, performance and handling improvements were readily adopted. In 1991 Ford GT40 and Jaguar D-type replicas were also offered but the firm was reorganised in 1995 and was up for sale in 1996.
MG

R.M. CLASSICS (RSA) c.1989–1990
R.M. Classics made copies of the Lamborghini Countach and the Westfield S.E. As soon as the R.M. Seven was imported into Britain in 1990, Caterham Cars instigated legal action for use of the name 'Seven' and Westfield claimed infringement of copyright over the chassis (Westfield had been successfully proceeded against by Caterham in 1987 for exactly the same reason). The importer, Tiger Cars, which had been assured that there would be no problems, lost heavily on the deal, but responded by building the Six, which was a completely new design.
ML

R.N.W. (GB) 1951–1954
R.N. Wellington & Co., Farnham, Surrey.
Advertised as Britain's cheapest car, costing only £285, the R.N.W. microcar offered rather more than the very basic 3-wheelers with which it competed. In looks it resembled a scaled-down proper car and had four wheels. Open aluminium and steel bodywork hid ifs, Duplex coil spring rear suspension and brakes on the rear wheels only. The engine was an 8bhp 197cc Villiers unit, giving a top speed of 45mph (72km/h).
CR

ROA (E) 1958
Industrias Motorizadas Onieva SA, Madrid.
This well-known motorcycle and sidecar manufacturer presented in 1958 a minicar which had a body resembling that of an Isetta and which was fitted with a single wheel at the rear and a Hispano-Villiers single-cylinder 197cc engine.
VCM

ROADCRAFT *see* SOUTHERN ROADCRAFT

ROADER (US) 1911–1912
Roader Car Co., Brockton, Massachusetts.

1920 R.L.C. 10.8hp 2-seater.
NATIONAL MOTOR MUSEUM

1920 Roamer (i) 6-54 tourer.
NICK BALDWIN

The Roader was offered initially in roadster form only, powered by a 20 or 30hp 4-cylinder engine. It bore some resemblance to a small MERCER Type 35. The 30hp was dropped for 1912, when a 2-seater foredoor runabout was made in addition to the starker roadster. Roader was a term for a high-spirited horse, but this one did not kick up its heels for long.
NG

ROADSTER CAR (F) 1985–c.1992
Roadster Car, Le Havre.
This was a conventional Porsche 356 Speedster replica sold complete and in kit form. It was subsequently made by P.G.O.
CR

ROAD & TRACK LeMANS COUPÉ (US) 1957–1960
Road & Track, Playa Del Ray, California.
Although R&T is one of the foremost American sports car magazines, they were also instrumental in the production of a short run of sports cars in the late 1950s. Editor John R. Bond published a series of articles on building an American car to run at Le Mans. It was called the Road & Track LeMans Coupé, and was styled by Strother McMinn. Several readers built cars to the R&T design, although they used other chassis than the one recommended. A mould was made and it appears that at least three, maybe more, fibreglass bodies were built. They were handsome coupés with pointed noses and tails.
HP

ROAMER (i) (US) 1916–1929
1916–1917 Barley Manufacturing Co., Streator, Illinois.
1917–1929 Roamer Motor Car Co., Kalamazoo, Michigan.
The Roamer was the result of a collaboration between Cloyd Y. Kenworthy, New York City distributor of the Rauch & Lang electric car and Albert C. Barley, manufacturer of the Halladay at Streator, Illinois, an assembled car with a radiator closely resembling that of the Rolls-Royce. The car was designed by Karl H. Martin, a New York City custom car body builder (and subsequently the designer of both the Deering-Magnetic and Kenworthy cars and later manufacturer of his own Wasp automobile). The Roamer was available either with a 6-cylinder Rutenber engine or a more powerful and more expensive line

1926 Robert Serf 1100 sports car.
NATIONAL MOTOR MUSEUM

fitted with the Rochester-Duesenberg four. In 1917, Barley left the Halladay company and moved to Kalamazoo, Michigan where he organised the Barley Motor Car Co. for Roamer production.

By 1920, the Roamer had attracted a clientele of its own and producing some 1600 cars priced between $2750 and $4500, that year changing its 6-cylinder engine to a Continental 9N L-head type. The Rochester-Duesenberg four would continue to power the more expensive Roamer series until 1926, the lower-priced 6-cylinder line using Continental engine types 9N, 12XD and 7U into 1926 when an 8-cylinder series with power by Lycoming would be added. The 6-cylinder Roamer would be discontinued later in 1926, production being restricted to Lycoming eights until the end of production in 1929.

In 1922, Albert Barley introduced a cheaper 6-cylinder car named after himself and with the Roamer, production peaked in 1923 with approximately 1900 units of both Roamer and Barley cars completed. Production dropped in 1924 and the Barley was continued as the Pennant taxi for one more year.

From 1926 the plant turned exclusively to Roamer production but from that point on, sales figures continued to drop, reaching a single figure in 1929, Roamer going out of business that year.

Total Roamer production is estimated as 11,850 cars built during its 14 years of activity.

KM

ROAMER (ii) (GB) 1992–c.1996
G.B. Restorations, Hawkesley Mill, Birmingham.
This Mini Moke-style utility car was one of dozens of kit-form cars of this sort built in Britain. The chassis was in square section steel tubing and the minimal bodywork was in mild steel. All the mechanicals derived from the Austin Metro, including its Hydragas suspension.
CR

RO-AN (A) 1921–1922
Rumpler & Ringer, Vienna.
The car was designed by Anton Rumpler, no relation to the German Edmund Rumpler, and had a 1-litre 10hp 2-cylinder engine.
HON

ROARING TWENTIES (US) c.1979–1997
Roaring Twenties Motor Car Co., El Cajon, California.
This kit car company was started by Mark Beals, who wanted to build a neoclassic car for himself. He named it the Corsair, and it proved so popular he put it into production. They were built on full-size Ford chassis with Ford V8 engines. The body was steel with the long, flowing fibreglass mudguards typical of neoclassic designs. Like many others, it used MG Midget doors and windscreen. The Peerless was another neoclassic design, this one based on 1930s Cadillac styling with late-model Cadillac running gear and chassis. The rear body section was Volkswagen Beetle instead of MG, attached to a long bonnet and the usual running boards. The Stiletto was a Ferrari 308 replica on a Chevrolet Camaro chassis and body. Front and rear fibreglass sections attached for an easy installation. In 1991 the Python was announced. It was to be a high-tech sports car with a stainless-steel honeycombed chassis and carbon-fibre bodywork. It was supposedly powered by a 10,185cc all-aluminium V8.
HP

ROBBINS (US) c.1987
Jim Robbins Co., Brownsburg, Indiana.
Robbins sold a kit for building a replica of the 1935 Miller-Ford 2-man racing car that ran at Indianapolis.
HP

ROBE (i) (US) 1914–1915
W.B. Robe & Co., Portsmouth, Ohio.
Having built three prototypes in three years, W.B. Robe put his cyclecar on the market late in 1914 as a 1915 model. It had a 1160cc 4-cylinder engine with 2-speed gearbox and shaft drive. The 48in (1218mm) tread put it in the cyclecar class, though a standard 56in (1421mm) track was available. A standard roadster cost $325, and a 4-door torpedo roadster $375.
NG

ROBE (ii) (US) 1923
Robe Motor Corp., Nansemond, Virginia.
This was W.B. Robe's second attempt at car building, financed by real-estate magnate J.D. Stone. Although announced as a six, the only Robe cars completed had 4-cylinder engines. The most unusual feature of the car was the suspension, by a pair of interlinked leaf springs running the length of the frame from front to rear axles. Some Model T Ford components were included in the prototype, such as the rear axle and the valves, though the engine itself was not a Ford. The cylinder blocks were said to be made of 'Robe metal' which was really aluminium. Only four Robes were made in all.
NG

ROBERTS (i) (US) 1915
Roberts Motor Co., Sandusky, Ohio.
Founded in Clyde, Ohio, in 1905, this company moved to Sandusky three years later. Their business was engine building, including units from three to 60hp, for marine and motor use, while they also made some early examples of aero-engines. For one season only they advertised a car powered by their 60hp pair-cast 6-cylinder engine.
NG

ROBERTS (ii) (CDN) 1921
Canadian Automobile Corp., Lachine, Quebec.
This company seems to have been an outgrowth of the Roberts Motor Works who were listed as suppliers and repairers of cars from 1913. They announced the Roberts Six and the Mercury Six, the former in tourer, sedan or coupé models selling for the high prices of CDN$4500–5800. Probably no more than a prototype was made, and the Mercury Six may never have been built at all.
NG

ROBERT SERF (F) 1925–1934
Automobiles Robert Serf, Colombey-les-Belles, Meurthe-et-Moselle.
The little-known Robert Serf cars were made in a small factory by Georges Didier who also sold Ford cars and Fordson tractors. The first model, which made up the bulk of production, had a 1470cc 4-cylinder side-valve engine manufactured in-house, made as a tourer, saloon or commercial travellers' car. This was of saloon shape but with an opening rear door. Two or three sports models were made as well. The bodies were built locally, though not in Didier's factory. Most sales were in the local region, and the cars were never seen at the Paris Salon, nor did they feature in most lists. In 1932 they were replaced by a smaller car, the 4CV with 600cc 2-cylinder 2-stroke engine, made only as a 2-seater. Total production of Robert Serf cars was about 80, of which only ten were of the 4CV. In 1935 Didier built a prototype front-wheel drive version of the 4CV, but it never went on sale. He carried on with garage work in new premises at Nancy-Vendeuvre, and died in 1942. The designer Robert Serf was still running a garage in the 1970s, when nearly 80 years old.
NG

Further Reading
'Les Automobiles Robert Serf', Serge Pozzoli,
l'Album du Fanatique, December 1976.

ROBERTS MOTOR COMPANY (US) c.1988

Roberts Motor Co., Kingsport, Tennessee.

This Ferrari Daytona replica was very similar to the ones built by Tom MCBURNIE for the *Miami Vice* television series. The Roberts Miami Spyder was also based on a Corvette chassis.

HP

ROBERTSON (GB) 1914–1916

James Robertson, Sale, Manchester.

The Robertson cyclecar was a 3-wheeler with single front wheel, not unlike the postwar L.A.D. in appearance. It was powered by an 8hp V-twin JAP or Precision engine, with 2-speed transmission by chains and chain final drive. Made also in delivery van form, the Robertson was said to be 'very steady on the road, and practically a non-skidder'.

NG

ROBIE (US) 1914

Robie Motor Car Co., Chicago, Illinois.

Fred Robie built no cars himself but commissioned two designs from other manufacturers. The first was a cyclecar with air-cooled 2-cylinder engine and staggered side by side seating. It was made for him by Massnick-Phipps of Detroit who were better-known as engine builders. It differed from the usual run of cyclecars in having more sweeping lines and disc wheels. Robie was apparently not pleased with this car, and planned to have another built by PULLMAN in York, Pennsylvania. This had a 4-cylinder Perkins engine and the same appearance as the previous model. Robie's money ran out before production could start.

NG

ROBIN HOOD (GB) 1984 to date

1984–1995 Robin Hood Engineering, Sherwood, Nottinghamshire.
1995 to date Robin Hood Engineering, Mansfield Woodhouse, Nottinghamshire.

One of the kit car industry's most successful names began with an intriguing Ferrari Daytona replica. Pundits had always said the Rover SD1 aped its styling from the Daytona, and Robin Hood proved it by converting SD1 saloons into Ferrari replicas by shortening the wheelbase and modifying the bodywork. Then a steel chassis and replica fibreglass body based around Jaguar V12 parts was offered before a bizarre version based on a stretched Triumph TR7. In 1989 the company took a very different direction with the S7, a very cheap and extremely popular Lotus 7 style kit. Early ones used TR7 or Dolomite mechanicals in a space frame steel chassis, though more popular was the Ford Cortina Mk IV option. A notable feature of all Robin Hoods was their polished stainless steel bodies. The 1993 S8 was Rover V8 powered. A folded steel monocoque body/chassis and Ford Sierra basis came later. Even cheaper kits followed: the abortive Go never reached production but the KAIG did under its own brand name.

CR

ROBINET (F) 1906–1907

F. Robinet et Cie, Nantes, Loire Inférieure.

The Robinet was a curious machine, an ancestor of the cyclecar made several years before the breed became common. It had a narrow wooden frame which seated two passengers in tandem with the driver at the rear. Between him and his passenger lay a 10hp V-twin Deckert engine driving through a 2-speed Bozier gearbox with final drive by chain.

NG

ROBINSON (i); POPE-ROBINSON (US) 1900–1904

1900–1901 John T. Robinson & Co., Hyde Park, Massachusetts.
1901–1902 Robinson Motor Vehicle Co., Hyde Park, Massachusetts.
1902–1904 Pope-Robinson Co., Hyde Park, Massachusetts.

John Tilden Robinson ran a successful company making paper and cardboard box machinery, which he had founded in 1880. From late 1898 to 1900 he made 3-wheeled cars in partnership with W.C. Bramwell, (see BRAMWELL-ROBINSON) but when he set up on his own he made 4-wheelers. These had 2464cc 2-cylinder engines under the seat, with double-chain drive. With the formation of the Robinson Motor Vehicle Co. in 1901 a more up-to-date car was built with 4928cc 4-cylinder engine at the front under a bonnet. One

1997 Robin Hood S7 sports car.
ROBIN HOOD ENGINEERING

1904 Robinson (i) 24hp tonneau.
NATIONAL MOTOR MUSEUM

reporter described it as a copy of the NAPIER. The 2-cylinder car continued, but it seems that practically all the company's efforts were devoted to the larger car.

In April 1902 two members of Albert Pope's family, his nephew Edward and son Harold, purchased a substantial interest in the Robinson Motor Vehicle Co., and the 1903 models were known as Pope-Robinsons. They were similar to the earlier 4-cylinder cars, though more expensive. At $6000, the 5-seater tonneau was the most expensive car in the Pope empire. 1904 was the last season for the Pope-Robinson. John T. died of a stroke in November, and this was given as the reason for the car's discontinuance, but if the Popes had wanted to they could have put more money into the company to keep production going. John T's son carried on with the box machinery company and the Pope-Robinson name was bought by Buick as a way of acquiring a Selden patent licence and membership of the A.L.A.M. (Association of Licenced Automobile Manufacturers). Robinson and Pope-Robinson production has been calculated at 59 cars.

NG

Further Reading
'Robinson Meets the Pope', Edward R. Peterson, *Automobile Quarterly*, Vol. 33, No. 1.

ROBINSON (ii) (GB) 1907

Charles Robinson, Kettering, Northamptonshire.

The Robinson had a 12hp 4-cylinder engine of Charles Robinson's own design, and was remarkable for its cooling system, which employed exhaust gases. The exhaust entered the 'radiator' at the bottom, and was cooled by a fan as it progressed to the header tank at the top. Here it was mixed with cool air which was drawn into the tank by a circular orifice, and passed to the finned cylinder heads by a sheet-iron cowl. While it must have reduced the cooling effect of the fresh air, the exhaust accelerated the flow of air to the cylinders. It must have been the only engine in which the radiator also acted as a silencer! Otherwise

1907 Robinson (ii) 12hp 2-seater.
NICK GEORGANO

1922 Rob Roy 8hp 2-seater.
NATIONAL MOTOR MUSEUM

the Robinson was quite conventional, with shaft drive and a 2-seater body. Only three were made, of which one survives.

NG

ROBINSON & HOLE (GB) 1906–1907

Robinson & Hole Ltd, Thames Ditton, Surrey.
This was a conventional car powered by a 16/20hp 4-cylinder T-head engine with shaft drive. Body styles were 2- and 5-seaters, but only six cars were made altogether. A planned 24/30hp car was never completed. They were designed by Angus Maitland who made the BEACON cyclecar a few years later.

NG

ROBINSON & PRICE (GB) 1905–1906; 1913

Robinson & Price Ltd, Liverpool.
This company was mainly involved in general engineering and repair work, but they made two ventures into car manufacture. In 1905 they announced two shaft-driven models with Fafnir engines, a 6½hp single-cylinder and a 10/12hp twin. Production was minimal and they concentrated on their regular business until 1913 when they were tempted by the cyclecar boom. Their contribution had a single-cylinder 6/8hp Coventry-Simplex engine, belt drive to a countershaft and thence by chain to the rear axle. It had a curious radiator in which the tubes made an inverted vee, meeting at the header tank. Designed by a Mr Lamb, who was said to have had several years experience with light cars, it was known as the R & P, a name sometimes applied to the earlier cars.

NG

ROBNELL (AUS) 1988 to date

Robnell Sports Cars Pty Ltd, Bayswater, Victoria.
A fibreglass Cobra replica by Rob Darnell, the Robnell was built on a space frame with coil and wishbone suspension front and rear while Ford V8 engines

were installed. The 302 had 4952cc, 281bhp and weighed 2548lb (1158kg) while the 429 had 7035cc, 398bhp and weighed (2750lb) 1250kg. Kevlar superseded fibreglass as material for the body, a 5-speed gearbox became standard and Halibrand-pattern wheels were fitted to complete cars.

MG

ROB ROY (GB) 1922–1926

Kennedy Motor Co. Ltd, Glasgow.
Named after Sir Walter Scott's outlaw hero, Rob Roy MacGregor, this light car was made by a company which made the Koh-I-Noor flat-twin engine, also used in the BOWSER and KINGSBURY JUNIOR cars. Naturally the Rob Roy also used this 1012cc unit in the cars seen for the first time at the 1922 Glasgow Show. By the time of the 1923 Show there was a 4-cylinder model as well, powered by a 1491cc 12/24hp Dorman 4MV side-valve unit, and in 1924 there was another 4-cylinder engine, a 1248cc 10/12hp Coventry Climax. All three models were listed in 1924, with bodywork made in-house. These included a 4-door saloon on the 12/24 chassis. The company went into liquidation in 1925, and it is probable that no more cars were made after 1924, although some may been assembled by the liquidator in 1925.

NG

Further Reading
'Cross Border Cousins', M. Worthington-Williams,
The Automobile, September 1999.

ROBSON (US) 1909

E.P. Robson Manufacturing Co., Galesburg, Illinois.
This was a revival of the GALE which had been made by the Western Tool Works of Galesburg from 1907 to 1909. The company was re-organised by Percy Robson under his own name, and three former Gales models were listed, an 8/10hp single-cylinder, 30/32hp 2-cylinder and 40/45hp 4-cylinder. The latter had been in the experimental stages when Gale closed down. However, the Robson was short-lived; no catalogues were issued, and the few that were made were assembled from Gale parts that were on hand. The company later specialised in spring starters and emery grinders.

NG

ROC *see* WALL

ROCA (GB) 1988–1990

ROCA Engineering, Cowes, Isle of Wight.
Based on an American design, the ROCA Alpha was a fibreglass-bodied Porsche 911 replica using Ford Sierra or Granada mechanicals, which the company said was suitable for front, mid or rear engines. Its purpose-designed suspension was fitted in an integral chassis.

CR

ROCABOY KIRCHNER (F) 1972–1980s

Les Ateliers de l'Automobile Réunis, Paris.
This operation displayed its first prototype at the 1972 Foire de Paris but did not actually enter series production until 1980. The 1972 Morvan prototype was a plastic-bodied pickup based on a Citroën Dyane chassis. The company then concentrated on electric vehicles. Its range of forward control electric vehicles included pickups, vans and leisure vehicles. Six 12-volt batteries powered the 6kW electric motor, fixed in the front of a tubular chassis. The bodywork was plastic.

CR

ROCHDALE (GB) 1952–1968

Rochdale Motor Panels & Engineering Co., Rochdale, Yorkshire.
Rochdale was founded in 1948 and its first road car project was a very basic fibreglass shell in 1952 – probably Britain's first. During the 1950s, several models were offered: the Type C, Type F, MkVI and ST. Its most successful model was the GT coupé (or Riviera in open form), intended for Ford E93A chassis. By far the most significant Rochdale was the Olympic of 1959. Only the world's second all-fibreglass monocoque (after the Lotus Elite), it was a smart and well-engineered coupé that one major magazine called a 'British Porsche'. Early examples used Riley 1.5 or Ford side-valve engines, while the 1962 Phase II

1966 Rochdale Olympic coupé.
NICK GEORGANO/NATIONAL MOTOR MUSEUM

had a hatchback, a choice of Ford Anglia, Cortina GT or MGA engines, disc front brakes and Triumph Spitfire front suspension. Kits were made until 1968, although bodyshells were available to special order until around 1977.

CR

ROCHE (US) 1924
Clifton R. Roche, Los Angeles, California.
Clifton Roche designed an advanced car with a 2-stroke V8 engine and front-wheel drive. He built a prototype with a tourer body, but did not succeed in finding any backing, and did not even form a company.

NG

ROCHÉ (GB) 1986
Sports Cars & Specials, Blackburn, Lancashire.
The M1 Roché was a replica of the Le Mans specification BMW M1, using a triangulated steel chassis designed for Renault V6 or Audi power. The fibreglass bodyshell cost £1675.

CR

ROCHE-BRAULT (F) 1898–1899
Sté Française d'Automobile Roch-Brault & Cie, Paris.
Maurice Roch-Brault made a few examples of an 8hp 2-cylinder car in collaboration with Gabriel MALLIARY who also built a car under his own name at Puteaux in 1901. The Roche-Brault design was also made in Belgium by VINCKE under the name Vincke-Roch-Brault.

NG

ROCHESTER (i) (US) 1901
Rochester Cycle & Manufacturing Co., Rochester, New York.
This company made a light steam car which was typical of its kind, with vertical 2-cylinder engine under the seat and single-chain drive to the rear axle. Steering was by tiller (replaced by a handle later in the season), and suspension by full-elliptic springs, a single transverse one at the front and two at the rear. Two body styles were offered, a 2-seater runabout at $750 and a 4-seater surrey at $1000.

NG

1903 Rochet 6hp 2-seater.
NATIONAL MOTOR MUSEUM

ROCHESTER (ii) (US) 1901–1902
Rochester Gasoline Carriage & Motor Co., Rochester, New York.
Operating at the same time as the above, this company also made a steamer, despite its name, as well as a petrol car. They were both simple, light machines and looked not unlike the Rochester Cycle company's car, though there was apparently no connection. The steamer had a 2-cylinder engine and was priced at $600 for a 2-seater. Details of the petrol car are not known. Rochester built some vehicles for a taxi service between Buffalo and Niagara Falls, but whether these were petrol or steam-powered is likewise unknown.

NG

ROCHET; ROCHET-PETIT (F) 1899–c.1905
Sté Rochet, Paris.
This cycle-making company purchased the rights to the cars designed by Édouard ROSSEL of Lille. The engines were 'of Daimler type', ie: vertical twins of 6/8hp, front-mounted and driving through 4-speed gearboxes and chain drive. A 12hp

c.1899 Rochet Frères *vis-à-vis.*
NICK GEORGANO

1895 Rochet-Schneider *vis-à-vis.*
NATIONAL MOTOR MUSEUM

1907 Rochet-Schneider 40hp coupé.
NATIONAL MOTOR MUSEUM

model was added in 1900. Their appearance was not Daimler-like; they had wrap-around radiators which made them look more like Wolseleys. Several body styles were available, including a 2-seater, 4-seater rear-entrance tonneau and enclosed limousine.

In 1902 there was a smaller model powered by a 4½hp single-cylinder Aster engine. In 1904 Danneels of Ghent acquired the licence to make Rochets for sale in Belgium, Holland and Great Britain.

NG

ROCHET FRÈRES (F) 1898–1901
Rochet Frères et Cie, Lyons.
This company had no known connection with the Parisian Rochet, or with the Rochet-Schneider also made in Lyons. They made light cars of De Dion-Bouton appearance, with De Dion engines, *vis-à-vis* 3-4-seater bodies, 3 speeds and belt final drive.

NG

ROCHET-SCHNEIDER (F) 1894–1932
SA des Éts Rochet-Schneider, Lyons.
One of France's better-known quality cars, the Rochet-Schneider was made by a company formed by Édouard Rochet who made bicycles with his father, and Théophile Schneider who was distantly related to the armaments family. Their first cars were modelled on the BENZ, with horizontal single-cylinder engines and belt drive. About 240 of these were made until 1901 when a new factory was erected and new models introduced. Again following a popular design, the new Rochet-Schneiders were on PANHARD lines, with front-mounted vertical 2- and 4-cylinder engines of 8 and 12hp, and chain final drive. These were only interim designs, for in 1903 the partners went for the latest fashion and introduced a range patterned closely on the MERCEDES. They had pair-cast 4-cylinder engines, 4-speed gearboxes and double-chain drive. The main difference between them and the German cars was that they used armoured wood frames until the 1904 season. Models included a 16hp, 20/22hp, 40hp and 55hp; the latter of 6113cc. Production reached 152 cars in 1903. Rochet-Schneider sold a number of licences to foreign firms, including to MARTINI in 1902, F.N. and MOYEA in 1904 and FLORENTIA in 1905. From 1904 to 1907 Rochet-Schneider was in British ownership, but this company was in liquidation in November 1907, and the firm was rescued by the Marseilles financiers Demetrius and Georges Zafiropulo. A subsidiary made Zenith carburettors which provided more than half the company's profits in some years.

A 4.4-litre 18hp with shaft drive joined the larger chain drive cars in 1906, and in 1907 the largest model was a 10.9-litre chain-driven six. More modern L-head fours appeared on the smaller models in 1908, and this layout spread up the range, being found on the 4846cc 25hp four and 5526cc 30/35hp six by 1911. The 1914 range covered six models, all with monobloc L-head engines, from a 2612cc 15hp four to a 7234cc 50hp four, as well as the 5526cc six, now called the 28hp. Production rose from less than 250 per year in 1906/07 to around 500 per year in 1910 and 600 in 1913. An important commercial vehicle department was opened in 1906, which was outlive the cars by nearly 20 years.

The first postwar models, of 12, 18 and 30hp, were essentially of prewar design, but ohvs arrived in 1923 on the 2612cc 12CV and 3969cc 20CV. In the late 1920s only two 6-cylinder models were made, the 3754cc 20CV and 4560cc 26CV. The latter had a 4-speed gearbox in unit with the engine, dual ignition and servo brakes, though wooden wheels were an old-fashioned feature. The smaller six often had wire wheels. The Depression hit Rochet-Schneider hard, and after rejecting plans to merge with another Lyons firm, COTTIN-DESGOUTTES, they decided to concentrate on commercial vehicles. They were successful with these up to 1951 when they were bought by BERLIET who discontinued the name. As happens sometimes, the company survived on paper, even after the merger between Berliet and Renault, and Rochet-Schneider was not formally dissolved until 3 June 1998.

NG

RÖCK (H) 1905–1914
István Röck Machine Works, Budapest.
The Röck factory never designed a car but was a car-maker nonetheless. They helped János CSONKA, pioneer Hungarian car-builder by making the necessary components (chassis, transmission, engine) for his first car, and partly assembling it. Between 1906 and 1908 the chassis of the Csonka designed passenger cars were also made at Röck. Up to 1912 the Csonka-Röck co-operation remained intact but in that year Csonka was forced to stop all automotive operations. The Röck company looked for another car to make, and they acquired the rights to

1930 Rochet-Schneider 26CV coupé.
NATIONAL MOTOR MUSEUM

make HANSA-LLOYD cars in Hungary. But World War I intervened, and only a few prototypes left the factory gates.

PN

ROCKAWAY (i) (US) 1902–1903

Mohler & Degress, Rockaway, New York.

This Rockaway was a light runabout with 5hp and 8hp single or 16hp 2-cylinder engine and shaft drive. Alexander Mohler and W.A. Degress had made a car in Mexico in 1896, almost certainly the first car built in that country. Mohler had made a car under his own name at Astoria, New York, in 1901.

NG

ROCKAWAY (ii) (US) 1903–1904

Rockaway Automobile Co., Rockaway, New Jersey.

No connection with Rockaway (i), this car took its name from a different town. It was a light 2-seater with single-cylinder engine and chain drive. It was sometimes called the Rambler or Rockaway Rambler, presumably to distinguish it from the Rockaway from New York, but these were unofficial names.

NG

ROCKEFELLER (US) c.1953

Rockefeller Sports Car Corp., Long Island, New York.

The Rockefeller Yankee was a fibreglass-bodied sports car with a modified 1948 Ford frame. Suspension was also Ford, and designer Warren Shiber recommended 100hp Ford V8 engines. However, any engine could be ordered. Price in 1953 was $2495 and the colour was impregnated into the gellcoat. Weight was about 2000lbs and the wide cockpit could accommodate up to five people. Upholstery was ribbed Naugahyde trimmed in brightly coloured plastic. Stewart-Warner instruments were used, and a dashboard plaque guaranteed the Yankee would do 100mph (161km/h).

HP

ROCKET (i) *see* SCRIPPS-BOOTH

ROCKET (ii) (US) 1948

Hewson Pacific Corp., Los Angeles, California.

The Rocket was a 3-wheeled car with an attractive aluminium body. The base 4-cylinder engine had 65hp, but an optional six produced 95hp. However, the

c.1912 Rochet-Schneider all-weather saloon by Audineau.
NICK BALDWIN

c.1923 Rochet-Schneider 12CV saloon.
FONDATION MARIUS BERLIET

prototype, which was the only Rocket made, used a Ford V8. An automatic transmission was standard and the front two wheels were partially skirted.

HP

Further Reading
'Hewson's Rotund Rocket', Richard Kelley, *Special Interest Autos*, May–June 1992.

1932 Rockne Six sedan.
NATIONAL MOTOR MUSEUM

ROCKET (iii) *see* LIGHT CAR CO.

ROCK FALLS (US) 1919–1925
Rock Falls Manufacturing Co., Sterling, Illinois.
Rock Falls was a well known manufacturer of funeral cars, and occasionally of ambulances, as far back as 1909. In 1919, the company decided to augment this speciality with a line of large, 8-seater limousines and formal sedans which were targeted for use in funeral processions. These cars had wheelbases of 132 (3350mm) and 136in (3452mm) and were fitted with Continental 6-cylinder L-head engines, the 9A and, after 1923, the 6T. As many as 50 of these large cars were produced annually. In addition to them, a handful of open roadsters and phaetons were also produced on special order only.
KM

ROCK HILL (US) 1910
Rock Hill Buggy Co., Rock Hill, South Carolina.
This was the first automotive venture of Gary Anderson, who later made the ANDERSON (ii), also in Rock Hill. He ran a successful buggy manufacturing business, and when he decided to enter the automobile field he bought a number of 35hp NORWALKs and fitted them with the Rock Hill badge. This practice was encouraged by Norwalk's president Arthur Skadden, who advertised 'We make most of the car and you finish it, then badge and sell it under whatever name suits you'. In fact, Anderson only bought 25 Norwalks, then returned to buggy making exclusively, until he tried again with the more successful Anderson.
NG

ROCKNE (US) 1932–1933
Rockne Motors Corp., Detroit, Michigan.
The Rockne was a small companion car to the Studebaker and named after the famed Knute Rockne, football coach at Notre Dame University in South Bend, Indiana and who, in addition to his athletic activities, had been named sales manager of the Studebaker Corp. which was also located in South Bend. The companion car had already been planned when Rockne was killed in a 1931 plane crash and the new car had been named accordingly. The Rockne, in a sense, was the companion car successor to the earlier Erskine which had become a lower-priced Studebaker in 1930. It had a 3.1-litre 6-cylinder engine and a full line of open and closed bodies priced from $585 to $675. Introduced in February 1932, it was discontinued 14 months later after a production of 30,293 units.
KM

ROCKWELL (US) 1909–1912
Bristol Engineering Co., Bristol, Connecticut.
The Rockwell was primarily built and marketed as a taxicab by the New Departure Manufacturing Co., prominent in the manufacture of brakes for bicycles. It also manufactured both the Allen-Kingston and Houpt-Rockwell cars in 1910. The Rockwell landaulet taxicab was a successful venture. The $3000 car had a 4-cylinder engine and 106in (2690mm) wheelbase and more than 200 of them operated in New York City during 1911. The Rockwell was also available to the public as a passenger car with a modicum of change from its taxicab form.
KM

ROCOURT-MERLIN (F) 1900
Éts Rocourt et Merlin fils, Marseilles.
A few light cars powered by Abeille engines were made under this name, but the company's main activity lay in coachbuilding.
NG

RODEFELD (US) 1909–1917
A.H. Rodefeld, Richmond, Indiana.
Rodefeld and his sons were blacksmiths who made about 25 cars and trucks powered by 4-cylinder air-cooled engines of their own construction. At least one had a transverse engine, but most were longitudinally placed. Final drive was by chains. All Rodefeld's vehicles were made to customer's order, and were sold locally. After 1917 the family made water pumps for Model T Fords.
NG

RODGERS (i) *see* IMPERIAL (ii)

RODGERS (ii) **(US)** 1921
Scientific Automotive Corp., New York, New York.
This was announced as a 36hp 4-cylinder tourer priced at $1295. The factory location is unknown, and the car was probably intended for export.
NG

RODLEY (GB) 1954–1956
Rodley Automobile Co. Ltd, Leeds, Yorkshire.
The Rodley 750 microcar quickly acquired a reputation as one of the worst cars available in its day. Its very boxy coupé bodywork was particularly ugly and, despite being advertised as a 4-seater, the rear seats were very cramped. The J.A.P. 750cc V-twin engine sat in the tail of the car, where cooling proved ineffectual and overheating and even fires were commonplace. Drive was by chain to the rear wheels and a top speed of 60mph (97km/h) was claimed. Production targets called for a manufacturing rate of 50 cars each week but in fact only 65 cars were ever built.
CR

ROEBLING-PLANCHE (US) 1909
Walter Automobile Co., Trenton, New Jersey.
This car was designed by French-born Etienne Planche who joined the WALTER (i) company when they were still in New York City. The wealthy Washington A. Roebling of the wire rope family who had built the Brooklyn Bridge commissioned Planche to design a monster racing car developing 140bhp, to be built by Walter. He planned to make ten, to sell for $12,000 each, but only one was completed. Early in 1909 William Walter left his company, and the 50hp Walter Model M was renamed a Roebling-Planche. Prices ran from $4500 to $5175, and there was also a smaller 20hp car selling for $3500. Although there were plans for a Roebling-Planche company to be set up, it was never incorporated. Instead, the Walter Automobile Co. was renamed Mercer Automobile Co. They made the MERCER car which became much more famous than either the Walter or Roebling-Planche ever were.
NG

ROGER (i) **(F)** 1888–1896
Émile Roger, Paris.
Though he did not make cars under his own name for long, Émile Roger played a vital part in establishing Carl Benz as a manufacturer. France was more open to new ideas than Germany in the 1880s, and Roger was Benz' first customer. He already had the Paris agency for Benz stationary engines, and bought a car, possibly the third that Benz had built, in 1888. He showed this under his own name at the 1889 Paris Exposition, and soon began selling the cars. By the end of 1892 he had sold about 25 3-wheelers and then turned to the 4-wheeled Viktoria. It is not certain how much, if any, of the cars were made in France, but they were sold under the Roger name. He drove one in the 1894 Paris-Rouen Trial but it finished last, which did not please Benz who was against competitions. However, there is no doubt that Roger sold more cars than Benz, certainly up to 1895 or 1896.
In 1895 Roger attacked the American market, selling three cars to prominent New York department stores, which earned him excellent publicity. Macy's entered

their car in the Chicago *Times-Herald* race, but it retired. Roger also sold cars in England under the name Anglo-French. His death in 1897 put an end to the Roger name in the car world.

NG

ROGER (ii) **(GB)** 1920–1924
Thomas Roger & Co. Ltd, Wolverhampton, Staffordshire.
This was a light car powered by a 1370cc 4-cylinder Coventry Climax engine, with friction transmission and chain final drive. Buyers of the 1923 models had the option of a conventional 3-speed gearbox and bevel rear axle. These components were by Meadows, while the chassis and other components came from Turner. The only body style was a 2-seater with leather upholstery, royal blue paintwork and disc wheels.

NG

ROGERS (i) **(US)** 1911–1912
Rogers Motor Car Co., Omaha, Nebraska.
Ralph F. Rogers made a high-wheeler with 18hp 2-cylinder engine and chain drive. He was very late on the scene, and if his car had no other distinction, it was the last new make of high-wheeler launched in the United States.

NG

ROGERS (ii) **(CDN)** 1984–c.1988
Rogers International Auto Inc, Vancouver, British Coumbia.
Much larger than most other 3-wheelers, the Rogers Rascal had a single front wheel and a front-mounted engine. Two body styles were available: a hatchback and a convertible, both featuring faired-in headlamps and an aerodynamic profile.

CR

ROGERS & HANFORD **(US)** 1899–1902
Rogers & Hanford Co., Cleveland, Ohio.
The prototype of this unusual car with 4-cylinder rotary engine was built by Frank Rogers and George Hanford in 1899. Two years later the partners put it on the market, with 2- or 4-seater bodies. Very few were made.

NG

ROGERS & THACHER **(US)** 1903
Rogers & Thacher Manufacturing Co., Cleveland, Ohio.
Built by George D. Rogers and A.Q. Thacher, this car had a 35hp 4-cylinder engine. It had a frontal bonnet and one would have expected an engine of that size to have been mounted under it, but instead it lived under the floorboards and the bonnet contained only the fuel and water tanks. It had a 2-speed gearbox and what was described as 'toggle shaft drive'. Its seating was nothing if not adaptable; the tonneau could be removed to make it into a 2-seater, and the passenger seat could then be removed to make it into a racing car. Despite these attractions the car never went into production.

NG

ROGNINI & BALBO **(I)** c.1927–1928
Rognini & Balbo, Milan.
This company specialised in electrically-driven hearses, made in both normal and forward-control models. In their 1927/28 catalogue they advertised electric passenger cars and delivery vans as well.

NG

RÖHR **(D)** 1927–1935
1927–1930 Röhr Automobilwerke AG, Ober-Ramstadt.
1930–1935 Neue Röhrwerke AG, Ober-Ramstadt.
Hans Gustav Röhr (1895–1937) was a leading World War I fighter pilot and also designed aero-engines. In the early 1920s he modified cars to use his ifs, and in 1926 acquired the factory which had formerly built the FALCON (iii). Here he put into production an advanced car with a small straight-8 engine of 1980cc and a sheet steel platform frame. Front suspension was independent by two transverse leaf springs, and there were cantilever springs at the rear, also giving independent suspension. Brakes were by Lockheed. At first only two body styles were offered, both made by Autenrieth. They were a 4-door saloon and a

1888 Roger (i) -Benz 3-wheeler.
NATIONAL MOTOR MUSEUM

1930 Röhr RA cabriolet.
NATIONAL MOTOR MUSEUM

1932 Röhr Type F 3.3-litre saloon.
HANS OTTO NEUBAUER

1933 Röhr Olympier 8 saloon by Authenrieth.
NICK GEORGANO

'cabrio-limousine' with roll top which enabled the car to be completely open. A 2-door roadster-cabriolet was added in 1928, when engine capacity went up to 2246cc. Röhr made about 1100 of these models, which were called the Typ R 8/40PS and 9/50PS, but the firm was badly hit by the Depression, and H.G. Röhr left to become technical director of ADLER and then to work for MERCEDES-BENZ. Negotiations with Thomas Godman of HAMPTON Cars to supply engines and chassis came to nothing, with only one engine delivered.

A reorganised company with largely Swiss capital brought out an enlarged version of the R called the RA with 2496cc 55bhp engine. The wheelbase was lengthened by 4in and a 4-speed ZF-Aphon gearbox with freewheel was available as an alternative to the 3-speed Warner unit. The same body styles were offered as before, and from 1932 appearance was modernised by a sloping radiator. In 1933 came a larger engine, the 75bhp 3287cc Typ F designed by Ferdinand Porsche, and this was further developed into the Typ FK in 1934, with supercharger,

RÖHR, HANS GUSTAV (1895–1937)

No qualified engineer himself, Hans Gustav Röhr had more influence on technical trends than many who had distinguished diplomas. Born on 10 February 1895 at Uerdingen, the son of a small lead-products manufacturer, he finished college in 1914 and joined the Rheinishchen Aerowerke as a trainee.

Drafted into the Royal Prussian Flying Troops in 1915, he had pilot training and made reconnaissance flights before becoming a fighter pilot. He was shot down in 1918 and spent the rest of the war in a field hospital. Home again, he found a job as an engine designer with Priamus Automobilwerke, where he created a radical prototype economy car with an air-cooled 4-cylinder engine and ifs, weighing only 761lb (346kg). He became joint managing director of Priamus but the firm went bankrupt in 1921 and Röhr moved to Berlin to join one of his wartime flying friends.

He kept on improving his car design and rented workshop space from Bolle & Fiedler to build his prototypes. His 1924 prototype had a 6-cylinder engine, low frame, and weighed only 1859lb (845kg). The following year he obtained the backing of Dr Hugo Greffenius of MIAG in Frankfurt to take over the failing Falcon Automobilwerke in Ober-Ramstadt.

It was reorganised as Röhr Auto AG on 10 October 1926, and production of the Röhr 8 began in 1927. The enterprise folded in 1930, but Röhr managed to sell the assets to a Swiss consortium. In May 1931 he joined Adlerwerke as chief engineer, becoming technical director in 1934. He brought with him a full engineering team, including Joseph Dauben, Willy Syring, Otto Winkelmann, Laurenz Niessen and Oberingenieur Engel.

Leaving Adler over a disagreement on sharing licence fees, he explained the situation to Emil von Stauss, chairman of the supervisory board of Daimler-Benz AG, who arranged for him to come to Stuttgart. He was given the title of technical director on 17 September 1935, and brought with him a team of about 25 engineers.

He aimed to make front-wheel drive cars, and designed the W-144, W-145 and W-146 with horizontally-opposed 4-, 6- and 8-cylinder engines. They never got to the production stage. He had to cope with the eternal conflict between the established Benz and Daimler engineers and his own ex-Adler team, plus the distrust of top management (because he had a French wife, he was never informed of the company's military projects).

He directed the design teams for the 1938 Mercedes-Benz 230 and 770, and began a V78 project. But his life and career were cut short on the way to the German Grand Prix at the Nürburgring in August 1937, when he caught a cold which turned to lung inflammation. He died on 10 August 1937, in the Marienhof Hospital at Koblenz.

JPN

c.1910 Rolland-Pilain 30hp tourer.
NICK BALDWIN

giving 100bhp. These were not made in large numbers, about 350 of the RA, 250 of the F and no more than 20 of the FK. The F and FK had wheelbases of 127 (3223mm) and 128in (3249mm), allowing for a 6-light pullman-limousine body as well as the sports saloons and cabriolets.

To supplement the limited sales of the straight-8s, Röhr acquired the licence to build the TATRA T.57 with 1485cc flat-4 engine and central tubular chassis. About 1700 of these were made between 1933 and 1935, and sold under the name Röhr Junior. The licence was then sold to STOEWER and Röhr discontinued cars. Agricultural machinery was later made in the factory.

NG

ROKKO (J) c.1935
Kawasaki Rolling Stock Co., Kawasaki.
This company made trucks from 1932 to 1942, and also announced a car with 4738cc 8-cylinder engine, made in saloon and tourer forms.

NG

ROLAND (i) (D) 1907
Kraftwagen-Gesellschaft Roland, Berlin-Wilmersdorf.
This company made two models of light car, powered by a single and a 2-cylinder engine. No further details are known.

HON

ROLAND (ii) (D) 1926
Firma Bertling, Dessau.
This company made a light car powered by a 4/24PS engine with a 2-seater body.

HON

ROLLAND-PILAIN (F) 1907–1931
1907–1928 SA des Éts Rolland-Pilain, Tours.
SA des Établissements Rolland-Pilain, Courbevoie, Seine.
This company, the most famous to come from the Tours region, was founded by François Rolland and Émile Pilain, (1880–1958), nephew of François Pilain who had founded the PILAIN company at Lyons. Their first car had a 20CV monobloc

1912 Rolland-Pilain 12hp roadster.
NATIONAL MOTOR MUSEUM

4-cylinder engine which the partners claimed was the first monobloc four in the world. It was called, logically, the Type A, and was followed in 1907 by the 40CV Type B. Three models were shown at the 1907 Paris Salon, the Type A now called a 20/28CV, Type B 35/45CV and a new Type C 12/16 intended mainly for town work. For 1909 they made a still smaller car, the 8/10CV Type D, but this did not sell as well as the Type C. In 1910 Rolland-Pilain experimented with both sleeve-valve engines and front-wheel brakes, the former going into production on the 18CV 6-cylinder car of 1911. They brought a suit against Argyll for infringement of patents on sleeve-valve engines, but were unsuccessful. In 1911, when about 150 cars were made, they were making a wide range of cars, from a 2211cc 12CV to a massive chain-driven 14,335cc 60CV. The latter, whose capacity beat both the Pierce-Arrow 66 and the Bugatti Royale, was not listed in 1912, when the largest engine was a 9025cc 40CV. Even this had gone by 1913,

1913 Rollo 8hp cyclecar.
NICK GEORGANO/NATIONAL MOTOR MUSEUM

when the range was topped by a 5195cc 20CV. However, the 40CV reappeared in the 1914 catalogue, with the option of shaft or chain drive. The smaller models of 1913/14, the 9 and 10CV Type RP, had pointed radiators, which were continued after the war. Most coachwork was made for Rolland-Pilain by Bernin, whose premises were just across the rue Victor Hugo from the factory. Rolland-Pilain also made a 5911cc 4-cylinder aero-engine at this time and motorboat engines from 11 to 20CV.

The marque took part in a number of sporting competitions between 1907 and 1914, and again after the war. Their first appearance was at the Meeting de Provence in 1907, when Émile Pilain drove a stripped touring car. They built a team of three 1526cc cars for the 1908 GP des Voiturettes, but they all finished well down the list. For the 1911 GP de France they entered specially-built cars with 6.1-litre 4-cylinder single-ohc engines and chain drive. They did not distinguish themselves, any more than did the similar cars with capacity enlarged to 6274cc entered in the 1912 French GP.

In 1918 there were plans for collaboration with the aero-engine maker Gnome et Rhône, and R-P may have had some input into the three large cars made by Gnome et Rhône in 1919. The Rolland-Pilain range in 1919 consisted of just two models, the 1924cc Type RP and 3969cc Type CR, the latter with electric lighting and starting as standard equipment. They were joined in 1920 by the 2270cc 6-cylinder Type M6, but a more advanced design came in 1922 with the 2235cc 4-cylinder Type R with ohvs, detachable head and 4-wheel brakes, hydraulic at the front and mechanical at the rear. This car was catalogued up to 1926. A team of three Grand Prix cars were built for the 1922 season; they had 1968cc straight-8 engines with twin ohcs and desmodromic valve operation, but did not distinguish themselves, any more than did the 1923 cars without the desmodromy, or a cuff-valve six that ran alongside them. In fact the only successes they had were the first two places in the 1923 Spanish GP, against weak opposition. The straight-8 engine was theoretically available in a road-going sports car, but how many were made is not known. Rolland-Pilain also ran 2-litre cars at Le Mans from 1923 to 1926, their best result being sixth in 1924.

In 1925 came a 1924cc ohv four with mechanical brakes all round, the Type B25, and the slightly larger 2008cc Type C23 which was the most popular Rolland-Pilain of the 1920s. A 1498cc model, the D26, was introduced for 1927, and for 1928 there was a new small six, the 2177cc Type F28 with overhead inlet and side-exhaust valves. This and the D26 remained in the catalogue until 1930, but production dropped after the Tours works were sold off in 1927 and the company moved to Courbevoie, where they took over the Bignan factory. It seems that they made 4- and 8-cylinder Bignan cars as well as their own. At the 1930 Salon two new models appeared, powered by side-valve Lycoming engines, the 3030cc six and 4040cc eight. They were bodied in saloon and cabriolet form by Macquet et Galvier, and used Chrysler 80 silencers. Very few of these were made, but they appeared again at the 1931 Salon, together with descendants of the D26 and F26. They shared a show stand with BNC and

LOMBARD, all three marques being owned by Charles de Ricou. There was certainly no production in 1932, but the Paris depot offered spare parts until the mid–1930s. Émile Pilain made light cars under his own name at Levallois until the end of 1931. Lucien Rolland, son of François, was involved in the O.T.I. microcar project in the late 1950s.

Including unrestored examples, it is thought that at least 32 Rolland-Pilain cars survive.
NG

Further Reading
Rolland Pilain, la Grande Aventure Automobile Tourangelle,
Gilles Blanchet and Claude Rouxel, Éditions Édijac, 1985.

ROLLERA (F) 1958–1959
Sté Rollera Française, Levallois, Seine.
Based on a BRÜTSCH design, the Rollera was a tiny open plastic-bodied single-seater with three wheels. Powered by a 125cc single-cylinder 2-stroke engine, it weighed only 123kg and could reach a speed of 50mph (80km/h).
CR

ROLLFIX (D) 1933–1936
1933–1934 Rollfix-Eilwagen GmbH, Hamburg-Wandsbek.
1934–1936 Rollfix-Werke Frederic Schroder KG, Hamburg-Wandsbek.
This small firm had some success with their 3-wheeled delivery vans which they made from 1927 to 1940. Reduced taxes on 3-wheeled cars in the early 1930s encouraged them to make a passenger car. It had a 200cc 2-cylinder 2-stroke Ilo engine driving the single rear wheel, and an attractive 2-seater coupé body. They also made a few cars on the pattern of the later vans with a single front wheel.
HON

ROLLIN (US) 1923–1925
Rollin Motor Co., Cleveland, Ohio.
This car was made by, and named for, Rollin Henry White (1872–1962) who had been chief engineer of the WHITE company. After leaving White he formed the Cleveland Tractor company in 1916 to make the Cletrac tractor, but was tempted by the car business again in the 1920s. He obtained financial support from Cleveland industrialist E.E. Allyne and hired as designer former Studebaker engineer Fred M. Zeder. For this reason the car was originally to be called the Allyne-Zeder, but the more attractive-sounding name Rollin was chosen. Zeder soon left the project to help design the new Chrysler, but the Rollin was well on its way by then.

Announced in the autumn of 1923 as a 1924 model, it had a 41bhp 2446cc 4-cylinder side-valve engine derived from that used in the tractor; some sources say that the first pilot models of the Rollin carried Cletrac badges. It had a 3-speed Muncie gearbox, and 4-wheel brakes were fitted, making Rollin something of a pioneer in this field as far as modestly priced cars went. Two models of tourer, a coupé-roadster and a sedan made up the range, and prices ran from $895 to $1275. 1924 sales were 3662 cars and in 1925 only 2088 Rollins found customers. It seems that the car's compact size went against it among American buyers. People expected a 6-cylinder car in its price range. Production ended in November 1925 and the company was declared bankrupt the following month. White returned to the tractor business, from which he retired at the age of 72 in 1944.
NG

Further Reading
'The White that Wasn't', Thomas S. Lamarre,
Automobile Quarterly, Vol. 31, No. 4.

ROLLING see DUPRESSOIR

ROLLO (GB) 1911–1913
Rollo Car Co. Ltd, Birmingham.
The Rollo company was early in the field as a cyclecar maker. Initially they offered two models, a monocar powered by a 4¼hp single-cylinder Precision engine and a tandem 2-seater powered by an 8hp JAP engine. Both models had belt final drive and tubular frames. The monocar, which weighed only 336lbs, was modestly priced at 70 guineas (£73.50), and the 2-seater cost £99.75 with tandem seating or £105 with side by side seating, which was introduced for 1913.
NG

ROLLAND PiLAIN

GEOW

LA VOITURE DES AS
L'AS DES VOITURES

SIÈGE SOCIAL
USINES & BUREAUX
44, PLACE RABELAIS, 44
TOURS
TÉLÉPHONE { 0-82
{ 4-85

TÉLÉGRAMMES : ROLLAND-PILAIN, TOURS
Succursale :
TOULOUSE : Square Roland
TÉL : 13-48

SUCCURSALE
ET
ATELIER DE RÉPARATIONS
83-85, ROUTE DE LA REVOLTE, 83-85
LEVALLOIS
TÉLÉPHONE : WAGRAM 12-57
TÉL.: ROLLANPILAIN, LEVALLOIS-PERRET
Magasin d'Exposition
PARIS : 46, Avenue Montaigne
TÉL : PASSY 42-57

1905 Rolls-Royce (i) 20hp Tourist Trophy tourer, Percy Northey at the wheel, C.S. Rolls behind him.
NICK BALDWIN

1908 Rolls-Royce (i) 40/50 landaulet by Hooper, with Queen Mary on the western front, 1917.
IMPERIAL WAR MUSEUM

ROLLSMOBILE (US) 1958–1960

Starts Manufacturing Co. and Horseless Carriage Corp., Fort Lauderdale, Florida.

This company made two replicas of early automobiles. One was of the 1901 Oldsmobile runabout and the other was an early Ford. Both were powered by a single-cylinder 3hp engine and had a top speed of 35mph (56km/h).

HP

ROLLS-ROYCE (i) (GB) 1904 to date

1904–1906 Royce Ltd, Manchester.
1906–1908 Rolls-Royce Ltd, Manchester.
1908–1945 Rolls-Royce Ltd, Derby.
1946–1971 Rolls-Royce Ltd, Crewe, Cheshire.
1971 to date Rolls-Royce Motors (1971) Ltd, Crewe, Cheshire.

The most famous partnership in motoring history came about through a meeting in a Manchester hotel between two very different characters, the aristocratic Honourable Charles Stewart Rolls and the workaholic engineer Frederick Henry Royce (see biographies). The 10hp 2-cylinder ROYCE car had already been running for more than a month when the fateful meeting took place, and it is

very likely that Rolls had seen another Royce two weeks earlier when it took part in sideslip trials in London, as he was on the trials committee. He was so impressed with Royce and his car that he offered to take the entire output of the company, on condition that they bore his name as well as Royce's.

The first Rolls-Royce car was ready by December 1904, although the two companies, C.S. Rolls & Co. and Royce Ltd remained independent until March 1906, when Rolls-Royce Ltd was formed. The first car was a 10hp vertical twin of 1809cc similar in size to the Royce though with a redesigned crankshaft and improved external finish. The most visible difference was that the flat-topped radiator of the Royce was replaced by a Grecian design not unlike the Parthenon in proportions, which has been carried by every Rolls-Royce car since 1904.

The first public showing of the Rolls-Royce took place in December 1904 at the Paris Salon, and a production run of 20 cars was begun. In fact only 16 were made, as Rolls thought that a 2-cylinder car did not suit the luxury image he wished to create. The last 10hp was built in 1906, by which time other models with 3, 4, 6 and 8-cylinders had been made. In fact, the stand at the Paris Salon also contained a 20hp 4-cylinder car, a chassis for the 15hp 3-cylinder car, and a 30hp 6-cylinder engine. All four models were listed in Rolls-Royce's first catalogue of January 1905. They were supplied as chassis only, but the recommended coachbuilder was Barker who made many bodies for Rolls-Royce up to their closure in 1938.

A four-model programme was ambitious for a new and small manufacturer, although production was simplified by using the same cylinder dimensions, (101.6 × 127mm) for all models. As the cylinders were cast in pairs, the 20hp four was made up of two twins, and the 30hp six of three. The exception was the 15hp 3-cylinder car which, although it had the same dimensions, had separately cast cylinders. The complications in making this engine was probably the reason for its being dropped at the end of 1905, after only six had been made. The 4-cylinder Twenty was the most successful of the early Rolls-Royces, selling 40 examples between 1905 and 1908. Its 4118cc engine developed at least its quoted 20bhp, and it was the only Rolls-Royce to play an important part in racing. Two tourers were entered in the first Tourist Trophy race, driven by Rolls and Percy Northey. They differed from the regular model in having a lighter chassis and a 4-speed gearbox, in which top was an overdrive, with third being the direct gear. This was later used on production cars, which were called the Light Twenty to distinguish them from the 3-speed Heavy Twenty. Rolls retired on the first lap, but Northey finished 2nd, and the following year Rolls won the TT in a car similar to the 1905 model, but with Rudge-Whitworth detachable wire wheels in place of artilleries. In December 1906 Rolls took one of the TT cars to the United States, where he won a race at Yonkers, NY. This did not result in many orders, and it was some years before the make became established in the US. As well as the different gearboxes, the 20hp was made in two wheelbases, 106 and 114in (2692 and 2896mm), and was fitted with a variety of bodies, closed as well as open.

The V8 was an aberration sometimes described as 'Royce's Brief Flirtation with Folly'. It was built in response to a suggestion by Rolls' partner Claude Johnson that they should cater for the town brougham market, for which a number of manufacturers were making both petrol and electric vehicles. The petrol ones tended to be very high, as the driver was perched over the engine in order to achieve a short wheelbase. Royce's solution was to design a wide-angle V8 engine which could be mounted below the floor on the passenger's side of the frame. The 3535cc engine had square dimensions of 82.6 × 82.6mm, and was the world's first V8 to be designed from scratch. Only three cars were completed, two underfloor-engined town cars and one with the engine mounted in front under a very low bonnet. This was ordered by the newspaper tycoon Lord Northcliffe who called it the Legalimit, as it could not exceed 20mph (32km/h) which was the speed limit in force in Britain. The V8 is the only Rolls-Royce model of which not a single example survives today.

The 40/50

The fourth member of the original range was the 30hp 6-cylinder car of 6177cc. This suffered from the torsional vibration that afflicted most 6-cylinder crankshafts at the time, and Henry Royce was determined to overcome this. He redesigned the engine so that it had two blocks of three cylinders rather than three blocks of two, and the blocks were back to back so that the third and fourth pistons rose and fell together. The diameters of the pins and journals were nearly twice those of the 30hp, and pressure lubrication replaced the splash system. The head was redesigned too, being of the familiar L-head layout rather than the F-head inlet-over-exhaust which had been used on all the Rolls-Royces up to 1906. The capacity was enlarged to 7036cc with square dimensions of 114 × 114mm. The output of the new engine was 48bhp, and it was initially called the 40hp, though the designation 40/50 was very soon adopted.

Two 40/50s were exhibited at the Olympia Show in December 1906, but it was nine months before any production cars reached the public. The intervening time was taken up with exhaustive testing which Claude Johnson insisted on to avoid embarrassing breakdowns in the hands of owners. The 13th chassis was completed in April 1907 and at Johnson's request, was fitted with a Barker tourer body painted silver and with silver fittings. It was christened The Silver Ghost, and so famous did it become that eventually the name was given to all 40/50s. This practice was not widespread until the model was replaced by the Phantom in 1925. When new, the cars were called 40/50s, or since they were the only model made until the arrival of the Twenty, simply as the Rolls-Royce.

Among the trials to which the 40/50 was subjected were a 2000 mile (3218km) run covering the course of the Scottish Reliability Trial, followed by the Trial itself, in which the Silver Ghost won a Gold Medal, and continuous driving between London and Glasgow until 15,000 miles (24,139km) had been covered. This was considered to be the equivalent of three years normal use. Production of the 40/50 began in September 1907, and soon four chassis per week were leaving the factory. The 20hp was quietly dropped, though it was not until March 1908 that Rolls-Royce finally decided to concentrate on a one-model policy. This was unusual at a time when most of their rivals such as Daimler, Napier and Mercedes, made wide ranges of cars.

The demand for the 40/50 necessitated a move to larger premises, which were found at Derby. The new factory was opened by Lord Montagu of Beaulieu in July 1908, and production rose to about seven chassis per week, remaining at this level until the outbreak of war in August 1914. The design was not greatly

Charles Stewart Rolls at the wheel of a 1906 TT Rolls-Royce.
NICK BALDWIN

ROLLS, CHARLES STEWART (1877–1910)

Charles Stewart Rolls was the third son of Lord and Lady Llangattock, prominent landowners of English descent living in Monmouthshire where they had a property of about 6000 acres. Charles was educated at Eton and Trinity College, Cambridge, where he read engineering. In 1896, when he was 19, he bought a 3½hp Peugeot, probably the first car to be seen in the university city, and certainly the first to be owned by an undergraduate. That Christmas he drove the car 180 miles from London to Monmouthshire. A less adventurous soul would have left the car in London for the vacation, or put it on a train, but Rolls thought that cars were for driving, and although the journey took him two days, including many hours spent working on it by the roadside, he arrived in time for the family's Christmas celebrations.

By the time he left Cambridge, Rolls was one of the most experienced and skilled motorists in the country. In 1899 he began his racing career, driving a Panhard in the Paris-Ostend and Paris-Boulogne Races, finishing second in the tourist class of the former, and 5th overall in the latter. He won a Gold Medal in the 1900 Thousand Mile Trial, and in 1901 he drove a Mors into 18th place in the gruelling Paris-Berlin Race. He was known as one of the Four Sporting Charlies, the others being racing driver Charles Jarrott, motor dealer Charles Friswell, and owner of the *Motor Car Journal* Charles Cordingley. By then he was well-known in motoring circles and also in London society, and did as much as anyone to introduce one group to the other. He had no need to earn a living, but could not spend all his life at the

wheel of a racing car. In 1902 his father set him up in business as a seller of imported cars; at first he held the agency for Panhard and Mors, supplemented later by the Gardner-Serpollet steam car and Belgian Minerva. He even dabbled in commercial vehicles; the only vehicle ever to bear the Rolls name was the Swiss-built C.I.E.M. truck and bus chassis. The absence of British cars in his showrooms was not for lack of patriotism, but there were few native-built cars of quality available. Those that were, such as Napier and Lanchester, were already represented. When he heard about the Royce car that had just been built in Manchester he was at first unimpressed as it had only two cylinders, and his customers were used to four. However, Royce director Henry Edmunds persuaded him to make the trip to Manchester, where he was so impressed by the little car's silence and smoothness of running that he agreed to take the entire output, so long as Royce's promise of 4- and 6-cylinder cars was put into effect, and that the cars should bear the name Rolls-Royce.

Rolls and his partner Claude Johnson were happy with the cars, the only problem being that there were too few of them. Rolls said of Royce a few years later, 'I won't say he has suited me in quantity for we could have sold double or treble the number, and I see no chance of getting satisfaction in this respect for a considerable time to come'.

For the first few years of the company Rolls devoted himself enthusiastically to selling Rolls-Royces, particularly where racing was involved. He drove a 20hp in the Tourist Trophy Races of 1905 and 1906, winning the second event, and in May 1906 he beat the record from Monte Carlo to London by 1½ minutes, despite losing more than three hours waiting for a boat at Boulogne. However, both Henry Royce and Claude Johnson were less than enthusiastic about competitions, seeing the company's future in smooth and comfortable cars for what Royce called 'the duchess trade'. Rolls was too restless a character to be happy selling cars to duchesses, and from 1906 onwards his energies were increasingly devoted to flying. During a sales trip to America in October 1906 he took part in a balloon race at Pittsfield, Massachusetts, and two years later he took up heavier-than-air flying with a Wright bi-plane. In April 1910 he resigned from his post as technical managing director of Rolls-Royce, becoming merely technical adviser. Three months later, on 12 July, his Wright bi-plane crashed during a flying display at Bournemouth, and he died almost instantly.

According to his contemporaries and biographers Charles Rolls was a curious man, cold and lacking in emotion, a 'natural solitary', who was more at home with children than adults. He did not pull rank through his title, though he could be impatient to the point of cruelty. When his mechanic Al Poole fell out of the Panhard during the 1000 Miles Trial, doubtless due to the driver cornering too enthusiastically, he warned him that if he fell out again he would not stop and pick him up. This might have been a joke, but according to Poole it was not. Charles Rolls never married.

NG

Further Reading
Rolls of Rolls-Royce, Lord Montagu of Beaulieu, Cassell, 1966.
'The Contrast between Rolls and Royce', Lord Montagu of Beaulieu, *Veteran & Vintage Magazine*, May 1971.

1913 Rolls-Royce (i) 40/50 tourer by Salmons.
NICK BALDWIN

1926 Rolls-Royce (i) Phantom I prototype Continental tourer by Barker.
NICK BALDWIN

changed during this time, though capacity went up to 7428cc (60bhp) in 1909, and in the same year the 4-speed box was replaced by a 3-speeder in which top was direct. This was in response to customers who complained the former overdrive top was too high for hill climbing; as most drivers hated changing gear they liked to hang on in top as long as possible. In 1913 a 4-speed box was again available, but this time a lower first gear was added, top still being direct.

A great variety of bodywork was built on the 40/50 chassis, which was available in four wheelbases. Tourers, landaulets and limousines made up the majority, but there were some 2-seaters, including one with 70bhp engine which Charles Rolls used for transporting his balloon. Two particular models were the London-Edinburgh and Alpine Eagle tourers. The former was developed from a car built for an RAC-observed run from London to Edinburgh in top gear, which had a raised cr and light 4-seater body. When fitted with a single-seater body and raised rear axle ratio it reached 101.8mph (163.82km/h) at Brooklands in 1912. A limited number of replicas were sold from 1912 to 1914. The Alpine Eagle was derived from the team cars which took part in the 1913 Austrian Alpine Trials. Failure to restart on a hill during the 1912 event had prompted the adoption of the lower first gear on all 1913 cars, and this, together with other improvements, enabled the Rolls-Royce team to dominate the 1913 Trials, winning the Archduke Leopold Cup and taking six other awards. The team cars had distinctive 'water towers' which were expansion chambers above the radiator. Replica Alpine Eagles did not have these, but shared the team cars' 70bhp engines with higher cr and larger choke carburettor. They were higher in appearance than the London-Edinburgh cars but no less handsome, and are among the most-desired 40/50s today.

Rolls-Royce cars played an important part in World War I, as staff cars for senior officers and royalty, supply vehicles for 750kg loads, and as armoured cars.

They were the most widely-used British armoured cars in the war, seeing service in France, Egypt, Palestine, Arabia and East Africa. By the spring of 1919 the chassis was back in production for civilian buyers, though demand easily outstripped supply, and prewar examples were selling for greatly inflated prices; a 1914 London-Edinburgh which cost £985 for the chassis plus around £400 for a body was priced at £3500 in December 1919. The postwar chassis was not greatly changed, though electric lighting and starting were standard equipment, whereas they had been extras in 1914. The lighting and starters were of Rolls-Royce's own make, as was practically every part of the car, save the tyres and, of course, the coachwork. It was not until the 1930s that the company would buy in items such as carburettors, fuel pumps and electrical equipment. In response to competition from rivals such as Hispano-Suiza, Rolls-Royce introduced 4-wheel brakes on their 1924 models. Although they were not standardised until well into the year, they could be installed at no expense to the customer on all cars ordered after November 1923. In May 1925 a new ohv engine was installed in the 40/50 chassis, which was given the name New Phantom. The previous models were then retrospectively called Silver Ghosts. Production at Manchester and Derby was 6173, together with 1703 American Silver Ghosts made at Springfield, Massachusetts between 1921 and 1926.

The Rolls-Royce Twenty

Once the pent-up demand for expensive cars had been satisfied, the position for Rolls-Royce looked less encouraging, as inflation pushed up prices and the incomes of the rich were threatened by taxation and the prospect of a Socialist government. Claude Johnson therefore asked Henry Royce to design a smaller and cheaper car which could be driven easily without a chauffeur. The result was the Twenty, which appeared in October 1922. It had a 3127cc 6-cylinder monobloc engine with ohvs and a detachable head, modern features compared with the bi-bloc side-valve fixed head 40/50 engine. However, there were other features which dismayed the traditionalists, such as coil ignition instead of magneto, and a 3-speed gearbox with central change.

J.T.C. Moore-Brabazon, the Edwardian racing driver who had acted as C.S. Rolls' mechanic in the 1903 Irish races, summed up these feelings when he described the Twenty as 'A very excellent vehicle of somewhat uninteresting American type.' In fact a 4-speed gearbox with right hand change was adopted on the Twenty from the 1925 season onwards, and the lever remained on the right on all Rolls-Royce cars until the steering column change on the 1949 Silver Dawn.

The Twenty had an adequate performance for a car of its day and kind, with a top speed of around 60mph (97km/h) so long as the coachwork was not too heavy. In fact a number of customers wanted heavy limousine bodies which did pull down the performance. And while more Twentys than Silver Ghosts were owner-driven, a considerable number were seen with chauffeurs at the wheel. The chassis price was £1100, compared with £1850 for a Silver Ghost.

The Twenty was made up to 1929, with few changes apart from the gearbox already mentioned, and the adoption of 4-wheel brakes in 1925. In October 1929 the engine was enlarged to 3669cc and the model renamed 20/25. The 20 engine was the longest-lived of all Royce's designs, for it was progressively developed and enlarged up to the late 1950s, by which time it displaced 4887cc and gave 178bhp, compared with the 53bhp of the original. The only dimension to remain unchanged over 37 years was the space between the centre of the cylinder bores, 105.4mm.

The 20/25 had a top speed of 65 to 78mph (105–125km/h) according to coachwork, and was made with little change until the 1936 season, when there was a further engine enlargement to 4257cc, a hypoid rear axle and a new name, 25/30. The last small prewar Rolls-Royce was the Wraith, introduced for 1939. The engine was the same size as the 25/30, but had larger valves and a redesigned crankshaft. The Wraith shared the Phantom III's coil-and-wishbone ifs.

These small Rolls-Royces did a great deal to keep the company going through the Depression. Though the aero-engine business was profitable and growing, the big Phantoms alone would not have made the car division viable, and without the smaller model to build their postwar range on there would almost certainly have been no Rolls-Royce cars today. A total of 8459 small Rolls-Royces were made between 1922 and 1939, as well as 2350 Bentleys derived from the 20/25 and 25/30. The exact breakdown was 2940 Twentys, 3827 20/25s, 1201 25/30s and 491 Wraiths.

The 1930s saw an increasing reliance on components from outside firms. Whereas in earlier times practically everything was made in the Rolls-Royce factory, they now bought carburettors from Zenith-Stromberg, fuel pumps

Henry Royce in the garden of his house at West Wittering.
NICK BALDWIN

ROYCE, HENRY (1863–1933)

A great engineer who preferred to call himself Henry Royce, Mechanic, Frederick Henry Royce was born on 27 March 1863 at Alwalton, Lincolnshire, where his father James Royce owned a flour mill. When Henry was four the business failed, and the family moved to London, but James Royce had no more success there. By the time Henry was nine he was sent out to earn his living, not unusual among poor families in the 1870s. His first job was selling newspapers for W.H. Smith, followed by one delivering telegrams. In 1878 his aunt enabled him to take up an apprenticeship at the Great Northern Railway workshops at Peterborough, for £20 a year. By day he worked on Stirling '8 footer' locomotives, so called because their driving wheels were 8 feet in diameter, and in the evenings he studied mathematics, foreign languages, and, especially, electricity. This was to give him his proper start in life. After three years his aunt could no longer afford the premium; after an ill-paid job with a firm of tool makers, Royce moved back to London and obtained a post with the Electrical Light & Power Co. After a short time he was transferred to their subsidiary, the Lancashire Maxim & Western Electricity Co. of Liverpool. There one of his jobs was to see that the lights were functioning in the city's many theatres and music halls. This was a complex task at a time when a decrease in load caused the dynamos to run too fast and transmit so many volts to the remaining lights that they burned out. Royce was now chief electrician, and would send a small boy around the theatres to see that all was well.

Unfortunately, all was not well with the Lancashire Maxim & Western Electric Co., which went into liquidation about 18 months after Royce joined it. He was tired of working for other people, and as he had saved £20 he went into partnership with a friend, Ernest Claremont. In 1884 they rented a small workshop in Cooke Street, Hulme, Manchester. It was described by Royce's biographer Sir Max Pemberton as 'a sorry den when the young men rented it', although it was greatly extended and improved over the years, and was to see the birth of the first Royce car, and of all subsequent models of Rolls-Royce up to 1908. The partners began in a modest way, doing subcontracting work for larger concerns for whom they made electric filaments and lamp holders. They then made electric bell sets which were becoming fashionable even in quite modest homes. They cost 1/6 (7½p), excluding batteries.

In 1891 they added Royce's patent sparkless drum-wound dynamo to their products, and in 1894 began to make electric cranes. These were a novelty in a world where all heavy lifting jobs in factories, mines, quarries, and building sites were performed by steam cranes, and lighter work by hand-cranked cranes. They were soon making a wide variety of lifting equipment up to large dockside cranes. F.H. Royce & Co. became a public company in 1894, and by the turn of the century was bringing in a good income for the partners, as well as for their employees.

It is not surprising that a man of Royce's mechanical interest should have bought a car as soon as they became available. His first was a De Dion-engined quadricycle, and in 1903 he bought a Decauville with 10hp vertical twin engine. He was not impressed with this, complaining of its 'terrible unreliability and bad design'. After working on it until he felt no further improvements could be made, he decided to make a car of his own. At first there was no question of this being a new line of business, so 'Pa' Royce as he was already being called, installed himself in a corner of the works, appropriated two of the most promising apprentices, and set to work.

The Royce car owed much to the Decauville, being also a vertical twin, but it had a two-throw crankshaft which gave a better-balanced engine, a less tortuous inlet pipe system, and a larger and more effective silencer. Above all he was fanatical about the fit and finish of all moving parts, and of the tooth formation in the gearbox, all of which contributed to the silence of running so much admired by Charles Rolls. The first car emerged onto the street on 1 April 1904, to the accompaniment of hammering on bench, anvil, and floor by the employees.

At first, like Carl Benz, Royce annoyed his fellow directors by taking time and staff away from their main business of making cranes, but once the Rolls contract was set up, cars became more important. After 1906 Royce & Co. continued as a separate business, making cranes and electrical equipment until its closure in 1933.

During this period, and indeed up to 1911, Royce took little care of his health. He never ate regular meals, and would walk round the factory followed by apprentices carrying glasses of milk which they would endeavour to persuade him to drink, while his food consisted of chunks of bread and eggs boiled on the furnace. He worked incredibly long hours, sometimes staying in the factory overnight and snatching, at the most, a couple of hours sleep. The result was that in 1911 he became gravely ill. His biographers have always been somewhat coy about the exact nature of his illness. Bowel cancer has been suggested, but it seems as likely that it was ulcerative colitis, a disease often associated with stress, and one for which there was little hope of cure in Edwardian days. In December 1912, while visiting the south of France where a house was being built for him, he was again taken very ill. He was rushed back to London for a major operation which left him a semi-invalid for the rest of his life. The doctors had given him three months to live, but he confounded them by living a further 22 years. However, everyone was insistent that he should not return to the factory, so Claude Johnson acted as a go-between and teams of engineers and draughtsmen would visit him at his homes in Crowborough (later West Wittering) Sussex or Le Canadel in France. There he supervised the design of the Twenty, and the Phantoms 1, 2 and 3, although he died before the latter was built. At first he was reluctant to become involved in aero-engines, but he worked on the Eagle and Falcon, and in the late 1920s on the 'R' engine which powered the Schneider Trophy-winning Supermarine seaplanes of 1927, 1929, and 1931. It was for his work on the victorious 1929 plane, and not for his cars, that he was created a baronet. Throughout this time he was cared for by his devoted nurse Ethel Aubin; without her and Claude Johnson it is unlikely that Royce would have lived long enough to produce half these designs.

Henry Royce married Minnie Punt, the daughter of a London printer, in 1893. They saw less and less of each other up to his illness, and after that he virtually lived the life of a bachelor. They had no children.

NG

Further Reading
The Life of Sir Henry Royce, Sir Max Pemberton, Selwyn & Blount, c.1934.
'The Contrast between Rolls and Royce', Lord Montagu of Beaulieu, *Veteran & Vintage Magazine*, May 1971.
'Royce, the Mechanic', John Bolster, *Classic & Sports Car*, September 1983.

1929 Left: Rolls-Royce (i) Phantom I saloon by Weymann, Right: Twenty saloon.
LAWRENCE DALTON

from SU, starters from Bijur and electrical equipment from Lucas, just like lesser manufacturers. This policy enabled costs to be kept down on the smaller models so that a 1936 25/30 cost £1050 for the chassis, to which a good saloon body by Barker or Hooper would add around £600. Cheaper bodies could be

had for half that figure, while a Phantom III cost £1850 for the chassis, and perhaps £800–1000 for a quality body.

The Phantoms

1925 saw a new 40/50 which was sufficiently different from the Silver Ghost to merit a new name. It was called the New Phantom and only after later models appeared did it acquire its present name, Phantom I. The engine had ohvs and a considerably larger capacity, of 7668cc. Output was not quoted, a policy Rolls-Royce have followed up to fairly recent times, but was around 90bhp in 1925, rising to 100bhp by 1929. The chassis was little changed from the last Silver Ghosts, with spiral-bevel final drive which had been adopted in 1923. Hypoid bevels came in with the Phantom IIi for 1930. The Phantom I was heavier and slower than the prewar Silver Ghost, and with the balloon tyres which were coming into fashion in the mid–1920s, its steering was heavy. Even with a light tourer body a Phantom I could not exceed 75mph (120km/h) at Brooklands, which did not compare very well with the 78.48mph (126.3km/h) achieved by a London–Edinburgh Silver Ghost in 1911. Matters improved with the Phantom II, particularly the Continental model.

After 2212 Phantom Is had been made, the model was replaced by the Phantom II in September 1929. This time it was the chassis which was changed, the engine remaining much the same apart from a redesigned cylinder head which increased power to about 120bhp. The new chassis was much lower,

NATIONAL MOTOR MUSEUM

HIVES, ERNEST WALTER (1886–1965)

Ernest Walter Hives was a man of action, a man who got things done. He was sure and quick in making decisions, and fearless about committing his company to major spending programmes once his mind was made up. His way of doing business was simple and direct. In 1943, when Rolls-Royce was making advances in turbojet development, and while Rover was under contract to build a turbojet engine for Frank Whittle, Hives took Spencer Wilks to dinner, and they talked of many things before the gas turbine topic came up; Hives said, 'Here's what we'll do. You give up the Whittle project, and we'll give you the contract for the Meteor tank engine'. It was settled in a matter of minutes.

He was born on 21 April 1886. His parents did not feel that he was destined for an academic career, so he started an apprenticeship with a garage in Reading, Berkshire, leaving in 1903 to go to London and work in the service department of C.S. Rolls & Co. at Lillie Hall, Fulham. A year later he joined Napier's automobile department and came to know S.F. Edge and A.J. Rowledge.

He joined Rolls-Royce Ltd as a chassis tester in 1908, and was responsible for the preparation (and sometimes driving) of cars for speed and fuel-consumption demonstration runs. At an early date he also became involved with testing aircraft engines. In 1914 he was promoted to head of the aircraft engine experimental department, which meant that nothing new would be cleared for production without his approval. He never acted as a brake on progress, however, just the contrary, for he had a way of finding the true cause of any delay and dealing with it promptly. He cut the development time for the Eagle V12 engine to six months, and by the end of World War I it was putting out three times the power of the first production unit.

After the war, when Henry Royce worked at his homes in West Wittering or Le Canadel, most of his written communications were addressed to Hives, who came to serve as an alter ego for Royce, and demonstrated his ability to operate at executive level. He became the de facto manager of aircraft engine design, development, and production, and launched the Kestrel engine in 1925. The famous V12 'R' engine which propelled the Supermarine S.6 seaplane to victory in the 1931 Schneider Trophy contest was a pure Henry Royce design, but it was Hives who directed its development into the Merlin which was installed in the Spitfire, Lancaster, Mosquito, and other RAF airplanes of World War II. Since Rolls-Royce lacked the capacity to fill the orders in time, the Merlin was also produced in important numbers by Packard and Ford in the USA. Hives also directed the development of the 1775hp 42,500cc X24 Vulture engine.

In 1946 he was named managing director of Rolls-Royce Ltd, which saddled him with the ultimate responsibility for a new range of cars to take over from the Silver Wraith and Bentley Mk VI, which were essentially prewar models.

He led the aircraft engine department into the gas turbine age, with a mixed programme of turbo-prop and turbojet engines (Welland, Derwent, Nene, Dart) and was raised to the peerage as Baron Hives in the King's honours list in 1950.

He was chairman of Rolls-Royce Ltd from 1950 until his retirement in 1958. He suffered a stroke in March 1963 and never regained consciousness. He died in a London hospital on 24 April 1965.

JPN

Further Reading
Rolls-Royce – Hives' Turbulent Barons, Alec Harvey-Bailey,
Sir Henry Royce Memorial Foundation, Historical Series No.20.

ROLLS-ROYCE
The Best Car in the World

ROLLS-ROYCE LTD. CONDUIT ST.
LONDON W.I. MAYFAIR 6201

1939 Rolls-Royce (i) Phantom III limousine de ville by Hooper.
LAWRENCE DALTON

1939 Rolls-Royce (i) Wraith limousine by Thrupp & Maberly.
LAWRENCE DALTON

1954 Rolls-Royce (i) Silver Wraith touring limousine by H.J. Mulliner.
NICK BALDWIN

and the cantilever rear springs were replaced by semi-elliptics, the same as at the front. Even with a formal limousine body the Phantom II was a low car, and many people think it the best-looking Rolls-Royce ever made. It was available in two wheelbases, 144 and 150in (3658 and 3810mm), the shorter being the

basis for the Continental sports saloon. This originated when Royce and Ivan Evernden sought to design a body on the lines of the new Riley Nine Monaco, but of course scaled up to fit a Phantom II chassis. Prototypes were built by Barker and Park Ward, and the latter's 4-light saloon became a recommended body, though other firms such as Hooper also built Continentals. The name was never strictly defined by Rolls-Royce, but according to the American Raymond Gentile, who is the recognised expert on the model, the two essential distinguishing points of the Continental are the 144in wheelbase and five flattened front spring leaves in place of the regular nine thinner leaves. A more raked steering column was fitted to some, though not all Continentals. Out of a total of 1681 Phantom IIs, 281 genuine Continentals were made.

By the early 1930s it was evident that Rolls-Royce would have to offer more than six cylinders if they were to maintain their reputation for smoothness and silence, in the face of competition from the V12 Daimler, Hispano-Suiza, Packard and Lincoln, and the V16 Cadillac. Henry Royce died in April 1933, so development of the new engine fell to A.G. Elliott and Ernest Hives. A prototype was running by early 1934, and the new model made its bow at the Olympia Show in October 1935. Christened the Phantom III, it had a 7340cc ohv V12 engine which developed about 165bhp, rising to 180bhp by 1938. The 4-speed gearbox with synchromesh on three upper speeds, was mounted further back in the chassis than on the Phantom II, to compensate for the heavier engine which was located further forward. This necessitated a forward move for the radiator, giving the car a less classic appearance, opulent rather than understated. The V12 engine was very complex and in particular the hydraulic rams that kept the tappet clearances automatically correct gave trouble unless they were supplied with ultra clean oil. In 1938 the hydraulic tappets were abandoned.

A variety of magnificent coachwork was fitted to the Phantom III, of which 710 were made, production ending at the outbreak of war. They were exported to 22 countries, of which the United States took the most (35), followed by France (27) and India (19).

The Postwar Rolls-Royce

In 1938 Rolls-Royce opened a new factory for aero-engine production at Crewe, Cheshire, and after the war car production was transferred there, as the Derby factory was more suited to aero-engines. The postwar model was named the Silver Wraith, sharing the prewar Wraith's cylinder block and gearbox, although the head was now an inlet-over-exhaust or F-head layout, a revival of

Henry Royce's first engine of 1904. The front-wheel brakes were now hydraulic, though at the rear there was still the traditional mechanical servo assistance. The Silver Wraith chassis cost £1835, and in prewar tradition, was supplied for outside coachbuilders to work on. However, the Bentley Mk VI, which was very similar to the Silver Wraith, was made with a steel body by the Pressed Steel Co., and in 1949 Rolls-Royce offered a similar body on the export-only Silver Dawn, which also had lhd and a steering column gearchange.

The steel body was not only cheaper, but also more suited to the variety of climates encountered in export markets than was the traditional ash frame with aluminium panels. A total of 761 Dawns were made, some with rhd, and the later ones having the 4566cc engine also used in the Silver Wraith and Bentley Mk VI from 1951.

The Silver Wraith remained in production until 1959, gaining a longer wheelbase in 1951 which, although it meant a heavier car more suited to chauffeur-drive, also allowed for more handsome coachwork. The 639 long-wheelbase Silver Wraiths carried the last flowering of the British coachbuilding industry, magnificent examples being made by Freestone & Webb, Hooper, H.J. Mulliner, Park Ward and James Young. A few were one-offs, but there were also several series of up to 50 of the same shape, though of course an infinite variety of different fitments could be had to the customer's choice. Automatic transmission of GM type was optional from late 1953, and from 1955 the engine was enlarged to 4887cc.

The larger engine was also used in the Dawn's successor, the Silver Cloud. This also had a Pressed Steel body designed by Rolls-Royce, with more flowing lines than its predecessor, and automatic transmission as standard. Power-assisted steering was optional from the 1957 season. The Cloud was identical to the S-type Bentley apart from the radiator, and £130 in price. It could still be supplied in chassis form, and there were some striking designs by Freestone & Webb and Hooper as well as the Harold Radford estate car built by H.J. Mulliner. In 1959 the Silver Cloud received a brand-new 6230cc V8 engine. Although larger in capacity, the V8 was about 10lb (4.5kg) lighter than its predecessor, thanks to the more extensive use of light alloys. With an identical body and chassis, the Silver Cloud II was 15mph (24km/h) faster than the Cloud I, with a top speed of 115mph (185km/h). The final development of the Cloud series was the III, made from 1963 to 1965 and recognisable by its four headlamps. Like the Clouds I (from 1957) and II it could be had in long-wheelbase form, and as a drophead coupé as well as saloon. Total production of the Clouds was 7365, the breakdown in series being as follows (long-wheelbase models in brackets): Cloud I, 2238 (121), Cloud II, 2417 (299), Cloud III, 2044 (253).

The Last of the Phantoms

When Phantom III production ended in 1939 it seemed as if there would never be another prestige Rolls-Royce to bear the name. However, in 1950 came the first of a very limited series called the Phantom IV. This had a 5675cc ioe straight-8 engine which was one of the family of engines known as the B Series, the 6-cylinder version powering the Silver Wraith. They had common cylinder dimensions and shared many components. One of these straight-8s was installed in a Bentley, and the Duke of Edinburgh was so impressed with its performance that he asked Rolls-Royce to make a limousine with the same engine, for himself and Princess Elizabeth. It was installed in a lengthened Silver Wraith chassis with 145in (3683mm) wheelbase and fitted with an H.J. Mulliner body. Though it was essentially a car for chauffeur-drive, the Duke took the wheel himself from time to time. This first Phantom IV was delivered in July 1950, and was followed by 17 others, all built for Heads of State. These included General Franco and the Shah of Iran who had two each, the Aga Khan, the Sheikh of Kuwait and Prince Talal Al Saud Ryak of Saudia Arabia. The only British Phantom IV owners were members of the Royal Family, Princess Margaret and the Duke of Gloucester. All Phantom IV coachwork was by Hooper or H.J. Mulliner, except for Prince Talal's, which was by the French coachbuilder Franay. They were all very stately cars, not always easily distinguishable from long-wheelbase Silver Wraiths, though they had an extra 12in (305mm) in the wheelbase.

In October 1959 came the Silver Wraith's successor, the Phantom V which had the 6230cc V8 engine in a wheelbase the same as the Phantom IV. Increased front and rear overhang made the Phantom V the longest Rolls-Royce ever made, at 245in (6240mm). At the 1959 Earls Court Show seven Phantom Vs were exhibited, carrying limousine coachwork by Hooper, H.J. Mulliner, Park Ward and James Young. Hooper soon closed down, having made just one Phantom V limousine, and Mulliner merged with Park Ward in 1961, most of

1960 Rolls-Royce (i) Silver Cloud II saloon.
NICK BALDWIN

1966 Rolls-Royce (i) Silver Shadow saloon.
NICK BALDWIN

1978 Rolls-Royce (i) Phantom VI limousine by H.J.Mulliner.
NICK BALDWIN

1989 Rolls-Royce (i) Corniche II convertible.
ROLLS-ROYCE MOTOR CARS

1994 Rolls-Royce (i) Silver Spirit III saloon.
ROLLS-ROYCE MOTOR CARS

1994 Rolls-Royce (i) limousine.
ROLLS-ROYCE MOTOR CARS

the subsequent Phantom Vs and VIs being bodied by the newly merged firm. However, James Young built a few models, including four sedanca de villes which must have been the last of this design made anywhere in the world. Unlike the Phantom IV, the V was available to anyone able to afford the price of £8905-9394, and a total of 793 were made up to 1968, when it was replaced by the Phantom VI. This was little changed apart from separate air-conditioning in the front and rear compartments. In 1978 it received the enlarged engine of 6750cc, and was made up to February 1992 though production dwindled to around two or three cars per year in the 1980s. No price was officially quoted after 1974, because it varied so much with the extra features required by customers. In 1982 the makers gave a figure of 'not less than £125,000' and an enquiry in July 1988 elicited the reply 'around £350,000'. 373 Phantom VIs were made.

Integral Construction

The Silver Cloud had hardly gone into production in 1955 when work began on its successor. A prototype was running in the summer of 1957, but the new car did not go into production until the end of 1965. Called the Silver Shadow, it had a completely new full-width saloon body, and was the first Rolls-Royce to have integral construction. The bodies were 7.75in (125mm) lower, 7in (180mm shorter) and 3.5in (90mm) narrower than those of the Cloud, making a less distinctive car which did not stand out so much in the car park. This was what customers wanted, according to Rolls-Royce research.

Other new features included irs and a self-levelling system whereby the car returned to its normal level a few seconds after passengers had entered the rear compartment or luggage had been loaded into the boot. There were disc brakes all round, with triple hydraulic circuits. The engine and transmission were the only major parts of the Shadow which were virtually unchanged from the Cloud III. Capacity remained at 6230cc to 1970, when it was enlarged to 6750cc. The Bentley T Series was identical to the Shadow apart from the radiator, and the price differential was only £60.

The Shadow was originally made only as a 4-door saloon, but James Young converted 35 to 2-doors, and in March 1966 H.J. Mulliner/Park Ward brought out a 2-door saloon, followed by a convertible in September 1967. With a more powerful engine, these were renamed Corniche in 1971, and were made up to 1977 before being replaced by the Corniche II. These were more expensive than the Shadow saloons, and were made in much smaller numbers. Between 1966 and 1977 there were 1351 2-door saloons and 1737 convertibles, compared with 19,493 Silver Shadows. These figures include 2776 long-wheelbase Shadows with optional limousine division. In 1977, when the ordinary saloon became the Shadow II, the longwheelbase version was named the Silver Wraith II. Improvements included rack and pinion steering, split-level air conditioning and a front spoiler. Production of these second generation models was 8422 Shadow IIs and 2144 Silver Wraith IIs.

Like the Shadows, the Corniches had Pressed Steel bodies, but they were modified by Mulliner/Park Ward at their Park Royal premises, as were the Silver Wraith IIs.

Change of Ownership

At the end of 1970 Rolls-Royce Ltd went bankrupt due to problems encountered with an aero-engine contract, and no fault of the cars, which were selling well. The aero-engine side of the business was nationalised, and in May 1971 a new public company, Rolls-Royce Motors Ltd was floated to concentrate on car manufacture. It was headed by David Plastow, the successful director of the former car division. It was independent until August 1980 when it was bought by the big engineering group, Vickers Ltd. In 1975 they took the bold step of launching a new model which was nearly £10,000 more expensive than the Corniche, and double the price of a Silver Shadow. There was a long waiting list for the Corniche, and the makers were prevented by government regulations from increasing the price by more than 10 per cent. There were no restrictions on the price of a new model, though, hence the Camargue, a 2-door saloon with different styling by Pininfarina which was later extended to all Rolls-Royces. The Camargue was neither roomier nor faster than the Corniche, but had a certain appeal thanks to its exclusivity (about one built per week) and price. Introduced at £29,250, its price rose to £83,122 in 1985, this figure being maintained until it was discontinued towards the end of 1986. A total of 531 Camargues were made.

The Silver Shadow/Bentley T Series was the most successful Rolls-Royce ever made, selling more than 32,000 units before it was replaced in the autumn of 1980 by the Silver Spirit/Bentley Mulsanne. This had a new body styled by the Austrian engineer Fritz Feller, with a heavier look to the front end which was reminiscent of the Camargue. It was a little longer and wider, but the window area was increased by 30 per cent. The engine was the same as that of the Shadow. The long-wheelbase (by 100mm) version, successor to the Silver Wraith II, was known as the Silver Spur. These models were made without major change up to 1998, though in 1994 the Spur gained a turbocharger to become the Flying Spur, and in 1996 the name Silver Dawn was revived for the non-turbo saloon, formerly Silver Spirit. The Corniche was not made after 1995, although the name was revived in 2000 for a convertible and coupé based on the Bentley Azure, and using that car's 6750cc V8 engine. To replace the Phantom VI a number of long-wheelbase limousine conversions were offered by such firms as Robert Jankel Design, Hooper and Park Ward. The latter was the closest to a standard model, having a 148.5in (3770mm) wheelbase, and a price of nearly £190,000.

Rolls-Royce sales reached a peak of 3333 in 1988 (including Bentleys), then dropped drastically to about 1660 in 1991, since when they have climbed gradually, reaching 1918 in 1997, though the workforce was halved to about 2500 over the same period. Vickers decided to sell Rolls-Royce during 1997, as a much-needed new range would have required more investment than they could provide. After lengthy negotiations they found a buyer in BMW in 1998, but in an extraordinary 'auction' they were outbid by Volkswagen. Two months later the two German firms came to an agreement in which VW would retain control of Rolls-Royce until the end of 2002, when it would pass to BMW. However, BMW will have to find a new factory for its 2003 model Rolls-Royce, as VW will retain the Crewe plant. Before the VW take-over Rolls had already contracted with BMW to supply their 5379cc V12 engine for the new Silver Seraph. This arrangement will continue despite VW ownership. Introduced in the spring of 1998, the Seraph had a restyled 4-door saloon body, and was later available in a longer version which allowed for a division between front and rear seats.

NG

1999 Rolls-Royce (i) Silver Seraph saloon.
ROLLS-ROYCE MOTOR CARS

Further Reading
The Edwardian Rolls-Royce, John Fasal and Bryan Goodman, Fasal, 1994.
Rolls-Royce, the Derby Phantoms, Lawrence Dalton, Dalton Watson, 1991.
Rolls-Royce Silver Shadow, Graham Robson, Crowood AutoClassics, 1997.
Rolls-Royce and Bentley, Sixty Years at Crewe, Malcolm Bobbitt, Sutton, 1999.
Those Elegant Rolls-Royce, Lawrence Dalton, Dalton Watson, 1967.
Rolls-Royce, the Elegance Continues, Lawrence Dalton, Dalton Watson, 1971.
Coachwork on Rolls-Royce 1906–1939, Lawrence Dalton,
Dalton Watson, 1975.
Rolls-Royce Silver Cloud, Graham Robson, Osprey, 1980.

ROLLS-ROYCE (ii) (US) 1921–1931
Rolls-Royce of America Inc, Springfield, Massachusetts.

Rolls-Royce cars had been sold in America in small numbers since 1906, but the idea of making cars there only arose after World War I. Claude Johnson felt that the American market had a better future than the British, but the cars were very expensive there because of import duties. An American factory was the answer, and in 1919, a plant was bought from the American Wire Wheel Co. of Springfield, Massachusetts.

Production began in 1921, the first 25 cars being identical to the Derby-built Silver Ghost, with all chassis components imported. After that American-made magnetos, starters, and wheels were used, while the coachwork was always locally made, by leading firms, mostly fairly close to Springfield such as Merrimac, Biddle & Smart, and Willoughby. In 1923 Rolls-Royce of America set up their own body-building plant at Springfield, and no longer farmed the work out, although there were always some special requests for bodies from other firms, and in December 1926 they bought up Brewster who made the majority of bodies for American Rolls-Royce from then on. Brewster chose very English names for their various body styles, the Newmarket convertible sedan, Piccadilly roadster, Kenilworth sedan, and Oxford tourer.

In 1924 the Springfield coachwork factory offered eleven styles, priced from $12,930 to $15,880. Despite the absence of import duties, these were still the highest prices in America. The most expensive American car, the Locomobile 48, cost from $7900 to $11,200, while Pierce-Arrows ranged from $5250 to

1923 Rolls-Royce (ii) Silver Ghost salamanca permanent town car.
NATIONAL MOTOR MUSEUM

1929 Rolls-Royce (ii) Phantom I Derby speedster by Brewster.
NATIONAL MOTOR MUSEUM

1932 Rolls-Royce (ii) Phantom II sport sedan by Brewster on LHD chassis imported from Derby.
NATIONAL MOTOR MUSEUM

1950 Rolux 125cc 2-seater.
NICK GEORGANO

1980 Rom Carmel 1301 saloon.
NICK GEORGANO

with cars being assembled from stocks of parts for a few years longer. The last was not delivered until 1935. Production was 1241.

The Phantom II was never made at Springfield, as the company could not afford to tool up for the new chassis, but between 1931 and 1934 Derby supplied 125 lhd chassis to Rolls Royce of America. These were bodied mainly by Brewster, and were among the best-looking American Rolls-Royces made. Styles included the Newmarket convertible sedan, Newport town car, and Henley roadster.

Rolls-Royce of America changed its name to the Springfield Manufacturing Co. in August 1934, and less than a year later the new company went bankrupt. Sales and service of Rolls-Royce cars was taken up by New York dealer J.S. Inskip who had been president of Rolls-Royce America from 1931. He built about 20 bodies on imported Phantom III chassis between 1936 and 1945. His last efforts were two sports roadster bodies on the postwar Silver Wraith chassis.

NG

Further Reading
Rolls Royce in America, John Webb de Campi, Dalton Watson, 1975.
The American Rolls-Royce, Arthur W. Soutter, Mowbray, 1976.

ROLT (F) 1982–1983
Rolt S.A., Saillans.
This was an entirely conventional microcar produced during the French boom period. Very compact, it was a 2-seater with a rear-mounted 49cc engine and automatic transmission.
CR

ROLUX (F) 1938–1952
1938–1947 New-Map, Lyon.
1947–1952 Sté Rolux, Clermont-Ferrand.
1952 Sté de Construction du Centre, Montferrand, Puy-de-Dome.
When it first appeared in 1938, the New-Map microcar from the well-known motorcycle manufacturer was something of a novelty, but it certainly found favour in the austere postwar period. It first had a 100cc Fichtel & Sachs engine, and was produced both in Lyon and post–1945 in Geneva. In 1947 the name was changed to Rolux VB60 (also known as Microcar Baby). From 1950 the engine grew to 125cc, while the VB61 had a 175cc engine (requiring a restricted driving licence). Both motors were single-cylinder, 2-stroke, air-cooled and mounted in the tail and transmission was via a 3-speed gearbox and chain drive to the rear axle. The chassis was made up of welded tubes, the front suspension was by transverse leaf springs and the rear by coil springs. There were no doors, though a big car look was engendered by a Ford-style front end. In 1946 a saloon version of the VB60 was shown but never reached production. Having produced around 300 cars, after 1952 the company continued to make motorcycles and small 3-wheeled commercial vehicles.
CR

ROMANAZZI (I) 1953
Romanazzi, Bari.
Based on the Piaggio Ape delivery trike, Romanazzi added an enclosed body with a bench rear seat for two passengers, behind the scooter-seated driver.
CR

ROMAN DESIGNS (US) c.1996 to date
Roman A.D., Newport Beach, California and Ontario, California.
The Roman EB 110 kit car was a replica of the Bugatti EB 100 supercar. The kit was based on Pontiac Fiero running gear and was initially priced at $9000 for the basic kit. They were also available in assembled form. In 1997 Roman moved to Ontario, California, where they continued to sell the B 110 and a Lamborghini Diablo replica. The body package price dropped to $5500.
HP

ROMANELLI (CDN) 1970
Romanelli Motors Ltd, Montréal, Québec.
Italian-born Francesco Romanelli planned to make an ambitious sports car using his own design of aluminium alloy 6-litre V12 engine developing 520bhp, with a 5-speed transaxle gearbox. The body was a fibreglass 2-seater coupé, and top speed was said to be 203mph (327km/h). A price of $9000 was quoted, but only one prototype was made.
NG

$8000. Sales of the Springfield Silver Ghost were quite creditable, considering the high prices; 135 in 1921, 230 in 1922, and between 325 and 365 each year from 1923 to 1926. The total was 1703.

In design the American Silver Ghost tended to lag behind the British one, none of the Ghosts having 4-wheel brakes, nor the Autovac introduced on the Derby cars in 1924. The 12-volt electric system was changed to a 6-volt on the Springfield cars in 1924, which seems a retrograde step. The most important development came with the switch to lhd on 1925 models. This was costly, and ate into the small profit made on each car. Also the old rhd cars which were traded in were hard to sell.

The Phantom I, or New Phantom, did not go into production at Springfield until 1926, a year later than in England, and 4-wheel brakes were not offered until early 1927. The first 66 rear-braked Phantoms were later recalled and updated. However, it did have centralised chassis lubrication operated from the dashboard, and thermostatic radiator vents, which the Derby-built cars did not. Prices were higher than the Silver Ghost, at $13,835 for a chassis so that a complete car cost from $18,000 upwards. As with the Ghost, the Springfield Phantom I had a longer life than its British counterpart, being made until 1931,

ROM CARMEL (IL) 1974–1981

Rom Carmel Industries, Haifa-Tirat Carmel.
This was a successor to the SABRA, and like the last of these it was powered by a 1296cc Triumph engine. It had a fibreglass 4-door saloon body with a rather ugly rectangular grill, and was also made in delivery van and pick-up versions. In its early years production ran at about 1600 vehicles per year, but in its last full year, 1980, only 540 were delivered.

NG

ROMER (US) 1921

Romer Motors Corp., Danvers, Massachusetts.
Albert J. Romer was a mechanical engineer who, in 1920 had been a designer of the NORTHWAY car, simultaneously serving as an engineer for the MURRAY Motor Car Co., when he decided to produce a car of his own. This was the Romer, frequently confused with the better known ROAMER being built in Kalamazoo, Michigan, at the same time. The Romer had little originality in its design, was powered by a Continental 6-cylinder 7R L-head engine and rode on a 120in (3046mm) wheelbase. A complete line of open and closed models were featured in the Romer prospectus but it is more than likely that Romer cars completed were all touring models priced at $1975. Albert Romer acquired the Peters Autocar company of Bethlehem, Pennsylvania which had been marketing the PETERS, a midget car, at the same time transferring his manufacturing operations to Taunton, Massachusetts. It is extremely doubtful that any production either of Romers or Peters midget cars occurred and by August 1921 Romer was out of business.

KM

ROMI-ISETTA (BR) 1956

Maquinas Agricolas Romi, São Paulo.
Americo Emilio Romi made these microcars in Brazil, under licence granted by ISO Spa of Italy. They were powered by a 9.4bhp engine and can be counted among the first Brazilian-made automobiles, along with DKW-VEMAGs.

ACT

RONART (GB) 1986 to date

Ronart Cars Ltd, Bretton, Peterborough, Cambridgeshire.
Arthur Wolstenholme's Ronart W152 was the summation of his fascination with Mercedes-Benz racers, although it was not a replica of any one particular car. Instead, it looked like an amalgam of the great Grand Prix racers of the 1950s. Spyder created the backbone space frame chassis and the beautiful bodywork could be ordered in fibreglass, Kevlar or aluminium. The mechanical basis was the Jaguar XJ series, with straight-6, V12 or Rover V8 engines all capable of being fitted. The chassis could handle very large power outputs (one even had a V16 engine installed). Ronart also displayed a tandem 2-seater model called the Grand Prix Racer with V8 power but by 1999 this had still not entered production.

CR

RONTEIX (F) 1906–1914

J. Ronteix, Levallois-Perret, Seine.
Though small, the Ronteix was always more of a light car than a cyclecar, and never featured engines of less than four cylinders. The first had a capacity of 905cc and had transverse leaf front suspension. Its gear change system was unusual; the shaft from the clutch ended in a bevel gear which could mesh with any of three rows of teeth on the crown wheel. Final drive was by single-chain. This system was replaced in 1913 by a conventional sliding gearbox. Ronteix cars were quite successful in cyclecar races, finishing 2nd in the 1913 Cyclecar GP at Amiens, and 1st in the similar event at Le Mans. For 1914 three engine sizes were offered, of 966, 1130 and 1460cc. They had shaft drive, but chain drive was available at a lower price. The two smaller models were sold in England under the name CUMMIKAR.

NG

ROO (AUS) 1917–1918

The Roo Motor Car Manufacturing Co., Sydney, New South Wales.
W.B. Foulis who had made engines for marine and automotive applications since 1909 drew together a firm, managed by ex-racing driver Rupert Jeffkins, to build a light car powered by a 10hp flat-twin engine of his design, incorporating

1912 Ronteix 8hp chummy 4-seater.
NATIONAL MOTOR MUSEUM

1929 Roosevelt Eight coupé.
JOHN A. CONDE

light alloy pistons. The underslung chassis had a wheelbase of 100in (2540mm), a 3-speed gearbox was employed and the weight was 1344lb (611kg). A proving and publicity run to Melbourne was made but only two examples were built before internal conflict ended the firm. Jeffkins attempted a revival at Geelong in 1930 while the later SOUTHERN CROSS project involved Bill Foulis.

MG

ROOSEVELT (US) 1929–1930

Marmon Motor Co., Indianapolis, Indiana.
The Roosevelt, named after Rough Rider and former President Theodore Roosevelt, claimed to be the first straight-8 in America to sell for less than $1000, the claim rightfully made – by just five dollars, the Roosevelt sedan selling for $995 f.o.b. Indianapolis. Designed by Count Alexis DeSakhnoffsky, the Roosevelt was a handsome car featuring a lightning-rod motif in chrome across the radiator core and horizontal bonnet louvres. The Roosevelt range comprised the sedan, coupé, victoria and convertible and sales were excellent for a completely new line, approaching somewhere 'less than 24,500 units' according to Marmon historians Dr and Mrs George P. Hanley. The name was changed to Marmon-Roosevelt for 1930 and the Roosevelt suffix dropped for the 1931 model which became the Marmon 70.

KM

ROOSTER (F) 1989

Automobiles Rooster, Montpellier.
The oddly-named Rooster was a 2-seater coupé based around the body and running gear of a Fiat Uno. The Rooster's extreme wedge fibreglass body panels were placed over the Uno's existing metal panels, with the rear section cut away to allow a fastback coupé profile. The Fiat's front seats and instrumentation were retained, but the rear seats removed. Only three cars were built.

CR

1902 Roots & Venables 4½hp tonneau.
MALCOLM JEAL

1930 Rosengart coupé.
ROBERT STRAUB

1938 Rosengart LR4-R saloon.
NICK GEORGANO

ROOTLIEB (US) c.1994

Rootlieb, Inc, Turlock, California.
The Rootlieb Model T Speedster was a kit to transform original Model T chassis and engines to the rare Speedster body style. Prices started at $2600.

HP

ROOTS & VENABLES (GB) 1896–1904

Roots Oil Motor & Motor Car Co., London.
This car was made by James Dennis Roots and Cuthbert Edward Venables. Roots was a pioneer of the heavy oil engine who is said to have had one running in 1886. One was installed in a boat in 1890, and Roots supplied a number of engines to Vospers, later famous for their association with Thornycroft when they merged under David Brown ownership in the 1960s to become Vosper-

Thornycroft. He is said to have supplied engines to other car makers in 1894, but who these could have been is a puzzle, as there were no production cars in Britain at that time, and there is no record of oil engines being used on the Continent. However Roots was certainly a pioneer among British car builders. He had a 3-wheeler on the road early in 1896; called the Petrocar, it had a 2¼hp vertical single-cylinder oil engine and tiller steering. By April 1897, in partnership with Venables, he was advertising three designs of 4-wheeler, 2- and 4-seaters and a delivery van, as well as passenger and van versions of the 3-wheeler. They had 3hp engines, chain drive and tiller steering. Roots was keen to point out that his were the only cars to use oil motors, all other so-called oil motors using benzolene spirit. He used only kerosene and paraffin with a flash point of 73 to 150 degrees. 'The oil motor is the only safe motor' he said, 'benzolene spirit is dangerous'.

At the time when Roots began advertising, the only other British firms making cars were Daimler, the Coventry Motor Co. (Coventry Bollée) and Petter. The first two were based on foreign designs and the third, also an oil-engined car, was made in even smaller numbers than the Roots & Venables. The latter's small premises at Lambeth were unable to make many of the car's components, so the work was contracted out to B.S.A. in Birmingham. From October 1902 Roots & Venables cars were made completely in the ARMSTRONG-WHITWORTH factory at Newcastle-on-Tyne. The 1902 range consisted of the old 3½hp rear-engined model on solid tyres, a 4½hp front-engined car, also on solids, and a 7hp front-engined car on pneumatics. Their last year of production was 1904, when two models were made, with 5hp single-cylinder and 12hp 2-cylinder engines. J.D. Roots later became a consulting engineer and patent specialist.

NG

ROPER-CORBET (GB) 1911–1912

A car of this name was sold by the London & Parisian Motor Co. Ltd whose managing director was a Captain Bertram Corbet, but its origin is uncertain. It was of conventional design, with a 2412cc 15.9hp 4-cylinder engine and a Rolls-Royce-type radiator. One was exhibited at the 1911 Olympia Show on the stand of the coachbuilders Melhuish & Co., with cabriolet body.

NG

ROSE NATIONAL see NATIONAL (ii)

ROSENBAUER (A) 1950

Konrad Rosenbauer, Linz.
This company started life in 1908 making motors for fire-fighting equipment, and produced the Trio 3-wheeled delivery wagon in the 1930s. In 1950 it made a 3-wheeled coupé with a single rear wheel, a rear-mounted 250cc 10bhp engine and a 3-speed gearbox. The 2-seater featured a sloping nose and tail and a roll-top roof.

CR

ROSENGART (F) 1928–1955

1928–1936 Automobiles L. Rosengart, Neuilly, Seine.
1936–1955 Sté Industrielle de l'Ouest Parisien (SIOP), Paris.
Lucien Rosengart (1881–1976) was one of the most influential figures in the French motor industry, being a first-rate publicist as well as an engineer. He started a business in 1909 making screws and nuts especially for the motor industry, with a workforce of 60. During World War I he made a patent shell fuse and his workforce rose to 4500. He worked closely on this with André Citroën, and in 1919 helped him over a financial crisis, forming the SADIF group to raise 20 million francs. Without this aid it is possible that Citroën would not have become a manufacturer, and Rosengart was rewarded with a seat on the board of the SA André Citroën.

From 1923 to 1926 Rosengart was commercial consultant to PEUGEOT, while still running his screw factory. During this time he organised the purchase of the BELLANGER and DE DION-BOUTON factories, which led to a customised De Dion-Bouton Model JP being marketed briefly as a Bellanger.

In 1928 Rosengart decided to make a car himself, and engaged the engineer Jules Salomon who had designed the original Citroëns and the LE ZÈBRE. Salomon recommended a car the size of the Austin Seven, a category recently vacated by Citroën when they dropped their 5CV. Rather than design a new car Rosengart took out a licence from the British company. Herbert Austin was

A TEMPS NOUVEAUX...
FORMULES NOUVELLES!

PUISSANCE ACCRUE
CONSOMMATION RÉDUITE

VOICI LA
8-40 CV

Moteur : **4** cylindres
Puissance effective : **40 C.V.**
Reprises foudroyantes.
Toutes les côtes
en prise directe, jusqu'à 8 %.
Vitesse réelle en palier :
110 Kms à l'heure

8 LITRES aux 100 Klm.

*la plus confortable et la plus
économique des voitures
de grande puissance*

Rosengart

1939 Rosengart Supertraction saloon.
NICK GEORGANO

given a seat on the board. The first 100 cars were assembled from British-made parts, but thereafter the Rosengart 5CV was entirely French. Apart from semi-elliptic rear springs in place of the Austin's quarter-elliptics, the main differences were in styling; the Rosengarts had ribbon radiators from the start. The bodies were semi-panelled or fabric saloons and tourers with a delivery van added in October 1928, and sports models offered from 1929.

Production began in March 1928 in the former Bellanger factory with an optimistic forecast of an output of 60,000 cars per year, but in fact only 11,000 were made in two years. Production was running at 28 cars per day in June 1930, probably the high point of Rosengart's output. In 1931 he was said to have 1500 agents across France, with 250 of these in the Paris area.

In 1932 Rosengart brought out a small six with 1097cc 25bhp engine. This bore the same relationship to the four as did the Wolseley Hornet to the Morris Minor, a lengthened bonnet and chassis but similar bodies. Also in 1932 Rosengart became attracted by front-wheel drive. Again, he did not originate his own design, for which his factory was unsuitable, but bought from ADLER the rights to the 1504cc Trumpf and 1645cc Primus. These were made in small numbers up to 1935, with German Ambi-Budd or French bodies. They did not sell well; in 1935 only167 front-drive cars were made out of a total of several thousand Rosengarts. These were mostly the 747cc Austin-derived cars, the 8CV small six and the Superdix which used the 1645cc Adler engine driving the rear wheels, and French-built bodies by SICAL. The 5CV was made up to the war, with bodywork very different from the Austin Seven. This featured a pointed radiator grill from 1936 and some quite elegant cabriolet bodies which featured in concours d'élégance. In 1939 it was the smallest and cheapest French car in regular production. Prices ran from 13,950 to 18,530 francs, compared with 20,900 francs for the Peugeot 202. The small six with similar styling to the four was still available, and at the top of the range was the Supertraction, a handsome 2-door saloon or cabriolet with front-wheel-drive based on the Citroën 11CV running gear. Not more than 150 of these were made in 1939, out of a total of 5650 Rosengarts, though about 30 more were made in the first half of 1940. A handful of 4-door Supertractions were made for government officials and one for Lucien Rosengart's personal use.

NATIONAL MOTOR MUSEUM

ROSENGART, LUCIEN (1881 – 1976)

Lucien Rosengart was born in Paris on 11 January 1881, the son of the owner of a small precision engineering works. He attended the Lycée Charlemagne, but proved such a poor student that his father took him out of school and trained him for every job in the machine shop. At the age of 16 he began

inventing things, aiming at the automation of manufacturing processes. From 1896 to 1901 he was actually running the factory for his father.

A licensed driver from 1898 , he bought his first car, a De Dion-Bouton, and set up his own business, in Paris, in 1906. From a modest beginning, making buttons, washers, nuts, and bolts, he was soon making electric lighting sets for bicycles, flashlights with integral hand-operated generators, and cycle motors.

His wartime activities brought him in contact with André Citroën, and during a chance meeting in 1919, he was invited to join Citroën as special director in charge of finance. He left in 1923 to join Peugeot and take charge of its reorganization.

In the spring of 1926 he went, with other motor engineers and executives on a study tour of the USA, during which he met W.C. Durant, making a preliminary agreement to produce the Peugeot 5CV in Durant's New Jersey plant, but the scheme fell through. Later in 1926 Rosengart founded Peugeot Maritime, and helped establish the Salon Nautique boat show, serving as its president until 1952.

Dismissed from Peugeot in 1927, he was approached by Robert Bellanger, who was keeping his big factory active by subcontracting with De Dion-Bouton for chassis assembly. Rosengart purchased the plant and founded the Societé de Automibiles Rosengart. He secured manufacturing rights to the Austin Seven, retooled the plant, and began production.

After a visit to Frankfurt in 1931, where he met Hans Gustav Röhr, he signed a licence agreement for the front-wheel-drive Adler, adding it to his production. Adler supplied the engines and front suspensions, Later, Rosengart used Citroën power trains.

Rosengart came close to bankruptcy in 1936, and he hurriedly transferred the company's assets to a new corporation, Societé Industrielle de l'Ouest Parisien, which continued production of the Rosengart cars until 1939.

Rosengart spent World War II in the USA with his wife. When they returned to Paris in 1944, they found the Levallois plant in no condition to produce cars. Rosengart wanted to produce front-wheel-drive cars with Mercury V8 engines, but the government suggested he should make taxis. Disappointed and tired, he retired to the French Riviera, and spent his time painting landscapes and indulging his other hobbies. He died on 27 July 1976.

JPN

1954 Rosengart Sagaie cabriolet.

During the war Rosengart made some electric conversions of the 5CV, which he called the Electrirod, and at the 1946 Paris Salon he showed a restyled version of the 5CV. He also showed an enlarged Supertraction powered by a 3917cc Mercury V8 engine, but only two of these were made, a saloon and a cabriolet. A new version of the 5CV appeared in 1951. Called the Ariette, it had a modern-looking slab-sided 2-door saloon body and hydraulic brakes, but the engine was still the old side-valve 747cc unit whose 21bhp did not give it a very exciting performance. At nearly twice the price of a 2CV Citroën it was no bargain either, and only 237 were sold in 1953. For 1954 SIOP came up with a modified Ariette body in fibreglass powered by a 748cc ohv flat-twin CEME engine as used in police motorcycles, called the Sagaie. It gave nearly twice the power of the former engine, and a top speed of 74mph (119km/h), but it was still too expensive and very few were sold. SIOP sold about 200 bodies to Panhard who fitted their own 850cc flat-twin engine and marketed the car as the Panhard Scarlet. The last cars made by SIOP were coupés with the TRIPPEL fibreglass body and Panhard engine mounted at the rear, of which about 50 were sold under the name MARATHON in 1954 and 1955.

NG

ROSIER (F) 1952–1955

Monte Carlo rally and Le Mans champion Louis Rosier attempted to make a sports car under his own name. He used Renault 4CV mechanicals in an elegant and lightweight coupé body designed and made by the Turin coachbuilder Motto. Its extremely high price prevented any commercial success but Rosier made a barquette open version which he raced at the 1953 Le Mans 24 Hours. His final model was a coupé built over Renault Frégate mechanicals in 1955.

CR

ROSS (i) (US) 1906–1909

Louis S. Ross, Newtonville, Massachusetts.
This was a large steam car made by Louis S. Ross (1877–1927) who had achieved fame driving Stanley Steamers at Daytona Beach. He was one of the first American drivers to cover a mile in less than a minute. In 1906 he turned manufacturer, though he never incorporated a company and his output must have been very small. His car had a large bonnet under which, unusually, the 2-cylinder double-acting engine, boiler and tanks for fuel and water all lived. The Ross steamer had shaft drive and was made with 5-seater tourer or 2-seater runabout bodies.

NG

ROSS (ii) (US) 1915–1918

Ross Automobile Co., Detroit, Michigan.
This car was made by an offshoot of the Ross & Young Machine Co. which had been long established in Detroit. The Ross Eight had a Herschell-Spillman V8 engine and was made only in 5-seater form in its first season. For 1916 the body range was expanded to six styles, including a sedan and a town car. New owners from New York took over in 1917 and announced that the V8 would be replaced by a 6-cylinder Continental engine, but shortly afterwards came the news that the V8 had been re-instated. Whatever its power unit, the Ross did not survive the 1918 season.

NG

1914 Rossel (ii) 12/14hp tourer.
NICK BALDWIN

1903 Rothwell 6hp 2-seater.
NATIONAL MOTOR MUSEUM

c.1909 Rothwell 14hp tourer.
NATIONAL MOTOR MUSEUM

ROSSEL (i) (F) 1898–1899
Édouard Rossel, Lille.
The first car built by Édouard Rossel had a Daimler vertical 2-cylinder engine, but in 1899 he built a car using an engine said to be of his own design. He sold the rights to this to ROCHET of Paris whose first cars were said to be 'of Daimler type', so he had probably not changed it greatly from his first car. After giving up car manufacture Rossel built at least one steam tractor specially designed for pulling canal barges.

NG

ROSSEL (ii) (F) 1903–1926
F. Rossel et Cie, Sochaux-Montbéliard, Doubs.
SA des Automobiles Rossel, Sochaux-Montbéliard, Doubs.
Frédéric Rossel had worked for several years for PEUGEOT, including managing their Audincourt factory, when he set up as a car maker himself. While many of his contemporaries started small with a voiturette or light car, Rossel went straight for an expensive car powered by a 3955cc 20/26CV 4-cylinder engine, with 4-speed gearbox and chain drive. Both from its appearance and its quality, it was nicknamed 'la Mercedes française'. An unusual aspect was that it used a carburettor of Rossel's own design and manufacture. Over the next three years Rossel increased the size of his engines, with a 28/35CV four and two sixes, of 60 and 80CV. These had pair-cast cylinders and T-head valves and the larger had a capacity of 12-litres. Though of undoubted quality the Rossel never became well-known; however by 1908 they had branches in Paris, Mulhouse, Lucerne and New York, and later they supplied taxicabs to Vienna, for which Rossel was never paid. This was a serious blow to his finances, and obliged him to sell his Suresnes factory to Peugeot. This factory was used for making aircraft engines in partnership with a Monsieur Verdet. It is thought that no cars were made there.

Like many other manufacturers Rossel turned to smaller cars from about 1910. These were of 10, 12 and 16CV, with 4-cylinder engines and shaft drive. However, one large chain-driven car, the 7460cc 40CV six with over-square cylinder dimensions (120 × 110mm) remained in the catalogue at least until 1913.

From 1914 to 1918 Rossel made shells for the war effort, and returned to car manufacture after the war. He listed no fewer than seven models, from 1690 to 5516cc in the early 1920s, but not all of them may have been built. They were of old-fashioned design with side-valves and long-stroke engines, and Rossel lacked the finance to introduce more up-to-date designs. The last new model was the 3½-litre 17/45CV six of 1923, but it attracted very few customers. Rossel sold his factory to Peugeot in 1926, and subsequently worked for Berliet, Donnet and Mathis. He died in December 1940.

NG

Further Reading
Franche Comté, Berceau de l'Automobile, Raymond Dornier, Éditions l'Est Republicain, 1987.

ROSSELLI (I) 1901–1904
Emmanuel A. Rosselli Fabbrica Italiana di Automobili, Turin.
Rosselli was a leading Italian manufacturer of motorcycles from 1901 to 1910, and made a few light cars powered by V-twin engines from 3 to 7hp.

NG

ROTARY (i) (US) 1903–1905
Rotary Motor Vehicle Co., Boston, Massachusetts.
Unlike the ADAMS-FARWELL this car did not have a genuine rotary engine, but its design was unorthodox enough. Its 8hp vertical single-cylinder engine had two connecting rods and two crankshafts which rotated in opposite directions. The latter were geared to a central shaft which drove a conventional gearbox and live axle. Body styles were a 2-seater or a 4-seater rear-entrance tonneau priced at $1250 and $1500 respectively. An alternative name for the car, of which very few were made, was Intrepid.

NG

ROTARY (ii) (US) 1922–1923
Bournonville Motors Co., Hoboken, New Jersey.
Eugene Bournonville, a Belgian engineer who is credited with the invention of oxyacetylene welding and cutting apparatus, and who had lived in the United States for several years, was the inventor of a 5-litre 6-cylinder rotary-valve engine designed for use in an automobile. Toward this goal he formed his Bournonville Motors Co., completing a pilot model in time for display in New York City's Automobile Show for 1922. In Bournonville's design the solid sleeve – which was the rule in the heads of most sleeve-valve engines – was changed to an adjustable sleeve and shoe which acted as a seal. The prototype featured a 7-seater body designed by Bournonville himself, had a wheelbase of 130in (3299mm) and was fitted with wire wheels, otherwise comprising standard parts throughout. The car attracted considerable attention at its debut and carried a price of $6000.

In the autumn of 1922, Bournonville and his son drove the car on an endurance run from New York City to San Francisco with considerable success and the same prototype reappeared at New York's Auto Show in 1923 but with its price reduced to $3800. During 1923, a few other cars were completed but his enterprise was not successful.

Bournonville returned to Belgium and attempted to interest Minerva in his rotary-valve engine but was unsuccessful and returned to the United States where he died several years later.

KM

ROTHWELL (GB) 1901–1916
Eclipse Machine Co. Ltd, Oldham, Lancashire.
Originally the partnership of Shepherd, Rothwell & Hough, this company dated back to 1872. They made a variety of products including phonograph parts for Thomas Edison, bicycles, sewing machines and ticket punches. In 1896 the brothers Fred and Tom Rothwell examined a Benz, and later made components for one of Edward Pennington's Raft-Victorias. In 1901 they built the first of their own cars, a 6hp single-cylinder light car, which was followed in 1904 by a 10/12hp twin and by larger 4-cylinder models of 12 and 15hp, some of which used Aster engines. Their most successful model was the 4150cc 20hp (called originally 25hp) made from 1910 to 1916. The 4-cylinder engines with dual ignition were designed by A.J. Adams who had joined the company in 1905 and was also responsible for some attractive coachwork which was built on the premises. About 600 Rothwells were built, including some commercial vehicles, and most were sold locally. However, a few were exported to India and South Africa. Fred and Tom Rothwell died within four years of each other, in 1914 and 1918, and this put an end to their cars. One cannot imagine the Rothwell surviving for long in the 1920s, without a completely new design.

NG

ROTOR (GB) 1999 to date
RoToR Motive, Glasgow.
An ultra-light sports car in the Caterham Super Seven mould, the RoToR JT7 had a mid-mounted 2-litre Ford engine, a simple open 2-seater body with rollbar, and could accelerate to 60mph (97km) in 4 seconds.

NG

ROTRAX (GB) 1988 to date
1988–1991 Adams Rotrax, Bradford-on-Avon, Wiltshire.
1991 to date J.S. Rotrax, Bristol, Avon.
Ex-Marcos designer Dennis Adams bravely made his debut as a car maker with the Rotrax. It echoed some previous designs Adams had done for Glenfrome but immediately found favour with the Tonka toy generation. It boasted an immensely strong chassis and a chunkily-styled fibreglass body, Ford Cortina mechanicals and a huge ground clearance for potential off-roading. The 4 × 4 DAKAR was also developed from the Rotrax. A long-wheelbase 4-seater was later developed (called the Rotrax Safari, the 2-seater being renamed Sport). A manufacturing licence was also issued to a South African company.

CR

ROTUS (US) c.1993 to date
Rotus Ltd, Frederick, Maryland.
The Rotus was a Lotus 7-type kit car with a fibreglass body. It was originally intended for Mazda rotary engines, hence the name. Later variations included V6 and even V8 engines. With a weight of about 1380lbs (627kg), it made a very quick street car.

HP

ROUGH see ROYAL HEREFORD

ROUQUET (F) c.1920–1927
Charles Rouquet, Pau; Paris.
There were two distinct types of Rouquet. At Pau Charles Rouquet had a cycle factory where he also made some motorcycles, 3-wheelers and quadricycles, powered by Zurcher, Indra, Aubier-Dunne and Wilier engines. These were made until the mid–1920s, and then in 1927 a light 4-wheeled car was announced from 15 rue Lorumel, Paris, by Charles Rouquet, presumably the same man though this has not been proved. It had a 4CV 2-cylinder engine, 3-speed gearbox and tubular integral frame. Open and closed 2-seater bodies were offered, and one of the former survives today. Charles Rouquet also designed the 1920 CYCLAUTO.

NG

1904 Rover 8hp 2-seater.
NICK BALDWIN

ROUSSEAU (F) 1982–1985
J.M. Rousseau, Vincennes.
Vaguely inspired by the SS 100, this was an ill-formed neo-classic based on a VW Beetle chassis with a fibreglass body, sold in kit form.

CR

ROUSSEL (F) c.1908–1914
Éts Roussel, Charleville, Ardennes.
This regional manufacturer made conventional light cars with 10 and 12hp 4-cylinder engines. They had 2- or 4-seater bodies.

NG

ROUSSEY (F) 1948–1950
Roussey Frères, Meudon, Seine-et-Oise.
The Roussey – produced by a bicycle parts company – was one of the most ambitious of the immediate postwar economy cars that mushroomed in France. It was a 4-seater saloon of very simple construction. It was powered not by a motorcycle engine, as most such cars were, but by a new flat-twin 700cc air-cooled 2-stroke engine, on which each cylinder was fed by an inverted carburettor that eliminated the need to mix oil and petrol. Drive was by chain via a 4-speed transmission to the front wheels. The curious design featured a bulbous front end and a canvas roof over the four passengers. It did not enter production.

CR

ROUSSON (F) c.1910–1914
Rousson et Chamoix, Feurs, Loire.
Another small regional make of car, the Rousson was made in five models, all with 4-cylinder monobloc engines. They ranged in size from the 1460cc 8CV to the 3632cc 16CV, and were available with 2- or 4/5-seater open bodywork. The make was listed in the 1920 Motor Car Red Book, but there is no other evidence of postwar production.

NG

ROUXEL (F) 1899
Rouxel et Cie, Boulogne-sur-Seine.
Few companies can have had a shorter life than Rouxel et Cie, which was founded on 4 August 1899 and dissolved on 22 December the same year. The car was a voiturette powered by a single-cylinder 2¼hp Aster engine, but few can have been made.

NG

ROVER (GB) 1904 to date
1904–1945 The Rover Co. Ltd, Coventry.
1920–1925 The Rover Co. Ltd, Birmingham.
1945–1973 The Rover Co. Ltd, Solihull, Warwickshire.
1973–1975 Rover British Leyland UK Ltd, Solihull, Warwickshire.
1975–1978 Leyland Cars, British Leyland UK Ltd, Solihull, Warwickshire.
1978–1980 Jaguar Rover Triumph Ltd, Solihull, Warwickshire.
1980–1986 Light Medium Cars Division, BL Ltd, Solihull, Warwickshire; Cowley, Oxford.
1986 to date Rover Group Ltd, Cowley, Oxford.

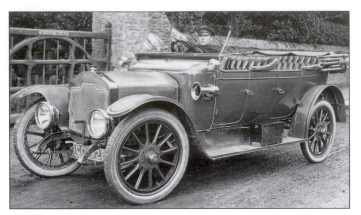

c.1912 Rover 12hp tourer.
NICK BALDWIN

c.1923 Rover 8hp coupé.
NATIONAL MOTOR MUSEUM

Rover is the oldest surviving name in the British vehicle industry, being seen first on a tricycle in 1884, while today it is the only name left from the conglomeration that made up British Leyland. The tricycles were made by the Coventry firm of Starley and Sutton, formed in 1877, which was the first Coventry factory to concentrate solely on cycles. 1885 saw one of the most significant machines in the history of transportation, John Kemp Starley's Safety bicycle. With its chain drive to the rear wheel and wheels of almost equal diameter it was a tremendous improvement over the traditional Ordinary bicycle, nicknamed the 'Penny-Farthing', and made cycling a practical proposition for millions of people.

Starley's business flourished in the l890s, and became a public company in 1896 as the Rover Cycle Co. Ltd. He had made a battery-powered tricycle in 1888, and nine years later he imported some Peugeot motorcycles with a view to starting production. This was delayed until after his death in 1901, but from November 1902 to late 1905 about 1250 2¾hp Rover motorcycles were made. 2-wheelers were revived in 1910, and made up to 1924, total production being 10,401. Pedal cycle production also ended in 1924, after 426,530 had been made.

Towards the end of 1903 Rover's new managing director Harry Smith decided to join the ranks of Coventry's car makers. Having no experience with cars or coachwork, he lured one of Daimler's designers, Edmund Lewis, to Rover. Lewis did not follow conventional lines, choosing a tubular backbone frame incorporating the 3-speed gearbox at the front, while the rear axle was bolted rigidly to the rear of the backbone. The engine was more conventional, an 8hp vertical single-cylinder unit of 1327cc. Lewis was appointed in December 1903, the first prototype was running by July 1904 and the 8hp went on sale in December 1904, at a price of £200. lt was soon joined by a cheaper and more conventional 6hp (780cc) with an armoured wood chassis which sold for £105. Lewis also designed larger cars for the 1905 season, the 4-cylinder 10/12hp and 16/20hp. The former was short-lived, but the 16/20 was made up to 1910. It provided Rover's first competition entries, when two cars ran in the 1905 Tourist Trophy, chief tester Ernest Courtis finishing 4th and Lewis 12th. Two years later Courtis won the TT, with a margin of 12 minutes over the 2nd place Humber. Harry Smith decided to withdraw from racing after this, and works-entered Rovers were not seen again on the circuits until the 1970s.

Edmund Lewis left Rover for Deasy at the end of 1905, but his designs persisted for several years. In 1908 Bernard Wright designed a 15hp car with four cylinders cast in pairs (Lewis' 16/20 had separately-cast cylinders) which was distinguished by a heart-shaped radiator which had first been seen on the 1907 TT cars. Two sleeve-valve engines were listed in 1911 and 1912, an 8hp

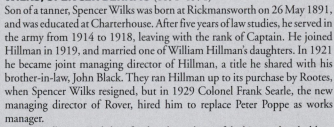

WILKS, SPENCER BERNAU (1891–1971)

Son of a tanner, Spencer Wilks was born at Rickmansworth on 26 May 1891, and was educated at Charterhouse. After five years of law studies, he served in the army from 1914 to 1918, leaving with the rank of Captain. He joined Hillman in 1919, and married one of William Hillman's daughters. In 1921 he became joint managing director of Hillman, a title he shared with his brother-in-law, John Black. They ran Hillman up to its purchase by Rootes, when Spencer Wilks resigned, but in 1929 Colonel Frank Searle, the new managing director of Rover, hired him to replace Peter Poppe as works manager.

W.D. Sudbury, a Yorkshire food trader and one of the biggest shareholders, was chairman of Rover. But neither Searle nor Sudbury were able to exercise adequate financial control and show a profit. Wilks was blamed for high production costs, but he convinced the board of directors to hire a chartered accountant, H.E. Graham, to come in and report on the costs; the losses were *not* caused in the factory. Graham was named finance director of Rover in 1932, and Spencer Wilks replaced Searle as managing director in January 1933. His steady hand brought Rover out of the economic depression, and he volunteered for the 'shadow factory' scheme in 1936.

After World War II, he ordered the development of the vehicle that became the Land Rover, secured a healthy budget for experimental gas turbine cars, and was named chairman of Rover in 1957.

He retired in 1962 and died in his home on the Scottish isle of Islay in 1971.
JPN

NICK BALDWIN

single and a 12hp twin. It is probable that components for these were supplied by Daimler as the cylinder dimensions (96 × 130mm) were used by Daimler; the reason why there was never a 4-cylinder sleeve-valve Rover was that Daimler would never have agreed to assisting a rival to their own fours. Very few sleeve-valve Rovers were made, and they were swept aside by Owen Clegg who arrived from Wolseley in 1910, and gave Rover one of their most successful designs. This was the Twelve, a 2297cc L-head monobloc four with a water-jacketed carburettor bolted directly to the cylinder block, worm final drive and electric lighting. It was a well-made conventional design, and by 1912 had replaced both the sleeve-valve models and the small single-cylinder cars. Sales jumped from 883 in 1911 to 1943 in 1914, all these being Twelves, though there was a short-lived 3307cc Eighteen, of which 150 were made in 1912 and 1913.

The Twelve was not considered large enough for military purposes, so Rover's wartime car production was devoted to the 12/16 hp Sunbeam, of which they built 1781, together with 500 Maudslay 3-ton trucks.

The Vintage Rovers
Owen Clegg left Rover for Darracq in 1912, but his Twelve was continued with little change up to 1924. The main differences between the pre- and postwar models was that the latter had detachable cylinder heads, and headlamps mounted on the side of the radiator shell rather than between the shell and the wings, as on most of its contemporaries. In 1920 Harry Smith and Jack Starley, son of J.K., decided to return to the light car market. They were put in touch with a young Birmingham engineer, Jack Sangster, who had designed an air-cooled flat-twin and was looking for a manufacturer. They bought an ex-Government factory in Birmingham where the chassis would be made, bodies to be fitted at Rover's Meteor works in Coventry. The car went into production early in 1920 as the Rover Eight. Between then and 1925 more than 17,000 were made, outselling the Twelve.

The Eight had a 998cc flat-twin engine whose cylinder heads projected through cut-outs in the bonnet sides. The final drive was by shaft to a worm gear rear axle. At £300 it was more expensive than the average cyclecar, but it was more of a real car. An electric starter was optional from 1923. The prices were steadily reduced so that the 1924 models, which had 1130cc engines, cost only £146. Body styles included open 2- and 4- seaters, a closed 2-seater coupé and a delivery van. Between 1921 and 1925 the basic design was made in Germany by PETER & MORITZ, though their capacity was slightly larger, and later models had water-cooling.

The Eight helped Rover to record sales, which reached 6466 in 1922 and 6749

1929 Rover Six 15.7hp fabric saloon.
NICK BALDWIN

in 1924. More than 5000 of the 1924 cars were Eights. However, the Eight had a deadly rival in the Austin Seven which offered four cylinders and was slightly cheaper, as well as having a much larger dealer network. At first Starley's response was to offer a car at the other end of the price range, a large and heavy 3446cc six costing £1050 whose only point of distinction was the use of front-wheel brakes. Shown at the 1923 London Motor Show it attracted no interest, and only three were made. Starley's next step was the more obvious one of putting a 4-cylinder engine in an enlarged Eight chassis. The engine was a conventional pushrod ohv unit of 1074cc developing 20bhp in its original form. It was known as the 9/20 from 1924 to 1927, and with capacity enlarged to 1185cc, as the 10/25 from 1928 to 1933. It was less distinctive than the air-cooled Eight, but kept the Rover company going through some very difficult years.

The designer of the 9/20 is not known, for Sangster had left Rover in 1922; it was probably the work of a committee working under works manager Mark Wild. There is however, no doubt about the authorship of Rover's other 1920s car, the 14/45. This was the work of Norwegian-born Peter Poppe, who had

WILKS, MAURICE FERNAND CARY (1904–1963)
Younger brother of Spencer Wilks, Maurice was born in Hayling Island on 19 August 1904, and educated at Malvern College. As a youngster of 13, he helped Don Francis design a motorcycle with a pressed-steel frame (which later formed the basis for the Francis-Barnett motorcycle).

He went to Detroit to get experience in the American motor industry, and worked for General Motors from 1926 to 1928. He joined Hillman as a planning engineer in 1928, and stayed on when his brother left. However, Spencer offered him the role of chief engineer if he would come to Rover, which he did in 1930.

Together they redirected company policy and gave the Rover name a new image. Engineering policy was turned around from a model line-up of frequently changing cars of widely scattered prices, to concentrate on a tight range of mid-range quality cars with continuity in concept and design. He modernised the Rover cars in 1947–48, led the creation of the P4 and the big P5, and supervised the development of gas turbine cars and the Land Rover range.

He died suddenly in his holiday-home on Anglesey on 8 September 1963.
JPN

NICK BALDWIN

1936 Rover Twelve sports saloon.
NICK BALDWIN

1947 Rover 12hp sports tourer.
NICK GEORGANO

been a partner in the engine building firm of White & Poppe and who, like Sangster, brought his design complete to Rover. It was an interesting unit, with a single high-mounted camshaft, valves inclined at 90 degrees and hemispherical combustion chambers. It should have been a recipe for high-performance, but the 2132cc unit developed little over 40bhp, and mounted in a heavy frame it seemed definitely underpowered. In its original 1925 form it was known as the 14/45, and when capacity was enlarged to 2413cc, as the 16/50. About 4140 were made between 1925 and 1928, some 14/45 chassis being fitted with 16/50 engines. The 14/45's chief claim to fame was that one made 50 consecutive ascents of Bwlch-y-Groes hill in Wales, thereby earning its makers the Dewar Trophy presented by the Royal Automobile Club (they were to win it again in 1950 for their first gas turbine car). Poppe's next design for Rover was a more conventional side-valve six of 2023cc. Launched at the end of 1927 it was cheaper to make and easier to service, as well as being smoother running. Known initially as the 2-litre, it evolved into the Light Six by 1930. This was a striking-looking 2-door saloon with raked windscreen and cycle-type wings which became known as the Blue Train Rover after one had beaten the famous *Train Bleu* from St Raphael to Calais in 1930. Like many Rovers of its time the Light Six had a Weymann fabric body, and the rapid deterioration of these earned the company a bad name.

The Wilks Era

By 1928 Rover's financial position was desperate; no dividend had been paid since 1923, and in January the shareholders called an angry meeting at which Colonel Wyley, the Chairman since 1909, resigned. Colonel Frank Searle was appointed joint managing director with Jack Starley, but the latter resigned in 1929, and Searle, with business experience but none of the motor industry, needed a general manager. Although he was not long with the company he probably saved it from extinction by his choice of general manager, Spencer Wilks. He had run Hillman from 1919 until it was acquired by the Rootes brothers in 1927. Also from Hillman came his younger brother Maurice who was an engineer, and and another engineer, B.H. Thomas, who provided Spencer Wilks with the car he needed to fill out the Rover range.

This was a small six, the 1410cc Pilot which came between the 10/25 and the 2-litre, and used an enlarged 10/25 engine in a slightly modified chassis. It had

little performance, even when the engine was enlarged to 1577cc from 1933, but it started a line of small sixes which were made up to 1938. 4396 Pilots were made in 1932 and 1933. There was also a high-performance version with the larger engine in a lowered chassis, known as the Speed Pilot, of which 204 were made in 1933 only. Wilks' philosophy was quite different from that of Searle; the latter believed that Rover should make larger numbers of relatively cheap cars, effectively competing with Morris and Austin, but Wilks saw the future in terms of medium-priced quality cars, and this was the policy followed once he became Managing Director, in January 1933. Searle's policy led to massive over-production; in 1930 the Rover factories were making 280 cars per week while the dealers could not sell more than 55 per week. In 1931 more Rovers were made than ever before, 10,144, but they simply piled up, unsold, in dealers' showrooms. Most production in the period 1929 to 1933 was devoted to the 10/25, which became the Family Ten and Ten Special in 1933. The Weymann bodies were replaced by a cheaper Pressed Steel saloon for 1931, and the chassis was lowered and widened, but still the cars did not sell. Total production was around 15,000.

Searle's other attempt to reach the mass market was the abortive Scarab, a return to the cyclecar theme. It had an 839cc air-cooled V-twin engine mounted at the rear of a ladder-type chassis with all independent suspension. The body was a simple open 4-seater, and the whole car was crude and devoid of frills, as it had to be to get the price down to the target of £85. In fact, when it was exhibited at the 1931 London Show it was priced at £89, still lower than any other British car. Searle had talked airily about a production of 30,000 per year, but public response was not favourable, and only six prototypes were ever made.

At the top of the range were the sixes, the Light Six which lasted for only the 1930 season, and the larger Meteor and Speed 20. There was a complex permutation of engines and chassis, with at least seven different body styles. The engines were 2023 and 2565cc, which in the Meteor powered mainly tourers, saloons and limousines, while the Speed 20 followed the familiar recipe of using the most powerful engine in the shortest chassis. By 1934 there were servo brakes and an underslung frame; the Speed 20 sports tourer looked more like a Lagonda than a Rover, and might have given serious competition to makes such as Alvis and Lagonda, but Wilks preferred to concentrate on saloons, and very few Speed 20s were made. They were assembled at Rover's London service depot.

Among the bodies available on the Speed 20, and also on the smaller Speed Pilot, was a 2-door coupé by Carbodies. One of these won the coachwork competition which concluded the 1933 RAC Rally at Hastings. It became known as the Hastings coupé, and so impressed the Wilks brothers that its lines were imitated on all the Rover sports saloons up to the end of the P3 series in 1949. If the Hastings coupé gave the impetus to Rover styling in the 1930s, the Wilks-era engineering was established in the 1934 models, 10, 12, 14 and Speed 14, which were announced in the autumn of 1933. They had new engines of 1389 and 1496cc in the 10 and 12, while the 14 used the ex-Pilot 1577cc six. The new engines had a common stroke of 100mm, and were designed to be 'stretchable', so that by increasing the bore and the number of cylinders a whole range of sizes from 10 to 20hp could be obtained. All the new Rovers had underslung frames, constant mesh 4-speed gearboxes with freewheels and spiral-bevel rear axles to replace the traditional worm. The 6-light saloon bodies on the 10 and 12 were still rather upright, but there were also sports saloons which had more of the Hastings coupé about them, and sports tourers. The 14 carried a wider range of bodies including 4- and 6-light streamlined saloons, and all models were available in chassis form for outside coachbuilders to work on.

For 1937 the Speed 14 was replaced by two new 6-cylinder engines in the 100mm family, the 2147cc 16 and the 2512cc Speed 20. With 4- or 6-light saloon bodies these carried Rover up to the outbreak of war, though a small number of Tickford drophead coupé bodies were made on the 14, 16 and Speed 20 chassis. The 12 also acquired the new styling, though not the drophead body, and only the 10 carried on with the older upright 6-light saloon body. The new styling reached the 10 for 1939, in saloon and fixed-head coupé forms. All these bodies were made for Rover by Pressed Steel. 1939 models featured synchromesh gearboxes, built-in jacks, automatic chassis lubrication and, on the top models, fitted suitcases. Spencer Wilks' plan had worked, aided by the design work of Maurice Wilks, B.H. Thomas and Robert Boyle. From the confused range and near bankruptcy of the early 1930s, Rover had emerged as a respected marque catering to the discriminating upper middle class market.

The
10' 25 h.p.
Rover

1958 Rover 90 saloon.
NICK BALDWIN

Sales rose encouragingly, from 4960 in 1933 to 11,103 in 1939, and profits over the same period from £7511 to £205,957.

The short-lived 1940 models were distinguished by disc wheels, and these were also seen on the postwar models. Rover's Coventry factory had been all but destroyed by bombing, so in 1945 they restarted car production in a shadow factory at Solihull which they had used during the war to make components for Bristol aero-engines. The new cars were very similar to the 1940 offerings, though the Speed 20 did not reappear. Nor did the Tickford dropheads, though a small number of sports tourers were made on the 12 chassis in 1947 only. A total of 13,335 were made of the 10, 12, 14, and 16 between December 1945 and January 1948, when they were replaced by the 60 and 75. Known as the P3 series, these were gap-fillers before an all-new postwar model could appear. In looks they were very like the previous models, but under the bonnet there were new inlet-over-exhaust engines of 1595 and 2103cc, the brakes were hydro-mechanical and front suspension was independent by coils. Although similar in appearance, the P3 bodies shared very few common panels with the earlier cars, being wider at the front and narrower at the back. They are always known as P3s, but the identity of the P1 and P2 is less certain. At one time it was thought that these designations referred to the first and second generation of Wilks cars (1934 and 1937), but it is now thought that P stands for Postwar. P1, therefore, is the original postwar model, and P2 a re-engined version of it which never went into production. Fewer P3s were made than P1, 9111 between February 1948 and October 1949.

The Auntie Rovers
In late September 1949 Rover launched the P4 which used the 2103cc 75 engine in an all-new body which owed its styling to the Raymond Leowy-designed Studebakers. Indeed Maurice Wilks was so impressed with the Studebaker that he imported a 1948 Champion and mounted its body on a P4 chassis during the latter's development trials. A feature not borrowed from Studebaker was the 3-headlamp arrangement, with a cyclops' eye in the centre of the grill. This, together with the slab-sided styling and column gear-change made the P4 the design that would last for fourteen years and about 130,000 cars. By the time the last of the series was withdrawn in 1964 the P4 had become one of Britain's best-loved cars known affectionately as the 'Auntie Rover' because its dignified way of going about things was associated with aunts and great-aunts.

Auntie's shape remained basically the same throughout her life, though there were several revisions to the front end, and 1955 models had a less sloping boot and larger rear window. The cyclops' eye was dropped early in 1952, and the gearchange was moved to the floor from 1954. Hydraulic brakes replaced the hydro-mechanicals in 1951, and vacuum-servo assistance arrived in 1955, with discs at the front from 1960. For the 1957 and 1958 seasons only, there was a 2-speed plus overdrive automatic transmission on the 105R. Otherwise most changes were concerned with the power unit, of which there were six different sizes and eight designations. The 75 was joined by a 4-cylinder 1997cc 60 from 1954 to 1959, and this gave way to the 80 (1960–62) which used the 2286cc Land Rover-based ohv engine. The 4-cylinder models were rather sluggish and are not highly sought-after today. The 90 (90bhp, 90mph = 145km/h) had a 2639cc 6-cylinder engine and was the first to have vacuum-servo brakes. The 105R was the automatic version, and the 105S had the same 2639cc engine with overdrive, two-tone paint and a speed of 100mph (161km/h). The final models were the 95 and 110, with 102 or 123bhp versions of the 2625cc engine, made from 1962 to 1964.

Larger and Faster Rovers
Successful though it was, the P4 catered for one market only, and during the 1950s Spencer Wilks considered making both smaller and larger cars to widen the marque's appeal. The smaller was quickly rejected (although the idea was revived in the 1960s), but work went ahead on a larger and more expensive model which was code-named P5. This appeared for 1959 as a 4-door saloon powered by a 115bhp 2995cc version of the familiar inlet-over-exhaust engine. The body bore a family resemblance to the P4s, but was wider and heavier, and was the first Rover to adopt unitary construction. It was well described by Michael Sedgwick as a 'hefty unitary barge beloved of British officialdom'. Early cars had drum brakes, but most had servo-assisted discs at the front, while power steering was available from 1961 models onwards. Output went up to 134bhp on the 1962-65 3-litre Mk 2 range, which included a coupé as well as the saloon. This was curiously named, for it had four doors, and was essentially a saloon with lowered roofline, a sharper slope to front and rear screens, and two-tone paintwork, although this was also available, in a different pattern, on the saloons.

The 3-litre was made up to 1967 (48,541 made, of which only 7983 were coupés), and for 1968 was replaced by the 3.5-litre, which used the 160bhp

1963 Rover 2000 saloon.
NICK BALDWIN

3528cc light alloy Buick V8 engine in the same bodies as the 3-litre. Rights to manufacture the V8 were acquired by Rover Managing Director William Martin-Hurst from General Motors in 1965; the Americans were only too glad to get further mileage out of the engine, which had been used in the Buick Special, Oldsmobile F-85 and Pontiac Tempest, but dropped after three years when the public turned away from compact cars. Available with automatic transmission only, the 3.5 had a top speed of 110mph (177km/h), and was made up to 1973. The proportion of coupés to saloons was much higher than in the 6-cylinder range, 9099 to 11,501.

The other new Rover of the 1960s was a complete break with tradition. A new generation of engineers came to the fore in the 1950s, among them David Bache, Spencer King and Peter Wilks, nephew of Spencer and Maurice. They saw the need for a cheaper Rover which would not be a downgraded P4, as the 60 was, but a compact and modern design in its own right, appealing to the younger executive and to the export market. Work on the P6 began in 1958, although it was not released to the public until October 1963. It featured an all-new single-ohc 4-cylinder engine of 1978cc developing 90bhp, with an all-synchromesh 4-speed gearbox, servo-assisted disc brakes all round, and a

'Spen' king at the wheel of the T.1. gas turbine car.
NATIONAL MOTOR MUSEUM

KING, CHARLES SPENCER (born 1925)

Charles Spencer King was the son of a solicitor and a nephew of Spencer Wilks of Rover. On leaving Haileybury School, he joined Rolls-Royce as an apprentice in 1942. At that time, no cars were made, but he had the opportunity to work on parts for the experimental Dart turbojet engine. He joined Rover in 1945 and assisted F.R. Bell in the JET 1 gas turbine car project, remaining in the experimental laboratories of Rover and helping to create the T.3 4-wheel drive turbine car in 1956. He was named head of Rover Advanced Vehicles but was taken off gas-turbine projects in 1959 when he was promoted to chief engineer of new vehicle projects.

He had nothing to do with the P5, but everything to do with the P6, which became the Rover 2000 production car in 1963. He led the Range Rover project, and then transferred to Standard-Triumph as director of engineering in 1968, leading the teams that created the TR6, Stag, and TR7. When British Leyland swallowed up Rover, he became a director and chief engineer of Rover-Triumph. On the formation of Leyland Cars in 1975, he was named director of engineering and development. But it was a time of regression for the company, and he had little outlet for his creative talent. One major accomplishment was the twin-cam cylinder head for the Triumph Dolomite Sprint.

In 1979 he was named vice chairman of BL Technology and developed the ECV 1, ECV 2, and ECV 3 prototypes.

He retired at the end of March 1985, but kept himself occupied as a consultant on gas turbines and aluminium vehicle structures.

JPN

Further Reading
'The Mind Knows No Bounds', David Burgess-Wise,
Automobile Quarterly, Vol. 33, No. 4.

1968 Rover P5B coupé.
NICK BALDWIN

De Dion rear axle. (Another link with De Dion was that, from 1964, the Société Franco-Britannic, who sold Rovers in France, had their service depot in the old De Dion-Bouton factory at Puteaux.) The body was lower than any previous Rover, and was made up of a steel skeleton to which the panels were fitted. The skeleton could be driven as a complete unit before the panels were installed. The idea had already been used by Citroën on their DS and ID models. Sold as the 2000, the P6 soon became the best-selling Rover ever, and a total of 327,808 were made up to 1972.

1966 saw the 2000TC with twin-carburettor engine giving 124bhp and 110mph (177km/h); this model was not available with the automatic transmission which could be had on the regular 2000. The fastest car to use the 2000 body was the 3500, also known as the Three Thousand Five, which was powered by the 3½-litre V8 engine, and could reach 117mph (188km/h) in its original form (1968–70), and 121mph (195km/h) in its final version, the 3500S made from 1972 to 1976. Total production of the P6B, as the V8s were officially known, was 80,100. These cars were very popular with the British police, as were their successors, the SD1 series. Only one body style was ever offered on the P6, a 4-door saloon, although FLM Panelcraft made about 150 estate car conversions on the 2000 and 3500, and one 2000 2-door convertible, and there were a few one-off coupés by Graber and Zagato.

The P6 gave Rover a car with which to re-enter the competition field. The works Competition Department was in fact founded in 1962, before the P6 appeared, and ran P5s in several international rallies including the 1962 East African Safari and Liège-Sofia-Liège in 1962 and 1963, 1962 RAC and the 1964 Spa-Sofia-Liège. Their best results were a class win and 6th overall in the 1962 Liège-Sofia-Liège (Ken James/Mike Hughes). The P6 was more suited to rallying, and from 1964 to 1966 there was a works team in many of the major international events. Roger Clark and Jim Porter finished 6th overall in the 1965 Monte Carlo, winning their class and the Production Touring Car category, while in the same year's Alpine Andrew Cowan and Brian Coyle came 3rd overall and first in the Grand Touring class in a 2000TC. Rover entered seven cars in the 1966 Monte Carlo, but the best place was only 10th, and they cancelled their entries for the rest of the season.

The Competitions Department was closed down, but four years later, now under the British Leyland flag, a 3500 was campaigned in saloon car racing. This had a 4.3-litre Traco-Oldsmobile engine, essentially a tuned version of the V8, and a new lightweight body with flared wings and wheel arches. Output was 360bhp, and Roy Pierpoint drove it to a number of victories in the 1970 season British Saloon Car Championship. A second car ran in 1971, and achieved the remarkable feat of leading the Marathon de la Route for 16 hours, having a three lap lead over the works Porsches, until severe propshaft vibration forced its retirement. Unfortunately BL closed its Competition Department before this car could prove itself. It was to be ten years before Rovers were again seen in racing.

Prototypes and Experimental Cars

The postwar years saw a number of interesting Rover prototypes, beginning with the little M-type coupé. Tested in 1945–6, this had a tiny 4-cylinder engine of 699cc and 28bhp, using the same inlet-over-exhaust layout as the larger engines.

NICK BALDWIN

BACHE, DAVID (1925–1994)

David Ernest Bache was the leading stylist at Rover during the years 1954 to 1981, when their most significant postwar models were being made. He was born in Worcestershire in June 1925, the son of the Aston Villa and England footballer Joe Bache who won an FA Cup winners' medal. David joined Austin as an engineering apprentice in 1948, and spent six years with the Birmingham firm before going to Rover's styling department where he worked on the P4, though he was allowed only limited scope, as Rovers were meant to be discreet, not eye-catching. He had more scope with the design of the P5 saloon. Working under the guidance of Maurice Wilks, he took his inspiration from the Pinin Farina prototypes on the P4, and produced a bulkier and more impressive design than the P4, eminently suitable for the ministerial transport than many P5s provided. His next commission was the advanced P6 saloon which was to give Rover a younger image and appeal to the up-and-coming executive who did not wish to drive a smaller version of the boss' car. An admirer of American cars, Bache drew some ideas from Virgil Exner's 1956 Chrysler Dart prototype, though Wilks talked him out of using tail fins, and the rounded front end was replaced by a low horizontal grill.

The successful and trend-setting P6 was followed by the even more significant Range Rover introduced in 1970. Bache and Spencer King had their work cut out to convince the cautious Rover management that there were many customers for 'a glorified Land Rover costing over £2000', but it turned out to be a highly influential design as well as successful aesthetically. It is the only car to have been exhibited as a work of art at the Louvre. Bache was also responsible for the SD1 hatchback, and for several designs which did not see production. These included the P8, a large saloon intended to replace the P5, and the mid-engined BS sports coupé.

He was perhaps less successful with more popular cars, and his work on the Metro and Maestro were worthy rather than inspiring. He also produced designs for Leyland trucks and buses.

In 1981 David Bache became disenchanted with the uncertain atmosphere at Leyland, and left to form his own international design consultancy, David Bache Associates.

He was married, with two sons and a daughter.
NG

NICK BALDWIN

NICK BALDWIN

DAY, GRAHAM (born 1933)

Graham Day was 53 years old before he had any connection with the motor industry, and was part of it for only five years, but became widely known for shrinking the British motor industry down to a single, manageable and profitable corporation – though too small to remain viable for long.

He was born on 3 May 1933, at Halifax, Nova Scotia, as the son of a former Essex stockbroker's clerk who had emigrated to Canada for health reasons. He attended Queen Elizabeth High School and graduated from Dalhousie University in Halifax in 1956, with a law degree. He joined a local firm as a clerk and became a defence lawyer in the supreme court of Nova Scotia within two years.

In 1964 he joined Canadian Pacific and worked in hotel management, truck fleet management, shipping, and vessel procurement. In 1971 he became chief executive of Cammell Laird Shipbuilders, leaving in 1975 to serve as vice president of the British government's organisational committee for shipbuilding, returning to Canada after two years. He became a professor of business administration and lectured on maritime transport at Dalhousie University.

In 1980 he became president of Chantiers Davie at Lauzon, Quebec, and vice president of Dome Petroleum. Three years later he was invited back to the UK as managing director of the state-owned British Shipbuilders. He streamlined it by closing 30 shipyards and workshops and cutting the payroll from 60,000 to 9000 in a little more than two years.

Under state ownership, British Leyland's losses and debts became a matter for decision-making at the highest level. Ford Motor Co. made a bid for Austin-Rover and General Motors made an offer for Land Rover. Prime Minister Margaret Thatcher refused to sell to foreigners, and picked Graham Day to sort things out. He was named president of British Leyland on 1 May 1986, and renamed it The Rover Group on 10 July 1986.

Under his leadership, Rover's dependence on Honda Motor Co. for its products became near total (except for Land Rover). In March 1988, the government agreed to sell its 99.8 per cent stake in the Rover Group to British Aerospace for £150m while agreeing to inject an additional £800m in aid to Rover.

Graham Day left in 1991, handing over to George Simpson.

JPN

EDWARDES, MICHAEL (born 1930)

If anyone could have saved British Leyland, it was Michael Edwardes. Clear-headed and fearless, he dared to draw the conclusions that his predecessors had evaded – but for reasons beyond his control, BL ended in failure.

Born and raised in South Africa, he went to work for the local branch of the Chloride group after getting a law degree, and made a career with Chloride, getting a seat on the board in 1969, becoming chief executive in 1972, and chairman in 1974. He tripled its profits in five years.

In October 1977 Leslie Murphy, chairman of the national Enterprise Board which held a 95 per cent stake in BL, decided that BL needed new management. Michael Edwardes accepted, on condition that he could remain non-executive chairman of the Chloride group during his three-year contract to reform BL.

Edwardes took office at BL on 1 November 1977, and gave himself just two weeks to size up the problems and draw up a strategy for survival. With uncommon alacrity, he set about cutting losses, and ordered the closing of the former Standard-Triumph plants at Speke Road (Merseyside) and Canley, the Coventry Engine plant, Vanden Plas, Rover's Solihull plant, and the MG factory at Abingdon. He kicked the Morris Marina, Triumph Toledo, Austin Maxi, and Allegro off the agenda.

Before the end of November 1977, he began talks with Chrysler about cooperative schemes, then turned to Vauxhall in 1978. They failed because GM planned to reinforce Vauxhall through Opel, and Chrysler was trying to forge a deal with Peugeot for the sale of all its European assets. He sold Alvis Ltd to United Scientific Holdings Ltd in May 1981, and offloaded Coventry Climax, Prestcold, and Aveling-Barford.

After pouring £1771 million into BL from 1975 to 1981, the British government spent another £900 million to modernise the Cowley plant for a joint venture with Honda Motor Co. Ltd. The deal with Honda gave BL new products and a lot of breathing space, but no final solution. Michael Edwardes did not stay on long enough to dispose of Jaguar and Rover, for he resigned from BL on 1 October 1982. His responsibilities were split in three: Sir Austin Bide of Glaxo food and pharmaceuticals was named chairman; Ray Horrocks was put in charge of cars, and David Andrews of commercial sales.

Edwardes returned to Chloride, but only briefly, for on 1 April 1984 he was appointed president of ICL (International Computers, Ltd).

JPN

1977 Rover SD1 3500 saloon.
NICK BALDWIN

1986 Rover 820Si saloon.
NICK BALDWIN

The 2-door body seated four passengers, and the car had a top speed of 60mph (97km/h). Several factors prevented it from going into production, including the Government's insistence on a flourishing export trade, for which the M would not have been suitable, and the change in taxation from a horsepower-based sliding scale to a flat rate in 1948. This eliminated one of the M's chief *raisons d'être*, and only three prototypes were made.

1950 saw the first of the Rover gas turbine cars, for which the company became more famous than any other European manufacturer. Their experience with gas turbines dated back to 1940, when they worked on Frank Whittle's original aero-engine, but in 1943 they exchanged this project with Rolls-Royce, receiving in return the contract for the Meteor tank engine. They retained their expertise, though, and in 1950 a small gas turbine was mounted in a P4 chassis. It was too bulky to fit under the bonnet, so was mounted behind the driver, which meant that the body became a 2-seater roadster. Registered as JET 1 it was demonstrated before the RAC's Technical Committee in March 1950, and earned the company their second Dewar Trophy. Two years later it was seen again, with an updated front end, and taken to Belgium where Spen King drove it at 152.2mph (244.93km/h). Two turbine-powered P4 saloons followed, T2 with a front-mounted engine and T2A whose turbine was mounted in the boot.

In 1953 a separate company, Rover Gas Turbines Ltd, was set up to develop turbine engines for fire pumps, emergency generators etc, and was responsible for the later cars. These included the T3 coupé of 1956, which had a purpose-designed fibreglass coupé body and 4-wheel drive, and the T4, a 4-door saloon of 1961 which had front-wheel drive and the body of a prototype P6. In 1962 the T4 was demonstrated at the Le Mans circuit, and the Automobile Club de France offered a prize for the first gas turbine car to average 93mph (150km/h) during the 24-hour race. Rover seized the opportunity, and in collaboration with BRM who supplied a spaceframe from a 1962 Grand Prix car, and Motor Bodies who provided an open 2-seater body, built the Rover-BRM in time for the 1963 race, in which it averaged 107.84mph (173.55km/h). The drivers were BRM team members Graham Hill and Ritchie Ginther. Had it been allowed to compete with other cars, this would have given it 8th place. A new Rover-BRM with more aerodynamic coupé body was entered for 1964, but was damaged when it fell from its trailer after practice. It did compete in 1965, driven by

Graham Hill and Jackie Stewart, but the engine overheated, and it could manage no higher than 10th. It never raced again as the Rover Competitions Department closed down in 1966.

Another interesting project, inspired in part by the Rover-BRM, was a mid-engined coupé known as the P6BS, which was powered by the 3528cc V8 engine and used P6 running gear. Tested in 1967, it had a top speed of 140mph (225km/h), and with development, could undoubtedly have been made faster still. Had it gone into production it would probably have carried an Alvis badge, as Rover owned the Alvis company which had a more sporting image. However, in 1967 Rover was acquired by Leyland, and a year later they merged with BMC to form the British Leyland Motor Corp. This meant that they were under the same umbrella as Jaguar. The idea of a serious rival to his E-type did not please Sir William Lyons, who used all his influence on the Leyland board to have the P6BS killed off. Two years later he did the same with the P8, a large saloon with 4.4-litre V8 engine which was intended to replace the P5. This would have competed head on with the Jaguar XJ saloons, so was dropped in 1971 after six prototypes had been made.

The SD1

In the early 1970s Rover needed a single car to replace a number of existing models; these were the P5 which was withdrawn in 1973, the P6 which would be going by the middle of the decade, and, since the ranges of Rover and Triumph were to be merged, the Triumph 2000/2500. With the dropping of the P8 at Sir William Lyons' insistence Rover had to come up with a new model which would cater for a number of markets yet not compete with Jaguar. The new car was code-named SD1 (Specialist Division One); work began on the styling in 1971, and it was launched in the summer of 1976. David Bache's styling was its most controversial feature, for it was a 5-door hatchback larger than any other, competing in the quality car field. The smooth sloping front was reminiscent of the Ferrari Daytona, though Bache denied any conscious imitation. There was a new 5-speed gearbox, but the engine was the familiar light alloy 3½-litre V8. Top speed was 125mph (200km/h).

Made in a new factory at Solihull, the SD1 3500 replaced the Rover P6 almost immediately, and the following year came the 2300 and 2600 which used single-ohc 6-cylinder Triumph-designed engines and replaced the Triumph 2000 and 2500. Although cheaper and more economical, the 2600 was nearly as fast (118mph/190km/h) as the 3500. In 1982 a 4-cylinder 1994cc Leyland O Series engine was used in the economy 2000, and the Italian-built 2393cc VM turbocharged diesel engine was also available in the SD1 bodyshell. Also in 1982 production was transferred from the new Solihull factory to the Morris factory at Cowley; Solihull was to have been sold off, but a change of plan resulted in all Land Rover and Range Rover production being concentrated there.

In 1980 British Leyland decided to enter a team of 3500S hatchbacks in saloon car racing. The engines had been developed for the Triumph TR7 rally cars, and developed over 200bhp. Only two races in the Tricentrol series were won in 1980, but the following year saw the cars prepared by Tom Walkinshaw Racing, and winning five championship races to take the big car class. The leading driver was Peter Lovett. In 1982 the Ford Capris were more of a threat, but the Rovers again just took the title in their class, Jeff Allam winning. In France René Metge won the French Championship. In 1983 the cars had to be homologated, and BL authorised the production of a high-performance version of the 3500 to make this possible. This was the 190bhp Vitesse which was the fastest (135mph/218km/h) and most expensive (nearly £15,000) Rover yet made. Rover completely dominated the 1983 British Saloon Car Championship, and the culmination of the season was victory in the Tourist Trophy for Steve Soper and René Metge. This was Rover's second TT victory, the first being in 1907!

Foreign Investment and Change of Ownership

British Leyland's links with Honda began in 1979, when an agreement was signed for the joint development of several ranges of car. The first to appear in Britain was the Triumph Acclaim, based on the Honda Ballade, although the Honda Quintet was sold in Australia as the Rover Quintet. In the summer of 1984 the Acclaim was replaced by a new car based on the current Honda Ballade and it was decided that this should carry a Rover badge. The family was to be called the Rover 200, the first model to appear being the 213 which differed from the Ballade only in its distinctive front end. Nine months later came the more powerful 216 which used the 1598cc BL S Series engine which also powered certain Austin Maestro and Montego models. Output was 86bhp with carburettor or 104bhp with fuel injection, the latter being used in the Vitesse model. Transmission was by Honda manual 5-speed box or ZF automatic. Despite being less of a Rover than any previous model, the 200 soon became popular, reaching 9th place in the British sales league for 1987, with more than 50,000 delivered.

In November 1981 Austin-Rover and Honda signed an agreement on the joint development of a new executive car, code named XX. Honda's version appeared in November 1985 as the Legend, while the Rover 800 was launched in July 1986. Although they shared a floorpan and internal panelling, in appearance they were quite different, the Legend being a 4-light saloon, while the 800 had additional rear quarter lights and crisper styling. Two engines were offered in the 800, a 1996cc twin-ohc 16-valve four designed and built by Rover, and a 2494cc Honda-built V6. Drive was to the front wheels by Honda 5-speed manual or automatic gearboxes. The models powered by the 4-cylinder engine were designated 820, while the V6 was used in the 825i Sterling. US-market cars, which differed from the 825i in their impact-absorbing bumpers, special alloy wheels and high intensity headlamps, were badged as Sterlings, with no mention of Rover, in order to avoid reminders of the unsuccessful US career of the SD1. For a while after their introduction, the Legend was built at Cowley and the 800 in Japan, but this came to an end in March 1988, as proposed changes in both models would not have been compatible with joint production. Also Rover wanted more factory space for their forthcoming mid-sized model, code-named R8.

In the spring of 1988 a 2676cc V6 was offered instead of the 2494cc. Its 177bhp was only 4bhp higher than the smaller engine, but it had much better mid-range torque. With manual gearbox the 827SLi had a top speed of 137mph (220km/h). May 1988 saw a return of the hatchback to the Rover range, with 5-door versions of the 800 series. There were six models, from the 100bhp 2-litre 820 to the 177bhp 2.7-litre Vitesse. With a claimed top speed of 140mph (225km/h) the Vitesse was advertised as the fastest production Rover ever made. The stress was on production, and ads showed the even faster Rover-BRM lurking in a corner.

Company changes in the 1980s served to bring the Rover name to the fore. In the spring of 1986 Canadian-born Graham Day took over as Chairman of British Leyland. One of his first steps was to change the name, as he felt that the British Leyland title was too much associated with controversy and failure. The new name was the Rover Group, with the cars being made by the Austin-Rover Division, and Land Rover and Range Rover by the Land Rover Division. The Austin name was played down, and Metros, Maestros and Montegos were re-named Rovers in 1989–90. In 1988 the former nationalised Rover Group was sold by the British Government to British Aerospace for £150 million. Six years later BAe sold it on to BMW for £800 million, leading to accusations that the original sale price had been too low, to the detriment of the taxpayers.

A new 200 series appeared in 1989, based on the Honda Concerto, with 1396cc Rover K-series or 1590cc Honda engines, both with 16-valves, the Rover having twin-ohc. The bodies were 5-door hatchbacks, but a saloon derivative called the 400 followed in 1990, joined by the high-performance 3-door 216GTi. This and the top 400 model used a 130bhp 1590cc twin-ohc Honda engine.

Of the carried-over Austin models, the Metro became the Rover 100 in 1994, and the Maestro and Montego were dropped in the same year. Some Maestros were sold in kit form to Bulgaria, and, surprisingly, the model returned to the UK market in 1998, offered by a private company in Ledbury, Herefordshire, who bought up 621 crated kits left over from the Bulgarian order. At £4995, they were the cheapest new cars on the market.

In mid–1991 Rover launched a revised 800 with a traditional radiator grill which eventually spread throughout the range. Offered with a choice of three engines, 1994cc Rover four, 2500cc VM turbo-diesel four and 2675cc Honda V6, it came in three body styles, 2-door coupé, 4-door saloon and 5-door hatchback. It was followed in April 1993 by the 600, a 4-door saloon using 1997cc Honda Accord engine and gearbox with a quite distinct British-styled and manufactured body. Summer 1995 saw a new 400; based on the 5-door Honda Civic, it was the last Rover to have input from the Japanese firm, as the BMW take-over put an end to the Honda link. The 400 was available in one body style but with three engines, 1396 and 1589cc twin-cam Rovers and a single-cam 1590cc Honda. It was followed by the new 200, the first 'all-Rover' model since the 1970s. Made as a 3- or 5-door hatchback it came with 1396 or

1989 Rover 216 Vitesse saloon.
AUSTIN ROVER

1990 Rover Metro 1.4GS hatchback.
ROVER

2000 Rover 25 hatchback.
ROVER

2000 Rover 45 saloon.
ROVER

1999 Rover 75 saloon.
ROVER

1947 Rovin D2 2CV 2-seater.
NICK BALDWIN

1949 Rovin D3 3CV 2-seater.
NATIONAL MOTOR MUSEUM

1589cc petrol or a 1994cc turbo-diesel engine. The most powerful model was the 200vi which combined the 3-door body with the 1796cc VVC engine from the MGF. The Rover 100 (ex-Metro) was dropped at the end of 1997, and an all-new medium-sized saloon appeared in October 1998. This was the 75, developed thanks to a £700 million investment by BMW. Styled by Richard Woolley, the new body retained a Rover family likeness in its grill. Four engines were offered, a 1795cc four, V6s of 1991 and 2497cc, and a 1951cc turbo-diesel. All had 4-valves per cylinder. The diesel came from BMW's Austrian factory, and the 5-link rear suspension was shared with the 3 Series, but otherwise the car was all-British. It went into production in May 1999, replacing the 600 and 800. An estate version was planned for a Spring 2000 launch, but this was later postponed to 2001. Later in 1999 the 200 and 400 were restyled with a family look shared with the 75, and renamed 25 and 45. They were not expected to be replaced until 2003.

In Spring 2000 BMW sold the Rover Group. After a deal with the venture capital firm, Alchemy Partners, fell through, in May they found a buyer (for a nominal £10) in the Phoenix Consortium, headed by former Rover executive John Towers. Phoenix planned to continue production at the Longbridge factory, including the 75, hitherto made at Cowley.

For Land Rover and Range Rover see LAND ROVER.

NG

Further Reading
The Rover Story, Graham Robson, Patrick Stephens Ltd, 1988.
Classic Rovers 1934–1977, a Collector's Guide, James Taylor, Motor Racing Publications, 1983.
Classic Rovers 1954–1986, a Collector's Guide, James Taylor, Motor Racing Publications, 1996.
Rover P4, James Taylor, Crowood AutoClassics, 1998.
Rover P5 and P5B, James Taylor, Crowood AutoClassics, 1997.
Rover SD1, Karen Pender, Crowood AutoClassics, 1998.

ROVIN (F) 1946–1961
Robert de Rovin, Saint-Denis, Seine; Colombes, Seine.
Having built cyclecars and motorcycles in the 1920s, brothers Robert and Raoul de Rovin installed themselves in the old Delaunay-Belleville works, where they established a production line in 1946. Their first model, the Rovin D2 was initially presented with a 260cc air-cooled 6.6bhp engine but in production form it sported a water-cooled 425cc flat-twin-cylinder 4-stroke engine mounted in the rear, from whose 10bhp a maximum speed of 40mph (64km/h) could be

expected. Into a unitary/backbone chassis were fitted all-independent suspension, chain/shaft drive and a 3-speed fully-synchronised gearbox. The stark doorless-bodied D2 lasted little more than one year, during which time about 200 were built. It was replaced by the D3 in 1948, with the same mechanical basis but smart all-new enveloping bodywork which was virtually symmetrical front to rear. In 1950 (after 922 of the D3 had been made), the car's engine size increased to 462cc and the power output rose to 13bhp. The new D4 had a top speed of 53mph (85km/h). It was externally distinguishable by its headlamps mounted high on the wings, as opposed to being on either side of the false front grill. The Rovin's heyday was the early 1950s, but cars continued to be offered on a much less enthusiastic basis until 1961.

CR

ROWLEY (US) c.1990–1995

Rowley Corvette, Rowley, Maine.
The Rowley GTC was a replica of the Ferrari Daytona Spyder. It was built on 1968–82 Corvette chassis and was sold in kit and assembled form. Turn-key GTCs were assembled on rebuilt Corvettes with the buyer's choice of engines and performance modifications.

HP

ROX (F) c.1985–c.1988

Rox Automobiles, Puteaux.
Stylistically inspired by the Willys Jeep, the Rox Roxy was created in [2/3] scale, so that it measured a minuscule 240cm long. The engines were equally puny, either 122cc or 190cc.

CR

ROYAL (i); ROYAL PRINCESS (US) 1904–1905

Royal Automobile Co., Chicago, Illinois.
This company made electric cars called Royal and petrol ones called Royal Princess. The Royal Electric was made in four body styles in 1904 and five in 1905; many companies included a victoria in their range, but Royal went one better and called theirs the Queen Victoria. This was the additional style for 1905. The Royals were very small, all being built on a 60in (1523mm) wheelbase, and had a guaranteed range of 75 miles per charge. The Royal Princess had a 16hp 2-cylinder engine with 2-speed epicyclic transmission and single-chain drive. It had an 82in (2081mm) wheelbase and tourer body.

NG

ROYAL (ii) (US) 1913

Royal Motor Co., Elkhart, Indiana.
This company listed two models for one season only, of 35 and 45hp, both tourers with 4-cylinder T-head engines.

NG

ROYAL (iii) (US) 1915

Royal Cyclecar Co., Bridgeport, Connecticut.
This was a late entry in the American cyclecar market, and an exceptionally small one, with 5/7hp single-cylinder engine and seating for one person only. It had friction transmission and belt final drive. The wheelbase was 75in (1903mm).

NG

ROYAL CONSORT (GB) 1904–c.1905

A. Cope & Co. Ltd, Manchester.
This was a tricar of conventional layout powered by a 3½hp W.A. Lloyd engine, with belt drive.

NG

ROYALE (i) (GB) 1981–1984

1981–1982 Ryder Designs Ltd, Coventry, Warwickshire.
1982–1984 Graham Autos, North Shields, Tyne & Wear.
1984 Sabre Cars, Wallsend, Tyne & Wear.
From 1981, the firm that took over the PELLAND Sports also made the Royale, a Morgan replica based on a VW Beetle chassis. The dummy rear fuel tank hid the engine, while the 'bonnet' at the front concealed the fuel tank and spare wheel.

CR

c.1990 Royale (ii) neo-classic roadster.
ROYALE

1997 Royale (iii) sports car.
ROYALE MOTOR CO.

ROYALE (ii) (GB) 1988–c.1993

1988–1991 Imperial Motor Car Co., Callington, Cornwall.
1991–1993 The Royale Motor Co., Preston, Lancashire.
Just as many specialist companies rebodied the Bentley MkVI, the Imperial was a neo-classic conversion – originally of American origin – for a Jaguar XJ6 or XJ12, with the alternative of Ford V8 power. Models offered included the Corsair and Royale – and indeed the whole enterprise was called Royale after 1991. The bodywork incorporated an MG windscreen and doors and was in steel and fibreglass reinforced with carbon fibre. All Jaguar XJ mechanicals were used, as well as XJ wheels, instruments and seats. Options included Wilton carpets, air conditioning and a rear luggage trunk, and prices started at £38,000.

CR

ROYALE (iii) (GB) 1991 to date

The Royale Motor Co., Preston, Lancashire.
This company's first model was the Royale Drophead, a superior kit car that evoked the sedate and charming 1930s era with a large tourer-style open body. The Jaguar XJ series donated its mechanical side into a substantial steel chassis, and there was space for up to five passengers inside. The Sabre of 1994 was much more sporting, but of equally exacting quality. Like the Drophead, the Sabre had a steel box section chassis and fibreglass bodywork, but the donor vehicle was less grand: either Ford Granada or Ford Sierra. Engine choice therefore stretched from 4-cylinder units up to the 2.9-litre V6. Options included an interchangeable hard-top and luxury trim. A third model, the 4-door Ford Granada-based Windsor, arrived in 1998 and was available in saloon and landaulet configurations.

CR

ROYAL ENFIELD (GB) 1901–1905

Enfield Cycle Co., Redditch, Worcestershire.
Royal Enfield was one of the best-known names among British motorcycles from 1900 to 1971, and the name survives on Indian-built machines today. Their involvement in cars was short-lived, and grew out of the quadricycles derived from the 2-wheelers. These were powered by 2¾ and 3½hp De Dion-

1904 Royal Enfield 8hp 2-seater.
NATIONAL MOTOR MUSEUM

c.1906 Royal Star 2-seater.
NATIONAL MOTOR MUSEUM

1910 Royal Tourist 48hp roadster.
NATIONAL MOTOR MUSEUM

Bouton engines. A few VINOT cars were imported and badged as Enfields in 1902, and native-built light cars appeared in 1903, powered by 6hp single-cylinder De Dion-Bouton or 10hp V-twin Ader engines. Some sources say that three complete Aders were imported and sold as Royal Enfields without authorisation. The order was for 50 but the balance were never taken up because of poor workmanship. In 1904 the Ader engine was replaced by a vertical-twin of Enfield's own manufacture. Two years later car making was separated from the rest of the company and set up as the Enfield Autocar Co. Ltd (see ENFIELD (i)).

NG

ROYAL HEREFORD (GB) 1899–1900
Rough & Co., Hereford.
The first, and almost the only, car made in Herefordshire was a light 2-seater powered by a horizontal 2-cylinder engine developing 2bhp, which drove a countershaft by 5 to 1 gearing and thence by pulleys to the rear axle. The car had solid tyres, with springs fitted beneath the seat and a coil spring at the front.

A 'silent exhaust' was fitted and so positioned that it acted as a foot warmer in winter. Mr Rough was to have driven the car in the 1900 Thousand Miles Trial, but did not do so. The company made Royal Hereford bicycles which were more successful commercially than the cars.

NG

ROYAL RUBY (GB) 1913–1914; 1927
Royal Ruby Cycle Co., Manchester.
This company built motorcycles from 1909 to 1933, latterly at Bolton, and had two short periods of car manufacture. The first came during the cyclecar boom, and had a 10hp V-twin JAP engine, with two speeds and shaft drive, but a belt-drive model was to be added later. Few cyclecars were made, and the next Royal Ruby car was a 3-wheeler announced in 1927. This was also JAP-powered but had half the number of cylinders and half the horsepower of the cyclecar. Production was minimal, but a modified form of the car appeared in 1928 as the M.E.B. made by Bromilow & Edwards of Bolton.

NG

ROYAL STAR (B) 1904–1910
Sté de Construction Mécanique, Antwerp.
This company was set up in 1902 to manufacture motorcycles, cars and industrial engines. The first cars appeared in 1904 in 2- and 4-cylinder models, and by 1906 they were making a wide range, five 4-cylinder models from the 1698cc 10/12CV to the 4940cc 25/30CV, and two sixes, the 6123cc 29CV and 7408cc 37CV. The 11/12CV had monobloc casting, the 17CV had bi-bloc casting, and the others all had separate cylinders. There was also a 680cc single 7CV which had many parts interchangeable with De Dion-Bouton. The factory had a capacity for 1500 motorcycles and 300 cars per annum.
    In 1910 the company was reorganised under the name Sté Anversoise pour la Fabrication de Voitures Automobiles, and the cars were renamed SAVA.

NG

ROYAL-TOLOSA (F) 1925
Automobiles Royal-Tolosa, Toulouse.
This car was announced in October 1925 with a 6/18CV 4-cylinder engine and saloon body. It was said to made throughout of 'celebrated Ugine steel', and had a top speed of 45mph (72km/h).

NG

ROYAL TOURIST (US) 1904–1911
1904–1906 Royal Motor Car Co., Cleveland, Ohio.
1906–1907 Royal Motor Car & Manufacturing Co., Cleveland, Ohio.
1908–1911 Royal Tourist Car Co., Cleveland, Ohio.
1911 Consolidated Motor Car Co., Cleveland, Ohio.
In November 1903 Edward Schurmer bought the HOFFMAN (i) Automobile Co., re-named it Royal and launched a new car called the Royal Tourist for the 1904 season. It was a tourer on a 90in (2284mm) wheelbase with 18/20hp 2-cylinder engine, and was joined a few weeks later by a 32/35hp four on the same wheelbase. 100 cars were made in the first season, and the Royal Tourist grew in size, luxury and price over the next few years. The twin was quickly dropped, and by 1906 prices of the 40hp Model F ran from $3500 to $5000. The company was re-organised in November 1906 and moved into larger premises with a workforce of 400 men. Plans for a large 6-cylinder model were frustrated by the slump of 1907, and the company went into receivership before being reorganised again in October 1908.
    For the rest of its life the Royal Tourist was a large 4-cylinder car, in 42 and 48hp models, on wheelbases from 114 (2893mm) to 126in (3198mm). The 1909 models had a horn button placed in the centre of the steering wheel, with the horn itself concealed under the bonnet. This was said to be the first example of this system in America. In March 1911 Royal Tourist merged with the CROXTON Motor Car Co. of Cleveland and the Acme Body & Veneer Co. of Rahway, New Jersey, to form the Consolidated Motor Co. A few months later the group was dissolved, and though Croxton survived for about 18 months, the Royal Tourist was discontinued.

NG

ROYAL WINDSOR see DOMINION (i)

225 GUINEAS.

ROYAL ENFIELD AUTOCAR.

— MODEL 21. —

WE purposely emphasise the price, as the ENFIELD 10-h.p. TWO CYLINDER AUTOCAR represents the greatest value in Cars for 1905.—NOT an ounce of waste weight!—NOT a foot pound of lost energy!—MECHANICAL Construction equal in every way to Cars costing twice the price.— NO grade is too steep or too long; most grades encountered can be taken on the direct drive, while the second gear, which is the hill-climbing gear, takes every grade, the low gear being only used for

DASH.

starting.—THIS dashing, graceful, noiseless Car is controlled by touching the throttle; it is instantly amenable to the will of the driver. INTERCHANGEABILITY of all parts. MECHANICAL OILING system, delivering oil direct to each cylinder. WATER COOLING—natural circulation—no pump troubles.

Mere statements are worthless, but facts proving indisputable evidence should find weight with every thinker. We offer facts! One short demonstration in a hilly district will convince. Send your name to-day for further information.

THE ENFIELD AUTOCAR CO.,
Enfield Works, Redditch.

1904 Royce 10hp tonneau.
NICK BALDWIN

1907 Roydale 20 or 25hp tourer.
NICK BALDWIN

ROYCE (GB) 1904

Royce Ltd, Manchester.

Frederick Henry Royce was manufacturing electric cranes at the turn of the century, but sales were hit by competition from cheaper imports, and he was looking around for new kinds of business. He was naturally fascinated by the motor car, and in 1903 bought a two-year old second hand DECAUVILLE. He tinkered with it until he could improve it no more, then set to making his own car, which owed a lot to the Decauville. It had a 1809cc vertical-twin inlet-over-exhaust engine, 3-speed gearbox and shaft drive. The wheelbase was 75in (1903mm) and a simple 2-seater body was fitted. Two further cars had rear-entrance tonneau bodies. Royce kept the 2-seater, gave one of the tonneaus to his partner Ernest Claremont and sold the other to Henry Edmunds, who was to introduce him and the car to the Hon C.S. Rolls in May 1904. As a result of this meeting Rolls agreed to take the whole output of Royce cars, so long as they bore the name ROLLS-ROYCE.

NG

Further Reading
The Edwardian Rolls-Royce, Bryan Goodman and John Fasal;
(preliminary article by Tom Clarke) published by John Fasal, 1994.

ROYDALE (GB) 1907–1909

Roydale Engineering Co. Ltd, Huddersfield, Yorkshire.

The Roydale was made by a subsidiary of Learoyd Brothers & Co. Ltd, makers of fancy worsted and woollen goods. Designed by Charles Binks (1864–1922) who had previously made the LEADER (i), it was a conventional 4-cylinder car with monobloc T-head engine, 3-speed gearbox and shaft drive. Two engine sizes were offered, a 3190cc 18/22hp and a 3920cc 25/30hp, and there was also a 7-litre 40/45hp six listed, which may never have been built. Roydale supplied only chassis, but various open and closed bodies were made by Rippon.

The Roydale should have been successful but its launch coincided with the serious trade recession of 1907. It seems that it was only a hobby for A.E. Learoyd whose wealth came from the textile business, and after about a dozen cars had been made, the make was discontinued. Binks set up a carburettor business at Eccles which was much more successful than either of his car-making ventures. Continued by his sons it became AMAL.

NG

Further Reading
'Roydale – British-built Throughout', Malcolm Jeal,
The Automobile, March 1992.

RPM (US) c.1994 to date

RPM Design Ltd, Newport, Rhode Island.

The RPM Saber was a Corvette rebody kit that looked a little like a Dodge Viper, although the lines were altered to avoid legal problems. It was sold in kit form or RPM would assemble the components on the buyer's 1968 to 1982 Corvette. RPM also sold a styling kit for 1982 to 1992 Pontiac Firebirds.

HP

R.S. (GB) 1990s

R.S. Panels, Nuneaton, Warwickshire.

This Jaguar C-Type replica maker also began making very high quality E-Type Lightweight replicas, in open and low-drag coupé body styles, from 1993.

CR

R-SPORT (U) 1955

Danree & Silveira, Montevideo.

This was a plastic-bodied sports car powered by a Renault 4CV engine. The engine and the rest of the mechanical components were imported from France and an unknown number of cars were made. Some of these vehicles still survive in Uruguay. They can be considered the first attempt at building and producing in series a genuinely Uruguayan car.

ACT

R.T.C. (GB) 1922–1923

René Tondeur Co. Ltd, Croydon, Surrey.

This was a cyclecar designed by a young Belgian engineer who had built a car in his own country in 1914, employing the automatic transmission that he used in the R.T.C. It had twin-belt drive whose ratio was automatically variable by a governor which enlarged and reduced the diameter of the pulleys, similar to the system used on the prewar Clyno motorcycle. The suspension was unusual too, employing a combination of cantilever and coil springs. The power unit was the familiar 1000cc Blackburne air-cooled V-twin. Only a handful were sold, possibly because the car was too unconventional, and also it was not a great bargain at £160, once the Austin Seven came on the market.

Tondeur later had more success with the Vici carburettor, which was used on many racing motorcycles in the 1930s.

NG

RUBAY see LÉON RUBAY

RUBINO (I) 1920–1923

Officine di Netro SA, Turin.

This was a conventional touring car powered by a 2.3-litre 4-cylinder side-valve engine designed by Lamberti who had worked for S.P.A. Though it was said to be an excellent hill climber, few were made. It was taken over by Pietro Scaglione's TAU concern.

NG

RUBURY-LINDSAY see R.L.C.

RUBY (F) 1910–c.1922

Godefroy et Levêque, Levallois-Perret, Seine.

The Ruby was one of the best-known proprietary engines made in France, and was supplied to a large number of customers. The makers, Godefroy and Levêque also built a number of light cars. Six models were on the market in 1912, three with single-cylinder engines and three fours from 6 to 12hp, all using friction transmission and chain drive. A cyclecar was sold in England under the name Elburn-Ruby up to 1912, and from then until 1914 as the Tweenie. It was marketed in England by Dunhills, the pipe makers. A surviving example, owned by Dunhills, has a 10hp V-twin Buchet engine, and another example in England has a Coventry-built Premier engine, surprising in view of Ruby's pre-eminence as engine builders. A few Ruby cars were made after the war, one of which Levêque drove into 2nd place in the 1920 Cyclecar GP at Le Mans. He also made his own cyclecar which he called the SUPER.

NG

RU CAR CRAFTERS (US) 1997 to date

RU Car Crafters, Sand Springs, Oklahoma.

This Cobra replica had a backbone-type frame with Ford suspension and running gear. It was engineered by Roger Upton and would accept Ford or Chevrolet engines.

HP

RUDGE (GB) 1912–1913

Rudge-Whitworth Ltd, Coventry.

1955 R-Sport 4CV convertible.
ALVARO CASAL TATLOCK

Rudge was one of the great names among British motorcycles, being made from 1911 to 1940. They were famous for the Rudge-Multi variable gear by expanding pulleys, and the few Rudge cyclecars used the same transmission. They had 750cc single-cylinder engines and belt final drive, with staggered 2-seater bodies. An underslung frame gave a very low appearance. The Rudge cyclecar was on the market for less than a year.

NG

RUGBY see STAR (v)

RUGER (US) 1969–1972

Sturm, Ruger & Co., Inc, Southport, Connecticut.

Famous gun manufacturer Sturm, Ruger got into the car business with a replica of the 1920s-era 4½-litre Bentley. The body was fibreglass and aluminium, and the cockpit area was covered with Naugahyde to simulate the fabric-covered Bentley body. It was a long car with a wheelbase of 130in (3299mm) and tall 18in wheels gave a proper vintage stance. A 7000cc Ford engine produced 425hp giving it a top speed of 110mph (177km/h). They were sold for $13,000.

HP

RUHL (B) 1901–1907

SA des Automobiles Ruhl, Verviers.

Adolphe Ruhl (1866–1913) made steam engines and weaving machinery, and in 1900 built a 3CV voiturette. He was sufficiently pleased with it to form a company and put it into production. It was followed in 1904 by larger cars with 4-cylinder engines of 14, 24 and 40CV, the latter having a capacity of 9.8-litres. They took part in a number of competitions, a 14CV defeating a Renault and a Panhard in a race meeting at Niort. Unfortunately, the failure of the Modera bank in which the company's money was placed brought production to an end in 1907. One Ruhl survived in regular use by a garage at least up to 1943.

NG

RULAND (CDN) 1975

Reputedly styled by a fashion designer, the Ruland was a plastic-bodied 1930s-style roadster that kicked off the craze for such machines based on VW Beetle chassis. Perhaps fortunately, it appears that an intended production run of 250 units per year did not materialise.

CR

RULER (US) 1917

Ruler Motor Car Co., Aurora, Illinois.

The Ruler was designed without a chassis or, in its promotion, 'frame-less'. The chassis was replaced by its patented 3-point cradle with two wheels as two points plus a ball and socket in the centre of the front transverse member as the third point. In the cradle were the clutch, transmission, and differential. The body of the Ruler was removable by unfastening the ball on the forward end of the cradle and disconnecting the brakes and rear springs. The 4-cylinder ohv engine featured a roller-type camshaft with lubrication by means of a flywheel rim. The Ruler completed prototypes but never reached the marketplace and was out of business in less than a year.

KM

1921 Rumpler saloon.
HANS-OTTO NEUBAUER

RULEX (GB) 1904

R.L. Motor Engineering Co. Ltd, London.

The Rulex voiturette was offered in two single-cylinder models, with 3¹/₂hp engine at 70 guineas (£73.50) and with 4¹/₂hp engine at 80 guineas (£84).

NG

RUMPF (B) 1899

Sté le Progres Industriel, Brussels.

This company was formed to make machine tools and engines as well as complete cars. Engines of 5, 7¹/₂, and 14hp were offered, with 4-speed gearboxes and double-chain drive. The 3-seater *vis-à-vis* body was made by d'Ieteren, soon to become one of Belgium's best-known coachbuilders.

NG

RUMPLER (D) 1921–1926

Rumpler Motoren Gesellschaft GmbH, Berlin.

Austrian-born Dr Edmund Rumpler (1872–1940) worked for the car manufacturers NESSELSDORFER and ADLER before turning to the infant aircraft industry. He made engines, the Rumpler Taube and other aircraft of which 3260 were delivered between 1910 and 1918. Forbidden to make aircraft under the terms of the Treaty of Versailles he turned to cars again after World War I. He had a prototype tourer running in 1919, and at the 1921 Berlin Motor Show he exhibited a very advanced car with streamlined saloon body and a 2310cc W6 engine made by Siemens & Halske. This had three rows of two cylinders in

W-formation, the pistons working on a common crankshaft. This was mounted in unit with a 3-speed gearbox at the rear of the perimeter frame which followed the lines of the body, tapering towards the rear. A larger engine of 2580cc followed in 1923, but because of cooling problems the W6 was abandoned in 1924 in favour of a 2610cc in-line four by Benz. Rumpler already had links with Benz when they bought a licence from him to make their *Tropfenwagen* racing and sports cars of 1922. The new car was longer than the old, with an impressive 131.5in (3338mm) wheelbase, and eight passengers could be carried at a pinch. A few of the Benz-powered Rumplers were used as taxis in Berlin, and a price of RM17,000 was quoted for sale to the public. 100 chassis were laid down, of which 60 were to be given saloon bodies and the rest tourers. Of these, no more than 80 were bodied, and even fewer sold.

In 1926 Rumpler changed direction and built a front-engined front-wheel drive car, using again the 2610cc Benz engine. Much of the body and the Z-section frame were made of Lautal aluminium. Though not making such extensive use of aluminium as the POMEROY, it has a good claim to be the first largely aluminium car built in Europe. Only a handful of saloons and a single tourer were made. They were Rumpler's last passenger cars, although he made one striking front-drive 6-wheeled van for the publishers Ullstein in 1931. He dissolved his consulting bureau in 1933, though he continued to work on various designs.

NG

Further Reading

'Edmund Rumpler – an Engineer's Life', Karl Ludvigsen,
The Automobile, May–August 1999.

RUSKA (NL) 1968 to date

Ruska Automobielen, Amsterdam.

Ruska presented itself as the first purely Dutch kit car maker, producing beach buggies from as early as 1968. While it continued to specialise in buggies, it offered several other kit-built models. The Sprinter and Classica were traditional/buggy cross-over styles, the former with two seats and the latter with four. The 1979 Regina was another Beetle-based kit, this time a Mercedes SSK inspired shell with four seats. The Sagitta from 1981 onwards was a licence-built version of the LINDBERG Auburn Speedster replica. Ruska also offered a Bugatti Type 35 replica, again with the inevitable Beetle engine in the tail (though a Porsche 6-cylinder unit could also be fitted).

CR

RUSSEL (US) 1921

S. Russel Co., Detroit, Michigan.

Under the direction of S. Russel of Detroit's Russel Wheel & Foundry Co., one known Russel car was completed as a prototype for a series of cars targeted to the export market. As such, it was equipped with right-hand steering. Whether the Russel export car was developed further is not known. The existing photo of the prototype depicts a small disc-wheeled touring car, typical of most of America's export cars built in the early 1920s.

KM

RUSSELL (i) (US) 1903–1904

Russell Motor Vehicle Co., Cleveland, Ohio.

E.L. Russell's light car had a number of advanced features including a very small 4-cylinder engine of 6hp, shaft drive and a lever which did duty for starting the engine when pushed forward, engaging low gear when pushed further forward and high gear when pushed further forward still. Pulling it backwards engaged reverse. With a 2-seater stanhope body it was priced at a reasonable $800, but production never started.

NG

RUSSELL (ii) (CDN) 1905–1915

1905–1910 Canada Cycle & Motor Co., Toronto, Ontario.
1912–1915 Russell Motor Car Co. Ltd, Toronto, Ontario.

The Canada Cycle & Motor Co. was founded in 1899, initially building bicycles and then adding tricycles and quadricycles powered by De Dion-Bouton engines. From 1903 to 1905 they made the IVANHOE electric car, then introduced a 14hp 2-cylinder car named after the company's general manager, T.A. 'Tommy' Russell (1877–1940). It had shaft drive and a steering column gearchange. It was phased out during 1906 after about 25 had been made, giving way to the 16hp Model B and 24hp 4-cylinder Model C. This was priced at $2500. Like so many other makes, Russells grew larger over the years; a 40hp 7-seater 4-cylinder car joined the range in 1907, and a 50hp in 1908.

In 1909 Tommy Russell took an important step by acquiring the sole Canadian rights to the Knight sleeve-valve engine. The Knight-powered car was offered in two sizes in 1910, 22 and 38hp, the engines actually being made by DAIMLER in Coventry. The 38 was a high-priced car at $5000. Fifteen body styles were offered in 1910 on three chassis, the old 30hp poppet-valve car and the two Knight-engined models. These were officially called Russell-Knights for the 1913 season, when two new models appeared, the 4-cylinder 28hp and a massive 42hp six on a 142in (3604mm) wheelbase. They had electric lighting and starting and lhd. Unfortunately, they had been rushed into production without sufficient time for testing, and proved unreliable. It was the beginning of the end for the Russell-Knight. They were continued into 1915 when a return to the poppet-valve and to cheaper cars was made with the Continental-powered 6-30 at $1750. This and the 32hp sleeve-valve car were offered for the 1916 season but the demands of wartime production took over, Also Russell received a very good offer for the Canadian sleeve-valve rights from John North Willys. By the end of 1915 production of Russell cars ended forever. Tommy Russell became president of Russell which controlled a number of important companies making components.

NG

RUSSO-BALTIQUE (RUS) 1909–1915

Russko-Baltiskji Vagonnji Zavod, Riga, Russia.

1908 Russell (ii) tourer.
NATIONAL MOTOR MUSEUM

1909 Russell (ii) Knight 22hp tourer.
NATIONAL MOTOR MUSEUM

1912 Russo-Baltic Type K tourer.
MARGUS H. KUUSE

The sizeable works in Riga specialised in railway rolling stock–like FONDU in Belgium. Fondu built automobiles as well and 'loaned' its automotive engineer Julien Potterat for setting up a similar production at RBVZ. The Swiss engineer had a staff of nearly 160 at his disposal and within a year the first model of 4500cc, called C 24/30 and patterned after a similar Fondu, was ready for a bodywork. That meant engine block cast in two parts, a 3-speed transmission and shaft drive. The exact date is known: 26 May 1909. There followed testing and two long-distance runs between Riga and St Petersburg. The updated model C 24/40 came in 1912, followed by a monobloc 2211cc four in the K 12/24.

1951 Russon 197cc 3-seater.
NATIONAL MOTOR MUSEUM

1921 Ruston-Hornsby 15.9hp tourer.
NICK BALDWIN

The same year a 7235cc model 40/60 appeared on a longest-ever 136in (3460mm) wheelbase and that was followed by a 3684cc Type E 15/35 for the last two years of the make's existence. The influence of another consultant, Dr Ernst Valentin of Rex-Simplex fame, was noticeable in later models. Various bodies were built on the Russo-Baltique chassis, including a few sporting and racing bodies, as well as tourers, landaulets and limousines. A gentleman driver and auto-aviation journalist Andrey Nagel won a special prize for his solo 196½ hours run from St Petersburg to Monte Carlo in the 1912 rally. He travelled extensively and far from Russia, finding the Riga-built cars most reliable. Historians are not sure about the overall number of Russo-Baltique cars and trucks built, but a figure like 600 must be quite close, including possible assembly of automobiles at other premises from the parts manufactured in Riga before machinery and tools were dismantled and transferred to St Petersburg and Moscow. Actually the first-ever Soviet automobile – the BTAZ-1 of 1922 – was nothing other than a prewar Russo-Baltique with a vee-radiator and disc wheels. Only one complete Russo is known to survive, a K-series model of 1911, on display at the Polytechnical Museum in Moscow.

MHK

Further Reading
'The Odyssey of the Russo-Baltique', Alec Ulmann,
Automobile Quarterly, Vol. 14, No. 2.

RUSSON (GB) 1951–1952
Russon Cars Ltd, Eaton Bray, Stanbridge, Bedfordshire.
The Russon Minicar was an attractively styled microcar that resembled a shrunken Triumph TR2 or Jaguar XK120. Produced by a publisher, it initially used a 197cc JAP engine but this proved underpowered for the size of the car and 250cc Excelsior Talisman engines were substituted. The open body (claimed to seat three abreast) was formed in aluminium over a wood frame, with a tubular chassis featuring all-independent suspension. A high purchase price of £491 and a lack of finance scuppered the project and only around ten cars were made. Some of the engineering was later incorporated in the FAIRTHORPE Atom.

CR

RUSTON-HORNSBY (GB) 1919–1924
Ruston & Hornsby Ltd, Lincoln.
This company was formed in September 1918 by a merger of two old-established engineering companies, Ruston Proctor which had been founded in 1840 and Richard Hornsby which dated back to 1815. Hornsby were well-known for oil engines in the 1890s, one being used to light the Statue of Liberty. They also made pioneer full-tracked vehicles which led to the development of the tank.

By the end of World War I the combined companies had a workforce of 13,000. In an attempt to keep them all busy they launched into furniture, van bodies and the Ruston-Hornsby car. Like the CUBITT this was seen as a suitable design for mass production, having a large 15.9hp 4-cylinder engine of 2614cc made by Dorman or a 20hp 3308cc engine made in-house, American-type central gearchange and a roomy tourer body. The Dorman-engined model was sold as the Standard and the 20hp as the De Luxe. Unfortunately, they were expensive for what they offered, at £650 and £750 respectively, and though by 1923 prices dropped in line with all other cars, they never achieved the large sales that the makers hoped for. About 1500 Ruston-Hornsbys were sold in all over five years, of which the 15.9hp accounted for 1050.

NG

RUTH (US) 1907
Ruth Automobile Co., North Webster, Indiana.
This car was made by three men all of whom had daughters called Ruth. It was a 2-seater high-wheeler with chain drive, and was made in limited numbers, all for local customers including North Webster's doctor.

NG

1930 Ruxton roadster.
NATIONAL MOTOR MUSEUM

RUTHERFORD (GB) 1907–1912

Highclere Motor Car Syndicate Ltd, Highclere, Newbury, Berkshire.

This car was designed by E.J.Y. Rutherford, and was at first known by his initials as the E.J.Y.R. He was a typical inventor, his accomplishments including a small howitzer gun in William Brittain's model soldiers series, and a burner for heating houses and cookers which was adopted by the army.

In 1906 he joined forces with the village postmaster, George Hamilton, who had previously been a coachbuilder and who also ran the Highclere Garage next door to the post office. Together they formed the Highclere Motor Car Syndicate Ltd to manufacture a steam car. The 30/40hp had a Serpollet-type flash boiler and 3-cylinder vertical single-acting engine. With shaft drive, a 5-seater tourer body and a Packard-type 'radiator' it had the appearance of a conventional petrol-engined car. They were exhibited at the Olympia Show in 1907 and 1908, but were not a financial success. Steam had very few fans in England at this time, not that this stopped some other companies such as BOLSOVER, FAWCETT-FOWLER and PEARSON-COX from having a go. A price reduction in 1911 from the original £575 to £400 for a larger-engined car did not save it. Rutherford's other claim to fame was that his father was agent to Lord Carnavon of Highclere Castle at the time of his discovery of King Tutankhamen's tomb in 1922.

NG

RÜTTGER (D) 1920–1921

Carl Rüttger Motorpflug- und Automobilwerke, Berlin-Hohenschönweide.

Rüttger made agricultural tractors and motor ploughs, and also built some prototypes of a 10PS light car, but no production resulted.

HON

RUXTON (US) 1929–1930

New Era Motors Inc., New York City; St Louis, Missouri;
Hartford, Wisconsin.

The Ruxton began life without a name and only '?' for a badge. Ironically, the man with whose name it was eventually christened, financier William Ruxton, elected not to invest in the project. Its innovative front-wheel drive chassis was designed by engineer William Muller, then employed by body builders Edward G. Budd Manufacturing Co. of Philadelphia. A prototype was completed in 1928, with a body designed by Budd's Joseph Ledwinka. Budd director Archie

1980 Rvia Sunrise roadster.
NATIONAL MOTOR MUSEUM

Andrews was also on the board of HUPP Motor Car Corp., and attempted to sell the car to them. Hupp declined. Andrews then formed his own New Era Motors Inc. to market the car.

Muller's drive axle was of De Dion configuration, made of molybdenum steel. Constant-velocity universal joints allowed a turning radius of 19ft, quite compact for a front-wheel drive car. In order to move the engine closer to the drive wheels, Muller split the gearbox, placing first and reverse ahead of the axle, second and third behind. The differential was of worm gear design. The engine was a Continental 18S in-line side-valve 8, of 4403cc and 100bhp. The Ruxton was visually distinctive because it was so low. Only 63.25in (1605mm) high, its body was channelled over the chassis; running boards and splash aprons were dispensed with. However, the car still had 10in ground clearance. Sedan bodies were by Budd, with stampings, from Budd dies, supplied by Pressed Steel Co. in England. Baker-Raulang Co. of Cleveland supplied roadsters and a one-off town car.

New Era Motors had a car, but, in the spring of 1929, still no place to build it. Talks were conducted with several midwestern auto companies; in June it was announced that GARDNER Motor Co. of St Louis would build the car. Ruxtons were exhibited at New York and Chicago, but then Gardner bowed out. MARMON was interested, but talks came to naught. Finally, in November, a deal

1903 Ryknield 10/12hp tonneau.
NATIONAL MOTOR MUSEUM

was made with another St Louis firm, the MOON Motor Car Co., which would also sell the Ruxton through the Moon dealer organisation. The Moon-Ruxton arrangement did not proceed smoothly. It was, in effect, a takeover of Moon by New Era, but Moon directors refused to vacate and seat Andrews on their board. In a coup of sorts, Andrews increased the number of directors, ousting the holdouts and installing Muller as president. Finding the Moon plant antiquated and inadequate, Andrews and Muller enlisted the KISSEL Motor Car Co. of Hartford, Wisconsin, to help with production. In June 1930 the first Ruxtons were produced in the Moon plant, although plans had been made to transfer production to Kissel's works and some tooling was sent there. Its $3195 price was competitive with America's other front-drive car, the CORD L29, but Cord had a head start on production. Then Kissel went into voluntary receivership, apparently to avoid falling into the complete control of Andrews. Moon halted Ruxton production in November 1930, because of shortages of parts made unavailable by the Kissel collapse. Moon soon followed Kissel into receivership. Total Ruxton production is believed to be about 300, some 27 at Kissel, 11 assembled in Philadelphia by Budd and the balance built by Moon. The legal tangles created by the rise and fall of New Era Motors were not cleared up until 1966.

KF

Further Reading
'Ruxton, a superb automobile that never had a chance', Jeffrey I. Godshall, *Automobile Quarterly*, Vol. 8, No. 2.
'William Muller Reminisces', William Muller, *Automobile Quarterly*, Vol. 8, No. 2.
'A genuine lowness ingeniously attained: Ruxton', Tom Meredith, *Automobile Quarterly*, Vol. 20, No. 2.

R.V. (GB) 1996 to date
R.V. Dynamics, Feering, Colchester, Essex.
The Nemesis was plainly inspired by the Ferrari Testarossa in the styling department. Under its high-quality fibreglass pastiche bodywork sat a multi-

tubular chassis with an aluminium floor, designed for Jaguar XJ12 suspension and power. Alternative engine choices were Rover V8 and American V8 units.

CR

RVIA (US) 1979–c.1983
Ross Vick, Des Moines, Washington.
Unlike many neo-classics which sought to recreate the style of a 1930s Mercedes-Benz, the Rvia Sunrise recalled the 3-litre Bentley in its radiator shape. The body was a 2-seater cabriolet and it was offered with choice of 4- and 6-cylinder Volvo or Ford V8 engines. Only the 4-cylinder model could be had with a manual gearbox.

NG

R. & V. KNIGHT (US) 1920–1924
R. & V. Division of the Root & Vandervoort Engineering Co., East Moline, Illinois.
The R. & V. Knight was the continuation of the Moline Knight which had been built since 1914 – itself a continuation of the Moline dating back to 1904. This was a relatively large car, its two series, the 4-cylinder Model R and the larger six-cylinder Model J powered by in-house engines utilising the Sleeve-Valve principle, the latter priced as high as $4000 for its most expensive closed style. Unfortunately, the recession of the early 1920s and outstanding financial obligations crippled R. & V. production which, like the Moline-Knight before it, never reached the annual goal of 1000 units. Production peaked in 1921 but dropped after that and the R. & V. was discontinued during 1924.

KM

R.W. (GB) 1982 to date
R.W. Kitcars Ltd, Melton Mowbray, Leicestershire.
Roger Woolley ran one of the UK's more prolific old-style kit car companies. Its main product was the Karma, a vaguely Ferrari Dino inspired coupé that was initially an American import brought in by A.D. but soon manufactured in

Britain. It could be rear-engined (using a VW Beetle floorpan), mid-engined (using a special chassis for a variety of 4-cylinder, 6-cylinder and V8 engines, or front-engined (using another chassis designed for Ford power). Another kit was a Cobra replica, launched in 1988, using a triangulated steel backbone chassis, Jaguar suspension, engines up to V8s. Alternatively a 427 shell was available for a VW Beetle floorpan, as well as a Countach replica called the Taurus and a VW-engined 3-wheeler 'chopper'.

CR

RWN (D) 1928–1929
Rudolf Weide Motorfahrzeugbau, Nordhausen.
This was a 3-wheeled 2-seater light car, with single front wheel, powered by a rear-mounted engine offered in three sizes, 200, 350 or 500cc. It was well-built but this was not enough to ensure success, and like so many others of its kind the RWN soon disappeared. Delivery vans were made for slightly longer, from 1927 to 1933.

HON

RYAN MOTORS (US) c.1996 to date
Ryan Motors, Vista, California.
Ryan Motors was already known as a Volkswagen engine builder for street and off-road cars, so building a line of VW-based kit cars was only natural. The Ryan 356 Speedster was a clone of the Porsche Speedster that used a VW floorpan and running gear. The 718 RS/60 Spyder replicated the 1960 Porsche racing car of the same name. It used a VW floorpan, or a mid-engine tube frame with a 4in longer wheelbase. The mid-engine chassis could also use Porsche 914 or 911 suspension. The Baja Hummer was an AMG Hummer-inspired VW kit car with open sides.

HP

RYCSA see GILDA

RYDE (GB) 1904–1906
Ryde Motors Ltd, West Ealing, Middlesex.
The Ryde was a conventional-looking car made in 2-seater or 4-seater rear-entrance tonneau styles, but was slightly unusual in having an in-line 3-cylinder engine of 14/16hp. It had a 3-speed gearbox and shaft drive, and there was also a delivery van version. Ryde also made a smaller car with 10hp flat-twin engine, but only for the 1904 season.

NG

RYDER see ROYALE (i)

RYJAN (F) 1920–1926
Grillet, Chatou, Seine-et-Oise (1920–1925); Nanterre, Seine (1925–1926).
Made by M. Grillet and sometimes known as the Ryjan-Grillet, this was a conventional car which used a variety of engines. The first was the well-known 1690cc single-ohc S.C.A.P. but for 1924 Grillet turned to less exciting power units, also by S.C.A.P., of 1614cc and with either side-valves or pushrod ohv. For its last two years the Ryjan had a 190cc pushrod Altos engine. Front-wheel brakes were standard, and the car was offered with saloon or 4-seater tourer bodies.

NG

RYKNIELD (GB) 1903–1906
Ryknield Engine Co. Ltd, Burton on-Trent, Staffordshire.
Named after the Roman road that passes through Burton-on-Trent, the Ryknield company was set up by Ernest Edward Baguley, who had been apprenticed at locomotive builders Hawthorn Leslie. He was financed by A. Clay, a director of the Bass brewery in the town, and most of Ryknield's output was of trucks for the brewing industry, and also some buses. Their first car had a 10/12hp vertical-twin engine and shaft drive, and was joined in 1905 by a 15hp 3-cylinder model and a 24hp 4-cylinder with a capacity of over six litres and chain drive. Initial plans called for production of 150 cars a week, which was clearly quite unrealistic. In fact, no more than 100 cars were made in the first year. The company collapsed in 1906 and no more Ryknield cars were made, though commercials were revived from 1909 to 1911. Baguley moved to B.S.A. where

1905 Ryknield 15hp tourer.
NATIONAL MOTOR MUSEUM

he designed a range of conventional 4-cylinder cars, then returned to Burton-on-Trent in 1911 and took over the now vacant Ryknield works to make a car under his own name.

NG

Further Reading
'Made in Burton-on-Trent', M. Worthington-Williams, *The Automobile*, September 1994.

RYLEY (i) (GB) 1901–1902
Ryley, Ward & Bradford, Coventry.
These three partners had experimented for two years before they announced their light car in September 1901. It had a 2¾hp M.M.C. single-cylinder engine, 2-speed gearbox, shaft drive and a tubular frame. In 1902 they offered a larger car with 5hp Aster engine and three speeds.

NG

RYLEY (ii) (GB) 1913
J.A. Ryley, Birmingham.
The short-lived Ryley cyclecar had a 6hp JAP V-twin engine and belt drive.

NG

RYNER-WILSON (GB) 1920–1921
Ryner-Wilson Motor Co. Ltd, Wimbledon, London.
Unlike many new car manufacturers who started up after World War I Ryner and Wilson did not rely on proprietary components, but used their own design of 2290cc 6-cylinder engine with ohvs grouped in sets of four on the heads of each pair of cylinders. There were two camshafts, one on each side of the cylinder block. It had two Vici carburettors (made by René Tondeur of the R.T.C. cyclecar) and the cone clutch could be adjusted from outside to make the car as suitable as possible for the owner-driver. Dry sump lubrication was used. Mr Ryner was an American who is said to have incorporated some ideas from his Buick into the car. The chassis price was £700, too high for Ryner to be able to afford one himself, and production did not exceed 12 cars.

NG

RYTECRAFT (GB) 1934–1940
1934–1939 British Motor Boat Manufacturing Co. Ltd, London.
1939–1940 B.M.B. Engineering, London.
This curious little car had its origin in a fairground 'dodgem car' and never entirely lost the appearance of one. It was designed by Jack Shillan who also made the Scoota-Boat, and was originally electrically-powered and tethered to a central pole to run in circles. When Shillan made a petrol version using a 98cc Villiers Midget engine he saw its possibilities as a road car. Put on the market in 1934 the Scootacar had a single speed, automatic clutch and no springs, relying on the balloon tyres to give a reasonably comfortable ride. Drive was to one rear wheel and a single band brake operated on the other.

By 1940 the Scootacar had been greatly improved, with a 250cc Villiers engine which gave a top speed of 40mph (64km/h) (the original could do no more than

1935 Rytecraft Scootacar with Jim Parkinson during his round the world trip.
NATIONAL MOTOR MUSEUM

15mph/24km/h), 3-speed and reverse gearbox, 2-seater body and electric lights. Some were built with the styling of Vauxhalls or Chrysler Airflows for publicity purposes, and there was also a commercial version, the Scootatruck. About 1000 Scootacars were made, including a few assembled after the war. One achieved fame in the 1960s when Jim Parkinson drove it round the world, covering 15,000 miles under its own power. This was all the more remarkable as it was a 98cc single-speed model.

NG

S1 (DK) 1949–1950

E. Sommer, Copenhagen.

The Jaguar distributor for Denmark conceived this 5-passenger 2-door saloon, which used a 25bhp Jowett Bradford 2-cylinder engine and resembled contemporary Opels in apperance. Three decades later, the Sommer family produced the SOMMER OScar.

CR

SAAB (S) 1949 to date

1949–1965 Svenska Aeroplan Aktiebolaget, Linköping and Trollhättan.
1965–1969 SAAB Aktiebolaget (alternatively Saab Aktiebolaget), Linköping and Trollhättan.
1969–1990 Saab Car Division, Saab-Scania AB, Linköping and Trollhättan.
1990 to date Saab Automobile AB, Trollhättan.

The name SAAB is an acronym of the corporate title, Svenska Aeroplan Aktie-Bolaget (Swedish Airplane plc or Inc.), registered on 26 April 1937 to make aeroplanes in factories at Linköping and Trollhättan.

Sweden's industrial leaders had been telling the government about the need for a domestic aircraft industry in correspondence, papers, and petitions dating back to 1925.

SJ Aeroplane, a subsidiary of Aktiebolaget Svenska Järnvägsverkstäderna (Swedish State Railways Manufacturing Branch) began producing the Viking I civilian aeroplane in 1931, and made a prototype land-based fighter and one seaplane in 1932, both powered by Wright Whirlwind R 975 engines. But without firm Defence department orders, production began slowly with such planes as the Raab-Katzenstein RK-26 trainer and the Tiger Moth.

By 1936, the inevitability of war in Europe became obvious, and the government promised support for a private-sector military aircraft venture. Three candidates came forth: the Götaverken shipbuilding yards; Järnvägsverkstäderna; and Bofors, the steel and arms giant.

Marcus Wallenberg (1864–1943) was at the helm of a financial empire built around Stockholm's Enskilda Banken, established in 1856, which controlled Bofors, and held wide industrial interests, including a stake in the State Railways Industrial Branch. Wallenberg met with the leaders of Nohab, a state-owned (since 1905) industrial group, originally founded in 1847 as Nydqvist & Holms Verkstäder to make steam locomotives at Trollhättan. This company later diversified into aircraft engines and changed its name into Nohab. Wallenberg and Nohab each put up 40 per cent of the share capital in Svenska Aeroplan AB, the remaining 20 per cent being held by Axel Wennergren and other stock-market investors.

Svenska Aeroplan AB immediately started plant construction next door to Nohab in Trollhättan. SAAB acquired a licence for the Ju 86 heavy bomber and at first assembled German-made parts. The first all-Swedish Ju 86 flew in August 1939.

Military orders were channelled through a Stockholm-based design and sales organisation, AB Förenade Flygverstäder (United Aircraft Works), and shared between SAAB and ASJ Aero. They merged in 1939, and SAAB moved its administration and technical offices into the former ASJ Aero headquarters at Linköping. The Trollhättan plant became a secondary production centre. By 1944, SAAB had completed 322 aeroplanes.

The flow of defence orders all but dried up, and SAAB began to develop aeroplanes for civil aviation, a market that, in 1945, was negligible and might not become commercially important for decades. At that time Ragner Wahrgren was president of SAAB, and began a search for a suitable alternative activity.

After brief consideration of going into household appliances and prefabricated houses, the company determined that it should stay in the transport sector and manufacture equipment that could get maximum benefits from its know-how and experience in aeronautical engineering. That meant passenger cars. The board of directors decided to make a study of the Scandinavian automobile market and the car makers likely to have new products on the market in the short-term future.

A positive conclusion having been reached, Gunnar Ljungström was placed in charge of the car project, with a 15-man group. He had graduated as a civil engineer in 1932, and went to work on the development of an automatic transmission invented by his father, and was associated with Rover and Triumph. Returning to Sweden in 1937, he joined SAAB as an airframe designer, later becoming a specialist on wing structures.

1950 Saab 92 saloon.
NATIONAL MOTOR MUSEUM

1965 Saab 95 estate car.
NICK BALDWIN

1967 Saab 96 saloon.
NICK BALDWIN

Without any previous automobile experience the SAAB engineers arrived at a radically different concept from Volvo's, even entering on paths subsequently trodden by Citroën. It was done with some elements of knowledge, plus intuition tempered by logic, and a heavy dose of luck.

Ljungström was familiar with the DKW, which had been a popular seller in Sweden from 1933 to 1939, with its 2-cylinder 2-stroke engine and front-wheel drive. It was clear from the beginning that the Saab would share those features. But Ljungström wanted an all-steel body, and since they worked in an aircraft company which had its own wind tunnel, it was also going to be streamlined.

Sweden's best-known industrial designer, Sixten Sason, was invited to submit styling proposals. Born in 1912 as Sixten Andersson, son of a stone mason, he began signing his artwork Sason, which led to the formal name change. His clients included Husqvarna, Electrolux and Hasselblad. He had also drawn aeroplanes.

c.1973 Saab Sonnet III coupé.
NICK GEORGANO

Sason's 1936–39 sketches show that he cleverly anticipated both the Isetta and the Messerschmitt Kabinenroller, and the basic shape of the Saab 92 was taken from sketches he had made in 1939. The first test cars were running in 1946, and a pre-production prototype was shown to the Swedish press on 10 June 1947.

Gunnar V. Philipson, Sweden's biggest auto importer and retailer, who had sold DKW and Chrysler before the war, placed an order for 8000 cars, and paid for them in advance, which enabled SAAB to go ahead and tool up the Trollhättan factory for car production.

The Saab 92 (the previous 91 design projects were aeroplanes) was a 2-door 4-5-seater saloon, standing on a 97.2in (2467mm) wheelbase, with an overall length of 154in (3908mm). The body had a torsional stiffness of 1742m/kg per degree and the car's aerodynamic drag coefficient was a record-low 0.32. There was luggage space behind the back seat, but the boot lid had been sacrificed, and it was accessible only by folding the rear seat. The complete car weighed 762kg.

All-independent suspension with torsion bars, rack-and-pinion steering, and Lockheed hydraulic brakes were the main chassis features. The 764cc engine was mounted transversely ahead of the front wheel axis to gain space within the wheelbase, driving the front wheels via a 3-speed gearbox with free-wheeling.

Although the Saab 93 was introduced on 1 December 1955, that did not spell an immediate end to production of the 92 which continued well into 1956 and reached a total of 29,128 cars. The Saab 93 was powered by a 3-cylinder 33hp 748cc 2-stroke engine mounted longitudinally, tilted about 20 degrees to the left, with a 3-speed gearbox, and coil-spring ifs. A rear axle with coil springs was introduced to cure roll-oversteer. This car had a top speed of 71.4mph (114.8km/h).

The Trollhättan plant turned out 457 Saab cars before the end of 1955, and 5640 in 1956. The Saab 93 B arrived in 1957, with better brakes and a one-piece curved-glass windshield, and production climbed to 9847 cars. A 45hp triple-Solex engine with 4-speed gearbox powered the 750 GT introduced in 1958, boosting that year's output to 13,968 cars.

A station wagon, Saab 95, built on the Saab 93 platform, went into production late in 1959 (only 55 being completed that year). The coach body was given front hinged doors and the model was renamed 93 F. It became the SAAB 96 in 1960, when the engine size was increased to 841cc and output to 38hp. The body was redesigned with a wider rear section, bigger boot and rear window. The arrival of the 93 F spurred production to a total of 17,836 cars.

Saab made 26,066 cars in 1960, including 19,391 96, 1634 95, and 5041 93 F. The Saab count totalled 52,731 cars at the end of production run. A 55hp Saab 96 Sport (also sold as the 850 GT) with 4-speed gearbox, front disc brakes, and a 93mph (150km/h) top speed, came on the market in 1962.

It turned out that Saab would need a 4-stroke engine before the Ricardo-Triumph unit could reach the production stage, and Saab made contact with Ford about using the Taunus M-15 V4. Gillbrand lived in Italy for a year, 1966–67, conducting secret tests of Saab cars powered by the Ford V4.

In 1966 Saab began mounting the Ford V4 engine in the Saab 95 and 96, in the same Taunus configuration, with the engine in the front overhang. The 1498cc V4 put out 65hp. Car weight increased to 885kg, but it would reach 94mph (151km/h). Internally, the 96 with the V4 was the Saab 98 but for marketing purposes the 96 label was retained.

The Ford-power period was just a stopgap for Saab, and Per Gillbrand worked in England from 1967 to 1970 as a liaison engineer with Triumph. Production of the Saab 99 began in November 1967, but only 25 cars were completed by the end of the year. The company still had to rely on the 95–96 combination to provide the income. The Trollhättan factory made 29,766 Saab 96 and 7243 Saab 95 in 1966, and the following year 37,622 Saab 96 and 7223 Saab 95.

The Saab Sonett sports car did not show up in the official production statistics until 1966, although six cars by that name had been made as early as 1956. It was Rolf Mellde's project, an open 2-seater roadster with an aluminium space frame and plastic body, weighing only 1100lb (500kg).

SAAB

GILLBRAND, PER S. (born 1934)

Saab has always gone its own way, and no manufacturer has done more to adapt turbocharging to the family car. The man behind the Saab Turbo is an engineer of independent thought and uninhibited opinion – Per Gillbrand. His career with Saab began in 1964, and his first task was a preliminary study on 4-cylinder 4-stroke engines for the Saab 96, followed by a period as project leader for the Saab version of an engine created in association with the Ricardo laboratories and Triumph. This work overlapped with test trips to Poland with Saab 99 experimental cars, and adapting the Ford V4 engine and the Saab 96 to each other.

His turbocharger research began because the 99 was considered underpowered for the US market, and management disliked the idea of buying a bigger engine from outside. Equipped with a Garrett T.3 turbocharger set to provide low boost over a wide rpm-band, the Saab 99 turbo made its debut at the IAA in Frankfurt in 1977. Later refinements developed by Per Gillbrand include anti-knock control, not by playing with the spark timing as other turbo-car makers did, but by electronic control of the boost pressure. He designed the 16-valve head for the Saab engine and led the development of Saab's 'direct ignition' system, with each spark plug carrying its own coil.

Per Gillbrand was born at Tidaholm on 23 March 1934, and had a fascination with engines, cars, and boats from an early age. He was 14 when he built his own racing hydroplane. He studied engineering at Chalmers Technical College in Göteborg. He met his future wife at Skövde, and their son became an electronics specialist with Saab. At time of writing their daughter was still at school.

JPN

1977 Saab 99GL Super Combi coupé.
NICK BALDWIN

The 748cc 3-cylinder engine had been tuned to put out 57.5hp and was installed in a reversed position from the 93 ie inside the wheelbase, with the gearbox in front. The Saab 94 Sonett was first exhibited at the Stockholm Bilsalong in 1956.

Karossverkstäderna in Katrineholm made the plastic bodies for a prototype plus a series of test cars, which were assembled by ASJ at Linköping. But the Saab management had no interest in it, and it was written off as a pure experiment.

For years Saab had a very successful rally team, and Mellde was always developing ways to make the cars go faster. Eric Carlsson, supported by his wife, the former Pat Moss, scored most victories, including the RAC Rally in 1960–1962, the Monte Carlo in 1962 and 1963, and the Targa Florio (Rally, not Race) in 1964. Simo Lampinen and John Davenport won the 1968 RAC in a V4 Saab. Sixten Sason began in 1963 to prepare designs for a new Saab sports car based on the 96 platform. His leading candidate was a T-roofed roadster with a coke-bottle shape. In 1965, there was a TV show on car design, with a scale-model coupé designed by Björn Karlström for MFI (Malmö Flyg-Industri), makers of light aeroplanes and plastic boat hulls.

Tryggve Holm saw it and sent Saab representatives to MFI. Björn Karlström had designed bicycles, mopeds, outboard motors, etc for the Nyman group, but when he offered Nyman a sports car design, he was turned down.

His automobile artwork came to life again when he went to work for MFI. Saab AB engaged ASJ for final assembly of the Sonett II at the Arlöv plant, with Saab 96 engines and platforms from Trollhättan and fibreglass-reinforced plastic bodies made by MFI. The Arlöv plant turned out 258 Saab Sonett II coupés with 2-stroke engines from 1966 to 1967 and then 1613 Sonett cars with Ford V4 engines from 1967 to 1969.

The 99 was Rolf Mellde's concept, and Sixten Sason began making sketches for it in 1958. Mellde wanted a wide-track car, and made a remarkable test car in 1960 by sawing a 96 body in two, straight down the middle, from front to back, welding in steel plates to fill the gaps in the floor and the roof.

He put a 3-cylinder engine transversely on each side of the gearbox, making a 1500cc 100hp 6-cylinder power train. Because of its flattened appearance this car was nicknamed Paddan (The Toad) by the crew in the experimental

1983 Saab 900GLS saloon.
SAAB

1989 Saab 9000 Carlsson saloon.
SAAB

1999 Saab 9-5 Aero saloon.
SAAB

shop. Mellde decided to put the 99 on a 54.8in (1391mm) front track, with a 55.3in (1044mm) rear track compared with 48.03in (1219mm) front and rear on the 96.

The general body shape of the 99 had been approved in 1962, but Sixten Sason kept polishing it right to the end. He died in May 1967, and Björn Envall, who had worked for Saab from 1960 to 1964, returned to take over the design studio. He was the son of a ship's captain from Härnösand in northern Sweden, who had learned his craft under Sixten Sason since he was 18. He was on leave of absence from Saab from 1964 to 1967, to broaden his experience, which he did in the Opel studios in Rüsselsheim.

With its stub nose and short deck, near-upright windshield and 178in (4518mm) overall length, the 99 2-door saloon did not have a streamlined look, but its aerodynamic drag coefficient was a respectable 0.37. The chassis featured all-coil suspension and 4-wheel disc brakes.

The 1709cc 4-cylinder engine was mounted longitudinally and canted 45 degrees to the left, with the 4-speed gearbox, differential and free-wheel alongside the crankcase. It delivered 80hp at 5200rpm and gave the car a top speed of 96mph (155km/h). Bosch K-Jetronic fuel injection and Borg-Warner Type 35 automatic became optional in August 1969. A 95hp 1850cc export version had been added earlier in the year, and a 4-door saloon was introduced as a 1970 model.

From 4190 Saab 99s built in 1968, the assembly line was speeded up to produce 19,411 99s in 1969 and 29,755 in 1970. To make room for the 99 at Trollhättan, assembly of the 95 and 96 was transferred to Saab-Valmet at Uusikaupunki (formerly Nystad) in Finland, a 50/50 joint venture set up in 1968 by Saab AB and the Valmet industrial group.

The 500,000th Saab built since 1949 was a 99 that rolled out in February 1970. The annual total for 1970 topped 70,000 cars for the first time (73,982 units).

In January 1969 Saab AB merged with Scania-Vabis (another Wallenberg controlled company) to form Saab-Scania AB. Erik Nilsson was named executive vice president for the Saab-Scania automotive group, with Bengt Akerlind as head of Saab car production.

In 1970 a corner of the big Scania-Vabis diesel-engine factory at Södertälje was set aside for a new shop to make car engines for Saab. Per Gillbrand left Coventry to take charge of the Saab engine laboratories there, and in 1972 the supply contract with Triumph was cancelled.

Disagreements between Mellde and Mileikowsky grew in both frequency and intensity for some time, until Mellde solved the problem by signing up with Volvo as technical director for passenger cars in February 1971. Henrik Gustafsson was transferred from the Scania bus division factory at Katrineholm to become Saab's chief engineer of passenger-car development.

The 99 EMS was added at the end of 1973, with a 110hp version of the 1850cc engine. The following year, Saab introduced the 99 Combi-Coupé, styled by Björn Envall.

He had nothing to do with the Sonett III sports coupé, which was designed by Sergio Coggiola and slightly retouched by Gunnar Sjögren in the Saab studio. Introduced in 1970, it inherited the 96 platform and the 65hp 1498cc V4 Ford engine, which grew to 1698cc in 1971 with no change in power output.

The production arrangement with ASJ at the Arlöv plant was adapted to the new model. All in all, the plant turned out 8365 Sonett III, including 2500 in 1974 alone, its final year. The Arlöv plant then began assembling the 96 in the summer of 1975.

The 95 had its best-selling year in 1968, when 11,478 were built. As demand fell off, production dropped to 7991 in 1973 and 3364 in 1976. It was discontinued in 1978 after a run of 110,527 units.

The popularity of the 96 held up for three years after the introduction of the 99 but in 1972, Saab-Valmet still turned out 28,795 saloons and did not drop below 20,000 a year until 1976. The last Saab 96 was built in May 1980, ending a production run of more than 20 years and 547,221 cars.

During 1976–77 Peter Wallenberg was negotiating with Volvo's management principal shareholders about a merger of AB Volvo with Saab-Scania AB. The Volvo side was strongly for it. Curt Mileikowski and Sten Wennlo, Saab's sales director, opposed it bitterly. The plan sank in August 1987, when the directors of the Scania Truck and bus divisions formed a strong anti-Volvo front.

Until then, Saab's turnover and profits had been more or less proportional with the number of cars produced. Since production capacity was small, unit cost was too high to compete against makes like Opel, Ford, VW and Renault. Sten Wennlo reasoned that Saab could only survive by going up-market, building cars packed with value, and selling at high prices, with a healthy profit margin, in direct competition with cars renowned for their luxury and quality. This led very quickly to an upgrading of the 99 into the 900, development of the Saab Turbo engine, and the start of the 9000 project.

The original 1985cc Saab Turbo engine came into being at Per Gillbrand's initiative and was first displayed at the Frankfurt Auto Show in September 1977, as an option for the 99. With K-Jetronic fuel injection and a Garrett turbocharger, it put out 145hp at 5000rpm. Very few changes were made in this power unit for three years.

The number of Saab 99 cars with turbocharged engines started modestly with 1064 units in 1977, grew to 10,490 in 1978, 12,174 in 1979, and 16,573 in 1980.

The Saab 900, introduced late in 1978, was essentially a 99 with the Combi-coupé body and lengthened front wings and bonnet. The 900 EMS and 900 Turbo added in August 1979, were offered with an optional 5-speed gearbox. A 900 formal (notchback) 4-door saloon was added for 1981 in three versions: GL, GLE and 900 Turbo. The 1981-model 1985cc engine was 11.5kg lighter and had accessory drives with separate shafts (on earlier engines the accessories were driven off the camshaft).

Late in 1981, turbo engines for the 99 and 900 (for the Scandinavian markets) were equipped with APC, a Gillbrand invention using microprocessor control of boost pressure to prevent detonation.

A 2-door 900i was added to the range in September 1983, with a 118hp aspirated engine and power steering. The 1984 900 Turbo was equipped with intercooling on the boost-air from the Garrett turbocharger and delivered 175hp.

In 1986 Saab introduced the 900 Convertible. The design came from ASC, Inc. (formerly American Sunroof Corp.) and production was assigned to Saab-Valmet. A total of 48,888 convertibles was produced to the end of 1993.

The 99-900 engine programme was co-ordinated with the needs of the 9000 project, since Saab could not afford a new engine programme while simultaneously preparing an entirely new car. In 1978 Saab came to an agreement with Fiat to join a car programme that would create three Italian cars (Lancia Thema, Fiat Croma and Alfa Romeo 164) and one Swedish model: the Saab 9000. At the outset, they would share the platform and most of the inner body structure, suspension and drive line components.

The Saab was the first into production, in May 1984, but it had only architectural and layout similarities with the Italian cars, sharing no components except for 12 small steel pressings. Yet Giugiaro (Ital Design), who had drawn the bodies for the Thema and Croma, was also brought in as a styling consultant for the 9000.

For the first 20 months, all 9000 cars were powered by 175hp Turbo engines. The first non-turbo version was the 9000i-16 introduced in March 1986, with Bosch LH-Jetronic injection and an output of 130hp at 5500rpm.

Henrik Gustafsson had been moved laterally to a more suitable office as director of quality control in 1981, and Gunnar Larsson was named technical director for Saab passenger cars. He was given overall responsibility for the 9000, and named Rolf Sarsten as project manager. Magnus Roland, who had fixed the suspension problems of the 99 was made chief engineer of chassis design for the 900 and 9000.

2000 Saab 9-5 Griffin estate.
SAAB

Sten Wennlo retired in 1986, and Peter Wallenberg installed Ake Norrman, who had led the Volkswagen-Sweden company from 1970 to 1983, as head of the Saab car division.

From 1978 to 1983, the president of Saab-Scania AB was Sten Gustafsson, formerly of Goodyear/Sweden, Astra Pharmaceuticals, and Incentive AB. He was replaced by Georg Karnsund, one of Wallenberg's finance men. Production of the Saab 99 ended in 1984, after a run of 588,643 units in a 17-year span.

Rolf Sandberg, plant director at Trollhättan at the age of 36, played a major role in making the 9000 a pure Saab rather than an Italian replica, but it also ended up more expensive to build, and about 200kg heavier than the Fiat Croma. He was transferred to Investor AB (a Wallenberg holding) in 1989, but kept a seat on the Saab-Scania board. Peter Möller became director of production.

When Gunnar Larsson defected to Volvo in 1986, Stig-Göran Larsson (no relation) who had been with Saab as an engine specialist since 1972, took over as technical director of the Saab car division. Georg Karnsund put Jan-Erik Larsson (no relation) into the car division presidency in May 1989 (replacing Ake Norrman).

In June 1989, Saab had 40,000 unsold cars stockpiled at Trollhättan, and was losing money at a precipitous rate. Jan-Erik Larsson did everything he could to keep Saab viable. He ordered the closing of the Arlöv plant, and bought a former Kockums shipbuilding yard in Malmö to set up a high-productivity assembly for export models of the Saab 900. But Peter Wallenberg read the financial map better than anyone, and decided to find a partner for Saab.

Ties to Lancia existed, for Saab's Swedish dealer organisation had been selling the Lancia Delta and Y-10 since they were new, and informal talks were opened with top-level Fiat officials. At the same time, Saab executives were talking with representatives of Mazda Motors about possible areas of collaboration. That led to rumours of a Ford takeover, which was denied by both sides. Yet talks with Mazda and Ford ended only in September 1989, when Ford's negotiators demanded a majority holding in Saab-Scania AB.

Volvo made an offer to take the passenger-car branch off Saab-Scania's hands, but the Saab-Scania management rejected it. Georg Karnsund favoured the Lancia connection, and a team of Saab-Scania negotiators had Fiat officials convinced that the deal was made in November 1989. Unbeknownst to the Fiat officials, Saab-Scania and Wallenberg had also been engaged in discussions with corporate officers of General Motors.

2000 Saab 9-5SE saloon.
SAAB

Saab Automobile AB was formed on 1 January 1990 when Saab-Scania AB transferred its passenger-car operations, including the development of engines and gearboxes to the new company. On 15 March 1990, as per earlier agreement, General Motors Corp. acquired 50 per cent of the capital stock in Saab Automobile AB for $600 million, and installed David J. Herman as president.

Stig Göran Larsson was promoted to vice president of product development, and Thomas Enquist became head of powertrain operations at Saab Automobile AB in 1990. Saab engineers had access to the GM technical centre in Rüsselsheim and the GM proving grounds at Dudenhofen and Millbrook.

Saab's purchasing department was integrated with the GM Global Sourcing Network of suppliers, and the Saab-Valmet plant at Nystad began assembly of the Opel Calibra.

Throughout this eventful period, the Saab model range evolved steadily. The Saab 9000 CD super-deluxe limousine with the 16-valve 175hp turbo engine, appeared early in 1988. In 1990 Saab added TCS to the 9000 turbo. TCS was an intelligent anti-wheelspin device for front-wheel drive cars, combined with the ABS and electronic accelerator linkage.

In September 1990 the 900i engine was bored out to 2088cc, raising output to 140hp. A 2290cc version was offered in the 9000, beginning in September 1989, as a 150hp 10.1:1 compression aspirated unit. A year later, the 2290cc engine was equipped with direct ignition, Garrett T3 turbocharger and APC boost control, 8.5:1 compression and Bosch LH-Jetronic fuel injection, to deliver 200hp at 5500rpm.

The Saab 9000 Aero saloon, with its aerodynamically optimised and spoiler-equipped body, appeared in September 1992. It also had an Ecosport low-emission 225hp version of the 2290cc turbo engine, and ACS automatic clutch system.

David J. Herman was a Harvard-trained lawyer who had held many international positions with General Motors, but sorting out the Saab situation proved to be a much slower process than he first thought. Saab declared losses of $900 million under his presidency. In August 1992 he was named president of GM Europe, and Keith Butler-Wheelhouse was airlifted in from South Africa to take charge of Saab.

Herman had found that the Malmö-assembled cars cost 40 per cent more than cars made at Trollhättan, and closed the Malmö plant in February 1991, after only 18 months' operation. He also cancelled plans for a new engine factory at Karlskrona.

In May 1992 he arranged the sale of Saab's stake in Saab-Valmet to the Valmet group, which reorganised it as Valmet Automotive, while Herman brought assembly of the Saab 900 back to Trolhättan. Herman also gave high priority to new-car programmes, such as a new-generation 900 based on the Opel Vectra platform. At first, Herman and Fritz Lohr, technical director of Opel, thought they could use the Omega platform (with rear-wheel drive) for the replacement model for the Saab 9000, but had to change their minds.

The old 900 was taken out of production in 1993, after a run of 908,810 units built over 15 years.

The new Saab 900 was developed over a 42-month period as Project 104, and 100 test cars racked up millions of miles. It was introduced in July 1993. Leif Karlsson was responsible for the engine development (and transverse installation). The basic engine was a 133hp 1985cc aspirated unit, with a 185hp turbo as optional. It was also offered with a 150hp aspirated 2290cc unit, and a 170hp 2498cc V6 made by General Motors in England.

Einar Hareide led the styling of the 900, with Kent Bovellan as executive engineer for body design and development. Production time for the car was 38 hours. In 1989 it took 120 hours to build a Saab 9000. GM experts cut that to 81 hours in 1991 and 55 hours in 1993. Peter Möller was promoted to vice president for technical development and manufacturing with Magnus Jonsson as chief engineer, product development. A new 900 convertible was introduced in spring 1994, with assembly by Valmet Automotive.

In August 1994 a 24-valve 2962cc GM V6 with variable intake manifold, delivering 210hp at 6200rpm, became optional in the CSE, CDE and Griffin versions of the Saab 9000. TCS (wheelspin control) and ABS were standard; buyers had a choice of a 5-speed gearbox or a GM 4-speed automatic transmission.

In September 1996, GM installed Robert W. Hendry as president of Saab automobile AB, replacing Keith Butler-Wheelhouse, who left the GM organisation, after putting Saab in the black (1995 was the first year of profits since 1988).

The Saab 9-5 replaced the 9000 in June 1997, after a production run of 521,000 cars. The unit-construction body did not have any Opel parts, and both front and rear suspension systems were mounted on subframes. Einar Hareide and Tony Catigani were responsible for the styling. The 4-door short-deck deluxe saloon stood on a 106.3in (2698mm) wheelbase and was 189in (4797mm) long, for a weight of 3276lb (1485kg). Engines included a 150hp 1985cc Ecopower unit with low-pressure turbocharging, a 170hp 2290cc unit with Trionic management and turbo-intercooling, and a 200hp 2962cc GM V6 with low-pressure turbocharging.

The 900 was renamed 9-3 in February 1998 and continued without major modifications. September 1998 saw the announcement of a new engine line-up, with three versions of the 1985cc engine, redesigned with 16 valves and two balance shafts throughout. The 200hp turbo-intercooled unit was reserved for cars with a manual gearbox, the 185hp turbo replaced the fuel-injected 2290cc engine. The 9-3 also became the first Saab offered with diesel power, a 115hp 16-valve 2171cc engine based on Opel technology but developed in Sweden for turbo-intercooling.

JPN

Further Reading
Saab, the Innovator, Mark Chatterton, David & Charles, 1980.
The Saab-Scania Story, Saab-Scania AB, 1987.
'A Short Journey for a Sporty Swede – the Saab Sonnett II', John Matras, *Special –Interest Autos*, Jan – Feb 1995.

S.A.B.A. (I) 1927–1928
Stà Automobili Brevetti Angelino, Milan.
The S.A.B.A. had a conventional 1-litre 4-cylinder engine, but apart from that its specification was very unusual. It had 4-wheel-drive and steering and a central backbone frame, while suspension was by transverse leaf springs front and rear. The brakes were on the front wheels and the transmission. It was said to be reaching the production stage in July 1927, but does not seem to have been built for sale. However, a conventional car, the S.A.B.A. Stelvio, was also made.
NG

SABELLA (GB) 1906–1914
Sabella Motor Car Co. Ltd, Camden Town, London.
Fritz Sabel's first car was hand-propelled, with a lever and chain which went over a free wheel on the back axle. To this he attached a 1hp engine and showed a development at the 1906 Stanley Show. He built one or two more cars, though possibly not for sale, and also another hand-powered machine, this time for six passengers. 'It will be found an exercise similar to rowing in a boat where no river is available' he said.

According to a statement given to *The Cyclecar* Mr Sabel introduced the BEDELIA into Great Britain. However, by 1912 he was making a cyclecar of his own, powered by a 10hp V-twin JAP engine, with chain drive to a countershaft and vee-belt drive to the rear wheels. The body was a 2-seater, with either side by side or tandem layout, and it was also available as a delivery van. The price was £115, reduced to £99 by the Spring of 1913.
NG

SABER (US) c.1977–1985
Saber Automotive, Waukesha, Wisconsin.
The only thing wrong with an Opel GT was its graceless body. The Saber GT kit car fixed all that with an aerodynamic and attractive body that used the Opel engine, transmission, suspension, brakes, windshield and many other parts. A steel tube frame was mounted to the fibreglass body at the factory and the Opel doors were reskinned with fibreglass panels. The Saber GT was easy to assemble and possibly the only Opel-based kit car ever built.
HP

SABLATNIG-BEUCHELT (D) 1925–1926
Beuchelt & Co., Grünberg.
This company specialised in building railway carriages and bus bodies, but made a short-lived foray into car manufacture. A tourer with 1496cc 6/30PS 4-cylinder engine was made for a few months.
HON

SABRA (IL) 1960–1974
Autocars Ltd, Haifa.
The Sabra has two firsts to its credit, Israel's first production car and the first of RELIANT's package motor industries, later employed in Greece (ATTICA CARMEL) and Turkey (ANADOL). Autocars Ltd was founded in 1954 to assemble Reliant 3-wheeled vans from kits. An initial batch of 100 was ordered, followed in 1960 by 500 of a 4-wheeled estate car called the Sussita. This was powered by a Ford Anglia 105E engine in a box-section frame, with 2-door fibreglass body. A more ambitious project was thought up by Autocar's managing director Mr Shubinsky, who wanted a car suitable for export, especially to the USA, which the Sussita clearly was not. He admired the Ashley fibreglass body for Ford and Austin Seven chassis and also Leslie Ballamy's chassis with transverse leaf suspension, and asked Reliant to marry the two. The result, with 1703cc Ford Consul engine, was called the Sabra, after an Israeli cactus, though it is also the name for a native-born Israeli as opposed to an immigrant. The first 100 were made by Reliant and exported directly to North America. It went into production at Haifa shortly afterwards. In 1961 it appeared on the Reliant stand at the Motor Show as the Sabre, the ancestor of a long line of Reliant sports cars culminating in the Scimitar GTC of 1986.

Meanwhile a new saloon had appeared to join the Sussita. Also Anglia-powered, the Carmel had more attractive line than the estate car, and soon gained a Cortina engine. A 4-door model, the Sabra Gilboa appeared in 1967, the year after Reliant ended their supply of components to Autocars. They then signed an agreement with British Leyland for the supply of Triumph Herald 12/50 engines, although Ford units as well as Triumphs were used up to 1969. At their

1963 Sabra sports car.

peak in the mid–1960s Autocars were turning out 60 cars and light commercials per week, or about 3000 per year, but this figure dropped to 1600 by 1974, when Autocars was bought by Rom Carmel Industries. The car's name was changed to ROM CARMEL that year and continued up to 1981. When the Editor-in-Chief visited Israel in 1984 Sabras and Rom Carmels were frequently encountered, but on another visit in 1998 not one was to be seen.

NG

Further Reading
The Scimitar and its Forebears, Don Pither, Court Publishing, 1987.

SABRE (GB) 1984–1987

1984–1986 Sabre Cars, Wallsend, Tyne & Wear.
1986–1987 D.C. Kit Cars, Newcastle, Tyne & Wear.
When the Sabre Sprint was launched, it was greeted as a fibreglass alternative to the Mini Metro. Conceived by a firm which made fibreglass sunbeds, it was a Mini-based fibreglass 4-seater with a glass tailgate. The Mini front subframe was used untouched in the monocoque but the rear one was swapped for a steel crossmember. The later Vario featured an interchangeable rear roof section allowing open or estate-type styles.

CR

SABRE AUTOMOTIVE (US) c.1997 to date

Sabre Automotive, Jensen Beach, Florida.
Sabre bought INTEGRITY COACHWORKS in 1997 and took over their production of the KVA GT40 replica. They were sold in various stages of completion, and used Corvette suspension components with Ford V8 engines and Porsche transaxles. They also continued with Integrity's 427 Cobra replica which used Ford engines and Corvette-based suspension.

HP

SACA (B) 1924–1927

Automobiles SACA, Etterbeek-Brussels.
This was one of several Belgian firms which modified the Ford Model T, in this case by lowering and lengthening the frame and fitting front-wheel brakes.

1963 Sabra Carmel saloon.

c.1970 Sabra Gilboa 12/50 saloon.

1906 Sage tourer.
BRYAN K. GOODMAN

They worked with second-hand as well as new Fords, and made trucks with engines converted to run on producer gas.

NG

SACHSENRING (DDR) 1956–1959

VEB Sachsenring Automobilwerke, Zwickau.
This car originated as the revived HORCH with 2407cc ohv 6-cylinder engine and 4-door saloon body. The name was soon changed to Sachsenring, after one of East Germany's racing circuits, and the model was called the P240. Apart from minor styling changes, it was made unaltered up to 1959. About 1500 were built, including some estate cars and a handful of 4-door cabriolet parade cars. Later the TRABANT was made in the same factory.

HON

SACKVILLE (GB) 1915

Sackville Motor Co., Tooting, London.
The Sackville was a light car with 10hp 4-cylinder engine and 2-seater body, priced at $126. Its life was short as it was introduced during the second year of World War I.

NG

SADO see ENTREPOSTO

S.A.F. (i) (F) 1908–c.1912

Sté Anon. des Ateliers du Furan, St Étienne, Loire.
The company that had made the JUSSY car from 1898 to 1900 returned to the field in 1908 with a tandem-seated tricar on similar lines to the RILEY and ROYAL ENFIELD. The 500cc 4¹/₂hp single-cylinder engine was mounted under the driver's seat and drove the rear wheel by chain. The two front wheels had independent suspension.

NG

S.A.F. (ii) (S) 1919–1922

AB Svenska Automobilfabriken, Bollnas.
The Swedish S.A.F. company was founded by Anders Jonsson to make an assembled car powered by a 4-cylinder G.B. & S. or Continental engine, with 3-speed gearbox. It had cantilever springs and the tourer body could seat six passengers. The components were imported from the USA, mainly from the makers of the PULLMAN (i). Plans called for production of 1000 cars per year, but far fewer, probably no more than 25, were made, and it lasted less that two years.

NG

SAFARI (DK) 1970s

This was a licence-built version of the Brazilian GURGEL, a Volkswagen-based jeep-style vehicle, constructed in Denmark.

CR

SAFETY (US) 1901–1902

Safety Steam Automobile Co., Ipswich, Massachusetts.
This company made a small steam runabout like so many others of its time, with single-cylinder engine, single-chain drive, tubular boiler, full-elliptic springs and tiller steering. In addition to the 2-seater runabout the company offered a 4-seater brake and a delivery van.

NG

SAFIR (i) (CH) 1906–c.1909

1906–1907 Schweizer Automobil Fabrik in Rheineck SAFIR, Rheineck.
1907–c.1909 SAFIR Automobile, Zürich.
Unlike most of the early automobile manufacturers, Safir did not start his business on a shoestring. Two experienced and affluent industrialists, Anton Dufour and Jakob Schmidheiny, founded this company and soon transfered it to spacious premises in Zürich equipped with up-to-date tool machinery. From the beginning Safir aimed at the top-class market and took out a licence for SAURER engines. Two models of 30 PS and 50 PS both had 4-cylinder in-line T-head engines, 4-speed gearbox with direct top and shaft drive. The Saurer compressed-air starter was a refinement not many competing cars offered. Top speed of the big model was nearing the 60mph (97km/h) mark. A few dozen cars were produced and sold. In 1908 the very first fast revving diesel engine, suitable for road vehicles and based on a Saurer petrol version, was completed in the Safir factory under the supervision of Rudolf Diesel, Hyppolyt Saurer and the engineers Duchamps and Seguin. Safir also produced some commercial vehicles but none of their efforts seems to have been economically successful and by about 1909 the dream of superior automobiles, lorries and buses had to be buried.

FH

SAFIR (ii) (GB) 1981 to date

Safir Engineering Ltd, Weybridge, Surrey.
This company, well-known for its Formula 3 racers, produced the world's first accurate Ford GT40 replica. With a simplified steel monocoque chassis designed by Len Bailey (ex of Ford Advanced Vehicles), it was so accurate that it was given the MkV designation (the last genuine GT40s were MkIVs) and even the chassis numbering sequence continued as if production were unbroken. A 350bhp 4.7-litre Ford V8 engine and ZF 5-speed gearbox were used, and a potential 200mph (320km/h) top speed was quoted. The car was also referred to as the Brooklands GT40.

CR

S.A.G. see PIC-PIC

SAGA (F) 1980–c.1994

Jean-Louis Baud Automobiles, Laon, Aisne.
This was a particularly pleasing replica of the 1932 Bugatti Type 55, reproduced in 9/10 scale. Many items were painstakingly recreated as per the original, including the wheels, grill, suspension and front axle. The mechanicals derived from Alfa Romeo, including the engine (from 1.3- to 2-litres), 5-speed transaxle, De Dion rear suspension and disc brakes. The bodywork was made of nine fibreglass panels and fitted over a tubular steel chassis. Another model was the P3, a replica of the Alfa P3 racer, which was intended more for track use. The aluminium and polyester body was mated to a tubular steel chassis and modern Alfa Romeo mechanicals. In 1994 the replica was still being made by Spirit Saga Concept of Clichy.

CR

SAGE (F) 1900–1906

Ateliers P. Sage, Paris.
This company made solid, fairly large cars powered by a variety of engines. Their suppliers included Abeille, Aster, Brouhot and Mutel, in sizes from 10 to 24hp, with 2- or 4-cylinders. They had gilled tube radiators to start with, and from 1904 used a round honeycomb radiator similar to that of the Hotchkiss. Final drive was by double chains. One model had forward control and an under seat engine. In 1906 a wide range from 10 to 50hp was offered, including some with Gassner petrol–electric drive.

NG

SAGER (CDN) 1910–1911

United Motors Ltd, Welland, Ontario.

This car was promoted by former Oldsmobile manager Frederick Sager, who originally planned to call it the Welland. It was a conventional car powered by a 30hp 4-cylinder engine and listed with tourer or roadster bodies. Despite Sager's enthusiastic promotion, there was little evidence of any cars being made. Possibly a few prototypes were built, but it is equally possible that no Sager ever saw the light of day.

NG

SAGESSE (GB) 1990–1991

Sagesse Motor Co., Gosforth, Newcastle, Tyne & Wear.

This ambitious Ford CVH mid-engined 2+2 coupé was called the Sagesse Helios. Its dramatic styling was created by Matt Ritson and incorporated lift-out T-roof panels. It clothed a tubular space frame chassis using Ford running gear. Only three were made.

CR

SAGINAW (i) (US) 1914

Valley Boat & Engine Co., Saginaw, Michigan.

Originally to be called the Faultless, the makers chose the more modest name of their home town. The car was a cyclecar with the usual 9/12hp V-twin engine, although they made it themselves rather than buying from De Luxe as so many of their rivals did. Friction transmission and belt drive were typical for cyclecars, but the Saginaw had more dashing lines than most, with swooping curved wings over the driving belts and headlamps mounted on the wings Pierce-Arrow style. With a wheelbase of 100.5in(2551mm) the Saginaw roadster sold for $395, but it did not survive the year of its launch.

NG

SAGINAW (ii) (US) 1916

Lehr Motor Co., Saginaw, Michigan.

This company announced the Saginaw Eight, a tourer to be powered by a Massnick-Phipps V8 engine and selling at the reasonable figure of $1050. Only a few were made, together with two examples of a 4-cylinder car.

NG

SAGINAW SPEEDSTER see DETROIT (iv)

SAIGA (F) 1910–1912

De la Salle et Lacombe, Poitiers.

The Saiga was a medium-sized car with a 12CV 4-cylinder engine made in very small numbers for a local clientele. About 15 were built, of which one survives today. This has an advanced, fully-enclosed saloon body.

NG

S.A.I.L. see SIPANI

S.A.L. see ESPERIA

SALATHE see MACH 1

SALEEN (US) 1984 to date

Saleen Autosport, Brea, California.

Steve Saleen began his career by racing Ford Mustangs in the Trans-Am series. In 1984 his company introduced a series of modified Mustangs for street use. They had arrangements with Ford that allowed them to receive technical and marketing help. The suspension was upgraded with heavy-duty pieces and special body trim parts differentiated it from a standard Mustang. By 1995 Saleen-modified Mustangs had 5700cc Ford engines with around 450 supercharged horsepower. They were sold through Ford dealers with a new-car warranty.

HP

SALMON (GB) 1914

Baguley Cars Ltd, Burton-on-Trent, Staffordshire.

This was a light car with 11.9hp 4-cylinder engine planned as a companion make to the bigger BAGULEY. It was named after P. Salmon who had been chief

1925 Salmson 10hp 2-seater.
NICK BALDWIN

1927 Salmson VAL 3 tourer.
NICK GEORGANO

engineer for the RYKNIELD Engine Works when they were taken over by Ernest Baguley. Only three Salmons were made, an open 2-seater, a coupé and a delivery van. Salmon also designed the smaller ACE (ii) for manufacture of which he formed a separate company, while the Salmon was made by Baguley.

NG

SALMSON (F) 1921–1957

Sté des Moteurs Salmson, Billancourt, Seine.

The Société des Moteurs Salmson was founded at Billancourt in 1912 by Émile Salmson (1859–1917), a civil engineer who turned to the manufacture of aero-engines when over fifty years old, becoming one of the first to make purpose-built engines. The war gave a tremendous boost to his business to which he added the manufacture of magnetos and complete aircraft. After his death in 1917 the company came under the control of M. Heinrich, manager of the Lyons branch factory, and it was he who had the task of keeping the business going after the Armistice. In fact aero-engine manufacture continued right through until World War II, but other work was needed as well. Heinrich tried wood-working machinery, car bodies and pumps, but only the latter flourished, and was soon hived off by Salmsons' sons who formed a separate company, the Société des Fils d'Émile Salmson, in 1922. Car bodies led Heinrich to consider the making of complete cars, and like many others in 1919, he saw a future in the light cyclecar. Having no one on his staff with experience of automobile engineering, he decided to make cars under licence, and for his model chose the British G.N., probably the most successful of all the cyclecars. Six cars were shown at the 1919 Paris Salon, and production got underway in 1920. They were identical to the British product, having 1086cc inlet-over-exhaust V-twin engines, dog clutches and chain drive. The contract was for 3000 cars, but only 1578 were built. Among customers for the G.N.-Salmson were the Paris police. It seems that Salmson built some cars for G.N.'s Paris agent to sell as G.N.s, presumably

1930 Salmson S4 saloon.
NICK BALDWIN

1933 Salmson S4-C saloon.
NICK BALDWIN

to supplement the British-built cars he was importing from Wandsworth. This was after Salmson had begun to make 4-cylinder cars of their own design.

The first Salmsons proper were the work of Émile Petit who had designed an ohv engine as long ago as 1902. He was introduced to Heinrich by André Lombard, an agent for the international sales company, Gaston, Williams & Wigmore, who also drove Salmsons in competitions. The engine that Petit brought Salmson was a 1087cc 4-cylinder unit with inclined ohvs and curious valve gear, in which a single pushrod per cylinder operated the exhaust valve in the normal way but acted as a pullrod to operate the inlet valve. The cams were recessed to allow a second spring to push the tappet into this recess at the right time so that the pushrod pulled the rocker down with it and so opened the inlet valve against a weaker spring. The engine was placed far back in the frame, final drive was by bevel gear with no differential, and the body was a light 2- or 3-seater. The car was christened the AL after André Lombard, and it was he who chose the St Andrew's Cross motif for the radiator.

Although Petit's push-pullrod engine was used on some Salmsons up to 1929, it was obvious that the engine had limitations and could not operate at high speeds. The prototype AL took part in the 1921 Swiss Six Day Trial with the push-pull unit, but on its return to Billancourt the engine was replaced by a new twin-ohc unit. Thus equipped it was raced by Lombard in the French Cyclecar GP at Le Mans, which it won easily, despite running out of fuel which necessitated a 2-mile sprint by the mechanic to get some more. Later in the year Lombard was 2nd in the 200 Mile Race at Brooklands (1100cc class), while in 1922 Salmsons won the GP des Voiturettes, Tour de France and their class in the 200 Mile Race.

The twin-ohc cars gained valuable publicity for Salmson, but it was the touring AL and its successors which earned the company's profits, and these were made in much larger numbers. By 1929 the touring models had accounted for 11,632 sales, compared with 2672 of the twin-cam cars. 1922 saw the D-type, a tourer with twin-cam engine, and the first of its type in the world. In fact, Salmson was not only a pioneer of twin-ohcs, but was the only company to make engines of this layout continuously for 36 years. From 1929 until they closed their doors in 1957 they made nothing else.

For 1923 the AL was joined by the VAL3 with semi-elliptic springs replacing the front quarter-elliptics, and in 1925 a cross member at the rear of the frame enabled 4-seater coachwork to be fitted. A differential finally arrived during the 1926 season. The engine size remained at 1087cc, but power rose from 18 to 22bhp. The twin-ohc D-type had a 1195cc engine, and from 1927 the D2 had a vee-radiator and longer wheelbase which could accommodate open and closed 4-seater bodies. Salmsons were sold to other firms for badge engineering; BIGNAN bought a number of AL3s in 1923 which they fitted with their own radiators though the rest of the car was pure Salmson, even the serial numbers of engine and chassis. In the late 1920s RALLY bought a number of Salmson GS sports cars, and in the early 1930s, S4 and S4Cs, which they sold under their own name.

Lombard left Salmson in 1923, later to make a car under his own name, but Petit stayed until the end of the decade, and designed some excellent little sports cars. The 1926 Grand Sport (sold as the Grand Prix in England) had a cowled radiator and front-wheel brakes, and was good for 70mph (112km/h), while the GS Special had full-pressure lubrication and a 4-speed gearbox, and could be bought with a Cozette supercharger, in which form top speed was 100mph (161km/h) Only 138 of these were made, between 1924 and 1927. The most powerful engine was the San Sebastian, with larger sump and twin magnetos.

The years 1925 to 1930 were Salmson's finest in sport. The 1926 catalogue listed the previous year's successes; 52 wins in France, six in Italy, five in Germany, four in Czechoslovkia, three in Austria and two each in Belgium, Spain and Switzerland. These included minor races and hill climbs, but it was nevertheless a remarkable roll of honour. Superchargers were used for the first time in 1926, when Casse won at Miramas ahead of the new 6-cylinder Amilcars. Petit's swan song for Salmson was the 1100cc twin-ohc straight-8 with desmodromic valve gear, twin Cozette superchargers and an output of 140bhp, later increased to 170bhp. This represented 150bhp per litre. Only two chassis and three engines were made before Heinrich closed down the competition department.

Although the sports Salmsons grabbed most of the headlines, the touring D-types were made in larger numbers, and made more profit for the firm. A 1630cc six was announced for 1929, but never reached the public. By 1929 Heinrich felt, correctly as it turned out, that the small French sports car had had its day, and did not sanction a replacement for the GS, the last of which was made in April 1930. This decision, and the closure of the racing department, so distressed Émile Petit that he left to become chief engineer at Ariès. The D-type's successor, in which Petit had a hand, was called the S4; the twin-ohc layout was retained, and capacity was slightly up at 1300cc. Other features carried over from the Ds included magneto ignition, gravity feed and thermo-syphon cooling. The S4 was both more refined and more robust than its predecessors, but in no way was it a sports car. Only closed bodies were offered, and top speed was around 65mph (105km/h).

The S4 acquired a 4-speed gearbox in 1932, when a handsome roadster was added to the range, and in 1933 came the S4C with 1465cc engine, longer wheelbase and Bendix brakes. Capable of 70mph (112km/h), the S4C was the basis of the l2hp BRITISH SALMSON made from 1934 to 1938. A Salmson-built Cotal electric gearbox was standard equipment from 1934 to 1936, but it was not very reliable, and from 1936 onwards a choice of 'genuine' Cotal box or Delahaye-built 4-speed synchromesh was offered. The S4D of 1935 had a larger engine of 1596cc, transverse-leaf ifs suspension and rack-and-pinion steering. The five body styles included 2- and 4-door aerodynamic saloons.

The S4 underwent few changes in the later 1930s, though coil ignition was adopted in 1937. For 1939 two models were made, the 1730cc S4-61 and the 2312cc S4E. The latter had hydraulic brakes, torsion bar front suspension instead of transverse springs and a slightly longer wheelbase, though body styles, now reduced to three, were similar, and there was little to distinguish the two models externally. More than 1000 were sold of the S4-61 and S4E, out of a total for the 1930s of around 6000. This was considerably less than the 14,000 cars sold between 1921 and 1930, but Salmson was increasingly turning to aero-engines in the years leading up to the war.

Postwar Developments

The two S4 models were revived after the war, and made up to 1950 with little change, apart from rounder wings and semi-enclosed headlamps, which were adopted on the S4E for 1948 and on the S4-61 a year later. The 1950 Paris Salon saw a new Salmson in the shape of the E72 Randonnée. This had the same twin-cam engine as the S4E, though slightly smaller at 2200cc, with an all-enveloping

1935 Salmson S4-D cabriolet.
NICK GEORGANO

1955 Salmson 2300 coupé.
NATIONAL MOTOR MUSEUM

4-door saloon body. This was heavier than its predecessor, with a top speed of 84mph (135km/h). It might have maintained the sales of the earlier cars, but Salmson had to increase the price by 40 per cent during its first year, which inevitably damaged its prospects, and only 630 Randonnées were sold. Nearly all were saloons, though there were a handful of 2-door cabriolets. By contrast, more than 2800 postwar S4s were made, their best year being 1950 when 1162 were delivered.

1952 was a very difficult year for Salmson. The market for their radial aero-engines was drying up as American flat-fours were taking over, and the Randonnée was not selling. The factory closed down for a while, and car deliveries were only 89 in 1952 and 61 in 1953. Heinrich retired during this period, after 36 years in charge of the company.

Despite their problems Salmson had an excellent technical staff, and these were put to work to design a new and more sporting car which appeared at the 1953 Salon. Called the 2300 Sport, it had a similar engine to the Randonnée's, but with capacity back at 2312cc, and output was now 105bhp. The Cotal gearbox was retained, and the body was a completely new 2+2 coupé styled by Eugène Martin. This was the only production 2300, though an open 2-seater was shown at the Salon. Salmson did not make these bodies; the first 39 were

made by Esclassan and the remaining 188 were by Chapron. The 2300 Sport had a good performance, with a top speed of 112mph (180km/h) which made it competitive with cars such as the Triumph TR2 and A.C. Aceca. They appeared at Le Mans in 1955, 1956 and 1957, the 1956 entry being a standard coupé with full upholstery and a radio, while the others were special open 2-seaters. They did not distinguish themselves, but in rallies they made a good showing, with 13 wins in 1954.

However, the sands were running out for all the French quality cars makers; Delage ceased production in 1953 and Delahaye in 1954, and Salmson managed only another three years. They hoped to augment the range with a 4-door saloon, but only prototypes were made, by Chapron in 1954 and Motto in 1956. 72 cars were made in 1955, and just eight in 1956. The last car to be delivered was a 2300 Sport which left the factory in February 1957. Renault subsequently took over the factory.

NG

Further Reading
The Salmson Story, Chris Draper, David & Charles, 1974.
Salmson, Histoire d'un Nom, Claude Chevalier, E.T.A.I., 1998.

SALOMON (F) 1931–1932

The famous engineer Jules Salomon, who was responsible for the first CITROËNS, the LE ZÈBRE and was adviser to Lucien ROSENGART, designed a small car to be sold either under his own name, or as the Le Cabri. It had a 386cc single-cylinder engine and a 2-seater body. Salomon thought that a motorcycle manufacturer would be the most appropriate firm to make it, but he never signed an agreement with anyone.

NG

SALTER (US) 1909–1915

W.A. Salter Motor Co., Kansas City, Missouri.
Salter's car was conventional enough with its 30hp 4-cylinder engine and 5-seater tourer or 2-seater roadster body, but its transmission was unusual. A 2-speed epicyclic system was not common on so large a car, and it incorporated no reverse gear, Instead, this was incorporated in the rear axle. Salter's output was not large, but lasted until 1915.

NG

SALVA (I) 1906–1907

Stà Anonima Lombarda Vetture Automobili, Milan.
Many of the short-lived Italian car companies of the time made light cars, but Salvas were large machines with 4-cylinder engines, the smallest of which was a 16/25hp, and others were a 28/45 and a 60/70hp. They are likely to have used chain drive.

NG

SALVADOR (i) (US) 1914

Salvador Motor Co., Boston, Massachusetts.
Named after Salvador J. Richards, this was a light 2-seater car powered by a 12hp 4-cylinder Farmer engine, with 3-speed gearbox and shaft drive. Production was due to start in June 1914, and a few may have been made, but in February 1915 Richards announced a new car to bear his initials, the S.J.R.

NG

SALVADOR (ii) (E) 1922

Automóviles Salvador, Barcelona.
Salvador Grau produced motorcycles, wheels and rims, but also built a typical cyclecar with MAG 2-cylinder engine, with double wishbone suspension at the front and shaft transmission. Only a few were made.

VCM

SALVATOR see UNDERBERG

SALVO (GB) 1906

Swan & Co., London.
This company exhibited a limousine with 24/30hp 4-cylinder engine at the 1906 Stanley Show. As Swan & Co. were dealers, it is possible that the Salvo represented bankrupt stock from another company.

NG

S.A.M. (I) 1924–1926

Stà Automobili e Motori, Legnano, Milan.
This company made a sporting light car in four models, the B23 and B24 with side-valve engines, and the C25 and V25 with 1100cc ohv engines which developed 22bhp. The company also supplied chassis and bodies to F.O.D.

NG

S.A.M.A.S. see YETI

S.A.M.C.A. (I) 1947–1949

Stà Applicazioni Meccaniche Costruzioni Automobilistiche, Parma.
This company produced the Atomo 3-wheeled microcar rolltop coupé. Into a tubular chassis was placed a 246cc 2-stroke twin engine in the tail, developing 10bhp, plus a 3-speed gearbox. It weighed only 190kg. After its presentation at the 1947 Milan show, a coachbuilder called Bertolini in Milan was enlisted and a modified version prepared, but the Atomo never entered production.

CR

SAMCO (US) 1968–1970

Sports Automobile Manufacturing Co., Manford, Oklahoma.
After the demise of the CORD 810 in 1966, this Oklahoma company resumed production of reduced-size replicas of the classic Cord shape. The SAMCO Cords were very different from the Glenn Pray replicas. They had two models with longer wheelbases and conventional front engine/rear-wheel drive chassis. The headlights, which had retracted on the original Cords and the Pray replicas, were mounted on the ends of the front mudguards on the SAMCO cars. There was a Ford V8-powered version called the Warrior based on a 108in (2741mm) wheelbase. Chassis choices included one based on a Ford Econoline van or a custom-built tube frame that used Jeep front suspension. The Royale version was longer at a 113in (2868mm) wheelbase, and it used a 7200cc Chrysler powerhouse.

HP

SAMIMI (US) c.1985

Samimi Corp., Encino, California.
Samimi built a replica of the Lotus Super 7 based on Toyota running gear.

HP

1932 Salomon Le Cabri 386cc 2-seater.
NICK BALDWIN

1914 Salvador (i) 12hp 2-seater.
NICK BALDWIN

SAMPSON (US) 1911

United States Motor Corp., Alden Sampson Division, Detroit, Michigan.
In 1911 the ALDEN SAMPSON Manufacturing Co. of Pittsfield, Massachusetts, was bought by Benjamin Briscoe's United States Motor Co. He decided that the Sampson name, which had been carried on trucks, should be used for a car again, and launched a conventional 35hp 4-cylinder tourer. It did not survive the collapse of United States Motor Co. in 1912.

NG

SAMSON (US) 1919

Samson Tractor Co. (Division of General Motors), Janesville, Wisconsin.
The Samson 'All-Family' car was one of the great curiosities of General Motors for, although planned for production in formidable numbers, its production was limited to a single car. A 9-seater touring car, the Samson was constructed for readily-simple removal of the rear and both jump seats and easy conversion to pick-up truck status. This was an attempt by GM under William C. Durant's presidency to further embellish GM's position in farm machinery, in this case a car which could be used by a large farm family for church transportation on Sundays and for carrying produce to markets on weekdays. The idea died before production and the projected 'All-Family' car was abandoned, the lone pilot model being sold to a farming family by the Janesville Samson Tractor dealer. The Samson used the same 6-cylinder engine as the Chevrolet and had a wheelbase of 118in (2995mm). Samson introduced two trucks the following year, both designed for farm use and continued production alongside tractor manufacture until the division was closed down in 1923, its factory being turned into a Chevrolet assembly plant.

KM

1998 San Streak convertible.
NICK BALDWIN

1906 Sanchis tricar.
NATIONAL MOTOR MUSEUM

1934 Sandford 1100cc 3-wheeler.
NICK BALDWIN

SAM'S SURPLUS (US) 1998 to date
Sam's Surplus, Stanton, Texas.
The Alley-Cat was a replica of the AMG Hummer. It was a kit car that used a Chevrolet pick-up truck or Suburban chassis and running gear. They planned to introduce Ford and Chrysler-based versions as well.
HP

SAMSUNG (ROK) 1995–1998
Samsung Motors Inc, Seoul.
For many years the industrial giant Samsung lobbied the Korean government to obtain the necessary dispensation to begin car production. It formed an alliance with Nissan to develop future products. In 1995 it displayed an unusual and rather frivolous open-sided design exercise, but its intentions were far more serious. It developed five conventionally-engineered passenger cars: the SM525V, SM520V, SM520 SE, SM520 and SM518. Ultimately the economic conditions in Asia that

forced Kia into such dire financial straits persuaded Samsung to abandon its plans for car manufacture in 1998.
CR

SAN (IND) 1997 to date
San Motors, Bangalore.
This company specialised in railways and branched out into car production with a pair of delightfully styled small sports cars. Both were designed in France by Le Mans Design and were fitted with 1.2-litre Renault Twingo engines. The first model was the Storm, a 2-door coupé, while the convertible was called the Streak. In Britain, Reliant collaborated with the project and was set to offer them through its own franchises.
CR

SANCHIS (F) c.1906–1912
Enrique Sanchis, Paris; Courbevoie, Seine.
In 1906 Enrique Sanchis was making a tricar with single rear wheel and combined frame and body of pressed steel. In 1907 he advertised a 14hp car and by 1910 was making what were described as 'voiturettes extra-légères' powered by 4½ to 10hp engines and weighing 880lbs. These were sold by L. Pierron, who also made the car known in England as the Mass.
NG

SANDBACH (GB) 1983–1984
Sandbach Replica Cars, Sandbach, Cheshire.
Various kits were imported from the USA by Sandbach, all exclusively for VW Beetle floorpans until Sandbach developed a chassis for Vauxhall Chevette suspension and a choice of Vauxhall or Ford engines. This chassis was adapted to fit the Saxon (an imported Austin-Healey 3000 replica) and the Duke (an imported SS100 replica).
CR

SANDERSON-ASTER (GB) 1905–1907
Henry Angus, Sanderson (Carlisle) Ltd, Carlisle, Cumberland.
This company took over the wagon-building works of William Lawson, and was an offshoot of coachbuilders Sir William Angus, Sanderson, who later built the ANGUS SANDERSON car in Newcastle. In 1905 they announced the Sanderson-Aster, with 18/22hp 4-cylinder Aster engine and coachwork made by themselves. Very few were made, possibly no more than three, and there are no references to the make after 1907.
NG

SANDFLY (AUS) 1924
Mitchell Brothers, Randwick, New South Wales.
The Mitchell brothers had been associated with establishing the Australian Six project but were in their own business when this little car appeared. Built on a 60in (1524mm wheelbase), it had a 2.25hp air-cooled 2-stroke engine which drove via a 2-speed gearbox and chain to a live rear axle. With quarter-elliptic springs all round, a 2-seater body and regulation electric lighting, it was claimed to be practical despite its small size, being registered for road use.
MG

SANDFORD (F) 1923–1939
1923–1925 S. Sandford, Paris.
1925–1939 S. Sandford, Levallois-Perret, Seine.
Though born in Birmingham, Malcolm Stuart Sandford (1889–1956) lived in France from the age of two. In the early 1920s he started to sell the MORGAN 3-wheeler in Paris, but lost sales to DARMONT who were assembling Morgans in Courbevoie. Sandford decided to make a Morgan-based 3-wheeler of his own, but of a higher quality than the Darmont. He built a prototype in 1921, using a Ruby engine, and remained faithful to that engine for the rest of his car's life. Production models appeared in 1923, and two years later he moved to Levallois-Perret. Though the Sandford name soon became well-known especially in competition circles, his output was strictly limited. A workforce of 12 men turned out no more than one car per fortnight. They were of better quality than the Darmont, but almost twice the price. They had front-wheel brakes from 1924 and three forward speeds, which Morgan themselves did not offer until 1931. In 1927

1906 San Giorgio 60hp tourer in Coppa d'Oro.
NATIONAL MOTOR MUSEUM

there were three models, the Tourisme, Sport and Super Sport, the latter with the 1088cc ohv Ruby engine which developed 50bhp in standard tune, but considerably more when supercharged. The Sandfords had a distinctive appearance, with pointed tail polished aluminium bodies which were bought from Lecanut.

In 1934 a cheaper 3-wheeler powered by a 954cc flat-twin Ruby was introduced, and also a 4-wheeler which was essentially a 4-cylinder 3-wheeler with an extra rear wheel, both being independently sprung. It cost 28,500 francs (34,000 with supercharger), compared with 21,500 for the 3-wheeler. It did not sell well against competition from sports cars like MG and Singer. Serge Pozzoli thinks no more than 30 were made. In 1936 Sandford brought out a new 4-wheeler which was no more than a Morgan 4/4 with different badging and radiator grill. A journalist who tested it against examples of MG TA, Singer Nine Le Mans, Georges Irat and Fiat 1100 pronounced it the best in terms of overall road holding and performance. For 1939 the same car was offered with 1100cc Ruby engine. However few were sold and the war put an end to Sandford's business. Plans to revive the cars after the war came to nothing, but Sandford kept busy selling Morgan and Standard cars, as well as James and Velocette motorcycles.
NG

SANDRINGHAM (GB) 1902–1905
Frank Morriss, King's Lynn, Norfolk.
Morriss styled himself 'official car repairer to King Edward VII', and as the Royal estate of Sandringham was only a few miles from the Morriss garage at King's Lynn, doubtless he was in demand to keep the royal wheels turning. As well as selling Benz and Daimler cars he made a speciality of modernising Daimlers, replacing hot tube ignition with battery and coil, converting tiller steering to wheel, rebuilding the gearbox and increasing the cylinder bore from 90 to 100mm. Cars sold under the Sandringham name were said to be of Morriss' own design, but owed a great deal to Daimler. More were sold as wagonettes and hotel buses than for private work. Later Morriss made steam cars under his own name in North London, and in the early 1920s was involved with the Crow-Elkhart-based MORRISS-LONDON.
NG

SANDUSKY (US) 1902–1904
Sandusky Automobile Manufacturing Co., Sandusky, Ohio.
The Sandusky was made only as a 2-seater, powered by a 5hp single-cylinder engine, with 2-speed epicyclic transmission and single-chain drive. The tiller-steered runabout sold for $700, but few were made. Some electric cars were made

as well, and in 1904 the company offered the larger COURIER (i) which was made into 1905.
NG

SANDWOOD (GB) 1983–1986
1983 Sandwood Automotive, Birmingham.
1983–1984 Sandwood Automotive, Tamworth, Staffordshire.
1984–1986 Sheldonhurst Ltd, Tyseley, Birmingham.
Terry Sands' first kit was a copy of the Porsche Speedster with the usual recipe of a shortened VW floorpan and fibreglass reproduction body, and a flared-arch Californian model was also sold. The first Cobra replica from Sandwood was the usual cocktail of Jaguar suspension and V8 power, but from 1984 it pioneered the development of a Ford-based backbone chassis for it, creating the first of the true budget Cobra kits. V6 or Rover V8 engines were recommended. Sandwood's next replica was an XK120 lookalike which was based on an American kit which, amazingly, used Datsun 240/260Z mechanicals. For the UK market Sandwood developed a box section steel tube ladder chassis for Jaguar XJ mechanicals. Other kits offered were the Mongoose and Gopher street rods, the Scorpione GT coupé and a Bugatti 59 replica. Sandwood was also known as Classic Reproductions, and in 1984 was absorbed by a company called Sheldonhurst.
CR

SANFENG (CHI) 1995
Sanfeng Minibus Corp. Ltd, Tianjin Municipality.
This Tianjin Bus Factory was erected in 1956. It produced minibuses from 1965. In 1993 the present company was established, and a small 3-door estate car, called Sanfeng (Three Peaks) TJ 6360, based upon the Xiali made in the same city, was designed in 1995.
EVIS

SAN GIORGIO (GB/I) 1906–1909
SA Industriale San Giorgio, Genoa.
The San Giorgio name was used for an Italian-built Napier assembled by a shipyard in which Fiat had an interest. Apparently the Turin firm did not object to its subsidiary making a small number of quasi-Napiers. Three 6-cylinder models were made, the 25, 40, and 60hp, and bodies came from a coachworks at Pistoia which built them under licence from Kellner in Paris. The supervisor of the Genoa works was the former Napier racing driver Arthur Macdonald.
NG

1923 San Giusto 748cc chassis.
NATIONAL MOTOR MUSEUM

1920 Santler Rushabout 3-wheeler.
NICK BALDWIN

1992 Sao Penza 1.3 hatchback.
NICK BALDWIN

SAN GIUSTO (I) 1922–1924

SA San Giusto, Milan; Trieste.

This was a most unconventional car designed by Guido Ucelli di Nemi. It had a 748cc 4-cylinder air-cooled engine mounted at the rear of a central backbone frame, with independent suspension all round by transverse leaves, and 4-wheel brakes. It did not go into production, but a chassis survives today in the Museo dell'Automobile in Turin.

NG

SAN JOSE CUSTOM COACHWORKS (US) c.1980

San Jose Custom Coachworks, Cupertino, California.

This company produced two kit cars. One was a replica of the Jaguar XK-120 and the other was a Mercedes 450SL replica based on a 1979–80 Ford Mustang or Mercury Capri.

HP

SANKOULE (CHI) 1993–1995

Huaibei Family Car Institute, Huaibei City, Anhui Province.

The Sankoule (Three Mouths, which means three persons) SKL 160 3-seater scootmobile was only 87in (2200mm) long. It used a 163cc engine. Two body variants were known. The Sankoule was designed by retired engineers of the Hongqi (First Auto) Works. After making VIP-limousines for years, the engineers wanted to design a real 'people's car' for the Chinese people.

EVIS

SANTA MATILDA (BR) 1977–1980s

Cia Industria Santa Matilda, Rio de Janeiro.

A 2+2 glassfibre-bodied sports coupé using Chevrolet (iii) mechanics in a conventional chassis, with a 4-speed gearbox. Disc brakes were standard from 1980.

NG

SANTAX (F) 1922–1926

Cyclecars Le Santax, Paris.

One of the smallest-engined cyclecars of the 1920s, this car earned its name from the fact that the owner was exempt from tax, as its capacity of the single-cylinder 2-stroke engine was below 125cc. He also did not have to pass a driving test. By 1926 this model had been superseded by one with a 500cc single-cylinder engine, 3-speed gearbox and final drive by very short chains. Front suspension was by a single transverse spring. It was remarkably cheap at Ffr5300, about one third the price of a 5CV Citroën.

NG

SANTLER (GB) 1889–c.1922

1889–1915 C. Santler & Co., Malvern Link, Worcestershire.
1915–c.1922 C. Santler & Co. Ltd, Malvern Link, Worcestershire.

The brothers Charles (1864–1940) and Walter (1867–1942) Santler, cycle makers and general engineers, have a good claim to the title of Britain's first car makers, for they built a steam car in 1889. It did not perform well and was later fitted with a gas engine fuelled by a cylinder of compressed gas, before appearing in its final form with a single-cylinder petrol engine in 1894. There has been much controversy about the date of the car in its original form. It still exists and has been dated 1894 by the Veteran Car Club of Great Britain, though the original petrol engine had disappeared and been replaced by a Benz unit. The brothers claimed the date of 1889 on a postcard issued in 1907 and published elsewhere. This in itself is not much proof, but Dr R.A. Sutton, the present owner of the car and author of a book on the Santlers, points out that they had nothing to gain by claiming a false date, and that there were many employees and others who would soon have exposed the deception, had there been one.

The car as it exists today has a very solid angle-iron frame, necessary to carry a boiler and compound expansion marine-type steam engine, transmission to fast-and-loose pulleys on a countershaft, and thence by chains to the rear axle. The Santlers built a second car in 1897, 'with all the improvements of the first one added' said Charles Santler in 1939, and there were several subsequent models, a front-engined car in 1902, a larger, 4-seater tourer in 1907 and a small series of light cars with 1093cc 10hp 4-cylinder Dorman engines and 2- or 4-seater bodies in 1914–15. These were the first Santlers to be advertised for commercial sale, their prices being £175 and £190 respectively.

The brothers lost a lot of money on a motor plough between 1910 and 1914, and finding that there was no market for it after the war, they hastily brought out a 3-wheeler which they called the Rushabout. This was superficially similar to the Morgan Runabout (the Morgan works were a short distance away from Santler's who had been subcontracted to do machining work for Morgan from time to time), with air-cooled V-twin engine and ifs (though by a different system from the Morgan's), but the transmission was by a 2-speed gearbox and single chain to the rear wheel, while the Morgan had two chains on different sized sprockets, which were brought into action by a sliding dog clutch, giving two forward speeds. About a dozen Rushabouts were made.

1928 S.A.R.A. 1.8-litre sports car.
NICK BALDWIN

The brothers called their original car the Malvernia, by which name it is generally known today, but all their other cars were called Santler.

NG

Further Reading
Malvernia, Dr R.A. Sutton, Michael Sedgwick Memorial Trust, 1987.

SANTOS DUMONT (US) 1902–1904
Columbus Motor Vehicle Co., Columbus, Ohio.
Named after the famous French balloonist, this car had a 12hp 2-cylinder engine mounted under the seat and chain drive. The body was a 4-seater rear-entrance tonneau, and it was priced at $1500 ($1800 in 1903). For 1903 it was joined by a 9hp single-cylinder 2-seater at $1250. The company was in financial trouble during 1903 and was reorganised to make a larger car with 20hp 4-cylinder engine under the bonnet, and a 5-seater side-entrance body. This was called either the Santos Dumont or Dumont. The new company was bankrupt before the end of 1904.

NG

SAO PENZA (ZA) 1991–1992
South African Motor Corp., Pretoria.
SAMCOR combined the South African activities of Ford and Mazda. The Mazda 323 was sold on the UK market in saloon and hatchback forms under the name Sao Penza in 1991 and 1992. SAMCOR also made the Mazda 626 which they sold as the Ford Telstar.

NG

S.A.R.A. (F) 1923–1930
Sté des Automobiles à Refroidissement par Air, Courbevoie, Seine; Puteaux, Seine.
The name of this company translates as Air-cooled Car Co., and they were one of the few European cars to make a success of air-cooling over several years. The first model was a low-built 2-seater powered by an 1100cc 4-cylinder ohv engine with centrifugal turbine blower impelling air into a jacket around the cylinders. It had a 3-speed gearbox and shaft drive to a differential-less rear axle, and front

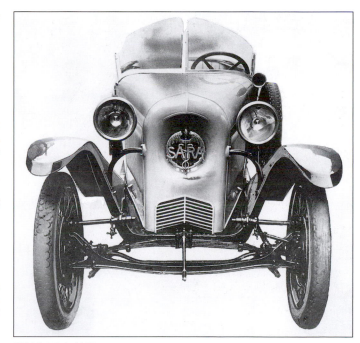

1924 S.A.R.A. 1100cc sports car.
NATIONAL MOTOR MUSEUM

suspension was by a transverse leaf spring. In 1925 it became a 4-seater and gained front-wheel brakes, and 1927 saw the arrival of a 4-speed gearbox.
In 1928 a new model appeared with 1806cc 6-cylinder engine. This was made as a low-slung sports car and as a more upright 4-door saloon or drophead coupé. It was said to have been made in Scotland as the SCOTSMAN, but it seems more likely that the few cars sold were imported from France and fitted with Scottish-made bodies.

NG

1941 Satam electric coupé.
NICK BALDWIN

1999 Saturn SCI coupé.
SATURN

SARALEGUI *see* MOT ET SARALEGUI

SARATOGA TOURIST *see* ELITE (i)

SARD (J) 1990s

The Sard MC-8 was a rebodying exercise on the second-generation Toyota MR2. The wheelbase was lengthened by 18in (460mm) to accommodate a 260bhp 4-litre Lexus V8 engine mounted centrally. The front and rear bodywork was completely changed, and a racing version was also offered.
CR

SAROUKH (LIB) 1999 to date

The Saroukh (Arabic for Rocket) was Libya's first car and was built to the orders of Colonel Muhammar Gadaffi. Dismayed by the number of road deaths in his country, Gadaffi planned it as a safety car, with a sharply pointed front end which would deflect two colliding cars, and make a head-on collision virtually impossible. If it was likely to roll over, a stabilising arm would shoot out from the side of the car to prevent it doing so. The body was a 4-door saloon, and it was powered by a 130bhp 16-valve 2-litre 4-cylinder engine driving the front wheels through a 5-speed gearbox. The Saroukh was available only in green, the traditional colour of Islam. A large factory was built on the outskirts of Tripoli, with a production capacity of 100,000 cars per year.
NG

S.A.S. (F) 1928–1929

Automobiles S.A.S., Paris.

This obscure car was listed with several different engines, all made by C.I.M.E., including a tiny six of 1215cc, a slightly larger one of 1491cc, and fours of 1494 and 1598cc. The former had a single-ohc, while the latter was a pushrod ohv unit. It was illustrated with a low 4-door saloon body, but how many were actually built is uncertain.
NG

S.A.T.A.M. (F) 1941

Éts Satam, La Courneuve, Seine.

One of many electric cars built in wartime France, this had a 2-seater coupé body and batteries divided between the bonnet and a space behind the seats. Top speed was 30mph (48km/h).
NG

S.A.T.M.E. (F) 1922–1923

Sté d'Appareils de Transports et de Manutentions Électriques, Paris.

This was a light 2-seater electric car with a bonnet fronted by a dummy radiator of Turcat-Méry shape. The motor and batteries lived under the bonnet, and drove via a conventional gearbox and propeller shaft to the rear axle. It is possible that the Electrix electric conversion of petrol cars and trucks was the work of the same company.
NG

SATURN (US) 1990 to date

Saturn Corp., Spring Hill, Tennessee.

In 1983 General Motors began exploring the idea of a new marque to confront imported cars head-on, instead of simply badging Japanese and Korean products with familiar names like Chevrolet and Pontiac. They chose the name Saturn in honour of America's moon rocket, and decided to locate the plant at a completely new site in Tennessee. Unlike GM plants which work in collaboration with others, using engines from one source, transmissions from another and steering gears from a third, the Saturn was produced entirely in one location, with its own foundry, body stamping and general assembly shops. No components were shared with other GM cars, although quite a number of components were bought in from specialist suppliers, including tyres, seats and sparking plugs.

The car was a conventional transverse-engine front-wheel drive sedan and coupé with a 1900cc 4-cylinder engine in two versions, a single-ohc developing 85bhp and a twin-cam 123bhp. The 104.2in (2645mm) wheelbase was almost identical to that of the Honda Accord and Toyota Camry, cars which the Saturn targeted. Production started on 31 July 1990, with dealers receiving their first cars in October. A station wagon was added for 1993.

Saturn sales were encouraging to start with, 171,000 in the model year 1992 and 244,000 in 1993. However, by 1997 Saturn was forced to cut weekly output from 6500 cars to 5500 as the cars struggled against imports and US-assembled Japanese products. 1997 sales were 250,810, down from 278,574 in 1996. There were no major changes in the cars since they were introduced, apart from minor styling alterations and increase in power to 101 and 126bhp, From 1997 the General Motors EV1 electric car was branded as a Saturn, though it was not made in the Spring Hill factory. 1997 sales were only 289 cars. A new Saturn model launched in April 1999 was the L-Series sedan and station wagon based on the Opel Vectra platform and powered by the 16-valve twin-ohc 2.2-litre Globa 4 engine intended for future Astras and Vectras. In 1999 Canadian-born Cynthia Trudell became the world's first woman head of a car division, when she took over at the helm of Saturn.
NG

Further Reading

'Saturn: GM's Final Frontier', Jonathan Stein, *Automobile Quarterly*, Vol. 31, No. 1.

SAUER (D) 1921–1922

Sauer Motorenwerke GmbH, Hamburg.

This firm offered a single model, with a 10/30PS 4-cylinder engine.
NG

SAUNDERS *see* MORRISS-LONDON

SAURER (CH) 1896–1917

Adolph Saurer, Fahrzeug- und Motorenfabrik, Arbon.

In 1886 Adolph Saurer (1841–1920) took over the textile machine company founded by his father in 1853. As a substitute for water power for driving the textile machines, Saurer in 1888 developed a stationary petroleum engine of 1.5hp. Improved versions were produced and in 1896 the first motor car was produced. It had a 5hp single-cylinder twin-opposed piston petroleum engine of 3140cc capacity, tiller steering (replaced by a wheel on the production models), a double-phaeton body and solid rubber tyres. A licence agreement was signed with Société des Automobiles KOCH, Neuilly, France. About 25 of these vehicles were made in France and mainly sold to French colonies overseas. In 1901 the Koch company went into liquidation but some of the sturdy cars were used for many years.

The next Saurer car, designed by Adolph's son Hyppolyt, an engineer, who graduated from the Technical University of Zürich, was launched in 1903. It had considerably more advanced specifications – 4-cylinder T-head petrol engine 24/30hp of 4398cc with liberal use of ball bearings, cone-clutch, 4-speed gearbox and chain drive. One year later Saurer patented a new, efficient engine exhaust-brake working by twisting the camshaft and shortly afterwards a compressed air starter for which Renault, Panhard & Levassor and Brasier took licences. After the initial batch of six cars all later Saurer cars obtained shaft drive. The engine was enlarged to 5321cc capacity and 30/35hp and later this model was joined by the 50/60hp with a similar engine of 9231cc. These heavy and fast luxury cars, often with coach-built tourer and limousine bodies by the leading Swiss company Geissberger of Zürich, were among the best money could buy in Switzerland. They were made in limited numbers. Up to 1911 total production reached 96 units. From 1903 onward Saurer also made several types of commercial vehicles and by 1917 this part of the programme had become so important that production of passenger cars was dropped.

Saurer was the largest and most innovative Swiss manufacturer of commercial vehicles, a pioneer of the diesel engine for road use, and had several branch companies and licence agreements in other countries. In 1982 Saurer was taken over by Daimler-Benz and by 1985 production of vehicles under their own make had ceased.

FH

Further Reading
Saurer, K. Sahli and J. Wiedmer, Buri Verlag, Bern, 1983.
Drei Generationen Saurer, M. Mäder, Verein für Wirtschaftshistorische Studien, Meilen, 1988.
Werkbesuch bei Saurer, Saurer Arbon, 1959.

SAUTEL ET SÉCHAUD (F) 1902–c.1904

Sautel et Séchaud, Gentilly, Seine.
This 3-wheeler bore some resemblance to the Léon Bollée, though it had side by side seating instead of tandem, and a vertical engine instead of horizontal. This was a single-cylinder unit of 3½hp, driving through a 2-speed gearbox and single chain to the rear wheel. All controls were on the steering column. To change gear the driver moved the steering column forward or backward.

NG

SAUTTER-HARLÉ (F) 1907–1912

1907–1908 Sté Sautter, Harlé et Cie, Paris.
1908–1912 Harlé et Cie, Paris.
Sautter, Harlé et Cie was established as a general engineering business in 1825, and at the turn of the century they made the heavy oil engines used in KOCH and SAURER cars. They brought out a car of their own in 1907, powered by 10/12 2-cylinder or 16/20hp 4-cylinder engines, with shaft drive and Renault-type bonnets, though the radiator was placed at the front, below the level of the bonnet. The 1911 range consisted of two fours, a 1944cc 12hp and 3053cc 18hp, and a 4580cc 24hp six. They still had the bonnet and radiator arrangement as before, and also a very compact gearbox with internally meshing gears. With this it was as easy to pass directly from first to fourth gear as from third to fourth, though *The Motor* warned '...naturally such a proceeding is not recommended for the transmission'.

NG

S.A.V.A. (B) 1910–1923

Sté Anversoise pour Fabrication de Voitures Automobiles, Antwerp.
This company was a reorganisation (with the help of the English David Brown gear makers) of the Société de Construction Mécanique which had made cars under the name ROYAL STAR. The range was continued into 1911 under the SAVA name, the smallest model having a 1692cc monobloc 4-cylinder engine made by Fondu. The marque employed constant-mesh gearboxes and worm-drive rear axles, the latter made by David Brown who represented SAVA in England. In 1913 the side-valve models were joined by two cars of sporting character with

1898 Saurer 6CV phaeton.
ERNEST SCHMID

1908 Saurer tourer.
ERNEST SCHMID

c.1914 S.A.V.A. cabriolet.
NICK BALDWIN

dual ignition and the unusual layout of overhead exhaust and side inlet valves. These were of 2956 and 5024cc. They had a number of sporting successes, including the fastest speed of 77mph (124km/h) achieved on a *pavé* road, of which Belgium had plenty at that time. In 1913 the previous flat radiator gave way to a rounded shape.

1914 Saxon 12hp 2-seater.
NICK BALDWIN

The factory was almost completely destroyed during World War I, but hesitant production of a prewar 20CV started, and these could be fitted with front-wheel brakes. They still had ohvs. At the December 1922 Brussels Salon SAVA showed a new model, with 2-litre all-ohv engine, 4-speed gearbox and optional front-wheel brakes. Few were made, and at the end of 1923 the SAVA factory was sold to MINERVA who used it as a repair depot and a store for spare parts.

NG

SAVAGE (i) *see* DAN PATCH

SAVAGE (ii) (US) c.1961
Savage Sports Car Manufacturing Co., Los Angeles, California.
Savage made a wildly styled kit car body that supposedly fitted 35 different chassis. A removable hard-top was optional. The low, 2-seat sports car-type body had tall fins on the rear and scallops on the front and rear mudguards. This body was later sold by LaDAWRI as the Centurion 21.

HP

SAVANT (GB) 1998
Sector 3 Ltd, Huddersfield, West Yorkshire.
This Lotus 7-style sports car, called the Savant 175, used double-wishbone suspension all round, an aluminium skinned stainless steel monocoque chassis and Ford Sierra mechanicals. Three slightly different body styles were offered. The project was quickly assumed by QUANTUM.

CR

S.A.V.E.L. (F) 1997 to date
1997 Sté Anonyme Véhicules Européens Légers, Aniche.
1998 to date Sté Anonyme Véhicules Européens Légers, Masny, Valenciennes.
This new operation took over the ERAD factory when that company liquidated in 1997. It continued production of the Spacia and Agora models under its own name and in 1998 it showed the Sisma, an individual-looking new microcar styled by the Institut Supérieur de Design. At a very compact 98in (2495mm) long, it used a twin-cylinder Lombardini 505cc diesel engine.

CR

SAVER (GB) 1912
Saver Clutch Co. Ltd, Manchester.
The Saver was a rare car powered by a rare engine, the 14hp Hewitt piston-valve unit also used in the DAVY and some models of CROWDY. It had a 2-speed gear incorporated in the clutch, on the strength of which it was called a car without a gearbox, and a worm-drive rear axle. It was exhibited at the 1912 Manchester Show with a curious boat-shaped body, but no price was quoted. It was probably built as a test bed for the combined clutch and gearbox rather than as a serious commercial proposition.

NG

SAVIO (I) 1965–c.1983
Savio Giuseppe Carrozzeria Automobili, Moncalieri, Turin.
Savio was very typical of Italian coachbuilders, creating special bodies for many different Fiat models, including the 500, 600, 850, 1600 and 2300. Like many small Italian coachbuilding companies, Savio – which was founded in 1919 – found a commercial niche producing 'torpedoes' or leisure/utility vehicles. The 1965 Giungla (later Jungla) was an open jeep-type 4-seater car based on Fiat/Seat 600 parts. This was replaced in 1974 by a new Jungla using Fiat 126 mechanicals. Some 3200 Junglas were made in total. A smaller jeep-style device was presented in 1967, called the Albarella and based on Fiat 500 parts. A further Fiat 127-based doorless open utility car was also marketed, but Savio turned more and more simply to modifying Fiats and building prototypes.

CR

SAXAN (GB) 1993–c.1996
I.J.F. Developments, Rishton, Lancashire.
The Saxan Warrior was an answer to the terminal rust problems faced by owners of Daihatsu F20/F50 4 × 4 vehicles. On to the Daihatsu separate ladder chassis, a fibreglass body was simply bolted, with all mechanicals left intact and unmodified. Several body styles were on offer, including an estate, pick-up and convertible. The Crusader was a restyled and more spacious later version.

CR

SAXON (US) 1913–1922
Saxon Motor Car Corp., Detroit, Michigan; Ypsilanti, Michigan.
The Saxon was one of America's more successful low-priced cars, reaching eighth place in US automobile production in 1915 and 1916 and seventh in 1917. It was formed in 1913 with its first cars surfacing for the 1914 models. The first cars were light wire-wheeled 2-seat runabouts. With 2-speed selective transmission, the small cars were powered by a 4-cylinder Ferro engine with carbide lights for illumination, electric lights being available at extra cost. The Saxon, priced at $357, was an instant success with more than 7000 finding buyers the first year of production. In 1915 electric lighting became standard and a touring car was added to Saxon offerings, and production increased to more than 11,000 units produced during the calendar year. In 1916 a 6-cylinder Saxon was introduced to augment the existing line, with production exceeding 21,000 cars. For 1917 a sedan – Saxon's first closed car – was added to the existing line and production peaked at more than 28,000. It would be the car's last year as a major producer.

The 4-cylinder Saxon was dropped for 1918. Also dropping was the car's production which, with 12,000+ units constituted a drop of more than 50 per cent. The company was now in financial difficulties as well as internal management problems. The sedan was dropped for 1919 with production plummeting to under 3500 cars.

Production increased to over 6000 units in 1920, a new ohv four was introduced and, termed the Duplex, augmented the existing six. Once again the sedan was included in the Saxon catalogue. Internal strife and increased financial instability continued, however. For 1921, the six was dropped. Also falling was production, with only 2100 cars sold.

With the company in precarious straits, the Saxon operations were moved to Ypsilanti, Michigan, where the company had leased the factory of the Ace automobile, itself in the final stages of operation. The move was to no avail and slightly more than 500 cars were the last Saxons to be built. The leftover Saxon Duplex open models, sedan and coupés, the latter introduced the previous year, were sold at cost as 1923 models.

KM

SAYERS (US) 1917–1924
Sayers & Scoville Co., Cincinatti, Ohio.
The Sayers & Scoville company had been a successful builder of funeral cars and ambulances since 1913, deciding to augment this line to include standard passenger cars, the first year of production limited to a 5-seater touring car priced at $1295. A roadster was added to the Sayers line for 1918, both types listing for $1695, reduced from $1765 and raised to $2195 and $2595 for the touring car and roadster, respectively, in 1921. In 1922 the touring car listed at $1795 and the roadster at $2095, these reduced to $1645 for both types in the Sayers' final year of 1923. A sedan was added to the Sayers offerings for $2795 in

1920 and, later that year, a limousine at the same figure. The limousine was dropped for 1921 and the sedan price was upped to $3295, dropping to $2995 for 1922 and to $2645 for its final year during which a coupé was added at $2645, the fluctuating prices being similar to a game of fiscal musical chairs. The production was minimal during the first three years of production, after which it levelled off at an estimated 185 to 200 cars per year. The Sayers changed little during its seven years of production and, although 1924 was regarded as an active year in most of the contemporary automotive rosters, it is almost certain that cars marketed that year were leftover 1923 units. The Sayers were powered by a Continental 7R 6-cylinder L-head engine until 1922, the last cars being fitted with the new Model 8R which afforded an increase of a meagre one-half of one per cent bhp. The wheelbase measured 118in (2995mm) throughout production. The otherwise rather insignificant looking Sayers was balanced by exceedingly fine coachwork. From 1921 to the end of production, body types were given such names as Avondale, Glendale, Brighton, Derby and Linwood, the first two being communities within Cincinnati or adjoining it. Shortly after the Sayers automobile operation was terminated, Sayers & Scoville introduced a line of sedans and limousines carrying the S. & S. badge and also identified by similar names, the Brighton being retained and augmented by Elmwood, Gotham and Lakewood.

KM

S.B. (D) 1920–1924

S.B. Automobilgesellschaft GmbH, Berlin.

The initials of this company stood for Slaby and Beringer. It was designed by Dr Rudolf Slaby and an engineer called Beringer (not Behringer as his name is sometimes rendered). Slaby favoured plywood construction, which he had used on aircraft, and his little car had a unitary construction plywood body/chassis. It was a single seater with batteries under the bonnet and motor close to, and driving, the rear wheels. To provide accommodation for an additional passenger a 2-wheeled trailer could be had, making a 6-wheeler with tandem seating for two. A later version had a wider body with side-by-side seating for two. The single-seater was sold in England by the London department store, Gamages, for £150.

Later the company was taken over by J.S. Rasmusssen and a 3PS DKW petrol engine fitted. These had either tandem or side by side seating.

HON

SBARRO (CH) 1967 to date

1967–1968 Franco Sbarro, Grandson.
1968 to date ACA Atelier d'Études et de Construction Automobiles Sàrl, Grandson.

Franco Sbarro was born in 1939 at Lecce, southern Italy, and he emigrated to Switzerland when 18 years of age. Two years later he built his first prototype with a Lancia engine. In 1963 he came in contact with Georges Filipinetti, who was the owner of an automobile museum at the Château de Grandson and had just founded the Scuderia Filipinetti. Sbarro was engaged as chief mechanic of the racing stable, took care of the restoration of vintage cars and designed the prototypes of FILIPINETTI sports coupés. Four years later Franco Sbarro, with the help of Filipinetti, set up his own workshop in a former blacksmith's premises in Les Tuileries-de-Grandson.

Apart from manufacturing sports racing cars for various formulas, he converted for road use two Ford GT40, which had taken part in the Le Mans 24-hour race. For the account of the Scuderia Filipinetti he co-operated with John Wyer and Zora Duntov of Detroit in the preparation of Ford GT40s and Corvettes for racing. In 1968 he founded together with Dr Herbert de Cadoga the new company ACA. The first ACA project was based on the NSU 1000 TT with a tuned engine delivering 102bhp. It was planned as a sports racing car for beginners but at the asking price of SFr 18,000, demand was not sufficient to warrant production.

For Lola owner Eric Broadley, Sbarro then converted a Lola racing car for street use, and purchased sufficient parts to produce from 1970 onward a total of 11 Sbarro Sloughi coupés, named after the greyhounds of North Africa. They were all made to buyers' individual requirements and could be fitted with various engines. Mainly big V8s were used but at least one each obtained a Ferrari V12 and a Porsche turbo engine. In 1971 three sports racing spyders for Group 7 events, which resembled scaled-down Can-Am cars, two with BMW engines and one with a Ford Cosworth engines, were completed. With the help

1921 Sayers Six Avondale tourer.
JOHN A. CONDE

1923 S.B. cyclecar.
NICK BALDWIN

1983 Sbarro-Mercedes 500 coupé , with Franco Sbarro.
NICK GEORGANO

and financial support of Uwe Hucke, a German who owned a fine automobile collection, a subsidiary of the ACA was formed.

From 1973 the marque Sbarro was used for production models, and ACA built prototypes only. At the Geneva Show of the same year, Sbarro exhibited the SV-1, a safety vehicle seating three, with gull-wing doors reminiscent of the Mercedes-Benz 300SL and powered by two NSU Ro 80 Wankel engines developing a total of 230bhp and a top speed of 155mph (249km/h). This was followed by the Sbarro Tiger, which was a high-performance coupé with a Mercedes-Benz V8 engine of 6322cc. Again, other engines, from Ford, Chevrolet or Chrysler, could be ordered. The price exeeded the SFr100,000 barrier. In 1974–75 a few Sbarro Stash coupés, developed from the SV-1 but with a VW K70 engine mounted midships, were completed. One of them became famous as it was decorated and put on show by Pierre Cardin, the Paris fashion designer.

1999 Sbarro Folia Tec roadster, based on VW Golf.
SBARRO

1985 Sbarro Challenge coupé.
SBARRO

The Sbarro replica of the BMW 328 was then launched. It had a tubular frame, a double fibreglass body shell and was available in three models with BMW engines ranging from 1573 to 3295cc and 85 to 200bhp. About 150 of these cars were sold in Europe and overseas. From 1977 Sbarro also produced a few electro town vehicles. Other Sbarro models styled after prewar classics were eight Mercedes-Benz 540K with the powerful V8 Mercedes engine of 4973cc and the Bugatti Royale limousine with two Rover V8 engines of 3500cc in tandem. Miniature Mercedes-Benz 540 and the BMW 328 replicas for children, with SACHS 50cc single-cylinder engines were also built. In 1978 Sbarro produced his first 4 × 4, the Wind Hound, which was made in various versions powered by Mercedes-Benz, BMW or American V8 engines. More exotic, and more expensive, was the single Wind Hawk 6 × 6, ordered by King Khaled of Saudi Arabia for hawking expeditions. An outstanding prototype was the Super Twelve of 1982 with two 6-cylinder Kawasaki motorcycle engines of 1300cc each and delivering 240bhp. Other incredibly 'hot saloons' were the VW Golf powered by a Porsche 345bhp turbo engine, the Super Eight with a Ferrari V8 engine, the Mercedes Bi-Turbo and 500SEL, both with gull-wings.

In the mid–1980s there were several prototypes and also replicas of the Mercedes-Benz 300SL and the Ferrari P4. At the 1987 Geneva Autoshow, Sbarro launched the Monster, a 4 × 4 based on a modified Range Rover chassis with a 6.9-litre Mercedes V8 engine and outsize tyres reputed to have been based on those of the Boeing 747. The Sbarro Robur was a small luxury car with a transverse-mounted Audi 5-cylinder turbocharged engine of about 200bhp. The Challenge was perhaps the most dramatic looking Sbarro so far. Its wedge-shaped body was very low and had the excellent drag coefficient of 0.25 CX only. In 1989 Sbarro invented the spokeless wheel covered by eight patents, which he applied to the Osmos V12 with a Jaguar engine of 350bhp placed midships, and absolutely fabulous looking motorcycles. One year later another small but very potent model, the Sbarro Chrono with the a BMW Procar M1 6-cylinder engine of 500 bhp was shown.

In 1992 Éspace Sbarro, a special school for automotive design, was opened and from then Sbarro presented numerous concept cars, prototypes and modifications based on Citroën, Alfa Romeo, Ferrari, Peugeot, Lancia, Renault elements, chassis and/or engines. Sbarro also built the famous Ellipsis, designed by Philippe Charbonneaux, with wheels arranged in a lozenge form and powered by a Porsche Carrera 3.6-litre engine. These often superbly styled Sbarro models were regularly highlights of the Geneva and Paris Shows – Isatis was a sports car; Urbi a small electro town car; Onix a restyled Citroën ZX pick-up, a simple utility vehicle for the farmers in Morocco; Oxalys a roadster prototype with a BMW engine; Mandarine was a small town car; Alcador a prototype based on the Ferrari V12, Gruau a fun car based on the Peugeot 106; Issima was an incredible twin-V6-engined Alfa Romeo roadster with about 500bhp; Ionos was an equally unlikely Lancia twin-5-cylinder coupé; Crisalys a convertible coupé with mid-engine by Peugeot, and there were some more in the late 1990s.

Franco Sbarro and his team are among the most innovative of today's designers, and their fertile minds have created, outstanding and unexpected studies and prototypes over the years

FH

S.B.K. (S) 1904–1906

Svenska Belysning-Kraft AB, Tidaholm.

This was a high wheel buggy type of vehicle, with single or 2-cylinder engine, tiller steering and chain drive. Only five were made.

NG

SCACCHI (I) 1911–1915

Scacchi & Cia, Fabbrika Automobili, Chivasso, Turin.

Made by Cesare Scacchi, this was a medium-sized car with a 4396cc 20/30hp 4-cylinder monobloc engine and 4-speed gearbox. Three wheelbases were available, 117.5in (2982mm), 124in (3147mm) and 127.5in (3236mm). There was also a 6283cc 24/80hp model. The 20/30 was sold in England by British & Foreign Motors who also handled the ITALA. Fewer cars were sold as Scacchis than were made, for Luigi Storero contracted to sell all Scacchi's production on condition that he could brand them with his own name. Some were sold under the name Caesar; these may have been Cesare Scacchi's outlet for the cars which did not pass through Storero's hands.

NG

1914 Scacchi 20/30hp landaulet.
NICK BALDWIN

SCAMP (i) (GB) 1965–1967

Scottish Aviation Ltd, Prestwick, Ayrshire.

The Scamp was one of many electric car projects of the late 1960s which was intended for eventual production but never made it. The first prototype was completed by Scottish Aviation based at Prestwick Airport in 1965 but the car's public debut did not come until the 1967 Ideal Homes Exhibition. A simple fibreglass-over-ash bodied 2-seater just under 84in (2132mm) long, it used twin series-wound ventilated DC 2.7hp electric motors which drove via chain to each rear wheel. It was claimed that the car could reach a top speed of 35mph (56km/h), while its maximum range was 26 miles. Although a price of £330 was announced, only a pilot run of around 12 vehicles was made, ten of the which were allocated for evaluation by various Electricity Boards, the remaining two being kept by Scottish Aviation. Vague plans to productionise the Scamp as 'the commuter car of the seventies' were never realised.

CR

1903 Scania 6hp tonneau.
NATIONAL MOTOR MUSEUM

SCAMP (ii) (GB) 1970 to date

1970–1974 Miller Mandry, Reading, Berkshire.
1974–1987 Robert Mandry Scamps (Connaught Garage Ltd), Woking, Surrey.
1987 to date The Scamp Motor Co, East Grinstead, West Sussex.

Robert Mandry was the man behind the amazingly successful Scamp, which first appeared in 1970. Its Moke-like construction was tough and hid the inevitable Mini subframes. The multi-tube spaceframe chassis was clothed with aluminium panels and could be ordered in 6-wheel, van, estate, pick-up or short wheelbase forms. The new Mk2 model of 1978 was squarer and uglier but had a tougher chassis and optional removable doors (initially gullwing). A Mk3 model was launched in 1990, again restyled. A simplified version was offered from 1993 under the name Grass Tracker, and there was a Suzuki SJ based version from 1995. Over 3000 Scamps of all types had been built by 1998.

CR

SCANIA (S) 1902–1912

Maskinfabriks AB Scania, Malmö.

This company was founded in 1900 to maker Humber bicycles under licence, and began experimenting with cars the following year. Their first was designed by Reinhard Thorssin, and had its engine under the seat. Thorssin soon left to join A.M.G. in Gothenburg. In 1902 six cars were completed, powered by German-made Kamper engines. A larger, 4-cylinder, model was ordered by Crown Prince Gustaf, but was not delivered until January 1904. In 1905 Scania began to make their own engines designed by the German engineer G. Wentzel. They ranged from a 5/6hp single-cylinder, through twins to a 25/30hp four. More were used in commercial vehicles than passenger cars; indeed only 31 cars were delivered between 1908 and 1912 all with 4-cylinder engines ranging from 12 to 30/36hp. In November 1910 Scania merged with VABIS of Södertälge. Car production was transferred to the Vabis factory, and the Malmö plant was devoted to commercial vehicles.

NG

1910 Scania 24/30hp tourer.
NATIONAL MOTOR MUSEUM

Further Reading
'Northern Lights, Dawn of the Swedish Automobile', Len Lonnegren, *Automobile Quarterly*, Vol. 31, No. 4.

1914 Scania-Vabis 22hp tourer.
NATIONAL MOTOR MUSEUM

1929 Scania-Vabis Type 1 2/22 saloon.
NATIONAL MOTOR MUSEUM

1927 S.C.A.P. Type Z 9CV tourer.
NICK BALDWIN

SCANIA-VABIS (S) 1911–1929
AB Scania-Vabis, Södertälge.

After the merger with Vabis, three types of passenger car were made, the 22hp Typ 1, 30/35hp Typ II (also known as Typ F4A) and 50hp Typ III, all with 4-cylinder engines. Scania's Per Nordmann was managing director and its designer Anton Svenson became chief engineer. The round-topped radiator was adopted in 1913. From 1913 to 1920 Scania-Vabis cars were also made in Denmark, including a 4.8-litre V8 in 1917 which was never part of the Swedish range. The 4-cylinder

cars were made with little change and in dwindling numbers until 1924, when commercial vehicles took over completely. In fact four more cars were made to special order of former customers, the last in 1929. This was assembled from components intended for trucks and other models of car, and was used by Scania-Vabis management for many years. Only 122 cars in all were made between 1921 and 1929, with a total of 840 for all Scania, Vabis and Scania-Vabis.

Scania-Vabis flourished in the commercial vehicle field, up to the 1960s, making heavier trucks than their rivals VOLVO. In 1968 they merged with car makers SAAB and dropped the Vabis part of the name. In August 1999 Scania was bought by Volvo, forming the world's second largest truck and bus manufacturer.
NG

Further Reading
'Northern Lights, Dawn of the Swedish Automobile', Len Lonnegren, *Automobile Quarterly*, Vol. 31, No. 4.

S.C.A.P. (F) 1912–1929
SA des Automobiles S.C.A.P., Billancourt, Seine.

S.C.A.P. (Société de Constructions Automobiles Parisiennes) was best known as a provider of proprietary engines to a large number of French car makers. Among their better known customers in the 1920s were Bignan, BNC, Derby, and Turcat-Méry. However they also made complete cars under their own name, starting with a range of side-valve monobloc fours between 8 and 15CV. These had Ballot engines as S.C.A.P. had not yet become engine makers. It was their war work making aero engines that led them to make proprietary power units, which were offered in great variety; at least 17 different models between 1920 and 1929.

Their first postwar car was the 10CV Type L which used an unusual rear suspension consisting of a transverse cantilever spring pivoted on the chassis at its centre and with two linked semi-elliptic springs. More conventional was the 6/7CV Type M of 1923, with 1100cc ohv engine. Engine manufacture became of increasing importance in the late 1920s, but one final car was made, with 1995cc ohv straight-8 engine, in 1928–29.
NG

S.C.A.R. (F) 1906–1915
Sté de Construction Automobile de Reims, Witry-les Reims, Marne.

This company was founded by Messieurs Rayet and Lienart in 1898, and in 1906 they built a conventional car with 18/20hp T-head 4-cylinder engine with separately-cast cylinders, 3-speed gearbox and shaft drive. It had a radiator reminiscent of a Mors or Brasier, but by 1910 a Renault-style dashboard radiator had been adopted, which was to characterise the S.C.A.R. for the rest of its life. They also had L-head 4-cylinder engines and 4-speed gearboxes. The smallest was a 1272cc 10/12hp twin, and there were two fours, a 2092cc 10/12hp and a 2412cc 15hp, and a 3617cc 20hp six. The twin and the six were not made after 1912, and the 1914 range consisted of the 10/12 four, now called the 11.9hp from its RAC rating, and the 3176cc 17.9hp. They were sold on the UK market by SCAR (London) Ltd, headed by Sydney Cummings who also sold the Ronteix cyclecar under the name Cummikar. S.C.A.R. also made engines for some early Voisin aeroplanes.

The village of Witry, about 4 miles from Rheims, was in the front line during the war. The marque's obituary was recorded in *Fletcher's Motor Car Index*: 'Works captured by Germans early in 1915, being blown up after occupation. Up to the present works have not been reconstructed'. The company survived the war, though, and ran a Mathis agency until 1925. They then became a general garage and repair business until they finally closed down in 1933.
NG

SCARAB (i) *see* STOUT

SCARAB (ii) (GB) 1972
Dragsport Cars, Yeadon, Yorkshire.

This was a bulbous little mid-engined Mini based sports coupé using a triangulated box-section frame. The fibreglass body was initially open-topped, later changed to a coupé design. This company also produced a Ford Model T hot rod kit.
CR

SCARAB (iii) (US) c.1975

Scarab, San Jose, California.

The Datsun 140/260/280Z was a good sports car, but Scarab felt it was underpowered. They installed modified Chevrolet V8 engines and extensively reworked the suspension and brakes to match the increased power. Their top model used a 5700cc Chevrolet with 425 turbocharged horsepower backed up with a 4-speed transmission. They were sold fully assembled for $35,000, or Scarab would perform the conversion on a customer's car.

HP

SCARLATTI (ZA) 1980s

Scarlatti Cars, Benoni.

A 4-seater coupé, the Scarlatti was based on Ford mechanicals, including a 3-litre V6 engine and manual or automatic transmissions. It employed the chassis of an American Ford.

CR

S.C.A.T. (I) 1906–1923

Stà Ceirano Automobili Torino, Turin.

This was another product of the Ceirano family, in this case Giovanni the younger (1865–1948) who had made the JUNIOR car before forming S.C.A.T. Under this name he built a range of T-head 4-cylinder cars which were quite small by contemporary Italian standards; the biggest was a 22/32hp of 3.8 litres, enlarged to 4.4 litres by 1910. The first monobloc four came in 1910, and a year later the old T-head designs had given way to L-heads. Compressed air starters were introduced in 1912.

By 1909 Ceirano had made 500 cars, and by 1912 production was running at 400 per year. The immediate prewar range consisted of 4-cylinder cars of 15, 18, 25 and 60/70hp, the latter with a capacity of 6280cc. S.C.A.T. had a number of sporting successes, including victories in the Targa Florio in 1911, 1912 and 1914. Ceirano hoped to raise production to 1000 a year in 1915, but the war intervened, and he found himself making trucks and Hispano-Suiza aero engines.

In 1917 Ceirano sold his company to a Hispano-Suiza-controlled group which continued production of the 2722cc 15hp and 4710cc 25hp models after the war, and introduced new, smaller fours of 1551 and 2951cc in 1922. The following year Ceirano regained control and started to make a 2296cc car which he sold under his own name.

NG

S.C.A.T.T. (F) 1978–1979

Sté de Construction Automobiles Tout-Terrain, Luxeuil-les-Bains.

Launched at the 1978 Paris Salon, the Gambade was a rather rough-and-ready all-terrain vehicle with enclosed plastic bodywork. The engine choice was Peugeot V6 petrol and Mercedes 220D/300D or Perkins diesel. The chassis was independently sprung by coils and featured 4-wheel drive. It is doubtful that production ever began.

CR

SCAVIANO (US) c.1960

Scaviano Vehicles, Warren, Michigan.

The Scaviano Scat was a jeep-like utility vehicle with a front-mounted, air-cooled 25hp engine. The body was made of angle-bent metal and it sold for $1390 in 1960.

HP

SCEPTRE (US) 1979–1980

Sceptre Motor Car Co., Santa Barbara, California.

This neo-classic kit car had a unique look, more along the lines of European pre-war sedans like the BMW 328 and Talbot Lagos than Packards and Duesenbergs. Shorter and more rounded, it was one of the best looking kits of its type. Mechanically, it was pretty much like the others, with a Mercury Cougar chassis and engine powering an MG Midget rear body section with a long bonnet. Sceptres were designed by Tom McBurnie and Ray Kinney and they were loaded with luxury features. This kit project was sold to GATSBY, who renamed it the Griffin.

HP

1906 S.C.A.R. 18/20hp tourer.
NATIONAL MOTOR MUSEUM

1912 S.C.A.T. 22hp landaulet.
NICK BALDWIN

S.C.H. (B) 1927–1928

This firm showed a light car at the 1927 Brussels Salon, powered by an 8CV 4-cylinder engine with 4-speed gearbox and independent suspension on all four wheels.

NG

SCHACHT (US) 1904–1913

1904–1909 Schacht Manufacturing Co., Cincinnati, Ohio.
1909–1913 Schacht Motor Car Co., Cincinnati, Ohio.

Gustav Schacht had been a buggy manufacturer for a number of years when he launched his first car. Predictably, it was a high-wheeler clearly betraying its buggy ancestry. It had a 10hp 2-cylinder engine, double-chain drive and solid tyres. Unlike many buggy makers, Schacht introduced a large tourer powered by a 40hp 4-cylinder engine in 1905, and this was continued alongside the buggies up to 1907. It cost $2850–3200, compared with $650–680 for the buggies. One of these was called the 'Three Purpose Car', being convertible from 2-seater runabout to 5-seater family car to delivery wagon. The high-wheelers became steadily more powerful as the years passed, and by 1910 were quoted at 24hp.

For 1911 Schacht returned to conventional 4-cylinder cars with the 40hp Model AA which sold for $1385. Variations on this theme were the only Schacht cars for 1912 and 1913, after which they concentrated on trucks which they made up to 1938.

NG

c.1906 Schacht 18/20hp high-wheeler.
NICK BALDWIN

1911 Schacht 35/40hp tourer.
NICK BALDWIN

1913 Schacht Model NS 45/50hp tourer.
JOHN A. CONDE

SCHARFF GEARLESS *see* PAINE

SCHAUDEL *see* MOTOBLOC

SCHAUM (US) 1900–1903
Schaum Automobile & Motor Manufacturing Co., Baltimore, Maryland.
This company made sparking plugs and other components, and also a chain-driven, light car powered by a 4/7hp single-cylinder engine. Unusually it could seat two, four, or six passengers. Even more unusually it had no brakes. Its builder William A. Schaum said that it could stop on any hill at any speed, but he did not explain how. He built 16 cars to sell under his own name, and 10 for the Autocarette Co. of Washington, D.C. After a disagreement with this company he left Baltimore, and surfaced again in Buffalo in 1906, calling himself William A. De Schaum. In 1908 he launched a car under that name.
NG

SCHEBERA *see* CYKLON

SCHEELE (D) 1899–1910
1899–1906 Heinrich Scheele, Cologne.
1906–1910 Kölner Elektromobil-Gesellschaft Heinrich Scheele, Cologne.
Heinrich Scheele was a pioneer builder of electric vehicles in Germany, making passenger cars, taxicabs, delivery vans and small buses. Cars in various models, particularly landaulets for town use, were made up to 1910. Scheele then saw that petrol was the coming power for passenger vehicles and concentrated his production on commercial vehicles.
HON

SCHEIBLER (D) 1900–1907
1900–1903 Motorenfabrikfabrik Fritz Scheibler, Aachen.
1903–1907 Scheibler Automobil-Industrie GmbH, Aachen.
When Scheibler started production of passenger cars he favoured flat-twin engines and friction transmission. These were soon superseded by 4-cylinder vertical engines of up to 6.9 litres and double-chain drive. The engines were also used in commercial vehicles. Smaller single and 2-cylinder models were made in 1906–07, after which Scheibler concentrated on commercial chassis. These were made up to 1909, after which the company was renamed and trucks marketed under the name Mulag.
HON

SCHILLING (D) 1906
V.Chr. Schilling, Suhl.
Schilling marketed a light car using a 6/12PS 4-cylinder Fafnir engine and Omnimobil components. They were also sold under the name V.C.S. The friction-driven LILIPUT cars were made under licence by Schilling.
HON

SCHLOSSER (US) 1912–1913
W.H. Schlosser Manufacturing Co., New York, New York.
This company was founded in 1906 to manufacture engines for boats, cars and trucks. They built a 32hp 4-cylinder car in 1910 but did not market it. Two years later they announced that they would make a car powered by one of their 40hp 4-cylinder T-head engines of 7718cc. It was offered in three models, runabout, tourer and limousine, at prices from $4200 to $5400. A few were made, but they did not sell well, and in 1913 they were being offered at the discount price of $2370.
NG

SCHMIDLIN (F) c.1925–1926
Constructions Jean Schmidlin, Paris.
This was a light car powered by a 985cc 4-cylinder Ruby engine, with 3-speed gearbox and shaft drive.
NG

SCHNADER *see* RIVIERA

SCHNEIDER *see* BRILLIÉ and TH. SCHNEIDER

SCHRAM (US) 1913–1914
Schram Motor Car Co., Seattle, Washington.
The first car offered by this company had a 38hp 6-cylinder engine and a 5-seater tourer body on a 130in (3299mm) wheelbase. It was priced at $2300, but nothing more was heard from the company until the autumn of 1914 when they said they would make 1000 light cars powered by 4-cylinder 20hp engines, to sell at $600. Nothing further was heard of this either.
NG

1899 Schuckert Electric victoria.
SIEMENS MUSEUM

SCHUCKERT (D) 1899–1900

Elektrizitäts-Aktiengesellschaft vorm. Schuckert & Co., Nuremburg.
The Schuckert electrical concern made electric vehicles for a short time. Both their passenger cars and delivery vans bore a close resemblance to horse-drawn vehicles. In 1903 they were bought by Siemens and re-appeared as a car make in 1906 under the name SIEMENS-SCHUCKERT.

HON

SCHULER (US) 1924

Schuler Motor Car Co., Milwaukee, Wisconsin.
'The Lowest Priced Light-Weight Car in the World' said the advertisement for the tiny Schuler roadster appearing in *The Milwaukee Journal* for 20 January 1924. It just might have been, too. The 2-seater featured a 78in (1980mm) wheelbase and a water-cooled V-twin-cylinder Mar-Tan engine. A coupé was also featured but probably not built, prices being $245 for the roadster and $295 for the coupé. Launched in January 1924 at the Wisconsin State Automobile Show in Milwaukee, the Schuler was guaranteed 50 miles to a gallon of petrol and a top speed of 45mph (72km/h). Despite some interest, the Schuler failed to capture the imagination of the buying public and the venture failed before the

end of the year. Minimal production was reported with an estimated 35 to 50 Schulers finding buyers.

KM

SCHULZ (D) 1904–1906

Maschinenfabrik G. Schulz, Magdeburg.
Not much is known about this make except that they exhibited 18 and 28hp cars at the 1904 Berlin Show, and took part in the 1905 Herkomer Trial.

HON

SCHUPPAN (GB) 1991–c.1994

Vern Schuppan Ltd, High Wycombe, Buckinghamshire.
Australian ex-patriate and Le Mans winner Vern Schuppan offered for sale a roadgoing version of the Porsche 962 racer, called the Schuppan 962CR. It shared its carbon-fibre chassis with Schuppan's Le Mans race cars. The 3.3-litre flat-6 twin-turbo modified Porsche engine was claimed to produce 600bhp and a top speed of 217mph (349km/h). The cost of the car was some £700,000 and the project was funded by the Art Corp. of Osaka, Japan. The coupé bodywork was designed by ex-Holden employee Mike Simcoe. A limited run of 50 cars was announced, each car priced at £770,000.

CR

1957 Scootacar 3-wheeler.
NICK BALDWIN

SCHURICHT (D) 1921–1925

1921–1924 Automobilwerk Walter Schuricht, Pasing.
1924–1925 Bayerisches Automobilwerk AG, Pasing.
Walter Schuricht built a small car with either a 4/12PS or 5/15PS 4-cylinder engine. They were available with 2- or 3-seater bodies.

HON

SCHUTTE-LANZ (D) 1922–1923

Schutte-Lanz Kleinautomobil GmbH, Zeesen.
This company was engaged in building airships during World War I, but could not continue with this as a result of the terms of the Treaty of Versailles. As they had long experience in wood-working techniques, they used wood for the construction of their small car. It had an exceptionally long wheelbase for its kind. Proper production did not begin, but the few owners who did take delivery praised the car's reliability.

HON

SCIMITAR (US) 1959

Brooks Stevens, Milwaukee, Wisconsin.
The Scimitar was a project designed by Brooks Stevens for Olin Aluminium. One set of dies could be used to form three body variations on this full-size sedan. These were a 5-seater hard-top convertible, a sedan and a phaeton that could be converted from a formal sedan into a convertible with a retractable hard-top. The body used much aluminium for weight reduction. The nose had a large V-shaped front bumper that had overtones of Edsel, but with more daring side treatment. Stevens tried to interest Studebaker in the project but failed.

HP

SCIOTO see ARBENZ

SCIREA (I) 1914–1927

Officine Scirea, Milan (1914–1915); Monza (1924–1927).
This aero-engine maker had two short-lived phases of car manufacture. In 1914 Antonio Scirea built a 1.2-litre 8/10hp light car with inlet-over-exhaust valves and a 3-speed gearbox, but the war prevented production from starting. He did not get back to cars until 1924, when he launched a 1500cc machine, still with overhead inlet valves, and now with a 4-speed gearbox. A sports version of this was announced in 1927.

NG

SCM (US) c.1988

SCM Motors, Seattle, Washington.
This company converted new Corvettes with a Ferrari Testarossa-style convertible body. The resulting car was called a Culebra. The rear mudguards and tail-light treatment were borrowed from the Ferrari, along with some similarity in the nose. A 6-year warranty was included, as were a wood dash and wide wheels. They sold for $85,000 in 1988.

HP

SC MOTORCAR CO. (US) c.1994

SC Motocar Co., Eucha, Oklahoma.
This was another Cobra replica manufacturer. Theirs used a ladder frame with Ford suspension, engine and running gear, and was sold in kit form.

HP

SCOIATTOLO (I) 1968–c.1982

Carrozzeria Arrigo Perini, Arco, Trento; Scoiattolo SpA, Riva de Garda.
This was a very basic open utility car in the same vein as the SAVIO Jungla. The first incarnation of the Scoiattolo (which means 'squirrel') used Fiat 500 mechanicals, a beam front axle and front disc brakes. The bodywork was very rudimentary and was composed of entirely flat surfaces. Later examples used a Seat 600 (767cc) engine, prior to the launch of a Fiat 126 engined example. In normal guise it had 2-wheel drive, but from 1970 a Super Scoiattolo model with 4-wheel drive was launched.

CR

SCOOTACAR (GB) 1957–1964

Scootacars Ltd, Leeds, Yorkshire.
An improbably tall 60in (1523mm) and narrow fibreglass body marked the Scootacar, which was a 3-wheeled microcar in the 'bubble car' tradition. The driver sat on the front end of a narrow tandem seat. A single passenger could sit astride the engine itself, rather like a motorcycle pillion, or two people could just squeeze in either side of it. Steering was by handlebars. The first Scootacars were equipped with a Villiers 9E 197cc single-cylinder 2-stroke 8bhp engine, driving the single rear wheel by chain. In 1960 came the MkII De Luxe version with its more bulbous front end and an elongated tail. The twin-cylinder 16bhp 324cc Scootacar MkIII De Luxe Twin arrived in 1961, boasting a top speed of 68mph (109km/h). Of the 1000 or so Scootacars built in total, a mere 20 or so were the more powerful De Luxe Twin variety. The manufacturer, a division of Hunslets, the railway locomotive makers, ended Scootacar production as microcars fell from fashion.

CR

SCOOTMOBILE (i) see MARTIN (ii)

SCOOTMOBILE (ii) (US) c.1946

Norman Anderson, Corunna, Michigan.
The Scootmobile was a small 3-wheeled economy car built around a war-surplus auxiliary bomber fuel tank. It used a 12hp air-cooled engine and was to sell for $350.

HP

SCORA (F) 1974 to date

1974–1992 Société Scora, Nantes.
1992 to date Scora, Mougin.
After the demise of his JIDÉ marque Jacques Durand set up a new company and revived the model, in modified form, as the Scora. It kept its Renault 8 basis – though it boasted R12 rear suspension – and the body styling and tubular chassis were modernised somewhat. Various engines could be fitted transversely at the rear, from the 1.6-litre R17 Gordini, to a Renault 1.8-litre engine with either normal carburation (178bhp) or fuel-injection (183bhp). A 5-speed gearbox, all-independent suspension featuring front torsion bars and disc brakes all round were standard. The Scora was sold only in kit form and was popular with rally drivers but its existence was – and indeed remains – almost something of a secret.

CR

SCORHILL (GB) 1988 to date

1988–1992 Scorhill Motors, Godalming, Surrey.
1992–1993 Scorhill Motors, Walton-on-Thames, Surrey.
1993–1996 Scorhill Motor Co, Chertsey, Surrey.
1996 to date Crestel Services, Chertsey, Surrey.
Scorhill Motors became a sort of elephant's graveyard of old kit car designs; it inherited various models from the DUTTON empire, the M.F.E. Magic and the CARISMA Century. The company also produced a replica of the Citroën Méhari called the El Cid, derived from a design called the Oasis Scorpion: it was a faithful replica, identical except for a strengthening roll-over bar, rhd and conventional woven mat type fibreglass rather than injected plastic. Scorhill also briefly offered its own design, the ME4, an imperfectly proportioned mid-engined Ford-based coupé. After the 1996 disappearance of Scorhill, Crestel continued to offer the Dutton Melos, El Cid and various Ford Model A hot rods.
CR

SCORPION (i) (GB) 1972–1975

1972–1974 Rycam Engineering Ltd, Sutton Coldfield, Warwickshire.
1974–1975 Rycam Engineering Ltd, Telford, Salop.
Tom Killeen was a pioneer of monocoque design (he claimed to have made the world's first monocoque in 1950), and one of his specials, the Imp-based K18, was initially scheduled to enter production as the Rycam Mirage. In fact it formed the basis for the production Scorpion. The bodywork was a semi-monocoque fibreglass structure (a later version featured steel instead). There was a tubular steel roll-cage surrounding the cockpit area, which dictated high sills. Pop-up headlamps and gullwing doors were fitted but they were poorly conceived. The rear-mounted engine was a twin-carburettor 998cc Imp Rallye unit developing 65bhp, good for 95mph (153km/h). It is believed that only 11 were made, but the design was later revived as the KESTREL Scorpion.
CR

SCORPION (ii) (GB) 1979–1981

A. Evans Mouldings, Stourbridge, West Midlands.
This fibreglass-bodied MG TF replica was based on Triumph Herald/Spitfire chassis, priced in kit form at £1775. Its creator had previously been responsible for the Delta fibreglass bodyshell of the 1950s.
CR

SCORPION MOTOR CO. (US) c.1969

Scorpion made Ford GT-40 replica kits called the Scorpion GT that resembled the KELLISON kits. These kits had been sold as the SEBRING Mk II. They made versions to fit Volkswagen Beetle floorpans, or a tube frame that would accept V8 engines. They also made dune buggies and Ford Mustang trim parts.
HP

SCOTIA (GB) c.1907

A car of this name with a 16/20hp 4-cylinder engine was built in Glasgow in 1907, but details of the manufacturer are not known.
NG

SCOTSMAN (i) (GB) 1922–1923

Scotsman Motor Car Co., Glasgow.
The first of two makes to bear the name Scotsman, this was a conventional light car made with a choice of three 4-cylinder engines, a 1460cc 10hp, 1492cc 11hp and 14/40hp 2310cc. The first two had side-valve engines but the 14/40, known as the Flying Scotsman, had an ohc Sage unit. Designed by the pioneer Scottish motorist, J. Hall Nicol, they were all on the same chassis, with Meadows 3-speed gearboxes. The radiator carried a Scottish thistle motif, and the famous singer Sir Harry Lauder sat on the board of directors.
NG

SCOTSMAN (ii) (GB) 1929–1930

Scotsman Motors Ltd, Gorgie, Edinburgh.
Two models were offered by this company, which had no longer a life than its predecessor. One used a 1496cc Meadows engine and was known as the Little Scotsman, while the other was based on the 6-cylinder air-cooled S.A.R.A. It was claimed that it was made under licence in Scotland, but it is more likely that the

1973 Scorpion (i) GT coupé.
NATIONAL MOTOR MUSEUM

1930 Scotsman (ii) Little Scotsman 11.9hp saloon.
NICK BALDWIN

chassis were imported from France, and only the bodies were Scottish-built. These included a 4-seater sports tourer with cut-away doors. Not more than 30–40 were made of both types of Scotsman.
NG

SCOTT (i) (US) 1900–1901

1900 Scott & Cooper Manufacturing Co., St Louis, Missouri.
1900–1901 Scott Automobile Co., St Louis, Missouri.
The brothers Ashley and Semple Scott built an 8-seater electric bus in 1898 and a runabout in 1899, but did not start any kind of production until 1900, when they were financed by Todd K. Cooper, and began making electric cars and a delivery van. Fresh finance from Charles Drummond brought about a change in company name and in 1901 they bought out the electric car side of A.L. Dyke's business. The cars previously known as Dyke or St Louis were now made under the Scott name, though Drummond liquidated the business before the end of the year.
NG

SCOTT (ii) (F) 1912

Scott et Cie, Paris.
This obscure company offered two models for the 1912 season only. Both with four cylinders, they were a 2120cc 15hp and a 3770cc 20hp.
NG

1924 Scott Sociable 3-wheeler.
NATIONAL MOTOR MUSEUM

1911 Scout (i) 15.9hp tourer.
NATIONAL MOTOR MUSEUM

SCOTT ELLIS RACING (GB) 1989–c.1993

Scott Ellis Race & Replica Engineering, Wimborne, Dorset.
Scott Ellis racing was the manufacturer behind the Chevron B8 and was also an agent for K.V.A.'s GT40 replica. It offered its own GT40 package based on the K.V.A. featuring an aluminium chassis and body and each car was built to individual specification.

CR

SCOTTISH ASTER see ST VINCENT

SCOTTISH REPLICARS & CLASSICS (GB) 1984

This company briefly offered conventional build-to-order replicas of two classics, the MG TF and Porsche Speedster.

CR

SCOTT-NEWCOMB see STANDARD (x)

SCOTT SOCIABLE (GB) 1921–1925

Scott Autocar Co. Ltd, Bradford, Yorkshire.
This unusual machine was made by Alfred Angas Scott, better known for his 2-stroke motorcycles which he first marketed in 1909. At the beginning of World War I he was making a sidecar machine gun carrier, and from this he developed a 3-wheeler for the same purpose with two wheels in line and the third beside the rear wheel, which gave it the superficial appearance of a sidecar, though it had wheel steering. The engine was a 578cc 2-stroke twin, and final drive was by shaft to a spiral bevel gear on the offside rear wheel.

Scott acquired a new factory to make this machine, but the War Office contract never materialised, and he decided to make a civilian version, which he called the Scott Sociable. It had a triangulated tubular steel frame and fibreboard body. This was announced in June 1916, but it did not go into production until after the war, when Scott set up a separate company at Bradford (his motorcycle works were at Shipley), called the Scott Autocar Co. Ltd. This was dedicated to Sociable production, and was capitalised at £30,000. The Sociable made its debut at the 1920 Olympia Motor Cycle Show, priced at £273 for a 'Family' model; the price was reduced to £215 in 1921 and to £135 in 1923, by which date it had the Austin Seven to compete with. Scott's death in August 1923 removed the driving force behind the car, and production ended in 1924 after about 200 had been made. Scott motorcycles continued to be made up to the early 1970s, latterly by Bert Houlder in Birmingham.

NG

SCOUT (i) (GB) 1904–1923

1904–1908 Dean & Burden Ltd, Salisbury, Wiltshire.
1908–1921 Scout Motors Ltd, Salisbury, Wiltshire.
1921–1923 Whatley & Co., Pewsey, Wilrshire.
William Burden, with his sons William and Albert, had been producing clocks in Salisbury since 1885, before diversifying into the production of marine and stationary engines in 1902. Their first motorcycle was made in 1903 and a prototype car, with 2-cylinder engine and pressed steel chassis, the following year, when Percy Dean, a landowner from Chitterne, helped finance the firm's expansion into a limited company. Auspicious early successes in the TT races, Percy Dean driving, enhanced the marque's local reputation and a range of new models was soon introduced, including the 25hp 6-cylinder of 4389cc shown at Olympia in 1906. Encouraging sales figures led to a move to larger premises in Bemerton Road in 1907 and an unusually large proportion of components was manufactured 'in-house', including the shaft transmissions and many of the bodies. The range of private cars available in 1909 ran from a 10hp 2-cylinder at £265 up to the 40hp 6-cylinder, priced from £730 according to bodywork. From 1910 onwards increasing emphasis was laid on commercial vehicles, for which the overhead worm rear axles were well-suited, and only sales of the medium-sized 4-cylinder private cars held up. Scout charabancs and buses became quite well-known and popular locally, often with IB (Armagh) registrations, while a 'Colonial' version of the 15.9hp car (rated at 12/14) was introduced in 1914. Spares were still being sold for this model to several countries in the 1950s.

Percy Dean left in 1911 and Clifford Radcliffe took his place on the board, shepherding the firm through World War I contracts for military workshop equipment, shells and magnetic mine mechanisms. The factory was expanded in 1915, but this became a mixed blessing after peace was declared and the extra capacity was not matched by demand for a car of prewar design, with 15,9hp fixed-head engine, separate gearbox and cone clutch, priced at £950 for a 4-seater tourer. This was the staple model, although three other 4-cylinder cars were listed briefly, including one of no less than 6333cc. In 1920 Radcliffe was killed in a furnace room accident and the moulders' strike also hit the firm hard. Massive price reductions were of little avail and too many parts were built in small numbers by the firm itself to make further cost savings feasible. Commercial vehicle sales were negligible due to the number of ex-service vehicles on the market and the firm remained in token production only up to 1921. Some 1500 vehicles had been constructed in total, of which only two or three cars survive. The works was taken over by the Eclipse Carburettor Co. and the stock of parts by a firm of water engineers who assembled perhaps four more vehicles. Albert Burden reverted to clockmaking.

DF

Further Reading
The History of Scout Motors Ltd of Salisbury, Jeremy P. Farrant, South Wiltshire Group of Industrial Archaeology, 1967.

SCOUT (ii) (US) 1914

Scout Cyclecar Co., Muskogee, Oklahoma.
This was a typical cyclecar in appearance, with tandem seating for two, and transmission by a very long belt. It did, however, have a 4-cylinder engine and selective gearbox. A price of $375 was quoted, but it is unlikely that production ever started.

NG

SCOUT (iii) (GB) 1983–1991

1983–1985 Import Export, Spalding, Lincolnshire.
1987–1988 Automotive Engineering & Manufacturing.
1990–1991 The Sun Motor Company, Solihull, West Midlands.
This was one of many Mini-based Moke style kits but it differed from most in respect of its all-steel monocoque and was available in both 4-wheel and 6-wheel

1915 Scripps-Booth Model C coupé.
JOHN A. CONDE

versions. It was first launched as the T.M.C. Scout, but was ambitiously revived in 1987 by a new firm (A.E.M.). Despite its tortuous production career, a fair number were made.

CR

SCRIPPS-BOOTH (US) 1912–1922

1912–1913 James Scripps Booth, Detroit, Michigan.
1914 Scripps-Booth Cyclecar Co., Detroit, Michigan.
1914–1916 Scripps-Booth Co., Detroit, Michigan.
1916–1918 Scripps-Booth Corp., Detroit, Michigan.
1918–1922 General Motors Corp., Detroit, Michigan.

Few automobile builders had a more fertile mind than James Scripps Booth (1889–1955). The son of a Detroit newspaper publisher, Booth had a fascination that led him to create some of the most beautiful, and bizarre, cars of his period.

The first, the Bi-Autogo, was more motorcycle than car, with large wheels fore and aft and small auxiliary wheels at the side for 'landings'. A massive 6309cc V8 sat at the front, its water-cooling effected not by a conventional radiator but with 450ft (≈137m) of copper tubing. Behind the engine was seating for three, two passengers being seated behind the driver. Only one was built, in 1912, at a cost of some $25,000, footed mostly by his uncle, William Scripps.

James Booth's next adventure was with a cyclecar, which he called the Rocket. A tandem seater, it owed much to the French BÉDÉLIA, including, on the prototype, a back-seat driving position. Production models moved the steering wheel to the front seat and used an air-cooled V-twin SPACKE engine with the characteristic cyclecar belt drive, a two-speed gearbox, and drum brakes on the rear. At $385, it was priced just below the Model T Ford runabout. The start of production in January 1914 coincided with the upswing of the cyclecar fad in the United States. About 400 were built before the cyclecar bubble burst at the end of the year, at which time the company was sold to Puritan Machine Co. of Detroit who continued to service the cars and sell spares.

Continuing in the lightweight vein, Booth now conceived a 'luxurious light car', and again approached his uncle, who provided more cash. A new company was organised, and a designer, William Stout, hired away from the Imp Cyclecar Co. The first examples of the car, the Scripps-Booth Model C, emerged in February 1915. A 2-passenger, staggered-seat roadster, the Model C had a 'step down'

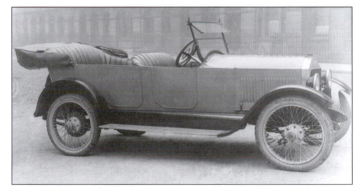

c.1919 Scripps-Booth Model Six-39 tourer.
NICK BALDWIN

floor below the chassis frame, a feature touted by Hudson as novel after World War II. A 4-cylinder ohv Sterling engine of 1700 cc produced about 20hp. The car's appeal was heightened by a German silver radiator and Houk wire wheels, but parts supply problems slowed production. Interestingly, about one third of Model C production was exported to England, and significant numbers of cars were shipped to Cuba.

A V8 car, the Model D, followed in late 1916. The engine, the Ferro unit, had been designed by Alanson Brush, erstwhile builder of the Brush car. Called a light eight by its makers, the Model D appeared as a 4-seat roadster (with novel removable hard-top), and, in limited quantities, as a town car. The Model C continued to be produced, and Scripps-Booth took over the Sterling Engine Co., but the 4-cylinder engine was proving very unreliable. The Scripps-Booth car was widely called, in the vernacular, 'slips loose'. The Sterling was then replaced with a Chevrolet engine as used in their 490 model, and the resulting car was called the Model G. Following a tiff with the directors in October 1916, James Scripps Booth left the company, never to return.

The production and reliability problems continued into 1917, by which time James's two uncles, financier William Scripps and company president Clarence Booth had also departed. By the end of the year, the Chevrolet company had

c.1923 Seabrook 12/24hp tourer.
NICK BALDWIN

taken over, and Scripps-Booth became part of General Motors when Chevrolet was absorbed in 1918.

Scripps-Booth cars soon became much less adventurous. Built on Oakland chassis, they were fitted with Northway 6-cylinder engines. They proved not to be an important part of the GM line, being discontinued at the insistence of chairman Alfred P. Sloan in 1922. About 60,000 Scripps-Booth cars were built. Ironically, the greatest rate of production was in the GM period, 1919–20, when 16,000 were produced. The factory was converted to build Buicks.

James Scripps Booth, however, was not finished with automobiles. Having moved to California, he had devoted his time almost entirely to painting, but eventually became fascinated with another car concept, which he called DA VINCI. Attempts to market the Da Vinci resulted in much heartache and a great deal of litigation. He made one last try at automobiles in 1930, with another cyclecar, the tandem-seat Da Vinci Pup, but only one prototype was ever built.

KM

Further Reading
'Artist's Conception, the Novel Cars of James Scripps Booth', Sam Medway, *Automobile Quarterly*, Vol. 13, No. 3.

S.D. (I) 1980s
Autocostruzioni di Salvatore Diomante, Turin.
Formed in 1970, this was a coachbuilding firm specialising in stretching saloons to become limousines. In the late 1980s it built a handful of exacting Bizzarrini replicas.

CR

S.D. 500 (GB) 1988 to date
1988–1990 Transformer Cars, Frant, East Sussex.
1990 to date Elmsett Road Racing Automobiles, Aldham, Suffolk.
Stan Daniel created one of the highest quality kit cars in the world with the S.D. 500, a highly convincing fibreglass-bodied 1955 Ferrari Mondial lookalike. The first S.D. 500 was built in 1986 and, after a brief spell with Transformer Cars, Stan Daniel began making them himself. The semi-spaceframe multi-tube chassis mimicked the original Ferrari, but used Alfa Romeo Alfetta parts, including the twin-cam engine, ZF 5-speed gearbox with reverse-position gate, hubs and disc brakes. Cars were marketed mostly in kit form.

CR

SEABROOK (GB) 1920–1928
Seabrook Bros Ltd, London.
The brothers Herbert and Percy Seabrook founded their business as cycle component factors in 1895, at premises in Great Eastern Street, London. It was a substantial firm with branches in Berlin and New York, and in 1911 they added cars to the lines, importing the American-made REGAL, which they sold as the RMC or Seabrook-RMC. During World War I they imported Napoleon trucks from America, which they sold under the Seabrook name. At the 1919 Olympia Show they exhibited a tourer of American origin powered by a 3.8-litre 6-cylinder engine; its make is unknown as it did not correspond to any model of Regal. Few, if any, were sold, and the following year they launched a light car of wholly British design.

The 11.9hp Seabrook had a 1795cc light-alloy 4-cylinder engine with shaft-driven single-ohc, said to have been made in London. They exhibited a chassis and two complete cars at the 1920 Olympia Show, but prices were very high, at £775 for a deluxe 2-seater. Possibly there were problems with the manufacture of the engine as well, for in 1921 they turned to a 1495cc Dorman engine with twin high-camshafts on the lines of the later Riley Nine. They ordered 41 of these engines, which probably marked the total for this model, as from 1923 onwards they bought 1496cc engines from Meadows, who already supplied the 4-speed gearboxes. Several body styles were offered, including a saloon and an attractive-looking sports model, and prices were more realistic at £395 for a 2-seater, and £275 for a smaller model, the 1247cc 9/19hp. Apart from the standard sporting 2-seater, Seabrook offered a special model in 1924 on the 12/24 chassis, with large outside exhaust pipe and a single headlamp at the buyer's request. 160 Meadows-engined cars were made, the majority before the Seabrooks retired in 1926. They sold the business to Frank Burgess who moved production to Chelsea, He only ordered three more Meadows engines after 1926, but may have made more cars than that by using up stock already bought by the Seabrooks. The make was listed up to 1928, but it is not certain if any cars were made that year.
NG

Further Reading
'Fragments on Forgotten Makes, the Seabrook', Bill Boddy, *Motor Sport*, April 1986.

SEABURY (US) 1904–1905
Howard Automobile Co., Morris Heights, New York.
In November 1904 Charles L. Seabury bought up William Howard's company and continued the largest model, a 24hp 4-cylinder tonneau, under his own name. A few modifications were made to the design by Budd G. Gray from the LaFrance Fire Engine Co., who also designed the SPEEDWAY car for Seabury. Both Seabury and Speedway were out of production before the end of 1905.
NG

SEAGRAVE (i) (US) 1914
The Seagrave Co., Columbus, Ohio.
Seagrave were among the best-known fire engine makers in America, being in business from 1907 until recently. In 1914 they made a few chief's cars, 2-seater roadsters for the use of fire chiefs. They were made with 28/30hp 4-cylinder or 40/45hp 6-cylinder engines. Production for sale to the general public was planned, but did not take place. Seagrave's next venture into passenger cars came in 1960.
NG

SEAGRAVE (ii) (US) 1960
Seagrave Fire Apparatus Co., Columbus, Ohio.
Although Seagrave primarily built fire fighting equipment, they also built three prototypes for a line of small economy cars. They were 2-door hard-top coupés with 65hp Continental engines, but they never made it into production.
HP

SEAGULL (GB) 1984
Seagull Cars, Ash Vale, Aldershot, Hampshire.
Design and execution were distinctly lacking in this Mini-based open-topped sports car kit. It used Mini subframes (the Mini engine being positioned in the rear), with fibreglass front and rear ends sandwiching an aluminium centre body section.
CR

SEAL (GB) 1912–1924

1912–1920 Haynes & Bradshaw, Manchester.
1920–1924 Seal Motors Ltd, Manchester.

The Seal was in the same class as the Scott Sociable, resembling a motorcycle and sidecar, but steered from the sidecar. On early models steering was by tiller, but from 1914 a wheel was provided. From 1912 to 1914 the power unit was a 770cc 6hp JAP V-twin driving through a Sturmey Archer hub gearbox with belt final drive, but the improved model made from 1914 onwards had a 980cc 8hp JAP engine, conventional 3-speed sliding gearbox and chain drive. A 1920 model had Seal's own gearbox and shaft drive, but the following year they returned to chain drive in conjunction with a Burman gearbox. Postwar models included 2-, 3-, and 4-seater cars, the latter being called the Family model. A goods carrying version was made at least from 1923, and production of this lasted longer than of the car. In about 1930 it was renamed Progress, in a new version with the driver on the motorcycle rather than in the sidecar, and in 1932 it became a more conventional 3-wheeler with single front wheel. A few passenger carrying versions of this were made under the Progress name. The makers were now called Haynes Economy Motors, so at least one of the original partners was still involved.

NG

1924 Seal Family 3-wheeler.
NATIONAL MOTOR MUSEUM

SEARCHMONT (US) 1900–1903

1900–1901 Searchmont Motor Co., Philadelphia, Pennsylvania.
1902–1903 Fournier-Searchmont Motor Co., Chester, Pennsylvania.

The Searchmont company was formed by a group of businessmen, headed by Theodore C. Search, (hence the name) who was president of the Stetson Hat Co. They bought out the KEYSTONE Motor Co. which was making a small car called the Wagonette. This was continued into 1902 under the name Searchmont Wagonette, with 5 or 10hp single-cylinder engines mounted at the rear, and tiller steering. In the winter of 1901/02 the famous French racing driver Henri Fournier visited Philadelphia, and became involved with a new design of Searchmont. How much input came from Fournier is not known, since most of the reworking of the design was due to Lee Sherman Chadwick and Edward B. Gallaher who had been head of Keystone and continued as manager of Searchmont. However, Fournier's name counted for a lot, and the company was actually renamed Fournier-Searchmont in 1902, by which time the Frenchman had returned to Europe. The new Searchmont had a front-mounted 2-cylinder engine, double-chain drive and a 4-seater tonneau body. The bonnet was similar to that of the Mors, which make Fournier drove in the European town-to-town races (he won Paris-Bordeaux and Paris-Berlin in 1901), so perhaps that was his contribution to the Searchmont. The 1903 10hp had a longer wheelbase, but was otherwise unchanged. Chadwick designed a 32hp four but the company failed before it was completed. However, he took a wagonload of components to a small foundry at Chester, where he assembled them into the first CHADWICK car.

NG

1903 Searchmont 10hp tonneau.
NICK BALDWIN

SEARS (US) 1908–1912

Sears Motor Car Works, Chicago, Illinois.

One of the best-known of the high-wheelers, the Sears was made for sale by the Sears Roebuck mail order company. It was designed by Alvaro S. Krotz, and the first year's models were made by the McCurdy buggy company in Evansville, Indiana. By late 1909 Sears had their own factory in Chicago, although the 10/12hp flat-twin engine was made by a small Ohio firm called Somers. It was mounted under the seat and drove through a friction transmission and double-chain drive. The wooden wheels were shod with solid tyres and top speed was only 25mph (40km/h). In their advertising the company claimed 'The Sears will do everything that a $5000 car will do except travel faster than 25mph'.

All Sears buggies used the same size of engine and 72in (1827mm) wheelbase, but there were several variations. The basic Model G ($325) had neither wings nor weather protection, the Model H ($365) had both, while the Model K ($475) had cushion tyres and the Model L ($475) had pneumatic tyres. The top of the range was the Model M 'cozy coupé' at $485. There was also a combined pleasure car/delivery van on an 87in (2208mm) wheelbase at $445. These are all 1911–12 prices.

The Sears was very popular with country folk whose tributes included the following: 'It beats a horse bad as it don't eat when I ain't working it and it stands

1910 Sears Model H high-wheeler.
NICK BALDWIN

without hitching, and best of all it don't get scared at automobiles'. Two factors caused Sears to discontinue their buggy after the 1912 season; they found that at their modest prices they were making no profit on the cars, and anyway the vogue for the high-wheeler was over. After making about 3500 cars the company ceased to offer them by mail order although they built a few vehicles, mostly commercials, for general sale under the name LINCOLN.

c.1956 Seat 1400 long-wheelbase saloon.
NICK GEORGANO

1968 Seat 850 Especial saloon.
NICK GEORGANO/NATIONAL MOTOR MUSEUM

1990 Seat Ibiza 1.5 hatchback.
SEAT

Sears Roebuck considered a return to cars in 1927 with a small car of Austin Seven size, the chassis to be made by Gardner and the bodies by Budd. However, they decided against it, a wise decision in view of the poor response to the American Austin launched two years later. In 1953 Sears tried again with the ALLSTATE.

NG

Further Reading
'Behold the High-Wheeler', Beverly Rae Kimes,
Automobile Quarterly, Vol. 9, No. 1.

SEAT (E) 1953 to date
Sociedad Española de Automóviles de Turismo, Barcelona.
In a poor Spain devastated by Civil War (1936–39) and isolated from World War II (1939–45), Wifredo Ricart created the biggest private car industry, signing a license with FIAT. In 1953 the first Spanish-built 1400 was presented. To reduce the expenses of imports, the company had to develop a new component industry, soon achieving 95 per cent national components. After the 1400 the rear-engined 600 was launched, in 1957. This was the car which put the whole nation on wheels. Over 800,000 of this small car were built. With these two models in production up to the 1960s, Seat was one of Spain's fastest growing companies. Already at this time, the company was developing some of its own designs. A diesel-engined 1400, a 4-door 600, called the 800, and the 1500, which used the body of a Fiat 1800 but the 1400 engine. In 1967 Seat signed a contract with Fiat that permitted it to export the car, using, in some countries, Fiat distributors. At the same time Fiat increased its stake from 7 per cent to 36 per cent.

600,000 850s and 900,000 124s were built in over ten years. In 1973 the company started to build the 132 and in 1974 presented the 133, a small car using the 843cc engine from the 127, the first car not designed by Fiat. It was sold to several foreign markets and also built in Egypt and Argentina. Other Spanish versions were the 850 4-door, 127 4-door and the 1430, based on the 124. In 1975 appeared the 1200/1430 Sport Coupé, based on the 127, and the 131. In 1977 came the 128 with engines from the 1200/1430 Sport, bigger than Fiats own, and in 1980 the company introduced the Panda, to be built first in Spain and than in Italy. The Panda and the Ritmo were the last designs developed

1986 Seat Malaga 1.7 Diesel GLX saloon.
SEAT

under Fiat licence. At the end of the 1970s production failed, Seat lost market shares and Fiat and Seat finished their collaboration.

In 1976 Seat had been obliged by the government to save the AUTHI plant at Pamplona. The economic crisis following the first oil-crisis in 1973 and the political problems following General Franco's death in 1975 made the situation very complicated for Seat: too many workers building old cars in old factories.

In order to continue production without Fiat licences, Seat developed the Ronda, a restyled Ritmo, and the Marbella, looking very like the Panda. The 127 was changed into the Fura. At the same time Seat developed a complete dealer network around Europe and got good penetration into several markets, including Italy. Fiat took Seat to court for imitating their cars, but Seat finally won, demonstrating that the Ronda was not the Ritmo. Nevertheless, a new generation of cars was necessary. At the same time Seat signed a contract with Volkswagen to build the Polo, Passat and Santana in Spain.

2000 Seat Toledo V5 saloon.
SEAT

The state-owned company spent a lot of money to prepare the new generation of cars, and with a design from Giorgio Giugiaro, later known as 'Mediterranean design', and engines developed by Porsche, introduced the Ibiza and Malaga, with different engines from 900c up to 1500cc. The company looked for a new partner, but Toyota was shocked by the debts, and the Volkswagen group only wanted to take shares when the company was in the black. In 1985 VW took over 51 per cent of the shares. In 1988 Seat built the new plant at Martorell, where by the end of the 1990s over 500,000 cars were built annually. These were very difficult years for Seat, as the company had to reduce the workforce and needed a lot of money to modernise production. But to demonstrate that Seat was back with new ideas, the company presented several concept cars, like the Ibiza Convertible in 1988, the Proto T in 1989 and the Proto C in 1990. The Ibiza, Malaga and Cordoba, and later the Toledo had such success that, in 1996, the company was finally solvent again. The range at the end of the 1990s started from the small VW Lupo-based Arosa, the Ibiza II – with engines from 999cc up to the 16-valve 1984cc engine giving 150bhp (and diesel engines from VAG), the Cordoba (Arosa, Ibiza and Cordoba using the same engine range), the Toledo II with 1595cc, 1781cc and the 5-cylinder 2324cc engine and the Alhambra MPV, built together with Volkswagen and Ford by the Portuguese Autolatina. A new model announced in the spring of 2000 was the Leon 5-door hatchback

2000 Seat Ibiza Vibe hatchback.
SEAT

1926 Seaton-Petter 10/18 tourer.
NICK BALDWIN

1910 Sebring Six tourer.
NICK BALDWIN

c.1975 Sebring–Vanguard Citycar.
NICK GEORGANO

with a choice of four engines, from 1.4 litres to the 180bhp 20VT, the latter combined with a 6-speed gearbox and 4-wheel drive.

VCM

SEATON-PETTER (GB) 1926–1927

British Dominions Car Co. Ltd, Yeovil, Somerset.

This company was run by Douglas Seaton, and his cars were made in the works of Petters, the oil-engine maker, who built some early cars under the name PETTER. The Seaton-Petter had a 1.3-litre vertical twin 2-stroke engine, three forward speeds, and quarter-elliptic springs all round. A 4-seater, the rear seats were removable to allow the car to be used as a light truck. The price was a very low £100.

NG

SEBRING (i) (US) 1910–1912

Sebring Motor Car Co., Sebring, Ohio.
This was a conventional car powered by a 35/40hp 6-cylinder engine and made in three styles of open body, a torpedo, a baby tonneau and a cross-country roadster, all 5-seaters, and priced identically at $2750. They were made from March 1910 to early 1912, but only 25 were turned out.

NG

SEBRING (ii) (GB) 1990 to date

Sebring International, Wisbech, Cambridgeshire.
Initially under the name Classic Roadsters, this Austin-Healey replica range was first imported from the United States, though licensed production under the name Sebring. Three models were offered: the SX was a straight copy of the original Healey, the MX had wide flared arches and the MXL was an MX set up for a Chevrolet small block V8 engine. All shared the same steel ladder chassis with Ford front uprights and specially-made wishbones, but the SX used a narrowed Jaguar rear axle, and the MX/MXL had a full-width Jaguar axle. Engine choices encompassed Ford 4-cylinder, Ford V6, Nissan straight-6, Rover V8, and Chevrolet V8.

CR

SEBRING Mk II (US) c.1967

Sports Racing Equipment, San Carlos, California.
This company made a Ford GT-40 kit that bolted to a VW floorpan called the Sebring Mk II. They also made a dune buggy called the Desert Rat. By 1969 these kits were being sold by the SCORPION MOTOR CO.

HP

SEBRING SPRITE (GB) 1993 to date

Archer's Garage, Birmingham.
From 1959, Austin-Healey Sprite owners wanting to go racing were offered parts after the race in which the model had such success. In 1993, a replica of the John Sprinzel bodied Sebring was launched, reviving a classic hard-top style of which only six were ever built. It was supplied as a conversion of any MG Midget or Austin Sprite, and you could select various body panels in any of three materials: fibreglass, Diolen, or Kevlar. You could retain your BMC engine, upgrade it to Sebring specification or fit a modern Rover K-series engine and Ford 5-speed gearbox. Also available were replica Mk1 Sprite bodyshells.

CR

SEBRING-VANGUARD (US) 1974–1978

Sebring-Vanguard Co., Columbus, Maryland.
The Sebring-Vanguard Citicar was a short, ugly electric car that sold very well in the late 1970s. It was about the size of a golf cart and had an angular, utilitarian 2-seat body. It used a 3.5hp electric motors with eight 6-volt batteries. Top speed was 38mph (61km/h) with a range of 40 to 50 miles. They also sold the Citivan, a lightweight utility truck conversion with a more powerful motor. About 2000 Citicars were built before Sebring-Vanguard was purchased by General Engines Co., who renamed it the COMUTA-CAR.

HP

S.E.C.M.A. (F) 1996 to date

Sté d'Étude et Construction Mécanique Automobile, Aniche.
Even among the *sans permis* microcars that proliferated in France, the S.E.C.M.A. Scootcar was extraordinarily small and basic. It was also unique in that it returned to the 3-wheeler pioneer days, however, with the single rear wheel supplemented by two small stabilising wheels. A Morini 49cc 2-stroke engine was used in conjunction with automatic transmission and there was MacPherson strut front suspension plus a cantilever-type rear end. A 4-wheeled 125 version with a 338cc

Lombardini single-cylinder 4-stroke engine was launched at the end of 1997, alongside an electric model with very close-set rear wheels. 500 cars had been supplied after only one year of trading. The open version was called the Fun Tech, while a further variation was the Fun Cab, with full weather protection and doors. In some markets these models were known as the Ma-Goo.

CR

SECOND CHANCE MOTORS *see* GIBBON

SECQUEVILLE-HOYAU (F) 1919–1924

SA des Anciens Établissements Secqueville et Hoyau, Gennevilliers, Seine.
This high quality light car was made by Alfred Secqueville and Gaston Hoyau who had started in business in 1911 as makers of aero engines and propellers. During World War I they ran a modern, well-equipped factory which made aero engines of Hispano-Suiza and Bugatti design. Before the war ended their chief engineer, M. Porney, designed a light car powered by a 1244cc 4-cylinder side-valve engine with aluminium pistons and tubular connecting rods, and a 3-bearing crankshaft. The 4-speed gearbox was in unit with the engine, and an unusual feature for a light car at that time was electric starting. Wire wheels and a Rolls-Royce shape radiator gave it an air of distinction, and four body styles were offered, a 4-seater tourer, 3-seater torpedo, saloon and coupé de ville, the latter unusual on so small a car. This was on the longest of three wheelbases, 94 (2386mm), 106 (2690mm) and 114in (2893mm). Everything about the S et H was attractive apart from the price, 20,000 francs, when comparable 8CV cars cost from 13,500 to 15,000 francs. Total production was just under 600 cars, of which only 80 were made in the last year, 1923, with a few being sold off from stock in 1924.

NG

Further Reading
'Secqueville et Hoyau', Serge Pozzoli, *l'Album du Fanatique*, February 1974.

SEDAN (GB) 1907–1910

Sedan Auto-Car Syndicate Ltd, Wolverhampton, Staffordshire.
This was a front-wheel drive forecarriage design articulated at the centre of the frame. It was powered by a 22hp flat-twin engine and was mostly seen as a commercial vehicle. However, at least one was made with 7-seater tourer body. Wolverhampton may have been an office address, as one old timer said that they were made at the Seaham Harbour Engine Works in County Durham, where Londonderry steam wagons had been made a few years earlier.

NG

SEETSTU (GB) 1905–1907

James McGeoch & Co., Paisley, Renfrewshire.
This was a 2-seater 3-wheeler powered by a 3hp 2-stroke engine, of which only six or seven were made. There are two explanations of the unusual name, 'seats two', and 'seestu', which means 'see you' in Paisley dialect.

NG

SEFTON (GB) 1903

Liverpool & Manchester Motor Manufacturing Co., Liverpool.
This company was a well-known car dealer, selling De Dietrich, Regal and other makes. In 1903 it was announced that they were going to make a voiturette, car and delivery van under the name Sefton. No details were given; and if any were made, they were probably assembled vehicles using Lacoste et Battmann components, as indeed did the Regal, one of the makes sold by the company.

NG

SEIDEL-AROP (D) 1925–1926

Arop GmbH, Automobilbau, Berlin.
This was a very short-lived light car powered by a 1020cc 8/25PS engine. It was designed by Ing. Seidel.

HON

SEKINE (US) 1923

I. Sekine & Co., New York, New York.
The Sekine was not 'just another' small car targeted to the export market. It differed considerably in its mechanical layout which featured no differential, its

1999 Secma Fun-Tech 2-seater.
SECMA

1920 Secqueville-Hoyau 10hp coupé de ville.
NATIONAL MOTOR MUSEUM

1907 Sedan front-drive articulated car.
NATIONAL MOTOR MUSEUM

1910 Selden 28hp limousine.
NICK BALDWIN

1920 Selve 6/24PS tourer.
HERMAN ERIKSSON

1928 Selve Selecta front-drive saloon.
NICK BALDWIN

drive being taken by a 4-cylinder engine of just under 2-litres capacity, angled at 17 degrees from the longitudinal axis of the car to the left rear wheel, thence to the right wheel via a shaft. Double transverse springs were substituted for conventional axles, the brake being connected to the right rear wheel. Production may have been limited to the lone touring car prototype which featured a 108in (2741mm) wheelbase.

KM

SELDEN (US) 1907–1914

Selden Motor Vehicle Co., Rochester, New York.

George Baldwin Selden (1846–1923) is better remembered for a single archaic vehicle that he built himself than for some 7400 cars made by his company. In 1877 he designed a carriage powered by a petrol engine which drove the front wheels on a swivelling forecarriage. He did not have the means to build it, although he applied for a patent in 1879 for a wide-ranging number of designs for a 'road locomotive' This was not granted until 1895, when the design

was already old-fashioned, and in 1899 the Electric Vehicle Co. of Hartford, Connecticut, makers of the Columbia electric, acquired the patent and tried to enforce a royalty from every maker of petrol cars in the United States. To make the claim more credible, in 1907 Selden built a car on the lines of his 1877 design, and even painted the date 1877 on the side. A similar vehicle was built by the Electric Vehicle Co.; both survive, Selden's in the Henry Ford Museum and the other in the Connecticut State Library at Hartford. It took until 1911 for the claim to be declared unenforceable, thanks to the tough attitude of Henry Ford.

Meanwhile Selden had become a manufacturer, building a 30hp 4-cylinder car designed by E.T. Birdsall. One of the company's slogans was 'Made by the Father of Them All', which many people probably believed, for it was some time before the false date of Selden's car was revealed. The Selden car was made in various sizes, all with 4-cylinder engines most of which were made by Continental. The usual body styles were offered, including a 7-seater limousine, and prices were in the $2000–3000 range, though the limousine cost $3750 from 1912 onwards. Passenger car production ended in 1914, but trucks were continued until 1932.

NG

SELF (S) 1916–1922

Axel H. and Per Weiertz, Svedala.

The Weiertz brothers made three prototypes of cyclecar with air-cooled engines; the first had a single-cylinder engine, the second, of 1919, had a 4-cylinder Phänomen engine and friction transmission close to the rear axle, with chain final drive, and the third, from 1922, used a V-twin. None was produced commercially, but the brothers later worked for Thulinverken where they designed the Thulin Typ B.

NG

SELLERS (US) 1909–1912

Sellers Motor Car Co., Hutchinson, Kansas.

This company was organised by O.G. Sellers and Harry Shoemaker who had previously made the SHOEMAKER at Elkhart, Indiana. The Sellers was a conventional car with 35hp 4-cylinder engine, 4-speed gearbox and shaft drive. The only body style offered was a 5-seater tourer which sold for $1700. Production ran at three cars per week, most being sold to Kansas customers, and this output was insufficient to make the business profitable, so it closed in June 1912.

NG

SELTZER (US) 1978–1985

Seltzer Motor Industries, Chatsworth, California.

The Seltzer Willow was a mid-engined kit car with a Targa-style top and low, race car lines. It used a Ford Pinto 2000cc engine and Fiesta transverse transaxle located behind the driver, and the suspension was a mixture of Porsche 914 at the rear and Triumph Spitfire in front. A racing-type spaceframe was equipped with a roll bar. With a weight of 1780lb (809kg) it was quick for its size. Kit prices started at $7320 with a fully assembled car selling for $18000.

HP

SELVE (D) 1919–1929

Selve Automobilwerk AG, Hamelin.

This company was a successor to the Norddeutsche Automobilwerke which had made COLIBRI and SPERBER cars before the war. They made engines under the name Basse & Selve, an aluminium specialist which took over NAW during the war, and in 1919 turned to complete cars with 1570 or 2086cc 4-cylinder side-valve engines. In 1923 came a 2091cc sports model with inlet-over-exhaust valves. This was designed by Ernst Lehmann who had worked for Daimler (i) and Métallurgique, and who was killed at the wheel of a Selve in the Teutoberger hill climb in 1924. He was succeeded by Karl Slevogt who came from Apollo.

All subsequent Selves had side-valve engines, and included a 2850cc 11/45PS six of 1925–27, and the 3075cc Selecta six made from 1928 to 1929. At the 1928 Berlin Motor Show Selve showed a low-slung front drive saloon powered by a 6-cylinder engine, but it never went into production. About 3000 Selves cars were made, and Basse & Selve continued to make engines up to 1932.

HON

S.E.M. (i) see MORISSE

S.E.M. (ii) (GB) 1988–1992

S.E.M. Cars, Poulton-le-Fylde, Lancashire.
During the 1980s, T.V.R. moved steadily away from its kit car roots but two
ex-T.V.R. staff (Tony Edwards and Terry Steptoe) decided to turn the clock back
by forming S.E.M. Cars and building the Saiga in nearby Poulton. In appearance
it recalled the T.V.R. 3000M. It had a tubular steel backbone space frame chassis
intended for Ford Cortina MkIII/IV parts. Very few Saigas were made.

CR

SENATOR (i) (US) 1907–1910

Victor Automobile Co., Ridgeville, Indiana.
Senator cars used air-cooled Carrico engines, a 20/24hp four which was built
throughout the make's short life, and a 14/16hp twin which was offered for the
1909 season only. Body styles included a tourer and a roadster on the 4-cylinder
chassis, both priced at $2000, and a $650 runabout on the 2-cylinder chassis.

NG

SENATOR (ii) (US) 1912

Senator Motor Car Co., Pittsburgh, Pennsylvania.
The short-lived Senator from Pittsburgh was offered in roadster or tourer form,
with a 40hp 4-cylinder engine. The company planned to build 1000 cars in 1912,
but actual output was undoubtedly much smaller.

NG

SENECA (US) 1917–1924

Seneca Motor Co., Fostoria, Ohio.
Formerly the FOSTORIA, the Seneca was a typical assembled car of its time.
The output of several hundred cars a year was limited exclusively to open models,
roadsters and touring cars, and its entire production was confined to 4-cylinders
– a Le Roi engine until 1921 and a Lycoming for its final three years. A small car,
the Seneca had a wheelbase of 108in (2741mm) until 1921 and 112in (2843mm)
thereafter. A curious aspect of the Seneca was that most, if not all, of its cars were
marketed in green with black running gear. Approximately one half of Seneca's
annual production was targeted to the export market, the other half sold primarily
in the Fostoria area. An estimated 5000 Senecas found buyers during the company's
eight years of existence.

KM

SÉNÉCHAL (F) 1921–1927

1921–1923 Sénéchal et Cie, Courbevoie, Seine.
1923–1927 Sté Industrielle et Commerciale, Gennevilliers, Seine.
The Sénéchal was one of France's best-known small sports cars, though it never
achieved the wide fame of its rivals the Amilcar and the Salmson. It was built by
Robert Sénéchal (1892–1985) who learnt to drive in 1907 on his father's 24hp
Gladiator, and served as a pilot in the French Air Force during World War I. He
then made a fortune selling ex-army trucks, his partner in this venture being
Louis Delage's son, Pierre. In 1921 he launched his own make from a small
factory at Courbevoie, with a *carrosserie* nearby. His first models used the well-
known 4-cylinder Ruby engine, made by his friends Godefroy and Levêque, and
95 per cent of all Sénéchals were Ruby-powered. A few of the early models had
Train V-twin engines, and some used Chapuis-Dornier 4-cylinder engines.

Two models were offered in 1921, the 904cc B4 with 2-speed gearbox and
the 3-speed 985cc B5S. Bodies were a 2-seater tourer and a pointed-tail sports
model. Sénéchal was a keen driver and raced his cars with great success, scoring
51 victories in 56 races in 1922 and 1923 alone. A larger engine of 1095cc was
added for the 1923 range, when 2-speed gearboxes were abandoned, and electric
lighting was featured.

By 1923 Sénéchals were selling so well that Robert needed a larger factory than
he had at 30 rue Louis Blanc in Courbevoie. He came to an agreement with
Chenard-Walcker, who wanted a small car in their range, by which a new
company would be set up to make cars of Sénéchal design in the Chenard factory.
The organisation was called the Société Industrielle et Commerciale, and the
cars continued to be sold under the Sénéchal name. In October 1923 the new
range was announced; the Type T touring model, the Types S and SS sports and
the GS Grand Sport. The latter was available in two sizes, the 750cc with Ruby
engine and the 1095cc with Chapuis-Dornier engine. There was a racing model

1924 Sénéchal Grand Sport.
NICK BALDWIN

of the latter, called the Acacias after an event won by Robert Sénéchal, and also
the Type C light van. In 1924 a 2-litre Sénéchal was announced, but it was in
fact a Chenard-Walcker rebadged and entered in the Touring Car GP. It was never
a production model.

From 1926 onwards the accent at Sénéchal was on more luxurious coachwork
rather than competitions (Robert Sénéchal himself was no longer available to
drive his own cars once he had become a member of the Delage works team in
1926. The following year he bought himself a 1½-litre Grand Prix Delage). The
1927 Type Z3 Sénéchal was very similar to the 7CV Chénard-Walcker, yet
prices for all but the basic torpedo were noticeably higher. In mid–1927 the 9CV
Type Y5 Sénéchal was renamed Chenard-Sénéchal and given a Chenard-type
radiator. In October 1927 the Y5 became the Y7 with a new Toutée-designed
engine with overhead inlet and side exhaust valves. The Sénéchal as such was no
longer listed, and very few Chénard-Sénéchals were made either. A single final
example was completed in about 1930 for the grandson of René Donnay, a
director of Chenard-Walcker. As the boy was only 12 it never left the gates of the
family estate.

Robert Sénéchal ran a garage in Paris selling Chenard-Walcker, Delage and
Ford cars, and servicing Bugattis. He was active in the Motor Cycle Club de
France, of which he became president, and in 1970 he was president of the
Amicales des Coureurs Automobiles de France and vice-president of the Fédération
Motocycliste de France.

NG

Further Reading
'Sénéchal ou Monsieur Cyclecar', François Jolly,
l'Album du Fanatique, September–December 1977, April–June 1978,
November–December 1978.
Chenard-Walcker-FAR, Claude Rouxel et Jacques Dorizon,
Histoire et Collections, 1998.

SENG ET HENRY (F) 1901–1902

This was a light car powered by a front-mounted vertical-twin engine, with a
4-speed gearbox and shaft drive. Movements of the steering column operated
both clutch and brakes.

NG

SENSAUD DE LAVAUD see DE LAVAUD

SEQUOIA (US) 1926

Gilbert H. Porter, Glendale, California.
The Sequoia was a 2-seater roadster with a vee-radiator not unlike that of a Bentley.
Gilbert Porter built two and sold them for $3000 each, but problems with a sub-
contractor prevented further production.

NG

SERA (F) 1959–1961

Sté d'Études et de Réalisations Automobiles, Porte de Villiers, Paris.
M.G. Rey formed SERA to manufacture a stylish 2-seater convertible with Panhard
running gear, first shown at the 1959 Paris Salon. Built in the old Motobloc
factory, the SERA Panhard had strong hints of Jaguar D-Type in its styling, and
held great promise. High production costs made the fibreglass-bodied SERA too
expensive though, and only 22 cars were built before the factory was shut down
in January 1961.

CR

1968 Serenissima coupé by Ghia.
NATIONAL MOTOR MUSEUM

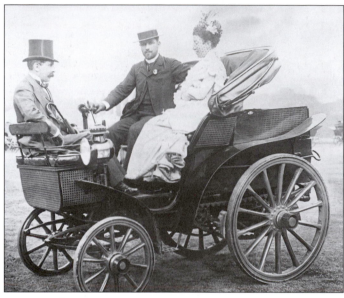

c.1895 Serpollet steam car.
NATIONAL MOTOR MUSEUM

1903 (Gardner) Serpollet 6-seater steam car for the Maharajah of Rewa.
NATIONAL MOTOR MUSEUM

SERAPH (GB) 1984–1987
1984–1985 Motorstyle, Bristol, Avon.
1985–1987 Seraph Cars Ltd, Bristol, Avon.

The first product of this operation was the Seraph Sports Racer, a dramatic but very boxy spaceframe chassis coupé designed for a mid-mounted Ford engine, and first shown in 1984. The following year it took over the BONITO.

CR

SERENISSIMA (I) 1965–1970
Scuderia Serenissima, Bologna.

Serenissima (the old name for the city-state of Venice) was an attempt by Count Volpi to salvage something from his disastrous ATS project. In 1965 Volpi revived the ATS road car with double-ohc heads replacing the original single-ohc layout. Customers were offered either a 300bhp 3-litre V8 or a 340bhp 3.5-litre version. A coupé with a Ghia body was offered in 1968 but there were few takers. The marque's little moments of fame came when a Serenissima ran unsuccessfully in the 1966 Le Mans race and McLaren occasionally used a 3-litre Serenissima engine in Formula One that year, also without success. In 1970 the project was sold on to Moreno Baldi, but nothing further was heard of it.

MJL

SERPENTINA (US) 1915
Claudius Mezzacasa, New York, New York.

This was one of that select band of 4-wheeled cars whose wheels were arranged in diamond pattern. The first was the Sunbeam-Mabley, and the Serpentina, as befitted a car some 14 years younger, was considerably more streamlined, with a torpedo-shaped 2-seater body. The front and rear wheels steered in opposite directions, so that the car could practically spin on its centre wheels. When approaching a New York policeman it was said to have performed 'a pirouette of the most amazing swiftness, and darted off in a right-angle direction before the startled policeman could open his mouth'.

NG

SERPOLLET (F) 1887–1907
1887–1900 Léon Serpollet, Paris.
1900–1907 Gardner-Serpollet, Paris.

Léon Serpollet (1858–1907) was the leading exponent of the steam car in France, although nearly all the cars made were built with finance from the American Frank Gardner, and were often known as Gardner-Serpollets, While working in Paris as a carpenter and pattern maker he built a steam tricycle in 1887, following this with another 3-wheeler of much heavier construction. Using a boiler and engine made by La Buire in Lyons, this was assembled for him by Armand Peugeot at Montbeliard, and is sometimes thought of as the first Peugeot car. It was exhibited on the Peugeot stand at the 1889 Paris Exposition. Peugeot decided against going into production with steam cars, and Serpollet obtained financial support from the wealthy sportsman Ernest Archdeacon who was later to be an important figure in the development of aviation in France. With Archdeacon's help Serpollet commissioned three more tricycles of the Peugeot pattern from the Parisian coachbuilder Jeantaud, still using mechanical elements from La Buire. He soon realised that the tricycle was top heavy and unwieldy, and in 1894 built his first 4-wheeled steam car. This had a multi-tube flash boiler, as had his 3-wheelers, but it used paraffin fuel instead of coke, and had a dual pump which fed water to the boiler and fuel to the burners.

Although he made a few isolated cars in the 1890s, most of Serpollet's vehicles were commercials and were built for him by Decauville. Steam trams and buses were built for use in Paris, Berlin, Geneva and Vienna.

In 1899 Serpollet met Frank Gardner who had made a fortune in Australian gold mines and had invested in the Anglo-French Motor Carriage Co., Paris agents for Benz. When this failed he made a few petrol cars under his own name (see GARDNER (i)) but had sufficient faith in steam to agree to manufacture Serpollet's cars in his large premises in the rue Stendhal which he had bought from Anglo-French. Production began in June 1899 of an improved Serpollet car with Longuemare burners and horizontally-opposed 4-cylinder engines. Made in 5, 6, and 10hp sizes, they ranged from relatively light 2-seaters to heavy landaulets used by the wealthy for long-distance journeys. Among customers were the Shah of Persia and several Indian Maharajahs. Serpollet publicised his cars by entering competitions, including the Nice Speed Week where, in 1902, he achieved 75mph (120km/h) over the flying kilometre. This was a new Land Speed Record. The car, called Easter Egg, was not only fast but dramatically streamlined. He entered teams in the 1903 Paris–Madrid and 1904 Gordon Bennett races, though without great success.

1905 (Gardner) Serpollet steam tourer.
NATIONAL MOTOR MUSEUM

The workforce in the rue Stendhal rose from about 60 to 140 between 1900 and 1904, when production was running at about 100 cars per year. This was small beer compared with Locomobile's 2750 in 1902, but it was more than any other European steam car manufacturer. For 1903 the water tank was moved to the front, located under a bonnet which gave the Serpollet the appearance of a petrol car. In 1904 the engine and boiler were also located at the front. A 9hp utility model was introduced for 1905, but by then the European vogue for steam cars, never great at the best of times, was waning to such a extent that Frank Gardner withdrew his support for Serpollet. He soon found another wealthy backer in the person of Alexandre Darracq, but their joint venture made no cars, only commercial chassis, mostly for bus work. Léon Serpollet died of tuberculosis in February 1907, and car production ceased very soon afterwards. His importance as a pioneer was recognised in 1911 when a statue was erected to him in the Place St Ferdinand des Ternes in Paris.

There were two foreign ventures in the manufacture of Serpollet vehicles. The British Power Traction and Lighting Co. of Leeds made a few cars from 1900 to 1903 which they sold under the name P.T.L., and in Italy Serpollet Italiana SA made some cars and commercial vehicles in the former plant of Ricordi e Molinari in Milan from 1906 to 1908. They also offered a light 8hp single-cylinder petrol car under the Serpollet Italiana name.

NG

SERRIFILE (US) 1921–1922

Serrifile Motor Co., Hollis, New York.

Whether the Serrifile car actually appeared in prototype form is a matter of conjecture. The company's administrative headquarters was listed at Hollis, New York, and presumably any operations would have been located in the factory of the former Mercury (v) which had gone out of business in 1920. The Serrifile was announced as being a large car, available only as a sedan, weighing 4100lb (1863kg), a wheelbase of 138in (3502mm) and priced at $5000. Further details are missing.

KM

SERTUM (I) 1935

Officine Meccaniche Fausto Alberti SA, Milan.

Sertum motorcycles were made from 1931 to 1952, and were among Italy's best regarded machines in the 1930s. In 1935 they offered a single-seater coupé with chain drive to the single front wheel. It probably did not pass the prototype stage, though the company also made some 3-wheeled delivery vehicles with two driven rear wheels.

NG

SERVICE (US) 1911

Service Motor Car Co., Kankakee, Illinois.

This company was better-known for their trucks, which were built from 1911 to 1926, but in their first year they made a 2-seater runabout with friction transmission and double-chain drive.

NG

SERVITOR (US) 1907

Barnes Manufacturing Co., Sandusky, Ohio.

The Barnes company made cars under their own name from 1907 to at least 1910, and for the first year only they offered under the name Servitor a roadster with 4-cylinder air-cooled engine and patented 2-speed epicyclic transmission.

NG

SERV-WELL (JAM) 1992

Serv-Well of Jamaica Ltd, Kingston.

A patio furniture manufacturer planned to become the first major Jamaican car maker with its Party leisure vehicle. A smartly styled 4-seater prototype appeared as the company's principal sales hope, a leisure car aimed at the tourist rental trade, but other plans called for a 4-door saloon, a sport-utility and a pick-up. The prototype had a Ford engine but Fiat or Suzuki power was being considered for production versions.

CR

1920 Severin Touring Sportster.
NICK GEORGANO

1912 S.G.V. limousine brougham.
NATIONAL MOTOR MUSEUM

SETA (GB) 1976–1978

Malcolm Wilson, Hayling Island, Hampshire.
There was nothing very sophisticated about the SETA kit car. Its uncompromisingly slab-sided fibreglass bodyshell sat on an unmodified VW Beetle floorpan. At £1000, the kit included wheels, carpets, a roll cage, wiring and a stereo as standard. The gullwing doors lifted on hydraulic struts. Seven cars were made and a planned revival under the name ZETA failed.

CR

SETHERA (S) 1980s–1990s

S.H. Design, Landskrona.
This was a kit car made in Sweden by Svenharry Akesson (previously involved in competition cars), with styling vaguely inspired by the Ford GT40. It was available in two basic versions: one for a VW Beetle floorpan, and a longer wheelbase version with its own spaceframe chassis and mid-mounted engine. In the latter case the front suspension uprights were Ford Cortina or Granada and the rear uprights were designed to accept Mercedes hubs and brakes. The design was also known as the Silver Hawk. A later version looked more like a Lamborghini Countach, sharing its scissor-opening door design.

CR

SEVEN LITTLE BUFFALOES (US) 1909

De Schaum Motor Syndicate Co., Buffalo, New York.
This colourfully-named car was the same vehicle that had been marketed in 1908 as the DE SCHAUM. It was made in two high-wheeler versions and two conventional models. The high-wheelers had 2-cylinder air-cooled engines and friction transmission, and were offered as a $500 runabout on a 72in (1827mm) wheelbase and a $600 stanhope on a 76in (1929mm) wheelbase. The conventional cars had 4-cylinder water-cooled engines and also used friction transmission. The range was made up of a tourer, town car and landaulet, all on an 87in (2208mm) wheelbase. Production of all models was just 54 units.

KM

SEVERIN (US) 1920–1922

Severin Motor Car Co., Kansas City, Missouri.
The Severin was a typical assembled car of brief duration and without any originality in design or choice of components. A touring car appears to have been the only model the company offered, these powered by a Continental 9N 6-cylinder engine. Production was probably somewhere between 200 and 250 cars completed in Severin's three years of production.

KM

SEVERN (GB) 1990–1991

A clever play-on-words cleared the makers of this plans-built sports car from legal action by Caterham Cars, the owners of the 'Seven' trademark, for this was a typical Lotus 7 style sports car.

CR

SEYMOUR-TURNER see TURNER (ii)

S.F.A.T. (F) 1903–1904

Sté Française des Autos Thermo-Pneumatiques, Paris.
This company built a car which combined a conventional 4-cylinder engine with a compressed air drive, in which the engine drove a compressor which forced air into a turbine which drove the rear wheels. It was one of many attempts to eliminate the conventional gearbox, but probably the power loss was so great that it was not a practical proposition. One was shown at the 1903 Paris Salon.

NG

S.G.V. (US) 1911–1915

1910–1911 The Acme Motor Car Co. S.G.V., Reading, Pennsylvania.
1911–1915 The S.G.V. Co., Reading, Pennsylvania.
The S.G.V. marque resulted from a reorganisation of the ACME (i) Motor Car Co., which had been in business in Reading since 1903. The name came from three Acme personnel, Herbert M. Sternberg, Robert E. Graham and Fred Van Tine. The first two were executives, while Van Tine was the shop manager and designer of the new car. This was a high-quality product, based on the Lancia, having a relatively small 25hp 4-cylinder engine with pressure lubrication and a hot water jacket over the inlet manifold to prevent icing of the carburettor. The low frame was upswept over the rear axle. A variety of bodies was offered, tourer, runabout, landaulet and limousine, and prices rose from $2500–3500 for the 1911 models up to $4250 for the more expensive styles of 1914. Custom coachwork by such firms as Quinby and Fleetwood could push prices as high as $12,000. The S.G.V. was thus a high-quality small car, in the same class as the Brewster, and sold to many prominent families such as the Astors and Vanderbilts. Suggestions (from a company brochure) that the cars were also bought by the King of England and Kaiser of Germany are unlikely to be true in view of the policy of those monarchs of always buying their own countries' products.

Though the company was not founded until August 1911, the design was first made in 1910, when the cars carried badges displaying both Acme and S.G.V. names. The design was little changed over the make's five-year life, although a larger engine rated at 35 or 36hp was listed from 1912. In 1914 they featured the Vulcan electric gearchange operated by push buttons in the centre of the steering wheel, but this did not work well, and many cars had to be recalled. The company failed in the summer of 1915, and the entire stock, including 32 chassis and 100 Quinby and Fleetwood bodies, was sold off to R.J. Metzler. He said he would continued the S.G.V., but instead, with a group of associates, he launched the PHIANNA in 1916.

NG

Further Reading
'S.G.V., Reading's Refined Roadster', Stuart W. Wells,
Automobile Quarterly, Vol. 35, No. 4.

S.H. see SETHERA

SHADO (GB) 1990–1992

The prototype of the Shado Sorrento was an enormous Jaguar V12 powered mid-engined coupé, but it was subsequently redesigned for Honda CBR motorbike power and its dimensions were toned down. Production cars were to have Ford Sierra engines, but further cars were not built.

CR

SHAD-WYCK (US) 1917–1918

Shadburne Brothers, Frankfurt, Indiana.

The Shad-Wyck was something of a curiosity of its time and though advertised, was never a reality. The Shadburne Brothers purchased the Bour-Davis Motor Car Co. of Detroit, Michigan and moved the operations to a recently acquired factory in Frankfurt, Indiana where Bour-Davis production continued. Simultaneously, the Shadburnes decided to build their own car which would be called the Shad-Wyck. Advertisements for the Shad-Wyck in various automotive journals were illustrated with pictures purportedly showing the Shad-Wyck design but which, to observant readers of those journals, were actually Roamers. The Shad-Wyck failed to even reach the prototype stage and all cars completed at the Frankfurt factory were Bour-Davis touring cars. Operations ceased in the winter of 1918. Bour-Davis interests, still in Detroit, were sold to a Louisiana group who founded the Louisiana Motor Car Co., moved operations to Shreveport, Louisiana, and continued Bour-Davis production into 1923. The Shadburnes moved to Chicago, Illinois where they formed a financial establishment and planned to revive the idea of the Shad-Wyck car, this time to be fitted with a 4-cylinder Rochester-Duesenberg engine and sold in the $4000 price range. The second coming of the Shad-Wyck never progressed beyond a listing of specifications in the contemporary automotive journals.

KM

SHAKA (ZA/USA) 1997 to date

Advanced Automotive Design, Pretoria; Glover Designs Inc., Oakland Park, Florida.

Conceived by two South Africans, Brian Glover and Rhys Edwards, the Shaka Nynya was a lightweight roadster in the Lotus Seven idiom but with modernised bodywork. The fibreglass body was bonded on to its tubular steel spaceframe chassis and then painted in South Africa before being shipped to the USA for completion (or for sale in kit form). The engine was a 5.7-litre Chevrolet LT1 V8 unit, although other powerplants such as the Oldsmobile Quad 4 and Buick V6 could be fitted. Tubular front wishbones and a live rear axle were employed, along with Chevrolet disc brakes.

CR

SHALAKO (US) c.1971

House of Shalako, La Habra, California.

The Shala was a race car-inspired gull-wing body that was mounted on a shortened 80in (2030mm) Volkswagen Beetle chassis. It had a low shovel nose with headlights mounted on top. A longer tail section was available to house a Corvair engine. The Shala-Vet was another kit that fitted the same shortened VW chassis. It resembled a caricature of a 1968 Stingray. It was sold in coupé and roadster form and doors were optional. Engine choices included VW, Corvair and the Ford V-4 Taunus. A longer version of the Shala-Vet to fit a 94.5in (2398mm) wheelbase was optional.

HP

SHAMROCK (i) (IRE) 1959

Shamrock Motors Ltd, Tralee, Kerry.

Although it was made in Ireland, the conception and intended market for the Shamrock was decidedly American, courtesy of William K. Curtis. Using the 1.5-litre engine, transmission and suspension of the Austin A55, Curtis constructed a sports-style 4-seater fibreglass body with a removable hard-top on a wheelbase of 98in (2487mm). Production of 3000 was planned for the first year, rising to 10,000 during the following two years, but only four cars were made. According to *Automobile Engineer* the maker's address was at Broad Street Green, Guildford, Surrey, 'while the Tralee factory is being equipped for production'. It is possible that no cars were made at Tralee.

CR

SHAMROCK (ii) (ZA) 1990s

Shamrock Automotive, Cape Town.

One of South Africa's first A.C. Cobra replicas was produced by Shamrock. It followed established Cobra replica practice and had an epoxy coated chassis and fibreglass bodywork. Another model was a Moke-style leisure vehicle using Volkswagen Golf mechanicals, while in 1998 a Dodge Viper replica was marketed.

CR

1959 Shamrock (i) hard-top convertible.
NATIONAL MOTOR MUSEUM

c.1972 Shanghai (i) SH 760 saloon.
ERIK VAN INGEN SCHENAU

c.1985 Shanghai (i) SH 7221 saloon.
ERIK VAN INGEN SCHENAU

SHANGHAI (i) (CHI) 1958–1993

1958–1991 Shanghai Auto Works, Shanghai Municipality.
1991–1993 Shanghai Shenlian Special Auto Works, Shanghai Municipality.

The Shanghai Auto Works produced, together with the First Auto Works, the first range of Chinese motor cars. In 1958 the Shanghai factory introduced the FENGHUANG motor car, accompanied by the 2 ton truck (the SH 130), by a Jeep (the type CJ 3A) and by a 1½ ton 3-wheel truck. In 1964 the Fenghuang was renamed the Shanghai SH 760. For ten years the SH 760 was China's most numerous motor car. The vehicle was based upon the Mercedes-Benz 220S saloon of 1957. It was driven by a 2232cc 6-cylinder engine, delivering 90hp at 4800rpm. The front and rear end were of contemporary American design. This saloon was used by all kinds of governmental organisations. In 1974 the front and rear end were updated, again influenced by American styling. The

c.1980 Shanghai (ii) SKL 720 saloon.
OLIVER BARNHAM

new car was called Shanghai SH 760 A. The A-type was built for 15 years, until 1989. Production numbers were always low, mostly around 2000–4000 units per year. Top production year was 1984 with 6010 units made. The car was modernised for a third time, but it was too old fashioned by then to have a chance, and the production of the last versions, the SH 7221 and SH 7231 (even the engine was somewhat updated at the end) ceased in 1991.

During all these production years the factory designed a lot of prototypes and pre-serial production vehicles, most of them meant as replacement for this saloon. In 1960 the SH 770 was made, which was in fact a 100 per cent copy of the Hongqi CA 770 limousine. In 1966 a small series of state convertibles were made, called the SH 761. They used the same engine as the standard saloon, but as the convertible was much bigger and heavier, the vehicle was terribly underpowered. A year later several prototypes of an ugly squared-off saloon were introduced. In 1975 the works showed a wooden mock-up of a Mercedes-Benz 230 copy, which was seen as prototype in 1978, then called the Shanghai SH 762. In the same year another Mercedes-Benz copy appeared, this time based upon the bigger 280S type. This Shanghai SH 771 was made in a small batch. In 1978 a new test vehicle, the SH 750, with a strong resemblance to the Ford Zephyr, was shown.

To open new markets, the Shanghai Auto Works asked Locomotors of the United Kingdom to design two pick-ups, a 3-seat single row version (the SH 760 C) and a 5-seat double row version (the SH 760 D). Shanghai Auto Works started to produce the double row version as the SH 1020 SP. But the Shanghai Volkswagen Santana production, which had started in a new joint venture in 1984 on the Shanghai Auto Works site, was very successful, and consumed the whole production capacity of the Shanghai Auto Works. Production of the SH 7221 and SH 1020 SP was then moved to a small local factory called the Shenlian Special Auto Works, where production ceased in 1993.

EVIS

SHANGHAI (ii) (CHI) 1979–1981
Shanghai Bus Works, Shanghai Municipality.
Shanghai Bus produced a small batch of mini cars, the Shanghai SK 720 in 1979. They used the Changjiang 750cc side-valve motorcycle engine.

EVIS

SHANGHAI (iii) (CHI) 1990
Shanghai Auto Research Institute, Shanghai Municipality.
Several years before Volkswagen of Germany produced their own spacewagon, the Shanghai Institute designed a model based upon a Shanghai-Volkswagen Santana platform. It was the Shanghai SH 7181 (originally named SVW 7181, until VW protested). The prototype was built by the Kunshan Xindong Auto Refit Works.

EVIS

SHANGHAI (iv) (CHI) 1991–1993
Shanghai Anting Bus Works, Shanghai Municipality.
Shanghai Dayuan Auto Refit Works, Shanghai Municipality.
Shanghai No. 3 Auto Chassis Works, Shanghai Municipality.
Kunshan Xindong Auto Refit Works, Kunshan City, Jiangsu Province.
These four factories produced station wagons based on the last version of the Shanghai saloon. They looked alike, but they had different designations and some were named differently. The Anting models were named SA 5020, the Dayuan models SQL 5020/4 (Jinfeng), the No. 3 Works models SQL 5024/9, the Kunshan models SQL 5027 (Haifeng).

EVIS

SHANGHAI-VOLKSWAGEN (CHI) 1984 to date
Shanghai-Volkswagen Auto Corp., Shanghai Municipality.
The joint venture between the Shanghai Auto Industry Corp. (35 per cent), Bank of China (15 per cent) and Volkswagen (50 per cent) was established in 1984. Since the beginning of the 1970s there were rumours that Volkswagen would start a Chinese factory. In 1983 the Shanghai Auto Works trial-assembled the Volkswagen Passat B2 3-volume saloon as the Shanghai-Volkswagen Santana. It was then decided that this should be the car to be produced by the joint venture. This car soon proved to be very successful in China, and production rose to 250,000 units per year by the end of 1999. From 1986 to 1988 a 1.8-litre Audi 100CC was assembled by this joint venture too, but production was soon moved to the First Auto Works in Changchun. The Santana Variant, the estate version, was introduced in 1986, but proper production only started years later, in 1991. Together with Volkswagen do Brasil, SVW developed a new Santana which came off the line in 1994. The Chinese version had a slightly longer wheelbase than the Brazilian version, to give extra leg room. This was the Santana 2000, produced with a 1781cc fuel-injection engine. The Shanghai Auto Works had to stop their production to make space for the Santana 2000 production. In 1999 the Volkswagen Passat B5 was introduced as the Shanghai Passat, with a 3.5in (90mm) longer wheelbase than the German version.

EVIS

SHAPECRAFT (GB) 1986–1989
C.V. Shapecraft, Northampton.
Clive Smart (who also made the BIRCHFIELD Sports) was responsible for the first Lotus 23 sports racer replica made in Britain. Called the Shapecraft SR, it followed the Lotus design fairly closely, having a space frame chassis, although the specially designed suspension used Ford uprights and the bodywork was in fibreglass. When Shapecraft stopped making kits in 1987, Lee Noble took the SR project over and the car became known as the NOBLE 23 (and later the AURIGA).

CR

SHARON see DRIGGS-SEABURY

SHARP (US) 1914
Sharp Engineering & Manufacturing Co., Detroit, Michigan.
Although announced as the S.E.M.(i), this light car had been renamed Sharp before it went on the market. It was powered by a 7hp air-cooled V-twin engine, with 2-speed gearbox and shaft drive. Only one body style was offered, a staggered 2-seater roadster, and the price was a very low $295. It was probably too low, for the makers were out of business before the year was out.

NG

SHARP ARROW (US) 1908–1910
Sharp Arrow Automobile Co., Trenton, New Jersey.
William H. Sharp was a photographer who dabbled in cars from at least 1905. In 1908 he built a powerful racing car with which he won his class in the Long Island Sweepstakes, and in December that year he formed the Sharp Arrow Automobile Co. He found a factory in part of the Walter Automobile Co. at Trenton, where the Mercer would be built later. The 40hp Sharp Arrow was built in four body styles, tourer, toy tonneau, runabout and speedabout, the latter being a stripped version of the runabout, and selling for $50 less. According to different sources, the 4-cylinder engine was either of Beaver or Continental manufacture. Sharp's slogan was 'Speed King of American Stock Cars', and

about 25 cars were made during 1909. There were plans for production to be moved to Stroudsberg, Pennsylvania, in 1910, but these never came about, and in November Sharp was killed in practice for the Savannah Grand Prize.

NG

SHARP IMAGE (US) c.1990
Sharp Image Motor Cars, Port St Lucie, Florida.
The Lamborghini Countach body was severely altered to get it to fit on a Volkswagen Beetle chassis by this kit car company. VW running gear could be used, or Sharp Image would install a Mazda rotary engine and 4-wheel disc brakes. They were sold in kit or turn-key form.

HP

SHATSWELL (US) 1901–1903
H.K. Shatswell & Co., Dedham, Massachusetts.
This company was mainly involved in supplying components for steam cars, including a complete kit for the home assembler. However, in 1901 they built a steamer powered by a 4-cylinder single-acting engine, and offered replicas at $750 each. Unlike many New England steamers it had wooden rather than wire wheels, which gave it a rather heavy appearance. It is not certain if more than one was made, and the larger cars at $1200–1500 almost certainly got no further than Shatswell's catalogue.

NG

SHAW (i) (US) 1920–1921
The Walden W. Shaw Livery Co., Chicago, Illinois.
The Shaw, a luxury range of automobiles augmenting the Shaw taxicab, made its debut at Hotel Congress, Chicago, during Chicago Automobile Show Week in February 1920. The car was equipped with a Rochester-Duesenberg G-1 engine, developing 81bhp at 2600rpm, had a wheelbase of 136in (3452mm) and disc wheels. The three available choices of coachwork included a 4-seater close-coupled phaeton, a 7-seater touring car and a roadster, all equally priced at $5000. Despite favourable, even glowing coverage in the automotive press, sales were few. In an attempt to change its image, the cars were re-equipped with a 12-cylinder Weidely ohv engine and rebadged, using the name 'Colonial' which, also proving unsuccessful in attracting buyers, reverted to Shaw. Sales were minimal, if any at all, and the company was taken over by John Hertz, a veteran taxicab operator, who would change his acquisition from the Walden W. Shaw company to that of Yellow Cab. The remaining cars would carry the Ambassador badge.

KM

SHAW (ii) (US) 1920–1930
Shaw Manufacturing Co., Galesburg, Kansas.
Stanley Shaw began in business in 1903 by making motorised units for bicycles, and made a few complete motorcycles in the years up to 1914. In the 1920s he offered a very small car, more suitable for children than adults, though he insisted that his speedster was 'not a toy but a real automobile'. It was powered by a 2½hp single-cylinder engine made by Shaw or Briggs & Stratton with no gearbox and final drive by chain or belt. Shaft drive was available from 1926. Production ended in 1930 but Shaw continued to offer it in kit form for a few years. He also made the Shaw Du-All mower which he built until 1962 when he sold his company to the makers of the Brush Hog rotary mower. This was still made in the 1990s.

NG

SHAWMUT (US) 1906–1908
Shawmut Motor Co., Stoneham, Massachusetts.
This company occupied the factory where the PHELPS had previously been made, and the 40hp 4-cylinder Shawmut was the same design as had been made to special order by Phelps (regular Phelps had 3-cylinder engines). It was an expensive car, costing $4750 for a roadster and $6500 for a landaulet. Sales must have been fairly restricted at these prices, but the final blow was a disastrous fire in November 1908 in which 10 finished cars and several half completed ones were destroyed.

NG

1909 Sharp Arrow S 2-seater runabout.
NICK GEORGANO

1921 Shaw (i) V12 tourer.
JOHN A. CONDE

SHAY (US) 1979–1980
The Model A & Model T Motor Car Reproduction Corp., Detroit, Michigan.
This company built fully-assembled replicas of famous Ford products which they marketed through Ford and Lincoln dealers. Their most popular replica was the Shay Model A Roadster, which was designed by Harry Shay and based on Ford Pinto running gear. It was very accurate in appearance even if the body was fibreglass. The Shay '55 Thunderbird replica was not as popular. It had a fibreglass body, a removable hard-top and an optional Ford V8 engine. When Shay closed they sold their inventory to SHELL VALLEY.

HP

SHEEN (GB) 1964–1965
Peter Sheen, Kingston, Surrey.
Wine merchant Peter Sheen created the Sheen Imperator GTS, an interesting Abarth-style coupé. The sleek bodywork was mated to a Hillman Imp floorpan and two rear-mounted engine choices were intended to be offered: a 70bhp Nathan-tuned version and a 105bhp 1147cc Emery version with a 5-speed gearbox. Production cars were to have had fibreglass bodywork but Rootes was unwilling to supply Imp parts, so only two aluminium prototypes were ever made.

CR

SHEEPBRIDGE (GB) c.1948–c.1953
Sheepbridge Engineers, Chesterfield, Derbyshire.
Various microcar prototypes were built by this engineering company at a time when the species was proliferating in continental Europe. All had tubular chassis and fibreglass bodies, some had three wheels and others four. However, no production run ensued.

CR

1919 Sheffield-Simplex 30hp coupé.
NICK BALDWIN

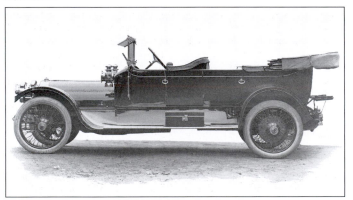

1911 Sheffield-Simplex 25hp tourer.
NICK BALDWIN

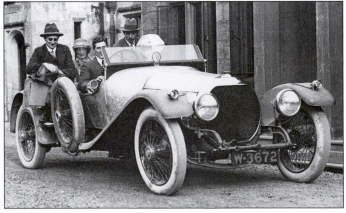

1914 Sheffield-Simplex 30hp tourer.
NATIONAL MOTOR MUSEUM

SHEFFIELD-SIMPLEX (GB) 1907–1920

Sheffield-Simplex Motor Works Ltd, Tinsley, Sheffield, Yorkshire.

The Sheffield-Simplex replaced the BROTHERHOOD-CROCKER which had originally been made in London, and from 1906 in a new factory built by the immensely wealthy coal magnate, Earl Fitzwilliam. Before the factory was completed the Brotherhoods pulled out, but a few 20hp Brotherhood cars were made under the Earl's ownership. In November 1907 the 1908 catalogue was introduced under the new name, Sheffield-Simplex Motor Works Ltd and describing the completely new 45hp model. Like the Brotherhood, it was designed by Percy Richardson, and had a 6978cc 6-cylinder engine with square dimensions (114 × 114mm) and, on the LA1 model, a 3-speed gearbox mounted immediately behind the engine. In the middle of 1908 this was supplemented by the LA2, the so-called 'gearless' car which in fact had two forward speeds and a reverse mounted in the rear axle. There were three crown wheels and two pinions, any one of which could be selected by the driver. In fact there was a separate crown wheel and pinion for each forward speed, and one crown wheel for reverse. The LA2 was intended for use with lighter bodies, and the conventional LA1 was retained for the heavier closed coachwork. The complicated transmission soon gave way to a conventional 2-speed sliding pinion gearbox, though this was still mounted by the rear axle. With a light body most hills could be tackled in top gear.

For 1910 the big sixes were joined by two new models built on Renault lines, complete with the characteristic dashboard radiator. They were the 2882cc 4-cylinder LA3 short wheelbase and LA4 long wheelbase, and the 4324cc 6-cylinder LA5 and LA6, again differentiated by their wheelbases. After only one season they were dropped in favour of a new six, the 4740cc 25hp Model LA7. This ran parallel with the LA1 and 2 for two years, when Sheffield-Simplex boasted that there was only one other factory in England that made six cylinder cars only. They meant Rolls-Royce, a make which Sheffield-Simplex thought was a worthy rival. In 1913 they opened London showrooms at 20 Conduit Street, only five doors away from Rolls-Royce. In 1913 came the 30hp Model LA7b, which shared the cylinder dimensions with the 25hp, but had a number of improvements to the engine. The old LA1 and LA2 were still in the catalogue, now sharing the wheelbase of the LA7. In October 1913 Percy Richardson announced electric starting on the LA7b, only months after Cadillac had introduced it in America.

1966 Shelby (ii) Cobra 427 sports car.
NATIONAL MOTOR MUSEUM

The LA1 and LA2 were dropped for 1914, leaving the 30hp LA7b as the only model in the last year of peace.

During the war Sheffield-Simplex built two types of armoured car on the 30hp chassis, with a single turret for the Belgian Army, and with twin turrets for the Russian. The 30hp was revived after the war and was exhibited at the 1919 Olympia Show. How many were made is not certain, but at the 1920 Show there appeared a new 50hp model, a dinosaur with six separately cast cylinders and the largest engine capacity of any Sheffield-Simplex, at 7778cc. It may not have been built at Sheffield, for a plate on the scuttle read 'Sheffield Simplex Kingston on Thames'; they had a factory at Kingston where the Neracar motorcycle was made. Although it appeared again at the 1921 Show it was not registered for the road until 1925. Fitted with a 2-seater body, it was the only one of its kind made. It is curious that it should have survived today, when of the c.1500 other models of Sheffield-Simplex, not more than two (one 45hp and one 30hp) still exist.

NG

Further Reading
Cars from Sheffield, Stephen Myers, Sheffield City Libraries, 1986.

SHELBY (i) (US) 1903
Shelby Motor Car Co., Shelby, Ohio.
Introduced at the New York Automobile Show in January 1903, the Shelby was made in two models, a 10hp single-cylinder runabout and a 20hp 2-cylinder rear-entrance tonneau. The engines were of the double-piston layout as on the Gobron-Brillié, but otherwise the cars were conventional, with De Dion-type bonnets and low-mounted radiators ahead of them.

NG

SHELBY (ii) (US) 1962–1970; 1998 to date
1962 Shelby-American Inc, Santa Fe Springs, California.
1962–1967 Shelby-American Inc, Venice, California.
1967–1968 Shelby-Automotive, Ionia, Michigan.
1968–1970 Ford Motor Co., Detroit, Michigan.
1986–1998 Shelby Automobiles Inc, Whittier, California.
1998 to date Shelby-American Inc, Las Vegas, Nevada.

Carroll Shelby was born in Leesburg, Texas, in 1923 and had a varied and successful career as a racing driver before he became a car manufacturer. From the late 1950s he explored the idea of a low-cost American sports car using a General Motors engine, but GM were not interested, doubtless seeing it as a competitor to the Corvette. He investigated cooperation with several European firms including Aston Martin, De Tomaso, Jensen and Maserati, but without success; then in September 1961 he heard that AC were no longer able to obtain the Bristol engine they had used in their Ace. He had admired the Ace in club racing so he suggested the new lightweight small-block 3621cc Ford V8 as a replacement. It was insufficiently powerful so Ford bored it out to 4260cc; and the first 75 Shelby Cobras used this unit before the engine grew again to 4736cc, the famous 289 engine (289 cubic inches) which powered 598 Cobras. Although Shelby admired the John Tojeiro-designed chassis (he described Tojeiro as 'a fabulous designer and very influential'), he found it inadequate for the power of the 289 engine, and had it completely redesigned. This work was shared between AC's Alan Turner and Shelby's Phil Remington. Shelby recalled 'It took a year and a half of testing and $1,500,000. AC didn't pay for any of that. I paid for it. It was a horrible chassis to put power through – the chassis tubes were too thin, the springs were too short'.

Shelby chose the name Cobra, said to have come to him in a dream, and resented the use of the name AC Cobra, though that is how they were marketed in the UK. They were homologated for US racing as Shelby-American. The first 30 were made at Shelby's original works at Santa Fe Springs, and in June 1962 he moved to larger premises at Venice, formerly used by Lance Reventlow for his Scarab racing cars. A further 45 Cobras were built with the 260 engine, after which the 289 took over. From 1965 the 6997cc 427 engine was also available in the Cobra, giving a top speed of 165mph (265km/h), or more when the engine was tuned to give up to 500bhp. Shelby himself admitted that the 427 was a bit of a handful. 'The 427 will kill you in a second' he said, 'On a Sunday afternoon I'd rather drive the 289, but if I'm on the freeway looking for some Porsches to blow away, I'll take the 427'. In 1965 the transverse leaf suspension was replaced by coil springs with double wishbones.

Ford were very helpful to Shelby, supplying engines on delayed credit and allowing him to use their dealer network, but after 1965 their attention was directed to the GT40 programme, and they withdrew their support for Shelby's

1969 Shelby (ii) Mustang GT350 coupé.
NATIONAL MOTOR MUSEUM

racing activities. The Daytona coupé version of the Cobra beat Ferrari in the international GT championship in 1967, a long-held ambition of Carroll Shelby. Production of the 427 ended in 1967, but AC made a few 289s in England up to 1969. Total Cobra production was 1183, of which 75 had the 260 engine, 598 the 289 and 510 the 427. The Cobra name became the property of Ford, and among the many replicas being made today, only one is officially allowed to use the name. This is the Autokraft made by Brian Angliss at Brooklands Track in Surrey, whose chassis use the same jigs as the original Cobra.

The Mustang GT-350

The arrival of the Ford Mustang in April 1964 gave Carroll Shelby a new car to work on. With the 289 engine the Mustang performed well, but lacked the handling to endear it to sports car enthusiasts. Shelby ordered 289 engines from Ford's San Jose, California, factory with certain modifications such as stiffer, stronger con rods and crankshafts, and his own design of camshaft. Further development took place at his own factory, including the fitting of a 4-barrel Holley carburettor, and improved exhaust manifolding. The soft suspension was beefed up with stiffer anti-roll bars, new steering arms and modified rear suspension. The rear seat was replaced by a shelf, and the steel bonnet was replaced by one in fibreglass. Externally the Shelby Mustangs could be distinguished by a blue stripe running from the front to the rear, along bonnet and roof. The price was $4567 compared with $2589 for the standard Mustang 289 fastback coupé. In standard form the Shelby GT-350 gave 306bhp, but competition versions, of which about 25 were made, gave 350bhp. These were SCCA Class B champions in 1966 and 1967. In 1966 Shelby sold 936 cars to the Hertz rental organisation. Known as the 350H, they had triangular rear quarter lights, whereas the regular Mustangs were strictly 2-light cars. Another special model made in 1966 only was the GT-350 convertible. Only six were made and all went as gifts to Shelby's friends or employees.

For 1967 the GT-350 was joined by the GT-500 which used the 7014cc 428 engine (not to be confused with the more powerful 427 used in the Cobra, though this was available as an option), and styling changes followed those of the Ford Mustang. A convertible joined the coupé in both sizes for 1968, and in the middle of the season the GT-500 was replaced by the GT-500KR. This stood for King of the Road, and had a more powerful version of the 428 engine. The GT-350 received a new 302 cubic inch (4949cc) engine. A 4-speed manual gearbox was standard in all these models, with automatic as an option. However, the GT-350H came with automatic only; Hertz presumably thought that hire car customers could not cope with manual gearboxes.

The lease on Shelby's Venice factory ran out at the end of 1967, and the 1968 engines were made in a Ford factory at Ionia, Michigan. Front end design was changed for 1969, in a style which was copied by Ford for their 1970/71 Mach 1 Mustang. This was the last year of Shelby Mustang production, although a number of cars were assembled from parts on hand and sold as 1970 models. The total number made was 14,769, of which 7483 had the 289 engine and 7286 the 427 or 428. This was considerably more than the Cobra, but a small figure when set against the 2,800,827 Mustangs built by Ford over the same period.

Shelby had received a lot of encouragement from Lee Iacocca when he was with Ford, and after he moved to Chrysler Shelby was contracted to create performance cars based on Dodge components. These were the Shelby Chargers made from mid–1983 to 1987 with improved performance and beefed up suspension. In February 1986 Shelby Automobiles Inc was formed at Whittier, California to make high-performance versions of other Dodge models such as the Omni and Lancer sedans and Shadow coupé. Shelby was also involved in the development of the Dodge Viper sports car.

In 1998 he made a dramatic return to car production under his own name with the Series 1. This was an open 2-seater sports car in the Cobra idiom, powered by a modified version of the 3995cc Northstar engine used in the Oldsmobile Aurora tuned to give 350bhp, and with a carbonfibre body weighing less than 100lbs. Transmission was a 6-speed ZF transaxle. The Series 1 was built alongside a replica Cobra with fibreglass body at a new factory by the Las Vegas Speedway.

NG

Further Reading
'The 427 Cobra S/C: Ford's Ultimate Better Idea', David Kimble, *Automobile Quarterly*, Vol. 22, No. 3.
'Striped Lightning – the Shelby Mustangs', Joe Oldham, *Automobile Quarterly*, Vol. 16, No. 3.

SHELDONHURST *see* SANDWOOD

SHELL VALLEY (US) c.1971 to date
Shell Valley Companies, Platte Center, Nebraska.
This fibreglass manufacturing company built a number of kit cars. Their 427 Cobra replicas were unusual in that Shell Valley made most of the parts used on them, including the shock absorbers and all fabricated metal parts like the chassis and suspension. Ford or Chevrolet V8s were optional. Shell Valley also made fibreglass replica bodies for Jeep, Lamborghini Countach and Ford Model A hot rod kits. They could be purchased in kit or turn-key form.
HP

SHELSLEY (GB) 1983–1984
1983 A.G. Thorpe Developments, Darley Abbey, Derby.
1983–1984 A.G. Thorpe Developments, Burton-on-Trent, Staffordshire.
Produced by a company already well-known for its fibreglass MG Midget panel kits, the Shelsley Spyder was a traditional-style kit-built sports car with boat-tailed fibreglass bodywork reminiscent of Alfa Romeo. The spaceframe chassis was race-developed and featured wishbone suspension and Triumph Vitesse rear uprights and differential. It was intended for Lotus Twin Cam power, although Ford engines were also possible and a version using a Triumph Vitesse chassis was also listed.
CR

SHELTER (NL) 1954–1958
Van de Groot, Terborg.
Since the demise of the Spyker, the Netherlands had effectively had no car industry until the Shelter. The first prototype was built by an aircraft engineer called van de Groot in 1947, consisting of two bicycle frames welded together, but a more serious attempt was made in 1954. Another 3-wheeler, it was an enclosed 2-seater with aluminium bodywork. The engine was an Ilo 200cc unit, although a specially-conceived 228cc single-cylinder engine was the intended eventual power source, along with a new 3-speed automatic-clutch gearbox. After government support for the project was diverted elsewhere, the project faltered with only four prototypes constructed.
CR

SHENJIAN (CHI) 1987 to date
State Operated Jiangbei Machinery Works, Jilin City, Jilin Province.
In 1987 the Jiangbei works started with the production of a plastic copy of the Japanese SUBARU Rex. This minicar, named Shenjian ('Magical Arrow') JJ 720 (later renamed JJ 7050/JJ 7060), was produced in small quantities of 50–150 units per year. The selling price was only Y40,000 ($5000). In 1992 this factory was one of the Chinese factories that started the 796cc Suzuki Alto licence production. It was sold as the Shenjian JJ 7080, but also as the Beifan Alto, as the works belongs to the Beifan Corp. (China North Industries), one of China's main ordnance industries.
EVIS

SHEPHARD (F) 1900

E.F. Shephard, Levallois-Perret, Seine.

The Shephard voiturette was powered by a 5hp 2-cylinder Doré engine mounted transversely under a bonnet perforated to give optimum cooling. It had shaft-drive to the gearbox, with chain final drive, and a 2-seater body.

NG

SHEPHERD (i) (GB) 1899–1900

W. Shepherd & Son, Exeter, Devonshire.

One of the few cars made in Devon, the Shepherd had a vertical 2-cylinder engine mounted transversely at the front of the frame. It was governed by cutting out one exhaust valve. The 2-speed drive was by belts and pulleys. Very few were made, but one survives, as does the company which made it.

NG

SHEPHERD (ii) (GB) 1985–1986

Jim Graham, Colne, Lancashire.

The Shepherd utility estate had frankly gawky flat-panel styling. It was based on Ford Cortina parts and its body was fabricated from plywood by a boatbuilder. Two and 4-seater versions could be built.

CR

SHEPMOBILE (US) 1903–1905

Shepmobile Auto-Engine Co., Los Angeles, California.

This company made a few single-cylinder runabouts with detachable tonneaus between December 1903 and April 1904, when they announced that they would concentrate on delivery wagons as they had received a contract for 50 of these. However, a new owner built a few more Shepmobile cars in 1905.

NG

SHEPPEE (GB) 1912

Sheppee Motor Co. & Engineering Co. Ltd, York.

Retired Indian Army officer Colonel F.H. Sheppee was an idealist builder of steam vehicles using high-pressure steam. He had a stake in the British Power Traction & Lighting Co., makers of the P.T.L. car which was based on the Serpollet, and when he left that firm in 1904 he took a number of workmen with him and set up his own company, mainly with the intention of making steam commercial vehicles. He built (or perhaps re-built) 14 vehicles over the next nine years, of which all but one or two were trucks or charabancs. None was identical, as he was conducting a quest for the ideal steam wagon, rather than seeking commercial success. In 1912 he made at least two passenger cars, a tourer and a limousine, both using the same flash boiler, double high-pressure single-acting engine and frontal condenser as the commercial chassis.

NG

SHERET see CARDEN

SHERIDAN (US) 1920–1921

Sheridan Motor Car Co., Muncie, Indiana.

The Sheridan was a short-lived car built under the umbrella of the General Motors Corp., ostensibly to fill the gap between GM's Chevrolet and Oakland cars. The Sheridan used a Northway 4-cylinder engine and was offered in both open and closed models. Plans were underway to introduce an 8-cylinder luxury line of cars in the $3250 to $4000 price range to complement the existing four which cost $1750 to $2500. Upon his appointment as president of General Motors to succeed W.C. Durant, Alfred P. Sloan Jr, 'cleaned house' with the existing range of GM cars in which both the Scripps-Booth and the Sheridan were discontinued, the Sheridan factory being sold to Durant who used it for the manufacture of his Durant Six cars and the stillborn Princeton.

KM

SHERPLEY (GB) 1997 to date

Sherpley Motor Co., Littleborough, Lancashire.

The imposing Sherpley Speed Six evoked the charms of a prewar Blower Bentley but was bizarrely based on Leyland Sherpa van running gear. The substantial ladder chassis accepted semi-elliptic springs, a beam front and solid rear axle and a Ford 2.3- or 2.8-litre V6 engine. The open tourer bodywork was in fibreglass that could be painted or covered in fabric.

CR

1912 Sheppee 35hp tourer.
NICK BALDWIN

1921 Sheridan Model B41 35hp tourer.
NICK BALDWIN

SHERWOOD (GB) 1984–1992

Sherwood Universal Vehicles, Pinxton, Nottinghamshire.

The makers of the SPARTAN branched out in a totally new direction with the Sherwood, forming a separate company to make and market it. The estate/pick-up design employed the centre section of a Ford Cortina MkIV, grafted on to a purpose-built chassis, on to which fibreglass body panels were then bolted. Both 3- and 5-door versions were offered. A 6-wheeled camper version called the Starcraft was also offered.

CR

SHIBAURA (J) 1954

This obscure minicar was exhibited at the 1954 Tokyo Motor Show, but seems to have got no further. It was powered by an air-cooled motorcycle engine.

CR

SHIELDS (AUS) 1906

W.J. Shields, Melbourne, Victoria.

Advertised as being built for the particular Australian requirements with special axles and springs, the Shields was offered in a range of models from 7 to 30hp, all with high tension magnetos. In 1907, however, its origin became clear when Brown Bros of London insisted that the cars should bear their name.

MG

SHIELS (AUS) 1933

L. Shiels, St Kilda, Victoria.

After a period as a journeyman at US motor factories, when he was obviously impressed by the Miller front-wheel drive system, Leo Shiels built a rakish roadster at Phoenix Motors. This roadster incorporated that feature, had a 6-cylinder 18hp engine, a wheelbase of 108in (2745mm) and it weighed 2015lb (916kg). Commercial intent is unknown but the Depression period was not the best time for fostering novel engineering, despite the model gaining much attention.

MG

1951 Siata (i) Daina 1400 coupé.
NICK BALDWIN

1954 Siata (i) Mitzi 400cc minicar.
NATIONAL MOTOR MUSEUM

1969 Siata (i) Spring 850 sports car.
NICK GEORGANO

SHOEMAKER (US) 1906–1908

1906–1907 Shoemaker Automobile Co., Freeport, Illinois.
1907–1908 Shoemaker Automobile Co., Elkhart, Indiana.
Designed by Charles Clinton Shoemaker and his son, Harry, this was a conventional car powered by a 30/35hp 4-cylinder engine and available only as a 5-seater tourer. After 25 cars had been built in Freeport Harry transferred production to Elkhart while his father remained in Freeport to make incubators which were the mainstay of his company. He listed two models for 1908, of 28 and 40hp, on the same 102in (2589mm) wheelbase, but few were made for the company closed down in February. It was revived later in the year as the St Joe Motor Car Co., but this name lasted only a few months before a new company was formed to make the SELLERS.

NG

SHOPPER (S) 1960s

Norsjö AB, Forshaga.
The Shopper Mopedbil was absolutely minimal transportation for a single passenger. It consisted of a polyester lower body with a luggage rack on the back and a single seat, protected from the elements by a canopy that swung sideways for entry. The handlebar steering and rear-mounted engine were taken from a moped.

CR

SHORT-ASHBY (GB) 1919–1923

1919–1921 Short Bros Ltd, Rochester, Kent.
1921–1923 Ashby Motors Ltd, Chorlton-cum-Hardy, Manchester.
The prototype of this cyclecar was designed by Victor Ashby and the car was put into production by aeroplane makers Short Brothers. It had a flat-twin Coventry-Victor engine of either 5/6 or 8hp, friction transmission and ifs. Fewer than 50 of these were made by Shorts, and the next design had a 970cc 4-cylinder Ruby engine and a choice of friction transmission or a Moss 3-speed gearbox. Some of these were also made by Shorts, but they abandoned it because of disappointing sales, and the design was taken up by a new company in Manchester. About 180 cars were made in all, under the names Short-Ashby or Ashby.

NG

S.H.W. (D) 1924–1925

Schwäbische Hüttenwerke AG, Böblingen.
This was an advanced design of small car by Professor Wunibald Kamm who was later famous for his work on streamlining at the Institute for Automobile Engineering in Stuttgart. The Schwäbische Hüttenwerke made three prototypes of his car which had cup-shaped integral construction bodies completely enclosed at the bottom. These aluminium bodies were made by the Zeppelin works. Power came from a 1030cc 4/20PS flat-twin engine driving the front wheels. There was no series production because a manufacturer could not be found to take up the design, and Kamm did not have a factory. The prototypes each ran for over 65,000 miles.

HON
Further Reading
'Pieces of a Puzzle', Jerry Sloniger, *Automobile Quarterly*, Vol. 26, No. 1.

S.I.A.M. (I) 1921–1923

Stà Italiana Automobili Milano, Milan.
The prototype of this car had a single-ohc 6-cylinder 2-litre engine, but production never started.

NG

SIATA (i) (I) 1926–1970

1926–1959 Stà Italiana Applicazione Transformazione Autobilistiche, Turin.
1959–1961 Siata-Abarth, Turin.
1961–1970 Siata Auto, Turin.
Società Italiana Applicazione Transformazione Autobilistiche was founded in 1926 by an amateur racing driver called Giorgio Ambrosini. Siata tuned cars and sold performance equipment, mainly for small Fiats. In 1948 Siata showed the 'Bersaglieri', a mid-engined 3-seat sports car (the driver sat in the middle), which had a tubular frame, a Siata double-ohc 4-cylinder 750cc engine, largely made from aluminium, a 2-speed rear axle, and independent suspension all round by coil springs and double wishbones.

If it sold at all, it was in tiny numbers, and the first successful Siata design was the Amica which was available as an open car or a coupé and had Fiat running gear in a tubular frame. A 750cc competition version of the Amica won the Italian Motor Racing Championship in 1948.

1950 saw the little company link with Fiat. The Siata Daina used Fiat 1400 running gear and 1951 saw the Fiat 1400-based Rallye, which copied the MG TD and a 5-speed gearbox was optional. The Daina and Rallye stayed in production until 1958.

In 1952, Siata began to build cars with American engines. There was an Amica fitted with a 720cc Crosley unit; and a large coupé, the America, which used a Chrysler V8 engine. 1952 also saw a Siata version of the Fiat 8V, with a Vignale body (with pop-up headlights, and available as a rag top or a coupé) which was sold as the Siata 208 until 1955.

Apart from a minicar called the Mitzi, from the mid–1950s Siata concentrated on cars based on the Fiat 600 and 1100 and its main seller was the 1100-103 fastback coupé, with a 52bhp engine.

In 1959 Siata joined forces with Abarth, to form a new company called Siata-Abarth, but no joint ventures came from this arrangement and both marques continued to sell their own models. The partnership ended in 1961 when Siata became Siata-Auto and concentrated on the Fiat 1300 and 1500 models. Most products were tuned versions of the standard cars, but a handsome GT body was also available. Production of all types peaked at 1400 examples in 1964.

The last Siata was the 'Spring' of 1968. It was a parody of the MG TD on a Fiat 850S floorpan. It was one of Siata's biggest sellers, but the company folded in 1970. The Spring was revived by ORSA in 1973 and was made in small numbers until 1976.

MJL

Further Reading
'Siata: the never-told tale of a very great little marque', Griffith Borgeson, *Automobile Quarterly*, Vol.23, No.2

SIATA (ii) (E) 1960–1973
Siata Española SA, Barcelona and Tarragona.
Created in Barcelona with the factory at Tarragona, the Spanish Siata specialised in bodies, engine conversions and special accessories for cars. The company developed special bodies for Seat, some under Italian licence, but also some of its own. The Seat 600 could be changed into the 750 (with more power, thanks to new pistons), the Ampurias, with a three-volume body, the Turisa with coupé or spider body, or the Tarraco, a sports-coupé with 750cc or 850cc engine. The company also built the Formichetta and the 2850 delivery van.

VCM

SIBLEY (US) 1910–1911
Sibley Motor Car Co., Detroit, Michigan.
The Sibley was a 2-seater roadster powered by a 3.6-litre 30hp 4-cylinder engine, with 3-speed gearbox and shaft drive. Few were made, and in January 1911 the venture came to an end when the owners of the factory sued for the recovery of their property. Eugene Sibley then moved to Connecticut, where he attempted to launch the SIBLEY-CURTISS.

NG

SIBLEY-CURTISS (US) 1911–1912
Sibley-Curtiss Motor Car Co., Simsbury, Connecticut.
This company was formed by Eugene Sibley and Joseph Curtiss, ostensibly to manufacture touring cars, though a local resident recalled that the true plan was to purchase the previous year's output of another Connecticut manufacturer and to sell them under the Sibley-Curtiss name. Only two cars were ever sold.

NG

SIBRAVA (CS) 1921–1929
Jaroslav Sibrava, tovarna motorovych vozidel, Praha.
When the Prague firm of J. Walter stopped the production of its 3-wheelers built from 1910 to 1918, this was taken over by J. Sibrava in 1921. His Trimobil had an air-cooled V-twin cylinder 1248cc 9bhp engine; later flat-twins with the same capacity but of 14bhp were used. These reliable tiller-steered vehicles were bodied as a 2-seater open sports car (type E2), a 4-seater family car (E4) with electric lights and a folding waterproof roof, a taxicab (EK4) with covered body and separate chauffeur-compartment, a light 2-seater pick-up (EN), and a light van (END).

Between 1925 and 1929 Sibrava produced his only 'real' cars powered by the flat-twins (as were his 3-wheelers) with 3-speed gearbox. Both rigid axles with semi-elliptic leaf springs were mounted on a rectangular steel frame, rear wheels were driven by a propeller shaft through a differential. Weight 700kg, top speed 37mph (60km/h), price 34,000 Kc. About 100 vehicles of both ranges were built.

MSH

S.I.C. (I) 1924
Stà Italiana Cyclecars, Chiavari.
Cyclecars were relatively rare in Italy, and the S.I.C. was one of the smallest, with a 500cc 2-cylinder 2-stroke engine and a 2-speed gearbox.

NG

c.1965 Siata (ii) Turisa coupé.
NICK GEORGANO

1905 Siddeley 6hp 2-seater.
NATIONAL MOTOR MUSEUM

SICAM (F) 1919–1922
Sté Industrielle de Construction d'Automobiles et de Moteurs, Pantin, Seine.
Built by Marcel Violet and R. Legras, this was a small cyclecar powered by a Violet-designed 496cc 2-cylinder 2-stroke engine. This prolific designer was involved with a number of makes, including the Sima-Violet which was developed from the Sicam. The Sicam had quite a neat 2-seater body and coil front suspension with a transverse leaf at the rear. Final drive was by belts on the earlier model, later replaced by a dog-clutch and chain drive as used by G.N. and Frazer Nash, though the Sicam system offered only two forward speeds. From 1922 the company made 98cc engines for attaching to bicycles and in 1924 it was reformed as the Société Industrielle de Matériel Automobile to make the Sima-Violet.

NG

SIDDELEY (GB) 1902–1904
1902–1903 Siddeley Autocar Co. Ltd, Coventry.
1903–1904 Vickers Sons & Maxim Ltd, Crayford, Kent.
The first cars offered by John Davenport Siddeley were thinly disguised Peugeots with front-mounted vertical engines, a 2.3-litre twin and a 3.3-litre four. In 1903 came a 6hp single-cylinder 2-seater which was made for Siddeley by Vickers, who supplied the same car as a Wolseley, but with that make's typical wrap-around radiator. Vickers at that time owned the Wolseley Tool & Motor Car Co., and Crayford was one of their factories. In 1905 Siddeley succeeded Herbert Austin as general manager of Wolseley.

NG

1913 Siddeley-Deasy 14/20hp landaulet.
NICK BALDWIN

SIDDELEY-DEASY (GB) 1912–1919

Siddeley-Deasy Motor Manufacturing Co. Ltd, Coventry.

In 1909 Captain H.H.P. Deasy left the company he had founded (see DEASY), his place being taken by J.D. Siddeley who had just left Wolseley. He became managing director in 1910 and introduced his own designs, a 2917cc 14hp and a 4082cc 18/28hp, known as Siddeley-J.D.S. They had dashboard radiators and the engines probably were supplied by Aster. A smaller four of 1944cc appeared in 1911 and became part of the Siddeley-Deasy range for 1912. Deasy soon adopted the Knight sleeve-valve engine in two sizes, the 3306cc 4-cylinder 18/24 and 4960cc 6-cylinder 24/30hp. The engines were bought from Daimler but were dismantled and re-built before being installed in Siddeley-Deasy chassis. They had an excellent reputation for silence, and earned the slogan 'As silent as the Sphinx'. They carried a Sphinx mascot, which became more famous after the war when it was used by Armstrong-Siddeley, which succeeded Siddeley-Deasy.

In 1912 J.D. Siddeley formed a separate company, Stoneleigh Motors Ltd, to make a smaller car called the Stoneleigh which was, in fact, a 13.9hp sleeve-valve B.S.A. This sold as a chassis for £275 whereas Siddeley-Deasy chassis prices ranged from £400 to £695. On the 1914 Siddeley-Deasys electric lighting was standard, and electric starting optional.

During the war Siddeley-Deasy made ambulances on their car chassis, and trucks under contract from Maudslay. They also developed the Beardmore-Halford-Pullinger aero-engine which became the Puma, and of which 3225 were in use by 1918. In May 1919 Sir W.G. Armstrong, Whitworth & Co. bought Siddeley-Deasy for £419,750 to form the Armstrong-Whitworth Development Co. Armstrong-Siddeley Motors was formed as a subsidiary, and a few months later the 30hp Armstrong-Siddeley car was launched.

NG

SIDÉA (F) 1912–1924

Sté Industrielle des Automobiles Sidéa, Mézières-Charleville, Ardennes.

This company made touring cars of no great originality, powered by 4-cylinder Chapuis-Dornier engines ranging in size from 6 to 14hp. Production did not

NICK BALDWIN

SIDDELEY, JOHN DAVENPORT (1866–1953)

As a captain of industry, John D. Siddeley was known as a strong personality with remarkable business acumen. Astute and self confident, he was a hard task master, with a tendency to dominate. Yet he had a kind and generous side. Devoutly religious, he became a great benefactor of Coventry Hospital and several local charities.

He was born on 5 August 1866, at Cheadle Hume, Manchester, the son of an Altrincham hosier, William Siddeley. He was a prominent member of the Humber cycling team and joined Humber as a draughtsman in 1892. His promising career came to the attention of Harvey du Cros who offered him a post in the Dunlop factory at Belfast. After starting the Dunlop Cycle Co. in Belfast, Siddeley returned to London as Dunlop representative.

In 1899 he became managing director of the Clipper Pneumatic Tyre Co. Ltd and he drove a Daimler in the 1000 Miles Trial of 1900. In 1901 he resigned from the tyre company to take on the Peugeot franchise for Great Britain. Early in 1902 he formed the Siddeley Autocar Co. in Garfield Road, Coventry. His first cars were patterned on Peugeot models and had Peugeot components. He secured the financial backing of Lionel de Rothschild for manufacturing a true British car to be called Siddeley.

He approached Vickers Sons & Maxim of Crayford in Kent about production facilities, and Vickers put him in touch with Wolseley, whose drawing office turned his specifications into blueprints for making a complete car. Vickers tooled up for its production at Crayford and began making the Wolseley-Siddeley in 1905. Early in 1905 Vickers arranged to take over the Siddeley Autocar Co. where he stayed on as Sales Manager. After Herbert Austin's resignation, he took over as general manager of Wolseley.

In April 1908 he learned of the resignation of Captain Henry Hugh Peter Deasy, who had taken over the defunct Iden Motor Co. at Parkside, Coventry, in 1906, and that the board of directors was looking for a new managing director. He left Wolseley, signed up as managing director of Deasy & Co. early in 1909, and redesigned the Deasy cars (originally designed by Edmund Woodward Lewis), which were renamed Siddeley-Deasy. Siddeley left London for Coventry, and took up residence at Hill Orchard, Meriden. Deasy & Co. undertook valuable military production projects during World War I, and in 1918 Siddeley was honoured with a CBE. He acquired Crackley Hall near Kenilworth and moved his family there.

He was a co-founder and director of Armstrong-Siddeley Motors Ltd, and the Armstrong-Siddeley Development Co. Ltd, and led their expansion for 17 years. He was knighted in 1932 and was appointed High Sheriff of Warwickshire. From 1933 to 1938 he also served as a Justice of the Peace for Coventry and Warwickshire. He retired from industry in 1936, and a year later became Baron Kenilworth, also purchasing Kenilworth Castle. Crackley Hall ended up as St Joseph's Convent School. His last years were spent in retirement on Jersey.

He was twice married. In 1893 to Mary Goodier, by whom he had a son, Cyril (born 1894). She died in about 1907, and he subsequently married Sarah Hall, by whom he had two sons, Ernest and Norman, and two daughters, Joan and Nancy.

Further Reading

'John Davenport Siddeley', Grahame Orme-Bannister, *Automotive History Review*, Winter 1999 – 2000.

JPN

get underway after the war until 1922, when they again made assembled cars, now with engines from Fivet (a side-valve 1496cc) or S.C.A.P. (a single-ohc 1690cc). The last models were marketed under the name Sidéa-Jouffret.

NG

SIDEWINDER STREET RODS (US) c.1988

Sidewinder Street Rods, div. Cobra Trikes, Jeffersonville, Indiana.
The Ultimate was a crude hot rod with no hood, doors or bodywork. It had a simple firewall between the engine and interior. There was a bench seat with room for three people perched above the rear axle and cycle-type mudguards. They were sold in kit and completed form.

HP

SIEGEL (D) 1908–1910

Theodor Siegel, Schönebeck.
The 8hp 2-cylinder Siegel was originally intended as a delivery van, but seeing a demand for a passenger car it was made in this form as well, with 2- or 4-seater bodies.

HON

SIEGFRIED see REISSIG

SIEMENS-SCHUCKERT (D) 1906–1910

Siemens-Schuckert GmbH, Automobilwerk, Nonnendamm, Berlin.
This well-known electrical concern entered car production in 1906, offering electric, petrol-electric and petrol powered vehicles. The petrol-electrics were made under Pieper licence. The petrol car used a 1½-litre 6/10PS Körting engine. Production did not last very long as the well-known PROTOS company was acquired in 1908, and all future petrol cars were marketed under this name. However, electric cars were continued under the Siemens-Schuckert name until 1910. Commercial vehicles were made until 1913, and the name was revived from 1928 to 1939 for 1½- and 2-ton electric vans.

HON

Further Reading
Autos aus Berlin, Hans-Otto Neubauer, Kohlhammer, 1983.

SIENNA (GB) 1988–1991; 1993–1994

1988–1989 Sienna Cars, Dorking, Surrey.
1989–1991 and 1993–1994 Sienna Cars, Sutton Veny, Warminster, Wiltshire.
A sheep farmer from New Zealand, Alan Booth improved on the Lamborghini Countach replica kit norm with high quality fibreglass bodywork, a sound chassis and proven rose-jointed suspension. Around 25 cars were built in all.

CR

S.I.F.T.T. (F) 1987–1989

Sté Industrielle Française de Tout-Terrain, Ardèche.
This was a serious and fairly large-scale operation to put an open plastic-bodied jeep-type car, the Katar, into production. The first Katar used a Citroën 2CV chassis fitted with a 652cc LN engine coupled with a Voisin 4 × 4 system. Later came a 4 × 2 model with a Peugeot 1769cc diesel engine, and a second 4 × 4 model based on the Citroën C.15 light van, with either petrol or diesel power. A prototype participated in the 1987 Paris-Dakar rally.

CR

SIGMA (i) (CH) 1909–1914

Sté industrielle genèvoise de mécanique et d'automobile, SIGMA, Geneva.
John Meynet (1883–1938) was a versatile and successful sportsman from Geneva. In 1908 he bought the former LUCIA factory and with the help of Robert Faech, an engineer, the first Sigma car was launched by him one year later. The name is derived from the company initials and the cars carried the Greek [Sigma] on their round radiators. It was a light car of 8/11hp with a 4-cylinder engine of 1592cc, a 4-speed gearbox and shaft drive. In 1910 this was supplemented by a 14/18hp model. De Prosperis, Sigma's representative in Sicily, took part in the Targa Florio and was runner up to Cariolato in a Franco. In 1911 the factory was enlarged and Sigma took over the exclusive agency for the American Knight sleeve-valve engines. In 1912 Sigma introduced two new models with 4-cylinder Knight engines of 18hp, 2612cc and 28hp, 4574cc.

1906 Siemens-Schuckert Typ B electric landaulet.
HANS-OTTO NEUBAUER

1913 Sigma (ii) 2-seater.
BRYAN K. GOODMAN

1919 Sigma (ii) 10hp tourer.
NICK GEORGANO

Sigma cars were successfully entered in Swiss competitions and Meynet himself drove an 18hp model in the 1912 Monte Carlo Rally. In addition to the sleeve-valve models, two poppet-valve 4-cylinders chassis of 15 and 25hp respectively were produced. Up to 1914 about 250 Sigma cars were made in Geneva. During World War I up to 2000 workers were employed producing various kinds of war material, and in 1918 John Meynet, who was by now a wealthy man, decided not to restart automobile production.

FH

SIGMA (ii) (F) 1913–1928

Sté des Automobiles Sigma, Levallois-Perret, Seine.
The Sigma was an assembled car of no great originality, though it survived for longer than many of its kind. Its greatest claim to fame was that one was owned by the famous World War I fighter pilot Georges Guynemer, whose flying stork mascot was adopted by Hispano-Suiza.

Prewar Sigmas, such as the one owned by Guynemer, had 4-cylinder Ballot engines in chassis by Malicet et Blin. The 8 and 11hp models were sold in England as Marlboroughs. After the war Ballot engines were again used, as well as various sizes of S.C.A.P. from 894 to 1610cc. The most sporting Sigma was the Model W of 1925, powered by a 1494cc single-ohc C.I.M.E. engine. Though staid in appearance it had a claimed top speed of 75mph (120km/h), compared with 45mph (72km/h) for the average Sigma. Production never exceeded 200 cars per year, and although this figure was just viable in the early 1920s, it was hopelessly limited eight years later, when Citroën and Peugeot were making cars just as good as the Sigma at considerably lower prices. The 1928 models, which were the last, used 1170 and 1614cc S.C.A.P. engines.

NG

SIGNET *see* FENTON

SILA (I) 1960
Stà Industriale Lavorazioni Acciai, Turin.
The Sila Autoretta was a curious attempt by a toy car factory to enter the world of true car production, although the result was so basic that it looked and felt like a go-kart. Like the old American buggies, there was no bodywork to speak of, only wings covering the four wheels, a frame to carry the steering wheel, two seats and an exposed fuel tank. It had a rear-mounted 200cc single-cylinder 2-stroke 15bhp engine driving only one rear wheel via a 4-speed gearbox, with a top speed of 46mph (74km/h).

CR

SILAOS (F) 1985–1988
Projet Plus sarl, Dieppe.
The Silaos Demoiselle was a replica of the tiny Bugatti Type 56 electric car used to ferry visitors around the Molsheim factory in the 1920s. Created by Joël Michel (one of the design team on the Renault 5 Turbo project), it used 47cc or 124cc petrol, 199cc or 430cc diesel or electric power. It weighed only 430lbs (195kg) and cost FFr39,900 in 1986. Silaos also offered a more conventional microcar under the name Type 3.

CR

SILENT KNIGHT (US) 1905–1907
Knight & Kilbourne Co., Chicago, Illinois.
Though few cars were made by this company, they were noteworthy in being the first to use the sleeve-valve engine invented by Charles Yale Knight. He went into partnership with L.D. Kilbourne to make a car with 30/40hp 4-cylinder engine. The chassis and gearbox came from Garford. With 5-seater tourer body (the only style offered), it sold for $3500, but the main purpose of building it was to demonstrate the sleeve-valve principle in order to induce other car makers to take up a licence. As the Silent Knight was a crude product, they did not succeed at first, but when Knight took a car to Europe he interested Daimler (ii) in England, followed by Minerva in Belgium, Panhard in France and Mercedes in Germany. This persuaded American car makers that there must be some merit in the system, and licences were sold to Stearns, Stoddard-Dayton and many others. The Silent Knight had served its purpose after all, and was soon dropped. Not more than 50 were made.

NG

Further Reading
'The Knight', R.L. Perrin, *Automobile Quarterly*, Vol. 4, No. 1.

SILENT SIOUX *see* FAWICK

SILHOUETTE (i) (GB) 1970–1973; 1978
1970–1973 Silhouette Cars Ltd, London.
1978 Adrian Wood, Lichfield, Staffordshire.
The Silhouette GS70 was a VW Beetle-based coupé kit car. The rather cumbersomely-styled fibreglass body initially had conventional doors but from 1971 there was the option of gullwing doors. The Silhouette disappeared in 1973 but was revived in 1978 without success. At least one of the dozen or so Silhouettes built was a convertible.

CR

SILHOUETTE (ii) (GB) 1987–1989
Silhouette Cars, Corby, Northamptonshire.
The Silhouette SC 5000S was one of a plethora of kit-form Lamborghini Countach replicas around this period. The recipe was familiar enough: a spaceframe chassis, independent suspension by unequal length wishbones, Renault 30 transaxle, steel floor, fibreglass body and V6, V8 or even a Jaguar V12 engine.

CR

SILURIAN (GB) 1992–c.1996
This was possibly the largest kit car ever made: a full 4-door, 5-seater convertible in a classic 1920s idiom, with full running boards and a vintage style soft-top. The mechanical basis was mainly Jaguar and the car was made in Wales.

CR

SILVA-CORONER (F) 1927
This obscure car was made by, or to the order of, a M. Silva-Coroner for an Egyptian clientele. It had a 2490cc ohv straight-8 engine, 3-speed gearbox and Perrot-Bendix brakes. Two versions were made, a saloon with lhd and a sports car with pointed tail and cycle-type wings, with rhd. It is thought that these were the only two Silva-Coroner cars made.

NG

SILVER (US) 1914–1919
C.T. Silver Motor Co., New York, New York.
Conover T. Silver was the New York City distributor for both Peerless and Willys-Overland cars. His headquarters was at Broadway & E. 56th Street where, as a designer, he introduced a number of exquisitely designed sporting cars of which his name appeared in hyphenated form alongside the make of car represented. Noted for his Silver-Knight roadsters on a Willys-Knight chassis and the Silver-Peerless, Conover Silver became New York's distributor for Apperson and Kissel cars in 1917 where he continued his designing prowess with his Silver-Apperson and Silver-Kissel roadsters. These cars were exhibited at the New York Auto Shows of the period and were highly publicised, their individuality of design being further emphasised by their hubcaps which carried the Silver name and address. Silver ceased his position as a distributor toward the end of 1918 and further examples of his designing talent coincided with it.

KM

SILVER ARROW (US) c.1992
Silver Arrow, Fargo, North Dakota.
Silver Arrow made the Mercedes 300SL Gullwing, 300SLR, 500K and 540K replicas that were sold by CLASSICS INTERNATIONAL. The 300SLR was not particularly accurate and could be purchased in coupé or roadster form. They were designed around Ford and Chevrolet V8 engines. Although Silver Arrow's manufacturing plant was in Florida, their business address was the same as Classics International in North Dakota.

HP

SILVER CROSS (GB) 1904
Thomas Hamlin & Co. Ltd, Bridgewater, Somerset.
Founded in 1896 this company made the Silver Cross bicycle, and in 1904 completed a car powered by a 7hp single-cylinder engine and fitted with a 4-seater tonneau body. It is not known how many other cars they made, and the firm did not feature in the national motoring press. However, they continued as general engineers, being active in both World Wars and are still in business today.

NG

SILVER HAWK (GB) 1920–1921
Silver Hawk Motors Ltd, Cobham, Surrey.
This sports car was made by Noel Campbell Macklin after he had ended his connection with Eric-Campbell. It used a 1498cc Coventry Simplex engine, rebuilt and lightened by Macklin's staff, with 3- or 4-speed gearbox and a 2-seater body. Some were very sporting in appearance, with pointed tail and a long external exhaust pipe, though at least one had a more sober 2-seater body with doors and a vertical windscreen. The radiator was similar to that of the later Invicta, with which Macklin was also involved. The Silver Hawks and prototypes of the Invicta were assembled in the garage attached to Macklin's private house. Not more

1920 Silver Hawk 10hp sports car.
NATIONAL MOTOR MUSEUM

than 12 Silver Hawks were made. Three took part in the 1920 Coupe des Voiturettes, being the only British team to do so (there was also a solitary G.N.). Two finished 6th and 7th against strong opposition from Bugatti and Bignan. The name Silver Hawk was also used for the SETHERA.

NG

SILVER STREAM (GB) 1907
Somerville-Large & Co., Kilcullen, County Kildare.
This was the result of Philip Somerville-Large'a ambition to build a high quality car in Ireland. The prototype had a 3-litre 6-cylinder Gnome engine, a Malicet et Blin chassis and a tourer body by Salmons. A price of £2000 was quoted, unrealistically high when a Rolls-Royce 40/50 chassis cost only £950, and only the prototype was ever made. It still exists today.

NG

SILVERTOWN (GB) 1905–c.1910
The Silvertown Co., Silvertown, London.
This was an electric car made by a subsidiary of the India Rubber, Gutta Percha & Telegraph Works Ltd, makers of batteries and instruments. W.F. Thorn bodies were used on many of the town cars. In 1908 a model was offered with electric motors on both front and rear axles, giving 4-wheel drive, though it could be used with the rear wheels only driven. It had a range of 50 miles.

NG

SIMA-STANDARD (F) 1929–1932
Automobiles Sima-Standard, Courbevoie, Seine.
This company grew out of S.I.M.A. (Société Industrielle de Matériel Automobile) which had made the Sima-Violet cyclecar. Whereas that had been unconventional the makers realised that the days of the cyclecar were over, and engaged Émile Dombret (formerly of Motobloc) to design a conventional small car. He combined the features of a number of rivals, using an 860cc engine very similar to the 5CV Citroën, some people say left over Citroën components, Citroën front axle and suspension, 6CV Amilcar gearbox and some other components from Renault.

1905 Silvertown electric landaulet.
NICK BALDWIN

The result was a not unattractive small car, made in roadster, cabriolet and 2- and 4-door saloon models, some of which featured in Concours d'Élégance.
In 1932 came a larger Sima Standard with 1306cc engine which did not correspond exactly to any Citroën, though the 68mm bore was shared with the B10. Few of these were made, and no more of any kind after 1932.

NG

SIMA-VIOLET (F) 1924–1929
Sté Industrielle de Matériel Automobile, Courbevoie, Seine.
This company was formed from the makers of the SICAM and used the same Marcel Violet-designed 496cc flat-twin engine as its predecessor. It was more

1451

1936 Simca (i) Simca-Fiat 6CV saloon.
NATIONAL MOTOR MUSEUM

1938 Simca (i) 8 coupé.
NICK BALDWIN

streamlined than the Sicam, with plywood body, tubular backbone frame and a 2-speed gearbox on the rear axle. A few were fitted with 750cc engines and took part in competitions, but a 1½-litre flat-4 Grand Prix car competed only once, when Violet finished 3rd in the 1926 Boulogne GP. The touring Sima-Violet design was also sold under other names including Alcyon and Labor. The latter was sold as a *camionette Normande* as well as a 2-seater car.

NG

SIMCA (i) (F) 1935–1980

1935–1961 Sté Industrielle de Mécanique et Carrosserie Automobile, Nanterre, Seine; 1954–1970 Poissy, Seine-et-Oise.
1970–1980 Chrysler France SA, Poissy, Seine-et-Oise.

The origins of Simca date back to 1924, when Teodoro Enrico Pigozzi (1898–1964) was sent by Giovanni Agnelli to France to buy up scrap metal for the Fiat works. He settled in France, changed his Christian names to Henri-Théodore, and in 1926 was appointed Fiat's main distributor in France. In 1932 he began manufacture of Fiat Balillas in a couple of hangars at Suresnes. It was really an assembly operation, for the engines were made by Chaise in Paris, coachwork by Manessius at Levallois, and gearboxes and transmissions by Renaudin & Losson at Suresnes. Nevertheless, he managed to make 29,000 cars up to the end of 1934, when he acquired the former DONNET factory at Nanterre, and formed the Société Industrielle de Mécanique et Carrosserie Automobile S.I.M.C.A.

After modernisation of the factory, production got underway in the spring of 1935. The first cars made were Balillas, sold under the name Simca-Fiat 6CV, and Arditas, sold as Simca-Fiat 11CV. They were almost identical to the Italian product, though the 11CV soon acquired more attractive styling. Seven body styles were available in the 6CV series, including an attractive 2-seater sports, while the 11CV was made only as a 4-door pillarless saloon or 2-door cabriolet.

The spring of 1936 saw the announcement of the 5CV, or Simca Cinq, alias the Fiat Topolino. Because of widespread industrial unrest that year, the Cinq did not go into production until September. It was joined in 1937 by the Huit,

Pigozzi's version of the Fiat 1100. The 11CV was dropped after 1937, so the Cinq and Huit made up the Simca range up to the outbreak of war. They were similar to their Italian equivalents, though for 1939 there was a 2-seater coupé on the Huit chassis which was unique to Simca. 1938 production was nearly 21,000 cars of which about two thirds were Cinqs.

Simca had many sporting successes, thanks to the attentions of Amédée Gordini, another French-domiciled Italian, nicknamed 'le Sorcier' (the Sorcerer). Prewar Simca-Gordinis were sports cars, but single-seaters arrived in 1946. The early postwar Simcas followed the Fiat theme. The Cinq was still a Topolino, and the Huit kept the prewar style of radiator whereas Turin had gone over to a vee-grill. The first sign of modernisation came with the 1948 Simca Six which had an ohv 570cc engine and a horizontal grill with inset headlamps. Simca was a step ahead of Fiat who adopted the ohv engine for 1948, but did not modernise their little car's appearance until the 1949 season. The 1949 Paris Salon saw an updated Huit, the Huit-1200 with 1221cc engine and a larger boot, also the Huit-Sport which had a completely new cabriolet body styled by Mario Revelli de Beaumont built for Simca by Façel Métallon. A higher cr gave an extra 10bhp on the 40bhp of the Huit saloon, but the cabriolet was also heavier, and top speed was only 84mph (135km/h). Bodily at any rate, the Huit-Sport was a breakaway from Fiat parentage, and was followed by a line of cabriolets and coupés which were made up to 1962. An average of 2000 per year were made, and at their peak, in 1951, Façel were turning out 20 per day.

The spring of 1951 saw the arrival of the Aronde, a 4-door saloon with contemporary slab-sided styling which marked a further step away from Fiat influence. The engine was the 1221cc unit from the Huit-1200, but the body was of unitary construction and (on 1952 models) there was a hypoid rear axle. Nanterre was now leading Turin, for both these features would be found on the Fiat 1100-103, introduced in 1953. For 1953 a station wagon and a Grand Large 2-door hard-top joined the saloon, and the Huit-Sport acquired the Aronde engine and running gear.

The Aronde proved a success from the start, and by March 1953 the 100,000th was delivered. In August a stock saloon set out to cover 100,000km at 100km/h at Montlhéry. When the run finished the car had covered 115,000km at an average of 64mph (103km/h). The Aronde was gradually improved during the 1950s, receiving smaller wheels (to achieve a lower appearance) and higher gearing for 1955, and a 48bhp 1290cc engine for 1956. The P60 model for 1959 was considerably restyled, with a new grill and a flash down the body sides, while the engine now gave up to 57bhp. In fact there were eight models of Aronde with four different power outputs, the base model being a 1090cc 40bhp unit. The last major improvement was a 5-bearing crankshaft for 1961. The Aronde was dropped after the 1963 season, total production being 1,274,859. From 1962 to 1965 the P60 was assembled in Keswick, Southern Australia, by Chrysler Australia Ltd. As well as the saloon, there was a locally-designed and built station wagon.

The Ford Influence

Simca's expansion in the 1950s involved the acquisition of several other companies. These included two truck builders, Unic and the French branch of Saurer, Ford France and Talbot. The most important from the point of view of future Simcas was the Ford purchase, which took place in November 1954. Not only did it bring a new design enabling Simca to enter a more expensive market, but it also brought a more modern factory at Poissy, into which eventually all Simca production would be transferred. In 1961 the Nanterre factory was sold to Citroën.

Shortly before the merger, Ford had brought out a new Vedette powered by a 2355cc V8 engine, featuring integral construction and MacPherson strut suspension. This was made in three models, the basic Trianon, mid-range Versailles and luxury Régence, the latter with wire wheels and two-tone paintwork. There was also a station wagon called the Marly. All these erstwhile Fords became part of the Simca range for 1955, being joined in 1957 by the Ariane which used the 1290cc Aronde engine in the Trianon hull. This was economical and could just reach 75mph (120km/h), but its acceleration was feeble. However, it found numerous customers, particularly in the wake of the Suez-induced fuel shortage. Many Arianes were sold as taxis, the Paris G7 company replacing all their Dyna Panhards with Arianes. For 1958 the V8s were renamed, and the more expensive models were restyled with more chrome and wrap-around windscreens. The Trianon became the Ariane 8, the Versailles became the Beaulieu and the Régence the Chambord. The 1958 Salon saw the most luxurious of all the V8s, the Présidence limousine which featured a radio-telephone and, for the first

1950 Simca (i) 8 sport coupé.
NATIONAL MOTOR MUSEUM

1955 Simca (i) Aronde saloon.
NATIONAL MOTOR MUSEUM

1956 Simca (i) Vedette estate car.
NATIONAL MOTOR MUSEUM

time in a European car, a television in the rear compartment. The Présidence could be distinguished by its externally-mounted spare wheel, also by its all-black finish. A few Présidence convertibles were made, one 4-door for Presidential use when foreign leaders came to Paris, and several 2-door cars for government officials. The run of Simca V8s came to an end in 1962, with a total of 166,895 having been made. Licence production in Brazil continued up to 1967, later models having ohv engines.

In 1958 the Chrysler Corp. took a 15 per cent stake in Simca, a step which would lead to total control by the American company in 1970. Meanwhile, at home, Pigozzi ordered a replacement for the Aronde, and work on a rear-engined prototype began in 1959. The car appeared for the 1962 season as the 1000; its 944cc 45bhp 5-bearing engine was mounted longitudinally with the radiator alongside it, and the specification included an all-synchromesh 4-speed gearbox and all-round independent suspension. With a top speed of 75mph (120km/h) and a price of FF6490 which undercut Citroën's Ami 6, the 1000 quickly became a best seller. The basic 1000 was made up to 1978, being joined in 1969 by the 1000GLS with 49bhp 1118cc engine and, from 1970, disc brakes at the front. There was also an economy version sold on the home market, called the Sim'4 (4CV) with 777cc engine. The most powerful versions of the rear-engined 1000 were the Simca-Abarths with 1135cc engines giving 55, 65 or 85bhp, and front-mounted radiators. They were announced in 1963 but Simca management refused to sanction the expense of a rally team, and so an interesting rival to the Renault 8 Gordini was lost. However, in the 1970s the Rallye 1, 2 and 3 models were made, with 1294cc engines from the front-drive 1100, giving speeds of 96mph (155km/h), 106mph (170km/h) and 112mph (180km/h). They were widely used by the S.R.T. (Simca Racing Team) which gave amateurs a chance to race without great expense. Total production of the rear-engined saloons was 1,642,091.

The S.R.T. also used the 1000 coupé, an attractive little 2+2 designed by Bertone which took over the role of the Sport models of the 1950s. All the coupés had disc brakes, and with the 52bhp engine top speed was around 90mph (145km/h). The 1000 coupé was made from 1962 to 1967, when it was replaced by the 1200S with 1204cc engine giving 80–85bhp and a top speed of 109mph (175km/h). Even more power was extracted from this engine by Abarth. A more specialised collaboration between Abarth and Simca was the 1300 coupé which used a twin-ohc 1288cc engine in a body of Abarth-shape using Simca floorpan, gearbox and suspension. It was a competition rather than a road car, and one averaged 93.3mph (150.132km/h) at Le Mans in 1962. Another Simca-based sports car was the C.G. made by Chappe Frères & Gesselin. Fibreglass-bodied roadsters and coupés were made in small numbers from 1967 to 1974, using various sizes of Simca engine from 944cc up. 24,752 Simca coupés were made between 1962 and 1971.

A car designed to replace both the Aronde and the Ariane was the 1300/1500 series, a conventional front-engined rear-drive saloon and estate car made from 1963 to 1966. The 1300 used the Aronde's 1290cc engine, while the 1500 had an enlarged version of 1498cc. Disc brakes featured on the 1500 from the start, reaching the smaller-engined car in 1966. The 1300 and 1500 were almost identical externally, apart from different radiator grills. In 1967 they were replaced by the 1301 and 1501, which had 1290 and 1475cc engines and larger luggage boots but were otherwise similar to their predecessors. The 1501 acquired servo brakes in 1969, and the series was made up to 1976, by which time a total of 1,342,907 had been made.

Inspired by the success of the Austin/Morris Mini, Henri Pigozzi had ordered work to begin on a transverse-engined front-drive Simca in 1962. Five years later, and three years after his death, the new car appeared under the title 1100. Its 1118cc pushrod ohv engine was mounted ahead of the front axle and inclined at an angle of 41 degrees to the rear. In the model LS the engine gave 53bhp, in the GL and GLS, 56bhp. Suspension was independent all-round by torsion bars, the front wheels were disc-braked, and three bodies were offered, 3- and 5-door hatchbacks, and a station wagon. Other engines were soon available, the 1204cc from the 1200S coupé in 1970, and a 1294cc version of this from 1973, while for the economy minded there was the 944cc unit from the old 1000. The 1100 in its various versions was made up to 1979, the last examples carrying Chrysler badges. To complicate matters further, the 1100 vans were badged as Dodges. The front end of the 1100 was used for the Matra-Simca Rancho, while the 1294cc engine powered another Matra product, the Bagheera sports coupé. Total 1100 production approached the two million mark.

The Chrysler Era
On 1 July 1970 the company name Simca was changed to Chrysler France. This had no immediate impact on the existing range of Simca cars, but a new 'international' model appeared at the Salon in October in the shape of the 160/180 saloons which had been designed at the British Chrysler (formerly Rootes Group) headquarters in Coventry. They were conventional rear-drive 4-door saloons powered by 1639 or 1796cc single-ohc 4-cylinder engines, with MacPherson strut suspension and disc brakes, on the front wheels in the 160, all-round in the 180. In January 1973 came a 2-litre version with automatic transmission. French production of these cars ended in 1976, though they were continued in reduced numbers at the Spanish Chrysler factory. The early 1970s were Simca's best years for production, which exceeded 500,000 annually in 1972 and 1973.

In August 1975 a new range of front-drive Simcas appeared, the 1307 and 1308. These 5-door hatchbacks with 1307 or 1442cc engines were made and sold in Britain as Chrysler Alpines. They were voted Car of the Year in 1976, and in 1978 were joined by the 1309 with automatic transmission. Another international car, badged as a Chrysler in Britain, was the Horizon introduced at the end of 1977. Smaller than the 1307 but also a 5-door hatchback, the Horizon came initially with engines of 1118 or 1294cc, joined a year later by the 1442cc GLS 1500. The Horizon was sold in America as the Dodge Omni and Plymouth Cricket.

In August 1978 Chrysler France and Chrysler UK were bought by Peugeot, and a new name was needed as there was no longer any American ownership. Simca was considered lacking in charisma, so Talbot was chosen, being a name with a renowned sporting history, and one which had international connections. The new owners had the right to the name as the French Talbot company had been bought by Simca in 1958.

September 1979 saw a revised 1307 appear under the name Talbot-Simca 1510, and the other cars in the range was also called Talbot-Simcas. A new model which arrived in March 1980 was the Solara, essentially a 1510 with a boot instead of a hatchback. The early examples of the Solara bore the Simca name at the rear, but when the 1981 season came round, Simca had disappeared.

NG

Further Reading
'Simca, de Fiat à Talbot', Michel G. Renou,
La Boutique du Collectionneur, 1999.

1960 Simca (i) Aronde P60 saloon.
NICK GEORGANO

c.1968 Simca (i) 1000LS saloon.
NICK BALDWIN

1969 Simca (i) 1200S coupé.
NICK GEORGANO

c.1974 Simca (i) 1100LX hatchback.
NICK BALDWIN

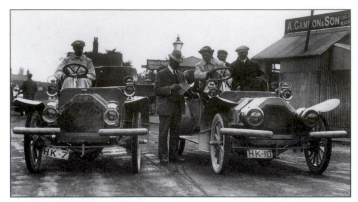

1905 Simms (i) Simms–Welbeck 20/24 tourers.
NICK BALDWIN

1912 Simplex (ii) 50hp runabout.
NATIONAL MOTOR MUSEUM

1913 Simplex (ii) limousine.
JOHN A. CONDE

1915 Simplex (ii) 50hp tourer.
NATIONAL MOTOR MUSEUM

SIMCA (ii) (BR) 1959 – 1969

Simca do Brasil, São Bernardo do Campo, SP.

Simca do Brasil was founded in 1958 as a subsidiary of the French Simca concern. The initial investment was $8 million and in 1959 the Simca Chambord 4-door saloon started production. It was derived from the French model and was powered by the old V8 flat-head engine introduced many years before in France by Ford. In the early 1960s a Simca cost about 20 per cent more than an Aero Willys, also made in Brazil. They were also more temperamental, experiencing frequent mechanical and electrical problems. However, Simca do Brasil continued production, aiming for a share of the luxury car market with the Presidence model introduced in 1960, of which only four a month were to be made. It had a continental spare wheel kit fitted. In 1962 a sporty version was introduced, this being the Rallye and in 1963 came the first Brazilian luxury station wagon, called Jangada. Other models were the Profissional and the Alvorada. The redesigned Esplanada was introduced in 1966. In 1967 Chrysler purchased Simca do Brasil and even though Simca cars continued to be built, the writing was on the wall. Simcas were dropped in 1969 and in 1970, Dodge cars were introduced. 42,910 Simca Chambord, 3992 Rallye, 2705 Jangada, 848 Presidence and 378 Alvorada cars were made.

ACT

SIMMS (i) (GB) 1901–1908

1901–1903 Simms Manufacturing Co. Ltd, Bermondsey, London.
1903–1908 Simms Manufacturing Co. Ltd, Kilburn, London.

This company was founded by Frederick Simms who had made important contributions to the start of the British motor industry (see biography). The first Simms car had a 3½hp single-cylinder engine of own manufacture, single-chain drive and an aluminium body. It was a one off and probably no further manufacture took place at the Bermondsey premises, though engines were supplied to other firms such as Clyde and Eastmead-Biggs. The company which was to make chassis for Simms, Donkin & Clinch, moved away from London and in 1903 Frederick Simms set up new premises at Kilburn in North London, where he was able to make complete cars. These had 2-cylinder engines of 10 and 12hp and 4-cylinder engines of 20/24 or 30/35hp, conventional chassis and shaft drive. The model name for these cars was Welbeck, and they were sometimes known as Simms-Welbecks. The engines were also made for supply to other manufacturers including Crawshaw-Williams, Dennis and General (i).

Some 1905 models were equipped with pneumatic bumpers which did not improve the car's appearance, but enabled them to escape unscathed from quite serious accidents. In 1907 a 30/35hp 6-cylinder car was introduced, but manufacture was suspended the following year so that the company could concentrate on magnetos which became their principal business. They became Simms Motor Units in 1913 and were major suppliers of magnetos in both World Wars, in the second for Bristol aero-engines.

NG

SIMMS (ii) (US) 1920

Simms Motor Corp., Atlanta, Georgia.

The Simms was a light car with a 4-cylinder valve-in-head engine of its own design and a wheelbase of 114in (2893mm). Disc wheels were standard and otherwise the Simms featured various standard components. A touring car was the only model planned and a projected price of $1015 was increased to $1200. Only pilot models were completed before the corporation filed for bankruptcy. The car subsequently surfaced under the direction of Henry L. Innes who had been the Simms production manager and who moved operations to Jacksonville, Florida and continued the car under his own name. (See INNES.)

KM

SIMPLEX (i) (NL) 1899–1919

N.V. Machine-, Rijwiel- en Automobielfabriek Simplex, Amsterdam.

In 1892 the first Simplex bicycle came off the production line with which the firm made a successful start, both in Holland and abroad. In 1898 the time came to join the motoring world. After first thinking about a tricycle the management changed this policy and the first prototype of a 4-wheel car with a single-cylinder Benz engine was seen on the road. Like so many first cars this one looked very much like the Benz. At the automobile show in Amsterdam they displayed a car, a van, and a 3-wheeler, all with Benz engines. After 1900 a 4-cylinder car was developed, and orders even came from the Dutch East Indies to deliver 24 cars with 2-cylinder engines within 2 years.

The 1902 model was available with the Belgian Vivinus engine, and later the German Fafnir engines were used in the production models. Bigger models were on display at the show in 1908, with 2-cylinder 8/10hp engines and 4-cylinder 16/18hp Fafnir engines in a double phaeton. New activities to produce a smaller car started in 1912, with the result that they showed a 2-seater with a 4-cylinder 10hp Fafnir engine of 1093cc. This engine had a Claudel carburettor and Bosch magneto ignition and, as usual with Dutch cars, a round-shaped radiator. During World War I a new assembly plant came into production. In 1915 they exported 32 small cars to the Dutch East Indies, but a year later car production finally stopped. After the war some prototype 3-wheelers, like early Morgans, were made, but they never went into production.

FBV

SIMPLEX (ii) (US) 1907–1917
1907–1913 Simplex Automobile Co. Inc, New York, New York.
1913–1917 New Brunswick, New Jersey.
This company grew out of Smith & Mabley who made the S & M SIMPLEX from 1904 to 1907. In that year Herman Broesel bought S & M and changed the name to Simplex Automobile Co. He acquired a new design which Edward Franquist had been working on, a 50hp T-head 4-cylinder car with square dimensions of 5.75 × 5.75in, giving a capacity of 9778cc. It was mounted in a massive and robust chassis with 4-speed gearbox and double-chain drive. Production from the factory on E. 83rd Street in New York City was limited, about 250 cars being made between 1907 and 1913. They were expensive, prices running from $5500 for a stark roadster which they called the 'speed car', to $6750 for a 7-seater landaulet or limousine. Bodies were made under contract to Simplex by some of the finest coachbuilders on the East Coast, such as Quinby, Healey, Holbrook and Brewster.

In 1911 Franquist brought out the smaller Model 38 with 7.8-litre engine and the choice of chain or shaft drive. Prices were a bit lower at $4850 for a 7-seater tourer. Herman Broiesel died in 1912 and the following year his sons sold the business to the New York firm of Goodrich, Lockhart and Smith, (the Goodrich brothers were sons of tyre maker B.F. Goodrich). Simplex production was moved out to New Jersey, and in 1914 the old 50 gave way to a new long-stroke engine of 9662cc, although a few 50s were assembled from stock for customers who wanted them. It was probably the last chain-driven car to be offered by an American manufacturer.

In the autumn of 1914 Simplex bought the Crane Motor Car Co. of Bayonne, New Jersey, which had been making a very expensive shaft-driven 6-cylinder car costing $8000 for the chassis alone. It was designed by Henry Middlebrook Crane who joined Simplex as a vice-president. His design went into production at New Brunswick at the slightly lower prices of $5000 for a chassis and $6500 for a complete tourer. It was known as the Simplex, Crane Model 5, which was often abbreviated to Crane Simplex. For the rest of the car's history, see CRANE-SIMPLEX.

NG

Further Reading
'The Simplex complex: Edgar Roy's miniatures', Bruce Feldman, *Automobile Quarterly*, Vol. 29, No. 1.
'Hare's today, gone tomorrow: Emlen Hare's failed empire', Tony Muldoon, *Automobile Quarterly*, Vol. 35, No. 3.

SIMPLEX (iii) (F) 1920
Appearances were deceptive with this car. It was an open 5-seater tourer with large bonnet fronted by a bullnose radiator, but under the bonnet there was a horizontal single-cylinder engine of only 735cc. A special balance weight coupled to the connecting rod and to an eccentric was supposed to eliminate the vibration inevitable with most single-cylinder engines. For a car of this limited power it was unusual in having front-wheel brakes.

NG

SIMPLEX PERFECTA (GB) 1900
Randolph Works, Normanton, Derby.
The 4hp Simplex Perfecta voiturette cost only £100, but prospective customers were asked to deposit this sum at the maker's bank before work on their car began.

1920 Simplic cyclecar.
NICK BALDWIN

As it lasted less than a year, one wonders how many customers there actually were, and if any of them lost their deposits.

NG

SIMPLIC (GB) 1914–1923
1914–1915 Wadden & West, Cobham, Surrey.
1920–1923 G.W. Wadden, Weybridge, Surrey.
George Wadden had been in partnership with a Mr Edmunds making the AUTOTRIX 3-wheeler at Weybridge, before setting up another partnership to make a simple 4-wheeled cyclecar powered by a 5/6hp air-cooled JAP engine. Transmission was by epicyclic gear and belt final drive. This was announced in June 1914, so probably few were made. In 1920 he revived the Simplic name and design, though the engine was slightly larger at 8/10hp, and final drive was by chain rather than belt. At £185 it was described as 'Positively the best value in Cycle Cars.'

NG

SIMPLICITY (i) (US) 1906–1911
Evansville Automobile Co., Evansville, Indiana.
This car was made by Willis Copeland who ran the Single Center Buggy Co., and had already offered four makes of car from this address, the Zentmobile, Single Center, Windsor (i) and Worth. The Simplicity had a 35/40hp 4-cylinder engine and friction transmission and double-chain final drive. It was a large and heavy car to have friction transmission, and apparently in wet weather the system completely failed to transmit power. Smaller engines of 20 and 30hp were also used, and it was these that Copeland renamed TRAVELER in 1909. He also enclosed the friction discs. However, the 40hp Simplicity was continued to 1911. Copeland then gave up car manufacture.

NG

SIMPLICITY (ii) (F) 1980
M. Delamour, Penchard.
This was a prototype for a microcar for two passengers. It had angular enclosed bodywork, a 5bhp 50cc engine, measured only 85in (2150mm) long and weighed 308lb (140kg).

CR

SIMPLICITY SIX (US) 1920
Simplicity Motors Corp., Seattle, Washington.
One of the relatively few attempts to build a car on the country's West Coast, this attempt to market a high-priced luxury car failed before production began. The Simplicity Six was fitted with a Beaver engine and coachwork mounted on a wheelbase of 134in (3401mm). Several pilot models were completed and used for promotion of the ill-fated make.

KM

SIMPLO (US) 1908–1909
Cook Motor Vehicle Co., St Louis, Missouri.
The Simplo used a 14/16hp 2-cylinder engine which was offered in either air-or water-cooled form, and the buyer could have solid or pneumatic tyres. All models

1900 Simpson (i) steam car.
NATIONAL MOTOR MUSEUM

1924 Simson Supra 2-litre tourer.
NATIONAL MOTOR MUSEUM

1984 Sinclair (ii) C5 3-wheeler.
NATIONAL MOTOR MUSEUM

had friction transmission and double-chain drive. The 1909 Model S had a slightly larger engine of 16/18hp, and a 4-seater surrey body with doors. The makers had been carriage builders before making the Simplo, and afterwards became car dealers.

NG

SIMPSON (i) (GB) 1897–1904

John Simpson, Stirling.
John Simpson was an inventive engineer who made about 20 steam cars of varying design, mainly for his own interest and use, though he sold some of

them. An early model had a 6hp 4-cylinder single-acting engine and double suspension – the chassis was sprung on the axles in the usual way, and the body was sprung on the chassis, as in the first RATIONAL (i) car. Later examples of Simpson's work had engines of 6, 10 and 12hp, flash boilers and automatic regulators for fuel and water.

NG

SIMPSON (ii) (US) 1998 to date

Simpson Design and Development, Langley, Washington.
Formerly BLUE RAY, this kit car company relocated to Washington state in 1998. The first project for the new company was a Mazda Miata rebody kit. It had a low, sloped nose with plexiglass covered headlights and a short tail with a spoiler. The lines resembled a shortened Ferrari 275 GTB/4 NART Spyder. The interior was upgraded with leather and wood, and these kits were sold in kit or assembled form.

HP

SIMS (I) 1908–1909

Stà Italiana Merz e Stinchi, Turin.
The 1767cc 10/12hp Sims had its four cylinders cast en-bloc, which was pretty advanced for its date, but the valves were arranged in the old-fashioned T-head layout. It had low-tension magneto and chain final drive. Only one model was offered.

NG

SIMSON; SIMSON-SUPRA (D) 1911–1934

Simson & Co., Suhl.
Simson was an armaments factory dating back to 1856 in the hands of the Simson family, though it was originally founded in 1741. In 1911 they began small-scale manufacture of cars, with two models, a 6/18 and a 10/30PS. They returned to full-time arms making during the war, and also made some trucks, but in 1919 revived their prewar car designs. The first new postwar designs came in 1920; still on conventional lines with inlet-over-exhaust valve engines, they were a 1570cc 6/32PS (Typ Bo), 2612cc 10/40PS (Typ Co) and 3538cc 14/45PS (Typ D). A more interesting model appeared in the summer of 1924-called the Simson-Supra Typ S, it had a 1950cc 4-cylinder engine with twin ohcs driven by a vertical shaft, and four valves per cylinder. It developed 50bhp at 4000 rpm (60 to 80bhp in sports models), compared with 40bhp at 1900rpm from the larger Typ Co engine. It was designed by Paul Henze who had worked for Cudell, Imperia and, during and immediately after the war, for Steiger. The Typ S's performance (75–90mph; 120–145km/h) gave it a number of sporting successes especially in hill climbs and long-distance trials. However, it was very expensive and only about 30 were made.

Alongside the S was the less powerful So which had the same size engine with a single-ohc. This was made in touring and saloon models, and about 750 were delivered between 1925 and 1929. Simson started a range of pushrod ohv 6-cylinder cars in 1926, the 3106cc Typ J, 3130cc Typ R and 3358cc Typ RJ, the latter being made up to the end of car production in 1934. Only 12 cars were completed in 1934. They were joined in 1931 by a side-valve straight-8, the 4673cc Typ A, of which not more than 20 were made. All models from 1924 onwards were called Simson-Supra. The company concentrated on armaments from 1934, and were nationalised in 1935. After the war they built motorcycles, and in the 1990s the HOTZENBLITZ electric car was made in the same factory.

HON

SINCLAIR (i) (GB) 1899–1902

E.H. Clift & Co., London.
The first of Clifts's cars was an electric called the Clift victoria, but petrol-engined cars were called Sinclair, after the road in Kensington (near Olympia) where they were made. They had 5 or 7hp rear-mounted horizontal engines, and there was also a 10hp with front-mounted vertical engine. All used shaft-drive.

HON

SINCLAIR (ii) (GB) 1984–1985

1984–1985 Sinclair Vehicles Ltd, Coventry, Warwickshire.
1985 T.P.D. Ltd, Coventry, Warwickshire.
1985 Sinclair Vehicles (Sales) Ltd, Coventry, Warwickshire.

Often regarded as one of the great flops of motoring history, the Sinclair C5 was, however, a brave attempt to produce ecological transport. Conceived by the computer magnate Sir Clive Sinclair, it was designed with help from Lotus and was built at a Hoover plant in Wales. The C5 was a 3-wheeler featuring a steel chassis and a polypropylene body – a world first – that the driver simply sat on top of, steering the car by handles placed underneath the seat. The electric power source was a modified Hoover washing machine motor and the transmission was by a reduction gearbox with toothed belt drive to the rear axle, which could be supplemented by human-powered pedals and chain. The brakes were cable-operated on the front and on one of the rear wheels, which were made of nylon composite. A top speed of 15mph (24km/h) was quoted with a range of 20 miles using a single 12V battery (a second battery was optional). Production hopes had been as high as 100,000 per annum but slow sales (possibly tempered by scare stories about safety) proved this to be wildly optimistic: when the receiver was called in in October 1985, only 9000 vehicles had been made. The demise of the C5 scuppered plans for intended larger 3-wheelers, the C.10 and C.15. Following the company's failure, Sinclair was bought by Amstrad but Sir Clive Sinclair continued researching the possibility of electrically-powered transport.

CR

SINGER (i) (GB) 1905–1970

1905–1927 Singer & Co., Coventry.
1927–1936 Singer & Co., Birmingham.
1936–1956 Singer Motors Ltd, Coventry.
1956–1970 Singer Motors Ltd, Ryton-on-Dunsmore, Warwickshire.

Like HUMBER, ROVER, SWIFT and others, the Singer company had its origins in the Coventry cycle industry. George Singer (1847–1908) worked with Coventry Machinists before starting his own firm in 1875, making bicycles and tricycles. In 1900 Singer acquired the rights to manufacture the Perks Motor Wheel, a self-contained powered wheel which could be fitted in place of the front or rear wheel of a bicycle or tricycle. These gave way to more conventional tricars which were made up to 1907, becoming more car like, with water-cooling and wheel steering.

The first 4-wheeled Singer car appeared for 1905; designed by Alexander Craig, it was a 2-cylinder version of the 15hp 3-cylinder car he had designed for Lea Francis. Two sizes were offered, a 1853cc 8hp and a 2471cc 12hp. The engine incorporated very long 32in (812mm) connecting rods, heavy flywheels at each end of the crankshaft, and chain drive. Lea Francis only sold two, and Singer were not much more successful. In 1906 an unspecified number of the Craig-designed cars were scrapped. Also in 1906 more conventional Singers appeared, with 10/15hp 4-cylinder Aster T-head engines. The following year the range had been extended to five models, an 8-10hp twin, 10hp 3-cylinder and 12/14hp 4-cylinder with White & Poppe engines, and larger fours of 15 and 20–22hp whose engines were made by Aster. Soon afterwards White & Poppe engines were standardised, a 16hp in 1909 and 15 and 20hp L-head engines in 1911. Singer was White & Poppe's best customer until William Morris began to place large orders from 1913 onwards. The largest White & Poppe-engined Singer was the 4710cc 20/25hp of 1910.

In 1912 Singer entered the light car market with their 1096cc Ten. This 4-cylinder L-head engine with pair-cast cylinders was Singer made, and drove through a 3-speed gearbox mounted on the rear axle. Though its weight qualified it as a cyclecar, it was a refined large car in miniature, and became Singer's first best selling product. Although larger models of 14, 15, 20 and 25hp were made up to the outbreak of World War I, the Ten was the mainstay of production. Manufacture continued at least up to 1916 as it was used by the armed forces, the 1915 models having rounded radiators and electric lighting. Of the larger Singers, the 2384cc 14hp had a Singer-made monobloc engine, while the 2610cc 15hp and 3307cc 20hp were still White & Poppe powered. Few of these were made.

Singer in the 1920s

The Ten was the only model to be made in the immediate postwar years, and sales reached 50–60 per week by 1920, when a 59mph (95km/h) sports model was made as well as the 2-seater tourer. The gearbox was moved forward to the conventional position in 1922, and for 1923 the car was redesigned, with an ohv engine in unit with the gearbox. In 1920 Singer bought the motorcycle and light car maker Coventry Premier, and for 1923 they offered a cheaper version of the Ten under the Coventry Premier name.

1910 Singer (i) 16/20hp tourer.
NICK BALDWIN

1914 Singer (i) Ten 2-seater.
NICK BALDWIN

1927 Singer (i) Junior tourer.
NATIONAL MOTOR MUSEUM

1932 Singer (i) Junior Special saloon.
NICK GEORGANO

1936 Singer (i) Bantam 2-seater.
NICK GEORGANO

1935 Singer (i) Nine Le Mans 4-seater.
NICK GEORGANO

1938 Singer (i) Super Nine saloon.
NICK BALDWIN

A larger model for 1922 was the 15hp 6-cylinder, Singer's first six if one discounts a prototype of 1906 which never went into production. It had a 1990cc L-head engine and sold for £695 compared with £395 for the Ten. It was made up to 1925 after which it was replaced by a smaller six of 1776cc. 6-cylinder cars in various sizes, mostly under 2 litres, would be part of the Singer range up to 1937. The Six acquired 4-wheel brakes in 1924 and the Ten followed suit in 1926.

September 1926 saw the arrival of one of Singer's most important and successful models, the 848cc Junior. It had a single-ohc engine, being the smallest British car so equipped, and was the ancestor of a long line of ohc engines which only came to an end after the Rootes Group takeover brought pushrod Hillman Minx engines into Singers. At £148 the Junior was excellent value, and by 1929 Singer were making 100 cars a day, mostly Juniors. This put them in third place amongst British manufacturers, behind Morris and Austin. The Junior acquired 4-wheel brakes in 1928, and was made with a variety of body styles including tourer, saloon, fabric coupé and sports 2-seater with pointed tail. Curiously only one model was fabric bodied, at a time when the material was at its most popular, yet a few years earlier Singer had used fabric extensively. Up to the 1930 season the Juniors wore disc wheels like their larger sisters, but in that year all Singers went over to wire wheels, which improved their appearance considerably. Another change for 1930 was the replacement of magneto ignition by coil. The Junior acquired a 4-speed gearbox in 1931, and in 1932, its last year, a new frame and smaller wheels. During 1932 a 972cc engine was put into this frame to make the Nine, and the Junior name was dropped. Production was about 25,000. Singer acquired two factories in the 1920s, the Coventry works of Calcott in 1926, and a Daimler/BSA plant in Birmingham in 1927. They retained this until 1936. They also bought Aster's Wembley factory to serve as their London service depot.

The introduction of the Junior caused the Ten to be re-named the Senior. Capacity had already gone up to 1308cc in the 1925 10-26hp, and for 1928 it was increased further to 1570cc. The Senior was dropped for 1930, but for 1931 the name was revived for a 1261cc four which was made up to 1932. The Singer range became very complex in the 1930s, with six basic models being listed for 1931, two with side-valve engines, two with pushrod ohv and two with chain-driven ohc. At the top of the range were two sixes, the side-valve 1792cc Six and

The AIRSTREAM **SINGER** ELEVEN

THE CAR OF TOMORROW—TODAY

1953 Singer (i) 4AD1500 roadster.
NICK BALDWIN

1954 Singer (i) SM1500 saloon.
NICK BALDWIN

1964 Singer (i) Chamois saloon.
NICK BALDWIN

The most successful models were the Nines and their successors, the Bantams. Synchromesh and freewheels came in 1934 with a more streamlined body and ifs in 1935. The Nine was replaced by the Bantam in 1936; this had the same 972cc ohc engine and a new body very similar to that of the rival Morris Eight, and made in the same styles of 2- and 4-door saloons, and 2-/4-seater tourers. A 3-speed synchromesh gearbox was featured, and 1938–40 models had larger engines of 1074cc and Easy clean wheels. 1939 saw the Bantam roadster with cutaway doors and 4-seater bodywork, which was revived after World War II, and with larger engines survived until 1955. Next up in size was the Eleven, which had a 1384cc ohc engine, enlarged to 1459cc for 1936, coil ifs and hydraulic brakes. Captain D.F.H. Fitzmaurice designed a striking streamlined saloon body for the Eleven which resembled a Chrysler Airflow, and was called the Airstream. A batch of 750 were laid down, but customers did not like its radical appearance; not more than 300 Airstreams were completed, the rest being bodied conventionally. Much publicity was gained when band leader Jack Payne bought 15 Airstreams to carry his band around the country. For 1937 the Eleven became the Twelve, with engine enlarged to 1525cc, while the ifs was replaced by semi-elliptic springs. The Singer range became much simpler in the last two years of peace, there being only three models, the Bantam, a new 1185cc Ten and the Twelve. The Ten was made only as a 4-door saloon, the Twelve as a saloon or drophead coupé.

The Sporting Singers

For much of its history Singer showed little interest in sport, though some cars ran at Brooklands before and just after World War I, and two 3-litre cars ran in the 1912 Coupe de l'Auto without success. The sports model of the Junior was pretty but not a performer, and the first serious sports Singer was the 4-seater Nine of 1933. This had the ohc engine and hydraulic brakes of the touring Nines, combined with a lowered frame and remote control gearbox and friction shock absorbers. It did well in trials, and was joined by the Le Mans Speed Special with engine tuned to give 42bhp and a slab-tank 2-seater body. The sports Nine was made as a coupé or tourer, good for 65mph (105km/h), while the Le Mans would do 75mph (120km/h). Encouraged by reliable performances in the 1934 Le Mans race, Singer prepared a team of lightweight 2-seaters for 1935. With a top speed of 90mph (145km/h) they won the Light Car Club Relay race at Brooklands and finished at Le Mans, but disaster struck in the TT when all three cars suffered steering arm failures, two of the cars crashing at the same spot, piling on top of each other. Singer promptly closed their competition department, although private owners continued to campaign the cars up to the war, collecting a number of prizes in rallies. The 1935 TT cars finished 4th and 8th in the 1937 TT, and at Le Mans in 1938 the best placed British car was the Savoye brothers' Singer in 8th place.

The Nine Le Mans was made from 1933 to 1937, and in 1934 was joined by the 1½-litre Le Mans, similar in appearance but powered by a 1493cc ohc 6-cylinder engine. It featured triple carburettors and a close ratio gearbox; all but the earliest cars had Scintilla magneto ignition in place of coil. Top speed was 84mph (135km/h), and at £375 the 6-cylinder Le Mans was good value. Singers were concentrating on more mundane machinery, though, and only 71 were made. The last sports Singer was a 1½-litre four of 1937 which never went into production. Its engine did, however, power the 1½-litre H.R.G.

Postwar Cars and the Rootes Take-over

The 1946 Singer range was a carry over from the 1939 models, though the Bantam saloon was not revived. The only car to use the 1074cc engine was the Nine roadster which was made up to 1952. It received a 4-speed gearbox on the 4A (1949–50), coil ifs, hydromechanical brakes and disc wheels on the 4AB (1951–52). The final development of the roadster was the SM (1951–55) which was a 4AB powered by the short stroke 1497cc engine of the SM1500 saloon. Singer attempted to modernise the roadster with the SMX of 1953. This was an SM with slab-sided fibreglass body and slightly smaller wheels. They experienced problems with the quality of the fibreglass panels, and the project was dropped after only four SMXs had been made. A total of 10,334 roadsters were made in the postwar years, and although not exciting performers they are today the most collectible of any postwar Singers.

Two prewar saloons were revived alongside the roadster, the Ten and Super Twelve, the latter with more chrome, hydraulic brakes and a projecting luggage boot. It took a long time to get into production, and fewer were made, 1098 compared with 10,497 Tens. For 1948 Singer brought out a brand new saloon, the SM1500 with slab sided styling reminiscent of the American Frazer and

the ohv 1920cc Super Six. A year later they had become the 2050cc Eighteen-Six and the 2160cc Silent Six. The latter was made as a standard saloon, coupé and Kaye Don saloon. The latter was styled by C.F. Beauvais who also worked for the Avon Body Co.; dual colour schemes, slightly skirted wings and a new grill gave the Kaye Don models quite a distinctive appearance. The same styling was available on the Nine saloon. There was also an undistinguished 1476cc side-valve Twelve Six made in 1932 only, and between 1933 and 1937 there were three different sizes of ohc six, 1493, 1611 and 1991cc, powering both touring and sports models. There is no doubt that this complexity and lack of direction harmed Singer, for short runs of different models were unlikely to generate profits, and they lost their high place in the sales league, falling far behind Austin and Morris, and being overtaken by Ford, Standard, Hillman and Vauxhall by 1939.

1959 Singer (i) Gazelle convertible.
NICK BALDWIN

Kaiser, and a short-stroke version of the ohc engine, which gave 48bhp compared with 43 from the Super Twelve, even though it was marginally smaller at 1506cc. The body, made by Pressed Steel at Oxford, was separate from the chassis, which incorporated coil-and-wishbone ifs made under licence from General Motors. The SM1500 was aimed directly at the export market, with more going to Australia than anywhere else. In 1953 some pick-ups were made in Australia on the SM1500 chassis. Another Australian Singer was a family tourer by Flood on the Super Ten and SM4AD chassis. The SM1500 did not reach the home market until May 1951, capacity being reduced to 1497cc. They sold well at first, with 6358 finding buyers in the eight months of 1951. However, it was expensive compared with rivals such as the Standard Vanguard and Vauxhall Velox, and two years later sales were down to 2000. They did achieve some bulk sales, to police forces and taxi companies, and total production of SM1500s was 17,382. They were mildly updated for 1953, with a larger rear window and 2-tone paintwork, and for 1954 the SM1500 gave way to the Hunter. This was the same car with a traditional vertical radiator grill and a fibreglass bonnet top. It was more lavishly equipped and more expensive (£125 more than Ford Zodiac), though Singer tried to broaden its appeal by offering a cheaper version as well without the walnut dash, leather seats, screenwash and foglamps. However, Hunter sales only reached 4772, and a proposed twin-cam version never went into production.

Singer was the sort of medium-sized company that could not survive the harshly competitive postwar climate, and the name was only kept going because the Rootes Group took over in 1955. A few Hunters were sold off under the new regime, and the first Rootes Singer was the Gazelle, a more luxuriously equipped Hillman Minx with a different radiator grill and, for a while, the Singer ohc engine. This lasted through the Mks I and 1II of 1955–58, with 5926 cars made, but the Mk IIA and III Gazelles had the Minx's 1494cc pushrod ohv engine, and the Singer identity was confined to the radiator grill. The Gazelle was made up to 1967, by which time it had become the Mk VI, following Minx development with a larger engine of 1592cc in 1961, front disc brakes in 1963 and a further engine enlargement to 1725cc in 1965. There then followed the New Gazelle, simply the Hillman Hunter-based New Minx with 1496 or 1725cc engines. Production figures are not known for the New Gazelle, but the earlier models with Minx engines totalled 80,142. This was far more than any genuine Singer model.

Two other Hillman designs carried Singer badges; the Vogue (Super Minx) and the Chamois (Imp). The Vogue was made as a saloon and estate car from 1962 to 1966, and then as the New Vogue (Hunter) to 1970, with an increase in engine size from 1592 to 1725cc in 1965. As with the Gazelles, interior trim was way above the Hillman class, and prices were not drastically higher (£845 cf £769 in 1965). The Chamois was similarly better equipped than the Imp, with walnut veneer, chrome trim down the body side and a frontal radiator grill. The fastest model was the Chamois Sport with 55bhp from the 875cc engine instead of the standard 39bhp. Some Chamois Sports took part in saloon car racing. There was also the Chamois coupé, alias Imp Californian, which like the Hillman had the standard engine. At 49,820, Chamois production was little more than 10 per cent of the Imp's.

With the Chrysler take-over of Rootes in 1970 the Singer name was dropped. The Birmingham factory had been closed for manufacture in 1956, and became a parts warehouse for the Rootes Group, while production was gradually moved from the two Coventry factories to Rootes' headquarters at Ryton-on-Dunsmore. This process was completed by May 1963. The last British-built Singer Vogue came off the line in March 1970, though they were assembled for a while in New Zealand from the remaining stock of parts.

NG

Further Reading
The Singer Story, Kevin Atkinson, Veloce, 1996.

SINGER (ii) (US) 1914–1920

1914–1919 Singer Motor Co. Inc., New York, New York and Long Island City, New York.
1919–1920 Mount Vernon New York.

The Singer was a successor to the PALMER-SINGER which had been built at Long Island City since 1908. A quality automobile, Singers used a 6-cylinder Herschell-Spellman engine developing 50bhp throughout their seven year existence, featured a wheelbase of 138in (3502mm) and a complete compliment of open and closed coach work initially priced from $3800 to $5350 until 1920 when prices were increased from $5250 to $7300.

The Singer standard line was augmented in 1920 by a more powerful series with a Weidely V12 engine developing 90bhp at 3000rpm priced from $6500 to $8800 plus custom offerings on order from $9000 up. All Singers were

1907 Sinpar (i) 8hp voiturette.
NICK GEORGANO

1914 Sirron 10/12hp 2-seater.
NICK BALDWIN

1973 Siva (ii) Llama 875cc.
NICK BALDWIN

distinguished by sharply pointed radiators. Historian Beverly Rae Kimes has noted that all Singer V12s went to Singer's dealer in Portland, Oregon and also that although the Singer remained among active listings in automotive trade publications, cars marketed in 1921 were remaining unsold 1920 models. An estimated 500 to 550 cars are believed to have been the Singer total output.

KM

SINGLE CENTER (US) 1906–1908

Single Center Buggy Co., Evansville, Indiana.

This was a product of Willis Copeland, who also made cars for Schuyler Zent (ZENTMOBILE) and J.A.Windsor (WINDSOR (i)), as well as the SIMPLICITY. He had made horse-drawn buggies for some time, and apparently made a few motorised versions which had no name, before he began to make them under the name Single Center. They had 2-cylinder engines of 12 or 15/17hp, chain drive and solid tyres.

NG

SINPAR (i) (F) 1907–1914

Automobiles Sinpar, Courbevoie, Seine.

The first cars made by this company had single-cylinder engines, a 4½hp De Dion-Bouton or 8hp Anzani, with dashboard radiators and shaft drive. In 1912 the Sinpar had an 8hp 4-cylinder monobloc engine. It was in fact identical to the 8hp DEMEESTER, though sold under the Sinpar name. In 1968 the same company revived the name for a Renault 4-based Jeep-type vehicle described under SINPAR (ii).

NG

SINPAR (ii) (F) 1968

Appareils Sinpar, Colombes.

Sinpar was synonymous with 4-wheel drive versions of Renaults, and its conversions even obtained factory approval. Above and beyond its most popular 4×4 conversion of the Renault 4, Sinpar offered its own bodywork conversions, usually open-air versions of the Renault 4 (it made the Plein Air for Renault). The 1968 Torpedo S was a completely new jeep-style car with a body created by Brissonneau & Lotz that did not enter production in France, but was however taken up the Renault concessionaire in the Philippines.

CR

SINTERA (GB) 1995

This was a prototype of a compact Ford-based coupé that appeared at the 1995 Newark Kit Car Show but was not seen again, probably due to its appalling quality and design.

CR

SINTZ (US) 1902–1904

Claude Sintz Inc, Grand Rapids, Michigan.

Though the Sintz name was famous for engines, only six cars were made. They were built by Claude Sintz, son of engine maker Clark who had built an experimental car in 1897, and who supplied engines to Reeves. In 1902 two separate companies were formed, Claude Sintz Inc for the manufacture of cars, and the Sintz Gas Engine Co. for engines for marine and industrial use, as well as for cars. Claude made only six cars powered by a 16hp 2-cylinder 2-stroke engines before both companies went bankrupt in 1904.

NG

S.I.O.P. see MARATHON

SIPANI (IND) 1975–1997

1975–1978 Sunrise Auto Industries Ltd, Bangalore.
1978–1997 Sipani Automobiles, Bangalore.

In economy-minded India, the Sunrise Badal was the most basic form of enclosed transport on offer. It was a curious 3-wheeled vehicle with an oddly-shaped fibreglass body whose most unusual feature was that it had two doors on the nearside but only one on the offside, which was described as 'futuristic'. Despite its size (over 120in (3046mm) long), it weighed only 882lbs (400kg). This meant the rear-mounted 198cc single-cylinder 10bhp engine could power it to a top speed of 47mph (75kh/h). There was room for four passengers, making it popular as a taxi. In 1981, the Badal gained an extra wheel at the front, but this could not hide the fact that it was basically a very crude and poorly-finished car and the model was withdrawn the same year in favour of licensed production of the British Reliant Kitten 4-wheeler. This was known as the Sipani Dolphin and was virtually identical in all respects to the Kitten. However, in addition to the 850cc Reliant engine, there was the option of a 1.5-litre diesel as used in the Hindustan Ambassador. A redesigned version called the Montana was later made in both 2- and 4-door forms. Sipani then turned to the D1, a modified Daihatsu Charade, and licensed production of the Austin Montego, which ultimately foundered.

CR

c.1913 Sizaire-Berwick 20hp tourer (left) with Sizaire-Naudin.
NICK BALDWIN

SIRRON (GB) 1909–1916

Cresswell, Norris & Co. Ltd, South Kensington, London.
Sirron Cars Ltd, Fulham, London; Southall, Middlesex.
This car derived its name from that of H.G. Norris, one of the promoters, spelt backwards. It was a conventional, medium-sized car with tourer or roadster bodies, powered by French-built proprietary engines of 2212cc (12/16hp) and 2553cc (16/20hp). Bother were rated at 15.9hp as they had the same cylinder bore of 80mm. There was also a smaller 1356cc 10/12hp whose engine was made by Alpha of Coventry. The first Sirrons were made in the unlikely location of Cornwall Gardens Mews, in the heart of residential South Kensington, though the firm soon moved to Fulham, and then further west to Southall.

NG

SIR VIVAL (US) 1959

Hollow Boring Corp., Worcester, Massachusetts.
Walter C. Jerome designed a number of safety devices for cars in the 1950s, and in 1959 built a complete car, which he described as 'The Car of the Future Here Today'. Taking a 1948 Hudson sedan, he cut it ahead of the passenger compartment, and constructed a raised driving tower with cylindrical rotating windscreen which rotated past a stationary blade to remove rain or dirt. Inside were a padded interior, passenger headrests and seatbelts, while on the exterior were side marker lights, all years before such items were required by US Federal regulations. A wrap-around rubber bumper, similar to those on amusement park 'bumper cars', cushioned any impact with moving or stationary objects. The power unit, a side-valve six from a later Hudson Hornet, sat in an articulated nose section, the idea being that the car would bend in a head-on crash, protecting the occupants. Drive was to the rear wheels, through a Hydra-Matic gearbox and several universal joints.

Jerome completed his car in 1959, and announced that his Hollow Boring Corp. would put it into production to sell for $10,000. Despite widespread appearances at car shows and at the 1964 New York World's Fair, no orders came in. The solitary car was put into storage at the Hollow Boring factory. After Jerome's death it was acquired by a Massachusetts collector, and presently awaits restoration.

KF

SIVA (i) (I) 1967–1970

Siva srl, Lecce.
The Italian Siva operation had no connection with its British namesake, but produced an interesting and ambitious targa-topped sports car. The Siva Sirio used a mid-mounted Ford of Germany 2-litre V6 engine, in 90bhp standard or 130bhp Conrero-tuned versions. All-round independent suspension and disc brakes were employed. The targa-roof 2-seater bodywork was realised by Stile Italia and featured cowled headlamps and Lamborghini Miura-style front air intakes.

CR

SIVA (ii) (GB) 1969–1976

1969–1974 Neville Trickett Design Ltd, Bryanston, Blandford, Dorset.
1970–1976 Siva Motor Car Co Ltd, Aylesbury, Buckinghamshire.
Neville Trickett designed and made plastic-bodied Edwardian pastiches on humble contemporary chassis. The first was the 1969 Roadster, a 2-seater based on a Ford Popular/Anglia chassis, complete with side-valve engine. Shortly after came the Tourer with an extra row of seats. Next were Raceabout and San Remo, both on VW Beetle chassis (2- and 4-seaters respectively), and the Parisienne on a Citroën 2CV chassis. 126 Edwardians were made in all. Siva branched out in 1970 with the Mule, an attempt to update the Mini Moke concept with a modern fibreglass body. In 1972, the design was modified for a rear-mounted Hillman Imp engine, the resultant machine being called Llama. Another Mini-based car was a front-engined beach buggy.

More serious intentions were courted with the Spyder of 1971. It had a VW Beetle chassis clothed in an exotic open body, quickly changed to become the S160 with gullwing doors. Its successor was the Saluki, introduced in 1973, offering even more exotic coupé styling on a Beetle floorpan. This project was later modified by EMBEESEA. Even more ambitious was the S530, also built in 1971. Aston Martin supplied the 5340cc fuel-injected V8 engine for this gullwing-doored coupé and even contemplated manufacturing it. Trickett tried productionising it with a Chevrolet V8 engine but Siva's other product lines took precedence. Siva also produced some more obscure models such as the Jeep-type utility Sierra using Ford Escort parts, and a Citroën Méhari replica.

CR

SIX see BARRON VIALE

SIXCYL see BREGUET

SIZAIRE-BERWICK (F/GB) 1913–1927

1913–1927 Sté Nouvelle des Autos Sizaire, Courbevoie, Seine.
1920–1925 F.W. Berwick & Co. Ltd, Park Royal, London.
London car dealer Frederick William Berwick was keen to get into manufacture when he was put in touch with the brothers Georges and Maurice Sizaire, who had been forced out of the company they had founded, Sizaire-Naudin. The go-between was the well-known Paris-based British journalist W.F. Bradley.

1913 Sizaire-Berwick 20hp limousine by Labourdette.
NICK BALDWIN

1920 Sizaire-Berwick 25/50hp tourer.
NICK BALDWIN

1927 Sizaire Fréres Six saloon.
NICK BALDWIN

A factory was found at Courbevoie, where production would be supervised by Georges Sizaire, while design was by Maurice. It was a conventional car with 4070cc 4-cylinder side-valve engine, a 4-speed gearbox and a Rolls-Royce shaped radiator. It is said that Berwick wanted to give the impression of a Rolls at less than half the price, £475 for a chassis against £985 for a Silver Ghost. The first few cars had 3014cc Decolange engines, which proved rather noisy, but it is possible that the larger 'Sizaire' units were made for them by Decolange. The factory was very small and most components were bought in. The Paris Salon and London Show car was bodied by Labourdette, but once production got underway, four-fifths of the chassis were exported to England, where they received bodies made at Berwick's factory at Highgate, in north London. A few were bodied by other firms such as Mulliner. Berwick's financial backer was Alexander Keiller of marmalade fame, while one of the test drivers who delivered chassis from Courbevoie to London was Jack Waters, later Jack Warner of *Dixon of Dock Green*.

By the outbreak of war in August 1914 139 Sizaire-Berwicks had been made, and they had acquired a good reputation, being said to be as smooth and silent as a 6-cylinder car. The few chassis which had not been bodied in London were fitted with armoured car bodies for the Royal Naval Air Service. In 1915 Berwick built a large factory at Park Royal, north west London, which became the home of the cars after the war. During the conflict it was used for the manufacture of De Havilland aircraft, and employed 5800 people.

In 1919 the British and French companies were separated; Berwick made an enlarged version of the prewar car at Park Royal, while the French operation was taken over by an American called Burke. He imported British-built cars for a while, then, when these were no longer available, turned to independent designs including one with an ohv version of the British car, and another with a straight-8 Lycoming engine. The postwar London-built car was known as the 25/50 and had a 4534cc engine in a much heavier chassis. This was the work of a former steamroller engineer called Greig, who was a relation of Alexander Keiller. The Rolls-Royce radiator had been replaced by one with a slight vee. Derby had not been able to object when the S-B chassis had been French-built, but now that it was British, pressure was brought on Berwick. However, when he set up a new company to make the Windsor car, its radiator was distinctly Rolls-Royce-shaped.

By the end of 1922 all the original partners had left Sizaire-Berwick. Maurice and Georges Sizaire made the Sizaire Frères car from 1923, and Berwick was involved with the Windsor. Two Austin directors joined the S-B board, and this resulted in some curious hybrids. The Sizaire-Berwick 13/26 was an Austin Twelve chassis with Park Royal-built body and Sizaire radiator, while the Austin Twenty with the same treatment was the 23/46. There was also a mysterious 3191cc six called the 26/52 which corresponded with no Austin model. Listed only in 1923, it may have used the engine from a still-born Austin Six. Few of the Austin-based cars were made, and the bulk of the 250 Sizaire-Berwicks made between 1920 and 1925 were 25/50s.

NG

Further Reading
'A History of the Sizaire-Berwick, 1913–1925', G.R.G. Berwick,
Motor Sport, July 1957.
'Sizaire-Berwick', Richard Mawer, *The Automobile*, July 1995.
'L'Histoire Phénoménale, Sizaire-Berwick, Sizaire Frères', Achille Devereux,
Automobile Quarterly, Vol. 18, No. 2.

SIZAIRE FRÈRES (F) 1923–1929

1923–1927 Automobiles Sizaire Frères, Courbevoie, Seine.
1927–1928 Sté Nouvelle des Autos Sizaire, Levallois-Perret, Seine.
1928–1929 SA de Gérance des Automobiles Sizaire, Levallois-Perret, Seine.
Georges and Maurice Sizaire registered a company called Sizaire Frères in 1920, while they were still working for F.W. Berwick, but they did not produce a car until 1923. When they did, it was an advanced design, with all-independent suspension by transverse leaves at front and rear. The engine was a 1993cc single-ohc unit with aluminium crankcase. In honour of the suspension, Maurice Sizaire called the car the 4RI (Quatre Roues Indépendentes). As before Maurice was the designer and Georges the production engineer who tried to keep prices at a fairly reasonable level. Financial support, without which they could not have run the business at all, was provided by Paul Dupuy, publisher of the popular magazines, *Le Petit Parisien* and *Le Miroir des Sports*.

The 4RI did not get into production until the autumn of 1924, and lasted until 1927, when about 900 had been made. Only bare chassis were sold, and the cost of having a body built (Letourneur et Marchand was a popular choice of coachbuilder) made the complete car more expensive than a Ballot 2LTS or Delage DIS. They were not particularly fast, but came into their own on rough ground. One came through the punishing 3725 mile Leningrad-Tiflis-Moscow Trial in 1925 without a single involuntary stop. They also did well in the Monte Carlo Rally between 1926 and 1930.

Paul Dupuy died in 1927 and the company was reorganised under new ownership with a new factory at Levallois. Though a 3-litre six, developed from the four, was tried in one prototype the new owners preferred proprietary engines, which usually cost less than an in-house unit. The new Sizaire Six for 1928 had a 2910cc Willys-Knight sleeve-valve engine in the same independently sprung chassis. About 150 of these were made, but in July 1928 ownership changed again, coming under control of the Garage Saint-Didier, which had been the

1907 Sizaire-Naudin roadster.
NICK BALDWIN

main agent for Sizaire cars. They chose another engine, the 2413cc Hotchkiss AM2 and made about 100 cars. Production at Courbevoie ended in 1929, but the design had further leases of life in Belgium as the BELGA RISE and in Poland as the RALF STETYZ.

Georges Sizaire died in 1934 but Maurice worked for the Tecalemit oil filter company until he retired at the age of 83. He then devoted the rest of his life to painting, dying in 1970 at the age of 92.

NG

Further Reading
'L'Histoire Phénoménale, Sizaire-Berwick, Sizaire Frères', Achille Devereux, *Automobile Quarterly*, Vol. 18, No. 2.

SIZAIRE-NAUDIN (F) 1905–1921

1905–1920 SA des Automobiles Sizaire et Naudin, Paris.
1920–1921 Sté des Nouveaux Établissements Sizaire et Naudin, Paris.
At the turn of the century two young men just out of their teens set up a small workshop in the Paris suburb of Puteaux. They were the brothers Maurice (1877–1970) and Georges (1880–1934) Sizaire, soon to be joined by Louis Naudin (1876–1913). Georges Sizaire and Louis Naudin had both worked for De Dion-Bouton. The nature of their business is not known, possibly furniture making, but there was no question of a car before 1902. Then they built a voiturette powered by a single-cylinder De Dion-Bouton engine, with tubular frame and belt drive. Where it differed from its contemporaries was the front suspension which was by a transverse leaf spring and sliding pillars. This featured on all Sizaire-Naudin cars up to 1912.

The company of Sizaire Frères et Naudin was registered on 1 June 1903, but no cars were built for sale until 1905. They were similar to the prototype, but had an unusual gearchange. This consisted of three spur cut pinions at the end of the driveshaft, each of a different diameter. The shaft could be moved both laterally and fore-and-aft, allowing the engagement of any of the pinions with the large diameter ring gear on the crown wheel.

1912 Sizaire-Naudin 12hp 2-seater.
NICK BALDWIN

The Sizaire-Naudin was shown to the public at the 1905 Paris Salon, and attracted more orders than the little workshop could cope with. However, they received financial backing from bicycle importers Hammond et Monnier, who paid for their move to a larger factory. Within a few months the voiturettes were being built at the rate of one per day, but once Hammond et Monnier had established the firm they sold it. The new owner was the Duc d'Uzes, whose wife was a pioneer lady motorist. From 1907 the cars wore the red and blue flag of the d'Uzes family above their radiators, at the front of the tubular fuel tank which characterised Sizaire-Naudin cars from 1907 onwards.

The first production cars had single-cylinder De Dion-Bouton engines of 1244cc, and this was increased to 1357cc for the cars entered in the Coupe des Voiturettes and other events of 1906. The largest single-cylinder engine in a racing car was a very long-stroke 1963cc unit (100×250mm), but the road cars did not run to more than 1583cc. Even this gave a distinct 'plop plop plop'

1921 Skelton Model 35 Seasonette tourer.
JOHN A. CONDE

1921 Skeoch 3¹/₂hp cyclecar.
RON SKEOCH

sound, and it was said that the engine gave one explosion per telegraph pole. The single was made up to 1912, and was joined by a four with an 1847cc 12hp Ballot engine in late 1910. Several larger fours were made, the biggest being the 3016cc 17hp of 1914. The singles had been very successful in racing, with victories in the 1906, 1907 and 1908 Coupes des Voiturettes, and the 1907 Sicilian Cup, but the supercharged 4-cylinder car finished no higher than 16th in the 1912 Coupe des Voitures Légères. In the same year the Duc d'Uzes dismissed Naudin and the Sizaire brothers. They soon got busy with the Sizaire-Berwick, but poor Naudin, who was already in bad health, died in 1913. The partners' names must have been of some value, for when a new company was organised in December 1920, it was called the Société des Nouveaux Établissements Sizaire et Naudin. Two prewar models, the 13 and 17hp were made, still using Ballot engines, and in 1921 the new company sought a return to the voiturette with a light sports car powered by a 1092cc 4-cylinder engine designed by Nemorin Causan. Three ran in the International Voiturette Cup at Le Mans in August 1921, but none finished the race. A few months later the directors decided to liquidate the company.

NG

Further Reading
'La Voiture Phénomene Sizaire & Naudin', Griffith Borgeson,
Automobile Quarterly, Vol. 18, No. 2.

S&J (GB) 1984–1986

S&J Motor Engineers, Battle, East Sussex.

An intriguing Alfa Romeo GTV conversion was the Milano. Almost all of the components from the GTV – including the front bulkhead, windscreen, dashboard and doors – were placed in a special multi-tube steel chassis. The open 4-seater bodywork was fibreglass and was inspired by Pininfarina's Jaguar XJS prototype. Most of the 40 or so cars built were sold in kit form. In 1986 a second model called the Sportiva was developed, a 2+2 convertible boasting more sophisticated body mouldings in a broadly similar layout but only five such cars were made.

CR

SJR *see* SALVADOR (i)

S.K. (GB) 1985–1986

S.K. Automotive, Langdon Hills, Essex.

In style the S.K. Roadster was inspired by the Allard at the front and the Morgan at the rear. Conceived by Steve Blakey and Kim Ford, both engineers at Ford, the S.K. used MGB parts bolted into a cruciform steel chassis. The bodywork was entirely of fibreglass, and kits cost from £1500.

CR

S.K.A.F. (PL) 1922

This was a prototype light car designed by Stefan Koslowski and Antoni Fraczkowski who gave their initials to the name. It had a 502cc engine developing 10bhp with thermo-syphon cooling and magneto ignition. The carburettor was of their own design, and the car had friction transmission with no differential. The mechanical brakes operated on the rear wheels only. The wheelbase was 86in (2200mm) and the prototype had an open 2-seater body. The designers planned closed bodies and a delivery van, but production never started.

RP

SKELTON (US) 1920–1922

Skelton Motor Car Co., St Louis, Missouri.

The Skelton was a typical assembled car of its time, named after Dr S.L. Skelton, an affluent and prominent Oklahoma physician and built by the St Louis Car Co., widely known as a major builder of railway coaches and tramcars. The shops of the St Louis Car Co. were deemed ideal for Skelton car manufacture, having been the production site for the earlier AMERICAN MORS (1906–909) and, in 1910, the STANDARD (iv). The Skelton was an assembled car, typical of its time, with pleasing lines, a 112in (2843mm) wheelbase, Lycoming K 4-cylinder engine and a price tag of $1295 for the touring car, f.o.b. St Louis. Like many of its peers, the Skelton was a victim of the 1920–22 recession and ended production in 1922 after the completion of approximately 450 units per year. Dr Skelton, whose financial assistance had made the car possible, died in 1921.

KM

SKENE (US) 1900–1901

Skene American Automobile Co., Lewiston, Maine.

James W. Skene was a bicycle maker who designed and built a steam carriage in 1900, and after gaining backing from R.H.B. Wharton he began manufacture of a typical light steamer with 5hp double-acting 2-cylinder engine and single-chain drive. Four body styles were offered, a stanhope, victoria, surrey and what was described as a Canadian surrey which was the most expensive at $1300. Wharton's headquarters were in Springfield, Massachusetts, but the factory remained in Lewiston, Maine. The company claimed that all parts were made in the factory. At least 20 cars were made before the money ran out. Skene later became a Rambler dealer.

NG

SKEOCH (GB) 1921

The Skeoch Utility Car Co., Dalbeattie, Kirkudbrightshire.

The only cyclecar commercially made in Scotland, the Skeoch was a very light machine powered by a 348cc single-cylinder Precision engine, with Burman 2-speed gearbox and single-chain drive. It had a simple ash frame with quarter-elliptic springs at front and rear. Lighting was by acetylene and the 'streamline coachbuilt body' was made by Sims & Wilson of Cathcart, who also bodied the GILCHRIST. At £180 complete it was the cheapest car at the 1921 Scottish Motor Show, but not more than 10 were made.

NG

Further Reading
'Scotland's One and Only', Michael Worthington-Williams,
The Automobile, May 2000.

SKIP (GB) 1988 to date

J.J. Calver, Crossgate Moor, Durham.

The Skip 1000 was a 3-wheeler conceived almost purely for trials use, although it was fully road-legal and could be driven to events. It was a kit car constructed around a Mini floorpan and space frame chassis clad with aluminium panels and topped off with a fibreglass upper section. All Mini parts were used, including the engine which sat exposed up front. The single rear wheel was suspended on a Mini arm in a special subframe.

CR

SKODA (CS/CZ) 1925 to date

1925–1929 Akciova spolecnost drive Skodovy zavody, Plzen, Mlada Boleslav.
1930–1939 ASAP – Akciova spolecnost pro automobilovy prumysl, Mlada Boleslav.
1939–1945 ASAP – Reichswerke-Hermann-Göring AG, Mlada Boleslav.
1945–1991 AZNP – Automobilove zavody, narodni podnik, Mlada Boleslav.
1991 to date Skoda, automobilova akciova spolecnost, Mlada Boleslav.

For more than 100 years Skoda has been one of the biggest engineering combines in Europe. It was founded by Baron Waldstein in Plzen in 1895, in the period of rapid industrial growth, but it was the extraordinary vision of Emil Skoda (1839–1900) who turned the original workshop into a company of outstanding reputation. During World War I the Skoda works with its 36,000 employees became the largest arms manufacturer in the Austro-Hungarian Empire. The end of war and formation of Czechoslovakia in 1918 were difficult times for the company as military production had to be dismantled and converted to comply with the requirements of the postwar reconstruction era. The programme included locomotives, ships, automobiles, aircraft, power stations, engineering plants, sugar refineries, breweries and distilleries, as well as bridges and various other constructions.

In the history of the motor industry, Skoda is one of the names that was in there almost from the start. Laurin & Klement started out in 1895 making bicycles, in 1905 the first car was produced, and in 1925 the company merged with the industrial giant Skoda, Plzen, with the cars taking the Skoda name.

The Skoda company had its own automobile department from 1919, producing heavy road tractors and Sentinel steam trucks, but it wanted to enter the lucrative passenger car market. Skoda bought a manufacturing licence for the production of French Hispano-Suiza cars which were being built in the company's new arms and machine works in Plzen from 1926 onwards. These Marc Birkigt designed cars had a 25-100hp 6-cylinder ohc engine of 6654cc capacity. The engines and chassis were built in Plzen, and bodywork of Skoda's own design in Mlada Boleslav plant, or custom built bodies by Brozik or Jech were used. Only about 29 cars were bodied in Mlada Boleslav. The first Skoda Hispano-Suiza 25-100hp was delivered in May 1926 to the President of Czechoslovakia, T.G. Masaryk, and the last one of a series of 100 cars was sold in January 1930.

By 1929 Skoda employed 3278 people making motor cars, and the new models of that year were the 4-cylinder type 4R with 1944cc 32bhp SV engine, of which 975 were built until 1930, and the 6-cylinder type 6R with 2916cc 50bhp engine (322 cars).

The 4R-types were later produced as the 422 (1930–32, 3435 cars made, 1195cc 22bhp engine), the 430 (1929–32, 3028 cars, 1661cc 30bhp), and the 430D (1930–36, 651 cars, 1802cc 32bhp). The 6-cylinder 6R-types were replaced by the 633 (1931–34, 504 cars, 1792cc 33bhp engine), the 637 (1932–33, 67 cars, 1961cc 37bhp, later – until 1935 – 45bhp engine), the 645 (1929–34, 758 cars, 2492cc 45bhp), and the 650 (1932–36, 58 cars, 2704cc 50bhp engine). The only pre-World War II 8-cylinder Skoda was the type 860 with 8-cylinder in-line 3880cc 60bhp engine. It was built in 49 examples from 1929 to 1932, as a limousine, cabriolet and faux-cabriolet.

In 1930 the ASAP (Automobile Industry Co. Ltd) was founded and the company was restructured. The early 1930's saw also the development of a rear-mounted flat-4 air-cooled prototypes 932 (1498cc, 30bhp) and the 935 (1995cc 55bhp), and the 911 Sagitta with V-twin air-cooled 845cc 15bhp engine placed in front of the front axle. None of these went into production.

The type 420 Standard of 1933–34 (995cc, 20bhp, 421 cars) and the 420 Rapid of 1933–34 (1195cc 26bhp, 480 cars) were of a more modern design with a chassis of a centre tubular layout and rear swing half-axles. It would become a trend-setter and was developed into the 420 Popular of 1934–38 with a 995cc 22bhp sv engine, from 1937 to 1938 with an ohv 27bhp engine with the same displacement, of which 5510 were produced.

From the late 1930s there were further developments of the Popular, Rapid and Superb models. It seems the Populars were the most popular Skoda cars of that period. The 995 type was produced again with a 22bhp 995cc sv engine, from 1939 even to 1946, and 1500 units were sold during the war years. The Populars

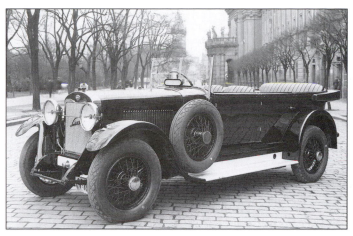
1925 Skoda Typ 350 3½-litre tourer.
NATIONAL MOTOR MUSEUM

1926 Skoda-Hispano-Suiza 6½-litre tourer.
NATIONAL MOTOR MUSEUM

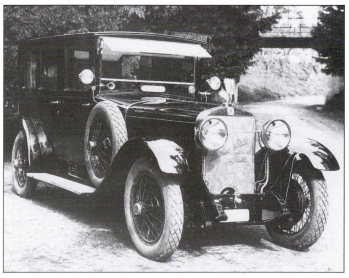
1926 Skoda-Hispano-Suiza 6½-litre limousine.
NATIONAL MOTOR MUSEUM

1934 Skoda Typ 650 2.7-litre saloon.
NATIONAL MOTOR MUSEUM

1937 Skoda Popular 1100 saloon.
NATIONAL MOTOR MUSEUM

1949 Skoda 1101 Tudor saloon.
NICK BALDWIN

of the 1938–44 era were the predecessors of the first postwar Skodas, the 1101 type. All of them were fitted with a 1089cc 30-32bhp engine, and more than 7600 cars were built, mostly as a sedan, tudor, cabriolet, roadster, light van and ambulance. Only 72 cars of the Popular Sport-Monte Carlo were assembled in 1935–38 being powered by the 1385cc 36bhp side-valve engine, and bodied as a streamlined coupé and roadster, on which sporting successes were achieved in the Monte Carlo and Olympic Games Rallies.

The Rapid range started in 1935 with 4-cylinder models with 1386cc 31bhp side-valve or 1564cc 42bhp ohv engines (until 1947 there were 4500 and 1804 cars built), and in 1941–42 the 6-cylinder 2199cc 60bhp ohv engine powered 34 cars bodied as sedans or cabriolets.

The largest engines were used in the Superb models: three 6-cylinder side-valve engines (1934–36, 201 cars, 2492cc, 55bhp; 1936–37, 53 cars, 2704cc, 60bhp; and 1936–39, 350 cars, 2916cc, 65bhp) were used, one 6-cylinder ohv engine (1938–49, 275 cars, 3137cc, 85bhp), and even one V8-cylinder 3991cc 96bhp ohv engine found its place in 10 limousines built in 1939 and 1940.

Fewer units were produced of the Favorit types: 169 cars were fitted with a 1802cc 38bhp sv engine, and 54 used a more advanced 2091cc 55bhp ohv engine. By 1938 Czechoslovakia had changed from rhd to lhd, and in the Mlada Boleslav plant 5642 people were employed. In 1939, Czechoslovakia was occupied by the German forces and Skoda was made to contribute to the German war effort. The whole Skoda concern and the car factory were incorporated into the German war-oriented industry, and suffered considerable damage due to military operations of the Allied Forces. The Skoda works were, however, destroyed by the Germans shortly after they had surrendered, on 9 May 1945.

Production of the small 1100 ohv based on the prewar Popular, and the larger Superb had resumed by late 1945. After the Communist take-over the company was nationalised in March 1946. The car division was separated from the rest of the Skoda Works and was renamed Automobilove zavody, narodni podnik (Automobile Works, National Enterprise) or AZNP Mlada Boleslav for short.

The 1946–49 front-engined, rear-driven Skoda 1101, with its 2-door body, called the Tudor, was the company's first car after the war. It had a steel body on a wooden frame mounted on a backbone chassis. The 1101 was available also as ambulance, police patrol car, estate, delivery van, roadster and even a jeep-like version 1101P for the armed forces. A 4-door version of the car become available by 1948. The engine was the 1089cc 4-cylinder unit which it inherited from the earlier Popular (and was used until the 1960s on the Octavia models!). Power output was 32bhp pushing the car to a top speed of 62mph (100km/h) through a 4-speed gearbox with synchromesh on third and fourth. Suspension was independent with transverse springs at the front, and swing axles to the rear. From 1948 the 1101 was known as 1102 when it received slightly modified bodywork. 66,904 cars of both types were built until 1952, and many of them were exported to most European countries as well as to Australia, South America and Africa. Motokov, a state-run organisation was set up to export Skoda vehicles from 1950.

1952 saw the 1221cc Skoda 1200 with 36bhp engine and all-steel body placed on a backbone frame. This was a new design with contemporary styling featuring a simple grill made of only two broad chrome horizontal bars, very low-set built-in headlamps and a split windscreen. Central chassis lubrication was carried over from the 1101/1102 models. The 1201 joined the 1200 in the Summer of 1955 and ran until 1961. It had the same bodyshell as the 1200 but had more power (45bhp) with some refinements. Efforts to sell the 1201 in the USA were to no avail but in some other export markets it enjoyed reasonable sales. That year production of some modifications of the 1200/1201 models was transferred to the subsidiary works of Vrchlabi (formerly the Petera coachbuilding firm) and the former Jawa works in Kvasiny where the ambulances and estate cars were assembled. The total production figures of both models show 15,594 units in Mlada Boleslav, 13,359 in Kvasiny and 38,118 in Vrchlabi.

Between 1951 and 1952 Skoda built 2100 Tatraplans in Mlada Boleslav. For some time after Tatra stopped its private car production between 1954 and 1957, Skoda was the only automobile producer in Czechoslovakia.

For 1955 the Skoda 1201 was joined by the entirely new 1089cc 40bhp Skoda 440 which featured a central backbone chassis and independent suspension all round. The 440 meant four cylinders and 40bhp, nevertheless the public liked to use names and soon christened this model the Spartak, using the name of the prototype. The Skoda 440 was in production until 1959 (75,417 were built), and the 445 type using the 1201 engine fitted into the basic 440 model sold 9375 from 1957 to 1959. The 1089cc engine, but with twin carburettors and producing 50bhp, was installed into a 2-seater convertible bodied Skoda 450, of which 1010 cars were assembled at the Kvasiny works.

In 1959 the front suspension using a transverse leaf spring was replaced by coil springs and telescopic dampers on all 440, 445 and 450 models. Together with some minor body refinements a new range of cars started: the 440 was renamed Octavia, the 445 became the Octavia Super and the 450 was sold as Felicia. Until production stopped in 1964, there were 229,531 Octavias, 79,479 Octavia Super and 14,863 Felicias built. About 2200 cars with 50bhp 1089cc engines or 55bhp 1221cc engines with the Octavia body were produced as the Octavia TS or Octavia 1200 TS respectively. The more powerful engine was used also in the Felicia Super and enabled them to reach a top speed of 80mph (129km/h).

At the Kvasiny plant the Octavia Combi STW was made from 1961 to 1971 (54,086 cars), and in Vrchlabi the Skoda 1202 as estate car, light delivery van, ambulance, pick-up and hearse was built from 1961 to 1973 (60,141 cars); both were fitted with a 1221cc 47–50bhp engine.

1964 Skoda Octavia saloon.
NICK BALDWIN

In the late 1950s the demand for new cars needed a radical solution. It was decided to build a large new modern factory complex. By 1964 the new complex was built on a 800,000 square metres site, with a production capacity designed for up to 600 cars a day. That year, the new 4-seater (later 5-seater) Skoda 1000 MB, with a 4-cylinder 998cc ohv 48bhp engine placed in the rear behind the final drive gear and a self supporting body, was introduced. Top speed of 77mph (124km/h), fuel consumption of 7 l/100km, and a price of 44,000 Czechoslovak crowns (the older Octavia cost 38,000 Kcs) made the S 1000 MB a suitable car for average motorists. More powerful engines of the same capacity but of 52bhp and with a twin carburettor were mounted to the MBG sedans and the MBX two-door models.

In 1967 the engine was increased to 1107cc and fitted into new models of the Skoda 1100 MB/MBX. Up to August 1969 419,540 of the 1000 MBs and 23,601 of 1100 MBs were made. During the factory summer holiday break, on 12 August 1969, a large fire started in one of the workshops and quickly damaged the whole old plant including expensive special machines and parts. Nevertheless, the production of the new types of 100/110 started on 25 August. The restyled body based on a 1000 MB/1100 MB body shell, and the old familiar 998 and 1107cc engines were used. The main technical improvements were front-wheel disc brakes and a twin circuit hydraulic brake system. Total production until 1976 was 819,787 S 100s and 219,864 S 110s. The 1100 LS (1971–76, 40,057 cars) had a more powerful 62bhp engine used also in the S 110 R coupé assembled in the Kvasiny works from 1970 to 1980 (56,902 cars). Some sports modifications were derived from these 1.1-litre models, as the 120 S, 120 S Rallye and 130 LR with sedan bodies, and the 130 RS with lightly restyled 110 R coupé body. These cars participated in both domestic and foreign races and rallies, winning many victories. About 350 were produced.

From 1976 the follow-up Skoda 105, S 120, S 125 and later on the S 130, S 135 and S 136 were built based on the S 1000 MB/S 100. The engines were of 1046cc and 45bhp (S 105) or 1174cc and 50bhp (S 120). A 2+2 2-door coupé followed in 1981 – the Skoda Rapid, in former Czechoslovakia also called Garde, with more powerful 55bhp engine capable of 93mph (150km/h). From 1976 to 1987 840,561 S 105s, 1,070,693 S 120s, and 11,179 Garde/Rapid (assembled in Kvasiny) were produced. The 130/135 range in the new M-series came in autumn

1973 Skoda 110R coupé.
NATIONAL MOTOR MUSEUM

1980 Skoda 105L Super Estelle saloon.
NICK BALDWIN

1993 Skoda Favorit LXi hatchback.
NATIONAL MOTOR MUSEUM

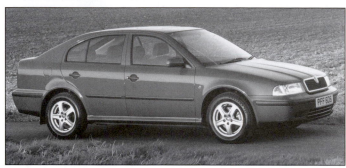

1999 Skoda Octavia saloon.
SKODA

2000 Skoda Fabia hatchback.
SKODA

1984 with a 1289cc 58bhp (S 130, 49,749 cars) or 62bhp (S 135, 1020 cars) engine, used also in the S 130 Rapid (22,475 cars) and S 135 Rapid (1272 cars) 2-door coupés. The S 136 models as Rapid 5-seater sedans and 4-seater coupés (1987–90, 1631 and 9708 cars respectively) were fitted with an all-alloy 1289cc ohv engine to be used in the new Favorit coming in 1988.

That year, a new era began in Mlada Boleslav. The first front-wheel drive car with a 5-seater 5-door hatchback body designed by the Carrozzeria Bertone, and many foreign components (such as the Pierburg carburettors, Lucas-Girling disc brakes, Porsche suspension engineering, electronic ignition, etc) left the production lines. Two basic types were sold: the S 135 Favorit with 58bhp engine and the S 136 Favorit with 62bhp engine. In 1990 the estate car Forman, and in 1991 the Pick-up completed the Favorit range. To 1995 there were 783,167 Favorits, 219,254 Formans and 60,744 pick-ups produced.

After the revolution in 1989 and in the new free-market environment, Skoda started to look for a strong foreign partner who would assure their competitiveness by investing capital and know-how in the company. After a keenly fought battle with Renault, the Volkswagen Group signed an investment memorandum of understanding to purchase Skoda on 16 April 1991. Skoda automobilova a.s. acquired the right to use the Skoda-symbol. To differentiate it from the other parts of Skoda, the words 'Skoda Auto' appear on the black border.

Skoda Auto launched its first new car under VW management, the compact 5-door Felicia hatchback range, in the autumn of 1994. A 5-door Combi (estate) and pick-up versions were also produced. The engine options were the 1289cc, 54bhp or 68bhp Skoda engine, the 1598cc 75bhp VW engine and the 1896cc 64bhp VW diesel with power steering. In February 1998 the last Felicia in the original version left the Mlada Boleslav plant, 793,376 cars being produced. Today models with body and interior modification, and with a front end similar to the new Octavia, are built.

In late autumn 1996 Skoda Auto launched its second new range, the Octavia. This was a mid-range saloon car based on VW's A+ platform. Available engines ranged from the 1.6-litre VW engine with 5-speed manual or 4-speed electronically managed automatic gearbox, through the 1.8 20V Audi A4 engine to the Audi 1.8 TDI diesel. In May 1998 the Octavia Combi (estate) appeared, also fitted with the above mentioned engines. The Octavia was entering the most competitive sector of the automotive market. In 1996 1168 and in 1997 60,690 Octavias were built. Skoda entered the supermini field in late 1999 with the Fabia, a 5-door hatchback on the platform of the next generation VW Polo. Engine options were 1.4-litre petrol or 1.9-litre diesel, with a turbo diesel to follow.

Skoda Auto's production in 1999 was 371,169 cars, and the target for 2000 was 437,700 vehicles. The firm was the largest Czech manufacturing concern, and its revenues in 1995 reached approximately DM 2.2 billion, and around half derived from domestic sales. The biggest markets abroad are those in Slovakia, Germany, Poland, Great Britain, Austria, France and Italy.

MSH

Further Reading
Od laurinky ke Skode 1000 MB, Adolf Babuska, Nadas, Praha, 1967.
Skoda, Laurin & Klement, Ivan Margolius and Charles Meisl, Osprey, London, 1992.
Laurin & Klement – Skoda 1895–1995, Petr Kozisek and Jan Kralik, Motorpress, Prague, 1995.
Skoda Automobile. Zukunft durch Tradition, Bernd-Wilfried Kiessler, Delius Klasing Verlag, Bielefeld, 1997.

SKORPION (GB) 1986–1988; 1994–1995

1986–1988 Skorpion Car Co. Ltd, Llanelli, Dyfed.
1994–1995 S.K. Distributors, Brackley, Northamptonshire.
Not many kit cars have been based on Skoda mechanicals, but the Skorpion Chikara was a brave effort. The body/chassis unit accepted any post–1964 rear-engined Skoda engine, gearbox and front axle. A variety of tuning parts was offered by the Skoda dealer that conceived the car. However, the 2+2 fibreglass coupé bodywork was rather unpleasantly styled and little interest was shown.

CR

SKRIVA (F) 1922–1924

Automobiles Skriva, Paris.
Only a few examples were made of the conventional Skriva, which was powered by a 2402cc side-valve Sergant engine.

NG

S.K. SIMPLEX (GB) 1908–1910

Smeddle & Kennedy Ltd, Newcastle-upon-Tyne.
This company listed light cars with single- or 2-cylinder engines, the latter a 10hp unit with single-ohc. It had a conventional gearbox and shaft-drive.

NG

SKYLINE (US) 1953

Skyline Inc, Jamaica, New York.
This sporty convertible was based on the Henry J, which it partially resembled. The grill was changed and the interior had such safety feature as high-backed seats, seat belts and a padded dash.

HP

SKY STREAK (US) c.1988

Charley Holecek, Coeur d'Alene, Idaho.
The Sky Streak was an eccentric 3-wheeled car that looked like an amusement park ride. It was built out of a golf cart, a Suzuki motorcycle, a Toyota differential and other parts. The body resembled a small aircraft with a tall tail spoiler and

short, thick wings to cover the two rear wheels. It had a top with open-side doors and headlights attached to the sides of the nose. Plans and a construction video were sold.

HP

SLEM *see* TWIKE

S.L.I.M. (F) 1920–1925
Sté Lyonnaise de l'Industrie Mécanique et Autos Pilain, Lyons.
The successor to the Société des Automobiles Pilain, this company began by making a few cars of prewar Pilain design, such as the 16/20, before bringing out their own car which was launched at the Lyons Fair in March 1920. Known as the Type AP, it was designed by M. Adenot and had a 1726cc 4-cylinder engine with 16 valves operated by twin camshafts, one operating the inlet valves and the other the exhausts. Drive was by shaft to a rear-axle-mounted 4-speed gearbox, and the rear suspension was unusual, in having two conventional semi-elliptic springs carried at their rear end by twin quarter-elliptic springs. 4-wheel brakes were provided and it was a modern-looking car with an attractive radiator and wire or disc wheels.

The AP was made until 1922, and it was succeeded by similar cars with larger engines of 1885, 2405 and 2613cc. A move to a new factory in 1925 did the company's balance sheet no good at all, and production ceased before the end of the year.

NG

S.L.M. (CH) 1899; 1934–1935
S.L.M. Schweizerische Lokomotiv- und Maschinenfabrik AG, Winterthur.
This well-known locomotive building company started to design internal-combustion engines in 1886 and by 1899 had built the prototype of a light 4-seater car with a single-cylinder opposed piston engine of 7hp. It is not known whether or not there was a small production of this vehicle. In 1906 steam trucks were made and a few petrol-engined commercial vehicles were produced from 1924 to 1932. In 1934 S.L.M. made a rather dramatic second venture in the passenger car field. Based on the drawings of Marquis de Pescara, who had built the NACIONAL-PESCARA sports and racing cars in Spain, the prototype SLM-Pescara was built. The V16 engine was constructed mainly of alloy. It had a capacity of about 3600cc, and fitted with a Roots blower it supplied 150bhp at 4000rpm. The chassis came from Chausson of Paris, and it obtained a good looking French coach-built 2-seater cabriolet body which was delivered to the Marquis de Pescara himself in 1935. Owing to the Spanish Civil War, this car was destroyed and two further engines which had been built, were lost.

FH

SLOANE (GB) 1907
Ruff, Walker & Co. (Sloane Motor Works), London.
This company advertised four models, with 6½ or 8hp single-cylinder De Dion-Bouton engines, a 10/12hp twin and 14/20hp four, the make of these larger engines being unspecified. They had shaft drive and top speed was quoted, uninformatively, to be 'as desired'. Their works were said to be at 91 Pimlico Road, near Sloane Square.

NG

S & M (US) 1913
S & M Motor Co., Detroit, Michigan.
These letters stood for (Edward E.) Stroebel and (Walter C.) Martin, two New Yorkers who employed R.C. Aland to design a car for them. It had a Continental 6-cylinder engine and a large tourer body on a 130in (3299mm) wheelbase. A roadster and a limousine were also listed, but may not have been built. Production did not get under way until late 1913, and by January 1914 the company was bankrupt. The assets were bought by George Benham who put his own name on the cars and sold them as BENHAMs. Prices were the same as for the S & M, of which no more than 40 were sold. Benham did even less well, with 19 sales and the dissolution of his company before the end of 1914. Aland also made a car under his own name, from 1916 to 1917.

NG

1923 S.L.I.M.
NICK BALDWIN

1935 SLM-Pescara 3-litre V16 drophead coupé.
ERNEST SCHMID

S & M SIMPLEX (US) 1904–1907
Smith & Mabley Manufacturing Co., New York, New York.
This company was formed by A.D. Proctor Smith and Carlton R. Mabley who were importers of some of the highest quality European cars, including C.G.V., Fiat, Panhard and Renault. They were behind the manufacture of the C.G.V. at Rome, New York, and in 1904 decided to make their own car which would be the equal of the imports in quality but would sell at a lower price because no duties would be levied on the components. They bought a 7-story (5 above ground, 2 below) factory on East 83rd Street in New York, and engaged Edward Franquist as their designer. His first car had a 30/35hp engine on Mercedes lines, with double-chain drive. Only a tourer was offered, on a 105in (2665mm) wheelbase, at $6750. Though expensive, it was less so than a 35hp Mercedes at $8400 or a 35/45hp Renault at $8200. There was also an 18hp chassis, on a 90.75in (2303mm) wheelbase, priced at $5250 for a 2-seater runabout and $5750 for a tourer. Few of these smaller cars were made, and they disappeared from the catalogue after the first year. Coachwork on both chassis was by Quinby, but practically all of the rest of the car was made in the factory, apart from coils, tyres and wheels. 73 cars were delivered in the first year.

The 30/35hp was continued into 1907, with a longer wheelbase of 113in (2868mm) added ('greater wheelbases available to order') and prices reduced to $5600. In that year Smith & Mabley were bought by their friend and customer, textile magnate Herman Broesel who changed the name of company and car to SIMPLEX. Total production of the S & M Simplex was about 225 cars.

NG

S.M. (GB) 1904–1905
S.M. Car Syndicate Ltd, Willesden Junction, London.
This car, otherwise known as the Shave-Morse, was a steamer designed by George J. Shave, formerly works manager of the Locomobile Co. of Great Britain, and Irving J. Morse. It had a 4-cylinder vertical single-acting engine under the bonnet, and a flash boiler at the rear, the opposite of the more logical Stanley system, where the boiler was at the front and the engine acted directly on the rear axle.

1999 Smart city car.
NICK GEORGANO

Final drive was by double chains. Two models were offered, of 8¹/₂ and 20hp, but very few were delivered. The company was better known for its steam trucks, which were made up to 1912. They also made an experimental car with Aster engine driving the front wheels, in 1909, and the FOY STEELE light car from 1913 to 1916.

NG

SMART (D) 1997 to date

Micro Compact Car GmbH, Rennlingen (factory at Hambach, France).
This was a 2-seater city car only 98in (2487mm) long, originally conceived by the Swiss maker of Swatch watches, Nicolas Hayek. After an abortive involvement with Volkswagen he formed a partnership with Daimler-Benz. They took 81 per cent of the shares in the joint venture, Micro Compact Car, with the balance being held by Swatch. Ownership became 100 per cent Daimler after the formation of Daimler Chrysler. A factory was built at Hambach in north-eastern France, and the production car was displayed at the 1997 Frankfurt Show. It had a 599cc 3-cylinder single-ohc engine developing 45bhp in standard form and 54bhp with turbocharger. The rear wheels were driven through a 6-speed sequential gearbox. Maximum speed of both models was limited to 80mph (129km/h), but the turbo version had slightly faster acceleration with a 0–60mph (0–97km/h) of 17.5 seconds, compared with 18.9 for the less powerful model. The start of production was delayed becauseof suspension modifications necessitated by the instability shown by the Mercedes-Benz A Class (the infamous 'elk test'), but Smarts began to come off the lines in July 1998. The factory had a capacity of 200,000 cars per year. A convertible was launched in Spring 2000, and further developments under consideration included a 4-door model and a roadster.

NG

S.M.B. (I) 1907–1910

Stà Meccanica Bresciana, Brescia.
This was a conventional medium-sized car with 4-cylinder T-head engine, offered in two sizes, 3.8 or 4.2 litres. Transmission was via a 4-speed gearbox and shaft drive, and it had a circular radiator.

NG

SMITH; GREAT SMITH (US) 1903–1911

Smith Automobile Co., Topeka, Kansas.
This company was founded by two brothers, Anton and Clement Smith, who ran a successful truss and artificial limb business which they had founded in 1885. They also stuffed birds and made bows and arrows. Helped by local engineer Terry Stafford, they built some experimental cars from 1897, and formed their company in 1903, their first products being buggy-type vehicles with 2-cylinder

engines, epicyclic transmission and chain drive. 2- and 4-seater bodies were provided; the latter was a rear-entrance tonneau which was described as the Veracity observation car. Veracity was the name used by the Smiths for their 2-cylinder cars, and was dropped when they began to make fours, from 1906 onwards. These had 24hp engines on a 98in (2487mm) wheelbase, but for 1907 the name Great Smith was adopted. One model was no greater than the previous year's, though it had a longer wheelbase, but there was also a 50/60hp 6-cylinder car on a 131in (3325mm) wheelbase which truly deserved the title 'great'. It lasted only one season, and production was limited to 10 cars. From 1908 onwards the Great Smith was a 4-cylinder car of 45hp, about 150 a year being made. Unfortunately the cars did not earn any money as they were too expensive to build.

In 1909 the brothers separated. Anton exchanged his portion of the Smith Truss Co. for Clement's share in the car company. He was now virtually sole owner, as he had bought out Terry Stafford. A Michigan furniture maker, C. Werneke, put in $90,000, but this could not save the Smith Automobile Co., which went into receivership at the end of 1910. About 25 cars, listed as 1911 models, were sold by the receiver. One of the last cars sold was a 60hp six, presumably assembled from 1907 parts, which went to Arthur Koppen, the Governor of Kansas. The factory was sold to the Perfection Metal Products Co. of Kansas City.

When it was all over Anton Smith, described as 'a rather cheerful individual', made a huge bonfire of all the company's records around which he and his family gathered and sang a song 'Broke, broke, absolutely broke. May sound funny but it ain't no joke'. He later moved to Buffalo, New York, where he built up another successful business with the 'Uncle Sam Truss'. He died in 1931. His brother Clement continued to make trusses in Topeka and died in 1947.

NG

SMITH FLYER (US) 1916–1919

The A.O. Smith Corp., Milwaukee, Wisconsin.
Originally bicycle makers, the A.O. Smith Corp. had become a major supplier of pressed steel frames to the motor industry by 1914, when they acquired the licence for the British-made Wall Auto Wheel. They supplied large numbers of these for the purpose of motorising bicycles, and noted that the American Motor Vehicle Co. of Lafayette, Indiana, made a light buckboard powered by an auto wheel at the back. Seeing the possibilities of this idea, they bought up the design and put it on the market in November 1916 as the Smith Flyer. Three years later they sold it to BRIGGS & STRATTON who made it for three years before selling it on to a New Jersey company who made it as the RED BUG or Auto Red Bug.

NG

SMUGGLER (US) c.1994

Smuggler Cobra Co. Ltd, Sebastopol, California.
The Smuggler Cobra replica used a square-tube frame with fabricated front suspension and a Ford live rear axle. Ford 5000cc engines were offered. They were sold in kit and fully assembled form.

HP

SMYK (PL) 1958

Szczecinska Fabryka Motocykli, Szczecin.
Of unauthodox design, with a tilting front entrance, this small saloon was powered by a 15hp 4-stroke motorcycle engine. Only 20 were built.

NG

SMZ (SU) 1958–1990

Serpukhovskji Motornnyi Zavod, Sarpukhovskji Avtomobilnji Zavod, Serpukhov.
As they were not the first priority, the handicapped veterans of World War II ('Great Patriotic War' as it was called in the USSR) only got their very first motorised transportation seven years after the Victory. In 1952 a motorbike works in Serpukhov launched an open 3-wheeler, a 275kg model S1L. Initally these light creations were powered by a 123cc (4.15bhp) motorbike engine, but the last model SZL was upgraded to a 346cc engine and the convenience of an electric starter. A 3-wheeler with three tracks and thence greater resistance in snow, sleet and mud was basically the wrong solution; therefore by 1958

appeared another open model SZA, a car-like creation with four wheels and two headlamps. This time top speed reached 25mph (40km/h) instead of 12.4mph (20km/h), front torsion suspension was attached to a tubular frame and the vehicle used 5 × 10 tyres instead of 4.5 × 9. Two differently equipped models were manufactured, SZA for driving with two hands, SZB for drivers with one hand and one leg. The following, modernised model with lots of glass and squarish closed bodywork was called the SZD. From 1990 re-named as SeAZ, the works assembled the VAZ-1111 Oka, again modified for the handicapped driver. Starting from 1500–2500 units per year, current production has reached 8000–11,000.

MHK

SN1 (GB) 1982–1987
1982–1984 Steaney Developments, Chalgrove, Oxfordshire.
1984–1985 Amplas Ltd, Chalgrove, Oxfordshire.
1985–1987 Lemazone, Leigh, Lancashire.
The SN1 started life as a Richard Oakes design for EMBEESEA. While that company pursued an alternative body style called the Eurocco, Steaney Developments developed it in notchback form to become the SN1. It was based on a VW Beetle floorpan and had 2+2 seating. Lemazone later restyled and renamed it the Comet.

CR

SNA (CH) 1903–1913
Sté Neuchâtelois d'Automobiles SNA, Boudry, Neuchâtel.
Fritz Henriod, together with his brother Charles Édouard, had constructed automobiles under their name from 1886 to 1898 in Bienne. When the two brothers went their separate ways, Fritz Henriod founded SNA in Boudry specializing in air-cooled engined automobiles. They were advertised as 'Automobiles sans eau'. The first model of 6/8hp, had a front-mounted opposed twin-cylinder engine, a special type clutch, 4-speed gearbox and shaft drive. In 1905 two additional models of 10/12hp and 18/20hp both with air-cooled 4-cylinder in-line engines were produced, and prices for complete cars ranged from SFr6,000 to 12,500. When exhibited at the Paris Show of 1906, the SNA obtained much attention and there were licence discussions with various manufacturers. From 1906 to 1913 the largest model was a 25/30hp with a 4-cylinder engine of 4941cc which had two large laterally placed fans for cooling the ribbed separate cylinders. Whereas side-valves were used for the intake, the exhaust valves were ohv with pushrods and rockers operated from the same camshaft. SNA cars had electric lighting as standard equipment. A few were fitted with the 'progressively working continuous speed changing flywheel', an early attempt at an automatic gearbox invented by Charles Éduoard Henriod. Some commerical vehicles and at least one snowmobile with twin longitudinally arranged propelling drums were built. The company was often in financial trouble but in 1913 these could not be solved and production ceased.

FH

S.N.D. see DUPORT

SNOECK (B) 1899–1902
Éts Snoeck, Ensival-Verviers.
This company was formed in 1863 to make textile machinery, and tried to get into the motor industry by acquiring the Belgian licence for the French DE RIANCEY *avant train*. It seems that they never put this into production, but in 1900 they bought another licence, for the BOLIDE, and made a number of these large cars with horizontal engines. They sold one to the racing driver Camille Jenatzy who, in February 1900, set a new petrol car record for the flying kilometre of 58.4mph (94km/h), though this was still short of the 65mph (105km/h) he had achieved with *La Jamais Contente* electric car the previous year.

In 1902 Snoeck exhibited some smaller cars of 8½hp 2-cylinders and 12, 16 and 24hp 4-cylinders all with shaft drive. These may also have been of Bolide design. They also made some heavy forward-control trucks, but by the end of 1902 they had reverted to textile machinery.

NG

SNYDER (i) (US) 1908–1909
D.D. Snyder & Co., Danville, Illinois.

c.1960 SMZ SZA 2-seater.
NICK GEORGANO/NATIONAL MOTOR MUSEUM

1912 SNA 25/30CV tourer.
ERNEST SCHMID

This buggy and carriage-building company made isolated examples of motorised buggies from 1906, but only started serious production in 1908. They followed the usual buggy formula of 10/12hp 2-cylinder engines, 2-speed epicyclic transmission and double-chain drive, and sold for $450. Not many were made before Snyder returned to full-time carriage making, though he did work as a painter and trimmer of car bodies.

NG

SNYDER (ii) (US) 1914
Snyder Motor & Manufacturing Co., Cleveland, Ohio.
This company offered a cyclecar in three models, with 9hp air-cooled V-twin engine for $390, with 12hp water-cooled 4-cylinder engine and 2-seater body at $425 or for four passengers at $450. Like most cyclecars firms, its life was short.

NG

SOAMES (GB) 1903–1904
Langdon-Davies Motor Co. Ltd, Southwark, London.
This was an unusual car powered by an 11hp 2-cylinder vertical engine which was mounted on a subframe separate from the chassis which supported the body. It drove via a constant-mesh gearbox and double-chain drive. Unlike most exponents of this system, the chains were mounted close together rather than near the wheels.

NG

SOÇÉMA-GRÉGOIRE see GRÉGOIRE

1904 Société Manufacture d'Armes 24/30hp landaulet.
MARK TIDY

1956 Soletta 750 saloon.
ERNEST SCHMID

SOCIÉTÉ DES PONTS MOTEURS (F) 1913–1914
Sté des Ponts Moteurs, Paris.

Avant train attachments to motorise horse-drawn vehicles were not unknown at the turn of the century, but 1913 was very late to launch such a device. This example had a 1100cc V-twin engine and a 3-speed gearbox, with a track which was adjustable to fit whatever type of horse carriage was being used.
NG

SOCIÉTÉ MANUFACTURE D'ARMES (F) 1904
Sté Manufacturiere d'Armes, St Étienne, Loire.

The evidence for this make lies in the name on the hubcaps of what is almost certainly the only surviving example. However, the SA de Constructions Méchaniques de la Loire, also of St Étienne, which was said to be a branch of the Manufacturiere d'Armes, made or sold two makes, the AUTOMOTO and the SVELTE. The surviving car has a 4-cylinder Aster 46NS engine, 4-speed gearbox and shaft drive. The body, by Sala, was originally on a Serpollet steam car.
NG

SOFRAVEL (F) 1948–1949
Sofravel, Annonay, Ardèche.

This miniature open 2-seater, baptised the Coccinelle (Beetle), attempted to evoke the style of much larger cars with its Americanesque steel body. It used a front-mounted 150cc 4-stroke single-cylinder 6.5bhp engine driving the rear wheels by chain through a 3-speed gearbox. A full production run was not forthcoming.
CR

SOLAR ELECTRIC (US) c.1994
Solar Electric, Santa Rosa, California.

This was one of the largest American electric vehicle manufacturers. They converted a wide range of vehicles, including cars, trucks and minivans. They also made an electric-powered Pontiac Fiero.
HP

SOLARWIND (US) c.1986
Solarwind, Sunset Beach, California.

This was a kit car with a difference, as it was powered by solar energy. It was an aerodynamic coupé with side by side seating, plain slab sides and enclosed wheels. It is not apparent if they were sold in kit or instruction form.
HP

SOLETTA (CH) 1956–1976
Ingenieurbureau für Fahrzeugbau, Solothurn.

Willy Ernst Salzmann graduated as an engineer at the Technical University of Zürich. As a student he developed a 3-wheeler microcar which was however not built. In order to exhibit at the Geneva Show of 1956 his ideas of a new type of 'elastic axle' which he designated as a 'live-swing-axle', he built a 4-wheel microcar. The name Soletta is the Italian version of Solothurn. It had a platform frame with tubular structure and a closed fibreglass 4-seater body. An improved Condor motorcycle air-cooled opposed twin-cylinder engine placed midship of 748cc and 22bhp allowed a top speed of a quite creditable 62mph (100km/h). It was also exhibited at the Paris Show and enjoyed much interest and praise from the press but no quantity production resulted. Salzmann then developed an unorthodox, very light 4-cylinder engine in X-configuration of about 30 to 40bhp but again it remained a prototype. In the 1970s he presented another engine with pistons in unit with the rods which was tested in 2- and 4-stroke form. Experiments for a modern light engine for microcars are believed to have been continued into the 1990s.
FH

SOLIDOR (D) 1905–1907
Beaulieu & Krone, Berlin.

This company marketed the French-built Passy-Thellier or Mendelssohn cars in Germany, using component parts or completed chassis, with the bodies being made in Berlin. A variety of models was offered, with single-, 2- and 4-cylinder engines, and in sizes from 8 to 30hp.
HON

SOLID STERLING (US) c.1996 to date
Solid Sterling, St Helens, Oregon.

The British Nova kit, called the Sterling in the US, was produced by this company after CALIFORNIA COMPONENT CARS had ceased production. It was pretty much the same as it had always been, with a VW floorpan and VW, Mazda rotary or Corvair engines.
HP

SOLIGNAC (F) 1900–c.1903
Sté des Voitures Électriques, Paris.

This was an electric *avant train* for the motorisation of horse-drawn carriages.
NG

SOLLER (CH) c.1904–1905
Eugen Soller, Basle.

Prior to manufacturing commercial vehicles of 1 to 5 tons payload, Soller apparently had made a few passenger cars but no details could be found.
FH

SOLOMOBIL (D) 1921–1923
Kraftwagenfabrik Solomobil GmbH, Berlin.

This company made two models of cyclecar, a 4/10PS 3-wheeler and a 6/12PS 4-wheeler. Both had air-cooled V-twin engines.
HON

SOLON (S) 1994–1995

Solon AB, Uddevalla.

Ulf Bolumlid's Solon 2000 was a rare example of an electric-powered sports car. In fact its power source was a hybrid, using a 54bhp (40kW) electric motor supplemented by a 16bhp diesel or petrol engine. A top speed of 68mph (109km/h) was claimed for the coupé, while its 400-mile range far exceeded other 'green' cars. The company was also working on a model powered by wood shavings. Features included an interior that seated three passengers abreast and scissor-gullwing doors.

CR

SOMÉA (B) 1921–1923

SA des Automobiles Leroux-Pisart, Brussels.

Leroux-Pisart made the A.L.P. car from 1919 to 1920, after which the design was taken over by a group called SOMEA. They continued it for a further season under the A.L.P. name, but Leroux left to work for Citroën, and the group hired Paul Bastien to design a new and more up-to-date car which they launched at the Brussels Salon in December 1921 under the name Soméa. It had a 2017cc single-ohc 4-cylinder engine, front-wheel brakes, and a handsome vee-radiator. Its advanced design attracted other manufacturers; among those who bought a Soméa to study were Métallurgique and Peugeot. A small number were sold, including a few to Holland and Switzerland, but manufacturing difficulties brought the project to an end in 1923. Bastien went to America where he designed the Vertical Eight for Stutz, while another Soméa employee, Germanes, went to Métallurgique, where he modified the Soméa into the 2-litre Métallurgique.

NG

SOMMER (i) (US) 1904–1905

Sommer Motor Co., Detroit, Michigan.

This design had been made as the HAMMER-SOMMER from 1902 to the spring of 1904 when Henry Hammer left to make a car under his own name. His brother Herman and William Sommer continued the same design under the Sommer name. It was a 5-seater tourer powered by a 15hp flat-twin engine with 2-speed epicyclic transmission. Priced at $1250, it lasted into 1905 but for no longer.

NG

SOMMER (ii) (US) 1910–1911

Sommer Motor Co., Bucyrus, Ohio.

This company had no connection with the Detroit firm of the same name. They had made engines in Aurora, Illinois, and on moving to Bucyrus they announced that they would take up the manufacture of complete cars. In November 1910 they announced that they had been making cars for several months, but specifications are not known. A few cars may have been made to special order into 1911.

NG

SOMMER (iii) (DK) 1971; 1982–c.1986

O. Sommer, Klampenborg.

Ole Sommer was a Volvo distributor and he produced the highly unusual Joker. Fittingly named, this Volvo-based car was uncompromisingly designed around straight lines. It had an external box-section steel frame and resembled a World War II look-out post. One unusual feature was an exhaust pipe that travelled under the car's running boards, then transversely across the car and out under the opposite running board. No less than seven Jokers were built. The OScar of 1982 was an AC Cobra 289 replica, using a fibreglass bodyshell supplied by B.R.A. of Great Britain. The OScar used its own substantial platform chassis into which Volvo 244 mechanicals were installed: 112bhp 2.3-litre 4-cylinder engine, 4-speed overdrive gearbox, disc brakes and suspension (modified with leaf springs). Turbocharged or 6-cylinder Volvo engines could also be fitted in a Mk II version with a revised chassis and a Danish-built body.

CR

SONÇIN (F) 1900–1902

Émile Ouzou et Cie, Paris.

This was a 2-seater voiturette powered by a 4½hp engine of Ouzou's own manufacture, which was also used to power racing tricycles. In 1903 the company became GRÉGOIRE (i).

NG

1922 Soriano-Pedroso 6/8CV sports car.
NICK GEORGANO

SONGHUAJIANG (CHI) 1993 to date

Haerbin Aircraft Corp., Haerbin City, Heilongjiang Province.

China Aviation Industry Corp. owns a large engine factory in Manchuria. Its main product was the 787cc DA 462 engine (Suzuki licence), making more than 100,000 units per year. The 4-seater Songhuajiang (the name is from the local river) HFJ 7080 was one of the mini cars that used this engine. In 1993 23 units were made, in 1994 only eight. In 1998 this factory started production of the Songhuajiang HFJ 6330 A, a licenced Korean DAEWOO Tico, which was also in production in Mengcheng district, Anhui Province, as the Anchi MC 6330.

EVIS

SORIANO-PEDROSO (F) 1919–1924

SA des Automobiles Soriano-Pedroso, Biarritz; Neuilly, Seine.

This delightfully-named car owes its title to two Spanish Marquises, Ivanrey de Soriano and San Carlos de Pedroso. The prototypes were made at Biarritz, close to the Spanish border, but production cars came from Neuilly. Three models were offered, the 6/8CV with 1130cc side-valve Ballot engine and 3-speed gearbox, the 8/10CV with 1590cc Ballot engine and 4-speed gearbox, and a *luxe sport* version of the 8/10CV with lighter pistons and a top speed of 70mph (113km/h). The 6/8CV was most unusual for its date in having double-chain drive, while the larger cars had conventional shaft drive to a differential. The cars were of very sporting appearance, the *luxe sport* often having two bucket seats for a body, but they did not feature in major sporting events. The three cars entered in the 1920 Coupe Internationale des Voiturettes at Le Mans failed to start, as did two entered in the 1921 Brooklands 200 Mile Race.

After they stopped making cars jointly, the two partners each made one-off cars of their own. The Soriano was a streamlined record breaking car powered by a 904cc Ruby engine, while the Pedroso was an impressive machine with a twin-ohc 3-litre straight-8 engine of the Marquis' own design. Both of these cars still exist, together with at least one Soriano-Pedroso.

NG

SORRELL (US) c.1955–1960

Sorrell Engineering, Inglewood, California.

Bob Sorrell's kit car company built two fibreglass bodies that were popular in the mid–1950s. The SR-100 (not to be confused with the Byers body by the same name) was an aggressive sports car body for cars with a 100in (2538mm) wheelbase. It had a smooth, rounded shape with a wide, flat grill across the front. Headlights were recessed and could be covered with plexiglass. A one-piece body sold for $500 in 1956. At least one was built on a KURTIS 500KK chassis with a GMC 6-cylinder engine, and another was fitted to an Allard J2. An attractive fastback removable top was optional. The other Sorrell body was the SR–190, a fibreglass coupé body shell that fitted on an Austin-Healey chassis. They resembled a Healey 100 with a Cobra-like grill and a fastback top. They were also sold in a longer length for use with 100in (2538mm) wheelbase chassis. The fastback top was available separately to fit on an Austin-Healey. This body cost $295 in 1956.

HP

1934 Southern Cross Airline saloon.
MICHAEL WORTHINGTON-WILLIAMS

SOURIAU (F) 1912–1914
A. Souriau et Cie, Montoire, Loire-et-Cher.
This was an unconventional 3-wheeler whose single front wheel both steered and drove. Two sizes of engine were offered, a 625cc 5hp single and a 1460cc 8hp four, and drive to the front wheel was by belt. It was also known as the Obus (shell).
NG

SOUTH BEND (US) 1913–1914
South Bend Motor Car Works, South Bend, Indiana.
This company specialised in trucks and fire engines, but made a few 38hp 6-cylinder roadsters and tourers, some on a long 136in (3452mm) wheelbase.
NG

SOUTHEASTERN REPLICARS (US) c.1977–1980
Southeastern Replicars, Largo, Florida.
This company mixed restoring original classic cars with building replicas of the Auburn. They built three models, the 2-seater Speedster, the 2+2 Phaeton and a long-wheelbase Phaeton. The bodies were very accurate in appearance and could be fitted to Ford or General Motors full size sedan chassis and running gear.
HP

SOUTHERN (i) (US) 1906–1908
Southern Automobile Manufacturing Co., Jacksonville, Florida.
This was a typical high-wheeler powered by a 12hp air-cooled or 20hp water-cooled 2-cylinder engine mounted under the seat. Less typical was its location; it was the first serious attempt at car production in Florida.
NG

SOUTHERN (ii) (US) 1909
Southern Motor Co., Jackson, Tennessee.
This company announced a car powered by a 30hp 4-cylinder engine, with 3-speed gearbox and shaft drive, to sell for $1500 for either a 5-seater tourer or 2-seater roadster. It is not certain if production ever started, despite the assurance that many of the most prominent businessmen in Jackson were behind the venture.
NG

SOUTHERN CROSS (AUS) 1933–1935
Marks Motor Construction Ltd, Burwood, New South Wales.

While Jim Marks was the son of Arthur Marks, backer of the earlier MARKS-MOIR, and both used forms of unitary construction with glued wood laminates, they were separate entities. Jim led the project and he involved the famous aviator Sir Charles Kingsford Smith, taking the name from 'Smithy's' trans-Pacific aircraft, and this proved to be most beneficial in gaining publicity. The design was by Bill Foulis, who favoured horizontally-opposed engines, as seen earlier with the ROO. The structure was of laminated wood, impregnated with waterproof glue and pressed. The 4-cylinder engine gave 60bhp, the gearbox included an overdrive and a McGill torque converter was later tried but found to absorb too much power. Wheelbase was 120in (2540mm), springs were semi-elliptic and wide tyres by Dunlop Australia were fitted to special wheels. A tourer was seen first but production was of a small number. The Airline saloon, fitted with a larger engine, achieved some sales in Victoria.
MG

SOUTHERN ROADCRAFT (GB) 1984 to date
1984–1987 Southern Roadcraft Ltd, Portslade, West Sussex.
1987–1994 Southern Roadcraft Ltd, Southwick, Brighton, West Sussex.
1994 Southern Roadcraft Ltd, Lancing, West Sussex.
1994 to date Roadcraft UK Ltd, Lancing, West Sussex.
The S.R. V8 was a fairly early A.C. Cobra replica with an accurate, high quality body and a multi-tube chassis with steel-panelled floors, transmission tunnel and bulkheads. Inevitably, Jaguar running gear and small or big block V8 power (usually Chevrolet) was specified. S.R. became the European agents for the McBURNIE Californian Daytona Spyder and in 1988 S.R. developed a Jaguar V12 version called the S.R. V12 (6-cylinder engines could also be fitted). The Jaguar donated all its running gear, mounted in a new backbone chassis with a tubular and sheet steel skeleton to support the fibreglass bodywork, plus a steel floorpan. In time, American V8 power plants became options. available in a Euro-spec chassis following the V12's successful German TUV testing.
CR

SOUTHERN SIX (i) (US) 1920
Southern Automobile Manufacturing Co., Memphis, Tennessee.
The Southern Six was designed by W.F. Drake, who would design the Drake Six which was to be built in Knoxville, Tennessee less than a year later, and marketed under his own name. Whether one or two of the Southern Six cars were completed is not certain. Conflicting accounts list both Continental and Herschell Spillman

6-cylinder engines as power for the make and it is likely that a Continental engine was used and that the Herschell-Spillman car identified as the Southern Six was mistakenly identified with the Drake, which used the latter engine. The one car which is known to have carried the Southern Six badge was badly damaged in a Memphis garage during a shootout between the Memphis police and bootleggers. Like the Drake of Knoxville, plans for the Southern also included trucks, tractors and tyres, this coincidence making a mix-up in the two cars likely. Production, however, was limited to one or two cars.

KM

SOUTHERN SIX (ii) (AUS) 1921–1922

Australian-British Motors Ltd, Sydney, New South Wales.

Cyril Maddocks, a former wartime aviator, favoured British parts for his assembled car, the Southern Six. The engine was an ohc 2385cc 6-cylinder Sage which developed 40bhp, the transmission was by Wrigley, electrics were Brolt, the magneto a B.T.H. and the carburettor a Zenith. On a 124in (3150mm) wheelbase, it was the centre of attraction at the 1922 Sydney Centenary Show but the company was liquidated later in the year so production was unlikely to have commenced.

MG

SOVAM (F) 1965–1969

Automobiles SOVAM, Parthenay, Deux Sèvres.

After years of building specialist coachwork for light commercial vehicle applications, Sovam launched its first (and only) passenger car project. Sovam's optimistically named GT was a fibreglass 2-seater coupé based on a Renault 4 drive train. The 845cc 45bhp engine made it very slow, so 1108cc 65bhp and 1300cc versions were soon added, while 4-wheel disc brakes were optional. The GT featured distinctive styling, with a steeply raked windscreen and a lift-out targa roof panel. The Sovam GT enjoyed modest commercial success in France (100 were sold in 1966 for example), but the project never made money, and Sovam returned to its core business of building specialist industrial vehicles in 1969. In 1999 Sovam still existed, making unusual people-moving machines for airport use.

CR

SOVEREIGN (US) 1906–1907

Matthews Motor Co., Camden, New Jersey.

This was a large car powered by a 48hp 4-cylinder engine with dual ignition and double-chain drive. The tourer body was of aluminium, and was claimed to seat eight passengers. The car was advertised as 'especially adapted for protracted touring'. The car was sometimes called the Matthews, after its makers, who bought out the Jones-Corbin Co. of Philadelphia in 1906. They lasted for a shorter time than Jones-Corbin, and were out of business before the end of 1907.

NG

S.O.V.R.A. (F) 1969 to date

S.O.V.R.A., Corbeilles-en-Gatinais.

Michel Landois' company claimed to be Europe's largest supplier of buggies, selling hundreds under the name Sunhill, Fiber Bug, Mini Bug, Dolliac and others. It also made convertible conversions of the Renault 5 and Peugeot 104, as well as producing two original designs. The first was the LM2, an angular buggy-style device with bug-eye headlamps and a fixed roll-over bar on a VW Beetle chassis. The other was the LM3, first seen in 1973 but relatively short-lived, a rear-engined fibreglass-bodied sports estate using VW Beetle mechanicals. Michel Landois was also behind the G.M.F.S.A.

CR

S.P. (i) (GB) 1972–1974

Hooe Garage (East Sussex) Ltd, Hooe, Sussex.

The S.P. Highwayman was built by an established restoration company with a specialisation in Bugatti, run by Derek Skilton and Jack Perkins. This was one of the first-ever specialist cars to use the Rover V8 engine, in this case in a tubular steel chassis. The front suspension consisted of a novel set-up of a tubular axle operating horizontal coil springs via rockers. The styling was 'sports' and inspired by the 1930s. Due to a lack of orders, only two cars were made, one open and one closed, the latter with an angular glass-panelled estate-type rear end and dubbed the SP2.

CR

1972 SP2 3½-litre estate car.
NATIONAL MOTOR MUSEUM

1909 S.P.A. 70/80hp tourer.
JOAQUIN CIURO GABARRO

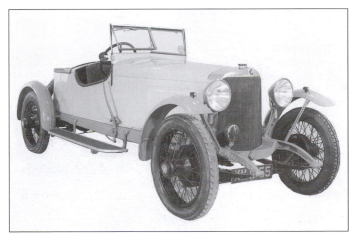

1922 S.P.A. Tipo 23S sports car.
NATIONAL MOTOR MUSEUM

S.P. (ii) (US) 1979–c.1983

Structural Plastics, Tulsa, Oklahoma.

The shape of the 3-wheeled Bond Bug could just be made out in the S.P. Spi-Tri, though the body was stretched front and rear. This was a fibreglass monocoque car, rather than a separate chassis design as per the original Bond. Early versions had electric power, weighed a ton and cost $12,000. Later versions could be ordered with petrol engines, but it is doubtful whether very many people bought one.

CR

S.P.A. (I) 1906–1926

Stà Ligure Piemontese Automobili, Turin.

This company was founded by Matteo Ceirano who had worked with his brother Giovanni Batista Ceirano and in 1904 had founded ITALA. The first S.P.A. cars were conventional 4-cylinder designs in the medium to large category, with 24

1980 Sparks Turbo roadster.
NATIONAL MOTOR MUSEUM

c.1975 Spartan (ii) roadster.
NICK GEORGANO

and 60hp T-head engines and shaft drive. 6-cylinder models arrived in 1907, including an enormous 11.7-litre 70/80hp with flywheel attached to the front end of the crankshaft, which was made up to 1912. In 1908 they merged with Fabbrica Ligure Automobili Genova (F.L.A.G.), but the S.P.A. name was retained. Smaller models were introduced, including a 10hp monobloc 2-cylinder, and in 1911 a 1.8-litre monobloc four. These had L-head engines in unit with gearboxes. Monobloc engines extended up to a 7.6-litre 50hp luxury car in 1911, when production was running at about 380 cars per year, in addition to trucks. These included army trucks made by a consortium with Fiat and Isotta-Fraschini, which built 450 starting in 1909. In 1912 500 cars were made. The 1914 range consisted of four 4-cylinder models, the 1846cc 12/15, 3176cc 18/25, 4396cc 25/30 and 7600cc 50hp.

About 3000 trucks were made during World War I, and commercials became increasingly important in the 1920s, being S.P.A.'s sole product after 1926. Several models of car were made at first, including the Tipo 23 with 2722cc 4-cylinder engine and the Tipo 24, a six with the same cylinder dimensions giving 4426cc. Sports models of both were made, with twin-ohc engines, aluminium pistons, four valves per cylinder and 4-wheel brakes. These were distinguished from the side-valve touring models by vee-radiators.

The collapse of the Banco di Sconto in 1922 seriously weakened S.P.A. and in 1926 they were acquired by Fiat. This led to an immediate end to passenger car production, but trucks were made up to 1948. Even later, the heavy truck division of Fiat was referred to as 'the S.P.A.' and the trucks carried the words 'Costruzione S.P.A.'.

NG

SPACKE (US) 1919–1920
Spacke Machine & Tool Co., Indianapolis, Indiana.
The Spacke was a minute 2-cylinder air-cooled car which featured a 2-speed planetary transmission with its drive to the right rear wheel. The 90in (2284mm) wheelbase Spacke was available only as a roadster, with passenger space limited to two bucket seats. It was priced at $295 and sales were few. For 1920 its only change was in the removal of its fuel tank from the rear deck to the front of the car in what resembled the radiator. Shortly thereafter, the name was changed to Brook (frequently misspelled as 'Brooke'), surviving briefly, subsequently being sold to the Peters Automobile Company of Pleasantville, New Jersey later that same year.

KM

S.P.A.G. (F) 1927–1928
Automobiles S.P.A.G., Asnières, Seine.
These initials represent those of the car's makers, A. Simille and G. Pequignot, suitably re-arranged to make them easier to remember. The car itself was an assembled machine, offered with a choice of 1100 or 1500cc engines by C.I.M.E. Chapuis-Dorner, Ruby or S.C.A.P., and with chassis by Rouget, rear axle by Sinpar or Malicet et Blin and brakes from Perrot-Piganeau. Five body styles were listed, but only two are definitely known to have been made, a 2-seater sports and a 2-door coupé by Weymann. The sports finished 6th in the 1927 Bol d'Or, driven by a man with the splendid name of Obsnibichine.

NG

SPARK (AUS) 1923–1924
Spark Motors Pty Ltd, Sydney, New South Wales.
A.E. Walker & Co had represented the RENOWN in New South Wales and carried on with its own Ford T rebadging when that faded. The Spark incorporated several of the after-market and customising items then current, such as a German silver radiator of Rolls-Royce shape and a 'California' top.

MG

SPARKS (US) 1980s
Ron Sparks Coachbuilders, San Mareos, California.
A neo-classic in the form of a victoria phaeton or a rumble-seat roadster. The fuel-injected engine was a 6-litre V8 Cadillac, with optional turbocharger, and Cadillac supplied the running gear.

NG

SPARLINGCO (US) c.1982
Sparlingco, Santa Ana, California.
Sparlingco made an 'antique' fun car with a choice of motorcycle engines. It looked like a caricature of an early 'horseless carriage' with a tall windscreen, skinny tyres and skimpy running boards. Top speed of this fibreglass-bodied runabout was 40mph (64km/h) and it returned 80mpg.

HP

SPARTAN (i) (US) 1910
C.W. Kelsey, Hartford, Connecticut.
The Spartan was a conventional 4-cylinder touring car with Maxwell overtones, plus the inclusion of front doors, something of a novelty in 1910. Designed by C.W. Kelsey, sales manager for the Maxwell-Briscoe Motor Co., initial plans were to build the car at Maxwell's factory in Rhode Island and badge it as the Pilgrim of Pawtucket. Although a good looking car for its price, the Spartan failed to get into production, first because its price was not competitive with its contemporaries – especially the Model T Ford, and second because at this time, Kelsey severed his connection with Maxwell-Briscoe and rented the factory of the moribund Cheney Silk Co. in Hartford, Connecticut. This would be the focal point for the production of the 3-wheeled Kelsey Motorette into 1914. During the period between the failure of the Motorette and the construction of a friction-drive car in 1917, the Spartan served as Kelsey's personal transportation. His friction-drive prototype would serve as the prototype for a series of friction-drive cars manufactured by the Kelsey Motor Co. of Newark, New Jersey in 1920. (See KELSEY.)

KM

SPARTAN (ii) (GB) 1973–1994
1973–1978 Spartan Car Co., Mapperley Plains, Nottinghamshire.
1978–1994 Spartan Car Co., Pinxton, Nottinghamshire.
Vintage-style 'replicars' became established with the Excalibur in the USA and Panther in the UK but the first budget kit-built example was the Spartan. The brainchild of Jim McIntyre, the design was obviously inspired by the MG TF, but was certainly not a replica. Early ones had suicide doors and most 1970s examples used Triumph Herald/Vitesse/Spitfire chassis; from 1974, there was a specially-designed chassis. From 1981 came a Ford Cortina based chassis intended for various Ford engines. The bodywork was in aluminium with fibreglass wings and a fibreglass lockable boot lid. Spartan also offered the Treka, a Ford Fiesta based jeep-type vehicle, and the Bandit, which was a Ford Cortina based fun car, as well as launching the SHERWOOD and Starcraft brands. Approximately 4000 Spartans were built in 21 years.

CR

SPARTAN (iii) (US) c.1983 to date

Spartan Motors, Santa Ana, California.
Spartan Motorcar Co., San Marcos, California.
Table Mountain Rancheria, Friant, Califonia.
One of the longest lived neoclassic kit cars was the Spartan. It was designed by Ron Sparks, and was based on a lengthened Datsun 280ZX chassis. A 25in (634mm) extension gave room to add a long bonnet and grill, and the Datsun cockpit area was retained. A new tail finished out the back, and the usual long, flowing running boards typical of neoclassics were added. Originally the Spartan was sold through Datsun dealers for $52,900, but later it was sold as a kit as well. The Spartan II was based on the Nissan 300ZX. In 1998 Spartan production was taken over by the Table Mountain Rancheria, an American Indian reservation, who intended to sell them fully assembled for $49,900.

HP

SPATZ (D) 1955–1957

Bayerische Autowerke GmbH, Traunreut.
This was a light car powered by a rear-mounted 250cc engine developing 14bhp. The fibreglass body accommodated three people on a bench seat. It was made by the Victoria motorcycle firm, and after 1957 was marketed under their name.

NG

SPAULDING (i) (US) 1902–1903

Spaulding Automobile & Motor Co., Buffalo, New York.
The Spaulding brothers had previously operated the Spaulding Machine Screw Co., and in January 1902 launched a small car powered by a 4hp single-cylinder engine. Both in its engine and springing it resembled the Curved Dash Oldsmobile, so much so that the Spauldings were forced to make some design changes. A larger car with tonneau body, wheel steering and 25hp 2-cylinder engine was listed for 1903. In March of that year the Spauldings were bankrupt, and the assets were bought by J.F. Morlock, who made a similar car to the small Spaulding under his own name.

NG

SPAULDING (ii) (US) 1910–1916

Spaulding Manufacturing Co., Grinnell, Iowa.
Henry W. Spaulding (1846–1937) was a blacksmith and carriage builder. In 1900 his business was said to be the oldest and largest maker of vehicles west of the Mississippi. He and his two sons launched their first car in 1910; it was a conventional 30hp 4-cylinder model, with either 2-speed epicyclic or 3-speed sliding gearbox, and shaft drive. It was offered in tourer, pony tonneau or roadster models, and these, or variations on them, made up the Spaulding range for the rest of the make's life. An unusual design, which predated the Nash by more than 20 years, was a Sleeping Car with front seats that folded down to make a bed. Spaulding never offered a closed model. Up to 1914 they used Rutenber engines, but changed to a 40hp Buda for the last three seasons. The difficulty of transporting components to Iowa was given as the reason for ending car production in 1916. By then 1481 cars had been made. The company continued in business making truck bodies.

NG

SPECFRAME (GB) 1983–1985

SpecframeVehicle Co. Ltd, Preston, Lancashire.
Road testers driving the Specframe Spectre sports kit roadster were impressed by the strength and finesse of the car's chassis (designed by an ex-T.V.R. engineer), but the 'chunky Californian inspired 2-seater' styling lacked any charm whatever. The mechanical basis was Ford Cortina and engines up to V6 could be fitted.

CR

SPECIALTY CARS (US) c.1985

Specialty Cars, Artesia, California.
This kit car company made fibreglass-bodied replicas of 1923 to 1932 Fords in hot rod form. They were intended for V8 engines.

HP

SPECIALTY MOTOR CARS (US) c.1995–1997

Specialty Motor Cars, Fayetteville, Arkansas.

1996 Spectre R42 coupé.
SPECTRE CARS

In addition to a 'normal' Cobra replica with a ladder frame and Ford-based suspension. SMC also built a very high-tech model called the IRS. It had a stiff monocoque chassis designed by engineer and former professional racing driver Richard Hudgins. Suspension was by fabricated aluminium rocker arms in front and a modified Ford Thunderbird irs in back. Cockpit-adjustable sway bars and racing shock absorbers made this one of the best handling Cobra replicas. The only engine choices were the Ford 5000cc or 5700cc V8. This design was later sold to PRECISION MOTORSPORTS.

HP

SPECTER (US) c.1993

Specter Automotive Corp., Forth Worth, Texas.
The Specter Turborossa was a Ferrari Testarossa replica based on Pontiac Firebird or Chevrolet Camaro running gear. Fibreglass panels were attached to the outside of the original body.

HP

SPECTRE (GB) 1994 to date

Spectre Supersports Ltd, Poole, Dorset.
This high performance coupé was originally presented as the G.T.D. R42 in 1994 but entered production as the Spectre R42 following the liquidation of G.T.D. The chassis was a Kevlar/composite and bonded aluminium sandwich monocoque derived from Group C racing practice. The suspension – again race-derived – consisted of front double wishbones and swivel joints, with rear A-arms and parallel radius rods. A 350bhp 4.6-litre V8 engine – sourced from Ford in North America – was mounted centrally, allied to either a 5- or 6-speed manual transmission. A top speed of 175mph (282km/h) was claimed. The company gained publicity from a starring role in the film *RPM*, and Swedish financial backing ensued. Estimates of R42 production vary from 16 to 36. An evolution model dubbed the R45 was launched at the 1997 London Motor Show, with a redesigned chassis featuring push-rod A-arm suspension, a better interior and redesigned bodywork including cowled headlamps rather than pop-ups.

CR

SPEED see BRISSONET

SPEEDFORD; SPEEDSPORT (B) 1924–1927

Bartsoen et Bonar, Brussels.
The partners Jean Bartsoen and Geo Bonar made modified Model T Fords, using the original engine and transmission but with front-wheel brakes, Hartford friction shock absorbers and new bodies. These were mostly 2-seater sports, sometimes with two additional wickerwork seats behind the aluminium ones, though some 2-door saloons and coupés were made from the end of 1925. They had a number of sporting successes, and one car with a 16-valve ohv conversion won the 3-litre class in the 1924 Belgian Grand Prix. About 100 cars were made in 1925, the company's best year. At about that time the name was changed from Speedford to Speedsport.

NG

c.1904 Speedwell (i) 6hp 2-seater.
NATIONAL MOTOR MUSEUM

1906 Speedwell (i) 14/16hp landaulet.
NICK BALDWIN

1910 Speedwell (iii) Series 10 tourer.
KEITH MARVIN

SPEEDWAY (US) 1904–1905

Gas Engine & Power Co., Morris Heights, New York.

This car was named after the road on the west bank of the Harlem River, overlooking the Bronx, where horsemen could exercise their steeds at speed. The car was a 5-seater tourer powered by a 28hp 4-cylinder engine, with shaft drive. Its price of $4700 was very high for such an unknown make, and no doubt inhibited sales. The makers supplied engines to W.S. Howard, maker of the HOWARD (ii) car, and who joined Gas Engine & Power as chief engineer in 1905, at about the time that the Speedway was discontinued.
NG

SPEEDWAY MOTORS (US) c.1980 to date

Speedway Motors, Lincoln, Nebraska.

Speedway sold a wide variety of hot rod and racing parts, including a number of kit cars. Initially they included Bugatti replicas and dune buggies, but later they specialised in hot rods and antique cars. Among their most popular kits were a Ford Model A replica called the Modern A, and a Ford Track Roadster with a cut-down Model T body on a ladder frame set up for V8 engines.
HP

SPEEDWELL (i) (GB) 1900–1908

1900–1906 Speedwell Motor & Engineering Co. Ltd, Reading Berkshire.
1906–1908 New Speedwell Motor Co. Ltd, London.

Speedwells were originally agents and factors in the cycle trade, diversifying into cars before the turn of the century, when they advertised several then popular models such as Léon Bollée, De Dion-Bouton, MMC and Renault. The Dew family, who owned the business, built a Rochet-based special, and also imported a few Hanzer cars which they sold as Speedwells, but the first cars assembled under the Speedwell name used Lacoste et Battmann chassis and De Dion 1-cylinder engines of 700cc. W.J. Warren, who worked for Speedwell and whose father had joined in 1898, later recalled that the main thrust around 1902 was in promoting the Gardner-Serpollet steam cars for which they also held an agency, but this did not prevent an increasing range of petrol vehicles being assembled under the Speedwell name. At the Crystal Palace show in January 1903, for example, 5 chassis were on offer, from 6hp to 40hp, with a wide variety of coachwork. The single cylinder model, with engine equivocally claimed to be 'of De Dion type' (possibly Volta, as was the 10hp 2-cylinder of the period), was available in 1904 at only 165 guineas (£173.25) with a 2-seater tonneau body. Chassis frames were variously tubular, re-inforced wood or conventional channel section for some larger models.

By 1905 a completely revised range of vehicles was on offer and Speedwells had started to commission their own castings for axle and gearbox parts. There were other changes such as a distinctive round radiator. A 2-cylinder Gnome-engined car rated at 10hp and a 4-cylinder 14hp of 2497cc ran in the TT. Prices ranged from £195 for the 6hp 2-seater up to £525 for the 18/22 double phaeton and more for a landaulet. An entry was again made in the 1906 TT, with a 4-cylinder of 3922cc, but around this time the firm was restructured and ambitious changes made to the specifications. The rear axle, split horizontally, was mounted on three-quarter elliptic springs with shackle-pin angles claimed to eliminate wear, whilst 'wheel wobble' was also ruled out. Other advanced features were a concealed spare wheel compartment, a fan belt tension adjuster and a multiple disc clutch with spring take-up in unit with the gearbox. A variety of Gnome engines were used, from the 10/12hp 2-cylinder through 3- and 4-cylinder models up to an imposing 40hp 6-cylinder 6136cc.

The original firm by now had been taken over by Brown Brothers and were once more concerned primarily with factoring and agencies. Further new models, with Aster engines, were on show at Olympia in November 1907 but sales did not reflect ambitions and production appears to have ceased soon after.
DF

SPEEDWELL (ii) see KUNZ

SPEEDWELL (iii) (US) 1907–1914

Speedwell Motor Car Co., Dayton, Ohio.

This Speedwell was a large, conventional tourer designed at first by Gilbert Loomis who had made cars under his own name in Westfield, Massachusetts from 1901 to 1904. The first models had 40hp 4- or 60hp 6-cylinder Rutenber engines, on wheelbases of 116 (2944mm) and 132in (3350mm), with roadster, tourer or limousine bodies. Only 25 were sold in 1907, so the company decided to concentrate on a one-model policy and to make their own engines. These were of 50hp and the cars had a wheelbase of 120in (3046mm). They made up for a single chassis by offering six body styles in 1909, and ten in 1911. These included roadsters, tourers, a limousine and a Duck Boat. Also that year they included a 132in (3350mm) wheelbase again, and from 1913 offered an all-6-cylinder range which included cars with poppet-valve and Mead sleeve-valve engines. The latter were not a success, and when the inventor Cyrus Mead was killed in a car crash the Speedwell directors had no one to turn to for improvements. In 1914 they suffered a disastrous flood at the factory which delayed deliveries for a long time, and the business never recovered. About 4000 Speedwell cars were made as well as a number of trucks.

NG

Further Reading
'The Speedwell from Dayton: A motor car worth remembering',
Beverly Rae Kimes, *Automobile Quarterly*, Vol. 13, No. 1.

SPEEDY (i) (GB) 1905
Jackson Brothers & Lord, Salford, Lancashire.
This was a light 3-wheeler powered by a 4hp engine with belt final drive and seating for two in tandem.

NG

SPEEDY (ii) (GB) 1920–1921
Pullinger Engineering Co. Ltd, Peckham, London.
The manufacturers had great hopes for the Speedy cyclecar, promising output of 5000 in the first year, but it probably never got beyond the prototype stage, and did not make its way into most sales guides. It was powered by an 8hp air-cooled V-twin engine, with 2-speed gearbox, belt final drive, and a streamlined 2-seater body. The projected price was £150, very reasonable when compared with a G.N. at £275. At first it was known as the Pullinger, after its makers.

NG

SPEIDEL (CH) 1914–1922
Paul Speidel, Geneva.
Speidel designed a voiturette making use of a well-known French Chapuis-Dornier 4-cylinder side-valve engine of 8hp with 3-speed gearbox and shaft drive. At least one had the two seats arranged in tandem fashion. Motorcycles with various proprietory engines were also made. In 1920 he resumed manufacture of voiturettes on a small scale but these were now fitted with a Swiss 8hp Müller-Vogel (MV) 4-cylinder engine and a 4-speed gearbox. For the Swiss voiturette GP of Meyrin, Geneva, in 1922, Speidel built a light racing car in just six weeks. It had a Müller-Vogel twin cylinder engine of 620cc and was capable of over 70mph (113km/h). This however was the end of a brave venture. A total of about 15 Speidel voiturettes were made.

FH

SPENCER (i) (US) 1901–1902
Christopher Spencer, Windsor and Hartford, Connecticut.
Christopher Miner Spencer built a steam wagon in 1862 in which he used to drive himself to work, and became a successful manufacturer of rifles. He built another experimental steamer in 1899, and from 1901 to 1902 he made nine more (seven in Windsor and two in Hartford). One was a delivery van for Macy's in New York City. These had four single-acting cylinders under the body, with the boiler slung behind. All were made for sale, though he never formed a company.

NG

SPENCER (ii) (US) 1921–1922
Research Engineering Co., Dayton, Ohio.
The Spencer was a small car, designed by O.H. Spencer, who headed the Research Engineering Co. With a wheelbase of 103in (2614mm) and powered by a 4-cylinder ohv engine, also designed by O.H. Spencer, the 5-seater touring car was the only body type produced. The car weighed 1500lb (682kg). Its original price of $1200 was reduced to $850 for 1922 which was its final year. Production of this short-lived car was minimal.

KM

1920 Speedy (ii) 8hp cyclecar.
NATIONAL MOTOR MUSEUM

SPENNY (US) 1913–1914
1913 Clarence A. Spenny, Tucson, Arizona.
1914 Spenny Motor Car Co., Holland, Michigan.
Clarence Spenny made three 6-cylinder cars in Tucson, but decided that Arizona was not the place to found an automobile industry, and headed for Michigan. There he set up a company and a few more cars were made, a 4/30 selling for $1075 and a 6/60 at $3750.

NG

SPERBER (D) 1911–1919
Norddeutsche Automobilwerke, Hamelin.
This company first made cars under the name COLIBRI from 1908 to 1910, then built a larger car which they called the Sperber. It had a 1592cc 6/15PS 4-cylinder L-head engine, 3-speed gearbox and shaft drive. In 1913 two smaller models appeared, the 1330cc 5/15PS Typ E and 1545cc 6/15PS Typ F. A very few were made after the war, before the factory was taken over by SELVE in 1919.

HON

SPERLING (US) 1921–1923
Associated Motors Corp., Elkhart, Indiana.
The Sperling was a car designed for export and built by the Crow Motor Car Co. of Elkhart, Indiana. It was built exclusively with right-hand steering, a 114in (2893mm) wheelbase and powered by a Supreme S4 4-cylinder L-head engine. The car was available as an open touring model at $980, a sedan at $1450, and in chassis form. The Sperling was distinguished by a slightly pointed radiator.

KM

SPERRY (US) 1898–1901
Sperry Engineering Co., Cleveland, Ohio.
Elmer A. Sperry was a well-known electrical pioneer in the fields of arc lamps and mining equipment, who formed his company in 1898, though the cars were built for him by the Cleveland Machine Screw Co. At first they were called Cleveland Electric, Sperry System, but from about 1900 simply as Sperry. They were powered by a 3½hp motor, and came in eight body styles, 2- and 4-seaters, open and closed. A single lever controlled steering, acceleration and braking; this later became the norm for electric vehicles, but was an innovation in 1898. The Cleveland Screw Co. had a French board of directors, and at least 100 Sperrys were exported to France.

In January 1901 the makers sold the design (and a few complete cars) to the American Bicycle Co. who incorporated some of its features in the WAVERLEY Electric. Cleveland then made a petrol-engined car from 1902 to 1904, while Elmer Sperry invented his famous gyroscope, made by the Sperry Gyroscope Co. which later became the Sperry Rand Corp. He died in 1930.

NG

SPEX (CDN) c.1981–c.1990
Spex, Montreal, Québec.
Founded by Paul Deutschman and Kell Warshaw, Spex produced the Gamine, a handsome small convertible car. It used front-wheel drive Honda mechanicals and had plastic bodywork. A prototype Spexster was also shown in 1988, a smooth-shaped open 2-seater sports car described as a Porsche Speedster for the year 2000, but this did not enter production.

CR

1908 S.P.O. 24hp roadster.
NICK GEORGANO

SPHINX (i) (F) 1912–1925

1912–1916 F. Terrier, Courbevoie, Seine.

1920–1925 Sphinx Automobiles Usines Perfecto, Puteaux, Seine.

The Sphinx was a French-built cyclecar designed by an Englishman, J.H. Forster. Some cars of similar design were made in England under the name GLOBE (ii). At least three engine options were available on the French-built cars, a 1038cc 8/10hp single-cylinder, an 1130cc 8/10hp in-line four and a 1327cc V-4. Chain or belt final drive was offered. In the 1920s engines were a 1400cc flat-twin or a 1323cc four. Mr Forster was still connected with the firm for they were sold in England under his name (FORSTER (ii)) and also as the ANGLO-SPHINX.

NG

SPHINX (ii) (US) 1914–1916

Sphinx Motor Car Co., York, Pennsylvania.

The promoter of this car, H.R. Averill, bought the factory formerly occupied by the Hart-Kraft Motor Car Co. and hired E.T. Gillard to design it. The Sphinx was a conventional 5-seater tourer or 2-seater roadster powered by an 18hp 4-cylinder Lycoming engine, and priced at $695. It was launched in late 1914 as a 1915 model but before that year was out it was announced that the company was being reorganised as the DuPont Motor Car Co. It is not certain if any cars were marketed under this name, or whether the plan was frustrated by the famous DuPont company of Delaware, who were to make cars of their own after the war. At all events, the 1916 cars announced in October 1915 were called Sphinx again. They were slightly lower in price, but otherwise identical to the 1915s. 123 cars were made in 1915 and 224 in 1916, before Averill gave up the motor business, selling part of his factory to his former employers, PULLMAN, and part to a consortium who would make the BELL (ii).

NG

SPHINX (iii) (D) 1920–1925

Sphinx Automobilwerke AG, Zwickau.

This firm produced only one model during its five-year lifespan, a light car with 1320cc 4-cylinder engine. In 1925 manufacture was taken over, or perhaps the company name was simply changed, as it became the Georg Kralapp Automobilwerke.

HON

SPIDOS (F) c.1921–1925

Cyclecars Spidos, Lyons.

This was a light car powered by a 1095cc ohv Ruby 4-cylinder engine. The make achieved a number of successes in hill climbs, driven by the designer de Vassiaux.

NG

SPIJKSTAAL (NL) 1980s

Spijkstaal BV, Spijkenisse.

From as early as 1930, this company specialised in the production of electric vehicles, both 3- and 4-wheeled, principally for commercial use. Some machines were made that can be classified as passenger cars, including people carriers and even motor homes, though most Spijkstaals were mobile shops or delivery vans, some with diesel engines. A very small single-seater electric saloon was also marketed during the 1980s.

CR

SPINELL (D) 1924–1925

Spinell Motorfahrzeuge GmbH Otto Krell Jr, Berlin.

The Spinell was an attractive-looking small sports car with engine and radiator set well back in the frame. It was powered by a 500cc 4/18PS Kuhne or 5/20PS Motosacoche engine.

HON

SPIRI EURODYNAMICS (US) c.1990

Spiri Eurodynamics, Sudbury, Maine.

The Ferrari 308 was the inspiration for this kit car based on the 1982 to 1990 Chevrolet Camaro.

HP

SPIRIT (GB) 1983–1987

1983–1986 Spirit Cars, London.

1986–1987 Daytona Classics, Clacton, Essex.

Kit car maker A.D. was the first company to make the Spirit, a vague 'replica' of the Mercedes SSK in the American vein with a VW Beetle floorpan and rear-mounted engine. A Ford Cortina-based chassis was also engineered shortly before the project passed to Spirit Cars of London, who offered it for three years until Daytona Classics took it on in 1986, renaming it the Gatsby.

CR

SPITZ (A) 1902–1906

Arnold Spitz, Vienna.

Spitz operated a successful business in Vienna selling well-known foreign makes such as De Dion-Bouton, Benz and Mercedes, Together with the engineer Otto Hieronimus he designed cars which were at first built for him by GRAF & STIFT. The early models used De Dion-Bouton engines of 8 and 12hp, but in 1905 a new model was introduced with a 24/30PS 4-cylinder engine; the chassis and engine were built by a railway wagon factory in Raab, Hungary. About 30 had been made when Spitz ran into financial difficulties. It is said that he was too generous with the prices paid for vehicles taken in part exchange, so no profit was made. He was declared bankrupt before the end of 1906.

HON

SPLINTER (US) c.1982–1990

Splinter Auto Works, Inc, Plymouth, Indiana.

The Woody wagon was a popular body style in the 1930s to 1950s. These station wagons had beautifully finished wood on the bodywork. Splinter made 9/10 scale replicas of a typical 1930s Chevrolet 'Woody' in station wagon and pick-up truck styles. They had fibreglass mudguards and nose with ash and marine birch bodywork. They were based on Chevrolet Chevette sedan running gear.

HP

S.P.M. (GB) 1990 to date

1990–1994 Specialist Performance Mouldings, Whitminster, Gloucestershire.
1994 to date Lakeside Carriages, Redditch, Worcestershire.

This was a Ferrari 308 GTB lookalike based on the Pontiac Fiero. Its 11-piece fibreglass body panel set fitted over the Fiero chassis. Options included a targa roof and a Ferrari BB512 Boxer body style.

CR

S.P.M.A. (F) 1908

Sté Parisienne de Mécanique Appliquee, Courbevoie, Seine.

This was a light car powered by a 10/12hp 4-cylinder engine. It had friction transmission by a small pulley which worked on two large discs.

NG

S.P.O. (F) 1908–1911

Sté Française de Petit Outillage, Courbevoie, Seine.

This company made a wide variety of components for the motor industry before building a complete car themselves. Two models were offered, a 16hp taxicab and a 24hp town car, both with L-head 4-cylinder engines. Several chassis were exported to America where they were fitted with roadster bodies. One of these survives today.

NG

SPOERER (US) 1909–1914

Carl Spoerer's Sons Co., Baltimore, Maryland.

Carl Spoerer was a carriage builder whose two sons Charles and Jacob decided to enter the car business in 1907, though their first production cars did not appear until the end of 1909 as 1910 models. They had 40hp 4-cylinder Herschell-Spillman engines, 3-speed gearboxes, shaft drive and Mercedes-like radiators. They seem to have been good quality cars but having little to distinguish them from any others, they sold mostly to local buyers, even though the makers tried to promote them as a national rather than a purely regional product. In 1911 a smaller car using a 25hp Excelsior engine was introduced. This and the 40hp remained on the market until 1914, when financial problems forced the company to close.

NG

SPORTECH see PIONTEK

SPORTS (GB) 1900–1901

Sports Motor Car Co., Kensington, London; Kilburn, London.

This name was used for at least three models of car which were imported rather than made in England, though the bodies may have been locally built. The 4-seater Sports Car had a 4½hp single-cylinder engine and chain drive, while the 4-seater Sports American Phaeton had an 8hp flat-twin engine 4-speed gearbox and shaft drive. The Phaeton used a Gautier-Wehrlé transmission and may have been of this make. A new model for 1901 was the 9hp with vertical twin engine and shaft drive. The Sports Motor Car Co. also sold other imported cars under the name Mayfair.

NG

SPORTSCAR (NL) 1974–1980

1974–1979 Sportscar, Cruquis, Haarlemmermeer.
1979–1980 Bart Holland, Zwammerdam.

This company rivalled Ruska in the production of beach buggies for the Dutch market and it also produced a licence-built version of the American TALON under the name Matula GT sports coupé. This consisted of a plastic body designed for a shortened VW Beetle chassis. It featured a flip-forward canopy for entry, close-set headlamps in cut-outs and a louvred rear end. Cars were sold principally in kit form.

CR

SPORTS CAR ENGINEERING (US) c.1958

Sports Car Engineering, Los Angeles, California.

The Spyder fibreglass body was the British Mistrale shell, built under licence. They came in two lengths. The Spyder 1 fitted an 88in (2233mm) to 94in (2386mm) wheelbase and cost $295. The Spyder 2 fitted a 94in (2386mm) to 102in (2589mm) wheelbase and was an extra $50. There were also two chassis designs in wheelbases to fit the bodies, one with A-arm front suspension and one with live axles at both ends.

HP

SPORTS CAR SERVICES (GB) 1985–1987

Sports Car Services, Peterborough, Cambridgeshire.

The S.C.S. 427 Cobra replica was given birth by engine tuner Stuart Titman. His aim was to offer a Cobra kit at a reasonable price. The recipe was familiar: a steel backbone/ladder chassis, Jaguar XJ steering and suspension, narrowed Jaguar drive shafts and power from Rover V8, American V8 or Jaguar V12. From 1986, it offered the Mako, a replica of the 1976–1978 Chevrolet Corvette using the 427 Cobra replica chassis.

CR

SPORTS CARS INC (US) c.1998

Sports Cars Inc, Kentucky.

This company made kit cars based on Pontiac Fiero or custom tube frame chassis. They sold replicas of the Ferrari F-50 called the XR-2000, a Lamborghini Diablo clone called the Executive, and a Lamborghini Countach copy called the Euro.

HP

SPRINGER (US) 1903–1905

Springer Motor Vehicle Co., New York, New York.

John H. Springer purchased the KIDDER Motor Vehicle Co. with the intention of continuing their steam car, but after a few had been made he turned to a petrol design by Frank T. Clark. His first was a 2-seater roadster powered by a 12hp 2-cylinder engine, followed by a 5-seater tourer with 40hp 4-cylinder engine. This in fact consisted of two 2-cylinder engines which could be run together or with one disconnected. Despite the presence of a bonnet, all Springer engines were mounted under the front seat.

NG

SPRINGFIELD (i) (US) 1903

Springfield Automobile Co., Springfield, Ohio.

This car was made by the Bramwells, father and son, who had formerly made the Bramwell-Robinson in Hyde Park, Massachusetts. The Springfield was fairly typical of a light car of the period, with 8hp single-cylinder 2-stroke engine, epicyclic transmission and single-chain drive. It was made only as a 2-seater, on a 72in (1827mm) wheelbase. Production was said to be running at three cars a week by the summer of 1903, but later in the year the Bramwells, who were managers, bought out the owners and changed the name of the car to BRAMWELL.

NG

SPRINGFIELD (ii) (US) 1907–1910

1907 Med-Bow Automobile Co., Springfield, Massachusetts.
1907–1909 H.C. Medcraft Automobile Co., Springfield, Massachusetts.
1909–1910 Springfield Motor Car Co., Springfield, Illinois.

The Med-Bow company was formed by Harry C. Medcraft and George G. Bowersox, hence the name, to make a conventional tourer with 35hp 4-cylinder Rutenber engine, and a 107in (2716mm) wheelbase. Before many cars had been made

1905 Spyker 4-wheel drive tourer (left) with a Thornycroft.
NICK BALDWIN

1987 Spyder Silverstone sports car.
NICK BALDWIN

Bowersox withdrew from the partnership, so the company was renamed after Medcraft. For 1908 the tourer was joined by a roadster, and in 1909 they moved to Springfield, Illinois, where some of the directors lived. The Illinois-built car had the same engine, but was on a longer wheelbase of 128in (3249mm). The company slogan was 'The Made-to-Order Car for 300 Exacting People', but even on the most generous estimate they never achieved this figure. Apparently 46 cars were built in Massachusetts, but figures for Illinois vary between 11 and 200! Before the end of 1910 the factory had been bought by the RAYFIELD Motor Car Co.

NG

SPRINGUEL (B) 1907–1914
SA des Automobiles Springuel, Liège.
Jules Springuel-Wilmotte began experimenting with cars in 1902, but did not offer one for sale until 1907. The 24/30CV had a 3768cc 4-cylinder engine with pair-cast cylinders, dual ignition, double-chain drive and a large tourer body. It was made up to 1910, by which time it had been joined by a smaller car, the 3052cc 16CV and a larger, the 4586cc 28/35CV, which was available in short, long and extra-long wheelbases. A smaller, and altogether more up to date model was the 2120cc 12/14CV of 1911, with monobloc casting of its four cylinders and overhead inlet valves. It was made as a sports car and as a taxicab. In 1912 Springuel's business was acquired by Imperia, and some models were known as Springuel-Imperia. The 1913/14 range consisted of five 4-cylinder models, from the 12/14 to the 28/35CV. Only the latter retained pair-casting of the cylinders. Production came to an end with the outbreak of World War I, but a few 18/24s were assembled from a stock of parts up to 1920.

NG

SPRITE (US) 1914
W.S. Frazier & Co., Aurora, Illinois.
The Sprite cyclecar was powered by a 4-cylinder Farmer engine, and had friction transmission and belt final drive. Frazier's main business was making racing sulkies, which was continued into the 1920s.

NG

SPURR (US) 1900–1901
Spurr Automobile Co., New York, New York.
Charles Spurr's car was a simple *dos-à-dos* buggy powered by a 2-cylinder engine that could be started from the seat. A 2-speed gearbox gave speeds of 8 and 24mph (13 and 39km/h). Steering by wheel was quite advanced for the period.

NG

SPYDER (GB) 1985–c.1992
Spydersport Ltd, Whittlesey, Peterborough, Cambridgeshire.
Spyder was the name behind the design and manufacture of numerous chassis for specialist and racing cars, as well as Lotus replacement chassis. The Silverstone was its first complete car design, reinterpreting the Lotus 7 theme in an original way. It had a steel backbone chassis with body panels made of metal and fibreglass, a smooth undertray, rakish body panels and a built-in roll-over bar, while the suspension was specially designed. The choice of engines included Ford Kent, Toyota twin cam, Saab 16V and Mazda rotary. There was an optional fibreglass hard-top with a tailgate. Some 40 cars were made up until 1989. Spyder's position as a manufacturer of Lotus replacement chassis put it in a strong position to make a replica of the Lotus Elite 501, which it called the Donington. Unlike the original, it could use a Rover V8 engine and Jaguar limited slip differential, though the suspension was original Lotus.

CR

SPYDER RSK (AUS) 1983–1985
Spyder Conversions, Boronia, Victoria.
At first, Richard Raftis intended to merely buy the bodies for the Spyder RSK from G.P. Vehicles in England, and to fit these to shortened VW platforms. However, he found that design rules and registration requirements were so stringent that he had to revise the shell to fit full-length floorpans. Eventually this resulted in a unique locally-made product. The roadster was sold in either kit or complete forms with a variety of engines, up to Mazda rotor or Porsche for top performance.

MG

SPYKER (NL) 1898–1925
1898–1915 N.V. Industriële Maatschappij 'Trompenburg'.
1915–1923 N.V. Nederlandsche Automobiel- en Vliegtuigfabriek Trompenburg.
1923–1925 N.V. Spyker Automobielfabriek.
In 1880 the brothers Jacobus and Hendrik Spijker set up in business as coachbuilders at Hilversum, south east of Amsterdam. In 1899 they drove the first Benz cars that entered the country and joined the rallies that began in those years. In their coachbuilding-shop they improved the car bodies for their customers and called them 'Spyker, genre Benz'. From this they got the idea to build cars themselves. In 1898 they founded the N.V. Industriële Maatschappij 'Trompenburg' and built a new production hall. Two years later at the 1900 Amsterdam show, the whole series of Spyker cars was on display. ('Spyker' instead of 'Spijker', for the export market.) Most of the 3hp and 5hp cars strongly resembled the famous Benz cars. The 5hp had a front-mounted air-cooled flat-twin engine, 2-speed and reverse gear, and shaft drive (Spyker never used chains). This car was not a commercial success. The bigger 20hp had a 5-bearing crankshaft and full-elliptic front suspension. The close fit of the bonnet was the first step towards the dust sealing that became a strong Spyker selling point (the 'Dustless' Spyker car), accentuated by the full undershielding of later models. For 1903 and the following years Spyker had a number of 4-cylinder cars in their programme: 14/16, 15/22, 20/28, 25/36, and 30/42hp models. Those models were especially important for the English market. At the London and Paris shows Spyker showed the first 6-cylinder, 4-wheel drive car with an 8.5-litre 60hp engine.

Conventional pair-cast cylinders and semi-elliptic front springs came in 1905, and in the same year round radiators were adopted. The 1906 Spykers had ball bearing crankshafts. The biggest of a range of four 4-cylinder cars was the 25/38 with the 7.9-litre engine. Pressed steel frames arrived on 1907 models, smallest of which was a short stroke (80 × 90) 10/15hp 4-cylinder (1809cc). The next big change came in 1909, when the company adopted Valentin Laviolette's ingenious T-head, transverse-camshaft layout, a feature of all the Spykers up to 1917. Of the 4-cylinders, from the 1.7-litre 12hp up to the 7.2-litre 40hp, all with thermo-syphon cooling, only the larger ones had four forward speeds,

1906 Spyker 2-cylinder 2-seater.
NICK BALDWIN

although all but the smallest had three-quarter elliptic springs at the rear. The 12hp had a 3-speed transaxle and in 1911 some models were available with Allen-Liversidge 4-wheel brakes as an optional extra, though these were apparently not a success. Electric lighting was available in 1913 and standard by 1915. The vee radiators appeared during 1914, when the company introduced a faster version of the 3.4-litre, being a 20hp Sport with light steel pistons, giving 52bhp and capable of 68mph (109km/h).

Production dropped sharply after 1916 because of shortage of material during World War I. The postwar Spykers reverted to an L-head layout, as well as making liberal use of American components like Delco coil ignition, Stewart vacuum feed, and Stromberg carburettors. The 13/30 3560cc had a 3-speed gearbox with central change. In 1920 the company tried to import MATHIS light cars from France and sell them with Spyker badges, but the last real Spyker was the Frits Koolhoven-designed 6-cylinder 30/40hp, of which approximately 150 were built. It featured a 5.7-litre side-valve Maybach engine with dual ignition, and there were four forward speeds. Front-wheel brakes came in 1923, but although Queen Wilhelmina of the Netherlands purchased in all ten Spyker cars, and S.F. Edge used a 2-seater for a successful attack on his Double 12-Hour record at Brooklands in 1922, there was little future for such an expensive car. The last Spyker car left the factory at the end of 1925.

In 2000 the name was revived for a sports car powered by a mid-mounted 4.2-litre Audi V8 engine.

FBV

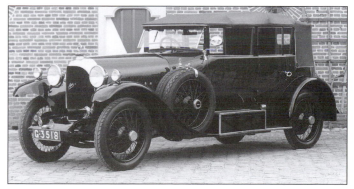

1922 Spyker C4 30/40hp tourer.
DUTCH NATIONAL AUTO MUSEUM

Further Reading
Spyker 1890–1926, Vincent van der Vinne, De Bataafsche Leeuw, 1998.
Spyker, made in Holland, Wim Oude Weernink, Institut Trompenberg Foundation, 1997.
'Dutch Treat: The inimitable Spyker', Wim Oude Weernink, *Automobile Quarterly*, Vol. 16, No. 4.

1936 Squire (i) 1½-litre sports car.
NATIONAL MOTOR MUSEUM

1936 Squire (i) with 'Skimpy' body by Markham.
NICK BALDWIN

SQUAL (F) 1961

Guy Mismaque and Bernhard Gouiran conceived what was probably the raciest car ever to be based on the Citroën 2CV. Its fibreglass coupé bodywork, only 112cm high, was made by Seveno. Weighing only 390kg its top speed was 81mph (130km/h). After being seen at the 1961 Paris Salon, the Squal never went into production.

CR

SQUIRE (i) (GB) 1934–1936

Squire Car Manufacturing Co. Ltd, Henley-on-Thames, Oxfordshire.
Few cars have generated more interest from a tiny production figure than the Squire. It was conceived by a young Englishman, Adrian Morgan Squire (1910–1940), who had worked out the basic design of the car, even issuing a 6-page catalogue, while still at school. At the age of 21, in 1931, he set up Squire Motors Ltd, a small company which sold, repaired and tuned sports cars, and in 1934 incorporated a separate company, the Squire Car Manufacturing Co., to build his dream car. Announced in September 1934 it was a low-slung 2-seater sports car powered by a twin-ohc supercharged 1496cc Anzani R1 engine which, when Squire had worked on it, developed 110bhp. The press never mentioned the Anzani origins, for Squire had his own trademark cast on the inlet manifold. The engine's designer, Douglas Ross, is reported to have said that Squire could call it anything he liked, so long as he paid for it. The engine drove through a Wilson 4-speed pre-selector gearbox in which the bottom gear band served as a clutch. The chassis was a very strong cruciform-braced structure, and the brakes, though

Lockheed actuated, were Squire's own design, with manganese alloy drums 15.5in (395mm) in diameter, which entirely filled the internal diameter of the wheels, with practically no daylight showing through. They were able to stop the car in under 10 metres from 30mph (48km/h), braking so powerful that sometimes the front spring shackles fractured.

Two wheelbases were offered, 102 or 125in (2589 or 3172mm), for 2- or 4-seater bodies, which were to be open or drop-head coupés by Vanden Plas. In fact the coupés were never made, and only two long wheelbase cars were ever delivered, together with five on the short wheelbase. There was nothing against the Squire but its price; this was £1220 for a Vanden Plas 2-seater, about double the cost of a contemporary Aston Martin or Frazer Nash, and nearly as much as a Type 55 Bugatti. Adrian Squire hoped to sell the cars through his friends, and several did become customers, but not enough to keep the little firm going. In an effort to reduce the price, a much cheaper body by Markham, with cycle-type wings, was offered in 1935, but even so it still cost £995. A single-seater, also bodied by Markham, was raced at Brooklands by Luis Fontes, but he never had much success with it. By May 1936 the price of the 'Skimpy', as the Markham 2-seater was nicknamed, had been reduced to £695, with a standard 2-seater at £795 and a 4-seater at £895. However, only two cars were delivered in 1936, a 'Skimpy' and a Vanden Plas 4-seater, and on 3 July 1936 the Squire Car Manufacturing Co. was wound up. Squire Motors continued as a garage, but Adrian Squire left to join Lagonda. He was working for the Bristol Aeroplane Co. when he was killed in an air raid in September 1940.

The Squire story did not end completely in 1936, for one of the customers, Val Zethrin, purchased all the remaining parts, and managed to build up two more short-chassis cars between 1937 and 1939. They were made by Squire mechanics working at the Henley-on-Thames premises. The first to be completed had a Corsica drophead body and the second was a Zethrin-designed open 2-seater. Zethrin also modified the Anzani engine to make it quieter. He hoped to resume production after the war, but could not obtain the patterns for the cylinder heads and blocks, and the cost of making new ones would have been unrealistic for a small run. Of the seven cars made by the Squire Car Manufacturing Co., six survive, as do both the Zethrin-assembled cars.

NG

Further Reading
The Squire, Jonathan Wood, Profile Publications, 1966.
'Bless the Squire and his relations', Bill Morgan,
Automobile Quarterly, Vol. 11, No. 3.

SQUIRE (ii) (US) c.1971–1976

Auto Sport Importers, Inc, Philadelphia, Pennsylvania.
This fibreglass-bodied Jaguar SS-100 replica was powered by a Ford engine and built by AUTOMOBILI INTERMECCANICA in Italy. It was a very accurate full-sized replica and used Dunlop wire wheels. A Ford 4100cc in-line 6-cylinder engine was coupled to a 4-speed manual or 3-speed automatic transmission and much of the suspension and the rear axle were Ford as well. The Squire was designed by Auto Sports Importers president Ed Felbin and partner Mike Wolf, but the frame was redesigned by Intermeccanica before production started. Fifty cars were sold in fully assembled form.

HP

SQUIRE (iii) (I) 1970s

An Italian company built a series of SS100-inspired 'replicars' mostly for export to the USA. They used the mechanical components of various American-market 6-cylinder Fords.

CR

SQUIRE (iv) (GB) 1984–1993

1984–1986 Squire Sports Car Co. Ltd, Hartlebury, Worcestershire.
1986–c.1988 Squire Sports Car Co. Ltd, Walsall, West Midlands.
c.1988–1993 Squire Sports Car Co. Ltd, Bridgnorth, Shropshire.
1993 Squire Motors Ltd, Crediton, Devon.
1993 Marlin Engineering, Crediton, Devon.
A replica of the exquisite 1935–1936 Squire — one of the great lost causes of motoring — was warmly welcomed by enthusiasts. Car restorer Phil Kennedy created a steel box section chassis using Ford Cortina mechanicals and later Alfa Romeo 1750cc twin cam or Rover V8 engines. The body construction echoed

vintage practice, using an ash frame and aluminium panels. An S Type version was also offered to duplicate more precisely the original Squire's features, including 18in (457mm) wheels, 10in (254mm) headlamps and 17in (431mm) steering wheel. Only 16 kits were built by the original maker.

CR

SQUIRE MOTOR CARS (US) c.1982–1990
Squire Motor Cars Ltd, Hamden, Connecticut.
Top-Notch Chop 'N' Rods, Hamden, Connecticut.
The Squire Roadster was the old DOVAL Shadow neo-classic 2-seater. The aluminium coachwork was replaced with fibreglass and an MGB cockpit area with doors was used. It was mounted on a Ford Cougar or LTD chassis and was sold in kit or fully assembled form. By 1990 the company had changed its name (and, we presume, its focus) to Top-Notch Chop 'N' Rods and renamed the Squire the Boattail Roadster.

HP

S.R. (i) *see* SOUTHERN ROADCRAFT

S.R. (ii) **(GB)** 1985–1986
S&R Sportscars, Wakefield, Yorkshire.
This was a revival of the EMBEESEA Eurocco. It was offered in two forms: the SR1 (2-seater) and SR2 (2+2), both over an unmodified VW Beetle floorpan.

CR

S.R.C. (E) 1921–1924
Stevenson, Romagosa y Cia, Barcelona.
MATAS decided to abandon car production and sold his car design to S.R.C., a well-known company representing Studebaker cars and Caledon trucks in Spain. S.R.C. continued with the car without any changes. The only new car was introduced in 1921, on the same base, but with a better finish.

VCM

S.R.K. (US) 1915
S.R.K. Motor Co., Detroit, Michigan.
Originally known as the Strouse, this car and company were renamed after the three men involved, Clarence B. Strouse, Frederick T. Ranney and Thomas D. Knight. It was a cyclecar powered by a 4-cylinder Hermann engine, with friction transmission and single-chain drive. A 2-seater was planned to sell for $300, but though a prototype was extensively tested, production never started.

NG

S. & S. (US) 1924–1930
Sayers & Scoville Co., Sandusky, Ohio.
The S. & S. automobiles were the linear successors of the earlier SAYERS cars. The change in name represented the winnowing down of cars previously on the general automotive roster to a category targeted to funeral cars and formal limousines, for which Sayers & Scoville had been noted for many years. The S. & S. passenger cars were built explicitly for the funeral trade, affording a formality in keeping with it and with a selection of large sedans and limousines for the use of pallbearers and members of a bereaved family. Over the years the S. & S. passenger cars used a series of Continental 6-cylinder engines, wheelbases from 132 to 143in (3350 to 3629mm) and a choice of disc or artillery wood wheels. The models carried specific designations as to type such as Brighton, Elmwood, Gotham, and Lakewood and were available to the general public in a range of prices up to and including $5000. After 1930, although the S. & S. badge continued with the funeral coaches, the large sedans and limousines were available only on special order.

KM

S.S. (i) (GB) 1900
S.S. Motor Car Co., London.
This was a light car powered by a 5½hp horizontal single-cylinder engine, with constant-mesh 3-speed gearbox and chain final drive. It was sold from offices in Holborn Viaduct, but the factory location is not known. Neither is the origin of the name, although the makers took advantage of it to promote their car as Simple, Silent, Speedy, Safe, with the adjectives entwined within the letters S.S. A 4-seater

1922 S.R.C. 11.9hp roadster.
NATIONAL MOTOR MUSEUM

1933 S.S.(ii) I tourer.
NICK GEORGANO

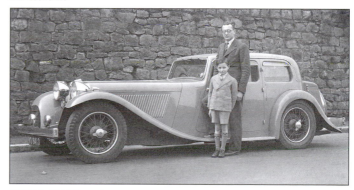

1935 S.S. (ii) I 20hp saloon.
NATIONAL MOTOR MUSEUM

took part in the Thousand Miles Trial of 1900, and in the programme the company advertised other cars including a 3hp 2-cylinder voiturette and a 3½hp car to seat two or three persons.

NG

S.S. (ii) (GB) 1931–1945
1931–1934 Swallow Coachbuilding Co. Ltd., Coventry, Warwickshire.
1934–1945 S.S. Cars Ltd., Coventry, Warwickshire.
When William Lyons and William Walmsley, neither having an engineering background, joined forces in 1922, they began manufacturing streamlined aluminium sidecars in humble first and second floor premises in Blackpool with a £1000 bank overdraft. Continuing this production which blossomed over the years to a profitable business, they also began to create sporting bodies for the Austin 7, which they called 'Swallow', followed by no less attractive individual

1937 S.S. (ii) 100 2½-litre sports car.
NATIONAL MOTOR MUSEUM

1998 SsangYong Chairman saloon.
SSANGYONG

1998 SsangYong Korando LS 2.9D estate car.
SSANGYONG

1998 SsangYong Musso GLS 2.9 Turbo Diesel estate car.
SSANGYONG

coachwork on Swift, Morris, Fiat and Standard (i) chassis. With the business developing positively, a move to Coventry was considered in 1928, where an elegant low-line saloon version of the 16hp Standard became the first model to be named S.S.I, launched in 1931. A special underslung frame was made, otherwise the car used Standard mechanical components throughout including the 2054cc 6-cylinder sv engine. Similar Swallow design treatment was applied to a Wolseley Hornet in 2- and also 4-seater versions. The typical appearance included a long bonnet, a diminutive coupé 2+2 body and helmet-type front wings which gave the £310 car a £1000-plus look. Added to the range was a 2552cc engine of 20hp rating, followed by the S.S.II based on the 1054 cc Standard Little Nine.

The S.S. had become an acknowledged marque by now, and production figures increased in spite of the economic crisis in the early '30s. The 1933 S.S. models looked even more beautiful due to being better proportioned, and a sports tourer was available for the first time, while the 1934 refinements included a new X-braced frame, syncromesh gearbox and more powerful engines like the 2663cc 68hp six. In 1935, the company offered their first sports car, although three S.S.I tourers had already been entered in the 1933 Alpine Trials, as well as in 1934 when they took the Team Prize. The 1935 S.S.90 Sports, with twin carburettors and featuring a shorter chassis and a slab tank, was a 90mph (145km/h) 2-seater getting considerable attention with sports car enthusiasts.

The model name Jaguar was first chosen by William Lyons, who had parted from Walmsley in late 1934, for a 4-door sports saloon in autumn 1935, powered by a 104hp 2663cc (though being referred to as a '2.5') Standard engine. Special treatment by Harry Weslake and William Heynes resulted in sports car performance with a top speed around 90mph (145km/h), while a short chassis 2-seater with the same engine, sold as Jaguar S.S.100, became the synonym for *the* successful British sports car and proved hard to beat in international rallies. In 1938, a 3485cc version of the ohv six, available for the saloon as well as for the S.S.100, made its debut and was successfully on its way to establishing the reputation of the Jaguar name, standing for peak performance and high reliability. The 4-door saloon was also available in 1½-litre form, at first a 1608cc side-valve (1936–1937), then a 1775cc ohv unit (1938–1940). Over 5000 cars were sold in the 1939 model year when war broke out and stopped car production.

In 1945, shortly after the war, the name of the company was changed to Jaguar Cars Ltd and the sidecar interests including the Swallow trade name rights were sold. Under new ownership the Swallow company was responsible for the Swallow Doretti in 1954.

HS

SSANGYONG (ROK) 1988 to date
SsangYong Motor Co. Ltd, Seoul.
Founded in 1939, the large engineering and oil refining conglomerate SsangYong entered the car industry in 1988 when it took over manufacture of the PANTHER Kallista. It added the Jeep-like Korando 4 × 4 and in 1995 launched its most ambitious project yet, the Musso 4 × 4 estate as a rival for the Range Rover and Jeep Cherokee. Powered by a 2874cc 5-cylinder Mercedes-Benz diesel made in Korea, the Musso (Korean for Rhino) had a 5-door body styled by former Aston Martin and Rolls-Royce designer Ken Greenley. More recently other engine options have been available in the Musso, including a 2299cc 4-cylinder diesel and two fuel-injection petrol engines, a 2295cc four and a 3199cc six.

In 1997 SsangYong launched the Chairman, a luxury saloon based on the Mercedes-Benz W124, with 3199cc 6-cylinder engine. In 1998 SsangYong merged with DAEWOO, but its own range continued alongside Daewoo's, at any rate for the time being.

NG

SSB (D) 1923–1926
Stuttgarter Strassenbahn AG, Stuttgart.
In the mid–1920s the Stuttgart Tram Co. was looking for fresh outlets for its skilled staff and high-quality machine tools. Their chief engineer Freund (ex-Daimler) designed a 2-seater with a 20bhp flat-twin engine, and other engines tried were a JAP V-twin and a Mathis four. Production was very limited, but apart from the use of the cars by the SSB staff, a few were sold to outside customers.

HON

Sheer beauty of line

. . . and unparalleled performance too—for the 1935 S.S. with high compression engine incorporating special induction system with 2 carburettors, provides exceptional acceleration with high cruising and maximum speeds. The S.S. for 1935 is a car designed to satisfy the demands of the most exacting sports car connoisseur. Below is the famous S.S. 1 Saloon, 16 h.p. £340 (20 h.p. £345).

S. S. CARS LTD. FOLESHILL COVENTRY

1914 Stabilia 2.7-litre 2-seater.
NICK BALDWIN

1920 Stafford (ii) 11.9hp tourer.
NICK BALDWIN

S.S.E. (US) 1916–1917

S.S.E Co., Philadelphia, Pennsylvania.

This car was openly promoted, at least by the Philadelphia Chamber of Commerce, as 'a rich man's toy'. It had a 30hp 6-cylinder engine of 4.7 litres capacity, and a wheelbase of 124in (3147mm). The chassis alone was priced at $5000, with complete cars costing from $6700 for a tourer and roadster to $8000 for a limousine or berline. The roadster had a claimed top speed of 115mph (185km/h), at a time when the world land speed record was only 17mph (27km/h) faster. The company was incorporated in May 1916 as the Emerson Motor Car Manufacturing Co., and renamed S.S.E. Co. four months later. In January 1917 a factory was said to be completed, and in May the press was told that although no cars had been made yet, they had orders for a full year ahead. In fact only one complete S.S.E. was ever made, together with components for several more. These still exist.

NG

SSZ (US) c.1993–1997

SSZ Motorcars, Ltd, Aniwa, Wisconsin.

SSZ was a real curiosity among American kit car manufacturers – they did not build a Cobra replica. The SSZ Stradale was based on reworked Alfa Romeo Sprint Speciale replica bodywork. It used a fabricated space frame with racing-derived adjustable suspension. They were only sold in rolling chassis or fully assembled form with Alfa Romeo V6 or Nissan 300ZX twin-turbocharged engines. The SSZ Shark was a kit car with a slightly modified DEVIN-style body and a 1968 to 1982 Corvette chassis and running gear. They were sold in kit and assembled form.

HP

STABILIA (F) 1907–1930

1907–1910 Automobiles Stabilia, Neuilly, Seine.
1911–1920 Giraldy et Vrard, Neuilly, Seine; Asnières, Seine.
1920–1930 Vrard et Cie, Asnières, Seine.

The Stabilia was the life's work of M. Vrard who realised earlier than most the advantages of a low-slung car. After working for Léon Bollée and De Dion-Bouton, he built a prototype in 1904 which he showed at the Paris Salon. Its main feature was an underslung chassis with complicated leaf springing which, according to its inventor, resulted in a centre of gravity 50 per cent lower than most contemporary cars. A company was formed in 1907 and at the 1908 Salon three 12/16hp 4-cylinder chassis and one coupé were shown. The cylinders were pair-cast and the engine was doubtless a proprietary unit, as Vrard's interests lay in

chassis and suspension rather than in engines. Three engines were listed in 1912, of 1.5, 1.7, and 2.7 litres, and the 1913 cars had unconventional rear suspension in which the coil springs were held in tension and connected to the bodywork by wire cables. Vrard claimed that this eliminated skidding, by allowing the body some sideways motion of its own.

The company was reformed in 1920, and Stabilia cars were offered for the next ten years, though production was very small. A 2815cc 14CV four was used in the 1920 models, which also had pump-and-fan cooling, 4-speed gearboxes and cantilever rear suspension. Ohv Altos engines of 1495 and 1990cc were used later in the decade, and some small Gobrons were sold under the Stabilia name when output of Stabilias virtually ceased in 1926. However, a new model was launched with the 1494cc single-ohc C.I.M.E. engine popular in many French sports cars. It was made as a 2-seater sports car, while the 2-litre Altos engine still powered the saloons which were made in tiny numbers up to 1930. In that year a Stabilia with 1492cc straight-8 S.C.A.P. engine and reversed quarter-elliptic rear suspension was announced, but probably no more than a prototype or two were made. The later cars carried the word *inversable* (non-capsisable) on their radiators.

NG

STABLE AUTO WORKS (US) c.1998 to date

Stable Auto Works, Richardson, Texas.

The F250 was a Ferrari 250GTO replica based on a Datsun Z-car chassis, and was similar to the kits built by ALPHA and VELLO ROSSA. It was sold in kit or complete form.

HP

STACK (GB) 1921–1925

G.F. Stack & Co., East Croydon, Surrey.

The Stack started life as a cyclecar with a 766cc V-twin engine, friction transmission and chain final drive. For 1923 a bored out engine increased capacity to 858cc, and the price had dropped from £198 to £137, but the car struggled in an overcrowded market, although it was prettier than many, with black wings and a lavender-fawn coloured body. The friction drive had an ingenious device which increased pressure of one disc on the other under heavy load or steep gradients. In 1925 they went over to a conventional 1526cc 4-cylinder engine, 3-speed gearbox and shaft drive, but production ceased at the end of the year. About 60 Stacks were made.

NG

S.T.A.E. see KRIEGER

STAFFORD (i) (US) 1908–1915

1908–1910 Stafford Motor Car Co., Topeka, Kansas.
1908–1915 Stafford Motor Car Co., Kansas City, Kansas.

This company was founded by Terry Stafford who had designed cars for the Smith brothers, sold under the names SMITH and GREAT SMITH. His own car had a 30hp 4-cylinder engine, unusual for its date in having a single-ohc. It was made as a roadster selling for $1900 or a tourer at $2350, and changed little over the years apart from styling updates. The most famous Stafford owner was future President Harry S. Truman, who converted his 1913 tourer into a hot-rod roadster and used it in his army camp during World War I. Total Stafford production was 499 cars.

NG

STAFFORD (ii) (GB) 1919–1921

Stafford Associated Engineering Co. Ltd, Battersea, London.

This was an assembled car which the makers hoped to build in large numbers for the car-hungry postwar market. They used a 1794cc Dorman 4MV engine, Zenith carburettor, Watford magnetos, Sankey wheels, Smiths electric starting, Powell & Hanmer lighting and other components from well-known suppliers. Perhaps the only part of the car made by Stafford was the body, and even then one cannot be sure. Photographs show both disc and artillery wheels on rather plain looking tourers. Though the factory was in London, the name possibly came from Dorman's home town of Stafford. A car with a 2613cc 16/20hp engine was also listed. Production is unknown, although only 12 cars were made in 1919–20.

NG

STAG (GB) 1913–1914

The Stag Co., Sherwood, Nottingham.
This company was better known for its engines, which were used in several cyclecars including Heybourn and L.A.D., but it also made a few cars of its own. The company had 763cc 5/6hp single-cylinder engines, Jardine 3-speed gearboxes and belt final drive. The vaned flywheel acted as a fan. The price was a modest 85 guineas (£89.25).

NG

STAIGER (D) 1923–1924

Automobilfabrik Staiger, Stuttgart.
Originally a car dealer, Staiger entered production with a 4/12PS cyclecar available with 2- or 4-seater bodies. It was no more successful than many other contemporary German makes.

HON

STAINES-SIMPLEX (GB) 1906–c.1912

Staines Motor Co. Ltd, Staines, Middlesex.
This car was first exhibited at the 1908 Cordingley Show in London, although *The Motor* said that the company 'have been specialising in car building for nearly two years past, and actually manufacture certain parts'. Production seems to have been quite limited, as *The Motor* also said that the company's main business was hiring out chauffeur-driven cars, and that when the hiring trade was slack the chauffeur/machinists assembled cars to order. They had Coventry-Simplex engines, either an 8/10hp 2-cylinder or 15/20hp 4-cylinder, shaft drive and Renault-style dashboard radiators. They were also known as the S.S.S. (Staines Silent Simplex).

NG

STALLION (i) (US) c.1984

Stallion Replicars, Nashotah, Wisconsin.
Not to be confused with the Stallion Cobra replicas built by EAGLE AMERICAN, the SR400 kit car was a replica of the Lamborghini Countach. It used a custom frame with independent suspension, 4-wheel disc brakes and a Z-F transaxle bolted to a Ford or Chevrolet V6 or V8 engine. They were sold as basic body kits or with the chassis and running gear installed.

HP

STALLION (ii) (GB) 1985–1986

S.P. Engineering, Redditch, Worcestershire.
Steven Povey made this vaguely vintage-style 4-seat tourer. Its styling was uncompromisingly ill-conceived, resembling a creation of Heath Robinson's, and despite its up-market Jaguar XJ basis it is hardly surprising that only one car was ever built.

CR

STAMM (US) 1901–1905

Frederick B. and George T. Stamm, Los Angeles, California.
Probably not more than three Stamms were made, two 4hp single-cylinder runabouts in 1901 by Frederick Stamms, and a larger car powered by a 40hp air-cooled 2-stroke 4-cylinder engine by his brother George in 1905. The latter planned a series production, but it never happened.

NG

STAMMOBILE (US) 1900–1901

Stammobile Manufacturing Co., Stamford, Connecticut.
This was a 4-seater steam car powered by a 2-cylinder engine, with single-chain drive and wood or wire wheels. The name Stammobile was sometimes given to the car built by George T. Stamm in Los Angeles.

NG

STANBURY (i) (GB) 1903

Stanbury & Co., Liverpool.
This well-known cycle and motor factory made at least one car, powered by a 12hp engine. It was said to have passed its tests with flying colours, but no more was heard of it.

NG

1907 Standard (ii) 30hp tourer.
NICK BALDWIN

1910 Standard (ii) 20hp landaulet.
NICK BALDWIN

STANBURY (ii) (GB) 1983–1986

1983–1985 Stanbury Design Services, Weston-super-Mare, Avon.
1985–1986 Stanbury Design, Worle, Avon.
Jan Quick was the force behind the Stanbury TT, although it was designed by her husband David. It was an extremely basic trials-style alloy-over-plywood roadster designed to fit over a Triumph Herald chassis. A body kit cost just £250 or you could save even more by building your own body from plans.

CR

STANDARD (i) (US) 1900–1901

Standard Motor Vehicle Co., Camden, New Jersey.
The first of fourteen makes of car called Standard was a light runabout powered by a 4½hp single-cylinder engine and selling for $500.

NG

STANDARD (ii) (GB) 1903–1963

Standard Motor Co. Ltd, Coventry.
Best known of the fourteen different motor manufacturing companies who chose the name Standard for their product, the Standard Motor Co. Ltd was founded by Reginald William Maudslay ((1871–1934) who came from a famous engineering family. His great-grandfather, Henry Maudslay (1771–1831), was one of the pioneers of the marine steam engine, and also the inventor of the screw-cutting lathe and micrometer. Reginald's brother Cyril set up the Maudslay Motor Co. in 1901, which later made cars and commercial vehicles, and Reginald himself founded his company in 1903, helped by backing of £3000 from Sir John Wolfe Barry, the designer of London's Tower Bridge, for whom Reginald had worked.

1913 Standard (ii) 9.5hp Ranelagh coupé.
NICK BALDWIN

1924 Standard (ii) 11hp Kenilworth tourer.
NATIONAL MOTOR MUSEUM

1925 Standard (ii) 14hp Pall Mall saloon.
NICK BALDWIN

The car's name was chosen because, as Maudslay put it, 'I want my car to be composed purely of those components whose principles have been tried and tested and accepted as reliable standards'. Maudslay had made sketches of the kind of car he wanted to build, but the actual design work was by Alexander Craig, who also designed Lea-Francis' and Singer's first cars. The Standard had an oversquare single-cylinder horizontal engine, with dimensions of 127 × 76.2mm, a 3-speed gearbox and shaft drive. The second car built had a similar short-stroke engine, but with two cylinders; exhibited at London's Crystal Palace Show in February 1904, it was the first Standard to be sold. More conventional cars with vertical engines under a bonnet were soon made, with 2-, 3-, and 4-cylinder

engines. An 18/20hp six was introduced in 1905, advertised as being available for installation in other cars or as a complete chassis. The only entry of a Standard car in a major race was by a one of these 18/20hp sixes, which ran in the 1905 Tourist Trophy, finishing 11th out of 18.

At a time when most 6-cylinder engines were found in large and expensive cars, the Standards were reasonably priced, the 18/20hp costing £625. There were also larger and more expensive models, the 30hp at £725 and 50hp at £850. From 1906 to 1911 the entire output of the Coventry factory was taken by the London dealer Charles Friswell, who was Chairman of Standards up to 1911. It was Friswell who arranged for Standards to be the sole make supplied for the Coronation of King George V as Emperor of India. This event, known as the Delhi Durbar, took place in December 1911, and involved 70 Standards, including some special models with 4-wheel drive, and several trucks for carrying beaters on tiger hunting expeditions. It was a considerable feat to secure such a contract for a relatively unknown company, and helped Standard in the export market.

Friswell left in 1911 after disagreement with Maudslay, his shares being bought by a Coventry solicitor, C.J. Band, and Siegfried Bettmann who owned the Triumph motorcycle company. Band's connection with Standard was to last until 1956 when he retired, aged 82. The next important step was the introduction of a quality light car, the 9.5hp Model S, in March 1913. This had a 1087cc 4-cylinder monobloc engine, and was in the same class as the Morris Oxford and Singer Ten. It was available with open 2-seater bodywork initially, this being later supplemented by drophead and fixed-head coupés. A total of 1933 were made up to May 1915, when war work took priority. The sixes had been dropped in 1912, and the 9.5's companions at the outbreak of World War I were two fours of 15 and 20hp of 2368 and 3336cc.

Standard in the 1920s

In 1916 Standard moved from the centre of Coventry to a new factory at Canley on the outskirts, which was to remain their home for the next 47 years. Large numbers of aircraft were made there, and in 1919 the Model S was put back into production. After 198 had been made it was replaced by the SLS which had a longer stroke, giving a capacity of 1328cc. July 1921 saw a larger car in the shape of the 1597cc SLO with exposed pushrod-operated ohvs, and a wheelbase long enough to take 4-seater coachwork. One of these was the all-weather tourer which had a very effective weatherproof hood and sidescreens. Three months later came the 1086cc 8hp, a low slung car with disc wheels. It was made in 2- or 4-seater form, but few were built, probably because of the unexpected success of the SLO. Demand was so great that a batch of 1000 was sanctioned, the first time a single batch of a Standard model had reached four figures. More than 4000 were delivered in 1923, and by the time production ended in 1928 more than 20,000 had been made. From 1922 capacity was increased to 1944cc, and the designation became SLO-4. In 1924 Standard began to give English place names to their body styles; the 11.4hp had the Canley and Coleshill 2-seaters, Kineton and Kenilworth 4-seaters and Piccadilly saloons, while the SLO-4 styles included the Warwick tourer and Pall Mall saloon. Front-wheel brakes were standard on the SLO-4 from 1926. A 2230cc 18hp six was made from 1927, but did not sell in large numbers.

The Standard Nine and its Successors

Despite the success of the SLO-4 Standard's finances were strained at the end of the 1920s, and they were borrowing heavily from Barclays Bank. A new smaller car seemed the answer, and this appeared for the 1928 season as the Nine. Designed by Ray Turner, it had an 1155cc side-valve engine and a worm drive rear axle, the latter also being used on the SLO-4. Originally made with a fabric saloon body (the Falmouth) only, it sold for £198.50. In February 1928 the range was increased by open 2- and 4-seaters, and by a Sports model with Gordon England body which was capable of over 68mph (110km/h) with a supercharger. September 1928 saw the longer wheelbase Teignmouth saloon with engine enlarged to 1287cc. All saloons at this time had sliding sunshine roofs; these remained of fabric construction even after the Teignmouth acquired a metal body in the Spring of 1929.

9000 Nines were sold in 1929 and 1930, and a new range of side-valve sixes appeared in 1929, which were continued up to 1940. The most important event of 1929, though, was the appearance of Captain John Black who joined the company from Hillman, becoming Managing Director in 1933. He brought financial aid and a dynamic reorganisation which led to all production being concentrated at Canley. Soon after Black joined Standard, Canley turned out 100 cars in one day. By 1934 annual production exceeded 20,000, and there were six models, Nine, Ten, Ten/Twelve, Twelve, Sixteen and Twenty, the latter two with 6-cylinder engines. The Ten/Twelve used a 45bhp twin-carburettor version of the 1608cc Twelve engine in a Ten chassis; dual colour bodies were featured, and the Speedline 2-door saloon foreshadowed the later Flying Standards. The traditional humped radiator and Union Jack badge disappeared in 1931, as did the worm drive which gave way to spiral bevel. Synchromesh, freewheels and Startix (a device which restarted the engine when it stalled) were seen on 1934 models.

Avons and Flying Standards

By far the best looking Standards of the 1930s were those fitted with Avon coachwork. The first of these was on a 1929 Nine chassis with styling by the Jensen brothers. The radiator and bonnet were lowered and the steering column raked, while wire wheels and cycle-type wings completed the sporting appearance. Coupés followed, on the Nine and Ensign Sixteen chassis; they were handsome cars, offering competition for another Standard-powered car, William Lyons' new S.S. The Avons, however, did not have the benefit of the lowered frame, which was made exclusively for Lyons. In 1933 Charles Beauvais took over as stylist for Avon, with the consequence of more flowing lines, dual colour schemes and disc wheels on the Avon Standards. The last of the series was the Wayfarer pillarless saloon on the 1937 Flying Twenty chassis, which cost £370 compared with £315 for the regular body. It was arguably as good looking as the S.S. Jaguar, but lacked that car's ohv engine and its performance.

The 1935 Olympia Show saw three new Standards added to the regular range. These were the Flying Standards with fastback bodies which completely enclosed the luggage boot and spare wheel. They were available on the Twelve, Sixteen, and Twenty chassis, and cost only £30 more than the older styles, or £40 in the case of the Twenty. The Flying Standards sold so well in 1936 that the older models were dropped for the next season, and the 1936 Show saw six Flying models, the Nine, Ten, Twelve, Fourteen, Twenty and V8. The latter was intended

1928 Standard (ii) 9hp Fulham saloon.
NATIONAL MOTOR MUSEUM

as a rival to the smaller Ford V8, and consisted of two Ten blocks on a common crankcase to give a capacity of 2686cc and a top speed of 82mph (132km/h). The saloon and drophead bodies were similar in styling to the Twenty. Also similar were the Bendix mechanical brakes, which were not up to the V8's performance, one reason why it did not sell well and was withdrawn after the 1938 season.

The other Flying Standards were continued up to World War II, with some restyling including new radiator grills and extended boots giving more luggage space on the touring saloons. Transverse leaf ifs was introduced for 1938, and was seen on the last prewar design, the Eight. New for 1939, this had a 1021cc long stroke (57 × 100mm) engine developing 31bhp, 3-speed gearbox and a top speed of 65mph (105km/h). Saloon, tourer and drophead coupé bodies were

Sir John Black in 1949 with journalist Kay Petre.
NICK BALDWIN

BLACK, SIR JOHN (1895–1965)

John Paul Black made his name as a dynamic leader of business, but there was an aggressive side to his character that made him a lot of enemies. Some of them complained that he was very quick to claim credit for the accomplishments of others. Those who admired him pointed to the acuity of his foresight and the scope of his vision.

He was born on 10 February 1895, at Kingston-on-Thames, the son of a municipal clerk, John George Black, and his wife, Ellen, née Smith. He studied law at London University, found a job in a lawyer's office, and in August 1914, volunteered for military service. He served in the Royal Navy Voluntary Reserve and was on board ship during the Battle of Gallipoli. Learning about the formation of a Royal Tank Regiment, he applied for a transfer, and by the end of the war, he was a captain in the Royal Armoured Corps.

Back in civilian life, he returned to law with a London firm of solicitors, but joined Hillman as sales manager in 1918, marrying Daisy Hillman in 1921. He was then appointed joint managing director of Hillman, the same title being held by his brother-in-law, Spencer Wilks. In 1928 he was also given seats on the boards of Humber Ltd, and Commer Car Ltd.

He resigned from all his offices within the Rootes group in 1929 to handle the reorganisation of the Standard Motor Co. Ltd for the aging Reginald W. Maudslay. He became managing director of Standard in 1933. In 1936 he was an eager supporter of the 'shadow factory' scheme, which led to contracts for Standard to operate two such plants during World War II. He was named chairman of the joint aero-engine committee in September 1939, and he was knighted in 1943.

The war was not yet over when he gave top priority to Project 200, which became the Standard Vanguard. He arranged the merger with Triumph, and began to diversify by entering an agreement for farm-tractor production with Harry Ferguson. In 1953, after the launch of the Triumph TR2, Sir John was elected chairman of Standard-Triumph. He sold the Ferguson tractor business to Massey-Harris and left the day-to-day running of Standard-Triumph to Alick S. Dick.

After an accident when being given a demonstration ride by Ken Richardson in a prototype Swallow Doretti (based on the TR2), his judgement and decision-making were no longer to be trusted. He developed an irrational fear that E.G. 'Ted' Grinham, the chief engineer he had himself brought in from Humber in 1930, was trying to push him out and take his job.

Grinham, Dick, and a majority of the board made a surprise call at the Black home one evening and forced him to sign a letter of resignation. He was given a generous settlement and retired to a peaceful life as a sheep-farmer.

He was taken ill suddenly and died at Cheadle Hospital, Cheshire, on 24 December 1965.

His first marriage was childless, and ended in divorce in about 1939. In 1943 he married Alison Joan Pears, whom he had met at the Ministry of Aircraft production; they had three sons: Hugo, Stuart, and Nicholas.

JPN

1933 Standard (ii) 16hp saloon.
NICK BALDWIN

1937 Standard (ii) Flying Nine with special drophead body.
NICK BALDWIN

1947 Standard (ii) Eight drophead coupé.
NICK BALDWIN

listed, with a 4-door saloon joining them for 1940. The Eight was modestly priced, at £125–159, and about 15,000 were sold up to early 1940, with a further 53,099 made after the war.

The Vanguard, a Car for the World

The Standard range was simplified after the war, with only three models made from 1946 to 1948. These were the Eight, similar to the 1939 models except for the adoption of a 4-speed gearbox, the Twelve and the Fourteen, the latter two sharing the same body and chassis, with engines of 1609 or 1776cc. An additional body style available on all three chassis was a wood-bodied estate car, introduced because of the shortage of steel, and because in Britain, such vehicles did not carry the 33 per cent Purchase Tax payable on all passenger cars. 9959 Twelves and 22,229 Fourteens were made up to September 1948.

Standard's all-new postwar car was announced in July 1947, although production did not begin for another twelve months. It had a 4-cylinder ohv engine, originally of 1850cc, though this was increased to 2088cc on production models, a 3-speed gearbox with column change, and hydraulic brakes. The body was a bulbous full-width 6-seater saloon suitable for export markets. 'It is a full-size car

equally suitable for home and overseas service' said *The Times*. The Vanguard's styling, which was not universally welcomed by traditionalists, was by Walter Belgrove who was also responsible for the Triumph TR series (Standard had bought up the Triumph company in 1945). The Vanguard sold well in export markets, both in Europe and further afield such as Australia. The first six months production all went abroad, and the proportion of Vanguards sold on the home market was very small until the early 1950s. The saloon was joined by an estate car, delivery van and pick-up in October 1948. There were no open models, though Tickford provided a roll-top roof at a cost of £60, and in Belgium the Imperia company made a few 2-door convertibles around 1950–51.

Optional overdrive was available from June 1950, and the Vanguard's appearance changed slightly with the addition of wheel spats on 1950 models, and of a lower bonnet and new grill for 1952. The first major change came with the Phase 2 Vanguard of 1953, on which the rounded back was replaced by

NATIONAL MOTOR MUSEUM

WEBSTER, HENRY GEORGE (born 1917)

Henry George Webster was born in Coventry on 27 May 1917 and educated at Welshpool County School and Coventry Technical College. He joined Standard Motor Co. as an apprentice in 1932 and became a member of the Standard engineering staff in 1935 under E.G.'Ted' Grinham. He was assistant technical engineer in 1938 and deputy chief inspector in 1940, when the plant was converting to military production.

From 1946 he was again an assistant technical engineer and worked on preliminary studies for the Vanguard. He was chief chassis engineer from 1948 to 1955, directing the design of the suspension, steering and brakes for the Standard 8, Vanguard II, Triumph TR2, and Vanguard III. He was chief engineer from 1955 to 1957, and technical director from 1958 to 1968.

The Herald frame and structure were his inventions, born of necessity from the loss of the company's traditional body shell supplier, leading to a long line of derivatives such as the Spitfire, GT6 and Vitesse. He masterminded the Triumph 2000 saloon of 1963, and led the development of the front-wheel drive Triumph 1300. He directed the evolution of the TR2 into TR3, TR4 and TR4A.

In June 1968 he became director and chief engineer for the Volume Car and Light Commercial Vehicle Division of British Leyland Motor Corp., which put him in control of the Morris and Austin car lines, plus badge-engineered MG, Riley and Wolseley derivatives. He led the development of the Morris Marina and the Austin Allegro. He also took a dim view of the prospects for the corporation and left in June 1974 to work as an engineering consultant with Automotive Products.

JPN

THE *Flying* STANDARD

BRITISH BUILT · · · FOR MOTORISTS WHO PUT QUALITY FIRST

1952 Standard (ii) Vanguard saloon.
NICK BALDWIN

1956 Standard (ii) Eight saloon.
NICK BALDWIN

1960 Standard (ii) Vanguard Luxury Six saloon.
NICK BALDWIN

a large luggage boot. In 1954 the Phase 2 could be had with a 2092cc diesel engine, the first of its kind catalogued in a British car. Top speed was no more than 65mph (105km/h), while a petrol-engined Vanguard could do 75mph (120km/h), but fleet owners and taxi operators appreciated the diesel's economy (50mpg if not pressed too hard). Nevertheless only 1973 diesels were sold, compared with 81,074 petrol-engined Phase 2s, and 184,799 Phase 1s.

The Vanguard was completely re-styled for 1956, with a lower and lighter body which had unitary construction for the first time. The same 2088cc engine was used, but gearing was higher, and the Phase 3 Vanguard had a top speed of 84mph (135km/h). Even faster was the limited production Vanguard Sportsman which had a 90bhp twin-carburettor engine, larger brakes and a front anti-roll bar. The Sportsman, which was recognisable by its MG-style grill, was good for 90mph (145km/h), but only 901 were made, in 1956 and 1957. The Ensign was an economy Vanguard with 1670cc engine and more austere trim, while for 1958 the regular Vanguard was restyled by Michelotti with a new grill and aluminium wheel discs. Michelotti's design was put into practical form by the coachbuilders Vignale, hence the name Vignale Vanguard, though the cars were entirely built at Canley. A 4-speed floor change was now an alternative to the 3-speed column change. The last Vanguard, made from 1961 to 1963, had a 1991cc 6-cylinder engine in the Vignale hull, with front disc brakes available from July 1961. Production of the Vanguard Six was only 9953 cars, while the 4-cylinder Vignale Vanguard sold 26,276. Both the Vanguard and the Standard name were dropped in May 1963 by the new owners, the Leyland Motors Group. The name chosen by Maudslay, which had connotations of high standards at the beginning of the century, now implied 'ordinary' as opposed to 'special' or 'de luxe', particularly on the American market.

The Small Postwar Standards

When the Vanguard was launched its makers made much of their one-model policy which would reduce manufacturing costs, but by 1953 they felt the need for a smaller car which would rival the Austin A30 and Morris Minor. This appeared at that year's Earls Court Show in the form of the Eight, a unit construction 4-door saloon powered by an 803cc ohv engine. The early ones were very basic, with sliding instead of wind-up windows, no hub caps and no external access to the luggage boot. Wind-up windows and hub caps were available on De Luxe models in 1954 and on all from 1955, while the rear-access luggage boot was introduced on the Ten which also had a larger 948cc engine. The Phase 2 Tens of 1957 offered automatic transmission called Standrive, as well as overdrive. The final development of the small Standards was the Pennant, a Ten with 2-tone paintwork, a new grill and little fins at the back. The Pennant was dropped in 1959, after 42,910 had been made, but the Eight and Ten lasted into 1960, their production figures being 136,317 and 172,500. The Eight and Pennant were made only as saloons, but there was an estate version of the Ten known as the Companion. On the American market they were sold as the Triumph Sedan and Estate Wagon, and when the small Standards were due for replacement, the new car was called the Triumph Herald. The name survived until 1980 in India, on a 4-door Triumph Herald called the Standard Gazel.

NG

Further Reading
The All-British Standard Motor Co. Ltd, Brian Long, Veloce, 1993.

STANDARD (iii) (US) 1904–1905

Standard Motor Construction Co., Jersey City, New Jersey.

This was a successor to the U.S. Long Distance, and was made in the same factory. It was a larger car than its predecessor, with a 25hp 4-cylinder engine and on a 95in (2411mm) wheelbase. It had a 3-speed gearbox and chain final drive. The 1904 model was sometimes known as the Standard Tourist U.S. Long Distance, and the 5-seater tourer was described as the Tourist. For 1905 the wheelbase was increased to 109in (2766mm), and the two body styles were called, more conventionally, touring and landaulet. They were quite expensive, at $3500 and $3900 respectively.

NG

STANDARD (iv) (I) 1906–1912

Fabbrica Automobili Standard, Turin.

This was a conventional car powered by a 14/20hp 4-cylinder engine, with a 4-speed gearbox. It was sometimes called the F.A.S. after the initials of the manufacturer.

NG

STANDARD (v) (US) 1909–1910

Standard Gas Electric Power Co., Philadelphia, Pennsylvania.

Despite its maker's name this was not a petrol-electric design as it used a 28hp 4-cylinder engine with 3-speed gearbox and shaft drive. It did, however, have electric operation of the gears by push button, as used by Edsel 50 years later. It also pre-dated Cadillac by two years in having an electric starter. Presumably neither of these systems worked well, as the car, sometimes known as the Standard G.E., had a very short life.

NG

STANDARD (vi) (US) 1910–1911

1910 St Louis Car Co., St Louis, Missouri.
1910–1911 St Louis Car Co., Wabash, Indiana.

The St Louis Car Co. was a well-known manufacturer of railway carriages which made the AMERICAN MORS from 1906 to 1909, and for 1910 launched a car of native design, the 50hp 6-cylinder Standard Six. It had a 3-speed gearbox and shaft drive, riding on a 124in (3147mm) wheelbase. Four body styles, a tourer, miniature tonneau and roadster at $3000, and a limousine at $4000, were offered. In 1910 manufacture was moved from St Louis to a subsidiary factory in Wabash, but production was discontinued before the year was out.

NG

STANDARD (vii) (D) 1911–1912

Standard Automobilfabrik GmbH, Berlin-Charlottenberg.

This company offered two models, a 10/28PS and 13/35PS, both with Henriod rotary valve engines. They did not prove successful.

HON

STANDARD (viii) (US) 1911–1915

Standard Electric Car Co., Jackson, Michigan.

This company made typical electric cars, mostly coupés, though it offered an open model which it called a runabout in 1913 and a roadster in 1914–15. They had a creditable range of 110 miles between charges. The controller gave six forward speeds, with a maximum of 20mph (32km/h). In some advertisements the company called its car the Standard Electrique.

NG

1917 Standard (x) Eight tourer.
NATIONAL MOTOR MUSEUM

1921 Standard (x) Eight sedan.
NICK BALDWIN

STANDARD (ix) (US) 1914

Standard Engineering Co., Chicago, Illinois.

When it was launched in January 1914 the Standard cyclecar had a 9/13hp V-twin engine, but three months later a 10/16hp 4-cylinder engine had been substituted. Otherwise the specification remained the same, with friction transmission and final drive by single chain. It had electric lighting and starting, unusual for a 1914 cyclecar, but production still did not last beyond the end of the year.

NG

STANDARD (x) (US) 1915–1923

Standard Steel Car Co., Butler, Pennsylvania.

This company was a well-known maker of railway carriages and wagons which built a brand new $2 million factory for car production. The prototype was a six, and a few of these were made up to the 1916 season, but the main product had a V8 engine. At 29hp and 4.6 litres, it was a smaller unit than the six, and the wheelbase was 5in shorter at 121in (3071mm). Prices were lower than the six as well, at $1735 for a tourer or roadster. By 1917, when 2318 cars were sold, there were two sizes of V8 engine, 29.3 and 33.8hp, and two wheelbases, 121 and 127in (3071 and 3223mm). Prices were still reasonable, although a 33hp limousine now cost $3500. The company slogan was 'Monarch of the Mountains' and every car was given a 25 mile test on local hills before delivery. From 1918 the only engine was the 5437cc 70bhp V8. Standard claimed that the engines were its own, but they carried a plate attributing manufacture to the Model Engine Works, and it is thought that they contained several components from Herschell-Spillman. In 1923 the car-making side of the business was reorganised and separated from the main company. The V8 was to be continued and a new small four to be introduced, but this never appeared, and all manufacture ceased before the end of the year. Production had exceeded 14,000 cars. The factory was later used for manufacture of the American Austin.

NG

1933 Standard (xii) Superior coupé.
NATIONAL MOTOR MUSEUM

1934 Standard (xii) Superior sports car.
NATIONAL MOTOR MUSEUM

1924 Standish sedan.
KEITH MARVIN

STANDARD (xi) (US) 1920–1921
Standard Engineering Co., St Louis, Missouri.
Frequently listed in contemporary automobile rosters as the Scott-Newcomb, this attractive steam car failed to achieve production, its estimated five to seven prototype touring cars of 1920 and 1921 representing completed units. Powered by a 2-cylinder kerosene-burning engine with boiler pressure of 600psi, its promotional flyer claimed the car could develop a full head of steam within one minute. The car had a wheelbase of 128in (3249mm) and a weight of 4200lb (1909kg). The Standard Steam Car carried a condenser closely resembling the radiator of the Roamer or Rolls-Royce.

KM

STANDARD (xii) (D) 1933–1935
Standard Fahrzeugfabrik GmbH, Ludwigsburg.
This light car was made by Wilhelm Gutbrod, who had made motorcycles since 1925, and who would use his own name for cars after World War II. The

Standard Superior was designed by Josef Ganz, and had a 396cc 12bhp 2-cylinder 2-stroke engine mounted at the rear of a tubular chassis with independent suspension all round. A 16bhp 496cc 4-stroke engine was also available. The body was a streamlined coupé, although a few roadsters were made as well. The car was promoted as the Volkswagen (People's Car), but Gutbrod was forced to give this name up when the Nazi Government adopted it for their own Porsche-designed car. The Standard Superior car was given up in 1935, but vans were made up to 1939. Ganz, who was Jewish, moved to Switzerland where he designed a light car for RAPID on generally similar lines to the Standard.

HON

STANDARD (xiii) (AUS) 1953–1963
1953–1959 Standard Motor Products Ltd, Port Melbourne, Victoria.
1959–1963 Australian Motor Industries Ltd, Port Melbourne, Victoria.
A branch of the Standard Motor Co. was established in Australia prior to World War II and a significant contribution to local content was being produced by 1952 when the Vanguard was a top seller and the Ferguson tractor, with the same engine, was market leader. No major variations resulted but the Vanguard Phase 2 was the Spacemaster with a kangaroo figure on the bonnet. With the Vanguard Phase 3 of 1955, this was the only year when it was identical with the home example, the 1959 Vignale restyle, for instance, being staged over two seasons. The car-type utility (pick-up) had a 614kg rating; which was greater than other car-based types. The locally produced 8 and 10hp models always had trunk lids and plated grills, and a utility was also offered but the restyled Pennant was not produced in Australia. As Standard's competitive ability waned, the plant took on the assembly of MERCEDES-BENZ, RAMBLER and TOYOTA, adopting the new name in 1959 but continuing to be the motor firm with the greatest degree of Australian ownership.

MG

STANDARD (xiv) (IND) 1961–1980
Standard Motor Products of India Ltd, Madras.
The Standard Gazel was a 4-door saloon version of the original 948cc Triumph Herald, a model made only in India.

NG

STANDISH (US) 1924–1925
Luxor Cab Manufacturing Co., Framingham, Massachusetts.
The Standish was the stillborn attempt by the Möller Motor Car Co., of Hagerstown, Maryland to market a car based on its DAGMAR automobiles, but to be made and sold regionally. The Luxor Cab, a Möller subsidiary, was being built in a wing of one of the BAY STATE car's factories. Like the Dagmar 6-70, the Standish was powered by a 6-cylinder Continental 6-J engine and shared other specifications with the Dagmar. Unlike the Dagmar, however, the Standish was fitted with a pointed radiator, but otherwise resembled the Dagmar even with that car's optional brass trim in place of standard nickel fittings. Plans for the continued manufacture of the Standish were abandoned after one sedan and possibly one phaeton had been completed. The pointed radiators featured on the Standish were later used on Möller's Elysée trucks.

KM

STANGA (I) 1949–c.1952
Officina Meccanica della Stanga, Manerbio.
Sandro Stanga's little Fiat-based sports cars achieved promising results in the 1950 and 1951 Mille Miglia events but the marque was short-lived. Most cars used Fiat-derived Giannini 750cc twin cam engines, though others had Fiat 600 engines. Carrozzeria Motto also built a Stanga coupé with a Fiat V8 engine.

CR

STANGUELLINI (I) 1946–1966
Officine Stanguellini Transformazioni Auto Sport Corsa, Modena.
Vittorio Stanguellini was a school pal of Enzo Ferrari and his father owned the first car to be registered in Modena. By the time that he took over the family engineering company in 1932, a Fiat agency was part of the operation. In 1936, Vittorio began to modify Fiats for competition, and was very successful. In 1938 he formed his own team, Squadra Stanguellini, and built a range of Fiat-based

1904 Stanley (i) 8hp runabout.
NICK BALDWIN

sports cars, often with very handsome aerodynamic bodies. For the rest of his manufacturing career Stanguellini would concentrate on competition cars but, just after World War II, the company offered some road cars.

In 1946 Vittorio founded Officine Stanguellini Transformazioni Auto Sport Corsa which, in the manner of small Italian makers, made tuning kits and built truck and van conversions, while its main business was the Fiat agency. In 1947 came a 4-seat berlinetta, with a Bertone body and the (tuned) running gear of a Fiat 1100 in a tubular chassis. A 1500cc version of this engine was available. The following year saw a 2-seat 750cc Fiat-based car.

By 1950 Stanguellini was making Bialbero (double-ohc) 750cc and 1100cc engines which were designed by Golfieri – they were not converted Fiat units. 60bhp was claimed for the smaller engine, 80bhp for the 1100, but these were exaggerated claims. Most of these engines were used in competition cars but a few road cars were built until 1956. The chassis, designed by Alberto Massimino, had transverse leaf spring and lower wishbone front suspension with a live rear axle suspended on coil springs. The 750cc Bialbero road car was claimed to do 112mph (180km/h), the 1100cc version, 118mph (190km/h).

Stanguellini dominated 750cc sports and single-seater racing in Italy in the mid–1950s, but the marque had no international success until Formula Junior was announced in 1957. The company made more than 100 examples of a Fiat-based front-engined car which set the standard until Lotus and Cooper arrived in 1960 and destroyed the opposition. Stanguellini tried to respond and produced the odd design until 1966 after which it concentrated on tuning equipment and subcontract work for other companies.

MJL

Further Reading
Stanguellini, il Mago dei Motori, Dante Candini and Nancia Manicardi, 2000.

STANHOPE (GB) 1919–1925

1919–1922 Stanhope Motors (Leeds) Ltd, Leeds, Yorkshire.
1922–1924 Bramham Motors Ltd, Leeds, Yorkshire.
1924–1925 Stanhope Brothers Ltd, Leeds, Yorkshire.
Designed by jeweller Harry Stanhope, this was an unusual cyclecar of which the prototype appeared in 1915. It had a single front wheel driven by an 8hp V-twin JAP engine via twin belts, and the wheel turned on a fixed axle. Transmission was

automatic by belts on pulleys whose inner flanges moved slightly sideways against pressure from strong coil springs. It was displayed at the London Motorcycle and Cyclecar Show in November 1920, where it was the only front-drive vehicle to be seen. Production was limited and came to an end when the backer Rowland Winn withdrew his support. However, it was taken over by wealthy butcher Walter Bramham who formed Bramham Motors Ltd in March 1922, and launched two models under his own name. In addition to the original design with automatic belt transmission there was another model with conventional 3-speed and reverse gearbox and chain drive. At £195 it was £30 more expensive than the belt-driven car. Bodies were mostly 2-seaters, though there was a single-seater sports Bramham, as well as a delivery van. For 1923 a Caton 4-speed gearbox was featured, and a tandem body capable of seating 'four small-girth people or two bulky persons'. The air-cooled JAP engine was supplemented by a 1098cc water-cooled Blackburne on the sports model.

At the same time as Bramham production was proceeding, the Stanhope brothers were making various experimental cars in the same factory. These had shaft drive to the front wheel and proprietary engines such as Singer, Triumph and Blackburne, and included at least one saloon. In 1924 Walter Bramham closed his business as he found he was making no money on the cars. The Stanhopes began to make cars under their own name again, but their output was very small and there was a great variety of designs. Many of these were probably one-offs, and included 3- and 4-wheelers, with 2- or 4-cylinder engines and chain or shaft drive in almost any permutation. Harry Stanhope's death from influenza in 1925 put an end to the business.

NG

Further Reading
'Front-Wheel Drive in Leeds; the Stanhope and the Bramham',
M. Worthington-Williams, *The Automobile*, February 1992.

STANLEY (i) (US) 1897–1927

1897–1902 Stanley Dry Plate Co., Newton, Massachusetts.
1902–1924 Stanley Motor Carriage Co., Newton, Massachusetts.
1924–1927 Steam Vehicle Corp. of America, Newton, Massachusetts.
The name Stanley has become almost synonymous with American steam automobiles. Though not the most productive of American steam car builders,

1908 Stanley (i) Model F 20hp tourer.
NICK BALDWIN

the Stanley firm produced steamers for the longest period of time, and the mystique of the Stanley brothers helped elevate their cars to legendary status.

The Stanleys, Francis Edgar (1849–1918) and Freelan Oscar (1849–1940), were identical twins endowed with the quality known as 'Yankee ingenuity'. They made their fortune in the photographic industry with a novel process for coating dry plates that revolutionised the field. The twins had become interested in self-propelled vehicles after seeing some early experimental cars, and after moving their plate business from their native Maine to Newton, Massachusetts, set about tinkering with a vehicle of their own. For power they chose steam, much the favoured concept in nineteenth century New England, and had a complete car constructed by the autumn of 1897. A nimble runabout, the car had an upright fire-tube boiler under the seat, and a two-cylinder 2.5 × 3.5in steam engine under just ahead of it, driving the rear axle with a chain. Suspension was by full-elliptic leaf springs, located front-to-rear with longitudinal 'perch rods'. Both boiler and engine were of lightweight design, the latter weighing just 35lb (16kg) and the former wound with piano wire to withstand higher pressures than used by most manufacturers.

New England's first automobile show was held in Boston in October 1898. The Stanleys were persuaded to take part in associated speed and timing trials held at the velodrome at Charles River Park. F.E. Stanley drove their car to a winning 2 minutes, 32 seconds mile, and won the hill climb by scaling a 30 per cent wooden incline. The twins had already built and sold several cars, but the Boston performance resulted in sufficient orders that they bought a bicycle plant adjacent to the photo plate works for manufacturing space. It has been estimated that as many as 200 were built by the end of 1899.

In February of that year, the Stanleys had been approached by John Brisben Walker, publisher of *Cosmopolitan* magazine. Walker wished to buy the enterprise, and the twins, intending to put him off, quoted the seemingly-astonomical price of $250,000 cash. To their surprise, Walker agreed, then raised the money by enticing asphalt tycoon Amzi Lorenzo Barber into the deal. The Stanleys agreed to exit the auto business for at least a year. Walker and Barber's Automobile Co. of America was launched in June, and soon renamed LOCOMOBILE Co. of America to avoid infringing on a company already using the other name. Disagreement between Walker and Barber led to the former's departure to build the MOBILE steamer at Tarrytown, New York, and Barber subsequently moved Locomobile to Bridgeport, Connecticut. The Stanleys retained some ties to the Locomobile firm, and F.O. and wife Flora gave the car lasting notoriety by making the first self-propelled ascent of Mount Washington in New Hampshire on 31 August 1899. In short order, the Locomobile was the best-selling American automobile.

The Stanleys bought back the Newton factory early in 1901, for a tenth of the price at which they had sold the company. They readied production of a new car, similar to the one they had sold, but changed the drive mechanism after some litigious wrangles, mounting the engine horizontally, fixed directly to the rear axle. This 700lb car sold for $650. The car business was spun off as the Stanley Motor Carriage Co. in the early part of 1902, and the photo plate operation was subsequently sold to George Eastman of Kodak fame.

By 1904, there were four models of Stanley steamers, catalogued by seating arrangement. In mid–1905, the boiler was moved to the front of the car, and covered with a coffin-like bonnet; soon the tiller steering was replaced with a

wheel. This was the definitive 'round nose' Stanley that would be produced for nearly a decade and be recognisable to the present day.

It was during this time that the Stanley acquired its lasting reputation for superlative performance. Privateer Louis Ross set a flying mile class record of 94.7mph (152.3km/h) with his twin-Stanley-engined Woggle Bug at Ormond-Daytona Beach, Florida in 1905. Two racers, with oversized engines and boilers, were built for the Vanderbilt Cup race of 1906, but were withdrawn. In January 1906, Stanley employee Fred Marriott drove a specially-built, streamlined Stanley Rocket to a record land speed record of 127.659mph (205.403km/h). The following year, in an attempt to raise the record, the revamped car flipped and broke apart, Marriott narrowly escaping with his life. It was estimated that the car was going 150mph (241km/h) at the time of the crash, but there was no measurement to confirm it. The Stanley Brothers hastily retired their firm from competitions. They did, however, continue to build the 'civilian' version of their 20hp racing car, the Model H Gentleman's Speedy Roadster, which offered 75mph (121km/h) performance for just $1000, and the 30hp engine of the Rocket was available for a short time in the Model K 'semi-racer'. (Stanley horsepower ratings are imprecise and based on boiler capacity, and are not translatable to either rated horsepower or brake horsepower.)

The peak year of Stanley production was 1907, with 775 cars built. The steam automobile era was waning, but the Stanleys took no notice. A line of updated cars was introduced for 1909, with sturdier chassis frame (still wood), and a larger bore engine, now running in an oiltight enclosure for better lubrication. Brakes were improved, with rear wheel drums replacing an inadequate differential brake. That year a commercial line was inaugurated, with a large, 9- or 12-seat, 30hp Mountain Wagon, conceived to transport guests to F.O. Stanley's new hotel in the mountains of Colorado.

Although the Stanleys detested complication, by 1914 they had to concede that steam cars really needed a condenser, to recycle used steam back into water and extend range. Their first condenser car was ready for 1915, rode a pressed-steel chassis frame and had semi-elliptic front springs – still retaining the perch rods to locate the full-elliptic rears. Lhd was finally adopted. The Stanley steamer was now much heavier, and more expensive than the cars of the previous decade. The 1915 Model 720 tourer weighed 3400lb and cost $1975, but it had the same engine as the 1350lb Gentleman's Speedy Roadster of 1907. Startling Stanley performance was a thing of the past.

Perhaps the brothers realised this – in any case they decided to retire, consigning the business to F.E.'s two sons-in-law, and production manager Carlton Stanley, their cousin, in 1917. F.E. then turned his attention to a steam-powered rail car, but was killed in a road accident the following year. F.O. Stanley devoted himself to his hotel business, living to age 91.

The vee-shaped condenser of 1915 was not fully satisfactory, so a flat, finned design was introduced in 1919, and a general restyling was accomplished for 1922. Sales were minuscule, and by 1923 the firm was bankrupt. The remnants were acquired by the Steam Vehicle Corp. of America in February 1924. The 1924 models featured semi-elliptic springing all round, and a new SV model for 1925 was smaller and lighter, but barely cheaper. The SV was even less well received, and few were built and sold in the next two years. The Massachusetts plant was sold in July 1925, and the Steam Vehicle Corp. finally liquidated in 1929.

KF

Further Reading
The Story of a Stanley Steamer, George Woodbury, W.W. Norton & Co., 1950.
'F.E. and F.O. Stanley – The Challenge from Steam', John F. Katz, *Automobile Quarterly*, Vol. 25, No. 1.

STANLEY (ii) **(US)** 1907–1910
1907–1908 Stanley Automobile Manufacturing Co., Mooreland, Indiana.
1909–1910 Troy Automobile & Buggy Co., Troy, Ohio.
James Stanley aimed to produce a 'people's car' that almost anyone could afford, his target price being $350. When he put his car on the market in 1907 he could not get the price below $575, but even so that was quite reasonable for a 20hp 2-cylinder car with epicyclic transmission and chain final drive. He planned to make a shaft-driven model, but it never appeared. In late 1908 he joined forces with Troy Automobile & Buggy Co. and made a few more cars there.

NG

STANLEY-WHITNEY *see* MCKAY *and* WHITNEY (i)

STANWOOD (US) 1920–1922

Stanwood Motor Car Co., St Louis, Missouri.

The Stanwood was a typical assembled car of its time assembled from standard components throughout and available as a touring car, roadster, and sedan. The engine was a Continental 7R six and the wheelbase measured 118in (2995mm). Wood artillery wheels were standard. Prices ranged from $1765 for both open types and $2750 for the sedan, although it is more than likely that no sedan was built. Production totalled an estimated 250 to 300 cars during Stanwood's three years in the field.

KM

STAR (i) (GB) 1898–1932

1898–1902 Star Motor Co., Wolverhampton, Staffordshire.
1902–1909 Star Engineering Co., Wolverhampton, Staffordshire.
1905–1909 Star Cycle Co., Wolverhampton, Staffordshire.
1909–1928 Star Engineering Co. Ltd, Wolverhampton, Staffordshire.
1928–1932 Star Motor Co. Ltd, Wolverhampton, Staffordshire.

The Star was one of the best-known and longest lived of the many makes of car from Wolverhampton, outshone only by Sunbeam. For most of its life it was guided by the Lisle family who had started in business in 1883 as cycle makers under the name Sharratt & Lisle. In 1896 Edward Lisle senior changed the name to the Star Cycle Co. Ltd, and in 1898, when car production was taken up, he formed the Star Motor Co., the Cycle company continuing in business to make bicycles and motorcycles and, at a later date, Starling and Stuart cars.

For several years Star relied on other designs for their cars. The first was the 3½hp Benz Velo but although the cars were sometimes called Star-Benz they were always manufactured at Wolverhampton. No components were imported from Mannheim, and the only parts bought in were the Brampton roller chains and Clipper tyres. Production was running at one car per week from October 1899, and the last Benz-based car did not leave the factory until 1902. By then other designs were being made, two De Dion-engined cars and three Panhard-like cars with 8 and 10hp twin and 20hp 4-cylinder engines. The 1904 Stars all had 4-cylinder engines, of 12, 18, and 24hp and were on Mercedes lines with honeycomb radiators, mechanically-operated inlet valves and pressed steel frames. There was also a 70hp racing car which was closely based on the Mercedes Sixty, but it had much less success than its German counterpart.

In 1905 the Star Cycle Co. entered the car market with a 2-seater powered by a 6hp De Dion engine, called the Starling. It had chain drive and an armoured wood frame. This company was run by Edward Lisle junior, and made Starlings in 8 and 10hp versions up to 1909. During 1906–08 they were joined by the 7hp shaft-driven Stuart which could be had in 2- or 4-seater forms. In 1909 the Star Cycle Co. changed its name to BRITON and became a separate make, still under Edward Lisle junior.

Meanwhile the Star Engineering Co. prospered with a range of conventional cars, the most successful of which was the Fifteen, made in various sizes, 3482cc from 1909 to 1911, 3052cc in 1911 and 1912, and as the 15.9hp 3014cc from 1913 to 1916. The 1909–11 model was unusual in being offered with bi-bloc or monobloc engines. The largest prewar model, and indeed the largest of all Stars apart from the 70hp racing car, was the 7698cc 30hp four, while there was also the 6977cc 40hp six, made in small numbers from 1907 to 1911. The larger models had dual ignition as standard, and rounded radiators were adopted for 1913 and detachable wheels for 1914. By 1914 Star was among the six largest British car makers, with annual output of more than 1000 passenger cars as well as a range of vans and trucks up to 4 tons capacity.

Star made a large number of trucks for the army during the war, as well as working on the abortive A.B.C. Dragonfly radial aero engine. In 1919 they resumed production with two prewar models, the 3014cc 15.9hp and the 3815cc 20.1hp, both with pair-cast cylinders. These were joined in 1922 by the 1794cc 11.9hp with monobloc cylinders and unit construction of engine and gearbox. Star was making about 1000 cars per year in the early 1920s, but the premises were very old fashioned, the workshops being in a series of buildings in cramped back streets. Edward Lisle senior's conservative personality was against the idea of mass production, even if they could have afforded to adopt it. 'I would rather build one good car a day than commit us to mass production', he said. Apart from the frames which came from Thompson of Bilston, practically all of the cars was made in-house, including the bodies. One of the more unusual orders for the body department was for eight harem wagons for King Ibn Saud of Saudi

1899 Star (i) 3½hp dog cart.
NICK BALDWIN

1905 Star (i) 7hp 2-seater.
NICK BALDWIN

1926 Star (i) 14/30hp tourer.
NICK BALDWIN

Arabia. He stipulated that no men were to enter the cars during their construction.

New models in the 1920s included the 2915cc 6-cylinder Eighteen which became the 3263cc 20/50 in 1925, and the 1924 12/25 which was an enlarged 11.9hp. An ohv version of this was the 12/40 sports with which Malcolm Campbell won a short handicap at Brooklands in 1925, although Star was by no means a sporting make, unlike its fellow Wolverhampton make, Sunbeam.

1930 Star (i) Comet/Planet saloon.
NATIONAL MOTOR MUSEUM

1932 Star (i) Little Comet sports car by Jensen.
NICK GEORGANO/NATIONAL MOTOR MUSEUM

In 1928 the Lisle family sold out to Sydney Guy, by then a sizeable maker of commercial vehicles, although he had made at few cars at the beginning of the decade. He was anxious to have a car range, and moved Star production from its cramped premises to the body plant at Bushbury, on the outskirts of Wolverhampton. New models for 1931 were the 2470cc 18hp Comet and 3180cc 21hp Planet, restyled versions of the earlier sixes, with silent third gearboxes, twin-plate clutches and a host of equipment such as thermostatically controlled radiator shutters, stop and reversing lights and Jackall built-in jacks. They were good value, but the old-fashioned machinery at Bushbury brought about a loss on each car made. The last new models were the 2100cc Comet Fourteen and 3620cc Planet Twenty Four introduced in 1931. Of these, 216 Comet Fourteen (or Little Comet) were made, but only nine Planet Twenty Fours. Of the others the Comet 18 accounted for 416 deliveries and the Planet 21 for 41. Production ended abruptly in March 1932. Although McKenzie & Denly of Birmingham took over the manufacturing rights and the Star lingered on in some Buyer's Guides until 1935, probably no more cars were made. The last entry in the order book, dated 2 April 1932, was for an 1898 Star-Benz, preserved at the works for 34 years, which went to a buyer in Birmingham for £5.

NG

Further Reading
Lost Causes of Motoring, Lord Montagu of Beaulieu, Cassell, 1960.
'Twilight of the Star', D.E.A. Evans,
Veteran & Vintage Magazine, December 1975.
'Star Cars', Mike Cotton, *Wolverhampton Express & Star*, 1996.

STAR (ii) (US) 1903–1904
1903–1904 Star Automobile Co., Cleveland, Ohio.
1904 H.S. Moore, Cleveland, Ohio.
The Star was made as a 2-seater with detachable tonneau to give two extra seats. It was powered by an 8½hp single-cylinder engine mounted under the floorboards, with epicyclic transmission and chain drive, on a 76in (1929mm) wheelbase. About 20 were made before the company was sold to Harry S. Moore. He made a few alterations, increasing power to 9hp, lengthening the wheelbase and giving

the car an oval-shaped bonnet and radiator, but he probably made fewer Stars that the original company.

NG

STAR (iii) (US) 1907–1908
Star Automobile Co., Chicago, Illinois.
This Star was a 2-seater runabout powered by a 10hp single-cylinder 2-stroke engine, with friction transmission. In this the shifting of the disc was by a secondary wheel on the steering column, giving the appearance of two steering wheels.

NG

STAR (iv) (US) 1908–1909
Model Automobile Co., Peru, Indiana.
This Star was the MODEL renamed, and was made in 2- and 4-cylinder versions, 24hp twins and 30, 35, and 50hp fours. In 1909 the company's owner E.A. Myers changed the name of company and car to GREAT WESTERN.

NG

STAR (v) (PL) 1912–1913
Auto Central Garage STAR Spolki Omnibusow Automobilowych, Krakow.
This company was the representative for Laurin & Klement vehicles in Krakow, and in order to service the buses which they sold to the town, they built well-equipped new workshops in 1912. This led the ambitious chief engineer Bogumil Bechyne to design a small car to be built in these workshops. It had a 1385cc 10/12hp 4-cylinder air-cooled engine mounted transversely as in the Mini, although drive was by chains to the rear wheels. It had a 2-speed gearbox and top speed of 40mph (64km/h). Bechyne planned to make 50 cars in 1913 and 100 in 1914, but only two prototypes and four production cars were made. The company continued as a Laurin & Klement agency.

NG

STAR (vi) (US) 1922–1928
Durant Motor Co. of New Jersey, Elizabeth, New Jersey,
also at Lansing, Michigan and Oakland, California.
The Star was the lowest-priced make in the automotive empire of William Crapo Durant. It followed the medium-priced Durant which had appeared in 1921, and was a budget-priced car aimed deliberately as a competitor for GM's Chevrolet. Durant had hoped to undercut Chevrolet and steal some customers from Ford, and the initial prices of his Star Four roadster and tourer exactly matched Ford's at $319 and $348 respectively. However, in mid-season Ford dropped his prices by $50 which Durant could not possibly match. Indeed he was forced to increase his 1923 prices, to $414 and $443 respectively. However, he did match Chevrolet's prices almost exactly for a few years.

The Star Four was a thoroughly conventional car powered by a 2137cc side-valve engine made by Continental. Orders for Star and Durant cars made Durant Continental's biggest customer in the mid–1920s, taking about 85 per cent of their annual output. Other bought-in components included Spicer universal joints and Timken axles. In 1923 Durant bought up the Adams Axle Co. to assure a satisfactory supply, and he also owned Warner, his gearbox suppliers. The gearbox location was the only unusual feature of the Star, for it was separate from the engine, not in unit as with most mass-produced American cars of the 1920s. Four body styles were offered initially, roadster, tourer, coupé and sedan, joined in 1923 by an open-sided station wagon, America's first production example of this body, and a panel delivery van. 1925 Stars were more expensive, at $540 for a roadster to $820 for a sedan, which put them slightly above Chevrolet.

Durant's sales held up well for several years, though, totalling 172,000 in 1923, 111,000 in 1924, 127,000 in 1925 and 125,000 in 1926. Stars accounted for more than 75,000 in 1923, and 60–80,000 of subsequent annual sales.

The first Stars were built in Durant's Long Island City factory, but most were made in the big plant at Elizabeth, New Jersey, which had formerly belonged to Willys. Other factories which saw Star production included those at Lansing, Michigan; Oakland, California, and Toronto, Canada. Stars enjoyed good export sales, being sold under the name Rugby in Britain and its Empire to avoid confusion with the Wolverhampton-built Star. A larger 4-cylinder engine of 2490cc was introduced for the 1926 season, as well as a 2774cc six, both units being Continental-built. The 1926 Star Four roadster could be converted to a pick-up by unbolting the dickey seat and replacing it with a box. There was

1922 Star (vi) Four tourer.
JOHN A. CONDE

also a larger commercial model, the Star Compound Fleetruck powered by the 6-cylinder engine. Front-wheel brakes were introduced for 1927, but the Star was on its way out. In April 1928 the four became the Durant Four, and the six the Durant Star or Durant Model 55. The same engines and wheelbases were made in 1929, now called the Durant M Series 4-40 and Model 55. Sales of all models were drastically down by this time, 47,716 in 1929, and only 20,900 in 1930. The Depression completely wiped out Durant's empire and personal fortune. The last cars were made in 1932 and Billy Durant was declared bankrupt in February 1936.

NG

STARBORNE *see* APAL

STARIN (US) 1903–1904
The Starin Co., North Tonawanda, New York.
This was a typical light runabout powered by a 6 or 8hp horizontal single-cylinder engine mounted under the seat, with 2-speed epicyclic transmission and single-chain drive. They were priced at $800 and $1000 respectively.

NG

STARLIGHT (US) 1959–1963
Kish Industries, Inc, Lansing, Michigan.
The Starlight was a small, 2-seater electric car with roadster bodywork.

HP

STARLING *see* STAR (i)

STARR (US) 1909–1910
This car was built in Minneapolis, although the name of the company which produced it is unknown. It was of conventional design, with a 24hp 4-cylinder or 36hp 6-cylinder Brownell engine, and was apparently made only in roadster form. Despite its slogan, 'The Wise Men of the East Followed the Star – the Wise Men of the West Ride in the Starr', not many did, and a planned factory move to Downing, Wisconsin did not happen.

NG

1924 Star (vi) 15.6hp station wagon.
NATIONAL MOTOR MUSEUM

1921 Start Type C 1460cc sports car.
NATIONAL MOTOR MUSEUM

1977 Status 365 coupé.
NATIONAL MOTOR MUSEUM

1989 Steadman S.S.100 sports car.
OTTERCRAFT

START (CS) 1921–1931

1919–1922 Petrasek a Vechet, tovarna motorovych automatu, Kukleny.
1922–1924 Frantisek Petrasek a spol., Hradec Kralove.
1924–1931 Ing. Fr. Petrasek, tovarna automobilu 'Start', Hradec Kralove.

In 1919, car producer Vojmir Vechet came to Kukleny from Nymburk and became Petrasek's partner. The PAV (Petrasek and Vechet) cars were planned to be produced at Kukleny Works but at the 1921 Prague Auto salon again the B type of the former Perfekt marque was exhibited, but now renamed 'Start'. It was soon followed by a bigger 4-seater of the type C with 4-cylinder 1460cc 6-20hp sv engine with aluminium pistons, bodied as an open tourer or closed taxicab. About 35 were sold until 1926 when the type D2 appeared, designed by a son of the firm's founder, Ing. Frantisek Petrasek, with flat twin-cylinder 1000cc 12bhp air-cooled engine. This was, however, underpowered and that is why the type E4 with 4-cylinder 1453cc 24bhp sv engine, was built from 1928 to 1931. No more than 10–15 cars with 2-door 4-seater open or closed bodies were sold. In 1932 158 Start passenger cars and 24 delivery vans were registered in Czechoslovakia. Petrasek later manufactured engines for fire pumps and had a large repair shop.

MSH

STATES (i) (US) 1914–1915

States Cyclecar Co., Detroit, Michigan.

This was a 2-seater cyclecar powered by a 4-cylinder engine on a 90in (2284mm) wheelbase. Unusually for such a car, it had artillery wheels.

NG

STATES (ii) (US) 1916–1918

States Motor Car Co., Kalamazoo, Michigan.

Although it had no connection with the Detroit-built States cyclecar, the States from Kalamazoo did come from a former cyclecar maker, Greyhound. The States was a conventional tourer on a 112in (2843mm) wheelbase, powered by a 32hp 4-cylinder engine. For 1918 it was joined by a 37hp six on the same wheelbase.

NG

STATUS (GB) 1971–1996

1971 Status Co., Norwich, Norfolk.
1971–1973 Status Motors, New Buckenham, Norfolk.
1973–1974 Motor Marianne, New Buckenham, Norfolk.
1974–1975 Status Co., New Buckenham, Norfolk.
1976–1977 Brian Luff Ltd, Nazeing, Essex.
c.1980–1981 Brian Luff Ltd, Jersey.
c.1985–1996 Brian Luff Ltd, Bawburgh, Norwich.

Ex-Lotus and Clan engineer Brian Luff set up Status to sell a Mini-based space frame chassis, mostly to autocross drivers. He then made his own fibreglass body for that chassis and so created the Status Symbol. Features included a right-hand mounted gear lever, independent double wishbone suspension all round, any BMC A-series engine driving through BMC 1100 driveshafts and soft- and hard-top options. Of 20 chassis supplied, only eight had Luff's bodyshell. Luff's next project was the 365, so named because it was designed to be used every day of the year. The styling was a curious mix between Clan Crusader and Lotus Elite 501. The fibreglass-and-wood bodywork (over Mini subframes) seated four and featured odd 3-piece front glass and a rear hatchback. Luff went on to develop the MINUS and his Mini-based Streaker and Abacus fun car kits were listed as early as 1985. The Streaker was a basic 2-seater sports car with an external steel chassis and fibreglass body tub. The 1992 Sabot was a squarish open Mini-based utility/fun car with a doorless fibreglass monocoque.

CR

STAUNAU (D) 1950–1951

Staunau-Werk, Hamburg-Harburg.

Considering the size of its engines, 500 or 750cc 2-cylinder 2-strokes, the Staunau had a very heavy saloon body with generous use of chrome on the grill. At 162in (4111mm) it was longer than an Opel Olympia. About 80 were made, of which 16 had the 750cc engine.

HON

STAVER; STAVER-CHICAGO (US) 1907–1914

1907–1911 Staver Carriage Co., Chicago, Illinois.
1911–1914 Staver Motor Co., Chicago, Illinois.

Harry C. Staver's first car was a high-wheeler powered by an 18/20hp 2-cylinder engine, with the usual epicyclic transmission and double-chain final drive. It was, however, on the expensive side at $1000, when the contemporary Sears cost from $370 to $495, and the Holsman $650 to $800. Nevertheless, Staver sold 800 of his buggies before switching to a conventional tourer with 4-cylinder engines, initially of 30 and 45hp. By 1912 he was making two models, the 30hp on a 112in (2842mm) wheelbase and the 40hp on a 124in (3147mm) wheelbase, with eight body styles on the 30hp chassis. The Stavers of 1913 had some fancy names recalling the smarter districts around Chicago, such as Englewood and Newport tourers, Lakeport roadster, South Shore Colonial Coupé and North Shore limousine. These were all on the 35hp chassis; the 40hp was listed with just one model, the Dictator tourer. Staver chose this name some 14 years before Studebaker started using it. The 1914 range included two fours and a 70bhp six. The factory was sold that year to the makers of the Partin-Palmer. Total Staver production, including the high-wheelers, was 5880 cars.

NG

STEADMAN (GB) 1986–c.1989

1986–1987 Traditional Sportscar Panels, Hayle, Cornwall.
1987–c.1989 Ottercraft Ltd, Hayle, Cornwall.

The TS 100 was not the usual insipid replica of a 1930s S.S. 100, as it offered a fairly high degree of accuracy and an all-aluminium body (though fibreglass wings were available to keep costs down). It used Jaguar XJ suspension and powertrain in a substantial box section steel ladder chassis. Cars were sold either complete or in kit form.

CR

STEAMOBILE (US) 1900–1902

Steamobile Co. of America, Keene, New Hampshire.

This company was a successor to the Trinity Cycle Manufacturing Co. which had made the KEENE STEAMOBILE car, and the design was carried on with little change. It was a typical light steamer powered by a 7/8hp vertical engine with single-chain drive. The 2-seater had a curved dash like that of the Oldsmobile, though it was higher built. By September 1901 25 had been sold, and two new models followed for 1902, a 4-seater *dos-à-dos* and a delivery wagon called the Transit, in which the driver sat behind the load. These evidently did not sell well, for in June 1902 it was reported that the company had a considerable number of vehicles in stock and would probably build no more. Later, 40 unsold cars were disposed of to the Standard Roller Bearing Co. of Philadelphia.

NG

STEARMAN (US) c.1984

Stearman Aircraft Products Corp., Valley Center, Kansas.

The Stearman Mini-Car was a midget car similar to the ones that were popular immediately after World War II. Although about the same size as a KING MIDGET, it had a monocoque chassis with leaf springs, automatic transmission and a rear mounted 18hp engine. A simple convertible body held two adults and two children in minimal comfort. It was designed for city, farm and ranch driving, or for use in underdeveloped countries. Two prototypes were made before the project was put up for sale in 1984.

HP

STEARNS (i); STEARNS-KNIGHT (US) 1899–1930

F.B. Stearns Co., Cleveland, Ohio.

Frank Ballou Stearns (1879–1955) built his first car in the basement of the family home on Euclid Avenue in Cleveland, when he was only 17, and formed F.B. Stearns & Co. two years later, with the help of the Owen brothers who would later make cars under their own name. The first production Stearns was a single-cylinder 2-seater runabout with wheel steering, which was quite advanced for that type of car at the turn of the century. The 1901 model had an enormous cylinder of 6.25 × 7.5in (158.25 × 190.5mm), giving a capacity of 3745cc, but by 1902 Stearns had progressed to a 5.5-litre 24hp 2-cylinder engine mounted under the bonnet, with a tonneau body and chain drive.

The first 50 cars had been made in a workshop behind the Stearns home, but in late 1900 Frank moved to a rented workshop also on Euclid Avenue. This site remained the home of Stearns cars for the next 30 years. After the Owens left, the business was renamed the F.B. Stearns Co. During 1901 the little company was helped by Frank's father-in-law Captain Thomas Wilson, founder of the Wilson Marine Trust Co. and the Central National Bank of Cleveland. In 1902 the company was reorganised with fresh capital totalling $200,000; Frank was president, general manager and treasurer, while his father F.M. Stearns was vice-president and secretary.

The 1904 range included the 24hp twin and a 36hp four which, with a 7-seater tourer body, cost $4150. From 1905 the Stearns became more European, with mechanically operated side valves, pair-cast cylinders and a Mercedes-style radiator. They also increased steadily in size and price, reaching a peak in the massive 45/90hp six introduced in 1908. The 13-litre engine was so long that it projected into the scuttle. Few were made of this model, which cost from $6400 for a tourer to $7500 for a limousine or landaulet. At the other end of the scale was the 'baby Stearns' introduced in 1909, with 4.8-litre 15/30hp 4-cylinder engine. This was also used as a taxicab.

In 1910 Frank Stearns sent his chief engineer, James G. Sterling, to England to study the Knight sleeve-valve engine as used by Daimler. After exhaustive testing Stearns adopted the Knight on a 28hp four in June 1911, followed by the whole range for 1912. A sleeve-valve six was added for 1913, when there were two engines, the 5.1-litre 28hp four and 6.8-litre 43.8hp six, offered with five wheelbases from 115in (2919mm) for the 4-cylinder roadster to 140in (3553mm) for the 6-cylinder 7-seater tourer, limousine or landaulet. All models had electric lighting and starting by 1914. For 1915 Stearns introduced a 22.5hp Light Four of only 4 litres capacity. This brought the company into a more popular market, and to satisfy demand a new 5-storey addition to the factory had to be built. The Light Four was priced from $1750 for a tourer to $2850 for a limousine, and raised sales from 2415 in 1914 to 3718 in 1917. By then there was also a 5.4-litre 34hp V8 in the range and the big six had been dropped.

1908 Stearns 45/90 tourer.
NICK GEORGANO

1923 Stearns-Knight 6-cylinder coupé.
NATIONAL MOTOR MUSEUM

1929 Stearns-Knight Model 8-90 cabriolet.
NATIONAL MOTOR MUSEUM

Frank Stearns retired at the age of 37 at the end of 1917 to devote himself to experiments with diesel engines; he later obtained 16 patents in connection with diesels, and sold an engine to the US Navy in 1935.

After Stearns' departure the company was reorganised under former St Louis agent George W. Booker. Rolls-Royce aero engines were made in 1917 and 1918, and although car production was not suspended, only 1450 were delivered in 1918. James G. Sterling left in 1920, taking with him several Stearns staff and set up his own business at Warren, Ohio making the STERLING-KNIGHT. This design was taken over by John N. Willys, who also bought Stearns in December 1925, to give him a prestige sleeve-valve car to add to the Willys-Knight that he was making. The two existing sixes, the 4077cc Model 6-C and 4728cc Model 6-S were continued for 1926, and for 1927 came a 6309cc straight-8 developing 100bhp. Prices ran from $3950 to $5800. For those prepared to pay more, Stearns had the exclusive US rights for the Daimler Double Six, which carried a $17,000 price tag.

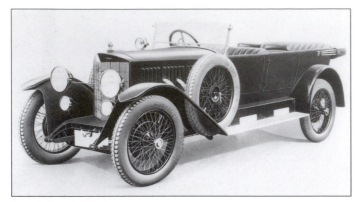

1923 Steiger 10/50PS tourer.
HALWART SCHRADER

1909 Stella (ii) 16/24CV tourer.
ERNEST SCHMID

1914 Stellite 9.5hp tourer.
NATIONAL MOTOR MUSEUM

Despite the initial euphoria Willys soon found that the Stearns-Knight was not a great money spinner. The inventory had been written up far beyond what it was worth, and dealers were disorganised and dispirited. Although it was a good car, the straight-8 was up against makes such as Lincoln and Packard, and sales were not exciting. In 1927 combined sales of the six and eight were only 927, though they rose to 1081 in 1928 and 1143 in 1929. That was the Stearns-Knight's last year, for production ended on 20 December 1929. A few cars were sold off as 1930 models during the first few months of the following year. A curious postscript to the Stearns-Knight story was provided by the three Stearns-based petrol-electrics built for Colonel Edward Green (see RAUCH & LANG).

NG

Further Reading
'Quest for Perfection: The motorcars of Frank Stearns', Thomas S. La Marre and Jonathan A. Stein, *Automobile Quarterly*, Vol. 30, No. 3.
'Power Up Its Sleeves', Arch Brown, *Special-Interest Autos*, June 1989.

STEARNS (ii) (US) 1899–1903
1899–1900 E.C. Stearns & Co., Syracuse, New York.
1900–1903 Stearns Steam Carriage Co., Syracuse, New York.
1903 Stearns Automobile Co., Syracuse, New York.
Edward Stearns ran a hardware store in Syracuse, and added bicycle manufacture to his business before making an electric car in 1899. It had three speeds, of 5, 8 and 12mph (8, 13, and 19km/h), and spur gear drive. A few were made up to the autumn of 1900, when Stearns formed a new company to make steam cars. These had 8hp 2-cylinder slide-valve engines, single-chain drive and tiller steering. Unusually, it was offered in nine body styles, including a 6-seater with three rows of seats and roll-down canvas sides, which could be considered as the world's first station wagon. Unfortunately Stearns became involved with Edward Joel Pennington, and like most who went into business with that gentleman, came off worse. The newly-formed Stearns Automobile Co. folded in the summer of 1903.

NG

STECO (US) 1914
The Stevens Co., Chicago, Illinois.
The Steco was a typical cyclecar powered by a 9hp air-cooled V-twin engine, with friction transmission and belt final drive. The frame was of ash and the body aluminium. This seated two in tandem, and the car cost $450.

NG

STEELE (US) 1915
The William Steele Co., Worcester, Massachusetts.
This company was best known for its trucks which were made from 1914 to 1919. The company was reported to have built a small number of 2-cylinder cyclecars in 1915, but details are lacking.

NG

STEEL SWALLOW (US) 1907–1908
Steel Swallow Auto Co., Jackson, Michigan.
This was a high-wheeler design, although unlike most of that kind it carried its 8hp air-cooled 2-cylinder engine under a bonnet. It had friction transmission and final drive by double chains. It was also made as a delivery van, including one for rural mail delivery.

NG

STEIGER (D) 1920–1928
1920–1925 Walter Steiger & Co., Burgrieden.
1925–1928 Steiger AG, Burgrieden.
Walter Steiger planned his car during World War I, with design by Paul Henze who later worked for SIMSON. He went into production in 1920 with a 2604cc 10/50PS 4-cylinder car with shaft-driven single-ohc, which made extensive use of lightweight metal. It was made as a 4-seater tourer on a 118in (2995mm) wheelbase, later increased to 128in (3249mm), and reduced to 102in (2589mm) on the sports model made from 1922. These later cars had bored-out engines giving 2826cc. Steiger built their own bodies and the bonnets were fronted by handsome Vee-radiators. In 1924 Walter Steiger and his brother took over the Swiss MARTINI company and designed the Martini-Steiger. Meanwhile Steiger production in Germany came to an end in 1925, although the Düsseldorf dealer assembled a few more from existing parts up to 1928.

HON

Further Reading
Steiger, die Geschichte einer Schwabischen Autofabrik, Michael Schick, 1999.

STEINMETZ (US) 1922–1923
Steinmetz Electric Motor Car Corp., Baltimore, Maryland.
Designed by the famous electrical engineer Charles P. Steinmetz, this was an electric sedan with a top speed of 40mph (64km/h) and a remarkable range of 200 miles per charge. Only four prototypes were made, as the company then concentrated on commercial vehicles which survived up to 1926. Although the company headquarters were in Baltimore, the four electric cars were made by the Thorne Machine Tool Co. of Syracuse, New York.

NG

1919 Stephens (ii) Salient Six tourer.
JOHN A. CONDE

STÉLA (F) 1941–1944
Véhicules Électriques Stéla, Villeurbanne, Lyons.
This company was formed by H. Pascal, an engineer from the École Centrale de Lyon, to provide electric vehicles for use during the time when petrol was virtually unobtainable. The first Stéla was an angular 2-door saloon with batteries on the wide running boards, but in 1942 came the RCA, a streamlined 4-door 5-seater saloon. Admiral Darlan, head of the Vichy Government in France, had two, while a number served as taxis, and two were still in service in 1953. The liberation and arrival of reasonable supplies of fuel put an end to Stéla cars, although commercial vehicles were continued up to 1948.
NG

STELKA (CS) 1922–1924
Rudolf Stelsovsky a spol., strojirna a slevarna, Pribram.
The first version of this simple car was developed from the track motor cars with petrol engines, built by the firm of Wohanka a spol. The 4-seater Stelka (named after the manufacturer, Stelsovsky) was designed by Jan Svejda in 1922, and one year later their light car (chassis weight 660lb/300kg) with twin-cylinder air-cooled 1145cc engine was the cheapest automobile at the Prague Autosalon – it cost 29,000 Kc. After also producing some light vans Stelsovsky formed a joint-stock company for production of ASPA cars in 1924.
MSH

STELLA (i) (F) 1900–1901
Sté de Constructions Mécaniques Stella, Levallois-Perret, Seine.
Aster or De Dion-Bouton engines of 2¹/₂hp were used to power this light voiturette with tubular frame. Transmission was by epicyclic gear with final drive by belts. It weighed only 336lb (153kg). It was announced in August 1900, and the company failed in February 1901.
NG

STELLA (ii) (CH) 1906–1913
Compagnie de l'Industrie Électrique et Mécanique, Geneva.
When CIEM abandonded petrol-electric vehicles, a range of conventional cars were made under the name Stella. The first Stella was a 10/12hp with a 4-cylinder cast in pairs engine of 3054cc. It was followed by a larger 14/18hp. From 1910 monobloc engines were used. The 14/16hp chassis, with an engine of 2813cc, cost SFr7800 in 1911 and the 18/20hp with 3052cc was available at SFr9000.

In 1912 the biggest Stella, a 24/30hp with 4070cc and a 4-speed gearbox and shaft drive, as on the smaller models, was launched. Open touring as well as coach-built limousine bodies were offered. The Stella radiator was round and rather similar to those on the Hotchkiss. About 200 Stella cars had been made when in 1913 production ceased. The company later was renamed SA des Ateliers Sécheron, Geneva, which did some coachbuilding in the early 1940s.
FH

STELLA (iii) (A) 1947–1948
Stella-Werk Wien 2, Vienna.
Franz Weidlich assembled a small number of cars which he called Aero Stella from components which he found by scouring the garages and breakers' yards countrywide. He also issued a catalogue for an advanced car with hydraulic brakes and swing-axle suspension. Two engines were specified, a 35bhp 4-cylinder ohv petrol unit and a 4-cylinder diesel. It is not known if this car was ever built.
HON

STELLITE (GB) 1913–1919
Electric & Ordnance Accessories Co. Ltd, Birmingham.
The Stellite light car was made by a subsidiary of Wolseley. It had a 1074cc monobloc 4-cylinder engine with overhead inlet valves and a detachable head. It had a 2-speed gearbox in unit with the rear axle, and an armoured wood frame. Two- and 4-seater bodies were available, and about 1500 were sold in the model's first year. Production was resumed in 1919, and in 1921–22 the Stellite name was revived for a less expensive version of the Wolseley Ten, without electric lighting or starting. This was a Wolseley model rather than a separate make.
NG

STEPHENS (i) (GB) 1898–1900
R. Stephens, Clevedon, Somerset.
Richard Stephens was a cycle and general engineer who made a few vehicles over a period of about three years. The prototype, which still exists, had an 8hp 2-cylinder horizontal engine built into the frame, with drive by belts to a countershaft and chains to the rear wheels. It had ifs with the wheels held in bicycle-type forks. The wheels were also of cycle type but later Stephens had artillery wheels. They included two 9-seater buses which operated a service between Clevedon and Portishead in 1900.
NG

1509

1922 Stephens (ii) Six sport roadster.
NATIONAL MOTOR MUSEUM

STEPHENS (ii) (US) 1916–1924

1916–1921 Moline Plow Co., Moline, Illinois.
1922–1924 Stephens Motor Car Co., Freeport, Illinois.
The Moline Plow Co. had been a well-known builder of buggies and farm implements for more than 40 years when it entered the automobile business due to diminishing sales of horse-drawn vehicles. Named after G.A. Stephens, company head, its pilot model was built and tested in 1916 with regular production following the next year. The first cars, powered by a 6-cylinder Continental engine and built on a wheelbase of 115in (2919mm) proved successful and for 1918 the wheelbase was lengthened by two inches. The Stephens proved a popular car and production would be consistent with the factory's capability, peaking in 1920 with nearly 3800 units completed. During 1918 the Continental engine was replaced by a smaller ohv in-house engine which would remain in all Stephens cars until the end of production. In 1920 the wheelbase was lengthened to 122in (3096mm) and both a coupé and a sedan were added to the Stephens line. Prices, which had started at $1150 in 1917 and had gradually risen through the first three or four years, reached $2400 to $3400 in 1921, dropping to the $1950 range for 1922 in which year the closed cars were temporarily phased out of the line.

In 1922 the company was reorganised as the Stephens Motor Car Co., operations were moved to Freeport, Illinois and the new models completely redesigned, the Salient Six Model 10 with a wheelbase of 117in (2969mm) and priced at $1295 for the touring car to $1895 for the 5-seater sedan and a larger Series 20 with the 122in (3096mm) wheelbase and priced from $1800 to $2850. Especially popular with the 'sporting set' was the sport phaeton, essentially the Model 10 touring car with cycle mudguards, step plates in place of running boards, bevelled glass windwings, a boot and painted in French grey with apple-green wire wheels. The Model 10 would, however, be dropped for 1924 in which the Model 20 was continued, 1924 being the final year of Stephens production, its seven years having produced an annual output averaging approximately 2900 cars.
KM

STERA (F) 1954

This enterprise produced an open plastic body for the Panhard Junior chassis. A revised model designed by Jean Bernadet appeared six months later.
CR

STERLING see NOVA (ii) and CALIFORNIA COMPONENT CARS

STERLING (i) (US) 1909–1911

Elkhart Motor Car Co., Elkhart, Indiana.
This was a conventional car powered by a 4-cylinder Model engine of either 30 or 40hp, and available as a tourer, runabout or surrey. The company was formed by Dr E.C. Crow, his son Martin, and Willard Sterling. Before even a car had been made the Crows left to make the CROW ELKHART, so Sterling carried on and used his own name for the car. He also made the KOMET which was similar to the Sterling in design. In 1911 a group of former Haynes officials took over the factory to make the Lohr car, but this was almost immediately renamed the ELMER. Total Sterling production was 862 cars.
NG

STERLING (ii) (GB) 1913

Sterling Engineering & Automobile Co., Leeds, Yorkshire.
This was an ephemeral cyclecar powered by an 8hp JAP V-twin engine, with vee-belt final drive. Another car of the same name was announced by the Warbrooke Engineering Co. of Kingsbury, north London, in 1923, but did not go into production.
NG

STERLING (iii) (US) 1915–1916

Sterling Motor Car Co., Brockton, Massachusetts.
Made by Alonzo C. Marsh who had built the MARSH (i) earlier in the twentieth century, this Sterling was a light car with a 13hp 4-cylinder engine and available as a tourer or runabout. Production began soon after the appearance of the prototype in June 1915, but ended in May of the following year.
NG

STERLING (iv) (US) 1919–1922

1919–1921 Consolidated Motor Car Co. Inc., Middlefield, Connecticut.
1922 Sterling Motor Car Co., Middlefield, Connecticut.
Albert E. and Bert E. Lazaro, with Frank J. Kenney, incorporated the Consolidated Motor Car Co. in October 1919. The early activities of the firm are not known, but in April 1921 it advertised a Sterling car, a 4-cylinder vehicle in 2- and 4-passenger configurations fully equipped at $1185. Also offered was a Sport Model B.E.L. (presumably for Bert E. Lazaro) 2-passenger roadster with complete equipment for $495.

The Sterling Motor Car Co. is listed in a 1922 directory as a dealer for Consolidated Motor Car Co., and also distributed the SENECA built in Ohio. Although geography and chronology suggest a link to STERLING-NEW YORK or AMS-STERLING, the relationship has not been documented.
KF

STERLING-KNIGHT (US) 1920–1926

1920–1922 Sterling-Knight Motors Co., Cleveland, Ohio.
1923–1926 Sterling-Knight Motors Co., Warren, Ohio.
The Sterling-Knight was a quality car featuring a Knight 6-cylinder sleeve-valve engine and other components purchased from specialists in various fields. It was designed by James G. Sterling, formerly chief engineer of the F.B. Stearns company. An estimated 40 to 50 cars were completed when the company moved its headquarters and manufacturing operations to a larger factory. Unfortunately, the economic recession of 1922 struck the company and production was curtailed for more than a year before sufficient financial backing could be obtained for reorganisation and resuming production in August 1923. The updated car was similar to that of 1921 and 1922 but with a shorter wheelbase of 124in (3147mm). A complete line of open and closed body styles was offered priced from $1985 to $2800 with an 'offset coupé' for $3200 launched in 1925. The company failed late in 1926. Total production from both locations saw about 500 cars completed.
KM

STERLING-NEW YORK, AMS-STERLING (US) 1915–1918

1915–1916 Sterling Automobile Manufacturing Co., New York, New York.
1916–1917 Sterling Automobile Manufacturing Co., Bridgeport, Connecticut.
1917–1918 Amston Motor Car Co., Amston, Connecticut.
The Sterling Automobile Manufacturing Co. was incorporated in 1915, with headquarters in New York City. Principals were Charles Chambers, William and Edward Adelson, and Henry Hyman. The car was produced in leased facilities in Paterson, New Jersey, and the first models appeared in mid-year. Christened Sterling-New York, it had a 1703cc ohv 4-cylinder water-cooled engine, a 3-speed sliding gear transmission, and was built on a 102in (2589mm) wheelbase. As its symbol, the car took the '£' from the British pound sterling; it sold for $595 'entirely equipped'. Its designer was freelance engineer Joseph Anglada, whose prior art included the LIBERTY cyclecar and who later worked on the ANDERSON. By December, the Sterling-New York was advertised with a 1970cc Sterling (Sterling Engine Co., Detroit) engine.

In September 1916, Charles W. Ams bought the firm, moving its headquarters to Bridgeport, Connecticut. The car was re-engineered to use a 2263cc side-valve 4-cylinder engine, probably a LeRoi, and its wheelbase lengthened to 110in (2792mm). Now called the Ams-Sterling, it sold for $825–845. Ams had moved production to a plant in his 'company town' of Amston in south-eastern Connecticut. A Royal Amston model was announced, but probably never built. The few Ams-Sterling cars produced are reported to have been unreliable and short-lived. The firm had stopped producing cars by January 1918.

KF

Further Reading
'Sterling: Standard of Fineness', Kit Foster,
Upper Hudson Valley Automobilist, July 1986.

STESROC (GB) 1905–1906

Johnson Brothers, Knaresborough, Yorkshire.
This firm was listed in the 1905 *Harrogate Directory* as makers of the Stesroc steam motor carriage, made in 8, 10, and 12hp tonneau models at prices from £200 to £400. They were never described or illustrated in the motoring press, nor was any explanation given of the unusual name. The pioneer motoring historian John Pollitt observed that, when reversed, the name spelt 'corsets'.

NG

STEUDEL (D) 1904–1909

Horst Steudel Motorwagenfabrik, Kamenz.
The first Steudel cars used De Dion-Bouton engines, but the later cars powered by 5/10PS 2-cylinder Aster and 6/12PS 4-cylinder Fafnir engines were better known. When Steudel gave up production of his own cars he turned to manufacturing engines for other car makers including Freia, Hagea-Moto, Hataz and Kenter.

NG

STEVENS (GB) 1976–1986

1976–1980 Anthony Stevens Design Ltd, Warwick.
1980–1983 Stevens Cars Ltd, Warwick.
1983–1984 Falcon Design, Birmingham.
1984–1986 Stevens Cars Ltd, Warwick.
Anthony Stevens began his manufacturing career making vintage-style vans on Ford Escort or Transit mechanicals from 1972, and also made Jaguar conversions in collaboration with coachbuilders Ladbroke Avon. His first passenger car was the Reliant Kitten-based Sienna of 1976, a fibreglass-bodied traditionally-styled roadster. Planned production did not begin. However, the 1980 Cipher open 2-seater did enter production. It was co-designed with Peter Bird of Falcon Design and again used Reliant Kitten mechanicals. The fibreglass body shape was extremely attractive and the separate steel frame was obviously strong, as the Cipher passed Type Approval crash tests. Some heralded it as the Frogeye Sprite reborn but finance never materialised for a production run. Instead, kits were offered from 1983 by Peter Bird's Falcon Design at £3500. A revised Ford-based car was later developed by Stevens but never reached production. Only eight Ciphers had been built.

CR

STEVENS-DURYEA (US) 1901–1915; 1919–1927

1901–1906 J. Stevens Arms & Tool Co., Chicopee Falls, Massachusetts.
1906–1915 Stevens-Duryea Co., Chicopee Falls, Massachusetts.
1919–1927 Stevens-Duryea Inc, Chicopee Falls, Massachusetts.
After J. Frank Duryea parted company with his brother Charles and the DURYEA Motor Wagon Co., he formed the Hampden Automobile & Launch Co. in Springfield, Massachusetts. The prototype Hampden car became the Stevens-Duryea when the J. Stevens Arms & Tool Co. acquired the interests in the car in the autumn of 1901. The Hampden firm then became a repair business.
The Hampden car had been a twin-cylinder 4-stroke runabout, of which only a few pre-production units were completed. By late in the year, the Stevens-Duryea 5hp runabout, a tiller-steered vehicle selling for $1200, had entered the market. It featured wire wheels and a sliding gear transmission. By 1904, Stevens-Duryea had pioneered three-point mounting of its engine; the following year a 4-cylinder car was introduced. The company touted its 'unit power plant' as 'combining strength with the greatest flexibility', thus protecting the engine bearings such that 'no road strain will wrench them'. A 6-cylinder model was

1911 Stevens-Duryea Model AA tourer.
NICK BALDWIN

1914 Stevens-Duryea Model C-Six limousine.
JOHN A. CONDE

added in 1906, a huge 9147cc 50hp car designated the Model S Big Six. It joined the Model R 20hp Four, and in 1907 a Model U 30/35hp Light Six of 5508cc was added to the line. Prices ranged from $2400 to $6000. A front-mounted flywheel on all models was divorced from the multiple disc leather-faced clutch, which was completely removable, without disturbing either engine or gearbox, through an opening in the top of its housing. A few runabouts were listed in the catalogues, but most production, about 100 cars annually, was of large touring cars and limousines.

The last year for the 4-cylinder car was 1912. In 1906, the Stevens-Duryea Co. had been spun off from the armaments and tool company, with capital stock of $300,000. But in January 1915 production was suspended due to cash flow problems. New York bankers are reported to have come to the rescue, but with demands that Stevens-Duryea undertake the manufacture of less expensive cars, a condition to which Frank Duryea would not agree. The Stevens plants were then sold to Westinghouse for war efforts.

In 1919, Ray S. Deering, Thomas Cowles and several former Stevens-Duryea employees purchased the name and goodwill of the company, and also acquired the buildings from Westinghouse. Reorganised as Stevens-Duryea Inc., the firm updated the old 6-cylinder car, now called Model E. Inflation had pushed the price upwards to the $8000-9500 range. In 1920, Ray Deering bought the electric car business of BAKER, RAUCH & LANG, of Cleveland, Ohio, which was moved to an adjacent factory in Chicopee Falls. A few R&L taxicabs were also built.

Receivership of Stevens-Duryea, however, followed in 1922, from which the firm emerged some 14 months later, after purchase by a syndicate headed by Ray M. Owen of OWEN-MAGNETIC. The cars built were designated Model G, but were virtually identical to Ray Deering's 80hp Model E of 1920–23. A full range of bodies was offered on the 138in wheelbase, but cars were built only to fill orders received. Thus only a handful had been completed by the time the company was wound up in 1927.

KF

1922 Steyr Typ IV 7/23PS tourer.
NICK BALDWIN

1926 Steyr Typ VIII 12/50PS saloon.
NICK BALDWIN

1929 Steyr Typ 30 8/40PS saloon.
NICK BALDWIN

STEWART (US) 1915–1916

Stewart Motors Corp., Buffalo, New York.

The Stewart was an attempt by the Stewart Motors Corp., a builder of trucks, to enter the passenger car field and, in so doing, introduced a car featuring a sloping bonnet similar to its trucks and both the contemporary Franklin and Renault automobiles. Like the Renault, the Stewart radiator was mounted directly in front of the dash. Two body styles made up the Stewart production – a 7-seater touring car and a roadster, both priced at $1950. Powered by a 6-cylinder Continental engine, the Stewart had a wheelbase of 127in (3223mm). However, sales of the Stewart car were disappointing and the car's production ceased at the close of its second season. Stewart then reverted to the exclusive production of commercial vehicles and its trucks were manufactured into 1941.

KM

STEWART & ARDERN see HAWK

STEWART-COATS see COATS

STEYR (A) 1920–1941; 1953–1977

1920–1926 Österreichische Waffenfabriks-Gesellschaft AG, Steyr.
1926–1935 Steyr-Werke AG, Steyr.
1935–1941 Steyr-Daimler-Puch AG, Steyr.
1953–1977 Steyr-Daimler-Puch AG, Graz.

Steyr was the leading Austrian make in terms of numbers made, though in quality they never challenged the luxury car makers Austro-Daimler or Graf & Stift. The history of the company dates back to the 1820s, when Leopold Werndl (1797–1855) founded an engineering business, which later concentrated on the manufacture of sporting and military rifles. The concentric circle of today's Steyr badge represents a target. By the end of the 19th century the Österreichische Waffenfabriks-Gesellschaft, as it had become, was the largest arms manufacturer in Europe, and their output was vastly increased by the advent of the World War I. They also made aero-engines and bicycles.

The terms of the 1919 Versailles Treaty took away all Steyr's business apart from the bicycles. The directors had foreseen during the war that this might happen, and in 1916 they decided to enter the car business. For a designer they chose Hans Ledwinka (1878–1967) who was at that time working for Nesselsdorf. For several months he worked at home on a design for Steyr, while still employed by Nesselsdorf, to which firm he was later to return when it had become Tatra. His first car went into production in 1920 as the Steyr Typ II Waffen-Auto (Arms Car) a medium-sized touring car powered by a 3325cc 6-cylinder single-ohc engine. This developed 40bhp at the recommended maximum speed of 2400rpm, but owners reckoned that it was safe up to 4000 or even 5000rpm. Ledwinka used 4-wheel brakes on the prototype, but not on production models.

The robust Typ II sold well considering the limited market offered by impoverished postwar Austria; 2150 were made up to 1924, and 1850 of the generally similar Typ V (1924–5). This was succeeded by the Typ VII which gave 60bhp from the same capacity, and had 4-wheel brakes. 2150 of these were made up to 1929, though only two cars were completed that year.

The Typ II was joined in 1922 by a smaller car, the 1814cc 4-cylinder side-valve Typ IV. Top speed was only 50mph (80km/h), but it sold quite well, in closed as well as open form, 950 being made up to 1925. More exciting were the sports derivatives of the Typ VI, with 4014, 4400 or 4890cc engines, the latter developing 153bhp in its most powerful version. Ferdinand Minoia finished 3rd in the 1923 Targa Florio in a car equipped with the 4890cc engine, and a team of three 4014cc Typ VIs with streamlined saloon bodies ran in the French Touring Car GP of 1924 and 1925, Gauderman finishing 2nd in 1925. The 4890cc engine was put into a production car, the Klausen Sport version of the Typ VI with shorter wheelbase. In the Klausen it developed 145bhp and in the SS-Klausen, 153bhp. These specialist sports cars, almost all bought with competitions in mind, were made in small numbers, 51 Klausens and nine SS-Klausens. They had many successes in hill climbs, often running without road equipment.

A new generation of smaller Steyrs began in 1926 with the introduction of the Typ XII with 1568cc single-ohc 6-cylinder engine and swing-axle rear suspension. It must have been the only car to combine this with a conventional beam front axle. It was lower and more up to date than its predecessors, with disc wheels and a flat radiator. At a quick glance it might have been a Fiat or Bianchi rather than a Germanic car. It was the best-selling Steyr yet, with 11,124 cars delivered between 1926 and 1929. Its successor, the Typ XX, was slightly larger in dimensions and capacity, with 2070cc and 40bhp.

In 1929 Ferdinand Porsche came to Steyr for what proved to be a short stay, bringing with him a new design of 6-cylinder engine which he had designed while with Daimler-Benz. This had pushrod ohvs and although the capacity was almost the same as the Typ XX, at 2078cc, it had a much shorter stroke. This engine was installed in a chassis similar to that of the Typ XX to make the Typ 30 (Roman numerals were abandoned as being too cumbersome), of which 2200 were made in 1930 and 1931. There was also a taxicab version, the Typ 45, of which 666 were made up to 1934. Several Typs 30 and 45 taxis were in service in Vienna up to the late 1950s.

Porsche's other design for Steyr was a large luxury car called the Austria. This had a 5295cc straight-8 ohv engine, swing-axle rear suspension and one-shot chassis lubrication. Porsche drove the show car to the 1929 Paris Salon, but while he was there he learnt of the merger between Steyr and Austro-Daimler. There

1938 Steyr Typ 220 cabriolet.
NATIONAL MOTOR MUSEUM

was no room for two rival luxury cars in the new group, and A-D already had their ADR-8 in the pipeline. Porsche resigned from Steyr, and only three Austrias were ever made.

Because of their financial problems Steyr built only 12 cars in 1930, four Typ 30s and eight Typ 45s. In 1931 they bounced back with 2688 deliveries, though this was still well below their 1929 figure of 4986 plus more than 1000 trucks.

After Porsche's departure, control of Steyr design passed to Karl Jenschke (1899–1969) who had been with the company since 1922, and was Porsche's deputy. For four years modified versions of the Typ 30 were made, the 30E, 30S and 30SL. They had more power (45bhp) thanks to improved carburation, 4-speed gearboxes made under ZF licence, and the 30SL had a longer wheelbase. 1018 were made, of which only 55 were the 30SL. Its final developments were the 2260cc Typ 530 of 1935–6, and 630 of 1937–9 of which 456 and 500 were made. Steyr also made 496 1.2-litre Opels under licence.

Jenschke's first design was the Typ 100 which used a 1385cc side-valve engine in a platform frame with ifs as well as rear. The body was an aerodynamic 4-door saloon or 2-door cabriolet, and 2850 were made from 1934 to 1936. It was succeeded by the generally similar 200 with 1498cc engine, of which 5040 were made from 1936 to 1940. The same styling and chassis layout was used for the 6-cylinder Typ 120 and 220, whose engines were derived from Porsche's Typ 30. They were good-looking cars, particularly the Glaser-bodied cabriolets which wore different grills from the standard models. The 220 was offered on the British market with Jensen body, and there were plans to make a Steyr-powered Jensen, though nothing came of them. Production of the 120 (1935–7) was 1200, and of the 220 (1937–41), 5900.

Jenschke joined Adler in November 1935, and his last design for Steyr was the Typ 50, a 2-door coupé which bore a superficial resemblance to the Fiat 500, and which, at 984cc, was the smallest-engined Steyr yet made. The engine was a 22bhp side-valve flat-four, a compact unit in which the radiator was mounted directly on the crankcase. Suspension was independent all round as on the larger Steyrs, and there was integral construction. The Typ 50 did not share the larger Steyr's hydraulic brakes, but with a speed of under 60mph (97km/h), perhaps this did not matter too much. In 1938 capacity was increased to 1158cc (25bhp)

on the Typ 55, but the rest of the car was unchanged though it could be had in dual colour schemes. Only one body style was offered, the 2-door coupé (the makers called it a roll-top saloon) which could just seat four people. Made from 1936 to 1940, the Typs 50 and 55 were the best-selling of all Steyrs, with exactly 13,000 being delivered.

The Fiat Alliance

Steyr's factories were almost destroyed during the war, and it was decided not to return to car production for the time being. Bicycles began to be made again in 1945, and Puch motorcycles and Steyr trucks and tractors in 1946.

Two years later Steyr reached an agreement with Fiat whereby they would assemble the Italian cars, paying for the components with tractors and raw materials to circumvent regulations which forbade export of Austrian currency. In 1953 they began to make the Steyr-Fiat 2000 which had a Steyr-built 2-litre engine of 65 or 85bhp in a Fiat 1900 hull. Car production was now at the former Puch factory at Graz, the Steyr premises being used for trucks and tractors.

The next Austro-Italian hybrid was the 500, which used Fiat's Nuova 500 hull with a Steyr 493cc vertical-twin engine. Introduced in 1957 it evolved into the 650T and TR with 643cc 40bhp engine. Austrian equivalents of the Mini Cooper, the Steyr 650 had many successes in rallies and hill climbs, particularly in the hands of Polish driver Sobieslaw Zasada who won the Polish Rally in 1964, was 2nd in 1965 and was European Rally Champion in 1966. Production ended in 1968 after about 50,000 of all Fiat 500-based Steyrs had been made. The last Steyr-built car was a Fiat 126 powered by the 643cc engine, which was made up to 1977. This engine also powered the Haflinger, a light 4 × 4 all-terrain vehicle which had been made since 1959, and which was replaced by the larger 2.5-litre Pinzgauer in 4 × 4 or 6 × 6 forms. Though cars are no longer made, Steyr is very active in the commercial vehicle field today, making a wide range of medium and heavy trucks and buses. In 1985 they also began making the G series of 4 × 4 vehicles for Mercedes-Benz.

NG

Further Reading
Steyr-Daimler-Puch 1864–1964, Josef Nagler, Mally & Co., 1964.

STICKNEY (US) 1914

Charles A. Stickney Co., St Paul, Minnesota.

Stickney's cyclecar, which he called a Motorette, used a 12/15hp 4-cylinder engine with friction transmission and final drive by double chains. Seating was for two passengers in tandem, but it was unusual among American cyclecars in following the French pattern of seating the driver in the rear seat. It was priced at $395, or $410 for a combination roadster/light delivery van.

NG

STIGLER (I) 1921–1925

Officine Meccaniche Stigler SA, Turin.

This company made small electric cars and delivery vans with dummy bonnets containing the batteries. The range between charges was 62 miles at an average of 22mph (35km/h). The cars were offered in 2- and 4-seater versions.

NG

STILL see CANADIAN MOTOR SYNDICATE

STILSON (US) 1907–1909

Stilson Motor Car Co., Pittsfield, Massachusetts.

Designed by Clarence P. Hollister and financed by jeweller Herbert M. Stilson, the Stilson was a large car powered by a 50/60hp 6-cylinder Herschell-Spillman engine and using a fluid clutch designed to prevent stripping of gears, which did not work well. In 1909 it was replaced by a conventional 4-speed gearbox, but that was the last year for the Stilson, although the company name survived into 1910. It shared premises with the BERKSHIRE which also used the fluid clutch. Two body styles were listed, tourer and limousine, and two wheelbases, 123 and 133in (3122 and 3376mm), and prices were as high as $5500.

NG

STIMSON (GB) 1970–1986

1970–1971 Design Developments, Chichester, Sussex.
1971–1972 Barrian Cars, Westbourne, Hampshire.
1972–1973 Barrian Cars, London.
1973 Lainston Investment Services Ltd, Sparsholt, Hampshire.
1973 Fauchan Plastics, Walburton, Sussex.
1974–1981 Noovoh Developments, Brighton, Sussex.
1981–1983 Nouveau Developments, Southsea, Hampshire.
1976–1977 J. Evans & Son, Portsmouth, Hampshire.
1977–1986 Mini Motors, Rochdale, Lancashire.
1983–1985 Sarronset Ltd, Birkenhead, Merseyside.

Prolific fun car designer Barrie Stimson's first kit car was the Mini Bug which, as its name suggests, was a buggy based on Mini parts. The style was certainly original, with the headlamps mounted just in front of the windscreen pillars. Underneath the basic open shell lay a space frame chassis into which Mini subframes bolted. The Mini Bug 2 of 1971 had more rounded lines and a lift-off targa bar. There was also a lightweight CS+1 racer, which transmuted into the CS+2 in 1976, then became the CS2 with Mini Motors of Rochdale, who also offered an electric version. The next Stimson project was the Safari Six of 1972. This was a modern 6-wheeled utility/buggy cross-over, again based on Mini mechanicals. By far the most extraordinary of Stimson's designs was the 3-wheeled Scorcher. In construction, it had a triangulated tubular steel chassis, a Mini front subframe and a fibreglass body that resembled a playground horse – indeed the driver and two tandem passengers sat astride it. The Mini engine sat exposed up front. Stimson's final kit car project was the Trek, something like a 4-wheeled Scorcher. It had a very tall roll-over cage and windscreen, and tandem seating (although the two rear passengers could sit side by side). Again the basis was Mini. Kits cost £924 and the options list included weather gear, boot and dash panel. Probably approaching 300 Stimson kits of all descriptions were built by a wide variety of companies.

CR

STIMULA (i) (F) 1907–1914

De la Chapelle Frères et Compagnie, St Chamond, Loire.

This company had its origins in 1900, when two brothers, Guy and Carl de la Chapelle in their early 20s, set up a small business in the family mill at Cormatin, Saône et Loire, to make bicycle parts. At the 1903 Salon it showed a powered

1976 Stimson CS+2 fun car.
CHRIS REES

1912 Stimula (i) 12/16hp 2-seater.
NICK BALDWIN

1978 Stimula (ii) roadster.
NICK BALDWIN

bicycle called the Autobicyclette Stimula, and followed this with complete motorcycles. In 1907 the company moved to St Chamond where it started car manufacture. Initially an 8hp single-cylinder model was offered, probably De Dion-Bouton powered, but 4-cylinder models were soon in the catalogue, from an 8CV of 1726cc to a 14CV of 2815cc. The last single-cylinder model was made in 1912. They were seen in competitions, including the 1907 Coupe des Voiturettes, although without great success. Production almost certainly ended in 1914, but the company was listed in 1920. About 1000 cars were made, a good number for a small regional firm.

In 1978 the Stimula name returned to the world of cars when Xavier de la Chapelle, great-nephew of Guy, launched a Bugatti 55-like replica.

NG

1897 Stirling-Daimler.
NATIONAL MOTOR MUSEUM

1901 Stirling victoria de luxe.
NATIONAL MOTOR MUSEUM

STIMULA (ii) (F) 1978–1982

Automobiles Stimula sarl, Brignais.

This exquisite replica of the Bugatti Type 55 was made by the De La Chapelle family, just as its eponymous predecessor of 1907–1914 had been. While the bodywork was of steel-reinforced fibreglass, the quality and attention to detail were impeccable. Mechanically the Stimula used Opel 6-cylinder engines (2.5 or 2.8 litres), changed in Series 2 form in 1981 to BMW 323i mechanicals. The company changed its name to DE LA CHAPELLE in 1985, by which time some 30 cars had been built.

CR

STIMULATOR (GB) 1989 to date

Stimulator Cars, Paignton, Devon.

Les Hindley built the Lotus 7-inspired Stimulator to order according to customer specification. All cars had a strong spaceframe chassis reputedly capable of handling power outputs up to 400bhp. Engine options included Rover V8, Alfa Romeo and small block V8. Overall dimensions were much grander than most Seven style cars and a distinguishing feature was the exposed suspension radius arms.

CR

STINGER (GB) 1994–1996

Tony Bradwell, Stratford-on-Avon, Warwickshire.

The Stinger was a sports 3-wheeler mating a BMW motorbike rear end with the front end of the Sylva Striker kit car. Its space frame chassis was mated to the BMW engine, rear wheel, shaft drive and gearbox. At the front end was inboard ifs. The prototype used aluminium side panels, but plans called for an all-fibreglass bodyshell to be sold in kit form, however this plan did not mature.

CR

STIRLING (GB) 1897–1903

1897–1898 J. & C. Stirling, Hamilton, Lanarkshire.
1898–1902 Stirling's Motor Carriages Ltd, Hamilton, Lanarkshire.
1902–1903 Hamilton's Motor Carriages Ltd, Granton, Edinburgh.

J. & C. Stirling was an old-established coachbuilding business dating back to at least 1850, and in January 1897 the firm took delivery of a Daimler from Coventry, which it fitted with a varnished walnut double phaeton body. In fact, the chassis was only partly Daimler, for the engine was a Paris-built Panhard. The first 'all-Daimler' chassis was delivered to Stirling in March 1897, and by October the firm had taken, and sold, more than a dozen. Stirling was Daimler's best customer at this time, and one feels that the balance sheet at Coventry would have been considerably less happy had it not been for the orders from north of the border. In July 1897, Stirling was advertising dog-carts, stanhopes, victorias, wagonettes and delivery vans. One of Scotland's pioneer motorists, T.R.B. Eliot, fitted his Stirling with pneumatic tyres in 1897, a very early use of this invention.

Stirling's Motor Carriages Ltd paid a dividend of 5 per cent to shareholders in December 1897, the first motor company to do so. In 1900 it began to import the Clément-Panhard from France. This was sold in Scotland as the Stirling-Panhard or Clément-Stirling; one model had a very tall closed coupé not seen on the French cars. This body, although perhaps not the open ones, was made at Hamilton. In 1901 the company made a light *vis-à-vis* powered by a 5hp single-cylinder MMC-De Dion engine driving the front wheels. At the Cordingley Show in March 1901 it also showed two larger victorias with 7hp vertical engines mounted 'about the centre of the channel steel frame'. These cannot have been Daimler-based, although larger cars on Daimler lines, with gilled tube radiators and rear-entrance tonneau bodies, were still being made in 1902. However, the company was becoming increasingly involved with commercial vehicles. It moved to Edinburgh in late 1902, and probably very few cars were made there. A number of Stirling buses ran in London, and, as Scott-Stirling, they were made at Twickenham from 1906 to 1908.

NG

ST JOE *see* SHOEMAKER

ST LAURENCE (GB) 1899–1902

John Tavendale, Laurencekirk, Kincardineshire.

John Tavendale was a millwright and bicycle maker who built a small number of cars. He called his first the Mearns Motor; it used engine castings made in Coventry by the Endurance Motor Co. and had a high dog-cart body. Later he made about six smaller cars powered by 6hp single-cylinder Accles & Turrell engines.

NG

ST LOUIS (i) (US) 1899–1907

1899–1905 St Louis Motor Carriage Co., St Louis, Missouri.
1905–1907 St Louis Motor Car Co., Peoria, Illinois.

Built by George Dorris and John L. French, the St Louis began as a light, tiller steered runabout powered by a rear-mounted single-cylinder engine, and made as a 2-seater runabout, delivery van and, later a 4-seater *dos-à-dos*. Wheel steering came in 1902 when there was a short-lived 24hp 4-cylinder model. This did not survive into 1903, when the range consisted of 8 and 9hp singles and a 16hp 2-cylinder victoria. In 1904 and 1905 24hp 3-cylinder engines were featured, as well as the singles, but in late 1905 the partners separated, French to move production to Peoria, Illinois and Dorris to remain in St Louis where he made cars under his own name for 20 years.

The Peoria-built St Louis was made only with 4-cylinder engines of increasing size, 30/34 and 32/36hp in 1906 and 35 and 45/50hp in 1907. They were not a success and production ceased before the end of 1907. In its day the St Louis was the biggest car-making company west of the Mississippi. About 900 cars were made in St Louis, but not more than 50 in Peoria.

NG

ST LOUIS (ii) (US) 1921–1923

1921–1922 Neskov-Mumperow Motor Car Co., St Louis, Missouri.
1922–1923 St Louis Automobile Co., St Louis, Missouri.

The Neskov-Mumperow Automobile Co. – the St Louis distributor for both the Anderson and Dort cars – decided to branch into manufacturing by introducing a car of the 'sporting type', assembling one phaeton and one 3-seater speedster just in time for the St Louis Automobile Exposition in October 1921. The cars were attractively designed and were listed with options of Rochester-Duesenberg 4-cylinder or Weidely 12-cylinder engines and a choice of wire or disc wheels plus a feature of the phaeton of a duplicate instrument panel for the enlightenment of tonneau passengers. Both cars featured aluminium step plates in place of running boards and wheelbases of 125in (3172mm). In addition to the exhibition, the cars were shown at both of the St Louis Automobile Shows in 1922 and 1923. A curious aspect of the car was that no price was set for either car or for possibly three others which may have been built during 1922, nor was one mentioned in the attractive, though unillustrated, brochure which carolled 'Built in St Louis by St Louisans' and terming it 'The Ultra Four' – possibly overlooking its engine options. 'Painted in colours to suit individual tastes', the brochure further claimed the St Louis was 'The Tailor-Made car you have been wishing for; a car to suit the most fastidious taste'. A tentative price of $2000 to $3000 was announced. Considering the factory cost for either Rochester-Duesenberg or Weidely engines plus the numerous other options, one is left wondering how such a low price could be imagined. More curious was the fact that despite the appeal the St Louis cars obviously had, no sales were apparently realised. It would not have mattered much, as the St Louis Automotive Co., which succeeded the former agency, filed for bankruptcy in August 1923. Among the articles to face disposal were 'five cars in storage' which, although they might all have been St Louis 'sporting type cars' were more likely the two cars known to have been completed and perhaps three leftover Andersons or Dorts previously consigned to the Neskov-Mumperow Agency. The fate of the St Louis cars is a mystery.

KM

STODDARD-DAYTON (US) 1904–1913

1904 Stoddard Manufacturing Co., Dayton, Ohio.
1904–1910 Dayton Motor Car Co., Dayton, Ohio.
1910–1913 U.S. Motor Co., Stoddard-Dayton Division, Dayton, Ohio.

The Stoddard Manufacturing Co. was formed in 1884, although the family had been in business for nine years before that, making hay rakes and agricultural implements of all kinds. Charles Stoddard became interested in cars as soon as they appeared, and in April 1904 he announced his first machine, which was designed by a young Englishman, H.S. Edwards. It had a 26hp 4-cylinder Rutenber engine and steering column gearchange. The company name was changed to Dayton Motor Car Co. in December 1904, when the agricultural side of the business was given up. Over the next few years the Stoddard-Dayton grew in size and price, and output grew as well. In 1905 125 cars were made, in 1906, 385, while in 1907 output grew to 1200. In 1908 four models were made, from an 18hp four on a 92in (2335mm) wheelbase to a 50/60hp six on a 128in (3249mm) wheelbase, selling for $4500 as a tourer. This lasted for only one year, and in 1909 the company launched a companion cheaper brand, the COURIER. Also designed by Edwards, it was made in a separate factory and by a separate company, the Courier Car Co. It was made up to 1912.

In 1910, when 30, 40 and 50hp 4-cylinder cars were being made, Stoddard made what turned out to be a fatal mistake in joining Benjamin Briscoe's U.S. Motors conglomerate. During the summer of 1911 they became the second American car maker, after Stearns, to adopt the Knight sleeve-valve engine, in this case an 8.6-litre 70hp six. At the end of 1912 U.S. Motors fell apart, and the only make to survive was Maxwell. Production of the Stoddard-Dayton ended in the first half of 1913, with the factory becoming a supplier of bodies, axles and castings for Maxwell.

NG

Further Reading
70 Years of Chrysler, George H. Dammann, Crestline Publishing, 1974.

1899 St Louis (i) stanhope.
JOHN A. CONDE

1911 Stoddard-Dayton Type 11-C roadster.
NICK BALDWIN

1908 Stoewer G4 6/12PS tourer.
HANS-OTTO NEUBAUER

'Mister Fisher's Stoddard-Dayton', John F. Katz, *Automobile Quarterly*, Vol. 23, No. 3.

STOEWER (D) 1899–1940

1899–1916 Gebr Stoewer, Fabrik für Motorfahrzeuge und Fahrradbestandteile, Stettin.
1916–1940 Stoewer Werke AG, Stettin.

The Stoewer was something of an anomaly in the German motor industry, being made in the Baltic port of Stettin, far from the traditional centres of car

1913 Stoewer C2 10/28PS tourer.
NICK BALDWIN

c.1922 Stoewer D10 10/50PS limousine.
NICK BALDWIN

1930 Stoewer Repräsentant sport-cabriolet.
NATIONAL MOTOR MUSEUM

manufacture, and never very well known, even in its homeland. Nevertheless, the make lasted for 40 years, building more than 35,000 cars as well as several thousand commercial vehicles.

The Stoewer brothers Emil (1873–1942) and Bernhard (1875–1937) worked for the family ironworks in Stettin, and in 1897 began to make De Dion-type tricycles and quadricycles. Their first full-sized car was on the road by the end of 1899. It was a 4-seater double phaeton powered by a rear-mounted 2.1-litre 2-cylinder engine, with chain drive. Buyers had the option of solid or pneumatic tyres. Probably not many of these were made, though one survives in a museum in Moscow, and the next Stoewers were on Panhard lines with front-mounted engines, a 10PS vertical twin (1902) and a 28PS four (1903). These were quickly followed by cars on Mercedes lines, with honeycomb radiators. Bernhard Stoewer drove a 40PS crypto-Mercedes from Stettin to Paris and back in 1903, although apparently he did not win any orders.

Shaft drive made its appearance on the 8/14PS twin in 1904, and as with other car makers, gradually spread up the Stoewer range until, by 1907, it was standardised. Stoewer's first six, the 8820cc 34/60PS with shaft drive and dual ignition appeared in 1906. The Stettin firm's first step towards national recognition came when Kaiser Wilhelm II bought one of these, while Bernhard Stoewer drove one in the 1907 Herkomer Trials. Stoewer was never a major sporting make, although both brothers drove in the 1908 Herkomer, and some 4-cylinder cars were prepared for the 1910 Prince Henry Trial.

A very modern design of small 4-cylinder car was introduced in 1907. The 1501cc Typ G4 had a monobloc engine with short-stroke dimensions of 75 × 85mm, and high-tension magneto ignition. It was made up to 1911, with larger capacity of 1546cc and a longer wheelbase from 1908. For 1912 it became the G5, with 4-speed gearbox, although these had been available on the British market G4s from 1910. The G5 had a good performance for its size, one covering a flying mile at Brooklands at 67.42mph (108.48km/h). In 1908 Stoewer made 200 G4s for NAG, which fitted its own radiators and bodies and sold them under the name NAG Puck. A second involvement with another firm came in 1910 when Émile Mathis made some 2-litre Stoewer B6s in his

Strasbourg factory, selling them under the name Stoewer-Mathis. This arrangement lasted until 1912 when Stoewer dropped the B6.

Stoewer opened an aero-engine department in 1911, under the direction of the Russian engineer Boris Loutsky, and this led to the Typ F4 or *Grosse Stoewer* with 8620cc single-ohc aero engine which developed 100bhp. It was, in fact, not all that large by the standards of the day, being smaller than a Mercedes 37/90PS or Isotta-Fraschini KM. By 1914 the F4 had full electric equipment and a Mercedes-like vee-radiator. Other Stoewers were more modest, the 1546cc Typ C, 2409cc Typ C2, and 4942cc Typ B4. Some B4 chassis were fitted with 4½-litre sleeve-valve engines made by the British Daimler company, but Stoewer did not pursue the valveless theme for long.

After a war devoted to staff cars, trucks and aero engines, Stoewer returned to car production with the C5, developed from the 1915 Typ C and with the same 1546cc engine. It now wore the vee-radiator fashionable on Germanic cars, though Stoewer's was handsomer and less aggressive than some. The first new models were the D series, the 4-cylinder 6/18PS D2, 8/24PS D3, and the 6-cylinder 12/38PS D5, 19/55PS D6 and 42/120PS D7. Some were little changed from prewar designs, the D2 being similar to the C and the D6 to the B4. The most exciting was the D7, an aero-engined monster whose engine was larger than that of any other European-made car. The single-ohc Argus engine displaced 11,160cc and developed 120bhp. It was the only member of the original D range to have shock absorbers, and was capable of 112mph (180km/h). Unfortunately, 2-wheel brakes meant that this performance could seldom be safely used. The price was inevitably very high, and only 20 D7s were made, all in 1921. One competed regularly in the Fanøe Speed Trials in Denmark from 1921 to 1924. Driven by Kordewan, its best performance was in the touring car class in 1922. Kordewan was sufficiently enamoured of large engines to have a special built in 1929, which used a D7 engine in a modified Gigant chassis, with sketchy 2-seater body.

The D series cars were made up to 1928. The best-looking were the sporting versions of the D3 and D10; with their wire wheels and vee-radiators they resembled Bentleys or Voisins, although their performances were not outstanding. For 1928 a completely new series of American-style straight-8 models was introduced, designed by Fritz Fiedler who was best known for his later work with BMW. It has been suggested that the larger straight-8 Stoewers were copied from the GARDNER, but Russell Gardner denied any links with the German firm, and it is more likely that Fiedler was simply following the American idiom which was popular with several German car makers in the late 1920s. The 8-cylinder series included the 1999cc S8, 2464cc S10, 3633cc G14 and 3974cc G15 Gigant. They all featured side-valve engines with detachable heads, 12-volt coil ignition, 4-wheel hydraulic brakes and low-pressure tyres. The closed bodies were often finished in dual colour schemes, and bore some resemblance to the Stutz Model AA. Two more straight-8s were added in 1930, the 2963cc Marschall and the 4806cc Repräsentant. The latter was an impressively large car on a 138in (3502mm) wheelbase, less expensive than a Mercedes-Benz Nürburg although slightly more expensive than a straight-8 Horch. The latter company was probably Stoewer's closest rival in their straight-8 era, and easily outsold them. Total production of the Fiedler straight-8s between 1928 and 1936 was 3074 cars, compared with about 12,000 Horchs between 1926 and 1934. Only 24 Repräsentants were made, 14 in 1930 and a second series of 10 in 1933.

Bernhard Stoewer had retired in 1921 to breed horses on his Pomeranian estate, but returned eight years later to oversee the introduction of the Marschall and Repräsentant, and later of a new small car, the V5. Designed by Ing. Pommer it had a 1192cc V4 side-valve engine driving the front wheels, 4-wheel independent suspension by transverse springs, hydraulic brakes inherited from the larger Stoewers, and a fabric 2-door saloon body not unlike that of the DKW. In 1932 it was also offered as a cabriolet and open roadster. There were plans to make the V5 in England at William Morris' Cowley plant, in return for licence manufacture of Morris Commercial trucks at Stettin, but nothing came of this. Development of the V5 was financed by the City of Stettin, which wanted to maintain full employment. In 1931, 1380 V5s were made and a further 720 in 1932 – not the sort of figures to worry firms such as DKW or Opel, with whom Stoewer were competing. For 1933 the V5 gave way to the R140, still with front-wheel drive but now with an in-line engine of 1355cc, later enlarged to 1488cc for 1934 and 1769cc for 1935. Total production of these models up to 1935 was 3760. Bernhard was also responsible for a larger front-drive car, the 2489cc V8 Greif with horizontal side-valves operated by a single camshaft between the blocks. It was a handsome car, made as a 4-door saloon or phaeton, or a 2-door cabriolet,

1935 Stoewer Greif V8 saloon.

and reasonably priced at RM5500. This was probably too low to enable a profit to be made, and only 825 Greifs were built in the four years 1934–37. The R140 and Greif were shown at the 1934 Brussels Salon by M. Dewaet, who hoped to sell them under the name D.S. (Dewaet-Stoewer), but nothing came of this.

Bernhard Stoewer left his firm for Opel in 1934, and the next Stoewer was not a native design but a licence-built Tatra 57. This air-cooled flat-4 had been made by Röhr up to 1932, and when that company closed down, Stoewer took over the licence for the German market. It had a backbone frame, all-round independent suspension, centralised chassis lubrication and hydraulic brakes. Stoewer called it the Greif Junior, and made 4000 of them between 1935 and 1939.

The last Stoewer passenger cars saw a reversion to a conventional rear-wheel drive layout. The 2406cc 4-cylinder Sedina and 3610cc 6-cylinder Arkona had pushrod ohv engines and 4-speed synchromesh gearboxes. They were designed by a team under Dr Karl Trefz (1890–1947), who had worked at Stoewer in the 1920s, then spent some time at Magirus and returned to Stoewer as manager in 1936. The Sedina and Arkona were good-looking cars but offered nothing original, and were undercut in price by rivals such as Hansa and Opel. Only 924 Sedinas and 201 Arkonas were made. Production continued into the war; the last Sedina was made in the spring of 1940. Stoewer was in the same position as Berliet and Unic in France, respected names but not specialists, and could not compete with the mass producers. However, the French companies had flourishing commercial vehicle departments, which Stoewer did not. The approaching war helped them, for they received a contract to make a command car with 4-wheel drive and steering. Up to 1944 the company delivered more than 7000 of these and a simplified version with 2-wheel steering.

After the war Stettin became part of Polish territory, and was renamed Szczecin. From 1956 to 1965 the former Stoewer factory made Junak motor cycles, and in 1957 they made a prototype of the Smyk minicar. In 1959, 20 more were made,

1924 Stoneleigh 9hp 2-seater.
NATIONAL MOTOR MUSEUM

1920 Storey 14.3hp Kent 2-seater.
MICHAEL WORTHINGTON-WILLIAMS

1926 Storey 17/70 2-seater.
MICHAEL WORTHINGTON-WILLIAMS

but the project was dropped, and since then the factory has made components for Polski Fiat.

NG

Further Reading
Stoewer, Automobile aus Pommern, Hans Falkenberg, 1986.

STOLLE (D) 1924–1927
Martin Stolle Motoren AG, Munich.
This car was of very modern design, with a low appearance and 1.5-litre 6/40PS 4-cylinder engine with shaft-driven single-ohc. A sleeve-valve engine was tried, but was not successful. Most were made with 2-seater sports bodies, although a 4-seater tourer was available. The Stolle company was a member of the Stinnes group and when that collapsed the promising Stolle sports car disappeared.

NG

STONEBOW see PAYNE & BATES

STONELEIGH (GB) 1912–1914; 1921–1924
Stoneleigh Motors Ltd, Coventry.
This name was used for two distinct types of car whose production was separated by World War I. The first was a close relative of the 13.9hp B.S.A. and although it was sold by the Siddeley-Deasy organisation, it was probably made in the B.S.A. factory. It had a 2014cc 4-cylinder sleeve-valve engine, and was offered with a chassis price of £275 which was £25 more than the B.S.A. Bodies were mostly 4/5-seater tourers. A few chassis for light truck and 14-seater bus bodies were made, using the same engine, and some were supplied as ambulances to Russia.

The next incarnation of the name came in late 1921 when Armstrong-Siddeley formed a separate company to make a light car powered by a 998cc air-cooled V-twin engine with 3-speed gearbox and shaft drive to a bevel rear axle without a differential. The driver sat centrally, with a passenger on each side and slightly behind him. A conventional 2-seater layout was adopted in 1924, and there was also a van version, some of which were used by the Royal Mail. It is thought that several hundred postwar Stoneleighs were made. The name came from Stoneleigh Park, a large estate near Coventry now used for the Royal Agricultural Society's annual show.

NG

STORCK (US) 1901–1902
Frank C. Storck, Red Bank, New Jersey.
Frank Storck was a cycle repairer and dealer who made a small number of steam cars. They had 2-cylinder vertical double-acting engines, and single-chain drive. The water tube boiler was said to raise steam in 2½ minutes, quite fast for the time. The 2-seater was priced at $725 for a wood body and $800 for one in steel. A 4-seater *dos-à-dos* cost $950. Storck offered to build cars and wagons of all kinds and to the customer's specification, but his activities lasted little over a year.

NG

STORERO (I) 1912–1919
Storero Fabbrica Automobili, Turin.
This company was founded by Luigi Storero, a close friend of Giovanni Agnelli and a co-founder of F.I.A.T. He was the first driver to race a F.I.A.T. outside Italy, in the 1903 Paris-Madrid Race, and he soon established a nationwide network of garages for selling and servicing the cars. In 1908 his company was taken over by Fiat (as it had become) and he took to making more luxuriously-equipped versions of the larger Fiats.

In 1912 he launched his own make; the Storero 20/30 was in fact made for Storero by Cesare SCACCHI who also made cars under his own name. It had a 4.4-litre 4-cylinder side-valve monobloc engine in unit with the 4-speed gearbox. This was unusual for the time in having direct drive on third gear, with top being an overdrive. Storeros were well-equipped and relatively expensive. At least one survives, in the Museo dell'Automobile, Turin.

NG

STOREY (GB) 1919–1930
1919–1920 Storey Machine Tool Co. Ltd, New Cross, London; Tonbridge, Kent.
1921–1925 Storey Motors, Clapham Park, London.
1925–1930 Storey Motors Ltd, Clapham Park, London.
The Storey family had been machine tool makers in south London for several years and formed the Storey Machine Tool Co. Ltd in 1916. William Storey was a car enthusiast and before World War I was over he experimented with prototypes using engines from Coventry Simplex and Wisconsin, as well as a rotary unit. In 1919 he acquired a 40-acre site at Tonbridge, and the following year went into production with a medium-sized car using 2296cc 14.3hp and 2995cc 20hp 4-cylinder Chapuis-Dornier engines and a 3-speed gearbox in unit with the overhead worm rear axle. The bodies were built in the London factory where chassis assembly also took place until the Tonbridge works was ready. Storey's own 1496cc engine was ready by the end of 1920, but Will Storey's company was bankrupt by the end of the year. He claimed to have made 1000 cars in the 12 months that he had been in business, but this seems a very high figure.

Will's brother Jack then came onto the scene. He had planned to make a car called the Winchester in partnership with Ernest Vernon Varley Grosssmith (see VARLEY WOODS), but this had come to nothing. He acquired a small premises at Clapham Park and began to assemble Storeys from components already on hand. He retained the characteristic oval radiator but obtained engines from wherever he could. At least one Storey had a 6-cylinder Buick engine, and others used various sizes of Meadows units. Although he formed a private limited company in 1925, output was very small. It has been estimated that no more than 50 cars left Clapham Park between 1921 and 1930 when the make finally disappeared. The business supplied spares for a while, then became a garage, moving to Norbury in south London. Will Storey returned to the machine tool business. He died in 1971.

NG

STORK KAR (US) 1919–1921
Norwalk Motor Car Co., Martinsburg, West Virginia.
Marketed by the Stork Kar Sales Co. of New York City, this was in fact a NORWALK with 35hp 4-cylinder Lycoming engine. The MARSHALL (ii) sold from a Chicago address was also a badge-engineered Norwalk. A 5-seater tourer was the only body style for either make. The last Storck Kars and Marshalls were made in the PIEDMONT factory at Lynchburg, Virginia.

NG

STORM (i) (E) c.1924–1925
Jose Boniquet Riera, Barcelona.
Dentist and racing enthusiast Boniquet Riera built the J.B.R. cyclecar from 1921 to 1923, and followed this with a more luxurious car which he called the Storm, after the initials Siempre Triumfante Optimo Rendiemente Motor (always triumphant, best output engine). It had a 6/8hp 4-cylinder Ruby engine, and was mostly made as a 2-seater. Boniquet was absent from the car world from 1925 to 1947, when he built a prototype 3-wheeler which carried his own name.

NG

STORM (ii) (US) c.1954
Sports Car Development Corp., Detroit, Michigan.
This company was started by Fred Zeder Jr, the son of a Chrysler executive. He was joined by Gene Casaroll, who would later build the DUAL GHIA. They proposed to build a Dodge-based sports car called the Zeder Storm Z-250. It had an attractive coupé body designed by Chrysler stylist Henry Kean and built in Italy by Bertone on a tubular chassis with Chrysler running gear. The effort failed owing to internal politics at Chrysler and only the prototype was built.

HP

STORMS (US) 1915
William E. Storms, Detroit, Michigan.
This was a rare example of an electric cyclecar. William Storms had been associated with two earlier makes of electric car, the Colonial and the Anderson Electric Car Co. who made the Detroit. Storms' cyclecar rode on a 90in (2284mm) wheelbase and was made in three models, a roadster, a closed coupé and a delivery van. A range of 40–50 miles per charge and top speed of 18mph (29km/h) were promised, but few people were interested and the Storms lasted less than 12 months. Its maker was later associated with the American Beauty electric car made at Jonesville, Michigan, but this lasted no longer than the Storms.

NG

STORY (i) (NL) 1940–1941
Internationale Automobiel Maatschappij, 's-Gravenhage.
During World War II it was difficult to get permission to drive a car with a petrol-engine. Most of them were used for military duties, others were equipped with gas-units on the roof or wood or coal boilers in the trunk or on a trailer. However, it was still possible to drive an electric car, and one of those designed to fill this need was the 3-wheeled Story. Earlier the importer of Studebaker cars and the originator of this project wanted to call it 'Study', but legal problems prevented this. The employees of the import firm designed the 2-seater and the order to make it was given to the coachbuilder, Pennock. The electrical equipment was designed by Utrechtse Electromotorenfabriek E.M.I., being a 24/30volt 1.3hp engine with a gear transmission on the left rear wheel. The top speed was about 15–18mph (25–29km/h), with a range of 50–60km. In the rear part of the body there was space for some luggage. Control of the car was very simple, with only

1920 Stork Kar Model M tourer.
KEITH MARVIN

1924 Storm (i) 6/8hp 2-seater.
NATIONAL MOTOR MUSEUM

1941 Story (i) electric 3-wheeler.
NATIONAL MOTOR MUSEUM

1936 Stout Scarab sedan.
NATIONAL MOTOR MUSEUM

NICK GEORGANO

STOUT, WILLIAM BUSHNELL (1880–1956)

William Bushnell Stout was born in 1880 at Quincy, Illinois the only son of an itinerant Methodist minister. He attended the Mechanical Arts High School in St Paul, Minnesota and built a model aeroplane that actually flew as early as 1898.

In 1910 he designed the Bi-Car 2-wheeler prototype, and was named chief engineer of the Schurmeir Motor Car Co. of St Paul for whom he designed two motorcycles. He devoted his spare time to technical writing, serving as aviation editor of the *Chicago Tribune* in 1912, writing reports for *Motor Age* and *Automobile*, and started publishing *Aerial Age* in 1914. William H. Mcintyre, builder of high-wheelers at Auburn, Indiana, hired him to design a cyclecar, which was produced as the Imp, notable for its all-independent suspension, from 1913 to 1915. In 1914 he linked up with James Scripps Booth of Detroit, for whom he designed a 4-cylinder car.

In 1916 he joined Packard as a consultant in the aircraft department, whose chief engineer he replaced in 1917. In 1919 he was called to Washington, D.C. as technical advisor to the War Aircraft Board which was dissolved shortly afterwards. He designed an all-metal twin-engine monoplane and founded Stout Metal Aircraft Corp. The prototype, however, was destroyed during a test flight by a navy pilot. His next design was a 3-engine monoplane, which was produced as the Ford Trimotor (popularly known as the Tin Goose) from 1925 to 1934.

In 1926 he started Stout Air Services with scheduled flights between Detroit and Grand Rapids, selling out to United Air Lines in 1929. In the meantime, he had been signed up as first secretary of Northwest Orient Airlines by Colonel Louis Brittin, but left to start his Stout Engineering Laboratories in Dearborn in 1930.

Turning his attention to cars, he became a frequent lecturer at meetings of the Society of Automobile Engineers, and in 1931 he designed the Skycar, a light easy-to-fly 3-passenger airplane with 4-wheeled landing gear in Lozenge formation, and began preliminary sketches for the futuristic Scarab car, whose prototype was exhibited in 1935. He set up the Stout Motor Car Co. to produce it, but only nine were made. However, he designed a 24-passenger rear-engine bus for Gar Wood Industries, Inc, producing a series of 30 vehicles. He also developed a streamlined railcar for the Pullman Co.

He was hired by Consolidated Vultee Aircraft Corp. in 1932 to organise a research division, which he directed until 1946. In the spring of 1944 he began working on a new Scarab, this time proposing a plastic body. The prototype body was made by Owens Corning Fiberglas Inc and a demonstration car took to the Detroit streets in 1945, but the industry showed nothing more than polite interest.

Stout continued to work as a private consultant in the Detroit area until 1951, when he retired to Phoenix, Arizona, where he died in 1956.

He was survived by his wife, Alma, née Raymond, whom he married in 1906.

JPN

two handles under the steering wheel. The first series of 50 cars sold very quickly, but after the start of the second series in 1941 shortage of material forced the company to discontinue production. In total about 75 Storys were produced. The Electrolux, a kind of 3-wheeled cycle-carrier for two passengers followed the Story for a short period, but unfavourable war-time conditions prevented more than a few being made before production ended in 1941.

FBV

STORY (ii) (US) c.1950–1951

Tom Story, Portland, Oregon.

The Story was a handsome metal-bodied sports car built on a lightweight frame. Chrome moly tubing was used for the body framework and the frame rails were chrome moly channel. Willys ifs and a live rear axle were combined with quick steering for agile performance. The body was made from mudguards body panels from several American sedans. The prototype had a modified Ford V8-60 engine, but other V8s could be ordered.

HP

STOUT (US) 1932–1946

Stout Engineering Laboratories, Dearborn, Michigan.

Bill Stout was an engineer who had been involved with the Ford Tri-Motor aircraft. He developed an aerodynamic sedan called the Scarab with a beetle-like duralumin body with no bonnet and a rounded body. A rear-mounted Ford engine and transmission were used. The first car was completed in 1932, followed by a revised version that was more practical for production. It was outwardly similar but had a steel body, different suspension and an even more stylised body with headlights hidden behind metal grills. It was first shown in 1935, and about nine production models were built. In 1946 a final Stout was built with a fibreglass body by Owens-Corning. It featured a short bonnet, a curved windscreen and door without handles. The engine was an air-cooled six and a monocoque chassis was used. This was one of the earliest fibreglass-bodied cars built in America, but it remained a one-off. Stout also designed a number of roadable aircraft called Skycars. The Skycar I was designed in 1931, and the Skycar II came out in 1940. Although Vultee Aircraft helped with redesigned versions, they were never developed into practical vehicles.

HP

Further Reading
'The Prophet. 1935 Stout Scarab', Richard Taylor,
Special-Interest Autos, January/February 1976.

STOVALL (US) c.1993

Stovall Automotive Engineering, Lighthouse Point, Florida.

Stovall built a Ferrari 308 replica on a Pontiac Fiero chassis. It differed from an original Ferrari in not having a Targa top. They were sold in kit form or completely assembled with Fiero or V8 engines.

HP

STRADA (GB) 1974–1975

Strada Cars Ltd, Saxmundham, Suffolk.

Developed by a light engineering company, the Strada 4/88 was a bold attempt at an all-new mid-engined sports car. It used a 2-tier spaceframe chassis fitted with Triumph GT6 suspension, an 88bhp Ford Escort Mexico engine and a reversed VW gearbox. The wedge-shaped 2-seater fibreglass body was designed by Specialized Design Associates to be fully removable and the car passed its full MIRA crash test as a prelude to volume sales. Despite plans to make 100 cars per year, only three cars were ever completed.

CR

STRAKER-SQUIRE (GB) 1906–1925

1906–1918 S. Straker & Squire Ltd, Fishponds, Bristol.
1918–1925 Straker-Squire Ltd, Edmonton, London.

Sidney Straker began his career with road vehicles in 1899 when he joined forces with Edward Bayley to make a steam wagon called the Bayley-Straker. Two years later he started a partnership with L.R.L. Squire in the Straker Steam Vehicle Co., and by 1906 about 200 Straker steam vehicles were in use, both trucks and buses. They also made petrol-engined chassis based on the German Büssing, and in 1906 entered the passenger car market with the French-built CORNILLEAU-

1974 Strada GT coupé.
NICK GEORGANO

1906 Straker-Squire CSB 25hp tourer.
NICK BALDWIN

If you want the BEST FIFTEEN h.p. purchase from the firm who make nothing else.

STRAKER-SQUIRE
15 H.P.

ONE MODEL ONLY.
(Various types of bodies.)

After four years' concentration on ONE MODEL, we now claim the perfection aimed at.

"I do not know another car of the same cylinder capacity that would perform quite like this one - she is really extraordinary."
—H. Massac Buist in "The Tatler."

LIMOUSINE, complete, ready for road, £470.
IMMEDIATE DELIVERY.

STRAKER-SQUIRE (Pleasure Car Dept.)
75-77, Shaftesbury Av., London, W.

1911 Straker-Squire 15hp limousine.
NICK BALDWIN

STE BEUVE. They imported this and sold it under the name Straker-Squire-C.S.B. There were plans to make it in England, but these never came about. Instead they took up a design by a young engineer, Roy Fedden, for a smaller car than the C.S.B. It had a 4-cylinder engine with oversquare dimensions of 87 × 85mm (2020cc). Fedden called it the Shamrock, possibly out of flattery to Straker-Squire's Irish technical director John Brazil, who eagerly adopted the car, which was exhibited at the 1907 Olympia Show. By the time of the following year's show it had a raised cr and other improvements, and was renamed the 14/16hp Straker Squire. For the 1910 season the stroke was lengthened to 120mm, giving a capacity of 2852cc. It was renamed the 15hp and became the staple model of Straker-Squire up to World War I. It was given a 4-speed gearbox

1920 Straker-Squire 20/25hp 2-seater.
NICK BALDWIN

NICK GEORGANO

FEDDEN, ROY (1885–1974)

One of Britain's most illustrious engine designers, A.H.R. Fedden was noted for his independent mind and for succeeding when using engineering principles which had brought failure to many others.

He was born into a well-to-do family in Bristol on 6 June 1885, and educated at Clifton College and the Bristol Merchant Venturer's Technical College. He was expected to pursue a military career, but when his father bought his first car in 1903, the 18-year-old Roy changed his mind and decided to be an automotive engineer, and started an apprenticeship with Bristol Engines Ltd. He designed his first car in 1905–06, and John P. Brazil, a prosperous Irish businessman, decided to finance its production under the Shamrock trade mark. In 1908, it was renamed Straker-Squire, and about 150 cars were produced at the Fishponds works in 1908–09. Roy Fedden designed a new model in 1909, the 15hp 4 cylinder 3-litre Straker-Squire, which was produced from 1910 to 1914.

He also designed a 3300cc version, with a gear-driven single-ohc for the Straker-Squire T.T. of 1914 and became technical director of the company and spent World War I at the Fishponds Works. In 1918 he designed a 6-cylinder 3920 cc ohc engine for the postwar Straker-Squire. The valves were splayed, with exposed valve springs, and the crankshaft ran in seven main bearings.

The Brazil-Straker partnership broke up in 1919, and the plant was sold to the Cosmos Engineering Co., in which Roy Fedden held an interest. He designed the C.A.R. (Cosmos Air-cooled Rotary) engine and chassis, with a 1206cc radial 3 cylinder power unit.

In 1920 the Cosmos Engineering Co. was sold to the Bristol Aeroplane Co., and Fedden served from 1920 to 1942 as chief engineer of aircraft engines. He was responsible for the 400hp 9-cylinder radial Jupiter engine, followed by the double-row radial Perseus engine which led directly to the Hercules 38,700cc 14 cylinder radial engines with forged light-alloy pistons in forged light-alloy cylinders and Burt-McCollum single sleeve-valves. In 1934 he adopted sodium-cooled exhaust valves for the Mercury and Pegasus engines.

After leaving Bristol in 1942, he linked up with Alex Moulton and Gordon Wilkins in a scheme to develop an advanced passenger-car for postwar production, leasing office space from the Dowty Group at Cheltenham. Like Tucker, Stout, Rapi of Isotta-Fraschini, and other contemporaries, Fedden placed the engine in the rear. Two different designs were prepared and prototypes were built, but the project went no further.

Fedden also served as a technical advisor to Churchill's government from 1943 to 1945 and in 1946 the Ministry of Supply gave him a contract to design the Cotswold airscrew-type of gas-turbine engine (turbo-prop), only to cancel it in 1947.

He had visited Wolfsburg in 1938, when the KdF (later VW) factory was under construction, and examined the prototype car. He went back with an S.M.M.T. delegation in 1945 for another look, and brought back a Volkswagen for the British motor industry to study. He even advanced a plan for producing a British version VW in a Bristol factory – a plan which foundered when George White opted for BMW technology in collaboration with H.J. Aldington (Frazer Nash).

From 1950 to 1952 Fedden was a technical advisor to NATO, and later served as director of research and development for Leyland Motors Ltd. He retired in 1955 and died during the winter of 1974.

JPN

Further Reading

'Britain's Forgotten Beetle', Graham Whyte, *Thoroughbred & Classic Car*, February 2000.

for 1914, when the bore was increased by 3mm, giving a capacity of 3052cc. The 15hp was well thought of and had a number of sporting successes including the Flying Mile and other records at Brooklands in a specially prepared car called P.D.Q. (Pretty Damned Quick).

All prewar car production took place at Bristol, and a factory acquired at Twickenham, Middlesex was intended for commercial vehicles only. Aero engines were made at Bristol during the war, and in 1919 the factory was bought by an American consortium called Cosmos. Car and commercial vehicle production was transferred to a redundant shell factory at Edmonton, north London, where the postwar Straker-Squire was built from 1920 onwards. Fedden was working on single-ohc engines before the war, both a 15hp and a 3918cc six, and the latter was the basis for the postwar car, sold as the 20/25 , later the 24/90. It was a powerful unit, but was old-fashioned in its exposed valve gear and six separately-cast cylinders. Fedden was no longer with Straker-Squire, having chosen to try his hand with the COSMOS (or C.A.R.) radial-engined light car, and the lack of his expertise was one reason for teething troubles with the new car. It was also very expensive, at £1200 for a chassis and about £1600 complete with tourer body. The prewar 15/20 was resurrected and made during 1922–23, but fewer were sold of these (40) than of the 6-cylinder car (67). Attempting to get into a lower-price market, Straker-Squire introduced in 1922 the 10/12hp with 1460cc 4-cylinder Meadows engine and 4-speed Meadows gearbox. It became the 10/20 in 1923 with little change, and the 11/28 in 1924 when it was given 4-wheel hydraulic brakes. These were also seen on the six from 1924, when it was renamed the 24/80. Total production of the Meadows-engined car was 92, but a few more may have been made with Aster engines. Straker-Squire's last year at Olympia was 1923, although cars were made up to 1925 or possibly 1926. The company was also active in the commercial field, making petrol-engined truck and bus chassis, and the Straker-Clough trolleybus. The Edmonton factory was sold to Rego Clothiers Ltd, and was destroyed in the Blitz in 1940.

NG

Further Reading
'Straker-Squire – the Car for the Connoisseur', M. Worthington-Williams, *The Automobile*, May and June 1990.

STRALE (I) 1966–1967
Strale SpA, Turin.
The man behind the Strale Daytona sports car was Eduardo Martini, an aeronautical engineer. At the 1966 Italian Grand Prix he presented his new GT coupé, which was an attractive short-nosed 2-seater intended for road use and Group 4 racing. It featured a 6.3-litre Chrysler V8 engine of up to 431bhp mounted at the front, a 4-speed gearbox and all-independent suspension featuring a De Dion rear axle, and the company claimed a 180mph (290km/h) top speed. The bodywork was designed by Carlo Bernasconi and was realised in aluminium and fibreglass by Neri & Bonacini of Modena. A more luxurious Grey Flash version was also listed.
CR

STRATHCARRON (GB) 1998 to date
Strathcarron Sports Cars, Tebworth, Bedfordshire.
A return to a simple, lightweight sports car ideal was the reasoning behind the Strathcarron SC-4. This open 2-seater was designed to be as lightweight as possible – weighing just 560kg – while its choice of 1200cc, 125bhp Triumph motorcycle power gave it an enviable power-to-weight ratio. The SC-4 was designed and chassis engineered by Reynard Motorsport and productionised by a company specialising in pre-production development for major car makers. The chassis was a monocoque made of composite materials and the doorless open body – styled by Simon Cox – was in 'Hylite' aluminium. A 6-speed sequential gearbox, high-ratio steering rack, Brembo ventilated disc brakes, unequal length wishbone front and De Dion/4-link rear suspension completed the picture. Production was scheduled to begin in the summer of 2000, to include the SC5A with tuned 140bhp Triumph engine, and for 2001 a de-tuned SC6 model was planned, to sell for under £20,000..
CR

STRATHMORE (US) 1899–1901
Strathmore Automobile Co., Boston, Massachusetts.
This company built steam and petrol cars, both with 6hp engines, chain drive and tiller steering. Suspension was by full elliptic springs all round. Delivery vans were also made, and it seems that more of these were sold than of passenger cars.
NG

1999 Strathcarron SC-4 sports car.
STRATHCARRON SPORTS CARS

STRATTAN (US) 1923
Strattan Motors Corp., Indianapolis, Indiana.
Frank E. Strattan was formerly vice-president of the Grant Motor Car Corp. of Findlay, Ohio, which had gone out of business during 1922, and who had ambitions of his own for automobile manufacturing. He acquired the assets of the Monroe car from an Indianapolis bank and formed the Strattan Motors Corp. The vice-president of the new concern was Frederick Barrows, president of the Premier Motor Corp. of Indianapolis, builder of the Premier car which was in financial difficulties. Frank Strattan had plans to produce his Strattan car in a $600 to $1000 price range and toward this aim had designed a prototype with a 4-cylinder in-house L-head engine with a potential of 23bhp and a wheelbase of 102in (2589mm).

Meanwhile, Barrows, who was also serving as controller of Premier, managed to persuade Strattan to sell him the Monroe assets. Strattan then concentrated fully on the development of his Strattan car but failed in his quest shortly thereafter, with two pilot models comprising the output that the Strattan had produced. Barrows introduced the Monroe as the Premier Model B but almost immediately following its debut Premier itself went out of business.
KM

STRATTON (US) 1909
C.H. Stratton Carriage Co., Muncie, Indiana.
Charles Stratton was a buggy manufacturer who, like many others, ventured into car production with a high-wheeler. It had a 14hp 2-cylinder engine under a bonnet, epicyclic transmission and double-chain drive. Lack of finance prevented the venture from being a success, but Stratton remained in the buggy and bodybuilding business until his death in 1913.
NG

STRATTON-BLISS (US) 1922
Stratton-Bliss Co., New York, New York.
The Stratton-Bliss Co. was a leading automobile dealership which was an agency for several cars including Dodge Brothers and which, in 1922, introduced a car carrying its own badge. The Stratton-Bliss used a conventional Dodge Brothers chassis on which was fitted a hand-crafted custom closed brougham or town car body. Features included step plates, square side lamps, disc wheels, and other styling items, usually associated with more expensive cars. One sport roadster is also known to have been built on special order. The Stratton closed cars were listed at $8000 each, these cars all being built and sold during the 1922 calendar year.
KM

STREETER & SMITH (ZA) 1913
Streeter & Smith, Cape Town.
This was a cyclecar whose 8hp air-cooled Precision engine, 3-speed Armstrong gearbox and belt final drive were typical of the breed. It was unusual in being made in South Africa, where all cars were imported at that time, and nearly all were larger and more substantial than a cyclecar. The price was £100, but it was not on the market for long.
NG

c.1922 Stringer-Smith 9hp 2-seater.
NICK BALDWIN

1996 Stromboli II electric saloon.
STROMBOLI

STRINGER (US) 1899–1902

Stringer Automobile Co., Marion, Ohio.

John W. Stringer made experimental cars powered by electricity and petrol in 1899, and formed his company to manufacture the latter, although in fact the first Stringer offered for sale had a 4-cylinder steam engine. This appeared in the summer of 1900, and was joined by a petrol model in December. By 1902 Stringer had run out of capital and production ended.

NG

STRINGER-WINCO; STRINGER-SMITH (GB) 1921–1928

Stringer & Co., Sheffield, Yorkshire.

John C. Stringer launched the WINCO cyclecar car in 1913, and after the war brought out a light car which he called the Stringer-Winco, and from 1923 as the Stringer-Smith. The Winco name came from the Wincobank Works owned by the Stringer family, which made crankshafts and other forgings. Smith's role is unknown, but possibly he was the designer. The car used a 1088cc 4-cylinder Alpha engine, with 3-speed gearbox and straight bevel final drive. A 2-seater body was provided, but there seem to have been a number of detail variations in the cars' appearance. On one, the radiator was set very far back in the frame, behind the front wheels. For 1924 a larger engine of 1330cc, also an Alpha, was available, and the two models, 9 and 11hp, were listed with prices up to 1928. The later cars were very reasonably priced, at £125 and £135.Some lists carried the marque up to 1932, although it is most unlikely that cars were made as late as that. Chassis numbers indicate that no more than 25–30 were made each year, with a possible peak of 100 in 1923.

NG

Further Reading
Cars from Sheffield, Stephen Myers, Sheffield City Libraries, 1986.

STROHM (D) 1992–1994

Automobilbau Strohm KG, Laichingen.

In appearance this was almost identical to the Lamborghini Countach, and indeed a few original Countach body parts were used. However the company made their own spaceframe and fibreglass body panels. The engine was a Renault Alpine A610 turbo, with an output of about 250bhp. The car was marketed under the name Strohm de Rella. Production figures are not known, but a reasonable estimate would be from 50 to 60 cars.

HON

STROMBOLI (CH) 1995 to date

Stromboli AG, Niederutzwil.

The prototype Stromboli 2-seater electric car was built in 1989, and the company went into production in 1995 with Stromboli 11, a 2+2-seater saloon powered by a 10kW (13bhp) motor and a choice of nickel/cadmium or lead/acid batteries. The chassis was of aluminium and the body fibreglass. Maximum range was 125 miles.

NG

STRØMMEN; STRØMMEN-DODGE (N) 1933–1940

AB Strømmen Værksted, Strømmen.

Norway's best-known bus manufacturer, Strømmen assembled Dodge cars from 1933 to 1940, and made some long-wheelbase 7-seater saloons from 1933 to 1936. These were known simply as Strømmen, while the standard cars were Strømmen-Dodge. Annual production of all models varied between 800 and 1000.

NG

STRONG & ROGERS (US) 1900–1901

Strong & Rogers, Cleveland, Ohio.

Built by Lewis H. Rogers and Edwin L. Strong, this was an electric stanhope with 2¹/₂hp motor mounted on the rear axle and with direct drive to the right-hand rear wheel. It offered six forward speeds, with a maximum of 16mph (26km/h) in top gear. There were also four reverse speeds. The standard model cost $1200, but for $2000 the buyer could have the de luxe version, with seat and tiller bar covered with goatskin, and the handle of pearl with sterling silver ferrules. Despite these attractions, the Strong & Rodgers was not made after 1901.

NG

STROUD (US) 1919

Stroud Motor Manufacturing Association, San Antonio, Texas.

This was a conventional car powered by a Continental engine, with components from well-known suppliers. The makers claimed that there was a demand in Texas for 100,000 cars and about 150,000 trucks and tractors, and that its aim was 'to keep Texas money in Texas for Texans'. Probably no more than a prototype car was built, although possibly some examples were made of the Stroud All-in-One Tractor.

NG

STROUSE see S.R.K.

STUART (i) see STAR (i)

STUART (ii) (US) 1961

Stuart Motors, Kalamazoo, Michigan.

The Stuart was a 2-passenger electric station wagon. It had a fibreglass body and used eight 6-volt batteries.

HP

STUART TAYLOR (GB) 1998 to date

Stuart Taylor, Nottingham.

One of a clutch of Austin-Healey Sprite MkI replicas that sprang up in 1998, the Stuart Taylor MkI differed substantially in its mechanical layout. It used a Ford engine in a perimeter spaceframe chassis with double wishbone front suspension based around Ford Sierra stub axles and a Bedford Rascal rear axle located by five links, with coil spring/dampers all round. The fibreglass bodywork was noted for its accurate reproduction of the Sprite. This company also produced chassis and semi-kit packages for the LOCOST Lotus 7 lookalike.

CR

NATIONAL MOTOR MUSEUM

LOEWY, RAYMOND (1893–1986)

Raymond Fernand Loewy was born on 5 November 1893 in Paris, the youngest of three brothers. One brother became a surgeon, another a banker and Raymond showed a lively interest in motorcars, airplanes and locomotives. He sketched them endlessly in school.

Young Raymond entered Paris University as a precocious 12-year-old and majored in electrical engineering. At 15, he won the J. Gordon Bennett prize for model aircraft, a design he patented, manufactured and sold in kit form.

In 1910, he enrolled at the Ecole de Laneau hoping to study for an advanced degree in engineering, but World War I intervened. Loewy enlisted in the French army as a private and came out in 1918 a captain. He was gassed and burned and received the Croix de Guerre with four citations plus an Inter-Allied medal. Toward the end of the war, he acted as a liaison officer to the U.S. Expeditionary Forces, which helped him learn English.

In 1919, after finishing college and with $40 in his pocket, he came to America. Aboard ship, he met the British consul in New York, who introduced Loewy to Conde Nast, publisher of Vogue and Vanity Fair. Nast hired him as a fashion illustrator. Between magazine assignments Loewy designed displays for Macy's and Saks Fifth Avenue and costumes for the Ziegfeld Follies.

He opened an industrial design office in 1927. His early clients included Gestetner office machines, Westinghouse and Hupmobile. To persuade Hupmobile's reluctant management to use his services, he had a custom $19,000 Hupp convertible sedan built at his own expense. Loewy entered this car in several French concours d'elegance, taking first prizes at Le Touquet, Trouville and Dieppe in 1931 and a grand prize for 'aerodynamic design' at Cannes in 1932. As a result, Hupp hired Loewy, who designed the cycle-fendered 1932 models. Loewy was also responsible for Hupmobile's advanced 1934 Aerodynamic series.

In the mid 1930s, Sears became a Loewy client, as did Studebaker. Loewy's influence appeared first in the 1938 Studebakers.

Loewy did not design things personally, but he had a knack for hiring talented designers and for landing lucrative accounts. He hired Clare Hodgman and Bob Bourke from GM and Sears and, in 1938, lured Virgil

Exner from Pontiac. Hodgman did the 1939 Studebaker Champion, and Exner designed the 1941 President and Commander Skyway Land Cruiser very much along GM lines.

Others who joined Loewy's Studebaker group included John Reinhart from Budd and Packard; Gordon Buehrig and Vince Gardner from Auburn-Cord-Duesenberg; Albrecht Goertz, Tucker Madawick, Joe Thompson, John Lutz, Stan Brom plus the mother/daughter team of Virginia and Nancy Spence.

After World War II, the trendsetting 1947 Studebaker emerged from wartime studies, based on designs by Virgil Exner, who worked for Loewy but did the car on his own. Bob Bourke created the stunning 1953 Loewy coupe, and a small, impromptu team consisting of Bob Andrews, Tom Kellogg and John Ebstein later created the 1963 Studebaker Avanti.

Raymond Loewy Associates (RLA) had incorporated in 1945 and occupied the penthouse and top floor of 580 Fifth Avenue in Manhattan, with branch offices in London, Paris, Sao Paolo, Los Angeles, Chicago and South Bend, Indiana. Loewy kept taking on new clients and hiring new designers so that by 1953 his staff numbered 200 and his firm had 125 accounts. Gross income topped $3 million a year.

RLA clients included Pepsodent, Coca Cola, Shell, Exxon, United Airlines, International Harvester, Pennsylvania Railroad, IBM and NASA. He won dozens of international design awards and citations.

Loewy himself was often mistaken for the debonair movie idol, Ronald Colman. He was 5ft 10in tall and kept his weight to 165lb (75kg) with careful dieting, fencing, boxing and hiking. He wore a medium moustache and, according to Life, changed clothes 'at least three times a day.' Loewy spoke in muted, French-accented tones (some felt he could enrich his accent at will) and presented different personalities in different situations.

One on one, he tended to be almost timid, yet he was always thoughtful, charming and outgoing. His conversation had an entertaining quality, and he could hold forth on a wide range of topics, art and design being only two of them. In business meetings or speeches, Loewy could hold a group spellbound by sheer force of personality. He rarely showed anger and had a very definite streak of kindness.

At age 56, 'Lucky Ramon' shed his wife of 14 years on friendly terms and married Viola Erickson, a former model exactly half his age. The Loewys maintained six homes: apartments in New York and Paris, houses in Palm Springs and Mexico, a red-tiled villa overlooking the Cote d'Azur at Saint-Tropez and a 16th-century chateau near Paris. His California home had an indoor/outdoor swimming pool that entered the living room under a glass wall. When a guest accidentally fell into the pool, Loewy jumped in after him, fully clothed, not to rescue him but merely to neutralize any embarrassment.

Bob Bourke called Loewy a 'good editor' and admired his abilities as a graphic designer. 'He could swing a script right in front of your eyes,' noted Bourke, 'but he couldn't draw automobiles; not at all. He was just ridiculous as far as cars were concerned, and he knew it.'

Loewy's right-hand man in the New York office–RLA's manager of transportation, packaging and product design–was A. Baker (Barney) Barnhart. Barney Barnhart often stood in for Loewy at meetings at Studebaker or attended with him when there were big decisions to be made. Barnhart had previously worked at GM and had a good sense for auto design.

For Studebaker board shows and important meetings, Loewy and Barnhart would arrive together in South Bend, often on the overnight train from New York. Loewy preferred the train to flying. Looking dapper and refreshed, Loewy would stop by Bob Bourke's office before a big meeting and tell Bob to listen for tough questions. If Loewy couldn't answer, he would drop his chin and stare at the floor. This signaled that he wanted Bourke to answer for him. And if the questions got too tough, or if Loewy wanted to escape from a meeting, Barnhart would leave the room and phone New York. The New York office would call back and tell Loewy that an 'emergency' needed his immediate attention, and Loewy would excuse himself. Everyone knew the ploy, but no one questioned it.

Raymond Loewy passed away in 1986.

ML

STUDEBAKER (US/CDN) 1902–1966

1902–1954 Studebaker Corp., South Bend, Indiana
(cars at Detroit, 1908 to 1928).
1954–1964 Studebaker-Packard Corp., South Bend, Indiana.
1964–1966 Studebaker Corp. of Canada Ltd, Hamilton, Ontario.

Studebaker was the oldest-established American company making motorcars, for the brothers Henry and Clem Studebaker (1826–1901 and 1831–1901) set up in business as blacksmiths in South Bend, Indiana in February 1852. That year they made two wagons, and gradually built up their business, aided from 1858 by their younger brother John Mohler Studebaker (1833–1917) who had

NICK GEORGANO

EXNER, VIRGIL (1909–1973)

Virgil Max Exner was born in Ann Arbor, Michigan on 24 September 1909. He was adopted by the Exner family in Buchanan, Michigan soon afterward and, as a youngster, learned woodworking and shop skills from his grandfather, a head machinist at Clark Equipment Company in Buchanan.

In 1926, Exner enrolled at Notre Dame, some 15 miles south in South Bend, Indiana, where he studied art and design. His teachers found he had considerable artistic talent and encouraged him to pursue art as a profession. He did well at Notre Dame but, after 2½ years, left when his money ran out.

Exner had an abiding interest in cars. He and some of his friends from school would take the train to the Chicago Salon to see the latest styles and, for his own amusement, he often made designs of cars that interested him. His son, Virgil M. Exner Jr, still has sketches that Ex did showing a modified Duesenberg Model A and a Kissel roadster. Exner was also an avid car-racing fan. When he was 16, he talked his father into taking him to his first Indy 500, and he never lost his enthusiasm for race cars.

After Notre Dame, Exner, then 19, interviewed for a job in South Bend with a firm called Advertising Artists. Not only did he get the job but, three years later, he married the secretary who'd interviewed him, Mildred Marie Eschleman.

In 1928, when Exner arrived there, Advertising Artists was producing brochures and catalogues for Studebaker. Exner began by painting picture backgrounds, but when his employer noticed how good he was, they asked Exner to illustrate Studebaker cars and trucks, too. Exner soon became a very adept, versatile commercial artist, excellent at quick sketches and particularly good with transparent watercolors. He also developed a knack for sculpting clay, all of which later helped him as a car designer.

In 1934, Exner heard that GM was looking for designers, so he drove to Detroit, interviewed and got hired into the Pontiac studio under Frank Hershey. Exner's quality of artwork set him apart even from those highly skilled artists at General Motors. His drawings had a style and a personality that made them instantly identifiable. When Hershey went over to Opel in 1937, Exner took his place as head of Pontiac design.

The year before, in 1936, Raymond Loewy had landed the Studebaker account and launched a talent search to service it. He did a little discreet corporate raiding and hired first Clare Hodgman at Sears-Roebuck, then Paul Zimmerman and Virgil Exner at GM. Earl pleaded with Exner to stay, because the two men got along so well, but Loewy's salary offer and the lure of New York were too strong. Exner, his wife and their young son moved to Long Island and lived there until mid 1941, when Studebaker insisted on having Loewy stylists on the premises in South Bend. This was like a homecoming for the Exners, who rented a small house on the Paul G. Hoffman estate. Hoffman was Studebaker's president.

At Studebaker, with Loewy's blessing, Exner built up a lively, talented and compatible design staff that eventually included Bob Bourke; Gordon Buehrig, John Reinhart and Vince Gardner (all ex-ACD); Bob Koto (ex-Briggs); Jack Aldrich, modelers Frank Ahlroth, Joe Thompson and John Lutz (all ex-GM). They were known collectively as the 'Loewy Gang', but Loewy rarely showed up in South Bend, having spread himself thin worldwide. Exner reported basically to Roy E. Cole, Studebaker's chief engineer.

During the development of the 1947 Studebaker, Exner became frustrated with Loewy's long absences plus the fact that Loewy gave Gordon Buehrig equal rank within their design group. Buehrig and Exner remained good friends, but Exner now felt that his allegiance was more to Studebaker than to Loewy and, with Roy Cole's encouragement, he and modeler Frank Ahlroth began to make a rival clay model of the 1947 Studebaker in Ex's basement at home. When Loewy found out, he accused Exner of insubordination and fired him. Studebaker, meanwhile, chose Exner's clay over Loewy's, and Cole put Exner on the Studebaker payroll the next day.

Cole, though, was nearing the end of his career, and he knew that Exner didn't stand a chance at Studebaker without his patronage. Thus, in early 1949, Cole began to search for a new job for Exner. One of Cole's first calls was to John Oswald, who'd just gone to Ford from Oldsmobile. Oswald very much wanted Exner and offered him a handsome welcoming salary. It all looked set: The Exners began to look for a house in Detroit and had almost signed the papers when Oswald called to say that Ford had taken on George Walker's firm and no longer needed Exner. Roy Cole then phoned K.T. Keller at Chrysler, and Keller hired Exner in the late summer of 1949--at a considerably lower salary than Oswald had offered. In time, Exner became Chrysler's design director, brought Chrysler's design department into modern times, built up a staff of 300 and, in 1957 was named Chrysler's first vice president of design.

All was going extremely well when Exner suffered a severe heart attack in 1956. Chrysler brought in William M. Schmidt, formerly Studebaker-Packard's styling vice president, as a temporary replacement. Exner returned to work a year later, but in November 1961, Chrysler president Lynn Townsend brought in Elwood Engel as corporate styling vice president. Exner took an early retirement and opened his own industrial design firm with his son but remained with Chrysler as a consultant until 1964. During that time, Townsend assigned Exner the task of developing a Jeep-like vehicle for Chrysler.

In his private firm, Exner generated artwork for an article that appeared in Esquire. The magazine drawings led to the design of the classic Stutz Blackhawk, the Duesenberg II and the Mercer Cobra. The Exners consulted with toymaker Renwall, who made scale plastic model kits of these cars. The Exner firm also did automotive designs for U.S. Steel, Dow Chemical and Ghia in Italy. The Ghia contract called for one design per month, and from those sketches came the Ghia 2100S, the Ghia Selene II, the Renault Floride (Caravelle in the U.S.) and the VW 1500 series.

Virgil Max Exner passed away two days before Christmas, 1973.
ML

made a fortune building wheelbarrows in California. The American Civil War (1861–1865) brought large orders to the company, and even when the war ended business did not drop because of the great trek westwards by countless Americans. By 1872 the Studebaker Wagon Works were the largest in the world, building a wagon every seven minutes, and their pre-eminent position lasted up to the turn of the century.

An experimental car, of which no details have survived, was built in 1897, and the company supplied a number of bodies to electric car manufacturers over the next few years. In 1902 the first of Studebaker's own electrics took to the road, designed by the great electrical engineer Thomas Alva Edison (1847–1931). 2-seaters were made at first, with single electric motors, leather wings and cycle-type wheels. Twenty cars were made in the first year, and by 1903 4-seaters and commercial vehicles were added, these having two motors and artillery wheels. The traditional 'china closet' closed electric coupé joined the Studebaker range in 1906, and electric cars were made up to 1912. A total of 1841 were made, quite a small proportion of the overall Studebaker output during the period.

In 1903 J.M. Studebaker's son-in-law Frederick Fish bought the defunct GENERAL Automobile Co. of Cleveland with the intention of entering the petrol car market, despite his father-in-law's opinion that such cars 'stink to high heaven'. The 25 Generals remaining at the time of the bankruptcy were completed and shipped to South Bend where they were sold as Model A Studebakers. They were typical light cars of the period, with 12hp flat-twin engines under the seat, and single-chain final drive. In 1904 Fish arranged for his chassis to be made by the GARFORD Co. of Elyria, Ohio, a contract that lasted until 1910. Bodies were made in the Studebaker factory. The cars are sometimes known today as Studebaker-Garfords but at the time they were plain Studebaker, for Garford were not allowed to use their own name on a car for the duration of the contract.

The 1904 Model B delivery wagon had Model A running gear, and the first Garford-built Studebaker was the Model C, with 16hp flat-twin engine mounted under the seat, planetary transmission and chain final drive. Bodies were 5-seater tonneau or delivery van. This was continued through 1905, when it was joined by a 20hp 4-cylinder Model 9503 with front-mounted engine and shaft drive. Only fours were made after 1905, in various sizes up to a 40hp of 6098cc (1908–1910) which, confusingly, was also offered under the Garford name until Studebaker reminded the Elyria company of the contract.

The Garford-built cars were expensive, at $2600–4000, and Fish decided that a cheaper line was essential if the company was to expand in the direction he wanted. Wagons and carriages were still made (and would be until 1921), but the market was obviously shrinking with the growing acceptance of the motorcar. Studebaker were still not ready to make their own chassis, so they contracted with the Everitt-Metzger-Flanders Co. who were making the EMF 30, a conventional car selling for $1250. They bought stock in EMF in 1908, and gained complete control in 1910, also acquiring several factories including those of the defunct car makers DE LUXE, NORTHERN and WAYNE, all in Detroit, and EMF's Canadian factory at Walkerville, Ontario. This began a connection with Canada which was to last beyond car manufacture in the United States. In 1909, a year after Studebaker signed an exclusive contract with EMF, they sold 7960 cars, and in 1910 when the Garford contract was terminated, sales reached 15,020, giving them 4th place in the US industry. 1911 was even better, with 26,827 sales and second place, being beaten only by Ford.

The EMF 30 had a 3703cc 4-cylinder L-head engine, and under Studebaker control prices were reduced to $1000 for a tourer or roadster, and $1400 for a coupé. In 1910 one of the EMF partners, Walter Flanders, persuaded Studebaker to make a still cheaper car using the De Luxe factory. The FLANDERS 20 had a 3153cc engine and cost $750–790 for a runabout or tourer. Between 1910 and 1912 30,707 Flanders 20s were made, considerably less than the 47,619 EMF 30s made from 1909 to 1912.

For the 1913 season Studebaker dropped the EMF and Flanders names, and for the first time manufactured complete cars. Three models were offered, the 4-cylinder 3153cc SA25, 4-cylinder 4378cc AA35, and the company's first six, the 4729cc Model E. This had a monobloc casting, being one of the first two such designs (the other was PREMIER) in America. The tourer cost $1550, leading to a claim that it was the first 6-cylinder car to sell for less than $2000. The AA35 was dropped for 1914 but the smaller four was continued to 1919. The six grew to 5798cc for 1916 and became known as the Big Six for 1918. Other models that year were the SH Light Four in its penultimate season, and the EH Light Six which used the same 4729cc engine as the original 1913 six. For 1920

c.1906 Studebaker Model 17 electric coupé.
NICK BALDWIN

1913 Studebaker AA35 tourer.
NICK BALDWIN

1923 Studebaker Big Six sedans.
NICK BALDWIN

1929 Studebaker Commander Eight sedan.
NICK GEORGANO

1931 Studebaker President Eight sedan.
NICK BALDWIN

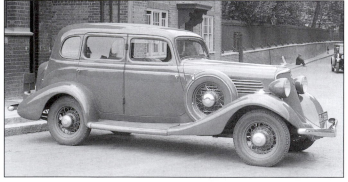

1934 Studebaker Commander Land Cruiser sedan.
NICK BALDWIN

was in charge of engineering, aided by Carl Breer and Owen Skelton. These three were later to set up their own design consultancy, their most famous work being the first Chrysler.

The three sixes, Light, Special and Big, made up Studebaker production to 1925, a period when output grew dramatically, from 48,831 in 1920 to 146,238 in 1923. Rivals' output grew also, though, and Studebaker was seldom higher than 7th in the production league. Technically they did not change greatly; the transaxle of earlier models was replaced in 1920 by a conventionally-located, though still separate, gearbox. Studebaker were among the last of the major American makes to adopt front-wheel brakes. As late as 1924 they were taking full-page advertisements to declare that front-wheel brakes were dangerous, but a year later they offered hydraulic front-wheel brakes as an option. For 1927 they were standard on all models except the Special Six, and in 1928 front-wheel brakes were standard on all models, though now mechanical rather than hydraulic. In price, Studebaker occupied the middle ground, though there was quite a wide variation, from $975 for the Light Six roadster to $2750 for the Big Six 7-seater sedan (1923). A new 3960cc Standard Six replaced the Light Six for 1925, and in mid–1927 it was renamed the Dictator Six. At the same time the Big Six was renamed Commander Six or President Six, names which were to be kept by Studebaker until 1942. An attempt to reach a lower-priced market was the Erskine, a compact car powered by a 2392cc 6-cylinder Continental engine, and made from 1926 to 1930 (see ERSKINE).

A Move up Market

In the mid–1920s Albert Erskine felt that Studebaker needed to brush up its image and compete in a higher-priced market. He introduced more stylish bodies and exhibited Sixes with custom bodies by well-known names at shows, but his most important step up-market was the introduction of the President Eight for 1928. The existing engineers did not favour an eight so Erskine replaced them with a new man, Delmar G. 'Barney' Roos who had plenty of experience with straight-8s, having designed Locomobile's Junior Eight and Marmon's Little Eight. His Studebaker President was a conventional side-valve unit of 5129cc which developed a healthy 100bhp. Eight body styles were available, from $1985 for the 5-seater sedan to $2450 for the 7-seater limousine. These were modest prices for cars which could rival a Cadillac or Lincoln in looks. In the first year's production (December 1927 to October 1928) 13,186 FA President Eights were made, and they were joined in June 1928 by the FB which had a larger engine of 5520cc. Power was up to 115bhp on the 1929 models, which had longer wheelbase double-drop frames of 125 and 135in (3175 and 3430mm). These went up still further to 130 and 136in (3300 and 3455mm) on the 1931 Presidents, which featured narrow vee-radiators and oval headlamps. The last of the big President Eights was the Speedway model of 1933, of which only 635 were made. Although the President name was continued, it was henceforth borne by a smaller car of 4096cc and 123in (3124mm) wheelbase.

The arrival of the President gave Studebaker an opportunity to engage in racing and record-breaking, which for six years they did to a greater extent than any other mass-produced American car maker. They were successful in stock car racing, hill climbing and at Indianapolis where their best result was Cliff Bergere's 3rd in 1932. For a major company to field a works team at Indianapolis was unknown at that time, or indeed any time since.

Merger and Receivership

In 1928 Erskine merged his company with Pierce-Arrow, the prestigious car makers from Buffalo, NY, which gave him access to the very top of the market. His cars now ranged from the $795 Erskine club sedan to the $8000 Pierce-Arrow French Landau. At first all seemed promising, with Pierce-Arrow recording record sales of 9840 in 1929, but the Depression forced Pierce's sales down to 2692 by 1932, and Studebaker's own finances were ailing. Profits were inevitably lower, but Erskine insisted on paying high dividends, drawing on capital to do so. By the beginning of 1933 liabilities exceeded assets by $15 million, and his only hope was a merger with the truck makers, White. However, White's directors vetoed this plan, and in March 1933 Studebaker went into the hands of a receiver. Erskine was personally bankrupt, and committed suicide three months later. Control of the company passed to Harold Vance and Paul Hoffman who had been vice-presidents in charge of sales and engineering respectively. They sold off Pierce-Arrow for $1 million, and the banks agreed to wait for the rest of the money owing, as indeed they really had no alternative. By March 1935 Studebaker had paid all their debts and were on course for another twenty years of successful trading.

the Light Six became the Special Six, and there was a new Light Six with 3394cc engine and more modern styling. A new $15 million factory was built at South Bend for Light Six manufacture, and the Detroit factories were gradually run down, though some Studebakers were made there up to 1928, and the properties were not finally disposed of until 1933.

Studebaker production had boomed during the last prewar years, reaching 65,536 in 1916. John Mohler Studebaker and Frederick Fish had resigned by then, the new president being Albert Russell Erskine (1871–1933). Fred Zeder

An amazing tribute to the
miracle-ride !

* THE ORIGINAL OF THIS LETTER CAN BE SEEN AT THE OFFICES OF STUDEBAKER DISTRIBUTORS LTD

Dear Sirs,
    Never in the course of my 250,000 miles of motoring have I experienced so unexpected a thrill as when I took the wheel of the latest 8 cyl. Studebaker saloon.

    I had been looking for a car which would be suitable for a Continental tour . . . a car in which one might maintain high speeds with comfort and without fatigue, whatever the road surfaces might be.

    I had tried out almost every suitable car under £800 and over £500 in price, when it occurred to me that at least I might try the Studebaker, in spite of what one might fear from its comparatively low price. I had not driven more than a few yards before I was surprised, nor a few miles before I was amazed at its performance. For acceleration, for road-holding and even for high speed, I had met nothing to better it.

    I took the car over Bishops Avenue at 50 m.p.h., deliberately driving into potholes and over manholes. Not once did the car deviate from its path and only once did we touch the rubber buffers, nor were shocks communicated through the steering, which is indeed a sheer delight. Then again, once on the open road, there is the over-top gear brought into action merely by momentary deceleration. At once the engine seems to disappear, one seems to be coasting, yet still the car has remarkable hill-climbing and accelerating capacity. One could hardly wish for a better car.

                    Yours truly,————, BSc., Consulting Engineer.

Do yourself the justice and pleasure of trying the Studebaker . . . at our expense . . . to-day. Immediate delivery. Art catalogue on request.
STUDEBAKER DISTRIBUTORS LTD., 155-157 GT. PORTLAND ST., W.1.   MUseum 7734

Saloons from
£298

STUDEBAKER

1941 Studebaker President sedan.
NATIONAL MOTOR MUSEUM

1941 Studebaker Champion sedan.
NICK GEORGANO

1950 Studebaker Champion coupé.
NICK BALDWIN

From 1932 to 1933 Studebaker again fielded a small companion make similar in conception to the Erskine. This time it was the ROCKNE (see own entry), but it did not fare much better than its predecessor, selling only 23,000 cars in two seasons. For 1934 the Rockne and Studebaker sixes were replaced by the Dictator Model A with 3364cc 6-cylinder engine and priced from $815–895. There were also two sizes of straight-8, the 3621cc 103bhp Commander and the 4103cc 110bhp President. The most expensive 1934 Studebaker cost only $1510, but this retreat from the higher-priced market did nothing but good for the company's finances. Their debts were cleared by the spring of 1935, and production rose from 43,024 in 1933 to 49,062 in 1935 and 85,026 in 1936.

In styling the 1930s Studebakers followed national trends, with skirted wings from 1933, inset headlamps in 1938 and low, horizontal grills in 1939. An unusual style was the 1934 Land Cruiser sedan with fastback 4-light body, tiny rear window and spatted wheels. This was available on the Commander and President series in 1934, and on all three in 1935. The latter also had transverse leaf ifs, while the President had automatic overdrive. A new feature for 1936 was the 'Hill Holder', which locked the brakes when the clutch was depressed to hold the car on a hill. This was an option on all Studebakers up to 1942. 1938 models saw the introduction of windscreen washers.

In 1936 Barney Roos left Studebaker to join the Rootes Group in England, being replaced by Roy E. Cole whose most notable contribution to Studebaker was the Champion. Launched for 1939, this was yet another attempt at a compact car, but unlike the Erskine and Rockne, the Champion was a resounding success, selling 215,117 units over the next four seasons. It had an all-new 2693cc 6-cylinder engine developing 78bhp, and shared the larger Studebakers' column gearchange and transverse ifs. Styling was by the Raymond Loewy studios, who also worked on the 1939 Commanders and Presidents, but the Champion was quite distinctive in appearance, although it was never marketed as a separate marque in the manner of the Erskine and Rockne. There were two Champion series, the Standard at $660–740 and the De Luxe at $720–800. These figures were slightly above those of Ford or Chevrolet, but the Champion's compact size and excellent fuel economy earned it many friends. They were only slightly restyled for 1940, but 1941 Champions were brought closer to the larger Studebakers in appearance. In 1941 Studebaker was America's best-selling independent make, with 119,325 sales.

'Coming or Going?'

Studebaker had very ambitious plans for postwar cars, but until their new models were ready, they revived the 1942 Champion with small styling changes, making 19,275 between December 1945 and March 1946 when the new Champions and Commanders burst upon the scene. Styled by the Raymond Loewy studios and Virgil Exner, they had full-width bodies with short bonnets and large boots, curved windscreens and rear windows. The 'coming or going' look was particularly noticeable in the coupés, so that one wondered where the engine was. The frame had in fact been engineered to take either a front or rear engine, though Studebaker were probably wise to opt for the conventional position. They also considered air- or water-cooled flat six engines and torsion bar suspension, but kept to their traditional power units and transverse leaf suspension. Two side-valve 6-cylinder engines were offered, 2779cc in the Champion and 3706cc in the Commander. The President eight was not revived.

The new Studebakers were a great success, for they were brand-new designs on the market in 1946, whereas most of their competitors would not bring out newly-styled cars until mid or late 1948. Sales reached a record 228,402 in 1949, and rose to 268,229 in 1950. The 1946 styling was continued with only minor face-lifting until the 1953 season, but under the skin the Commander engine was enlarged to 4024cc in 1949, and transverse leaves gave way to coil ifs in 1950. For 1951 the Commander received a new 3811cc ohv V8 engine with wedge-shaped combustion chambers.

Studebaker celebrated their centenary in 1952, having built 7,130,874 vehicles since that first wagon rolled out of Henry and Clem's blacksmith shop. As well as the main manufacturing plant at South Bend, Studebaker had many assembly plants around the world; in the early postwar years these included Belgium, Denmark, Sweden, Ireland, India, Brazil, Argentina, South Africa and the Phillipines.

The 1953 models were again newly styled, by Bob Bourke and Holden Koto working under the direction of Raymond Loewy. They were long, wide and low, and for their day had very little chrome ornamentation. The Starlight coupé, in particular, was one of the best-looking of any postwar American cars. Unfortunately the company had underestimated the demand for these coupés, and there were long delays in delivery which made customers turn elsewhere. Also, the market was becoming more competitive, and favoured the Big Three with their massive resources for research and development as well as investment in new plant. Studebaker's sales dropped drastically from 186,484 in 1953 to 85,252 in 1954, and although they recovered somewhat later, particularly with the introduction of another compact, the Lark, they never regained the heady heights of the early 1950s.

1955 Champions had larger engines of 3031cc, while the Commanders had a 3676cc V8 at the beginning of the season, later enlarged to 4248cc. The latter also went into an up-market Commander for which the name President was revived. The regular 1956-58 Studebaker sedans and station wagons had undistinguished styling, but the 1955 lines were continued in the Hawk series of coupés. These used the President chassis and came in four models, the Flight Hawk with 101bhp 6-cylinder Champion engine, the Power and Sky Hawks with 179bhp Commander or 210bhp President V8 engines, and the Golden Hawk with 275bhp 5768cc Packard V8 engine. With a top speed of 130mph (210km/h), this was an early muscle car, though the term would not be applied for another ten years. Just over 4000 Packard-powered Golden Hawks were

1953 Studebaker Champion coupé.
NICK GEORGANO

sold, in the 1956 season only, for the next year the name was used for the most powerful of the Studebaker-engined coupés, with 4736cc engine.

In 1954 Studebaker merged with Packard, which resulted in the Golden Hawk gaining a Packard engine, and the 1957-58 Packards becoming badge-engineered Studebakers. No lasting benefit came to either company from the merger, and in 1956 the Studebaker-Packard Corp. was bought by the Curtiss-Wright aircraft company, primarily as a tax loss operation. Under Curtiss-Wright guidance, Studebaker-Packard gained a new president in Harold Churchill who had been with the company since 1926. He followed his predecessors in going for a compact car which appeared in late 1958 under the name Lark. This had the Champion's old 2779cc 6-cylinder engine (Lark VI) or the Commander's 4248cc V8 (Lark VIII) in completely new sedan and coupé bodies on a shorter wheelbase, 108in, (2743mm) than even the original Champion.

The Lark attacked on two fronts, for the 6-cylinder model was more economical than AMC's Rambler six, and the V8 Lark outperformed the Rambler V8s. 138,000 were built in the calendar year 1959, out of a total Studebaker production of 153,823. The Lark remained in production until December 1963, gaining a convertible body for 1960, a 4736cc V8 engine and four headlamps for 1961, Mercedes-Benz-style grill for 1962, and new, more conventional styling for 1964. The Hawk was also continued to 1963 as the Gran Turismo Hawk. The 2779cc engine was used in export models only, while home-market Hawks had the choice of 4247 or 4736cc V8s. The latter could be had in tuned and supercharged form as used in the Avanti, to give a maximum of 335bhp. The GT Hawk, which was styled by Brooks Stevens, was made in relatively small numbers, 14,519 in three years.

In 1960 Churchill resigned as president, being replaced by Sherwood Egbert who had been vice-president of McCulloch Superchargers. He was responsible for the last, and one of the most striking of all Studebakers, the Avanti coupé. This used a shortened Lark frame and 4736cc engine clothed in a new Loewy-styled fibreglass body with razor-edged front wings leading through to a jacked-up tail, large rear window and complete absence of a radiator grill (the air intake

1961 Studebaker Lark VI Cruiser sedan.
NICK GEORGANO

1963 Studebaker Avanti coupé.
NICK BALDWIN

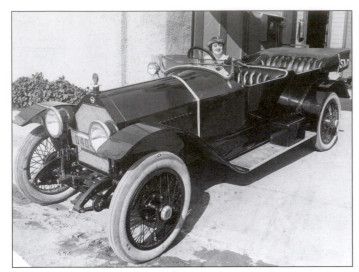

1915 Stutz (i) tourer.
JOHN A. CONDE

1923 Stutz (i) Speedway Four coupé.
JOHN A. CONDE

1928 Stutz (i) Series BB Black Hawk speedster.
NICK BALDWIN

was concealed under the front bumper). In base form the engine gave 240bhp, but the supercharged R2 gave 290bhp and the R3, bored out to 4990cc, gave 335bhp. Top speed of the 240bhp Avanti was 124mph (200km/h).

In order to publicise the Avanti, Egbert had a special car prepared with which Andy Granatelli broke 29 stock car records in October 1962. His best flying kilometre was covered at 168.24mph (270.75km/h), beating all other American stock cars. In 1963 Granatelli returned to Bonneville with an even more powerful Avanti, whose twin-supercharged engine gave 575bhp. The car was christened Due Cento, Italian for Two Hundred, as they hoped to exceed 200mph (322km/h), but the best time achieved was 196.6mph (316.42km/h).

Unfortunately the Avanti did not move so quickly in the showrooms. Problems were encountered with distortion of the fibreglass, and Studebaker had to set up their own fibreglass production. This caused delays, and by the time the Avanti was ready for the public, many potential customers had given up and bought Corvettes instead. Only 3834 were built in 1963, and 809 in 1964. The design was revived a year later by two South Bend Studebaker dealers, who bought the rights to the Avanti and put it into small scale production in a corner of the Studebaker factory, using Corvette engines (see AVANTI).

Move to Canada

Studebaker sales dropped badly in 1963, to only 69,555. In November the ailing Sherwood Egbert resigned, and was replaced by Byers Burlingame who decided to close down the South Bend plant and concentrate production at the Canadian plant at Hamilton, Ontario. The last Lark left the production line on 9 December 1963, though South Bend continued to make engines through the 1964 season. The Hawk, Avanti and truck lines were discontinued, so that the only models to go into production at Hamilton were the 6- and 8-cylinder Larks, known as the Challenger, Commander and Daytona. The Lark name was not stressed in the 1964 range, and some lists do not quote the name at all after 1963.

The 1965 Studebakers were almost unchanged in appearance, apart from having four headlamps. But as the supply of engines from South Bend had ceased, they used Canadian-built General Motors McKinnon engines based on Chevrolet designs, a 3180cc 120bhp six and a 4638cc 195bhp V8. The models' names were Commander, Cruiser and Daytona, and body styles 2-door sedan, 4-door sedan, 2-door coupé and station wagon. For 1966 they were mildly restyled, but the same engines and body styles were offered. However, the cars did not make the necessary profits, and in March 1966 the Hamilton plant was closed. Only 28,382 General Motors-powered cars were made in 18 months.

The Studebaker name survived through a merger with Wagner Electric and Worthington Corp., to become Studebaker-Worthington in 1967. Twelve years later it was absorbed by the Illinois-based McGraw Edison Co.
NG

Further Reading
The Studebaker Century, Asa Hall and Richard Langworth, Dragonwyck Publishing, 1983.
'One Can Do a Lot of Remembering in South Bend', Maurice Hendry, *Automobile Quarterly*, Vol. 10, No. 3.
'The Big Presidents. Studebaker in the Classic Era', Bevery Rae Kimes, *Automobile Quarterly*, Vol.18, Nos 1 and 4.
'Going out in Style – Studebaker and the Avanti', Patrick R. Foster, *Automobile Quarterly*, Vol. 37, No. 1.

STURGES *see* MORRISON (i)

STURMEY *see* LOTIS

STURTEVANT (US) 1904–1907
Sturtevant Mill Co., Boston, Massachusetts.
This company built several experimental cars from 1902, and with the third, made in 1905, it decided to go into manufacture. It had a large 6-cylinder engine rated at 40/50hp and used the Sturtevant patent transmission. This consisted of a series of disc clutches operated by centrifugal force to provide three forward speeds, and a sliding gear for reverse. Sturtevant hoped to sell this idea to other manufacturers, and the cars were made as demonstrators of the system. For 1906–07 the two listed models were a 30/35hp four with one body style, the Flying Roadster, and the 40/50hp six tourer. This was sometimes called the Sturtevant Automatic or Automatic Sturtevant. The Sturtevant Mill Co. is still in business making industrial machinery.
NG

STUTZ (i) (US) 1911–1935
1911–1916 Ideal Motor Car Co., Indianapolis, Indiana.
1916–1935 Stutz Motor Car Co. of America, Indianapolis, Indiana.
One of America's most famous sporting makes, the Stutz is always thought of in connection with the Bearcat and its rivalry with the Mercer Type 35, though Stutz made a greater variety of cars than Mercer, and in larger numbers. Harry Clayton Stutz (1876–1930) was born on a farm in Ausonia, Ohio, and built

1931 Stutz (i) DV32 Monte Carlo sedan.
NICK BALDWIN

his first home-made car in 1898, following it with one or two more in 1900–02. Between 1902 and 1910 he worked for a variety of motor companies in Indianapolis. In 1910 he formed the Stutz Auto Parts Co., primarily to make a combined rear axle and gearbox which he had invented, and the following year he built a racing car using his transmission and powered by a Wisconsin 4-cylinder T-head engine. It was completed in five weeks and entered for the first Indianapolis 500 Mile race. Driven by Gil Anderson, it finished 11th out of 22, and Stutz was sufficiently encouraged to make replicas, using the slogan 'The Car That Made Good in a Day'. He formed a separate company for car manufacture, the Ideal Motor Car Co., and renting a 3-storey factory on North Capital Avenue in Indianapolis, he began to turn out cars in August 1911.

The first Stutz cars were close replicas of the Indianapolis machine, with 6374cc Wisconsin engines, and the Stutz patent transaxle. Three body styles were offered, 2-seater roadster, 4-seater toy tonneau and 5-seater tourer, all selling at the same price of $2000. The range was enlarged in November by a coupé at $2500, and during 1912 Stutz added their most famous model, the Bearcat. This was a more spartan version of the roadster, without doors, still priced at $2000. The body consisted of two bucket seats ahead of an enormous bolster fuel tank, and behind that a toolbox and two spare tyres. Top speed was around 72mph (115km/h), for which the small brakes were grossly inadequate. Bearcat purchasers had the option of wire or artillery wheels. Also in 1912 Stutz added a 6-cylinder engine of nearly 7-litres capacity as an alternative; it was mainly ordered in the touring models, as customers for the roadster and Bearcat did not object to the fierce and noisy four. Prices for the six ran from $2125 to $2250. For the 1915 season Stutz offered a smaller and cheaper version of the Bearcat, called after his initials, the H.C.S. Not to be confused with the later H.C.S. which was a separate make, the H.C.S. roadster had a 23hp 4-cylinder engine and cost only $1475. Not many were sold and it lasted only one year. At the other end of the range was a fully-enclosed sedan at $3675 with 4-cylinder engine and $3800 with the six.

From 1912 to 1918 Stutz had many sporting successes, from amateurs competing in stock Bearcats to the specialised ohc racing cars campaigned by the White Squadron. Victories on track and hill climbs undoubtedly helped Stutz sales, which rose from 266 in 1912 to 1079 in 1915 and 2207 in 1917. By 1918 the great years of the speedster were over. Most customers demanded greater comfort, and although the Bearcat name was kept going until 1925, the later

cars had doors, windscreens and bumpers, while the famous bolster fuel tank was no more.

In 1915 the company had come under the control of a young financier, Alan Ryan, and Harry Stutz became increasingly disillusioned with the way in which Ryan's interest lay in stock market manipulation rather than making motorcars. Stutz resigned in 1919, going off to found two independent companies, the HCS Motor Co. which made cars up to 1925, and the Stutz Fire Engine Co., which was in business until 1928. Ryan, meanwhile, fell foul of the New York Stock Exchange, and in 1920 lost the company to the steel magnate Charles M. Schwab.

Car design stagnated during the early 1920s, for Schwab and his associates were not motor industry men, and were slow to bring in new ideas. The company had made its own engines since 1917, a 5012cc 16-valve T-head four similar to the Wisconsin unit they had used previously, joined in 1923 by a 4398cc six designed by Charles Crawford who had formerly been with Cole. Stutz went over to lhd in 1922, initially on closed models only; this was late compared with most of the rest of the industry. Up to 1923 Stutz bodies were mostly open, but with the arrival of the six sedans were offered as well. They were well-made and performed well, but by 1925 had fallen behind their rivals in the upper middle class field, who were offering eight cylinders.

The Safety Stutz

At the end of 1925 a new manager was brought in, Hungarian-born Frederick E. Moscovics, who scrapped the existing models and commissioned a completely new car. Known as the Safety Stutz or Vertical Eight, it had a 4730cc single-ohc straight-8 engine developing 92bhp. This was designed by Swiss-born Charles Greuter who had built a cars of his own as early as 1896, and had later worked for the Holyoke and Matheson companies. The chassis featured central lubrication, and had underslung worm drive which allowed for very low bodies. The name Safety Stutz was earned by the use of wire-reinforced glass in the windscreen. Five body styles were offered, Stutz-made but to Brewster designs. Following prewar practices they were offered at a single price of $2995, whether open or closed, 2- or 4-seaters. This was considerably lower than the older Stutzes which cost up to $4785.

The new Stutz was an immediate success; more than $3 million worth of orders were taken in a single day at the dealer's convention in December 1925, and sales for 1926 were a record 5000, compared with 2000 in 1925. For 1927 engine

1975 Stutz (ii) Blackhawk coupé.
FRANS VRIJALDENHOVEN

capacity went up to 4893cc (95bhp), and on the 1928 BB models the same engine was uprated to 115bhp at the higher speed of 3600rpm. Styling was improved with larger headlamps and more gracefully swept wings, while a longer wheelbase encouraged custom coachbuilders such as LeBaron to work on Stutz chassis. Most of the factory bodies were of Weymann fabric construction, and in the spring of 1928 Moscovics contracted with Charles Weymann to take all his American output of bodies.

Moscovics was quick to enter his new car in stock car races, winning all but one of the 1927 events organised by the AAA (American Automobile Association). In 1928 Gil Anderson set a new US Stock Car record of 106.53mph (171.43km/h) at Daytona, and in the same year Moscovics challenged Weymann to a 24-hour run at Indianapolis. Weymann entered a Hispano-Suiza of nearly 8-litres capacity, and a much more expensive car. The Stutz dropped out with valve trouble after 19 hours, losing Moscovics a bet of $25,000, but later another Stutz defeated the Hispano in a 3½ hour race. The cars used in the contest with Hispano were Black Hawk boat-tailed speedsters which were developed with the help of racing driver Frank Lockhart. Striking-looking cars, they were made in 2- and 4-seater versions selling for $4895 and $4945 respectively, compared with $3495-3995 for the standard touring Stutzes. Custom bodied cars were more expensive, running up to $6895 for a LeBaron town car.

Moscovics withdrew from competitions after his friend Frank Lockhart was killed in a Land Speed Record attempt in April 1928. However, Weymann was sufficiently impressed with Stutz cars to enter cars at Le Mans in 1928 and 1929. Their best place was second in 1928, behind a Speed Six Bentley.

The immediate success of the Vertical Eight was not repeated in subsequent years, possibly because most of the potential customers had bought their cars in 1926, and were not disposed to replace them quickly. Whatever the reason, sales dropped to 2900 in 1927 and 2400 in 1928. Criticism of Moskovics' leadership led to his resignation in January 1929, the year in which Stutz introduced a cheaper line of car, the Blackhawk. The name was chosen to capitalise on the glamour of the Black Hawk speedsters, but on the cheaper cars it was always spelt as one word. (see BLACKHAWK (ii)). The Blackhawk was marketed as a separate make, in the manner of Buick's Marquette and Marmon's Roosevelt, but it was not a success, selling only 1310 units in 1929, when sales of the Stutz proper were a disappointing 2320. 1930 was even worse, but the big cars still outsold the Blackhawks, figures being 510 and 210 respectively.

The Blackhawk did not last beyond 1930, being absorbed into the Stutz range for 1931, but the company tried very hard with their other cars, Over the next four years they produced some of their finest designs though distressingly few people bought them. The engine had been increased to 5277cc in 1929, and the 1931 models were known as the SV16 (single inlet and exhaust valves per cylinder, total of 16 valves). The companion model was the DV32, with twin-ohcs and dual inlet and exhaust valves, 32 in all. With hemispherical combustion chambers, the DV32 engine gave 156bhp, compared with 113bhp from the SV16. A very wide range of bodies was offered in these series, 12 on the 134.5in (3416mm) wheelbase and 20 on the 145in (3683mm) wheelbase. Prices ran up to $5775 for the short-wheelbase SV16, and from $3895 to $7495 on the long-wheelbase. The DV32 engine was theoretically available on all models, at an extra cost of $1000. The Bearcat name was revived for a 2-seater on the short-wheelbase and as the Super Bearcat on an extra-short wheelbase of 116in (2946mm). Both models were priced at $5895.

The magnificent SV16 and DV32 range were made with little change from 1931 to 1934. A cheaper 3-speed gearbox replaced the Warner 4-speed 'box for 1933, enabling prices to be reduced by $400 on some models, but this was not enough to save the company. Sales dwindled from 310 in 1931 to 80 in 1933, and just six in 1934. The make was still quoted on the British market in 1935. Any '1935' Stutzes were probably older chassis bodied and sold in 1935, as Stutz had issued a statement in January of that year that they would not continue manufacture and sale of the Stutz car. They subsequently made a number of rear-engined delivery vans called Pak-Age-Car, but this lasted only to 1937 when Stutz were declared bankrupt.

NG

Further Reading
'Harry Clayton Stutz, the Man, the Enigma and the Legend', Dave Emanuel, *Automobile Quarterly*, Vol. 20, No. 3.
Series of Articles on Stutz, *Automobile Quarterly*, Vol. 8, No. 3.

STUTZ (ii) (US) 1970–1985
Stutz Motor Car of America Inc, New York, New York.
The Stutz name was revived for this updated version based on Pontiac running gear. It had a rakish body with exaggerated lines created by ex-Chrysler stylist Virgil Exner. The metal bodies were built in Italy and power was by Pontiac V8s.

The first body type was a coupé called the Blackhawk. In 1972 a limousine version was offered, based on Cadillac chassis and running gear, but it was discontinued in 1974. The Stutz was very expensive, which led to low sales totals. However, they were popular with movie stars. In 1979 the IV Porte, a 4-door sedan, was added to the line, as well as the Bearcat convertible. In 1980 a new limousine, the Royale, was introduced at $235,000. The Porte sedan was replaced by a longer version, the Victoria, in 1984. Total sales were reported to be 60 units.

HP

STUTZNACKER *see* REGENT

STUYVESANT (US) 1911–1912

Stuyvesant Motor Car Co., Cleveland, Ohio.

This car was made by Frank C. Stiverson, who in 1909 organised the Stiverson Motor Car Co. to make it. Before it went on the market he decided to change the name of car and company to the more aristocratic-sounding Stuyvesant. For the 1911 season he announced the Stuyvesant 6-60 with 9.4-litre 60hp 6-cylinder engine on a 128in (3249mm) wheelbase, and also the 40/45hp four on a 120in (3046mm) wheelbase, which was in fact the previous year's GAETH, as he had taken over Paul Gaeth's company. Only the four was listed for 1912, when the company was owned by the Grant-Lees Machine Co. which made gearboxes. In 1913 Stiverson changed his own name to Stuyvesant, but by then he was only making accessories.

NG

ST VINCENT (GB) 1903–1910

William McLean (St Vincent Cycle & Motor Works), Glasgow.

McLean was a bicycle maker who ran a general garage and repair works, and assembled a few cars and commercial vehicles from time to time, though there was no regular production. He used 2- and 4-cylinder Aster engines from 12 to 40hp, and the vehicles were sometimes known as Scottish-Aster. Bodies were built in the works. Cars were not made after 1910, though some taxicabs were assembled for a few years longer.

NG

SUBARU (J) 1958 to date

Fuji Heavy Industries Ltd, Tokyo.

Less well-known than Japanese makes such as Honda, Nissan or Toyota, Subaru nevertheless makes more than half a million cars per year, and lies 8th in the Japanese production league. The parent company is Fuji Heavy Industries which was formed in 1953 as an amalgamation of six engineering firms, all of which had originally been part of the giant Nakajima Aircraft Co. The name Subaru is Japanese for the Pleiades, or six stars in Taurus constellation, representing the six companies which made up Fuji Industries.

Fuji began to make Rabbit motor scooters in 1956, and two years later they launched their first car. The Subaru 360 had a rear-mounted 356cc flat-twin air-cooled 2-stroke engine, and 3-speed all-synchromesh gearbox. 4-wheel independent suspension by torsion bars was advanced for a minicar of that era. The body was a fibreglass 2-door saloon, and a station wagon was later added. The 360 sold well in its home country, being made up to 1971, but it was not so well-received abroad. Malcolm Bricklin, the Canadian maker of the Bricklin sports car, imported Subarus into the United States, until the 360 was named by Consumer Report as 'the most unsafe car on the market'. Subsequent small Subarus were not exported; they included the R-2 (1970–72) which had a redesigned body and 4-speed gearbox, and the front-engined front-wheel drive Rex (1972–92) which received a 4-stroke engine in 1973, progressively enlarged to 490, 544 and 665cc. 3- and 5-door hatchbacks became available in 1981, and other developments in the Rex range included a turbocharger in 1984 (41bhp at 6000rpm) and 4-wheel drive in 1986. In 1992 it gave way to the Vivio.

1966 saw the first full-sized Subaru, the FF-1 with 977cc flat-four engine, all-synchromesh 4-speed gearbox and front-wheel drive. Four bodies were available, 2- and 4-door saloons and station wagons. Capacity was increased to 1088cc in 1968 and to 1267cc in 1970, when the most powerful version gave 80bhp and a speed of 100mph (160km/h). For 1972 the FF-1 was replaced by the Leone with redesigned body and a choice of 1088 or 1361cc flat-four engines. This model was progressively developed with restyling in 1979 and 1984, and engines enlarged to 1595 and 1781cc. The Leone name was not used in some export

1906 St Vincent tourer.
NICK BALDWIN

1959 Subaru 360 coupé.
NICK BALDWIN

1979 Subaru 1600 GFT coupé.
NICK BALDWIN

1989 Subaru Justy 4×4 hatchback.
SUBARU (UK)

1990 Subaru XT Turbo 4 × 4 coupé.
SUBARU (UK)

1990 Subaru Legacy 4 × 4 saloon.
SUBARU (UK)

1998 Subaru Legacy 2.5GX estate.
SUBARU (UK)

markets, including Great Britain, where they were known as the Subaru 1600 and 1800. The most important development was the introduction of the option of 4-wheel drive in 1973. This gave the Subaru a definite market advantage when most other 4-wheel drive vehicles such as the Land Rover and Range Rover were more expensive and less car-like. Alternatives to the 4-door saloon were 3-door hatchback, station wagon and pick-up. A turbocharged 1800 appeared in 1981.

In 1984 Subaru joined the 'supermini' class with the Justy, a 3- or 5-door hatchback powered by a transverse 997cc 55bhp 3-cylinder engine (later also 1189cc and 68bhp) driving the front wheels, with the option of 4-wheel drive which was selected by the driver, not permanently engaged. Transmission was by 5-speed gearbox or automatic CVT (continuously variable transmission) made under DAF patents. The 1189cc engine had an unusual 3-valves per cylinder layout.

A new departure for Subaru appeared in 1985, the XT or Alcyone sports coupé. This had a completely new 2-door 2+2 coupé body but used the floorpan, engine and transmission of the 1800. With the 134bhp turbocharged engine, top speed was 125mph (200km/h), but the XT's origins were evident in the high ground clearance which affected handling, and it was not competitive with cars such as the Mazda RX-7 or Toyota Supra. A 2672cc 150bhp flat-six engine became available, and this engine, enlarged to 3.3 litres with twin-ohc and 24-valves, powered the Alcyone's replacement, the SVX introduced in 1991. This luxury coupé had a top speed of 144mph (232km/h) and came, like all Subarus, with permanent 4-wheel drive. It sold 24,000 units before being discontinued in 1997.

The Rex's replacement was the Vivio whose name concealed the capacity of its 4-cylinder engine (VI-VI-0, or 660cc). It was available in 3- or 5-door forms, with choice of 44 or, with supercharger, 64bhp engines, the latter being the highest power allowed for a Japanese K-class car. It was still made in 1999 when variants included the T-Top coupé, Pleo mini-MPV and retro-styled Bistro. Like the Justy it had a vertical engine, whereas the larger Subaru units were all flat-4s.

The Justy was continued until 1995, and the following year the name reappeared, but it was now a rebadged Suzuki Swift equipped with 4-wheel drive. It was made for the European market in Hungary. Higher up the range was the Impreza, a 4-door saloon/5-door estate which replaced the 1800 in 1992 and was powered by 1597cc single-ohc or 1994cc twin-ohc engines. In turbocharged form (made from 1994) the latter gave 211bhp. The most powerful version was the Impreza Prodrive coupé with tuned 2212cc engine giving 280bhp. This was a limited production model in the same class as the Mitsubishi Evo VI. Prodrive was the UK-based rally and racing arm of Subaru. Initially they rallied the Legacy, but came to prominence with the Impreza, from 1994 onwards. They notched up three manufacturers' titles from 1995 to 1997, and in 1995 Colin McRae became Britain's first World Drivers' Champion. In 1999 Richard Burns won five world rallies, giving Subaru second place in the Manufacturers' Championship. Burns started the 2000 season well, with victory in the East African Safari, Portugal and Argentina rallies, putting Subaru in first place in the Manufacturers' championship.

The larger engine also powered the top of the range Legacy saloon, introduced in 1989 and restyled in 1993. This could also be had with a 128bhp 2212cc engine which Japanese buyers could have in 230bhp turbocharged form. The Legacy was made in estate form as well as saloon, while for off-road work there was a higher-built estate, the Legacy Outback with larger engine of 2457cc. This engine went into a new 4×4 Legacy saloon launched in 1999. Another off-roader appeared in 1997; the Forester, a 4×4 estate in the Isuzu Trooper class, powered by a 1994cc flat-4 engine.

Fuji has been linked with Nissan since 1968, and assemble a number of models for Nissan as demand requires. These included, for instance, 70,000 Cherries in 1984. Small commercial vehicles were assembled in Taiwan, New Zealand and Spain, and the Taiwanese factory began making the Justy in 1989 and the Impreza in 1998.

NG

SUBURBAN LIMITED (US) 1911–1912
1910–1911 De Schaum Motor Car Co., Detroit, Michigan.
1911–1912 Suburban Motor Car Co., Detroit, Michigan.
This was another venture of William de Schaum who had previously made a high-wheeler in Buffalo. The Suburban Limited was to be made in 2-seater roadster form only, with the choice of a 20hp 4-cylinder or 28hp 6-cylinder engine. The wheelbases of the two models were almost identical, at 106 and 108in (2690 and 2741mm), and the prices were the same, at $1200. There was a grand scheme to build the cars on a large site outside Detroit, with a model village for the workers, but it fizzled out with no more than 25 cars made. De Schaum's next venture was the TIGER cyclecar.

NG

SUCCÈS (B) 1952
Constructiewerkhuisen NV Succès, Antwerp.
At the January 1952 Brussels Motor Show, Succès showed a 2-seater 3-wheeled microcar. Its open bodywork was made of wood with imitation leather covering, plus steel wings over the two front wheels. It was powered by a rear-mounted 2-cylinder 2-stroke engine, but production did not ensue.

CR

SUCCESS (US) 1906–1909
Success Auto-Buggy Manufacturing Co., St Louis, Missouri.
The Success began as one of the simplest and cheapest high-wheelers on the market. It had a 2/3hp single-cylinder engine, when most high-wheelers had flat-twins of 10hp or more, with 2-speed epicyclic transmission and final drive by chain to a sprocket on the right-hand rear wheel only. The price was $250. The single was offered again for 1904, with quoted power up to 4hp and the price increased to $275, and there was also a 10hp 2-cylinder engine in a car selling for $400. By 1909 the single was no more, the twins were of 12, 16, and 18hp, and there was a 24hp 4-cylinder runabout selling for $800. This move upmarket, while probably inevitable in order to keep up with the competition, did not help Success sales, and the company went out of business during 1909. About 600 cars were made.

NG

1998 Subaru Forester S-Turbo estate.
SUBARU (UK)

2000 Subaru Impreza P1 coupé.
SUBARU (UK)

2000 Subaru Legacy 2.0GL AWD saloon.
SUBARU (UK)

1922 Suère 10CV tourer.
NICK BALDWIN

1910 Sultan 12/15hp landaulet.
NICK BALDWIN

SUÈRE (F) 1909–1930
Automobiles J. Suère, Paris.
Although the makers lasted for more than 20 years, Suère cars were not widely known, and hardly at all outside France, although they were represented in England during the 1920s. The company made engines from at least 1905, and complete cars from 1909. These had 8CV single-cylinder engines, and 8 and 10CV fours, with 3-speed gearboxes and shaft drive. In 1914 Suère broke new ground with a tiny V8 engine of only 1408cc. This was only a prototype, but it was offered for sale in 1919, though how many were actually made is not certain. Suères of the 1920s had 4-cylinder engines including an 1194cc introduced in 1925, and larger fours of 1843cc, as well as a 1984cc six. Several body styles were offered, including open 2- and 4-seaters, a saloon and a light truck. Production came to an end around 1930 but like a number of firms Suère went out in glory with a 3.2-litre straight-8 which never progressed beyond the prototype stage.
NG

SUFFIELD & BROWN see NEW CENTURY (i)

SUFFOLK (GB) 1995 to date
1995–1998 Suffolk Sports Cars, Woolpit, Suffolk.
1998 to date Suffolk Sportscar Engineering, Bury St Edmunds, Suffolk.
This company assumed control of the highly convincing TRAC SS100 replica, and put it through Single Vehicle Approval testing. It also built a replica of the Jaguar E-Type Lightweight racer, again based on Jaguar components.
CR

SUFFOLK ROYAL (GB) 1920
Woodbridge Engineering Co. Ltd, Woodbridge, Suffolk.
This is a shadowy make which was not written up in the press, although a catalogue was issued, and eye-witnesses attest to at least two or three cars having being made. It was powered by a 15.64hp 6-cylinder Sage engine with separately cast cylinders designed by Gordon Forsyth, hence the name Model F or Forsyth for the car. The catalogue showed a drawing of a large and imposing tourer with chauffeur at the wheel, but what the car looked like in reality is not known.
NG

SUI TONG (TAIWAN) 1982–c.1984
In collaboration with CONVENIENT MACHINES in New York, USA, Sui Tong was founded to manufacture the Cub 3-wheeler at the highly ambitious rate of 10,000 units in the first year. It looked like a modern bubble car, though its single wheel was at the front. The rear wheels were enclosed in removable spats and there was an opening rear hatch.
CR

SULMAN (AUS) 1923
Lloyd & Sulman, Camperdown, New South Wales.
Tom Sulman built his first car while still at Technical College – a cyclecar with an Excelsior 'Big-X' motorcycle engine. It went so well that it was decided to produce it, and his father-in-law assisted the formation of a company. Spacke 13½bhp air-cooled V-twin engines, made for cyclecars, were obtained and an example of the Simplex was completed, and gained publicity by performing well in events. An ash frame of 78in (1981mm) wheelbase, weight of 895lb (407kg), transverse leaf ifs, wire and bobbin steering and transmission via a 2-speed gearbox and final chain were main features. The arrival of the Austin 7 caused the backers to withdraw finance and the business was wound up after five cars had been made. Tom had a long career in motor sport and was part of the Kangaroo Stable Aston Martin racing team in Europe in the 1950s.
MG

SULTAN (US) 1908–1912
Sultan Motor Co., Springfield, Massachusetts.
This company was set up in New York City in 1904 to promote the licensed manufacture of the French SULTANE. The factory was that of the Elektron Manufacturing Co. of Springfield, and for several years only taxicabs were made. When it wanted to include passenger cars it had a prototype built by the Otis Elevator Co., also of Springfield, but later set up its own factory. Made with runabout, limousine or landaulet bodies, the cars used the same engine as the taxicabs, a 12/15hp 4-cylinder, with 3-speed gearbox and shaft drive. Many components were imported from France. A 6-cylinder model was planned but not built.
NG

SULTANE (F) 1903–1912
Lethimonnier et Compagnie, Paris.
The first Sultane car was a conventional tourer powered by a 2.4-litre 10/14hp 4-cylinder engine, with a Mercedes-like radiator. Larger models were offered over the next few years; in 1907 there were five 4-cylinder engines from a 1.8-litre 9/12hp to a 7.8-litre 45/60hp, as well as a 7/9hp twin. Two of the 45/60s ran in the 1907 Kaiserpreis Eliminating Trials under the name Martin-Lethimonnier, but did not get into the final race. A 2.2-litre four was made in America, mainly as a taxicab, under the name SULTAN. Production ended in 1912 for both the French and American ventures.
NG

SUMIDA (J) 1933–1937
Jidosha Kogyo Co. Ltd, Tokyo.
The Sumida name was more widely associated with commercial vehicles than with cars, being used from 1923 for the trucks made by the Ishikawajima Shipbuilding and Engineering Co. Most of the Sumida cars made between 1933 and 1937 were for military uses as staff cars. They included the Model H 4-door saloon, generally similar to the contemporary La Salle, the Model K-93 6-wheel tourer possibly inspired by the 6-wheeled Hudsons supplied to the Japanese Army, and the Model JC 4×4 staff car.
In 1937 Jidosha Togyo merged with Tokyo Gas & Electric, and the name Sumida (a river flowing through Tokyo) was dropped in favour of ISUZU, still familiar today. No Isuzu cars were made until 1953.
NG

SUMINOE (J) 1954–1955
Suminoe Engineering Works Ltd, Tokyo.
This company built bodies for Datsun before making its own design, called the Flying Feather. This was an extremely lightweight small 2-seater with a roll-top roof and tall, motorcycle-type wheels. In a transverse-sprung chassis, the V-twin air-cooled engine of 350cc capacity and 12.5bhp was mounted in the tail driving through a 3-speed transmission, and a top speed of 40mph (64km/h) was claimed. A pre-production batch of cars was produced but Suminoe decided to pursue other activities.
CR

1936 Sumida K93 6x4 tourer.
NICK BALDWIN

SUMMERFIELD (GB) 1993–1994
Summerfield Car Co., Craven Arms, Shropshire.
The Summerfield Solar was a replica of the 1958–62 Lola Mk1 racer. It used a spaceframe chassis with aluminium inner panelling. Suspension was bespoke, the outer bodywork was fibreglass, and the mechanical side derived from the Alfa Romeo GTV (up to 2-litre twin cam).
CR

SUMMERS *see* MOLL

SUMMERS & HARDING (GB) 1913
This cyclecar was powered by an 8hp v-twin JAP engine and had belt final drive. Late in 1913 it was renamed the Flyer, but few were made under either name.
NG

SUMMIT (i) (US) 1907–1909
Summit Carriage-Mobile Co., Waterloo, Iowa.
In appearance the Summit Carriage-Mobile was not unlike many other high-wheelers, but its engine was highly unusual. Each cylinder had a hollow piston with mechanically operated valves placed in a stationary head and running in guides as in the cross-head of a steam engine. The piston was said to help with the cooling, and the makers called it the Caldwell cylinderless self-cooling engine. Versions were offered with one, two, three or four pistons, giving from 8 to 40hp. The steering was on the archaic centre pivot system. How many of these strange vehicles were made is not known, and it is not even certain that the engine ran at all. In its first season it was known as the Farmer-Mobile, and thereafter as the Summit.
NG

SUMMIT (ii) (AUS) 1923–1926
Kelly Motors Ltd, Sydney, New South Wales.
An assembled car of US components, the Summit offered an unusual feature with Fredriksen's patent Acme triplex springing which Kelly had promoted earlier. Comprising two cantilever springs bearing on the axles, coupled midway along the chassis by a semi-elliptic, it claimed superior comfort. The engine was

1924 Summit (ii) tourer.
NICK BALDWIN

a 4-cylinder 3384cc Lycoming, with a Zenith carburettor, which drove through a 3-speed gearbox in a chassis of 112in (2845mm) wheelbase. Fitted with many accessories, roadster and tourer bodies, also with 'California' tops, were offered but a sedan was shown in 1924. Several hundred Summits were built.
MG
Further Reading
'Summit: The Car from Three Continents', Dennis Harrison, *Automobile Quarterly*, Vol. 29, No. 3.

SUN (i) (D) 1906–1908
Sun Motorwagen-Gesellschaft mbH E. Jeannin & Co. KG, Berlin.
The founder of this company was Émile Jeannin, brother of Henri Jeannin, who was the maker of the AAG and Argus cars. Émile had some experience with these firms before setting up on his own to make a range of relatively large cars. The smallest was an 18/22PS four, followed by a larger four of 28/32PS and two sixes of 40/50 and 65/75PS.
HON

1901 Sunbeam (i) Type A tonneau.
NICK BALDWIN

1902 Sunbeam (i) Mabley 2¾ hp light car.
NATIONAL MOTOR MUSEUM

SUN (ii) (US) 1916–1917

Sun Motor Car Co., Elkhart, Indiana.

The Sun was a conventional car with 23hp 6-cylinder Beaver engine and 3-speed gearbox, offered in four body styles, 5- and 7-seater tourers, roadster and sedan. It was designed by ex-Haynes engineer Roscoe C. Hoffman, while the company president was another former Haynes employee, R. Crawford. The company was organised in Buffalo, but before production started there it moved into the former Sterling and Elmer plant in Elkhart. It ordered 3500 engines from Beaver, but only managed to make 1063 cars before going into receivership in September 1917.

NG

SUN (iii) (D) 1920–1924

1920–1923 Sun Automobil-Kleinkraftwagen GmbH, Berlin-Charlottenberg.
1923–1924 Sun Motorfahrzeuge Henri Jeannin, Berlin-Schöneberg.

This light car was made by Henri Jeannin, brother of Émile of SUN (i). Powered by an air-cooled V-twin engine, it was made only in small numbers.

HON

SUN (iv) (US) 1921–1922

The Automotive Corp., Toledo, Ohio.

The Automotive Corp. of Toledo, Ohio had purchased the assets of the Sun automobile, produced in Elkhart, Indiana, which had been a small car manufacturer in 1916 and 1917. The small Sun made its debut in 1921 and, although it was in no way like the earlier car of the same name, the Automotive Corp. decided to retain the earlier car's badge and other nomenclature in advertising and otherwise promoting the new venture. The second Sun was powered by a 4-cylinder air-cooled L-head engine designed by Everett Cameron, builder of the Cameron car, plus a wheelbase of a scant 98in (2487mm). Although both open and closed styles were theoretically available, all promotion centred on the tiny 2-seater roadster which the corporation claimed could get 50 miles per gallon of petrol and attain a speed of 50mph (80km/h). This 2-seater weighted 90lb (41kg) and was priced at $375. The Sun attracted few buyers and production ended after one year.

KM

SUN (v) (GB) 1993 to date

Coupés of London, London.

T.V.R. specialists Coupés of London were behind this replica of the Vignale-Fiat Gamine, dubbed the Sun Roadster (actually it was launched as the Noddi!). A ladder chassis contained Fiat 126 mechanicals. The open fibreglass replica body could be fitted with optional soft- or hard-tops, or a novel delivery wagon version.

CR

SUNBEAM (i) (GB) 1899–1937

1899–1905 John Marston Ltd, Wolverhampton, Staffordshire.
1905–1935 Sunbeam Motor Car Co. Ltd, Wolverhampton, Staffordshire.
1935–1937 Sunbeam Motors Ltd, London.

One of the most respected British cars for more than thirty years, Sunbeam grew out of the bicycle industry, though not like so many others in Coventry but further west in Wolverhampton. John Marston (1836–1918) founded his Sunbeamland Cycle Co. in 1887, and in 1899 one of his most trusted assistants, Thomas Cureton, began to build a car of his own design, aided by one man and a boy. It had a vertical single-cylinder engine mounted at the front, belt drive and solid tyres. Marston was sufficiently impressed with it to sanction a second machine, which had a horizontal engine and was actually catalogued in 1900. It was not made in series, though, because Marston was attracted by a most unconventional car designed by Mr. Mabberly-Smith. This had four wheels in diamond pattern with three seats facing sideways and outwards in the manner of a Victorian sofa. It was powered by a 2¾hp De Dion-Bouton engine driving the centre axle by belt pulleys and chain. Unlike most eccentric designs the Sunbeam-Mabley as it was called, sold quite well, about 150 in three years, at a modest price of £130. At least three still exist.

A 2-cylinder front-engined car with wheel steering was shown alongside the Mabley at the 1901 Crystal Palace Motor Show, but does not seem to have gone into production. The next series of Sunbeam cars were the work of Thomas C. Pullinger who suggested that Marston should base his designs on the French BERLIET. Complete chassis were imported at first, but soon Sunbeam built the chassis to receive Berliet engines and gearboxes. Chain drive was used, with the chains running in oil bath cases as used in Sunbeam bicycles. The engine was a 10/12hp 2412cc 4-cylinder unit, and the car was sold as the Sunbeam 12hp. The Mabley was soon dropped, and the 12hp was the mainstay of Sunbeam production until the arrival of the 3400cc 16/20hp designed by Angus Shaw at the end of 1905. A 6-cylinder car was announced in February 1904, but few if any were sold, and the first production six was the 5100cc 25/30hp, also a Shaw design, of 1907.

The Coatalen Era

Although the early Sunbeams were well-made and good performers, the company did not come to prominence until the arrival of the young French engineer Louis Coatalen (1880–1962) who had previously worked for Humber and Hillman. He was a keen driver as well as a designer, and supervised the manufacture and personally tested every car that left the works. He redesigned the 16/20hp, enlarging the engine to 3825cc, and introduced a smaller model, the 12/16hp, which had the same dimensions and capacity as the original Berliet design (80 × 120mm, 2412cc). The 12/16 was an immediate success, and of the 511 Sunbeams made in 1910, 350 of them were 12/16s. For 1912 it received a monobloc L-head engine in place of the original pair-cast T-head. Other Coatalen designs were two sixes, the 3618cc 18/22hp and the 6104cc 25/30hp, and a short-lived big four, the 4673cc 25/30hp of 1910–11. At the outbreak of war the range consisted of the 12/16 in standard and sporting forms, the 16/20 and the 6-cylinder 25/30, all offered with electric lighting. Under the Coatalen regime, profits rose from just £90 in 1909 to £95,000 in 1913.

Louis Hervé Coatalen, second from left, with VW staff, c.1959.
NICK BALDWIN

COATALEN, LOUIS HERVÉ (1879–1962)

Louis Hervé Coatalen's life was a fairy-tale story of a boy from a small fishing town who rose to fame by designing aircraft engines and racing cars, making a fortune, which he split between wise investments and squandering on his own amusements. The fishing town was Concarneau, France's third-biggest, measured by the weight of the catch, where he was born on 11 September 1879. He went to college in Brest and graduated from the École des Arts et Métiers of Cluny. He did his military service, not in the Navy as most of his schoolmates, but in the French Army.

He was drawn to fast cars and held jobs with De Dion-Bouton, Clément, and Panhard-Levassor prior to 1900. He went to England in 1900 and worked for the Crowden Motor Car Co. for a few months before securing a position with the Humber Co. at Coventry, as chief engineer for motor cars, when Walter Philips was general manager. He formed a partnership with William Hillman to build the Hillman-Coatalen car in 1907.

In 1909 he went to Wolverhampton as chief engineer of Sunbeam, where he designed the 12/16 touring car and the 16/20, which formed the basis for Sunbeam's racing programme.

He began experimental work on aircraft engines in 1913 and a year later was appointed joint managing director (with W.M. Iliff holding the same title). During World War I, he designed a series of very ambitious multicylinder aircraft engines, drawing on techniques developed in racing cars. In August 1920, Coatalen, W.M. Iliff, and Thomas Cureton became directors of the newly formed STD Motors Ltd under James Todd as chairman. As chief engineer of Sunbeam, he devoted more attention to the racing cars than the production models, which in the long run was justified by technology transfer to the benefit of the latter.

He designed the 350hp 18,322cc, V12 speed-record car himself in 1921, but engaged Ernest Henri to help him with the 1922 Grand Prix car, and lured Bertarione away from Fiat to prepare the 1923 Grand Prix Sunbeam. Both Bertarione and Henri worked with Coatalen on the supercharged 1988cc 6-cylinder Grand Prix car for the 1924 season. He hired J.S. Irving to help with the 16/50 of 1924-25 and the 1925 3-litre, and gave Irving the assignment of a speed-record car with a 300hp supercharged 3977cc engine in 1925.

He was also a director of a new subsidiary, Sunbeam Commercial Vehicles Ltd which specialised in trolley-buses, but he paid scant attention to this sideline. In1926 the racing activities of STD Motors Ltd were transferred from Wolverhampton to Suresnes, which led Coatalen to make business arrangements permitting him to spend most of his time in Paris. Yet the 1927 1000hp Sunbeam, sporting two 22,444cc Matable V12 engines, was designed by J.S. Irving and built in Britain, and was the first car in the world to exceed 200mph (322km/h).

In 1929 Sunbeam built another speed-record car, the Silver Bullet, for Kaye Don, with a Coatalen-designed 48,000cc 50 degrees V12, reputed to produce 4000hp, but it was a dismal failure. By 1931, STD Motors Ltd was bankrupt and the entire board of directors was dismissed. Settlement was tied up in the courts until 1934, when the Suresnes branch was sold to Tony Lago and the London (Talbot) and Wolverhampton (Sunbeam) branches fell into the hands of Rootes Securities Ltd.

Coatalen did well out of his STD shares, and used the proceeds to buy control of the French subsidiary of Lockheed brakes, which was the prime supplier of hydraulic brake systems to a growing number of European car makers. This gave him an income which permitted him to maintain a lavish lifestyle, with a villa on the Isle of Capri, and a yacht that was frequently moored in Monaco. He was also a director of KLG (spark plugs). He was still an engineer at heart and had a drawing board to hand wherever he went. In 1936 he designed a V12 Diesel engine for aircraft, with a centrifugal blower running at 10 times crankshaft speed. A test unit was built in France and put out 575hp at 2000rpm.

As a British citizen, he was not safe in his native land during the German occupation, and he sat out the war in Britain. In 1945 he returned to Paris and concentrated on rebuilding the Lockheed enterprise. As late as 1958 he was busy with the design of disc brakes. He died in Paris on 23 May 1962.

He was married four times. In 1907 to a daughter of William Hillman (marriage dissolved in 1909); in 1910 to Olive Bath, daughter of a director of Sunbeam (marriage dissolved in 1922); in 1923 to a widow, Florence van Raalte (marriage dissolved about 1932); and in 1934 to Amy Bridson, who survived him.

JPN

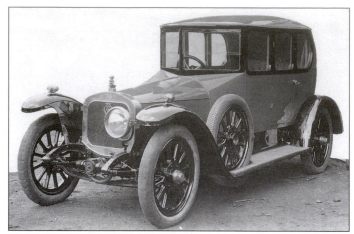

1913 Sunbeam (i) 25/30 saloon.
NICK BALDWIN

1921 Sunbeam (i) 16hp coupé.
NICK BALDWIN

1924 Sunbeam (i) 24/70 tourer.
NICK BALDWIN

Coatalen was quick to realise the sporting potential of his cars, particularly the 12/16, and he had a number of successes in sprints and hill climbs in 1909 and 1910. That year he built a curious machine especially for Brooklands racing. It was named Nautilus and had a 4256cc ohv engine with a conical nose and radiator behind the seat, and chain drive. It overheated and did not do well, but 1911 saw its successor, Toodles II which had a single-ohc engine and shaft drive. This won three races at Brooklands with Coatalen at the wheel, and covered a mile at 86mph (138.66km/h). Its successor Toodles IV, had a 30hp side-valve

engine and in the hands of Dario Resta gained the World's Hour Record at 92.45mph (148.78km/h).

More important than the Brooklands achievements was the entry of a 3-litre car in the 1911 Coupe de l'Auto. This had a 58bhp monobloc engine with straight bevel in place of worm drive, and a 4-speed gearbox with overdrive top. The body was an ungainly streamlined 2-seater, and the car retired in the race. Coatalen was sufficiently encouraged to try again in 1912. This time he used a narrower body with pointed tail and the same engines, now giving 74bhp. The Coupe de l'Auto, for 3-litre cars, was run concurrently with the French Grand Prix; Rigal, Resta and Caillois took the first three places in the Coupe and finished 3rd, 4th and 5th in the Grand Prix, defeating cars with twice the engine capacity. This was Britain's first important continental victory since S.F. Edge's Gordon Bennett win in 1902, and earned Sunbeam very welcome publicity. They never did so well again, although they returned in 1913 with more powerful cars with differential-less axles, Kenelm Lee Guinness finishing 3rd. 4-litre 6-cylinder cars ran in the 1913 and 1914 Grands Prix, finishing 3rd and 6th in 1913, and 5th in 1914. The 1914 GP cars had Peugeot-inspired twin-ohc engines with hemispherical combustion chambers and four valves per cylinder. This layout was also used on the smaller 3.3-litre cars entered in the 1914 Tourist Trophy, which Guinness won at 56.37mph (90.77km/h), setting a record lap for the Isle of Man course at 59.26mph (95.43km/h). In 1913 Coatalen turned his attention to aero-engines, and some of these were used in record-breaking cars, foreshadowing Sunbeam's postwar achievements in this field. A car fitted with a 9-litre V12 engine took many records at Brooklands, including an hour at 107.85mph (173.68km/h).

The design work on the Coupe de L'Auto cars had some valuable spin-offs for the road cars. A new 12/16 appeared at the 1911 Olympia Show, with the monobloc L-head engine developed for the Coupe de l'Auto, and a capacity of 3016cc. As well as the rather staid tourer, there was a sporting tourer with wire wheels, priced at £425, £50 more than the standard model. The 1913 sporting tourers had the lipped radiator of the 1912 racing cars, and low 2- or 4-seater bodies designed by J. Keele Ltd of London. No more than 12 of these were made.

The Vintage Years: Touring Cars

During the war the Sunbeam factory concentrated on aero-engines, and manufacture of the 12/16 was farmed out to Rover. This and the 24hp 6-cylinder car were revived in 1919, with very little change from the 1914 models. There was an important change of ownership, though, for in August 1920 the Sunbeam Motor Car Co. amalgamated with A. Darracq & Co. (1905) Ltd which had acquired the London-based Clement-Talbot Co. the previous year. The resultant group was called S.T.D. Motors Ltd. Although British-built Talbots and French Darracqs soon had much in common, the merger had little immediate effect on Sunbeam. In the long run, though, they suffered by the concentration of sporting support on the Darracq factory, and the loss of Coatalen to France in 1926.

The 16 and 24hp Sunbeams received ohvs and detachable heads for 1922, being re-named 16/40 and 24/60, the implied brake horsepowers being slightly optimistic. 4-wheel brakes were optional on the larger car for 1923, and standard for 1924, when it was known as the 24/70. Sporting models of both 4- and 6-cylinder cars were announced in August 1921; these had what was called the OV engine, with inclined ohvs, four per cylinder, operated by a single-ohc. They should have been good performers, with the 6-cylinder car a worthy rival for the Vauxhall 30/98, but very few, if any reached the public, and no performance figures were ever published.

The first really new postwar model was the 14hp (later 14/40) introduced for 1922. This had a 1954cc 4-cylinder pushrod ohv engine which differed from the 16/40 in having a monobloc aluminium casting for the cylinder block and top half of the crankcase. It was the first Sunbeam engine to have the inlet and exhaust ports on the same side of the head. Capacity was increased to 2120cc for 1924 when the designation 14/40 was used, and this excellent touring car was made up to the end of the 1926 season. It was joined by a smaller version, the 1598cc 12/30 of which few were made, and two sixes, the 2540cc 16/50 and the 3181cc 20/60. These replaced the old 16/40 and 24/60 models. 4-wheel brakes were standardised on all Sunbeams from 1925 onwards.

In 1925 came a new sporting model which owed more to the Grand Prix Sunbeams than any touring designs. This was the 2916cc 3-litre, the only Sunbeam to follow Bentley's practice of using litreage in the name. The engine had gear-driven twin-ohcs with hemispherical combustion chambers, and developed

ACROSS SYRIA TO BAGHDAD

A JOURNEY TO IRAQ ON A
25 H.P. SUNBEAM

1932 Sunbeam (i) Sixteen coupé.
NICK BALDWIN

1934 Sunbeam (i) Long 25 saloon.
NICK GEORGANO

1934 Sunbeam (i) Dawn saloon.
NICK GEORGANO

90bhp at 3800rpm. The frame was basically a touring design, and was long at 130in (3296mm). The 3-litre was announced in the spring of 1925, but none was available to the public until much later in the year. At £1125 for a simple 4-seater tourer, the 3-litre was much more expensive than other Sunbeams, and initially only 25 chassis were sanctioned. In June 1925 Jean Chassagne and S.C.H. Davis drove one into 2nd place at Le Mans, which gave a great boost to the car's reputation. Series production began in the autumn, and about 315 were made up to 1930. Most had open 4-seater bodies with cycle-type wings, but a Weymann saloon was also available from the factory, and custom coachbuilders made open 2-seaters and fixed head coupés. A supercharged version giving 138bhp was announced for 1928, but only six were made. It was raced at Phoenix Park in 1929 and 1930, but retired on both occasions. In fact the 3-litre's sporting career did not live up to its promising start. The chassis was too long and fragile for strenuous competitions, and funds were not available for developing a shorter version. Had it appeared in 1922 or 1923, when Coatalen was still in charge and the racing department was active, it might have been a different story.

Another new departure in 1926 was the straight-8, originally of 4826cc, later enlarged to 5447cc for use with heavier closed bodies. It had a similar pushrod ohv engine to the smaller models, but shared with the 3-litre a slightly vee-radiator, which was adopted on all Sunbeams from 1927. Also shared with the 3-litre a gearbox-drive mechanical servo for the 4-wheel brakes.

The 4-cylinder Sunbeams were dropped after 1926, and a new range known as the Sixteen, Twenty and Twenty Five was introduced. The straight-8 was called the Thirty or Thirty Five according to engine size. The sixes had capacities of 2040, 2916 and 3619cc and were continued into the 1930s with little change. The Sixteen had coil ignition, and all the larger models magneto up to 1930, and dual ignition thereafter.

The Vintage Years: Racing and Record Breaking
For the first half of the 1920s Sunbeam were very active in racing, and the decade saw five successful attempts on the Land Speed Record. The first postwar racing car was the 350hp of 1920, powered by a 18,322cc V12 aero-engine. René Thomas made FTD at Gaillon in 1920 with this monster, and two years

later Kenelm Lee Guinness raised the Land Speed Record to 133.7mph (215.18 km/h) at Brooklands. Malcolm Campbell took over the 350hp in 1923, raising the record twice, at Saltburn, England, and Fanøe, Denmark, though both speeds were disallowed by the FIA as the approved timing apparatus was not used. In 1924, however, Campbell did achieve an approved time of 146.2mph (235.3km/h), at Pendine, Wales, following this with 150.88mph (242.81km/h) in 1925. The 350hp was retired after that, but can still be seen at the National Motor Museum at Beaulieu, one of four LSR cars on display.

In 1921 Sunbeam built three twin-ohc 3-litre cars with dry sump lubrication and front-wheel brakes for the Grand Prix. They were withdrawn from the race, but Talbot-Darracqs of similar design finished 5th, 8th and 9th. In slightly modified form they ran in the 1922 Tourist Trophy, Chassagne winning. One of these 3-litre cars was also driven at Indianapolis in 1921 under the Talbot label, finishing 5th. Two of the chassis were fittted with 5-litre engines for 1922, Segrave driving one of these into 2nd place in the Coppa Florio. Another development of the 3-litre engine was that Coatalen used half of it in the successful Talbot-Darracq voiturettes.

The 1922 4-cylinder 2-litre GP Sunbeams were not successful, and in 1923 a new designer, Vincent Bertarione, produced a twin-ohc 6-cylinder engine which was mounted in the 1922 chassis. He had previously worked for Fiat, and the cars were unkindly dubbed 'Fiats in green paint'. They triumphed in the French GP, finishing 1st, (Segrave), 2nd (Divo) and 4th (Lee Guinness). Segrave's victory was the first by a British car in a European Grand Prix, and was not to be repeated for another 32 years. Divo also won the Spanish GP.

For 1924 a lowered chassis and supercharged engine were used, but they were not so successful as in 1923. The only win was Segrave's in the San Sebastian GP, and Giulio Masetti finished 3rd in the 1925 French GP. The transfer of racing activities to the Talbot factory at Suresnes meant the end of Sunbeam's participation in Grand Prix racing, although the 2-litre 6-cylinder cars were raced at Brooklands, and took over 30 international class records by 1930.

Although their Grand Prix days were over, Sunbeam built two more successful Land Speed Record contenders. The first had a supercharged 3976cc V12 engine consisting of two 2-litre blocks, giving 296bhp. Segrave raised the record to 184mph (296.113km/h). Compared with the monsters that preceded and followed it, this Sunbeam Tiger was a compact and normal-looking racing car; it was the last LSR contender which could also be raced, competing at Brooklands, San Sebastian and Boulogne. Malcolm Campbell was still racing it in 1934. In order to beat the magic 200mph (322km/h) figure Sunbeam built an enormous car for Sir Henry Segrave to drive in 1927. This had two Sunbeam Matabele V12 aero-engines totalling nearly 45 litres. They developed about 400bhp each, but the car was called the 1000hp Sunbeam for publicity purposes, and this has remained its name ever since. One was mounted at the front of the chassis, the other at the rear, there was a 3-speed gearbox and final drive was by chains. The tyres were specially made by Dunlop who would only guarantee them for 3½ minutes running time at the expected speed of 200mph (322km/h). Segrave took the car to Daytona Beach in Florida in March 1927, where he achieved a speed of 203.79mph (327.94km/h).

Over the next two years Segrave's record was broken three times, once by Segrave himself in the Napier-powered Golden Arrow. Sunbeam determined to try again, and Coatalen designed a completely new car with purpose-built V12 engines totalling 48-litres, and said to give 2000bhp each. They were mounted in tandem in the chassis, but final drive was by a propeller shaft on each side of the driving seat, each with its own straight-bevel drive to the rear axle. Named the Silver Bullet, the car was taken to Daytona by Kaye Don, but his best speed was only 186mph (299.4km/h). Silver Bullet never ran again.

Decline and Bankruptcy
Sunbeam's decline can be ascribed as much as anything to the departure of Coatalen to Suresnes in 1926. Although he was responsible for the Silver Bullet in 1930 he played no part in the engineering of the road cars, and his successor Hugh Rose (later with Riley and Lea-Francis) was mainly concerned with commercial vehicles. From Rose's departure in 1932 to the arrival two years later of H.C.M. Stevens, the company had no Chief Engineer, and design was carried on by the drawing office along previously established lines. The few changes made merely kept up with contemporary trends, such as the adoption of coil ignition and synchromesh on the higher ratios in 1933. Stevens' Dawn was more innovative, with ifs, wet liners and aluminium cylinder block, but it was too late and too expensive. The 1930 models were continued with increases in engine size

1938 Sunbeam-Talbot 3-litre saloon.
NICK BALDWIN

1951 Sunbeam-Talbot 90 drophead coupé.
NICK BALDWIN

necessitated by heavier bodies and lower axle ratios. Thus the Sixteen went up from 2040 to 2193cc in 1931, becoming the Twenty in 1934, and getting a larger engine of 2762cc for 1935. Meanwhile the old Twenty was increased from 2916 to 3317cc, and the stock of 2916cc engines used up in a shorter chassis Speed Model which carried some very handsome coachwork, both factory and by outside firms.

It did not get synchromesh until 1935, but this was thought not to matter too much on a sporting car. When the supply of 2916cc engines ran out, some 3317cc were also used in the Speed Model, which was renamed the Twenty One Sports for 1935. The old 3619cc Twenty Five was continued to 1932, and the name was revived in 1934 for an upgraded Twenty with the 3317cc engine and a new, lower chassis. These last Sunbeams, though excellent cars with beautiful workmanship, were put together from whatever components might be to hand, so there was no standard specification. Most Speed models, like earlier Sunbeams, had right hand gearchange, but at least one had a central lever.

H.C.M. Stevens came from Singer, bringing a number of designers and draughtsmen with him, but by the time he arrived in 1932 there was no money left for fresh large cars. His contribution to Sunbeam was a new smaller car, originally to have been called the Auk, but renamed the Dawn. Sunbeam's first 4-cylinder car since 1926, it had a 1627cc pushrod ohv engine with combined aluminium block and crankcase, like the 1922 14hp, a 4-speed Wilson preselector gearbox, and ifs by a transverse leaf spring. With low gear ratios and only 49bhp, the Dawn was not a great performer, and at £485 for a six-light saloon it was expensive. An obvious rival, the Daimler Fifteen, cost only £450. Nevertheless, 570 Dawns were sold between its introduction at the end of 1933 and the closure of the company in the summer of 1935. The last season Dawns had synchromesh in place of the preselector, central gear levers and 4-light saloon bodies.

The whole S.T.D. combine went into receivership in the spring of 1935, and production of cars at Wolverhampton ended in the early summer. The Rootes Group acquired the assets of both Sunbeam and the British Talbot, combining the names in a new range of cars which appeared in 1938. There was one final

1960 Sunbeam (ii) Alpine sports car.
NICK BALDWIN

1964 Sunbeam (ii) Rapier IV coupé.
NICK BALDWIN

Sunbeam, though, an advanced 4504cc straight-8 designed by Georges Roesch of Talbot, with transverse leaf ifs and wheelbases of 124in (3150mm) or 136in (3460mm) to accommodate formal coachwork. The prototypes were put together in the Talbot works, and three were shown at the 1936 Olympia Show, but the car was never produced in series.

NG

Further Reading
Motoring Entente, Ian Nichols and Kent Karslake, Cassell, 1956.
'Sunbeams Between the Wars', Anthony Heal,
Motor Sport, December 1949 and January 1950.

SUNBEAM-TALBOT; SUNBEAM (ii) (GB) 1938–1954; 1953–1976

1938–1945 Sunbeam-Talbot Ltd, London.
1946–1970 Sunbeam-Talbot Ltd, Ryton on Dunsmore, Warwickshire.
1970–1976 Chrysler UK Ltd, Ryton-on-Dunsmore, Warwickshire.

The first cars marketed under the Sunbeam-Talbot name were Rootes-built Talbots renamed for the 1939 season. The Ten and the 3-litre were based respectively on the Hillman Minx and Humber Snipe, though with prettier bodies and better equipment such as, on the 3-litre, dual windtone horns, three ashtrays and a cigar lighter. Styling was by Ted White, who was also responsible for the postwar 80 and 90. A new model for 1939, not part of the old Talbot range, was the 4-litre, which used the 4086cc engine of the Humber Super Snipe and was offered in a wider range of bodies than the 3-litre, including a limousine. Apart from the engine, it was similar to the 3-litre, but fewer were made, only 229, compared with 1266 3-litres and 3603 Tens. Some of the more expensive bodies on the 3- and 4-litre chassis were made by Thrupp & Maberly. A new model for 1940, of which very few were made before the war, was the 2-litre, which used the 1944cc Hillman Fourteen engine in a slightly lengthened Ten chassis and the same bodies. The chief engineer on these Sunbeam-Talbots was Dawn designer H.C.M. Stevens.

The Ten and 2-litre were revived after the war with little change, though production was moved from Talbot's London factory to the large plant at Ryton-on-Dunsmore where Hillmans and Humbers were also made. There was no longer a Hillman Fourteen, so the 2-litre's engine was shared with the Humber Hawk. Production of the Ten reached 3718 and of the 2-litre 1124 before they were replaced in 1948 by the 80 and 90. These had ohv versions of the previous engines giving an extra 6bhp in the 80 and 12bhp in the 90, and completely restyled bodies with flowing wings and spatted rear wheels. Although the cars were built at the main Rootes factory the styling of the 80 and 90 was carried out at the old Talbot works in London, being the work of Ted White. They still had beam front axles, but September 1950 saw the 90 Mk II with coil-and-wishbone ifs, hypoid rear axle, and a more powerful 2267cc engine. The Mk II was identified by small horizontal grills next to the traditional vertical grill. It is said that the Raymond Loewy studios, who did the interior of the 80 and 90, wanted to do away with the vertical grill, but White and his staff were adamant that it should stay, and it lasted until 1957. The 80 was dropped when the Mk II 90 appeared. For 1953 the Mk II became the IIA with improved steering and brakes, ventilated disc wheels and no rear wheel spats. All these improvements were the result of rallying experience with earlier 90s.

The Alpine and a Return to Sport

The postwar Sunbeam-Talbots were sold in France as Sunbeams to avoid confusion with the native Talbot-Lago, and when a new sports model was announced in 1953, it carried the Sunbeam name alone. This was the Alpine, a Mark IIA with 2-seater body, high compression 80bhp engine, higher-geared steering and optional overdrive. Inevitably for a car derived from a touring design, the Alpine was heavier than purpose-built rivals such as the Austin Healey 100 and Triumph TR2, and its top speed was little over 93mph (150km/h). However, it was a valuable publicity machine for the Rootes Group through a string of rally successes.

The Sunbeam-Talbot 90 had begun to shine in rallies from the year of its introduction, 1948, when Murray Frame won a Coupe des Alpes. In 1952 Stirling Moss was 2nd in the Monte Carlo Rally, and later in the year took 10th place in the Alpine, the team winning three Coupes des Alpes. In 1953 Rootes team manager Norman Garrad fielded six Alpines in the rally after which it had been named, Moss finishing 6th and the team bringing home four Coupes des Alpes. Other successes that year were team prizes in the Monte Carlo and Great American Mountain Rallies and outright victory in the Victorian Alpine Rally in Australia. Successes continued in 1954 and 1955, with Stirling Moss becoming the second driver to win an Alpine Gold Cup for three unpenalised events in succession (the first was Ian Appleyard in a Jaguar XK120), and Sheila Van Damm winning the ladies' prizes in the 1954 Alpine, Tulip, Geneva, Viking and Austrian Rallies. In 1955 the Norwegian private entrants Malling and Fadum won the Monte Carlo outright in a Sunbeam Mk III saloon, and works driver Peter Harper was 3rd in the 1956 Monte Carlo Rally.

These rallying activities brought valuable input to the production cars, in the fields of brakes, cooling and chassis strength. For 1955 the Sunbeam-Talbot Mk IIA became the Sunbeam Mk III, with similar body and engine, though a revised cylinder head increased power from 77 to 80bhp, overdrive was an option, and competition brake linings were fitted. The Mk III was made up to February 1957, 2250 being built, and after manufacture ceased a batch of about 40 were acquired by Castles of Leicester who fitted a high compression head, straight-through exhaust and floor gearchange, selling the result as the Mk IIIS. The Alpine was also made in Mk III form, with overdrive standardised, but the model was dropped at the end of 1955, after about 3000 had been made of all Alpines. These included 120 Alpine Specials, replicas of the works rally cars with overdrive and uprated engines.

The replacement for the Alpine, and ultimately for the saloon as well, was an unlikely car called the Rapier. In the tradition of the original Talbot Ten, this was a Hillman Minx in a prettier body, a 2-door sports saloon with a family resemblance to the Minx Californian hard-top. The 1395cc gave a top speed of 80mph (130km/h), but the Rapier improved with the Mk II of 1958, which had 1494cc, a higher axle ratio, bigger brakes, a floor-mounted gearchange and a square Sunbeam grill to give it more identity. The Mk III (1959–61) had front disc brakes and a hypoid rear axle, while the Mk IIIA (1961–63) had these improvements plus a 1592cc engine giving 80bhp and a 90mph (145km/h) top speed. The Rapier was made up to 1967, by which time it had an all-synchromesh gearbox and 1725cc engine. Despite its humble origins, the Rapier turned out to be a very successful rally car, with countless class wins in the years

1956–60, and an outright victory in the 1958 RAC Rally. Events in which Rapiers dominated their class included Tulip, Scottish, Liège-Rome-Liège, Acropolis and East African Safari. They won the 1961 and 1962 Irish Rallies outright. They were also successful in racing, Peter Harper and Sheila Van Damm finishing 2nd and 3rd in class in the 1956 Mille Miglia, and Harper winning the BRSCC Saloon Car Championship in 1961.

Alpine and Tiger

To fill the gap left by the original Alpine, the Rootes Group brought out a new Alpine for the 1960 season. This had a completely fresh body styled by Kenneth Howes, but the rest of the car owed much to existing Rootes cars. The engine and transmission were those of the Rapier, though output of the 1494cc unit was upped from 68 to 83bhp, thanks to twin carburettors, while the chassis was essentially that of the Hillman Husky estate car, strengthened with cross bracing. It was not a startling performer, with a top speed of 101mph (163km/h) and 0–60mph (97km/h) in just under 14 seconds, but its attractive lines pleased many customers, and it was gradually improved through five series up to 1968. Capacity went up to 1592cc on the Mk II (1960–63), which also had a better ride and interior trim, while the Mk III (1963) was offered with a hard-top, servo brakes and a larger fuel tank. Automatic transmission as an alternative to an overdrive gearbox came on the Mk IV (1964–5), while the 1965 models gained the all-synchromesh box also seen on the Minx and Rapier. The final Alpine Mk V of 1965–8 had the larger 1725cc engine developing 92bhp and good for over 105mph (170km/h). Total production of the standard Alpine was 58,091, and there were also some special versions. Two were offered by the coachbuilders Thomas Harrington of Hove; the Series A Harrington Alpine coupé had a fastback fibreglass roof giving extra headroom (the Alpine was a nominal 4-seater), while the Series B Harrington Le Mans was similar in concept but was more radically modified, with the roof, boot, rear panel and wing tops being moulded in one giant piece. The rear window opened as in a modern hatchback. 150 of the first design were made, in 1961, and 250 of the second, in 1962–3.

Another Alpine variant was the Venezia, a 4-seater coupé by Touring of Italy, with tubular frame and aluminium panels. 145 were made from 1963 to 1965.

From the start Rootes were aware of the Alpine's lack of power, but they did not have the resources to develop a more suitable engine. They therefore took the obvious route of installing a big American V8, as Carroll Shelby had done with the AC Ace to make the Cobra. Shelby in fact played a part in the creation of the Tiger, as the V8 Alpine was called, for Norman Garrad's son Ian, asked him to supervise the transplant of the Ford 260 (4261cc) into the Alpine bodyshell. New rack-and-pinion steering was needed, on the prototype taken from an MGA. Shelby was paid $8700 for his work on the prototype, but received a royalty on all Tigers sold.

The prototype Tiger was shown to Lord Rootes in 1963, and he gave an enthusiastic go ahead to the project, placing the largest order for engines that Ford had ever received from an outside firm, 4000 initially, and eventually taking 6495 of the 260, and 571 of the 4736cc, 289 for the Tiger II. The Tigers were assembled at the Jensen factory, and the first cars reached the US and Canadian market in the summer of 1964. Rhd cars for the British market were not available until March 1965, and only 800 were ever sold in Britain. The Tiger was threatened and ultimately doomed by the take-over of Rootes by Chrysler in 1964, as the new owners were hardly likely to favour a car powered by engines from a rival firm. However, Tiger production continued until 1967. The larger engine was introduced in December 1966, raising top speed to more than 125mph (200km/h). Other changes were the replacement of the dynamo by an alternator, and a wide ratio gearbox. Externally, the Tiger II was identified by a new 'egg-crate' grill and stick-on stripes down the side of the body. Officially the Mk II was never sold in Britain, but it is thought that 17 slipped through the net, six of these being used by the police. All Tiger production ended on June 30th 1967.

The Alpine had numerous rally successes, largely taking over from the Rapier as the spearhead of the Rootes Group with class wins in the 1962 RAC Rally and Tour de France, and outright victory in the 1961 Scottish Rally. An Alpine also won the Index of Thermal Efficiency at Le Mans in 1961. It was perhaps this success that led Rootes to enter two Tigers prepared by Brian Lister with Shelby-tuned engines for Le Mans in 1965. They had streamlined coupé bodies and a theoretical top speed of 170mph (275km/h), but both retired. Later one of the cars was fitted with a 289 engine and raced with some success. Peter Harper's Tiger

1969 Sunbeam (ii) Rapier H120 coupé.
NICK BALDWIN

c.1985 Suncar sports car.
DAVID FILSELL

was 4th in the 1965 Monte Carlo Rally, and he seemed set to win the Alpine when he was disqualified on a technicality.

The Last Sunbeams

The old-style Rapier was replaced in 1967 by a new model which had a fastback coupé body styled after the Plymouth Barracuda, a Hillman Hunter floorpan and the 1725cc engine. Manual or automatic transmission was available, and there were disc brakes on the front wheels. The most exciting model was the Rapier H120, with Holbay-tuned 105bhp engine, twin Weber carburettors, close-ratio gearbox and higher-geared final drive. Top speed was 105mph (170km/h). This, together with the standard Rapier and an austerity version for which the Alpine name was resurrected, were made up to 1976. Total production of all models was 46,204.

The other Sunbeams were badge-engineered versions of the Hillman Imp. The Sunbeam Imp Sport had a 50bhp engine giving 90mph (145km/h), and was also badged as the Singer Chamois. Some were Rally models, with 998cc in place of the usual 875cc, and 65bhp. The Sunbeam Stiletto was their version of the fastback Hillman Californian with the 50bhp engine. Just to confuse matters, on some export markets all Imps were sold under the Sunbeam name. There was also a very short-lived Sunbeam Vogue, sister to the Singer Vogue, which lasted for only six months in 1970.

The Sunbeam name was dropped completely in 1976, although it was revived two years later as a model name for Chrysler's hatchback, which in 1979 became the Talbot Sunbeam.

NG

Further Reading

'Supreme Sunbeam?', Jonathan Wood, *The Automobile*, December 1999.
Alpine, the Classic Sunbeam, Chris McGovern, Gentry, 1980.
Sunbeam Alpine and Tiger, Graham Robson, Crowood AutoClassics, 1996.
Tiger, the Making of a Sports Car, Mike Taylor, Foulis, 1991.

SUNCAR

SUNCAR (F) 1980–c.1986

1980–1983 Suncar sarl, Annecy, Haute-Savoie.

1983–c.1985 Kamouth International, Clermont-Ferrand.

The stylistic inspiration for the Suncar Arpège 2+2 roadster – created by Guy Duport of the DUPORT microcar company – came from the 1930s, though its bodywork was made of fibreglass. It used a 1.3-litre Renault 5 engine mounted in a tubular steel frame that boasted all-independent suspension. Van and 4-seater versions were also presented and Suncar additionally attempted a jeep-style vehicle called the Charade.

CR

SUNPACER (ZA) 1990s

Sunpacer Manufacturing, Port Elizabeth.

A range of boxy-shaped leisure and utility vehicles with fibreglass bodywork was offered by this company. All used Volkswagen Golf mechanicals mounted in a sheet steel monocoque chassis with a wheelbase some 300mm shorter than the Golf's. Cars were supplied either in kit form or fully-built.

CR

SUN RAY (US) c.1993 to date

Sun Ray Products Corp., Minneapolis, Minnesota.

This kit car company resumed production of the BRADLEY GT, which they sold in kit form or assembled with 4-wheel disc brakes and 5-speed transaxles. They also introduced a restyled version of the same kit with an air dam, aerodynamic side panels and a tall, slotted tail. A kit called the Tornado with a similar body and tube frame was being developed. Sun Ray also sold electric drivetrains for their kits.

HP

SUNRISE (i) *see* SIPANI

SUNRISE (ii) **(US)** c.1982 to date

Sunrise Automobile Corp., Des Moines, Washington.

The Sunrise M-3 was a simple 3-wheeler kit styled like 1920s British and French trikes. It used Honda or Yamaha motorcycle running gear. Sunrise also made a series of neoclassic kits. The Ross Speedster was a typical neo with Ford 5000cc engine. The Sunrise El Grande and Executive were neos with Cadillac cockpits stretched to limousine proportions. The Royal was another neoclassic based on a standard-length 1977 Cadillac body. They were sold in coupé and convertible form. In 1998 they built the Sunrise Classic, another neoclassic kit based on Cadillac running gear.

HP

SUNSET (US) 1900–1913

1900–1906 Sunset Automobile Co., San Francisco, California.

1906–1912 Victory Motor Car Co., San Jose, California.

1912–1913 California Motor Car Co., San Jose, California.

The first Sunset car was a steamer very similar in layout and appearance to a Locomobile, with a Mason vertical 2-cylinder engine, Dyke chassis, tiller steering and single-chain drive. The company manager, Dorville Libby Jr, also built an electric car, but his main interest was in internal combustion, and once he had raised enough money by sales of the steamer, he replaced it with a petrol car powered by a front-mounted 2-cylinder 2-stroke engine. This was joined by a 4-cylinder model for 1906. Cars of Sunset design were built under licence by Harry Knox of Springfield, Massachusetts, under the name ATLAS (ii). The San Francisco factory was destroyed in the 1906 earthquake and production restarted in San Jose, where cars with 2- and 3-cylinder engines were made. By the end of 1908 the new factory was making eight cars a month, and more than 230 Sunsets were in use in San Jose alone. A new model for 1909 was the 30 which used a 4-cylinder Continental engine. Production continued in a small way up to 1913. By 1917 only 37 Sunsets were registered on the roads of California.

NG

SUN VALLEY AUTOTECH (US) c.1998 to date

Sun Valley Autotech Inc., Scottsdale, Arizona.

The Veepster was a Volkswagen-based kit car that resembled the World War II Willys Jeep. It had a tubular frame and was the same body dimensions as the original Jeep so standard Jeep tops and trim would fit. They were designed to accept VW, Corvair, Mazda, Toyota and Ford Pinto engines in the rear.

HP

S.U.P. (F) 1919–1922

Sté des Usines du Paquis, Cons-la Granville, Ardennes.

This company was founded in 1908, although its activities of making chassis frames and accessories dated back at least to 1905. It was run by the Hainon family and soon became a major force in the French motor industry. Among its customers were Delaunay-Belleville, Lorraine-Dietrich, Peugeot and, in Holland, Spyker. In 1910 they acquired another factory at Asnières where it made engines for the Le Zèbre company.

After World War I Albert Hainon decided to make complete cars which were sold under the name S.U.P. (Société des Usines du Paquis). They had a variety of engines including Altos, Ballot, Chapuis-Dornier and Janvier, with gearboxes supplied by Malicet et Blin. Tourer and saloon bodies were featured, and were made at the rate of four or five per day. They were also sold under the name GUILICK from an address in Maubeuge, although they were probably the same car. Hainon also made about 700 HINSTIN cyclecars for Jacques Hinstin from 1921–23 or early 1924. The Usines du Paquis is still in existence making components for major manufacturers such as Peugeot and Renault.

NG

SUPA SPORT (AUS) 1968–1973

Supa Sport Products, Mount Gravatt, Queensland.

As the maker of fibreglass beach, dune, sand and street buggies for VW platforms shortened to 80in (2032mm) wheelbase, Supa Sport Products also promoted a 4-seater on the full-length floorpan as the 'family buggy'. The revised, sharply styled, Mk 3 buggy arrived in 1972.

MG

SUPER (F) 1912–1914

H. Godefroy et Levêque, Levallois-Perret, Seine.

The Super was a tandem-seated cyclecar with final drive by long belts, providing seven forward speeds. Unlike its contemporary, the BÉDÉLIA, the driver sat in the front seat. Two engines were offered, a 540cc 5hp single-cylinder Anzani and a 977cc V-twin described as a Super, but almost certainly a Ruby as Godefroy et Levêque were the makers of this well-known engine. This engine was also fitted to the RUBY car, which was a side by side 2-seater and was sold in England as the Tweenie.

NG

SUPERIOR (i) **(D)** 1905–1906

Superior Fahrrad- und Maschinen-Industrie Hans Hartmann, Eisenach.

This bicycle maker was one of several firms which chose to enter car manufacture by using Omnimobil components. The 2- and 4-cylinder engines were by Fafnir.

HON

SUPERIOR (ii) **(CDN)** 1910

Petrolia Motor Car Co., Petrolia, Ontario.

This company built mainly light trucks which were versions of those made by the Superior Motor Car Co. of Detroit. They had 25hp 4-cylinder engines, epicyclic transmission and shaft drive. A few were fitted with extra seats in place of the load carrying area. In 1912 the factory was destroyed by fire. Estimates of Superior production run from 25 to 50, but most of these were trucks.

NG

SUPERIOR (iii) **(US)** 1914

Crescent Motor Co., St Louis, Missouri.

This was a light car with 4-cylinder engine on a 116in (2944mm) wheelbase, made in roadster and tourer form. It was launched as the Crescent, but after only three had been made, the company announced a change of name to Superior, this applying retrospectively to the already delivered cars. Not many more were made before the company went out of business.

NG

SUPERIOR CUSTOM CLASSICS (US) c.1985

Superior Custom Classics, Port Richey, Florida.

Superior made a 427 Cobra replica based on a rectangular steel tube frame with a Ford or Chevrolet V8 engine. Suspension was Ford-based.

HP

SUPER KAR (US) 1946

Louis Enrod, Cleveland, Ohio.

This small 3-wheeled economy car had a rear-mounted 18hp air-cooled engine.

HP

SUPER STEAMER (US) 1918–1919

Peterson-Culp Gearless Steam Automobile Co., Denver, Colorado.

The conventional looking Super Steamer had a 4-cylinder steam engine connected to the rear axle in such a way as to provide each wheel with its own power, which the makers claimed would avoid skidding. Only one prototype was built.

NG

SUPER TWO (GB) 1960–1965

Super Accessories Ltd, Bromley, Kent.

Offered by a firm which made a wide variety of accessories for Austin Seven and Ford Ten enthusiasts, the Super Two kit sports car cost £99 without engine. The chassis, suspension, and many other items came from Bowden Engineering of Ottery St Mary, Devon, while the simple aluminium bodies came from Hamblin Ltd. About 200 Super Twos were delivered during the make's five year life. Some were sold under the name Bowden.

NG

SURAHAMMAR see VABIS

SURANYI (H) 1946–1949

Endre Surányi, Budapest.

Endre Surányi was an army officer and also a racer of motorcycles and motorboats. In 1946 he completed his first microcar, a 50cc 2-seater which was barely able to move. So he quickly created a bigger model with a body made from steel. It was powered by a 125cc Fichtel & Sachs engine. The 2.3 metre-long car weighed only 86kg. The engine was built right into the rear axle to lighten the construction. No one believed it would work, but it did, although the ride was a bit shaky. An upgraded model, with a 250cc DKW motorcycle engine was also completed. Shortage of raw materials, fuel and the ban on car ownership made it impossible to fulfil the creator's dream of seeing his cars reach series-production.

PN

SURREY (i) (GB) 1920–1930

1920–1923 West London Scientific Apparatus Co. Ltd, Putney, London.
1923–1927 Surrey Service Ltd, Putney, London.
1927–1930 Surrey Light Cars, Putney, London.

This was an assembled car made originally by Charles Alfred West, using a 1498cc Coventry-Simplex 4-cylinder engine, Meadows gearbox, Model T Ford front axle and steering, and Moss or Wrigley rear axle. Some cars had friction transmission and chain final drive; 2- and 4-seater open bodies were available. West was said to have orders for 200 cars, but the company was in receivership in 1923. It was rescued by a new concern named the Surrey Service company, which continued the cars into 1925. About 80 were made, including two with Dorman engines, and then a change was made to Meadows engines. Only 11 were ordered by Surrey, being either 1247 or 1496cc units. The new cars were known as Victory models, which was sometimes regarded as a separate make. The last few years of Surrey are hard to trace, and few cars were probably made after 1927. A 2176cc 6-cylinder car was listed, but it is not known whether any were made. There may have been a link with PALLADIUM, which also made a model named Victory, but this make was not listed after 1925. The Surrey Victory was possibly a remaindered Palladium; its prices were more than £100 lower than those quoted for the Palladium, suggesting this was the case.

NG

SURREY (ii) (US) 1958–1960

E.W. Bliss Co., Canton, Ohio.

1961 Super Two sports car.
NATIONAL MOTOR MUSEUM

1923 Surrey (i) 10½hp 4-seater tourer.
NICK BALDWIN

This was a replica of the 1903 Curved Dash Oldsmobile with a single-cylinder air-cooled 4hp Cushman engine. There was also a Deluxe model with 8hp engine.

HP

SURRIDGE (GB) 1912–1913

Robert Surridge, Camberwell, London.

The Surridge was quite an attractive-looking cyclecar powered by an 8hp V-twin Fafnir engine, which was an unusual power unit for a British cyclecar. It had friction transmission and final drive by chain to the offside rear wheel. The frame was of ash wood reinforced by steel plates. Priced at a modest £110, it made an appearance at the Olympia Show in November 1912, but had little impact on the market.

NG

SUTOL (GB) 1986–1992

Sutol Motorsport, Billborough, Sleaford, Lincolnshire.

True to its origins as a replica of the Lotus 23, it was intended mainly for race use, although owners did prepare them for the road too. Standard specification included a replica tubular steel space frame chassis, full race suspension and dimensionally accurate fibreglass bodywork. The Ford crossflow engine (1100, 1300 or 1600) was centrally mounted, driving through a VW/Hewland transaxle; other engine options were possible.

CR

SUTTON (AUS) 1899–1901

Sutton's Cycle Agency, Melbourne, Victoria.

Henry Sutton was a brilliant inventor who was abreast of scientific developments in photography, electricity and telephony and his vacuum pump was taken up for the manufacture of electric lamp bulbs. His interest in motors centred on the

1967 Suzuki Fronte 360 coupé.
NATIONAL MOTOR MUSEUM

1981 Suzuki SC100GX coupé.
NATIONAL MOTOR MUSEUM

1990 Suzuki Vitara JLX 4x4.
SUZUKI

means of burning safe lamp oil; his opposition to surface carburation of petrol was implacable. His first engine went on a tandem cycle and his first car, with a 4hp air-cooled engine, had a front-drive, rear-steering layout and became known as the Autocar owing to his regular reports appearing in the journal of the same name. A 6hp model, with a water-cooled 1565cc motor and a 4-seater tonneau body, appeared in 1901. Although several motors were fitted with the Sutton low-grade fuel system, there is no record of any further vehicles being made.

MG

SUZUKI (J) 1956 to date
Suzuki Motor Co. Ltd, Hamamatsu.

The origins of today's great Suzuki empire lay in making power looms for cotton weaving, which was begun in 1909. Motorcycles were added in 1952, tiny 36cc

powered bicycles at first, though Suzuki are now one of Japan's Big Three motorcycle makers, with Honda and Yamaha. Car production began in 1956 with the Suzulight, a small saloon with 360cc air-cooled 2-stroke 2-cylinder engine driving the front wheels. Only 43 of the original Suzulights were made, and proper production did not begin until 1961 with a new model which had similar mechanical specification and a completely revised body. By the end of 1961 production was running at 200 per month, compared with 11,000 mopeds and light motorcycles, and 3000 engines for bicycles.

A prototype of a larger car with 800cc engine was shown at the 1962 Tokyo Show, but this did not go into production until 1964, when it was called the Fronte 800. It had a 785cc 3-cylinder 2-stroke engine driving the front wheels through an all-synchromesh 4-speed gearbox, independent suspension all round and integral construction. It was joined in 1967 by a new small car to replace the Suzulight, called the Fronte 360. This had a rear-mounted 3-cylinder 2-stroke engine with a carburettor for each cylinder, which developed 25bhp at 5000rpm in the standard version, and 36bhp at 7000rpm in the high-performance SS version. Top speeds were 68 and 78mph (110 and 125km/h) respectively. Although the 359cc engine was retained for the Japanese market, where small displacements gain valuable tax advantages, the engine was enlarged in 1977 to 539cc for both domestic and export markets, and two years later to 970cc and 4-cylinders in the Cervo, a neat little coupé which sold in some numbers in European markets under the name SC100.

In 1970 the 359cc 2-stroke engine was installed in the front of a small utility vehicle called the Jimny. With 4-wheel drive and the appearance of a mini-Jeep, the Jimny was a new departure for Suzuki, but a very significant one, as its descendants are probably better known than the saloons. Capacity went up to 539 and then 797cc during the 1970s, and to 970cc and 4-cylinders in 1979 with the SJ-410 which was the first of the 4 × 4 Suzukis to be sold in Europe. It was supplemented in 1984 by the 1324cc SJ-413, and descendants were still in production in 1999. The SJ was known as the Samurai in some markets, including France. European-market SJs are sourced from Land Rover's Spanish factory.

The SJ found an important niche in the market as a small and reasonably priced 4 × 4 vehicle. 1990 saw a larger model in two wheelbases called the Vitara. Made in 5-door closed as well as open form, it had a choice of two petrol engines, a 1590cc four or a 1998cc V6, and two diesels, 1905 or 1998cc. The latter was a turbocharged unit made by Mazda. Unlike the SJ the Vitara was made only in Japan.

The Cervo/SC100 was totally redesigned for 1982, with front engine and front-wheel drive; a high-performance version for 1983 was the Cervo De Tomaso Turbo with 40bhp from its 543cc engine. This was only for the Japanese market, but a development of the front-engined Cervo was the Alto 5-door hatchback which was sold internationally. It had 3-cylinder single-ohc engines of 543 or 796cc, the latter being used in the export models. Automatic transmission was optional from 1983, and a 4 × 4 version was available in Japan. The Cervo was updated for 1988, with 547cc 3-cylinder engine and option of 5-speed manual or 3-speed automatic transmissions.

In 1981 Suzuki entered an important deal with General Motors for the manufacture of small cars for sale on the US market. The result emerged in 1983 as the Suzuki Cultus when sold in Japan and Chevrolet Sprint or Pontiac Firefly in the US. When they reached European markets in 1984 they were named Suzuki Swift. A new 993cc 3-cylinder single-ohc engine was used, driving the front wheels through a 4- or 5-speed manual gearbox or 3-speed automatic. 3- or 5-door hatchback bodies were offered. For 1985 the 3-cylinder engine was joined by a 1324cc 4-cylinder unit, and for 1986 by a 1298cc twin-ohc 16-valve all-alloy engine in the 1.3GTi.

The Alto also had its high-performance version, the 547cc twin-ohc turbocharged 12-valve Works. For 1989 the Alto and Swift were updated with new bodies, the Swift's being very aerodynamic with a drag factor of only 0.32. The Alto had a minimal rear seat for children only, which gave it a tax advantage in Japan, while for the same car with more generous rear seats the name Fronte was revived. Engines were 12-valve 3-cylinder units of 547cc, with single- or twin-ohc, and outputs from 32 to 65bhp.

Like other Japanese companies, Suzuki produced a number of interesting concept cars which appeared at the Tokyo Show, some of them being seen subsequently at European shows. In 1981 there was the CVI, a 50cc bubblecar only 75in (1905mm) long, while 1985 saw two sports cars, the front-engined R/P2 with

1993 Suzuki Cappucino sports car.
SUZUKI

800cc turbocharged and intercooled 3-cylinder 12-valve engine and 4-wheel drive, and the mid-engined R/Si with 1300cc 16-valve 4-cylinder engine. The R/P2 had a production derivative in the Cappuccino made from 1991 to 1995. Capacity was reduced to 660cc and drive was to the rear wheels only. The mid-engined theme was productionised in 1992 as the Cara. The 660cc engine was mounted transversely, and the coupé had gull-wing doors. It was also made as the Mazda AZ-i.

Another concept which saw production was the Wagon R+, launched in 1993. A high-roof mini-MPV, it was powered by the same 660cc 3-cylinder engine used in the Cappuccino and Cara, though the European-market Wagon R+, available from 1997, used a 996cc twin-ohc 16-valve 4-cylinder engine. A new Wagon R+ with 1.3-litre 4-cylinder engine was due to go into production at Suzuki's Hungarian plant in spring 2000, This was very similar to the Polish-built Opel/Vauxhall Agila, with which it shared a number of body panels, though its engine was larger. Another new model was the Wagon RR Limited with 657cc 3-cylinder turbocharged engine. This engine was also used, mounted amidships and driving the rear wheels, in the MR Wagon shown at the 1999 Tokyo Show and due for production in 2000.

The Alto had sold almost two million units by 1996, when production of the current 4-cylinder model was switched to the Maruti factory in India. Cars for the local market were sold as the Maruti Zen, and for European markets as the Suzuki Alto. 3- and 5-door models were offered, both with a 996cc engine. Maruti also made the previous generation 3-cylinder Alto 800, which was continued alongside the Zen, and the Suzuki Baleno under the name Esteem. The Swift was continued into 1998, with choice of 993cc 3-cylinder or 1298cc four, European market cars being made in Hungary. It was also made in Canada for the North American market as the Geo Metro. The largest saloon was the Baleno (Cultus Crescent in Japan), made in 3-door hatchback or 4-door saloon models, with 1298cc single-cam or 1590cc twin-cam engines.

In addition to the Japanese factories, only one of which is devoted to passenger cars, and the Indian, Spanish, Hungarian and Canadian operation mentioned, Suzuki has assembly plants in China and Pakistan.
NG

S.V.A. (I) 1949
Stà Valdostana per la Costruzione di Motori, Aosta.
This was a prototype powered by a 813cc supercharged flat-4 engine driving through a 5-speed gearbox.
CR

SVELTE (F) 1904–1907
Sté de Constructions Mécaniques de la Loire, St Étienne, Loire.

1998 Suzuki Wagon R+.
SUZUKI

Well-known manufacturers of firearms and bicycles, this company made a small number of conventional cars in five different sizes from 16 to 50hp. The company was apparently the same as (or a branch of) Société Manufacturiere d'Armes, which made a car under that name in 1904. Later examples of the AUTOMOTO were made by the same company as the Svelte, and both these marques ended car production in 1907.
NG

S.V.J. (DK) 1965–1967
S.V. Jensen Bil A/B, Copenhagen.
S. Jensen's ill-fated S.V.J. 1000 GT Coupé was intended to address the absence of a true Danish-built sports car. Using an Auto Union 1000 S as its base, the S.V.J. was a spacious 4-seater with an Alfa Romeo-esque 3-box coupé body. The original Auto Union engine was later replaced by a rotary NSU Ro80 motor. Despite the S.V.J.'s promising specification and attractive contemporary styling, Jensen failed to raise enough funding to produce his fibreglass-bodied 1000 GT, and only one example was ever built.
CR

S.V.P. (F) 1905–1906
Sté des Voitures Populaires, Paris.
This was a light 2-seater powered by an 8hp 2-cylinder engine driving via a flat belt to a countershaft, annd thence by reduction gearing to the rear wheels.
NG

2000 Suzuki MR-Wagon.
SUZUKI

1955 Swallow (ii) Doretti sports car.
NATIONAL MOTOR MUSEUM

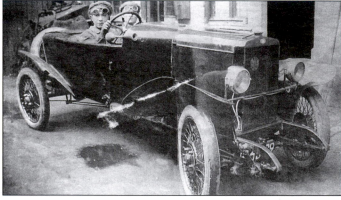

1923 Swan sporting 2-seater.
NICK BALDWIN

SWALLOW (i) (GB) 1921–1922

Sir J.F. Payne-Gallwey, Brown & Co. Ltd, London.

This car was marketed by the same company as the EDMOND and NORTH STAR. Its place of manufacture is uncertain, although it could have been the factory at Lee Green, where these two cyclecars were built. The Swallow was larger than these, and was offered with the choice of a 1100cc Blackburne V-twin or a 4-cylinder Dorman 4ML of the same capacity. It had a 2-speed epicyclic gearbox and shaft drive to a worm rear axle. With the 2-cylinder engine the only body style was a 2-seater, but with the Dorman four the Swallow had a family body for two adults and two children.

NG

SWALLOW (ii) (GB) 1954–1955

Swallow Coachbuilding Co. (1935) Ltd, Walsall, Staffordshire.

Swallow began as the Swallow Sidecars Co., founded in Blackpool in 1922 by William Lyons and William Walmsley. As the name suggests, it made motorcycle sidecars but, before long, car bodies were added. Then came the S.S.1 sports car and, in 1935, Lyons launched S.S. Cars Ltd as a public company – it would become Jaguar – while the original firm became Swallow Coachbuilding Co. (1935) Ltd under Lyons' ownership.

Lyons sold it in 1945 and it became part of the Tube Investments group. Sales of sidecars were flagging in the early 1950s so, to take up the slack, it was decided to build a sports car. Designed by Frank Rainbow, it had a tubular chassis made from Reynolds 531 tubing, Triumph TR2 running gear and suspension, and a body made of aluminium on a mild steel frame. It was a pretty, well appointed car, with a heater and fitted luggage as standard. In terms of price, it was pitched in the market between the TR2 and the Austin-Healey, but was less uncompromising than either.

It found an enthusiastic importer in California and was named Doretti for the importer's daughter, Dorothy. Dorettis were raced only occasionally, and then without much success, but the American racing driver Max Balchowsky was impressed by the strength of the Doretti's chassis and he began to transplant American V8 engines in second-hand Dorettis. In all he converted six cars, usually with a Buick engine. They achieved little success in racing but were exceptional road cars. Sir John Black, chairman of Standard-Triumph began negotiations to take over production but that came to nothing when he was seriously injured in a road crash.

Production eventually reached about 10 cars a week and a 2+2 coupé, the Sabre, with improved cockpit and luggage space and a De Dion rear axle, was running as a prototype when the project closed after 276 cars had been made.

William Lyons did not take kindly to Tube Investments marketing a rival sports car and asked whether TI would like to build cars or would it like Jaguar to continue as a customer for items like bumpers and door locks. Production ceased abruptly, without a public statement, which is why it has often been assumed that the Doretti was a failure. Instead, it was its success which caused its demise.

MJL

Further Reading
Articles by Mike Lawrence, *Motor Sport*, October 1984;
Classic & Sportscar, September 1988.

SWAN (F) 1922–1923

Bloch et Compagnie, Neuilly-sur-Seine.

The Swan was a light car powered by Altos engines, either 1244 or 1994cc, with 3-speed gearbox and shaft drive. At least one was made with sporting body and flared wings, and all models had electric lighting and starting. It is not known why a French firm should have chosen an English name for their car, when they could have called it 'Le Cygne'.

NG

SWEET (US) c.1991

Sweet T-Bird, Windham, New Hampshire.

The Sweet T-Bird was a replica of the 1955 Ford Thunderbird that fitted on a Volkswagen Beetle chassis. Unlike some similar kits that shortened the Thunderbird body to fit the shorter VW pan, the Sweet kit used a frame extender to make the chassis match the original length body. A removable hard-top was optional.

HP

SWIFT (i) (GB) 1900–1931

1900–1902; 1912–1914 Swift Cycle Co. Ltd, Coventry.
1902–1919 Swift Motor Co. Ltd, Coventry.
1919–1931 Swift of Coventry Ltd, Coventry.

The origins of the Swift dated back to 1869 and the formation of the Coventry Machinists Co. who made sewing machines, followed by bicycles. The Swift Cycle Co. was founded in 1896 to acquire Coventry Machinists whose works manager was James Starley, one of the leading figures in the nineteenth century cycle industry. The DuCros family who held the Dunlop patents were on the Swift board, so it had an abundance of talent and connections with the cycle and subsequent motor industry, extending to the Continent with the DuCros' links with CLÉMENT.

1900 Swift (i) voiturette with Swift tricycle.
NICK BALDWIN

A De Dion-Bouton-powered tricycle was introduced under the Swift name in 1898, very similar to the equivalent Ariel, and a quadricycle appeared two years later. Also in 1900 came a voiturette powered by a front-mounted 5½hp MMC-De Dion water-cooled engine, with Crypto 2-speed gear and final drive by single chain to the rear axle. A 3-seater body was offered. This and an 8hp model were continued into the 1902 season, but there was also a new, smaller 2-seater with a 4½hp engine, described as a 'genuine De Dion', and an unusual gearchange with two rings of teeth on the crown wheel, and two pinions, but no reverse gear.

The Swift Motor Co. was formed as a subsidiary of the cycle company in 1902, and car production was concentrated at a new factory in the Cheylesmore district of Coventry, although the cycle company made cyclecars from 1912 to 1914. Two- and 3-cylinder engines of Swift's own manufacture were offered from 1904, and larger fours of up to 16/20hp from 1905. The biggest was the 4940cc 25/30, listed only for 1908. In 1909–10 there was a Clement-type 1099cc 7hp single-cylinder 2-seater which was also badged as an AUSTIN because of the DuCros family's links with both firms. Of the 1030 built, 182 had Austin radiators. Other Swifts of the prewar era included an 1813cc 10/12hp twin and fours from a 1794cc 11.9hp to a 3052cc 16/20hp. There was also the cyclecar built by the Swift Cycle Co. in their own factory. This had a tubular frame instead of the pressed steel units of the other Swifts, and a 972cc 2-cylinder engine. It was quite a civilised little car with 3-speed gearbox and shaft drive, and sold for £125. Swifts were popular in several export markets, especially those where the bicycles had already made the name well known.

Although the factory was busy with war contracts, such as stretcher carriers, fuse caps, shells and military bicycles, cars were continued into 1916. In 1919 the car and cycle firms were combined, called Swift of Coventry Ltd. Car production concentrated on the 1122cc prewar Ten and a new 1944cc Twelve. Both had side-valve 4-cylinder engines which, like most of the rest of the car, were made in-house. The Ten had a 3-speed gearbox, the Twelve, four speeds. Bodies were mostly open 2- or 4-seaters, but there was a Pytchley saloon on the Twelve chassis. It was made until 1925, but the Ten gave way to a new Q Type Ten for 1923. This had a smaller engine of 1097cc and coil ignition in place of magneto. Together with the 1190cc 4-speed P Type which replaced it in 1926, it was the staple Swift of the 1920s, and about 4500 were made up to 1931. In the late 1920s, body styles had attractive names such as Nomad, Fleetwing, Migrant and Paladin,

1908 Swift (i) 25/30hp limousine.
NICK BALDWIN

1913 Swift (i) 7hp cyclecar.
NICK BALDWIN

1925 Swift (i) 10hp tourer.
NICK BALDWIN

while about 150 were given Swallow 2-door saloon coachwork similar to that on Fiat and Standard chassis.

In 1925 the old Twelve was replaced by the 12/35, later 14/40, with 1954cc engine in unit with a 4-speed gearbox. A 2950cc 18/50 was announced at the 1924 Olympia Show, but probably got no further than a prototype. In the mid–1920s the factories had an annual capacity of more than 5000 cars, but only about half this number was ever made. By 1930 Swift was in serious trouble, and it tried to help matters by launching a small car in the Austin Seven/Morris Minor class. The Cadet had an 847cc Coventry-Climax engine, a shorter wheelbase and either 2-door saloon or tourer bodies. Not more than 250 were made before the makers went into liquidation in April 1931.

NG

SWIFT (ii) (CDN) 1910
Swift Motor Car Co. of Canada Ltd, Chatham, Ontario.
This ephemeral car was made or sold by Frank Mount, who had been involved with the American ANHUT company and which had taken over the factory where the CHATHAM car had been built. He offered one or two Swifts for sale during 1910, but these may have been Anhuts re-badged. From 1911 onwards the Swift name was seen only on marine engines.

NG

SWIFT (iii) (US) 1959–1960
WM Manufacturing Co., San Diego, California.
Swift made two replicas of antique cars. The T resembled a Ford Model T while the Cat was modelled after the Stutz Bearcat. They were made to a smaller size than the original.

HP

SWIFT (iv) (GB) 1983–1985
Swift Cars Ltd, Silkstone, Barnsley, South Yorkshire.
John Swift designed this pleasant-looking and substantial vintage-style roadster, intended for Ford Granada power. It had a backbone steel chassis and all-aluminium bodywork. At £12,500 in complete kit form, it was too expensive to have any impact.

CR

SWIFT CLASSICS (GB) 1988
This company displayed a V12 powered Ferrari Daytona Spyder replica at the 1988 Stoneleigh kit car show but no more was heard of the project.

CR

SWIFTSURE (AUS) 1906
Isaac Phizackerley, Sydney, New South Wales.
A brand sold by this early cycle and motor house, the Swiftsure seems to have been an unidentified British make to which the famous warship name was applied. There was a range of sizes, from a 2-cylinder 10hp, to 4-cylinder 16 and 18hp models, and to a big 24hp. The name was only current during 1906.

MG

SWINDON SPORTSCARS see VINCENT and SYLVA

SWINNERTON (AUS) 1907–1914
A.J. Swinnerton's Foundry, Rozelle, New South Wales.
Alfred Swinnerton was an engineer who had risen to a foreman's position by 19 years of age, and who later established his own business, which built marine and other engines. His first car, a single-cylinder runabout of 1907, was innovative by having no chassis frame, the body structure being designed to have all components attached to it. Very little is known of its mechanical detail except that it was registered as a 6hp Kelicon, possibly indicating that its engine was a Kelecom. His later vehicle was a low-slung roadster with final drive by belts in the manner of the then popular cyclecars. Unlike the usual cyclecar, however, its engine was an 11hp 4-cylinder unit which had been produced at the Swinnerton works. He would have been disappointed if he had held commercial expectations, but he did obtain ten years of service from his 1914 vehicle.

MG

SWISS BUGGY (CH) 1972–1976
René Schmid, Fahrzeugbau AG, Otelfingen ZH.
As was the case with the majority of buggies, the Swiss Buggy was based on the Volkswagen platform frame which was modified to a wheelbase of 79in (2000mm).

The various VW flat-four engines from 1192cc to 1584cc with up to 54bhp could be ordered. The body consisted of two fibreglass shells. In 1973 production reached about 20 cars monthly and by the end of 1974, a total of about 300 Swiss Buggy cars had been sold. By 1975 demand dropped sharply and one year later this series small production was stopped. The Swiss Buggy remained available custom made and on firm orders only for some time.

FH

SYCAR (GB) 1915

R.R. Bertram, Gorebridge, Scotland.

As its name implies, the Sycar was a 3-wheeler on motorcycle and sidecar lines, similar to the Seal except that the sidecar and front wheel were coupled together. It had a tubular frame and two bucket seats between the rear wheels, the rear axle being driven by belt. It was powered by a 4¹/₂hp air-cooled engine. A price of £58 was quoted, but it does not seem to have gone into production.

NG

SYLPHE (F) 1920

Sté S.E.D.A.S., Bois-Colombes, Seine.

This short-lived light car had a very small 4-cylinder engine of unknown make. It should not be confused with Le Sylphe, which was the name given to the Carden Monocar sold in France by Jouvé et Compagnie in 1914.

NG

SYLVA (GB) 1982 to date

1982–1986 Sylva Autokits, Milford-on-Sea, Hampshire.
1985–1989 Swindon Sportscars, Swindon, Wiltshire.
1986–1988 Sylva Autokits, Lymington, Hampshire.
1988 to date Sylva Autokits, Louth, Lincolnshire.
1989–1991 Robley Motors, Worthen, Shropshire.
1994 to date Fisher Sportscars, Marden, Kent.
1997 to date Specialist Sports Cars, Woking, Surrey.

Draughtsman Jeremy Phillips was behind the individual-looking Star, a sort of modern interpretation of the Lotus 7. The chassis was a tubular steel space frame affair with stressed sheet steel panelling, and fibreglass body panels fitted at either end. Unusually the Leader was designed around Vauxhall Viva or Chevette components, though engine options also included Ford crossflow and Fiat twin cam. The Vauxhall suspension, pedals and rear axle were all modified. Low kit prices meant competition for Dutton. A revised all-fibreglass Leader replaced it in 1984, from 1985 made by Swindon Sports Cars, then Robley. In 1986 Sylva launched the Striker, a bare-boned sports car kit. It had a new space-frame chassis designed for Ford Escort parts, and was clothed with aluminium-and-fibreglass bodywork. Examples won the Kit Car race championship three times. In 1989 came the Mk4 (or Clubman's) which had an enveloping body and either Vauxhall Chevette or Escort mechanicals. The Lotus 7 style body remained the more popular choice thanks to low prices. The 1992 Sylva Fury's body was a heavily modified Mk4, underneath which was a new chassis designed for Escort MkI/II components (or optional Fiat twin cam power). Fisher Sportcars took over Fury manufacture in 1994, Sylva concentrating on a new model, the Stylus. The styling was an evolution of the Fury, though it had a one-piece fibreglass body, a small bonnet instead of the complete lift-up front of the Fury and Porsche 911 headlamps. The steel tube spaceframe chassis used stressed sheet metal and accepted a Ford Sierra rear end. This was taken over by Specialist Sports Cars in 1997, as Sylva pursued another variant of its clubman's body style, the Phoenix. Sylva Autokits took a very different direction with the Jester in 1997, a very short doorless open fun car that its manufacturers described as 'halfway between a Morris Minor and a Lotus 7'. In its spaceframe chassis went Ford Fiesta mechanicals. The Jester project was taken over in 1998 by Harlequin Autokits of Stroud, Gloucestershire.

CR

SYME see MUMFORD-SYME

SYMÉTRIC (F) 1951–1953; 1957–1958

1951–1953 Frères Loubière, Paris.
1957–1958 Automobiles François Arbel, Paris.

1983 Sylva Star sports car.
NICK BALDWIN

The Loubière brothers were behind this highly unusual project, first presented as early as the 1951 Geneva Salon as the Symétric. In form it was very distinctive, having a barrel-shaped body built around three grand hoops, each fixed to a central backbone tube that doubled up as the fuel tank; the plastic panels for the front and rear ends were identical, hence the name Symétric. Power came from a 6CV 1100cc 4-cylinder engine which in turn fed four electric motors, one for each wheel. Only one pedal was provided, which took care of acceleration and braking. This was an extremely heavy device that could hardly reach its top speed of 50mph (80km/h). The car reappeared at the 1953 Paris Salon but then went quiet for 4¹/₂ years. In March 1958 it was relaunched as the Symétric-Paris-Arbel with a number of extraordinary and, frankly, quite implausible features. A sumptuous catalogue described such features as Electric-Drive transmission, Thermogum suspension, phosphorescent bumpers and Polystic (plastic) coachwork. Most unlikely of all was the choice of powerplant: either rotary petrol, Genestat gas turbine or – most preposterously of all – a Genestatom nuclear reactor! The Arbel quickly disappeared in a haze of unpaid debts.

CR

SYNNESTVEDT (US) 1904–1905

Synnestvedt Machine Co., Pittsburgh, Pennsylvania.

This car was made by a Chicago lawyer, Paul Synnestvedt, who began to design an electric car in 1893, although it was ten years before he got anything on the market. Most Synnestvedt electrics were delivery vans or sightseeing buses, but a few 2-seater chain driven stanhopes with 8hp motors and 4-speed controllers were made for less than two years. Commercial vehicles lasted a little longer, to 1907.

NG

SYRACUSE (US) 1899–1903

Syracuse Automobile Co., Syracuse, New York.

This car was made by William H. Birdsall who later designed several other makes including the Buckmobile, Regas and Mora. It was a petrol-engined car but further details of its design are lacking. One was driven from Buffalo to New York City in 1901.

NG

SYRENA see FSO

SZA see SMZ

SZAWE (D) 1920–1922

Szabo & Wechselmann Automobilfabrik, Berlin.

Coachbuilders since 1919, Szabo & Wechselmann entered into the manufacture of complete cars with two models, the 4-cylinder 10/38PS and 6-cylinder 10/50PS. The former used a chassis and engine from NAG, the latter from EHRHARDT. They were not particularly distinguished mechanically but had very distinctive coachwork which appealed particularly to the *nouveaux riches*. The radiator was of hammered German silver, pipes and linkages were nickel plated and the chassis were polished. Many of the bodies were designed by Ernst Neumann-Neander. Some were boat-shaped and of wooden construction. In 1922 Szawe amalgamated with Ehrhardt, and for two years cars were sold under the name Ehrhardt-Szawe.

HON

1997 Sylva Jester sports car.
SYLVA AUTOKITS

SZB; SZD *see* SMZ

SZEKELY (H) 1928
Mihály Székely, Szentendre.
Székely was a fan of motor vehicles. In his autobiography he later said 'I learnt to fly in an aeroplane I built and learnt to drive in a car I built'. The latter was completed in 1928 with a 500cc motorcycle engine. The search for a would-be investor led to a press presentation, but despite the media blitz no one showed any interest.
PN

SZL *see* SMZ

T-3 (US) c.1996 to date

T-3, Littleton, Colorado.

This company built a Ford GT-40 replica that was sold in partially assembled form. It had a tubular frame with Ford Mustang front suspension and a Ford Thunderbird-based independent rear end. Engine choices were Ford and Chevrolet V8s.

HP

T.A. (i) *see* N.G.

T.A. (ii) **(GB)** 1989–1991

T.A. Design & Development, Wakefield, Yorkshire.

The T.A. Spirit began life as a one-off called the Ynot that was later put into production from 1989 on Escort/Cortina parts. It was an extraordinary swoopy, slab-sided sports car in the Sylva Star vein. Another sports car, the Phantom, was launched in 1990: the body was an ASHLEY using an MGB windscreen and a spaceframe chassis. Probably only one prototype was made.

CR

T&A (GB) 1990

T&A Sports Cars, Woodston, Peterborough, Cambridgeshire.

The Predator was a short-lived and conventional kit-form Cobra 427 replica using a ladder frame or backbone chassis and mechanicals from the Jaguar XJ range. V8 or V12 engines were recommended.

CR

TAAGER (US) c.1995

Taager Auto Co., Ocala, Florida.

The Taager T-99 was a small sports car built from a set of plans. It used Volkswagen running gear bolted to a simple steel chassis and clothed in a simple, slab-sided body built from plywood sheets.

HP

TAFCO (US) 1979–1980s

Tafco Design and Engineering, Dearborn, Michigan.

The Tafco Baronta 2-seater coupé had a tubular spaceframe designed to accept GM mechanical components. Top speed was quoted as 150mph (241km/h).

NG

TAHOE CARS (US) c.1983–1995

Tahoe Cars Ltd, Stateline, Nevada.

Tahoe T, Port Angeles, Washington.

This down-sized Ford Model T hot rod was certainly not the usual cup of 'T'. It was a kit car that used front-mounted 750cc and larger motorcycle engines with a chain drive to the rear axle. Suspension and brakes were borrowed from midget racing cars. By 1994 production had switched to Washington state.

HP

TAIFUN (D) c.1906

Two models of this car were offered in 1906, an 8/10hp 2-cylinder and 10/12hp 4-cylinder, sold by the London firm of Bowle Evans of Regent Street. They were said to be of German origin, but the identity of the maker is uncertain. In 1913 the Taifun name was listed in the *Radmarkt Adressbuch* as a maker of motor-boats in Werda. It is not known if there was a connection with the cars made seven years earlier.

NG

TAKEOKA (J) 1990 to date

The Takeoka Abbey, produced by the Takeoka Auto Craft Co., was Japan's only domestic microcar for some years, made by a company founded as early as 1981. It was a very small (85in/2150mm long) enclosed saloon weighing only 319lb (145kg) and was powered by a 49cc engine. Some 1500 units had been sold by 1997, when a new model called the Rookie was released.

CR

TAKURI (J) 1907–1909

Tokyo Jidosha Seisakusho, Tokyo.

1908 Talbot (i) 25hp landaulet.
NICK BALDWIN

The Takuri is believed to have been the first commercially produced petrol-engined car in Japan. It had a 12hp 4-cylinder engine and chain drive. The 4-seater tourer body had a roof on which there was a luggage rack, but no side windows. Lighting was by a single large acetylene headlamp. It was also known as the Yoshida, named after the company president. A total of 17 were built.

NG

TALBO *see* TLC

TALBOT (i) **(GB)** 1903–1938

Clement Talbot Ltd, North Kensington, London.

The Talbot name has been used for three quite distinct makes of car, the London-built British Talbot, the French Talbot or Talbot-Lago, and the Anglo-French Talbots of the 1980s, which were Chryslers renamed after Peugeot had taken over Chrysler's European operations.

The makers of the first, Clement Talbot Ltd, were formed in October 1902. Initially they imported the French-made Clément-Bayard into Britain until their factory was ready for manufacture. The Talbot part of the name came from the Earl of Shrewsbury and Talbot, a director and leading shareholder, who had been importing Clément cars since 1900, in partnership with Daniel M. Weigel who became general manager of Clement Talbot, and who was later to build cars under his own name. During 1904 they imported a 6hp single-cylinder car, an 11hp twin and three fours of 14, 20 and 27hp. They had T-head engines apart from the largest, which used the inlet over exhaust valve layout. By late 1904 their large factory in Barlby Road, North Kensington, was sufficiently complete to allow for the assembly of cars from French components, and by the end of the year the Clement part of the name had been dropped for the cars, though the company name remained Clement Talbot Ltd right up to the Rootes Group days in the late 1930s. In January 1905 the company exhibited a range of four 2-cylinder models and five fours, from a 7/8hp twin to a 35/50hp four of 6.3 litres.

The first all-British Talbot appeared in 1906. Designed by C.R. Garrard, it had a 3.8-litre 4-cylinder T-head engine, and was joined by other fours of similar design, the 2.7-litre 12/16 and 4.4-litre 24/30hp, while the 6.3-litre now called a 35/45, was still listed up to 1908. Talbot's first six was the 3.6-litre 20hp, made from 1910 to 1914. By 1910 the Talbot factory employed nearly 600 men, and could turn out between 50 and 60 cars a month. Talbots were beginning to make a name for themselves in speed and reliability trials, but greater sporting glory came their way after the arrival in 1911 of a new designer, George W.A. Brown. He had formerly worked for Argyll, Humber and Austin, and set to work redesigning the 4155cc 25hp T-head engine. Capacity was increased to 4530cc and valves were relocated in the more modern L-head position. The new engine probably gave around 50bhp in standard form, at any rate it was advertised as the 25/50, but when tuned by Brown and fitted with light tubular connecting

1914 Talbot (i) 20/30hp tourer.
NICK BALDWIN

1924 Talbot (i) 10/23 tourer.
NICK GEORGANO

1927 Talbot (i) 14/45 tourer.
NICK BALDWIN

rods, output went up to 120bhp at the very high speed of 3000rpm. It was this car which was chosen by Brown's friend Percy Lambert for his attempt to cover 100 miles (160.93km) in the hour, a very different task from reaching the speed of 100mph for a few minutes, which had been achieved in 1904. After one unsuccessful attempt, Lambert achieved his ambition in February 1913, covering 103.84 miles (167.1km) in the hour. The record was broken shortly afterwards by Jules Goux in a Grand Prix Peugeot, and in attempting to wrest it back from Goux, Lambert suffered a burst tyre, skidded over the top of the Brooklands banking and was killed instantly. This marked the end of Talbot's record breaking activities, and apart from some hill climb successes in 1914, the company played little further part in sport until 1930.

The Georges Roesch Era

In 1916 George Brown left Talbot for Coventry Premier, and was succeeded as chief engineer by Swiss-born Georges Roesch (1891–1969) who had gained plenty of experience working for Grégoire, Delaunay-Belleville, Renault and Daimler. His first design for Talbot was a 1750cc single-ohc car called the A12, which never went into production. This was because of major changes in company ownership just after the war. The Earl of Shrewsbury and his partner Oddenino sold their holdings in Talbot to the Darracq company which, although Paris based, was British owned. Shortly afterwards Darracq bought up Sunbeam, forming Sunbeam-Talbot-Darracq Motors Ltd. There was no immediate call for new Talbot designs; the prewar 15 and 25/50hp models were carried on, though there was no longer a sporting model of the latter, and for a small car Talbot used the 970cc Darracq which was fitted with a Talbot radiator and sold as the 8/18. It had an ohv engine and a lively performance, although economy in its construction was evident by a gearbox of only three speeds and lack of a differential. It was at its best as a 2-seater, but customers wanted 4-seats and even closed bodywork, so Roesch enlarged the engine to 1074cc, and lengthened the wheelbase, to make the 10/23. This had a differential, though still only a 3-speed gearbox. These two small Talbots were made from 1923 to 1926, joined by an obscure small six, the 12/30, which used the same cylinder dimensions as the 8/18, and a larger six, the 2538cc 16/50, renamed 18/55 for 1925. The big 25/50 was dropped after 1925, as were the 8/18 and 10/23 the following year, making way for Roesch's most important contribution to Talbot's history.

The 14/45 and its Descendants

Talbot was at a very low ebb in 1926, with out of date models which were barely selling at all. Had the new model not been a success the marque would almost certainly have disappeared; as it was it became more popular than its designer or makers could have hoped. The 14/45 was a small six of the type that was becoming fashionable, and used the same stroke (95mm) as the 12/30, but with a larger bore to give a capacity of 1665cc. The reciprocating parts were very light; the pushrods were slimmer than normal and yet very strong. Their resemblance to knitting needles was not coincidental, for they were made by a Birmingham needle factory. The light components permitted an unusually high engine speed for a touring car, 4500rpm, at which speed output was 41bhp. Advanced features of the design included the lubrication of the gearbox (now a 4-speed) by warm engine oil, and an oil pressure warning light in place of a gauge. The 14/45 was in no way a sports car, so customers were quite happy with a top speed of around 62mph (100km/h). Bodies were mostly open two or 4-seaters, or fabric saloons. The 14/45 was made up to 1932, when it was renamed the 65, and as such production continued to 1935. A total of 11,851 were made.

In 1929 a short-chassis 14/45 called the Scout appeared, and in 1930 a new 2276cc engine was dropped into a Scout chassis to make the 90 sports model. The same engine was used in the 14/45 chassis to make the 75 which carried a wide variety of saloon and coupé bodies, and was made up to 1935. Production was 2757, of which the first 119 chassis were called 70s; the name was changed because the car was capable of 75mph (120km/h). The 90 was made in much smaller numbers, only 216 from 1930 to 1933, but it was the car with which Talbot made a dramatic return to motor sport.

The Talbot 90s were prepared for and entered in competitions by Fox & Nicholl of Tolworth, Surrey. They and their successors the 105s were remarkable for their quietness compared with such thunderous monsters as the Blower Bentleys and Mercedes-Benz SSKs, and their reliability. Talbot 90s were 3rd and 4th in the 1930 Le Mans race, and took first three places in their class in the TT and in the 500 Mile Race at Brooklands.

For 1931 the engine was enlarged to 2969cc, giving 140bhp in competition form. These cars were known as the 105s, and among the achievements of the Fox & Nicholl team were 2nd in the Brooklands 500, 3rd at Le Mans and in the Irish GP, 4th in the TT, and 1-2-3 in the 3-litre class of the Brooklands Double Twelve. More successes followed in 1932, including 3rd again at Le Mans. Fox & Nicholl also entered the cars in the Alpine Trials, winning Glacier and Alpine Cups in 1931, 1932 and 1934.

Like the 90, the 105 was available with a variety of touring bodies, open and closed, including a fastback Airline saloon. Top speed of a touring 105 was around 84mph (135km/h). The final development of the Roesch Talbots was the 110, whose engine was enlarged to 3377cc giving a top speed of over 93mph (150km/h). The frame was a double dropped design, though the wheelbase was the same 120in (3050mm) as the original 14/45. Also unchanged from the 14/45

NATIONAL MOTOR MUSEUM

ROESCH, GEORGES HENRI (1891–1969)

Georges Henri Roesch was a meticulous engineer who loved mechanical precision but also had a much broader understanding of engineering. He was always in favour of technological advance, but never forgot his responsibility in terms of making a profit, which meant that cost was constantly on his mind.

He was born in Geneva on 15 April 1891, the son of a German-born blacksmith, wagon repairman, and bicycle racer, and his French-born wife. His father's business branched out into auto repair work when motoring came to the Rhône, Savoy, Vaud, and Valais regions. His first motoring experience dated from 1897 when he rode, at the age of 6, with his father in a Benz he had repaired. He was strictly brought up, attending local schools and serving an apprenticeship in his father's shop, finally graduating from the College of Geneva. He set off for Paris at the age of 18, his desire for personal independence reinforcing the sheer pluck of his venture.

He joined Automobiles Grégoire at Poissy, where he soon demonstrated that there was nothing he could learn on the shop floor, and was put to work in the drawing office. He served briefly as a draughtsman with Delaunay-Belleville before securing employment with Renault in 1911. At that time the Billancourt works were terribly busy with all kinds of projects, and full of engineering talent. He met Serre, Viet, de Ram, and others, all working in an environment of speed and productivity. A little over three years later, he felt he had learned all there was to learn from Renault.

He had seen British cars on the streets of Paris and was impressed with some of them: Sunbeam, Crossley, Daimler, Wolseley, and Napier. Through business connections, he made the acquaintance of Henry W. Watts, chief engineer of the Coventry Chain Co., who promised to smooth his way into Britain's motor industry. Georges left Renault and arrived in England with his eyes wide open and little more, just as he had arrived in Paris in 1909. The Watts family gave him a home as well as finding him a place in the drawing office of the Daimler Co. What they could not have known was that in World

War I, Daimler's production would have very little to do with cars, but everything to do with military tractors and trucks, tank engines, shells, and aircraft engines. Roesch felt stifled.

Suddenly in 1916, Clement Talbot Ltd put an advertisement in the newspapers for a chief engineer. At 25, Roesch had the temerity to apply for the job – and he got it. He had no great fluency in French or German, and a profoundly flawed knowledge of English when he came to Barlby Road. In view of his limited use of words, he had to let his drawing board speak for him. The best engine designers had one thing uppermost in their minds in 1916, and it was a more powerful aircraft engine. Daringly, Roesch took the approach that multi-row radials, W-engines, and X-engines, created more problems than they solved, and proposed an engine with axial pistons working in two circles of nine cylinders, aiming at 600hp from more than 50,000cc at a theoretical 1300rpm, within a compact and lightweight package. Prototypes were built and demonstrated to the War Office, but no orders came through.

A year later, there was no doubt about the outcome of the war, and Roesch turned his attention to postwar cars. He designed a 1750cc 4-cylinder model called the A.12 with a single rear passenger's seat and enough technical innovations to result in a flow of patent applications. He filed them in his own name only, but the Clement Talbot directors insisted that all the rights belonged to the company. They settled on a compromise–joint filing–but full trust was never re-established between Roesch and his employers.

Bad feelings got worse when the A.12 never made it into production. This was due to the company's inclusion in the S.T.D. combine, formed in 1920 to merge Clement Talbot Ltd of London with Sunbeam of Wolverhampton and Darracq of Suresnes. An initial plan for Darracq and Talbot to produce the same cars to designs by Owen Clegg was abandoned in favour of a new plan by Louis Coatalen to mount new ohv engines of his design in all models of all three makes.

Impressed with Roesch's work on the 4-cylinder units, Coatalen agreed to leave him in charge of those, while engines for the new 6-cylinder Talbot 12/30 would be designed by Darracq engineers in Paris. In fact, Roesch was himself detailed to the Suresnes drawing office from 1923 to 1925.

Back in London, Roesch created the Talbot 14/45, which went into production in 1926 and lived on to 1935. This compact 6-cylinder model stemmed from Roesch's idea of building a car that was like a Rolls-Royce 20/25 in terms of refinement, quality, and performance, but half the size, half the weight, and half the price.

During his period in Paris, Roesch had begun filing his patents in the name of Henry Watts, in whom he had complete trust, to keep the rights away from the STD combine, and this arrangement proved satisfactory, if not highly remunerative.

Fox & Nicholl wanted a competition version of the 14/45 and thus was born, in 1930, the Talbot 90. Roesch went on to create the 105 and 110 before his career was again put in the shade of greater events. The STD combine collapsed and Clement Talbot Ltd was put up for sale. He thought he would stay on when the company was purchased in January 1935, by Rootes Securities Ltd, and planned new models with lightweight frames and independent suspension, taking the best of the existing Talbot engine range. He even designed an in-line 8-cylinder 4503cc ohv engine for Sunbeam in 1935, planned for installation in a Humber-based chassis. But it was vetoed for production, and he never designed another engine for Rootes, although he stayed on until 1937. But when Rootes took a Hillman Aero Minx and a Humber Snipe, fitted Talbot radiator shells, and called them Sunbeam-Talbots, he resigned in disgust.

He joined Power Jets Ltd in 1942 to work on gas turbines and their gear systems for Frank Whittle. Two years later he became chief mechanical engineer at the National Gas Turbine Establishment. As late as 1958 he was an official advisor to the Ministry of Supply on small industrial gas turbines. He died in November 1969.

JPN

Further Reading
Georges Roesch and the Invincible Talbot, Anthony Blight,
Grenville, 1970.

1931 Talbot (i) 75 Cheriton saloon by Martin Walter.
NICK BALDWIN

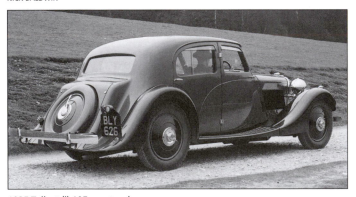

1935 Talbot (i) 105 sports saloon.
NICK BALDWIN

1936 Talbot (i) Ten saloon.
NICK BALDWIN

was the quarter-elliptic rear suspension These later Talbots had Wilson pre-selector gearboxes and 'traffic clutches', which advanced the gear selector one notch each time the clutch was depressed. Thus the lever needed to be used for downward changes only. Apart from the sporting 90, 105 and 110, there was the 95 which used a detuned 105 engine in the double dropped frame, and the limousine, the only one of the family to have a longer wheelbase (136in/3454mm). As the name implies, this was available with formal coachwork only, and a choice of 2969 or 3377cc engines. To allow a low seating position the rear axle was a double reduction unit originally designed for the Talbot ambulance, of which 216 were made between 1930 and 1937, powered by 75,95 or 110 engines. Production of the other Talbots was 806 95s, 335 105s and 154 110s.

The Rootes Takeover

In the spring of 1935 S.T.D. Motors fell into the hands of the receiver, from whom they were bought by the Rootes Group. The classic Talbots were continued, at any rate in name, to 1937, but they were mostly assembled from parts already to hand. As well as the 110 and the limousine, there was a 105 Speed which used a 105 engine in the 110's double dropped frame. By 1936 cost cutting measures were creeping in; the 75 lost its pre-selector gearbox to a synchromesh unit with unpleasantly wide ratios, and the 105 lost its aluminium finned brake drums. The last of the real Talbots was the 3½-litre, essentially a 110 with softer springing and a Humber synchromesh gearbox, though the preselector could be had for £25 extra. It was made with an attractive range of bodies up to the end of the 1937 season.

At the 1935 Olympia Show Rootes launched their new Talbot Ten, a pretty looking little car with styling by Ted White which echoed that of the 110. The engine and chassis, though, were from the Hillman Minx, albeit Georges Roesch extracted an additional 10bhp with improved combustion chambers and a higher compression ratio. Saloon, drophead coupé and sports tourer bodies were offered in the Ten, advertised as 'Britain's Most Exclusive Light Car'. 1748 were made up to 1938, in which year wire wheels were replaced by discs concealing Hillman pressed steel wheels. At the 1938 Show the Talbot Ten

still 'invincible'...for speed, comfort, endurance

The lessons of over 30 years successful racing experience bear full fruit to-day in Talbot's traditional speed, comfort and endurance.
As long ago as 1904 Talbot shattered 5 World's records and they have been achieving successes ever since . . . motorists expect this of Talbot . . . no wonder they talk of Talbot's brilliant engineering and of Talbot workmanship.

TALBOT

TRUE TO TRADITION

The Talbot '75' Special Sports Saloon £565

C L E M E N T   T A L B O T   L T D . ,   L O N D O N ,   W . 1 0
WORLD EXPORTERS: ROOTES LTD., DEVONSHIRE HOUSE, PICCADILLY, LONDON, W.1

BUY A CAR MADE IN THE UNITED KINGDOM

1927 Talbot (ii) 20/98 tourer by Jarvis.
NATIONAL MOTOR MUSEUM

1930 Talbot (ii) Type K75 cabriolet.
NICK GEORGANO

1938 Talbot (ii) 15CV cabriolet.
NICK GEORGANO

1939 Talbot (ii) Lago SS sports car at Goodwood in 1954.
NATIONAL MOTOR MUSEUM

reappeared as the Sunbeam-Talbot, and the Talbot name died, though the cars continued to be made at the Barlby Road factory until the outbreak of war. The only other Talbot in 1938 was the 3-litre, a combination of Talbot coachwork with Humber Snipe mechanical units, which also became a Sunbeam-Talbot for 1939. Georges Roesch could not bring himself to work for the new regime with its lower standards, and left at the end of 1938 to join David Brown as chief engineer to the tractor division.

NG

Further Reading
Motoring Entente, Ian Nichols and Kent Karslake, Cassell, 1956.
Georges Roesch and the Invincible Talbot, Anthony Blight, Grenville, 1970.

TALBOT (ii) **(F)** 1919–1959
Automobiles Talbot, Suresnes.
In 1919 the British directors of Darracq began building an automotive empire with the acquisition of the London-based Clément Talbot company, following this up in 1920 by buying two more companies, Sunbeam of Wolverhampton and the London-based commercial vehicle makers W & G du Cros. A large issue of shares was necessary to form the new combine, which was called S.T.D. Motors Ltd.

Also in 1920 the Darracq company was renamed Automobiles Talbot and the former French Darracq cars went under the Talbot name, though in Britain they were generally called Darracqs up to World War II, to avoid confusion with the London-built Talbots.

The first French Talbots were the old Clegg-designed 16 and a new 4½-litre V8 with coil ignition, spiral bevel final drive and front-wheel brakes. In 1922 they brought out a small 4-cylinder car with 970cc ohv engine. This was almost identical to the London-made Talbot 8/18 though the French car did boast a differential. A larger Talbot, with no exact British equivalent, was the DS introduced in 1924. This had a 2120cc 4-cylinder engine and the front-wheel brakes which were standardised across the range from that year. In sports form it had wire wheels and often carried pointed tail bodies. These 4-cylinder Talbots, which were made up to 1928, were strong and reliable cars, and many were still giving good service into the 1950s.

The first of a long line of ohv sixes was announced for 1926. Made in various sizes from 1999 to 2867cc, they were produced up to the mid–1930s with, at first, 3-speed gearboxes and magneto ignition. Coil ignition appeared on the 1928 2-litre M67, and four speeds were generally adopted by 1930. Apart from the sporting DS most Talbots of this era had wooden wheels which gave them a rather heavy appearance. After 1930 wire wheels and, from 1933, ribbon radiators, brought their looks up to date. The T150 3-litre sports tourer of 1935 looked very like an SS1. In 1930 two straight 8s were added to the range, the 19CV 3536cc Atlantic and the 22CV 3823cc Pacific. These were made in small numbers, the Pacific only to 1932, and the Atlantic to 1935, latterly under the name Superfulgur or T8. A few Pacific engines were supplied to the Belgian makers of the Belga Rise car.

From 1923 Talbot design was in the hands of an Italian trio who had been lured away from Fiat, Vincent Bertarione, Edmond Moglia and Walter Becchia. Their good designs were not helped by the chaotic management of the S.T.D. Group, whose problems were compounded by making too many models which competed against each other. In 1935 S.T.D. collapsed; Sunbeam and British Talbot passed into the hands of the Rootes brothers, and the French Talbot was acquired by the man who had been managing the company for a year, Italian-born Tony Lago. He was helped by finance from his component suppliers who were naturally anxious to see the firm carry on. The existing models were continued for 1935, but with an eye on competitions he commissioned from Becchia a new cylinder head with hemispherical combustion chambers, larger valves and centrally mounted sparking plugs. Valve operation was by cross pushrods from a single camshaft, on the lines of the BMW 328. This 110bhp 3-litre unit became known as the Grand Sport, and the less powerful 80bhp model as the Baby Sport. Wilson pre-selector gearboxes were used on the more expensive models, and all had ifs.

These new models were generally known as Lago Talbots, though this name never had any official blessing. By 1939 Lago Talbots were made in eleven models, with four engine sizes and three wheelbases. Engines ranged from the Minor, a 2323cc 62bhp four, to the 3996cc six used in the Major, Master and Lago Special models. In its most powerful 3-carburettor version this gave 140bhp, increased to 170 and 190bhp after the war. Bodies were cabriolets and

1949 Talbot (ii) Lago Grand Sport coupé by Saoutchik.
NATIONAL MOTOR MUSEUM

2- or 4-door saloons, while the Lago SS, which was supplied in chassis form only, was mostly bodied by Figoni et Falaschi with a very striking streamlined coupé. This was built as a replica by the American firm TLC in the 1990s. Lago Talbots ran in a number of sports car events between 1936 and 1939. The best they could do at Le Mans was 3rd in 1938, but they finished 1-2-3 in the French GP for sports cars in 1937.

During the war Lago was exiled from his factory, but returned in 1946 to launch his postwar range. The smaller engines were not revived, and the only power unit was a 4482cc six derived from the prewar competition engine. The cross pushrods were now operated by twin camshafts mounted high in the block, and output was 170bhp. Factory coachwork was very similar to prewar designs, and consisted of saloons, a 2-door coupé and a cabriolet. A bare chassis was available for special coachwork, and some fine examples, mainly of cabriolets, were built by firms such as Saoutchik, Chapron and Pourtout, as well as Graber in Switzerland and Pinin Farina in Italy. Saoutchik also built two 4-door parade cars, one for French President Vincent Auriol and the other for the Bey of Tunis, and an armoured limousine for King Saud of Saudi Arabia.

Single-seater Lago Talbots were very successful in Grands Prix between 1948 and 1950. Louis Rosier won at Le Mans in 1950 in what was virtually a road-equipped Grand Prix car, and Pierre Levegh led the field for most of the 24 hours in 1952. A replacement for the Lago SS appeared at the 1948 Paris Salon. The wheelbase was shortened from 123in (3130mm) to 104in (2650mm), and power was increased to 190bhp. Its top speed was 124mph (200km/h), which made it probably the fastest road car in the world at the time, though soon to be at least equalled by the much cheaper Jaguar XK120. Price was a great drawback of the postwar Talbots, as was also the French taxation system, which imposed an exorbitant tax on any engine of more than 15CV rating. Up to this figure annual tax was the equivalent of £23, but it then jumped to £79. This severely damaged the home market, and while Belgians and Swiss bought a few Talbots, sales were not sufficient to keep the company going. Talbot made only about 1200 cars between 1947 and 1953 compared with an annual prewar figure of 1000. Their best year was 1950, with 433 cars delivered.

In an attempt to beat the tax threshold Tony Lago brought out the 15CV Baby in 1949. This used a new short-stroke 2690cc 4-cylinder engine in a shorter chassis and with a 4-door saloon body styled on the lines of the bigger cars. Unfortunately it was underpowered and rough; one critic said that 'it rode like a brick and sounded and felt like a 5-ton truck'. The Baby did a lot of harm to Talbot's reputation just when they could have done with a good, cheaper car to

back up the expensive big sixes. For its size the Baby was not particularly cheap either, at 1,300,700 francs when a 15CV Citroën could be had for 754,000 francs.

Automobiles Talbot went into liquidation in 1951, but were soon rescued by outside financial interests. New models were launched, which had fresh slab-sided 4-door saloon bodies on identical chassis, the choice of engines being the 2690cc Baby or 4482cc Record. With a heavier body the Baby was more underpowered than ever, and anyway sales of all luxury French cars were dropping drastically. In 1951 Talbot sold only 80 cars, less than 20 per cent of their 1950 figure, and thereafter they were lucky to sell one a week.

In 1955 Tony Lago produced what was to be his final model which replaced the Baby and Record. The Grand Sport was a 2-door coupé, much more up to date than its predecessors, with a new, shorter chassis and a ZF gearbox to replace the old Wilson pre-selector. The engine was the 4½-litre six from the Record boosted to 200bhp, and top speed was 118mph (190km/h). With really good looks it should have sold at least as well as its forebears, but its price was against it – 2,775,000 francs when a Jaguar X120 sold in France for 1,900,000 francs. Lago next tried a smaller version of the Baby engine (2491cc), but performance was inevitably lower and the price was still more than 2 million francs. No more than 70 Grand Sports with both engines were sold from 1953 to 1955. Lago desperately needed a more powerful engine; for the first time he went to an outside manufacturer. After trying a Raymond Mays-converted British Ford Zephyr 2½-1itre six he chose a 2476cc BMW V8 which developed 125bhp. The engine apart, the new car was almost identical to the Grand Sport. Launched at the 1957 Salon, only 12 of these Lago Americas were made. A large part of the Talbot factory was let out to other firms, notably Hotchkiss and Velam, makers of the French-built Isetta.

The 1958 Salon was Talbot's last. Lago had sold out to Simca, and a coupé in the familiar style was shown, but it was on the Simca stand, and under the bonnet was a 2158cc side-valve V8 from Simca, the old small-block Ford V8. Power was sadly down at only 95bhp, and one wonders why Simca gave it a stand space, for it clearly had no hope of sales.

The final car to bear the Talbot name (until the revival of the 1970s) was a curious coupé on a Simca Aronde chassis, designed by the American stylist Virgil Exner and built by Simca apprentices. Called the Talbot Star Six, it appeared at the 1959 Salon.

NG

Further Reading
Talbot, Jacques Borge and Nicolas Viasnoff, Éditions Henri Veyrier, 1980.

1981 Talbot (iii) Tagora 2.2GL saloon.
NICK BALDWIN

1983 Talbot (iii) Samba cabriolet.
TALBOT

1983 Talbot (iii) Alpine GLS hatchback.
TALBOT

TALBOT (iii) (F/GB/E) 1979–1986
Automobiles Talbot, Poissy, Seine et Oise.
Chrysler UK Ltd, Ryton-on-Dunsmore, Coventry and Linwood, Glasgow.
Chrysler Espana SA, Madrid.
The Talbot name was revived by Peugeot after their purchase of Chrysler's European operations in 1978. These consisted of the former Simca plant at Poissy, the Chrysler UK operations at Ryton-on-Dunsmore, near Coventry and at Linwood in Scotland, and Chrysler Espana in Spain. Four models, the Sunbeam, Avenger, Horizon and Alpine, were inherited from the Chrysler range. Of these, the Sunbeam and Avenger were made only in the British factories, the Horizon and Alpine in both Britain and France, and also in Spain where two older Simca designs, the 1200 and the 180, were carried on for a few years under the Talbot name.

The Sunbeam was a 3-door hatchback based on a shortened Avenger floorpan, with three engine options, a 928cc single-ohc, which was an enlarged Imp unit, or pushrod ohvs of 1295 or 1598cc as used in the Avenger. A more sporting version was the 1600TI with twin-carburettor 1598cc engine giving 100bhp and 105mph (169km/h), but the really hot Sunbeam was the Lotus. This was built as a rally

homologation special in the mould of the Ford Escort RS models or Vauxhall Chevette HS2300, and like these became a popular road car. The engine was a 2174cc 16-valve twin-ohc Lotus giving 150bhp, mated to a ZF 5-speed gearbox. Apart from the engine and transmission, and improved suspension and brakes, the car was a stock Sunbeam. Its chief drawback was its price, for at just under £7000 it was over £1000 more expensive than the Ford or Vauxhall. Although Lotus was contracted by Talbot to supply 4500 engines over three years, only 2308 Sunbeam-Lotuses were made.

They made a substantial, though brief, mark on the rally scene; in 1980 24-year old Henry Toivonen became the youngest driver to win a World Championship event (the RAC), and in 1981 Talbot took the Championship with one win and four second places. The team consisted of Toivonen, Russell Brookes, Guy Frequelin and, from Talbot-Sweden, Stig Blomqvist. The company withdrew at the end of the season, intending to develop a new Group B car for the mid–1980s. This never appeared as a Talbot, but the Peugeot 205 Turbo 16 carried the parent company's flag high during 1984–86.

The Sunbeam was made at the Scottish factory at Linwood, near Glasgow, which had been built for Hillman Imp manufacture. After many problems this was closed in 1981, ending production of the Sunbeam after 105,847 of the basic models and 10,113 1500TIs had been made. The other British factories at Ryton and Stoke, both near Coventry, concentrated on the Alpine and assembling Horizons from French-built kits. The Horizon was a 5-door hatchback with choice of four petrol engines and one diesel. It was made up to 1986, when replaced by the Peugeot 309. The Avenger was dropped in 1981, but the Alpine was continued, and joined in 1980 by the Solara which was the same car with a boot in place of the hatchback. These also gave way to the Peugeot 309. A larger car which was badged only as a Talbot was the Tagora, a 6-light saloon with choice of 2155cc Peugeot ohc four, 2304cc turbo diesel or 2664cc V6 Douvrin engine made by the Peugeot-Renault-Volvo group. The anonymous-looking Tagora never really caught on, and only 19,000 were made from 1981 to the end of 1983.

More successful, though never really a big seller, was the Samba, a 3-door hatchback which used the same floorpan and running gear as the short-wheelbase Peugeot 104. Engines were Peugeot's 954, 1124, or 1360cc, and a convertible was available as well as the hatchback. Sambas were made in France and Spain, but not in Britain. They were dropped in 1986, along with other Talbot models. The only other car to carry the Talbot name was the former Matra-Simca Rancho estate car, which was badged as a Talbot-Matra up to 1984 when it was discontinued.
NG

TALON (US) c.1977–1982
Talon Automotive Products, Panorama City, California.
The Talon kit car was a development of the Matula, a 2-seat kit car that found a new life in Holland after being discontinued in the US. While the Matula was only a 2-seater, the Talon was a 2+2, which made it unusual among VW-based kits. The extra room was courtesy of using the standard-length VW chassis and enclosing it with a tall, wedge-shaped body. A steel subframe strengthened the chassis, and access was via a liftable canopy that pivoted up jet-fighter style from the back. It was designed by Ed Matula and could be purchased in kit, partially-assembled or complete form.
HP

T.A.M. (F) 1908–c.1925
Sté de Travaux Mécanique Automobile, Courbevoie, Seine.
H. Gendron, Boulogne-sur-Seine.
This company began by making a light car with 12hp 4-cylinder engine. By 1913 three models, a Chapuis-Dornier-engined 10/12hp with vee-radiator, a Decolange-engined 12/14hp with flat radiator, and a 16/20hp, were listed. The postwar range was made up of the 10/12 and 12/14, the latter now powered by a Sergant engine, which was the successor to Decolange. Some took part in touring car races, and they were also made in taxicab and delivery van forms.
NG

TAMA (J) 1947–1951
1947–1949 Tokyo Electric Motorcar Co., Tachikawa.
1949–1951 Tama Electric Motorcar Co., Tachikawa.

The Tama electric car achieved some popularity during a period of acute shortage of petrol in postwar Japan. The first was the E4S-47, a 2-door saloon based on the contemporary Datsun. It was followed in 1948 by two new saloons with improved performance and all-enveloping slab-sided styling. Called the Junior and the Senior, the latter had a 5-seater body and 5.5hp motor giving a top speed of 35mph (56km/h) and a range of 125 miles (200km/h) per charge. When petrol supplies improved, Tama abandoned electric cars at the end of 1951 and were re-formed as Prince Motors, launching the PRINCE car in 1952.

NG

TAMAG (D) 1933

E.W. Taschner GmbH, Krefeld.

This was an aerodynamic 3-wheeled coupé powered by a 200cc engine driving the front wheels. It was one of several German cars designed to take advantage of tax concessions on 3-wheelers. When this was withdrawn, the main reason for buying a 3-wheeler disappeared.

HON

TAMM (D) 1922

This was a cyclecar powered by an air-cooled 2-cylinder engine, with friction transmission and shaft drive to the right-hand rear wheel.

HON

TAMPLIN (GB) 1919–1925

1919–1923 Tamplin Motors, Staines, Middlesex.
1924–1925 Tamplin Motors, Chertsey, Surrey.

Edward A. Tamplin was a member of the well-known Sussex brewing family, and ran a garage near Staines station. In 1919 he was agent for the CARDEN tandem cyclecar, and before the end of the year he had acquired a licence to manufacture them. They were powered by a 980cc air-cooled V-twin JAP engine mounted on the side of the body, and driving a Sturmey-Archer 3-speed gearbox with belt final drive to the rear axle. The seating was more '1½' than 2-seater, for the passenger seat was very narrow, and his, or her, legs extended beside the driver. Bill Boddy, editor of *Motor Sport*, rode in one in the 1953 London-Exeter Trial, and found it exceedingly uncomfortable. The body was made of fibreboard impregnated with linseed oil, supplied by Sundeala of Sunbury, and the bodies were made by three separate concerns at Ascot, Ashford and Teddington. The top of the bonnet was formed by the fuel tank.

Production ran at between 6 and 12 cars per week from the end of 1919, and a few had Blackburne or M.A.G. engines. In 1924 Tamplin moved to Chertsey, and in October of that year he announced a new cyclecar with front-mounted JAP engine, proper bonnet and dummy radiator, and side by side seating. The body was still of fibreboard, although one sports model was made with aluminium body. Production at Chertsey was much lower than at Staines. Although six a week were made at best, this lasted only from the end of 1924 into the first half of 1925. Edward Tamplin claimed that he made 1896 cars in all, but the actual figure may have been somewhat less. He later became a dealer for Chevrolet, and then Bedford, trucks.

NG

Further Reading
'Fragments on Forgotten Makes, the Tamplin', Bill Boddy,
Motor Sport, May 1962.

TAND'CAR (F) c.1937–1941

Automobiles Tand'Car, Saint-Maur, Seine.

Tand'Car started, like Mochet, as a maker of pedal cars. In 1937 it listed three pedal models, the Evasion at 4995 francs, the Camping at 6745 francs and the Labeur with 2-speed gears at 7500 francs. For only 500 francs more one could get a powered version with 175cc engine, which seems good value. However, three electric models cost 17,500–18,500 francs, which was very expensive when compared with the cheapest Simca Cinq at 13,980 francs. These electrics were still listed in the 1940 catalogue, at the same prices, but the company said that as it was a new type of vehicle, not covered under the law, it could not give a firm assurance that no driving licence was needed. This would indicate that the company had not sold many. Helpfully, it said that as the police were ignorant of the car's classification, they were content to turn a blind eye. The electric Tand'Car had chain drive, a top speed of only 12mph (19km/h) and a fabric body.

NG

1925 T.A.M. Type AL74 2-litre sports car.
NATIONAL MOTOR MUSEUM

1948 Tama Junior electric saloon.
NATIONAL MOTOR MUSEUM

1921 Tamplin 8/10hp cyclecar.
NICK BALDWIN

TANKETTE (GB) 1919–1920

Ronald Trist & Co. Ltd, Watford, Hertfordshire.
Tankette Ltd, London.

The Tankette was an unusual cyclecar powered by a 2¾hp single-cylinder 2-stroke Union engine driving a 2-speed Burman gearbox, with chain final drive to the twin rear wheels which were mounted so close together as to give the impression

1920 Tankette 3-wheeler.
MICHAEL WORTHINGTON-WILLIAMS

1907 Tarrant 14/16hp 2-seater.
NATIONAL MOTOR MUSEUM

of a single wheel. The frame consisted of flat steel strips on either side of ash members, while the front axle consisted of concentric steel tubes which enabled the wheels to be pushed inwards, allowing the car to pass through a 3ft doorway.

NG

TARANTULA see NOVA

TARCHINI (I) 1966

The Jaguar distributor for the north of Italy hoped to disseminate copies of the Marcello Gandini-designed Bertone FT coupé, which used Jaguar 420 components. However, this imposing show car remained a one-off.

CR

TARKINGTON (US) 1922–1923

Tarkington Motor Car Co., Rockford, Illinois.
Despite an auspicious start in the planning stage and its seemingly favourable debut, the Tarkington vanished from the marketplace before even entering it. J. Arthur Tarkington was one of many entering the automotive milieu at the time and his product was a good looking car with lithe lines and set off with wire wheels. The car was introduced at Chicago during Auto Show Week in early 1923. Surprisingly, the Tarkington never exceeded its six pilot models and the company was out of business less than six months later. The reason for its failure appears to have been the waning interest of its previously enthusiastic backers. The Tarkington prototypes were all 5-seater touring cars, powered by an in-house 6-cylinder ohv engine developing 54bhp at 2600rpm and a displacement of

4257cc. Carburettor was by Rayfield and ignition by Elco. Tragically, J. Arthur Tarkington was shattered by the failure of the car and not long afterwards he disappeared. He was never heard from again. None of the six prototypes survives.

KM

TARRANT (AUS) 1899–1907

Tarrant Motor & Engineering Co., South Melbourne, Victoria.
Harley Tarrant started an interest in cars via an engine for driving farm and mine machines which could be transported by pack saddle. His first car, with a 2-cylinder engine of his own make, was unsuccessful. Then Mr O'Farrell returned from a European trip with the Benz agency and, with a similar 6hp engine, a car was built, with belt primary and chain final drive. This found a buyer in 1901 and gave years of service. The agreement with O'Farrell to handle sales had lapsed by 1902, when a car with a 5hp horizontal engine, 3-speed gearbox and a live axle appeared. Howard Lewis and Stewart Ross (formerly with Argyll) had joined Tarrant, bringing with them managerial and designing skills. Orders for one 25hp and two 12hp cars were taken in 1903. These were models with pair-cast cylinders and mechanical valve operation. A twin-cylinder 'balance' engine was fitted to a high-wheeled car for country use and the 4-cylinder powered an imposing convertible brougham.

In 1905 a smaller 8hp twin, of 1440cc, with separate cylinders, appeared and was joined the following year by a 16hp 4-cylinder of similar design, displacing 3192cc and installed in a long wheelbase chassis. This form of engine and chassis became the regular production, although a 12hp, with a White & Poppe engine was seen in 1907.

Marine engines were also made but the high cost of local car building could not be sustained and was discontinued at that time. It is believed that at least 12 vehicles were produced while the marketing of imported types became a big operation, particularly after the Ford franchise was accepted. The volume of Ford work grew rapidly, especially bodybuilding and the subsidiary company, Melbourne Motor Body Works, became a major operator and was one of the many in the group which traded until the onset of the Depression.

MG

TASCO (US) 1948

The American Sports Car Co., Hartford, Connecticut.
Gordon Buehrig was a legendary stylist, having designed the Cord 810 and Auburn 851, when he joined a consortium to develop an American sports car. The prototype was built on a shortened 1948 Mercury chassis, and a modified Mercury V8 was used for power. The body was radical for its day, with an enclosed aircraft-style cockpit and the first use of two removable Targa style tops. It had fibreglass front mudguards that turned with the wheels. In order to reduce the unsprung weight, the wheels were cast from magnesium by Dow Corning. The body was built by the Derham Body Co. Although the project showed much promise, the partners ran out of money and Tasco closed its doors after making only the one prototype. The removable roof panels later showed up on the 1968 Corvette.

HP

TASSO (I) 1998 to date

Tasso Engineering, Atessa (CH).
The Tasso ('badger') was one of a new wave of Italian microcars taking advantage of tax and licensing advantages. Innovative styling was realised using computer design techniques. Two engines were offered: air-cooled single-cylinder Yanmar 296cc or a Lombardini 505cc 2-cylinder diesel, while a further offering was an electric version. The standard transmission was variable automatic and the suspension was by MacPherson struts at the front and longitudinal arms at the rear.

CR

TATA (IND) 1998 to date

Tata Engineering & Locomotive Co. Ltd, Mumbai.
As the name implies, Tata was a large engineering conglomerate which entered vehicle production with licence built Mercedes-Benz trucks and buses in 1954. They went under the name of Tata-Mercedes-Benz up to 1971 and plain Tata thereafter. In the 1980s they began to make pick-ups and Land Rover-like 4 × 4 vehicles, made in short- and long-wheelbase forms, and their first passenger car

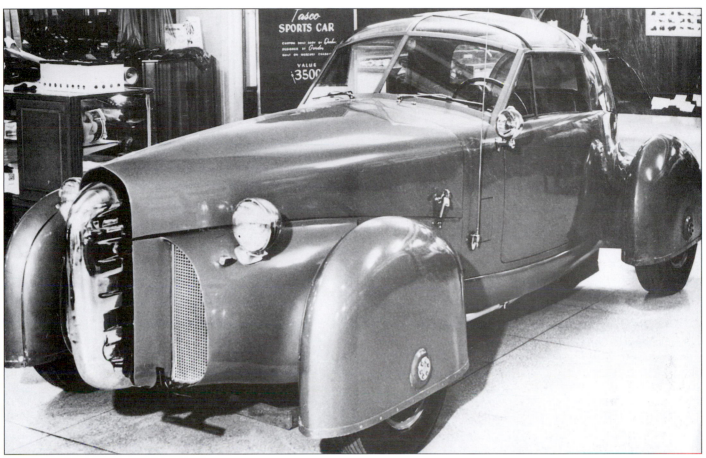

1948 Tasco coupé.
NICK GEORGANO

appeared in February 1998. Known as the Mint, later Indica, it was a 5-door hatchback powered by a transverse 1405cc 4-cylinder engine driving the front wheels. It was available in petrol or diesel forms. At the 2000 Geneva Show Tata announced a 2-seater sports car in the Mazda MX-5 class, but with front-wheel drive. It was called the Aria, and was planned to have a 1.8- or 2-litre engine and sequential gearbox.

NG

TATE (CDN) 1912–1913
Tate Electrics Ltd, Windsor, Ontario.
Tate Electrics was a subsidiary of the Tate Accumulator Co. of Canada which made the most efficient and powerful battery on the market. In 1912 it decided to go into the car business, rather than just selling its batteries to other manufacturers. It showed two unfinished prototypes at the 1912 Toronto and Montreal Shows, and during the following year it had a range of two passenger cars and four trucks for sale. The cars were a coupé at $3600 and a roadster at $2700. Both had shaft drive and a 108in (2741mm) wheelbase. They were apparently very good of their kind, but falling popularity of the electric car led to them being dropped before the end of 1914.

NG

TATIN (F) 1899
V. Tatin, Paris.
Victor Tatin built a light 3-wheeler powered by a 2.5hp horizontal single-cylinder engine.

NG

TATONKA PRODUCTS (US) 1998 to date
Tatonka Products, Salt Lake City, Utah.
The Bummer was a fibreglass-bodied full-sized replica of the AMG Hummer sports-utility vehicle. It was based on a 1973–1991 General Motors truck, Blazer

1999 Tata Indica hatchback.
TATA

1999 Tata Safari 4 x 4 estate car.
TATA

1923 Tatra T.10 sports tourer.
NATIONAL MOTOR MUSEUM

1923 Tatra T.11 tourer.
NATIONAL MOTOR MUSEUM

1932 Tatra T.57 cabriolet.
NATIONAL MOTOR MUSEUM

or Suburban chassis and running gear. They could be ordered with a variety of engines and interior options and were sold in kit form.

HP

TATRA (CS) 1919–1998

1919–1927 Koprivnicka vozovka, a.s., Koprivnice.
1927–1936 Tatra, a.s. pro stavbu automobilu a zeleznicnich vozu, Koprivnice.
1936–1945 Zavody Ringhoffer-Tatra, a.s., Koprivnice.
1946–1990 Tatra, narodni podnik, Koprivnice.
1990–1998 Tatra, a.s., Koprivnice.
In 1918, the Austro-Hungarian Empire was no more, Czechoslovakia was a newly created country, and the Moravian town of Nesselsdorf had become Koprivnice. The Nesselsdorfer Wagenbau was now called Koprivnicka vozovka (Koprivnice

Wagon Works). The name TATRA replaced the NW marque for the first time on 29 March 1919. The Tatra name comes from the High Tatra Mountains (Vysoke Tatry) in Slovakia where one day in the Winter of 1918–19 an NW car featuring 4-wheel brakes was tested. This involved passing a sleigh on the snow-covered road and surprising its occupants as to how an automobile could cope in such conditions, prompting a statement to the effect of 'This is a car for the Tatras!'.

Tatra management was changed, Erhard Kobel was replaced by Leopold Pasching, and Hans Ledwinka returned to Tatra in 1921 for good. He was installed in the position of chief engineer. In 1923 the construction of a new factory for car manufacture was completed, and production of the new Tatra T 11 was begun. The T 11, designed by H. Ledwinka, was the first car constructed as a Tatra from the outset, and was the 'people's car'. It was a relatively small car and actually quite progressive in its design. Featuring irs using swing axles and torsionally rigid backbone chassis construction (the drive-shaft ran inside a central tube to which components were bolted), it offered a comfortable ride. Its rear wheels were powered by a front-mounted 1056cc air-cooled 2-cylinder 12bhp engine, and it held a top speed of 56mph (90km/h). Until 1926 3540 T 11s were produced, when it was replaced by the evolutionary T 12, which was very similar except for an upgrade 4-wheel brakes. 7525 of the T 12s were sold until 1933. About 500 of these were assembled by the Hungarian Unitas company between 1928 and 1933.

In 1926 appeared a larger T 17 touring car constructed on the lines of the T 11/T 12 but with fully independent front and rear suspension. The engine was a 1930cc ohc water-cooled 6-cylinder with an output of 35bhp, capable 75mph (121km/h). Later on, it was joined by the T 17/31 differing only in its engine which was increased to 2310cc in capacity and 40bhp in output. Production of both models ceased in 1928 with 205 and 450 cars. Also in 1926 the production of the T 30, powered by an air-cooled 1678cc 4-cylinder 35bhp engine, started and 900 cars were made until 1933.

In the early 1930s Tatra introduced the T 52, T 54 and T 57 models, all with air-cooled 4-cylinder ohv engines placed in front. The T 52 (1930–1938, 1687 units) had a 1910cc 30bhp engine, while the T 54 (1931–1934, 1510 units) was fitted with a 1462cc 22bhp engine. The T 57 was one of Tatra's most popular models and remained in production until after World War II. Introduced in 1931, the T 57 had a 1154cc 18bhp engine, and in 1936 it was replaced by the T 57a with the same engine but of 20bhp output. The T 57b came in 1938 having a 1256cc 25bhp engine. About 22,000 cars of these types were made until 1949; exact figures are known only for 1946 (1147) and 1947 (1719 cars).

In the 1930s, Tatra had its heyday, with models in all price ranges from the small T 57 cars to the bigger T 75 (1933–1942, 1688cc air-cooled 29bhp ohv 4-cylinder, 4501 units), 6-cylinder T 70 (1931–1932, 3408 c water-cooled 64bhp ohc engine, 50 units) and the T 70a (1934–1936, 3847cc water-cooled 70bhp ohc engine, 70 units).

In 1925 in Frankfurt am Main, Germany, the Deutsche Lizenz-Tatra-Automobile Betriebs GmbH was set up which produced and sold the T 11, T 12 and T 57 cars under the name Detra or Delta. The T 57 and T 75 cars were also built under licence by the German firms of Neue Rohr-Werke (1933–1935, under the name Junior), and Stoewer Werke (1935–1939, as Stoewer Greif Junior).

The glamorous T 80 with 5990cc V 12, 119bhp SV engine and 93mph (150km/h) top speed, embodied the end of a long development line of Tatra models. With this largest model Ledwinka had proved that his original concept of the central tubular chassis and swinging half-axles was suitable for large cars as well as for the small and medium cars. The T 80 belonged to the largest cars: the chassis weight was at 1200kg, but with a spacious body the weight increased to almost 2500kg. The bodies – saloon, cabriolet or a landaulet – were built in the Tatra works, or by Josef Sodomka in Vysoke Myto. Only 25 cars were produced between 1931 and 1935. At the 1933 London Olympia Show the chassis price was £1950, and in Germany the basic price for the whole car was RM 28,500. The first President of the Czechoslovak Republic, T.G. Masaryk, and the Minister of Foreign Affairs, E. Benes, were owners of this Tatra.

Following automobile evolution, and always keeping one step ahead, Tatra started experimenting with car aerodynamics in the early 1930s. Tatra engineers, led by Hans Ledwinka and E. Ubelacker, started working on a small streamlined car with a rear-engine layout in a backbone frame. In 1933, Tatra presented the V 570 prototype (854cc flat-twin, 50mph/80km/h), and although it never came into production, it was used as a study object for the streamlining era which was to come in Tatra. Another streamlined car, although designed outside the Tatra factory, was the T 57 Fitzmaurice, a work of the British Tatra importer Captain D. Fitzmaurice. The T 75-based chassis had a streamlined body designed by Thomas Harrington Ltd of Hove, Sussex. This car was exhibited at the 1933 Olympia Motor Show in London, but no further cars were built.

Tatra started work on an automobile design on which decades of future Tatra cars were based. This car was first presented on 5 March 1934, and was called the Tatra T 77, having the honour of being the world's first serially produced aerodynamically styled automobile powered by an air-cooled rear-mounted engine. The T 77 had a relatively small 2968cc 59bhp engine propelling it to a top speed of over 87mph (140km/h). This massive and roomy 6-seater luxury car had an exceptionally low drag coefficient of about 0.21. The steering wheel was situated centrally at the front, the windshield was slanted at 45 degrees, and there was lots of luggage space above the rear suspension and in the nose.

In 1935 followed the improved T 77a with an extra central headlight, and with a 3377cc 75bhp V8 engine and top speed of 93mph (150km/h). The production of the T 77 and T 77a was very limited, numbering 105 and about 150 respectively.

1936 brought the company yet another name change. Baron Hans von Ringhoffer, the proprietor of the Tatra works since 1923, decided to combine Tatra with his Prague-Smichov wagon factory to create the Ringhoffer-Tatra concern.

The remarkable T 87, Hans Ledwinka's favourite Tatra, also bowed out in 1936 as a direct response to the critics of the previous model's unexceptional handling

1932 Tatra T.80 V12 De Luxe cabriolet.
NICK BALDWIN

abilities. The weight was reduced to 1370kg (a saving of over 400kg), accomplished by mounting a smaller 2968cc 75bhp V8 made of alloy and by decreasing the length of the car (the wheelbase went from 124in to 112in/3150mm to 2850mm). The drag coefficient was 0.36 which was still exceptional in its day. The windshield was flanked by small windows inserted at the A-pillars giving the driver, now

NATIONAL MOTOR MUSEUM

LEDWINKA, HANS (1878–1967)

Hans Ledwinka was one of the most original and logical thinkers ever to work in the motor industry, whose creations in such varied areas as engine design, frame and structures, suspension systems, and aerodynamics attracted worldwide attention.

Born at Klosterneuburg near Vienna on 14 February 1878, he attended the Volksschule der Schulbrüder in Wien-Fünfhaus from 1884 to 1889, and then spent three years in the Bürgerschule. From 1892 to 1895 he worked as an apprentice with Johann Zwiauer, mechanic and toolmaker, who was married to his father's sister. Next, he put in two years of studies at the Werkmeisterschule der Staatsgewerbeschule in Vienna, and then joined the Nesselsdorfer Waggonfabrik as a draughtsman. He played a small part in the design of the first Nesselsdorfer car in 1897, and worked on several other prototypes in 1898–1900.

He thought the Benz-style internal combustion engine was a crude piece of work, and returned to Vienna in 1901 to design steam cars for Professor Richard Knoller and Alexander Friedmann. He changed his mind about the internal combustion engine and returned to Nesselsdorf in 1905. He was the chief designer of their cars until 1916, when the management board cancelled two earlier decisions to leave automobiles alone to concentrate on railway carriages and equipment, and approved a plan to put up a spacious new automobile factory. However, because of World War I, it did not happen.

It was in a bitter mood that he left Nesselsdorf and moved to Steyr, the firearms factory whose management was then (1917) making plans for a postwar future as automobile manufacturers. Drawing heavily on the same designs he had made at Nesselsdorf, he created the first Steyr car in 1918.

When the war came to an end, the Nesselsdorf enterprise came under new management. The car factory plans were taken off the shelf and feelers were made to Ledwinka about returning to Nesselsdorf. It took him until 1921 to get the contract written on his terms. In the meantime, Nesselsdorf had been reorganised as the Tatra-Werke, and he was placed in complete charge of technical matters. He designed the Tatra 11 and 12, then the 30, and a succession of trucks, all the time remaining on the best of terms with the Steyr management and acting as a consultant to Steyr, supplying designs for the Steyr IV, V, and VI.

All Tatra vehicles were designed under his direction up to 1945. He favoured air-cooling for car engines, but alternated between air- and water-cooling for truck engines until about 1939. He took no interest in front-wheel drive, but made a number of designs for rear-engine cars. He embraced wind-tunnel testing and streamlining with great enthusiasm as early as 1932.

He held a government-appointed office during World War II, supervising the engineering and production of military vehicles, which resulted in a 6-year internment in postwar Czechoslovakia, finally regaining his freedom in 1951. He left Czechoslovakia and moved to Steyr, where his son Erich was chief engineer. For some time he acted as an engineering consultant to Robert Bosch AG, and assisted his son with new vehicle projects for Steyr.

He died in Munich on 2 March 1967.

JPN

Further Reading
Great Designers and their Work, edited by Ronald Barker and Anthony Harding, David & Charles, 1970.

1936 Tatra T.57A saloon.
CHRIS BACKLUND

1935 Tatra T.77 V8 saloon.
NATIONAL MOTOR MUSEUM

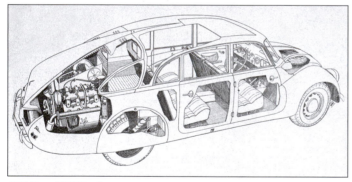

1939 Tatra T.87 V8 saloon.
NICK BALDWIN

1947 Tatra T.2-107 saloon, pre-production model of T.600.
NATIONAL MOTOR MUSEUM

positioned in the conventional fashion, exceptional visibility. The T 87 attained a top speed of 100mph (161km/h), had good acceleration and a fuel consumption of 12–13 l/100km. The company sold 3056 T 87s until 1950. Among their varied customers were racing driver Elizabeth Junek (1939), American novelist John Steinbeck (1947), King Farouk of Egypt (1947), Archbishop Beran of Prague (1948) and Czech President Klement Gottwald (1948).

Erich Ledwinka, one of Hans's sons, who replaced E. Ubelacker as chief engineer, was responsible for the T 97 which looked very much like a scaled-down T 87 except for the missing central headlight, a flat windshield and rear glass split window. A 40bhp 1749cc 4-cylinder unit allowed 81mph (130km/h).

In 1938 Tatra fell under German control due to the annexation of part of Czechoslovakia by the Germans. After the outbreak of World War II in 1939, Tatra was forced to produce military vehicles, only the T 87 was allowed into limited production for civilian use. Production of the T 57 and T 97 was forbidden due to their closeness to Porsche's Volkswagen design. Only 508 examples of the T 97 were produced between 1936 and 1939.

After World War II Tatra found itself stranded behind the Iron Curtain. In 1945 Hans Ledwinka was accused of collaborating with the Nazis and was imprisoned until 1951, when he returned to Austria. The factory was led by chief designer Ing. Julius Mackerle from 1946 onwards. Tatra worked hard to have their new streamlined model, first called T 107, ready for the 1947 Prague Auto salon. The production version was called the T 600 Tatraplan. (Note: After 1946 three figure numbers were used and altered to specific marking. 100 was reserved for goods vehicles, 200 for delivery vans, 300 for railway stock, 400 for trolleybuses, 500 for buses and coaches, 600 for passenger cars, and 800 for special purpose vehicles. 700 was not used.)

The Tatra 600 Tatraplan, with a body based on the T 97, was equipped with a 1952cc 4-cylinder air-cooled engine placed behind the rear axle. The good streamlining (cD 0.32) gave the car a top speed of 81mph (130km/h). More than half of the 4242 Tatraplans produced at Tatra were exported to many countries all over the world. In 1951 production of the Tatraplans was moved to Skoda, Mlada Boleslav, where another 2100 cars were built, for export only, until 1952. Special versions of the Tatraplan include the T 600 Diesel, T 601 Monte Carlo, T 201 ambulance and pick-up, convertible bodied by Sodomka (later given to Stalin for his birthday) and the T 602 Sport.

After production had ceased, there were no more luxury cars being produced in Czechoslovakia. When the centrally planned economy appointed Tatra to be the manufacturer for big automobiles, work started on the Tatra T 603.

The man responsible for the design of the car was again Julius Mackerle, while Jiri Klos was responsible for the engine. Tatra chose to use the 603 engine (2545cc V8 air-cooled ohv, 94bhp) that had already been developed several years ago and tested in the racing single-seater T 607 and sports cars T 602. The Tatra T 603 was unveiled to the public for the first time at the 1955 International six-day motor event in Zlin, and in 1956 it was also exhibited at the International Fair in Brno. Production started in 1957 when the T 603 was rolling out the factory at a speed of 2 cars per day. The T 603 could not be bought by private customers, it was only for Communist officials and Presidents in the Eastern-European countries and even in Cuba. Until 1962 nothing was changed on the car. In that year the engine was changed from the 603F to the 603G (2472cc, 105hp). In 1963 the T603-1, whose total production run had been 5992 cars, was followed by the T 603-2, with 4-headlight unit instead of the T 603 distinctive 3-headlight front. In 1969 the T 603-2 was equipped with disc brakes and cosmetic changes on the body were done. During the 18 years of series production from 1957 to 1975 20,422 cars were built. Special versions of the T 603 include the T 2-603 GTI racing cars, saloon and ambulance prototypes (T 603A), the NSU Ro80-like prototype T 603X, the small racing car T 605, the single-seater Formula 1 T 607, and the racing car Tatra Delfin.

In the late 1960s it became time to start work on the design of a new car to take over the role of flagship for the communist officials. The new model was called the T 613, and was the first Tatra styled outside the Tatra factory. Carrozzeria Vignale of Italy was responsible for the design of the T 613's body and interior. The T 613 did remain faithful to the general layout and unconventional design, and was equipped with a 3495cc air-cooled V8 165hp mounted on top of the rear axle giving the car a top speed of 118mph (190km/h). The T 613 was also intended to be used by government officials in Czechoslovakia and other communist countries. The original Vignale design stayed in production from 1973 to 1980 when the car was updated to the T 613-2, and several updates

1967 Tatra T.603 MkII saloon.
NICK BALDWIN

1989 Tatra T.613 Mk3 saloon.
MOTOKOV

followed during the years with the introduction of the T 613-3, -4 and -5. Production of the Tatra T 613 reached a total of 11,009 cars, having its peak in the late 1970s with over 1000 to 1500 cars produced each year. During the 1980s production decreased to a few hundred cars per year. After the fall of the communist regime in Czechoslovakia sales of the T 613 decreased rapidly. In 1996 only 11 cars were made and Tatra decided to stop its production. Several special versions of the T 613 appeared over the years such as the T 613 Long, Landaulet, ambulances, and first aid vehicles.

On 9 April 1996 the new T 700 was introduced, with the same layout and general body lines as the T 613. The T 700 originated one year earlier, when British designer Geoff Wardle was asked by Tatra to update the the original body structure. The V8 engine had a capacity of 3495cc, power output 200hp, and a really up-to-date powerplant with electronic multipoint fuel injection and a three-way catalytic convertor. Modernised chassis, bodywork with safety features, and the interior with leather upholstery and wooden dash were standard in this car. The T 700s were custom built to meet the exact requirements

of the customers. Howerver, customers were hard to find, and Tatra made only seven cars in 1998, the last in September. The factory was closed, but they would probably make one if anybody asked.

MSH

Further Reading
Tatra. The Legacy of Hans Ledwinka, Ivan Margolius and John G. Henry, SAF (Publishing), Harrow, 1990.
Osobní automobily Tatra 1897–1972 (Tatra passenger cars), Karel Rosenkranz, Tatra, Koprivnice, 1972.
Tatra. Die Geschichte der Tatra Automobile, Wolfgang Schmarbeck, Uhle & Kleimann, Lubbecke, 1989.
Tatra 100 Years. Passenger Cars, Karel Rosenkranz, Motormedia, Prague, 1997.
'Tatra: The constant Czech', B.P.B. de Dube,
Automobile Quarterly, Vol. 7, No. 3.

TAU (I) 1925–1927
Pietro Scaglione, Turin.
This car originated as the RUBINO, the design of which Scaglione took over. Launching the car at the 1925 Geneva Show, he retained the 2297cc 4-cylinder engine, but the L-head side-valve engine was replaced by a T-head layout (old-fashioned for the 1920s) on the touring Tipo 95, and pushrod-ohv on the 90 Sport, which gave 50bhp and a top speed of 75mph (121km/h). All Taus had 4-speed gearboxes and bodies were similar to those of the Lancia Lambda, although they did not have the Lambda's semi-integral construction. About 100 were made.
NG

TAUNTON (i) (US) 1901–1903
Taunton Automobile Co., Taunton, Massachusetts.
This company was managed by Everitt S. Cameron, who had designed the ECLIPSE steam car and would later make cars under his own name. Like the Eclipse, the Taunton had a water-tube boiler and a 3-cylinder engine operating directly on the rear axle. Runabout and tourer bodies were offered. About 25 cars were made and some of them were sold under the Cameron name.
NG

TAUNTON (ii) (US) 1904–1905

Taunton Motor Carriage Co., Taunton, Massachusetts.

Although made in the same factory as the previous Taunton, there was no business connection between the two firms. The Motor Carriage company made a petrol-engined car powered by a 7hp single-cylinder engine, and with a 68in (1726mm) wheelbase. The body was a 2-seater with two folding front seats, and the price was $850. It had steering by vertical tiller and artillery wheels. In 1905 the company was reorganised to make engines for cars and marine purposes.

NG

TAUNTON (iii) (GB/B) 1912–1920

Taunton Cars Ltd; Twickenham, Middlesex; Liége.

This Taunton was named after a man, not a place. John Bernard Taunton designed a cyclecar with 8hp 4-cylinder monobloc engine in 1912, but quickly turned to a more ambitious car, with 2358cc 14.4hp 4-cylinder engine with overhead inlet and side exhaust valves. The underslung frame incorporated all the cross members, sump, lower half of the crankcase and gearbox casing in a single stamping, so it was effectively a metal punt. It had a 3-speed gearbox and underslung worm drive, giving a low appearance. Taunton obviously had good connections, for he secured the bank note maker Sir Evelyn de la Rue as chairman and backer, while shareholders included the Marquess of Anglesey, the Earl of Lytton, the Duke of Rutland and his daughter Lady Diana Manners, later the well-known actress and socialite Lady Diana Cooper. A 1914 advertisement listed her, the Marchioness of Anglesey, the Countess of Lytton and Field-Marshal Lord Kitchener as having ordered Taunton cars.

The cyclecar and four prototypes with 2- or 4-seater bodies were made in a small workshop in Twickenham, but Taunton hoped to have the cars built in the Paisley factory then recently vacated by Arrol-Johnston. When this fell through, he looked abroad and settled on the factory near Liège, where the Hermes car had been made a few years earlier. This had a good complement of machine tools, and a potential capacity of 1500 cars a year. Unfortunately, only two Tauntons had been made and were on their way to England when the German army invaded Belgium and took over the Liège factory. The car was advertised after the war, but the only postwar Taunton was a 1914 model updated with disc wheels and a more modern body. John Taunton's doctor brother used it until well into the 1930s.

NG

Further Reading

'Taunton Cars', Nick Baldwin, *Old Motor*, Vol. 9, No. 6.
'Ahead of its Time', M. Worthington-Williams, *The Automobile*, April 1989.

TAUNUS (D) 1907–1909

Taunus Automobilfabrik GmbH, Frankfurt am Main.

This company was mainly concerned with the manufacture of commercial vehicles, but they offered a single model of passenger car, with 6/12PS proprietary engine. The name Taunus was better known on German Ford cars, being used from 1939 to 1967 and again in the 1980s.

HON

TAURINIA (I) 1902–1908

1902–1907 Stà Taurinia, Turin.
1907–1908 Taurinia Fabbrica Automobili, Turin.

This company began by making light cars with 9.5hp single-cylinder De Dion-Bouton engines and shaft drive. By 1905 a larger car with 10/12hp 4-cylinder Fafnir engine was on offer, and from 1907 a reorganised company made a 14/18hp with a side-valve engine and low-tension magneto ignition.

NG

TAUZIN (F) 1899

Tauzin et Compagnie, Levallois-Perret, Seine.

The Tauzin was a light 2-seater voiturette powered by a 3.5hp V-twin engine mounted at the front, with a 3-speed gearbox and shaft drive.

NG

TAYLOR (GB) 1922–1924

Taylor Motors Ltd, Newcastle-upon-Tyne.

1914 Taunton (iii) 2-seater.
NICK BALDWIN

Also rendered as Taylor's Motors, this company made a very limited number of conventional light cars. The prototype used a 1498cc 4-cylinder side-valve Coventry-Simplex engine with 3-speed gearbox and shaft drive to a spiral bevel rear axle. They then announced two models with ohv Meadows engines, a 11.9 and a 13.9hp, but as Meadows' sales ledgers record only four engines delivered to Taylor, one can hardly describe them as production cars.

NG

TAYLOR-DUNN (US) 1949–1966

Taylor-Dunn Manufacturing Co., Anaheim, California.

Taylor-Dunn made a wide range of electric utility vehicles in 3- and 4-wheeled forms and some were for passenger use.

HP

TAYLOR-SWETNAM (GB) 1913

Taylor, Swetnam & Co., Coventry.

This company was unusual for a small concern in that it made its own water-cooled 2-cylinder engine, which it installed in a light car with 3-speed gearbox and shaft-drive. It had a streamlined 2-seater body and cost £140. For 1914 the company was said to be bringing out a car with a French-built 4-cylinder engine.

NG

T.B. (GB) 1920–1924

Thompson Brothers (Bilston) Ltd, Bilston, Staffordshire.

Thompson Brothers were (and are) well-known boiler makers with a history dating back to 1810. The company made pressed steel chassis for several car manufacturers, and after World War I decided to enter the car market itself. The T.B. was a well-made 3-wheeler powered by a 961cc V-twin JAP engine although some Blackburne or MAG engines were also used, with a 2- or 3-speed

c.1920 T.B. 8/10hp 3-wheeler.
BRYAN K. GOODMAN

1989 Tecoplan Leo city car.
NICK BALDWIN

gearbox made in-house and shaft-drive to the single rear wheel. It had a Bugatti-shaped radiator, and was offered with either disc or wire wheels. The bodies were a 2-seater tourer with one door, or a hipbath-like sports model with no doors. About 500 were made.

NG

Further Reading
'Fragments on Forgotten Makes: the T.B.', John Coombes, *Motor Sport*, April 1969.

TD 2000 (AUS) 1986–1996
1986–1988 Marshall Car Co. Australia Pty Ltd, Sydney, New South Wales.
1994–1996 TD 2000 Pty Ltd, Gisborne, Victoria
This M.G. TD replica used a Nissan Pintara engine and drive-line. It had the support of Nissan because there were prospects of gaining credits from export sales, to use against its own component imports. All design rules were met and local content of 95 per cent was achieved by 1988, when the firm failed. The contracted builder formed a new company in 1994 to continue the TD 2000 but the withdrawal of Nissan from Australia was the final blow.

MG

T.D.C. (i) *see* CROMPTON (ii)

T.D.C. (ii) (GB) c.1951
Dick Staddon, general works manager at Ransomes, Sims & Jefferies, built his own idea of an Italian-British open sports car based on Fiat parts. Initially its all-alloy body had cycle wings but was soon updated with flowing wings, in which style it was productionised.

CR

TEAL (GB) 1984 to date
1984–1986 Teal Cars, Burscough, Lancashire (sales: Andover, Hampshire).
1986–1998 Teal Cars, Timperley, Altrincham, Cheshire.
1998 to date Teal Cars, Bisley, Surrey.
When ex-Daimler engineer Ian Foster's Teal Type 35 replica first appeared in 1984, it was virtually unique in that it had a front-mounted engine (most replicas had Beetle floorpans). Initially the twin rail chassis accepted Morris Marina parts, although other options included Nissan Silvia turbo and Triumph straight-6. Early cars had fibreglass bodywork but this was soon changed to hand-crafted aluminium and correct-looking 18in wire wheels. A Tourer 4-seater version was marketed from 1986, while the Type 44 replica arrived in 1988. The Type 59 of 1991 was larger than the 35, with a longer bonnet, folded steel chassis, Ford-based wishbone suspension, MGB rear axle and Jaguar 6-cylinder engine. It was engineered and built for Teal by vintage van makers Projects of Distinction and was initially sold under the G.P.B. brand name.

CR

TECHNIC (GB) 1987 to date
Technic Ltd (TRAC Services), Martin & Walker Ltd, Andover, Hampshire.
This company began producing a highly accurate kit-form Porsche 550 Spyder replica. Its round tube space frame chassis was designed to accept VW Beetle front suspension (or a double wishbone set-up), a De Dion rear end and mid-mounted Alfasud or Beetle/Porsche power. Further models were then launched, including a 356 Speedster replica in 1997 and 356 Coupé in 1998. Most desirable of all was the GTS, a Porsche 911-powered replica of the 1964 Porsche racer, sold only in fully-built form.

CR

TECO (i) (GB) 1905
Thornton Engineering Co. Ltd, Bradford, Yorkshire.
The Teco light car was assembled mainly from French-made components, including a Bailleul engine. It was said that only one was made. In 1919, *The Autocar*, which incorrectly described the car as a Tesco, reported that the makers had received an order for spare parts, 'showing the length of service obtainable from a British-built car'.

NG

TECO (ii) (D) 1924–1925
Teco-Werke GmbH, Stettin.
This company made a light car powered by a 5/30PS 4-cylinder engine.

HON

TECOPLAN (D) 1985–1992
Tecoplan Prototypenbau & Entwicklung GmbH, Munich.
The Tecoplan Leo was an ambitious plan for a pan-European city car which preceded the SMART by almost a decade. The company made components for prototypes, its main client being BMW. In 1987 the whole organisation was bought by Erich Graf von Waldburg-Zeil, a member of a German noble family. He brought with him Hungarian-born Ervin Gross, who soon became managing director. Waldburg's plan was for a fibreglass-bodied city car, no more than 100in (2538mm) long, powered by an eco-friendly engine and with a luxurious interior. He also envisaged special railway wagons in which the cars could be stored in the lower part, while the upper part would contain plush seats and a bar. With this system, owners could commute from city to city without leaving their cars. He invited ex-Porsche engineer Hans-Georg Kasten to be the designer. Gross suggested the Hungarian company which later made the PULI to provide mechanical components, but it proved unreliable, and the well-known Hungarian bus manufacturer, Ikarus, was asked instead.

The first complete Tecoplan Leo was exhibited at the 1989 Geneva Show, with 750cc Fiat Panda engine, Renault 5 suspension components and a Hungarian-made fibreglass body. It was later converted to electric power. A third model, using a 1.1-litre Volkswagen Polo engine was also made, along with another electric car. The latter used high-tech batteries in conjunction with a prototype high-frequency electric power train supplied by Siemens. The project would have required far more money than Waldburg was able to raise, and also the technology did not exist to make the fibreglass bodies in the desired quantity. By 1992 Waldburg abandoned the idea and retired from the automobile business.

PN

TEILHOL (F) 1970–1993
1970–1972 Les Ateliers de Construction du Libradois et les Établissements Teilhol, Arlanc.
1972–1981 Teilhol Voiture Électrique (Sté des Établissements Teilhol), Ambert, Puy-de-Dôme.
1981–1990 Teilhol SA, Courpière..
1990–1992 Automobiles Page Penouty, Courpière.
1992–1993 Centuri Automobiles, Courpière.
This firm began life as A.C.L., producing a model that subsequently became the Rodeo for Renault. It also made military vehicles, but Teilhol went on to specialise in electric microcars. Its first prototype appeared as early as 1972, an angular open-topped 3- or 4-wheeled car that, in production form, was intended to be a polyester monocoque. Teilhol's eventual first production car was the Citadine 3-wheeler. In layout it was a reinvention of the Isetta bubble car, with its single front-mounted door, though it hinged at the top. The body shape was an almost precise triangle. A centrally-mounted 48V motor drove the single rear wheel by chain, and there were hydromechanical brakes. The Handicar was a 4-wheeled version for the disabled, featuring a remote-operated rear door for wheelchair access and hydraulic brakes. Other models included the Messagette leisure car/commercial range and the Citacom pick-up. The 1981 Simply was Teilhol's first petrol car, a 50cc Motobécane powered open 4-wheeler, later offered with 125cc petrol and 325cc diesel engines. Its intriguing Dominique Delamour-styled body featured double headlamps and external door frames. Electric power had been abandoned completely by the mid–1980s.

In 1987 a new avenue was explored with the Tangara, the spiritual successor to the Citroën Méhari, launched just as the Méhari was dropped and a year after Teilhol had ceased producing the Rodeo. It had an open jeep-type body on a 2CV floorpan and the option of Voisin 4-wheel drive, and 800 examples were made in 1988 alone. A new generation of microcars was launched for 1989, the individualistic TXA series. The Theva, also in 1989, was an open leisure vehicle based on Citroën AX mechanicals. Teilhol went into liquidation in 1990 but its TXA range was twice revived by A.P.P. and Centuri.
CR

TEMPELHOF see BMF

TEMPERINO (I) 1919–1924
1919–1922 Vetturette Temperino SA, Turin.
1922–1924 Fratelli Temperino SA, Turin.
With his two brothers, Maurizio Temperino (1888–1975) opened a bicycle repair shop in 1907 and made an experimental car the following year. The brothers then made motorcycles powered by British-built Precision engines. In 1919 they turned to cars again, planning to mass produce a light car powered by a 1-litre 2-cylinder air-cooled engine bought from the Della Ferrera motorcycle makers, with chassis and final assembly by Antonio Opessi and bodies from Farina. Giovanni Farina was a director of the company. Transmission was unusual, being by shaft to a rear-axle gearbox which drove only the offside rear wheel. Lighting was by acetylene at first, replaced by electricity in 1922. In that year Opessi withdrew, and the company was reorganised as Fratelli Temperino (Temperino brothers), with financial backing from the Banca Nazionale di Sconto. The collapse of this bank in 1924 virtually wiped out Temperino, after about 1000 cars had been made. Plans to make the cars in England came to nothing.

Maurizio tried to make a comeback to car manufacture in 1928, but got no further than a prototype. He then devoted himself to inventions, including ways of producing electricity economically.
NG
Further Reading
'Temperino of Torino', Angelo Tito Anselmi, *Automobile Quarterly*, Vol 17, No. 2.

TEMPERO (NZ) 1981 to date
Tempero Coach & Motor Co., Oamaru, South Island.
The first production from this company was a Jaguar D-type replica, with semi-monocoque construction and aluminium-alloy panels, and 48 had been made by 1995, inclusive of long-nosed and XK SS variations. Replicas of the Aston Martin DBR 2, Lister Jaguar and Jaguar Lightweight E-type have also been made. In 1994 a replica Jaguar XJ13 followed, powered by a 5.3-litre V12 engine, and the first three examples were exported to the United States.
MG

1978 Teilhol Citadine electric 3-wheeler.
TONY BEADLE

1988 Teilhol Break 32STD.
CHRIS REES

TEMPEST (GB) 1988–1997
1988–1990 Tempest Cars, Burscough, Lancashire.
1992–1997 Thoroughbred Projects, Carnforth, Lancashire.
Originated by Lancashire-based Ian Foster (of TEAL) and John Box (ex-T.V.R.), the Tempest vintage-style kit car was unusual in its choice of donor vehicle: the Reliant Kitten/Fox. It had a simple twin-rail box section chassis and alloy-panelled bodywork in two variations: in road form with doors and a galvanised steel floorpan, and in trials-type TT form with a doorless step-over body and aluminium floorpan. Higher-powered versions of the Reliant 848cc engine were available, or another alternative was the 928cc Chrysler Sunbeam engine.
CR

TEMPLAR (US) 1917–1924
1917–1923 Templar Motors Corp., Cleveland, Ohio.
1923–1924 Templar Motor Car Co., Cleveland, Ohio.
Sold as the Super Fine Small Car, the Templar was a light car with flair. Designed by A.M. Dean, formerly of POPE-HARTFORD and MATHESON, the Templar was mostly an assembled car, although the firm built its own engines. Chassis engineering was fairly straightforward, with semi-elliptic leaf spring suspension, Hotchkiss drive, and a semi-floating live-drive axle.

The first Templar was introduced in July 1917, but production was soon interrupted by war work at its factory in a Cleveland suburb. Some 1800 had been built by the end of 1919, however. In that year endurance driver 'Cannon Ball' Baker set a new record of 26 hours, 50 minutes for the New York to Chicago run in a Templar, besting the previous mark by over 6 hours.

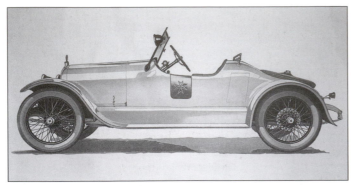

1919 Templar Model 4-45 roadster.
MICHAEL WORTHINGTON-WILLIAMS

1894 Tenting at the start of the Paris – Rouen Trial.
NATIONAL MOTOR MUSEUM

The Templar's Vitalic Top-Valve engine boasted ohvs enclosed in an aluminium case; displacement was 3229cc and the unit developed 43bhp. Touring, roadster and sedan bodies were offered on a 118in (2995mm) wheelbase, initially at a price of $1850 for any of the open models. Some models came equipped with a compass and Kodak camera.

Although the Armistice allowed production to resume at respectable levels the postwar economic condition took its toll. A disgruntled shareholder petitioned for receivership in 1920, but that action was dismissed by the court. However, sales were not healthy. Of some 1850 cars built in 1920, six-month sales declined to 128, although they rebounded somewhat for the remainder of 1921. Then a severe fire hit the factory, crippling production again. A supplier brought another action for receivership in 1922, this time granted, and a reorganised Templar Motor Car Co. emerged.

A 6-cylinder line, with 4-wheel brakes, was introduced in 1924, on a longer, 122in (3096mm) wheelbase. That autumn, after producing a total of 6000 cars, the firm was deemed in default on a loan and was taken over by its bank. Automotive manufacture ceased at that point.

KF

Further Reading
'Tarnished Knights: The Templar Motor Car Co.', Thomas F. Seal,
Automobile Quarterly, Vol. 31, No. 4.

TEMPLETON-DUBRIE (US) 1910

Templeton-Dubrie Car Co., Detroit, Michigan.
This company made a combination passenger and delivery car powered by an unusual 20hp 2-cylinder 2-stroke engine said to resemble a steam engine in some respects. Transmission was by epicyclic gears and shaft final drive. Only a few were made, selling for $1250 each.

NG

TEMPLE-WESTCOTT (US) 1921–1922

Temple Brothers, Framingham, Massachusetts.
Factual information surrounding the Temple-Westcott car was, until recently, almost non-existent, comprising for the most part bare, incomplete material based on hearsay, and it is important to review this at the outset. It was thought to have been built by the Bela Body Co. of Framingham, and limited to either ten or twenty units, depending on numerous accounts, all of which, however, specified that it was powered by an 8-cylinder engine of undetermined manufacture. These reports, with the exception of a few radiator badges in private collections, constituted such information until 1995. That year contact was established with one who knew the builders of the car and who had colour photos of a Temple-Westcott, which survives in pieces. The information provided by him was that the car was built by the Temple Brothers who operated a machine shop in the Amesbury-Framingham area where several prestigious custom coachwork concerns were located. The car was indeed fabricated by the Bela Body Co., one of the smaller custom body specialists of the area. Known specifications include the power plant to have been a Herschell-Spillman V8 engine, wood spoked artillery wheels and a wheelbase of 125 to 130 inches (3172 to 3299mm). The name 'Westcott' was after a local physician or dentist who put up money to make production possible. The existing car had been a coupé and the source of the information and pictures was not certain about the bodies on the other cars which he believes numbered at least six. Other facts surrounding the car listed a heat-treated steering wheel and a brass dashboard. American automotive historian Beverly Rae Kimes suggests the possibility of the car's having been produced on special order for a dealership in the area, but further noted that no such dealerships existed there at this time.

KM

TEMPO (i) (D) 1933–1956

Vidal & Sohn Tempo Werk, Hamburg-Harburg.
The first vehicles produced by Vidal under the Tempo name were 3-wheeled delivery vans, starting in 1926 with front-loaders derived from motorcycles, followed by models with a single front wheel in 1933. This layout was also used for a 2-seater passenger model powered by a 200cc single-cylinder Ilo engine. Later a successful range of combination cars for passengers or goods were made on these lines, followed by 4-wheelers introduced in 1936. These had 600cc 2-cylinder Ilo engines and front-wheel drive. An unusual design was the twin-engined G1200, with a 600cc engine at either end of the chassis, each driving an axle, and also offering 4-wheel steering. This was made mostly for military purposes.

Tempo did not revive passenger cars after World War II, although estate versions of their 3- and 4-wheeled vans were offered up to 1956. In 1955 Oscar Vidal sold a 50 per cent stake in his company to Rheinstahl-Hanomag, and ten years later they gained complete control. In 1970 the company became part of Daimler-Benz, and vans of Tempo shape were made under the Mercedes name until 1977.

HON

TEMPO (ii) *see* BAJAJ

TENNANT (US) 1914–1915

Tennant Motors Co., Chicago, Illinois.
W.G. Tennant sold several makes of car, including Peerless and Marmon, and for 1915 only he offered a conventional 30/35hp 4-cylinder car with 2-seater roadster or 5-seater tourer bodies.

NG

TENTING (F) 1891–1899

Sté Nationale de Construction de Moteurs H. Tenting, Boulogne-sur-Seine.
Established in 1884 to make stationary gas engines, this company made its first car in 1891, being a pioneer French make contemporary with Panhard, Peugeot and Serpollet. It had a 4hp rear-mounted horizontal 2-cylinder engine, friction transmission (surely the first example of this system) and final drive by chain to the offside rear wheel. It was steered by swivelling fore-carriage, but subsequent models had conventional steering and V-twin engines. Tenting entered a 4-seater car in the 1894 Paris–Rouen Trial, but it did not finish. It also entered cars in the Paris–Nantes–Paris and Paris–Marseilles–Paris Races in 1896, but made no impression.

In 1899 Tenting was said to be building a 26-seater bus powered by a 16hp 4-cylinder engine. No cars were made after February 1899, although the company continued in business making engines.

NG

TERAM (RA) 1956

Teram SRL, San Isidro, Buenos Aires.

When the military took power after ousting President Peron, in 1955, they rapidly dropped the JUSTICIALISTA, with its politically oriented name, from the IAME production line. The assets were sold to Teram SRL in late 1955. A number of incomplete Justicialista sports cars were included in the deal. The Teram was also known as Puntero and as Porsche-Teram, and had significant differences from the Justicialista. The Porsche engine was rear-mounted and the front-end was modified to give it a Porsche look. Three versions, with engines developing from 56bhp to 102bhp, were offered. About 100 Teram sports cars were made.

ACT

TERRAPLANE (US) 1932–1938

Hudson Motor Car Co., Detroit, Michigan.

The Terraplane was HUDSON's second 'companion car', successor to the ESSEX and derived from it. In fact, for the marque's first two years it was officially a model of Essex, designated Essex-Terraplane. Smaller, lighter and less expensive than the rest of the Essex line, it was also more refined.

While the Terraplane drive train was a modest evolution from that of the Essex, the body and chassis frame were all new. Where previously Hudson and Essex frames had been heavy conventional 'ladder' arrangements, Terraplane's was neatly tapered, given a cruciform centre section for strength, and bolted to the body at 23 points. A short (106in/2690mm) wheelbase and narrow track reduced weight by some 500lbs (225kg). The Essex-derived side-valve six featured downdraft carburation, and was enlarged to 3164cc, good for 70bhp. Hudson advertised the Terraplane as having the 'highest ratio of power to weight of any production car…', and the car gained a reputation for lively performance. Priced at $425 to $610, it competed with Ford, Chevrolet and Plymouth. Introduced by aviatrix Amelia Earhart at a July 1932 media event in Detroit, the Terraplane, whose name was said to mean 'Land Flying', vastly improved the fortunes of the company. Terraplane completely replaced the Essex for the 1933 model year, at which time it became a marque in its own right.

An 8-cylinder Terraplane was added in 1933, using a small bore version of the Hudson 8. Performing even better than the six, it proved serious competition for the Ford V8, and won a number of competition events, including record-setting times at Pike's Peak and Daytona. Its chassis was the basis for the first models of the Anglo-American hybrid RAILTON. The 1932 Terraplanes had appeared somewhat stubby, so a wider track was adopted for 1933, and a 113in (2868mm) wheelbase given to Deluxe Sixes and Eights. The popularity of Hudson in Britain, carried through to Terraplane, whose low price (as low as £275) and excellent performance earned it praise in the press. Tax considerations, however, dictated wide use of a small-bore 2560cc engine, though these 16.9hp-rated cars proved rather underpowered.

In 1934, all Hudson products adopted the Terraplane's lightweight chassis frame concept, and the 8-cylinder Terraplane was dropped. The following year Terraplane sales of over 70,000 lifted the company back to profitability. The side-valve six was enlarged to 3475cc, which would suffice for the duration of the Terraplane badge. The marque shared all the Hudson features, such as 'Electric Hand' remote gear selector, Baker 'Axleflex' ifs and, in 1936, 'Duo-automatic' hydraulic brakes with mechanical backup.

Longer, lower, wider bodies in 1937 made Terraplane all the more like parent Hudson. For 1938, it became, in effect, a model of Hudson, badged Hudson-Terraplane, and its place as the entry-level corporate car was taken by a new, smaller model, the Hudson 112. The Terraplane name was retired completely at the end of the 1938 model year.

KF

Further Reading
History of Hudson, Don Butler, Motorbooks International, Crestline series, 1992.
Land Flying, the Terraplane, James Fack, Railton Owners' Club, 1992.
'Terraplane – Flying by Land', Kit Foster, *Automobile Quarterly*, Vol. 39, No. 1.

1934 Terraplane Six coach.
NATIONAL MOTOR MUSEUM

1937 Terraplane Six coupé.
NICK GEORGANO/NATIONAL MOTOR MUSEUM

c.1960 Terrier MkII sports car.
NATIONAL MOTOR MUSEUM

TERRIER (GB) 1959–c.1963

L. Terry, Winchmore Hill, London.

In the 1950s, Len Terry dabbled in club racing, built a number of specials and convinced himself he was not likely to become World Champion. The cars he built, however, became his equivalent of a CV and enabled him to join Lotus as Colin Chapman's right-hand man. In his spare time, he made the Terrier Mk II with which Brian Hart walked away with the 1172 Championship in 1959, and won almost every other race he entered. On paper, it had a conventional specification but the secret was the complicated, and very stiff, spaceframe with the body panels acting as a stressed skin.

Production of this car was taken over by another firm and, like the Lotus Seven, it was offered both as a road and as a racing car. Unfortunately, the new firm tried to cut corners in making the cars and upset the careful thinking behind the design. This caused buyers to wonder why their cars were not as good as those which had been produced by Brian Hart. Terry washed his hands of the project and later Terrier cars had nothing to do the firm which made the production Terrier Mk IIs.

1902 Teste et Moret La Mouche voiturette.
NATIONAL MOTOR MUSEUM

The Terrier chassis was used by Falcon Shells for its Sports model (and also the associated Peregrine). Colin Chapman was not pleased to see his draughtsman's private enterprise beat Lotus cars on the track and as a result Terry was sacked. He went on to design cars for, among others, Gilby, Shelby, Eagle, BRM, Leda, Lotus (again), and BMW.

Prior to Len Terry, virtually all British competition cars were either designed by the founder of a marque – such as Colin Chapman at Lotus – or else were drawn by people who had long-term prospects within a manufacturer which decided to go racing, such as Jaguar. Len Terry was the first of a long line of designers who began with a small racing car maker and then went on to others.
ML

TERROT (F) 1912–1914
SA des Établissement Terrot, Dijon, Cote d'Or.
Terrot was one of France's best-known motorcycle makers, in business from 1901 to the 1960s, when it was absorbed by Peugeot. It made a few experimental voiturettes in 1900 and 1902 and a small series of conventional cars during 1912–14. They had 4-cylinder monobloc side-valve engines in two sizes, 1244cc 8CV and 1460cc 10CV. Both had shaft drive.
NG

TESTE ET MORET (F) 1898–1903
Teste et Moret, Lyons-Vaise.
Teste et Moret were manufacturers of steel tubes which, not surprisingly, they used in the construction of their voiturettes. Known by the trade name La Mouche (the fly), they had single-cylinder De Dion-Bouton engines, friction transmission and chain drive. Up to 1900 they had tiller steering, but that year's models had a wheel on a vertical column. 2- and 4-seater bodies were offered, the latter being a *vis-à-vis* similar to the contemporary De Dion-Bouton. They were designed by T.C. Pullinger who went to Sunbeam after Test et Moret ceased making cars to concentrate on machine tools. About 300 were made, of which at least seven survive.
NG

TEXAN (US) 1918–1922
Texan Motor Car Association, Forth Worth, Texas.
The Texan was a typical assembled car of its time powered by a Lycoming 4-cylinder L-head engine and other standard components. Priced between $1195 and $1495, production was limited to roadster and touring models. Plagued by lack of sufficient funds and other internal strife, the company was reorganised in 1921 after a total of about 150 cars and a handful of trucks including a light delivery type, a light stake model and a 'Light Oil Field Special', the term relating to the Texas oil fields for which use the truck was presumably built. The passenger cars, like their commercial peers, were equipped with oversize tyres and advertised by the company for use 'In Texas Oil Fields, where the goin' is rough'.
KM

TEXAS (US) 1920
Texas Truck and Tractor Co., Dallas, Texas.
This was a conventional assembled car which was offered for one year only.
NG

TEXMOBILE (US) 1919–1921
Little Motor Kar Co., Grand Prairie, Texas.
The saga of the Texmobile is illustrative of a stock manipulation which backfired for its instigator, William S. Livezey, who obtained the use of a factory in Grand Prairie, Texas for the construction of a small, good looking car. When the first Texmobile – a roadster – was launched at the Dallas Fair in October 1919, it attracted a good deal of attention and admiration by the public – a public which apparently did not look too closely at its construction or components. The Texmobile was a small 4-cylinder car on a 109in (2766mm) wheelbase and sporting wire wheels plus two side-mounted spare wheels as well. Livezey claimed to have another factory at Havre de Grace, Maryland and that the car's engine was of his own design. Early in 1920, charges were made against Livezey that the operation of the Texmobile company was in defiance of the law in several places and in April 1920 Livezey and some of his assistants were arrested on charges of defrauding the mails. Livezey and the company went to trial at Dallas in February 1921 when it was discovered that there existed only a handful of Texmobiles in various stages of construction, that no two cars bore any similarity with the others and that some of the components used had been made by local blacksmiths. In addition, one of the brake drums on hand was found to be that of a Ford. Livezey was found guilty as charged and sentenced to five years imprisonment in the Federal Penitentiary at Leavenworth, Kansas. The Little Motor Kar Co. continued as a maker of road equipment and a small truck called the Little.
KM

T.G.E. see CHIYODA

T. GREEN (US) c.1994
T. Green Enterprises, Indianapolis, Indiana.
This kit car company built a Lamborghini Countach replica based on a Pontiac Fiero or a custom fabricated tube frame. The custom frame had special A-arms and coil-over-shock suspension. It used Cadillac or Ford SHO V6 engines with Porsche or Z-F transaxles. They also sold 427 Cobra kits.
HP

T.H. (E) 1915–1922
Fábrica Española de Automóviles y Aeroplanes,
Talleres Hereter SA, Barcelona.
In 1917 the company that built the IDEAL cyclecar raised capital to form a new business building cars and aeroplanes. The 12/15hp car used a 4-cylinder 2120cc engine with inclined valves and had 4-wheel-brakes. T.H. also prepared industrial engines and built an aeroplane called the España, equipped with a French Caudron engine. The company moved to a larger workshop but the political situation in Spain finished the business.
VCM

THAMES (GB) 1906–1911
Thames Ironworks, Shipbuilding & Engineering Co. Ltd,
Greenwich, London.
A substantial shipbuilding firm, this company was founded in 1857 and among their achievements were building Queen Victoria's yacht, *Fairy*, and the first seagoing ironclad, *Warrior*, which was started in 1858. By 1910 they had made 900 ships, and their works near the London docks covered 30 acres. In 1898 they absorbed the marine engine firm, John Penn & Sons, who had made a steam carriage in 1835, and in 1902 started to build steam wagons. These and the cars were made at the former Penn works in Greenwich, a few miles down river from the main shipbuilding yards at Millwall. They were followed by petrol-engined vans, and in 1906 passenger cars appeared. The first was a large car with a 6977cc 6-cylinder engine called a 45hp. It was followed by the even larger 50hp of 7774cc and 60hp of 9648cc. One of the latter took records at Brooklands in 1907, driven by Clifford Earp who sold Thames cars from his own agency. These were designed by Charles K. Edwards, formerly of Napier, and the engines were very Napier-like in their conception. Smaller models followed in 1908, a 1960cc 12hp twin and a 3920cc 24hp four. In 1910 they moved smaller still,

1910 Thames 60hp limousine, The Emperor.
NICK BALDWIN

1910 Thames 12hp coupé, The Chirurgeon.
NICK BALDWIN

1933 Theis 3-wheeler coupé.
HANS-OTTO NEUBAUER

with an 8hp single-cylinder model of 1296cc. This had the same cylinder dimensions (102×127mm) as the 45hp six.

1910 Thames were given unusual names such as The Chirurgeon for the small coupé (appropriate for a doctor) and The Emperor for the limousine. The range was at its widest that year, including the 8hp single, 12hp twin which was made in taxicab form, 15.9hp monobloc four, 24hp four and the old 60hp six. 1911 was the last year for the cars, and the commercials survived for only two more years.

NG

THANET *see* WHITEHEAD-THANET

THEIN & GOLDBERGER (A) 1907–1908
Thein & Goldberger, Vienna.
This company was founded in 1898 and specialised in repairs for any make of car on the market. They also made motorcycles from 1903 to 1905, and built a voiturette with 8hp air-cooled engine from 1907 to 1908.

NG

THEIS (D) 1933
Dipl. Ing. K. Theis, Berlin-Charlottenburg.
This was one of several 3-wheelers which appeared in Germany to take advantage of the reduced tax rate on such cars. It had a 200cc engine driving the front wheels, and an aerodynamic coupé body. Few were made.

HON

THEYER ROTHMUND (A) 1900
Theyer, Rothmund & Co., Vienna.
This company made a small number of electric cars.

HON

THIEULIN (F) 1906–1908
Automobiles Thieulin, Besançon, Doubs.
Louis Thieulin founded a general engineering business at Besançon in 1886. Three years later he built a one-off steam car to a customer's order. He was also one of the first to maker a motor scythe, and in 1906, with his two sons Émile

and Joseph, started Thieulin et Compagnie to make small cars. They had 4-cylinder engines and 2-seater bodies, one running in the 1908 Coupe des Voiturettes, though without great success. Joseph soon became more interested in aviation, and car production ended in 1908.

NG

Further Reading
Franche-Comté, Berceau de l'Automobile, Raymond Dornier, l'Est Republicain, 1987.

TH!NK *see* PIVCO

THOLOMÉ (i) (F) c.1920–1922
M. Tholomé, St Ouen, Seine.
This was a cyclecar made with 2- and 4-cylinder engines, the latter being a 1095cc Ruby. Transmission was by friction discs, with chain final drive, though a conventional 2-speed gearbox was also available. The 2-seater body was known as 'un carrosserie bateau'.

NG

THOLOMÉ (ii) (F) 1948
Produced in Aubagne, the Tholomé was a small open economy 2-seater powered by a 2-cylinder engine. Its bodywork was more or less symmetrical front-to-back but even its cheap price did not prevent an early demise.

CR

THOMAS (i) (US) 1902–1919
1902–1911 E.R. Thomas Motor Co., Buffalo, New York.
1911–1919 E.R. Thomas Motor Car Co., Buffalo, New York.
One of America's greatest cars of the first two decades of the century, the Thomas Flyer grew out of the bicycle and motorcycle business run by Erwin Ross Thomas (1850–1936). He had begun his career in the railway business, and then manufactured the Cleveland bicycle in Ohio and Toronto. In 1900 he set up the Thomas Auto-Bi Co. in Buffalo to make motorcycles, followed by cars which he called the Buffalo Junior and Senior (see BUFFALO (i)). Two years later he changed the name to the E.R. Thomas Motor Co., and made the Thomas Model 16 with 8hp single-cylinder engine under the front seat, and a 5-seater tonneau body. In July 1903 he brought out a larger car with 24hp 3-cylinder engine. Like the Type 16 it had a De Dion-type bonnet with radiator mounted low in front, but by November this had been replaced by a conventional bonnet and radiator. This was the first Thomas to bear the name Flyer, and was made as a tonneau at $2500 and a limousine on a longer wheelbase at $3000. For 1905 the Flyer was still larger and more expensive, two engine sizes being offered, 40 and 50hp, and three wheelbases, 106, 110, and 114in (2690, 2792, and 2893mm) In three years the Thomas had passed from being a light car which differed little from many others to being one of America's quality makes, worthy to be considered alongside Locomobile and Pierce-Arrow.

More than 400 cars were sold in the 1903/04 season, and by November 1906 the company had made 1014 cars of 40hp or more, and there were orders for 1514 more. This was double the number made by Thomas' Buffalo rival, Pierce-Arrow. A 60hp six was listed for 1905, but probably only a handful were made. One took part in the eliminating trials for the 1905 Vanderbilt Cup, but it did not qualify for the race itself. The first listed production six appeared in 1908, the K-6-70 with 12.8-litre 72hp engine on a 140in (3553mm) wheelbase and priced at $6000. The company's best sporting achievement also came in 1908, when a specially-prepared stock 8554cc 4-cylinder Model DX tourer won the epic New York to Paris Race. With George Schuster and Montagu Roberts, the car made the trip in 169 days, defeating their nearest rival the German Protos. The car was sold at auction in 1913 for $200; today it is priceless.

For 1909 Thomas turned to shaft drive on their smaller models, the 2916cc 18hp Model G 4-cylinder (introduced in 1908 as a taxicab chassis) and 4375cc 31hp Model L 6-cylinder. The big chain-driven Model K was continued through the 1912 season. Despite the successful sales of the 14/16hp taxicab, Thomas' finances began to suffer from 1910 onwards. The 'small six' Model L was a disappointment ('leaky, slow and noisy' said George Schuster), and as it was intended to be the spearhead of an eventual production of 7500 cars per year, this was a serious blow. In fact, Thomas' output never exceeded the 1036 cars made in 1909. E.R. Thomas left in 1911, and in August 1912 the company

1907 Thomas (i) Flyer 60hp tourer.
NICK BALDWIN

1910 Thomas (i) Flyer 6-70 tourer.
NICK BALDWIN

went into receivership, No more than a dozen cars were made up to February 1913, when the company was auctioned, being bought by C.A. Finnegan of the Empire Smelting Co. He had plans to move production to Louisville, Kentucky, but instead cars continued to be made at the Buffalo plant, though in very small numbers. The last year for which records exist was 1913, when 313 were made. The make was listed to 1918, and possibly 1919. The last model was the MCX, with 43hp 6-cylinder engine and shaft drive. It was listed with six body styles, though whether all were built is not known. Out of about 7000 Thomas cars made, no more than 30 survive today.

NG

Further Reading
'The New York–Paris Thomas Flyer', Maurice Hendry, *Automobile Quarterly*, Vol. 8, No. 4.
'Flying High; touring Pennsylvania's back roads in a 1909 Thomas Flyer', John F. Katz, *Special Interest Autos*, November/December 1999.

THOMAS (ii) (GB) 1903
W.F. Thomas, Birmingham.
This short-lived car was powered by a front-mounted 8hp 2-cylinder engine, with friction transmission and chain drive. Two other models were planned, a 6hp single and a 10hp twin, but were not built.

NG

THOMAS-DETROIT (US) 1906–1908
E.R. Thomas-Detroit Co., Detroit, Michigan.
This car was marketed by E.R. Thomas but made in Detroit by former Oldsmobile personnel, designer Howard E. Coffin and sales manager Roy D. Chapin. It had a 40hp 4-cylinder engine, shaft drive and was offered in four body styles at $2750 to $3750. This was appreciably cheaper than the Thomas from Buffalo, and gave E.R. Thomas a good foothold in a lower-price market. It might have lasted longer if Coffin and Chapin had not wanted complete control. They encouraged Hugh Chalmers, a highly successful salesman who was working for

1970 Thomassima V12 coupé.
NICK GEORGANO

1947 Thomson (iv) 7.2hp 2-stroke tourer.
BRUCE LINDSAY

1904 Thor (i) 7hp 2-seater.
MICHAEL WORTHINGTON-WILLIAMS

the National Cash Register Co., to buy Thomas out, and in June 1908 the Thomas-Detroit became the Chalmers New Detroit. A month later this was abbreviated to Chalmers-Detroit, and in late 1910 the names of both car and company were changed to Chalmers. Meanwhile Coffin and Chapin had joined forces with department store owner J.L. Hudson to make a car named after him.

NG

THOMASSIMA (I) c.1966–1970

Tom Meade, Modena.

American enthusiast Tom Meade began re-bodying sports/racing cars for road use in 1961, operating from a small workshop in Modena. A Maserati 350 was followed by a series of Ferrrari-based cars which he called Thomassimas. The Virginia was based on the Ferrari GTO, with 5-speed ZF gearbox. The aluminium coupé body was only 40in (1015mm) high, the same as the Ford GT40. Top speed was 170mph (274km/h). Although the Virginia was built for his own use, Meade received at least two orders for replicas, which he sold for $15,000 each.

NG

THOMOND (IRL) 1925–1929

J.A. Jones, Dublin.

The Thomond was said to have been the first car to be made in the Irish Free State (now Eire). The first model of 1925 had a 1750cc 4-cylinder ohv engine, a 4-speed gearbox and either saloon or tourer bodywork. A surviving photo of the tourer shows it to be of very Germanic appearance with pointed vee-radiator and artillery wheels. A later Thomond of 1929, the 12/48hp, was better-looking, with fabric coupé body, wire wheels and a Bentley-like radiator. It was probably powered by a Meadows 4ED engine.

NG

THOMPSON (i) (US) 1901–1902

Andrew C. Thompson, Plainfield, New Jersey.

Though he never formed a company, Andrew Thompson made a number of light electric cars for sale. There were two models, a runabout with 1¼ hp motor and a top speed of 12mph (19km/h), and a stanhope with 2½hp motor and speed of 18mph (29km/h). The former was priced at $800, the latter at $1600. His cars were equipped with electric headlights and an electric gong. Though he did not make many cars, he was later in business making the MACKLE-THOMPSON petrol car in Elizabeth, New Jersey.

NG

THOMPSON (ii) (US) 1901–1907

Thompson Automobile Co., Providence, Rhode Island.

This company made steamers, most of them commercial vehicles. However the 7-seater wagonette was sold for private use, and even the 8- to 10-seater version might have suited a large family. They had Tonkin boilers and 8/10hp Fitzheney engines. There was also a 6-seater surrey, with *dos-à-dos* seating for the rear four passengers.

NG

THOMSON (i) (AUS) 1899–1904

The Thomson Motor Car Co. Ltd, Armadale, Victoria.

An engineering prodigy, Herbert Thomson had made model steam engines since childhood and his steamboat was on the river while he was a teenager. It was reported in 1895 that his small engines and boilers were commendable and his next step was to apply them to the road, and a vehicle of some kind was tested by runs on rural lanes during 1896. A purpose-built phaeton with *vis-à-vis* seating, a 5hp engine and the then novel pneumatic tyres was finished in time for display at the 1899 Melbourne Show. The favourable reception accorded this effort led to the formation of a company and several orders were received. These were aided by the satisfactory first overland automobile run from Bathurst in New South Wales to Melbourne in 1900, after exhibition at Sydney and Bathurst Shows. A light 4-seater steam buggy with a 2-cylinder 10hp engine and wire wheels was the production type, of which about 12 were sold. A delivery van version was made and steam power was applied to other vehicles until 1904, when selling imported types was found to be more profitable.

MG

THOMSON (ii) (US) 1900–1903

Thomson Automobile Co., Philadelphia, Pennsylvania.

This was a neat little car powered by a 5hp single-cylinder engine mounted under the seat and driving the rear wheels by double chains. This was unusual when most cars of that size and power made do with a single chain. The runabout was priced at $500, and there was also a physician's phaeton at $650 and a surrey at $800. By early 1901 production was running at two cars per week, and may have continued at this rate, though William Thomson admitted in January 1903 that 'some mistakes have been made'.

NG

1900 Thornton 3½hp 3-wheeler.
RODNEY FOWLER

THOMSON (iii) (F) 1913–1928

Éts Industriels Raymond Thomas, Talence, Gironde.

This company supplied components to the motor industry, and also made marine engines, but when they turned to cars they bought their engines in from well-known suppliers. These included Aster who provided a 1496cc four, and Altos whose engines were of 1495 and 1990cc. Thomson also listed a car powered by the 6594cc 40CV 4-cylinder Janvier engine, with side-valves in a T-head and a very long stroke of 100 × 210mm. Old-fashioned even in 1914 when it was introduced, this engine was archaic by 1926, when Thomson still listed it. Production was doubtless what the French call 'très confidentielle'.

NG

THOMSON (iv) (AUS) 1947–1949

Wiles Manufacturing Co. Ltd, Mile End, South Australia.

In 1938–39 Jack Thomson built a small 4-seater tourer not unlike an Austin 8 in appearance, powered by a 700cc 2-cylinder 2-stroke engine. He was aided by Harold Clisby, who had built a Villiers-powered runabout for his own use in 1927, and made a quad-cam V6 Formula One engine in the 1960s. Only one of the prewar cars was made, but in 1947 Thomson designed a chassisless 2-seater tourer which was taken up by the Wiles brothers who had made a fortune with army field kitchens. Known as the Wiles-Thomson, it was powered by a completely rebuilt DKW 2-stroke engine which drove the rear wheels via a 3-speed gearbox. The body was considered to be ugly, and Wiles Engineering made two more cars with more attractive lines in 1948–49. They then dropped the project, but Thomson started work on a further car, a sports tourer with cut-away doors and a Ford Ten engine. He was still at work on this when he died in 1952, and the car was completed by his son-in-law Doug Giles. This still exists.

NG

Further Reading
'Death of an Aussie Dream', Bruce Lindsay. *Australian Sports & Classic Cars.*

THOR (i) (GB) 1904–c.1906

Thor Motor Car Co., London.

This was a somewhat rustic-looking 2-seater with 6/8hp single-cylinder Simms engine, 3-speed gearbox and shaft drive. Its solid tyres were quite old-fashioned for 1904, but were retained on the 12/14hp 2-cylinder car offered in 1905. This

had final drive by double chains, again an old-fashioned feature for a relatively small car of that date. Delivery vans were also made.

NG

THOR (ii) (US) 1907–1909

Aurora Automatic Machinery Co., Aurora, Illinois.

The well-known Thor motorcycles company, in business from 1903 to 1916, made four large 6-cylinder tourers which were copies of the French Hotchkiss.

NG

THOR (iii) (GB) 1919–c.1921

Simpson, Taylor Ltd, London.

Though they both came from the Westminster district of London, there is no known connection between this company and the makers of the THOR (i). The car sold by Simpson Taylor probably had an American chassis, considering its components, a 2333cc 4-cylinder LeRoi engine, Allis Chalmers lighting, and Schebler carburettor. The bevel rear axle, on the other hand, was by Mepsted & Hayward, a north London firm who made a few taxicabs under the name Mepward. The Thor's old-fashioned coupé body looked distinctly English.

NG

THORN ET HOGAN (F) 1901–1902

Thorn, Hogan et Cie, Puteaux, Seine.

The English-sounding partners in this company were in fact American, and aimed to make cars more suitable for British and American roads than the average light voiturette being made in France. Their car had a 10hp vertical-twin engine and shaft drive. The 4-seater tonneau had the general appearance of a Panhard.

NG

THORNTON (GB) 1900

Thornton Motor Co. Ltd, Hulme, Manchester.

This was a short-lived venture into car making by John Thornton (1865–1940) who was much better known for his partnership in the Thornton-Pickard company which made high-grade cameras from the 1880s to the late 1920s. Thornton formed his motor company in 1897, but it was three years before he had a car ready for the road. This was a 3-wheeler, superficially similar to a Léon

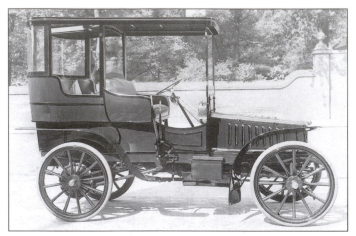

1904 Thornycroft 20hp tonneau.
NICK BALDWIN

1911 Thornycroft 18hp 2-seater.
NICK BALDWIN

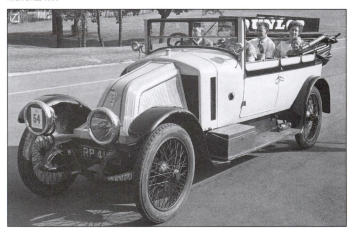

1912 Th. Schneider 18/22hp cabriolet.
NICK BALDWIN

Bollée, with 3½hp single-cylinder engine of Thornton's own manufacture, with variable belt transmission and chain drive to the rear wheel. The car was running during 1900, and he also planned a 4-wheeler with 2-cylinder engine. He also planned to make a 5hp heavy oil engine and a 10hp 2-cylinder 'lurry'. Very few 3-wheelers were made, possibly no more than two. The company was wound up in 1903, but no cars were made as late as that.

NG

Further Reading
'From Cameras to Cars', Tom Clark, *Veteran Car*, January 1999.

THORNYCROFT (GB) 1903–1913
John I. Thornycroft & Co. Ltd, Basingstoke, Hampshire.

One of Britain's best-known commercial vehicle makers for more than 60 years, Thornycroft had a relatively brief spell at car making, which roughly paralleled that of their rival, Dennis. The company was founded in 1864 as a ship builder. Their works were on the Thames at Chiswick and they made a great variety of craft from tugboats to destroyers, and also the Nile cruisers operated by Thomas Cook. In 1896 they built a steam van with front-wheel drive and rear-wheel steering (which still exists), and in 1898 moved vehicle-building to a new factory at Basingstoke. There they made steam wagons, followed by petrol ones and, in 1903, their first passenger cars. Two models were made, a 10hp twin and a 20hp four, both with automatic inlet valves, gilled-tube radiators and shaft drive. By 1905 they were of more modern appearance, with honeycomb radiators and mechanically-operated inlet valves. The 20hp had been uprated to 24hp, and for 1906 there was a new 14hp four with monobloc engine and ohvs. From 1906 to 1909 Thornycroft cars were sold under licence in Italy by F.L.A.G., but suggestions that they were made there, or that the F.L.A.G. car was a copy of the Thornycroft, were hotly denied by the Italians

In 1909 there were three models of Thornycroft, an 18 and a 30hp four and a 45hp six, all with monobloc casting and ohvs. They were of good quality and well thought of, but the increasing demands of commercial vehicle production, which enjoyed a flourishing export market as well as home sales, forced the directors to end car production in 1913. Only one model, the 18hp four, was made during the last year. About 450 Thornycroft cars were made in ten years, out of total production of 1360 vehicles.

Trucks and buses were made in great variety up to the mid 1960s, after which Thornycroft specialised in airport fire engines. These were made until 1977 when they were rebadged as Scammells.

NG

THOROUGHBRED CARS (US) c.1982 to date
Thoroughbred Cars, Redmond, Washington.
Thoroughbred Coach Builders, Mount Dora, Florida.
Thoroughbred Motorcars, Redmond, Washington.
This company made a number of kit cars in its Washington factory and sold them through their operations in Florida. They made replicas of the Mercedes 540K, 1956 300SL Gullwing and a cobbled up 300SLR. They also sold replicas of the 1936 pick-up truck and the British Witton Tiger kit. They used ladder frames with Ford or Chevrolet engines.

HP

THRIFT-T (US) 1947–1955
Tri-Wheel Motor Corp., Oxford, North Carolina and Springfield, Massachusetts.
Lightweight utility vehicles were the products of this company. They built 3-wheelers with Onan 10hp petrol engines mounted at the rear.

HP

THRIGE (DK) 1911–1918
Thomas B. Thrige AS, Odense.
Founded in 1894 this company was a well-known maker of electric motors and their first road vehicles were electric trucks. Their cars were petrol-engined, however, using Ballot or Daimler-Knight 4-cylinder engines, while Thrige bought in engines from White & Poppe, Continental and Hercules for their trucks. In 1914 a run of 50 light cars was made, using a 4/12hp Ballot engine. They had 3-speed gearboxes and shaft drive to a bevel rear axle without differential. Larger Thriges of the period 1914–18 had 8/22hp Ballot engines. In 1918 Thrige merged with two other Danish car makers, Anglo-Dane and Jan to form DeForenede Dansk Automobilfabriker AS. This company made trucks and buses under the name Triangel up to 1950, but no more passenger cars were built.

NG

THRUPP & MABERLY (GB) c.1896
Thrupp & Maberly, London.
This well-known carriage builder was founded in 1858, though Joseph Thrupp set up his business in 1760. In 1896 they fitted an electric motor to one of their victorias, which was bought by the Queen of Spain. They may have motorised a few other carriages in this way, as did another London coachbuilder, Offord.

NG

1923 Th. Schneider 15hp tourer.
NICK BALDWIN

TH. SCHNEIDER (F) 1910–1931

Automobiles Th. Schneider, Besançon, Doubs; Billancourt, Seine.

Théophile Schneider (NB An alternative rendering of the maker's name was Théodore) was one of the founders of Rochet-Schneider, and in 1910 he moved into the factory at Besançon where Messrs Chapuis and Amstoutz were making engines. Chapuis moved to Nanterre, where he later made the famous Chapuis-Dornier engines. Schneider's first product was a conventional 1846cc 10/12CV 4-cylinder car distinguished by a dashboard radiator. It was followed by a 3180cc 15CV six on similar lines, and the range was gradually expanded until by 1914 there were six 4-cylinder models from 1846 to 6079cc. They entered cars in the 1912 Coupe de l'Auto and Grand Prix de France, and in the Grand Prix de l'A.C.F. (the official French Grand Prix) in 1913 and 1914. Their best position was 2nd in the 1912 Grand Prix de France. In 1913 Schneider bought the REP (Robert Esnault-Pelterie) aircraft and engine factory at Billancourt. This was used for engine manufacture and assembly of other components made at Besançon. Output of Th. Schneider cars averaged 200 per annum in the years up to 1914.

During the war some ambulances were made on car chassis, but the main activity of the factories was the manufacture of shells. A few cars left the factory at the end of 1918; they had 1692cc 10CV 4-cylinder and 2538cc 16CV 6-cylinder engines, with ohvs and frontal radiators. A 4480cc six was listed up to 1924. In 1922 came their most important postwar model, the 1953cc 2-litre with 4-cylinder side-valve engine, 4-speed gearbox and (from 1925) 4-wheel Perrot type brakes. Ohvs also appeared in 1925. This was made up to the end of car manufacture in 1929, and examples were still being sold off in 1931. Smaller cars were made as well, the 1170cc VL (Voiture Légère) from 1926, which received ohvs in 1927. Like O.M., Th. Schneider lingered on paper long after production ended; the British concessionaires were still listing the 2-litre in 1938. The factory made tractors under the name SADIM until 1939.

NG

Further Reading
Franche-Comté, Berceau de l'Automobile, Raymond Dornier, l'Est Republicain, 1987.

THULIN (S) 1920–1928

AB Thulinwerken, Landskrona.

This company made aero-engines and complete aircraft during World War I, and had to look for fresh business after the war. They entered car manufacture with a 4-cylinder design which was based on the 1418cc 6/16PS AGA, though all components were made in Sweden. It was typically Germanic in appearance, with a sharply pointed vee-radiator and concave sides to the body. Thulin hoped to make at least 1000 of these cars, but only 300 had been completed before bankruptcy in 1924.

No cars were made until 1927 when the firm was reorganised by the brothers Axel and Per Weiertz who had built three prototype cyclecars under the name Self. They designed an up-to-date car called the Type B; this had a 1.7-litre 4-cylinder ohv engine, 4-wheel brakes of which those at the rear were mounted inboard, and a low 4-door saloon body with all seats between the axles. Only 13 were made (one fitted with a 6-cylinder Hupmobile engine), before competition from cheap imports and from the newly formed Volvo company forced Thulin out of business.

NG

THUNDER RANCH (US) 1995 to date

Thunder Ranch, El Cajon, California.

Tom McBurnie had been involved with a number of kit car projects in the past, including the EXOTIC ENTERPRISES Ferrari Daytona replicas. He produced a number of interesting kits at his later company, Thunder Ranch. The most popular kit was the Riot, a modern roadster body for the Volkswagen Beetle chassis, that was introduced in 1995. It had a low, sloping nose with projector-beam headlights. The Lightening was another unusual kit. It was a hot rod kit that resembled a Ford roadster but with a modern chassis and mid-mounted Oldsmobile Aurora or Cadillac Northstar V8 engines. The 959 was a replica of the Porsche Speedster with Porsche 959-style mudguards and spoilers grafted on. It was based on the VW chassis. The TR 250 was a Ferrari 250 GTO replica that was built on a Datsun 240Z chassis and running gear. The '32 Ford roadster

1999 Tianlong 2QZ 5020 XYLC 'grandfathers' car' (neo-classic).
ERIK VAN INGEN SCHENAU

1972 TiCi 848cc 2-seater.
NATIONAL MOTOR MUSEUM

was a conventional front-engined hot rod kit. Thunder Ranch also bought the rights to the BECK line of Porsche 550 Spyder replicas.

HP

THURLOW (GB) 1920–1921
Thurlow & Co., Wimbledon, London.
The prototype Thurlow 3-wheeler was built in 1914, but production did not get under way until 1920, and even then, few were made. It had a 10hp V-twin Precision engine which drove by chain to a 3-speed Sturmey-Archer gearbox, final drive to the rear wheel being by belt. Front suspension was by quarter-elliptics, with helical coils at the rear. The engine could be started from the seat, with a decompressor which lifted the exhaust valves during the first part of the starting lever's travel.

NG

THURNER (D) 1970–1973
Rudolf Thurner, Bernbeuren.
This 2-seater sports coupé featured a fibreglass body with gull-wing doors and a NSU TT 1200 engine. Production amounted to about 100 units.

HON

T.I. (GB) 1985–1987
1985–1986 T.I. Motors, Greenfields, Bedfordshire.
1986–1987 T.I. Motors, Shefford, Bedfordshire.
Tim Ivory's AC Cobra replica was called the Tuscan and was an early example of a 'budget' kit (costing only £1750). It had a steel box section ladder chassis for Ford Cortina front suspension (modified to accept coil/spring dampers) and a Capri rear end. The recommended engine was either Ford V6 or Rover V8.

CR

TIANJIN (CHI) 1968–1975
Tianjin Auto Works, Tianjin Municipality.

The Tianjin Auto Works started in 1965 with the production of cross country vehicles which were designed by the Beijing Auto Works. In 1968 a 1800 cc Tianjin TJ 740 4-door 4-seater was introduced with production in 1974 at 100 units. In 1986 the first DAIHATSU Charade was assembled by this factory under the XIALI name.

EVIS

TIANLONG (CHI) 1998 to date
China National Special Automobile Corporation Binzhou Company, Binzhou City, Shandong Province.
The Binzhou company produced a 'grandfathers car', a classic fantasy car in open and closed version, named Tianlong ('Dragon') ZQZ 5020 XYLC. The chassis was from the Jiefang CA 1021U2, the engine a Toyota 4Y.

EVIS

TIANMA (CHI) 1995–1998
Tianma Auto Works (People's Liberation Army Works No. 9506), Baoding City, Hebei Province.
The Tianma (Heavenly Horse) Army factory in Baoding specialised in station wagons and pick-ups based on the Beijing Jeep chassis. Several models of a small mini car were made, most of them using the 376Q engine.

EVIS

TIANYANG (CHI) 1997 to date
Guangzhou Auto Corporation, Guangzhou City, Guangdong Province.
In 1985 the Guangzhou Peugeot Auto Corp. started in a part of the old Guangzhou Auto Works the assembly of the Peugeot 504 pick-up, soon followed by the Peugeot 505 estate car. From 1990 to 1997 the Peugeot 505 saloon was made here, under the name of Guangzhou-Peugeot GP 7202/7203. In the top year 1992 GPAC produced 20,000 vehicles, but mostly the yearly production was around 2000–4000 cars. In 1997 Peugeot retreated from Guangzhou. Honda took over, to produce the Guangzhou-Honda Accord HG 7230 saloon. Production of the 505 saloon and estae car was continued under Chinese names: the estate car as Tianyang GP 7222 with a locally built diesel engine, the saloon as Tianyang GP 7200.

EVIS

TIBICAR (I) 1978–c.1988
Tibicar srp, Rome.
The Tibicar Bella 125 was a very basic 3-wheeled microcar with a single front wheel. It was powered by a 123cc BCB 2-stroke 5.5bhp engine, driving the front wheel via a 4-speed gearbox. The independent suspension used hydro-pneumatic damping and there was a front disc brake. The simple bodywork came with removable rear-hinged doors and a lift-out targa roof panel. Among its listed uses was as a hunting vehicle!

CR

TICI (GB) 1972–1973
TiCi Sales Ltd, Sutton-in-Ashfield, Nottinghamshire.
Design lecturer Anthony Hill made his first TiCi city car prototype in 1969: a tiny (72in/1827mm long) microcar powered by a Triumph Daytona 500cc motorcycle engine. The production kit-form TiCi (pronounced tichy) arrived in 1972. It was slightly bigger and featured a striking open-topped fibreglass monocoque body design. It used a Mini front subframe and engine mounted in the rear, and there were removable hard-top and solid door options. Many famous names were involved in the project, including ex-B.R.M. sponsor Raymond Mays and Stirling Moss, while Clive Sinclair was one of 40 customers for the car.

CR

TIC-TAC (F) 1920–1924
F. Dumoulin, Puteaux, Seine.
This cyclecar was powered by a 985cc 4-cylinder Ruby engine and had chain drive. Later models had larger engines by Chapuis-Dornier or Janvier, and were shaft-driven. One had a 1½-litre engine with three valves per cylinder. An early model was driven by its maker in the 1920 Coupe des Voiturettes. *The Autocar* remarked disparagingly 'The Tic-Tac did not have a ghost of a chance in the race, and was a nuisance to the faster machines'. However, at least it had a nice name!

NG

Th Schneider
Models

Sole Concessionaires for
Great Britain & Ireland
and British Possessions :

Th Schneider Automobiles (Eng.)
(WELBECK AGENCY)

**138 LONG ACRE,
LONDON —— W.C.**

'Phone :   Telegrams :
Regent 3322   Autoschnid Rand
London

1997 Tiger (ii) Cub sports car.
TIGER RACING

1990 Tilbury sports car.
LA ROCHELLE AUTO-LOISIRS

TIDAHOLM (S) 1906–1913

Tidaholm Bruks AB, Tidaholm.

This company had a longer history than any other car making firm, for it could trace its origin to the foundation of a mill in 1403. They made trucks from 1903, and these were always the mainstay of their production. From 1906 they made estate bus or shooting brake bodies on their 1-ton truck chassis. One was supplied to King Gustav V. In 1909 a Tidaholm car was announced with an ohc 4-cylinder engine said to have been designed, or inspired, by Ettore Bugatti, but nothing seems to have come of this. After 1913 the company concentrated on trucks and buses, one of their last products being a 6-wheeled bus with a capacity for 72 passengers, the largest bus made in Scandinavia at the time. Production ended in 1932.

NG

TIELONG (CHI) 1993–1994

Tielong Hongda Auto Refit Works, Kaiyan City, Liaoning Province.

This plant specialised in the moulding of fibreglass-reinforced plastic castings for motor cars. It assembled mini cars as well. The Tielong THD 7080 used a Suzuki F8A engine. Its length was 155in (3955mm), its wheelbase 91in (2320mm).

EVIS

TIFFANY (US) 1913–1914

Tiffany Electric Car Co., Flint, Michigan.

This electric car succeeded the FLANDERS (ii) electric, but only lasted for six months. Set up in October 1913, it had rejoined the Flanders fold by March of the following year. Its backer C. Leroy Pelletier, said that his ambition was to become the Henry Ford of the electric automobile industry, but fell sadly short of the mark. Three models were listed, the Mignon and De Luxe coupés at $2500 and $2750, and the Bijou roadster at a very low $750. Pelletier aimed his advertising at women, or rather their husbands, saying 'Of all the things she'd like, she'd like a Tiffany best'.

NG

TIGER (i) (US) 1914–1915

Automobile Cycle Car Co., Detroit, Michigan.

This cyclecar was the last automotive venture of William A. de Schaum who had several unsuccessful cars behind him including the De Schaum and the Suburban. It was originally to be a single-seater called the Auto Cyclecar, but when it appeared in June 1914 it was renamed Tiger and had side by side seating and a 4-cylinder Farmer engine. There was also a 4-seater and a delivery van. More car-like than some cyclecars, it had a 3-speed gearbox and shaft drive. De Schaum died in February 1915, and the Tiger died with him.

NG

TIGER (ii) (GB) 1990 to date

1990–1998 Tiger Cars Ltd, London.
1998 to date Tiger Sportscars Ltd, Thorney Toll, Cambridgeshire.

After trying unsuccessfully to import the South African R.M. Seven, Jim Dudley designed his own Lotus 7-style car. It used a spaceframe chassis with VW Golf-based front suspension and a Ford Cortina live rear axle. The Super Six model had a different nose and a power bulge on the bonnet. A Ford Sierra-based SSi was launched in 1993, featuring an improved chassis, irs and more aggressive styling. A V8 Super Six was also available. A budget model called the Cub arrived in 1996, available with a rounded nose. Tiger also produced a Jaguar D-Type replica, a Ferrari 250LM replica and – new for 1999 – the Storm, a racing-orientated sports car based on the Super Six chassis.

CR

T.I.G.E.R see CARTEL

TILBROOK (AUS) 1953

Tilbrook Motorcycles, Kensington, South Australia.

Rex Tilbrook became prominent with his motorcycles and sidecars in the postwar years. At the 1953 Adelaide Show a 3-wheeled minicar was exhibited. This was powered by a rear-mounted 197cc Villiers 2-stroke engine driving through a 4-speed gearbox. Built on a tubular chassis with a fully independent suspension and rack-and-pinion steering, its body was aluminium. Although it attracted a buyer, no further examples were built owing to the demand for motorcycles and sidecars.

MG

TILBURY (F) 1986 to date

1986–1988 Stylisme et Mécanique Sportive, Coignières.
1988–1990 La Rochelle Auto-Loisirs, La Rochelle.
1990–1996 Martin Production, Olonne-sur-Mer.
1996 to date Vibraction, Roanne.

The Tilbury was a vaguely Morganesque 1930s style plastic-bodied roadster kit based on Renault 4 parts, conceived by Yves Charles. Kits and complete cars were marketed. As Martin took over production, a new MkII version based on Renault 5 parts was launched, although it retained the R4 chassis. To address more modern needs, in 1998 a new version using Peugeot parts was developed.

CR

TILEY (US) 1904–1913

The Tiley-Pratt Co., Essex, Connecticut.

This company was primarily a manufacturer of bicycle parts, but they made a few cars to special order over a number of years. Built by Charles B. Tiley and his two brothers, they had mostly 32/36hp 4-cylinder Rutenber engines, though a few sixes were made as well. All had shaft drive. Not more than 24 Tileys were made altogether.

NG

TILIKUM (US) 1914

Tilikum Cyclecar Co., Seattle, Washington.

This cyclecar was powered by a 10/14hp air-cooled V-twin engine and had an unusual transmission in which a variable pulley system provided 12 forward speeds. A belt tightener moved the entire rear axle forwards or backwards by about 3in (76mm), a system also used on the first Bédélias. The word Tilikum means 'friend' in the Chinook language, but the cyclecar won few friends in Seattle, and probably did not progress beyond the prototype stage.

NG

TILKE (AUS) 1987–1996

Tilke Engineering, Riverstone, New South Wales.

Keith Tilke's experience with car building dated from 1958, when he built a fibreglass special in England. His first Australian effort was the Steed, a roadster of classic lines on a Toyota Crown chassis powered by a Leyland Australia alloy V8. The more affordable Amaroo Clubman followed in 1988, and this used Ford Escort, Holden Gemini and Toyota Corolla parts. It was also made in racing trim as the Sprinter. A Morgan-like roadster, the KTW 2XL, was a kit offering of 1990. The 1993 KTW Sting, a mid-engined targa-top, fitted supercharged Toyota 1.6-litre twin-cam power into a spaceframe. A Ford GT40 replica followed which mated 5-litre Ford V8 power to a Porsche transaxle. The KTW Echo of 1996 was a fibreglass-carbon fibre bodied roadster on a backbone frame chassis, with a 312bhp Lexus V8 engine and automatic transmission. With fully independent suspension, it was built on a wheelbase of 100in (2550mm), was notably wide and weighed 2596lb (1180kg).

MG

TILLI (AUS) 1957–1958

Tilli Motor Co., Moonee Ponds, Victoria.

Reg Tilley was the maker of after-market motor fittings. He entered the miniature car field with his 3-wheeled Capton, which was built on a chassis supplied by EDITH maker, Gray & Harper. On a wheelbase of 75in (1829mm), it used a more powerful 2-cylinder 350cc British Anzani engine giving 16bhp. It was clothed in attractive fibreglass bodies of roadster or hard-top types but it was obviously not received with enthusiasm as only four chassis were supplied. The fibreglass working abilities were applied to boats and he soon returned to South Australia.

MG

TIME MACHINE (US) c.1993–1995

Time Machine Motorcar Co., Brooksville, Florida.

The Time Machine 38 Special was a replica of the Jaguar SS100. It used Ford Pinto or Mustang suspension and a variety of engines, from 4-cylinder Fords to Chevrolet V8s, were optional. It had a fibreglass body, a steel tube frame and was sold in kit form. The 659 Speedster was a customised Porsche Speedster replica with a slotted nose and tail spoiler. It was based on Volkswagen running gear. The Starfighter was a typical Lamborghini Countach replica kit that fitted on a Pontiac Fiero chassis. The Decepzione Starfighter was the same Lamborghini-replica bodywork on a custom spaceframe with Corvette-derived suspension.

HP

TIMMIS (CDN) 1968 to date

Timmis Motor Co., Victoria, British Columbia.

One of the world's first – and certainly longest-lived – replicars, the Timmis recreated in extraordinary detail the 1934 Ford V8 Model 40 roadster. Unusually, it used a mixture of old, new and remanufactured parts, including a 3.9-litre Mercury 239 V8 engine from the 1939–48 period. The transmission, differential and brakes originated from Ford of Canada production cars of the 1949–54 period. The bodywork was unerringly modern, being made of fibreglass. Each recreation reputedly took one year to build.

CR

TIMOR (RI) 1996–1998

PT Timor Putra Nasional, Jakarta.

Indonesia's national car maker was founded by Tommy Suharto, son of the President Suharto, whose other car interests included ownership of Lamborghini and, for a while, Vector. The Timor S-515 was a slightly modified Kia Sephia saloon, and sold 6042 units in its first year of production. Nearly 19,000 were registered by the end of 1997, but the economic crisis that swept south-east Asia, together with the fall of the Suharto regime, was a fatal blow for the Timor, exacerbated by the simultaneous and unrelated bankruptcy of Kia Motors. At the end of 1998 14,000 cars remained unsold, and perhaps as many as 6000 were virtually scrap due to being stored in the open air.

NG

TINCHER (US) 1903–1909

1903–1906 Chicago Coach & Carriage Co., Chicago, Illinois.
1906–1909 Tincher Motor Car Co., South Bend, Indiana.

1959 Tippen Delta invalid car.
NICK GEORGANO/NATIONAL MOTOR MUSEUM

George Tincher made large and expensive cars which were originally built for him by the Chicago Coach & Carriage Co., and after his move to South Bend, in his own factory. His first car had an 18hp 4-cylinder engine, and was remarkable for its engine-driven air pump which compressed air to operate the brakes, and also to pump up the tyres and operate a whistle which took the place of the horn. For 1904 he offered a 45hp tourer for $5000 and a 90hp race car [sic] on the same 90in (2284mm) wheelbase, selling for no less than $12,000. For 1905 the tourer had a 60hp engine and wheelbase was increased to 125in (3172mm). The 60hp (sometimes rendered as 50hp, but probably the same unit) was continued to the end of production in 1909, and was joined in 1908 only by a 90hp six. Prices were as high as $7000. All Tinchers had chain drive. They were made in very small numbers, not more than six per year. The major stockholders in the Tincher Motor Car Co. at South Bend were the Studebaker brothers.

NG

TINY (GB) 1912–1915

Nanson, Barker & Co., Esholt, Yorkshire.

George Barker was a fellmonger, or dealer in skins and hides, and it was in a corner of his doubtless malodorous premises that his son Norman and friend Guy Nanson set up their car business. The first Tiny was a cyclecar powered by an 8hp air-cooled V-twin JAP engine, with 3-speed gearbox and final drive by chains. With a coachbuilt aluminium body, it sold for 98 guineas (£102.90). This car was shown at the Motorcycle Show at Olympia in November 1912, and the following year there was a new model with water-cooled Precision engine and shaft drive, priced at £135. This in turn gave way in mid–1914 to a further development with 10hp 4-cylinder Dorman engine. The Tiny was now a genuine light car, though few of these were made because of the war. How many Tinys were made altogether is uncertain. Some sources claim only three, but that would mean only one of each type, which is unlikely given that at least three were made of the first model, one being a delivery van. Certainly output was pretty limited. It did not survive the war and a new, larger, car called the Airedale was made by Nanson, Barker from 1919.

NG

Further Reading
'The Tiny and the Tyke from Esholt', M. Worthington-Williams, *The Automobile*, October 1995.

TIPPEN (GB) c.1950–c.1970

Frank Tippen & Sons, Coventry.

This company began by making conventional open invalid tricycles powered by a 147cc single-cylinder Villiers engine, with 3-speed gearbox and drive to one rear wheel. More distinctive was their Delta introduced in 1956, which had a narrow fibreglass body with a forward sliding door and roll-back hood. Like the rival INVACAR, the Delta was powered by a 197cc Villiers engine, with 4-speed gearbox. Two models were made, the first with a single headlamp, the second, the MOH Model 49, with twin headlamps. The standard colour was ice blue.

NG

c.1985 T.M.C.-Costin sports car.
NICK BALDWIN

TISCHER (US) 1914

Linton G. Tischer Tri-Car Co., Peoria, Illinois.
Linton Tischer ran a bicycle shop in the same building as the drugstore operated by his father, and assembled a few examples of a curious 3-wheeled cyclecar. It had a single front wheel, behind which was a 9hp air-cooled V-twin engine which drove the rear wheels by a long belt. It was priced at $425, later reduced to $350.
NG

TITAN (GB) 1911

Titan Motor Wheel Co., Coventry.
This could be considered as an early example of a cyclecar. It was a 3-wheeler powered by a 5¼hp single-cylinder Fafnir engine, with 2-speed epicyclic transmission and chain drive to the rear wheel. The frame was of ash, and the price was £78.75.
NG

TITANIA (I) 1966

Titania, Turin.
The main claim to fame of this unusual, swoopy 2-seater sports coupé was that it was designed by Franco Scaglione. It used a front-mounted Ford Cortina GT engine and was displayed at the Turin Racing Car Show and Turin Motor Show, but unfortunately did not enter production.
CR

TIVY (US) 1901–1903

Tivy Cycle Manufacturing Co., Williamsport, Pennsylvania.
This was a typical light steam runabout with wire wheels and full-elliptic suspension at front and rear. It was designed by Harry Rantz and built by a cycle maker.
NG

T&J (GB) 1989 to date

1989–1992 T&J Sportscars, Rotherham, Yorkshire.
1992 to date B.W.E. Sports Cars, Barnsley, South Yorkshire.
This company took over the Midge and Locust kit/plans built cars from J.C. in 1989. It then developed the Hornet in 1991 as an easier-to-build sister model, with a bigger cabin and a taller body. It was based entirely around Ford Cortina parts, although the front wishbones were replaced by specially fabricated items. Almost any engine could fit under the bonnet, the most popular being Ford, Toyota and Fiat.
CR

TLC CARROSSIERS (US) c.1992 to date

TLC Carrossiers Inc., Riviera Beach, Florida.
The Talbo was an exceptional replica of the Figoni et Falaschi-bodied 1938 Talbot-Lago. It was based on a perimeter frame with fabricated front suspension and a Ford Thunderbird independent system at rear. Power was from a Ford 5000cc V8 and manual or automatic transmissions. The body was a very convincing copy with correct trim and an inviting luxury interior. They were only sold in fully assembled form for $106,000 and were custom tailored for the buyer.
HP

T.M.C. (IRE) 1983–1988

Thompson Manufacturing Co., Castlebridge, Co. Wexford.
Frank Costin, the famous aerodynamicist whose work included the Lotus Mk 8, 9 and 11, Vanwall and Marcos, was asked by engineer Peter Thompson to design this Irish equivalent of a Caterham Seven. Costin's spaceframe chassis was widely admired, the ifs, self-levelling oleopneumatic rear end and ride quality being particularly praised. The initial choice of Vauxhall Chevette engines was questioned, however, and most in fact used Ford engines (84bhp 1600, 110bhp XR2 or 130bhp Cosworth BDR). Unusually for Costin, the fibreglass/Kevlar/ aluminium body looked awkward and unhappy and the standard fixed hard-top and upward-hinging doors made entry difficult. A targa- top and glass rear hatch were standard. Cars were sold in kit form at around £6000 and some 26 cars were built in all. Some notable racing success was also gained and the chassis design later evolved into the PANOZ.
CR

T.M.; T.M.F. (US) 1906–1909

1906 Termaat and Monahan, Oshkosh, Wisconsin.
1909 Badger Manufacturing Co., Oshkosh, Wisconsin.
In 1906 J.D. Termaat and Louis J. Monahan built a typical high-wheeler, unusual only in having lhd. A few were made for local customers, and in 1909 the two partners were joined by a third. H. Homer Fahrney was a wealthy young man who provided the cash to form the Badger company. This was going to make another high-wheeler under the name T.M.F., but production barely started.
NG

TOBOGGAN (GB) 1905–1906

Toboggan Tri-Car Co. Ltd, London.
Although it was called a tri-car, the Toboggan was more car-like than most of its kind, for it had wheel steering and proper seats for driver and passenger. A choice of engines was offered, a 4½hp Aster or 6hp Fafnir. Transmission was by friction discs and single-chain final drive.
NG

TOJEIRO (GB) 1954–1962

Tojeiro Automotive Developments Ltd, Barkway, Royston, Hertfordshire.
After serving in the Fleet Air Arm in World War II, John Tojeiro set himself up in a small workshop to undertake light engineering work. He was inspired by the MG Specials built by a neighbour, Harry Lester, to build a car on similar lines.
Tojeiro's next inspiration was a Cooper-MG owned by Brian Lister, who allowed him to take measurements from it. Tojeiro built a car on similar lines which he planned to race. While it was under construction, Chris Sears made him an offer and Tojeiro ceased being a special builder and became a constructor.
Tojeiro provided a ladderframe with all independent suspension, by transverse springs and lower wishbones, and alloy wheels supplied by Turner. About a dozen chassis was supplied and buyers arranged their own engines and bodies. Consequently, no two Tojeiros were alike. The Sears car had cycle-wings and somebody else fitted the body from a V12 Lagonda Project 115 which he discovered in a scrapyard. Brian Lister bought a chassis and fitted a skimpy body and a V-twin JAP engine. Nicknamed 'Asteroid'. this car launched the career of the great Archie Scott Brown.
The most successful of the ladderframe cars, LOY 500, had a Bristol engine and a body which copied the *barchetta* shell which Touring devised for the Ferrari 166. By a circuitous route, this became the AC Ace and, hence, the Cobra 289.
After selling the rights of his ladderframe car to AC, for £5 for each of the first 100 chassis, in 1955 Tojeiro produced a new design with a spaceframe, de Dion rear axle, and front suspension by coil springs and wishbones, and set up a company called Tojeiro Automotive Developments Ltd. Two cars were built that year, one with a Bristol engine, the other with a 2½-litre Lea-Francis unit, but a Jaguar engine was later substituted.
An improved, lighter, frame followed in 1956 and four were made, two with Bristol engines, one with a Coventry Climax FWA unit, and one with a flat-four, air-cooled, AJB engine. With outfits like Cooper, Lotus and Lister in the field, none of these cars achieved much success.

A wealthy amateur racer, John Ogier, commissioned a lightweight Jaguar-engined car. Subsequently three others were made, but none could compete with the Lister-Jaguar. Many of Tojeiro's post-ladderframe cars were styled by Cavendish Morton, an artist, who would paint a picture of the body which was then made up by Mo Gomm.

AC commissioned a special Bristol-engined car for Le Mans in 1958, which Tojeiro made along the lines of his 'production' models. Unfortunately, it was not as quick as the standard Ace.

In 1958 Tojeiro designed the BRITANNIA (iii) GT car, and to drum up interest, Britannia also commissioned him to build some Formula Junior cars. These appeared as both Britannias and Tojeiros, but were off the pace. Tojeiro's 'Bandit' sports car, designed for BERKELEY, was widely admired, bur Berkeley went into receivership before production could begin.

Finally, Ecurie Ecosse commissioned two cars for 1962 and one can claim to be the grandfather of all mid-engined GTs. Neither achieved success at international level, but one helped bring Jackie Stewart to prominence in 1963.

During the 1980s John Tojeiro became associated with the kit car company, D.J. Sportscars whose products included a copy of the Cobra 427. This was marketed under the name, Dax Tojeiro, though there was only the most tenuous link between Tojeiro and the Cobra 427.

MJL

TOLEDO (i) (US) 1901–1903
International Motor Car Co., Toledo, Ohio.

This began as a light steam car made by the American Bicycle Co. under the name Billings after its designer Frederick Billings. Early in 1901 the American Bicycle Co. was reorganised as the International Motor Car Co., making two models of steam car, the Toledo and the Westchester. By the end of the year the marque name had been changed to Toledo, and the Westchester was dropped. The steamer was powered by a 6¼ hp vertical 2-cylinder engine, with tiller steering and single-chain drive. Five body styles were offered, from $800 for the Junior Runabout to $1600 for a 4-seater surrey. In 1902 a new model was introduced with 16hp 3-cylinder petrol engine, 50 of which were made that year. For 1903 more petrol models were offered, a 12hp 2-cylinder and 24hp 3-cylinder, and the steamer range was scaled down.

In May 1903 the International Motor Car Co. was succeeded by the Pope Motor Car Co. The steamers were discontinued and the petrol cars continued under the name POPE-TOLEDO.

NG

TOLEDO (ii) (US) 1913–1914
Toledo Auto-Cycle Car Co., Toledo, Ohio.

This was a typical cyclecar with 9hp V-twin engine, friction transmission with belt final drive and tandem seating.

NG

TOM see FERBEDO

TOMASZO (A) 1977–c.1995
Tomaszo GmbH, Achau.

Beginning life in 1977 as a maker of fibreglass panels and accessories, this constructor pursued a wide variety of specialist product lines in Austria. Most popular were replicas and hot rods based on the 1932 and 1934 Ford Model A, plus an MG TF replica. There was also a Mercedes SSK replica, usually based on a VW Beetle chassis but also available with a special chassis designed for Ford Taunus and Sierra or Opel Kadett and Ascona mechanicals. More convincing were replicas of the Alfa Romeo P3 and P36 using Alfetta engines and rear transaxles. An Alfa P35 version was also offered with a VW Beetle engine. Tomaszo also engaged in the manufacture of beach buggies and VW Beetle body transformations, and made the fibreglass bodies for LEDL, a compatriot enterprise.

CR

TOMCAR (F) 1983–1985
Tomcar, St-Just-en-Chaussée.

Inherent in the Tomcar's flat-panel styling was a cartoon-like sense of humour, its bug-eyed headlamps and separate wings hinting at a bygone age. A 49cc Peugeot engine was used initially, but later BCB 125cc petrol and Lombardini

1953 Tojeiro-Bristol sports car.
NATIONAL MOTOR MUSEUM

1955 Tojeiro-Bristol sports car.
NATIONAL MOTOR MUSEUM

1902 Toledo (i) 6¼hp steam car.
NICK BALDWIN

325cc diesel options were added. Novelties included front-wheel drive and 4-wheel disc brakes. Two body styles were offered: an enclosed *berline* and a cabriolet. The design reappeared in Spain in 1986 as the Pypper.

CR

TOMCAT (GB) 1986; 1993–1994
1986 Hardy Racing Organisation, Nuthall, Nottingham.
1993–1994 Tomcat Cars, Nottingham.

Details of Alan Hardy's mid-engined sports coupé emerged as early as 1986 but it only appeared (at several kit car shows) during 1993 and 1994. It was an ambitiously styled fibreglass coupé built over a steel spaceframe chassis with custom-fabricated independent suspension. Planned production never commenced.

CR

1903 Tony Huber 8hp tonneau.
NICK GEORGANO

TOMITA (J/GB) 1996–1999
Tomita Auto UK, Hingham, Norfolk

Yoshikazu Tomita and Kikuo Kaira, whose company, Tomita, modified production cars, wanted to build a sports car, but owing to restrictions and regulations in their native Japan, this was not feasible. They therefore established a factory in Norfolk – Britain seemed the natural place to build specialist sports cars and Norfolk was where their hero, Colin Chapman, had located Lotus.

The Tomita Tommy Kaira ZZ was a mid-engined two-seater sports car powered by a 183bhp 1998cc Nissan in-line 4-cylinder engine. Top speed was a claimed 140mph (225km/h) with 0–60mph (97km/h) in 4.6 seconds. Production was limited to six cars a week and most cars were exported to Japan. At one time there was a waiting list delay of about 18 months on new orders, but the Japanese economic crisis ruined the market, and Tomita went into liquidation early in 1999.

MJL

TOM POUCE (F) 1920–1924
1920–1923 Blanc et Guillon, Puteaux, Seine.
1923–1924 Garage Ernault, Dommartin, Somme.

The Tom Pouce (Tom Thumb) cyclecar was powered initially by a 750cc 4-cylinder engine made by Lemaitre et Gérard, who also supplied this unit to Dalila, Zévaco and other small firms. Later Tom Pouces used the larger 1095cc Ruby engine. They had conventional gearboxes and shaft drive. Some of the earlier Tom Pouce cars had staggered seating.

NG

TONELLO (I) 1921–1923
Automobili Guido Meregalli, Milan.

This was a sports car powered by a 1.7-litre single-ohc 4-cylinder engine which developed 50bhp and gave the car a top speed of 80mph (129km/h). Interesting features of the design included dual magneto ignition and a steering column with adjustable rake. Its maker Guido Meregalli was a successful racing driver, winning the 1920 Targa Florio in a six-year old Nazzaro, and the Circuit of Garda in 1922, 1923, and 1924 in a Diatto.

NG

TONGBAO (CHI) 1996–1997
Yuanhu Special Vehicle No. 3 Works, Anhui Province.

The Tongbao No. 3 was one of the many Chinese small saloons with a fibreglass body. These vehicles were very popular in the early 1990s. Production was always on a very small scale – around 100 units per year.

EVIS

TONTALA (AUS) 1955
Tontala Motor Co., Canterbury, Victoria.

Early on the scene with a fibreglass body, this concept of Tony Theiler (pronounced Tyler, giving rise to Tontala) was the first such sports coupé to employ Holden components. The engine had valve modifications and two carburettors for

91bhp, its wheelbase was 102in (2590mm) and its weight 866kg. Exhibited at the Melbourne Motor Show, it attracted 40 orders, caused a sensation and became the focus of intense media attention. Achieving production, however, was an entirely different matter and the problems finally proved to be insurmountable. The next year saw the offer to supply the body and specific items for customer construction, but that scheme also failed.

MG

TONY HUBER (F) 1902–1906
Automobiles Tony Huber, Billancourt, Seine.

Tony Huber was born in 1874, and after an engineering training formed the MORISSE company. He also made proprietary engines under his own name, and in 1902 launched a range of complete cars with Arbel steel frames. These included 8 and 11hp 2-cylinder models, the latter with chain drive, though all other models, larger as well as smaller, were shaft-driven. The 4-cylinder models included 14, 16/18, and 20/25hp cars. Although his output was relatively small there are two surviving 8hp cars in England today. In February 1905 Huber formed a company with Armand Peugeot to make engines, motor boats and electrical equipment. A 1912 advertisement advised customers 're-engine your car cheaply and efficiently with the famous Tony Huber engine'. The Peugeot link was dissolved in 1912, but in 1920. Tony Huber et Compagnie was listed at a different address as a maker of motor boats.

NG

TOQUET (US) 1905
Toquet Motor Car Construction Co., Saugatuck, Connecticut.

B.L. Toquet designed a large and advanced car with 7.5-litre 45hp 4-cylinder T-head engine with detachable cylinder head and a flyball governor so connected that the clutch and brake pedals also operated the accelerator. The gearbox had only two speeds, and final drive was by shaft. A 5-seater tourer was made in very small numbers.

NG

TORBENSEN (US) 1902–1906
Torbensen Gear Co., Bloomfield, New Jersey.

This company was better known for transmissions than for its cars, but a small runabout was made in 1902, and a few others were completed over the next four years. In 1905 Torbensen built a tourer with 20hp air-cooled 6-cylinder engine, and a 14hp 3-cylinder delivery van. Commercial vehicles may have been built up to 1911, and the company later became a major supplier of axles to the motor industry.

NG

TORINO (RA) 1966–1992
1966–1968 Industrias Kaiser Argentina SAIC, Cordoba.
1968–1975 IKA Renault SA, Cordoba.
1975–1992 Renault Argentina SA, Cordoba.

A diversity of foreign designs were made by this company. Among them, the JEEP, KAISER, BERGANTIN and RAMBLER. Since the fusion with RENAULT, it also made these cars. The Torino is considered entirely Argentinian, but in fact was a Rambler derivative. It was a Rambler redesigned by Pininfarina. In 1966 the Torino was presented in three versions: 380W, 380 and 300. The 380 line was powered by a 3.8-litre ohc 6-cylinder engine, had coil spring suspension all around and ZF manual gearbox with three forward speeds (4-speed standard from 1970). These cars were also fitted with front disc brakes. The body was a hard-top coupé. The 300 was a 4-door saloon with the same basic engine but with only 3-litre capacity.

Torinos became very popular, being the 'in' car for many Argentine sportsmen of the 1960s. The most coveted model was the 380W with three Weber carburettors and 176 to 250bhp, depending on its state of tune. In the first year of production only six 380W coupés were made, while 158 380 coupés and 293 300 saloons came out of the Cordoba plant. By 1971, 1241 380W coupés had been made and 12,208 380 coupés. The 380W coupés were raced widely. In February 1967, the first Turismo Carretera road race of the year was won by Héctor Luis Gradassi, driving a 380W coupé. Torinos even tried their luck at the Nürburgring circuit in 1969, where they were rewarded with a class win. In 1972 the larger engine was standardised.

1966 Torino 380 coupé.
NICK GEORGANO/NATIONAL MOTOR MUSEUM

In the final years of production, Torinos could only be obtained to special order. By then, the coupé version had become a cult car in Argentina, and when the last Torino came out of the Cordoba plant in 1992, some models were already collector's items. Not long afterwards, a Torino owner's club was founded.

ACT

TORNADO (i) (GB) 1958–1964

1958–1963 Tornado Cars Ltd, Rickmansworth, Hertfordshire.
1963–1964 Tornado Cars (1963) Ltd, Rickmansworth, Hertfordshire.

In the late 1950s, Bill Woodhouse bought a kit car and found that it was almost impossible to assemble so he designed one which could be easily assembled. It had a simple ladder frame and a body which, while not a thing of beauty, was well-made and practical. The chassis cost £70, the body £130 and, at its launch, Woodhouse produced receipts to prove that he had built his car for less then £250, including the cost of the donor car.

The basic Ford-powered kit, the Typhoon sold about 400 examples, between 1958 and 1962. It could be had as a 2- or 4-seater, a hard-top was available as was the world's first production sports estate car.

The Tempest of 1960 was a Typhoon to take more modern engines from Ford, BMC and Triumph. It had rack-and-pinion steering and Triumph Herald front suspension and brakes. About 15 were made. The Thunderbolt was intended to take Triumph TR or Ford Consul engines, but it remained a one-off because it was nearly impossible to drive.

Kit cars disappeared from the range in 1962 as Tornado introduced the Talisman, a 2+2 GT available in component form, or as a finished car. The ladder frame had coil spring suspension all round, with a live rear axle and Triumph Herald front suspension.

Various Ford engines were offered in a range of tune from 55 to 85bhp and the Talisman was the first road car to have an engine tuned by Cosworth.

The Talisman handled well, was quick for its day, and was comfortable, practical, and well-finished. It promised much – Lotus even considered taking over the design – but Tornado encountered cash-flow problems and went into liquidation after making 186 Talismans.

MJL

1963 Tornado (i) Talisman coupé.
NICK BALDWIN

TORNADO (ii) (GB) 1987 to date

Tornado Sports Cars, Kidderminster, Worcestershire.

Tornado's first offering was a McLaren M6GT replica, unpromisingly based on a VW Beetle floorpan. Later versions gained a tubular spaceframe chassis intended for mid-mounted Renault V6, Rover or small block V8 power. Production was always very limited and the company was more successful with its TS40, a replica of the Ford GT40. Its specification consisted of a spaceframe chassis, original-style double wishbone front and A-frame/double radius arm rear suspension, Rover or small block V8 engines and a Renault transaxle. Optional rose-jointed suspension was intended for competition use. An authentic but rare replica monocoque version became available from 1992, hand-built either in steel (as per the original) or lightweight aluminium. Bolt-on subframes supported the bodywork, and there was unique suspension. A brand new V8 sports model was launched in 1998 – a clubman's car with all-independent suspension and Rover V8 power.

CR

1934 Tornax Rex 700cc sports car.
HANS-OTTO NEUBAUER

1999 Torrelaro replica Mercedes Benz SSK sports car.
NICK GEORGANO

TORNAX (D) 1934–1937
Tornax Fahrzeug- und Apparatenbau GmbH, Wuppertal-Langerfeld.
Makers of motorcycles since 1925, Tornax launched a small sports car called the Rex. It used the complete front end, engine and drive system of the 700cc DKW. It had a central tubular frame and independent suspension all round. It was an economical and reasonably-priced sports car, though not a startling performer. After car production ended Tornax continued to make motorcycles until 1955.
HON

TORPEDO (i) (A) 1906–1907
Frantisek Trojan a Alois Nagl, tovarna na motocykly a automobily, Kolin.
This motorcycle factory produced a small number of voiturettes with V-twin-cylinder sv 7bhp engines of their own design and manufacture, as an attempt to enlarge their successful motorcycle manufacture.
MSH

TORPEDO (ii) (GB) 1909
F. Hopper & Co. Ltd, Barton-on-Humber, Lincolnshire.
Though sold under the name Torpedo, these cars were in fact made by the STAR (i) Cycle Co., only the finishing touches being made by Hopper. A 6hp single-cylinder model was first made, which gave way to a 2-cylinder car. They also made motorcycles from 1910 to 1920, and bicycles into the 1960s.
NG

TORPILLE (B) 1920
M.M. Schoofs et Compagnie, Brussels-Ixelles.
Called by its makers an 'automobilette Torpille', this was a 3-wheeler with tandem seating, powered by a 1-litre V-twin JAP engine or a slightly smaller Train unit. It was expensive for what it offered, and very few were made.
NG

TORRELARO (U) 1989 to date
Guitolar SRL, Montevideo.
Thirty Torrelaro automobiles had been made by 1999. These were Mercedes-Benz powered replicas of the famed SSK sports-roadsters. The Torrelaro bodies and chassis were made entirely of stainless steel. Body panels were hammered

by craftsmen over wooden dies. The engine used was the Mercedes type W114, 6-cylinder, 2.5-litre. The bodies were open 2-seaters, with or without doors. Lhd versions were exported to Germany and rhd versions to the UK.
ACT

TOSAPE PUBLISHING (US) c.1952
Tosape Publishing Co., Aurora, Missouri.
This company sold a book called *How to Build Your Own Sports Car*. It showed how to build a custom car based on body panels and running gear from prewar American sedans. Their prototype was built by Charles Martz, and it was a handsome 2-seat convertible based on parts from two old Hudson sedans. This car was featured on the cover of *Motor Trend* magazine along with a feature article on the construction. A number of similar cars were built from the instructions.
HP

TOTAL PERFORMANCE (US) c.1971 to date
Total Performance, Wallingford, Connecticut.
This company first made parts for hot rods. This logically led to the production of hot rod kits in 1980. Some of the many Ford models that they have replicated in 'hot-rodded' form were the Model A, 1923 Model T Roadster, 1930 Phaeton and the 1932 Highboy. Total performance also bought the GLASSIC line of Model A replicas. These were very popular kits and included frames, trim and performance parts. They were designed for Ford and Chevrolet V8 engines.
HP

TOTEM (i) (US) 1921–1922
Davis Car Co., Seattle, Washington.
This was a tourer powered by a 38hp 4-cylinder Herschell-Spillman engine. Unusually for a car of this size and date, it used friction disc transmission.
NG

TOTEM (ii) (I) 1974–c.1977
This was a licence-built version of the NOVA with the distinction of conventional doors rather than a clamshell canopy. It predated the PUMA.
CR

TOURAINE (US) 1912–1916
1912 Nance Motor Car Co., Philadelphia, Pennsylvania.
1913–1915 Touraine Co., Philadelphia, Pennsylvania.
This car was the Nance renamed, because of additional finance from a Mr Touraine. It retained the 6½-litre 35/40hp 6-cylinder engine and 124in (3147mm) wheelbase, although prices were higher by $350 for the two models, tourer and runabout. From 1913 to 1916 the engine was rated as a 45/50hp and an additional 134in (3401mm) wheelbase was offered. In 1914 there were six body styles on the 134in (3401mm) chassis, and prices were up to $4350. A cyclecar called the VIM was made in 1914, but more important for the company's future were the trucks, also called Vim. In November 1915 Touraine announced that they would abandon cars for trucks, though 1916 Touraines had been made, and that the company name would be changed to the Vim Motor Truck Co. This lasted until 1923.
NG

TOURAND (F) 1900–1907
Tourand et Cie, Le Havre, Seine Inférieure; Suresnes, Seine.
Tourand made a car in 1900 with a front-mounted 6hp 2-cylinder Crozet-type engine and double-chain drive. There was no trace of cars for a few years, but in 1905 a range of shaft-driven 4-cylinder cars was introduced. These were of 16, 18, 40, 60, and 70hp. As with a number of these small French firms, one wonders if all these were actually built, although an 80hp Tourand racing car was advertised second-hand in *The Autocar* in 1912. It was said to have been specially built for the Coupe de la Presse, though when was not divulged.
NG

TOURETTE (GB) 1956–1957
The Progress Supreme Co., Purley, Surrey.
The egg-shaped Tourette, first displayed at the 1956 Earls Court Motor Show, bore a striking resemblance to the German Brütsch. Having built some fibreglass-bodied

scooters, the Tourette trike was a new departure for the parent company. A Villiers 197cc engine sat just in front of the single rear wheel. The 102in (2590mm) plastic-bodied car weighed only 430lbs (195kg) and was claimed to reach a top speed of 55mph (88kh/h). Soft- and hard-tops were available to cover the occupants – the manufacturers optimistically stated that three adults could fit in the cockpit. Only a handful of Tourettes were built during 1957.

CR

TOUREY (F) 1898
Jules Tourey, Paris.
This little car had a rear-mounted 4hp single-cylinder horizontal engine with a choice of two bodies, a 3-seater light carriage and a 4-seater Petit Duc. Probably only prototypes were made.

NG

TOURIST (i) (US) 1902–1910
The Auto Vehicle Co., Los Angeles, California.
The best-known West Coast make of the pre-World War I era, the Tourist began life as a 2-seater with detachable tonneau and with a 7hp single-cylinder engine under the seat, and single-chain drive. It looked similar to the contemporary Ford or Cadillac, though unlike these it had tiller steering. It was apparently not a success, and a 12hp 2-cylinder engine was substituted for 1904, when the Tourist had a front-mounted radiator similar to that of a Peugeot, though the engine was still under the seat. 75 cars were made in 1904, and 150 in 1905. In 1906, when production reached 487, a 35hp 4-cylinder engine was available as well as the 20hp twin.

From 1906 to 1910 2- and 4-cylinder models were made, the latter growing in size to reach 45/50hp on a 118in (2995mm) wheelbase in 1909. However all was not well with the company, which had difficulty in obtaining parts, and in November 1909 they sold out to the newly-formed California Automobile Co. Volney Beardsley, who had been president of the Auto Vehicle Co., became president of the new organisation, which made both California and Tourist cars during 1910. In September of that year both makes were discontinued; California became a dealership and the Tourist factory was taken over by former works manager William J. Burt, who would provide spare parts for owners of Tourist cars. In 1914 the California company entered car manufacture again with the BEARDSLEY electric. A total of 2692 Tourist cars were made.

NG

TOURIST (ii) (D) 1907–1920
1907–1911 Tourist Automobilwerk GmbH, Berlin-Tempelhof.
1911–1920 Berliner Automobilfabrik 'Torpedo' Georg Beck & Co., Berlin.
This was a 3-wheeler with single front wheel behind which was a 7PS air-cooled V-twin engine, which drove a separate 2-speed gearbox by shaft, with final drive by chains. A 5/10PS 4-cylinder engine was also available. The bodies were open 2-, 3-, or 4-seaters at first, while later models were offered with closed bodies, and a delivery van was also catalogued.

HON

TOWANDA (US) 1902–1904
Towanda Motor Vehicle Co., Towanda, Pennsylvania.
This company was organised by Charles Lindstrom who had been making the NIAGARA electric car in Buffalo. The Towanda was also an electric, but although he may have made the running gear, the body and frame probably came from suppliers such as BORBEIN or BRECHT. A workforce of 20 men assembled only seven Towandas during 1902; there was then an interval of a year before Lindstrom offered the same sort of vehicle as he had bought from Borbein or Brecht two years before, i.e.: a frame with wheels and seats, to which the buyer could fit his own engine.

NG

TOWNE SHOPPER (US) 1948
International Motor Car Co., San Diego, California.
This economy car was designed for short trips to the store rather than for highway use. This was a good idea, considering it only had a 10hp Onan 2-cylinder engine. It had a simple aluminium body with no doors.

HP

1957 Tourette Supreme 3-wheeler.
NICK GEORGANO/NATIONAL MOTOR MUSEUM

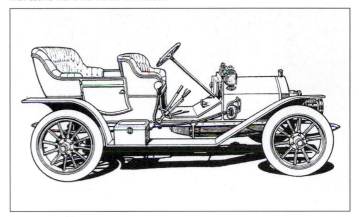

1909 Tourist (i) Type G tourer.
NICK GEORGANO

TOYOTA (i) (J) 1936 to date
1936 Toyota Automatic Loom Works, Kariya City.
1937 to date Toyota Motor Corp., Toyota City.
Today the world's largest vehicle manufacturer, with an annual output of over four million cars and commercial vehicles, Toyota began as a small offshoot of the Toyota Loom Works. Car development was started by Kiichiro Toyota (1894–1952), son of the company's founder Sakichi Toyota, and his first car was an amalgam of American designs. The 3389cc 6-cylinder engine, gearbox and frame were based on a Chevrolet, while the styling was a close copy of the Chrysler Airflow, although the Toyota's headlamps were mounted separately instead of being faired into the wings. The prototype was known as the A-i and appeared in 1935. Only three were made, but production started in 1936 of the generally similar AA. The Toyota Motor Corp. was founded in August 1937, the name being chosen in preference to Toyoda, although that is the Japanese pronunciation. The AA was made up to 1943, along with a 4-door tourer version called the AB. Production was 1404 of the AA and 353 of the AB. In 1943 a more powerful engine was used in the similarly styled AC, of which 115 were made. As this was the middle of the war, presumably most became military staff cars. Several other prototypes were built between 1939 and 1944, including the AE with 2258cc 4-cylinder engine, and several models of the B which had an 85bhp version of the Chevrolet-based engine. American influence was still strong, and the 1944 BC saloon looked very like the 1942 Chevrolet. None of these was made in series, because of the demands of war production.

Toyota resumed truck production soon after the end of the war, but permission for passenger cars was not forthcoming from the occupying forces until 1949.

1949 Toyota Toyopet SD saloon.
NICK BALDWIN

1962 Toyota 700 Publica saloon.
NICK BALDWIN

1971 Toyota Crown 2600 saloon.
NICK BALDWIN

1972 Toyota Corolla 1200 De Luxe saloon.
NICK BALDWIN

The Toyota SA of that year was a complete breakaway from previous designs, being a small 2-door saloon powered by a 995cc 4-cylinder engine with backbone frame and coil ifsn. The body was slightly reminiscent of the Volkswagen, though the engine was front-mounted. With 27bhp, the SA had a top speed of 54mph (87km/h). Car production was very limited at this time, and only 215 SAs were made up to 1952, when it was replaced by the SC, SD and SF with more modern styling. Only the latter was made in reasonable numbers, 3653 between 1951 and 1953; many were used as taxis. 1953 saw a larger engine of 1453cc and 48bhp in the RH, which had a similar 4-door saloon body to the SF. In 1955 the RH was succeeded by the Crown, this being the first Toyota to bear a name, and one which is still used today. The 1955 Crown had a wrap-around rear window and the appearance of a scaled-down 1955 Plymouth, with the same 1453cc engine as the RH.

The Crown was the first Toyota to be exported to the United States, beginning in August 1957. The first exports to Europe went to Denmark in 1962. Production figures rose dramatically during the 1950s, from 1857 in 1950 to 12,000 in 1956 and more than 30,000 by the end of the decade. In 1963 it reached 129,000, and two years later 230,000 cars were made. In 1969 the figure was not far short of a million, at 964,000. The million mark was passed in 1970, and the two million in 1978.

The Crown acquired a 1879cc engine in 1960, and received an all-new, wider body in 1962. In 1965 a 6-cylinder 1988cc engine was available, and the Crown soon became the top model of what was a growing range of cars. The smallest was the Publica, an economy car powered by a 697cc 2-cylinder air-cooled engine (1000cc in export models) which had been introduced in 1961, and was made as a 2-door saloon, convertible, station wagon and pick-up. From 1965 there was also a sports version called the Sport 800, with 790cc 45bhp engine and a top speed of 96mph (155km/h). The 790cc engine was used in all home-market Publicas from 1966, and 4-cylinder engines were soon available, of 933 and 1166cc. The simple Publica remained in production until 1978, with some 1,350,000 being made. The coupé version was called the Starlet, and this name was given to the Publica's replacement range of saloon and hatchbacks.

Next up in size from the Publica was the Corona, introduced in 1957 to cater for the smaller 4-cylinder market as the Crown was growing in size. The first Corona had a 33bhp 995cc 4-cylinder engine and 4-door saloon body. It was restyled in 1960 and again in 1964, when integral construction was featured for the first time. Capacity went up to 1453cc in 1961 and to 1490cc in 1964. This third-generation Corona was the first to become familiar in Europe, with its slant grill and four headlamps. It was made up to 1972, with larger engines of 1587 and 1858cc, the latter with single-ohc, and a choice of 4-door saloon, coupé or station wagon bodies. In 1969 the American magazine *Road Test* judged the Corona the best imported car of the year, and two years later a new Corona won a similar accolade from *Road & Track*. The Corona name was still current in 1999, though latterly only on home-market cars. Coronas grew larger during the 1970s and acquired transverse engines and front-wheel drive in 1983. By 1984 more than 5.6 million Coronas had been made.

Although a very large proportion of all Toyotas made have been family saloons, the few sports models have attracted a disproportionate amount of attention. The first was the little Sports 800, of which 3120 were made from 1965 to 1969, but the one which made an international impression was the 2000GT. Because Toyota were fully committed to making other models, they entrusted the development and manufacture of the 2000GT to the motorcycle makers Yamaha. The engine was a twin-cam version of the 1988cc six used in the Crown, giving 150bhp at 6600rpm. Transmission was by a 5-speed gearbox with direct drive 4th and overdrive 5th. The chassis was a backbone frame forked at the front to accommodate the engine and at the rear for the differential, similar to the Lotus Elan design, while the body was an attractive 2-seater coupé not unlike the E-type Jaguar, especially from the rear. Top speed was 127mph (205km/h), and handling excellent. With all these attributes the 2000GT should have been a great success, yet production ended early in 1969, less than three years after it began. Yamaha had limited facilities for making cars, and only turned out about 360 GTs. This made them expensive; on the US market they cost $6800, when you could get an E-type for $6000.

It was to be more than ten years before Toyota again made a sports car, but during the 1970s they had a very successful 'ponycar' or sports coupé in the style of Ford's Mustang and, in Europe, Capri. This was the Celica, a 2-door 4-seater coupé based on the Carina with 1588 or 1968cc engines (2134cc for the US

Eiji Toyota (right).
NICK BALDWIN

TOYOTA, EIJI (born 1913)

Eiji Toyota (Toyota is pronounced Toyoda in Japan) was the second son of Heikichi Toyota, younger brother of Sakich Toyota who founded the Toyota Spinning & Weaving Co. Ltd in 1918 (Toyota Loom Works from 1926). After graduating from Nagoya High School, he studied mechanical engineering at Tokyo Imperial University, specialising in the internal combustion engine. He graduated in 1936, coincidentally the year in which the first Toyota car went into production. He joined the family loom works, but was assigned to a research laboratory to study car design. They purchased a DKW from Germany, and built a prototype with 2-cylinder 2-stroke engine driving the front wheels, and a wooden body. This was clearly close to the DKW design. Meanwhile production Toyotas were more conventional rear-drive designs.

In 1937 Eiji spent three months in the army, stationed in Shanghai, China, then returned to the company, concentrating on the newly introduced conveyor belt systems, and also on quality control. He stayed with the firm throughout World War II, joining the board of directors in May 1945, and becoming a managing director in July 1950. He spent some time in the United States, particularly studying at the Ford factories, but also visiting many machine and parts makers. When he left, he said 'I realise that this is the way to produce perfect cars. Toyota has much to learn here . . . Because we are such a little company, we managers have to be involved in all the manufacturing areas'.

Toyota soon improved on American methods. Stamping machines used to make the same parts for weeks at a time, leading to stockpiling, because they could not be changed easily. In the 1960s Toyota's production manager Taiichi Ohno developed machines that could be changed easily, in a few minutes compared with several hours for American machinery.

Eiji Toyota was promoted to vice-president in February 1960, and became president in October 1967. He held this post for nearly 15 years before becoming chairman of the board in July 1982. This was a very important period for the expansion of the company, in which he played a key role. He retreated from day-to-day management which he handed over to his nephews Shoichiro and Tatsuro, but was very much a presence behind the scenes, his role perhaps like that of Deng Xiao-Ping in China. In June 1999, at the age of nearly 86, he was given the title of Supreme Adviser.

Toyota married Kazuko Takahashi in October 1939 and lives with her today in Toyota City.

NG (Thanks to Kazuo Kurita for most of the information in this biography.)

1975 Toyota Land Cruiser estate wagon.
NICK BALDWIN

1977 Toyota Cressida saloon.
NICK BALDWIN

1979 Toyota Starlet 5-door hatchback.
NICK GEORGANO

1982 Toyota Tercel GL 3-door hatchback.
TOYOTA

1982 Toyota Celica 2.0SY lift-back coupé.
TOYOTA

1990 Toyota Starlet 1.3 hatchback.
TOYOTA

1998 Toyota Rav 4 4 x 4 soft-top.
TOYOTA

market). These were originally single-ohc units, but some twin-cam engines were available as well in the GT models. Other improvements over the years included a 5-speed gearbox in 1974 and a liftback (hatchback) version in 1976. A second-generation Celica was made from 1977 to 1982 with notchback or liftback bodies and a choice of engines, 1588 and 1968cc 4-cylinder, and 1988 and 2564cc 6-cylinder. The largest-engined model was known as the Celica Supra (from 1979), the first use of a name which would later become a separate line.

The third generation of Celicas were basically similar, but had larger engines ranging from 1588 to 2759cc. The next generation of Celicas was introduced in 1985, and was completely new, having transverse engines driving the front wheels, and a new, more aerodynamic body. Like previous Celicas, this was derived from the Carina saloon range, which went over to front-wheel drive at the same time. The Celicas, however, used a twin-ohc head giving 147bhp from the 1988cc engine, with a top speed of 130mph (210km/h), much faster than any previous Celica. It was also the first Celica to be offered in convertible form. A 4 × 4 version came in the late 1980s, and a completely new Celica was launched in 1999.

Designed in Toyota's California studio, this seventh-generation Celica had crisper styling and was powered by a new 1.8-litre 16-valve engine co-developed with Yamaha.

The old-style Celica Supra was continued under the name Supra (as it had always been called in the USA and Britain). From 1986 it had a larger 24-valve engine of 2910cc, giving over 200bhp and a speed of 135mph (218km/h). Japanese-market models developed 230bhp, thanks to an intercooler. A less sporting but more luxuriously equipped coupé was the Soarer, a longer and heavier car available with 1988cc four or 2954cc six engines. It had computer-controlled air-suspension and very sophisticated dashboard displays which monitored suspension rates and could visualise cassette-borne maps.

In 1984 Toyota launched a new sports car in a lower price range than the Celica. This was the MR2, (Mid-ship Runabout 2-seater) a mid-engined 2-seater similar in concept to the Fiat X1/9, with a choice of 1482cc 83bhp single-ohc Corolla engine or 1587cc twin-ohc giving up to 130bhp. Thus, like the Ford Mustang, the MR2 could be either a personal small car or a hot sports car, according to power unit. Transmission, also from the Corolla, was 5-speed manual or 3-speed automatic. 4-wheel drive rally versions and the possibility of V8 power were considered, but the MR2 remained a simple, popularly priced sports car. After 166,104 had been sold, it was replaced in 1989 by a second-generation MR2; this was 9in (230mm) longer and had more rounded lines, losing the quirky slab-sided appearance of the original MR2 which people either loved or hated. The 2-litre engine was offered in several degrees of tune, from 119 to 150bhp, the latter with turbocharger. It was made without major change, though handling was improved, up to 1999, when it gave way to a new model, a smaller car more in the spirit of the original MR2, powered by an all-new 1.8-litre twin-ohc 16-valve engine.

Trying to cover a wide market, Toyota has produced a complex range of saloons since the 1970s. As well as the Corona and Crown already described, these have been (in ascending order of size), the Starlet, Corolla, Tercel, Carina, Camry, Cressida and Century.

The Starlet was a straightforward 3/5-door hatchback in the Ford Fiesta/Austin Metro class, but with rear-wheel drive. Engines were 993, 1166 or 1290cc, and 5-speed gearboxes were available on all but the cheapest models. For 1985 the original design was replaced by an up-to-date Starlet with front-wheel drive and 12-valve single-ohc engines of 999, 1296 or 1453cc, the latter a diesel. The last of 2.3 million Starlets was made in July 1999, when it gave way to the Yaris. The Corolla was one size up from the Publica/Starlet, being in the Ford Escort class, and has been made in a wide variety of models since its introduction in 1966. Originally with a 1166cc engine, it has since had larger power units of 1407 and 1588cc, and has been made in saloon, estate car and coupé. The latter, called the Levin, was the only performance model in the original Corolla series, with a number of race wins and the 1975 1000 Lakes Rally to its credit. Although the rear-drive Corolla was made in estate car form until 1987, the rest of the range was replaced in 1983 by a new series with transverse single-ohc engines and front-drive. These were updated in 1987 with longer, restyled bodies, and included a hot hatch GTi version with 120bhp 1587cc twin-cam 16-valve engine, and a top speed of 118mph (190km/h). The new Corolla was also available in 4-wheel drive form, though not the GTi. The twin-cam engine was available in a coupé for the US market, called the Corolla Twin Cam 16 coupé. The Corolla is the world's best-selling car in current production, more than 12.5 million having been sold since 1966.

Made from 1978 to 1988, the Tercel was Toyota's first front-drive car, and was a saloon or hatchback with 1295 or 1452cc Corolla engines. Unlike later front-wheel drive Toyotas, the Tercel's engine was mounted longitudinally. The estate car, which had 4-wheel drive, had a distinctive deep rear window. The Carina was one step up again from the Corolla, with engines from 1407 to 1588cc, made in rear-wheel drive form up to 1984, when a new model appeared with transverse engines and front-wheel drive. In size it corresponded to the Ford Cortina, and the 1977–84 models were quite similar in appearance as well. The Carina floorpan and running gear have been used as a basis for the Celica coupés, from the latter's appearance up to current models. The Carina was the first model to be made at Toyota's British plant in Derbyshire; production began in 1992, and in 1997 it was replaced by the Avensis, a similar-sized saloon/hatchback/estate with four engines from 1597 to 1998cc.

Next up from the Carina was the Camry, a relatively new model which was Toyota's first transverse-engined front-wheel drive car when it appeared for 1980.

1996 Toyota MR2 GT T-Bar coupé.
TOYOTA

Made as a 4-door notchback or a 5-door hatchback, the Camry was made with petrol or diesel engines, from 1588 to 1998cc. Restyled for 1987, the Camry II range included a 1998cc 16-valve twin-cam engine developing 160bhp, while a 4-wheel drive model was available. The Cressida grew out of the Corona range, the first appearing in 1968 with a slightly longer wheelbase. It was restyled in 1972 to make it more distinct from the Corona, engines now being fours and sixes from 1808 to 2253cc, and again in 1977, when the largest engine went up to 2563cc. Body styles were saloon, hard-top coupé and estate car. Near the top of the saloon range was the Crown, which grew in size during the 1970s and acquired a diesel option (Toyota's first diesel) in 1977. By the end of the decade the biggest engine in the Crown was a 2798cc six. Current Crowns, which are the seventh generation since 1955, have a 2446cc 4-cylinder diesel, or 6-cylinder petrol engines from 1988 to 2492cc. They have not sold widely in European or North American markets as they could not compete with cars like the Ford Scorpio or Opel Omega. The largest Toyota saloon is the Century, which was made with various sizes of V8 engine from 1967. It began with 2981cc and 150bhp, and by the 1990s had grown to 3994cc and 190bhp. In 1999 it received a 4996cc V12 developing 280bhp. It is sold only on the domestic market, and is made in comparatively small numbers.

Up to 1988 Toyota had never sought to compete internationally above the upper-middle market represented by the Crown, but this changed when they launched a competitor for BMW and Mercedes-Benz in the form of the LEXUS.

In 1998 Toyota launched an important new small car. Called the Vitz on the home market and the Yaris elesehere, it was a distinctively-styled 3- or 5-door hatchback powered by a 998cc or 1299cc 16-valve engine. In an *Autocar* survey in October 1999 it was voted the best of all cars on the UK market. For 2000 it was joined by the Yaris Verso, a mini-MPV on a Yaris frame lengthened by 5in (127mm). Also Yaris-based was the WiLL Vi, a quirkily-styled 4-door saloon intended to be marketed in conjunction with other WiLL-branded goods, including microwaves, cosmetics, and beer. Another significant Toyota was the Prius hybrid launched in 1997. It was a 4-door saloon powered by a 1497cc 16-valve engine with a planetary transmission in which the petrol engine acted on the shaft, the generator for starting and feeding the battery on the sun wheel and the electric motor on the planet wheel. By January 1998 it was selling very well on the home market, and by June production was up to 2000 a month.

1998 Toyota Land Cruiser 4 x 4.
TOYOTA

Land Cruiser and Space Cruiser

Toyota began competing in the off-road market in 1951, making them the third oldest firm in this field, after Jeep and Land Rover. The first 4 × 4 was called the BJ, and was made to special order only, but from 1953 it went into regular production under the name Land Cruiser. Initially it had a 3.4-litre 6-cylinder engine, enlarged to 3.9 litres in 1959, and 4.2 litres in 1975. Since 1972 diesel-engined Land Cruisers have also been made. For many years the Land Cruiser was available in 3-wheelbases, and with station wagon, canvas top or truck bodies. It underwent a major re-styling in 1980, and again in 1996. Engine options in 1999 were a 2982cc turbo-diesel four, 3378cc V6 and 4664cc V8. It was sold officially in 95 countries, unofficially in several others, and was assembled in 15 countries. Most foreign assemblies were similar to the Japanese product, but the Brazilian Bandeirante had a 3784cc Mercedes-Benz diesel engine and an older-style body, while the Portuguese version had a 5-cylinder 2½-litre Italian-made VM turbo-diesel engine. Total production of Land Cruisers is well over 1.5 million. Other 4 × 4 Toyotas were the Blizzard, a short-wheelbase vehicle based on the

1999 Toyota Yaris hatchback.
TOYOTA

1998 Toyota Corolla 1.3GS 3-door hatchback.
TOYOTA

1998 Toyota Prius hybrid saloon.
TOYOTA

Daihatsu Rugger (1980 to date) and the 4-Runner, a station wagon derived from the Hi lux pick-up with 2366cc four or 2958cc V6 engines, introduced in 1987. In 1994 came the RAV4, a 4 × 4 shorter than the Land Cruiser and made in 3- or 5-door models. Standard engine was a 1998cc four, mounted transversely unlike the Land Cruiser, and a small number of electric versions were made.

In 1983 Toyota launched their contribution to the 'people carrier' or MPV market, as a rival to Nissan's Prairie and Mitsubishi's Space Wagon. Called the Space Cruiser, it was more radical than the others, having forward control which allowed spacious accommodation for seven passengers. The engine was originally an 1812cc 78bhp unit, later replaced by one of 1998cc and 87bhp. In 1990 the Space Cruiser gave way to the larger and more sophisticated Previa, powered by a twin-ohc 2438cc 4-cylinder engine mounted almost horizontally under the cabin floor. Despite Toyota's impressive range of power units, this engine was designed specifically for the Previa, and was joined by a turbo-diesel version. A smaller MPV was the Picnic, launched in 1996, with transverse engine as opposed to the Previa's longitudinal one. The Previa's successor for 2000 had a hybrid-drive system with optional 4-wheel drive by a second electric motor on the rear differential.

A Worldwide Company

Toyota is today the world's largest company selling vehicles under one name (General Motors is larger in total output, but their products are sold under several names, Buick, Cadillac, Opel, Vauxhall, etc). Production in 1986 was over four million vehicles, or about one every four seconds of a 16-hour day. In September 1988 Toyota built its 60-millionth vehicle, being the first Japanese manufacturer, and the fourth world manufacturer, to reach this figure. It was achieved in 51 years, of which not more than 35 years saw serious quantity production, whereas rivals General Motors, Ford and Chrysler took considerably longer to reach their 60 million. Of this figure, 69 per cent were passenger cars. By September 1999 they had made 100 million passenger cars.

Toyota has seventeen assembly plants for cars worldwide, and their American operations are particularly important. Factories in Kentucky and Canada build about 200,000 and 50,000 cars per year respectively, and there is also a Californian plant jointly owned by Toyota and General Motors. The company is called NUMMI (New United Motor Manufacturing Inc) and makes a car based on the

Toyota Corolla marketed as the Chevrolet Nova. In 1987 American-built Toyotas (not including the Nova) took 6.9 per cent of the domestic car market. Toyota also owns two Japanese vehicle makers, Daihatsu and Hino.

In 1992 Toyota opened their first European factory at Burnaston, Derbyshire. Initially Carinas were made there, and from 1997 Avensis and the 5-door Corolla, for the UK and European markets, the latter taking about 70 per cent of output. Engines were supplied to Burnaston from a separate factory on Deeside, North Wales. The 750,000th British-built Toyota came off the line on 25 October 1999. A second European factory, at Valenciennes in France, was due to open in 2001 for production of the Yaris.

NG

TOYOTA (ii) (BR) 1958 to date

Toyota do Brasil, São Paulo.

In 1958, when the 50th anniversary of the start of Japanese immigration to Brazil was celebrated, Toyota do Brasil was founded in São Bernardo do Campo, in the State of São Paulo. A few months later, assembly of the Toyota Land Cruiser started there. Later, local production of Land Cruisers and Bandeirantes got going. In 1998 Toyota invested £100 million to start automobile production in Indaituba, in the State of São Paulo. Corollas were being produced there in 1999, but only for the Brazilian market.

ACT

TOYOTA (iii) (AUS) 1978 to date

Toyota Motor Co. Australia, Port Melbourne, Victoria.

Growing out of assembly by Australian Motor Industries (formerly Standard Australia) alongside Mercedes-Benz, Rambler and Standard-Triumph models in the early 1960s, the Toyota presence came to dominate. Some unique models, such as the Corona with the Holden Starfire 4-cylinder engine, arose due to local imperatives. The decision to manufacture in Australia was taken in 1978 and a 75 hectare greenfield site was developed by Toyota Manufacturing at Altona, with exports of components to Japan starting in 1982. Front-wheel drive appeared in 1985 with a delayed Corolla.

The earlier purchase of the former Standard holding was completed when the residual was bought out. AMI became wholly owned in 1987, when the front-drive Camry went into production. In 1988 a model-sharing programme with HOLDEN, as United Australian Automotive Industries, began, and Holden sold Corolla and Camry clones as the Nova and Apollo. Toyota badged its version of the Commodore as Lexcen (named after the designer of the winged keel for racing yachts). That joint venture survived until 1997 and complete manufacture of Corolla and Camry was achieved; exports to several markets became a pivotal factor. Production of the Corolla ceased in 1998 and production of the Avalon, a model sized closer to the market-leading Ford Falcon and Holden Commodore, initiated.

MG

TRABANT (DDR) 1958–1991

VEB Sachsenring Automobilwerk, Zwickau.

The Trabant succeeded the ZWICKAU P-70 as the small car built by the nationalised industry of the German Democratic Republic. Like its predecessor, it had a 2-cylinder 2-stroke engine, slightly smaller at 500cc and 18bhp, driving the front wheels. The only body style initially was a fibreglass 2-door saloon, but this was joined by an estate car in 1960, when output was raised to 20bhp. In 1963 the engine was enlarged to 594cc (23bhp), and remained at this size up to the end of 2-stroke production in 1990, when output was 26bhp.

Very few changes were made to the Trabant in its 33-year life, and it was still recognisably the same car as it was on its introduction in August 1958. Among the more important improvements were the replacement of the crash gearbox by a fully synchronised one in 1962, a restyled body in 1964, optional Hycomat automatic transmission in 1965, dual braking system in 1967, the 26bhp engine in 1969, higher rear axle ratio in October 1974 and in 1988 the replacement of the rear swing axles and transverse leaf spring by coil springs. In 1979 an open 4-seater without doors called the Tramp was added to the saloon and Kombi estate car. The most important change came very near the end of production. In May 1990 the ancient 2-stroke was replaced by a 1043cc VW Polo engine, and disc brakes were provided. About 10,000 of these were made, mostly for export to Hungary, but all Trabant production came to an end in May 1991. The factory was later

2000 Toyota MR2 roadster.
TOYOTA

2000 Toyota Celica coupé.
TOYOTA

2000 Toyota Avensis D4-D SR saloon.
TOYOTA

1962 Trabant 500 saloon.
NICK GEORGANO/NATIONAL MOTOR MUSEUM

1975 Trabant 601 saloon.
NATIONAL MOTOR MUSEUM

1929 Tracta 1100cc sports car.
NICK BALDWIN

used for manufacture of complete Polos. Only 1800 cars were made in 1958, but between then and 1962 production reached 140,000, and the millionth Trabant was delivered in 1973. The final figure was around three million. Most Trabants were sold in the German Democratic Republic and other Comecom countries, though it was available on the West German market during the 1960s.

NG

Further Reading
Trabant, Duroplast in Pastel Colours, Jurgen Schiebert, Veloce, 1998.

TRAC (i) *see* TECHNIC

TRAC (ii) (GB) 1991–1995
TRAC Products, Colchester, Essex.
Since this company restored genuine examples of the SS100, it was superbly qualified to produce a replica, and its effort was extremely accurate. The dimensions were correct and a host of reproduction parts gave all the details an authentic finish. Jaguar XJ6 running gear and engines were used in a ladder chassis, while the bodywork was one-piece fibreglass. The project was taken over by SUFFOLK in 1995.

CR

TRACFORT (F) 1934–1935
Automobiles Tracfort, Courbevoie, Seine.
This light car was designed by ex-Derby engineer A. Bourbonnet, and appropriately, it had front-wheel drive. The power unit was a 933cc Model Y Ford, with engine and gearbox reversed, and the suspension, though still the Ford-type transverse

springs, was independent at the front. The wheelbase was lengthened from the Ford's 90in (2284mm) to 104in (2640mm), allowing more attractive coachwork to be fitted. There were two styles, the Type Irlande 2/3-seater sports and the Type Mouette 2-door 4-seater saloon. Despite strong links with Ford France (Tracfort's managing director Louis Carle was on the board of Ford) the Tracfort had a short life.

NG

TRACKSON (AUS) 1901
Trackson Bros Ltd, Brisbane, Queensland.
This electrical contractor held the premier position in its field and developed an early interest in motors as James Trackson was one of Queensland's pioneer motorists. Trackson's workshop, under foreman Harold Green, completed what was claimed to be the first motorcar made in the northern state. Built in 1901, it closely followed the pattern of a De Dion-Bouton owned by Philange Trackson. A press report then stated that it had a dog-cart body, a 5hp gasoline engine, ran at 10mph (16km/h) and that the firm intended to devote part of its works to motors. Although it is doubtful whether further cars were made, motor-bicycles with Minerva engines were. A subsidiary, Trackson Transport, applied itself to outback haulage with traction engines and steam lorries also produced.

MG

TRACTA (F) 1926–1934
SA des Automobiles Tracta, Asnières, Seine.
The Tracta was the first successful front-wheel drive car made in any numbers. It was designed by Jean-Albert Grégoire (1899–1992) and financed by Pierre Fenaille whose wealth came from petroleum products. The first Tractas were built primarily for competitions, having 1100cc 4-cylinder S.C.A.P. engines, later replaced by 1200 and 1600cc units. As well as front-wheel drive they had ifs by sliding pillars and a Cozette supercharger was optional. These early cars were made in the Garage des Chantiers at Versailles, but Grégoire soon moved to a small factory at Asnières which he continued to occupy long after he stopped making Tractas, well into his old age, in fact.

After making about 140 cars with S.C.A.P. engines, Grégoire turned to larger power units, including a 15CV 2.7-litre Continental side-valve six and a 17 or 20CV (3- or 3.3-litre) Hotchkiss six with ohv. He found that these were no more expensive than the S.C.A.P.s. With this change of engine came a change in the direction of the company, from stark race and hill climb-orientated sports cars to elegant coupés and saloons which had some success in Concours d'Élégances. Some had four doors and included a town car by Letourneur et Marchand on a long wheelbase, which was specially made for Mme Fenaille. Other bodies for Tracta were made by Chapron, Duval and Mignon et Billebault. About 90 6-cylinder cars were made but Grégoire made little if any profit from them, and abandoned car production in 1934. He tried to claim patent royalties for front-wheel drive from Adler and DKW in Germany, and from Chenard-Walcker and Citroën in France, but with little success. For his later activities, see GRÉGOIRE (ii).

NG

Further Reading
50 Ans d'Automobile, J.-A. Grégoire, Flammarion, Paris 1974.

TRACTAVANT (F) 1951
Aviation and electrical engineer Henri Lanoy conceived the Tractavant 3-wheeled economy car. A single door gave entry to the open-topped cabin, where the driver sat alone in front, with 1–2 passengers behind; the car was very narrow as a result. The single front wheel was on a motorcycle-type fork, though steered by a wheel, and was driven via chain by either an Aubier Dunne 125cc or Sachs 150cc engine.

CR

TRACTION AÉRIENNE (F) 1921–c.1926
Sté la Traction Aérienne, Neuilly, Seine.
This was a propeller-driven car powered by a 1526cc flat-twin engine which drove a 4-bladed propeller at the front of the car. It had a tandem 2-seater saloon body, and overall weight was only 670lbs. It had 4-wheel brakes and front-wheel steering, unlike the contemporary LEYAT which steered by the rear wheels. It was said to ride surprisingly comfortably over rough ground, but on the debit side it was noisy and had slow acceleration. Later models went under the names Eolia and Hélica.

NG

TRACTOBILE (US) 1900–1902

Pennsylvania Steam Vehicle Co. Inc, Carlisle, Pennsylvania.

Avant-train attachments for motorising horse-drawn vehicles were not unknown at the turn of the century, but the Tractobile was unusual in that it was powered by steam. The boiler was made up of five separate units, each with 40 small tubes. Two vertical cylinders acted directly on each front wheel, although this is difficult to see in surviving photographs. Complete vehicles were also provided, a 2-seater stanhope at $500, a 4-seater surrey at $650 and a 6-seater depot wagon at $850. Output of Tractobiles is not known, but was probably pretty small, given that the notorious E.J. Pennington was behind the company.

NG

TRAEGER (D) 1923

Traeger, Freiburg (Silesia).

This was a small car powered by a 5/18PS 4-cylinder engine. Further details are not known.

HON

TRAIN (F) 1924–1925

Motorcycles et Moteurs Train, Courbevoie, Seine.

This company was better known for small proprietary engines, and for motorcycles which were made from 1920 to 1939, but they also offered a few complete cars powered, naturally, by their own 344cc single-cylinder engines.

NG

TRAKKA (GB) 1984

C.L. Cars Ltd, Salford, Manchester.

This was a jeep/utility kit car in the style of the Renault Rodeo, using completely unaltered Renault 4 parts.

CR

TRANSFORMER (i) (GB) 1986–1996

Transformer Cars, Frant, East Sussex.

This exacting replica of one of the greatest rally legends of all time, the idiosyncratic Lancia Stratos, proved extremely popular. The Transformer HF2000 duplicated the original structure in fibreglass, using mostly Lancia Beta mechanicals, mirroring the original car in most respects. Group 4 wide-arch bodywork was optional. Engine options encompassed Honda/Rover and even Ferrari V6s and V8s; there was also an Alfa V6 option (the more up-market versions were called HF3000). Chassis improvements in 1994 made it a better all-round car. This company also briefly produced the S.D. 500. Founder Gerry Hawkridge formed another company, HAWK, and launched production of an equivalent Stratos replica with that enterprise.

CR

TRANSFORMER (ii) *see* E.A.C.

TRASK-DETROIT (US) 1922–1923

Detroit Steam Motor Co., Detroit, Michigan.

In December 1921, O.C. Trask of Detroit, Michigan, distributor for the Stanley Steam Car, announced that he was entering the automobile business with a 2-cylinder steam car to be named after himself and that the car would sell in the $1000 range. Pilot models followed soon afterwards, the touring car which was used for exhibition purposes and three others which were used for preliminary testing. The cars had a wheelbase of 110in (2792mm) and were equipped with disc wheels. Trask, who had planned to export some of his production to Canada, announced that the cars sold north of the border would be badged under the name Windsor, subsequently further deciding to manufacture the cars at Windsor, Ontario. Neither the export of the cars or their actual manufacture in Canada came to pass and it is doubtful that any of the Trask-Detroits carried the Windsor badge. For 1923, Trask changed the car's name to the Detroit Steam Car, lengthened it to a 115in (2919mm) wheelbase and increased the price of the touring model to $1585. The venture failed to reach its anticipated production and the company went out of business later in 1923 with only the four prototypes marking Trask's career as an automobile manufacturer.

KM

TRAVELER (i) (US) 1907

Bellefontaine Automobile Co., Bellefontaine, Ohio.

This was the ZENT renamed, with a 24/32hp 4-cylinder engine made in either air- or water-cooled form. In 1908 the car became larger and more expensive, and was called the BELLEFONTAINE.

NG

TRAVELER (ii) (US) 1910–1911

Traveler Automobile Co., Evansville, Indiana.

Formerly known as the SIMPLICITY, this Traveler was a conventional-looking 4-cylinder car, made as a runabout or tourer. It had friction disc transmission which had proved troublesome in the Simplicity, hence the change of name. Surprisingly, manufacturer Willis Copeland continued the Simplicity name on a larger car, but both this and the Traveler were out of production by 1912.

NG

TRAVELER (iii) (US) 1913–1914

Traveler Motor Car Co., Detroit, Michigan.

The Traveler was a conventional 4-cylinder car made by J.P. LaVigne alongside the cyclecar which he named after himself. It was offered with a choice of Beaver engines of 36 and 48hp on wheelbases of 120 and 130in (3046 and 3299mm) respectively.

NG

TRAX *see* INTERSTATE

TREBERT (US) 1907–1908

Trebert Gas Engine Co., Rochester, New York.

Henry L. Trebert began making engines in 1902 and within a few years was offering units from 2hp to 40hp. In 1907 he offered a complete car, a 5-seater tourer powered by a 30hp 4-cylinder T-head engine, with 3-speed gearbox and shaft drive. Trebert made very few cars under his own name as he soon went into partnership with another Rochester engine maker, F.A. Brownell. Three Brownell cars were made, but the partners soon realised that engine building was more profitable.

NG

TREKKA (NZ) 1967–1970

Motor Holdings Group Ltd, Auckland, North Island.

A basic utility-type vehicle with a wide range of body types, inclusive of a station wagon, it was based on the SKODA Octavia which the company also assembled. Being 2-wheel drive, a limited slip differential was standard fitting to enhance off-road capability. It was exported to Australia and the Pacific Islands and served with New Zealand medical teams during the Vietnam War.

MG

TRESCOWTHICK (AUS) 1903

C.H. Trescowthick, Adelaide, South Australia.

Charles Trescowthick's business centred on installation of acetylene gas lighting plans in homes and small country towns. He was proficient with electricity and motors and was known to have constructed at least two motor vehicles. His car had a 330cc air-cooled De Dion-Bouton engine, the power being transmitted by a primary belt and chain final drive, while wire wheels were fitted. It proved to be unsatisfactory, and the motor was installed in a tricar with a fore-carriage. Motorcycles continued to be built.

MG

TRESER (D) 1987–1988

Walter Treser, Berlin.

Well-known for his conversions to Audi cars such as his Quattro roadster and Largo long-wheelbase limousine, Treser announced his own car in 1987. It was a 2-seater sports car powered by a mid-mounted 1.8-litre 16-valve VW engine, and featured a fully-retractable metal roof. Production was planned for the summer of 1988, but Treser could not find the necessary financial support.

NG

1992 Triad (ii) 3-wheeler.
CHRIS REES

1908 Tribelhorn electric victoria.
ERNEST SCHMID

c.1910 Tribet 14hp coupé.
NICK BALDWIN

TRESKOW (D) 1906–1908

Robert Treskow Motorwagenfabrik, Schönebeck.

This bicycle and motorcycle maker built a small number of light cars powered by a 10PS 2-cylinder engine, with 2-speed epicyclic transmission and chain drive.

HON

TREVETHAN (AUS) 1904–1905

T. Trevethan's Coach Works, Toowoomba, Queensland.

This coachbuilder was unusual in that it built bicycles and used machine tools in its workshop. It was thus able to readily take up motors when sons, Walter and Thomas Jr, came into control of the business. Their first vehicle was a high-wheeled buggy with a 4.5hp De Dion-Bouton engine. The transmission and running gear were of their own production. It was named 'Ly. E. Moon', after a coastal

steamship which had been wrecked in 1886. It made the first motor journey over the ranges to the coast. The second vehicle was made in 1905 and this also, in consideration of the operating conditions, had high wheels and solid tyres. The firm took the Napier agency and, as Town & Country Motors in Brisbane, became the state distributor.

MG

TRIA (I) 1990–1992

Tria Design, Verderio Inferiore, Como.

Tria Design was founded in 1986, specialising in prototype work and styling kits. At the 1990 Turin Show, it attempted a microcar design that was intended to become commercially available, the MOD 01. Only 102in (2600mm) long, its chassis was formed of plastic and steel and its open 2-seater bodywork was surmounted by a tubular roll-over bar. Four Lombardini engine options were envisaged: 500cc and 900cc petrol units (2- and 3-cylinder respectively) and two diesel units, driving through an automatic transmission. At the 1992 Geneva Salon, a sports car model was presented, whose chassis was designed to be used as the basis for kit cars, but no manufacturer took up that option.

CR

TRIAD (i) (AUS) 1984

Hi-Tech Car Co., Smithfield, New South Wales.

A mid-engined sports coupé in the Lotus Esprit mould, the Triad took its name from the three main instigators, Cliff Trefry and twin Hadley brothers, Bob and Wal, who had learned their bodybuilding skills at Hoopers in England. Built on a backbone frame with body of kevlar and divinycell sandwich, its power derived from a 154bhp Volvo V6 engine which drove through a Citroën SM 5-speed transmission. Weight was quoted at 1030kg. The necessary funding for production could not be obtained and it was decided in 1985 to offer it as a kit, into which owners could fit their own power packs. This design team then moved on to develop the BRABHAM in 1985 and the Morgan-style Smithfield kit car in 1986.

MG

TRIAD (ii) (GB) 1992–1998

Malvern Autocraft, Malvern, Worcestershire.

This peculiar little trike was a lightly updated version of the MOSQUITO, notably gaining a new chassis and minor body modifications. It retained a Mini subframe up front, now mounted in a space frame chassis, with a single Mini trailing arm and coil/spring damper at the back. The doorless fibreglass bodywork was open, with an optional windscreen and weather gear, plus a lightweight Warrior version intended for competition (having aero screens and a hard tonneau on the passenger's side). Some 14 kits had been supplied by 1996.

CR

TRIBELHORN (CH) 1902–1920

1902–1919 A. Tribelhorn & Co. AG, Feldbach, Zürich.
1919–1920 Elektrische Fahrzeuge AG (EFAG), Zürich.

The first Tribelhorn electric car was completed in 1902. It was an open 2-seater with front-wheel drive. The main production was electric commercial vehicles. In 1906 however, regular production of passenger cars was started, the 'light doctor's car' found a good market in both Switzerland and Germany. Many of the heavier models received pleasant coach-built double-phaeton, landaulet and limousine bodies by Geissberger, Zürich. With mock engine bonnets and radiators they looked very much like petrol-engined luxury cars. Tribelhorn cars were fairly expensive, prices ranging from SFr7100 for the 2-seater to SFr12,600 for the landaulet, which seated six. In 1914 a neat 2-seater drophead coupé was launched and at the end of World War I a semi-streamlined torpedo Nautilus was introduced. Over 100 Tribelhorn passenger cars were registered in use in Switzerland in 1918. When the company was taken over by EFAG, the production of passenger cars and heavy commercial vehicles ceased and the new owners concentrated on light delivery and postal vehicles. This production continued into the 1980s.

FH

TRIBET (F) 1909–1914

Tribet et Compagnie, Villeneuve-la Garenne, Seine.

Built by Camille Tribet, this was a conventional car with 8/10hp 4-cylinder and 12/16hp 6-cylinder engines, and shaft drive. In 1913 only fours were listed, of 8, 10, and 12hp. With a round radiator, the Tribet was said to 'embody all the refinements of large live-axle cars, and is a reproduction in miniature of the same'.

NG

TRIBUNE (US) 1913

Tribune Motor Co., Detroit, Michigan.

This car was made by Louis G. Hupp, brother of the better-known Robert C. Hupp who made the Hupmobile. It was a 5-seater tourer powered by a 4-cylinder Buda engine. The planned price was $1250 but production never started, and before the end of 1913 the factory had been leased to the makers of the MERCURY (iv) cyclecar.

NG

TRI-CAR (US) 1955

The Tri-Car Co., Wheatland, Pennsylvania.

This tiny 3-wheeler had a fibreglass coupé body and a 2-cylinder Lycoming engine.

HP

TRICOLET (US) 1904–1906

Pokorney & Richards Automobile & Gas Engine Co., Indianapolis, Indiana.
Also known as the Pokorney after its designer H. Pokorney, this was a light 3-wheeler with single front wheel steered by tiller, and 6hp air-cooled 2-cylinder engine mounted at the rear. The 2-speed epicyclic transmission did not incorporate a reverse gear as the car had a 14-foot turning circle. The wheelbase was only 66in (1675mm). As a 3-wheeler it cost $425, but an additional front wheel could be had for only $25 extra.

NG

TRIDENT (i) (F/GB) 1919–1920

Trident Federated Exporters Ltd, London.

This was a somewhat mysterious car as the prototype(s) were built in France, and production in England by Vickers Ltd never got under way. It was an unusual design, a 3-wheeler with single front wheel on which was mounted the 8hp vertical-twin engine, with 3-speed gearbox which also carried the magneto on the other side of the wheel. There were, in fact, twin front wheels but mounted so close together as to give the appearance of single wheel. Presumably two were needed to support the weight of the engine, gearbox and magneto. There were twin side-mounted radiators, and the body seated two in tandem. Projected bodies included a one-passenger taxicab and a delivery van, but it is doubtful if these were built. Suspension was by four laterally-mounted and interlinked cantilever springs. When the Trident was announced in August 1919 deliveries were promised in six to eight months, at a price of £160 which was very reasonable for the period.

NG

TRIDENT (ii) (GB) 1965–1978

1965–1968 Trident Cars Ltd, Woodbridge, Suffolk.
1968–1974 Trident Cars Ltd, Ipswich, Suffolk.
1976–1978 Trident Motor Co Ltd, Ipswich, Suffolk.
The Trident Clipper was originally a TVR prototype, with styling by Trevor Fiore, which was shown at the 1965 Geneva Motor Show. TVR then hit one of its periodic crises and the project was sold to one of its dealers, Bill Last, who was then making the Peel Trident as the Viking Minisport. Although the Trident was one of the 'prettiest' cars of its time, production never reached expected levels. Early Clippers had a TVR Grantura Mk III chassis and the later versions had Austin-Healey 3000 chassis with a 390bhp 4.7-litre Ford V8. It was a good performer in a straight line, but less so when it came to stopping or turning corners. A convertible was offered, but most were coupés. From 1969 a modified Triumph TR6 chassis was used because production of the Austin-Healey had ended, and two other models were offered.

The Venturer V6 used the Triumph chassis with a 3-litre Ford V6 engine while the Tycoon had the 150 bhp fuel injected TR6 engine but this was a stop-gap because Ford engines were temporarily unavailable due to a strike.

The company moved premises in 1968, then folded in 1974 in the wake of the energy crisis and new American regulations. It was revived with new backing in

1967 Trident (ii) Clipper V8 coupé.
NICK BALDWIN

1985 Trihawk 3-wheeler.
ELLIOTT KAHN

1976, when the Triumph irs was dropped in favour of a live rear axle. Production finally ended in 1978. About 120 Tridents of all types were made.

MJL

Further Reading
'Thrust of the Trident', Jonathan Stein, *Automobile Quarterly*, Vol. 39, No. 1.

TRIDENT (iii) (US) c.1993–1997

Trident Group Inc., Winter Park, Florida.

The Trident Spyder was a replica of the Ferrari Daytona Spyder built on Corvette convertible running gear. They also sold the T.F.A., a Lamborghini Countach replica based on a Pontiac Fiero chassis. These were stretched to give more realistic proportions. Trident kits were sold in kit and assembled form.

HP

TRIDENT (iv) (GB) 1998–1999

P.B. Design International Ltd, Swaffham, Cambridgeshire.

The Trident name was unexpectedly revived at the 1998 Birmingham Motor Show with an all-new V8-powered open 2-seater sports car. Financial problems had apparently sunk the project by early 1999.

CR

TRIHAWK (US) 1983–c.1987

1983–1985 McKee Engineering, Dana Point, California.
1985–c.1987 Trihawk Inc, Milwaukee, Wisconsin.
One of the most highly-regarded 3-wheelers ever was the Trihawk, conceived by CanAm race engineer Bob McKee and designed by ex-GM stylist David Stollery. In construction it consisted of a tubular steel perimeter frame with a roll-over bar and open doorless fibreglass bodywork. A Citroën GSA 1299cc engine and 5-speed gearbox was front-mounted, and suspension was by unequal length double A-arms up front and a single rear trailing arm; coil over dampers were used all round. *Road & Track* magazine tested a Trihawk and rated it as one of the best two cornering vehicles it had ever driven, partly due to a very low centre of

1981 Triking 950cc 3-wheeler.
NICK GEORGANO

c.1950 Trilox invalid 3-wheeler.
PHIL LOMAX

gravity. Harley-Davidson was sufficiently impressed by the design to acquire the rights to produce it, but it shelved the project because of fears over product liability and its own precarious financial condition at the time. Around 250 Trihawks were made.

CR

TRIKING (GB) 1978 to date

Triking, Marlingford, Norfolk.

Draughtsman and Morgan trike fanatic Tony Divey was behind the Triking, the first of a string of modern-day re-interpretations of the Morgan 3-wheeler. A strong backbone chassis with a steel spaceframe carried stressed alloy body panels with a fibreglass bonnet, rear section and cycle wings. The wishbone coil spring/damper front suspension used Lotus Esprit uprights; at the back end, the single rear wheel was suspended on a swinging fork and was driven by shaft from an exposed front-mounted Moto Guzzi V-Twin engine. The standard 844cc 68bhp or 85bhp engine could be changed for a 950cc 71bhp Guzzi unit, in which case 121mph (195km/h) and 0–60mph (0–97km/h) in 7.8 seconds was possible. Both complete cars and kits were sold. A linear Moto Guzzi gearbox was standard, or Toyota 5-speed and automatic transmissions were optional (both providing a reverse gear). The 100th Triking was built in 1992.

CR

TRILLIUM (CDN) 1987–1988

Triullium Factory, Toronto, Ontario.

This was a typical MG TD replica powered by a 1600cc 4-cylinder engine.

CR

TRILOX (GB) 1950s

Trowbridge, Wiltshire.

This company made a number of invalid tricycles, hand-propelled as well as petrol and electric-powered. On some of the motor tricycles the body was made of heavy plywood to provide a seat, footwell and leg covering with a small hinged door at the side. It was one of the heaviest vehicles of its kind, and never approved by the Ministry of Health. A surviving example has a Villiers engine, but others may have been used as well. The front forks are a cut-down version of the Royal Enfield CO. Gearbox was 2-speed, with a hand-crank start.

NG

TRI-MAGNUM (US) c.1985

Tri-Magnum Sales, Irvine, California.

The Tri-Magnum was originally a plan-set by QUINCY-LYNN Enterprises, but it was also sold in kit form by this company. Any motorcycle from 400cc to 1300cc could provide the running gear for this futuristic enclosed 3-wheeler. Front suspension was VW and the body was fibreglass.

HP

TRIMAX (US) c.1987
MPV Inc., San Antonio, Texas.
This 3-wheeler was a simple kit convertible with a steel frame that bolted to a motorcycle chassis and running gear. It added a VW front suspension system and a fibreglass nose cone. The interior pod seated two and had a short windshield. The motorcycle frame and seat remained in place for another rider or two out back.
HP

TRIMOBILE see AVON

TRI-MOTO (US) 1900–1901
Western Wheel Works, Chicago, Illinois.
This 3-wheeler had a mixed background. It was designed by Englishman Harry Lawson, the same design being made in England as the Lawson Motor Wheel, sponsored by the American Bicycle Co., made by the Western Wheel Works, and marketed by the Crescent organisation. It had a 2¼hp single-cylinder engine mounted over, and driving, the single front wheel. The whole engine and transmission turned with the steering, which was by tiller. Top speed was 12mph (19km/h) and the price was $425. Despite the doubtful business methods of Harry Lawson, it seems that quite a number of Tri-Motos were made.
NG

TRIO (GB) 1993 to date
Trio Cars, Wareham, Dorset.
The Trio 3-wheeler was the brainchild of Ken Hallett, as a part-time project sold mostly as a set of plans for customers to make their own cars. It used a Mini subframe and A-series engine with a wide cocktail of other Austin parts. The open body was extremely basic and made of wood skinned in aluminium and vinyl. The fold-forward bonnet and front cycle wings were fibreglass, however, which could be supplied for a very meagre sum. In shape, the body was classical barrel-back, with the spare wheel mounted right on the end. By 1996 some 25 plan sets had been sold, plus a couple of chassis.
CR

TRIOULEYRES (F) 1896
Compagnie Générale des Automobiles Paris.
Like the better-known ROGER, this was a French version of the BENZ, having a 5hp horizontal engine at the rear, belt transmission to the countershaft and final drive by chains. Examples of 2- and 4-seaters ran in the 1896 Paris–Nantes– Paris and Paris–Marseilles–Paris races, though they did not finish in either event.
NG

TRIPACER (GB) 1994 to date
Classic Car Panels, Frome, Somerset.
Before producing the Tripacer, this metalwork specialist built a number of one-off cars, including a Jaguar-based roadster called the Aleat, replicas of which were offered for sale. The Tripacer 3-wheeler used a lightly modified Citroën 2CV chassis and had hand-rolled aluminium bodywork built up over a steel tube frame. There was also a 4-wheeler version with a narrow-set pair of rear wheels, called the Somerset.
CR

TRI-PED see AMERICAN MICROCAR

TRIPLE C see CHALLENGER

TRIPLER (US) 1900–1901
Tripler Liquid Air Co., New York, New York.
This was a light 2-seater runabout which resembled a contemporary steamer, but was powered by a liquid air engine. Expansion of the air was said to operate the pistons in the same way as in a steam engine. Any chances of success that it might have had were doomed by the scandal surrounding another liquid air car, made by the Liquid Air Power & Automobile Co. of Boston.
NG

1943 Trippel amphibious car.
NATIONAL MOTOR MUSEUM

TRIPLEX (US) 1954–1955
Ketcham's Automotive Corp., Chicago, Illinois.
The Triplex had been known as the CHICAGOAN, but the name was changed in 1954. It was a fibreglass-bodied kit sports car with the buyer's choice of engines. The chassis was called the Triplex K-Type Safety Frame.
HP

TRIPOD (GB) 1985–1987
Heron Suzuki, Crawley, Sussex.
The British Suzuki motorcycle importer built a number of prototypes of an enclosed 3-wheeled microcar based on moped parts. John Mockett designed the Tripod, which used an advanced aluminium honeycomb chassis and fibreglass 2-seater open bodywork. It had two front wheels and chain drive to the single rear wheel. Escalating costs quashed a planned production run.
CR

TRIPOS (GB) 1984–1992
1984–1991 Tripos R+D Ltd, London.
1992 Cobretti Engineering, Wallington, Surrey.
The Tripos R81 was conceived as a one-off for architect Laurie Abbott, using Alfa Romeo parts. However, A.S.D. engineered a Ford-based kit version using double wishbone front suspension, 5-link Ford live rear axle, Ford crossflow engine, disc front brakes and a spaceframe chassis. The fibreglass doorless body was a round-tailed cycle wing style, in the manner of an updated Lotus 7. Only six cars were made.
CR

TRIPPEL (D) 1934–1944; 1950–1953
1934–1940 Trippelwerk, Homburg/Saar.
1940–1944 Trippelwerke GmbH, Molsheim.
1950–1952 Protek Gesellschaft für Industrie-entwicklungen mbH, Tuttlingen; Stuttgart.
Hanns Trippel was a specialist in amphibious cars, probably the world's leading exponent of the type. After experiments beginning in 1932 he began small scale production in 1934 with a 4-wheel drive Adler-powered car, the SG6. This was later fitted with an Opel engine , and was followed by the SK6 with 2-litre Adler engine and front-wheel drive. His work was given a boost by World War II when the army issued a contract for amphibious cars which Trippel built in the former Bugatti works at Molsheim. These had 2473cc 6-cylinder Opel engines, 5-speed gearboxes and 4×2 or 4×4 drive. About 1000 were made, together with a few of the SG7 with Tatra air-cooled V8 engine and 4-wheel drive.
In 1950 Trippel introduced a new car, not amphibious this time, with rear-mounted 600cc 2-stroke Horex motorcycle engine and 2-seater coupé body. Called the SK10, it had gull-wing doors which were patented by Trippel; it is said that the design was bought by Daimler-Benz for the Mercedes-Benz 300SL gull-wing coupé. Trippel was not able to get the SK10 into production, though it appeared at a number of motor shows between 1950 and 1952. In 1953 it was finally built

1907 Triumph (ii) 30hp roadster.
NICK BALDWIN

1928 Triumph (iii) Super Seven saloon.
NICK BALDWIN

1932 Triumph (iii) Super Seven pillarless saloon.
NICK BALDWIN

in a small series by MARATHON in France. It was also to be made in Norway as the TROLL (i), but never went into production there. A similar design was made in Germany under the name Weidner Condor. Trippel then made the AMPHICAR, of which about 800 were built.

HON

Further Reading
'Hanns Trippel – Fahren ohne Grenzen', Matthias Pfannmuller, *Automobilhistorische Nachrichter*, No. 2.

TRISHUL (IND) 1982–c.1995
1982–1991 Trishul Autocrafts Private Ltd, Patna.
1991–c.1995 Phooltas Transmotives Pvt Ltd, Patna.
This was a basic miniature jeep-style vehicle, only three metres long, powered by a front-mounted 12bhp Lombardini 510cc diesel engine driving the rear wheels. Despite a weight of only 600kg, performance was sluggish, the top speed being

listed at 40mph (64km/h). The tubular steel chassis was leaf-sprung and several 6-seater steel body styles were offered, including open, 4-door and taxi variants. The marque name changed to Phooltas, under whose aegis was produced a range of larger jeep-style vehicles under the name Champion, with 3.15-litre Perkins diesel engines.

CR

TRISPORT (GB) 1990
Motorsport Components, Bolton, Lancashire.
The TriSport Scorpion emerged from a manufacturer of components for Formula One and Group C racing teams. The idea was to build a modern 3-wheeled racer using a Japanese superbike engine and, taking a Yamaha FZR1000, creators Dennis Aldred and George Holt removed its front forks and simply bolted the unmodified superbike frame to a spaceframe chassis designed for two front wheels, plus aluminium cladding. The front suspension was an ingenious pushrod system using a single shock absorber mounted horizontally to rocker arms and interconnected by a Watts linkage. The top speed was in excess of 145mph (233km/h). Intending to offer it in kit form as a racer, in fact more interest was shown in a possible road version but stability problems led the founders to lose interest before production began.

CR

TRI-TECH (GB) 1996 to date
Tri-Tech Autocraft UK Ltd, Bamber Bridge, Preston, Lancashire.
As this company specialised in bubble car restorations, it was a short step for it to offer replicas of classic microcars. The first was the Zetta, a copy of the BMW Isetta on a ladder chassis using Bedford Rascal van front suspension and Mini brakes. The second was the Schmitt, an accurate replica of the Messerschmitt KR. This used separate steel subframes front and rear. Both cars featured fibreglass bodies, motorcycle engines (typically Honda 250cc or 400cc) and 6-speed sequential motorcycle transmission.

CR

TRITON (GB) 1963
David Johnson-Webb, Hampton Court, Middlesex.
As a side-line to the Johnson Racing Team, the Triton was a roadgoing coupé. Its round-tube spaceframe chassis was powered, in prototype form, by a modified 1580cc BMC B-series engine, so that a top speed of 140mph (225km/h) was claimed. Two further cars were built with slightly differing fibreglass bodies.

CR

TRIUMPH (i) (US) 1900–1901
Triumph Motor Vehicle Co., Chicago, Illinois.
This company made a neat-looking electric stanhope described as 'a swell carriage for professional men, ladies or family use'. They also advertised that they would make steam or petrol cars, but so far as is known only the electrics were built, and very few of them.

NG

TRIUMPH (ii) (US) 1907–1912
Triumph Motor Car Co., Chicago, Illinois.
This Triumph was made in several versions of 4-cylinder car, from 30 to 45hp and various wheelbases from 108 (2741mm) to 118in (2995mm). Tourer and roadster bodies were offered, with a limousine for 1909 only. What marked out the Triumph out from its contemporaries was its compressed air self-starter. This was operated by storing the exhaust gases in a tank under the seat, at a pressure of 125psi. This gas could be bled back into the cylinders for starting.

NG

TRIUMPH (iii) (GB) 1923–1984
1923–1929 Triumph Cycle Co. Ltd, Coventry.
1930–1972 Triumph Motor Co. Ltd, Coventry.
1972–1984 British Leyland (UK) Ltd; BL Cars Ltd, Coventry.
The Triumph name originated on the bicycles sold by German-born Siegfried Bettmann (1863–1951) in Coventry, at first made for him and, from 1887, made by him in his own factory. Motorcycles were added in 1902, and during World War I Triumph was a major supplier of 2-wheelers to the British and other Armies.

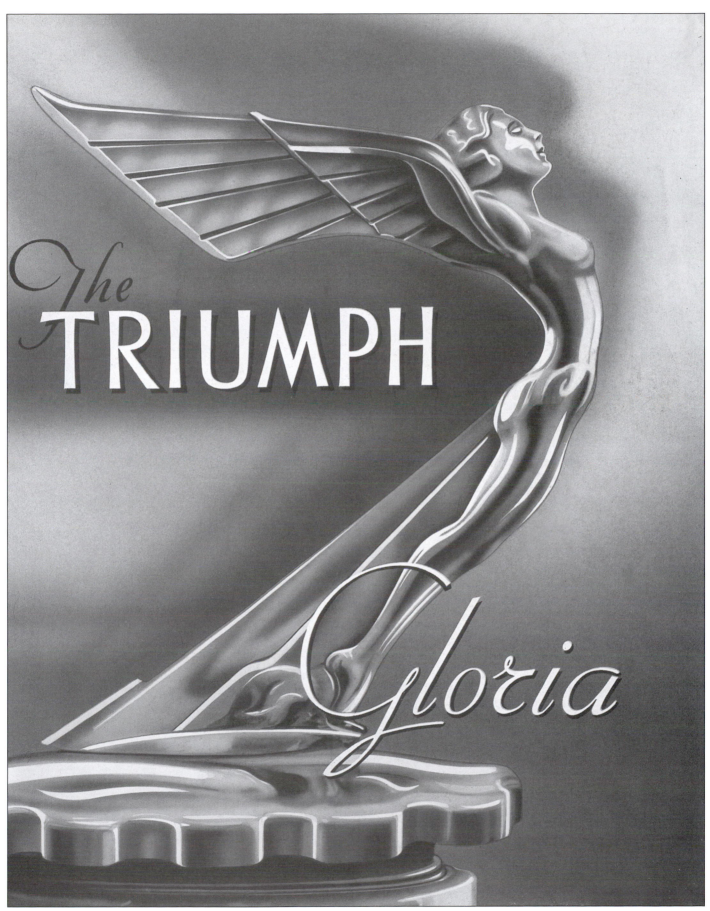

The TRIUMPH
Gloria

1933 Triumph (iii) Southern Cross sports tourer.
NICK BALDWIN

1935 Triumph (iii) Gloria sports tourer.
NICK BALDWIN

After the war Bettmann was persuaded by his new general manager, Claude Holbrook, to enter the car market, and they purchased the Coventry factory of the defunct Dawson Car Co. in 1921. Two years later appeared the first Triumph car, the 10/20 with 1393cc 4-cylinder engine and 4-speed gearbox. It was designed by Arthur Alderson who worked for Lea-Francis, so Triumph had to pay Lea-Francis a royalty on every car made. Perhaps this contributed to the unrealistically high price of £430–460. The 10/20 was listed until the end of the 1925 season, but in 1924 it was joined by a more important car, the 1872cc 13/35 which was the first British car to have Lockheed hydraulic brakes on all four wheels. 1926 saw an enlarged version of this, the 2169cc 15/50, better known as the Fifteen. This was the sole model for 1926 and 1927, and was made in larger numbers than the earlier Triumphs. Prices were £395 for a tourer and £495 for a saloon.

For 1928 Triumph introduced a new model which was to make their name and lift them above the ranks of the worthy but unexceptional cars which they had made so far. Designed by Stanley Edge who had helped Herbert Austin with his Seven, the Triumph Super Seven had a 4-cylinder side-valve engine of 832cc which developed only 21bhp in its original form. It had worm final drive, and shared the hydraulic brakes of the larger Triumphs, giving it a distinct advantage over the poorly-braked Austin Seven. The Triumph was not all that much more expensive, at £149 and £187 for tourer and saloon, compared with £135 and £150 for the Austin. Numerous body styles were available on the Super Seven, some made in Triumph's own coachworks, others by outside firms including Gordon England whose fabric saloons were well-known. A pillarless 4-door saloon was offered from 1931, and there were also sports models including a supercharged 747cc version capable of 80mph (130km/h). (A standard Super Seven tourer was hard put to exceed 60mph (97km/h.) They did not enjoy the racing successes of the Austin Seven or MG Midget, but Donald Healey finished 7th in the 1930 Monte Carlo Rally, and in Australia Super Sevens took three of the first four places in the 1930 Royal Australian Automobile Club Trials, and broke the Brisbane-Sydney light car record in 1931. About 17,000 Super Sevens were made in five years, 1928–1932, compared with around 2000 for all previous Triumphs.

HOLBROOK, CLAUDE VIVIAN (1886–1979)

Son of newspaper tycoon Sir Arthur Holbrook, Claude Holbrook grew up in a wealthy home and was privately educated. Volunteering for military service in 1914, he served in the forerunner of the Royal Army Service Corps before being called back from the field to head a military procurement office in Whitehall.

Transport equipment was part of his responsibilities, and one of his suppliers was Siegfried Bettmann, maker of the Triumph motorcycles in Coventry. During World War I, Whitehall was Triumph's biggest customer. In 1919 Holbrook resigned his commission and joined Triumph as works manager, replacing the co-founder, M.J. Schulte. Bettman was content to make motorcycles; Holbrook wanted to build Triumph cars. In 1921 he was able to arrange the purchase of the idle Dawson plant in Clay Lane, Stoke, Coventry, and began producing a car designed by Arthur Alderson in 1922 (the Triumph Ten). He also hired Frank G. Parnell as chief engineer, to prepare a range of new models.

For years, Triumph operated one car factory and one motorcycle factory, both producing (on balance) a profit. Holbrook, however, was not a man for 2-wheeled transport, and began arguing for selling off the motorcycle branch. He just did not have the power as long as Bettmann held the Triumph reins. That changed in 1933, when Bettmann stepped down and took the title of vice chairman, while Holbrook became managing director. He sold the Triumph motorcycle branch to Jack Sangster, who made Ariel motorcycles in Birmingham.

Holbrook named Charles Ridley director and general manager of the car operations and hired Donald Healey as chief engineer for Triumph cars. But he made the mistake of discarding Bettmann's cost-accounting system, and suddenly, at mid-year 1933, had the unpleasant surprise of hearing from his accountants that Triumph was running in the red. Ironically, Bettmann had a considerable personal fortune and in 1936 bought Triumph's motorcycle operations from Sangster.

In 1936 Holbrook was elected chairman of the board of the Triumph Co. Ltd, while Maurice Newnham, the prominent Triumph agent in London, assumed the duties of general manager. In 1938 Triumph was bankrupt. Holbrook stepped down and never played any further role in the motor industry. He died in 1979.

JPN

1937 Triumph (iii) Vitesse saloon.
NICK BALDWIN

1931 saw the first 6-cylinder Triumph; called the Scorpion, it bore the same relationship to the Super Seven as did the Wolseley Hornet to the Morris Minor, two extra cylinders in a slightly lengthened frame without any serious strengthening. Capacity was 1203cc and top speed around 60mph (97km/h), but the Scorpion handled poorly, and even the addition of a 4-speed gearbox and lengthened chassis for 1933 did not improve the car's appeal. Not more than 1500 were sold in three seasons.

Claude Holbrook had never really liked small cars, and realised that it was not worth pursuing the Super Seven theme when rivals such as Austin, Ford and Morris had much larger production capacity. He therefore moved upmarket in the 1930s, buying his engines from Coventry-Climax rather than spending a lot of money on developing larger in-house engines. The first model to use a Coventry- Climax engine was the Super Nine of 1932–33, essentially a late Super Seven chassis with the same wheelbase as the early Scorpion, and a 1018cc engine with inlet-over-exhaust valves. A sports version on a longer wheelbase was called the Southern Cross, and from 1934 this could be had in saloon or sports tourer form with a 1122cc engine. Although the Southern Cross has been touted as 'the pioneer Triumph sports car', it was not remarkable in performance (and surely the supercharged Super Seven deserved the title anyway?), with a top speed of around 68mph (110km/h).

Glorias and Dolomites

For 1934 Triumph brought out a completely new range of cars which fulfilled Holbrook's ambitions, and took on such cars as the Rileys, smaller Alvises and SS. Known as the Glorias, they had 4- or 6-cylinder Coventry-Climax engines of 1087 and 1476cc, cruciform-braced frames underslung at the rear, and spiral bevel rear axles. The engines were considerably reworked by Triumph, giving 42 or 50bhp in 4-cylinder form, and 55 or 60bhp from the 6-cylinder unit. From 1935 capacity of the Gloria Four went up to 1232cc, (though the smaller unit was still available) and of the Six to 1991cc. The handsome bodies were styled by Frank Warner and later improved by Walter Belgrove who was to be responsible for the postwar Renown and TR2. The Southern Cross name was revived for a short-chassis slab tank 2-seater sports available with 1232 or 1991cc engines. The latter had a top speed of 80mph (130km/h).

1937 Triumph (iii) Vitesse drophead coupé.
NICK BALDWIN

1938 Triumph (iii) Dolomite roadster.
NICK BALDWIN

1946 Triumph (iii) 1800 roadster.
NICK BALDWIN

1952 Triumph (iii) Mayflower saloon.
NICK BALDWIN

At the 1934 Olympia Show Triumph exhibited their most ambitious car, and the first to bear the name Dolomite. It had a 1991cc twin-ohc straight-8 engine closely based on the larger Alfa Romeo 2300. Suggestions that Triumph copied this design without permission, and were forced to drop the project because of threats from Alfa Romeo are unfounded. Alfa's designer Vittorio Jano knew all about it, and it is possible that a trade-off whereby the Italian company would make Triumph motorcycles was considered. The Dolomite had a Roots-type supercharger built by Triumph, giving 120bhp at 5500rpm, and a top speed of around 110mph (177km/h). Transmission was by an Armstrong-Siddeley-built pre-selector gearbox, and the Dolomite had a stark and functional 2-seater body. The chassis price was £1050, and a complete range of bodies was planned, including a 4-door saloon on a longer wheelbase. However, Holbrook cancelled the project in April 1935, after only three chassis had been made. One was driven by Donald Healey in the 1935 Monte Carlo Rally, but was wrecked at a level crossing in Denmark. Two incomplete chassis and five or six engines were bought by Tony Rolt, and were assembled by David Scott-Moncrieff and Robert Arbuthnot with Corsica bodies and sold under the name HSM (High Speed Motors).

The 1937 models saw a return to Triumph-built engines designed by Donald Healey with all ohvs in three sizes, 1496 and 1767cc fours and a 1991cc six. The 1232cc Coventry-Climax was continued in the cheapest Gloria, so the range was a complex one: 1.2-, and 1.5-litre Gloria fours, 1.8-litre four and 2-litre sixes called Vitesse or Dolomite. The Vitesse had traditional styling while the Dolomite wore a fencers' mask grill copied from the 1936 Hudson, and had more rounded body lines similar to those of the SS Jaguar. It was clearly aimed at the Jaguar market; at £368 the 2-litre saloon cost £73 more than a 1½-litre Jaguar and £7 less than the 2½-litre version. The most striking of the Dolomites were the roadsters which seated three abreast with double dickey seat. They were available with 1.8- and 2-litre engines, and about 200 were made out of total Dolomite production of c.6000. A fixed-head coupé was shown at the 1938 Earls Court Show, but never went into production. For those who appreciated the Dolomite's quality and performance but disliked its looks, there was the Continental with traditional Vitesse radiator.

Triumph's financial position was not happy in the mid–1930s, with a large loss in 1936, which was not entirely compensated by the sale of the motorcycle division to Jack Sangster of Ariel. A new lower-priced Twelve with 1496cc engine, made only as a 4-door saloon, was launched for 1939, but capital investment for this model resulted in another loss, and in June 1939 Triumph went into receivership. Only 50 Twelves were made, some of them by the steel makers Thomas Ward & Co. who bought the company from the receivers. One of the factories was sold to the government, and the other was let to the Armstrong-Whitworth Aircraft Co. It was badly damaged during the war, and in 1944 was acquired, together with rights to the Triumph name, by Sir John Black of Standard. He quickly sold the factory, but planned a new range of Triumph cars to rival the Jaguar, and which would be built in his factory at Canley, near Coventry.

The first Standard-built Triumphs were known as the 1800 saloon and roadster, and shared most mechanical components, though their appearance was quite distinct. Announced in March 1946, they had a 1776cc ohv 4-cylinder engine which was also supplied to Jaguar for their 1½-litre models. Because sheet steel was in short supply, the chassis were of tubular steel, and aluminium was extensively used in the bodies, The saloon had razor-edge styling similar to that favoured by custom coachbuilders, while the roadster was more rounded, with large wings and a boot which concealed a 2-passenger dickey seat. Both bodies

NICK BALDWIN

STOKES, DONALD GRESHAM (born 1914)

Donald Stokes was a truck-industry executive who did more than anyone to consolidate the British passenger-car industry-under his own leadership. But without a master plan, without a grand vision, it added up to full-scale failure.

Born on 9 March 1914, at Bexley, Kent, he was educated at Blundell's School and joined Leyland Motors as a student engineering apprentice in 1930. He stayed on with Leyland and held a succession of posts up to 1939, when he joined the army. He was attached to a transport group and became a technical service engineer for Leyland-built tanks, and was demobilised in 1946 with the rank of lieutenant-colonel.

were made by Mulliners of Birmingham. The original models were made from 1946 to 1948, production being 4000 saloons and 2501 roadsters. They were replaced by the 2000 series which used the 2088cc Standard Vanguard engine. Slightly more power was offset by the loss of a gear ratio, as they also used the Vanguard's 3-speed 'box. About 2000 each were made of the 2000, and there were no further models of the roadster, but the saloon was continued up to 1954 under the name Renown. This had a similar appearance to the earlier cars, but there was a modified Vanguard box section frame in place of the tubes, and coil spring ifs was featured instead of transverse leaves. Overdrive was offered from June 1950, and the Mk II Renown of 1952–54 had an extra 3in (76mm) wheelbase. On this chassis was built the rare Renown limousine with sliding division between front and rear seats. Only 190 were made, while Renown saloon production reached 9301.

The 1949 Earls Court Show saw two new Triumphs which attracted a lot of attention, One was the TRX, a bulbous roadster intended to replace the original postwar design. Vanguard-powered, it had a stressed-skin full-width body with retractable headlamps, and hydro-electric assistance for the overdrive, seats, windows, hood and radio aerial. Its appearance was against it, as well as the complexity of the hydro-electrics and the vulnerable body. Only three prototypes were made, of which two survive today.

1958 Triumph (iii) TR3A sports car.
NICK BALDWIN

1966 Triumph (iii) TR4A sports car.
NICK BALDWIN

Returning to Leyland, he became export development director, later becoming export director. In 1949 he was assigned to Scammell as director of sales and service. He never put a foot wrong, which earmarked him for promotion, and he was elected to Leyland's board of directors in 1953. His boss, Sir Henry Spurrier, began expanding by acquisition in 1958, buying control of Beans Industries Ltd, Mulliners Ltd, and the Forward Radiator Co. Ltd. In March 1961 Leyland Motors made a bid for control of Standard-Triumph International, which was successfully concluded.

In 1963 Donald Stokes became managing director and vice chairman of Leyland Motors, and before the end of the year, took on the additional role of chairman of Standard-Triumph International.

He killed off the Standard brand and built up Triumph with a spreading model range. In 1966–67 he had members of the Government's Industrial Reorganisation Corp. coming to his London flat for informal talks, which resulted in getting Leyland the green light to take control of British Motor Holdings, created in 1966 by British Motor Corp.'s take-over of Jaguar. British Leyland Motor Corp. was formed in 1968 with Donald Stokes as chairman and managing director, nearly 200,000 people on the payroll, and a sales target of £1 billion a year. In the Queen's honours list of 1969, he was given a life peerage and took the title of Lord Stokes of Leyland.

He announced a 5-year plan for the wholesale renewal of BL's entire passenger-car model range, and began pouring money into Austin-Morris at an annual rate of £125million. That gave birth to the Morris Marina and Austin Allegro, which were given a lukewarm reception in the market place. Even in the face of dwindling income and rising inventories, Lord Stokes steadfastly maintained his long-term investment programme.

The financial situation continued to worsen, and in December 1974 Lord Stokes applied for government aid for BL. The secretary of state for industry, Anthony Wedgwood Benn, responded that he could offer loan guarantees up to £121 million, but no direct aid without an equity stake in the corporation. Lord Stokes reacted by taking drastic steps to cut costs. The Waterloo plant in Australia was closed, the Authi factory at Valladolid shut its doors and was eventually sold to VW, and the car-making subsidiary of Innocenti was put into liquidation. In June 1975 the UK government refused to take Austin-Morris off BL's portfolio at the knockdown price of £1.

When British Leyland was nationalised, lock, stock, and barrel, in 1975, Lord Stokes resigned and joined Jack Barclay, London distributors for Rolls-Royce, where he became chairman.

JPN

The other newcomer was much more successful. The Mayflower saloon was an attempt to make a quality small car with razor-edge styling, using the 1247cc engine and gearbox from a prewar Standard Ten, though with only 3-speeds and column gearchange. The body was Triumph's first unitary construction, and the styling was criticised for being unsuited to such a short wheelbase. Nevertheless, the Mayflower sold quite well, about 35,000 in four seasons, of which reputedly half were exported. Ten drophead Mayflowers were made, of which it is thought that none survive.

The TR Series

The TRX was abandoned in mid–1951, but Sir John Black had not given up the idea of a sporting Triumph. He decided to make a simple sports car in the idiom of the MG TD and Morgan Plus Four, but with more up-to-date styling. He was not prepared to spend a lot of money on the project, and engineer Harry Webster and stylist Walter Belgrove had to work to a very tight budget. This meant using existing components wherever possible. As several hundred prewar Standard Flying Nine frames were still unused, Black decreed that these should form the basis of the new sports car, together with Mayflower suspension and rear axle, with a slightly reduced track. The engine was a Vanguard, reduced to 1991cc to put it in the 2-litre class for competitions, and endowed with twin carburettors to give 75bhp. Belgrove's body was a simple open 2-seater with exposed spare wheel and characteristic frontal cavity with the grill set inside. The prototype was running early in 1952, but tests showed that the Standard frame was inadequate, and it was considerably strengthened before the car's first public showing at the 1952 Earls Court Show. It was called the Triumph Sports Car, or 20TS, and only in retrospect has it been christened the TR1. Only one was made, and it was subsequently scrapped.

The frame was still inadequate, and Ken Richardson was hired from B.R.M. to sort out the car. When he drove it he pronounced it to be 'a bloody death trap'. Five prototypes of a new car which became the TR2 were built in early 1953, with much-strengthened frame, engine output increased from 75 to 90bhp and a longer tail which concealed the spare wheel and allowed for some luggage space. The second prototype was taken to the Jabbeke motorway in Belgium in

1963 Triumph (iii) Herald saloon.
NICK BALDWIN

1971 Triumph (iii) 2000 MkII saloon.
ANNABEL HOLMES

May 1953, where it achieved 125mph (201km/h) in speed trim, with undershield and no screen or hood, and 115mph (184.9km/h) in overdrive with undershield and touring trim. The production TR2, with overdrive, had a top speed of 102.5mph (165km/h). The history of the TR series can be summarised as follows:

TR2 Production, August 1953–October 1955: 8628 made.

Only 248 cars delivered in 1953, of which 198 went for export. A high proportion were equipped with overdrive, at first on top gear only, later on all but first gear. Centre-lock wire wheels optional. Early cars had doors which extended to the bottom of the body; from autumn 1954 the 'short doors' were introduced, with a small sill below them which made them less vulnerable to damage when being opened at the kerbside. A hard-top was also available from autumn 1954.

TR3 Production, October 1955–September 1957: 13,377 made.

Essentially the same as TR2, but with power increased to 95bhp and disc brakes on front-wheels. They were the first British production car to have disc brakes, and only the second in Europe (after Citroën DS19). Easily identified by the 'egg-crate' grill over the frontal cavity. Occasional rear seat with very limited leg room available. Nearly 90 per cent exported.

TR3A Production, September 1957–October 1961: 58,236 made.

Identified by full-width grill, more recessed headlamps and exterior door handles. Same seating and hard-top options as for TR3. 100bhp engine which had also been seen on late TR3s. Conversion kit enlarging engine to 2138cc available from 1959; this was originally developed by Ken Richardson for rallying, giving greater torque though little extra power.

TR3B Production, March–October 1962: 3331 made.

A special batch of TR3As built at the request of North American dealers who felt that the TR4 was too civilised for their traditional customers. Similar to TR3A, with both sizes of engine available, but had TR4's all-synchromesh gearbox. Bodies were built by the Forward Radiator Co., whereas all previous TR bodies were by Mulliner. TR3A and TR3B were not official factory designations, and the cars were badged simply as TR3s.

TR4 Production, August 1961–January 1965: 40,253 made.

2138cc engine only, and a completely new body styled by Michelotti and built in the new Standard-Triumph factory at Speke, near Liverpool. Same wheelbase as TR3, but 2.6in (66mm) longer and 2in (50mm) wider. Rack-and-pinion steering and all-synchromesh gearbox.

TR4A Production, January 1965–August 1967: 28,465 made.

Externally similar to TR4, though with new radiator grill, bonnet badge and combined side-lamp housing and decorative wing flash. Main engineering change was irs by coil and semi-trailing arms, in place of the semi-elliptics which had been used since the first TR2s. This added about 100lbs (45kg) to weight, but the 104bhp engine gave a top speed of 109mph (175km/h). On the US market, irs was an option, and many buyers preferred the old semi-elliptics, which were cheaper and simpler to maintain. Irs gave no great advantage on straight roads.

TR5 Production, October 1967–November 1968: 2947 made.

Similar styling to TR4A, but all-new fuel-injection 2498cc 6-cylinder engine developed from the 1996cc unit used in the Standard Vanguard Six and Triumph 2000 saloons. 150bhp and 118mph (190km/h). Rostyle wheels standard, wire wheels optional.

TR250 Production, August 1967–December 1968: 8494 made.

This was the TR5 made for the North American market, with carburettor engine in place of fuel injection, to meet the new emission laws, and correspondingly lower output of 104bhp. Distinguished externally by special colour schemes, including transverse stripes across the front of the bonnet.

TR6 Production, November 1968–July 1976: 94,619 made.

New body styled by Karmann with full-width front, the first of the TRs to have headlamps at the corners, and redesigned tail with wrap-around lamps. No separate designation for US models, which had same twin-carburettor engine as TR250. European market TR6s had 150bhp to 1973, then reduced to 124bhp. The most important change made in the lifetime of the TR6 (longer than any other TR), was a completely new overdrive for 1973, which replaced the Laycock de Normanville system which had been used since the first TR2s. It had a slightly higher step-up ratio of 0.797:1 compared with 0.82:1; optional at first, it was standardised from the 1974 model year. The optional wire wheels were discontinued in May 1973.

TR7 Production, September 1974–October 1981: 112,368 made.

Completely new model with wedge-shaped integral construction body and inclined 1998cc 4-cylinder single-ohc engine. This was a new unit, of the same family as the 1709cc unit used in the Saab 99, and having the same dimensions as the Dolomite Sprint, though the latter's 16-valve head was never seen in the TR7, to the disappointment of enthusiasts. The engine gave 105bhp in European form, and no more than 92bhp in Federalised form for the North American market. 4-speed gearbox at first, but 5-speeds and automatics optional from late 1976, and 4-speeds dropped by 1979. The TR7 was a controversial car from the start, and sold disappointingly on the US market at which it was aimed. Labour problems, particularly at the Speke factory where it was originally made, interfered with production, and prevented the 16-valve engine from reaching the public. Manufacture at Speke ended in March 1978, body pressings being transferred to BL's Pressed Steel Fisher factory at Swindon, with final assembly at Canley, Coventry. Then in 1980, in a rationalisation of Rover and Triumph production, the assembly of TR7/8 was transferred to the Rover factory at Solihull. The only TR7 body style up to 1979 was a 2-seater coupé, but a convertible was then added. From 1978 to 1980 a very small number of TR7s were fitted with the 3528cc Rover V8 engine for rallying. They had disc brakes all round, and should not be confused with the export-only TR8, which used the same engine but was not marketed until 1980.

TR8 Production, September 1979–October 1981: 2722 made.

Triumph dropped the 3528cc Rover V8 engine in the TR7 hull to make this export-only model, which was much more highly rated than the TR7. Output was 135bhp, even in Federalised form, giving a top speed of 121mph (195km/h). Coupés and convertibles made, the latter being more common, whereas the reverse was true of the TR7. Eighteen rhd cars were built for the UK market. Had it appeared two years earlier it might have saved the model, but it was too late, and could not redeem the poor reputation of the TR7.

Special-bodied TRs

A number of special-bodied versions of various TR models were built for commercial sale. In chronological order, these were the Francorchamps, a Belgian hard-top version of the TR2, of which 22 were made in 1954/5, the Italia, a TR3 fixed-head coupé styled by Michelotti and built by Vignale, of which several hundred were made in 1959–63, and the Dove, a 4-seater coupé conversion of the TR4, of which about 55 were made by Harrington for sale by Doves of Wimbledon. Unlike the Italia which had its own body, the Dove was a coupé top on an existing TR4. So far as is known, no TR4As were converted. Several other makes used TR engines, including Swallow Doretti, Peerless and Warwick.

The TR in Competition

Standard-Triumph had no competition department and took little interest in motor sport before the arrival of the TR2. The TR's first successes were achieved by private owners, notable being victory in the 1954 RAC Rally by Johnny Wallwork/John Cooper's TR2. The first works entry was in the 1954 Mille Miglia, and in that year's Alpine Rally Maurice Gatsonides and Rob Slotemaker won a Coupe des Alpes and the factory took the team prize. They also took the team prize in the TT. The 1955 TR2s for Le Mans had disc brakes, foreshadowing the production TR3s, while Ken Richardson was 5th overall in the 1955 Liège-Rome-Liège. In the later 1950s the TR3 and TR3A had numerous successes in rallies, particularly the Alpine and Liège-Rome-Liège, though they never won outright. This was partly because of their size, but also because Richardson did not believe in tuning the works entries too highly. They were always fairly close to production cars, and sometimes less potent than those of private owners. In 1959 Annie Soisbault tied with Evy Rosqvist in a Volvo for the Ladies' Rally

1975 Triumph (iii) Stag coupé.
NICK BALDWIN

1975 Triumph (iii) Toledo 2-door saloon.
NICK BALDWIN

1976 Triumph (iii) Dolomite Sprint saloon.
NICK BALDWIN

Championship. In the 1960s the increasingly rough terrain used for special stages put the low-slung Triumph sports cars at a disadvantage in international rallying. TR4s won team prizes in the 1962 RAC, 1963 Tulip and 1964 Canadian Shell 4000 Rallies, but after that Triumph entered 2000 saloons in rallies. However, the TRs were enormously successful in club rallies and races throughout the 1960s. In America, Bob Tullius won numerous SCCA races in TR4s, TR5s and TR6s.

From 1959 to 1961 special TR3s with twin-cam engines ran at Le Mans. They were not particularly successful in 1959 and 1960, but in 1961 the TRS with special fibreglass bodies won the team prize, the best finisher being the car of Keith Ballisat and Peter Bolton in 9th place.

A more specialised car developed in 1960–61 was the Conrero TRS, with Michelotti-styled closed coupé body and engine tuned by Conrero. This would probably have been Triumph's entry for Le Mans in 1962, had not the competition department been closed down.

In 1976 British Leyland used the TR7 as the spearhead of their rallying programme. Works cars used the 16-valve Dolomite Sprint engine and, later,

1977 Triumph (iii) TR7 sports car.
NICK BALDWIN

the Rover V8. All the rally cars had disc brakes all round and fat alloy wheels. Tony Pond won the 1977 Boucle de Spa and 1978 Ypres 24-Hours Rally, while Pond and Gallagher won the 1980 Manx Rally. The TR7s were successful on tarmac, but were hampered on forest stages by restricted visibility and unwieldy handling.

Spitfire and GT6

If the TRs were seen as rivals to the Austin Healey 100, Triumph's answer to the Sprite was the Spitfire, which appeared some months after its rival from BMC. It was essentially a sports version of the Herald saloon, using the same 1147cc engine, chassis and swing-axle rear suspension. The 2-seater body was styled by Michelotti. There were five marks of Spitfire, summarised as follows:

Mk I, Production 1962–1965: 45,753 made.

Twin carburettor version of the Herald 12/50 engine, developing 63bhp. Top speed 90mph (145km/h). Front disc brakes standard. From 1964 available with hard-top, centre-lock wire wheels and overdrive.

Mk II, Production 1965–1967: 37,409 made.

More power (67bhp) thanks to a hotter camshaft, and top speed now 92mph (148km/h). Better interior finish, but no major changes from Mk I.

Mk III, Production 1967–1970: 65,320 made.

Engine size increased to 1296cc and 75bhp, top speed 95mph (153km/h). Easily identified by larger and higher bumpers which covered radiator grill. Wire wheels, overdrive and hard-top still available.

Mk IV, Production 1970–1974: 70,021 made.

Restyled body with smoother nose and squared-off tail. 1493cc engine for the US market in 1973 and 1974, to cope with increasingly strict emission regulations. All-synchromesh gearbox, and new rear suspension which improved road-holding. 1973 models were the last with wire wheel option.

1500, Production 1974–1980: 95,829 made.

The 1493 engine now available for all markets. 71bhp and 100mph (160km/h), but only 93mph (150km/h) from US-market models. No important changes during its seven-year life, as British Leyland was concentrating development money on the TR7.

GT6 Mk I, Production 1966–1968: 15,818 made.

Conceived as a rival to the MGB GT, this was a Spitfire with fastback coupé body in the style of the E-type Jaguar, and a 1998cc 6-cylinder Triumph Vitesse engine. As with Spitfire, wire wheels and overdrive options. Top speed 105mph (170km/h), but handling alarming due to unmodified Herald rear axle.

GT6 Mk II, Production 1968–1970: 12,066 made.

Improved rear suspension from Vitesse Mk II, and higher bumpers as on Spitfire Mk III. 105bhp and 110mph (177km/h).

GT6 Mk III, Production 1970–1973: 13,042 made.

Same engine and performance, but restyled along lines of Spitfire Mk IV. US market cars much less powerful, only 79bhp, so sales were poor, main reason for discontinuing the model.

Herald and Vitesse

When Standard-Triumph replaced the Standard Eight and Ten they decided to badge the new small car as a Triumph. Christened the Herald, it used the 948cc engine from the Standard Ten, uprated to 38bhp, in an all-new chassis and body, the latter styled by Michelotti. A 2-door saloon, coupé and convertible were the initial models, joined in 1961 by an estate car, when capacity went up to 1147cc. The chassis had all-independent suspension, unusual for a popularly-priced British family car. Swing axles at the rear made for somewhat alarming cornering, more noticeable in the more powerful Vitesse and Spitfire. Front disc brakes were optional from late 1960. They were standard in the Herald 12/50 (1962–67) and 13/60 (1967–71), the latter with engine enlarged to 1296cc and 61bhp. The coupés were dropped in 1964, but the convertibles and estate cars were continued alongside the saloons up to the end of Herald production in 1971. The total made was 525,797, making the Herald the best-selling of any Triumph model.

In 1962 Triumph revived their prewar Scorpion theme in putting a small 6-cylinder engine into a 4-cylinder chassis. The Vitesse had a 1596cc engine in a lengthened Herald frame, with similar body and modified front end incorporating four headlamps. Saloons and convertibles were the only body styles, though a few estates were made unofficially. Disc brakes were standard on all Vitesses, and overdrive optional. Capacity went up to 1998cc on the Vitesse 2-litre Mk I (1966–68), while the best of the series was the 2-litre Mk II (1968–71) which had improved rear suspension to cope with the 100mph (160km/h) top speed. Total Vitesse production was 51,182, of which 15,391 were convertibles.

Triumph Saloons, 1963–1984

As well as the Heralds, Triumph built two ranges of larger saloon cars during the 1960s and 1970s. The first to appear was the 2000, which used a 1998cc twin-carburettor Standard Vanguard Six engine in a new unitary construction 6-light saloon body, with all-synchromesh gearbox, disc brakes on front wheels and independent suspension all round. It was made as a saloon and estate car in Mk I form from 1963 to 1969, when it was replaced by the Mk II with modified front end and bigger boot, which was made up to 1977. The estate cars were quite rare, accounting for only 14,906 out of a total of 219,816 2000s. In 1968 the 2498cc fuel-injected six of the TR5 was dropped into the 2000 hull to make the 2.5 PI, a high-performance saloon with a top speed of 105mph (170km/h). Relatively few were made with the original styling, as 1969 saw the Mk II with the same body modifications as the 2000 Mk II; this was made up to 1975 when it gave way to the 2500TC and 2500S. These used the 2498cc engine, but abandoned the fuel injection which had proved troublesome. In the TC the engine gave 99bhp, and in the S, 106bhp. They were the best of the 2000/2500 series, but were not made for long, as the Rover 2600 replaced them for 1978. Production of the fuel injection cars was 56,484, and of the 2500s, 40,656.

An interesting development of the 2000, which never realised its full potential, was the Stag coupé and convertible. It was conceived as a short-chassis version of the 2000, but when it reached production it was powered by a unique 2997cc ohc V8 which was not used in any other car. It developed 145bhp, and gave the 2+2-seater Stag a top speed of 115mph (185km/h). There were power assisted disc brakes on the front wheels, and overdrive or automatic gearboxes were available. Many Stags were equipped with automatics. Triumph hoped to sell 12,000 Stags a year, but they sold little more than twice that (25,877) in seven years, 1970 to 1977. The engine proved unreliable, and more than 50 per cent of Stags sold in the US had to receive major engine work under warranty, thus using up all the profit the makers hoped to earn on each car. Had the Stag been given the 3528cc Rover V8, it might have been a different story.

The line of smaller Triumph saloons began with the 1300, made from 1965 to 1970. This used a 1296cc Herald-type engine turned round to drive the front wheels via an all-synchromesh gearbox mounted underneath the engine. The body was an integral 4-door saloon, and unlike the Herald there were no convertible or estate versions. Top speed was around 78mph (125km/h), but the twin-carburettor 1300TC introduced in 1967 could do 90mph (145km/h). A larger-engined, though not more powerful version, was the 1500, which used a 1493cc single-carburettor engine later to go into the MG Midget. A total of 214,703 of the front-drive saloons were made, and in 1970 they were joined by the Toledo, which used the 1296cc engine with conventional rear-wheel drive in the 1300 body shell. Originally only made as a 2-door saloon, the Toledo acquired four doors in 1972, and for some export markets the 1493cc engine was fitted. This engine also powered the 1500TC, a rear-driven car which replaced the front-drive 1500 in 1973, and continued the same 4-headlamp layout which identified it from the Toledo.

In 1976 the Toledo became the Dolomite 1300 and the 1500TC the Dolomite 1500 (two headlamps) and 1500HL (four headlamps). There were also more powerful Dolomites with single-ohc engines, the 1854cc 1850 and the 1998cc Sprint. The latter was a really high-performance saloon with many credits in racing and rallying, powered by a slant-four 16-valve engine giving 127bhp and a top speed of 115mph (185km/h). The Sprint did not win any major rallies, but did well in Class 1 sections for less highly tuned engines. Brian Culcheth's win in Class 1 of the 1975 RAC was one example. However, it did not have a very long rallying life, as BL replaced it with the TR7 in 1977. Production of the Sprint was 22,941, compared with 79,010 1850s and 75,286 of the 1300/1500.

The Dolomites were made up to 1980, but no further saloons were planned, as BL's Sir Michael Edwardes favoured Rover as the saloon marque for the Group. He did not favour sports cars at all, so the Spitfire died in 1980 and the TR7/8 in 1981. The Triumph name had one last lease of life on a badge-engineered Honda Ballade christened the Triumph Acclaim. This used a Japanese-built 1335cc engine, transmission and front-drive assembly, with a 4-door saloon body styled after the Ballade but built at BL's Pressed Steel factory at Cowley, Oxford. Final assembly took place in the old Morris Motors factory, also at Cowley. The Acclaim was made from November 1981 to June 1984, with 133,000 being built, more than Honda made of the Ballade during the same period. It was replaced by another Honda-based car, sold under the name Rover 213.

NG

1958 Triver 197cc minicar.
NICK GEORGANO/NATIONAL MOTOR MUSEUM

Further Reading
Triumph Cars, the Complete 75-Year History, Richard Langworth and Graham Robson, Motor Racing Publications, 1979.
The Complete Guide to the Triumph TR7 and TR8, William Kimberley, Dalton Watson, 1981.
Triumph TRs, Graham Robson, Crowood AutoClassics, 1991.
Triumph Stag, the Complete History, James Taylor and Dave Jell, Windrow & Green, 1993.
Triumph 2000 and 2.5PI, Graham Robson, Crowood AutoClassics, 1995.
Triumph Herald and Vitesse, Graham Robson, Crowood AutoClassics, 1997.
Illustrated Triumph Buyers' Guide, Richard Newton, Motor Books International, 1984.

TRIUMPH (iv) (D) 1933

Triumph Werke AG, Nuremburg.
Well-known for their motorcycles from 1903 to 1957, this company made a few 3-wheeled coupés to take advantage of tax concessions for such vehicles. They were powered by 350cc engines driving the rear wheels.

NG

TRIUMPH (v) (AUS) 1951–1973

Standard Motor Products and Australian Motor Industries Ltd, Port Melbourne, Victoria.
Teasing out the strands of Triumph from Standard can be confusing but, in Australia, the Mayflower was built as a car-type utility (pick-up). In 1964, after a marketing debacle with the Herald, an attempt was made to keep the type alive by introducing the 12/50, with two carburettors, disc front brakes and the twin-headlamp frontal styling used on the home market Vitesse – a model not offered in Australia. An Australian version of the 2000 was the MD, an overtly sporting package with three carburettors, overdrive and wire wheels.

MG

TRIVER (E) 1957–1963

Construcciones Acoracadas SA, Bilbao.
This was an all-Spanish bubble car, produced by a manufacturer of strongboxes, which doubtless explained why its sheet metal bodywork was fully 3mm thick. It had side doors in contrast to the single front door of the Isetta and Heinkel and could seat 2+2 passengers. It measured only 105in (2670mm) long and weighed 500kg (1100lb). Early cars had a rear-mounted 339cc Fraso 2-stroke twin engine but later a Hispano-Villiers 14bhp engine was substituted, raising the top speed by 11mph (18km/h) to 48mph (77km/h).

CR

1922 Trojan (ii)10hp utility car.
NICK BALDWIN

1927 Trojan (ii) 10hp tourer.
NICK BALDWIN

1930 Trojan (ii) 10hp Purley saloon.
NICK BALDWIN

TRI-VETTE (US) 1975–1995
Bob Keyes, Sunnyvale, California.
Vigilante, San Jose, California.
Trans-Tech, Santa Rosa, California.
The Tri-Vette was a 3-wheeler kit car designed and built by Bob Keyes. The first series had Fiat 903cc engines and weighed 1140lbs. The single wheel was in the

front and the car looked like an AMC Gremlin that had been put in a vice and squashed to half width. 24 of the first series cars were built from 1975 to 1980. In 1980 the Tri-Vette was renamed the Vigilante and upgraded to Ford Fiesta 1588cc engines which could be run on gas or methanol. Weight was reduced to 980lbs. They were sold as kits or fully assembled to individuals and to city municipal departments that were experimenting with methanol fuels. In 1994 Keyes re-engineered the car again with a new, jet-like body and composite and aluminium construction. A Chevrolet V8 was to replace the Ford engine.
HP

TRI-X (US) c.1981
Gallati-Tenold Ent. Inc., Rogers, Minnesota.
This 3-wheeled commuter car carried two passengers in a stylish fibreglass coupé body. It had a steel chassis, independent suspension and a choice of petrol or diesel power. They were sold in kit and completed form.
HP

TROJAN (i) (US) 1903
Trojan Launch & Automobile Works, Troy, New York.
This company was run by William S. Howard who made a car under his own name, the HOWARD (ii), and also another which he called the Trojan. It was a runabout with 2-cylinder engine and sliding gearbox, and was made only for a few months before Howard moved to Yonkers, New York.
NG

TROJAN (ii) (GB) 1922–1936; 1962–1965
1922–1928 Leyland Motors Ltd, Kingston-on-Thames, Surrey.
1928–1965 Trojan Ltd, Croydon, Surrey.
The Trojan was a rare example of an unconventional and in many ways old-fashioned design which sold well and had a loyal following among British motorists for a number of years. It was a one-man design, that man being Leslie Hayward Hounsfield (1877–1957). He worked for several well-known British engineering firms including Ransomes, Sims & Jefferies, and the Crompton Electrical Co., and after service in the Boer War he set up a small engineering works in Clapham, south London, which he called the Polygon Engineering Works. In 1914 he changed the name to Trojan Ltd, but he had started work on his first car two or three years earlier.

His main concerns were with simplicity of driving and maintenance, and he drew up his specification with these objects in view. The engine was a 4-cylinder 2-stroke in which each pair of cylinders had a common combustion chamber. Company advertising made great play of the fact that the engine had only seven moving parts – four pistons, two vee-shaped con rods, and a crankshaft. Transmission was by a 2-speed epicyclic gearbox and final drive by duplex chain to the offside rear wheel. On the first two cars the engine was mounted vertically between the seats, but thereafter it was horizontal beneath the floorboards. To avoid the frequent problems of punctured tyres, Hounsfield used solid tyres, which had been abandoned by most car makers ten years before. However, two pairs of very long cantilever springs gave a reasonable ride at the low speed of the Trojan.

The short-bonneted prototype No. 1 (which still exists) was first driven in August 1913, and was followed by another on generally similar lines. War work followed, mostly the manufacture of gauges, specialised taps, dies, cutters and powder pellet moulds. It was not until 1920 that Hounsfield built another car. A series of six, known as the T cars because they carried T registrations, were made in 1920 at Croydon, and were very similar to the production cars which appeared at the 1922 Olympia Show. Hounsfield would never have been able to establish series production had it not been for the interest shown in the car by Leyland Motors, who wanted to try the car market at the other end of the scale from their luxurious Leyland Eight. They agreed to put the Trojan into production at the Kingston-on-Thames factory where they had been reconditioning their ex-RAF trucks. The first order was for 100 cars; over the next seven years Kingston was to build about 16,800 Trojans, of which nearly 11,000 were passenger cars and 6724 were vans. The latter included the large fleet of Brooke Bond tea vans which were a familiar sight up and down the country.

When first announced the Trojan Utility Car, as it was called, cost £230, but by June 1925 this had been reduced to £125, the same as the Model T Ford (which paid twice as much tax) and £24 less than an Austin Seven. Leyland adopted the

THE TROJAN ACHILLES FABRIC SALOON

(*Sole Concessionaires for the Sales and Service throughout Great Britain of Trojan Vehicles*)

PURLEY WAY, CROYDON

1913 True 10hp cyclecar.
JOHN A. CONDE

slogan 'Can You Afford to Walk' and published some ingenious calculations to prove that over 200 miles a Trojan cost less than one would spend on shoe leather and socks. For 1926 came an improved engine with roller bearing big ends, the XL, which had a capacity reduced from 1527 to 1488cc, to bring it within the 1½-litre class. A new body style introduced at the same time was the Three-Door Tourer, which seated five passengers, and could be had with a drop-down back for load carrying. Pneumatic tyres were optional from 1924, and most Three-Door Tourers were supplied with pneumatics. At this date Trojans were being made at the rate of 80 to 100 per week; with two parallel runways a car could be completed in 45 minutes. Iron castings came from Leyland's foundry at Farington, Lancashire, but the rest of the car, including the body, was made at Kingston.

In 1928 the arrangement with Leyland came to an end as they wanted the Kingston factory for a new smaller truck, which appeared three years later as the Cub. Trojan production was transferred to Croydon where the T-cars had been made, though not to the same premises. Leyland-made parts were used for some time, and it was not until January 1930 that an entirely Croydon-built Trojan car came off the lines. A new body style was a 4-door fabric saloon called the Achilles, or Apollo when it had a sun roof.

However, car sales were dropping, though the vans continued to sell well. At the 1929 Motor Show Trojan introduced the RE model in an attempt to bring the marque up to date. The bodies, a 2-door saloon and tourer built by D.M. Davies Ltd, were quite modern-looking, but the engine, now mounted vertically in the boot, was still the same old 1488cc 2-stroke, final drive was still by chain, and when it was announced it had neither front-wheel brakes nor an electric starter. At £198 for the saloon it was competing with cars like the Standard Nine and Singer Junior whose buyers could expect such amenities as a matter of course by 1930. Sales of the RE were disappointing, 250 between 1930 and 1934. This was less than the total for the old underfloor-engined model, which sold about 350 over a slightly longer period. In 1933 there was hybrid called the Wayfarer. This had the familiar engine under the floor, but worm drive rather than chain, an electric starter, 3-speed gearbox, and an RE radiator

grill. Only three were made. Though vans dominated output in the 1930s, the old-style car was available for anyone who wanted one; the last was built specially for a lady in Gloucestershire in 1937. The only other Trojan car of the 1930s was the Mastra, with rear-mounted 2232cc 6-cylinder 2-stroke engine. Saloon and drophead coupés by Ranelagh were announced, but only one of each was made.

Leslie Hounsfield resigned from Trojan in November 1930 and set up a small company to make a folding camp bed which had been produced in the Trojan factory, and also the Hounsfield Tensometer metal testing instrument. He was still operating his small factory in 1953, at the age of 76. Trojan made vans up to 1939, and also experimented with a light agricultural tractor, and made marine engines and hospital equipment. During the war they made bomb racks, incendiary bomb carriers and supply containers in which essential goods could be dropped to troops by parachute.

In the postwar period Trojan concentrated on a new van, powered originally by a 4-cylinder 2-stroke engine, then by Perkins diesel engines from 1952 onwards. In 1959 Trojan was bought by Peter Agg who had been the British distributor for the Lambretta motor scooter since 1950. From 1960 to 1965 the HEINKEL bubble car was made under licence at Croydon, and sold under the name Trojan 200, while from 1966 to 1968 the ELVA Courier sports car was assembled there. Unlike the Heinkel, this never carried the Trojan name. After the Elva, Trojan took on the contract to build Formula 5000 and Group 7 racing cars for McLaren, this continuing until 1973. Its last car building venture was an unsuccessful Formula 1 car driven by Tim Schenken in 1974.

NG

Further Reading
'Can You Afford to Walk?, the Saga of the Trojan Car', Nick Georgano, *Automobile Quarterly*, Vol. 18, No. 3.
Can You Afford to Walk? The History of the Hounsfield Trojan, Eric Rance and Don Williams, Bookmarque, 1999.

TROLL (i) (N) 1955–1957
Troll Plastik og Bilindustri, Lunde i Telemark.
The first Norwegian postwar car was formulated when Per Kohl Larsen obtained a licence to make the TRIPPEL in his native country. However, the necessary parts never arrived from Germany and so instead the chassis and mechanical parts were purchased from the defunct GUTBROD concern. The chassis was lengthened by 5in and, rather than the intended rear-mounted engine used in the Trippel, a Gutbrod 663cc 2-cylinder 2-stroke engine developing 30bhp was installed in the front, fore of the axle (the first prototype had a Saab 748cc engine, but it was too expensive to use in production). The chassis incorporated independent suspension, with coil sprung double A-arms at the front. The fibreglass 2+2 seater coupé body was derived from that seen in the Trippel. Only six cars were ever made.

CR

TROLL (ii) (GB) 1987 to date
Troll Engineering Co. Ltd, Minehead, Somerset.
The Troll is the spiritual heir to dual-purpose road/trials cars such as the Dellow. The prototype was built in 1980 by Peter James who then received requests for replicas. A delighted customer put the project on a businesslike footing in 1987 and, since then, it has been made in small numbers, but on a regular basis. The Troll Mk6B has a spaceframe, a simple cycle-winged aluminium and fibreglass body, coil spring and double wishbone front suspension and a securely located live rear axle. To take part in trials, ground clearance is 8in, yet handling on the open road is excellent. Power usually comes from a 115bhp 1700cc Ford engine which translates into 0–62mph (0-100km/h) in a little over 6 seconds.

The Troll Mk6B has been exceptionally successful in traditional trials, taking the British national championships on many occasions and, more often than not, filling most of the support places. It continues to fill a niche.

MJL

TRUE (US) 1913
Badger Brass Manufacturing Co., Kenosha, Wisconsin.
The True was a typical cyclecar powered by a 10hp V-twin Spacke engine, with belt drive and tandem seating for two. The driver sat in the rear seat. Priced at $400, it never entered serious production.

NG

TRUFFAULT (F) 1907–1908

Sté des Automobiles Truffault, Paris.
This was a belt-driven light car powered by a single-cylinder engine, probably a De Dion-Bouton. Examples ran in the Coupe des Voiturettes of 1907 and 1908, but were never high in the results lists.

NG

TRUMBULL (US) 1913–1915

1913–1914 American Cyclecar Co., Bridgeport, Connecticut.
1914–1915 Trumbull Motor Car Co., Bridgeport, Connecticut.
One of the best of the American cyclecars, the Trumbull had a 1704cc 14/18hp 4-cylinder engine, friction transmission and shaft drive. It was to have been made by the American Cyclecar Co. and sold as the American, but few, if any, were made before the Trumbull brothers bought the company and the design in January 1914, and made the car under their own name. It was available as a roadster at $425 and a coupé at $600. The 1915 models had conventional 3-speed gearboxes, which should have made them even more acceptable to the general car buying market, but the cyclecar had earned a bad name in America, and most Trumbulls were exported. Of about 2000 made, 1500 were sold in Europe or Australia. In May 1915 Isaac Trumbull was lost in the sinking of the Lusitania, together with 20 Trumbull cars en route to England. His death brought about the end of the company.

The Trumbull name was also used for some cars made by the Trumbull Manufacturing Co. of Warren, Ohio (see PENDLETON).

NG

TRUNER (GB) 1913

Turner & Co., Willesden, London.
The Truner cyclecar was powered by an 8hp V-twin JAP engine mounted parallel with the frame, and driving by chain to a 2-speed dog-clutch gearbox and thence by single chain to the offside rear wheel. It had an ash frame and 2-seater body, and was priced at 80 guineas (£84). The makers chose the name Truner rather than their own to avoid confusion with the better-known Turner car from Wolverhampton.

NG

TRYLON; TRYON (US) 1989 to date

1989–1996 Trylon Inc, Arlington, Illinois.
1997 to date Glass Masters, Mesa, Arizona.
Given its extraordinary styling, it was no surprise that the Trylon was the brainchild of a Star Trek fanatic. A giant 'clam-shell' canopy lifted for entry to the tandem 2-seater cockpit. Very narrow at the front and very wide at the rear, the Trylon was based on nothing more galactic than VW Beetle components, including the engine (or optional Mazda RX-7), gearbox, rear suspension and steering. A strong box section steel cage was encased in the lengthy fibreglass bodyshell, and the front suspension was based on motorbike components. Inside, the dashboard featured 'space-age' instruments and aircraft-style steering controls. In the first five years of production around 250 kits and complete cars were sold, in two versions: the standard Shuttle and the Viper, the latter including a body kit. The model was relaunched in 1997 as the Tryon.

CR

T.S.T. (GB) 1922

This was an unusual 3-wheeler steered from a sidecar, like the Seal, and powered by a single-cylinder Blackburne engine. Transmission was by a motorcycle gearbox and chain final drive.

NG

TSUKUBA (J) 1935–c.1937

Tokyo Jidosha Seizo Co. Ltd, Tokyo.
The Tsukuba superficially resembled contemporary Japanese light cars such as the Datsun or Ohta, but was less conventional in having a 750cc V4 engine and drive to the front wheels. It had a 3-speed gearbox and was made in three body styles, 2-seater roadster, 4-seater tourer and saloon. Only 50 cars were made.

NG

TUAR (F) 1913–1925

A. Morin, Thouars, Deux-Sèvres.

1915 Trumbull 10hp 2-seater.
NICK GEORGANO/NATIONAL MOTOR MUSEUM

1990 Trylon 3-wheeler coupé.
CHRIS REES

Adrien Morin was the son of a country solicitor who was intended to follow the law, but fell in love with the automobile whilst serving his articles in Angers. He promptly went to Paris, then the motor capital of the world, and worked first for Vinot et Deguingand and later for Decauville and Cornilleau-Ste-Beuve. He claimed to have been a director of the latter two firms. In 1906 he opened his own dealership, in partnership with a M. Mounal, in Boulogne-Billancourt. Vehicles were offered briefly in 1907 under Morin's own name, but it is not known how many were assembled or sold. He returned to his native area in 1912, setting up the 'Garage Moderne' near the centre of Thouars before commencing production there of a straightforward but robust light car, deemed suitable for local conditions. Two models were marketed – the 1726cc 1A and the 1244cc 2B. It was always Morin's policy to market a simple, orthodox and inexpensive chassis, using proprietary parts, but to clothe it with elegant and good quality bodywork.

During World War I the works was closed, but reactivated in 1917 to manufacture shells. Car construction recommenced in 1919 with the Chapuis-Dornier engined B1 model of 1244cc (60 × 100mm). The heavy postwar demand led to almost instant success and despite the intended local bias of sales, some exports were achieved, even to the USA. In 1921 he moved to larger premises, still within the town. The best year was 1922, when there were over 50 employees, turning out a finished car every day. Publicity was gained by sporting successes. Morin himself usually drove and, when interviewed in 1956, he produced photos of the lightened Ruby-engined car which he habitually ran in sand races at La Baule. A more robust car was courageously entered for the 1921 Coupe des Voiturettes at Le Mans, but retired with the failure of a bearing in the rear axle. The unusual rear suspension of this model, with leaf spring secured within the frame channel, was illustrated in the contemporary *Light Car and Cyclecar*.

The basic specification embraced Malicet et Blin chassis parts, a 4-cylinder side-valve engine, DF fixed wheels and an attractive but 'no frills' body. A B1 with 3-seater bodywork could cost as little as FFr7650, but one would have to pay extra for Michelin detachable wheels, any form of lighting, self-starter, Gleason

1948 Tucker sedan.
NATIONAL MOTOR MUSEUM

1948 Tucker sedan.
NATIONAL MOTOR MUSEUM

axle or (later) 4-wheel brakes. Every conceivable type of bodywork was offered, from light commercials to luxurious 'conduite intérieures', priced in excess of FFr20,000. The last model made, the D1 of 1925, had a 1601cc ohc CIME engine, and the list of models compiled by Griff Borgeson noted no less than 10 different engines. Even this list excluded the special racing Ruby motor, the 6-cylinder CIME version that Morin recalled in 1956, and the 68 × 100mm type of 1924 that was the only model recorded in the British 'Stone and Cox' listings.

The firm did not fail. Morin heeded the warning shots fired by the 'big battalions' – the major manufacturers achieving price cuts through mass production – and closed down his operations, selling out the mechanical facilities and the coachbuilding side separately to ex-employees. Some 800 vehicles in total had been sold. Morin remained in Thouars and was still proudly offering his services there in 1956 as motor expert, consultant and insurance assessor. He died in 1968.

DF

Further Reading
'Les Automobiles Tuar', Griffith Borgeson, *l'Album du Fanatique*.

TUCK (US) 1904–1905

Tuck Petroleum Motor Co., Brooklyn, New York.
The Tuck was an extraordinary car, and from the press description it is difficult to see how the engine worked at all. It ran on paraffin, which was not vaporised before being admitted to the cylinder, in which no explosion took place. The maker claimed that high torque was developed at low speed, so there was no need for gears. There was no reverse gear, as the driver could reverse the direction of the engine, although to do this he had to stop the engine and pull a lever which 'shifted the cams in such a manner that the direction of rotation is changed'. Final drive was by side-chains to the rear axle. An easily impressed reporter said that the Tuck was 'full of very novel ideas, of which much is expected', but it is not surprising that nothing more was heard of it.

NG

TUCKER (i) (US) 1900–1908

John O. Tucker, Santa Clara, California.
John Tucker ran a photographic studio, and built cars sporadically there. Several were made around 1900, though details of their design are not known. His 1908 car, probably his last, had a 16hp flat-twin engine and a 4-seater roadster body. Some of these cars were referred to as Tuckermobiles.

NG

TUCKER (ii) (US) 1946–1948

The Tucker Corp., Chicago, Illinois.
The most exciting and innovative car of the early postwar American scene was the work of Preston Thomas Tucker (1903–1956), a salesman whose background included being office boy for Cadillac boss D. McCall White, and a spell in the Detroit Police Force. In the 1930s he was a partner with racing car designer Harry A. Miller in Tucker-Miller Inc. He designed a revolutionary armoured car with a claimed top speed of 115mph (185km/h), and was running the Ypsilanti Tool & Machine Co. in Michigan when he conceived his plans for a totally new car to meet the pent-up demand for new cars caused by the cessation of production during World War II.

Work began on the Tucker Torpedo in late 1945. Much of the inspiration came from Miller, though he had died in 1943. It differed from conventional practice in almost every way. The engine, rear mounted, was an enormous all-aluminium horizontally-opposed six of 9652cc designed by Ben Parsons, with fuel injection and hydraulically-operated valves. Output was only 150bhp, but at the low speed of 1800rpm it was estimated that it would run for over 185,000 miles (300,000km) before any overhaul was needed. Initially, there was no gearbox, transmission being by a pair of torque converters connected to the rear wheels directly from the engine. The body was a streamlined coupé designed by Alex Tremulis who had worked for Auburn-Cord-Duesenberg, with central driving position and three headlamps, the outer two mounted in fenders which turned with the steering. Other features of the design included all-independent suspension, disc brakes all round, and a 24volt electrical system. Safety features were front and rear seat belts, a padded dashboard and pop-out windscreen.

This original design, unkindly nicknamed the Tin Goose, proved unsatisfactory and quite impractical to manufacture. The A589 (for 589 cubic inches) engine worked poorly, and only three or four were made.

The car would not run in reverse, giving rise to the rumour that the later Tuckers were also incapable of reversing, which was quite untrue. Preston Tucker set about radically redesigning his car, although he retained some features such as the rear engine location, independent suspension, padded dashboard and pop-out windscreen. The seat belts were dropped, as his vice president Fred Rockelman felt that they would imply that the Tucker was unsafe. The A589 was replaced by a much smaller flat six engine, a 5475cc Franklin 6ALV335 made by Air Cooled Motors of Syracuse, New York, whose predecessor had made the Franklin car. Tucker later bought Air Cooled Motors, which enabled him to reduce the unit cost of his engines considerably. The engine was designed for aircraft use, and was greatly modified by Tucker and his staff, including conversion to water-cooling. Output was 166bhp, which gave the Tucker a remarkable top speed of 121mph (195km/h). One car averaged 131.56mph (211.85km/h) in three runs on the Bonneville Salt Flats in 1950.

The torque converter was replaced by an automatic transmission called the R-1, though most Tuckers used a simpler pre-selector transmission called the Y-1. This used components from the Cord 810, and Tucker scoured the country to buy up Cords for their transmissions. Other items of the original design that were sacrificed for practicality and cost accounting were the disc brakes, central steering wheel and the swivelling mudguards/headlamps. However, the 3-lamp layout was retained, the central one turning with the steering. Tremulis redesigned the body to make it a 6-seater sedan. It was a large car, at 219in (5563mm), nearly as long as a Cadillac 75.

Tucker had ambitious plans for the manufacture of his car, and leased the largest single-building factory in the world, the Chicago plant used by Dodge to build aircraft engines. He had no great personal wealth, and raised finance by selling franchises to nearly 1000 dealers, and by a $20 million stock offer, which was never fully taken up. He also sold accessories to those who had paid deposits on their cars. His money-raising activities attracted the attention of the Securities and Exchange Commission, a Government organisation which monitored stock exchange offers. They accused him of fraud in that the car he was selling differed materially from the one he originally advertised. It is widely believed that the legal problems Tucker encountered were fostered by supporters of the Detroit car makers, who feared that he would make serious inroads into their markets. However, the late 1940s were a powerful sellers' market, and the Big Three bosses were hardly likely to worry about a way-out design from an unknown manufacturer.

Tucker was undoubtedly naive, though, both in his ambitions and in carelessness in some financial matters. He was eventually cleared of all criminal charges, but the factory was closed down while the hearings were taking place, and Tucker was not allowed to raise finance from any other source. Another government agency, the Reconstruction Finance Corp. was advised by the SEC to refuse him a loan. By the time he was cleared in 1950, the Tucker Corp. had gone into voluntary liquidation. Production was just 51 cars, of which 49 survive.

A few years later Tucker planned to make a small sporty car in Brazil, using a body designed by Alex de Sakhnoffsky and a rear-mounted engine. While he was attempting to raise finance for his new project he died of lung cancer.

NG

Further Reading
'Tucker – Design and Destiny', Philip S. Egan,
Automobile Quarterly, Vol. 26, No. 3.
'Tucker – The Man, the Myth, the Movie', Lisa E. Cowan,
Automobile Quarterly, Vol. 26, No. 3.

1981 Tulia Tulieta coupé.
NICK BALDWIN

TUDHOPE (CDN) 1908–1913
1908–1909 Tudhope-McIntyre Co., Orillia, Ontario.
1910–1913 Tudhope Motor Co. Ltd, Orillia, Ontario.
William Tudhope made hardware, harness and wagon parts, and from 1876 wheels for wagons and carriages, soon followed by complete carriages. By the turn of the century William Tudhope & Son was the biggest carriage and wagon builder in Ontario. In 1908 they entered car production with the Tudhope-McIntyre high-wheeler. This used parts from the MCINTYRE Co. of Auburn, Indiana, assembled at Orillia and fitted with locally-built bodies. The specification included a 13hp flat-twin engine, epicyclic transmission and double-chain drive. Priced at $550, the Tudhope-McIntyre sold well until the factory was destroyed by fire in August 1909. The Tudhopes built a new factory but decided against continuing the high-wheeler. Instead they acquired the licence to make the EVERITT 30, a conventional 3910cc 30hp 4-cylinder car made in tourer and roadster forms. They were called Everitts for the 1911 season, then for 1912 the Tudhope name was revived for a an updated and improved car with stronger differential, a speedometer, Bosch ignition, a running board tool box and nickel trim. Alongside this was an all-new 6-cylinder car, Canada's first regular production six. The 6-48 had a 5866cc engine and a 127in (3223mm) wheelbase, and was offered in 2-, 5- and 6-seater versions. For 1913 it had electric lighting and starting. However, it was too expensive, and the 4-cylinder car too old-fashioned. Sales were only moderate, and in the summer of 1913 the Tudhope Motor Co. Ltd was bankrupt. Their assets were acquired by the Fisher Motor Car Co. which sold cars of Tudhope design under the FISHER name for two years. Tudhope's carriage businesses survived, and later prospered for a while making car and truck bodies.

NG

TULIA (RA) 1969–1980s
Tulia Crespi srl, Buenos Aires.
The Tulia was a fastback coupé using 6-cylinder IKA-Renault, Chevrolet, Dodge, or Ford engines. The Tulieta coupé and cabriolet were offered from 1975, with 4-cylinder Renault engines.

NG

TULSA (US) 1918–1922
Tulsa Automobile Co., Tulsa, Oklahoma.
The Tulsa was a typical assembled car which targeted its advertising on its success in Oklahoma's oil fields, even offering an Oil Field Runabout. The original Tulsa line featured a 4-cylinder Lycoming engine, this being supplanted in 1920 by a Herschell-Spillman 7000, also a four. Fours would continue to power all Tulsa cars with the exception of a six in 1922, fitted with a Herschell-Spillman 10001 motor. Wheelbases on all Tulsa cars were 117½in (2982mm) excepting the six which was 119in (3020mm). Prices ranged from $985 for the earlier cars, subsequently reaching $1385 for the fours and $1595 for the six. Tulsa production averaged about 250 cars annually and body styles were limited to the Oil Field Runabout, roadster, and 5-seater touring car. Production ceased in 1922, the final cars being marketed as 1923 models later that year.

KM

c.1910 Turcat-Méry tourer.
NATIONAL MOTOR MUSEUM

1913 Turcat-Méry 25hp tourer by Guffault.
NATIONAL MOTOR MUSEUM

1925 Turcat-Méry Type UG tourer.
LUCIEN LOREILLE

T.U.M. (F) 1979

T.U.M., Nantes.

The T.U.M. (Transport Urbain Minimal) city car was the brainwave of M. Agaise. With assistance from l'École Nationale Supérieure de Mécanique de Nantes, Agaise built a prototype with a view to raising finance to produce the car. Sadly sufficient funding was never found to build the advanced one-box, front-wheel drive, Citroën 2CV-powered car.

CR

TUNISON (US) 1921

Tunison Motors Co., Oakland, California.

M.C. Tunison designed a sporty-looking roadster with laminated spruce frame and a V8 engine, of which he hoped to build 250 per month, later increasing this to 1000. Probably no more than a prototype was made. Murray Tunison returned to the car field in 1923 with the PARAMOUNT (i), but only three of these were made.

NG

TURBO (i) (CH) 1921–1922

1921–1922 Automobilfabrik G.W. Müller, Zürich.

The Turbo was quite an unconventional light car with a 5-cylinder radial engine of over-square dimensions 70 × 75mm, 1442cc and 27bhp. It had ohvs operated by pushrods and rockers. Vertically mounted in the front of the tubular chassis, the engine was air-cooled by a big four-blade fan and copper fins were fitted to the cylinders, their heads were of bronze. Power was transmitted via multi-plate clutch, 3-speed gearbox and shaft to the rear axle. On request a Soden 4-speed gearbox with small speed selector on the dashboard, could be fitted. Front and rear axle were suspended on coil springs. Brakes were on the rear-wheel drums only and steel disc wheels were used. Weight of the complete torpedo was less than 600kg and top speed about 60mph (97km/h). The Turbo was available with open or closed 2- and 4-seater bodies. The Torpedo fully equipped cost SFr7500. In January 1923 the Turbo was no longer listed. Müller transfered the operation to Germany were the Turbo was made in 1923–24 by TURBO (ii) Motoren AG, Stuttgart.

FH

TURBO (ii) (D) 1923–1924

Turbo Motoren AG, Stuttgart.

The German-made Turbo cars followed closely the design of the Swiss cars of the same name, being engineered by G.W. Müller who moved to Germany when production ended in his own country. Two models of the air-cooled rotary engine were made, the 1540cc 6/25PS and the 1980cc 8/32PS. Neither was a success.

HON

TURCAT-MÉRY (F) 1899–1928

1899–1921 Sté des Ateliers de Construction d'Automobiles Turcat, Méry et Cie, Marseilles.
1921–1928 Automobiles Turcat-Méry SA, Marseilles.

Léon Turcat and Simon Méry were brothers-in-law, (some sources say they were cousins) both born in 1874, who experimented with Panhard and Peugeot cars before building a prototype of their own in 1896. It had a front-mounted horizontal 4-cylinder engine with coil ignition, chain drive and pneumatic tyres. One or two others may have been made in the next two years, using components supplied by local engineering firms. The first they offered for sale was made in 1899, though news of it did not reach *The Autocar* until September 1900. It had a 2.6-litre vertical 4-cylinder engine, Bosch magneto ignition and chain drive. It was clearly based on established cars such as Panhard, but unusual features were the use of two radiators, ahead of and behind the engine, and a 5-speed gearbox, with two reverse speeds. Few were sold, and by 1901 a more modest car with 2-cylinder engine was on offer. However the partners were very short of working capital, and might well have gone under had they not met Baron Adrien de Turckheim of DE DIETRICH. They drew up an agreement whereby they would design cars for De Dietrich at Lunéville, receiving 5 per cent of the retail price of each car. At the same time cars of similar design were made at their Marseilles factory under the direction of Simon's brother Louis Méry and chairman Henri Estier, a financier who was also on the board of De Dietrich. Although not always identical, the cars made at Lunéville and Marseilles were very close in design.

An unusual car was the 6-wheeler with inter-connected suspension and chain drive to the centre axle, which was made in both factories. Their first six was an L-head design of 10.2-litres which appeared in 1907. Léon Turcat helped to design De Dietrich's new factory at the Paris suburb of Argenteuil, opened in 1907 (by then the cars were known as Lorraine-Dietrich) and retained their links with the firm until 1913 when he and Méry returned to Marseilles on a permanent basis. Their cars had 4-cylinder monobloc engines with magneto ignition, 4-speed gearboxes and shaft drive. Capacities were of 2.6, 3.3, 4.1, 4.7 and 6.3 litres. The larger models had pressure lubrication and elegant vee-radiators. On the 35hp a bell gave warning of low oil pressure.

Turcat-Mérys were active in sport; one finished 9th in the 1903 Paris–Madrid Race, and Rougier finished 3rd in the 1904 Gordon Bennett Race, in which identical De Dietrichs took part. In 1911 Rougier won the first Monte Carlo Rally in a 25hp saloon. They also competed after the war, fielding a team of three in the 1921 Circuit de Corse; Rougier was 2nd, and other examples of the make finished 3rd, 4th, 5th, and 6th.

Like so many French regional makes, Turcat-Méry declined in the 1920s. The firm collapsed in 1921, and the partners resigned. It was reorganised as a limited company and reorganised again in 1924. At first a prewar design of 2977cc side-valve four was made, but a more modern 2848cc single-ohc four came in 1923. This had a detachable cylinder head, dual coil ignition and uncoupled 4-wheel brakes. It gave way to a 2388cc four, also with single-ohc, but this had a fixed head and proper coupled brakes which were used on all subsequent Turcat-Mérys. It was known as the 16/60 in England. In 1926 there was yet another reorganisation, when the company was taken over by Louis Mouren, a former employee who raised the necessary funds with the help of the Berliet representative in Nice. Under the new regime proprietary engines were used for the first time; these included a 1200cc C.I.M.E. and a 1614cc S.C.A.P. both 4-cylinder pushrod units. For 1927 a 1215cc side-valve six by C.I.M.E. and a 2340cc ohv straight-8 by S.C.A.P. were offered, but few of these later cars were made. Turcat-Méry collapsed again in 1928 and was taken over by J. Monnerot-Dumaine. Cars were listed up to 1933 but were probably left over stock or built up from spares. The factory was subsequently used by a refrigeration firm. Léon Turcat became an insurance agent; his grandson André was chief test pilot for Sud Aviation and was the first man to take a Concorde into the sky in 1976. In 1991 the Municipality of Marseilles named a newly-created thoroughfare the 'Allée Turcat-Méry'.

NG

Further Reading
'Turcat Méry', W.S. Jaro, *Antique Automobile*, September 1957.
'Masterpieces from Marseilles', Finbar Corry,
The Automobile, April–May 1991.

TURGAN-FOY (F) 1899–1906

Turgan, Foy et Cie, Levallois-Perret, Seine.

Turgan-Foy began by making cars powered by the unusual Filtz engine, which was an air-cooled flat-twin, with each cylinder connected to a vertical crankshaft, the latter being geared at their upper ends to a third vertical shaft, running at half engine speed, and having at its lower end a large horizontal flywheel consisting of a heavy steel rim and wire spokes, which acted as a fan to cool the engine. Transmission was by belt to a 4-speed gear system, with final drive by single or double chains. The first engines developed 4½hp, later increased to 6 or 8hp.

After 1902 the Filtz engine was dropped, to be replaced by conventional 4-cylinder engines of 16 or 24hp, driving through a propeller shaft. By 1905 24 or 60hp chain-drive models were offered, but probably very few were made as the company was concentrating on commercial vehicles, both steam and petrol. Even in 1903 *Le Grand Album Illustré de l'Industrie Automobile* gave a detailed description of steam wagons, and made no mention of passenger cars at all.

NG

TURICUM (i) (CH) 1904–1914

1904–1906 Martin Fischer, Zürich.
1907–1914 Automobilfabrik Turicum AG, Uster, Zürich.

Martin Fischer (born 1866) was a trained watchmaker who in 1904 built the prototype of a miniature single-seater car with an air-cooled motorcycle engine. Final drive was by a long chain and steering by two pedals. It looked like the forerunner of a go-kart. He was assisted by Paul Vorbrodt and the popular light car manufacturing venture was financed by the German Dr Hommel, living in Zürich. The second model, also a low built single-seater with pedal steering but

1925 Turcat-Méry 16/60 Pullman saloon.
NATIONAL MOTOR MUSEUM

1899 Turgan-Foy 4 1/2hp voiturette.
NATIONAL MOTOR MUSEUM

with a rudimentary body, was the first to have the innovative friction-drive which was to remain a hallmark for Turicum. Both created curiosity but not much serious interest.

Fischer then designed the first real light car and called it 'Turicum', the Latin name of Zürich, and launched it at the Paris Show in 1905. The voiturette type A and later A1 had a 7hp air-cooled single-cylinder engine of square dimensions, 100 × 100mm, with 785cc capacity and an automatic inlet valve. The mock-radiator, which gave the car the appearance of a normal water-cooled model, served as a petrol tank. The friction-drive worked as follows: the crankshaft was linked to a large diameter cast-steel disc; another slightly smaller disc was fixed on a shaft under the seats and was set at a 90 degree angle; it was leather shod and could be moved from the centre of the driving disc towards the periphery, thus enabling an unlimited number of 'speeds'. Final drive of the rear wheels was by single chain.

Chassis and steering were conventional, suspension was by a new type of full-elliptic springs and the steel wheels with nine spokes had pneumatic tyres. This model was offered with 2-seater phaeton body only. It immediatedly met with success in the home country as well as in important export markets. Serial production was started in the new factory, and in 1907 a total of 127 chassis were completed. One year later the new 10/12hp model B1 with 4-cylinder monobloc L-head engine of 1385cc supplemented the programme. The single-cylinder engine was enlarged to 1045cc. Both were offered with open and closed 2- and 4-seater bodies. Prices ranged from SFr4500 to SFr6500.

A branch company was founded in Paris and agencies were set up in most European countries as well as in Transvaal and Argentina. In 1909 Martin Fischer left the company to form his own.

A few of the light cars obtained 4/8hp twin-cylinder engines of 971cc. The new 8/16hp model D received 4-cylinder engines of 1470cc, 1725cc or 1940cc. In 1912 three Turicums were ordered by the King of Egypt and about 50 were exported to Italy. A new 16/26hp model of 2613cc was announced. This could also be delivered, on request, with conventional gearbox and shaft drive, which perhaps mirrors the limitations of friction drive. Production in 1911 reached 200 chassis and was said to have steadily increased until the outbreak of World War I. However, the company ran into financial problems and had to close its doors in 1914.

FH

1904 Turicum (i) light car with foot steering; Martin Fischer seated in car.
ERNEST SCHMID

1909 Turicum (i) 16CV tourer.
NICK GEORGANO

TURICUM (ii) (A) 1912
Slatinanske tovarny automobilu, R.A. Smekal, Slatinany.
Before World War I the Smekal works, famous for their fire engine production, built limited numbers of light cars under licence, although contemporary advertisements described purely Czech, products. These cars were assembled from the parts bought from the Swiss Turicum Works in Uster, Zürich. The most remarkable item on these vehicles was a friction gearing. It seems the original type D with 4-cylinder 8–18hp was a pattern for Czech manufacture.

MSH

TURNBULL (NZ) 1989 to date
Turnbull Engineering, Bunnythorpe, North Island.
Although the Saker SV 1 was a sports-racing type coupé, Bruce Turnbull ensured that it had all the necessary interior conveniences to allow it to be used as a road car. The mid-mounted engines ranged from 4-cylinder types to 5-litre Ford or Chevrolet V8 units; the lightweight 3.9-litre Rover V8 being a favoured installation. In 1995 the Rouzy and Sambar 4-wheel drive models, with Subaru mechanicals fitted into galvanised chassis, were introduced. The bodywork was fibreglass and the range included a safari wagon.

MG

TURNER (i) (US) 1901–1903
Turner Automobile Co., Philadelphia, Pennsylvania.
George T. Turner made a number of very light cars in 3- and 4-wheeled form. The former was called the Liliputian and had a 1¼hp engine mounted under the seat. It had a tubular frame, virtually no bodywork and tiller steering. The wheelbase was only 51in (1294mm). The 4-wheeler was called the Gadabout and was of similar construction, but had a 3hp engine and 90in (2284mm) wheelbase.

NG

TURNER (ii) (GB) 1902–1930
Turner's Motor Manufacturing Co. Ltd, Wolverhampton, Staffordshire.
William Turner & Co. was an engineering firm which dated back to 1800. In 1902 they acquired a licence to make the Belgian Miesse steam car which they sold under the name Turner-Miesse. This had a flash-type boiler mounted under the bonnet, and a 3-cylinder engine under floor. The condenser was mounted at the front, at first slung between the dumb-irons as on a De Dion-Bouton petrol car, and later ahead of the bonnet, again as in contemporary petrol cars. The first model of 1902 was a 10hp, but later larger engines were

provided, including a 16hp which powered quite substantial cars, with 5-seater tourer or heavy landaulet bodies. The frames were of armoured wood and final drive was by side chains. In 1910 there was a cheaper shaft-drive 2-seater at £295, and the last Turner-Miesses were made in 1913, in 10, 15, and 20hp models, all shaft-driven. They outlasted the Belgian-built Miesse steamer by seven years.

In 1906 Turner had a brief fling with a 20/25hp 4-cylinder petrol car which they built for the London dealers, Seymours Ltd who sold it under the name Seymour-Turner. It was offered for only two seasons, but in 1911 Turner took up another petrol car, a light car with 1144cc V-twin engine, 2-speed constant-mesh gearbox, shaft drive and tubular frame. It was followed by the 1130cc 4-cylinder Ten of 1912, and some larger fours, the 1644cc Twelve, 2176cc 12/20 and 2120cc Fifteen. The Ten was made for sale by John Birch Ltd under the name J.B. with a higher ground clearance for colonial use, and both the Ten and the 12/20 were also sold under the Universal name. There was also a sporting version of the Ten with 4-speed gearbox, a vee-radiator and the unusual combination of wire wheels and detachable rims.

After World War I Turner made chassis for VARLEY-WOODS and ROGER. In 1920 they revived their prewar Ten, 12/20 and Fifteen models, and in 1923 listed a 1496cc 12/20 and a 2303cc 14/30. The former was probably a Dorman unit, as Turner ordered 40 of these between 1922 and 1924. A single Meadows engine was bought in 1922, and the other units are presumed to be of Turner's own manufacture. Production was very small in the 1920s and although the make was listed to 1930, output had probably ceased before then. Turner continued as an engineering firm, and in 1954 returned to road vehicles with a front-wheel drive minibus powered by their own 1.4-litre 2-cylinder 2-stroke supercharged diesel engine. They also made the Austrian-designed List diesel engine under licence; a V4 version of this powered Turner's Yeoman agricultural tractor made in the 1950s. Later they specialised in gearboxes and made transmissions of American Spicer and German ZF design.

NG

TURNER (iii) (GB) 1951–1966

Turner Sports Cars Ltd, Wolverhampton, Staffordshire.

Jack Turner built a special and was asked to make others. His first model was the Sports of 1951 which was built on similar lines to contemporary Tojeiro and Coopers; with a (lozenge-shaped) twin tube ladder frame, all-round independent suspension by transverse leaf springs and lower wishbones, and Turner alloy wheels, which were also used by Tojeiro. Seven chassis were supplied for road use – customers arranged their own bodies and engines – while an eighth formed the basis of an unsuccessful Formula 2 car.

Turner tuned engines and made a 4-cylinder, water-cooled double-ohc 500cc engine. Kieft planned to use this unit in a production sports car, but it fell short of its expected performance.

In 1955 Turner unveiled his A30 Sports, a 2-seater with an enveloping fibreglass body, a light tubular frame, Austin A30 front suspension, hydro-mech brakes, engine and gearbox; and a live rear axle suspended by trailing arms and torsion bars. With 81mph (130km/h) and 45mpg, it was the Austin-Healey Sprite before the Sprite.

BMC thought so and refused to supply Turner directly, so he had to buy components from Austin dealers which increased the price and restricted sales. In 1957, it was replaced by the 950 Sports which had fully hydraulic brakes and a 948cc Austin A35 engine. A few were fitted with the 75bhp 1100cc Coventry Climax FWA engine and these had wire wheels and front disc brakes. Almost all were exported, mainly to the United States and South Africa.

By 1959 Turner had made 260 of these cars when he introduced a new body on the established chassis. Front disc brakes were an option on all models and the 90bhp 1220cc Coventry Climax FWE engine was also available. Very successful in production sports car racing, it put Turner on the map.

The established chassis was used until the end of the Turner line although, from 1960, the A30 front suspension was replaced by Triumph Herald coil spring and double wishbone units. The main change until production ceased in 1966 was the replacement of BMC units with Ford engines, but Climax FWA and FWE units were optional. In all 660 examples of the line were made.

The Turner GT of 1961 was intended to be a fall-back, should sales of the Sports falter. It had a fibreglass monocoque centre section with a steel floorpan bonded in, and square-tube sections front and rear. Triumph Herald front suspension and the usual Turner rear end completed the outline while engines were either Ford or Climax. Just nine were made.

1904 Turner-Miesse steam tonneau.
NATIONAL MOTOR MUSEUM

1913 Turner (ii) 10hp coupé.
NICK BALDWIN

1956 Turner (iii) A30 sports car.
NATIONAL MOTOR MUSEUM

1960 Turner (iii) Mk II sports car.
NICK GEORGANO

1958 T.V.R. Grantura I coupé.
NICK BALDWIN

1973 T.V.R. 3000M coupé.
NICK BALDWIN

1986 T.V.R. 280i sports car.
T.V.R.

1990 T.V.R. S.2 sports car.
T.V.R.

Many BMC-engined Turners were tuned by Alexander Engineering who, in 1961 commissioned a one-off coupé body on a Turner Sports chassis which was very successful in British racing. In 1966, Jack Turner suffered a heart attack and, since he had no management structure, the business went into receivership. In the later 1980s, a company called M.C. made a Turner lookalike kit car. Called the Acer, the project was taken over by Carlton Automotive in 1989.

MJL

TURNER-MIESSE *see* TURNER (ii)

TURRELL *see* ACCLES-TURRELL

T.V.D. (B) 1920–1925
Éts Thiriar et Van den Daele, Brussels.
Announced in 1920 the T.V.D. was a light car with a 1095cc 4-cylinder Dambiermont engine, 4-speed gearbox and shaft drive. Wire or disc wheels were available, and the radiator was of Rolls-Royce shape. From 1922 it was powered by a 1496cc engine of French origin, possibly a Fivet. Larger engines were offered in 1924, a 10/12 and a 15/16CV, but output of all models was small.

NG

T.V.R. (GB) 1954 to date
1954–1957 Layton Engineering, Blackpool, Lancashire.
1957–1962 Layton Sports Cars Ltd, Blackpool, Lancashire.
1962–1963 Grantura Engineering Ltd, Blackpool, Lancashire.
1965–1965 T.V.R. Cars Ltd, Blackpool, Lancashire.
1965 to date T.V.R. Engineering Ltd, Blackpool, Lancashire.
In 1947 Trevor Wilkinson founded a small garage business called Trevcar Motors in his home town of Blackpool. He built a series of specials, selling each to finance the next and by 1954 T.V.R. (from TreVoR) Engineering was ready to market a kit car using proprietary fibreglass bodies. A new tubular backbone chassis was designed in 1955 and, the following year, three competition sports cars went to America where they were called Jomars, after the children of the American importer, JOhn and MARgaret Seidel.

During 1957, the first GT coupés were made with a notch-back body and a tubular backbone frame with VW torsion bar and trailing arm independent suspension at both ends. Engine options were wide, a few lightweight cars were built for racing, and most T.V.R.s sold in Britain were kits.

The first series production car, the 1958 Grantura had a conventional fastback and set T.V.R.'s style for years. Although the car was well-received, the company was not well-run and went into liquidation in 1962.

Under new management, after Trevor Wilkinson left, production was slow to get into its stride, but the Grantura Mk III had a new multi-tubular backbone chassis with independent suspension all round by coil springs and wishbones. As before, the most popular engine choice was MG.

An American, Jack Griffith, imported T.V.R. body/chassis units into which he installed the 4727cc Ford V8, and 4-speed Ford manual gearbox – and badged them as Griffiths. Power ranged between 191 and 271bhp and up to 140mph (225km/h) was possible – for the very brave only because the heavier engine upset the car's balance and made it difficult to handle.

Although the Grantura continued to be T.V.R.'s mainstay, the company attempted a number of prototypes, most notably the Trident, which was produced separately. T.V.R. was going through a rough time economically, and did not gain financial stability until the Lilley family acquired control in 1965. Quality improved and T.V.R. strengthened its hold on the market with the Vixen, a revised version of the Grantura which specified a 1.6-litre Ford engine. In 1967, T.V.R. made the Tuscan, with the same engine options as the Griffith, but the dubious reputation of the Griffith meant few V8 Tuscans were sold, although a version with a 3-litre Ford engine enjoyed better fortune.

With VAT looming, T.V.R. began to drop kit cars and its most popular models had 2.5-litre Triumph straight-6 engines or the 3-litre Ford V6.

The M-series of 1972 was the first wholly new car made under the new management, it had a stiffer chassis and a revised body style. The company survived both VAT and the OPEC oil crisis because it moved up-market, yet still offered reasonably priced cars with excellent fuel economy. In 1975 T.V.R. became one of the first makers to offer turbocharging, but poor fuel economy meant there were few buyers.

1999 T.V.R. Cerbera 4.5 V8 coupé.
T.V.R.

T.V.R. had to withdraw from the American market in 1977 when Triumph stopped making the 2.5-litre engine and the Ford unit did not meet emission laws.

With the Tasmin of 1980, T.V.R. finally broke away from the Grantura with a wedge shape with pop-up headlights. It was built on the existing chassis with the wheelbase extended by 4in and the irs was by fixed length drive shafts and lower wishbones. Originally launched as a 2-seater coupé, within a year it was joined by a 2+2 coupé and a convertible, all on the same chassis. At first Ford's 160bhp fuel injected 2.8-litre V6 was fitted and since that met US regulations, exports began again in 1983.

T.V.R. was taken over by Peter Wheeler in 1982. He wanted the cars to have more power and found it with the Rover V8. In 1984 the name Tasmin was dropped and cars were designated by engine size. Over the next few years the T.V.R.-developed Rover engine was offered in sizes up to 4.5-litres and Ford units were dropped in 1987. With the 4.5-litre engine, 155mph (249km/h) possible, with 0–62mph (0–100km/h) in 4.8 seconds.

A new model, the S, launched in 1986, was a 2-seat sports car whose style caught the essence of the old T.V.R. The chassis was similar to the larger cars, but used semi-trailing arm irs. It was fitted with the 2.8-litre Ford V6 engine and Ford 5-speed gearbox and helped double T.V.R.'s production. By the time it ended production in 1993, a Rover V8 was an option.

The Tuscan Sports of 1988 was made only as a competition model without type approval. This did not prevent some buyers from exploiting loopholes in the laws of their country and some were registered for road use. Power came from a 400bhp 4.4-litre Rover V8 which gave a top speed of 165mph (265km/h) (0–62mph (0–100km/h) in 3.8 seconds).

A new model, the Griffith went into production in 1992 with a new chassis, based on the competition Tuscan and a curvaceous body and new interior. It was cheaper than the wedge-shaped cars which were dropped, and was the model which took T.V.R. to new levels of success. Initially offered with 4-litre and 4.2-litre engines in 1993 it received a 340bhp 5-litre unit and was renamed the Griffith 500.

By then it had been joined by the Chimaera, which had a new body, which was intended to be the entry model while the Griffith was destined to receive T.V.R.'s own AJP V8 engine. That took longer than expected to develop, and the

1999 T.V.R. Speed 12 V12 coupé.
T.V.R.

Chimaera became the model with the wider appeal, being more softly sprung with a large boot. Most buyers chose the 4-litre. The AJP engine finally appeared in the 1996 Cerbera, a 2+2 coupé based on a lengthened Chimaera chassis. The light and powerful engine (420bhp in 4.5-litre form) gave the Cerbera a top speed close to 186mph (299km/h) and 0–100mph (0–161km/h) acceleration in under 9 seconds. The V8 engine is one of a family of three – a V12 first shown in 1997 and a 3996cc 'four valve' straight-6 which went into production in the Tuscan Speed-Six in 1999.

T.V.R. began with a simple special made from scrap parts and is now the largest British-owned car manufacturer, its products out-perform much more expensive rivals and, remarkably for so small a concern, it now makes three distinct engines. In its 2000 version the 7.7-litre V12 gave 880bhp, and promised to challenge the McLaren F1 as Britain's fastest accelerating car.

MJL

1999 Twike 3-wheeler.
TWIKE

1914 Twombly 10hp cyclecar.
NATIONAL MOTOR MUSEUM

Further Reading
TVR Gold Portfolio 1959–1986, Booklands Books, 1986.
TVR Performance Portfolio 1986–1994, Booklands Books, 1994.
TVR, a Collector's Guide (2 volumes), Graham Robson,
Motor Racing Publications, 1993.
TVR, the Complete Story, John Tipler, Crowood AutoClassics, 1994.
'The kit car that grew up – a history of TVR', David Owen,
Automobile Quarterly, Vol. 15, No. 2.

TWEENIE *see* SUPER

TWENTIETH CENTURY *see* OWEN (i)

TWIKE (CH) 1996 to date
Twike AG, Sissach.
The Twike was an ultra-light (550lb/250kg) 3-wheeler powered by a 5kW electric motor which could be assisted by pedals. Thus the makers claimed that as well as helping the environment, the Twike provided healthy exercise. The chassis was of aluminium spaceframe construction, with thermoplastic body panels, and steering was by a joystick. A similar design, without the Twike name, was sold as the SLEM (Swiss Light Electromobile), by a separate company, S-LEM AG of Lyss.
NG

TWIN CITY (US) 1914
Twin City Cyclecar Co., Minneapolis, Minnesota.
This was an unconventional cyclecar powered by a 4-cylinder piston-valve air-cooled engine and with suspension by double coil springs at front and rear. Those at the front were mounted transversely, those at the rear in the normal longitudinal position. The body provided side by side seating for two, with the wings acting as armrests. Its designer C.H. Scholer fixed a price of $425, but it is not known if any more than the prototype were made.
NG

TWOMBLY (US) 1904–1915
1904–1910 Twombly Motor Carriage Co., New York, New York.
1910–1911 Twombly Motors Co., New York, New York.
1911–1915 Twombly Car Corp., Nutley, New Jersey.
Willard Irving Twombly made three attempts at car manufacture, but only the third resulted in any serious production. He began in 1904 with a large steam car powered by a front-mounted 4-cylinder engine which could be converted from a 28hp single-acting unit to a 12hp compound. Prices were as high as $3000, expensive compared with most other steamers. Probably only one was made, and Twombly followed it with a 30hp petrol-engined car with pneumatic suspension. This was never marketed, and he set to work on a new design which appeared in 1910. This was his 'quick detachable car', whose engine could be replaced in five minutes, and whose body could be converted from limousine to tourer. It was also steam-powered, and Twombly planned it for use by taxicab operators; a rescue wagon with replacement engine could be sent to any stranded cab which could be put on its way within five minutes, with minimum inconvenience to the passengers. Twombly planned a large factory at Long Island City, but, as with his first steamer, only one prototype was made.
In 1913 he turned to the cyclecar market, building a $350 tandem 2-seater powered by a 7hp V-twin engine, with friction transmission and double-chain drive. For 1914 a 10hp 4-cylinder piston-valve engine was used, and for 1915 he chose a 16hp poppet-valve unit. 2- and 4-seater bodies were offered with this engine, as well as a taxicab. The latter was made by Twombly at Nutley, but the cars were made for him by the Driggs-Seabury Co. in Sharon, Pennsylvania. He placed an

1910 Twombly landaulet.
NICK BALDWIN

order with Driggs for 3000 cars, but did not take anything like this number. The last were made in February 1915.

NG

TWYFORD (US) 1899–1907

1899–1902 Twyford Motor Vehicle Co., Pittsburgh, Pennsylvania.
1902–1907 Twyford Motor Car Co., Brookville, Pennsylvania.
Robert Twyford was an early proponent of 4-wheel drive. His first car was of complex design, with a rear-mounted engine driving a long shaft to power the front wheels, with two pairs of friction clutches within the shaft meshing with gears to provide drive for all four wheels. Another set of bevel gears provided a crude form of power-assisted steering. Probably no more than one example of this was built in Pittsburgh over the three years 1899–1902. Twyford was next heard of in Brookville where he made a few cars with 20hp 2-cylinder 2-stroke engines and, again 4-wheel drive. 1907 models were announced but never built. He later planned to make 4×4 cars and trucks in Texas, but nothing came of this plan.

NG

T.X. (GB) 1970–1986

1970–1981 Technical Exponents Ltd, London
(Works: Denham, Buckinghamshire).
1983–1984 Tripper Cars, Isleworth, Middlesex.
1985–1986 Tripper Cars, Bangor, Gwynedd.
Torix Bennett, son of the founder of FAIRTHORPE, formed Technical Exponents to market the T.X. Tripper. The head office was in London but the cars were made at the Fairthorpe factory at Denham. The Tripper was a doorless 4-seater buggy/ sports car cross-over using a Triumph Spitfire chassis with a choice of Triumph

1972 T.X. Tripper 2500 DeLux.
NATIONAL MOTOR MUSEUM

1.3-, 2.0-, or 2.5-litre engines, or Ford 1600. Kits cost £180, complete cars cost from £740, and a hard-top was optional. The Tripper was twice revived by separate concerns with little success, and probably around 80 cars were made in total.

CR

TX-101 (US) c.1988

Maurice Bourne Jr, Marquez, Texas.
This was an aircraft-inspired 3-wheeler with two wheels in front. It used MGB front suspension with motorcycle running gear out back. The body had a pointed nose and sliding canopy for tandem seating. Kits were offered at $2995 while a completed car was $10,000.

HP

1912 Tyseley 8/10hp coupé.
NATIONAL MOTOR MUSEUM

TYLER (GB) 1994–1998

Tyler Industrial Mouldings, Hoo, Kent.

A fibreglass moulding specialist, Tyler initially assumed control of the B.R.A. 289 project. It then used the B.R.A. chassis in conjunction with a Daimler SP250 replica body to create the SP350, which used mostly MGB mechanicals with a choice of MG, Rover V8, American V8 or Daimler V8 engines. Ford Sierra irs and Ford Granada V6 power were also options. The company joined forces with Roadcraft (ex-SOUTHERN ROADCRAFT) but the alliance did not last long.

CR

TYNE (GB) 1904

W. Galloway & Co. Ltd, Gateshead, County Durham.

This company advertised two models of car, one with 6.5hp single-cylinder engine and double-chain drive, and the other with 12hp 2-cylinder engine and shaft drive. Galloway were nowhere listed as manufacturers, and it is likely that both cars were foreign imports.

NG

TYSELEY (GB) 1912–1913

Tyseley Car Co., Tyseley, Birmingham.

The Tyseley was more of a light car than a cyclecar, though it appeared in the middle of the cyclecar boom. It had a 1090cc 8/10hp water-cooled 2-cylinder engine made by the company, a 2-speed gearbox and shaft drive. In addition to the open 2-seater, a closed coupé was offered, unusual for such a small car.

NG

T.Z. (E) 1956–c.1969

Talleres Zaragoza, Zaragoza.

The T.Z. Líder (later renamed Síder) was the longest-lived of the many Spanish microcars that flourished in postwar times, although the exact date it left production is uncertain – it was listed as late as 1969. It succeeded in offering modern big car virtues in a small and cheap package. Its sophisticated specification included integral body/chassis construction, front-wheel drive, coil springs all round, ifs and rack-and-pinion steering. The 4-seater saloon body measured 128in (3260mm) long and weighed only 450kg (992lb). It was powered by a 350cc 2-cylinder engine developing 14.8bhp (later 18bhp), which drove the front wheels via a 4-speed manual transmission. A top speed of 59mph (95km/h) was claimed.

CR

UAZ (SU) 1954 to date
Ulyanovskji Avtomobilnji Zavod, Uljanovsk.
From 1954 onwards production of GAZ's second-generation down-to-earth 4-wheel drive vehicle was gradually transferred to Ulyanovsk. Two models were manufactured – GAZ-69 with eight seats and GAZ-69A, a 5-seater. The GAZ-M20 Pobeda engine developed 55bhp working together with a 3-speed gearbox and a 2-speed transfer box (2.78: 1.15). Rather small in length (152in/3850mm) and with a very good ground clearance of almost 14in (350mm) (under axles 8in / 210mm), fitted with all-terrain 6.50-16 tyres, the car was capable in almost any environment and found favour in numerous countries, including South America. The car, re-named UAZ-69, was Ulyanovsk Works' very own from 1956. When the production run ended in 1972, over 634,000 units had been made at two factories. The model was also assembled in foreign countries, such as Romania and North Korea.

The next model, called UAZ-469 came in 1965 and was about the same size and weight. Despite its more powerful (70bhp) engine, it consumed in off-road conditions up to 30 per cent less petrol and top speed was up to 62mph (100km/h).

As wheel reduction (1.94) was introduced, ground clearance came up by almost 3in (70mm). Window area was much bigger, and a highly effective heating system was an important feature. There was much more room inside. The Volga saloon engine was mated with a 4-speed gearbox from the UAZ-452 light truck and 8.40-15 tyres were used (6.50-16 on Model 69). The cars found great favour with the Armed Forces and in March 1965 both UAZ-469 and a model with all steel closed bodywork, UAZ-468, were put in service with the Soviet Army. One of those ageless designs, the model was gradually modernised from about 1980. Telescopic shock absorbers appeared, different rear suspension and steering, and a reworked heating unit.

A major update brought along new numbering: UAZ-31512 (civil version) and UAZ-3151 (for the army). A percentage of cars had front coil suspension.

Over 25 years something like 1.3 million UAZ off-roaders were built, various powerplants of 77–100bhp found their way to the engine bay and finally a 110bhp 2.9-litre motor with Bosch fuel injection became a champion. A small quantity of cars have been fitted with foreign (Peugeot, VM) diesels.

The first handful of a totally new model UAZ-3160 were produced in 1997. Two wheelbase lengths became available, 94in or 109in (2400mm or 2760mm). Overall length of these 7–9-seater all-terrain vehicles was now either 167in or 187in (4247 or 4754mm). The production figures for the second half of the 1990s remained comparatively stable: 1995: 44, 880; 1997: 51,411; 1998: 31,932.
MHK

UHER (H) 1921
Uher Automobilgyár, Budapest.
Ödön Uher made a plain looking tourer with a 1-litre engine in 1921, and with help from his friends he was able to set up a workshop. But nothing much happened and the company folded shortly afterwards.
PN

UHERECZKY (H) 1929
Ferenc Uhereczky, Budapest.
A successful bicycle racer, Uhereczky tried to attract the Hungarian public with his small car at the 1929 Budapest International Fair. It was powered by a 500cc motorcycle engine (for similar Hungarian efforts, see HA, MERAY, and SZEKELY). Just like others, he failed through lack of interest.
PN

UIRAPURU (BR) 1966–1968
Sociedad Tecnica de Veiculos SA, São Paulo.
The Uirapuru was first shown at the 1966 São Paulo Auto Show. In fact, it was a badge-engineered BRASINCA with only one difference: a convertible version was included alongside the coupé.
ACT

ULMANN (D) 1903
Edmund Ulmann, Berlin.
The main activity of this firm was the importation of the Curved Dash Oldsmobile, but a 12hp car of Ulmann's own design was also reported to have been made.
HON

1997 Ultima (ii) Spyder sports car.
ULTIMA SPORTS

ULTIMA (i) (F) 1912–1914
B. Bournay, Levallois-Perret, Seine.
Two models, a 954cc 10hp single-cylinder, and a 2120cc 10/12hp 4-cylinder, were made under the Ultima name. Both had friction transmission and final drive by chain.
NG

ULTIMA (ii) (GB) 1992 to date
Ultima Sports Ltd, Hinckley, Leicestershire.
The NOBLE Ultima in its post-1987 revamped guise, was taken over by Ted Marlow in 1992. This was a serious supercar, with engine options extending up to mid-mounted small block V8s. Options included carbon-fibre bodywork, Tig-welded chassis, various suspension packages, and a Porsche 5-speed transaxle in place of the usual Renault item. A Mk4 model, developed with road use more in mind than competition, and a cheaper roofless Spyder model also became available. McLaren chose an Ultima chassis to test components for its F1 road car programme.
CR

ULTRAMOBIL (D) 1904–1908
Deutsche Ultramobil GmbH, Berlin-Halensee.
This company was a selling agent for the German-built Curved Dash Oldsmobile, and the cars were made by two manufacturers, Fahrzeugfabrik Eisenach (1904–06) and by W.A. Boese & Co. of Berlin (1906–08). An additional model with front-mounted 2-cylinder engine appeared in 1906.
HON

ULTRAMOBILE (F) 1908
Voitures Ultramobile, Paris.
The Ultramobile light car was powered by a 6/12hp 4-cylinder engine with cylinders cast in one block, with 2-speed transmission, as the engine was said to be as flexible as a steam engine. Final drive was by shaft. There were two wheelbase lengths, to suit either 2- or 4-seater bodywork. The suspension was by long springs running the length of the frame on either side. This was a feature of the Curved Dash Oldsmobile, and suggests a possible link with the German Ultramobil, which was definitely a Curved Dash clone. However, the front-mounted 4-cylinder engine gives the lie to this, and the last year for the Curved Dash was 1907.
NG

U.M.A.P. (F) 1957–1959
Usine Moderne d'Applications Plastiques, Bernon, Aube.
This was a plastic-bodied 2+2 coupé based on a Citroën 2CV chassis. As an alternative to the standard 425cc engine, 435cc and 500cc units with single or double carburettors were offered. A U.M.A.P. was the only French car classed in the Liège-Brescia–Liège rally. Production was extremely limited.
CR

U.M.M. (P) 1978–1995
U.M.M., Lisbon.
This 4 × 4 utility vehicle began life as a Portuguese-built version of the French COURNIL, using 2498cc Peugeot diesel engines in standard or turbo forms. It was made as an estate car with metal panelled or detachable fabric soft-top body in 6- and 8-seater versions, and also as a panelled delivery van or pick-up

1957 U.M.A.P. 2CV coupé.
NICK GEORGANO

1991 U.M.M. Alter II 4x4.
NICK BALDWIN

1907 Unic 16/20hp tourer.
NATIONAL MOTOR MUSEUM

truck. It was little changed over the years, although a long-wheelbase model appeared in 1990, and by the mid-90s had become too rustic to compete with more sophisticated competition from Land Rover and the Japanese firms.

NG

UNDERBERG (F) 1899–1909
Underberg et Compagnie, Nantes, Loire-Inférieure.

The Underberg was made away from the main centres of French car manufacture, at Nantes on the west coast. It began life as a light 2-seater voiturette with 3hp air-cooled single-cylinder Gaillardet engine mounted at the front. By 1901 the range had expanded to include a 6/8hp twin and two fours, of 12/15 and 28/40hp. The latter was a larger 4-seater tonneau with chain drive, gilled-tube radiator and a Panhard-like appearance. These and subsequent cars were often sold under the name Salvator. By 1906 the cars sported round radiators, and came in three sizes of 4-cylinder engine, 12, 16, and 24hp. All had armoured wood frames, with shaft drive on the two smaller models and chains on the 24hp. This was still listed in 1909.

NG

UNIC (F) 1904–1939
1904–1906 SA des Anciens Établissements Georges Richard, Paris.
1906–1939 SA des Automobiles Unic, Puteaux, Seine.

Georges Richard (1863–1922) founded this company in October 1904 after ending his partnership with Henri Brasier. He was financed by Baron Dr Henri de Rothschild who had made the PASCAL car in 1902–03, and on whose land the large factory for the manufacture of Unic cars was erected in 1906. This factory was an extension of the premises used for making BARDON cars and commercial vehicles. Richard's original product had a 1727cc 10hp vertical twin engine, 3-speed gearbox and shaft drive. He planned a one-model policy, hence the name Unic (unique), but soon found a demand for larger 4-cylinder cars. Listed in 1906 were two fours, a 1943cc 12hp and a 2614cc 14hp. These were joined by a 3790cc 22hp four in 1907, which could run on petrol or alcohol fuel, and in 1908 by a 4084cc 35hp six. As early as 1906 the 2-cylinder chassis was fitted

1640

with taxicab coachwork and the name soon became generally associated with cabs. Of the 7292 Unic vehicles sold from 1906 to the end of September 1913, half were taxicabs. In both London and Paris, Unic ranked second only to Renault in cab numbers. One of the London firms operating them was the National Motor Cab Co. which employed W.O. Bentley in 1910–11. In his autobiography he commented, 'Nothing the English built at the time could stand up to the treatment nor show such economic running figures as the Unic'. Other cities using Unic cabs included Monte Carlo and Buenos Aires.

Several models of conventional 4-cylinder car were made from 1908 to 1913, when production rose from 598 to 1657 (figures for 1914 are not available, and would have been curtailed as a result of the war). The largest was a 4900cc 25hp, but more typical were the 1460cc 10/12hp and 2120cc 12/16hp. Unic made their own bodies for the smaller models. One of Unic's employees was Jules Salomon whose Le Zèbre car was made in the Unic factory until Salomon was able to set up his own business at Suresnes.

World War I saw shells and bombs being made at Puteaux, as well as some trucks and ambulances. Georges Richard's second son, Raymond, was killed in aerial combat in 1916, and the eldest son Jean contracted tuberculosis from which he died in 1923. His father had died the year before, as a result of an accident while testing a chassis with front-wheel brakes. Georges Dubois, who had been with the company from the beginning, took over the reins. The mainstay of postwar production was the 1847cc 10CV Type L, an unexciting car, although it did have unit construction of engine and gearbox and, from 1923, front-wheel brakes. Other features were a cone clutch, 4-speed gearbox and spiral bevel rear axle. Rear suspension was by a combination of cantilever and quarter-elliptic springs. A new model for 1923 was the 1997cc 11CV Sport with ohvs and a top speed of 70mph (113km/h). Like the smaller car and the taxicabs, which were still made in large numbers, it had a vee-radiator. Wire wheels distinguished it from the more pedestrian models. There were also two larger models, of 2603 and 2963cc, the latter with very long-stroke dimensions of 80 × 148mm.

The 1928 Paris Salon saw several straight-8 models, including Amilcar, Ballot, Chaigneau-Brasier and Renault. Unic also had an eight on display, which had been under development for four years, and would doubtless have appeared earlier had not the company given priority to commercial chassis. Designed by Marzloff who was also responsible for the straight-8 Ballot, the H1 had a 2492cc ohv engine with nine main bearings, giving 65bhp. Top speed, even with a saloon body, was 70mph (113km/h). Continuing Unic's interest in rear suspensions, the H1 had transverse springs located above and below the axle. At the 1930 Salon capacity was increased to 2650cc on the H3. It was made in small numbers up to 1934, but during the depression years most of Unic's activity was devoted to commercial vehicles. It acquired a licence to make Mercedes-Benz diesel trucks which proved very successful, and also offered lighter petrol-engined truck and bus chassis. Taxicabs were no longer made; the last were a small series assembled at Unic's London depot in 1928–30 and destined for London streets only. With bodies by Jones or Goode & Cooper, some survived into the early 1950s.

A new car range appeared for 1934. The U4 had a 1997cc engine based on the 11CV unit from the 1920s, but with side-valves instead of ohv, a double reduction rear axle which gave a low chassis, and an unusual ifs by crossed half axles bolted to semi-elliptic springs. Two body styles were available, a 4-door saloon and a 2-door cabriolet. At the 1935 Salon the U4 was joined by the U6 with 2994cc engine and a similar appearance to the U4 apart from a longer bonnet. The U6 wheelbase was a lengthy 131in (3325mm), and allowed for a 7-seater limousine body as well as the saloon and cabriolet. For 1936 the U6 Sport had ohvs, giving 85bhp, 15 more than the side-valve unit. Cotal gearboxes were optional across the range for 1936. Standard bodies were by Autobineau, but custom coachbuilders, in particular Chapron, De Villars, Letourneur et Marchand and Pourtout built some striking styles, especially on the U6. At the 1937 Salon the U6 had a fresh 'fencer's mask' grill designed by Letourneur et Marchand, while the U4 had a more conservative style. In July 1938, Unic announced that it was to give up passenger car production, but four cars were shown at the Salon in October, and it is believed that a handful were made into 1939.

No cars were made after World War II, but truck production flourished up to the 1980s, latterly as part of the Iveco group, so that from the 1970s Unics resembled Fiats apart from their badging.

NG

1908 Unic 10/12hp Doctor's Brougham.
NICK BALDWIN

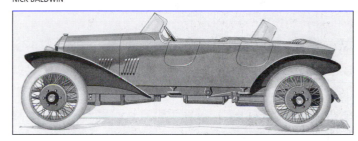
1924 Unic 11CV Torpedo Sport.
NICK BALDWIN

c.1929 Unic 14/28 saloon.
BRYAN K.GOODMAN

1931 Unic 15CV straight-8 coupé.
NATIONAL MOTOR MUSEUM

1936 Unic U6 Sport 2-door sedan.
NATIONAL MOTOR MUSEUM

1935 Unic U6 coupé de ville.
NATIONAL MOTOR MUSEUM

Further Reading
Unic passe avant tout, Dominique Dubarry, Jacques Grancher, Paris 1982.

UNICAR *see* OPPERMAN

UNICORN (GB) 1987
The Blee Unicorn was a very short-lived kit car that echoed the style of the Lotus Seven.
CR

UNION (i) (US) 1902–1905
1902–1905 Union Automobile Co., Union City, Indiana.
1905 Union Automobile Co., Anderson, Indiana.
The first of several cars to bear the name Union, this was designed by John W. Lambert, who had made an experimental 3-wheeler as early as 1891. It had an 8hp 2-cylinder engine available in air- or water-cooled form, with friction transmission and final drive by double chain. The only body style was a 2-seater with folding front seat to carry two more passengers. A 5-seater tonneau model was made for 1904–05, with 10hp engine in 1904 and 12 or 16hp in 1905. In that year production was concentrated in Anderson, where the engines and transmissions had always been made, and in the same year the name was changed to LAMBERT. About 300 Unions were made.
NG

UNION (ii) (US) 1905
Union Automobile Manufacturing Co., St Louis, Missouri.
This company was the St Louis agent for the Union built in Anderson, Indiana, and offered a similar range of 12 and 16hp cars on wheelbases of 81 and 94in (2056 and 2386mm), respectively. Their prices were somewhat lower, at $1125 for a 16hp tonneau, compared with $1200 for the same car from Anderson. When that company changed the car's name to Lambert, it is believed that the St Louis venture became a dealership for Lambert.
NG

UNION (iii) (US) 1908–1909
Union Carriage Co., St Louis, Missouri.
This company had no connection with the makers of the UNION (ii). It was a carriage builders which announced a motor buggy powered by a 12hp 2-cylinder engine selling for $650. It planned to make a runabout and tourer with front-mounted engines in 1909, but the high-wheel buggy was its only product.
NG

UNION (iv) (US) 1911–1912
Union Sales Co., Columbus, Ohio.
This company was to have been called the Eagle Motor Co., but in view of the many other American cars using this name, the makers changed to Union and called its car the Union 25. It was made only in roadster form, with a 25hp 4-cylinder engine, 3-speed gearbox and shaft drive.
NG

UNION (v) (US) 1916
Union Automobile Co., Auburn, Indiana.
This was a 4-cylinder version of the AUBURN (i), made by a separate company headed by John Zimmerman, who had made cars under his own name until he was taken over by Auburn. The only car made under the Union name was a 24hp made in tourer or roadster form.
NG

UNION CITY SIX (US) 1916
Union City Carriage Manufacturing Co., Union City, Indiana.
This company had been in business as a carriage maker since about 1900, and offered cars for one season only. They had 48/52hp 6-cylinder engines, and only one body style, a 7-seater tourer. The company was later bought by Auburn, and became the Union City Body Co., which made bodies for Cord and Duesenberg under the name La Grande.
NG

UNIPOWER (GB) 1966–1970

1966–1968 Universal Power Drives Ltd, Perivale, Middlesex.
1968–1970 U.W.F. Automotive (Unipower Cars), London.
Designed by BMC works driver Andrew Hedges and Tim Powell, the Unipower GT was made by a manufacturer of 4×4 forestry tractors. Its extremely low fibreglass coupé body was only 40in (1015mm) high and was bonded on to a tubular space frame chassis. Either a Mini-Cooper or Cooper S engine was mounted just ahead of the rear axle. Suspension was independent by wishbones and coil springs, there were front disc brakes and a right-hand gearchange. Only around 75 cars were made. A Unipower MkII was designed by Peter Bohanna but this evolved into the Diablo, itself later becoming the A.C. ME3000.

CR

UNIQUE (GB) 1916

The Motor Carrier and Cycle Co., Clapham, London.
The middle of World War I was not the best time to launch a car, and the Unique had less than a year of life. It was a cyclecar powered by a 1034cc 8/10hp 2-cylinder engine of the company's own manufacture, with a 3-speed gearbox and shaft drive. The price was £165.

NG

UNISPORT (US) 1974/1980s

Unicar Corp., Anaheim, California.
The first product of this company was the Duo Delta of 1974, a 3-wheeler designed by Walter Korff. It mated a motorcycle rear end with a 2-seater fibreglass cabin with doors and a sunroof. The powerplant was a 750cc motorcycle unit with continuously variable automatic transmission to the rear wheel. A top speed of 98mph (158km/h) and fuel consumption of 56mpg were claimed. It was sold in kit form and complete. This was followed up in the 1980s by a leaning 3-wheeler with two front and a single rear wheel. A tandem 2-seater, it was based on a steel tube frame clothed with fibreglass bodywork. Clever suspension consisting of sliding pillars with linear actuators from the steering wheel allowed the trike to lean into corners. It was priced at $3000 and the company claimed to make 50 cars per month.

CR

UNIT (GB) 1920–1923

Rotary Units Co. Ltd, Wooburn Green, Buckinghamshire.
This was a venture of Arthur G. Grice, the 'G' of G.W.K., who formed a separate company in 1912 to make 5-cylinder pumping units. He parted from G.W.K. in 1920, and started to make a light car on G.W.K. lines, with a 998cc air-cooled flat-twin engine behind the driver and passenger, friction transmission and chain final drive. Few of these were made, and by 1921 the engine was positioned at the front. A few of the flat-twins may have been used, but otherwise the new Unit had a 1247cc 4-cylinder Coventry-Climax engine. To make it more car-like still a conventional 3-speed gearbox was offered, although friction drive was still available. There was no standard model of Unit, and Grice clearly used whatever components were available. After about 50 cars had been made he returned to G.W.K. who took a few Units to sell off themselves.

NG

UNITED (US) 1914

National United Service Co., Detroit, Michigan.
This company made a cyclecar powered by a 12hp 4-cylinder engine, with friction transmission and double-chain final drive. It was made as a 2-seater and a light delivery van. The company also sold the ARROW and BEISEL cyclecars.

NG

UNITED POWER (US) 1901

United Power Vehicle Co., Springfield, Massachusetts;
Rutland, Vermont; Stamford, Connecticut.
This company had grand pretensions, advertising a wide range of vehicles from a runabout to a 60-seater Palatial Coach. Three motive powers were listed, each from a different factory. The steamers were to be made in the former KLOCK factory at Stamford, petrol cars in Springfield and electrics in Rutland.

NG

1966 Unipower GT coupé.
NATIONAL MOTOR MUSEUM

1923 Unit 10hp 2-seater.
NATIONAL MOTOR MUSEUM

UNITED STATES (US) 1899–1903

United States Automobile Co., Attleboro, Massachusetts.
Frank Mossberg began making light electric cars under this name in his bicycle bell factory. In 1902 he made five petrol-engined cars for the WEBSTER Automobile Co. of New York City, while other Attleboro businessmen made a petrol-engined car designed by James Blake in the same factory. In 1903 Mossberg regained control, and made a few more cars, both United States electrics and Blakes.

NG

UNITO (US) 1909

United Factories Co., Cleveland, Ohio.
This company made buggy hoods and for less than one season built a typical high-wheel buggy with flat-twin engine under the seat and chain drive.

NG

UNIVERSAL (i) (US) 1914

Universal Motor Co., Washington, Pennsylvania.
When production of the CROXTON ended the factory began to make the Universal light car. This was a 2-seater powered by an 18hp 4-cylinder engine, with 3-speed gearbox and shaft drive. Few were made, and the factory was sold at a sheriff's auction in February 1915.

NG

UNIVERSAL (ii) see TURNER (ii)

UNIVERSAL COACHWORKS (US) c.1985

Universal Coachworks, Sun Valley, California.
The Machette was a simple Volkswagen-based kit car with open wheels and a slender body with side pods. The VW chassis was shortened, but otherwise this was a simple kit to build. The Machette kit was later picked up by REDHEAD ROADSTERS.

HP

UNIVERSAL PLASTICS (US) c.1965

Universal Plastics, San Carlos, California.

This shadowy kit car company never showed photographs of their cars in their advertisements or their literature. The GT Monza was a replica of the sensational 1963 Corvair Monza GT show car and was intended to fit on a Volkswagen floorpan. It weighed 150lb (68kg) and cost $695. The Sebring GT-2 was a Ford GT-40 look-alike that was also for VW running gear. It included bucket seats and a dashboard. The Monza GP Roadster was a VW-based replica of the Chevrolet Monza S.S. show car that was the roadster companion to the Monza GT. These were two of the most striking show cars of all time but it is unknown if the kits did them justice. The Universal Plastics Cougar GT was a replica of the Ford Cougar show car. The kit version was based on Triumph, MG or Austin-Healey chassis. They also offered a custom-built chassis that could be adapted to VW, Corvair or other suspension options. Mounts could be installed for V8 engines and transaxles and lightweight competition bodies were optional.

HP

UNIVERSITY see CONTINENTAL (ii)

UNO (S) 1989

The Uno 001 sports coupé was designed by Uno Johansson. It was a handsome 2-seater powered by a mid-mounted Saab 900 T16 turbocharged engine, good for 250bhp. A 0–62mph (0–100km/h) time of 6.0 seconds was quoted, and the company announced its intention of building 50 cars per year.

CR

UPPERCU CADILLAC (US) 1923–1925

Cadillac Motor Car Co. Division, General Motors Corp., Detroit, Michigan.

These cars, marketed by Inglis Uppercu, New York City distributor for Cadillac, had an individuality of their own, not only by their own radiators which had little in common with the standard Cadillac shape but with the name and address of the Inglis Uppercu Agency worked into the badges of the cars. These cars were sold exclusively at Uppercu's sumptuous showrooms on New York's 57th Street. They featured custom coachwork to Uppercu's designs by both Hollander & Morrill of Amesbury, Massachusetts and Healey & Co. of New York City at considerably higher prices than those of both the standard Cadillac line and many of the Cadillac semi-customs by other coachbuilders. The Uppercu Cadillacs were available in all body styles and sold to a small but exclusive and consistent clientele for more than two years.

KM

UPSTATE SUPER REPLICARS (US) 1998 to date

Upstate Super Replicars Inc., Newtonville, New York.

The only product of this kit car company was a Cobra Daytona Coupé replica. It used a ladder-style frame with either Jaguar irs or a Ford live rear axle. Ford V8 engines were offered and they were sold in kit and fully assembled form.

HP

UPTON (i) (US) 1902–1903

Upton Machine Co., Beverly, Massachusetts.

Former merchant seaman Colcord Upton formed this company in 1900 for the manufacture of an epicyclic transmission he had invented, and built a runabout powered by a 3¹/₂hp De Dion-Bouton engine to demonstrate the system. Two more were made in 1901, and in 1902 Upton began to make cars for sale. As well as the runabout, he made a 16hp 4-cylinder car which he priced at $3500. Only one of these seems to have been built, and in 1904 it was re-issued in modified form as the BEVERLY. Meanwhile, Upton had left in July 1903, and moved to New York City, and then to Lebanon, Pennsylvania, where he built another car bearing his name.

NG

UPTON (ii) (US) 1905–1907

1905 Upton Motor Co., Lebanon, Pennsylvania.
1905–1907 Lebanon Motor Works, Lebanon, Pennsylvania.

Colcord Upton spent about a year and a half in New York working on a gearbox and a water pump before he was invited to Lebanon by Milton Schnader to manufacture the pump in his factory. They soon decided to make a car as well.

It was a conventional tourer powered by a 30hp 4-cylinder Continental engine, with chain final drive. By August 1905 only seven cars had been made in as many months, and the company was reorganised with much greater capital as the Lebanon Motor Works. About eight more 30hp Uptons were made, and for 1906 a larger shaft-driven car with 40hp engine was announced. Thirty-three of these were made during 1906, including a twin-engined runabout. Schnader also built a smaller car of his own design called the RIVIERA in the same factory, but both makes disappeared during 1907.

NG

URBANINA (I) 1965–c.1973

Bargagli e Cristani SpA, Pisa; Urbanina SpA, Santa Croce sull'Arno, Pisa.

First presented at the 1965 Turin Motor Show, this was a tiny (76in/1940mm long) city car conceived and designed by the Marquis Piergirolamo Bargagli. The idea was for a simple platform, powered by a 175cc single-cylinder 2-stroke engine, to be fitted with a variety of different bodywork, some of which featured the extraordinary ability to swivel around in order to maximise convenience. The bodywork varied from completely open, with only the scantiest wickerwork coachwork, to fully-enclosed cylindrical structures. Model names spanned Primavera (completely open), Quattro Stagioni (convertible) and Invernale (fully enclosed). Later versions acquired Innocenti 198cc air-cooled 2-stroke 3.75bhp petrol engines or Bosch 1kW/2kW (1.3/2.7bhp) electric motors fed by 24V of charge. Most production cars had more conventional non-swivelling bodywork, including the Minigip, a tiny utility car in the style of a jeep.

CR

URBANISER (GB) 1993–1995

Concept Car Co. Ltd, Oxford.

Designed by brothers Chris and Andy Mynheer, this was a small open car, a cross between a city car and a beach buggy, powered by a 1.4-litre Rover Metro engine. The prototype was built in Oxford, and there were plans for production to take place in Chesterfield, Derbyshire, with financial backing from Anglo-American Ventures. Nothing came of this, and the Urbaniser never went into production. However, the Mynheer brothers then set up a successful business tuning and providing body kits for Rover 200, 400, and 600 models.

NG

URBANIX see LEPOIX

URBAN MFG (US) 1998 to date

Urban Manufacturing Inc., Wickliffe, Ohio.

The aptly named Urban Gorilla was a metal-bodied replica of the AMG Hummer. It was a wild kit, designed to fit on Ford, Dodge and Chevrolet full-sized pick-up truck chassis. 2- and 4-door body kits were offered and they were sold in kit form only.

HP

URBANUS see HAGEN

URECAR (GB) 1923

Urecar Motor Co., Bournemouth, Hampshire.

One of a handful of cars made in the seaside resort of Bournemouth, the Urecar was a light car powered by a 9.8hp 4-cylinder Dorman engine, with 3-speed chain and dog clutch transmission similar to that used in the Frazer Nash.

NG

UREN (GB) 1967–1974

Jeff Uren Ltd, Hanwell, London.

Jeff Uren produced several modified Fords, of which the best-known was the Savage based on the Mk II and the III Cortina. This was recognised by the RAC as a Series Production Car, and was listed by *Autocar* and *Motor* as an independent make. Modifications included the installation of a 3-litre V6 engine as used in the Ford Zodiac, and major changes to the suspension to cope with the extra weight, also a more powerful battery and servo brakes. The Mk III-based Savage had the same engine but it was mated to a 3-litre Capri gearbox. A 218bhp Weslake-tuned V6 Savage tested by *Motor Sport* in 1972 had a top speed of 125mph (201km/h), and its 0–60 (0–97km/h) time of 6.7 seconds equalled that of a V12 E-type Jaguar.

1970 Uren Savage (left) and two Apaches.
JEFF UREN

Other Urens included Apache (3-litre V6-powered Escort), Comanche (3-litre V6-powered Capri), Navajo (2-litre Pinto-powered Escort), Stampede (5-litre V8-powered Capri), and Seneca (3-litre Granada in 170, 180, 190, or 220bhp forms). About 1700 Urens were made in all.

NG

URI (NAMIBIA) c.1997 to date

The only vehicle built in Namibia, the Uri was a passenger/utility vehicle powered by a Peugeot diesel engine. It was intended for safari use, and unlike many vehicles of its type, had only 2-wheel drive as its makers did not think the complications and expense of 4-wheel drive were necessary.

NG

URSUS (F) 1908

G. Mené;gault-Basset, Arcueil, Seine.

The Ursus was a light car with 8hp single-cylinder engine and friction transmission. A 2-seater was the only body style offered.

NG

U.S. (US) 1907–1908

U.S. Motor Car Co., Upper Sandusky, Ohio.

This car was presumably named after its home town of Upper Sandusky rather than the United States, although either derivation would have been appropriate. It had a 1.8-litre 12hp air-cooled 4-cylinder engine, with 3-speed gearbox and shaft drive. The frame was of hickory and the only body style was a 2-seater selling for $750. For 1908 the wheelbase was lengthened from 90 (2284mm) to 96in (2436mm), and the price increased to $900.

NG

U.S. BREVETS MATHIEU see MATHIEU

U.S. FIBERGLASS (US) c.1956

U.S. Fiberglass, Norwood, New Jersey.

The U.S. Mk II was a fibreglass-bodied kit sports car that was based on American sedan parts. The 2-seat roadster body fitted on 100–118in (2538–2995mm) frames and could be purchased in kit or assembled form. Styling was rounded but uninspired, with exterior door hinges.

HP

U.S. LONG DISTANCE (US) 1901–1903

U.S. Long Distance Automobile Co., Jersey City, New Jersey.

Although this company was formed in 1900, the first Long Distance car was not announced until April 1901. It was a tiller-steered runabout powered by a 7hp single-cylinder engine, with 2-speed epicyclic gearbox and chain drive. It was soon joined by larger cars with 10 or 12hp 2-cylinder engines, and a 20hp 3-cylinder with tonneau body. By November 1901 the company was turning out 10 to 12 cars a week, and said that they were willing to make racing machines to order. The runabout gained wheel-steering for the 1903 season, the other models being wheel-steered anyway. In January 1904 the company changed its name to the Standard Motor Construction Co., and subsequent cars were sold under the name STANDARD (ii).

NG

USRC (US) c.1994

United States Reproduction Corp., Ocoee, Florida.

The USRC 1936 Ford Pickup truck replica could be ordered in standard form or with a 'chopped', or lowered, top. It was built on a custom ladder frame with a Ford V8 engine. Custom A-arm suspension was used at the front, with a Ford live axle at the back. They were sold in kit and fully assembled form.

HP

UTIL (F) 1922

Pelgrin et Schuller, St Ouen, Seine.

This was a conventional 2-seater cyclecar with 2-cylinder engine and chain final drive.

NG

UTILE (GB) 1904

Utile Motor Manufacturing Co. Ltd, Kew Gardens, Surrey.

Known as the Utile-Simplex, this was a light 2-seater powered by an 8hp single-cylinder engine said to be 'of De Dion-Bouton type'. It had a 2-speed gearbox, with direct drive on top, although one was said to be sufficient for all normal running, and shaft final drive.

NG

UTILIS (F) 1921–1924

Lafarge et Pauillac, Paris.

The makers of this ultra-light cyclecar intended it as a replacement for the motorcycle and sidecar. It was made in single- or 2-cylinder models, using Train engines of 344 or 688cc, with 2-speed transmission and belt final drive to the centre of the rear axle. Its frame was of wooden slats without suspension, as on the Briggs & Stratton Flyer, but the seats were suspended on the frame by coil springs. *Omnia* was rather dismissive of the Utilis in its report on the 1922 Salon: 'It is perhaps amusing for a tour of Longchamp in very fine weather, but a bit hard on pavé'.

NG

1922 Utilis 2½hp cyclecar.
NATIONAL MOTOR MUSEUM

1986 UVA F33 Can-Am.
UVA

UTILITAS (D) 1920–1921

Utilitas-Gesellschaft Ritze GmbH, Berlin.

The first products of this company were cyclecars with single or 2-cylinder engines. Later, 4-cylinder engines were used, a 4/10PS in a tandem 2-seater, and a 5/14PS in a 4-seater.

HON

UTILITY FOUR (US) 1921–1922

Victor W. Page Motors Corp., Stamford, Connecticut.

The Utility Four was projected as a lower-priced companion car to the Victor Page Motors corporation's Aero-Type Four, at the time being built in the corporation's plant at Stamford, Connecticut. By mid–1921, four prototypes had been completed – a roadster, a touring car, a station wagon, and a stake truck. Designed with a 4-cylinder engine, the Utility was equipped with disc wheels and with a wheelbase of 119in (3020mm). Projected price of the touring car was $1450 but further plans to build the Utility were scrapped before production began.

KM

UTOPIAN (GB) 1914

Utopian Motor Works, Leicester.

This company was a bicycle maker, but in 1914 it made an unusual 2-seater car with single front wheel and steering by side tiller, which even Lanchester had abandoned by 1914. The 2-cylinder water-cooled engine lived under the seat, and drove the rear axle by shaft. It was built for a local clergyman, and possibly only the one Utopian was made.

NG

UTTÖR (H) 1954

Schadek János, Debrecen.

János (John) Schadek was a mechanical engineer who built two cars before World War II. He was also one of the many talented people who built their own microcar in Hungary during the early 1950s. The Úttör (Pioneer) was completed in 1954 with Csepel 250cc motorbike engine, placed on the rear axle. Parts were of mixed origin: gears from a motorcycle, wheels from a barrow, etc. It differed from other one-off creations in that the Ministry of Light Industry saw the potential and decided to research the possibility of producing it in small series as an intermediate type between a passenger car (production of which was banned in Hungary) and a motorcycle. The car received much publicity during 1954–55 and was scrutinised by the Hungarian Research Institute of Automobile Transport, but when they sent the car back to Debrecen the creator lost interest in it so it was shipped to Székesfehérvár where an ambitious microcar project was just shaping up (ALBA REGIA and BALATON).

PN

U.V.A. (GB) 1983–1995

1983 The Unique Vehicle & Accessory Co. Ltd, Curridge, Berkshire.
1983–1990 The Unique Vehicle & Accessory Co. Ltd, Newbury, Berkshire.
1990–1991 The Unique Vehicle & Accessory Co. Ltd, Whitchurch, Hampshire.
1992–1993 TAG Automotive Ltd, Whitchurch, Hampshire.
1993–1995 Laser Cars, Whitchurch, Hampshire.

U.V.A., as an importer of Volkswagen upgrade parts, launched the Fugitive as either a pure off-road 'sand rail' or as a fun road car. It used a rear-mounted VW engine in a very tough exposed tubular chassis cage and was extremely lightweight. With plain metal panelling inside and the absolute minimum of fibreglass bodywork outside, it was stark in the extreme. Two and 4-seater versions were listed. A Rover V8 mid-engined version called the F30 arrived in 1985, with very similar styling to the Fugitive and similar VW-based suspension, but a new spaceframe chassis. In 1986 came the F33 Can-Am, with more enclosed bodywork on the F30 chassis. On another tack entirely, U.V.A. imported the Montage McLaren M6GT replica from Manta Cars in America, then made it under licence. In 1986 the original VW-based version was re-engineered to create the M6GTR. This has a fibreglass monocoque centre section with tubular steel front and rear subframes, designed to accept the Rover V8 engine and VW transmission.

CR

U-WAGEN (A) 1919–1923

U-Wagen Ing. Ulmann, Vienna.

This company built a prototype cyclecar with 480cc 2-cylinder engine, but production cars had 760cc 7/18PS 4-cylinder engines. Most were supplied in 2-seater roadster form.

HON

V200 (I) 1953
Microcar, Milan.

With styling influenced by Detroit, the V200 was a convertible microcar with aluminium bodywork and an optional transparent plastic hard-top. It was powered by a rear-mounted 2-stroke 200cc 4-cylinder engine developing 12bhp.

CR

V2N see FRANCE-JET

V-8 ARCHIE (US) c.1994 to date
V-8 Archie, Niles, Michigan.

Although this company specialised in making conversion kits to install V8 Chevrolet engines into Pontiac Fieros and Fiero-based kit cars, they also sold kits themselves. The V-8 Archie CA-TR was a Ferrari Testarossa replica based, of course, on a V8 powered Fiero. The V-8 Archie F-40 replicated the Ferrari F-40 on the same running gear. They were sold in kit or completely assembled form.

HP

VABIS (S) 1898–1911
Vagnfabrik AB Södertälge, Södertälje.

This company was established in 1891 as a subsidiary of the railway carriage manufacturers Surahammars Bruk. In 1896 a motorcar department was set up under the management of Gustav Eriksson, who had been with Surahammars for several years. His first car was ready for trials by April 1898. It had a rear-mounted V-4 2-stroke engine running on paraffin fuel, and using hot-tube ignition. The body was a 4-seater of Benz-like appearance, and steering by tiller with vertical column. Apparently it ran poorly and the steering was almost impossible to handle. It was sometimes known as the Surahammar. Eriksson scrapped it and built another in 1899, followed by two petrol engines, a single cylinder and a twin. The smaller was used to power a railcar.

Vehicle production was sporadic until 1906, with more commercial vehicles than cars being made. From 1906 to 1910 about 85 cars were made, and these varied in size from a 6hp 2-cylinder to a 40hp 4-cylinder. Motorised rail trolleys and marine engines were also made. Eriksson left the company in 1910, and the following year it merged with Maskinenfabrik AB Scania. Henceforth the cars and trucks would be called SCANIA-VABIS. The Vabis factory at Södertälge was used for car and engine manufacture, while Scania's Malmö plant was devoted to commercial vehicles, which became more important in the range.

NG

Further Reading

'Northern Lights: Dawn of the Swedish Automobile', Len Lonnegren, *Automobile Quarterly*, Vol. 31, No. 4.

VAGHI (I) 1920–1924
1920–1922 Ditta Lodovico Boltri di Mezzi, Ganna & Compagnia, Milan.
1922–1924 Motovetturette Vaghi SA, Milan.

Also known as the M.V. (Motovetturette Vaghi) and in England as the Bambina, this was a 3-wheeler with single front wheel, powered by a 1077cc air-cooled V-twin engine. This was mounted with a bonnet and drove via a 3-speed gearbox and propeller shaft to the rear axle which was equipped with a differential. Thus it was more sophisticated than many cyclecars, but few were made. The poor roads of Italy were not encouraging for any makers of light cars, and exports were limited. The British concessionaires, the Bambina Motor Co. Ltd, apparently sold only two, of which one survives. Both open and closed 3-seater bodies were offered, with wire or artillery wheels. It was much better looking with the former. A 4-wheeled version was taken over by S.A.M. after Vaghi collapsed.

NG

Further Reading

'MV Bambina, an Italian Cyclecar', Alan Brierley, *The Automobile*, May 1990.

VAGNON ET CANET (F) 1898–c.1900
Vagnon et Canet, Lyons.

In May 1898 this company announced that it would make to order cars of any design or power. A few were built up to about 1900, but details of their design are not known. The company also made trucks and motorcycles.

NG

1898 Vabis 4-seater.
NATIONAL MOTOR MUSEUM

1910 Vabis Type G4 12hp tourer.
NATIONAL MOTOR MUSEUM

1923 Vaghi Bambina 3-wheeled saloon.
NATIONAL MOTOR MUSEUM

VAGOVA (F) 1924–1925
Vareille et Godet, Levallois-Perret, Seine.

The engineer Vareille was better known for his design of the LOMBARD engine than for his own cars. These used a very small 6-cylinder engine of only 745cc which nevertheless gave 40bhp at 6000rpm. The ohvs were desmodromically operated (positively closed as well as opened) and a supercharger made in-house was used. The car had Hallot 4-wheel brakes. Production was very limited, although one was a racing car which was entered for the 1924 Brooklands 200 Mile Race. A non-supercharged road-going chassis and a cabriolet were exhibited

1933 Vale Special sports car.
NICK BALDWIN

at the 1924 Paris and 1925 Brussels Salons. Nothing more was heard of the Vagova, but the Michel Aviation engine used by D'YRSAN was derived from that of the Vagova.

NG

VAILLANT (F) 1922–1924
Cyclecars Vaillant, Lyons.
Although the maker called its car a cyclecar, it was more of a light car, using a 5CV 4-cylinder Chapuis-Dorner engine and shaft drive.

NG

VAJA (CS) 1929
Jaroslav Vales, Praha-Kobylisy.
The Vaja cyclecars (for Vales and JAP) used either 4-stroke Czech Itar 750cc 12bhp motorcycle engines (weight 748lb/340kg, top speed 37mph/60km/h) or more successful 1-litre JAP engines that were capable of 47mph (76km/h). These cheap vehicles (18,000 Kc for the simplest outfit for the JAP-engined type with Bosch starter) could be bought by customers with a 2- or 3-passenger roadster body or as a 3-seater 2-door saloon. All body styles were of wooden construction covered by leatherette; only the mudguards were of pressed steel. About 30–40 Vaja cyclecars were sold during the one year of their existence.

MSH

V.A.L. (GB) 1913–1914
V.A.L. Motor Co. Ltd, Birmingham.
The V.A.L. was a cyclecar powered by a 8.9hp water-cooled V-twin Precision engine, with friction transmission and final drive by chain.

NG

VALE (i) (GB) 1932–1935
Vale Engineering Co. Ltd, Maida Vale, London.
Sometimes known as the Vale Special, this low-slung sports car was designed by the Hon. P.E. Pellow, later the ninth Viscount Exmouth. It was powered initially by an 832cc Triumph Super Seven engine in an underslung frame by Rubury Owen with a simple 2-seater body. The hydraulic brakes and worm-drive rear axle also came from Triumph. The low centre of gravity gave it excellent cornering, but a top speed of barely 65mph (105km/h) ruled it out of serious competitions, and its low ground clearance made it unsuitable for trials. From 1933 a 1098cc Coventry-Climax engine was fitted, and there was a 4-seater version named the Tourette. In 1934 the company said that it would install this engine or a 1476cc Coventry-Climax six in existing cars to improve their performance, and at least one car was re-engined with a 1242cc Meadows four. Just over 100 Vales were made.

NG

VALE (ii) (US) c.1953
Vale Wright Co., Berkeley, California.
Vale Wright was a designer/architect who raced cars for a hobby and wanted a special body for his MG-TC. He built a stylish roadster that appears to have drawn inspiration from the Cisitalia Nuvolari Spyder. It had an attractive shape, and the fibreglass body was soon in production for $800 in kit form. At first it was only designed for the MG-TC and TD chassis, but was soon modified to fit any chassis under 100in (2538mm) wheelbase. Some were built with Renault Dauphine running gear.

HP

VALENTINI (I) 1998 to date
Valentini Autoveicoli srl, Ortona.
This company produced the Jadim, a conventional microcar with a steel chassis, MacPherson strut front suspension, coil spring rear suspension, automatic transmission and simple fibreglass bodywork. It was powered by a 505cc 2-cylinder diesel engine or a 523cc Yanmar twin. Later the model was renamed the Smile.

CR

VALERIA (B) 1972
Only two examples of the Valeria 002 sports car were made. Both used a MÉAN Liberta chassis as their basis.

CR

VALIANT (i) see PLYMOUTH (ii)

VALIANT (ii) (RA) 1962–1969
Chrysler Fevre Argentina SA, San Justo, Buenos Aires.
Julio Fevre y Compania started their operations in 1910, when they imported Mors, Delage, Ariès, Delahaye, Berliet, and Delaugère-Clayette automobiles. In 1926 they started to distribute Dodge vehicles in Argentina. In 1928, the company became Fevre & Basset Ltda, commencing the assembly of Chrysler and Dodge vehicles in 1932. In 1959 they associated with Chrysler Argentina SA in order to get under way a local automobile industry. In 1960 Chrysler Fevre Argentina SA started to produce Dodge lorries and in 1962 production of the Valiant I saloon commenced too. The Valiant was identical to the American version, powered by a 6-cylinder 2790cc engine, developing 101bhp. Only the 4-door saloon was available at first. In 1968 badge-engineering policies led to the addition of the Dodge name to the marque, giving birth to the Dodge Valiant. Thereafter all the Chrysler Fevre Argentina SA automobiles would be Dodges, ranging from the Dodge Polara powered by a 6-cylinder 3687cc engine, to the small Dodge 1500cc saloons and pick-up trucks.

ACT

VALIANT (iii) (AUS) 1971–1978
Chrysler Australia Ltd, Tonsley Park, South Australia.
Originally a 1960 Plymouth compact, the Valiant was selected to compete against the runaway Holden success and the Ford Falcon. In Australia it differed by having 14in wheels and an iron block 3.7-litre engine, common to local trucks, rather than the alloy variety as in the US. It was received with enthusiasm, its local content gradually increased and it diverged from home market models but remained a Chrysler until the VH, which was unique to Australia, arrived in 1971, on a 111in (2820mm) wheelbase and fitted with the locally-made 'hemi' engine. A long 115in (2921mm) wheelbase version was the Chrysler CH, while the Mitsubishi Galant and Lancer were badged as Valiant. The 6-cylinder engine was made in 3.5-, 4.0- and 4.3-litre sizes and a short, 105in (2667mm) wheelbase 2-door, the Charger, attracted much attention. The energy crisis favoured the Japanese models but savaged the big cars. The Valiant faded by 1978. Mitsubishi took over in 1980.

MG

VALIENTE (US) 1980s
York Coachworks Inc., Olneg, Illinois.
A convertible 2-seater neo-classic with twin exposed spare wheels. The Classic was designed to accept Lincoln running gear and a 7.5-litre V8 engine.

NG

1899 Vallée (i) 'Slipper'.
NATIONAL MOTOR MUSEUM

VALKYRIE (GB) 1900

Springfield Cycle Co. Ltd, Sandiacre, Nottinghamshire.
The Valkyrie light car resembled a contemporary French voiturette, with 3½hp De Dion-Bouton engine mounted in front under a small bonnet, 3-speed gearbox and shaft drive.

NG

VALLÉE (i) (F) 1895–1902

Sté des Automobiles Vallée, Le Mans, Sarthe.
Born in 1865, Henri Vallée worked with the Bollée family in the 1880s and was chosen by the Marquis de Broc as the engineer responsible for maintaining the steam mail coach which Bollée had made for him in 1885. In 1890 he began to make high-quality bicycles, and five years later built his first car. It had a horizontal 2-cylinder engine made by Vallée himself, a 4-speed gearbox, chain final drive, coil ignition and a tubular frame. The front wheels were located in a modified form of bicycle forks, and the headlights turned with the wheels, surely the first example of this practice. This car was exhibited at the 1895 Cycle Salon in Paris, and the following year Vallée showed two new models, a 4-seater *vis-à-vis* and a larger car made as a 4-seater victoria with all seats facing forwards, or a 6-seater break.

By 1897 Vallée was making cars with engines of 3, 4, 5 or 7hp, and final drive by chains or belts. In 1899 he built an extraordinary racing car which was nicknamed La Pantoufle (the Slipper). It had a 7598cc horizontal 4-cylinder engine developing 16bhp. It had no gearbox as Vallée said that the engine was sufficiently flexible and powerful to make gears unnecessary. Final drive was by a single wide belt to the rear axle. Its best sporting result was Dr Lehwess' fifth place in the Paris–St Malo Race in July 1899. La Pantoufle was a one-off, but Vallée built smaller cars with horizontal 2- or 4-cylinder engines up to 1902, when falling sales brought about the end of the Vallée car. He made motorcycles for a few years from 1905, and later operated a ferry service on the River Sarthe. In July 1916 he drowned in the river after losing his footing on his boat.

NG

1910 Valveless 25hp tourer.
NICK BALDWIN

Further Reading
L'Invention de l'Automobile, Jean-Pierre Delaperrelle, Éditions Cénomane, 1986.

VALLÉE (ii) *see* P. VALLÉE

VALVELESS; LUCAS VALVELESS (GB) 1901–1914

1901–1908 Ralph Lucas, Blackheath, London.
1908–1914 Valveless Cars Ltd, Huddersfield, Yorkshire.
Ralph Lucas was a pioneer of the 2-stroke engine, which he first installed in a car in 1901. It was a vertical twin with a common combustion chamber and transverse crankshafts. There was no reverse gear as this was obtained by reversing the direction of the engine, but on later models an epicyclic reverse gear was provided. An epicyclic gearbox provided two forward speeds, and final drive was

1961 Vanden Plas Princess limousine.
NATIONAL MOTOR MUSEUM

by chain. The cars were bonnetless as the engine was centrally mounted. Lucas worked quietly on his cars for six years without forming a company or selling any, but in 1907 he formed Valveless Cars Ltd with an office in St Martin's Lane, London, and works at Blackheath. One car, by then with a conventional bonnet, although the engine was still under the seats, was exhibited at the 1907 Olympia Show on the stand of Crawshay-Williams which had made cars in 1904–06, and was presumably hoping to sell the Lucas Valveless.

Nothing came of the association with Crawshay-Williams, and no Valveless cars were made commercially until the design was taken up by David Brown of Huddersfield. The car it made had the same basic engine design as Lucas' prototypes, but it was now mounted at the front with longitudinal crankshafts, and drove through a 3-speed gearbox to a worm rear axle. The man chiefly responsible for the David Brown version was Frank Burgess, who later went to Humber and was instrumental in the design of the first 3-litre Bentley. The 3888cc 25hp Valveless was made through the 1911 season, and was then replaced by smaller models of 15 and 20hp (2501 and 3216cc). Several hundred Valveless cars were made up to 1914, but the design was not revived after World War I, and David Brown had no further involvement with car manufacture until it bought Aston Martin and Lagonda in 1947.

NG

VAN (US) 1911–1912
Van Motor Car Co., Grand Haven, Michigan.
Advertised as 'The Car for You', or 'One Best Bet in the Small Car Class', the Van 22 was a roadster powered by a 22hp ohv 4-cylinder engine, with 3-speed gearbox and shaft drive. The company closed its doors in April 1912 after making only a few cars. A planned revival under the name Pioneer never happened.

NG

VANCLEE (B/GB/F) 1978–1996
1978–c.1992 Vanclee Buggy, Egem, Pittem.
1996 Garage Central, Pernes en Artois.
Vanclee's main business was producing beach buggies, an interesting variation on which was the Highway, with its gullwing removable hard-top. From 1978 it also produced a Citroën Méhari style utility car based on a 2CV floorpan. This was variously called the Mungo, Emu/2, Emmet and Rusler. It featured plastic 2-door bodywork in estate, open-top or pick-up configurations. Options included a removable rear hard-top, soft-top and solid fibreglass or soft vinyl doors. Between 1983 and 1992 a company called Van Clee Motors in Belfast (later Lisburn), Northern Ireland, produced the Vanclee under licence with the name Land Ranger and the last cars were made in France.

CR

VANDENBRINK (NL) 1997 to date
Vandenbrink B.V., Rotterdam.
Vandenbrink began conceptual development of a small, lightweight 3-wheeled commuter vehicle in the late 1990s. Initially planned as an eco-friendly commuter vehicle, blending the comfort of a car with the agility and width of a motorcycle, Vandenbrink quickly realised that its trike stood more chance of

commercial success as a fun leisure vehicle than as a serious city car. Thus, in 1998 the project changed direction, and the new Carver used a rear-mounted Honda 660cc turbo K-car engine, developing 64bhp. The Carver had a closed cockpit with tandem seating for two, yet on the road the car handled more like a motorbike, with the front pivoting cab section leaning into bends to give occupants a bike-like sensation. Around 50 Carvers were scheduled for production.

CR

VANDEN PLAS (GB) 1960–1980
1960–1970 Vanden Plas (England) Ltd, London.
1970–1979 Austin-Morris Division, British Leyland Motor Corp. Ltd; BL Cars Ltd, London.
1979–1980 BL Cars Ltd, Abingdon, Oxford.
Vanden Plas was unusual in being a coachbuilder which became a make of car within the British Motor Corp. (later British Leyland). The name originated in Belgium in 1884. In 1946 the British branch of the company, which had been in business at Kingsbury, North London, since 1923, was bought by Austin, and the factory was given over exclusively to making bodies for the Princess luxury saloon, known originally as the A120, but when fitted with the 3995cc engine, as the A135.

In 1952 a long-wheelbase limousine was added to the Princess range, and it was this model that became the first to be badged as a Vanden Plas, in 1960. It was a substantial car, 215in (5460mm) long and weighing 4800lb (2182kg), and offered luxurious and spacious transport at less than half the cost of an equivalent Rolls-Royce. The first two production examples of 1952 were purchased by Her Majesty the Queen, and the limousines were popular with foreign rulers, British ambassadors and mayors in all parts of Britain. They were also used by funeral directors, and quite a number were bodied as hearses, and also as ambulances. The standard body was a limousine with division, but there were also saloons without division, and 18 landaulets built to special order. From about August 1958 the limousine's chassis was also assembled at the Kingsbury works. Total production of the long-wheelbase Princess was 3350, of which 2100 were made under the Vanden Plas name. The model was dropped in 1968, being replaced by the Daimler DS420 limousine which was finished and trimmed by Vanden Plas.

The limousine was the only model unique to Vanden Plas, but several other BMC models have been sold under the Vanden Plas Princess name, including one with a unique engine transplant. From 1959 to 1964 there was the Princess 3-litre, a luxurious version of the 2912cc Austin Westminster. The MkI (1959–61) was based on the A99, and the MkII (1961–64) on the A110 with high-lift camshaft, twin exhausts and floor gearchange. In 1964 the 3-litre hull received a 3909cc 6-cylinder Rolls-Royce B60 engine. This was derived from a Rolls engine for military vehicles, and was never used in a Rolls-Royce car. It was the only example of the prestigious Crewe firm supplying their engines to another car maker, and also the only time for many years that they have quoted the power output, in this case, 175bhp. Also the Borg Warner D8 automatic transmission was fitted for the first time as standard equipment on a British car. The suspension was modified, and the 4-litre rode on smaller wheels than the 3-litre. It could also be distinguished by more rounded rear wings without fins and its own dual colour schemes. Top speed was 112mph (180km/h), and the Princess R, as it was called, promised to be a big seller. Unfortunately, it proved unreliable, and production at the rate of 120 a week was far greater than dealers could cope with. The model was quietly dropped in 1968 after 6555 had been made. This was fewer than the 12,615 3-litre Princesses made.

The other two Vanden Plas models were closely based on BMC designs. The 1100 and 1300 were luxury versions of the AD016, with veneer and leather interior, armrests, picnic tables and other features expected of Vanden Plas. They were made from 1963 to 1968 (1100), and 1967–1974 (1300). Total production of both models was 43,741. The last car to be badged as a Vanden Plas was the Austin Allegro, sold as the Vanden Plas 1500 from 1974 to 1980 (11,842 made). Later models had the 1748cc engine, and in late 1979 assembly was moved from Kingsbury to the MG factory at Abingdon.

Vanden Plas versions of other models were built in prototype form, including the Austin 1800, the front-drive 3-litre and the Princess 18/22, but none of these saw production.

NG

Further Reading
Vanden Plas Coachbuilders, Brian Smith, Dalton Watson, 1979.

1964 Vanden Plas Princess R saloon.
ROVER GROUP/BMIHT/NATIONAL MOTOR MUSEUM

VANDY (GB) 1920–1921

Vandys Ltd, Notting Hill, London.

Major Frank and Lt Percy Vandervell, of the famous C.A.V. company, formed Vandys Ltd in 1919 to sell the Italian-made Chiribiri and S.P.A. cars, and only a year later did they advertise a car of their own. It was a large American-type tourer with a 3772cc 6-cylinder Rutenber engine and in-unit 4-speed gearbox. The radiator, axles and chassis resembled closely the COMMONWEALTH (ii) made in Joliet, Illinois, and the Vandy may well have been the short-lived Commonwealth Victory Six, revamped and with a slightly longer wheelbase. The Vandy's bodies were London-built, and only a 5-seater tourer and all-weather tourer with bulbous back were offered. The car was greatly overpriced at £1050 and although prices were reduced later, sales must have been hard to come by. Estimates of production are as high as 150, but in reality may have been much less. Three found their way to a Carmarthen dealer. The 'works' address at 27A Pembridge Villas, near Notting Hill Gate, was used by Jack Bartlett to sell sports cars in the 1930s.

NG

Further Reading

'What was the Vandy?', M. Worthington-Williams, *The Automobile*, August 1992.

VAN GINK (NL) 1899–1900

Van Gink, Otto Bultman & Co., Amsterdam.

The Van Gink light car was powered by two 2½hp air-cooled engines mounted at the rear, which could be used together or separately. The car, sometimes known as the Hinde, had a tubular frame and a 4-seater body.

NG

VAN LANGENDONCK (B) 1901–1902

Compagnie Générale d'Automobiles Brussels.

A small number of light cars were made (or sold) by this company, with 5hp De Dion-Bouton or 8hp Buchet engines mounted in the front of the frame, and driving by shaft to the rear wheels; 2- and 4-seater bodies were offered.

NG

VANNOD (F) 1958

L. Vannod, Neuilly, Seine.

One of a series of follies at the Paris Motor Show during the 1950s, the Vannod followed an often-tried but always-dismissed idea for a diamond pattern to the wheel layout. The single front and single rear wheel steered, while the two centre wheels provided traction. A Sachs 200cc 2-stroke 10bhp single-cylinder engine was rear-mounted and drove via chain. The driver sat in a central position at the front and two passengers could sit behind him on a bench seat. Entry was gained via a door that swung out on parallelogram hinges.

CR

VANTAGE MOTORSPORTS *see* COMPOSITE AUTO

VAN WAGONER (US) 1899

Barnes Cycle Co., Syracuse, New York.

The Van Wagoner electric car was made in two models, a 2-seater runabout and a 6-seater tourer. Few were built because the Barnes Cycle Co. was sold to the American Bicycle Co. in mid-1899. Designer William Van Wagoner moved to the American Bicycle Co.'s Ohio plant, but returned to Syracuse to make steam, petrol and electric cars under the name CENTURY.

NG

VANWALL (GB) 1991

Vandervell Ltd, Maidenhead, Berkshire.

A famous Grand Prix name was set to be revived as a mid-engined roadgoing supercar project in 1991 by the then-owners of the name, Vandervell Ltd. A scale model was produced for wind tunnel testing and Frank Costin was called in to help with aerodynamics; the coupé bodywork was styled by Simon Saunders. Production was due to begin in 1993 with a V8 engine but the general downturn in interest in such cars forced the abandonment of the revival.

CR

1903 Vapomobile 12hp steam car.
NATIONAL MOTOR MUSEUM

1924 Var 300cc 2-seater.
NICK BALDWIN

1920 Varley-Woods 11.9hp tourer.
NICK BALDWIN

VAN WALLEGHEM (B) 1902

Van Walleghem et Compagnie, Brussels.
This company specialised in the maintenance and repair of motor cars, but assembled a few voiturettes with 6hp De Dion-Bouton engines and 3-speed gearboxes.
NG

VAN WAMBEKE (US) 1907–1909

H.F. Van Wambeke, Elgin, Illinois.
Van Wambeke and his sons ran a grocery store, at the rear of which they assembled eight high-wheelers powered by 2-cylinder 10hp engines, with epicyclic transmission and chain final drive. Most were completed as delivery wagons, although a few were runabouts.
NG

VAPOMOBILE (GB) 1902–1904

Motor Construction Co. Ltd, Nottingham.
This was a light steam car designed very much on American lines, although the makers claimed that it was manufactured entirely in England and was consequently very much stronger than the American steamers. However, the 12hp model was known to use an American-built Mason engine. It had wheel steering, while the smaller 5hp and 7hp Vapomobiles were tiller steered. In 1903 the makers said that they used both American and English engines, quoting a higher price for the latter.
NG

VAR (A) 1924

Gianni Varrone, Hard, Vorarlberg.
Varrone was an Italian-Swiss engineer who designed a small car powered by a 300cc flat-twin 2-stroke engine with wooden chassis and body panels of imitation leather. This gave a very light weight of 616lb (280kg), but as the engine developed only 6.5bhp, top speed was no more than 25mph (40km/h). Varrone planned to build a more powerful car with 4-stroke engine, but could get no backing for his projects. These involved a pre-series of 10 cars and an initial production run of 100, but only one prototype was ever made.
NG

VARLEY-WOODS (GB) 1918–1921

1918–1919 High Speed Tool Co. Ltd, Acton, London.
1919–1920 H.S. Motors Ltd, Acton, London; Wolverhampton, Staffordshire.
1920–1921 Turner's Motor Manufacturing Co. Ltd, Wolverhampton, Staffordshire.
The men behind the Varley-Woods were more colourful than the car itself, which was an assembled machine of no great distinction. Ernest Vernon Varley Grossmith was a member of the theatrical and perfumery family and related to George and Weedon Grossmith, authors of the immortal *Diary of a Nobody*. His own talents were more commercial, and included the manufacture of tinned soup and mouth organs, and dealing in Government surplus goods. In 1918, before the war ended, he formed the High Speed Tool Co., operating from a disused laundry in Acton. One of his partners was an African river trader, John Robert Woods, who had returned to England in the hope of making the fortune which seemed to have eluded him in Nyasaland. In October 1918 Grossmith resigned from High Speed Tools (the kind of tools or how many they made is not known), dropped his German-sounding last name, and as Ernest Varley planned to make a car called the Varley-Woods. High Speed Tools became High Speed Motors and a few cars were assembled using French components such as Decolonge engines acquired from the STOREY company. The chassis were supplied by TURNER (ii) of Wolverhampton.

H.S. Motors was soon in financial difficulties, and, threatened by bailiffs in the summer of 1919, it moved all the machine tools from the laundry to premises in Wolverhampton. Here it continued to use Turner-made chassis, and bought its engines from Dorman of Stafford. These were the 1794cc 4-cylinder KNO model, with pushrod ohvs, which were used in conjunction with a 4-speed gearbox of Varley-Woods' own manufacture. Final drive was by shaft to an overhead worm rear axle.

In mid-1920 a change of engine was made, the new unit being a 2303cc side-valve Tylor. There was no particular advantage in this change, because the new engine had a larger bore and therefore attracted a higher tax rate. The most likely reason was that Varley-Woods had run out of credit at Dorman. The new cars were very expensive, at £725 for a tourer and £1200 for a limousine. By October 1920 the company was unable to pay the rent on the Wolverhampton factory and the Receiver was called in. Probably a few more cars were made by Turner's, which was also doubtless owed money. About 160 Dorman-engined cars were made, and an undisclosed, but very small, number with the Tylor engine.

After the debacle Varley sold his large country house and moved to a cottage in Cornwall. Woods returned to Nyasaland where he was eaten by a lion.
NG
Further Reading
'The Other VW', Peter Wallage, *The Automobile*, July 1988.

VARSITY (US) 1910

University Motor Car Co., Detroit, Michigan.
This company planned to make a 4-cylinder car selling for around $1300–$1350. Pilot models were made, but production never started. The name Varsity was also used for a model of the ADAMS (ii).

NG

VASKO (E) 1996–1998

Replicas Vasko, Tenerife, Canary Islands.
Two German fibreglass specialists offered different convertibles on a Volkswagen platform, as well as buggies, speedsters and trikes. The special Serpiente was a Cobra lookalike on a Beetle chassis using a Golf engine of 105bhp. Bodies were made of plastic and fibreglass.

VCM

V.A.T.E. (F) 1908

Voitures Automobiles de Transmission Électrique, Paris.
This short-lived car was unusual in that it combined a small 2-cylinder engine with petrol-electric transmission. The 10hp engine drove a combination dynamo and motor mounted in the flywheel, from which power was taken by propeller shaft to the rear axle.

NG

VAUCELLE (F) 1952–1953

This was a steel-bodied convertible microcar with four wheels, the front pair on swing axles and the rear pair on a differential-less rigid axle. A front-mounted 125cc Aubier & Dunne single-cylinder 2-stroke engine was used.

CR

VAUGHAN (US) 1910–1914

1910–1912 Wyckoff, Church & Partridge Inc., Kingston, New York.
1914 Vaughan Car Co., Kingston, New York.
Guy Vaughan was a dirt track racing driver who drove for Chadwick and Stearns. He designed a large touring car on a 120in (3046mm) wheelbase, powered by a 30hp 4-cylinder engine. The first firm he chose to manufacture the car, the W.A. Wood Manufacturing Co., folded before a single car was made, and then merged with Wyckoff, Church & Partridge who were also planning to make the British Commer truck under licence. They were soon in trouble as well, though a few cars were made. Guy Vaughan left to join Oldsmobile, followed by Stearns. In 1914 a new car, designed by Fred Moskovics, appeared under the Vaughan name; it was a 34hp six on a 138in (3502mm) wheelbase, made as a roadster or tourer. That lasted only a year, with few cars completed. Moskovics did much better with the Safety Stutz in the 1920s.

NG

VAUGHN (i) (US) 1921, 1923

1921 American-Southern Motors Corp., Greensboro, North Carolina.
1923 Irving Automobile Co., Greensboro, North Carolina.
The American-Southern Motors Corp. was formed to assemble the AMERICAN of Plainfield, New Jersey, for distribution in the southern United States in 1920. A year later, the decision was made to market a new high-powered luxury automobile to be named the Vaughn after a Greensboro banker, Robert G. Vaughn, agreed to finance such a car. Following a period of road testing, the Vaughn was launched at the 'Made in Carolinas' Exposition at Greensboro in September 1921. The Vaughn was a 5-seater sport-touring model powered by a Weidely V12 engine and riding on a wheelbase of 127in (3223mm). The Vaughn weighed nearly 5000lbs (2273kg) and was priced at $3995. Production was scheduled with both the Weidely-powered series and a companion line which would feature a Rochester-Duesenberg 4-cylinder engine. But production did not follow for either series. In December 1921 American-Southern Motors became a dealership – the Irving Automobile Co. Nothing further appeared concerning the Vaughn throughout 1922, the name resurfacing in the Spring of 1923 when further production was announced. It never came, although the new, lower-priced Vaughn did reach the prototype stage.

KM

1907 Vauxhall (i) 18hp landaulet.
NICK BALDWIN

VAUGHN (ii) (US) c.1952–1954

Vaughn Motors, New York, New York.
Bill Vaughn had an imported car dealership in New York and dabbled in limited-edition speciality cars based on his imports. The 1952 Vaughn-Singer was a GLASSPAR-bodied Singer. They intended to build a line of sports and competition cars based on a magnesium-block engine developing 129hp. This was to have been mounted in a tubular frame. Vaughn claimed to be moulding the fibreglass bodies at plants in California, Florida and Massachusetts, so perhaps he was building them under licence from Glasspar. The 1954 Vaughn V8 Wildcat was a Ghia-bodied Abarth chassis with an ohc 1500cc V8 of unspecified origin, most likely Fiat. It was a bulbous coupé with partially shrouded wheels. Optional engines included a 1300cc V8 and a 750cc 4-cylinder. Price was to be $3000 for the top-of-the-line V8 coupé.

HP

VAUTRIN (F) 1951

Productions M. Vautrin, Choisy-le-Roi.
The Vautrin was a handsome 2- to 3-seater convertible of very compact dimensions (only 104in (2650mm) long and weighing 330lb/150kg). It was powered by engines of 125, 175, 250 or 350cc and could attain a maximum speed of up to 56mph (90km/h) depending on which engine was fitted.

CR

VAUXHALL (i) (GB) 1903 to date

1903–1904 Vauxhall Iron Works Ltd, London.
1905–1906 Vauxhall Iron Works Ltd, Luton, Bedfordshire.
1906–1907 Vauxhall & West Hydraulic Engineering Co. Ltd, Luton, Bedfordshire.
1907 to date Vauxhall Motors Ltd, Luton Bedfordshire; Ellesmere Port, Cheshire.
Vauxhall Motors Ltd is today the British branch of General Motors, and the second largest vehicle producer in Great Britain. Their history as car makers dates back to 1903, but the parent company began making marine engines in 1857. The name comes from Vauxhall Gardens, which was located near the works in south London, and is a corruption of Fulk's Hall, named after a 13th century knight, Fulk le Breant, who owned the land. By a curious coincidence, when Vauxhall Motors moved to Luton in 1907, it turned out that the land on which they built their factory had also been part of Fulk le Breant's property. The Griffin, chosen as the trademark of Vauxhall Motors, was le Breant's crest.

The parent company was Alex Wilson & Co., founded by Scottish engineer Alexander Wilson to make a variety of engines for the river craft of the Thames, though they later became suppliers to the Royal Navy as well. The name was changed to Vauxhall Iron Works Ltd in 1897, and shortly afterwards they began to experiment with petrol engines, one of which was fitted to a river launch. It was a development of this single-cylinder unit which went into the first Vauxhall

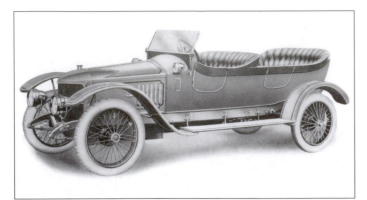

1913 Vauxhall (i) C-type Prince Henry tourer.
NICK BALDWIN

1913 Vauxhall (i) D-type 25hp Norfolk tourer.
NICK BALDWIN

1921 Vauxhall (i) D-type 25hp Warwick landaulet by Grosvenor.
NICK BALDWIN

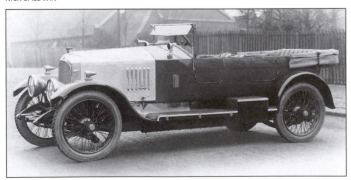

1922 Vauxhall (i) OE-type 30/98 tourer by Grosvenor.
NATIONAL MOTOR MUSEUM

car, made in 1903. Designed by F.W. Hodges and J.H. Chambers, who later made the CHAMBERS car in Belfast, it had a horizontal engine of 978cc, with trembler coil ignition, 2-speed epicyclic gearbox (without reverse) and single-chain drive. The armoured wood frame was suspended on coil springs at each corner, and steering was by tiller. In many ways it was more typical of American practice than European, though the engine was located under the short bonnet, not under the seat as in most small American cars.

About 70 cars were sold during the first year of trading, and in 1904 improvements included wheel steering, a reverse gear and a larger engine of 1029cc, justifying a change of name from 5 to 6hp. The 2-seater cost £136, but for an extra £6 one could have a front seat over the engine, for one adult or two children. Total production of the single-cylinder Vauxhalls was about 105, and they were not made after the end of 1904. Instead the company joined the ranks of the 3-cylinder protagonists; the in-line three was a fashionable layout in 1905, supporters including Panhard and Rolls-Royce. The Vauxhall engine was a T-head unit made in three sizes, 1293cc (7/9hp), 1435cc (9hp) and 2431cc (12/14hp). They now had three forward speeds as well as reverse, and double-chain drive. 2- or 4-seater bodies were made, and the chassis was also used for two designs of taxicab. In one the driver was seated over the engine, but the other placed him behind the passengers in the hansom cab position. Five of these actually saw service in London, but were not very popular with passengers. As *The Commercial Motor* said, 'even to hardened motorists, the apparent rushing straight into danger without being able to see that the driver is doing anything to avert it must be at times disconcerting'. Total production of all the 3-cylinder models was about 110.

Luton and 4-cylinder Cars

The premises of the Vauxhall Iron Works were very cramped, as marine engines were still made, and final assembly of the cars had to take place in the yard of a neighbouring brewery. In 1905, therefore, they moved to a new factory built on open land at Luton. Marine engines were continued, even though the new premises were a long way from the River Thames, but doubtless the fact that a railway siding ran straight into the works helped with deliveries. At the Motor Show in November 1905 Vauxhall showed their first 4-cylinder car, the 3336cc 18hp. This still had the T-head layout, with separately cast cylinders, and chain drive, though bevel was offered as an alternative, and was soon standardised. Hodges also experimented with six cylinders around 1905, but the chain-driven car with what seems to be two 3-cylinder units in line never saw production. For 1907 the 18 was replaced by a slightly smaller four with only 3-speeds, the 2354cc 12/16. About 100 were made of both types in three seasons, so production was still modest. Vauxhall was, however, on the verge of greater things.

Prince Henry and 30/98

In the winter of 1907–08 chief engineer Hodges took a long holiday in Egypt, and during his absence managing director Percy Kidner decided to enter three cars in the RAC 2000 Mile Trial. The task of extracting reasonable performance was given to a 24-year old draughtsman, Laurence Pomeroy (1883–1941). He redesigned the existing power unit completely, with a single camshaft operating the valves in an L-head, and monobloc casting of the cylinders. The 3054cc engine gave 40bhp, compared with about 23bhp from the previous 3336cc unit. Three cars were entered in the Trial, and Kidner's was victorious, defeating a Rolls-Royce 40/50. This marked the end of Hodges' regime, and for the next eleven years the engineering department was headed by Laurence Pomeroy.

The 20hp, or A-type, was made up to 1914, about 950 being built, and carried a wide variety of coachwork from landaulets to streamlined racing shells. The first of the latter appeared in 1909; based on a 20hp chassis whose output had been increased from 40 to 52bhp, it had a long pointed nose leading to a narrow single-seater body, and disc wheels. On the nose was painted its name, KN (as hot as cayenne pepper). With this car works driver A.J. Hancock covered a flying half mile at 88.62mph (142.62km/h).

Several other streamlined Vauxhalls competed at Brooklands in the years 1910 to 1913, their achievements including a flying half mile at 100.06 mph (161.03km/h) (October 1910), and a series of World and Class records including four hours at 91.64mph (147.47km/h) in 1913. The latter were achieved by KN2, powered by a 3969cc engine as used in the C-type Prince Henry.

Encouraged by the 2000 Mile Trial success, Kidner decided to enter two cars in the 1910 Prince Henry Trials. Pomeroy worked their output up to about 60bhp at 2800rpm and they carried narrow doorless 4-seater bodies fronted by pointed vee-radiators. They were no match for the much bigger Austro-

NICK BALDWIN

POMEROY, LAURENCE (1883–1941)

One of Britain's most distinguished motor engineers, and designer of two very different cars, the Prince Henry Vauxhall and the 30hp Double Six Daimler, Laurence Henry Pomeroy was born in London and served an apprenticeship with the North London Railway Co. After completing his day's work he would walk several miles to study at a technical institute, and was seldom in bed before midnight. His first motor industry job was as a junior draughtsman with Thornycroft at Basingstoke, and in 1905 he joined Vauxhall Motors, which had recently moved to Luton, again as a junior draughtsman. When their chief engineer F. W. Hodges left for a long holiday in Egypt in the winter of 1907–08 Pomeroy took the opportunity to press ahead with his 16/20hp 4-cylinder car. With 40bhp, monobloc casting, pressure lubrication and running at up to 2500rpm, when many designers were content with half that speed, it was an advanced design. Three took part in the RAC's 2000 Mile Trial when the example driven by Percy Kidner put up the best performance at Brooklands, lapping at 46.13mph (74.22km/h) as well as recording the best fuel consumption in its class. *The Motor Car Journal* commented 'That performance brought Vauxhall from a comparatively uninteresting background into the full glare of public interest', while the great historian Michael Sedgwick wrote 'Nobody would dismiss Luton again as merely the home of the straw hat'.

One hopes that Hodges enjoyed his Egyptian holiday, for on his return he was rapidly replaced by Pomeroy, who was made Works Manager, and was effectively in charge of design work for the next ten years. In 1913, at the age of 30, he was elected a full member of the Institution of Mechanical Engineers, the youngest man ever to achieve this distinction.

The 3-litre 20hp engine powered a number of sporting cars, including streamlined models which took many records at Brooklands, an entry in the 1911 Coupe des Voitures Légères, and three 4-seater doorless sporting tourers which were entered in the 1910 Prince Henry Trials in Germany. Output was now 60bhp with no increase in engine size. Trouble-free runs encouraged the makers to offer the cars to the public for the 1911 season. It has a good claim to be the first sports car, for its performance was achieved by carefully thought-out design rather than just by increasing engine size. Pomeroy *did* increase the capacity in 1913, to 4 litres, and then to 4½ litres on the Prince Henry's successor, the 30/98. This gave 90bhp and became one of Britain's best-known sports cars in the 1920s.

Pomeroy was also responsible for Vauxhall's touring cars, including the D-type which was so widely used as a staff car in World War I. Throughout the war he was active, not only at Vauxhall but also in the Institute of Automobile Engineers, of which he became president in 1934–35. Early in the war he spoke to the Institute, complaining about the poor quality of steel from British suppliers, which he said was greatly inferior to Continental steel.

In 1919 Pomeroy left Vauxhall, apparently because they allowed budgetary constraints to interfere with interesting lines of investigation. At the time of his departure he was working on an ohc six and L-head V12, neither of which was favoured by the board. His resignation prompted Fred Lanchester to suggest that Daimler approach him. 'If I had shares in Vauxhall', he said 'I would sell them quick. I do not know who they have got there capable of running the business. It was as nearly a one-man show as anything in the country'. Pomeroy did go to Daimler eventually, but only after a seven-year stint in America.

There he worked for the Aluminium Co. of America (Alcoa), trying to perfect a car which used a high proportion of aluminium alloy. It was not 'all aluminium' as had been claimed, for the engine had cast-iron sleeves in an aluminium block. The bodies were all aluminium, and were built by the American Body Co. in Buffalo, New York. Pomeroy persuaded them to include Vauxhall-like bonnet Flutes. Four cars were made at Cleveland, where Pomeroy was assisted by Forrest Cameron, and three more by Pierce-Arrow at Buffalo. Pomeroy said of Alcoa that 'they do not allow financial considerations to interfere when they think that any line of investigation has a reasonable chance of leading to success'. They apparently spent several hundred thousand dollars on the aluminium cars, but the project was wound up in 1924.

In 1926 an association was set up between Daimler and AEC (Associated Equipment Co.), makers of London's buses, the new concern being called Associated Daimler. Percy Martin of Daimler heard that Pomeroy would soon be looking for fresh work, and a month before ADC was formed he cabled him in America inviting him to be consultant to Daimler, the Associated Equipment Co. and the London General Omnibus Co. He was invited to name his terms which were a salary of £4000 per annum after income tax, or £3000 plus commission. He and Martin settled on £3500 plus a bonus to be arranged as early as possible, and he took up his post in October 1926, succeeding Algernon Berriman. He was not responsible for the original Double Six, which was announced in the same month that he arrived at Daimler, but he worked on the smaller 30hp model, as well as the low-chassis Double Six of which only three of four were made. He also designed the advanced CF6 coach chassis which made extensive use of aluminium alloys, and the CG6 bus chassis in 1930, followed in 1932 by the poppet-valve engined CP6. The ADC combine lasted only until 1928, but the following year Pomeroy became Managing Director of Daimler. He was responsible for the introduction of the fluid flywheel, initially in conjunction with a conventional 3-speed gearbox, and then with a self-changing epicyclic transmission which proved much more satisfactory.

Daimler's acquisition of Lanchester in 1931 was very satisfying to Pomeroy, who now had access to a medium-sized poppet-valve engine, the 15/18hp Lanchester unit. He also launched the smaller 1.8-litre Daimler Fifteen, but this proved to be his undoing, or rather it gave the opportunity to those who thought the company's future lay with larger cars to work against him. Percy Martin retired in 1935 and the new chairman Geoffrey Burton forced Pomeroy's resignation in May 1936. He then joined De Havilland Aircraft as general manager of their engine division; then, in November 1938, set up on his own as a patent consultant. This cannot have been very profitable, for he joined the Claudel Hobson carburettor company. He died in May 1941 of a heart attack, aged 58. In his obituary *The Autocar* said that he had a brilliant wit, and would have won fame as a KC if he had chosen the law instead of engineering.

Laurence Pomeroy had one son, also named Laurence, who became a well-known technical journalist and author of several definitive books including *The Grand Prix Car, 1906–1939*. He died in 1966, at the same age and of the same ailment as his father.

NG

c.1925 Vauxhall (i) OD-type 23/60 coupé.
NICK BALDWIN

1928 Vauxhall (i) R-type 20/60 saloon.
NICK BALDWIN

Daimlers, but two of the three cars made non-stop runs. Replicas went on sale towards the end of 1911; officially they were known as the C-type, but they have gone down in history as the Prince Henry model. The standard model had no doors and a bulbous back, but the factory also offered a model with small doors

which extended about half way down the body sides, and a straighter back. With a top speed of around 75mph (120km/h), and a price of £580 they were good value, and acquired a reputation for good handling and flexible performance on top gear. They were widely used in hill climbs and reliability trials; among their better achievements abroad were a penalty-free performance in the 1911 St Petersburg–Sebastopol Trials, and two clear runs for Kidner and local driver Klellgren in the 1912 Swedish Winter Trials. Their Russian successes earned them a significant foothold in the market there; Tsar Nicholas II had at least two, and of the 13 prewar 30/98s, three found their way to St Petersburg.

For 1913 the Prince Henry's engine capacity was enlarged to 3969cc, giving the same power at a lower speed of 2500rpm. Electric lighting was standard, and starters were available from 1914. The model was made up to early 1915, total production being 140 cars, compared with 50 of the smaller-engined Prince Henry. Although it had a satisfactory enough performance for most people, the Prince Henry could not compete with the fastest machinery in hill climbs and sprints, and at the suggestion of a well-known sportsman, John Higginson, Pomeroy developed a larger engine of 4525cc to be used in the Prince Henry chassis. This was known as the 30/98, probably because it developed 30bhp at 1000rpm, and a theoretical 98bhp at its maximum speed of 3000rpm. Also the cylinder bore was 98mm.

The Prince Henry's vee-radiator was abandoned as it was not a very efficient cooler, and the 30/98 had a flat radiator which characterised all Vauxhalls made after the war. Only 13 were made before the war, and they were not on general sale. Some were kept by the works, and the others were sold only to proven competition drivers who could be trusted to enhance Vauxhall's reputation. The price of £900 would have kept sales low, anyway.

Vauxhall entered a number of international races between 1912 and 1914, though without great success. For the 1911 Coupe de Voitures Légères and 1912 Coupe de l'Auto they used Prince Henry engines destroked to bring them within the 3-litre limit, but did not finish in either year. For the 1913 Coupe de l'Auto they used similar cars with 30/98-style radiators, and Hancock managed 4th place. Pomeroy designed some advanced cars for the Grand Prix and TT of

1914. They had bevel-driven twin-ohc engines, hydraulic shock absorbers and cantilever rear suspension. The inlet manifold was warmed by water from the radiator, a practice also seen on the Coupe de l'Auto Sunbeams. Engine capacity was 3.3-litres for the TT and 4¹/₂-litres for the Grand Prix, but both events were disasters for Vauxhalls, with no cars among the finishers. The TT cars did redeem themselves at Brooklands after the war, however.

There were only three touring models during the years 1910 to 1914, the A-type, a large 4525cc six, later enlarged to 5103cc, called the B-type, and the Prince Henry-derived D-type. The prototype B-type had a 3473cc monobloc engine, but all the cars that reached the public had cylinders cast in threes. It was a large and expensive car, with wheelbases up to 144in (3655mm) and costing as much as £1070 for a limousine. About 75 were made, compared with 950 A-types. The D-type had the same engine dimensions as the larger Prince Henry, but output was only 60bhp and it always came with a flat radiator. As with its sporting sister, electric lighting was standard, and a starter optional from 1914, standard from 1919. Although they overlapped for two seasons, the D-type took over the A-type's role, and was made in much larger numbers than any previous Vauxhalls, thanks to substantial orders from the War Office. In open and closed form it was the standard British staff car, and saw service on the Western Front and in the Middle East. A D-type was the first car to cross the Rhine into Germany after the signing of the Armistice in 1918. It remained in production until 1922, with more than 4500 being made.

The Vintage Vauxhalls

In 1919 Laurence Pomeroy left Vauxhall to work for the Aluminium Co. of America. Before he left he had designed two new engines, a 4.4-litre single-ohc six and a 3¹/₂-litre L-head V12; both ran in experimental cars but neither saw production. His successor was C.E. King who improved on the prewar designs but produced no startling innovations, apart from a twin-ohc racing car which never fulfilled its promise, and a sleeve-valve six which sold only 50 units. Immediate postwar production was confined to the D-type for touring or closed coachwork, and the E-type 30/98 for the sportsman. The latter was one of the finest fast tourers of the decade, with a slow-revving engine and high axle ratio (3.08:1) which enabled 80mph (129km/h) to be reached without undue stress. The brakes were less satisfactory, but on the uncrowded roads of the early 1920s this did not matter too much. The standard body was an open 4-seater called the Velox, but 2-seaters were also made, and the later OE 30/98 could be had with a pointed tail 4-seater body with flared wings, called the Wensum. This was also factory-made, but cost an extra £150. A few 2-door saloons by Grosvenor were made. The OE was introduced in 1922, and had a slightly smaller engine (4224cc) with ohvs which developed 112bhp to the E-type's 90bhp. A lower rear axle ratio of 3.3:1 was used, so performance was about the same. The straight bevel axle was replaced by a spiral bevel. Front-wheel brakes were available from mid-1923, at a cost of £25, and in 1926 hydraulic brakes became standard equipment. Production of the 30/98 dwindled after 1924, with the occasional batch of 50 or so chassis being put through, but the last was not completed until early 1927. Deliveries continued through the year. Total 30/98 production was 596, of which 13 were made before the war, 270 were E-types and 313, OE-types. More than 170 survive, especially in Australia where they were very popular, and they are among the most highly prized vintage cars.

The 30/98 was not raced to anything like the extent of the Bentley, and never appeared at Le Mans. This was because the makers regarded it as a fast tourer rather than a sports car, and did not maintain a competition department except for the short-lived TT racing car. Private owners, however, had many successes with their 30/98s, in particular Humphrey Cook whose 2-seater *Rouge et Noir* was an outstanding hill climber of its day. Although they did not race the 30/98, the works did guarantee 100mph (161km/h) from any stripped example, and they did build one or two racing cars to customers' orders.

The only car for which they set up a competition department was the 3-litre TT model of 1922. This may have been designed with the 1921 Grand Prix in mind, for the specification fitted with the GP regulations, but it was not ready until 1922. It was an advanced design, with gear-driven twin-ohcs operating four valves per cylinder, roller bearing big ends, 4-wheel brakes (uncoupled though they were air-assisted) and a differential-less rear axle. Two ran in the TT, but the best place was 3rd, and the works did not race them again. Several years later, one of the TT cars was used by Raymond Mays and Amhurst Villiers for their experiments with supercharging, and developed more than 200bhp with twin blowers. Known as the Vauxhall Villiers or Villiers Supercharge, it

1931 Vauxhall (i) Cadet saloon.
NICK BALDWIN

1936 Vauxhall (i) DX saloon.
NICK BALDWIN

enabled Mays to reduce the Shelsley Walsh hill climb record steadily between 1928 and 1933.

The other Vauxhalls of the 1920s were all touring models. In an effort to reach a wider market and to avoid the penalties of the £1 per horsepower tax, King introduced the 14/40 M-type for 1922. This had a 2297cc engine with detachable head, spiral-bevel rear axle and disc wheels. 1922 prices ran from £720 to £750, whereas a D cost £1100 and an E, £1195. In 1924 it became the LM with 4-speed gearbox, balloon tyres and wire wheels. A wider range of bodies was offered, with attractive names such as the Princeton tourer, Melton 2-seater, Bedford saloon, Kimberley limousine, Wyvern landaulet and Grafton coupé. Most of these were made by Grosvenor, who were Vauxhall's 'tame coachbuilders' between the wars, and were also available on the 23/60 chassis. About 5300 14/40s were made between 1922 and 1927. In 1922 the D-type received ohvs, becoming the OD or 23/60, and about 1400 were made up to 1926. Largest and rarest of the touring models was the S-type 25/70 which replaced the OD and had a 3881cc 6-cylinder sleeve-valve engine built to Burt McCollum patents. It was a large and heavy car, weighing more than 5600lb (2540kg) with closed coachwork, and cost £1350 for a tourer, £200 more than a 30/98. It was launched at the 1925 Olympia Show, just as General Motors were about to take control of Vauxhall, and was not the sort of car at all which the American giant wanted from their British subsidiary. Nevertheless, about 50 were made up to 1928, just as 30/98 production was allowed to trickle on while GM prepared their new model.

The General Motors Era

In his inimitable way Michael Sedgwick summed up the effect of the GM take-over by saying, 'Between 1925 and 1937 fun went out the door, and black ink appeared in the ledgers'. It is not quite fair to imply that there was a lot of red ink

1939 Vauxhall (i) GL 25hp limousine by Grosvenor.
NICK BALDWIN

1939 Vauxhall (i) J 14hp saloon.
NICK BALDWIN

1955 Vauxhall (i) E-type Velox saloon.
NICK BALDWIN

1957 Vauxhall (i) F-type Victor saloon.
NICK BALDWIN

before, for Vauxhall had made a good profit in 1924/5, and were just in the black for 1925/6. However, it is quite likely that without the GM involvement, they would not have weathered the Depression, and they would certainly not have survived to be the major car maker they are today.

The first Vauxhall planned under GM control was the R-type 20/60, which was launched for 1928. It had a 2762cc 6-cylinder ohv engine with coil ignition, central gearchange for the 4-speed gearbox, artillery or wire wheels and a wide range of conventional-looking bodywork, some of which bore the same names as those on the 14/40. The standard tourers and saloons were made by Vauxhall, but Grosvenor contributed a number of 'semi-custom' styles, as they continued to do during the next decade. Capacity went up to 2916cc for 1929, when a long-wheelbase chassis was available. The 20/60 was £100 cheaper than the 14/40, and sold quite well, 4228 in 1928 and 1929. It was replaced for 1930 by the generally similar T-type which had a higher radiator and mechanical pump feed in place of Autovac. All T-types had wire wheels, and among the large number of bodies offered was the Hurlingham 2-seater sports, the only sporting model offered prewar under the GM regime.

For 1931 the T became the T80 with 3317cc engine. Only 1172 Ts and 624 T80s were made, because Vauxhall were getting into production with a smaller and cheaper car, the Cadet. If the 20/60 was the first GM Vauxhall, the Cadet established the Luton marque in the popular field, and was the beginning of a line of small 6-cylinder cars which lasted until after World War II. It had a 2048cc engine and 107in (2718mm) wheelbase, compared with 123in or 130in (3124 or 3302mm) for the 20/60. The gearbox had only 3-speeds, but from 1932 it offered synchromesh, Britain's first, which was only fitting, coming from the corporation which had launched synchromesh on the world in the 1929 Cadillac and La Salle. Cadet prices started at £275 for a tourer. With an eye to exports, the Cadet was the first Vauxhall to be offered with lhd. An export special was the VX model powered by a 3180cc engine shared with the Bedford truck. The Cadet was made from 1931 to 1933, with 9691 being delivered. This figure was exceeded by the Light Six which arrived in May 1933, and of which 23,294 were made of the original ASY/ASX models, and 59,563 of later derivatives. They had two sizes of engine, 1530cc in the Y series and 1781cc in the X series, the latter being made in much larger numbers. 4-speed gearboxes were now featured, and Dubonnet coil ifs appeared on the DY/DX of 1935. The mid-1930s was the peak period for special bodies on Vauxhalls, and many varying styles were offered on the Light Six, not only by Grosvenor, but also by Abbey, Duple, Offord, Whittingham & Mitchel and others. Some of the Grosvenor coupés were similar to Opels, although it would be a long time before the two European GM products became almost indistinguishable, as they are today. In 1935 V.C. Cars of Streatham offered a 4-seater sports tourer with a body by Abbott on the DX14/6 chassis, with raked steering column, shallower radiator, and flattened rear springs.

The Light Six's larger companion was the Big Six (1934–36), which became the Twenty Five in 1937. This had the more rounded body and forward engine mounting of the 1935 DY/DX Light Six, though not its ifs. Two engines were offered, 2393cc in the BY and 3180cc in the BX, and features included built-in trafficators, automatic chassis lubrication and 'pedomatic' starting, effected by depressing the accelerator; the latter was familiar on American-made GM products. There was also a long-wheelbase Big Six for formal coachwork, called the BXL. This was only available with the bigger engine, and 796 were made. Sales of the BX and BY were 227 and 3561 respectively, a reversal of the Light Six sales where the bigger engine was much more popular. For 1937 the Big Six became the Twenty Five with slightly larger engine of 3215cc (no smaller option now), hydraulic brakes and torsion bar front suspension. It shared the vee-grill and pressed steel wheels with the contemporary Light Six, and was made in two wheelbases, 110 or 130in (2794 or 3302mm). Grosvenor built limousines and even a few sedanca de villes and landaulets on the long chassis, while there were also some ambulances by Lomas. These were practically the only commercial vehicles to carry Vauxhall badges, as all the car-based vans made at Luton were sold as Bedfords. The Twenty Five, like its smaller sisters, was exported to Australia in chassis form, where some local body styles were made by Holden. These included the fastback coupés known as 'slopers', also seen on Chevrolet, Oldsmobile and Pontiac chassis. Total production of all Twenty Fives was 6822. They were the last Vauxhalls to have a separate chassis, apart from a few Australian specials.

The New

VAUXHALL

10

FOUR

1960 Vauxhall (i) PA-type Velox saloon.
NICK BALDWIN

1963 Vauxhall (i) HA Viva saloon.
NICK BALDWIN

Integral Construction

Integral construction had been pioneered in GM cars with the Opel Olympia, and the 1937 Earls Court Show saw the debut of Vauxhall's H-type Ten. This took Vauxhall into a new field, being a rival to the Ford and Morris Tens and Hillman Minx. It had a 1203cc 4-cylinder ohv engine, 3-speed gearbox, hydraulic brakes and the same torsion bar ifs as the Twenty Five. The great majority were 4-door 4-light saloons, but there were a few 2-door coupés as well. With a top speed of 65mph (105km/h), and a price of £182 the Ten was good value, and sold 42,245 up to 1940. For 1939 it was joined by the Twelve-Four, a lengthened Ten with 6-light body and 1442cc engine, and by the Fourteen-Six. This replaced the DX Light Six, using the same 1781cc engine in an new unitary construction hull in the same style as the smaller Vauxhalls. A bonus for Fourteen-Six customers was synchromesh on bottom gear. It was revived after the war, total production up to 1948 being 45,499 cars.

The 1930s had seen a remarkable growth in Vauxhall production, from 1277 cars in 1930 to 34,367 in 1939. The 1930 figure represented less than 1 per cent of all UK production, but in 1939 Vauxhalls accounted for more than 10 per cent.

Fourteens and Twenty Fives were widely used as staff cars in World War II, just as the D-type had been in the previous conflict, and Vauxhall were quick to get back into production. Their postwar range, announced in December 1945, consisted of the Ten-Four, Twelve-Four and Fourteen-Six, little changed from prewar models, though the Ten now had an external spare wheel. At first the

Twelve used the prewar 6-light body, but it was soon decided that three body shells was an extravagance that could not be supported in the austerity years, and from March 1946 it had the 1442cc engine in the same body as the Ten. The smaller engine was dropped in the summer of 1947, leaving the Twelve and Fourteen to carry on until new models appeared in the summer of 1948. Combined production of the Ten and Twelve was 44,047.

The first postwar designs were also the first Vauxhalls for some time to carry model names. The Wyvern and Velox shared a 4-light saloon body with horizontal grill and faired-in headlamps, larger luggage boot and steering column gear change. The Wyvern had the old Twelve's 1442cc 4-cylinder engine, but the Velox was powered by a new 2275cc six giving a top speed of over 75mph (120km/h). On the debit side, it was less roomy than the old Fourteen, and no longer had synchromesh on bottom gear. Externally the models could be distinguished by the over-riders on the bumpers of the Velox. They were made in larger numbers than any prewar Vauxhalls, 55,409 Wyverns and 76,919 Veloxes, and a high proportion went for export. In the summer of 1951 they were replaced by new models bearing the same names but with completely redesigned bodies, full-width in the American idiom and with room for six passengers. They had coil-and-wishbone ifs and hypoid rear axles. The first examples had the same engines as before, but from the Spring of 1952 all-new short-stroke engines of 1508 and 2262cc were featured, dimensions being identical to those of the Ford Consul and Zephyr. They were made with only minor styling changes up to 1957, being joined in 1955 by the Cresta. This had dual colour schemes and extra interior refinements, being Vauxhall's answer to the Ford Zodiac. The 4-door saloon was the only style available from the factory in Britain, though Grosvenor and Martin Walter both offered estate car conversions, and Australians could have a pick-up or the Vagabond 2-door convertible, both bodied by Holden. In 1957 there was a further complete restyling on the PA series, with longer and lower bodies which featured wrap-around windscreens and rear windows. The 4-cylinder Wyvern was dropped, and only the Velox and Cresta survived, the latter identified as before by better equipment, though no longer by dual colours, which the Velox had as well. A new engine with square dimensions and 2651cc came for 1960, when other improvements included disc brakes at the front, overdrive or Hydramatic automatic transmission.

For 1962 the Velox and Cresta were restyled again, on the lines of the smaller Victor with more conventional bodies which no longer featured wrap-arounds at either front or rear. Capacity went up to 3294cc on the 1965 models, which were only Crestas. The engine was, in fact, a Chevrolet. The final model in this series was the Viscount, which had the same 3294cc engine and body shell with larger wheels, power steering, reclining seats and other luxuries. It and the Cresta were made up to 1972, but the Viscount was relatively rare, only 7025 built compared with 53,912 Crestas over the same period. Total production of the Velox and Cresta since the PA series was 314,723.

Smaller Vauxhalls, Victor and Viva

Up to 1957 the Velox had always outsold its 4-cylinder sister the Wyvern, and in order to boost the image of the smaller-engined car it was decided to make it an individual model, rather than using the same body shell for both cars. The result was the F Series Victor which used the Wyvern's 1508cc engine in a new body shell, very American in style, with wrap-around screen and rear window. For the first time since 1905 there were no flutes on the bonnet; they survived as part of the side trim, but on the next Victor they disappeared altogether. Other features of the Victor included synchromesh on bottom gear, and from early 1958, optional automatic transmission. Although criticised by some for its Transatlantic appearance, the Victor sold very well, more than 100,000 in its first 15 months, and a total of 390,747 in the four seasons before it was replaced by the FB Victor. This had more conventional styling, with a return to flat screen and rear window, and for 1964 engine capacity was increased to 1595cc. A high performance version of the FB Victor was the VX4/90, with twin carburettors which increased power from 69 to 71bhp, and later to 85bhp. The VX4/90 had individual front seats with a floor gear change, and front disc brakes, and was the first of the Vauxhalls aimed at the sporting driver, which became widespread in the 1970s.

The FC Victor (1964–67) was an improved FB, but the FD (1967–72) had new engines of 1599 and 1975cc, with hemispherical combustion chambers and cogged-belt drive ohc, and restyled bodies. When fitted with the 3294cc Chevrolet engine, the Victor became the Ventora, being made up to 1975. The last Victors were the FE series which had larger engines of 1759 and 2279cc, and were made up to 1978, though for 1977–8 they were renamed VX1800 and VX2300. There were VX4/90s in both FD and FE ranges, the last ones (1977–78) giving 116bhp from 2279cc, and a top speed of over 100mph (160km/h). They had 5-speed Getrag gearboxes with direct drive on top. Production of the later Victor series was 328,640 FBs, 219,814 FCs, 198,085 FDs (including Ventoras), and 130,886 FEs. Figures are not available for the original VX4/90, but later series were 13,449 FCs, 14,277 FDs, and 18,042 FEs.

Popular though Vauxhalls were in the 1960s, the company had no competitor in the small car field for the Ford Anglia, Triumph Herald or Austin 1100. The gap was filled in 1963 with the Viva, an Anglicised Opel Kadett with 44bhp 1057cc ohv engine, 4-speed all-synchromesh gearbox and rack-and-pinion steering, a novelty for Vauxhall. The body was an angular, rather utilitarian looking 2-door saloon, uninspired compared with the Anglia or 1100, but it was a dependable and simple design. It beat the Victor's record by selling 100,000 in ten months, and total production of the first series was 309,538. There was an estate car version, but this was sold as a Bedford Beagle. The first steps towards high performance were taken with the HA90, (1965–66) whose 60bhp high-compression head gave a top speed of over 80mph (130km/h).

The restyled HB Viva appeared in 1966; it had a bigger engine of 1159cc, revised suspension front and rear (coils in place of transverse-leaf ifs and semi-elliptics at the rear) and gave rise to several sporting versions. These included the 60bhp HB90, the 70bhp Brabham Viva, and the Viva GT which had the 104bhp 1975cc engine from the FD Victor, and a top speed of over 100mph (160km/h). The HB was also available as a 4-door saloon, and a total of 566,391 were made up to 1970. These figures do not include 78,296 HB90s, 13,517 HB1600s with 1599cc Victor engine, and 4606 Viva GTs. To cope with Viva production, Vauxhall opened a new factory at Ellesmere Port in 1963.

July 1971 saw the delivery of the millionth Viva, which was now the HC. This was again restyled, and over the next nine years was made with four different engines, the old 1159 and 1256cc pushrod ohv units, and the single-ohc Victor engines of 1759 and 2279cc. In 1974 the larger-engined Vivas were renamed Magnum to distance them from the humbler varieties. They were made as 2- or 4-door saloons, coupés and estate cars. The coupé began life in 1972 as the Firenza, an attractive 2-door 2+2 seater derived from the Viva. It was available with 1256, 1759 and 2279cc engines, the latter giving 110bhp and 102mph (165km/h). A rare and today much-prized variant of the Firenza was the 'droop snoot', with fibreglass panel at the front and boot-mounted spoiler. The engine was the 2279cc ohc four, tuned to give 131bhp, which meant a top speed of over 118mph (190km/h). The gearbox was a 5-speed ZF. The droop snoot was launched at the 1973 Earls Court Show, and Vauxhall said that there was

1976 Vauxhall (i) Chevette hatchback.
NICK BALDWIN

1976 Vauxhall (i) Cavalier GL coupé.
NICK BALDWIN

1989 Vauxhall (i) Astra GTE convertible.
VAUXHALL

capacity for between 20,000 and 50,000 to be made. In fact, just over 200 were delivered before the project was dropped in October 1975. It had proved too expensive to make, and it is most unlikely that the market could have absorbed enough to make it competitive. Although it was never homologated for racing, Gerry Marshall had many successes with droop snoots, including one with a V8 engine named Baby Bertha. From 1974 to 1975 about 200 Magnum estates were fitted with left-over droop snoot noses and sold under the name Sport Hatch.

Part of an International Range

From the mid-1970s the links between Vauxhalls and the international General Motors range became much more obvious, leading to today's situation where there is little but badging to distinguish Vauxhalls from Opels. The Chevette, or T-car as it was known by the planners in Detroit, first saw the light of day in Brazil in 1974, with Vauxhall's version being unveiled at the 1975 Geneva Show. It had the 1256cc Viva engine in an Opel Kadett floorpan with its own distinctive nose. Originally made only as a hatchback, the Chevette received 2- and 4-door saloons and estate versions in 1976. It gradually replaced the Viva,

1989 Vauxhall (i) Senator 2.5i saloon.
VAUXHALL

1995 Vauxhall (i) Calibra ES3 coupé.
VAUXHALL

1998 Vauxhall (i) Corsa Breeze hatchback.
VAUXHALL

2000 Vauxhall (i) Astra coupé.
VAUXHALL

though the latter was made until 1979, and by the time it was dropped in 1984 415,608 had been made. Opel Kadetts were made with a choice of engines, but the only alternative in the Chevette was the 2279cc ohc unit which went into the HS2300, a homologation special derived from the rally cars. This had a Vauxhall-designed 16-valve twin-ohc head and Getrag 5-speed gearbox, though the early team cars had Lotus heads and ZF gearboxes. The engine developed 135bhp, giving the HS a top speed of over 118mph (190km/h). Such performance did not come cheaply, and the 1978 price for a HS was £5312, compared with £2341 for the simplest Chevette L. Production of the HS was just 400 cars, and there were also 50 HSRs, developments of the HS with flared wheel arches and side skirts, 150bhp and a price tag of £7146. Most HSRs were converted from unsold HSs.

The HS and HSR gave Vauxhall a brief but very successful competition career. DTV (Dealer Team Vauxhall) had been formed in 1971 to enter cars for saloon racing, and in 1977 they began to enter the HS in rallies. As the name implies the team was organised by dealers rather than by the factory, the development of the cars being in the hands of Bill Blydenstein who had been tuning Vauxhalls since the 1960s. The first major rallying success for DTV came in 1977 when Pentti Airikkala won the Welsh Rally, followed by the Manx Trophy the same year. 1978 saw four wins, three by Airikkala and one by Chris Sclater, the International Hankiralli, Mintex International Douze Heures de l'Est (Sclater) and Hitachi International Rallysprint. In 1979 Airikkala won four British events to become British Open Rally Champion, and in 1980 there were five major wins, four by Jimmy McRae and one by Airikkala. 1981 was the last really successful season, with five wins again, all achieved by Tony Pond. The last major victory for the DTV Chevettes (usually HSRs after 1980) was by Russell Brookes in the 1983 Circuit of Ireland. Lack of finance and the advent of the 4-wheel drive Audi Quattros rendered the Chevettes uncompetitive. In 1982 DTV merged with DOT (Dealer Opel Team) to form GM Dealer Sport which prepared the Rothmans-sponsored Opel Asconas and Mantas.

In 1976 Vauxhall launched the Cavalier, an Anglicised Opel Ascona made in 2-door saloon, 4-door saloon and coupé models. The original Cavaliers were Belgian-assembled, and used 1584 or 1897cc Opel engines, but the 1256cc Vauxhall engine was available from February 1977, and assembly at Luton began in August of that year. A 1979cc engine was available from April 1978, in which year Crayford offered their Centaur convertible version. This did not have an Opel equivalent. Cavalier production totalled 248,440 between 1976 and 1981, and the model did much to restore Vauxhall's reputation which had been suffering from the presence of outdated models such as the Viva and Victor.

The Victor was replaced by the Carlton in 1978; this was an Opel Rekord with Vauxhall's plain front instead of Opel's grill and was made with three engines, including Vauxhall's first diesel, a 2260cc unit. The Carlton was made at Luton, unlike the Royale and Viceroy which were Opel Senators, Monzas and Commodores imported from Rüsselsheim.

The early 1980s saw three new Vauxhall models, all with equivalents in the international GM range, and all with front-wheel drive. The first was the Astra of 1980, sister to the Opel Kadett with 1196 or 1297cc petrol engines and a 1598cc diesel added in 1981 and a petrol unit of similar size in 1982. It was made until the 1985 season when it was replaced by a new Astra with more aerodynamic bodies and a choice of four engines from 1196cc and 55bhp to 1796cc and 115bhp, the latter being the 125mph (200km/h) GTE. 1981 saw the new Cavalier, part of the GM J-car range which included the Chevrolet Cavalier, Opel Ascona and Holden Camira. The third new model was the supermini-sized Nova, built in GM's Spanish factory and sold on the Continent as the Opel Corsa. As in Germany, models included a high-performance version, badged in Britain as the Nova 1.6i GTE and in Germany as the Corsa GSi.

These three new models did wonders for Vauxhall's fortunes. UK sales of all models rose from 110,208 in 1980 to 174,183 in 1982 and 270,437 in 1984. Between 1980 and 1984 their market share more than doubled, from 7.28 per cent to 16.17 per cent. In February 1984 the Cavalier was the best-selling model in Britain, the first time a Vauxhall was in this position for more than ten years. Vauxhall/Opel have twice won the European Car of the Year award, in 1985 with the Astra/Kadett and in 1987 for the Carlton/Omega. 1988 models, with their Opel equivalents, were the Nova (Corsa), Astra (Kadett fastback), Belmont (Kadett saloons), Cavalier (Ascona), Carlton (Omega), and Senator (Senator). Of these, the Nova was made in Zaragoza, Spain, the Astra at Ellesmere Port, except for the GTE 16-valve (Rüsselsheim) and the convertible (Karmann at

2000 Vauxhall (i) Vectra saloon.
VAUXHALL

Osnabrück), the Belmont at Ellesmere Port, the Cavalier at Luton, except the 4 × 4 model (Rüsselsheim), and the Carlton and Senator at Rüsselsheim.

During the 1990s the Vauxhall and Opel ranges became increasingly similar. Important models common to both included the Calibra coupé with 1998cc engine in 8- or 16-valve forms, with a 2498cc V6 engine and a 4 × 4 option added in 1994. This was dropped in 1997, to be replaced for 2000 by an Astra coupé powered by a 188bhp 2-litre turbo engine, with bodyshell built by Bertone in a new plant in Italy. The entry-level Nova was renamed Corsa to bring it into line with the Opel product in 1993, when a restyled version appeared. Other common models were the Corsa-based Tigra coupé, the medium-class Vectra made in saloon and estate froms, and the top-of-the-range rear-drive Omega saloons, as well as the Sintra and Zafira MPVs and Isuzu-derived Frontera 4 × 4 estate models. In these the engines were Opel-built, the gearboxes, chassis and bodies came from Isuzu. A completely new model announced in late 1999 was the VX220 Speedster, a mid-engined 2-seater described as 'a civilised Lotus Elise', powered by a 2198cc 16-valve engine. It was to be made in the Lotus factory, and carry Opel and Vauxhall badging. Another new Vauxhall/Opel model was the Agila high-roof city car, to be built at a new plant at Gliwice, Poland, as a joint venture with Suzuki. Powered by a choice of 1- or 1.2-litre engines, it was due to go on sale in the summer of 2000.

NG

Further Reading
Vauxhall, Michael Sedgwick, Dalton Watson/Beaulieu Books, 1981.
The Vauxhall 30/98, Nic Portway, New Wensum Publishing, 1995.
Vauxhall, the Postwar Years, Trevor Alder, Foulis, 1991.
The Vauxhall File, All Models Since 1903, Eric Dymock, Dove, 1999.

VAUXHALL (ii) **(AUS)** 1938–1957
General Motors-Holdens Ltd, Port Melbourne, Victoria.
Although the prewar Ten had unitary construction as a major advance, it was also offered with a chassis. The Australian selection was the locally-built 6-window

2000 Vauxhall (i) Omega Elite estate car.
VAUXHALL

2000 Vauxhall (i) Agila hatchback
VAUXHALL

2000 Vauxhall (i) Astra Sxi hatchback.
VAUXHALL

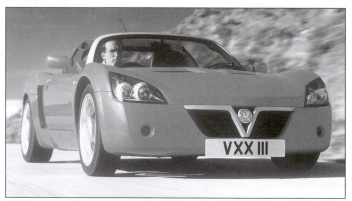

2000 Vauxhall (i) VX 220 sports car.
VAUXHALL

2000 Vauxhall (i) Corsa hatchback.
VAUXHALL

1972 Vaz-2102 estate car.
MARGUS H. KUUSE

saloon, a tourer (the Caleche) and utility (pick-up, badged as Bedford) with bodies fitted. The unitary construction for the Fourteen was made in Australia, the first such programme for Holdens which provided experience for the postwar HOLDEN. In 1949 the L-series arrived, with both 4- and 6-cylinder engines, being a development of the prewar Ten and offered with similar local bodies which were sold alongside the imported unitary models. As with the wholly new E-series, it was also obtainable with a chassis frame, and a local tourer, the Vagabond, and car-type utility, sold as a Vauxhall rather than Bedford, were offered.

MG

VAUZELLE-MOREL (F) 1902
Émile Vauzelle, Morel et Compagnie, Paris.
The Vauzelle-Morel voiturette had a small sloping bonnet of De Dion-Bouton pattern, though the 5hp Aster engine was mounted under the seat. Final drive was by a 2-speed Bozier gearbox to the rear axle.

NG

VAZ (SU) 1970 to date
Volszhkji Avtomobilnji Zavod, AvtoVAZ, Togliatti.
The Ford Motor Co. saved the day for the Soviet auto industry in the early 1930s, and the same can be said of FIAT about four decades later. The Turin giant signed an agreement to assist in the formation of a large factory, capable of putting together some 660,000 modern small cars per year, training the people and providing its successful model Fiat 124 as a prototype. The factory was erected near the town on the river Volga, fittingly re-named Togliatti after the former leader of the Italian Communist Party, Palmiro Togliatti, who died in Yalta. Initially there was just one model to be built, a slightly re-designed Fiat 124. Ground clearance was improved somewhat, the rear disc brakes were replaced with more mundane drums, and the engine was reworked. The forerunner of all Togliatti's automobiles was called VAZ-2101, a small 160in (4073mm) long car, weighing in at 2101lb (955kg) and running on 6.15-13 tyres. The engine developed 62 (later 64)bhp and 'zero-one' as it was called by people achieved 90mph (145km/h). Production started officially in August 1970. The next model, estate-bodied VAZ-2102 came two years later. By that time the third main assembly line was completed as well and each of those was capable of turning out 220,000 cars per year. The two were joined by a deluxe model VAZ-2103 with a 1452cc engine of 75bhp (as had the Moskvich-412), top speed 93mph (150km/h). The first modification of the base model, now called VAZ-21011 brought along a 1.3-litre engine with additional 5bhp, and two seconds were sliced off its 0–62mph (0–100km/h) time (now 20 seconds). During 1976–77 two new models were added to the range – the luxury VAZ-2106, and the first totally original vehicle, a 3-door VAZ-2121 Niva (field, crop). The former was treated with four headlamps and a 1569cc engine of 80bhp. With more modern interior and rich-looking exterior, the car was considered 'chic' among wealthier buyers. The Niva was a welcome effort to help transportation problems in rural areas which continued to suffer from an undeveloped roads system. The new off-roader was the first modern vehicle available to townspeople with active lifestyle, fishermen and travellers. Niva was rather heavy for its 146in (3720mm) length and the 80bhp engine was the same as fitted to model 2106. Permanent 4-wheel drive was supplemented by a 2-speed transfer case (1.2: 2.135). The tyres were 6.95-16 or 175/80 R 16 and speed equalled 81mph (130km/h). Fuel consumption was heavy: 9.8 litres per 100 km at 50mph (80km/h) against 7.3 by VAZ-2106.

The ultimate boxcar came with a base model of the second generation automobiles – VAZ-2105, soon to be joined by an estate model VAZ-2104 and a luxury VAZ-2107. The lack of design ideas was crowned in this case with a hang on 'Lincoln grill'. The second generation VAZ cars really lost their image.

The first comparatively modern product was created in 1985 by the sizeable Engineering Centre of VAZ – a front-wheel drive VAZ-2108 Samara (also Sputinik). The 3-door hatchback was developed with the help of Porsche, it was 156in (4006mm) long and weighed 1980lb (900kg). A 63.7bhp 1.3-litre engine was mounted transversely, joined to a 4-speed or 5-speed gearbox. Front suspension was of MacPherson variety this time and the rear was independent as well. A rack-and-pinion steering replaced the usual VAZ worm and roller. Split brake circuits, vacuum booster and front disc brakes were employed. The new family grew with addition of a 5-door VAZ-2109 and 4-door VAZ-21099. The latter

1980 Vaz-2121 Niva 4x4.
MARGUS H. KUUSE

gained in length about 8in (200mm). Engines of both smaller and bigger capacity were added to the original models.

The next generation of cars was developed and introduced slowly over many years, and moved up-market. The VAZ-2110 saloon had a 98in (2482mm) wheelbase and 168in (4277mm) overall length. Pilot production started finally in 1995, but quality problems hampered this really significant effort. Also, the styling of the model, possibly fresh and original during its creation in the 1980s, looked childish and outdated in late 1990s traffic. A 5-door car was added, called VAZ-2111 and a minivan acquired the number 2120 and a name Nadeshda (hope). In 1987 Lada's Mini appeared – only 126in (3200mm) long and weighing 635kg. VAZ-1111 Oka secured once again more affordable transportation on the lines of the original ZAZ-965. Its 2-cylinder engine gave 30 to 35bhp and the car was good for 75mph (121km/h). Production of the Oka was also to be transferred to other locations, like KamAZ truck works on the Kama river and motorbike works in Serpukhov, fittingly renamed SeAZ (or Serpukhov Auto Works). The latter was scheduled to equip Okas for handicapped drivers. Production of Oka cars at VAZ was stable during 1997–98, at 18–19,000 per year.

The second generation Niva was built on an elongated 96in (2450mm) wheelbase, the car's overall length (less spare wheel) growing to 154in (3900mm). The VAZ engine selection was really multi-faceted, involving GM fuel injection and multivalve arrangements, not to mention two-chamber rotaries of 120bhp, installed in VAZ-2108, 2109, and 21099 bodies.

For a short time the Uusikaupunki works in Finland tried its hand at making a Euro-Samara, but found other more attractive vehicles to develop.

The forthcoming engine programme calls for unified 82mm bore for mostly 16-valve engines of 1499, 1596, 1774, and 1997cc capacity, and modern engines with fuel injection, detonation sensors, catalytic converters – and even adjustable valve timing in some cases. These engines must be capable of producing competitive power, torque and fuel consumption figures and comply with Euro III emission regulations.

AvtoVAZ has been a rare car manufacturer of the former USSR (along with GAZ, essentially) which has not reduced output by a significant margin. In 1990 over 740,000 cars were manufactured and the same level was reached again in 1997. Even the 1998 result of 594,000 was honourable in Russia's economic

c.1982 Vaz-2107 saloon.
MARGUS H. KUUSE

1985 Vaz-2108 Samara hatchback.
MARGUS H. KUUSE

1988 Vaz-1111 Oka hatchback.
MARGUS H. KUUSE

1989 Vaz-2108 Samara 1500 SLX hatchback.
R.M.COMMUNICATIONS

1990 Vaz-1111 Oka hatchback.
MARGUS H. KUUSE

1998 Vaz Lada Niva 2123 4x4.
V. ARTEV

crisis. There was a sound alternative, of course – to revert to assembly of foreign designs. One plan called for manufacturing 200,000 Opel Astras and 300,000 Opel engines per year. However, the possibility remained of prototypes like the VAZ-1119 once more appearing on VAZ's assembly lines.

MHK

V.C.S. see SCHILLING

VDB see GEORGES IRAT

V.E. (US) 1901–1906
Vehicle Equipment Co., Brooklyn, New York (1901–1904);
Long Island City, New York (1905–1906).
This company was better known for electric sightseeing buses and heavy trucks than it was for cars, although these were made in a variety of models including a victoria with the chauffeur seated behind the two passengers, hansom, brougham and landaulet. The Brooklyn factory was destroyed by fire in July 1904 and the company built new premises in Long Island City, where production resumed in 1905. The Franco-American VIQUEOT car was made by a subsidiary of V.E.C. After bankruptcy in 1906, the company was reorganised as the General Vehicle Co., which made only trucks up to 1920.

NG

VECHET (A) 1911–1912
Vojmir Vechet a spol., Nymburk.
V. Vechet (1884–1953) was a machine locksmith working first as a railwayman and then at the Laurin & Klement Works. At the 1911 Prague Auto Show he introduced his light type DC with 3-seater torpedo body driven by a 2-cylinder 1108cc 10/12hp sv engine, priced at 5000K. In 1912 it was followed by a bigger type FF double phaeton for 4–6 passengers fitted with 4-cylinder 2108cc 20/24hp engine, priced 9000K. Car manufacturing was stopped that year and Vechet and Co. turned to 2- and 4-stroke stationary engine production. After World War I, V. Vechet became a partner of Frantisek Petrasek and planned to build the PAV (Petrasek and Vechet) – cars later manufactured under the name Start. Vechet also constructed the first Czechoslovak caterpillar carrier with DC type 10/12hp engine but it was underpowered and therefore not suitable for army purposes.

MSH

VECTOR (US) 1977 to date
Vehicle Design Ford, Venice, California.
Vector Aeromotive Corp., Jacksonville, Florida
Jerry Wiegert was a man with a vision. He wanted to build an American supercar to rival the best from Europe, and began with the Vector W8 Twinturbo. A prototype was shown in 1977, but the first production models did not roll off the line until 1991. The W8 was a mid-engined sports car with a transversely-mounted 6000cc V8 with twin turbochargers and 625hp. It proved to be one of the fastest production cars in the world, but financial problems, coupled with a price of over $450,000, resulted in only 14 cars. In 1992 an improved model, the Avtech WX-3, replaced the W8. The Avtech had more rounded styling and a 7000cc V8. The price was announced at a startling $765,000. Apparently only the prototype was built before Vector was taken over by new financial backers and Wiegert was replaced at the helm. The new owners, Mega Tech Ltd, an Indonesian company that also owned Lamborghini, relocated the company to Florida. The new M12 was a restyled and improved Avtech, but with a Lamborghini V12 engine, thus negating the all-American GT angle. It used a Z-F transaxle and scissor-opening doors. The price was down to $184,000, which was less than the Lamborghini with the same engine.

HP

VEDRINE (F) 1904–c.1910
La Voiture Électrique Vedrine, Neuilly, Seine.
Vedrine were primarily coachbuilders whose work was seen on some of the highest-quality French cars, such as Panhard and Hotchkiss. They had works at Courbevoie and Rouen, and also had an electric vehicle department which built a number of town cars of the usual brougham and landaulet fashion. Their motors were mounted just ahead of the rear axle and some had dropped frames to allow easy

access to the body. In 1906 Vedrine production was recorded as 1500 vehicles, but this figure may have included coachwork.

NG

VEE GEE (GB) 1913

Vernon Gash & Co., Leeds, Yorkshire.

Named after its maker's initials, this was a cyclecar powered by an 8hp air-cooled V-twin JAP engine. The frame was tubular, but unlike most of its kind, it had a conventional 3-speed gearbox and shaft drive to a worm-gear rear axle. It was claimed that the bench seat was sufficiently wide to seat three people. A price of 110 guineas (£115.50) was quoted for the touring model, and there was to be a racing model whose price had not been determined at the time of announcement in April 1913.

NG

VEEBIRDS (US) c.1980

Veebirds Inc., Colorado Springs, Colorado.

One of the weirdest concepts in kit car history was the idea that you could (or should) put a 1957 Thunderbird body on a Volkswagen chassis. Veebirds did just that by shortening the body to fit the VW chassis, using the boot as the engine compartment and the underbonnet room for storage. An optional hard-top had porthole windows. This kit was later sold to BRADLEY.

HP

VEEP (US) c.1977–1980

Hadley Engineering, Costa Mesa, California.

The Veep was a replica of the World War II-style Willys Jeep, but built on Volkswagen running gear. A box-section frame was included. Similar kit cars were later sold by SUN VALLEY.

HP

VEERAC (US) 1905

Frank H. Merrill, Plainfield, New Jersey.

Frank Merrill invented a 2-stroke engine which he called Veerac after the words 'valveless explosion every revolution, air cooled', and installed in a simple 2-seater car. Having built it in New Jersey, he tried to raise money for the project in Springfield, Massachusetts, but had no luck. It was eight years before the Veerac went into production, and then it was a truck made in Anoka, Minnesota. About 100 were built in 1913.

NG

VÉHEL (F) 1899–1901

M. et A. Dulac, Paris.

The Véhel was a light car made with a 6hp single-cylinder or an 8hp 2-cylinder engine mounted at the front under a pointed bonnet, with 3-speed gearboxes and final drive by chain. In 1901 they were sold in England under the name Torpedo, but this had no connection with the British car of that name made at Barton-on-Humber in 1909.

NG

VEHMA (CDN) 1989

Vehma International, Richmond Hill, Ontario.

Part of the Magna International group, Vehma was heavily involved in automotive components supply as well as prototype development, and the Torrero was presented at the 1989 Geneva Motor Show as a representation of what it could achieve. It was a fearsome beast, with rippling sport-utility styling reminiscent of something out of *Captain Scarlet*. It measured a substantial 189in (4800mm) long and 79in (2000mm) wide. Into its tubular steel chassis were fitted all-independent suspension by coil springs and a 4-wheel drive system. Most impressive of all was its powerplant, a specially-developed 8132cc V8 all-aluminium twin cam unit with four valves per cylinder, and a power output of 535bhp. It was built by Magna's Eagle Engine Co. A top speed of 150mph (241km/h) was claimed. A limited production run was envisaged but it is believed that this never occurred.

CR

V.E.L. (F) 1947–1948

Sté V.E.L. Paris.

1904 Vedrine electric cab.
NATIONAL MOTOR MUSEUM

1989 Vehma Torrero station wagon.
VEHMA INTERNATIONAL

This was a very small minicar, even by the standards of postwar France, powered by a single-cylinder Train engine rated at only 1CV. Unusually, this drove the front wheels, via a 3-speed gearbox. Top speed was 40mph (64km/h).

NG

VÉLAM (F) 1955–1957/1961

Vélam, Suresnes.

Having conceived the Isetta bubble car in 1953, Iso began to sell licences to other companies, including BMW in Germany and Vélam in France. The Vélam differed in numerous ways from the Italian Isetta, notably the smooth shape of its flanks and the extended front wheel arches. It undercut the price of Citroën's 2CV by 15 per cent at FFr297,000. Its engine was the Iso 236cc single-cylinder 10bhp unit driving through very close-set rear wheels. There was also a convertible version with a fold-down rear section. To combat falling sales, Vélam launched a luxury version called the Écrin in 1957, with a fixed roof, improved suspension and redesigned bodywork. After the demise of the Isetta, in 1961 Vélam developed a prototype of a very compact 6-seater car under the name TA 6 for the Israeli company Kaiser-Ilin. It measured only 130in (3300mm) long and was powered by a 640cc air-cooled twin engine. However, the TA 6 did not enter production.

CR

VELIE (US) 1909–1928

1909–1916 Velie Motor Vehicle Co., Moline, Illinois.
1916–1928 Velie Motor Corp., Moline, Illinois.

This company had close links with the John Deere plough and agricultural equipment firm, dating back to 1860 when Stephen Velie married John Deere's

1909 Velie Model A tourer.
JOHN A. CONDE

1919 Velie Model 38 roadster.
JOHN A. CONDE

1927 Velie Model 60 Royal sedan.
JOHN A. CONDE

Model H torpedo roadster on a 115in (2919mm) wheelbase at $1900 to the Model L 6-seater torpedo tourer on a 121in (3071mm) wheelbase selling for $2750. In 1914 Velie announced its first six, which used a 34hp Continental engine. Trucks were made from 1911 by a separate company, but the two companies merged in 1916 to form Velie Motor Corp. The cars were so popular in Louisiana that a small community north of Shreveport named itself Velie, which still survives. Velies were mostly of conventional appearance, but a striking model was the Sport Car of 1918–19, a 4-seater with wire wheels and external exhaust pipes.

Production reached a peak of 7738 in 1920, after which it settled down to between 4000 and 4500 in the 1920s. Velie used either Falls or Continental 6-cylinder engines up to the end of 1922, then switched to its own make, the units being built in Marion, Indiana, until 1925 when production was moved to Moline. They were 3205 or 3333cc ohv sixes to start with, although sizes varied over the years, and the 1927 60 displaced 3626cc. For 1928 the company adopted a 3670cc Lycoming 4MD side-valve straight-8 as a companion model to its own ohv sixes. A larger Lycoming 4HM straight-8 of 4893cc was listed for 1929, but by then Velie was almost out of business. The appointment of an 'efficiency expert', Edwin McEwan, in 1924 had led to a serious loss of morale. Willard Velie had handed over the reins to McEwan during a period of ill health, and on his return in 1927 things picked up for a while. However, he died suddenly in October 1928 and was succeeded by his son Willard Velie Jr. He also died suddenly in March 1929, and without any Velies at the helm the company soon went under. However, it would probably not have survived the Depression, being a relatively small company competing with major players such as Buick and Chrysler. The factory reverted to John Deere & Co., while the grandiose 46-room mansion that Willard Velie had built in 1913 later became a high-class restaurant.

NG

Further Reading
'The Velies of Moline, Father, Son and Motorcar', Beverly Rae Kimes, *Automobile Quarterly*, Vol. 15, No. 4.
'Who's Who in Automobilia – Velie', Walter O. MacIlvain, *Bulb Horn*, Nov–Dec 1975.

VELLO ROSSA (US) c.1997 to date
VR Engineering, Tempe, Arizona.
VR built a line of kit cars that were based on the Datsun Z-car platforms. The Velo Rossa Spyder was a Ferrari 250GTO replica, but it was made into a convertible. The Daytona ZX Spyder was a similar rebody that looked like a Ferrari Daytona. The Z-IMSA was not a replica, but a kit of body panels similar to those used on racing Datsuns. This included spoilers, a smooth nose, air dams and wide wheel flares. The Subtle Z was a mild restyling job on a Datsun 240Z, with a short tail spoiler, an air dam and narrow wheel flares. They were sold as kits or VR would assemble them on the buyer's car.

HP

VELOCAR *see* MOCHET

VELOCE (GB) 1908
Veloce Ltd, Birmingham.
Founded as Taylor Gue Ltd in 1904, this company became well known as the makers of the Velocette motorcycle. In 1908 it announced two models of 4-cylinder car, an 18/20 and a 24/26hp. The engines were of its own design and both cars had shaft drive. Intended for colonial use they had high ground clearance and larger than usual radiators. Only only one car was made, an 18/24hp.

NG

VELOMOBIL (D) 1905–1907
1905–1906 Motorfahrzeugfabrik Hermann Dettmann, Berlin.
1906–1907 Velomobil Kraftfahrzeugfabrik, Berlin.
This was a small 3-wheeler with drive by a proprietary engine of unknown origin to the single front wheel. It was available with 2- or 3-seater bodies.

HON

VELOREX (CS) 1950–1974
Vyrobni druzstvo Velorex, Solnice.

daughter. Their three sons all worked for Deere, but in 1902 the youngest, Willard Lamb Velie, set up on his own, forming the Velie Carriage Co. This soon became the largest such firm in the Middle West, with an output of 25,000 carriages a year. Most of the directors were also on the board of John Deere, which handled sales through its numerous dealerships.

In July 1908 the Velie Motor Vehicle Co. was formed, and a batch of 1000 cars was laid down for the 1909 season. They had 30/35hp 4-cylinder engines made by the American & British Manufacturing Co. in Bridgeport, Connecticut, which later built the PORTER (ii). They had Brown-Lipe gearboxes and Timken axles. The factory tooling came from the MONARCH Motor Car Co. of Chicago, which had made cars in 1907–09. This was transferred to Moline in 1910. The Velie was competitively priced, at $1750 for a tourer or roadster, and sold well thanks to the use of John Deere dealerships. The cars were listed in John Deere catalogues up to 1915. Production reached 3628 in 1912, when five models were made, all powered by a 40hp 4-cylinder engine. They ranged from the

1962 Velorex 250cc 3-wheeler.
NICK GEORGANO/NATIONAL MOTOR MUSEUM

In Czechoslovakia after World War II there were many people who had lost arms and legs, and there was a great need for a means of making them independently mobile. Frantisek Stransky with his brother Mojmir had already constructed a basic cyclecar for a disabled person in 1942. It had a simple frame of tubular construction with a seat beside an engine, and about ten were sold in the local area. Later Stransky and his brother designed a covered-in 3-wheeler which was a direct forerunner of the Velorex. To avoid the then high cost of metal, the body had a waterproof woven material similar to leather-cloth, stretched over a tubular frame very reminiscent of the motorcycle sidecars of the day. Dimensions were 3100 × 1400 × 1240mm, weight 451lb (205kg). In 1950 the government took over production using a co-operative called Velo (later to become Velorex), and with the assistance of the Stransky brothers production was started in 1950. They produced the 250cc Jawa engined Oskar which had two seats, 16in wheels and a limited amount of luggage space. By 1951 around 120 were made and in 1952 about 180. At the same time the 175cc engined vehicle was produced, and in 1954 the Oskar became known as the Velorex. This spartanly equipped, draughty vehicle with two front wheels was made available to disabled people at a very reasonable cost, sponsored by the Invalids' Organization. In 1960 the car became known as the Velorex 16/250 and the 350cc which was being developed was to be the 16/350. This finally went into mass production in 1963 when the production of 250cc version was stopped. The 16/350 was capable of 53mph (85km/h), weighed 682lb (310kg) and had a 12V electric starter. Of the Oskar and Velorex 16/175 800 were made, of the 250cc version about 2500, and of the Velorex 16/350 about 12,000 units.

In 1971 3-wheeler production ceased and was replaced immediately by a 4-wheeled vehicle. It was called the Velorex 435 and had a fibreglass body with leatherette rear panels on a tubular frame and a 350cc 17bhp Jawa engine. They made 1380 of these until 1974 when production was stopped because the car was deemed to be too slow and unsafe.

About half the Velorex 435 production (7540 vehicles) was exported to the GDR, Poland, Hungary and Bulgaria. In 1999 Velorex was making fibreglass sidecars which were exported to France, USA, Sweden, England, and Belgium.
MSH

1972 Velorex 435 350cc saloon.
MARIAN SUMAN-HREBLAY

1903 Miniature Velox (i) 3½hp 2-seater.
NICK GEORGANO/NATIONAL MOTOR MUSEUM

VELOX (i) (GB) 1902–1904

Velox Motor Co. Ltd, Coventry.
Built in part of the premises at Parkside of the Amalgamated Tyre Co., Velox cars used a number of different proprietary engines. The 1902 model had a 10hp

1903 Velox (i) 20hp tourer with pneumatic disc wheels.
NATIONAL MOTOR MUSEUM

1990 Venturi coupé.
M.V.S.

1999 Venturi 300 coupé.
VENTURI

Abeille 2-cylinder engine with 4-speed gearbox and shaft drive. For 1903, two models were offered, the Miniature Velox which used a 4.5hp single-cylinder Aster engine in a very low frame, and a larger car with 10hp 4-cylinder Forman engine. Towards the end of 1903 a 20hp four was announced, shaft driven like the others, but the company was soon to be wound up. Only 21 cars were made in all, although 15 more were in the course of construction at the time of the company's closure. A 1903 Miniature Velox survives.

NG

VELOX (ii) (A) 1907–1910

Prazska tovarna automobilu 'Velox', Praha-Karlin.

The Velox Co. started in 1906 as the owner of large garages and a repair shop for 100 motorcycles and 50 cars placed in the viaducts of the Austro-Hungarian State Railways in the Prague Karlin quarter. One year later the first taxicabs of their own design were introduced in Prague, either with 2-cylinder 12/14hp engine for 3–5 passengers or with 4-cylinder 25/30hp for 4–6 passengers. The

most successful was a 2+1 seater vehicle called Russian type owing to deliveries of taxicabs to St Peterburg and Moscow. A water-cooled vertical single-cylinder 1020cc 10bhp engine was placed under the driver's seat and rear wheels were driven by a chain through a differential gear. Due to expensive fares, taxicabs were not wide-spread at that time, and Velox stopped their production in 1910 remaining as a repair shop until 1914.

MSH

VENOM (GB) 1985–1987

T.K.H. Ltd, Manchester, Lancashire.

This was the first ever truly accurate Lamborghini Countach replica, launching a worldwide industry. The fibreglass body was reputedly moulded from a genuine Countach obtained through a hire company. G.T.D. supplied the chassis but financial troubles sank the project after only six cars had been sold. Almost all went on to form the basis of other Countach replicas.

CR

VENTURI (F) 1984–2000

1984–1990 Manufacture de Voitures de Sport, Cholet, Maine et Loire.
1990–1994 Manufacture de Voitures de Sport, Nantes Couëron.
1994–1996 Venturi SA, Nantes Couëron.
1996–2000 Venturi Paris SA, Nantes Couëron.

In the absence of a truly independent French sports car marque, ex-Alpine engineer Claude Poiraud and ex-Peugeot designer Gérard Godfroy collaborated to create a car initially called the M.V.S. Venturi. Two years later, in 1986, a revised model was shown under the name Venturi and productionised in April the following year. While the original prototype had been powered by a 200bhp 4-cylinder engine, the production version used a 200bhp Peugeot 505 Turbo V6, mounted centrally. Various other components from French cars were used, including Renault 25 front brakes, Peugeot power steering and mostly Renault Fuego glass. The chassis had front and rear box sections and all-independent suspension by double wishbones at the front and five links at the rear. A Cabriolet model was added in 1988, shortly before the company was acquired by the Swiss group Primwest, under the auspices of specialist car constructor Xavier De La Chapelle, the first of many changes of ownership. In 1990, new versions were launched: the 260 Coupé and Cabriolet, powered by 260bhp turbocharged 2.85-litre Renault V6 engines; the open-topped model was later badged the Transcup. A new factory and racing circuit were built near Nantes in 1991 as part of a dramatic expansion, including the launch of the Venturi-Larrousse F1 team in January 1992. Venturis also competed at Le Mans. In 1992 came the 400GT model, initially launched as part of a single-make racing series but offered in roadgoing form from 1994. As the name suggested, it had 400bhp from its twin-turbo V6 engine but it also scored a world first for a road car in having carbon-fibre disc brakes. Another change of ownership came in 1994, when a consortium of French industrialists and bankers assumed control. Then two years later they sold the company to a Thai entrepreneur, Seree Rakvit of Nakarin Benz but that association was even less durable, for in 1998 he sold out to the Australian group Auto Americas. By that stage, Venturi's staff level had plummeted to 30 from a high of 150 employees. A new model, the restyled Atlantique with a 3-litre 281bhp Renault V6 engine, arrived in 1994 (offered from 1997 with optional automatic transmission) and a more powerful 310bhp version of the twin turbocharged engine was presented in 1998. The 1999 range consisted of the Atlantique 300 and 400, and the 400GT. Venturi went into liquidation again in February 2000, and this time no saviours came forward. Five incomplete cars remained in the factory.

CR

VENTURINA (I) 1962

In America a number of companies produced miniature replicas of early Oldsmobiles. The Venturina was a peculiarly Italian reinterpretation of this theme by a certain Dr Franco. It was a tiny 73in (1850mm long) car recalling the style of the early 1900s, with spoked wheels, florid mudguards, a tall folding roof, and vertical windscreen. It used a rear-mounted Fiat 500 engine.

CR

VENUS (US) 1954

Venus, Houston, Texas.

1948 Veritas 2-litre sports car.
NATIONAL MOTOR MUSEUM

The Venus was a fibreglass-bodied kit sports car. It was a large body, intended to fit onto full size American sedan chassis, usually the 1949-51 Ford. It was a convertible with only two seats and long fins on the rear mudguards, a bonnet scoop and exposed door hinges. The prototype was powered by a 1949 Ford V8 with high-performance heads, intake manifold and exhaust system. It was built and designed by K.W. McLeod, D.Y. Gorman and E.F. Rockett. The Venus was to be sold as a simple body shell or a complete kit ready for installation.

HP

VERA (US) 1912

Vera Motor Car Co., Providence, Rhode Island.
Lasting less than a year, the Vera was a well-made high-quality car powered by a 7-litre 50hp 6-cylinder T-head engine, and made in tourer and roadster models. Several ex-Alco staff were involved in it, but they could not ensure its success.

NG

VERACITY see SMITH

VERCO (US) c.1985–1987

Verco Inc., Greensburg, Indiana.
The 1985 Verco Dream Machine 1 was a set of plans for an uninspired body that could be built on Ford Pinto running gear. Verco sold instructions for this angular car that was to be built from fibreglass and foam-core materials. Verco also sold a line of Ford Model A replicas in speedster, roadster, phaeton, and woodie body styles. These were custom frames with Ford Pinto running gear. In 1987 Verco added a fibreglass-bodied Lamborghini Countach replica built on a custom tubular frame with a General Motors 3800cc V6 engine. They were sold in turn-key form for $25,000 and many options were available.

HP

VERITAS (D) 1947–1953

1947–1948 Veritas GmbH, Hausern.
1948–1949 Veritas GmbH, Messkirch.
1949–1950 Veritas Badische Automobilwerke GmbH, Rastatt.
1950–1953 Automobilwerke Ernst Loof GmbH, Nürburgring.

1949 Veritas Komet coupé.
NICK GEORGANO

During the German occupation of Paris, three soldiers with motor sport backgrounds met and planned their ideal sports car for the postwar era. They were Ernst Loof, who had been a motorcycle champion and manager of BMW's sports department, Georg Meier, winner of the 1939 motorcycle TT, and BMW employee Lorenz Dietrich. As all three had strong links with BMW, it was natural that they would base their own car on the famous Bavarian make. There was also the fact that the BMW 328 was the only modest-sized German sports car which they could use, and as the occupying forces would not allow the manufacture of engines over 1-litre capacity, they began by acquiring old 328s and rebuilding them.

In effect the customer went to the small factory at Hausern, Bavaria, with the engine, gearbox and transmission of a 328, plus DM35,000, and a few weeks later collected his BMW-Veritas, as the cars were originally called. The engine was completely rebuilt, with a modified cylinder head, larger valves and a newly ground crankshaft, some of these being roller bearing units, while the bodies were slab-sided 2-seaters intended for racing, with a cover over the passenger's seat. The first car went to Karl Kling, who won at Hockenheim in the summer of 1947, and went on to become German 2-litre champion that year.

1898 Vermorel 4-seater.
NICK BALDWIN

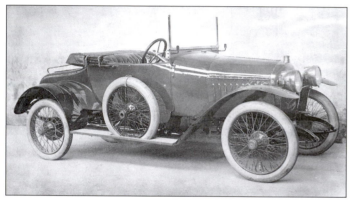

1914 Vermorel 12/16hp 2-seater.
BRYAN K. GOODMAN

1922 Vermorel 12/16hp town car.
NICK BALDWIN

The partners chose the name Veritas (Latin for Truth) from a French company which tested technical products. After only a handful of cars had been made, BMW objected to the use of their name on the cars. Dietrich, who was sales manager of the small firm, was not upset, as he wanted to promote Veritas as a make in its own right. Finding the American authorities difficult to work with, the company moved to Messkirch in the French zone in March 1948, and by the end of the year they had built 17 Rennsport or RS as the sports/racers were called. Specifications varied from car to car, with parts bought up all over Germany, wherever they could be found. The cars became more individual, with tubular space frames, and although engines retained the basic BMW layout with cross-over pushrods, some had smaller capacities to bring them within the 1½-litre

class. Racing successes continued in 1948 and 1949, Georg Meier winning the 1948 German single-seater title, and in 1949 Helm Glockler was 1½-litre champion and Kling 2-litre champion.

Veritas cars dominated German racing at the time, and at Nürburgring in 1949, ten out of twelve starters in the 2-litre race were Veritas. As Veritas was known to be a German make, some of the cars raced in France and Belgium were called Meteors, a name also given to the Formula 2 single-seater, which was raced with diminishing success from 1950 to 1952.

Veritas for the Road

Lorenz Dietrich had always dreamed of making cars in large numbers, which could never be achieved simply with competition machinery, and when he was asked for road-going versions of the Veritas he was only too pleased to comply. In 1949 he launched the Komet coupé. This was little more than an RS with a turret-like top grafted on, but later models were more comfortable. They included the Saturn coupé and Scorpion cabriolet, both with 2+2 seating and three engine options, the 55bhp BMW 326, the same engine with alloy head, larger valves and twin carburettors (65bhp), and the 80bhp BMW 328. Also in the range was the Komet sports car, in 100 or 150bhp forms. Coachwork came from the well-known firm of Spohn.

During 1949 Veritas moved again, to Meggensturm near Rastatt in Baden, and set up a larger factory with aid from the Baden state government. In recognition of this, the company name was changed to Veritas Badische Automobilwerke GmbH.

The first cars built at Meggensturm had BMW engines, but most used a new 1988cc single-ohc six designed by Erik Zipprich and built by Heinkel. This suffered from lack of development, and brought many complaints from customers. Dietrich returned from the 1950 Geneva Show with 200 orders, but could not get enough credit to buy the necessary components. The Baden government was unwilling to loan any more, but they persuaded a consortium of Jesuits, an Archbishop and the Prince von Fürstenburg to come up with DM500,000. Unfortunately Veritas needed three times this amount to fulfill their orders, and an approach to the Federal Government in Bonn was turned down. Production at Meggensturm virtually came to an end in 1950, but Dietrich had a second string in the shape of the Dyna-Panhard, which he fitted with coupé or convertible bodies by Baur of Stuttgart, and sold as the Dyna Veritas. Dietrich financed this operation out of his own pocket, and sold 184 cars between 1950 and 1952, mostly convertibles. Whether he made a profit is not known. The total number of Veritas cars made in all three factories was 78.

Meanwhile Ernst Loof had remained at Messkirch where he concentrated on tuning cars for competition. He then moved to the Nürburgring, where he rented premises that had been the old Auto Union workshops in prewar days. He set up a new company, Automobilwerke Ernst Loof GmbH, and launched a new line of Veritas cars, still with Heinkel engines but on two wheelbases, with attractive saloon or cabriolet coachwork which was wider than the previous models, still made by Spohn. Unfortunately he was even more under-capitalised than Dietrich, and could not make a success of his venture. The number of Veritas-Nürburgrings made is not known, some say as low as six, and the highest estimate is 20. He ran out of engines while several bodies were complete, so the final cars had Ford or Opel engines. Loof joined BMW as a development engineer, but built one final car in the Nürburgring works, a 2-seater sports on a BMW 302 chassis which was intended as a rival to Albrech Goertz design for the 507. However, the Goertz design was chosen. Loof died of a brain tumour in 1956, but his partners Meier and Dietrich had successful careers in car sales.

NG

Further Reading
'Winners, Losers, Might-have-beens – the Cars called Veritas', Jerry Sloniger, *Automobile Quarterly*, Vol. 14, No. 1.

VERMOREL (F) 1898–1930
Éts V. Vermorel, Villefranche-sur-Saône, Rhône.
The Vermorel was a typical French provincial make which enjoyed its best years before 1914, went into gentle decline in the 1920s and expired at the time of the Depression. The company was a maker of woodworking and agricultural machinery dating back to 1850, and in 1891 it set up a research institute to study the application of machinery to farming, as did Henry Ford later. In 1898 Victor Vermorel hired François Pilain, who had worked with Léon Serpollet and was later to make cars of his own, to launch his company into car manufacture. Pilain had already been working on a car at Lyons, and he moved his machinery

17 miles north to Villefranche and began to make a similar design there. It had a horizontal 2-cylinder engine and belt final drive, though for Vermorel he replaced it with chain drive.

Only a handful of experimental cars were made under Pilain's direction, and in August 1901 he returned to Lyons to set up the Société des Automobiles Pilain. Vermorel did not make another car until 1908, when it launched a conventional machine with 1.8-litre T-head 4-cylinder engine and shaft drive. It also experimented with a curious annular wing biplane designed by M. Givaudan, but wisely did not proceed with this. The cars sold well, and by 1911 Vermorel had 800 employees, although this was the total workforce, many of whom would have been engaged in the agricultural and wine-making machinery side of the business. The 1914 range consisted of three models, all with 4 cylinder L-head monobloc engines, the 1505cc 10/12hp, 2064cc 12/16hp and 2298cc 15/18hp. Light commercial vehicles were made on all three chassis; the larger was a basis for some fire engines, one of which was still at the Vermorel factory when it was finally closed in 1965.

The 15/18 reappeared after the war, and was joined by a 1603cc model with foot transmission brake, although 4-wheel brakes were available. The 4-speed gearbox had central change. More interesting was the 1843cc 12CV with ohvs and wire wheels. Both models acquired coupled brakes and full-pressure lubrication in 1925. Vermorel was never a sporting make, yet it entered two cars with twin-ohc 6-cylinder engines in the 1924 Touring Car Grand Prix. The cars never turned up, and there is some doubt that they ever existed, except on paper.

The first, and only, production 6-cylinder Vermorel came in 1928. The Type AH3 had a 2-litre ohv engine in unit with a 4-speed gearbox with central change, and spiral bevel final drive. It was made in small numbers until production ended in 1930. There was also a smaller Vermorel with 1131cc side-valve engine which was announced in 1927. Annual production in the 1920s varied between 350 and 400 vehicles, including some light commercials which were made as ambulances and postal vans. Victor Vermorel died in 1927, but his son Édouard carried on the agricultural machinery business. During World War II the company made gunsights and producer-gas conversions for trucks, then reverted to their original business. Édouard died in 1957, after which the company passed out of the Vermorel family, changing hands several times before it was finally closed in 1965.

NG

VERNANDI (F) 1928–1929
Automobiles Vernandi, Garches, Seine-et-Oise.
Designed by the famous engineer Nemorin Causan, the Vernandi was a very low sports/racing car powered by a 1494cc ohv V8 with twin superchargers. Although it is believed that only one complete car and two engines were ever made, a catalogue was issued showing the car with a 2-seater racing body and no road equipment. It listed numerous sporting successes achieved in 1928. They were mostly in hill climbs and included the infamous slow hill climb at Montmartre. The Vernandi covered the 4km 592m climb in one hour.

KB

VERNON (i) (US) 1911
Vernon Motor Car Co., Detroit, Michigan.
Named for the company's owner Vernon C. Fry, the Vernon 30 was a continuation of the DETROIT-DEARBORN but with a wider range of bodies: tourer, demi-tonneau, roadster, torpedo and coupé. They were priced at $400 less than the Detroit-Dearborns, but failed to last out the year of their introduction.

NG

VERNON (ii) (US) 1918–1921
Vernon Automobile Corp., Mount Vernon, New York.
The Vernon was the outgrowth of the Able Engine Co., of Mount Vernon, New York and consisted of two lines of cars, a 4-cylinder series and a more expensive V8, both featuring Able engines, and a wheelbase of 115in (2919mm). Production was not large and consisted of open models exclusively including 2- and 3-seater roadsters and touring cars for four or five. The 5-seater touring car was the predominant style in popularity, the four selling for $845 and the V8 exactly twice that price. Apart from the engine, components varied, consisting of standard wares from various speciality manufacturers. Wooden artillery wheels were used on the 4-cylinder cars, wire types being optional on the V8. Production was

c.1955 Vernon (iii) Vi-car invalid car.
NICK GEORGANO

terminated in 1920, leftover cars being marketed as 1921 models. Norton L. Dods, production and sales manager of the Vernon later surfaced with the novel CAVALIER 'pony car' in 1926, also in Mount Vernon. The Cavalier failed to survive the prototype stage.

KM

VERNON (iii) (GB) 1952–c.1958
Vernon Industries Ltd, Bidston, Cheshire.
A subsidiary of Vernons football pools, this company made a number of invalid cars. At first it made INVACARs under licence for the Ministry of Health, and in 1952 launched its own design, named the Vi-Car. Like most of its kind it was a 3-wheeler with single front wheel, and was powered by a 197cc single-cylinder Villiers 2-stroke engine mounted on the offside of the body, with a large luggage boot behind. Final drive was by chain to the offside rear wheel. A later version had a Siba Dynastart starter. In 1954 the Vi-Car was developed into a 3-wheeler for the general market, which was sold as the GORDON (iii), still with the side-mounted 197cc engine.

NG

VERNON-DERBY see DERBY

VERNON 30 see DETROIT-DEARBORN

VERONAC (CDN) 1981–c.1984
Veronac Automobile Enterprises Ltd, London, Ontario.
This company made ambitious replicas to order. Models included the Auburn Speedster, Cord 812 Phaeton and various Duesenberg J and SJ models. The standard engine choice was a 400bhp GM V8, but Veronac was said to be developing its own twin-ohc straight-8 engine.

CR

VESPA (i) (I) 1913–1916
G. Antonelli, Modena.
This was a light car powered by a 1460cc 4-cylinder side-valve engine, with a 4-speed gearbox and shaft drive. It had a top speed of 55mph (89km/h).

NG

VESPA (ii) (F/I) 1957–1961
Ateliers de Construction des Motocycles et Automobiles, Fourchambault, Nièvre.
The Vespa range of scooters is world-renowned but less well-known is its brave economy car project. Due to Piaggio's deference to Fiat that the Torinese giant's dominance should not be challenged, it decided not to produce the car in Italy but in a factory in France. The Vespa 400 was a pleasingly styled 2+2 coupé with unitary construction, a rolltop roof, all-independent coil spring suspension, hydraulic brakes and a 3-speed gearbox (4-speed all-synchromesh from 1960 onward). Its rear-mounted engine, an air-cooled vertical twin 393cc 2-stroke unit, developed 14bhp and could power the car to a top speed of 55mph (89km/h).

1960 Vespa (ii) 400 coupé.
NATIONAL MOTOR MUSEUM

1961 V.H. (ii) 400cc minicar.
NATIONAL MOTOR MUSEUM

1910 Via (i) 24/30hp tourer.
NICK BALDWIN

To its credit, the Vespa was a well-finished and competent car in a totally different class from most other microcars. Considering it was competing with Fiat's 500, it is a great credit to the Vespa that about 34,000 cars were built.

CR

VETCOR (US) c.1994

Vetcor Enterprises Inc., Dayton, Ohio.
The Vetcor I was a kit car that looked like a 1984 and onwards Corvette built on General Motors' mid-size sedan chassis.

HP

VETTA VENTURA (US) 1964–1966

Vanguard Inc, Dallas, Texas.
The Vetta Ventura was made in small numbers between 1964 and 1966. It was identical to the Apollo GT and the coupé bodies were supplied by Intermeccanica, the Italian company which made bodies for Apollo. The Ventura faded during 1966.

HP

VETTE-ROD (US) c.1998

Vette-Rod, Mandeville, Louisiana.
Vette-Rod built replicas of 1956 to 1960 Corvettes on custom frames with Chevrolet running gear. They were sold in kit form with a basic package including steering, disc brakes, a spaceframe, the full interior and a convertible top. Chevrolet V8 engines were used.

HP

VEXEL (E) 1999 to date

Vehículos Extremeños Especiales Ligeros SL, Madrid.
This was a very light car built specially for invalids but also prepared as a city-car. It used 49cc 5.4bhp, 125cc 9.8bhp petrol, or 600cc 18bhp diesel engines.

VCM

VEYRAT (F) 1990 to date

Veyrat Automobiles, La Garenne Colombes.
Conceived by a Parisian florist, the Veyrat was a brave attempt to create an extremely fast, pure, yet practical mid-engined sports car. In construction it consisted of a tubular chassis with an aluminium floor and fibreglass/carbon-fibre bodywork. The design was broadly wedge-shaped with an open roof and roll-over bar. The centrally-mounted engine was a 3-litre V6 taken from the Alfa Romeo 164. The high price of the Veyrat 630 kept production to a trickle.

CR

V.H. (i) see F.D. (i)

V.H. (ii) (E) 1961

Pedro Vargas Hernandez, Villafranca de los Barros.
Named after the initials of its builder, this was a 3-wheeled microcar powered by a 400cc vertical-twin 2-stroke engine driving the single rear wheel. Vargas Hernandez did not buy his engine from a proprietary supplier, like so many of his contemporary microcar makers in Spain and elsewhere, but designed his own. Only one car was made.

NG

VIA (i) (GB) 1910

Norburys Ltd, Manchester.
This company exhibited a 24/30hp 6-cylinder car at the Manchester Motor Show in February 1910. It had a dashboard radiator and was said to be 'largely on Renault lines'. However, its 3205cc short stroke (86 × 92mm) engine had no equivalent in the Renault range. They also listed 2- and 4-cylinder cars with the same cylinder dimensions.

NG

VIA (ii) (H) 1921

Villamos Autogar Reszvenytarsasag, Budapest.
This was a small electric car seating two passengers in tandem, with a top speed of 25mph (40km/h). Only a handful were made.

NG

VIBRACTION see TILBURY & PACHIAUDI

VICENTE (P) 1989–1990

The bodywork of the Vicente recalled certain Bugatti models of the 1930s, even though its use of Volkswagen Beetle mechanics was hopelessly inappropriate.

CR

VICEROY (GB) 1914–1915

Viceroy Sidecar Co. Ltd, New Basford, Nottingham.

Viceroy were well-known makers of motorcycle sidecars, but their car venture was short-lived, being cut short by World War I. It was a light car powered by an 8/10hp 4-cylinder Chapuis-Dornier engine, with shaft drive.

NG

VICI (GB) 1906–1907
Vici Motors Ltd, West Kilburn, London.
Little is known about the Vici car, except that a 12/16hp 4-cylinder model ran in the 1906 Tourist Trophy race. It was eliminated by running into a ditch. The company said that future Vicis would be all British, but that to get the TT car ready in time, 'some Continental fittings had to be used, so the car could not be described as of all-British manufacture'. The company had an office in Shaftesbury Avenue, where it traded as the British United Engineering Co., and a workshop in West Kilburn. They planned to build, or acquire, a factory at Walsall, Staffordshire, but this never came about. Possibly the TT car was the only Vici made.

NG

VICKERS (US) 1910–1911
Vickers Auto Car Co., Coshocton, Ohio.
Carl Vickers ran a repair shop in Coshocton, where in 1910 he built a runabout powered by a 20/24hp 4-cylinder 2-stroke engine of his own design. With financial backing from a friend he formed a company in May 1910 and began to manufacture the car on a small scale, selling it at the reasonable price of $650. Just 12 months later the company was in receivership, and no more cars were made.

NG

VICKSTOW (GB) 1913–1914
Vickers, Bristow & Co., London.
The only known address for this company was the Norwich Union Building in Piccadilly, so the factory location is unknown. It was listed as having a 1959cc 4-cylinder engine.

NG

VICOMTE (CDN) 1977–1979
Vicomte Classic Coachbuilders Inc., St Sauveur des Monts, Québec.
One of a small number of neoclassics made in Canada, the Vicomte had a convertible victoria body in early 1930s style, with a radiator that was a cross between that of a Duesenberg and a De Vaux. It was powered by a 6.6-litre Ford V8 engine with automatic transmission.

NG

VICTOR (i) (US) 1899–1903
1899–1900 Overman Wheel Co., Chicopee Falls, Massachusetts.
1901–1903 Overman Automobile Co., Chicopee Falls, Massachusetts.
The Overman Wheel Co. made three experimental petrol-engined cars between 1895 and 1898, but when A.H. Overman decided to start manufacture he chose a steam car which he called the Victor, after the bicycles that he made. It was typical of its kind, with a 4hp vertical 2-cylinder engine and single-chain drive. In 1900 the Victor bicycle business was sold to the Stevens Arms & Tool Co., and for a few months Overman leased the top floor of the building for the assembly of Victor cars. In January 1901 a new company was formed which took over space in another factory at Chicopee Falls, where the steamers continued to be built. His vacated premises were used by J. Frank Duryea for the manufacture of the STEVENS-DURYEA. About 50 Victor steamers had been made by November 1901, and they continued to be made with little change of design until early 1903. Meanwhile, Overman had been joined by A.L. Riker who designed the first petrol-powered LOCOMOBILE at Chicopee Falls, although it was put into production at Bridgeport, Connecticut. Overman merged his company with Locomobile.

NG

VICTOR (ii) (GB) c.1904
The Motor Works Co., Balsall Heath, Birmingham.
This company made frames for all kinds of cars, in tubular, angle steel or channel steel, saying that steel Bollée frames were a speciality. It also offered a light 3-wheeler either in kit form or completely assembled, for which the price was a modest £63. The engine was a 3⅛hp single cylinder Auto-Moto with water-

1914 Victor (vi) 965cc cyclecar.
NICK GEORGANO

cooled head, which drove through a 2-speed constant-mesh gearbox and chain-final drive to the single rear wheel. The wheelbase was only 60in (1523mm) and the overall length 108in (2741mm). The usual body was a tandem 2-seater with the passenger in front in the normal tricar position, but the makers said that for those who objected to tandem seats, a side by side body could be provided, the track and wheelbase being increased to suit, and the engine placed under a bonnet. They also offered a single-seater runabout and a delivery van.

NG

VICTOR (iii) (US) 1905–1911
1905–1910 Victor Automobile Manufacturing Co., St Louis, Missouri.
1910–1911 Victor Motor Car Co., St Louis, Missouri.
For most of its life this Victor was a typical high-wheeler, first with a 6hp single-cylinder engine and, from 1908–10, with a 14/20hp 2-cylinder engine. Transmission was by friction discs, and final drive by chain. It acquired a short bonnet in 1909 and for 1911 became a conventional tourer with front-mounted 40hp 4-cylinder engine and shaft drive. This was made for only one season, and the high-wheelers, with solid or pneumatic tyres, were continued alongside it.

NG

VICTOR (iv) (US) 1913–1917
Victor Motor Car Co., Philadelphia, Pennsylvania, etc.
Designed and promoted by C.V. Stahl, the Victor was a light car powered by a 16.9hp 4-cylinder engine, with 3-speed gearbox and shaft drive to a bevel rear axle. Originally riding on a 90in (2284mm) wheelbase and selling for $475, by January 1914 the wheelbase had been extended to 98in (2487mm), and the price raised to $500. Stahl moved around in attempts to find fresh funding for his business, first to Greenville, South Carolina, then to Wilmington, Delaware, Jenkintown, Pennsylvania and finally, in 1917, to York, Pennsylvania. It is unlikely that much, if any, production took place in these locations.

NG

VICTOR (v) (US) 1914–1915
Richmond Cyclecar Manufacturing Co., Richmond, Virginia.
This Victor was a typical cyclecar powered by an air-cooled V-twin engine by either De Luxe or Spacke, with friction transmission and belt final drive. The price was a very low $285, and this was reduced to $245 early in 1915, in an effort to unload stock before new models appeared. They never did.

NG

VICTOR (vi) (GB) 1914–c.1920
1914–1915 Victor Motors Ltd, Eynsford, Kent.
1915–c.1920 Tyler Apparatus (Victor Motor Department), Ealing, London.
Formerly the Dew, this was a cyclecar powered by a 965cc 8.96hp V-twin Precision engine with belt final drive. In 1915 an 1100cc 4-cylinder engine was used, still with belt final drive. About 24 cars were delivered after the war, probably assembled from existing parts.

NG

c.1921 Victoria (iv) sports car.
NATIONAL MOTOR MUSEUM

VICTOR (vii) (US) c.1982–1983

Victor Antique Auto, Rochester, New York.

The Victor TF–1800 was an exceptionally accurate replica of the MG-TF using MGB running gear. A steel tube frame mounted the MG engine and suspension. The body was fibreglass and authentic MG-TF trim parts were used. This kit was later passed on to GREAT LAKES.

HP

VICTORIA (i) (D) 1900–1909; 1957–1958

1900–1909 Victoria Fahrradwerke Frankenberger & Ottenstein AG, Nuremburg.
1957–1958 Victoria-Werke AG, Nuremburg.

A well-known bicycle maker from the 1890s, Victoria was renowned for motorcycles also, which were made from 1904. Car production began earlier, starting in 1900 with a voiturette powered by a 483 or 596cc single-cylinder engine, developing 4 and 5bhp respectively. In 1905 these were superseded by cars with 2-cylinder engines of 804 and 1248cc (8 and 10bhp). Later a 2680cc four was made, but after 1909 Victoria returned to 2-wheelers. These were made with great success up to the 1960s, and in 1957 Victoria returned briefly to the car market. Instead of designing a car itself, it bought the design of the SPATZ microcar, an open 3-seater powered by a 191cc single-cylinder Fichtel & Sachs or a 248cc 14bhp engine of Victoria'a own design, mounted in the rear. This car was refined for production by the famous Czech engineer Hans Ledwinka.

HON

VICTORIA (ii) (GB) 1907

Victoria Motor Works, Godalming, Surrey.

Assembled in a small garage, this Victoria was a tourer powered by a 10/12hp 4-cylinder Fafnir engine with overhead inlet valves. It had shaft drive and was priced at £300.

NG

VICTORIA (iii) (E) 1908

Automóviles Victoria, Barcelona.

Little is known about this car, but it was introduced at the Grand Prix International of the Catalonian Cup in 1908. The company announced three different models, a 2-cylinder 4hp, a 4-cylinder 16hp, and a 4-cylinder 18hp. There is no connection with the later Madrid-built Victoria.

VCM

VICTORIA (iv) (E) 1919–1924

Talleres Moderno Garage Franco Español, Madrid.

This was a small car using a 950cc ohv 4-cylinder engine designed by Arturo Elizalde with 4-wheel brakes. The company prepared touring and sports models, but only 100 were completed. The company also built the B (1020cc), the C (1093cc), and the D (1130cc). In 1924 Gwynne's Engineering bought the company, and especially the engine, which was used in the GWYNNE Eight.

VCM

VICTORIA COMBINATION see PARISIENNE

VICTORIAN (CDN) 1900

John MacArthur, Hopewell, Nova Scotia.

The first car to be made in the Maritime Provinces, the Victorian, or Victorian Motor Carriage to give it its full name, was a primitive car powered by a flat-twin engine which MacArthur purchased on a visit to New York, and was said to be of German manufacture. The engine was mounted beneath the seat, and drove the rear axle by flat belts. The tubular frame was of 1in pipe, a section of which also served as a carburettor, having petrol vaporised in it by in-rushing air. Steering was by tiller.

The belt drive proved unsatisfactory and was replaced by chains, but is still did not work well. It seems that MacArthur did intend to make replicas for sale, but he could never improve it enough to make it fit for the market. The solitary Victorian still exists.

NG

VICTORIOSA (F) c.1903

Albert Bauer, Paris.

Victoriosa cars were listed in several models of 6, 9, 12, and 16hp. The smallest was De Dion-Bouton-powered, but Aster and Brouhot engines were available in the larger cars. The 6hp was shaft-driven, but all the others used chain drive.

NG

VICTOR PAGÉ (US) 1922–1923

Victor Pagé Motors Corp., Farmingdale, New York.

Victor Pagé was a prominent author of textbooks surrounding mechanical subjects and magazine articles on technical matters. An ardent enthusiast of air-cooled engines, Pagé completed four small air-cooled vehicles which he badged the Utility Four, as a projected companion line of cars to a larger, more luxurious automobile. His design for the larger car – to be called the Victor Pagé – occupied all his attention and towards the completion of the first car, he abandoned any idea of continuing the Utility Four. Pagé, who continued to use his title of major to which rank he was commissioned during World War I, designed a 4-cylinder air-cooled ohv engine developing 30bhp to power the Victor Pagé. The car itself rode on a 117in (2969mm) wheelbase, featured an attractive vee false radiator, and disc wheels as standard equipment. It was vigorously promoted as the Victor Pagé Aero-Type Four throughout the automotive press in feature articles and its advertising included a picture of the Major plus a short biographical sketch. The car was marketed in both open and closed types as well as a taxicab and light commercial cars with prices from $1100 to $1750. According to automotive historian Beverly Rae Kimes, 128 Victor Pagés were completed.

KM

VICTORY (i) (AUS) 1916

Keep Bros & Wood, Melbourne, Victoria.

Having unsuccessfully tried to entice the horse-drawn vehicle coachbuilding trade to motors earlier with a motor-buggy named FRANKLINITE, this company engaged in the motor trade at this point with the light TRUMBULL and a car made by the Pontiac Chassis Co. which was sold under its own brand name. The intention was to label it Anzac (after the Australian & New Zealand Army Corps) but this was disallowed as the Government had protected it – so Victory it became. This was a conventional vehicle with a 17hp 4-cylinder Perkins engine of 2448cc and a 3-speed gearbox in a chassis of 106in (2692mm) wheelbase. Keep Bros & Wood built tourer and roadster bodies for both makes, which had short lives due to the war.

MG

VICTORY (ii) (US) 1920–1921

Victory Motor Car Co., Boston, Massachusetts.

The Victory was a curio in American motordom being, in point of fact, a reworked Model T Ford in camouflage which gave it an almost sporting appearance. The Victory was basically a rebuilt Ford equipped with a Rajo head, nicely set off with a wheelbase increased to 115in (2919mm), cycle mudguards and a square radiator plus disc wheels. Debuted at the Boston Automobile Show in 1920 and available as a roadster and 4-seater brougham, the Victory met with little success in the marketplace and production was terminated during 1921.

KM

VICTRESS (US) 1953–1961

Victress Manufacturing Co., North Hollywood, California.

Victress was one of the US' major kit car companies. It was founded by William 'Doc' Boyce-Smith, who had learned about fibreglass while working in the aerospace industry. He was joined by stylist Merrill Powell and production manager Bill Powell, and the threesome developed their first design, the S-1a. It was a beautiful car, with lines similar to the Ferrari 375. It was very aerodynamic and was used to set the fastest sports car record at Bonneville at 203.15mph (326.87km/h) in 1953. The S-5 was essentially the same body but smaller, and was intended to fit MG and similar imported chassis. The S-4 was a more angular shape intended for American sedan chassis. It was a handsome design with a vaguely Aston-Martin look in the grill. The C-2 was a coupé design to fit MG and VW chassis, and the C-3 was a larger version. These coupés were attractive with fastback tops and clean lines and Victress added a hatchback version of this design. They also made a dragster body. In 1960 they bought the SR-100 and CR-90 bodies from BYERS. All Victress bodies sold well. However, in 1961 Victress sold their entire automotive line to LaDAWRI.

HP

VICTRIX (i) (GB) 1902–c.1904

Victrix Motor Car Works, Kendal, Westmoreland.

The only car known to have been made in the county of Westmoreland, the Victrix was advertised with 6 or 8hp De Dion-Bouton engines. In 1903 larger cars with 12hp 2-cylinder and 24hp 4-cylinder engines were listed. The Victrix was also advertised by Farnan Frères of Paris, which would indicate a French origin.

NG

VICTRIX (ii) (I) 1911–1913

Officine Meccaniche Torinese, Turin.

When PEUGEOT-CROIZAT gave up their licence manufacture of Peugeot designs, this company took over and marketed the cars under the Victrix name. They also made a 695cc single-cylinder voiturette with 3-speed gearbox and shaft drive.

NG

VICTRIX (iii) (F) 1921–c.1924

Automobiles Victrix, Les Lilas, Seine.

This was an obscure car about which very little was published. It had a 15hp 4-cylinder engine and several body styles were offered: saloon, torpedo tourer, limousine landaulet, coupé and delivery van. It is unlikely that all of these were actually built.

NG

VIGILANTE/VIGILLANTE (US) 1974–1978; 1994 to date

1974–1978 Vigilante, San Jose, California.
1994 to date Vigillante Corp., Binghamton, New York.

Physicist Bob Keyes was behind the Vigilante Tri-Vette, an economy-driven enclosed 2-seater 3-wheeler. The first prototype examples used a Fiat 850 engine, gearbox, rear suspension and brakes but a Ford Fiesta 1600cc engine could also later be installed. It looked something like a slice of cheddar cheese with its razor-sharp nose and wedgey rear. It was short, ultra-narrow and a true lightweight at around 1000lb (450kg). Construction was by tubular steel space frame with steel side reinforcements, on to which was fitted the double laminated fibreglass body. To get into the tandem 2-seater interior, you would lift the gullwing door placed on one side; on the other side there was a convertible canopy. One strange feature was the positioning of the headlamps and indicators on the rear wings because the narrow front end had hardly enough space to fit even the single front wheel. A high speed pursuit vehicle was built for the California Highway Patrol but then production stopped. In 1994, the newly-spelt Vigillante completely swapped priorities, taking advantage of light weight and aerodynamics in a much longer shell to produce one of the world's fastest cars: a claimed top speed of over 215mph (346km/h) and 0–60mph (97km/h) in under 3 seconds. This time the powerplant was a Chevrolet V8, tuned to anything up to 700bhp.

CR

VIKING (i) (US) 1907–1908

The Viking Co., Boston, Massachusetts.

1903 Victrix (i) 6hp 2-seater.
NATIONAL MOTOR MUSEUM

1929 Viking (iii) Eight sedan.
NICK BALDWIN

This car was made by Arthur Bangs, who was the Boston representative for Franklin cars. Unlike the cars he sold, his own was not air-cooled, but used a 40hp 4-cylinder Rutenber engine, and was made as a 7-seater tourer on a 126in (3198mm) wheelbase. It was priced at $2500 and was made in small numbers only.

NG

VIKING (ii) (GB) 1914

Viking Motors Ltd, Coventry.

This was a light car powered by a 4-cylinder engine by Ballot or Mathis. It had shaft drive and Lanchester-type springs with long radius rods at the rear. The only body style was a 2-seater, priced at £160.

NG

VIKING (iii) (US) 1929–1930

Olds Motor Works, Lansing, Michigan.

The Viking was a sub-marque made by the Oldsmobile Division of General Motors, in the same way that Oakland had launched the Pontiac, Cadillac, the La Salle and Buick, the Marquette. The difference was that while the others were cheaper lines than the parent company built, the Viking was a move up-market, selling for $1595–1755 when Oldsmobile prices ran from $945 to $1035. The engine was an all-new 4252cc V8, the first side-valve V8 in America to be cast *en bloc*, and the valves were horizontal, which made for very easy maintenance. The same valve layout was used in the Oakland V8, though otherwise the two engines were quite different.

The rest of the Viking was strictly conventional, with a 3-speed non-synchromesh gearbox, spiral bevel rear axle and three body styles, 4-light sedan, 6-light sedan, and convertible coupé. In appearance the Viking somewhat resembled the La Salle, though it was in a slightly lower price range so as not to rival the Cadillac Division's product. Production began in April 1929 at the rate of 125 cars a day, and Olds announced that they would make 5000 a month from May onwards. Unfortunately customers did not come forward in large numbers, probably distrusting a new and untried engine, and in the whole of 1929 only 5259 Vikings were sold. The figure for 1930 was only 2738, and

1901 Vilain 6.8hp tonneau.

production was suspended in October of that year. 353 unsold cars were marketed as 1931 models. The Wall Street Crash in October 1929 has been blamed for the Viking's demise, but sales were disappointing even in the optimistic months before the Crash, so it is unlikely that the car would have succeeded anyway. Several Olds dealers went out of business on account of the Viking, and it is surprising that the parent company weathered the situation as well as they did.

NG

VIKING (iv) (GB) 1966

1966 Peel Engineering, Peel, Isle of Man.
1966 Viking Performance, Woodbridge, Suffolk.

It was the Manx firm of PEEL that conceived this car, which was originally called the Trident Mini. It was an odd-looking fibreglass 2+2 coupé designed for Mini subframes in a square tube steel chassis. The Mini windscreen and modified fibreglass Mini doors were retained. It was launched at the 1966 Racing Car Show, but only two were made before Bill Last of Viking Performance assumed production and renamed the car the Viking Minisport. Last's involvement with the ex-T.V.R. Trident led to him abandoning production in late 1966. Around 25 cars were made in all.

CR

VIKING (v) (GB) 1980–1983

1980–1982 Classic Cars of Coventry (Viking Cars), Blaby, Leicestershire.
1982–1983 Viking Cars, Narborough, Leicestershire.

A Jaguar specialist conceived the Viking. Its inspiration was the pre-war SS100, although it was not a replica. Into the box section chassis fitted Jaguar XJ6 suspension and any Jaguar XK 6-cylinder engine. The bodywork was made from aluminium with flowing fibreglass wings. It was offered as an up-market kit. The same company also offered World War II Mercedes staff car replicas on Jaguar parts. A break-up

of the original team led to another firm called Leaping Cats offering the same car, and this second operation also offered an expensive Jaguar C-Type replica.

CR

VIKING-CRAFT (US) c.1952–1955

Viking-Craft Manufacturing Corp., Anaheim, California.

Viking-Craft bought the rights to the Scorpion kit car built by the WILRO Corp. It was a tiny fibreglass-bodied sports car designed for modified Crosley sedan or station wagon chassis. It had no doors, a sparse interior and a tail section that pivoted up for access to luggage. A Super Scorpion was added, which looked similar but had doors and a conventional trunk lid. It was designed to fit the Crosley Super Sports, Renault, Morris and other small chassis. Either Scorpion model could be re-engined with a Ford V8-60. Company president Doug Caruthers also designed a sports car body for front- or rear-engined cars like the VW, Porsche, Austin, and MG. It was to be called the Cheetah and was an attractive design spoiled by clumsy detailing in the grill. Viking-Craft's main business was manufacturing house trailers, and they turned over sales of the Scorpions to Holloway Sports Car Center in California. Viking also made a runabout designed for children, but usable for short errands by adults. It had a Cushman engine and was considered for production in Japan where there was a strong market for small runabouts. It was sold in the US as a kit, with body, floorpan and frame selling for $79.50. All that was needed for completion was a Cushman motor scooter to provide running gear.

HP

VILAIN (F) 1900–1902

Vilain Frères, Paris.

This company made cars with horizontal engines, at first mounted at the rear, but from early 1901 in the centre of the frame. They had 6/8hp 2-cylinder engines with friction cone transmission and double belt or chain drive. A feature was the automatic lubrication box which, when once filled with oil, 'no further attention need be paid to the oiling of the engine parts for a considerable time'. Wire or artillery wheels were available. Models of 1902 had a special carburettor which was said to function equally well on petrol, paraffin, alcohol or a mixture of any two of these fuels. A Monsieur Vilain drove Prunel cars in the 1902 and 1903 Circuit des Ardennes, and 1903 Paris–Madrid Races, probably after he and his brother gave up making cars themselves.

NG

VILLAGE SMITHY (US) c.1987
The Village Smithy, Titusville, Florida.

This company made all-steel rebody kits for mini-pick-up trucks. The '06 Pie Wagon, '06 Huckster Wagon and '09 Limousine were caricatures of early commercial vehicles intended for use as delivery or promotion vehicles for businesses. They were sold in kit or assembled form.

HP

VILLARD (F) 1925–1935
Sté des Automobiles Villard, Janville, Oise.

The Villard was a relatively long-lived 3-wheeled cyclecar. Its single front wheel and low power made it unsuitable for high performance so it provided no competition to the Darmont and Sandford, but it was popular both as a passenger car and as a delivery van. For most of its life it was powered by a 345cc single-cylinder 2-stroke Chaise engine, which drove the front wheel via a friction transmission giving six speeds, and a single chain. In 1927 a few 4-wheelers were made, using a 500cc 2-cylinder engine, still driving the front wheels, and in 1931 there was an 'export' model with 500cc V4 engine and conventional gearbox. These were said to be destined for the United States, but they seem rather improbable cars for the American market, although the prototype still survives in the US.

Villards were made mostly as open 4-seaters, but at least one carried an elegant cabriolet body by Felber, whose work was usually seen on luxury chassis such as Hispano-Suiza. Villard's last appearance at a Paris Salon was in 1934, when it showed the Aero 34 coupé. This had a streamlined fastback 2-seater body and was available with single-cylinder engines of 250 or 350cc and conventional 3-speed gearbox. Suspension was by horizontal coil springs at the front, and semi-elliptic leaf springs at the rear. It also offered an older style open 2-seater which was said to be suitable for the handicapped driver (Type 29) and a delivery van (Type 33). Production ceased during 1935.

NG

VINCENT (i) (GB) c.1955
Vincent Engineers (Stevenage) Ltd, Stevenage, Hertfordshire.

Phil Vincent made some of the most desirable British motorcycles of the 1950s. When sales of these began to decline he experimented with a 3-wheeler, a 2-seater with no weather protection powered by a 1000cc V-twin Vincent engine driving the single rear wheel by chain. No production resulted, and Vincent went out of business in 1956.

NG

VINCENT (ii) (GB) 1982 to date
The Vincent brothers conceived the Hurricane in 1982. It was a clever rebodying exercise on a Triumph Spitfire/GT6 chassis. The stressed fibreglass body sported a hinge-forward front end and was a virtual monocoque. Hurricane production transferred to Domino, and ultimately to Caburn. The next Vincent model was a Riley MPH replica based on a simple ladder chassis designed for Ford Escort (later Cortina) parts, though the front suspension was Triumph Herald/Vitesse. Power options spanned Ford, Fiat, MG, Triumph, and Rover V8. The main body tub was in fibreglass, with an aluminium bonnet and engine side panels. Two versions were offered: the Brooklands with cycle wings and the MPH with flowing wings and running boards. New owners Dwornik developed the models (adding doors, for example) and renamed them Rallye and Sports respectively in 1993.

CR

VINCKE (B) 1894–1904
1894–1895 Vincke & Delmer, Malines.
1895–1904 Manufacture de Voitures Automobiles N. Vincke, Malines.

1987 Vincent (ii) MPH sports car.
CHRIS REES

Nicolas Vincke ran an important carpet and upholstery business, founded in 1852 and responsible for much of the furnishings on deluxe railway coaches such as those used by the Compagnie Internationale des Wagons-Lits et des Grands Express Européens. In 1894, in partnership with a French engineer, Louis Delmer, he built a 4-seater victoria with rear-mounted engine, very similar to a Benz in layout and appearance. A 2-cylinder Benz engine was used in the first car, but later the engines were made in Vincke & Delmer's factory. One of their cars took part in the 1895 Paris-Bordeaux-Paris Race, but retired. It was the first appearance of a Belgian-made car in competitions.

Six cars and two motorcycles were exhibited by the partners at the Salon du Cycle in Brussels at the beginning of 1896, but in the course of the year Delmer left to make cars in Brunn, Austria (now Brno, Czech Republic) although it is not known if he succeeded. The Benz-type cars were made up to 1898, when they gave way to a front-engined design on Panhard lines. Two such cars were shown at the Brussels Salon in March 1899, a coupé and a 6-seater brake, alongside an older Benz-style victoria and a quadricycle. Vincke built a 4-cylinder car in 1899 and a number of 8hp twins and 16hp fours up to 1903. His cars were sold in France under the name Vincke-Roch-Brault and in England under the name Vincke-Halcrow, the latter with 9hp 2-cylinder Aster engines. In 1904 Vincke abandoned cars to concentrate on his main business of furnishing, which included tramways and boats as well as railway coaches.

NG

VINDEC see ALLRIGHT

VINDELICA (D) 1899–1900
Heinle & Wegelin, Oberhausen.

Well known in the bicycle field, this company made a few light cars powered by 3.5hp engines with 3-speed gearboxes. They were sold in England by the P.T.S. Co. of Finsbury, London, under the name Liliput.

NG

VINDICATOR (GB) 1989 to date
Vindicator Cars, Halesowen, West Midlands.

The very first Vindicator, the Concept Coupé, was a 2-door coupé using a roof section taken from a Bond Bug. This was impractical, so a more Lotus 7-style car, the Sprint, was offered from 1991. The specification included Ford Sierra irs, Cortina-based front suspension (or special wishbone units), a stressed aluminium main body, and fibreglass wings, boot and front end. A full spaceframe chassis was offered from 1994. A further model was the Vulcan, introduced in 1998, with an enveloping doorless body and Ford Sierra parts. However, more importance was placed on the Shadow, also launched in 1998, which was a 2-seater open sports car using Ford Sierra components and a choice of Ford 4/V6 cylinder or Rover V8 engines.

CR

VINET (F) 1900–c.1904
Automobiles Vinet, Neuilly, Seine.

Vinet was a coachbuilder which entered the car field in the middle of 1900 with a 3.5hp De Dion-Bouton-powered voiturette with belt drive and a tubular frame.

1900 Vinet 3½hp voiturette.
NATIONAL MOTOR MUSEUM

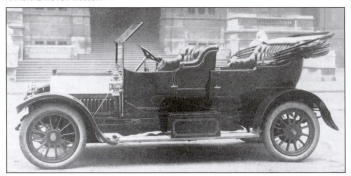

1909 Vinot 24hp tourer.
NICK BALDWIN

1914 Vinot 15/20hp landaulet.
NATIONAL MOTOR MUSEUM

As rendered in the original drawing it had a pointed bonnet like a Vauxhall with headlamps faired into it. This may never have been built, as photographs show a conventional bonnet fronted by a large gilled-tube radiator. By 1902 the Vinet had larger 12hp 2-cylinder or 16/20hp 4-cylinder Aster engines. They had low bonnets which were offset in the closed cars by the very tall limousine bodies.

NG

VINOT; VINOT-DEGUINGAND (F) 1901–1926

1901–1926 Vinot et Deguingand, Puteaux, Seine;
1919–1926 Nanterre, Seine.

This company was founded in 1898, to make bicycles, by Lucien-Marie Vinot-Préfontaine (1858–1915) and Albert Deguingand (1872–1943). The double-barrelled name Vinot-Deguingand was only used early in the company's history; once the cars became established they were always known simply as Vinots. The first cars, which were sold in England under the name La Silencieuse, had 5 or 7hp

vertical twin engines of 1475 and 1784cc respectively, with automatic inlet valves, front mounted and driving through belt primary and chain final drive. It had a vertical-gear gate change which was a feature of the marque for many years. By 1903 armoured wood frames and double-chain drive were adopted, and engines included a 10hp twin and two fours, the 3.3-litre 14hp Type H and 18hp Type F. In 1905 honeycomb radiators and pressed steel frames on the larger cars, which had grown to 5.8-litres and 30hp, were introduced. Vinot's first six came in 1906. This was a 6.5-litre car with pair-cast cylinders.

There was a considerable increase of capital in 1907, when the British Ducros family invested in Vinot as well as in CLÉMENT (i) and GLADIATOR. Two years later Gladiators were made in the Vinot factory and for the next 11 years two identical ranges were sold, even the catalogue prices being the same. Only the 24hp was peculiar to Vinot; this had shaft drive from 1909, but the largest Vinot/Gladiator, the 4153cc 35/40hp, retained chain drive until 1911. The year 1912 saw a more modern design, the 1692cc monobloc four with pressure lubrication, sold as a 10/12hp Gladiator and a 12/14hp Vinot. Town carriage versions of this had a double-reduction rear axle, and were popular as taxicabs. Some Vinot cabs of this era were still in use in London in the 1930s. There were four models in the 1914 Vinot/Gladiator range, those with Vinot badges being the 1689cc 12.1hp, 2208cc 15.9hp, 2610cc 15/20hp and 4166cc 25/30hp. In 1913, the last full year of production, the company made about 650 cars.

The Gladiator name did not survive 1920, and Vinots were made in a new factory at Nanterre, bought by Lucien-Marie Vinot-Préfontaine shortly before his death in 1915. The postwar cars resembled their predecessors of 1914, apart from electric lighting, but the full range was not made after 1920. Only the 15/20 survived, joined by a new 1847cc 10CV with pushrod ohv and aluminium pistons in 1921, which was made in declining numbers over the next few years. It received front-wheel brakes in 1924, which some sources say marked the end of production, although it was carried on lists up to 1926. In that year the factory was sold to DONNET. Albert Deguingand made cars under his own name from 1927 to 1930.

NG

VINTAGE JAG WORKS (US) c.1991

Vintage Jag Works, Murray, Utah.

This C-Type replica was a very accurate re-creation of the Jaguar sports racing car. It used a fibreglass body made from moulds pulled off an original car. They used a spaceframe that was supposedly identical to the original, with a Jaguar live axle at the rear and rhd steering. Jaguar engines with 240hp and Moss gearboxes completed the vintage illusion. Higher performance versions were optional. These cars were sold in kit or completed form.

HP

VINTAGE MOTOR WORKS (US) c.1985–1988

Vintage Motor Works, Sonoma, California.

The Hunter was a sports car kit that was formerly built by HATHAWAY. It was a traditional sports car that mimicked the Morgan and BMW 328 style. They were built on Triumph TR-4 and TR-6 chassis. This kit was later sold to HS ENGINEERING.

HP

VINTAGE SPEEDSTERS/SPYDERS (US) c.1994 to date

Vintage Speedsters/Spyders, Hawaiian Gardens, California.

This kit car company changed their name depending on the product being sold. They specialised in Porsche replicas built on Volkswagen Beetle running gear. The Vintage Porsche Speedster was built on a Volkswagen chassis. They also sold a version with big wheel flares for fitting wider rims. The Vintage 550 Spyder replicated the 1950s racing car and was based on a custom spaceframe with a mid-mounted VW or Porsche 914 engine. It had formerly been built by AUTO CLASSICS INTERNATIONAL.

HP

VIOLET-BOGEY (F) 1913–1914

Marcel Violet, Paris.

Achille Marcel Violet was one of the most prolific designers of small cars, and at least nine makes of car were largely or wholly his work, dating from the early years of the century to the 1950s. Only two, the SIMA-Violet and the Violet-

1914 Vinot 12/14hp tourer.
NICK BALDWIN

Bogey, actually bore his name. Although he was mostly concerned with the 2-stroke engine, the Violet-Bogey had a 1088cc vertical-twin 4-stroke engine with overhead inlet valves. Transmission was by friction discs, with final drive by single chain. Violet himself drove his car in several cyclecar races in 1913, finishing second in the Cyclecar Grand Prix at Le Mans.

The Violet-Bogey did not survive the war, but in the 1920s Violet was involved in the Major, Mourre, SICAM, SIMA-Violet, Weler, Galba and Huascar, while after World War II, Violet designed the front-drive Bernadet.

NG

V.I.P. (US) c.1986
Vehicle Improvement Products, Scottsdale, Arizona.
V.I.P. built a very believable replica of the Ferrari 250 Testarossa race car. Principals Chuck Rahn and Bob Shaw began with a partially completed project started by Doug Champlin and Dave Klem. They made a fibreglass body that was very similar to an original and mounted it on a tubular frame with 4-wheel independent suspension and powered with a Chevrolet V8. Although V.I.P. initially planned to build them in series, the legal problems associated with building Ferrari replicas caused them to cease production after four were made. One car ended up in the hands of Chuck BECK, who advertised in 1997 that he would sell replicas if there was sufficient demand. At one time the V.I.P. moulds were in the hands of EXCALIBUR, but none were produced by them.

HP

VIPEN (GB) 1898–c.1904
Easy Riding Cycle Co., Hull, Yorkshire.
This company sold cars under the names Vipen and Holderness, but they were probably imported machines. Early Vipens were heavy-looking cars similar in appearance to the MMC or Panhard, while in 1902 the company advertised a range of vehicles from a 1.5hp motorcycle to a car with 12hp 2-cylinder engine. The 1903 offering was a 4-seater tonneau on De Dion-Bouton lines.

NG

VIQUEOT (F/US) 1905–1906
The Viqueot Co., Long Island City, New York.
This company was a subsidiary of the Vehicle Equipment Co., makers of the V.E. cars and commercial vehicles. They were all electrics, but the Viqueot was a substantial petrol car with 28/32 or 40/45hp 4-cylinder engine, 3-speed gearbox and chain drive. The chassis were made in France at Puteaux, in a factory owned by Viqueot's president, Hector H.G. Havernmeyer, and bodies were built and fitted in the plant at Long Island City. The collapse of the Vehicle Equipment Co. brought an end to the Viqueot company as well.

NG

VIRATELLE (F) 1919–1924
Sté des Moteurs et Automobiles Viratelle, Lyons.
This company was listed as a car maker from 1919, and it also made large motorcycles with 686cc engines from 1922 to 1924. Probably the few cyclecars made also used these engines.

NG

VIRGINIAN (US) 1911–1912
Richmond Iron Works, Richmond, Virginia.
An old-established association of small iron foundries entered the car market with a conventional 6.4-litre 50hp 4-cylinder car made as a 4-seater roadster or 7-seater tourer. Both were priced at $3000. The venture was short-lived, and by February 1912 was in receivership.

NG

VISCOUNT (GB) 1985–1986
Viscount Motors, Bury St Edmunds, Suffolk.
The Viscount TC was a rather plain-looking 1930s style roadster kit. It used Triumph Herald or Vitesse parts mounted in a special twin rail chassis, with modifications to the brake pedal, fuel tank, gear lever and front springs. The bodywork was virtually all in unpainted fibreglass and cycle wings were standard, though flowing wings were listed among the options.

CR

VITREX (F) 1974–1980
Vitrex Industries SA, Paris.
The first product of this operation was the Riboud, a very basic 3- or 4-wheeled open microcar designed by architect Jacques Riboud, using a 2.4bhp 47cc Sachs engine. It was the cheapest microcar in France at FFr6430 in 1979. While the Riboud was made by MARLAND, the firm's other model, the Addax, was

c.1980 Vitrex Addax microcar.
NICK BALDWIN

1900 Vivinus 3½hp voiturette.
NATIONAL MOTOR MUSEUM

1907 Vivinus 22/28hp tourer.
NATIONAL MOTOR MUSEUM

sub-contracted to a firm called E.C.A.M. in Chambly. This was even more basic than the Riboud, and was offered exclusively in 3-wheeled format, using 47cc or 50cc engines with automatic and 3-speed gearboxes respectively. As well as importing the ALL CARS Snuggy, Vitrex also launched the Garbo at the 1980 Paris Salon: this was a rather snout-nosed enclosed 2-seater with a 49cc Peugeot engine, automatic transmission and disc brakes. After Vitrex ceased trading, the Garbo was revived as the PUMA.
CR

VITTORIA (I) 1914–1915
Giorgio Ambrosini, Turin.
This was a conventional car powered by a 3.2-litre side-valve monobloc 4-cylinder engine with 4-speed gearbox. The engine was made in-house, but bodies and other components were bought in from outside suppliers.
NG

VIVINUS (B) 1899–1912
1899–1911 Ateliers Vivinus SA., Schaerbeek, Brussels.
1911–1912 SA d'Automobiles Vivinus, Schaerbeek, Brussels.
Alexis Vivinus (1860–1929) was born in France where he worked originally as a naval engineer. In the 1890s he set up as a bicycle maker in Brussels, and in 1895 he started to import Benz cars, later using their engines in two cars of his own construction. He also made a 1hp motor for attachment to a bicycle. In 1899 he began car manufacture with financial support from Count de Liederkerke. His product was a light 2-seater voiturette with a front-mounted 785cc air-cooled single-cylinder engine, with 2-speed belt transmission and tubular frame. It proved very popular, selling 152 units between July 1899 and the beginning of 1901. More important than the domestic sales were the licences that he sold to foreign countries. His voiturette was made by De Dietrich in Germany, Georges Richard in France and Burford & Van Toll in England, who sold it under the name New Orleans.

These licence agreements brought BFr400,000 to Vivinus, who used the revenue to finance larger models with 2- and then 4-cylinder water-cooled engines, and shaft drive. In 1905 the company moved to a new factory where 250 workers produced six chassis a week. The foreign licence agreements had all expired by 1907, which was understandable with the general move towards multi-cylinder engines, but it meant a serious drop in income. From then onwards the Vivinus was a conventional car with 4-cylinder engines of 12/14, 20/24, 22/28, and 24/30CV. The smallest chassis was popular as a taxicab, examples running in Brussels, Liège, Vienna, Bucharest, Stockholm, and Rio de Janeiro. Vivinus also made motorcycles and aero engines; one of the latter was used in a Farman biplane in which Roger Sommer took the world duration record in 1909 (2 hours 27 minutes and 15 seconds). In 1910 a smaller 4-cylinder engine was produced, the 1943cc 10/12CV Type P, but at the end of 1911 the original company was put into liquidation, and Vivinus left to become the Belgian agent for Clément-Bayard. The new company exhibited cars at the Brussels Salon in January 1912, but few were made. Vivinus later joined Minerva where his greatest work was the design of the 40CV straight-8.
NG

VIXEN (US) 1914–1916
Davis Manufacturing Co., Milwaukee, Wisconsin.
The Davis company had been making engines for cars and tractors for some time before they launched their Vixen cyclecar. Naturally it used a Davis engine, a 15hp four in conjunction with friction transmission and shaft final drive. The frame was of reinforced ash, and the wheelbase long for a cyclecar at 106in (2690mm). Four body styles were offered, a 2-seater, 3-seater with side by side seating at the rear, a racing monocar and a delivery van, all priced at $395.
NG

V.L.S. (TAIWAN) 1981
A Taiwanese enterprise took up the rights to make the Pilcar, designed by Franco SBARRO in Switzerland. Instead of electric power, though, V.L.S. fitted the car with a 250cc motorcycle petrol engine in the tail.
CR

VOGTLAND (D) 1910–1912
Maschinen- und Automobilfabrik Endesfelder & Weiss, Plauen.
Vogtland cars were made in small numbers and sold mainly in the Vogtland district of eastern Germany. Two models of 4-cylinder car were made, a 6/12PS and a 10/20PS, with various bodies from 2- to 6-seaters.
HON

1923 Voisin 18hp coupé de ville by Belvalette.
NICK BALDWIN

VOGUE (US) 1921–1922

Vogue Motor Co., Tiffin, Ohio.

The Vogue was the linear descendent of the Economy-Vogue of 1920 which, in turn, had been badged as the Economy for the four previous years. The Vogue was an attractive car with slanted louvres on the bonnet and with wire wheels as optional equipment. Powered either by Continental 9N or Herschell-Spillman 11000 6-cylinder engines, the car was available in both open and closed types with prices from $2285 to $3250. In the two years of production, fewer than 100 units were completed.

KM

1925 Voisin 18hp tourer.
NICK BALDWIN

VOISIN (i) (F) 1919–1939

SA des Aéroplanes G. Voisin, Issy-les-Moulineaux, Seine.

Among the great characters of automobile history, few stand higher than Gabriel Voisin. He was a major manufacturer of aeroplanes during World War I, and the end of the war saw him with a large fortune and an equally large factory, but with a very small market for aeroplanes. He therefore decided to become a car manufacturer, and acquired a ready-made engine design, a 3969cc sleeve-valve four designed by Artaud and Dufresne, which had been considered by Citroën and turned down as unsuited to mass production. It could be said that Voisin stumbled upon the sleeve-valve principle by chance, but he remained faithful to it for the rest of his time as a car maker. Artaud and Dufresne later moved to Peugeot who also made large sleeve-valve engines. The Voisin engine, in fact, was on traditional Knight principles, and Voisin had to pay royalties to Charles Knight for each engine made. Aluminium pistons enabled it to develop 80bhp in its original 1919 form, the C1, later increased to 100bhp on the C3 of 1922 and to 140bhp in the C5, made from 1923 to 1926.

The rest of the C1 was conventional, with a 4-speed gearbox and brakes on the rear wheels only. At the front there was a handsome vee-radiator, topped from 1922 by a striking art-deco bird mascot, as distinctive as Hispano-Suiza's *Cigogne Volante*. The C1 was in production in 1919, and over the next two years more than 1000 were made.

Voisin's fertile mind was not content with a single design, and one that had originated with others. Among his designs of the period 1919 to 1921 were a 500cc 2-seater cyclecar called le Sulky, and a 7.4-litre light-alloy narrow-angle V12 which was shown at the 1921 Salon under the type designation C2. This had a remarkable braking system, each wheel having a closed hydraulic circuit of its own, with a small pump driven by the wheel itself. This had the effect of anti-lock braking, and was exceptionally light to operate. The clutch consisted of two opposed turbines in oil, with an electronic lock at the end of its travel, while

1927 Voisin 14hp saloon.
NICK BALDWIN

there was hydraulic control for the rear springs. Three prototypes of the C2 were built, but it would have been impossibly expensive to put into production.

The C1 was replaced by the C3 in 1921, the first model being the short-chassis C3C, followed the next year by the longer C3L. By raising the cr Voisin increased output to 100bhp, a remarkable figure of 25bhp per litre. Later competition versions of the CS engines gave as much as 140bhp or 35bhp/litre. This compares very favourably with the 25.3bhp/litre of the 8-litre Boulogne Hispano-Suiza.

For many years Voisin advertised that he would pay FFr500,000 to any manufacturer who could present a car of the same size which could match the performance and efficiency of a Voisin. There were no challengers. The competition engines had a cr of 8:1, very high for the time, and were used in the 1922 Touring Car GP entrants. These had light aluminium 4-seater bodies, and finished 1-2-3 (Rougier, Duray, Gaudermans). For the 1924 race, Voisin came up with a slab-sided unitary construction design, powered by 2- and 4-litre engines. Ironically, the race was won by a sleeve-valve Peugeot, designed by Voisin's original helpers Artaud and Dufresne, but Voisin cars were 2nd, 3rd, and 4th. This was the last year in which he raced his touring cars, but he entered a team in the 1923 Grand Prix.

Although the C1 and C3 sold well Voisin wanted to enter the quality small car field as well, and he commissioned from his engineer Marius Bernard a 4-cylinder car, still with sleeve-valves, which was launched as the C4 in mid-1921. It had a capacity of 1243cc. The main differences from the larger unit were thermo-syphon cooling in place of a pump, and only two bearings instead of five. This reflected Voisin's philosophy of 'infinite simplicity', with no more than the necessary minimum of any components. One of these small Voisins, with a very light open body of rivetted aluminium and little shelves for wings, was driven from Paris to Milan by Dominic Lamberjack to beat the Orient Express. It had an auxiliary epicyclic gearbox which doubled the available speeds. Originally operated mechanically, it became pneumatic, and eventually electric in actuation on later Voisins. In 1924 the small engine was increased to 1328cc (C4S), and in 1925 it became the 1550cc C7. All these increases were obtained by enlarging the bore, while the stroke remained constant at 110mm. This dimension was chosen for the first 6-cylinder Voisin, the 2326cc C11, which had the same cylinder dimensions as the C7. In fact the 110mm stroke was continued on Voisin engines up to the late 1930s.

The C11 was probably the best-selling of all Voisins, though exact figures are not known. Gabriel Voisin's own estimates of his total car production varied from

NICK BALDWIN

VOISIN, GABRIEL (1880–1973)

Probably the most idiosyncratic of all car makers, Gabriel Voisin had a role in aviation history more important than in that of cars. He was born on 5 February 1880, the son of Georges Voisin, a foundryman. Educated at the École des Beaux Arts in Lyons, he studied architecture at first, and an interest in the subject is evident in some of the styling of his coachwork. With his younger brother Charles he built an experimental car in 1899, but flying soon attracted them more. They built kites at first, then gliders, and in 1907 set up Voisin Frères in the Paris suburb of Issy-les-Moulineaux. In that year Gabriel Voisin built an aircraft which took off under its own power, and flew for about 80 yards. At this time the Wright aeroplanes still needed a catapult to become airborne, which is why Voisin claimed to have built the first proper aeroplane. With their partners Henri Farman, Léon Delegrange, and Captain Ferber they began to build bi-planes, being the first company to offer aeroplanes for sale. An early customer was J.T.C. Moore-Brabazon who bought a plane in October 1908, and with it became the first person to exceed 250 yards of powered flight in Britain, in 1909. By 1911 there were 59 Voisins owned by registered aviators, but the following year Charles was killed in a car crash, and the company was wound up. It was soon revived, and after various changes of name it became the S.A. des Aeroplanes G. Voisin in 1917. A large factory was built opposite the flying ground at Issy-les-Moulineaux, and a total of 10,700 bi-planes were made during World War I, as well as Hispano-Suiza and Salmson aero-engines.

In 1919 he found himself with a large factory, 2000 employees, and no orders for aeroplanes. He tried to diversity into prefabricated housing and motors for assisting bicycles, but became more famous for his cars. Falling sales led to loss of control of his company in 1932, although he regained it two years later, only to lose it again in 1937. It is surprising that he had as many customers as he did, for he had a low opinion of the average motorist, which he did not conceal. In a handbook he wrote 'We have divided this manual into two distinct parts; the first, short, incomplete, will, perhaps, be read, but the second, which represents an enormous amount of work, will doubtless never be opened'. To those who complained about some aspect of cars, he suggested that they buy another make. He was particularly contemptuous of American-style advertising, which used hype rather than hard facts, and of the people who fell for it. He was, however, sympathetic to other manufacturers in a smaller way of business. Charles Delfosse approached Voisin to ask if he might use the moulds for the differential housing which Arbel were supplying to Voisin for his 8CV. He replied 'I am fond of little chaps like yourself who are in the soup and trying to get out of it. Come and see me on Monday and you can use the moulds for your cars'.

He was constantly working on new ideas, including steam cars, of which he had owned several before World War I, but the only postwar design which went into production was the Biscooter minicar, and that was built in Spain rather than France. The last vehicle to bear his name was a tiny 6-wheeled truck powered by a 200cc engine, which was shown at the 1958 Paris Salon. In his old age he had a stream of visitors and correspondents but he complained that they were less interested in his aeroplanes than in his love life (which was extensive). He could not understand why people should be interested in his cars; to one young man who visited him with a vintage Voisin, he said 'Why are you bothering with old crocks like that? At your age you should be spending your time and money on pretty girls'.

Voisin was married, but separated from his wife in 1926. They had a daughter, Janine, In about 1950 he was married again to a Spanish girl of about 18. Her elder sister was her duenna and 'came as part of her dowry'. He lived with these two ladies for the rest of his long life, dying on Christmas Day 1973.

NG

Further Reading
Men, Women and 10,000 Kites (autobiography), Putnam, 1963.
Automobiles Voisin 1919–1958, Pascal Courtault, White Mouse Editions, 1991.
'A Visit with Gabriel Voisin', L. Scott Bailey, *Automobile Quarterly*, Vol, 13, No. 4.
'Gabriel Voisin, Archetype of Constructors', Griffith Borgeson, *Automobile Quarterly*, Vol.13, No.4.

1935 Voisin C25 Aérodyne saloon.
NICK BALDWIN

27,000 to 65,000 units, according to who he was talking to, and even the lower figure is probably on the high side. Nevertheless, production of the C11 and its successors, which were made up to 1936, must have run to around 4000.

Famous Owners

By the mid-1920s the Voisin was established as a fashionable and chic car, and numbered among its customers entertainers Maurice Chevalier and Josephine Baker, film star Rudolph Valentino who had three, two in Paris and one in Hollywood, novelists Anatole France and H.G. Wells, and the architect Le Corbusier who was a friend of Voisin's, and who designed the door handles on the early cars. Whenever he wanted to use a car in his architectural sketches, Le Corbusier always featured a Voisin.

In the late 1920s Voisin coachwork became more distinctive, and some were really bizarre. The most characteristic was the Lumineuse, a saloon with very large glass area and squared-off contours. Its lines followed those of some Weymann designs, and Voisin was an admirer of the Weymann system, although for its wood and fabric he substituted aluminium.

Voisin was a pioneer of the streamlined body, and his Aérodyne 4-door saloons had fastback bodies and wings which mirrored the bodies' lines.

Even more dramatic was the Aérosport 2-door saloon of 1936 in which the wings flowed straight through to the rear of the car, in the all-enveloping style which did not become common until the late 1940s.

Larger cylinder bores gave increases in capacity to 2994cc in 1931 and to 3318cc in 1936, by which date production of the traditional Voisins was practically at an end. To supplement dwindling sales the company bought in second-hand models and completely rebuilt them, selling them as 'voitures revisées' at considerably lower prices than new cars, though they carried the full works guarantee. In 1935 a new Voisin cost from FFr88–90,000, but the prices for the revisées ran from FFr16,000 for a 2-door saloon about eight years old to FFr50,000 for a year-old 4-door saloon. Improvements on the later 6-cylinder cars included an electric fuel pump, Cotal gearbox in place of the electrically-operated 2-speed axle, and hydraulic brakes. There were also some much larger 6-cylinder engines, the 4331cc C12 (1927–1930) and the 5830cc C16 and C22 (1930–c.1932). Some 5.8-litre engines were fitted in the underslung frames used for the V12s.

1930 Voisin V12 Myra saloon.
NICK BALDWIN

V12s and Straight-12s

In 1929 Voisin built a single-seater car to run at Montlhéry for 24,840 miles (40,000km), powered by an 11,660cc V12 engine. It was not successful, but Voisin was sufficiently enthused by the V12 layout to offer a smaller unit in a production car. Two sizes were listed, 3850 and 4860cc, though the majority of cars had the larger unit. It was offered in a conventional frame, and also in a very low underslung frame based on that of the record car. The entire frame was suspended under both axles, hanging by its semi-elliptic springs. This model, known as the C20 Simoun, was listed in the October 1929 catalogue, though the prototype was not running until the summer of 1930. It had a 2-door coupé body, but this was never commercialised. Those few underslung V12s that were sold were 2- or 4-door saloons and a cabriolet, known respectively as the Mylord, Myra, and Myrte. They were very expensive, at FFr180,000 (a Type 46 Bugatti cost only FFr100,000 at the time), production figures are uncertain, though it is thought that not more than 12 underslung V12s were made (the chassis was also available with the big six engine). Voisin himself said that he thought he had made 50–60 V12 engines, so presumably the balance went into conventional chassis, apart from two which he sold to the Bucciali brothers for their front-wheel drive cars.

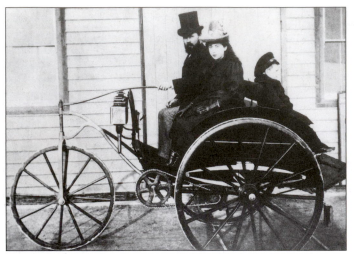

1887 Volk electric carriage.
NATIONAL MOTOR MUSEUM

These expensive and uneconomic cars combined with the Depression to put Voisin's finances in a very bad way; the millionaire of 1919 was comparatively poor by 1931, and so was his company. It was taken over by a Belgian group who wanted to form a European General Motors, and one of their first moves was to axe the V12s. However, he regained control in 1934, in time to work on a new design, this being the world's only straight-12. Voisin had tried an 8-litre straight-8 engine in one of his light Aérosport bodies, following this with a V12, but he found that the forward position of the heavy engine made for very unsafe handling. The idea of a straight-12 was to get the weight closer to the centre of gravity. Two 2994cc 6-cylinder blocks were used in tandem, the rear one projecting into the driving compartment, and transmission was by a 4-speed Cotal gearbox. The body was the standard Aérosport 2-door coupé. Top speed was 106mph (170km/h), and Voisin drove it frequently between Paris and Macon. A second straight-12 was built, with 4-door saloon bodywork, but production never started. He also designed other prototypes, including a front-wheel drive powered by a transversely-mounted V8 in 1930, and a saloon with diamond-pattern wheels like the Sunbeam-Mabley, powered by a sleeve-valve radial engine, in 1934. Neither of these was built, nor was a 6-wheeled bus with steering on the front and rear axles.

In 1937 Voisin again lost control of his company to a financial consortium, from whom a French Armenian, M. Garabeddian, bought up the remaining pontoon frames used for the Aérosport. Abandoning sleeve-valves he chose the American-built 3560cc Graham 6-cylinder engine, which could be had with a supercharger to increase power from 90 to 116bhp. Two bodies were offered, a 4-door saloon and a 2-door cabriolet. Gabriel Voisin had nothing to do with this car, whose engine he called 'a sorry piece of machinery'. It was launched at the 1937 Salon, and a year later the range was augmented by a 2-door coupé on a shorter wheelbase, but fewer than 20 of these C30s were sold altogether.

During World War II the Société des Aéroplanes Voisin was taken over by the large aeronautical firm, Gnome et Rhône, but Gabriel Voisin remained as a technical consultant. After the war, and still under Gnome et Rhône control, he designed an ultra light 2-seater powered by a 125cc Gnome et Rhône engine driving the front wheels. Baptised the Biscooter, it was shown at the 1950 Salon, and two years later was followed by a rear-engined model. Neither of these saw production in France, but the front-drive design was taken up by Autonacional in Barcelona who made several thousand of them between 1951 and 1958 (see BISCUTER).

Voisin continued to be interested in all forms of transport, including space travel, up to the time of his death at the age of 93. The last vehicle to bear his name was a tiny 6-wheeled truck powered by a 200cc engine, which was shown at the 1958 Paris Salon.

NG

Further Reading
Automobiles Voisin 1919–1958, Pascal Courteault,
White Mouse Editions, 1991.
'Gabriel Voisin, Archetype of Constructors', Griffith Borgeson,
Automobile Quarterly, Vol. 13, No. 4.

VOISIN (ii) (F) 1984–1985

S.A.R.L. Voisin Tout-Terrain, Livet.
Marc Voisin made a name for himself converting Citroën 2CVs into 4-wheel drives. His only foray into car production was the Lynx of 1984–85, a very basic open jeep-style device based on a 2CV chassis but powered by Citroën Visa/GS engines of 652cc or 1015cc. It came with its own 4-wheel drive system. However, the design did not enter production.

CR

VOITURE ÉLECTRONIQUE (F) 1968–1976

La Voiture Électronique, Paris.
Few cars have ever been as simply conceived as La Voiture Électronique. It consisted of a plastic triangle with moulded-in seats, between which sat a single joystick to control acceleration, braking and steering. Twin Jarrett electric motors drove the rear wheels. The car weighed only 440lb (198kg), and its top speed of just 15mph (24km/h) and the limited 40-mile range betrayed its intended role as a factory run-around and shopping car. By 1972 a leisure version, oddly called the Porquerolles, was available, while a Cab version was also sold with a hard-top.

CR

VOLGA *see* GAZ

VOLK (GB) 1887–c.1895

Volk's Electric Tramway, Brighton, Sussex.
Magnus Volk (1852–1937) built the electric railway which runs along the sea front at Brighton, as it has successfully done for more than 110 years. In 1887 he built an electric dog-cart with a single front wheel, chain drive and *dos-à-dos* seating for four people. It was an assembled car, for the 0.5hp motor came from the Acme & Immisch Electric Works of London, and the walnut wood body was built by local coachbuilder Job Pack of the Sussex Coach Works. On a smooth level road it could reach 9mph (15km/h), but any loose surface brought the speed down to 4mph (6km/h), and it could not cope with a gradient of more than 1 in 30. In 1895 he built a second car, to the order of Sultan Abdul Hamid II of Turkey. The engine was also by Acme & Immisch, now of 1hp, and instead of the single front wheel there were two set close together, with centre-pivot steering. The Sultan was sufficiently impressed to order another car, with body by Thrupp & Maberly, but Volk had less to do with this, and it is probably more accurate to call it an Immisch. They may have made a handful more, but there was insufficient demand to justify anything which one could call production.

NG

VOLKSWAGEN (i) (D) 1936 to date

1936–1937 Dr Ing h.c.F. Porsche GmbH, Stuttgart.
1937–1938 Gesellschaft zur Vorbereitung der Volkswagens, Berlin; Stadt der KdF Wagens.
1938–1960 Volkswagenwerk GmbH, Berlin; Wolfsburg.
1960 to date Volkswagenwerk AG, Wolfsburg.
The car which has sold in larger numbers than any other model, more than 20,700,000 to date, had its origins in a small design studio at 24 Kronenstrasse, Stuttgart, belonging to Dr Ferdinand Porsche. Despite the expensive cars with which his name was associated, Austro-Daimler Prince Henry and S series Mercedes-Benz, Porsche had a lifelong interest in a small car which could be bought by the average working man, perhaps because of his own humble background. Soon after he set up his Bureau, Porsche undertook the design of a family saloon powered by a rear-mounted 5-cylinder radial engine for the motorcycle firm Zündapp. Three prototypes were built, but the engines proved troublesome, and were probably too complex for mass production anyway. Zündapp withdrew their support, but Porsche soon found a backer for another design in another motorcycle maker, NSU. The prototype he built for them came closer to the design which was to appear as the Volkswagen shortly afterwards. The Zündapp (Project No.12) had a rear-engine and rounded back, but the NSU (No.32) added to these features a flat-four air-cooled engine, torsion bar suspension and a more rounded front as well as a fastback. The 1470cc engine was designed by Josef Kales, a member of Porsche's Bureau, while body styling was by another member, Erwin Komenda. Three No.32s were made, a steel saloon bodied by Drauz, and two fabric saloons bodied by Reutter.

1938 Volkswagen (i) VW38 pre-series saloon and tourer.
NICK BALDWIN

The 32 had no better fate than the 12, it is said because NSU realised that their contract with Fiat prevented them from making cars, but surely they would have been aware of this obstacle before commissioning the project? However, Porsche soon found another supporter, in the newly elected Chancellor, Adolf Hitler. Less than a month after coming to power, at the opening of the Berlin Motor Show in February 1933, Hitler said 'Without motorcars, sound films and wireless, there is no victory of National Socialism'. A year later, at the opening of the next Show, he said 'I see no reason why millions of good hard-working people should be excluded from car ownership'. By then Porsche was already at work on a new design, and Hitler took a keen interest in it, even suggesting a more rounded front than Porsche's June 1934 sketches showed. He may have originated the name 'beetle' for the car, for he said 'It should look like a beetle; you've only got to look to nature to find out what streamlining is'.

On 22 June 1934 Porsche signed a detailed contract for the development of the Volkswagen (People's Car). Porsche agreed with Hitler's request that it should cruise at 62mph (100km/h) and have a fuel consumption at touring speeds of 40 miles per gallon, but he was not so happy about the suggested selling price of RM995 (a contemporary 1.2-litre Opel cost RM1880, and even the 2-cylinder DKW was RM1750). The low price was adhered to when the VW was offered for sale in 1938, although the car could only be bought on a subscription scheme of a minimum payment of RM5 per month. At that rate it would have taken 16 years to buy a VW, as the car was not to be delivered until the full amount had been paid. In fact no ordinary citizens took delivery before World War II broke out.

Several designs of engine were proposed, and the first running prototype had a flat-twin power unit, but it proved excessively noisy. The flat-four was suggested by Austrian-born Franz Xavier Reimspiess who was also responsible for the VW monogram. His E-Motor, as it was called, had a capacity of 984cc, aluminium cylinder heads and a centrally-mounted chain-driven camshaft actuating eight enclosed pushrods which operated the ohvs. Although capacity has been increased several times, the basic layout of Reimspiess' engine has been

1956 Volkswagen (i) saloon.
NICK BALDWIN

followed in all the VW Beetles and commercial derivatives made up to the present. Porsche's original designs, Nos 12 and 32, were made by the companies who had commissioned them, but no one came forward to build the first Volkswagen. His design bureau was simply an office with no manufacturing facilities, so the first five cars were built in the garage of Porsche's home, some construction work spilling over into the garden. The first two cars, V1 and V2 (V=Versuchswagen, experimental car) were a saloon and a cabriolet, with bodies by Reutter and Drauz respectively. They were ready for testing by early 1936, and covered many thousands of miles in the hands of the Porsche family and members of the Bureau. Meanwhile three more cars were built, code-named

NATIONAL MOTOR MUSEUM

PORSCHE, FERDINAND (1875–1951)

'Father' of the Volkswagen, Ferdinand Porsche had earlier created a number of Austro-Daimler, Mercedes, Mercedes-Benz, and Steyr cars. He was an engineering consultant to Auto Union AG, Röhr, Mathis, Alfa Romeo, and others, but barely lived to see his own name on a car.

Born at Maffersdorf near Reichenberg in Bohemia on 4 September 1875, he learned his first lessons in mechanics in his father's workshop. His formal schooling was brief, as he was apprenticed to a metal-worker at the age of 15.

He joined Elektrizitäts-AG Bela Egger in Vienna as a mechanic in 1884, and was a design engineer when he left the company two years later. He signed up with Jacob Lohner GmbH in 1896 and designed battery-electric vehicles at first, adding a line of petrol-electric ones in 1898-99.

He was chief engineer of Jacob Löhner GmbH until 1906, when he signed up as technical director of the Oesterreichische Daimler-Werke AG. Here he designed the Maja car (named after Maja Jellinek, sister of Mercedes) one of which he drove to victory in the Prince Henry Trial of 1909. From 1910 to 1917 he created a range of Austro-Daimler aircraft engines. During the period 1991 to 1916 he was also associated with the Skoda Works, for whom he designed heavy military vehicles, such as artillery tractors, road trains, and armoured cars, propelled by the Löhner-Porsche system of petrol-electric motors built into the wheel hubs. In 1915 he was appointed managing director of Oesterreichische Daimler-Werke AG, and two years later, the Vienna Technical University conferred upon him an honorary doctor's degree in engineering.

In 1923 he accepted an invitation from the management of Daimler Motoren Werke and took office at Stuttgart-Unterturkheim as technical director on 18 June 1923. He designed a racing car for the Targa Florio and continued Paul Daimler's work on supercharging. His attention was focused on engines, which grew in size and power, at the expense of chassis development.

After the Daimler company's merger with Benz, he came in for much criticism, and several former Benz directors, including Friedrich Nallinger, were determined to oust him. In return, Porsche grew increasingly irritable, and his term with Daimler-Benz came to an end in November 1928. On 1 January 1929, he signed up as technical director of Steyr. He designed the Steyr Typ 30, based on a new car project he had started for Mercedes-Benz, and then created a 5297cc straight-eight model tentatively named Austria, but it was never put into production.

There was much disagreement between the Steyr management and Porsche, who saw his contract terminated in 1930. He returned to Stuttgart and opened an independent consulting-engineering office, Porsche Konstruktionen GmbH, in partnership with Adolf Rosenberger (1900–1968) on 31 January 1931, 'for the design of engines, motor vehicles, aircraft and ships', according to the Porsche prospectus. His first client was Wanderer, for whom he designed two small (1692cc and 1963cc) 6-cylinder engines which went into the W20 and W40, respectively, in 1933.

Rosenberger had driven the Benz Tropfenwagen and suggested that Porsche use its concept for a modern racing car. Rosenberger and Hans Baron Veyder-Malberg then founded Hochleistungsfahrzeug GmbH (high performance vehicle company) in Stuttgart to promote and finance the project, which was known as the P-Wagen before it was sold to Auto Union. Rosenberger left Porsche in 1932, however, and went to live in France in 1933 (when Hitler came to power).

Porsche got along with Hitler, who responded favourably to Porsche's exposition of a concept for an economy car that everyone could afford. One prototype (Porsche 12) had been built by Zündapp in 1932, and another (Porsche 32) was built by NSU. What became the KdF-Wagen or Volkswagen started as the Porsche 60 in 1935. Over the following five years, Porsche divided his time between the development and production plans for the Volkswagen and military vehicle projects. In 1940 Hitler named him head of the Panzer Commission, an engineering office (Krupp had pressured Hitler into removing Kniepkamp, Porsche's predecessor in that office).

Among Porsche's wartime duties was the conversion of the Peugeot factories to German military needs, a matter to which he paid scant attention, but which had fateful consequences. In 1944 Porsche moved his office from Stuttgart to Gmünd in Austria to escape bombing raids, and remained there when war ended. But on 15 December 1945, when attending a meeting at Baden-Baden, accompanied by his son, Ferry, and son-in-law, Anton Piëch, they were arrested by civil servants of the French ministry of justice, and accused of being instrumental in the deportation of Peugeot production workers (French citizens) to the Volkswagen plant at Wolfsburg. Ferry was released six months later, but Ferdinand Porsche and Piëch were incarcerated in a Dijon prison.

On 2 May 1946, Porsche was transferred to the Paris area and kept under house arrest in a comfortable villa. Here he was interviewed by executives and engineers of the Regie Nationale des Usines Renault, who wanted his advice on the 4CV (a project started by Louis Renault after seeing the Volkswagen at the Berlin Motor Show in February 1939). He did not give them much help, although he did point out that the Billancourt works did not seem well suited for the mass production of a small car.

On 17 February 1947, Porsche was transferred briefly to the Meudon prison before being taken to a prison in Reims to await trial. The trial never took place, and he was liberated on 1 August 1947, returning to Austria. His son paid the French authorities a ransom of FFr1million for his release, which had been arranged by a long chain of meetings and communications, involving Carlo Abarth, Rudolf Hruska, Tazio Nuvolari, Count Lurani, Louis Chiron, and Charles Faroux. Pierio Dusio put up the cash as payment to Porsche for the design (Porsche 360) of a 4-wheel drive 12-cylinder 1500cc racing car (Cisitalia). Charles Faroux, guiding spirit of motor racing regulations and journalist, had some clout in Paris and was able to open doors at ministerial level.

But the ageing engineer never recovered from his ordeal. His creative force was spent, and his health was failing. He died on 30 January 1951.

Ferdinand Porsche married Aloisia Kais in 1902. They had two children, Louise (b.1904) and Ferdinand ('Ferry') (1909–1998). Louise married Anton Piëch; their son Ferdinand is the present head of Volkswagen. Ferry was closely involved in the design of the first Porsche sports cars, and was chairman of the board of Porsche for many years.

JPN

VW3. These had saloon bodies of slightly modified design, built by Daimler-Benz (two coachbuilt, one pressed steel), platform steel frames incorporating the tubular backbone chassis in place of the wooden floorboards of the V1/2, and all three had the flat-four E-Motor. The V1/2 had been tested with a variety of engines, but were re-engined with the E-Motor towards the end of 1936. The VW3s were handed over to the RDA (Reichsverband der Deutsche Automobilindustrie) for testing. This organisation of manufacturers was not keen on the Volkswagen project, seeing the car as an obvious rival to Ford, DKW, Opel and other makes. However, they issued a fair report on the trials in January 1937, and Hitler ordered that the project should go ahead. Disagreement arose over the projected price, and this led Hitler to take the project away from the RDA, doubtless to their relief.

In May 1937 Hitler assigned the project to the Gesellschaft zur Vorbereitung der Volkswagens, known by its abbreviation of 'Gezuvor'. This had its offices on the fourth floor of Porsche's Stuttgart Bureau, but came under the control of the vast Deutsche Arbeit Front (German Labour Front) which replaced the disbanded trade unions. A batch of 30 cars, code numbered VW30 from the number made, was built by Daimler-Benz during 1937. These were the first to have headlamps mounted in the wings, and were therefore closer to the final design, but they still lacked rear windows, having a row of horizontal louvres over the engine compartment. They were extensively tested by members of the SS, each car covering at least 50,000 miles and the lessons learnt were incorporated in the next batch of prototypes. These were called VW38, and were also Daimler-Benz-built. They were very close to the postwar production cars, having front-hinged doors, a divided rear window, small running board, hubcaps and bumpers, all features lacking on the VW30. Forty-four of the VW38 were ready by early 1938, but an even more important event was the laying of the foundation stone for the new factory, on 26 May. A site was chosen near Fallersleben, about 50 miles east of Hanover, and Hitler announced that the town built to house the workers would be called KdF Stadt, after the motto of the DAF's leisure section, Kraft durch Freude (Strength through Joy). Only after the war did the town take on its present name of Wolfsburg, after a nearby castle. The savings stamp scheme was initiated on 1 January 1939, and in the remaining months of peace attracted more than 335,000 subscribers. Of these, about 70 per cent had never owned a car before. A further batch of 50 cars was ordered from Daimler-Benz, and were completed by July, though none reached a private buyer. Three body styles were offered, saloon, roll-top saloon and cabriolet, although the latter was cancelled soon after the announcement, and very few were made. A special model was the Typ 64 streamlined coupé which was built for the 1939 Berlin–Rome–Berlin race, curtailed by the outbreak of war. The Typ 64, of which three were built, had a highly aerodynamic 2-seater body with enclosed front and rear wheels, and looked quite similar to the Porsche 356. It was, in effect, a Porsche rather than a VW, as were the projected mid-engined cars, one with a V10 engine, which were never built. The idea of sports cars did not appeal to the DAF, though one would imagine that Hitler and his Minister for Sport, Adolf Huhnlein, would have been pleased with any racing successes that might have come their way.

Wartime Production

The first car did not actually leave the factory until 15 August 1940, and production continued until 1944, totalling only 630 cars. This was because the bulk of the factory was given over to two military derivatives, the Typ 82 Kübelwagen and the Typ 166 Schwimmwagen. The Kübelwagen (bucket car) was a Jeep-type open 4-seater of a type also made by Opel, Daimler-Benz, Ford and other German companies. The bodies were made by Ambi Budd in Berlin, and production ran from January 1940 to early 1945, by which time 50,435 had been made. An important step in 1943 was the adoption of an engine enlarged to 1131cc, as this was the standard size for the postwar Volkswagen car. The Schwimmwagen was an amphibious car, with doorless 4-seater body, a 5-speed gearbox, 4-wheel drive and a retractable gear-driven propeller. It was a much more sophisticated vehicle than the Kübelwagen, and production was lower, only 14,283 between the end of 1942 and 1944.

Even in the midst of war, Porsche was considering improvements to the Volkswagen, and among his projects were 4-wheel drive, supercharging, turbo-charging, diesel and sleeve-valve engines and an all-synchromesh gearbox (the production cars had no synchromesh at all until October 1952). These were carried on at his Stuttgart premises, which now included workshops, and indeed some Schwimmwagen were also made there. The KdF factory made not only

1961 Volkswagen (i) 1500 saloon.
NATIONAL MOTOR MUSEUM

1962 Volkswagen (i) Karmann Ghia 1200 coupé.
NICK BALDWIN

1972 Volkswagen (i) 411LE saloon.
NATIONAL MOTOR MUSEUM

1973 Volkswagen (i) Passat 2-door coupé.
NATIONAL MOTOR MUSEUM

1975 Volkswagen (i) Polo L hatchback.
NICK BALDWIN

c.1972 Volkswagen (i) Type 181 4-seater.
NICK GEORGANO

1979 Volkswagen (i) Golf L hatchback.
NATIONAL MOTOR MUSEUM

vehicles but also aircraft and aero-engine components, stoves and, from September 1943, the pilotless flying bomb known as the V1. The factory was 75 per cent destroyed by bombing, and when the Allied forces entered it in April 1945 there was little to encourage them. The first to arrive were American soldiers, though it soon passed under British control.

The Postwar Years

There have been few greater misjudgments than the opinions of British and American car makers on the Volkswagen. Ernest Breech of Ford said 'I don't think what we are being offered here is worth a damn', while the British commission under Sir William Rootes said the same thing in a more roundabout way: 'The vehicle does not meet the fundamental technical requirements of a motor car'. Nevertheless the British soldier in charge of the factory from August 1945, Major Ivan Hirst, sanctioned production of the Volkswagen saloon (the very first vehicles to leave the factory were Kübelwagens, of which 138 were assembled in June 1945; by the end of the year 522 were made). There was also the Typ 51, a saloon body on the Kübelwagen chassis, of which 703 were made in 1945, compared with only 58 standard saloons. In 1946, 7787 vehicles emerged from Wolfsburg, of which 7677 were standard saloons and the remainder Typ 51s or trailers. Of these the great majority went to the Allied military forces in Germany or abroad. They could be bought in Germany for the equivalent of about £100. Although official exports did not start until 1947, 3000 saloons went to France in 1946, and 50 to Russia. In 1947, 8987 saloons were made, and the first commercial exports began, two cars which went to Holland in October. By the end of the year the Netherlands had taken 56 VWs. Exports to the USA, which was to become a very important market, began in January 1949. In July 1949 the first export model appeared, with more chrome on running boards, waistline and bonnet. This was also available on the domestic market, at DM5450, compared with DM4800 for the standard saloon. By 1951 VWs were being exported to 29 countries, of which the most important markets were Belgium, Sweden, Switzerland, Holland, Finland and Brazil. It was not until the mid-1950s that Americans were converted to the advantages of the small car, but the US soon became VW's leading export market, with 500,000 sold there by June 1960.

An important development in 1948 was the appointment as General Manager of Heinz Nordhoff (1899–1968), formerly manager of Opel's truck factory at

Brandenburg. He was to direct the company through the vital years of its growth, and was one of the leading architects of Germany's 'Economic Miracle'. It was Nordhoff's decision not to change the Beetle's appearance, and he resisted all suggestions to that effect. In September 1948 the British military control of Volkswagen came to an end, and ownership of the company passed to the state of Lower Saxony.

Development of the Beetle, 1946 to date

Today's Beetle, still made in Mexico, is a clearly recognisable descendant of the 1936 model, yet according to Beetle expert Hans-Rudiger Etzold, only one single component has remained unchanged, the cross-section of the metal channel holding the rubber strip that seals the bonnet and boot. Otherwise, the Beetle has undergone 78,000 modifications, of which the most significant are listed in order here.

Note: these are calendar year changes, not model year

1946–48: one standard model, 1131cc 25bhp, non-synchromesh 4-speed gearbox.

1949: additional models include export saloon with additional chrome, 2-seater cabriolet by Hebmüller, 4-seater cabriolet by Karmann (see next section).

1950: hydraulic brakes (export model). Opening rear side windows, optional roll-top roof.

1951: ventilation flaps ahead of front doors, Wolfsburg crest on the bonnet front (export model only).

1952: synchromesh on 2nd, 3rd, and 4th gears (export model). Quarter light in doors.

1953: one-piece oval rear window replaces divided type. Many older models were retro-fitted with the oval window, making two-piece windows rare. 1192cc 30bhp engine from December 1953.

1955: twin exhaust pipes.

1956: tubeless tyres on all models.

1957: enlarged rear window, now rectangular rather than oval.

1960: semaphore arm direction indicators replaced by lights. Output increased to 34bhp. Synchromesh on bottom gear (export models). Optional Saxomat automatic clutch (to 1968).

1962: Wolfsburg badge removed from bonnet front.

1964: slimmer pillars and a gently curving windscreen give greater window area. Standard model gains all-synchromesh gearbox.

1965: 1300 model with 1285cc 40bhp engine added to range.

1966: 1500 model with 1493cc 44bhp engine added to range.

1967: optional semi-automatic 3-speed gearbox on 1500. Redesigned bumpers and front wings with vertical headlamps.

1968: optional automatic transmission and front disc brakes on 1300 and 1500.

1969: export models for the US have 47bhp 1584cc Transporter engine.

1970: new 1302 model with MacPherson strut ifs replacing torsion bars, easily identified by more prominent nose giving greater luggage accommodation. Available with 34 or 44bhp 1293cc or 50bhp 1584cc engines. Old-style 1200 and 1300 models still made (to 1977).

1971: rear window enlarged again, and more louvres in engine cover.

1972: 1303 model has curved windscreen.

1973: alternator on engines above 1300.

1974: more spartan 1200 without hub caps.

1975: 1303 saloons discontinued, so all Beetles of old-type appearance. Only cabriolet continued with long nose.

1978: German production ends. Beetles now imported from Mexico, with smaller rear windows of pre-1971 design.

1980: cabriolet discontinued.

1985: last consignment of Mexican-built Beetles arrives in Germany. Production for local market continues, though at a reduced rate.

Production and Exports

The sales success of the Beetle was phenomenal, and must have astounded those who were so contemptuous of the car just after the war. The 100,000th car was delivered on 4 March 1950, the 500,000th on 3rd July 1953, and the millionth on 5 August 1955. In honour of this achievement, just ten years after the first postwar model was made, Heinz Nordhoff was made a freeman of the city of Wolfsburg. 1955 was the first year in which average daily production exceeded 1000 units. By 1965 Beetle production was exceeding a million cars a year, and this was maintained each year to 1973, apart from 1967, when it dipped to 'only' 925,787. A long-awaited landmark occurred on 17 February 1972, when the 15,007,034th Beetle came off the line, beating the record for a single model which had been held by the Ford Model T.

NATIONAL MOTOR MUSEUM

HIRST, IVAN (1916–2000)

As a British soldier in war-torn Germany, Ivan Hirst played a unique role in establishing production of the Volkswagen Beetle. Without his vision this world-beating car might never have emerged from the ruins of Wolfsburg.

Hirst was born in Saddleworth, Yorkshire, and was educated at the local grammar school and at Manchester University. He joined the family firm which made optical instruments, and was also active in the Territorial Army. During World War II he was promoted to major in the Duke of Wellington's regiment, later transferring to REME (Royal Electrical and Mechanical Engineers). After D-day he managed a tank repair shop in Brussels before being sent to Wolfsburg, as the Nazi's KdF Stadt had been renamed.

The pundits in the British motor industry had little time for the curious rear-engined air-cooled car. Sir William Rootes told Hirst 'If you think you're going to build cars in this place, you're a bloody fool, young man'. However Hirst was encouraged by his commanding officer, Colonel Michael McEvoy, who had made superchargers and had been involved in the Hatton-McEvoy luxury car project in 1930. They rigged up a prototype and gained some orders from military personnel. 'Nobody gave me a real brief', Hirst said, 'I was just told to go there and do something'. Staffing was a huge problem as many of the workforce were Russian slave labourers who had to be sent home, while some of the management were Nazi sympathisers who were unacceptable to the occupying forces. However returning German PoWs were keen to work there, though at first they lived in huts and survived on potato soup. By the end of 1946 Hirst had a workforce of 8000 who were making 1000 Beetles a month. He introduced valuable lessons he had learnt in the Army, and ensured that spare parts were readily available.

For all his success Hirst's role was only that of a caretaker, for some time management would have to be handed over to Germans. He himself recruited his successor, Heinz Nordhoff, who was appointed managing director in January 1948, though Hirst did not leave Wolfsburg until August, a month before the company was formally handed over to a trust run by the state of Lower Saxony.

He subsequently worked for the German section of the Foreign Office before joining the secretariat of the OECD (Organisation for Economic Cooperation and Development) in Paris. He worked there until he retired to the Pennines in 1975.

He was married to Marjorie, who predeceased him, and died on 10 March 2000; they had no children.

NG

1983 Volkswagen (i) Scirocco GL coupé.
VOLKSWAGEN

1984 Volkswagen (i) Scirocco GTL coupé.
NATIONAL MOTOR MUSEUM

1990 Volkswagen (i) Golf cabriolet.
VOLKSWAGEN

To cope with the demand, VW opened other factories in Germany, at Hanover and Emden, and also through their acquisition of Auto Union in 1965, at Ingoldstadt. The Karmann body factory at Osnabrück could also be considered as a VW supplier, making all the convertibles as well as the Karmann Ghia coupé and convertible. The last Beetle left the line at Wolfsburg at 11.19 on 1 July 1974, but manufacture continued at Emden until 19 January 1978.

The Beetle was exported to over 100 countries during its lifetime, and was also assembled in 19 countries. These included Belgium, Portugal, Ireland and Yugoslavia in Europe, and numerous countries in Asia, Australasia, Africa, and Latin America. The Brazilian factory was particularly important, as it gave rise to a distinct family of Volkswagen described in their own entry. Beetle production continued in several countries after it ended in Germany, including Uruguay and the Phillipines (to 1982), Brazil (to 1986), Peru (to 1987), Nigeria, and Mexico, where it was still made in late 1999. These were available in England from an importer in Sway, Hampshire. Despite the Beetle's record sales in the USA, where it converted a nation to small cars and paved the way for

the success of other European and Japanese cars, it was never made there. The Pennsylvania factory only made Golfs.

Cabriolets, Coupés and Specials
The first open version of the Beetle was made in 1938, but very few were completed (just one survives). After the war Nordhoff wanted to revive the idea of an open Beetle, but decided to subcontract the work to outside coachbuilders. The firms that were awarded contracts were Hebmüller of Wulfrath for a 2-seater, and Karmann of Osnabrück for a 4-seater. The Hebmüller design did not last long, due to a fire and subsequent bankruptcy of the firm. 750 were made, between 1948 and 1953, of which the last few were built by Karmann. The latter's 4-seater was much more successful, and remained in production until 1980, two years longer than the saloon. It was a full 4-seater, providing the same accommodation as the saloon, and having the same roofline. In the days when there were standard and export models, the cabriolets incorporated the improvements

NICK BALDWIN

NORDHOFF, HEINZ (1899–1968)
Heinz Nordhoff was the man who made Volkswagen an industrial force and an important tool in drawing refugees from Eastern Germany into the Western economy by finding jobs for them at Wolfsburg. His political role in the preparation for the reunification of Germany was far bigger than was realised on either side of the Iron Curtain at the time.

Born in Hildesheim on 6 January 1899, he attended local schools and served in the Kaiser's Army for two years in World War I, and was wounded in action. He went back to school and graduated in 1925 from the Technical College of Charlottenburg in Berlin.

His first job was in the drafting office of the aircraft engine department of BMW in Munich. In1929 he went to Adam Opel AG as service manager, which meant coping with warranty claims, issuing service bulletins to the dealers, and providing feedback from the field to the product development engineers. He made several visits to the GM Institute and the GM car divisions in Detroit to learn American techniques, also picking up the essentials of American machine-tools and production methods. In 1934 he became a technical advisor to the made on the export cars, though not always straightaway. The export saloons gained hydraulic brakes in April 1950, the cabriolets not until December. From 1966 the cabriolet had the 1300 engine, followed in the 1970s by the 1500 and 1600, while from 1975 it was the only model to retain the longer bonnet. In its last few years nearly all cabriolet production went to the USA, where it was something of a cult car. The last of 331,847 left the production line at Osnabrück on 10 January 1980.

Another, more distinctive, car emerged from the Karmann works in May 1956. This was the Karmann Ghia coupé, an attractive 2-seater styled by Luigi Serge of Ghia on a slightly modified export chassis. The platform was a little wider than the saloon's, and there was an anti-roll bar at the front, which the saloon gained in 1960. The engine was the normal 1192cc unit, but better aerodynamics gave the coupé a higher top speed, 77mph (124kmh) compared with 68mph (110km/h). At 1808lb (814kg) it was 176lb (80kg) heavier than

management of Opel; in 1937 he was elected to the board of directors, and in 1939 he was delegated to the Berlin office which dealt with financial and political affairs.

In 1942 (at a time when GM had lost control of Opel to the Nazi government), he was named managing director of the Opel factory at Brandenburg, then the biggest truck factory in Europe. In 1945, after the Brandenburg plant had been lost to the Soviet occupation forces, he fled to the West and looked for work in Hamburg where he became service manager in a local garage. In 1947 he was spotted by British military officers who were looking for qualified leaders to run the Volkswagen plant in Wolfsburg. In January 1948 the British Military Government appointed him managing director of the Wolfsburg plant, whose buildings were more than 60 per cent destroyed, although the tooling, for the most part, was intact. During his first year in office he doubled the output to 19,244 cars.

Business analysts have accused him of over-doing a one-model policy, which was always a false accusation. From the beginning, he encouraged outside coachbuilders such as Hebmüller and Karmann to make VW convertibles and coupés. He managed to get the Type 2 van in production in 1950, cleverly sharing the complete basic platform as the Type 1 (Beetle). He made the same platform available to Porsche, who began buildings sports cars in 1949, but refused to supply even a single chassis to Ghia, where Mario Felice Boano had designed a sports coupé for it in 1950. The Ghia design became a big commercial success after Ghia got a chassis by buying a complete VW in Paris, and Karmann was engaged to handle its production.

Due to its KdF origin, Volkswagenwerk had no legal owner for years. That did not bother Nordhoff, who just kept up a growth rate that baffled the competition, the financial world, and politicians alike. He did it by rigid quality control and making sure that VW dealers around the world always had spare parts and trained service personnel. He was also shrewd enough to select David Ogilvie to handle worldwide advertising. The ownership question was settled on 22 August 1960, after the original KdF coupon-savers had been paid off, with the federal government in Bonn taking a one-third share of the DM600m share capital, the state government of Lower Saxony taking an equal stake, and the remaining one-third allowed to float on the stock market.

By a stroke of brilliance, Nordhoff set up a manufacturing plant in Brazil in 1953 (after an agreement with Renault and Fiat that they would stay out of Brazil as long as VW left the Argentinian market to them).

His downfall came because of an exclusive contract with the Porsche organisation for technical research and new-model programmes. When the 'Beetle' market showed signs of collapsing, Nordhoff hired engineers (Werner Holste, Albert Grotewohl) to work at Wolfsburg in competition with Porsche toward the creation of a durable 'Beetle' successor. But no viable solution was found in his lifetime.

He died on 12 April 1968 in the Wolfsburg hospital. The 'Beetle' successor eventually came from Audi-NSU.

JPN

the saloon, which made for slower acceleration. A convertible version joined the coupé in 1958, and in 1962 the 1500 engine was used in the Type 3 Karmann Ghia coupé with restyled body. This featured four headlamps and a more angular rear body, and was generally thought to be less attractive than the original. No convertible versions of the Type 3 were sold, though at least one was built for display purposes. The Type 3 was made alongside the earlier model up to July 1969, but the original Karmann Ghia remained in production until June 1974. Production was 364,401 coupés, 80,899 convertibles, and 42,498 Type 3 coupés.

A curiosity which was made at Hanover from 1969 to 1973, and later in Mexico, was the Type 181, an open 4-seater loosely based on the wartime Kübelwagen, with 1500 engine (1600 from 1974). It was intended as a fun car (Americans nicknamed it The Thing), though 2000 were supplied to the German Army in 1969/70, and others went to the Dutch and Belgian forces.

Hebmüller and Karmann were the only coachbuilders to produce officially-approved models, but numerous other firms made special versions of the Beetle. Rometsch made convertibles, coupés and a 4-door saloon version for taxi use, Meisen built an ambulance version, and Papler a doorless open 4-seater for the police (Hebmüller made some of these as well). Other firms who made special bodies, mostly coupés and convertibles, included Dannenhauer & Strauss, Spohn who made Germany's first fibreglass body in 1954, and, in Switzerland, Beutler and Ghia-Aigle. The Beetle platform was the basis of countless small makes of car such as the Australian Ascort, Swiss Enzmann, Austrian Denzel, Brazilian Gurgel and Puma and many others. The British kit car industry was largely founded on VW-based cars, before other donor cars such as Ford and Mini took over, while two other types of vehicle owe their origin to the Beetle, the Formula Vee racing car and the beach buggy.

The Beetle Grows Up

In 1961 Volkswagen broke their one model policy, though not drastically as the new car still used the rear-mounted air-cooled flat-four, slightly enlarged to 1493cc. The new car was called the 1500, and had a very different appearance from the Beetle, with a more conventional bonnet and a notchback rear end. It was made as a 2-door saloon and estate car, the latter called the Variant. An all-synchromesh gearbox was used, this being featured on the Beetle from 1964. With an extra carburettor it became the 1500S (1963–65), with a 9bhp increase to 54bhp, and a top speed of 84mph (135km/h). From 1966 it received the 1584cc engine to become the 1600; also featured were front disc brakes, while electronic fuel injection, dual circuit brakes and optional automatic transmission arrived in 1968. A fastback coupé was an additional body style in the 1600 range, which was made up to 1973. Total production of all 1500/1600s was 738,010 saloons, 601,286 coupés, and 203,046 Variants.

The final extension of the Beetle theme was the 411 which had a still larger engine of 1679cc (never used in any Beetle) and for the first time in a production Volkswagen, a 4-door saloon body. It also broke with tradition in having MacPherson strut ifs (adopted on the Beetle in 1970) and integral construction. A 2-door 411 was also available, and from 1970, a Variant estate car. Transmission was 4-speed manual or 3-speed automatic. With a 1795cc engine it became the 412 in 1972, made up to 1974. It was not the hoped-for sales success, perhaps because the market for cars of that size shied away from an air-cooled flat four with its distinctive sound which reminded people of its Beetle ancestry. Sales were 355,200 in seven seasons, low by Volkswagen standards.

Water-cooling at Last

Heinz Nordhoff died in April 1968, while still head of Volkswagen, but even had he lived it is likely that the loyalty to rear engines and air-cooling would have wavered soon. The disappointing sales of the 411 dictated that a more conventional car was needed quickly, so with no time to design a brand new model, VW adopted the K70 which had been designed by NSU, a company recently acquired by VW. It used a similar body shell to that of the Wankel-engined Ro80, but had a conventional 1605cc water-cooled single-ohc engine, front mounted and driving the front wheels. Suspension was all independent, and there were disc brakes on the front wheels. Unlike the Ro80, the K70 did not have automatic transmission. For 1974 and 1975 the engine was enlarged to 1807cc, giving 100bhp and a top speed around 100mph (161km/h), but the K70 never sold well (211,100 in six seasons), and was replaced by the Passat which overlapped it in production by two years.

The Passat of 1973 was the start of a whole new range of medium-sized Volkswagens, still made in updated form today. Its design came by courtesy of

1990 Volkswagen (i) Passat GT saloon.
VOLKSWAGEN

another acquisition company, Audi, for the Passat was based on the Audi 80. Initially made with 1296 or 1470cc single-ohc Audi engines, it had Giugiaro-styled bodies in 2-, 3-, 4-, and 5-door versions, saloons, hatchbacks and estates. A larger engine of 1588cc was available from 1975, and a 1470cc diesel from 1979. A total of 1,769,700 were made up to 1980, when it was replaced by the restyled Passat 2. This had a body shell completely different from the Audi 80/90, though some engines and transmissions were shared, as was the front suspension. The new Passat could be had with a wide range of engines over the years, from 1272 to 1994cc, including Audi's unusual 5-cylinder units, and a 1588cc diesel. From 1983 to 1985 there was a booted version of the Passat called the Santana. This had the same choice of engines, and after 1985 was reabsorbed into the Passat range. It chief claim to fame is that it was the first VW model to be made in China (from 1983), and it was also made by Nissan in Japan. 1988 saw a new range of Passats with more aerodynamic bodies and transverse engines of 1595, 1781 and 1984cc (petrol) and a 1588cc turbo-diesel.

Golf, Scirocco and Jetta

In 1974 VW announced the first loss in their history, a very serious one of DM807 million. The effects of the Arab-Israeli war, the downturn in the German economy and disappointing sales of the ageing Beetle all contributed to this, but fortunately the company had waiting in the wings the car which would save the situation. In May 1974 the Golf was announced, a successor to the Beetle in the popular-priced market, and a throughly up-to-date car with transverse front-mounted engine and front-wheel drive, originally in 1093 (50bhp) and 1471cc (70bhp) forms. The body was a crisply-styled 3- or 5-door hatchback designed by Giugiaro of Ital Design. The only thing the Golf had in common with the Beetle was the 95in (2411mm) wheelbase. At prices from DM8000 to DM10,790 it was very close to the Opel Kadett. The Golf displaced the Beetle from the production lines at Wolfsburg on 1 July. Production got under way very quickly, and by October 1976 the millionth Golf had been built. September 1975 saw the arrival of a high-performance Golf, the GTi, with 1588cc 110bhp fuel-injected engine. With a top speed of 112mph (180km/h) and excellent handling, the GTi won many friends, and led to numerous imitators in what became known as the 'hot hatchback' market. VW management was not initially very keen on the idea, and sanctioned only 5000 examples in order to gain homologation for Group 1 racing. It was, of course, a

new direction for VW, who had never stressed high-performance before, but they never had cause to regret the GTi. A larger 1781cc engine came for 1983; power was not much greater at 112bhp but was achieved at a lower engine speed. For those who wanted higher performance there were plenty of tuning firms offering various degrees of improvement. Oettinger of Friedrichsdorf made a 16-valve head which gave 136bhp at 8000rpm, and a top speed of 125mph (200km/h). Other firms offered styling improvements such as skirts, spoilers and special grills. Improving the Golf became quite a specialist industry, although only a relatively small proportion of GTis made were subject to conversion. In 1985 VW offered their own twin-cam 16-valve version, giving 139bhp and 123mph (198km/h). This was only available with the 3-door body, but the 8-valve GTi could be had with five as well as three doors.

Meanwhile a Karmann-built convertible version of the regular Golf had appeared in 1979, taking the place of the Beetle convertible at the Osnabrück factory. The hatchbacks came with a wider range of engines, including 1470 and 1588cc diesels, the first of these in 1976. For 1984 there was a major redesign of the body, with more rounded front ends and a longer wheelbase. This did not apply to the convertibles, as the Karmann factory did not tool up for the new body; even in 1989 the convertibles still used the old-style Golf front end, which some people considered more attractive. A new Golf for 1986 was the Synchro, with 4-wheel drive which had variable distribution between front and rear wheels according to the steepness or surface of the road. There was also a Golf Country Special, a 4×4 5-door hatchback with higher ground clearance made for VW by Steyr-Puch.

To meet the growing demand for a conventional saloon with luggage boot, VW brought out the Jetta in 1980. This was derived from the Golf, and was made with the same engines, petrol and diesel, though not in GTi form. For 1984 it was updated in styling along with the Golf, and later additions to the Jetta range included synchro 4-wheel drive (1986) and a twin-cam 16-valve engine (1987). In 1992 the Jetta was succeeded by the Vento, also a notchback saloon derived from the third generation Golf announced six months earlier.

The Golf succeeded magnificently in restoring VW's fortunes, and production reached 10 million in June 1988, and 19.3 million in June 1999. In 1980 it was the best-selling car in West Germany, Austria, Switzerland and Belgium. An American factory at New Scranton, Pennsylvania, opened in 1978, US-market

Golfs being known as Rabbits. By April 1981 500,000 had been made, and at their peak the factory was making 400,000 Rabbits per year. They concentrated on hatchbacks and never made the GTi or convertible, though they did also make a Golf-based pick-up that was unique to the US factory. The Scranton factory closed in 1988.

The Golf's floorpan and engines were also used for a coupé called the Scirocco, which in fact appeared three months before the Golf. It was made in the Karmann factory, and was effectively a replacement for the Karmann Ghia versions of the Beetle. Three engines were available initially, a 50bhp 1093cc and 70 or 85bhp versions of the 1471cc. In 1976 the 1588cc Golf GTi engine became available in the Scirocco, giving a 115mph (185km/h) top speed. Production had reached 504,200 when the original Scirocco was replaced in 1981 by a second generation model with a wider and roomier body. This was made with a variety of engines from the basic 70bhp up to the 139bhp twin-cam 16-valve. For 1989 it gave way to the Corrado, also a 2+2 coupé and using the twin-cam 16-valve 1781cc Golf GTi engine and a supercharged version of the single-cam 8-valve engine. Like

NATIONAL MOTOR MUSEUM

PIËCH, FERDINAND (born 1937)

A grandson of Ferdinand Porsche, Ferdinand Piëch was a brilliant engineer, if obsessive about details. A ruthless business leader, he turned companies around from loss to profit-first Audi, and then Volkswagen.

He was born on 17 April 1937 in Vienna, the son of Dr Anton Piëch, lawyer (1894–1952), and his wife Louise née Porsche. He was unremarkable in his early schooling, but gained entrance to the Polytechnic University of Zürich from which he graduated in 1963. Later that year he went to work for Porsche as an engine tester.

His first task was to find a solution to the oil-cooler problem with the 904. Next, he was put in charge of developing that flat-six engine for the 911. By 1966 he was head of the testing department, and in 1968 assumed the additional duties of product development, with a staff of 700. In 1971 he became technical manager of Porsche, having led the team that created the 917 racing cars (Le Mans, Canam), and supervising the company's non-automotive projects as well.

Then his mother and uncle (Ferry Porsche) decided that members of the Porsche and Piëch families should no longer hold positions of leadership with the Porsche company (while maintaining strict financial control). For five months he worked as an independent consulting engineer, 'making lots of money but at a very high risk', as he put it, before joining Audi-NSU Auto Union AG in 1972 as head of special projects.

A year later he was in charge of all test operations, and in 1974 became head of product development, attaining the title of Technical Director in 1975. In 1983 he became a member of the Audi management board and its deputy chairman, taking over the chairman's seat in 1988. His chief accomplishments at Audi were the development of lightweight body-shell construction and 5-cylinder engines, aerodynamic shapes, turbo-intercooling, permanent 4-wheel drive, full-zinc body coating, and advances in safety systems.

He was given a seat on the VW management board in 1992, and in January 1993 succeeded Carl Horst Hahn as chairman. Volkswagen was then in deep trouble, with an excessive unit cost, too-high a breakeven point, long lead times, and a dropping sales curve. Piëch told the press: 'VW is a duck that's grown too fat to fly'. Hahn had also gone way over budget in his commitments to new factory construction.

In March 1993 he ousted three of the eight board members, and in April he hired Jose Ignacio Lopez de Arriortua, former purchasing vice president of General Motors, as director of purchasing and production. 'Inaki' Lopez brought with him a heavy load of confidential GM documents on pricing and product planning, which led to civil and criminal lawsuits, forcing Lopez to resign from VW before the end of 1996. Lopez had to pay a penalty fee, and VW paid $100m in damages to GM, as well as agreeing to buy $1b worth of components from GM over a 7-year period. The contribution Lopez made to VW's balance sheet was to force suppliers to cut prices. Piëch cut the payroll by 41,000 jobs within two years and cut the number of high-volume car platforms from 16 to four in four years.

He was a hard taskmaster, and did not tolerate anything he perceived as under-performance by his executives. Some left due to a clash of personalities, such as Daniel Goeudevert, who had expected to succeed Hahn but agreed to stay on under Piëch only to walk out in July 1993. The VW production manager, Günther Hartwich, left soon afterwards. On 1 October 1993, Piëch dismissed Seat's president Juan Antonio Diaz Alvarez, blaming him for the loss of $1b. Piëch had picked Franz-Josef Kortüm (from Mercedes-Benz) in 1991 to be chairman of the Audi board, only to push him out in February 1994. Herbert Demel, an engineer was hired away from Bosch in 1990, only to be driven out in December 1996. Werner P. Schmidt, VW finance chief, who had come to Wolfsburg in 1967, was ousted in October 1994. Ulrich Seiffert served nine years as research director before being placed in charge of all engine programmes in 1987; he departed in December 1995. In 1996 Piëch chose Volkhart Koehler to succeed Ludvik Klima (who was killed in a traffic accident) as chairman of Skoda, and then dismissed him in March 1997.

When Nicholas Hayek, rebuffed by Peugeot, offered his Swatchmobile to VW, Piëch had the wisdom to reject it. It was later made by Daimler-Benz as the Smart. In November 1997 he opened negotiations with Vickers plc for the purchase of Rolls-Royce Motor Cars and ended up paying £479m but losing the rights to the Rolls-Royce name from 2003 (since the owners, Rolls-Royce plc, the aircraft engine makers, had sold it to BMW for £40m), leaving VW with a run-down plant at Crewe and the Bentley trade mark. A tentative offer to buy BMW in 1998 found no ear in Munich. Piëch then arranged the $110m purchase by Audi AG of Automobili Lamborghini, and secured the rights to the Bugatti trade mark. Later, Piëch announced the acquisition of real-estate in Molsheim and production plans for new Bugatti models.

VW shareholders, the press, and the public talked a lot about Piëch and megalomania, but in fact he never neglected the bread-and-butter models, be it Skoda, Seat, Audi, or VW. Shareholder discontent, however, kept the price of VW shares depressed for years, with an unfavourable knock-on effect whenever VW needed bank loans or planned a new stock issue.

JPN

1999 Volkswagen (i) Polo Match hatchback.
VOLKSWAGEN

1999 Volkswagen (i) Golf hatchback.
VOLKSWAGEN

1999 Volkswagen (i) Lupo S hatchback.
VOLKSWAGEN

Lancia, VW chose a supercharger in preference to a turbocharger to avoid the acceleration lag of the turbo. Top speed was 140mph (225km/h), though the Corrado's acceleration was no better than the 16-valve Golf as the coupé was 330lbs heavier than the hatchback, and the supercharger absorbed 16bhp. Like the Scirocco, the Corrado was made by Karmann.

In 1975 VW brought out a smaller car than the Golf, to tackle the supermini market. Called the Polo, it was clearly a member of the same family, with transverse 4-cylinder engine driving the front wheels, but the engine was only of 895cc (40bhp), and the only body style was a 3-door hatchback. Later, engines of 1093 and 1272cc became available in the Polo, and an alternative body was a 2-door booted saloon called the Derby. Production up to 1981 was 768,200 Polos and 303,900 Derbys. They were then replaced by a new series of Polos

with three bodies, an estate-like hatchback, a sloping hatchback called the coupé, and a saloon called the Polo Classic. Engines were 1043 and 1272cc petrol, and (from October 1986) a 1272cc diesel. The 1985 Frankfurt Show saw a high-performance Polo, the Coupé G40, with a 115bhp version of the 1272cc engine giving a top speed of 122mph (195km/h), faster than the 8-valve Golf GTi. A third generation Polo appeared in 1994, with restyled 3- and 5-door hatchback bodies and choice of 999, 1390, and 1598cc engines. In 1996 came 16-valve versions of the 1.4- and 1.6-litre engines, and a more powerful 120bhp version of the 1.6 came in 1998. Diesel engines were also available, and there were 4-door saloon and estate versions called Polo Flight which were, in fact, rebadged SEAT Cordobas.

The third generation Golf appeared in 1991 and the fourth in 1997. The bodies were updated, particularly in the third generation, and technical milestones included a 174bhp 2792cc V6 engine in the VR6 model of 1991, which replaced the GTi (though the name was revived later), and an innovative 2324cc narrow-angle V5 engine in 1999. This also had 4-wheel drive and a 6-speed gearbox. The most powerful Golf was launched in June 1999; the 2796cc V6 engine gave over 200bhp and had the same transmission and 4 × 4 drive as the VR6. Larger VWs included the Vento's successor called the Bora, a 4-door saloon available with three petrol and two diesel engines, and from 1999 with the 4-Motion 4-wheel drive shared with the Golf, and a completely restyled Passat. Launched in 1994, this was offered with four petrol engines, two fours, the V5 and V6, and two diesels, the largest being a 2496cc V6 also used by Audi. The 2781cc petrol V6 model came with 4-wheel drive, and there were also estate versions of the Passat.

In 1998 VW launched a new model below the Polo in size; similar to the SEAT Arosa, the Lupo was a 3-door hatchback offered initially with three petrol engines and one diesel, similar to those in the Polo. In autumn 1998 they launched the TDI powered by a 1196cc 3-cylinder diesel which achieved the magic consumption figure of 3 litres per 100km. In contrast, a hot Lupo was planned for 2000, with 4-wheel drive and turbocharged V4 engine developing over 200bhp.

Another new model in 1998 was the New Beetle; Mexican-built and using the Golf floorpan and drive with a 1984cc petrol or 1896cc turbo-diesel, it was a 2-door saloon with strong echos of the original Beetle, first seen as a concept car. A convertible version was planned for 2000, as well as a 150bhp 1781cc turbo-petrol option shared with the Golf GTi and Audi A3 1.8T. VW also had their version of the Ford Galaxy/SEAT Alhambra MPV, called the Sharan. For 2000 the Sharan had revised styling, as did the other two MPVs, to fit the corporate look of their manufacturers, though the common platform remained unchanged.

An Exciting Future
VW built their 61 millionth car in 1999 (world-wide sales for the whole VW Group are now 100 million), are now the third largest car makers in the world, and look set to continue their success into the next century. Their ambitious chief, Ferdinand Piech, made some dramatic purchases in the late 1990s, including Rolls-Royce, Bentley, Lamborghini, and Bugatti. Future plans for the VW range include a luxury saloon to rival the Mercedes-Benz S Series, powered by a 450bhp 6-litre W12 engine and viscous-coupled 4-wheel drive, and a luxury 4×4 estate using the same engine. A 5.6-litre version is already used in the top model of the Audi A8. Other engines planned for future VWs include a 4-litre V10 turbo-diesel and a 3.7-litre W8.

NG

Further Reading
The VW Story, Jerry Sloniger, Patrick Stephens Ltd, 1980.
The People's Car. An Investigation into the design and performance of Civilian and Military Volkswagens 1938–1946, Her Majesty's Stationery Office, 1996.
Battle for the Beetle, Karl Ludvigsen, Bentley Publishing, 2000.
The Beetle, Chronicles of the People's Car, Hans-Ruediger Etzold, Haynes, 1988.
The VW Beetle, a Collector's Guide, Jonathan Wood, Motor Racing Publications, 1983.
Small Wonder, the Amazing Story of the Volkswagen, Walter Henry Nelson, Hutchinson, 1967.
Volkswagen, Beetle and Derivatives, Hans-Otto Neubauer, Dalton Watson, 1979.
Volkswagen Golf, a Collector's Guide, John Blunsden, Motor Racing Publications, 1992
Volkswagen Karmann Ghia, Malcolm Bobbit, Veloce, 1995.

1999 Volkswagen (i) New Beetle saloon.
VOLKSWAGEN

VOLKSWAGEN (ii) (BR) 1957 to date

Volkswagen do Brasil, São Bernardo do Campo, São Paulo.

At the beginning of the 1950s José Thomson, the Brazilian Chrysler importer, suggested to Volkswagen the suitability of the Volkswagen Beetle for the Brazilian market. Volkswagen do Brasil was founded in March 1953, becoming the first, and subsequently the largest, manufacturing subsidiary outside Germany for Volkswagenwerk AG.

At first, only kits shipped from Germany, were assembled in the suburbs of São Paulo. In 1956, when 2820 cars had been assembled, a larger plant was built, with the intention of manufacturing rather than just assembling vehicles.

On 2 September 1957, covered by a Brazilian flag, the first Volkswagen Kombi came off the production line in São Bernardo do Campo. It had more than 50 per cent local content. Not until 7 January 1959 would the first Beetle with 54 per cent of its parts locally made make its appearance. Originally, Beetles were made at a rate of about five a day. In 1962, production of Karmann Ghia models was started. The cars had lower compression engines and stronger suspension, in comparison to their German counterparts.

Mr Thomson was right: the Beetle and the Kombi were well suited to the market, and in 1963 the 500,000th Brazilian Volkswagen was built. The one millionth came in 1967. By then, Brazilian Volkswagens had almost entirely local content. In 1967 Rudolf Leiding was sent from Germany to improve the company's performance by developing specifically Brazilian models. The first was a 4-door version of the 1600 saloon. A fastback version of this car was added in 1971. In 1972, in the elegant Rio de Janeiro premises of the Automovel Club do Brasil, the SP series of fastback GT coupés, with front disc brakes and 1.7-litre engines, was presented. In 1973, when Volkswagen do Brasil built its one millionth Beetle, they also introduced the 1.6-litre Brasilia saloon, based on a German prototype and available in 2-door, 4-door, and hatchback styles. Brazilian Passats were launched in 1974. The range included a low-priced version called the Surf, aimed at younger buyers. When Volkswagen opened their Nigerian assembly plant in 1975, the first cars to be assembled there were Brasilia and Passat kits from Brazil.

In 1979 Brazilian production passed the 5 million mark, and an alcohol-fuelled Beetle was being produced. Brazil could produce alcohol fuel in abundance from surplus sugar cane production. Hence, there was a pressing interest in using alcohol, to ease dependence on oil imports. From 1979, Volkswagen do Brasil built alcohol-fuelled cars in increasing numbers.

1999 Volkswagen (i) Passat TDI saloon.
VOLKSWAGEN

1990 Volkswagen (ii) Gol coupé.
VOLKSWAGEN DO BRASIL

The Beetle, nicknamed Fusca in Brazil, was dropped from the line in 1987. However, seven years later Brazilian President Itamar Franco, prompted, it is said, by an ex-girlfriend, suggested the Fusca production should be resumed. This was duly done, but from then on production was very limited.

1999 Volkswagen (ii) Parati Geracao III estate car.
VOLKSWAGEN DO BRASIL

1999 Volkswagen (ii) Gol Geracao III saloon.
VOLKSWAGEN DO BRASIL

1946 Volugrafo Bimbo 125cc microcar.
NICK GEORGANO

The Gol is another Brazilian model, which was introduced in 1984. It used the Beetle engine plus front-wheel drive. A water-cooled version of the Gol was called the Voyage and the Parati was an estate. The top of the range was the Santana.

The 1999 Gol was quite different from the early models. It was a 2-door hatchback or 4-door saloon, powered by engines which ranged from a 4-cylinder, 1000cc 62.5bhp unit, to a 4-cylinder 1600cc 88.5bhp unit. There was also the Quantum, powered by a 4-cylinder 2000cc 112bhp engine.

ACT

VOLKSWAGEN (iii) (AUS) 1959–1970
Volkswagen (Australasia) Pty Ltd, Clayton, Victoria.

Shortly after its arrival in Australia, local assembly of Volkswagen by Martin & King commenced and an Australian company was formed in conjunction with state distributors. In 1959 this company took over the Martin & King facility and expanded it to become the third centre of complete manufacture, after Germany and Brazil, and having, like them, a master body jig to ensure body panel accuracy. This outlay for relatively low production later caused delays to the introduction of overseas revisions. In 1968 a type unique to Australia, the Country Buggy, appeared.

Differing from similar models made elsewhere, it was an open runabout with the rear seat area easily converted to a load-carrying space and it incorporated the commercial's final drive units for better ground clearance. By 1970, when VW ceased production in Australia, 1119 Country Buggies had been built. Volkswagen took part in the development of a motor industry in the Philippines and Country Buggy production continued there as the Sakbayan 817. The Clayton plant continued under the Motor Producers title, assembling Nissan and Volvo models, eventually becoming the manufacturing base of Nissan Australia.

MG

VOLKSWAGEN-PORSCHE (D) 1969–1975
VW-Porsche Vertriebsgesellschaft mbH, Ludwigsburg.

This joint effort between two famous car makers was intended to provide would-be Porsche owners with a more affordable car. This first model, the 914, cost DM12,250 compared with more than DM21,000 for a standard 911. It had a mid-mounted VW-type engine offered in three sizes: 1679, 1795, and 1971cc. The latter gave 100bhp and a 120mph (193km/h) top speed. Transmission was by a 5-speed gearbox or Sportomatic, and it had disc brakes all round. More desirable, but also more expensive, was the 914/6 which was powered by a 1991cc flat-six engine as used in the Porsche 911T. It cost almost as much as a 911T, and relatively few were sold, only 3300, compared with 115,600 of the 914. Even rarer was the 916 which used a 2341cc flat-six from the Porsche 911S, which gave 190bhp and a top speed of 145mph (233km/h). Only 20 were made in 1971, and officially it did not exist as it was dropped just before the launch. The next joint venture was the front-engined 924, but this only carried the Porsche name.

NG

VOLPE (I) 1947
Anonima Lombarda Cabotaggio Aero, Milan.

The Volpe ('Fox') was an aesthetically successful attempt to recreate big car styling on a miniature level – and it certainly was miniature at only 98.5in (2500mm) long. A 2-seater convertible, it was powered by a 6bhp 2-cylinder 2-stroke 124cc air-cooled engine driving through an electro-magnetic 4-speed gearbox with a claimed top speed of 47mph (76km/h). The project came to an unfortunate demise with a legal battle over lost deposits.

CR

VOLTA CAR (US) 1914–1916
Cycolectric Car Co., New York, New York.

One of the few electric cyclecars ever made (another was the STORMS), the Volta Car was powered by a General Electric motor, with a range of 35 to 50 miles, and a top speed of 15mph (24km/h). Most Volta Cars were delivery vans, but a few roadsters were sold.

NG

VOLTOR (F) 1922–1925
Constructions Électriques Voltor, St Etienne, Loire.

This company specialised in the manufacture of batteries and electric chargers, but made a few cars in the early 1920s, one of which took part in an endurance run between St Etienne and Avignon in 1923. Car production did not last beyond 1925, but the firm showed a light electric van at the 1939 Lyons Fair.

NG

VOLTRA (US) 1961
Voltra Inc, New York, New York.

The Voltra was a large electric car with a 106in (2690mm) wheelbase and a General Electric motor.

HP

1960 Volkswagen-Porsche 914 sports car.
VOLKSWAGEN-PORSCHE

VOLUGRAFO (I) 1945–1948

A Torinese racing driver called Belmondo designed and built the Volugrafo Bimbo, described as the 'smallest car in the world'. It featured a tubular chassis and an aluminium one-piece body with straight-through sides and no doors. It resembled a dodgem car in shape, measured only 94in (2380mm) long and weighed only 275lb (125kg). Power came from a 125cc ohv 5bhp motorcycle engine driving through a 3-speed gearbox to the left-hand rear wheel only.

CR

VOLVO (i) (S) 1927 to date

1927–1979/80 AB Volvo, Gothenburg.
1979/80–1999 Volvo Car Corp., AB Volvo, Gothenburg.
1999 to date Volvo Car Corporation, Ford Motor Co, Gothenburg.
A company called AB Volvo was registered on 22 June 1915, as a subsidiary of SKF (Svenksa Kullager-Fabriken). Volvo became a trade mark for a type of ball bearing but went out of use in 1919, and AB Volvo became an empty shell company that existed only on paper.

A prominent SKF executive, Assar Gabrielsson, and an SKF engineer, Gustav Larson, met in 1924 and privately began to discuss car-making in Sweden. Gabrielsson had been SKF's operations manager in France from 1920 to 1922 and was amazed at the motoring scene there and the thriving auto industry. Larson had been an engine designer with White & Poppe from 1911 to 1913 and was well aware of the place of the automobile in Britain's society and economy. In August 1924 they made a verbal agreement to build cars in Sweden, which was formalised by a written contract on 16 December 1925. By that time, both had resigned from SKF.

As early as June 1925, Larson and his assistant Jan G. Smith, who had been a draftsman with car makers in the USA, were able to show detailed drawings of their car to potential backers, but no one wanted to invest in this scheme. Undaunted, Gabrielsson and Larson were able to obtain personal bank loans substantial enough to build ten pre-production cars between June and November 1926. Five of them had torpedo bodies by Freyschuss of Stockholm. Only one had a closed body, of Weymann-type construction.

1927 Volvo (i) P4 saloon.
NICK BALDWIN

1929 Volvo (i) PV651 coupé.
NICK BALDWIN

1936 Volvo (i) PV36 saloon.
NATIONAL MOTOR MUSEUM

1945 Volvo (i) PV60 saloon.
NICK BALDWIN

On seeing these cars, the investors changed their tune. SKF alone put up $40,000 and leased them the idle plant of Nordiska Kullager AB at Lundby, on the west side of the Göta river, just outside Gothenburg. SKF also made them a gift of the AB Volvo corporate identity.

The first production-model Volvo car was completed on 14 April 1927. It was powered by a 1940cc L-head cylinder engine delivering 28hp at 2800rpm, and looked like most moderately priced European cars of the 1921–24 period. The styling was credited to Helmer Mas'Olle, an artist painter with no automotive experience, who happened to be the brother-in-law of an SKF director.

At first, the Volvo factory was strictly an assembly plant. Engine production was subcontracted to AB Pentaverken at Skövde, and gearbox production to Köpings Mekaniska Verkstad.

Gabrielsson planned a pre-series of 1000 cars to be placed with selected customers. Production was to begin with 1000 cars the first year, 4000 cars the second year, and 8000 cars the third year. His targets soon proved over-ambitious. Volvo produced 996 cars with 4-cylinder engines from 1927 to 1930 (less than 300 in 1927, over 500 in 1928).

On the advice of Ivan Örnberg, assistant chief engineer of Hupmobile since 1915, who visited his native Sweden in 1926, Larson began to draw up a 6-cylinder engine. He did not copy the Chrysler six, but consulted with Continental Motors of Detroit. Volvo's DB six was ready in 1929, a 3010cc L-head unit with seven main bearings and a peak output of 55hp at 3000rpm. It was mounted in the PV-650 chassis first presented as a 5-seater saloon in April 1929, typically American in appearance. Steel pressings for the body were produced by Svenska Staalpressnings AB of Olofström, originally founded in 1735. Volvo built 376 cars in 1929.

The 1931 models were equipped with Lockheed hydraulic brakes, the gearbox had synchromesh on second and third (plus free-wheeling). For 1932 the engine was bored out to 3366cc, raising its output to 65hp at 3200rpm.

Gabrielsson wanted tighter control over the main Swedish supplier firms and in 1931 AB Volvo bought a minority stake in Pentaverken AB, which had been founded in 1868 by J. Grönwall as Skövde Gjuteri & Mekaniska Verkstad (Skövde Foundry and Engineering Works). The factory made farm implements,

steam winches, sawmill machinery, and water turbines. The first engine was a single cylinder 3hp marine engine sold with the Penta trade mark. The company was re-organised as Pentaverken AB in 1917 by Fritz Egnell. In 1934 Volvo purchased the outstanding shares and a year later, the enterprise was integrated as AB Volvo Pentaverken.

At the same time, Gabrielsson attracted new investors who bought out SKF's stake in AB Volvo, and purchased title to the Lundby factory and surrounding land. Volvo's profits came from trucks (1007 4- and 6-cylinder trucks were made in 1929), and probably did not break even on the cars. By May 1932, Volvo had produced 10,000 motor vehicles, but only 3800 (approximately) were cars.

In January 1933 Ivan Örnberg left Detroit and joined Volvo as chief engineer. At his initiative, Bofors began supplying crankshafts with integral counterweights. He modernised the Volvo's appearance, mainly by putting a stylish shell around the radiator, and drew on his contacts with the Budd Co. for assistance in developing all-steel bodies. He had no connection, however, with a much-publicised full-width slab-sided semi-streamliner on a PV 650 chassis. It was a one-off, designed by Gustaf L.M. Ericsson and built by Nordbergs Vagnfabrik in Stockholm, without any involvement on Volvo's part.

Örnberg was designing his own streamliner, which went into production in 1935 as the PV 36. It had a new X-braced frame, ifs with coil springs, and a bigger 6-cylinder engine (3670cc) delivering 86hp at 3400rpm on a 6.1:1 cr.

NICK BALDWIN

GABRIELSSON, ASSAR (1891–1964)

Born at Korsberga on 13 August 1891, Assar Gabrielsson attended local schools and aimed for a career in business. In 1909 he was accepted at the High Commercial College in Stockholm. His first job, in 1912, was serving as a shorthand clerk in Sweden's Riksdag (parliament). In 1916 he joined SKF (Bearings) in the sales department. Rising in the ranks, he served as director of SKF Operations in France from 1920–1922.

In partnership with Gustaf Larson, he made plans for automobile production in Sweden. He became managing director of AB Volvo in 1926 and led Volvo until his retirement in 1956.

JPN

1949 Volvo (i) PV444 saloon.
NICK BALDWIN

The PV 36 was very heavy (3652lb/1660kg) and high-priced (SEK8500, compared with SEK6900 for the PV 650). It was built in a series limited to 500 units. Total car production in 1935 reached 800 units (compared with over 2000 trucks).

Before his untimely death in August 1936, Örnberg had a new, lighter, lower-priced PV 51/52 ready for production. The styling was a sober derivative of the PV 36. It had the same 86hp engine, but an orthodox front axle with semi-elliptic leaf springs. It weighed 1500kg and was much livelier than the PV 36. Produced from December 1936 to October 1938, the PV 51/52 reached a total of 2800 units. It was facelifted for 1939 with a rounded-off front end and a built-in boot, offered in four models: PV 53 standard saloon, PV 54 with bigger boot, PV 55 deluxe saloon, and PV 56 deluxe saloon with bigger boot. A total of 3625 such cars were made, plus 275 chassis for other types of bodywork.

A Swedish-born GM engineer, Olle Schjolin, came to Volvo as Örnberg's successor, and started a number of experimental projects, but returned to the USA in 1940.

Volvo car and truck production continued throughout World War II, but much curtailed, due to material shortages and isolation from foreign suppliers. However, two new car projects were put on the drawing board in 1942: the PV 60, planned as a replacement for the PV 53/56 range, and the PV 444, a compact family car with a 4-cylinder engine.

The PV 60 had a new American-style body, ifs with coil springs, a 90hp version of the 3670cc L-head six, and a 3-speed gearbox with column-shift. Volvo made approximately 3000 PV 60 plus 500 chassis from 1946 to 1950.

The PV 444 was Helmer Petterson's idea. He was a Swedish engineer who had worked for years in the USA, starting with Excelsior motorcycles in Chicago about 1927. On his return to Sweden, war clouds were gathering and he knew that meant a shortage of motor fuel for Sweden. He developed a new type of wood-burning gas generator, whose production brought him in contact with Volvo. Gabrielsson hired him as a consultant, which gave him the opportunity to discuss all sorts of projects at the highest level inside Volvo.

Gustaf Larson had engaged an ex-Hanomag engineer, the Swedish-born Erik Jern, in 1941 and he became the *de facto* project manager for the PV 444. He agreed with Helmer Petterson that the car ought to have front-wheel drive, and Petterson also wanted a flat-four engine (à la Steyr). But Gustaf Larson overruled them. The engine would be an in-line four, mounted in front, driving a live rear axle.

At Erik Jern's recommendation, Volvo bought a 1939 Hanomag 1.3-litre model to study its unit-construction body. It is not so strange that the PV 444 engine also ended up with a strong resemblance to Hanomag's. Designed by Erik Jern and Gotthard Österberg, it had the same layout, with a 3-bearing crankshaft and gear-driven camshaft, pushrods and rocker arms to vertical in-line ohvs. There was one difference: Hanomag had removable cylinder liners in a cast-iron block; Volvo's block was unlined, like Fiat's and Opel's.

The Hanomag was smaller (1299cc vs 1414cc) but both were shortstroke designs (71×82mm vs 75×80mm). Volvo had higher compression (6.5 vs 6.0:1) and got higher output: 40hp at 3800rpm vs 32hp at 3600rpm.

Sven Viberg led a 10-man group that was responsible for suspension, steering and brakes. The PV 444 had all-coil suspension, independent in front. Spicer supplied the rear axle, Delco the dampers, Ross the steering, and Wagner Electric the brakes. The gearbox was designed by Stig Hallgren and built by AB Volvo Köpingverken (Volvo took over Köpings Mekaniska Verstad in 1943).

Edward Lindberg, who had worked in the USA for ten years and had body-engineering experience from Studebaker, was in charge of a 20-man group responsible for the unit-construction body, including styling. The complete body shell was welded up at Olofström and shipped by rail to Gothenburg. It was built only as a 2-door coach, and the complete car weighed 900kg.

Both the PV 444 and the PV 60 were first displayed in Stockholm in September 1944. Production could not begin until the flow of supplies was assured.

Erik Jern who was a keen, hard driver, used the delay to put the PV 444 through the most thorough road-testing ever done by Volvo, which paid off in terms of better quality and fewer warranty claims. Helmer Petterson, who had raced motorcycles in his youth, also took test cars on high-speed long-distance runs.

The 900 cars built in 1946 were all PV 60s, but PV 444 production finally got under way in February 1947. The first series of 12,504 cars built up to September

1962 Volvo (i) P1800 coupé.
NICK BALDWIN

1964 Volvo (i) 122B-18 saloon.
NICK BALDWIN

1950 had the 40hp engine. Then a new camshaft was fitted, raising output to 44hp at 4000rpm. At the same time a PV 445 station wagon, with the rear axle on parallel leaf springs, was added. The 25,000th PV 444 rolled off the line in January 1952, and the 100,000th on 24 January 1956.

A high-compression (7.3:1) export-model engine was added in December 1955, delivering 51hp at 4500rpm, and a new 60hp 1583cc version appeared in the PV 444 L-series in 1957. At the same time, a 4-speed gearbox designed by Inge Rosen was adopted for the export models.

Visiting the USA in 1954, Assar Gabrielsson thought it would be a good idea to build a Volvo sports car for the American market. He met with Bill Tritt, owner of Glasspar in Montecito, California, who made the plastic bodies for the Kaiser-Darrin, and Jerry Niger, managing director of Glasspar.

Gabrielsson gave them a styling contract for a roadster, which was very pretty, and Åke Zachrisson was delegated to study Glasspar's production methods, so that he could direct plastic body production in Sweden. Raymond Eknor and Erik Quistgaard designed a new frame with tubular cross-members and side members drilled for lightness, to be made by Motala Verkstad.

Erling Kurt developed a 70hp twin-SU version of the 1414cc engine, with 7.8:1 compression, matched with a 5-speed gearbox. Glasspar made individual pieces for the body, which Volvo put together. After three prototypes, production

began. But Volvo changed top management in 1956, when Gabrielsson retired and Gunnar Engellau took his place. Engellau ordered an immediate stop to Volvo Sport production and only 69 cars were completed. Gustav Larson retired in 1951 (although he was still influential as a consultant), to be succeeded as technical director by Anders Rydell.

The 6-cylinder Volvo passenger car was not out of the picture yet, for alongside the PV 60, the factory built a PV 820 limousine and chassis for ambulances, etc. Its original front-end styling was taken from the trucks, but late in 1950 it was renamed 830, facelifted with a variant of the PV 444 grill. The 820/830 could be ordered with a truck-type front axle or ifs. About 4500 of these vehicles had been built when production ceased in 1957.

Gunnar Engellau (1908–88) was born in Stockholm, the son of a lawyer. He graduated from the Stockholm Technological University in the worst days of Sweden's economy and joined the state railways as a roundhouse mechanic. After he married, he found a job with a general engineering firm building bridges and locomotives, and in 1939 joined Electrolux.

When Assor Gabrielsson asked him to become technical director of AB Svenksa Flygmotor at Trollhättan, he said 'no thanks'. Two years later, he accepted, at one-third the salary he was making at Elecrolux. He became general manager of Svenksa Flygmotor, spending 13 years there before he was invited to take over the presidency of AB Volvo. There was a sudden change when he came to Gothenburg. Gabrielsson's autocratic rule quickly gave way to a youthful 20-man management team.

Engellau saw Volvo's truck-and-bus market as a local matter, but wanted to explore the potential of Volvo cars in international markets. First he ordered big investments in the car production plants, and reinforced the export sales department under the direction of Rolf Hanson.

He encouraged modernisation of the PV 444 and rejected dozens of restyling proposals, while also promoting a more modern approach which finally surfaced as the Volvo Amazon. Tor Berthelius, chief engineer, held overall responsibility for it; a 4-door saloon of contemporary styling by Jan Wilsgaard, 175in (4441.5mm) in overall length, on a 102.5in (2601mm) wheelbase. Wilsgaard had joined Volvo upon graduation as an interior architect from the Art Industry School in Gothenburg in 1950, when he was 20.

The Amazon shared power trains with the PV 444, but had different front and rear suspension, although using coil springs all around. Amazon production began in October 1956, but perhaps only 20 cars were completed by the end of the year. It was assembled at the Lundby works, sharing the line with the PV 444. Approximately 3100 were made in 1957 and 2000 in 1958. Then Kreidler of Stuttgart sued Volvo for illegal use of the Amazon name, which Kreidler had registered for a motorcycle.

In the meantime (August 1958) the PV 444 had given way to the PV 544, with a one-piece curved-glass windshield and bigger engines (1583cc) in two versions: 60hp B 16 A with a single carburettor and 85hp B 16 B with twin SU's. The M 4 4-speed gearbox became standard on PV 544's and the Amazon. The Amazon was renamed 121 with the B 16 A engine, and 122s with the B 16 B. Over 21,000 121/122s were produced in 1959.

Helmer Petterson still had an office at Volvo, but he did not enjoy the same privileged relationship with Engellau and the new technical director Tord Lidmalm as he had had with Gabrielsson and Larson. But Engellau was keen on Petterson's ideas for a new sports car.

1968 Volvo (i) 164 saloon.
NICK BALDWIN

1972 Volvo (i) 1800ES sporting estate car.
NICK GEORGANO

1975 Volvo (i) 264GLE saloon.
NICK BALDWIN

NICK BALDWIN

LARSON, GUSTAF (1887–1968)

Gustaf Larson was born into a farming family at Vintrosa near Orebro, studied mechanical engineering at Orebro Technical Institute, and went to work for White & Poppe in Coventry as a graduate apprentice.

Returning to Sweden in 1913, he attended the Royal Institute of Technology in Stockholm, graduating in 1917.

For the next three years he worked for SKF (Bearings) in Gothenburg and Katrineholm. He went to Stockholm in 1920 as technical director of Nya AB Galco, makers of sheet-metal presses and bearing materials. His first car, later to be the first Volvo, was designed in his Galco office.

He became technical director of AB Volvo in 1926 and held that position until his retirement on 31 July 1951. He remained a consultant to Volvo and, seeing Gabrielsson's diffidence towards the Amazon, he declared that it was 'just the job' and argued strongly for putting it into production.

He died on 4 July 1968.

JPN

Helmer Petterson's son Pelle was then studying industrial design at Pratt Institute in Brooklyn, and sent some sketches to his father. Petterson demonstrated that, apart from a special body shell, the sports car could be made with standard components, and Gunnar Engellau gave it the green light in April 1957. Pelle Petterson's scale model was selected in competition with rival designs from Ghia and Frua, and Frua agreed to build a running P1800 prototype to Petterson's design.

Production director Bengt Darnfors, with Engellau's support, wanted Karmann to produce the body and assemble the car, but the Volkswagen management vetoed it in February 1958. By May 1959, Volvo signed a contract for P1800 body shell production by the Pressed Steel Co. Ltd at Linwood, Scotland, and a separate contract for assembling the car with Jensen Motors of West Bromwich.

A P1800 prototype was displayed at the Brussels' Salon in January 1960. A bigger engine (1778cc) with a 5-bearing crankshaft had been developed, and the twin-SU-equipped B 18 B delivered 100hp at 5500rpm. It became standard in the P1800.

c.1980 Volvo (i) 262C coupé.
NICK GEORGANO

1986 Volvo (i) 240GL saloon.
VOLVO

Helmer Petterson had calculated with a weight of 2200lb (1000kg) but it ended up at 1111kg. Volvo planned production of 3000 units in 1961, however, it was May 1961 before Jensen was building the car at scheduled rates. Volvo expected demand for 7500 a year, but annual production settled between 4000 and 4500 units.

In 1963, when Jensen had delivered 6000 cars, Volvo cancelled the contract. Production of the PV 544 and 121/122-S had been transferred to a new plant at Torslanda, further west of Gothenburg, leaving capacity for the P1800 at Lundby. The contract with the Pressed Steel Co. Ltd was altered, so that instead of complete body shells, the Linwood plant simply shipped the individual stampings, for Volvo to handle the welding and painting in Sweden.

Designed by Folke Zachrisson and Erling Kurt, new B 18 engines also replaced B 16 A and B 16 B engines in the PV 544 and 121/122-S. The basic B 18 A put out 75hp at 4500rpm, and the first-series B 18 D put out 90hp at 5500rpm. For the second-series B 18 D, the cr was raised from 8.5 to 8.7:1 and output went up to 95hp.

The last PV 544 was made on 20 October 1965. In 21 years of building the PV 444, 445 and 544, more than 450,000 cars had been turned out. Production of the 121/122-S lasted from 1956 to 1970, with a total of 667,323 cars. The P1800 had a 12-year production life, with a total of 39,314 cars. The final one was built on 27 June 1973.

In 1960 the P 660 project went on the drawing board, as a longer roomier family car than the 121. Ghia and Frua were invited to submit styling proposals, but in the end it was Jan Wilsgaard's boxy but crisp design that was approved. Marketed as the 144, it went into production early in 1967 with 85hp and 115hp versions of the B 18 engine. The 2-door appeared in June 1967, and a 145 station wagon was added in March 1968. The total number of cars built until the end of 1974 was 1,205,111.

After the 830 was discontinued in 1958, Volvo lacked a 6-cylinder model. Ambitious studies for an all-new car were started in 1959, but soon given up, since the expected sales volume would not justify the costs. By 1962 the planning zeroed in on a lengthened 144, with a new front end and an in-line 6-cylinder engine.

The 82hp B 20 A and 107hp B 20 B 4-cylinder engines went into the 140-series and P1800 models in the autumn of 1968, forming the basis for the 2978cc B 30 with the same bore and stroke and an extra pair of cylinders. It put out 130hp at 5000rpm. The Volvo 164 went into production late in 1968 and 153,023 units were made over a 7½-year span.

The 140-series evolved into the 240 in September 1974, and at the same time, the 264 replaced the 164. These were products of a new planning and engineering team, and top management had also changed. Gunnar Engellau retired in May 1971 and was succeeded as managing director by his son-in-law, Pehr Gustav Gyllenhammar. Born in Gothenburg in 1935, he studied law and medicine at Lund University where he met and married Cristina Engellau.

After training jobs with law firms and insurance companies in London, he came to Amphion Insurance in 1961 and moved to Skandia Insurance Co. in 1965, becoming its chairman and chief executive in 1970. He was elected chairman of Volvo in August 1983, but did not appoint a managing director until Christer Zetterberg, a banker, was given that title in October 1960. Gyllenhammar then changed his own title to Executive President.

Tor Berthelius retired in 1965, and Gunnar L. Johansson succeeded him as chief engineer of Volvo passenger cars. Born in Eskilstuna in 1928, he held a masters degree in Mechanical Engineering from the Royal Institute of Technology in Stockholm, and joined the Volvo organisation in 1955 at Köpings Mekaniska Verkstad. He was transferred to Gothenburg in April 1962, as manager of production engineering.

Dan Werbin was manager of product programmes in 1972–73. Born at Linköping in 1944, he graduated from Chalmers University of Technology in 1969 as a Master of Science. He built 23 different sports cars he called Reva, most of them with Porsche engines, steel spaceframes and plastic bodies. Joining Volvo in 1970, he was assigned to experimental safety cars.

Rolf Mellde, who left Saab to take over what he thought was the top job at Volvo, found himself sidelined into new-technology research.

On 28 June 1971, Volvo entered an equal-share 3-way joint venture with Peugeot and Renault to develop and produce V6 engines at Douvrin near Lille. This gave Volvo a 2664cc 125hp engine for the 264. For the first year, the 140 series cars continued with the B 20 A and B, but the 1976 models were powered by B 21 engines with belt-driven ohcs and aluminium crossflow heads. The carburetted B 21 A was rated at 97hp and the fuel-injected B 21 E at 123hp.

A 265 DL station wagon was also added in 1976, and Volvo contracted with Bertone for production of the 262 C coupé, built from 1977 to 1980 (approximately 5000 cars).

The 1979 D-24 was a 244 or 245 powered by a Volkswagen-supplied 82hp 2383cc 6-cylinder diesel engine. Volvo's Swedish plants had two major personnel problems: absenteeism and high labour turnover. The Swedish government was ready to pay for social experimentation, and Gyllenhammar was eager to co-operate. Kalmar Verkstads AB was a state-owned enterprise which formerly made fork-lift trucks and railway equipment, and in 1970 was occupied with small-scale production of DAF-powered delivery vans. Volvo stepped in, taking over the factory in July 1971 and rebuilding it in 1972–73 for a capacity of 30,000 cars a year in a new humanised production system with decentralised assembly points to get away from the monotony of the assembly line. Teams of 15 built a car from components and sub-assemblies brought by computer-guided carriers. The first Volvo cars from Kalmar appeared in 1974.

The Kalmar plant had lower productivity and higher costs than Torslanda, yet quality was no better. Volvo also got pressured into taking over the state's idle shipbuilding yards at Uddevalla (with heavy subsidies) and retooling them for car production. The Uddevalla plant came on stream in 1989, assembling the 940.

Gyllenhammar's absolute priority was money, not motor vehicles. In May 1978, Gyllenhammar made a deal with the Norwegian government for access to North Sea oil exploration in return for a 40 per cent stake in AB Volvo. Norway's Storting (parliament) agreed. But the Volvo shareholders voted it down. In 1981 he again led Volvo down the diversification trail, diverting Volvo's finances into investments in foodstuffs, energy, transport and non-automotive technology.

Peter Wallenberg had proposed a merger with Volvo in 1969, shortly after he had merged Saab and Scania, but at that time Engellau was not interested. Secret talks between Wallenberg and Gyllenhammar began in February 1977 towards the same end. On 6 May 1977, the boards of Volvo and Saab-Scania met for a joint session to approve the formation of Volvo-Saab-Scania AB. Late in August 1977, however, the whole idea was called off. The management of Saab-Scania were against it, the labour unions were against it and shareholders of both companies came out against it.

It was in 1979/80 that the Volvo Car Division was established as a separate subsidiary, Volvo Car Corp., charged with the conception, design, development, production, marketing, sales, and service of Volvo cars. The former car division had no responsibility for production, which had rested with the parent organisation. The former Svenska Staalpressnings-AB at Olofström, taken over by Volvo in 1969, was integrated with Volvo Car Corp., which also assumed control of foreign subsidiaries such as Volvo Europa Car BV of Gent, Belgium where assembly operations began in 1963, and Volvo Car BV of Born in The Netherlands (see VOLVO (ii)).

Lennart Jeansson became the first president of Volvo Car Corp. after years in various executive positions, succeeded in 1985 by Roger Holtback. Jan Christer Persson became technical director of Volvo Car Corp. He had joined Volvo in 1970 as a project co-ordinator at the age of 27 and worked in planning, purchasing and engine production.

The Volvo 760 replaced the 264 in May 1982. The V6 had grown to 2847cc and 156hp. There was also a 173hp turbo-intercooled 2316cc 4-cylinder engine, and the 110hp VW 6-cylinder turbodiesel. But it was still an orthodox car with rear-axle drive, and the angular styling by Jan Wilsgaard reinforced the feeling of obsolescence.

A companion model, the 740, arrived in January 1984, combining the 760 body shell with the engine options from the 244. It had a new rear suspension, however, with the axle carried by a central bridge-like sub-frame.

A 160hp turbo-intercooled B 23 E became optional in 1985. The 745 station wagon went into production in May 1985. In March 1988 the 740 was offered as a GLT with a 16-valve 2316cc 4-cylinder engine delivering 159hp at 5800rpm. Bertone had begun styling work on the 780 coupé in August 1981. Body engineering began in May 1982, and production got under way in February 1985, with the 156hp 2847cc V6.

In September 1987, when Rune Gustafsson was director of vehicle engineering, the 760/780 were updated with irs (vertical coil springs on trailing arms, and transverse multi-link rods).

Dan Werbin had been named executive vice president of Volvo Car Corp. in 1984, with responsibility for product planning, and Gerhard Salinger became chief engineer for product planning. Salinger had been chief experimental engineer since approximately 1955, and developed the chassis for the Amazon, P-1800, and 140-series. Ulf Lundqvist was manager of 4-cylinder engine systems and Aake Grandinson manager of 6-cylinder engine systems. Jan Wilsgaard had been promoted to director of styling, with Stig Weiertz as chief body engineer. When Wilsgaard retired in 1988, Stefan Juthage took over, with Stig Falck as head of the exterior studio and the interior studio under Lasse Petterson.

The 960 replaced the 760 in September 1989. In October 1989, Volvo broke off from the PRV joint venture for V6 engines in effect since 1971, and developed a 2922cc vertical in-line six for the 960, with twin-ohcs and four valves per cylinder, delivering 204hp at 6000rpm. The saloon had the irs from the latest 760, but the station wagon inherited the back axle from the earlier 760.

The 940 followed a year later, with the 960 body shell and the chassis components from the 240. Engine options were Volvo's own 4-cylinder 111hp 1986cc and 130hp 2316cc units, and the 122hp VW 6-cylinder turbodiesel. Together or singly, production of the 240/260 had lasted 18 years and the final count approached 3 million cars.

In 1990 Volvo AB suffered its first loss in 60 years. It dawned on Gyllenhammar that Volvo was too small to stay alive as a car company without a strong partner.

Volvo's relationship with Renault started with an agreement signed on 27 September 1990. This resulted in a cross-shareholding arrangement taking effect in February 1991. On 6 September 1993, Renault proposed a full merger project in which Renault would have 65 per cent control. Opposition from Sweden was voiced on 5 October 1993, and within weeks the joint venture was scuttled. Swedish investors and Volvo workers rejoiced. Pehr Gyllenhammar resigned on 2 December 1993. The split was formalised in February 1994, and on 31 July 1997, Volvo sold its last stake in Renault.

Practically the whole board of directors resigned when Gyllenhammar left. Sören Gyll had no automotive experience at all when he was brought into Volvo from Procordia (food and pharmaceuticals) in 1990. Yet he was the man who put in place a new strategy of shedding Volvo's non-core acquisitions and concentrating

1993 Volvo (i) 940S Highlander estate car.
VOLVO

1997 Volvo (i) V70 Bi-Fuel estate car.
VOLVO

2000 Volvo (i) V70 estate car.
VOLVO

2000 Volvo (i) V70 XC Cross Country 4 × 4 estate car.
VOLVO

2000 Volvo (i) S80 saloon.
VOLVO

1999 Volvo (i) C70 convertible.
VOLVO

on motor vehicles. He became chief executive and Volvo group chairman at the end of 1993. Roger Holtback resigned in 1990 and Per-Erik Mohlin took over as president of Volvo Car Corp.

During the years of Renault involvement, the French had been pushing for closure of the Kalmar and Uddevalla plants. Operations at Uddevalla were suspended in the summer of 1993 and car production at Kalmar ceased in June 1994. Production of the 960 was brought back to Torslanda and the car renamed S 90.

The Volvo 850 GLT was announced in June 1991, and production began at the Gent plant in October of that year. It was planned as a front-wheel drive successor to the 240-series, with transverse engine and all-independent suspension. Preliminary studies had been made by Jan C. Persson and Inge Rosen, the latter now in retirement but still active as a consultant. Lars Erik Lundin was chief engineer for the 850 platform, with Peter Augustsson as manufacturing project manager. Olle Englund was project manager for the power trains.

The 5-cylinder aluminium-block engine had twin-ohcs, 20 valves, and put out 170hp from 2435cc. A short-stroke 1984cc 5-cylinder unit rated at 143hp became optional in 1992. The turbo-intercooled 850 T5 with a 225hp 2319cc 20-valve unit was added in the spring of 1994, to be joined five months later by an economy version (five cylinders and ten valves, 1991cc and 126hp). In June

1995, a 140hp 2461cc Audi 5-cylinder turbodiesel became available in the 850 TDI.

Jan Christer Persson left Volvo in 1993 for an academic career at the IVF Institute of Mechanical Engineering in Gothenburg, and was succeeded by Martin Rybeck. Two years on, however, Rybeck was delegated to TWR to supervise the development of special car projects, and Sven Eckerstein was named technical director after five years as a car-programme manager. Born in 1945, he had graduated from Chalmers Institute of Technology in 1971 with a degree in electronics engineering, and went to work for Volvo's truck division. He came to Volvo Car Corp. in 1982 and served as director of the 240 programme from 1987 to 1991.

In 1995 Mohlin acceded to a vice presidency in the AB Volvo parent organisation, and Tuve Johannesson became chief executive of Volvo Car Corp. Mohlin had led the discussions with Tom Walkinshaw that led to the establishment of a joint venture, Autonova, in January 1995. Autonova then moved into the Uddevalla plant, with a target of making 20,000 cars a year. Its first product was the 850 T5R, an ultra-high-performance model, followed by the 850 AWD Kombi (193hp 2435cc turbo-intercooled engine and 4-wheel drive) in May 1996.

The Volvo C 70 coupé, unveiled in October 1996, was an Autonova development with styling by Ian Callum of TWR, and a new platform derived from the 850s.

In February 1997 the S 70 saloon estate car (both styled by Peter Horbury) replaced the 850 line, inheriting its line-up of engine options. The 70-series cars were assembled at the Gent plant. V 70 models with 4-wheel drive were added in August 1997. In the spring of 2000 came the V 70 XC (Cross Country), a larger and wider 4×4 estate with higher ground clearance and greater off-road capability.

Sören Gyll, having accomplished his task at AB Volvo, retired in April 1997, and was succeeded by Leif Johansson, formerly president of Electrolux. Hans Carlstedt became technical director of Volvo Car Corp., and Hans Wikman was named project manager for the S 80, the replacement for the rear-wheel drive S 90 (960 renamed).

Sharing the S 70 platform (with longer wheelbase), the S 80 went into production at Torslanda in May 1998, with a 204hp 2922cc transverse in-line six driving the front wheels. Five-cylinder options were borrowed from the S 70, and a 272hp twin-turbo 2783cc six was developed as a top-performance option. The 140hp 2461cc 5-cylinder turbodiesel was supplied by Audi.

At the beginning of April 1999, AB Volvo sold Volvo Car Corp. to the Ford Motor Co. for $6.4 million.

JPN

1986 Volvo (ii) 480ES coupé.
VOLVO

Further Reading
The Story of Volvo Cars, Graham Robson, Patrick Stephens, 1983.
The Volvo 1800 and Family, Andrew Whyte, Osprey, 1984.
Volvo Cars, 1920s to 1980s, Bjorn-Eric Lindh, Norden AB, 1984.
'Sport, style and speed: A history of the Volvo 1800', Lowell C. Paddock,
Automobile Quarterly, Vol. 22, No. 4.
'Before the eleven-year car: Prewar Volvo', Len Lonnegren,
Automobile Quarterly, Vol. 35, Nos 1 and 3.
'Swede success, Volvo PV 444 and 544', Len Lonnegren,
Automobile Quarterly, Vol. 37, No. 4.

VOLVO (ii) **(NL)** 1975 to date

1975–1991 Volvo Car BV, Born.
1992–2000 Netherlands Car BV, Born.

On 29 September 1972, AB Volvo acquired a 33 per cent stake in DAF Car BV, which had built the Born assembly plant, for $19 million. When it opened on 27 June 1968, it had capacity for 100,000 cars a year.

AB Volvo increased its stake to 55 per cent in January 1975 for $16 million and named the company Volvo Car BV with Helge Castell as chief executive officer. The Dutch National Investment Bank held 26.66 per cent of it and DSM (De Staats Mijnen–National Mining Corp.) 18.34 per cent.

The 1967 DAF 55 grew into a DAF 66 in September 1972, with a 1108cc Renault engine, Variomatic drive, De Dion suspension and MacPherson front suspension, developed by J. van der Brugghen. In 1976 it was renamed Volvo 66.

Volvo took over the DAF 77 project and turned it into a Volvo 343, which went into production in September 1976, with a 70hp Renault engine and Variomatic drive. Volvo engineers made it available with a Renault 4-speed gearbox bolted to the engine in 1978. The 343 styling came from the ex-DAF studio led by John de Vries, with an input from Trevor Fiore, design consultant, and refined by Rob Koch. A 345 estate car followed. They were renamed the 340 Series in 1982.

Volvo vice president Robert Dethorey had steered Pehr Gyllenhammar to DAF in order to acquire small car technology. What they bought was a loss-making car factory, so deep in debts that in May 1981 Volvo was able to obtain state aid for saving the jobs of 5500 workers. But Volvo's stake in the establishment was cut back to 30 per cent, with state agencies holding 70 per cent ownership. Helge Castell returned to Sweden and André Delaye took his place. A civil engineer who had been with Ford since 1965, he joined Volvo in 1967 at the Gent factory.

1982 Volvo (ii) 340 saloon.
VOLVO

1990 Volvo (ii) 440GL saloon.
VOLVO

The next new car was the 360, which was not offered with Variomatic but had a 5-speed transaxle, and 117hp 1982cc Volvo engine. It was launched in October 1982. A 1596cc Renault Diesel engine became optional in September 1984. It was taken out of production in the spring of 1991.

1999 Volvo (ii) S40 saloon.
VOLVO

Dan Werbin went to work on a front-wheel drive car, project E 12, for the Born factory in 1979. His power-train was first seen in the Volvo LCP prototype in 1983, and went into production for the 480 ES in March 1986, with a 109hp 1721cc Renault engine mounted transversely.

The sports-wagon aerodeck styling came from Geoffrey Wright, an ex-Sunbeam ex-Chrysler designer who joined Volvo Car BV in 1980. Peter Horbury was responsible for the interiors. Jan Maes was director of product planning with Pim de Ruigh as product manager, and Rob Kochas manager of the styling department.

In April 1988 the Volvo 480 Turbo appeared with a 120hp 1721cc turbo-intercooled Renault engine. June 1988 saw the arrival of the 330 saloon, based on the 340/360 platform with longer wheelbase and wider track. The body was styled in consultation with Giugiaro (Ital Design) and the standard engine was a 95hp 1721cc Renault unit. The Volvo 460, launched in February 1990, was a formal sedan based on the 440, and a prototype 480 cabriolet was shown in March 1990 but did not go into production. The entire 400 series was a market failure which cost Volvo SEK 1 billion a year.

In March 1991, AB Volvo reached an agreement with Mitsubishi Motors Corp. to expand the Born plant to a capacity of 200,000 cars a year and produce models of both makes sharing a platform and basic body structure.

On 6 January 1992 Volvo Car BV was officially changed to Netherlands Car BV (Nedcar for short), a 3-way joint venture between AB Volvo, Mitsubishi Motors Corp., and the Netherlands government, holding equal one-third shares.

André Delaye stepped down after 11 years as president and chairman of Volvo Car BV, and Frans Sevenstern became the first president of Nedcar. The surprise announcement of a Japanese partner did not sit too well with the French executives who were then drawing up the plans for the proposed Renault-Volvo merger, and certainly contributed to its being called off.

The Volvo S40 project was planned as a long-overdue replacement for the 400-series, with Dan Werbin as project manager. To make economical sense, it had to be a sister model of the Mitsubishi Carisma. Styled by Peter Horbury, the S40 saloon made its debut in September 1995, followed by the V 40 estate car three months later. Volvo-built 4-cylinder engines of 1731 and 1948cc, with an output range from 105 to 160hp, were offered. The 200hp S 40 T4 with a turbo-intercooled 1855cc engine was added in 1997. Renault supplied the 90hp 1870cc turbodiesel engine.

Volvo's stake in Nedcar BV became the property of Ford Motor Co. in April 1999, when AB Volvo sold Volvo Car Corp. The joint venture with Mitsubishi came to an end in March 2000, with DaimlerChrysler's acquisition of a controlling interest in Mitsubishi. The S40 was likely to be made in another European Ford factory.

JPN

VOODOO (GB) 1971–1975
Normandale Products, Long Itchington, Warwickshire.
Geoff Neale and John Arnold built the first Voodoo in 1971, and the prototype appeared at the 1971 Earls Court Motor Show, where a financier offered the money to begin a production run. The Voodoo had a space frame chassis, a 998cc Imp Sport engine, Vauxhall Viva front suspension and a dramatic and beautiful fibreglass body only 35in (888mm) high. Entry was via a forward-hinging canopy which incorporated a Chevron B16 windscreen. Kits were scheduled to be sold at £2000, but John Arnold's death sealed the car's fate, and only three were ever made.

CR

VOPARD (US) c.1974–1986
Vopard Industries, Suisun City, California.
Vopard's first kit car, the Vokaro, was a simple 2-seat sports car based on a shortened Volkswagen Beetle floorpan. It was a very basic and inexpensive kit with a simple roadster body that barely covered the running gear. A stretched 4-seater Vokaro was added later. The Vopard Ginetta G12P was an interesting kit based on a one-off sports car built by Richard Petit in 1966. Petit was head of the Ford Advanced Vehicles studio, and had built a fibreglass-bodied sports coupé based on a Ginetta G12 chassis with a Lotus Twincam engine and Hewland transaxle. Vopard bought the car and the moulds and intended to sell a variation in kit form. Unfortunately, it proved to be difficult to manufacture and not many were sold. They did not have the Ginetta chassis, and a variety of engines and transaxles were used in the few that were built. The car and moulds were later sold to someone in England. The Vokaro kits were later sold by REDHEAD ROADSTERS.
HP

VORAN (D) 1926–1928
Voran Automobilbau AG, Berlin.
This company was run by Richard Bussien who was a pioneer of front-wheel drive. He produced a limited number of light cars which were mostly existing cars transformed from rear- to front-drive, and powered by Pluto engines. Bussien's main aim was to sell licences to other manufacturers, of commercial vehicles as well as cars. In 1928 the company was bought by NAG, and this purchase resulted in the production of NAG-Voran cars in 1933 and 1934.
HON

VOUSEMOI (F) 1904
The Vousemoi, whose name means 'you and I', was appropriately a 2-seater. It was offered for one year only, with a choice of two engines, a 10hp 2-cylinder or 16/20hp 4-cylinder Gnome. Transmission was by a 3-speed gearbox with final drive by shaft.
NG

VOX (GB) 1912–1915
Lloyd & Plaister Ltd, Wood Green, London.
The Vox was the last of several cars in which Lewis Lloyd (1877–1923) was involved. His previous ventures were the HURST & LLOYD and LLOYD & PLAISTER. It was a light car powered by a 770cc 2-cylinder 2-stroke engine designed by Harry Ricardo who had been responsible for the DOLPHIN, also a 2-stroke, for which Lloyd & Plaister had supplied some components. The engine had one pumping cylinder and one working cylinder; the mixture was admitted to the latter by a leaf-spring valve. Final drive was by shaft and 2-seater bodies were fitted. A one-off was made of basket cane for an Indian tea planter. About 50 Voxes were made.
NG

VOYAGER (GB) 1984–1985
Lakes Sports Cars, Lorton, Cumbria.
Very few cars start life with an engine at one end, then switch to the other. The Voyager was one of them. The prototype of this 1930s style open roadster was based on a Volkswagen Beetle, and even incorporated fibreglass mouldings of its rear wings. After adverse comment, the company switched tack and opted for Vauxhall Viva mechanicals and a front-mounted engine.
CR

V.P. (F) 1952–1958
Vernet et Pairard, Paris.
Vernet et Pairard created an Antem-bodied aerodynamic record-breaker on Renault 4CV parts in 1952, succeeding in taking eight records at Montlhéry and impressing Renault enough for it to display the car on its stand at the 1952 Paris Salon. Road cars were subsequently built with low coupé roof-lines and Renault 4CV (later Dauphine) mechanicals. V.P.'s activities were publicised by consistent entries in the 24 Heures du Mans.
CR

VROUM (F) 1970
M. Viscardy, Ardennes.
This was a Mini Moke lookalike based on a Citroën 2CV, with steel bodywork.
CR

1914 Vulcan (i) 25/30hp tourer.
NICK BALDWIN

VSE (US) c.1990 to date

Very Special Equipment, Carmel, California.

VSE was started by former General Motors engineer and successful racing car constructor Herb Adams and his son Matt. In addition to selling performance suspension parts for street cars, VSE also built a number of successful kit cars. They made an aluminium monocoque chassis for use under Cobra replica bodies supplied by VSE or the customer. They had several suspension options including irs. The VSE Jackrabbit was a lightweight kit car based on Volkswagen Rabbit or Scirocco running gear in a tubular steel frame. It was easy to assemble and was available in four body variations. The Speedster was a basic body with a short windscreen and non-opening doors. The Roadster had doors that scissored up Lamborghini-style and a full-height windshield. The Coupé was a Roadster with a hard-top bolted on, and the Convertible had a soft-top, side windows and a roll cage. A special version of the Jackrabbit Speedster called the Wild Hare was built in 1991 with a lightweight aluminium chassis and modified engine. In 1995 a prototype of a Chevrolet-based sports car called the Blitz was built. It used the VSE Cobra chassis but with all Chevrolet running gear and a wedge-shaped body looking a bit like a larger Jackrabbit.

HP

VULCAN (i) (GB) 1902–1928

1902–1903 Vulcan Motor and Engineering Co. Ltd,
Southport, Lancashire.
1903–1906 Vulcan Motor Manufacturing & Engineering Co. Ltd,
Southport, Lancashire.
1906–1916 Vulcan Motor & Engineering Co. (1906) Ltd,
Southport, Lancashire.
1915–1928 Vulcan Motor Engineering Co. (1916) Ltd,
Southport, Lancashire.

The brothers Thomas and Joseph Hampson built a prototype car with a front-mounted 4.5hp single-cylinder engine in Bolton in 1899. Some say they made an earlier car at Wigan. It is not certain if they called this a Vulcan, but three years later they formed their Vulcan company with a factory at Southport on the Lancashire coast. They had previously traded as C. & J. Hampson Ltd from the same premises. The first car the company offered for sale also had a front-mounted

single-cylinder engine, but was less top-heavy looking than the prototype. It had radiators on the side of the bonnet as in contemporary Renaults, a 2-speed gearbox and final drive by single belt to the centre of the rear axle. The 1903 model was improved in several ways; the engine was now of 6 or 9hp, and mechanically operated inlet valves. There were three speeds and shaft drive, while the tubular frame gave way to armoured wood, and the wire wheels to artillery. For 1904 the Renault-like radiators were replaced by a frontal honeycomb type, and a 10hp 2-cylinder engine was offered. Fours of 12/14, 18/20, and 25/30hp followed in 1905.

Vulcan made their first six in 1906. This had a 4.8-litre T-head engine with dual ignition. Capacity rose to six litres in 1908, and sixes in various sizes were offered up to 1914. Production was running at six cars a week in 1909 in a new, palatial factory at Crossens, Southport. The first proprietary engine was seen in 1911, when a light car using a 1960cc 2-cylinder Aster engine was introduced. The 1914 range consisted of three 4-cylinder models with L-head engines, the 2409cc 10/15, 2610cc 15.9 and 3012cc 15/20hp, together with a 4476cc 25/30hp six. Bodies, which Vulcan made itself, included some luxurious types such as the Fulwood limousine on the 15/20 and 25/30hp chassis, and all 1914 Vulcans had bullnose radiators.

War work included the manufacture of gun limbers and the Be2d and Re8 aircraft. The Hampsons left after another reorganisation in 1916 (Thomas later became Mayor of Southport), and the company was run by C.B. Wardman who made a number of unwise decisions. One was to invest £150,000 of the company's share capital in the Harper Bean group, which involved Bean, A.B.C. and Swift cars, and Wallace tractors. Grandly called the British Motor Trading Corp., this conglomerate was soon in trouble, and did not do good to any of its participating companies. Wardman also sanctioned at least three car designs in the early 1920s, none of which saw production yet they must have wasted a lot of money. They were a 3.5-litre V8 of 1919, and in 1922 a 1398cc Howard cuff-valve flat-twin and a 3560cc four, also with Howard cuff-valve engine. A Vulcan subsidiary also made the CHILTERN car at Dunstable, Bedfordshire. This used a Dorman engine, and was probably a Vulcan chassis fitted with Chiltern radiator and bodywork. Vulcan's production cars were also Dorman-engined at first, a 1794cc ohv Twelve and a 2612cc side-valve 16/20, Dorman engines also being used in Vulcan's commercial vehicles which were becoming of growing importance

1926 Vulcan (i) 12hp saloon.
NICK BALDWIN

to the firm. Vulcan used other engines in the 1920s, including a 3306cc fixed head side-valve of its own manufacture and a unit with the same dimensions and a detachable head made by Hick Hargreaves of Bolton. This was used more in Vulcan light commercials and taxicabs, although it was listed for the 16/20 car in the early 1920s; 1496cc side-valve Anzani and 1795cc ohv Meadows units were also used.

Vulcan managed to extricate itself from the British Motor Trading Corp. and in 1923 Wardman brought about a link with LEA-FRANCIS, in which the two companies pooled their dealer network, and some Vulcan models were sold under the Lea-Francis name. These included an Anzani-engined Twelve and a Meadows-engined Fourteen in 1926. Vulcan made some Lea-Francis bodywork, and Lea-Francis in turn supplied gearboxes and steering gears to Vulcan. The makes also shared the disastrous 1696cc twin-ohc six designed by A.O. Lord. These were made in the Vulcan factory but, ironically, only five bore Vulcan badges compared with 340 sold under the Lea-Francis name. An enlarged version with 1990cc capacity was known as the 16/60, and many of the lubrication problems of the original six were cured. The Meadows-engined cars were last listed in 1927, and for 1928 only the sixes were on offer, the 1696cc as the Short or Long Six 14/40, and the 1990cc as the 16/60. Coachwork was still made by Vulcan, and one of the 16/60s destined for C.B. Wardman's personal use had an

unusual full-width 6-light fabric saloon body with enclosed luggage compartment and spare wheel. Called the Gainsborough, it was exhibited at the 1927 Olympia Show.

Vulcan discontinued its cars at the end of 1928, although it continued to make cars for Lea-Francis up to 1930. Thereafter it concentrated on commercial vehicles. In 1937 it was acquired by Tilling-Stevens, which transferred production to its Maidstone, Kent, factory, and in turn was absorbed into the Rootes Group in 1950. The last Vulcan trucks were made in 1953.

NG

Further Reading
'Vulcan engines', M. Worthington-Williams, *The Automobile*, June 1991.
'Made in Southport – the Vulcan', M. Worthington-Williams,
The Automobile, September and October 1996.

VULCAN (ii) (US) 1913–1915

1913 Vulcan Motor Car Co., Painsville, Ohio.
1913–1915 Vulcan Manufacturing Co., Painsville, Ohio.
This was a light car powered by a 27hp 4-cylinder Buda engine, with 3-speed gearbox and shaft drive. Body styles were a roadster on a 105in (2665mm) wheelbase and a tourer on 115in (2919mm). Although company headquarters were in Painsville, the cars were made in the DRIGGS-SEABURY factory at Sharon, Pennsylvania.

NG

VULKAN (D) 1899–1905

Vulkan Automobilgesellschaft mbH, Berlin.
The well-known designer Robert Schwenke was behind this company which made a small number of electric cars and trucks. He was later involved in front-wheel drive vehicles.

HON

VULPÈS (F) 1905–c.1910

1905–1907 Automobiles Vulpès, Paris;
1907–c.1910 Clichy, Seine.
The Vulpès was made in several models from a voiturette powered by an 8hp single-cylinder De Dion-Bouton engine to large cars with 4-cylinder Janus engines of up to 30/40hp. An unusual feature of these engines was that they had a transverse camshaft located between the two pairs of cylinders.

NG

W. (GB) 1920
W.T. Aked & Co. Ltd, St Anne's on Sea, Lancashire.
This was an improved Model T Ford, with coachwork by W.T. Aked and a Hampton-like radiator. Not more than half a dozen were sold.
NG

WAAIJENBERG (NL) 1986 to date
Waaijenberg Mobiliteit BV, Veenendaal.
Waaijenberg began constructing 4-wheeled microcars in the late–1980s, aimed primarily at the disabled driver, with able-bodied driver models also available. The first Waaijenberg had a box-shaped fibreglass body with a choice of Japanese 2-cylinder motor cycle engines. By the mid–1990s Waaijenberg's production had reach a few hundred vehicles per annum. In 1996 Waaijenberg's second-generation microcar, the Canta, was launched. The twin-cylinder Canta had a metal frame structure clothed in a more modern, but exceptionally narrow, one-box fibreglass body with intimate seating for two.
CR

WACHEUX (F) 1903–1905
The exact maker's name of this car is unknown, but the factory is known to have been in Calais. A surviving example of the Wacheux has a front-mounted 502cc single-cylinder De Dion-Bouton engine with automatic inlet valve, 4-speed gearbox, a tubular frame reinforced with wood and a gilled-tube radiator.
NG

WACO (US) 1915–1917
Western Automobile Co., Seattle, Washington.
The Waco was a very conventional assembled car powered by a 22.5hp 4-cylinder G.B. & S. engine, with tourer or roadster bodies, both priced at $950. It was only unusual in the place of manufacture, convenient for the 'fight for Pacific coast trade' as *Motor West* magazine proclaimed, though it was not a very successful fight.
NG

WADDINGTON (GB) 1903–1904
Waddington & Sons, Middlesborough, Yorkshire.
This company listed two cars, one with a 6.5hp single-cylinder engine 'of De Dion type' and 2-seater body, the other with 10hp 2-cylinder engine and 4-seater tonneau body. Both had shaft drive. They are likely to have been imports, possibly variants on the Lacoste et Battmann theme.
NG

WADE (US) c.1986–1990
Wade Motor Co., Waco, Texas.
The Wade Panache was a neoclassic coupé built from a 1976 to 1979 Cadillac Seville cockpit and running gear. The chassis was stretched and a long fibreglass bonnet with chrome grill and flowing mudguards were attached to the Cadillac cockpit section. Two body styles were offered, the Opera Coupé was a 2-door and the Panache sedan was a 4-door version. The Panache could also be adapted to fit other General Motors sedans. The Wade Sundance was a neoclassic pickup truck that fitted 1973 to 1986 Chevrolet pick-ups and Blazers, but could be adapted to Ford and Dodge trucks. It had a neoclassic nose, side-mount spare tyres and mudguards like the Panache with a pick-up truck cab and bed. All were sold in kit or assembled form.
HP

WAF (A) 1911–1925
Wiener Automobilfabrik GmbH, Vienna.
This company was founded by the engineer Ferdinand Trummer who had formerly worked for BOCK & HOLLANDER. His 25 and 35PS models were continued under the WAF name, and a new 2.8-litre 45PS called the Alpentyp took part in the 1914 Austrian Alpine Trial. After the war the 11/35PS was revived, and complemented by a 21/50PS 6-cylinder car. The most interesting postwar model was the 4-litre 15/45PS straight-8, whose engine consisted of two fours in line, each with its own carburettor and ignition. All WAFs were expensive, the straight-8 especially, and few were sold, despite their high quality.
HON

1998 Waaijenberg Canta LX microcar.
NICK GEORGANO

1903 Waddington 6hp 2-seater.
NATIONAL MOTOR MUSEUM

WAGENHALS (US) 1910–1915
1910 Wagenhals Manufacturing Co., St Louis, Missouri.
1910–1915 Wagenhals Motor Co., Detroit, Michigan.
W.G. Wagenhals designed a 3-wheeler with 14hp 2-cylinder engine mounted transversely between the front wheels, with epicyclic transmission and final drive by chain to the rear wheel. Despite the engine's location, there was quite a long bonnet projecting ahead of the front wheels, with Renault-style coal-scuttle shape. A number of 2-seaters and taxicabs were made along these lines, but more Wagenhals were supplied as delivery vans, in which case the driver sat further back and the bonnet was replaced by a large parcel-carrying box. Several of these were bought by the US Post Office. For 1915 a 4-cylinder engine replaced the twin and there was also an electric version. At least 200 Wagenhals were made altogether.
NG

WAHL (US) 1913–1914
Wahl Motor Car Co., Detroit, Michigan.
The 'Name-it-yourself' idea of selling automobiles was the idea of George Wahl who based his plan on his own name, Wahl being the German word for 'choice'. Wahl reasoned that there might be a viable market in building a standard type of roadster and touring model and selling it in small numbers to those who might attach their own names to the cars. With this idea in mind, he ran advertisements in various automobile magazines illustrating an automobile radiator (where a badge of any name could be affixed), basic specifications and the suggestion 'Attention, Automobile Dealers, Sell this car with your own trademark on the radiator'. The car itself was as generic as a car could be at the time featuring a 3.3-litre 4-cylinder Hazard engine, 108in (2741mm) wheelbase, 4-speed transmission and right-hand steering. Attractive as the idea was to Wahl, this

1913 Wall (ii) 3-wheeler.
NICK BALDWIN

novel approach in selling cars failed to interest many purchasers and finances dwindled. Depressed by the failure of his car to catch on, George Wahl committed suicide. The company was reorganised and continued into 1914, but the business closed and the premises were sold up before the end of the year.

KM

WALCO (GB) 1905

W.A.Lloyd's Cycle Fittings Ltd, Birmingham.
This company made a few motorcycles from 1903, and in 1905 announced a 3-wheeler powered by a 4hp Stevens engine. Few, if any, were sold.

NG

WALCYCAR see WALL (ii)

WALDRON (US) 1909–1911

1908 Waldron Runabout Manufacturing Co., Waldron, Illinois.
1909–1911 Waldron Automobile Manufacturing Co., Kankakee, Illinois.
The Waldron was a high-wheeler powered by an air-cooled 2-cylinder engine, of 14hp up to the end of the 1909 season, and of 18/20hp thereafter. All had friction transmissions and double-chain drive. It was made as a runabout, surrey or tourer, and production totalled several hundred. Apparently the later models were better than those made at Waldron, which were described as 'noisy, under powered and no good'.

NG

WALKER (i) (US) 1905–1906

Walker Motor Car Co., Detroit, Michigan.
Charles L. Walker's car was a 2-seater runabout powered by a 10hp 2-cylinder engine, with 2-speed epicyclic transmission and shaft drive. It was priced at $550, but Walker sold few before his company closed in the late spring of 1906.

NG

WALKER (ii) (US) 1910

Walker Motor Car Co., Detroit, Michigan.
Though the company name and city of manufacture were the same as for Charles Walker's venture of four years earlier there was no connection between these two companies. The Walker Six had a T-head engine and rode on a 127in (3223mm) wheelbase. A prototype chassis was shown in Detroit, but production never started.

NG

WALKER (iii) (NZ) 1967–1970

Pacific Auto Industries Ltd, Auckland, North Island.
Hamilton Walker of Whangarei invented a new form of rotary engine, in which oscillating heads acted with an elliptical rotor to provide two power impulses per revolution. It did not infringe existing patents, had a wide torque band and produced peak power at lower speed than the Wankel. A small unit, the equivalent of a 1500cc conventional engine, produced 65bhp, which led to plans being made to produce a car to be powered by it. The prominent manufacturing firm, UEB Industries, backed the project by taking holdings in both the engine developer, Rotarymotive Developments, and the vehicle producer. A prototype, with a fibreglass body styled by Ferris De Joux, on a wheelbase of 96in (2438mm), was completed in 1969. The transmission was by infinitely variable belt, disc brakes were fitted at the front and suspension was independent all round. It was estimated in 1970 that it would be on sale within two years, but no more was heard.

MG

WALKER & HUTTON (GB) 1902

Walker & Hutton, Electrical and Mechanical Engineers, Scarborough, Yorkshire.
These partners, who apparently never formed a company, advertised a light car powered by a 4hp engine, presumably a 2-stroke as they advertised that it had no valves, which would run on petrol or paraffin. Final drive was by belt on one model, though there was also a chain-driven car. This had four seats, the front ones being ahead of the driver. Walker & Hutton advertised that they would 'build carriages driven by oil, steam or electricity to customer's requirements'.

NG

WALKINS (US) 1896

Bay State Motive Power Co., Springfield, Massachusetts.
L.E. Walkins was a civil engineer from Boston who designed petrol and electric cars for production by the Bay State Motive Power Co. They planned to make 10 electrics, 10 cars powered by compressed air, and 30 petrol vehicles, both passenger and commercial. Some were built, but fewer than the planned 50.

NG

WALL (i) (US) 1900–1903

R.C. Wall Manufacturing Co., Philadelphia, Pennsylvania.
This company made petrol engines and running gear before they launched a complete car in 1901. This was a tiller-steered light runabout with 4hp 2-cylinder engine under the seat. By 1903 the runabout had a front-mounted engine under a bonnet, and a steering wheel. Wall also made a larger car with 9hp 3-cylinder engine and tonneau body. After 1903 the Walls turned to customising work; their son Alfred Sinclair Wall became well-known for his customising of cars such as Auburn and Hupmobile in the 1930s.

NG

WALL (ii) (GB) 1911–1915

A.W. Wall Ltd, Tyseley, Birmingham.
The Wall was an unusual 3-wheeler with 2-seater body of sidecar appearance, described as a coachbuilt side-entrance sociable. Steering was by long tiller to the single front wheel. It was powered by a 4/5hp single-cylinder or 6hp V-twin Precision engine mounted behind the front wheel and driving the rear axle by shaft. In March 1914 wheel steering was available. The company also made the Walcycar, a 4-wheeled cyclecar powered by an 8hp V-twin JAP engine, with 2-speed gearbox and shaft drive. It was priced at 95 guineas (£99.75), while the 3-wheeler cost 90 or 97 guineas (£94.50 or £101.85) according to the engine used. This was also known as the Roc, after the Roc Motor Works where the cars were made.

NG

WALMOBIL (D) 1920

Maschinenfabrik Walter Loebel, Leipzig.
This was a single-seater 3-wheeled cyclecar powered by a 3.7PS 2-cylinder engine mounted over, and driving, the single front wheel. Advertising referred to the System Loebel-Landgrebe, which would indicate a link with the LANDGREBE, also a 3-wheeler.

HON

1902 Walter (i) 12hp tonneau.
WALTER

WALTER (i) (US) 1902–1909

1902–1906 American Chocolate Machinery Co., New York, New York.
1906–1909 Walter Automobile Co., Trenton, New Jersey.

Walter cars were only made for a short time, unlike the trucks which have had a 91-year history and are still going strong, but they were linked with the birth of the famous MERCER. William Walter (1862–1945) was born in Switzerland, one of 13 children, and came to the United States at the age of 21. In 1898 he imported a 3-wheeled car, probably an Egg & Eggli, from his native land, but was dissatisfied with it, and built a car of his own later that year. After four years of experiments he was ready to put a car on the market. Named the Waltobile, it was made in the factory of Walter's American Chocolate Machinery Co. on West 66th Street in New York City. It had a front-mounted 12hp 2-cylinder engine and shaft drive. With a 4-seater rear-entrance tonneau body, it sold for $3000, quite a high price for a 2-cylinder car. A 24hp four joined it in 1903 and in January 1904 Walter launched his 30hp four on a longer wheelbase with a side-entrance tourer body and a $4000 price tag. Still larger cars followed in 1905 and 1906, with 40 and 50hp engines on 110 and 122in (2792 and 3092mm) wheelbases. A 1906 50hp limousine cost $5500, and the company's slogan was 'The Aristocrat of Motordom'.

Production at the six-storey building in Manhattan was small (about 50 cars altogether), as presumably the chocolate machinery was being made alongside the cars, and early in 1906 the newly formed Walter Automobile Co. moved to Trenton, New Jersey. There the existing range was continued, prices rising to $6300 for a 7-seater limousine in 1907. Etienne Planche was their chief engineer, and in 1909 Washington A. Roebling of the Roebling wire-rope family commissioned Planche to design a large racing car which would be built in the Walter factory. Only one was made but a few 50hp Walters were completed under the Roebling-Planche name. There was never a Roebling-Planche company as on 31 May 1909 the Walter Automobile Co. became the Mercer Automobile Co. William Walter returned to Manhattan where he began to make trucks. These spread the family name much wider than the cars ever did; they were pioneers of 4-wheel drive in 1911, and were famous for fire engines both for highway and, latterly, airport use. They left the West 66th Street factory in 1923, and from 1957 were made at Voorheesville, New York.

NG

WALTER (ii) (A/CS) 1908–1937

1908–1911 Josef Walter, Praha-Smichov.
1911–1919 Josef Walter a spol., s.r.o., Praha-Smichov, Praha-Jinonice.
1919–1932 Akciova tovarna automobilu Josef Walter a spol., Praha-Jinonice.
1932–1937 Akciova spol. Walter, tovarna na automobily a letecke motory, Praha-Jinonice.

In the history of the Czechoslovak automobile industry one of the most important places belongs to Walter. The founder of this company was Josef Walter (born in 1873), a talented craftsman who, as a 24-year-old in 1898, began a small workshop to repair weighing machines and cycles, then produced cycles using BSA parts, and in 1902, the first motorcycle was developed (motorcycles were made until 1924). But the most glorious product of the time was a 3-wheeler of the 1908–14 period of which about 220 were made, with 4-stroke V-twin 1240cc 9bhp engine. Automatic inlet valves had a relief cock. The air-cooling was sustained by a fan, lubrication with hand-operated pump, 2-speed gearbox without reverse. The fixed rear axle was driven by the propeller shaft and cone wheels to the 3-satellite differential. The vehicle was steered by handlebar with a gas and advanced ignition levers, and a tubular frame was used. These 3-wheelers were exported to Russia, too, but with a 3-speed + reverse gearbox.

In 1913 the Walter factory moved to Jinonice (a suburb of Prague) where the first real cars were made. The first was a water-cooled 4-cylinder 1243cc sv engined 14bhp W I type, and the W II with 1846cc 24bhp engine. A series of 10 cars of each types were sold. The biggest of this range, the W III with 2630cc 28bhp engine, was built until 1914, about 60 cars being sold.

From 1919 Walter was registered as a joint stock company, and in 1920, the WZ with 1545cc 18bhp engine was introduced. In 1922 Josef Walter left the director's chair and the factory and in Praha-Kosire he founded his own factory for gearwheels and car parts. The new chief was Vitezslav Kumpera, who launched the new type named WIZ with modern ohv 1544cc 20bhp engine, and a series of 200 cars was produced. This one was soon completed, with the WIZI with 2120cc 25bhp engine but with side-valves again.

In 1923 aircraft piston engine production began, first under the BMW licence, and soon of their own design. In the 'Motorlet' era from 1946 until today, piston and jet engines were made.

1910 Walter (ii) 7hp 3-wheeler.
NATIONAL MOTOR MUSEUM

1920 Walter (ii) WZ 2-seater.
NATIONAL MOTOR MUSEUM

1931 Walter (ii) Royal V12 cabriolet.
NATIONAL MOTOR MUSEUM

The new P-range started in 1924 and included the ohv engined P I (1544cc, 20bhp), the P II (1544cc, 24bhp) and after 1927 the P III (1945cc, 30bhp) and P IV (2368cc, 36bhp, 72mph/116km/h). In 1928 F. Barvitius designed two new types: the 4B with 4-cylinder ohv 1663cc 30bhp engine, and the 6B with 6-cylinder in-line 2494cc 50bhp, later a 2863cc 60bhp engine. This first 6-cylinder Walter was bodied as a luxurious 4-door faux-cabriolet, open 4–5-seater tourer, 6-seater limousine with chauffeur compartment, one of which was delivered to the President of Czechoslovakia. Some were bodied by Sodomka. Walter produced 1393 cars in 1928, and 1498 in 1929. Walter 6B was a successful type and new types Standard (1931–34, 2863cc, 60bhp, 89,800 Kc for sedan, 98,000 Kc for cabriolet), Standard S (1934, 3257cc, 85bhp, 90mph (145km/h), sports roadster), Super (1931–34, 2863cc, 70bhp, 99,800 Kc for a sedan, 112,000 Kc for a cabriolet) and Regent (3257cc, 80bhp, 125,000 Kc for a sedan, 137,000 Kc for a work's cabriolet, and more for those bodied by Brozik, Uhlik, Sodomka and Petera) were based on its construction features.

The most expensive Czechoslovak car of all times was the Walter Royal, a true 'king' among automobiles. Introduced in 1931, it was powered by a V12 5879cc 120bhp ohv engine, weighed 1980 – 2050kg depending on the body style, and was capable of 87mph (140km/h) at 26 l/100km fuel consumption. Its wheelbase was 142in (3600mm). The chassis cost 145,000 Kc, sedan 188,000 Kc, and cabriolet 198,000 Kc, and a special 4-door cabriolet by Petera cost 208,000 Kc in 1932. Only 3 cars were sold, and about 15 Royal engines served in the Walter D-Bus.

Walter Works after 1930 were busy with the production of aircraft engines and development of new passenger cars was restricted. Then Walter bought a licence for assembling FIAT cars, the first being the type 514 called Walter Bijou (1931–35, 4-cylinder 1438cc 32bhp sv engine, 2-door 49,800 Kc, sedan 52,000 Kc, cabriolet 62,000 Kc). Type 508 Balilla was renamed Walter Junior (1932–36, 4-cylinder 995cc 24bhp SV engine, 2-door 29,500 Kc), sports car FIAT 508 S was Walter Junior S (1934–1935, 4-cylinder 995cc 30bhp sv engine, 72mph/116km/h), later sold as the Junior SS with 995cc 36bhp ohv engine, capable of 78mph (125km/h). In 1933–37 the last two types, the Prince and the Lord with the same 6-cylinder 2491cc 55bhp sv engines but with a chassis of different length, priced 65,000 Kc and 79,800 Kc respectively, were produced. Passenger car production at Walter Works declined: in 1933 it was 471 units, in 1934–469, in 1935–262, in 1936–101, and in 1937 only 13 cars were made. Walter produced the 2.5-ton trucks and aircraft engines only, for military purposes.

After World War II, Walter was nationalised and renamed Motorlet, and produced the last few PN 2.5-ton trucks, and some truck engines for the destroyed Praga Works. Automobile production ended in 1951 when the last Jawa-designed Aero-Minor cars were delivered.

MSH

Further Reading
Walter, Vaclav Petrik, Auto Album Archiv, Brno, 1988.

WALTHAM (i) (US) 1898–1900
Waltham Automobile Co., Waltham, Massachusetts.
John Piper and George Tinker built a light steam car with 4hp engine in a corner of the bicycle factory run by Charles Herman Metz (see METZ and WALTHAM (ii)). They built two more which went by the name Piper & Tinker, as well as an Orient Electric, then struck out on their own in another factory also in Waltham, where they made a steam stanhope that sold for $750.
NG

WALTHAM (ii) (US) 1902–1908
Waltham Manufacturing Co., Waltham, Massachusetts.
This company was formed in 1893 by C.H. Metz to make bicycles under the name Orient. In 1899 an electric car was designed by John Piper and George Tinker; only one was made, and Metz turned to petrol vehicles. He began importing Aster engines and De Dion-Bouton tricycles and quads, followed by manufacture of tricycles, and then of his own engines. In 1902 he brought out a single-cylinder 8hp runabout, of which about 400 were sold. After disagreements with his partners Metz left Waltham to become technical editor of the *Cycle & Automobile Trade Journal*. The company's best-known product was designed by Leonard B. Gaylor. It was called the Orient Buckboard and had a frame of wooden slats without any springing, and powered by a rear-mounted 4hp single-cylinder engine geared directly to the rear axle. Originally there was only one forward speed and no reverse. In 1904 a 3-seater model and a delivery van were offered, and from 1905 there was a surrey with seating for four on two bench seats. The Buckboard became a little more civilised, with wheel steering and a small bonnet to cover the driver's feet, though there was still nothing that one could call a body. Nevertheless, they sold quite well, costing only $375 in their most basic form.

Though the Buckboard was made up to 1907 a more conventional car had been announced two years before. This had a front-mounted 16hp 4-cylinder engine, friction transmission and chain drive. They were made up to 1908 when Metz regained control of his company and launched the kit cars which he sold under the Metz Plan. This marked the end of the Waltham Orient cars.
NG

WALTHAM (iii) (US) 1922
Waltham Motor Manufacturers, Inc., Waltham, Massachusetts.
The Waltham company was a reorganisation of the former Waltham Manufacturing Co. which had previously built the Waltham Orient and the Metz. The car had

a Rutenber 6-cylinder L-head engine and a 120in (3045mm) wheelbase. Its models were restricted to a roadster and a 5-seater touring car. A handful of pilot models were completed but the company failed before production began.

KM

WALTON SPECIAL (US) 1917

Walton Body Corp., New York, New York.

This company built a 2-seater roadster based on the contemporary Hudson Six. It was designed by Wirt M. Walton who hoped to manufacture it, but was frustrated by the entry of the US into World War I. However, he did become a car maker after the war, with the NOMA which was made by a subsidiary of the Walton Body Corp., and which bore quite a close resemblance to the Walton Special.

NG

WALWORTH (US) 1904–1905

A.O. Walworth & Co., Chicago, Illinois.

This company made a short-lived rear-entrance tonneau powered by a 14hp 2-cylinder engine, with 2-speed epicyclic transmission and shaft drive. It was priced at $1500.

NG

W.A.M. (GB) 1996 to date

W.A.M. Classic Cars and Replicas (Bill Monk Classic Cars),
Bromyard, Herefordshire

From a classic car restoration company came the extraordinary W.A.M., a car that was half way between a sports car and a single-seater racer. Emphasising its role as a potential racing car, it had narrow bodywork, front and rear aerofoils and a Perspex wraparound screen, but it was also a full road car, with tandem seating for two, full lighting, and cycle wings. It was designed to accept Fiat running gear and engines. In 1998 the company offered its original project for sale and moved on to making replicas of the classic Aston Martin DB3S racer under the name W.A.M. 3S. Initially this was offered in complete form only but later kits were produced. BMW 4- or 6-cylinder engines were fitted in an exactly authentic replica.

CR

WANDERER (D) 1911–1942

1911–1917 Wanderer Fahrradwerke vorm. Winkelhofer & Jaenicke, Schönau-Chemnitz.
1917–1942 Wanderer Werke AG, Siegmar.

The Wanderer was a well-respected mid-class car which became part of the Auto Union group in 1932. The parent company, Winkelhofer & Jaenicke, was formed in 1885, and made milling machinery and typewriters. The name Wanderer was first used for their bicycles, which appeared in the 1890s. Motorcycles followed in 1902, being made up to 1939; the famous Czech Jawa motorcycles were originally of Wanderer design, their name coming from Janacek, the owner of the factory, and Wanderer. An experimental 2-cylinder car called the Wanderermobil was made in 1904, and a 4-cylinder one in 1907. Ettore Bugatti tried to interest the company in his small car which was later taken up by Peugeot as the Bébé, but by then they were almost ready with their own design, which was put on the market in 1911.

This first Wanderer car was a light 2-seater with tandem seating, a layout used in some cyclecars, but the Wanderer Typ W1 5/12PS was much more than a cyclecar, having a 4-cylinder monobloc engine of 1147cc, a conventional 3-speed gearbox and shaft drive. The engine was somewhat unusual in having overhead inlet and side exhaust valves. The little Wanderer was familiarly known as the Puppchen (doll), and sold well. For 1914 the engine was enlarged to 1220cc, and a side by side 2-seater was available in addition to the tandem. Capacity went up again to 1286cc in mid 1914, and remained at this size during the war, when Wanderers were made for military use.

An increase in cylinder bore from 64 to 64.5mm gave a capacity of 1306cc on the postwar models, which now had all ohvs. The small 4-cylinder engine remained in production until 1926, by which time about 9000 had been made altogether. Postwar models were the W4 5/15PS and W8 5/20PS. In 1921 a larger four, the 1551cc W6, appeared, becoming the W9 in 1923, W10/1 in 1926 and 1940cc W10/11 in 1927. They were conventional cars with 4-speed gearboxes, and were unusual in that they must have been almost the only German cars of

1936 Walter (ii) Lord saloon.
NATIONAL MOTOR MUSEUM

1905 Waltham (ii) Orient 16hp tourer.
NATIONAL MOTOR MUSEUM

1906 Waltham (ii) Orient buckboard.
NATIONAL MOTOR MUSEUM

1918 Walton Special roadster.
D. J. KAVA

1918 Wanderer W3 5/15PS tandem 2-seater.
NATIONAL MOTOR MUSEUM

1927 Wanderer W10 6/30PS tourer.
NICK GEORGANO/NATIONAL MOTOR MUSEUM

1930 Wanderer W10 6/30PS saloon.
NATIONAL MOTOR MUSEUM

their time not to sport the fashionable vee-radiator. A few sports models were made with single-ohc; the most successful driver of these was Huldrich Heusser who later achieved fame with Steyr cars.

Towards the end of 1928 Wanderer moved up-market with their first six, the 2540cc 50bhp W11 with 7-bearing crankshaft and hydraulic brakes. This came with seven body styles including three saloons, one by Lindner and two by Gläser. The gearbox was originally a 3-speed Wanderer, but from 1930 a 4-speed ZF-Aphon with synchromesh on the two upper ratios was used. Some cars of W11 design were built under licence by Martini in Switzerland from 1930 to 1932.

For 1931 the W11 engine was increased to 2970cc to make the W14. This was only available with Gläser cabriolet coachwork, and had the ZF gearbox and an optional Maybach *schnellgang* or 2-speed auxiliary transmission. It had a lower frame and was a very handsome car, with a top speed of 78mph (125km/h). However, its price was against it, RM12,900 compared with RM8450 for the W11 with the same body, and only 24 W14s were made. By contrast, more than 5000 W11s were sold, and 12,500 of the 4-cylinder W10. In 1928 the Wanderer factory had a capacity of 20 cars per day. In the years 1929 to 1932 Wanderer competed regularly in long distance events, especially the Alpine Trial.

The Porsche Influence

In 1931 Wanderer called in Ferdinand Porsche to design a new range of 6-cylinder cars. This was in fact, the first commission for the newly established Porsche Bureau. They had 7-bearing crankshafts and light metal cylinder blocks, resembling the Type XXX which he had designed for Steyr. They also had the Steyr's rear suspension by swinging half axles. Front suspension was by conventional semi-elliptics until 1936 when it became independent by transverse leaf springs. With 1690 and 1950cc engines these cars made up Wanderer production up to 1936 (W21, W25, W40), and some were continued to 1938. A larger engine of 2257cc (W245, W250) was added to the range in 1935. Porsche also designed an advanced 3½-litre straight-8 which never went into production as Wanderer joined the Auto Union group in 1932, and Horch was the marque to which the larger car projects were allocated. The one straight-8 made had a streamlined coupé body by Reutter, and provided Dr Porsche with personal transport for several years. At one time it was fitted with a supercharger.

The first signs of fresh styling appeared on the W25K of 1936. This was a 1950cc 2-seater sports car intended to rival the BMW 328, though it was not a serious threat to the Munich cars, being heavier and slower, with a particularly difficult gearchange which it is said even Grand Prix driver Bernd Rosemeyer could not master. The 'K' in its title indicated a supercharger which gave the elegant 2-seater a top speed of 90mph (145km/h). Initially cheaper than the BMW, at RM6800, its price went up to RM7950 in 1937/38, while the BMW sold for RM7400. A total of 258 W25Ks were made, some of the last being delivered without superchargers.

The W25K's grill was used for the touring Wanderers made from 1937. These had side-valve engines in two sizes, the 1767cc W24 and the 2651cc W23 and W26. The W26 had a longer wheelbase, and carried upright 7-seater coachwork, at first with the old-style grill and wings, although it was updated to match its cheaper sisters for 1939. Standard bodies on these were two or 4-door saloons and a cabriolet. The W24 2-door saloon was also used on the DKW Sonderklasse. Unlike the Porsche-designed cars the last Wanderers had synchromesh on all speeds but bottom. The were in general production up to early 1940, and 100 W23 cabriolets were built from late 1941 to early 1942 for government use.

Total production was about 8000 W23s, 23,000 W24s and 1800 W26s. After the war all Auto Union factories fell into the Eastern zone of Germany, and manufacture of Wanderer cars was not resumed.
NG

WARD (i) **(US)** 1914
Ward Cyclecar Co., Milwaukee, Wisconsin.
Ward Butler built the prototype of his cyclecar in Chicago, but for production he took a factory in Milwaukee, conveniently close to the plant where his engines were made. They were a 9hp twin and a 12hp four, both mounted in an underslung frame which gave the Ward cyclecar an attractive appearance. Transmission was by friction discs and final drive by vee-belt. Ten cars had been completed by the late summer of 1914, and a production run of 100 was planned for the next few months. It is unlikely that this figure was reached.
NG

1938 Wanderer W23 cabriolet by Gläser.
NICK BALDWIN

WARD (ii) (US) 1913–1916

1913–1915 Ward Motor Vehicle Co., Bronx, New York.
1915–1916 Ward Motor Vehicle Co., Mount Vernon, New York.
Charles A. Ward's company was always better-known for its electric vans and trucks, but he made a small number of passenger cars. Only one style was offered, a 4-seater coupé with low dropped frame and a commendable range of 100 miles between charges. After his move to Mount Vernon he reduced the price from $2100 to $1295, possibly to unload stock which was taking up valuable factory space. This was needed for the commercial vehicles which were made up to 1937. Ward then continued as truck bodybuilders until 1965.

NG

WARD LEONARD (US) 1903

Ward Leonard Electrical Co., Bronxville, New York.
Harry Ward Leonard had already designed two cars, the CENTURY TOURIST and the KNICKERBOCKER, before he brought out a car under his own name. The was a sizeable 30hp 4-cylinder machine with roadster or tonneau bodies and a Renault-type bonnet with side radiators. Few were made, as Ward Leonard was more interested in electrical inventions.

NG

WARD MOTORSPORTS see KURTIS

WAREENA (AUS) 1912

Auto-Import Co., Sydney, New South Wales.
A US-made type of unknown identity, the Wareena first appeared at the Sydney Show as a 4-cylinder 25hp torpedo and a 30hp touring car. Also advertised were 4-cylinder roadster and runabout models. Clearly a re-labelling of some other make – WARREN is an immediate candidate – except that it did not list a 25hp engine.

MG

WARFIELD (GB) 1903

Warfield Motor Car Co., Teddington, Middlesex.
Conveniently located on the Thames, this company made engines for steam launches, and briefly offered a steam car with a special design of flash boiler said

1937 Wanderer W40 saloon.
IMPERIAL WAR MUSEUM

to be capable of resisting a pressure of 3000psi. The makers had no stand at the 1903 Show, but a car was said to be running in the yard outside.

NG

WARLOCK (US) c.1996 to date

Warlock Designs, Chino, California.
Imaginary Fiberglass (I.F.G.), Chino, California.
This company had two names, depending on which model of Lamborghini replica kit it was selling. Warlock cloned the Lamborghini Diablo, calling it the Phantom. The Phantom VT was a coupé with several chassis variations, all based on the Pontiac Fiero. One allowed a Chevrolet V8 to be mounted longitudinally with a Porsche 914 transaxle. The others used transversely mounted Pontiac or Chevrolet engines. The Phantom Roadster was a convertible version. The I.F.G. division sold replicas of the Lamborghini Countach, which they called the Interceptor. There were two models, one replicating the 5000S model and the

1911 Warren-Detroit 30 runabout.
NICK BALDWIN

1913 Warren Resolute Six tourer.
J. P. NORBYE

1920 Warren-Lambert 10hp 2-seater.
NATIONAL MOTOR MUSEUM

other the 25th anniversary model Lamborghini. Both I.F.G. models were Fiero-based and less expensive than the Warlock models. Warlock briefly built replicas of the Ferrari F355 Coupé and Spyder, but quickly dropped them.

HP

WARMOUTH see APOLLO (v)

WARNE (GB) 1913–1915
Pearsall Warne Ltd, Letchworth, Hertfordshire.
The Warne was a cyclecar powered by an 8hp V-twin JAP engine, with belt final drive. Although the engine was air-cooled, the Warne had a dummy radiator, which gave it the appearance of a large car in miniature. It was priced at £99, and in mid–1913 production was running at six cars a week.

In May 1913 an emergency low gear was available at a cost of only £7 extra, for adventurous cyclecarists who wanted to climb 1 in 3 hills.

NG

WARP FIVE (US) c.1992 to date
Warp Five Inc., Blue Springs, Missouri.
Warp Five resumed production of the MANTA Mirage and Montage kits. They were updated to Ford Mustang II front suspension, and the Mirage was renamed the Manta GT. It was redesigned to take a Porsche transaxle to replace the Corvair unit used in the original. The Montage could be configured for the same running gear. Warp Five also sold the Starship, a revival of the old OSWOSSO Pulse. This was a small tandem 2-seater commuter with motorcycle running gear. It had four wheels in a diamond pattern and looked like a fighter plane cockpit with stubby wings.

HP

WARREN (US) 1911–1913
Warren Motor Car Co., Detroit, Michigan.
Sometimes known as the Warren-Detroit, this was a conventional car which used 4-cylinder engines for most of its life. In its first season, 1911, it was offered with a 30hp engine and no fewer than eight body styles on a single wheelbase. 1912 saw three wheelbases but fewer styles, only a tourer and a roadster. The 1913 models carried colourful names such as Wolverine, a 35hp on a 112in (2843mm) wheelbase, Pilgrim 40hp on a 116in (2944mm) wheelbase, and the Resolute which had a 50hp 6-cylinder engine on a 130in (3299mm) wheelbase. One of the engineers, W.H. Radford, later designed the PILGRIM (ii) and BALBOA cars.

NG

WARREN-LAMBERT (GB) 1913–1922
1913–1915 Warren-Lambert Engineering Co. Ltd, Shepherd's Bush, London.
1915–1922 Warren-Lambert Engineering Co. Ltd, Richmond, Surrey.
The prototype of this light car was called the Lambert & West, but when it went into production in the autumn of 1913 it bore solely the name of its maker, A. Warren Lambert (his name had no hyphen, but the car did). The first car had a Precision V-twin engine, but this soon gave way to a Blumfield, also a V-twin. In October 1914 a 1093cc 4-cylinder Dorman engine was announced. Production continued into 1915, despite the outbreak of war and Warren Lambert's departure for the front. About 200 cars had been made when production finally ceased, most of them with 2-cylinder engines.

Warren Lambert returned from the war with the rank of Major, acquired a new factory at Richmond, and a new engine for his cars. This was a 1330cc Alpha which was used in the touring 2-seaters, but there was also a striking sports car with burnished copper exhaust pipe that ran the length of the car from the bonnet to behind the rear axle. This used a 1498cc Coventry-Simplex engine, and had a top speed of 65mph (105km/h). Warren-Lamberts were particularly good at hill climbs, a prewar 2-cylinder car having defeated the notorious Nailsworth Ladder in Gloucestershire, but this did not save the firm. They were too expensive compared with rivals, particularly Morris, and they had no 4-seater in their range. Production ended some time in 1922.

NG
Further Reading
'Warren-Lambert, the Mountain Climber', M. Worthington-Williams, *The Automobile*, March 1991.

WARRIGAL (AUS) 1954
Fibreglass Custom Bodies Pty Ltd, Sydney, New South Wales.
Australia's first fibreglass motor body was not the usual sports roadster but a 2-door pillarless saloon fitted to the 108in (2743mm) wheelbase chassis of a Triumph Renown. Although both a company and a trademark were registered and the intention declared to commence production if successful, there is a possibility that it was a publicity exercise by the providers of fibreglass materials. It is believed that only one was made, this being named after the native Australian wild dog.

MG

WARRIOR (US) c.1964
Vanguard Products, Dallas, Texas.
The Warrior was a proposed mid-engined sports car built along Ford Mustang 1 prototype lines. Like the Mustang prototype, it used a Ford V4 engine. A fibreglass coupé body had a removable roof panel. Apparently only the prototype was built.

HP

1964 Wartburg (ii) 1000 President saloon.
NATIONAL MOTOR MUSEUM

WARSZAWA *see* FSO

WARTBURG (i) **(D)** 1898–1904

Fahrzeugfabrik Eisenach, Eisenach.

The Fahrzeugfabrik Eisenach was founded by Heinrich Ehrhardt in 1896 to make horse-drawn army vehicles such as gun carriages, field kitchens and sanitary wagons. This was followed by the manufacture of bicycles and in 1898 Ehrhardt took out a licence to build the French Decauville Voiturelle. This had a 3.5PS air-cooled 2-cylinder engine mounted at the rear, and was unusual in having independent suspension of the front wheels, and no rear suspension at all. A 5PS water-cooled engine followed in 1899, and in 1902 came a 5.5PS front-engined shaft-driven 2-seater resembling the Peugeot Bébé. This was followed by larger cars with 2- or 4-cylinder engines of up to 45PS. In 1904 Ehrhardt left to make cars under his own name, and subsequent cars from the Eisenach factory went under the name DIXI.

In 1930 the Wartburg name was briefly revived for a sports model of the Austin Seven-based Dixi which, by that time, was being made by BMW. The name, which was also used for the postwar 3-cylinder cars, came from a famous local castle.

NG

WARTBURG (ii) **(DDR)** 1956–1990

VEB Automobilwerk Eisenach, Eisenach.

In 1955 the State-owned VEB Automobilwerk Eisenach decided to update their 3-cylinder car which had been made since 1950 under the title IFA F9. For the new model they revived the ancient name of Wartburg, which had been carried by cars made in Eisenach in the early years of the century. The Wartburg retained the 900cc DKW-inspired in-line 3-cylinder 2-stroke engine, but output was raised from 30bhp at 3800rpm to 37bhp at 4000rpm. Front-wheel drive was retained, as was the unsynchronised 4-speed gearbox. The main change was in

1972 Wartburg (ii) Knight estate car.
NICK BALDWIN

the body, which was a completely new and wider 6-light saloon, capable of seating six, thanks to steering column gearchange. It was 12in (305mm) longer than its predecessor, and 132lb (60kg) heavier.

The Wartburg was launched at the 1956 Leipzig Spring Fair in three models, saloon, cabriolet and estate car (Kombi). Prices ran from DM-Ost 14,700 to 16,370, which translated to DM5300–7100 when the Wartburg came on the West German market in 1958. This was higher than the cheapest VW Beetle, but lower than a Ford Taunus or Opel Olympia, while none of these makes offered four doors at the time. The Wartburg's appeal then, as later, and on other West European markets, was that it offered a lot of car for the money, for which buyers were prepared to overlook unexciting performance and indifferent handling. Actually its performance was not too bad at the time of its introduction, its top

1960 Warwick (ii) GT coupé.
NICK BALDWIN

speed of 70mph (114km/h) being a bit faster than that of a VW Beetle 1200, but it changed little during more than 30 years' lifetime. A sports coupé/cabriolet with 50bhp and a top speed of 87mph (140km/h) was briefly offered from 1957 to 1959, but thereafter the Wartburg had no sporting ambitions.

From 1958 the gearbox acquired synchromesh on the two upper ratios and in 1962 capacity went up to 992cc in the Wartburg 1000. In 1966 the body was restyled in a shape which remained unchanged for the rest of the car's life. It was now a 4-light saloon or Kombi (no cabriolets offered) with more headroom, and synchromesh on all four speeds. Power was up to 45bhp, giving a speed of 78mph (125km/h). The beam rear axle was replaced by semi-trailing arm independent suspension. Apart from a further increase in power to 50bhp in 1969, and disc brakes on the front wheels in 1974, very few changes were made to the Wartburg up to 1988 when the two-stroke gave way to a 1.3-litre 4-cylinder Volkswagen unit, and a 5-speed gearbox was provided. Bodies were the same saloon or estate car, the latter being called the Tourist. Although they were exported quite widely at one time, from the mid-70s Wartburg sales were largely confined to the DDR and neighbouring Comecon countries. In 1990 the Eisenach plant began to make the Opel Vectra, for a very short time, alongside the Wartburgs.

NG

WARWICK (i) (US) 1901–1905

Warwick Cycle & Automobile Co., Springfield, Massachusetts.
This company had made bicycles for several years when they launched their first car (their catalogue referred to 'the ever faithful and true Warwick bicycle'). The car had the appearance of a typical light steamer, but it was powered by a single-cylinder De Dion-Bouton engine of 3.5 or 6hp, with 2-speed gearbox and drive geared to the rear axle. The frame was tubular and steering was by vertical tiller. In 1902 the 6hp model was available with a folding front seat, and for 1903 Warwick made their own 6hp engine and a longer wheelbase. 1904 models were considerably larger with front-mounted engines of 14hp 2-cylinder and 18hp 3-cylinder, and side-entrance tonneau bodies.

NG

WARWICK (ii) (GB) 1960–1962

Bernard Rodger Developments Ltd, Colnbrook, Buckinghamshire.
After the failure of the Peerless GT in 1960, the designer, Bernie Rodger, modified the concept and marketed it as the Warwick, the project's original name. Externally, the main differences to the Peerless were moulded rain gutters and a different headlight treatment, but Rodger also shed about 80lb while making the frame stiffer. Among the improvements were a revised dashboard and a one-piece forward-hinging bonnet. As with the Peerless, Triumph TR3 running gear was installed in a spaceframe with a De Dion back axle suspended on semi-elliptic springs.

The venture was under-financed, the car was not made to the highest standards, and production was from only late 1960 to late 1961. Towards the end of the Warwick's short life, a 3.5-litre Buick V8 engine was fitted to a prototype and it was intended to be offered as an option. That idea was the essence of the Gordon Keeble.

A variant was built by Chris Lawrence from Peerless and Warwick components. Called the Peewick, it was Lawrence's idea of what the car should have been and it had a new frame with a shorter wheelbase, lightly revised suspension and a Lawrencetune TR3A engine. A top speed of 134mph (216km/h) was claimed, but the Peewick remained a prototype.

MJL

WASHINGTON (i) (US) 1909–1912

1909–1912 Carter Motor Car Corp., Hyattsville, Maryland.
1911 Washington Motor Car Co., Hyattsville, Maryland.
1912 Independence Motor Co., Hyattsville, Maryland.
The Washington was designed by A. Gary Carter, brother of Howard O. Carter who had made the CARTER TWIN ENGINE, and was built in the same factory with a slight change of company name. It was a conventional car made in three sizes of 4-cylinder engine, 30, 35 and 45hp, with four open body styles, 3-seater roadster, 4-seater tourabout, 4-seater baby tonneau, and 5-seater tourer. Though orthodox it sold hardly any better than the unorthodox Carter Twin Engine. In 1912 the company was reorganised as the Washington Motor Car Co., but soon after that its name changed again to the Independence Motor Co. Under this name a wider range of cars was announced, with 2-, 4- and 6-cylinder engines. Only prototypes were made. The Carters were later involved with the HARVARD, MONARCH (vi), C.B. and CARTERMOBILE.

NG

WASHINGTON (ii) (US) 1921–1924

1921–1924 Washington Motor Co., Eaton, Ohio.
1924 Washington Motor Co., Middletown, Ohio.
This Washington was a conventional assembled car. Prototypes used a 3198cc ohv Falls X9000 6-cylinder engine, but it was found to consume too much oil, so a 3670cc side-valve Continental 7R was substituted for the 1921 production model, replaced by a 3957cc Continental 8R for 1922 and 1923. Four open and closed bodies were listed for these years at prices from $1785 for a tourer to $2385 for a sedan. Estimates of Washington production vary between 35 and 65 units. In 1924 they moved to a new factory at Middletown, where a few more petrol cars were built, and three examples of a steamer. This was made only as a tourer, which was priced at $1785, the same as the petrol version which it generally resembled, apart from having disc wheels instead of artillery.

NG

WASP (i) (GB) 1907–1908

Thames Bank Wharf Motor Works, London.
This company was listed as making a large car with 11,144cc 50/60hp 6-cylinder Mutel engine with pair-cast cylinders, a 3-speed gearbox and shaft drive. The bodies listed included a phaeton and a pullman-limousine. No prices were quoted, and it is unlikely that many, if any, were sold. There was said to be a link with the Euston Motor Co., who sold an imported car which they called the COURIER (i).

NG

WASP (ii) (US) 1919–1924

Martin-Wasp Corp., Bennington, Vermont.
Karl H. Martin, designer of the Wasp, had been a successful coachbuilder in New York City as well as the designer of the ROAMER, DEERING MAGNETIC and KENWORTHY cars. Between the summer of 1919 and the summer of 1924, a total of 18 Wasps were constructed with sharply pointed wings, rickshaw-type bodies and costing between $5000 and $10,000. Earlier models were 4-cylinder types with Wisconsin T-head engines; the later cars used a Continental 6T 6-cylinder unit. The Wasp was the only car ever built in the United States which carried a St Christopher medal on its dashboard. The bronze medallion was also fabricated and cast by Martin.

KM

Further Reading
Automobiles Wasp. Keith Marvin, published by the author, 1962.
'We were impractical, it is true … Karl Martin and his Wasp', Keith Marvin, *Automobile Quarterly*, Vol.17, No.2.

WATANI (MA) 1955

Éts France-Auto, Casablanca.
The Watani was a modified version of Gabriel Voisin's minimalist Biscooter, intended for mass production under licence in Morocco. The soft-top Watani

Karl Martin standing by a 1920 Wasp (ii) 4-cylinder tourer.
KEITH MARVIN

MARTIN, KARL (1888–1954)

Karl Hamlen Martin, custom car coachbuilder, designer and manufacturer, was born in Buffalo, New York, on 31 January 1888, the son of Dr Truman J. Martin, a prominent automotive pioneer, tourist and the first president of the Buffalo Automobile Club. Young Karl learned to drive, service and repair a Columbia electric at the age of nine, and with his father drove postmen around the city of Buffalo for mail deliveries. He graduated from St Paul's School, Concord, New Hampshire, in 1905 and planned to enter Yale, but he decided to try the oil business, in which he was active from 1908-12.

After a year's study of body design in New York he set up his own custom coachbuilding establishment. He did not work through any distributors, but direct with his customers. Most of his work was on foreign chassis, the only American one which he used being Locomobile. In 1916 he made his debut as a designer of complete cars when he penned the Roamer for Albert Barley. It was an instant success in the marketplace, and the following year a sporting model was introduced. His design of the Roamer attracted a group of Chicago businessmen who were planning a high-priced luxury car using Entz magnetic transmission employed in the Owen Magnetic. Martin was hired for the design of the car, which was called the Deering Magnetic. Unfortunately, shortage of materials hampered its success, and production ceased in early 1919.

Immediately after World War I he joined Cloyd Kenworthy in Mishawaka, Indiana, as a body designer for the Kenworthy car. This lasted only until 1919; after providing Kenworthy with his designs, but probably before any cars were built, Martin returned east, and set up home in Bennington, Vermont, in Hamlen House, the home of his maternal grandparents. He launched his Wasp car at the Hotel Commodore in New York in January 1920. Soon afterwards, hearing that Cloyd Kenworthy was having little success with his car, he invited him to move to Bennington as general manager of the Martin-Wasp Corp. This was to no avail, and Martin never heard from him again.

Martin made 18 Wasps between 1920 and 1925. He had received financial backing from a prominent businessman from Atlanta, Georgia, and when this man died, the money supply ended and no more Wasps were made. The corporation continued as a builder of custom furniture and engraved custom stationery for several years.

A 6-cylinder chassis ordered by the Atlanta businessman was never bodied, and remained the property of Karl Martin until 1954 when it was acquired by an Ohio collector who spent seven years restoring it and building a body from the original blueprints. It was widely shown in Ohio, New York and New England, and in November 1982 it was presented to the Bennington Museum where it is on permanent display in its own gallery.

Karl Martin married Elizabeth Jennings; they had a son, Karl Martin Jr, and he had a son, Karl H. Martin III. When the latter married, the 6-cylinder Wasp was used as his wedding car.

KM

1907 Pope-Waverley electric stanhope.
NICK BALDWIN

1915 Waverley (i) Model 109 electric brougham.
NICK BALDWIN

had four seats and a 197cc engine which its makers, France-Auto, claimed could be stretched to an optimistic top speed of 55mph (89km/h). France-Auto's ambitious production plans were never fulfilled with only one Watani prototype being built.

CR

WATFORD (GB) 1959–1962
Watford Sports Cars Ltd, Watford, Hertfordshire.
The Watford Cheetah was a very typical sports car of the kit-built 'specials' variety. However, it differed from most in that it was not simply a fibreglass shell: the company made chassis as well as open and hard-top sports bodies. Its tubular chassis featured ifs and was designed to accept Ford side-valve engines. All-round independent suspension was also available.

CR

WATLING (GB) 1959–1961
Watling Cars, Parkstreet Village, St Albans, Hertfordshire.

Watling produced a particularly inelegant fibreglass shell range, encompassing two and 4-seaters and open cars and saloons. Complete kits were also sold with a tubular ladder chassis with coil spring ifs in two different wheelbase lengths, designed for a variety of mechanicals, including Ford E93A, 100E and 105E, or Morris Minor.

CR

WATROUS (US) 1905
Watrous Automobile Co., Elmira, New York.
Made by Thomas M. Watrous, this was an unsuccessful car powered by a 12hp 2-cylinder air-cooled engine with friction transmission, made in two body styles, a 2-seater runabout on a 80in (2030mm) wheelbase and a 5-seater tourer whose wheelbase was 85in (2157mm). It had solid tyres which by 1905 were very old-fashioned except for a high-wheeler, which the Watrous was not. Production, such as it was, lasted less than six months. Locals called it the 'waterless, powerless, useless Watrous'.

NG

WATT (US) 1910
Watt Motor Co., Detroit, Michigan.
This company had ambitious plans to make a range of cars, runabouts, tourers and delivery vans, powered by a 45hp 'reversible' 6-cylinder engine. In the event, only two examples of the tourer were made. It had a very long bonnet, big enough to hold a straight-8 engine, and a 132in (3350mm) wheelbase, which gave it an impressive appearance, but the company lasted only a few months, and was bankrupt by May 1910.

NG

WATTEL-MORTIER (F) 1921
Made by an unknown company in Paris, the Wattel-Mortier used a 2362cc 6-cylinder engine of the maker's own design, with piston valves and a crankshaft which was made up of two pieces bolted together. It had flywheel lubrication, as on the Model T Ford, and a conventional 3-speed gearbox. The specification included 4-wheel brakes with Hallot servo assistance, still rare in 1921 except on luxury cars such as Hispano-Suiza. The Wattel-Mortier probably never passed the prototype stage.

NG

WAUKESHA (US) 1906–1910
Waukesha Motor Co., Waukesha, Wisconsin.
This famous engine company was founded in 1906 to make marine engines, and became very well-known as a supplier of proprietary engines to a wide variety of car and truck makers. A few complete cars were built, tourers and roadsters, for local customers.

NG

WAVERLEY (i) (US) 1898–1916
1898–1899 Indiana Bicycle Co., Indianapolis, Indiana.
1900–1901 American Bicycle Co., Indianapolis, Indiana.
1901–1903 International Motor Car Co., Indianapolis, Indiana.
1904–1908 Waverley Dept, Pope Motor Car Co., Indianapolis, Indiana.
1908–1916 Waverley Co., Indianapolis, Indiana.
Though there were several different company names, the Waverley electric was part of Colonel A.A. Pope's empire up to 1908. The first cars were introduced following a merger between the American Electric Vehicle Co. of Chicago and the Pope-owned Indiana Bicycle Co. They were light runabouts to start with, but by 1902 more substantial 4-seaters were made. From 1904 to 1908 they were known as Pope-Waverleys, and during this time the range was expanded to include ten models from a Road Wagon 2-seater at $850 to a coupé with special Edison battery at $2250. The Pope empire was foundering by 1908, but the Waverley was rescued by a group of Indianapolis businessmen who organised a new company. They continued the range, and from 1912 made a bonnetted roadster with the appearance of a petrol car. In 1912 they called this the Sheltered Roadster, but dropped this charming name for 1913, when it became simply the Model 90. In 1915 the closed models were called the Front Drive Four and Rear Drive Four, but this did not refer the driven wheels, simply the position of the controls, at the front or rear of the coupé body.

NG

WAVERLEY (ii) (GB) 1901–1904

Scottish Motor Co., Edinburgh; New Rossleigh Motor & Cycle Co. Ltd, Edinburgh.

Named The Pride of the North this was a light car powered by a 9hp single-cylinder De Dion-Bouton engine in a chassis and body made in Edinburgh. It cost £280 in 1902.

NG

WAVERLEY (iii) (GB) 1910–1931

1910–1915 Light Cars Ltd, Willesden, London.
1915–1931 Waverley Cars Ltd, Willesden, London.

The Waverley name first appeared at the Olympia Show in 1910, but the previous year Vernon Trier had exhibited under his own name, and on the MARLBOROUGH stand, a cyclecar powered by a 9hp V-twin JAP engine. Trier was also involved in the Trier & Martin carburettor company, and he and Martin set up Light Cars Ltd in 1910. Their first Waverley car was a more substantial machine than the Trier cyclecar, with a 1460cc 10hp 4-cylinder Chapuis-Dornier engine and 3-speed gearbox. The 2-and 4-seater bodies was made by E.B. Hall whose premises were close to the Light Cars factory in Waldo Road, Willesden. Sales were still handled by T.B. André who made the Marlborough, and it was not until 1913 that Waverleys were shown on their own stand. By then they had larger engines of 1843 and 2116cc (both known as the 12/15) still by Chapuis-Dornier. These were listed up to 1916, when the supply of Chapuis-Dornier engines dried up, and the factory was turned over to munitions work.

The company name was changed to Waverley Cars in 1915, and in 1919 they moved into a new factory at Trenmar Gardens, off the Harrow Road, still in Willesden. They adopted the 2303cc 14.3hp Tylor engine (as used by ANGUS SANDERSON) in the early postwar cars which were expensive, running to £750 for a coupé in 1919 and £960 for an all-weather coupé in 1920. The bodies were still made by E.B. Hall. A smaller and cheaper car came in 1922, powered by a 1504cc 10.8hp Coventry-Simplex engine selling for £325 in its cheapest form. This helped Waverley to sell 65 cars in 1923, not an impressive figure, but probably one of their best in the 1920s. A 1496cc Burt McCollum sleeve-valve engine was used in a few cars in 1924, and for 1925 Waverley announced their Light Six powered by a 1991cc ohv Coventry Climax engine, which was made up to the end of production in 1931. A variety of bodies was offered on this chassis, saloons, both coachbuilt and Weymann-type, a coupé, a 7-seater limousine-landaulet and a 4-seater sports with vee-windscreen and dual-cowl phaeton body. Aluminium pistons and a special camshaft gave it a top speed of 70mph (113km/h). Production figures for the Light Six are not known, but probably very few were made. If surviving cars are anything to go by, at least four pre–1916 cars are still around but none from the 1920s.

At the other end of the scale Waverley chose to enter the £100 market with a 4-seater cyclecar powered by a rear-mounted 901cc Coventry-Victor flat-twin engine, with friction transmission and spiral gears to the rear axle. It was exhibited at the 1926 Olympia Show, but only three were made. Though some lists carried the Light Six 16/50 up to 1935, the last was almost certainly made four years earlier. Waverley continued in business for many years, making trailers and doing general engineering work. As late as 1969 they were still listed in the London Post Office Directory as 'motor car manufacturers'. In 1970 they changed their name to Waverley Components & Products Ltd, still at the Trenmar Gardens address, and remained there until 1973.

NG

Further Reading
'The Waverley Story', M. Worthington-Williams,
The Automobile, August 1990.

WAYLAND (GB) 1895–1903

Wayland Works, Watton, Norfolk.
Samual Burr Joyce built a few 3-wheelers with rear-mounted engine, single front wheel and wickerwork seats.

NG

WAYNE (i) (US) 1904–1908

Wayne Automobile Co., Detroit, Michigan.
Designed by William E. Kelly, who had made an experimental car in 1901, the first Wayne had a 16hp 2-cylinder engine under the front seat, and a 5-seater

1919 Waverley (iii) 15hp tourer.
NICK BALDWIN

1921 Waverley (iii) 15hp coupé cabriolet.
NICK BALDWIN

1927 Waverley (iii) 16/50 fabric saloon.
NICK BALDWIN

tourer body. For 1905 the company made a greater variety, continuing the 16hp on two wheelbases and adding a 24hp 4-cylinder model. For 1906 larger fours were added, of 24/28, 35 and 50hp. The latter was a sizeable car, on a 117in (2969mm) wheelbase and costing $3500. It was continued into 1907, along with the 35hp, but the smaller Waynes were dropped. In 1907 nearly 600 cars were made, but in 1908 Wayne merged with NORTHERN and production ended in the summer of that year. Later the E.M.F. was made in the factory, also designed by William Kelly.

NG

WAYNE (ii) see RICHMOND (ii)

WEARWELL; WOLF (GB) 1899–1905

Wearwell Motor Carriage Co. Ltd, Wolverhampton, Staffordshire.
This company was well-known for its Wolf motorcycles, which were made from 1901 to 1939. In 1899 they announced a voiturette not unlike a Decauville voiturelle in appearance, with 2-cylinder air-cooled engine under the seat. Very

1922 Webb Super Nine all-weather 4-seater.
NICK BALDWIN

1902 Weber victoria.
ERNEST SCHMID

c.1920 Wege 2-seater.
MICHAEL WORTHINGTON-WILLIAMS

few were made, and it was not until 1904 that any other vehicle resembling a car was made. This was a tricar with a coachbuilt body and the 6hp water-cooled 2-cylinder engine placed vertically between the front and rear seats. Final drive was by shaft. The same design was made in 1905 with a 7/8hp engine.

NG

WEBB (GB) 1922–1923
V.P. Webb & Co. Ltd, Stourport, Worcestershire.
Victor Webb, a member of the well-known Webb seed family, planned to make a 2-cylinder 2-stroke motorcycle, but this got no further than a few prototypes. He then turned to four wheels, and in 1922 launched the Webb Super Nine. It was powered by a 1088cc 4-cylinder Alpha engine, with 3-speed gearbox and shaft drive, both the 'box and rear axle being supplied by Moss. Only one body style was offered, a chummy designed for three adults or two adults and two children. It cost £220, and with all-weather hood, £240. The bodies were built in the Webb works. The cars did not sell well, having little to offer compared with many rivals, and acquiring a bad reputation in the transmission department. Just under 100 were made in two years.

Webb later made some bodies for CALTHORPE, and also for small country buses and charabancs, and before they closed in the late 1920s they made milk churns. Victor Webb then emigrated to Australia.

NG

Further Reading
'The Webb Super Nine', A.B. Demaus, *The Automobile*, June 1992.

WEBB JAY (US) 1908
Webb Jay Motor Co., Chicago, Illinois.
Webb Jay was a well-known driver of White steam racing cars, but after a serious accident in 1906 he decided to turn to safer activities. First he became a White dealer in Chicago, where his brother Frank was selling the rival Stanley. In 1908 they became car makers themselves, building a large and expensive steam car powered by a 30hp 2-cylinder compound engine. This and the boiler were mounted under the bonnet, transmission was via a 2-speed gearbox with final drive by chains. With a spacious tourer body it sold for $4000. *The Steam and Electric Car Review* said '…the car is bound to leap into immediate popularity', but few were made. Webb subsequently invented a vacuum tank which was bought by Stewart Warner, enabling him to retire comfortably, while Frank became a vice-president of Stanley.

NG

WEBER (CH) 1899–1906
J. Weber & Co., Uster, Zürich.
The company had specialised in manufacturing of machinery for the textile industry well before the turn of the century. In 1899 the younger son of the owner, Johann Weber, was very much interested in taking up automobile production. Supported by Franz Brozincevic, a member of the executive staff and later founder of the famous F.B.W. commercial vehicle manufacturing company, he obtained a licence agreement from EGG & EGLI for their 3-wheeler.

They built a limited number of these vehicles but soon found that more up-to-date designs and four wheels were needed. Less than one year later they launched their own first light car with a tubular chassis and a big horizontal single-cylinder engine of 8bhp and 2510cc, usually placed in the rear. Transmission of power was by belts with variable diameter belt-pulleys, rather similar to the Variomatic of DAF of about half a century later. The bodies, *vis-à-vis*, victoria and phaeton, were made by local coachbuilders. The early models had steel-spoke wheels, but later with even bigger engines up to 12bhp and heavier bodies, wooden-spoke wheels were fitted.

Production was at a rate of about 60 cars annually and the majority was sold in export markets. The price of SFr12,000 was above the average and made it difficult to sell in Switzerland. By 1906 new models would have been required, but the whole venture was stopped for financial reasons. One fine example with a victoria body is preserved by the Swiss Transport Museum in Lucerne.

FH

WEBSTER (US) 1902–1903
Webster Automobile Co., Attleboro, Massachusetts.
This was a 16hp 4-cylinder tonneau with shaft drive. The prototype may have been built in New York City, but the five production cars were made in Frank Mossburg's bicycle bell factory at Attleboro, where the U.S. ELECTRIC was also made.

NG

WEEBER (US) 1898–1905
Christian F. Weeber, Albany, New York.
Weeber was a bicycle maker who built his first car in 1898. Called the Weebermobile, it was a 2-seater with single-cylinder engine under the floorboards, though a small bonnet gave the impression of a front engine. This car is still in existence today, but later Weebers, with larger engines of 4.5 to 8hp, have not survived in their entirety, though some components can be seen in the New York State Museum at Albany, together with the Weebermobile.

NG

WEGE (AUS) 1920–1925
The Wege Motor Ltd, Adelaide, South Australia.
The patented invention of W.J.F. Wege was to connect three cylinders of a 2-stroke

1909 Weigel 20hp tourer.

engine, having pistons of greater diameter at their bottoms than at their tops, by passages to allow each to charge its neighbour. The system only worked with groups of three cylinders and the initial car engine was a 24hp V6 exhibited at the Adelaide Motor Show and installed in a vehicle for testing. A company was formed which sent Bill Wege to England, where a 3-cylinder 11hp-engined roadster was built on a M.A.B. chassis, and licences were arranged with William Beardmore for aircraft and ships, Karrier Motors for trucks, Chambers Bros in Belfast for cars, and The Economic Power Co. for suction gas plants. Wege returned to Australia with the 3-cylinder car and unsuccessful attempts were made, including in other states up until 1925, to finance production. A racing hydroplane was Wege-powered, while farm and industrial engines were made in three sizes, all of iron rather than the car type's alloy.

MG

WEGMANN (D) 1925

Wagonfabrik Wegmann & Co., Kassel.

This company was mainly concerned with making railway carriages, but in 1925 they announced a small car with 3-seater tourer body and a 1016cc 4/20PS 4-cylinder engine. It had a 3-speed gearbox and final drive was by shaft.

HON

WEGO (US) 1916

Wego Motor Co., Jackson, Michigan.

The Wego lasted less than a year, and was a short episode in the history of the ARGO (ii). Built by Benjamin Briscoe, it was a larger car than the Argo, with a 22hp 4-cylinder engine, and was made in tourer and roadster forms. Before the end of 1916 Briscoe sold his company to Mansell Hackett, who renamed the car the Argo, as well as building his own HACKETT cars.

NG

WEICHELT (D) 1908

H. Weichelt Automobil- und Motorenfabrik, Leipzig.

This company offered two light cars with 10PS 2-cylinder or 16PS 4-cylinder engines, and the choice of air- or water-cooling on both models.

NG

WEIDE see RWN

WEIDNER CONDOR (D) 1957

Weidner AG, Schwabisch Hall.

This was the last manifestation of the TRIPPEL, and had a 600cc 2-stroke engine in the rear of a streamlined coupé body. It was similar in design to the TROLL (i) which was to have been made in Norway, but never saw production.

NG

WEI'ER (CHI) 1996–1997

People's Liberation Army Works No. 5720.

The Wei'er (Military Power) saloon was a 4-door 4-seater saloon with a maximum speed of 86mph (139km/h).

EVIS

WEIGEL (GB) 1906–1909

1906–1907 Weigel Motors Ltd, Goswell Street, London.
1907–1909 Weigel Motors Ltd, North Kensington, London.

D.M. (Danny) Weigel was chosen by the Earl of Shrewsbury and Talbot as the first managing director of Clement-Talbot Ltd. In 1906 he left to form his own company, with premises at Goswell Street in the City of London. The first Weigel car was shown in October; it was a large machine with 40hp 4-cylinder engine, described by *Motoring Illustrated* as being on the lines of an Italian Mercedes. This sounded like an Itala, and as Weigel's premises were described as being more of a depot than a factory, it seems that Weigel Motors made little of the cars themselves. The chassis were finished by the Wilkinson Sword Co. of Acton, and bodies were by the English branch of Rothschild, of which Weigel was a director.

Production figures for Weigel are uncertain, but in January 1907 25 cars were said to be 'under construction' at Goswell Street, as well as six complete cars. Later in 1907 a 25hp four and a 60hp six were announced. One of the latter, with a luxurious limousine body by Rothschild, was supplied to the Earl of Wilton. Weigel also made some unsuccessful Grand Prix cars, two 15-litre straight-8s in 1907 and three 13-litre fours in 1908. The eight's engine consisted of two 40hp fours coupled together, and the gearbox had only two speeds. Although they retired in the French GP, they finished 5th and 6th in the Circuit des Ardennes.

Weigel Motors was reorganised in 1907, and late in the year they moved to new premises in Latimer Road, North Kensington. 20, 30, and 40hp cars were listed, but in October 1909 it went into receivership, and was taken over by A.E. Crowdy

1946 Pente (Weiss Manfred) 600cc saloon.
PAL NEGYESI

c.1930 Weiss Manfred saloon.
PAL NEGYESI

1909 Welch 80hp touring limousine by Hume of Boston.
NICK BALDWIN

who had been manager of Wolseley sales in Lancashire. He continued 20/30 and 30/40hp cars of Weigel design under his own name, and also brought out a smaller car with 12/14hp Hewitt piston valve engine.

NG

WEISE (D) 1933
Weise GmbH, Berlin.
This company was better-known for 3-wheeled delivery vans with single driven front wheel, which were made from 1929 to 1939. In 1933 they launched a 4-seater saloon on the same lines, powered by a 196cc 5bhp Rinne engine. As can be imagined, the performance was not very impressive, and Weise soon returned to commercial vehicles, which included, in 1939, a 4-wheeled diesel-engined truck.

HON

WEISS (D) 1902–1905
1902–1904 Maschinenfabrik Otto Weiss GmbH, Berlin.
1904–1905 Automobil- und Motorenfabrik vorm. Otto Weiss, Berlin.
Weiss built friction-drive cars which were almost exact copies of the MAURER system. They used French-built Herald engines of 10/14PS (2-cylinder) and 10/22PS 4-cylinder. Production was given up after patent suits by Maurer.

HON

WEISS MANFRÉD (H) 1927–1932; 1946
Weiss Manfréd Steel and Metalworks, Csepel-Budapest.
The Weiss Manfréd company should really be compared to big industrial concerns, like Skoda. But Hungary was no Czech Republic, and the market offered little potential for expansion. The Weiss factory was established back in the 19th century and World War I brought them prosperity. However, the end of the war and the short period of communism in 1919 changed all that. But they survived and by the mid–1920s the Weiss family, which still managed the company, were looking for new products. One of them was the automobile. It is amazing that an industrial concern with vast resources can make such bad decisions. First they bought an Italian FIAM and copied the design. It proved to be unsuccessful, so the search continued. The Weymann-type body gained popularity in France, so to save costs they used that. It was a very simple method: bolting false leather onto a wooden frame. Further cost-saving was achieved with the 4-cylinder 875cc engine because it was 2-stroke. The car had to be cheap to have an impact on the Hungarian market, but the structure was not rigid and the engine was unreliable. Despite this, Viktor Szmik finished second in the 1929 Monte Carlo Rally. In those years all state-owned companies and taxi operators were forced to use Hungarian-made vehicles. So the Hungarian Post Office and various taxis used WM cars. Later the 2-stroke engine was dropped in favour of a 4-stroke, 4-cylinder unit made after Ford patterns. But the management soon realised there was no way they could make profit out of cars, so they shut down production. The small 100cc mopeds which came afterwards were a runaway success, so Weiss Manfréd found its niche in the Hungarian car and motorcycle market, and behind the scenes became a major supplier of army trucks, lorries, etc.

After World War II, before the company became state-owned and renamed Csepel Múvek, there was a more serious attempt to produce a passenger car suited to Hungarian tastes. János Pentelényi, one of the chief engineers at the company studied car-making abroad, and after the war established a realistic plan to make a Topolino-sized family car in Hungary. Only two prototypes of the Pente are recorded to have been made: one with a 500cc and the other with a 600cc engine. The latter survived, along with the plans for other body styles. The company was on the way to setting up the manufacturing lines when the communists took over control. Weiss Manfréd became the Csepel Múvek, and made trucks. Pentelényi was transferred there and worked on commercial vehicles afterwards.

PN

WEITZ (US) c.1979
John Weitz, New York, New York.
The X-600 was a one-off sports car with Chevrolet Camaro Z-28 running gear. Weitz was a well-known fashion designer and amateur racing driver who wanted to display his design talents for mechanical objects. It had a radical angular aluminium roadster body with a truncated tail and partially shrouded wheels. The body was built by Mallalieu Cars in England, and limited production in the $60,000 bracket was envisaged. It received a great deal of publicity. Weitz also considered building a smaller, less expensive sports car in the $9,000 price range.

HP

WEIXING (CHI) 1958–1960
Qinghua University, Beijing Municipality.
As a replacement for remaining rickshaws, the Qinghua University – which had a large Automobile & Tractor Department – started serial production of tiny motor cars. Small batches of different types were made, such as an open 4-seater, which had a length of 94in (2400mm), and a single-cylinder 4-stroke engine. In 1958 the first model was introduced, and a year later 33 were produced. In May 1960 a batch of 40 taxis was made. Later in 1960, at least seven different models were seen, of which 126 units were made. Weixing means 'Satellite'. From 1970 to 1972 – during the Cultural Revolution – a truck with a 4-ton payload, called

1905 Welch 30/36hp landaulet.
JOHN A. CONDE

July 27 (later renamed QH 140) was built in the college workshop. In the 1990s Qinghua University developed electric vehicles like the EV 6580 bus and the 704lb (320kg) Huoxinghao vehicle powered by solar energy.

EVIS

WELCH (US) 1903–1911
1903–1904 Chelsea Manufacturing Co., Chelsea, Michigan.
1904–1911 Welch Motor Car Co., Pontiac, Michigan.
1909–1911 The Welch Co., Detroit, Michigan.

A.R. Welch and his brother Fred built their first car in 1901. It had a 20hp 2-cylinder engine with ohvs and hemispherical combustion chambers, a very advanced feature, and almost certainly the world's first example of the 'hemi' head. The engine was under the seat and steering was by tiller, but in 1903 the bicycle-making Chelsea Manufacturing Co. put the car into production as the Welch Tourist. The engine was now in front under a bonnet and it had a steering wheel. The wheelbase was 78in (1980mm). Only 15 were made before lack of capital brought the venture to an end. Welch moved to Pontiac where he found fresh finance, and began offering a larger car with 30/36hp 4-cylinder engine on a 114in (2893mm) wheelbase. This was priced at $4000, and the Welch grew in size and prestige from then onwards. A 50hp came in 1906 and a 70hp six in 1907 on a 138in (3502mm) wheelbase and priced at $7000 for a limousine. From 1906 the ohvs were operated by an ohc, another first claimed by the Welch brothers, and justifiably, though the short-lived Finch Limited also made in 1906, had single-ohc as well.

In 1909 a new factory was set up in Detroit to make a smaller car with 40hp 4-cylinder engine called the Welch-Detroit. This was designed by A.B.C. Hardy who had been responsible for the FLINT (i). In 1909 the Welch companies became affiliated with General Motors, and in 1910 were formally taken over. Production at both factories ended in 1911, and the machinery was moved to the Saginaw, Michigan plant where the RAINIER had been made. There a new car was launched for 1912, said to combine features of both Welch and Welch-Detroit. It was called the MARQUETTE (i).

NG

1911 Welch Model 4-R 70hp limousine.
JOHN A. CONDE

WEL-DOER (CDN) 1914
Welker-Doerr Co., Berlin, Ontario.

A rare example of a Canadian cyclecar, the Wel-Doer was powered by a 9/13hp air-cooled V-twin engine, with friction transmission and final drive by belts. Suspension was by three-quarter elliptic springs all round. It must have been well-publicised, for the makers received an enquiry from St Petersburg, Russia, but the outbreak of war put an end to the project after only one pilot model had been made.

NG

WELER (F) 1921–1922
Made in, or advertised from, an address in Levallois-Perret, the Weler was another of Marcel Violet's creations. At the 1921 Paris Salon there was a Weler with an 8/10hp 2-cylinder 2-stroke engine by SICAM (also a Violet design), 3-speed gearbox and shaft drive. Also mentioned, but not ready for the Salon, was a rear-

1903 Weller 20hp tourer.
NATIONAL MOTOR MUSEUM

engined machine with 5/6hp engine and belt drive. Two front-engined Welers ran in the 1921 Coupe des Voiturettes, the one driven by 'Sabipa' (pseudonym for Louis Charavel) finishing in 4th place.

NG

WELLER (GB) 1903

Weller Brothers Ltd, West Norwood, London.
John Weller designed an advanced car powered by a 20hp 4-cylinder engine which, with the gearbox, was mounted on a detachable underframe which was separate from the chassis. Final drive was by double chains. When the clutch was fully depressed reverse gear was automatically engaged, providing an emergency brake. The Weller would have been expensive to make commercially, so its backer, butcher John Portwine, suggested a much cheaper machine which appeared as the Autocarrier, a trade carrier whose passenger version was the A.C. Sociable.

NG

WELLEYES see CEIRANO (i)

WELLINGTON (GB) 1900–1901

F.F. Wellington, London.
Frank Wellington built a very light voiturette powered by a 2.5hp air-cooled single-cylinder engine. He presumably hoped to commercialise it but apparently did not do so. He was an agent for Phébus-Aster and other makes of car.

NG

WENDAX (D) 1950–1951

Wendax Fahrzeugbau GmbH, Hamburg.
This company made 3-wheeled trade carriers from 1929 to 1949 under the name Freund, and in 1949 changed the name to Wendax. A 4-wheeled forward-control light truck was offered, and also passenger cars, originally powered by reconditioned VW engines. In 1951 the makers turned to a 2-seater microcar powered by a 750cc 2-cylinder 2-stroke Ilo engine driving by chain to the right rear wheel. They also made an extraordinary-looking pillarless 4-door saloon. Production was limited, and even the commercials had disappeared by 1952.

HON

WENKELMOBIL (D) 1904–1907

Automobilwerk Schneider GmbH, Berlin.
Max Wenkel designed the prototypes of his cars in Java, probably the first cars to be built in the Far East. In 1904 the Schneider company took up the design, and a small number of friction-driven cars with single- or 2-cylinder engines, and air- or water-cooling, were made under the name Wenkelmobil.

HON

WERBELL (GB) 1907–1909

W. and E. Raikes-Bell, Dundee.
This was a conventional tourer with 20/24hp 4-cylinder engine, named after its makers, the brothers William and Edward Raikes-Bell. They listed a six, also quoted as a 20/24hp, with the same top speed (57mph/92km/h), same dimensions and costing only £50 more. It is doubtful if it was built, and indeed only eight Werbells were made altogether. The makers were exceptionally modest; *The Car to Buy*, had a space at the end for manufacturers to mention 'a Few Users'. Most listed various titled people, major-generals and bishops, but the Raikes-Bells simply said 'A few local people whose names would not be of any particular interest'.

NG

WERNER (F) 1906–1914

Werner Frères et Cie, Billancourt, Seine.
Werner was a name famous in the motorcycle world, the brothers making their first example in 1898. Of Russian descent, Michel and Eugène Werner also made cameras and typewriters, and became car manufacturers via tricars based on their 2-wheelers. Their first car proper was made in 1906. It had a 7hp 2-cylinder engine and shaft drive. A 12/15hp 4-cylinder car came in 1907, and in 1909 they used a 1.3-litre 4-cylinder De Dion-Bouton engine in a light car. Racing voiturettes powered by long-stroke De Dion-Bouton engines took part in voiturette races between 1907 and 1909; their best result was Soyez' 3rd in the 1909 Catalan Cup.

Ironically, although they had been pioneers of the motorcycle, they stopped building these in 1908, but continued cars for six years longer. Their 1913 models ranged from an 850cc 8hp single to a 4070cc 20/30hp four. They had unusual sloping radiators.

NG

WESCOTT'S AUTO RESTYLING (US) c.1985

Wescott's Auto Restyling, Boring, Ohio.
Wescott built replicas of 1928 to 1940 Fords designed to take V8 engines.

HP

WESEN (D) c.1900

Fahrzeugfabrik Wesen GmbH, Wesen bei Lindau.
This company made a small number of light cars with 4.5hp single-cylinder engines and *vis-à-vis* seating. They also made trucks.

NG

WESNIG (D) 1920–1925

Dipl. Ing. Erwin Wesnig, Berlin.
Wesnig made a few 3-wheelers with streamlined bodies and single driven rear wheel. They were powered by very small engines, a single-cylinder 1.8PS BMW or 1.35PS Kuhne.

HON

WESTALL (GB) 1922

Sidney C. Westall, London.
Westall owned, or operated from, a showroom in Chester Street, Grosvenor Place, and announced that he was to make a cyclecar powered by an 865cc single-cylinder engine to sell for £130. So far as is known he never formed a company, and probably only a prototype or two were made.

NG

WEST-ASTER; WEST (GB) 1904–1913

1904–1913 E.J. West & Co. Ltd, Coventry.
1906–1908 West Ltd, Coventry.
Enoch John West (1864–1937) entered the cycle industry working for Singer, then formed Calcott Bros & West in 1888 and the Progress Cycle Co. in 1896. Progress cars were made from 1898 to 1903, and the cars made under the West name from 1904 were, to start with, very similar to the last Progress. They had 10/12hp 2-cylinder Aster engines. They were said to be 'motor chassis for the trade only' according to *Bicycling News & Motor Review*, and certainly over the next few years West supplied engines to a number of other firms, including Academy, Heron, Nordenfeldt in Belgium, Pilot (i), Scout, and Singer (i). He also supplied rear axles to Calthorpe and steering gear to the Scottish truck makers, Belhaven. As well as the Aster engines he used a few from White & Poppe, while the two chassis supplied to Nordenfeldt had Barriquand et Marre engines.

In 1906 he formed a separate company to make Aster-engined cars which were generally sold under the name West-Aster. The first models had 16/20 and 20/22hp engines, but later a wider range was offered, from an 1842cc 12/14hp twin to a 35hp four of 5320cc, and a 24/30hp six. Delivery vans and taxicabs were also made;

a West-Aster was the first British-made taxi to pass the Scotland Yard tests for the London area. In 1908 parts were bought and assembled for an order of 100 taxis for Australia. When this fell through West Ltd was put into receivership.

This was not the end of West cars, though, for in May 1911 a reformed E.J. West & Co. Ltd announced a new light car powered by an 830cc 7/9hp single-cylinder engine, with friction drive. This was very similar to the Pilot light car. Few were made, and in December 1912 West announced a cyclecar powered by a 965cc 2-cylinder Chater-Lea engine. Helped by financial support from the Imperial Typewriter Co., Goddard's Plate Powder Co., and others, West acquired a new factory for this, the major part of the Centaur Works in Coventry which had made bicycles and a few cars at the beginning of the century. In March 1913 the cyclecar's name was changed to RANGER.

NG

WESTCAR (GB) 1922–1926

Strode Engineering Works, Herne, Kent.

The specification of the Westcar was conventional enough, with a 1496cc 11.9hp 4-cylinder Dorman engine, 3- (later 4-)speed Meadows gearbox and shaft drive to a Moss spiral bevel rear axle, but its background was unusual. It was built on a large country estate, Strode Park in Kent, being assembled in outbuildings of the big house, and wood for the bodies came from the estate. Probably most of the workforce came from the estate as well, while the brackets were made by the local blacksmith. The man behind it was Major Charles Prescott-Westcar, OBE, who also made the very unconventional HERON (ii), which also went under the name Westcar Colonial tourer. The Westcar was unable to compete with mass-produced cars in the same class, and the Major discontinued production after fewer than 100 had been made. The last vehicle to emerge from the Strode Park works was a motor tram which ran on Herne Bay pier for more than 20 years.

NG

WESTCHESTER FIBERGLASS (US) c.1982–1995

Westchester Fiberglass, Port Chester, New York.

The Corvarri was a Ferrari Daytona replica built on a Corvette chassis. The fibreglass panels bonded onto a 1968 to 1982 Corvette coupé or convertible. Westchester later made a Ferrari Testarossa replica that was also Corvette-based.

HP

WEST COAST CAR SALES *see* GULL-WING

WEST COAST COBRA (US) c.1980 to date

West Coast Cobra, Sun Valley, California.
West Coast Cobra, Detroit, Michigan.
West Coast Cobra, Ontario, Canada.
West Coast Cobra, Sterling Heights, Michigan.

This company built a conventional 427 Cobra replica with a spaceframe and a Ford or Chevrolet V8 engine. It had the longer nose and wheelbase of the Stallion-type Cobra replicas. They were sold in kit or completed form.

HP

WESTCOASTER (US) 1960

Westcoast Machinery, Stockton, California.

The Westcoaster was an electric-powered runabout with a fibreglass 2-seat body. It was a coupé and was primarily sold for use as a golf cart.

HP

WESTCOTT (US) 1909–1925

1909–1916 Westcott Car Co., Richmond, Indiana.
1916–1925 Westcott Car Co., Springfield, Ohio.

The Westcott was one of the more highly regarded independent American automobiles throughout its 17 years of production. Founded by Burton J. Westcott, president of the Westcott Carriage Co., the first car was a high-wheeled type, a more conventional design for subsequent Westcotts being adopted a few months later. The 1910 series was powered by a Continental 4-cylinder engine and it is noteworthy that all Westcott cars would use Continental engines throughout the company's existence. The carriage manufacturing was phased out shortly after the car's introduction and in 1913 a 6-cylinder series was added to the existing

1907 West-Aster 28/32hp landaulet.
NICK BALDWIN

1924 Westcar Colonial tourer.
MICHAEL WORTHINGTON-WILLIAMS

1923 Westcott Model B44 permanent-top tourer.
G. MARSHALL NAUL

four, the latter being phased out during 1916. In 1916 Westcott operations were moved to a larger factory in Springfield, Ohio where all cars would be produced until production was terminated. As to production itself, this was never high, peaking in 1921 with more than 1700 cars completed. Throughout the 1920s Westcott produced at least two series of cars – as many as four in 1922 – powered by Continental Series 9N and 7R engines until 1922 and 8N plus 12X from 1923 on. In 1924 the company offered 4-wheel brakes and balloon tyres on an optional basis, these becoming standard equipment on the 1925 models. This was its final year during which Westcott went out of business after building an estimated 15,000 units.

KM

Further Reading
'Westcott: Keys to the city', Karla A. Rosenbusch,
Automobile Quarterly, Vol. 35, No. 2.

1990 Westfield (ii) Sei sports car.
WESTFIELD

1912 Westinghouse (i) Limousine fitted with Westinghouse air springs.
NICK BALDWIN

WESTERN FRONT (US) c.1982

Western Front, San Antonio, Texas.

The XK-1 was an unusual 3-wheeled car with a fibreglass coupé body. The manufacturer recommended a 16 to 30hp Onan or Briggs & Stratton engine, but others could be substituted. They were to be sold in several stages of assembly, but only a handful were made.

HP

WESTFALIA (i) (D) 1906–1914

Ramesohl & Schmidt AG, Oelde; Bielefeld.

This company was a well-established producer of farming equipment and dairy apparatus. They entered car production in 1906 with De Dion-Bouton and Fafnir engines. Only a small number of cars were made up to 1911, when a new factory was built at Bielefeld and four new models were made, using their own engines, of 6/16, 8/20, 10/25 and 12/50PS. However, production remained small and the Bielefeld factory was sold to Hansa. Production of the 6/16 and 10/25PS lingered on at Oelde for another year.

HON

WESTFALIA (ii) (D) 1954

Fahrzeugfabrik H.W. Voltmann, Bad Oeynhausen.

This company made a tiller-steered invalid car, the M50, powered by a 125cc Ilo 2-stroke engine.

HON

WESTFIELD (i) (US) 1902–1903

The C.J. Moore Manufacturing Co., Westfield, Massachusetts.

Charles J. Moore built a steam car of his own before starting a company to manufacture them in 1902. It was powered by a 6hp 2-cylinder engine. Early in 1903 he announced a petrol car powered by a 16hp 4-cylinder engine. It seems that this was built for demonstration purposes only, and there were no successors. The steamer was made in small numbers, but Moore was more interested in selling running gear with either chain or shaft drive, and runabout, tourer or delivery van bodies, for the customer to fit his own engine.

NG

WESTFIELD (ii) (GB) 1982 to date

1982–1985 Westfield Sports Cars, Dudley, West Midlands.
1985 to date Westfield Sports Cars, Kingswinford, West Midlands.

Lotus racer and classic car dealer Chris Smith made his first Lotus XI replica in 1982, thereby founding the Westfield dynasty. It used a metal-panelled space frame chassis allied to MG Midget mechanicals and accurate fibreglass bodywork. Alternative power choices were BL A-series, Ford crossflow and even Rover V8. The Eleven was dropped, but a restyled Sports of 1990 used a lengthened SEi chassis and Ford CVH power. It was to another Lotus that Chris Smith next turned: the legendary Seven. Initially, he made a copy of the Series 1 Seven, based around a multi-tube chassis with a Midget rear axle and engine (later Ford), plus special suspension. This time the bodywork was in aluminium with fibreglass wings and nose. Next came a Seven S3 replica, the SE of 1986, with its Ford Escort rear axle. Its S3 body was too close to the Caterham Seven, as affirmed by the courts. Westfield was forced to redesign its product and came up with the SE and SEi in November 1987, significantly restyled with more rounded all-fibreglass gel-coated bodywork and sporting a revised spaceframe chassis. The SEi had irs, the SE an Escort MkI/II live axle, and most were fitted with Ford crossflow or CVH engines. A hard-top option arrived in 1988 (also with a gullwing door option), and a wide-bodied model followed in 1989. As the ZEi, the model was type approved and sold fully-built. With a Rover V8 engine fitted in a redesigned chassis, the SEiGHT resulted. With a T.V.R. Power 330bhp 4.5-litre V8 engine, a SEiGHT rocketed to a world record-beating 0–60mph (0–97km/h) of 3.5 secs and 0–100mph (0–161km/h) in 7.7 secs. In response to numerous cut-price Seven clone kits, in 1994 Westfield launched a cheaper SE-based model called the SP; irs SPi and more fully-built SPa versions followed. Westfield also pursued other avenues, including the Sports 2000 and a Mini-lookalike racer (both mostly for competition work) and in 1988 the Topaz mid-engined coupé prototype (re-invented as the XEi in 1994 but still not productionised). A radical new departure at the 1998 Birmingham Motor Show was the FW 400 (indicating Feather Weight 880lb/400kg). This was an ingeniously constructed sports car, made entirely of carbon fibre, and was designed by former Lotus F1 designer Martin Ogilvie. It used a tuned 190bhp Rover K-series 1.8-litre engine and rear-mounted transaxle. Its specification was pared down to the bone to cut weight.

CR

WESTINGHOUSE (i) (F) 1904–1912

Sté des Automobiles Westinghouse, Le Havre.

Westinghouse SA was formed in 1901 as an amalgamation of the French brake and electrical interests of the massive American group founded by George Westinghouse. In 1904 a subsidiary began to make high-quality cars with 4-cylinder pair-cast engines of 20/24 and 30/40hp, and double-chain drive. They mostly carried heavy touring or limousine bodies which were built in Paris on chassis driven from Le Havre. Smaller shaft-driven cars with 16/20 and 20/30hp engines were made towards the end of production, though the big chain-driven 35/40 was still made. In 1908 Westinghouse set up a branch in Arad, Hungary, which made commercial vehicles to start with, then cars under the name MARTA.

NG

WESTINGHOUSE (ii) (US) 1967–1968

Westinghouse Electric Corp., Pittsburgh, Philadelphia.

The Westinghouse Markette was a boxy-bodied electric car measuring only 116in (2944mm) long. It was powered by twelve 6-volt batteries and the projected price was set at only $2000.

CR

WESTLAKE (GB) 1907

Westlake Motor Syndicate Ltd, Maidenhead, Berkshire.

The Westlake was an unusual car in that it had a 24hp 6-cylinder air-cooled engine which must have developed reasonable power, yet final drive was by a single chain, more usually associated with runabouts and light steamers. Transmission was by a 2-speed epicyclic gearbox. A water-cooled model was said to be available as well, but quite possibly only one Westlake was ever made. Exhibited at the Birmingham Motor Show in January 1907, it was designed by H.B. Lyon of Taplow, a few miles from Maidenhead.

NG

WESTMINSTER (GB) 1906–1908

Westminster Motor Works, London.

Like the Badminton and Beaufort, this was one of those makes with very British names which used largely foreign components. The 1906 Westminster had a 10hp French-made engine, while the 1908 30/35hp had a Prunel chassis with English body.

NG

WESTON (GB) 1914

'R' Development Syndicate, London.

The Weston light car was powered by a 773cc 2-cylinder 2-stroke engine of the Dolphin type. designed by Harry Ricardo. The Ricardo connection would indicate that it was probably the same engine that was used in the VOX, whose capacity was given as 770cc. The 'R' in the company name probably stood for Ricardo. No more than two cars were made, with 2-speed gearboxes and shaft drive.

The name Weston was also used for GROUT steam cars sold in England.

NG

WESTONE (US) 1914

Westone Cyclecar Co., Los Angeles, California.

The Westone was unusual for a cyclecar in having front-wheel drive. Deriving its name from that of its maker, Walter E. Stone, it had a 15hp 4-cylinder Pacific engine which drove the front wheels through chains. These wheels were braked too. Although a price of $375 was quoted, possibly no more than one Westone was made. The make has been erroneously listed as Van Stone.

NG

1925 Westwood 14hp tourer.
NICK BALDWIN

WESTWOOD (GB) 1919–1925

1919–1924 Westwood Motor Co. Ltd, Wigan, Lancashire.
1924–1925 Westwood-Ince Ltd, Wigan, Lancashire.

The Westwood was a conventional assembled car using the 1795cc Dorman KNO ohv 4-cylinder engine, with 3-speed gearbox and spiral bevel rear axle. The gearbox was made at first by Westwoods themselves. Body styles included a 2-seater, tourer and coupé priced from £550 to £675 which made it on the expensive side. Dorman's records show that only 57 engines were supplied up to 1923 when the company was reorganised as the Westwood Engineering Co. (Wigan) Ltd. There was a change in engine suppliers, to Meadows, although the capacity was the same as the Dorman, and a 4-speed gearbox was provided.

In 1924 the company name changed again to Westwood-Ince Ltd. Ince was the district in Wigan where the cars were built. A larger engine was used, a 2121cc Meadows and the gearbox, also by Meadows, was in unit with the engine. The rear axle was now by Timken, so Westwood were making less and less of the car themselves. A saloon was added to the range of bodies, as was an attractive sports model with wire wheels, polished aluminium body, tangerine wings, a vee-windscreen and pointed tail. It was said to be good for 70mph (113km/h), and was described in advertising as 'A Perfect Car for the Sportsman'. Apart from the sports car most Westwoods had artillery wheels, though wire ones were apparently an option in 1924 and 1925. Fewer of the Meadows engined cars were made, just 36, making a total of 93 in all. Some lists carried the Westwood to 1926, but it seems that no cars were made after 1925, and there was probably no serious production after 1924.

NG

Further Reading
'Westwood Ho!', M. Worthington-Williams,
The Automobile, September 1998.

WEYHER et RICHEMOND (F) 1905–c.1910

Automobiles Weyher et Richemond, Pantin, Seine.

This company made steam fire engines, both horse-drawn and self propelled, rather as Merryweather did in England. They also made a few steam wagons, and at the end of 1905 launched a steam car with tubular flash boiler of Serpollet design and a 25/32hp horizontally-opposed 4-cylinder engine based on Austrian Knoller-Friedman patents. Final drive was by double chains, and the Weyher-Richemond had the appearance of a petrol car. Four-wheel brakes were fitted, but abandoned as the makers said that the public did not like them. Some were sold in England under the name Rexer.

For the 1908 season the steamer gave way to a range of petrol-engined cars; there were four models, from a 2112cc 10/15hp four to a 5120cc 28/32hp four, and including a 4385cc 25/30hp six. They also made petrol cars sold under the name LABOR.

NG

WFM FAFIK (PL) 1958

Warszawa Fabrika Motorcykli, Warsaw.

This motorcycle maker was in business from 1951 to 1965, and in 1958 launched a bubble car with 148cc 6bhp single-cylinder 2-stroke engine as used in the Osa scooter. It had a 3-speed gearbox and a 3-seater all-steel body. Top speed was 44mph (70km/h). The project was soon dropped so that the company could concentrate on motorcycles.

RP

1921 Wherwell 7hp cyclecar.
PETER ROBERTS COLLECTION

1904 White (i) Model D 10hp steam tonneau.
P. WHITE

W.F.S. (US) 1911–1912
W.F.S. Motor Car Co., Philadelphia, Pennsylvania.
Made by W.F. Shetzline, this was originally made as a 25hp tourer, with 3-speed gearbox mounted on the rear axle. For 1912 the engine was of 40hp and a wider range of bodies was offered, from a raceabout at $2400 to a limousine at $3200.
NG

WHARTON (US) 1922–1923
Wharton Motors Co., Dallas, Texas.
'Southern Money for Southern Development' was the cry of Thomas B. Wharton, a Dallas promoter, whose grandiose plans, backed by a group of Dallas bankers and professional men, envisaged a potentially large company to start the production of 8-cylinder cars followed by additional lines of automobiles. The first stage of Wharton's plan was the manufacture of a large, powerful car equipped with the revamped Curtiss OX-5 engine, this being readily available from a large leftover unused stock at the time of the Armistice and already in use by such low production cars as the Curtiss and the Prado. Prices would fall, so ran the promotion, in the $3500 to $5000 price range with a complete line of both open and closed types available. A roadster was completed and used for promotion. Expense appeared as the name of the game for 1922, Wharton announcing that the V8 series of Whartons would be augmented by two other less-expensive series, one a four – the other a six. Moreover, it was rumoured that the overall plans would include a line of tractors. When Wharton failed, it had little to show despite its announcements, elaborate brochures and the OX-5-powered roadster which was more than likely the only car to actually wear a Wharton badge.
KM

WHEELER (US) 1900–1902
Wheeler Automobile Manufacturing Co., Marlboro, Massachusetts.
E.O. Wheeler designed these cars, which were built in the machine shop owned by his father. They had single-cylinder engines, the third being a 4.5hp De Dion-Bouton, though the origin of the first two is not known. Possibly it was made by Wheeler himself and was not satisfactory, which is why he turned to the well-tried French engine. Two cars had runabout bodies and the third was a 4-seater rear-entrance tonneau. The Wheelers were promised support from a Boston bank, but the bankers were alarmed by the activities of a dishonest car promoter and withdrew.
NG

WHERWELL (GB) 1920–1921
Thompson & Son, Wherwell, Andover, Hampshire.
Made in a small village garage, this was a simple cyclecar powered by a 5/7hp air-cooled flat-twin Coventry-Victor engine, with a 4-speed friction transmission and final drive by single chain. Unlike many air-cooled cars the Wherwell had no dummy radiator, so the engine could take full advantage of the oncoming air. The bonnet sides were open as well. A price of £130 was quoted, but only three Wherwells were made.
NG

WHIPPET see WILLYS

WHISPER (DK) 1984–1987
Hope Automobil Industri (Whisper Electric Car) AS, Hadsund.
The Hope Whisper was an attempt to make a Volkswagen Polo-based electric car. The chassis of the first prototype was a light multi-tube affair using Volkswagen Polo suspension, brakes and steering. Then came a distinctly different version, the 1986 Whisper II with completely restyled bodywork, featuring doors derived from the Polo, though the rest of the bodywork was in plastic. Twelve 12V batteries supplied a 6kW (8bhp) electric motor driving the front wheels. A lengthy range of 100 miles was quoted. Vastly over-ambitious plans to produce 225,000 cars in eight years were announced, but production did not begin.
CR

WHITBY (GB) 1983–1986
Whitby Engineering, Crewe, Cheshire.
The Mini-Warrior produced by Whitby was a very robust Mini-based utility vehicle. The bodywork consisted of all-flat panels in aluminium over a box section steel chassis, and could be had in fully open, convertible, pick-up cab, van, tilt, estate, half-door and full-door forms. Whitby's main trade was building ice-cream vans.
CR

WHITE (i) (US) 1900–1918
1900–1906 White Sewing Machine Co., Cleveland, Ohio.
1906–1918 The White Co., Cleveland, Ohio.
The history of the White Sewing Machine Co. dated back to 1866 when Thomas H. White, who worked for the Grout Sewing Machine Co. in Orange, Massachusetts, formed his own company and moved his business to Cleveland. From an initial production of 25 machines a month the business grew to 8000 a month by 1881. The company also made bicycles, roller skates, lathes and screw cutters. In 1900 Thomas White's second son Rollin (1872–1962) moved the company into car production with a light steamer whose boiler he had been working on for several years. This was of the semi-flash type, in which the generator (White preferred this term to boiler) consisted of a series of coils of seamless steel tubing in which water was pumped into the top coil and flashed into steam about half way down. It was superheated in the lower coils before being admitted to the cylinders.
A prototype was running in the autumn of 1899, and a production stanhope was ready for the public six months later. It was a light 2-seater with horizontal engine under the floor and single-chain drive. Eighteen were sold that year, including White's first commercial vehicle, the ancestor of a vast family made up to the 1980s. It was a delivery van for the Denver Dry Goods Co. These early steamers were long-lived; one 1900 stanhope was still being operated by its owner in Michigan in 1930. White made 191 stanhopes in 1901 and 387 in 1902. By then a large rectangular frontal condenser was used, although this identifying

1906 White (i) Model F 18hp steam tourer.
NICK BALDWIN

feature had been seen on some 1901 cars and even on the delivery van of 1900. A larger car with four seats and the engine mounted under a bonnet was made in 1902. Nicknamed the 'White Elephant' it was not made in series, but was the prototype for the 1903 Model C which also had a front-mounted engine, a 4-seater tonneau body, wheel steering and shaft drive. It was the first White to have a compound engine, in which the steam is condensed and re-used in a lower-pressure cylinder. The generally similar Model D of 1904 offered an enclosed limousine as well as a tonneau, both still with rear-entrance bodies. The 1905 Model was more like a petrol car in appearance, and had a wheelbase 13in (330mm) longer at 93in (2360mm). For 1906 this was extended to 118in (2995mm), which enabled side-entrance bodies to be used. 1534 cars were made in 1906, the peak year for steamer production. In that year Theodore Roosevelt became the first US President to drive a car, when he took the wheel of a White during a visit to Puerto Rico. His successor William Howard Taft included a White when he set up the White House automobile fleet in 1909.

In 1906 the car-making side of the business was separated from the Sewing Machine company, and a new company capitalised at $2.5m set up in a new factory with 1000 workers. The White steamer grew in power and price; a 1910 Model M-M had a 40hp engine, a 122in (3096mm) wheelbase and a price tag of $5000 for a limousine or landaulet. There was also a smaller Model O-O on a 110in (2792mm) wheelbase, priced between $2000 and $3300. On this the condenser was set further back in the frame. This gave a lower and less front-heavy appearance than on the bigger Whites. Joy valve motion replaced the Stephenson link on 1909 models. The valves were operated directly by the connecting rods, which halved the number of working parts.

Steamers were continued into 1911, but they had been joined in 1910 by two models of petrol car, the 30hp Models G-A and G-B, and (for 1911) the 40hp Model E. Their 4-cylinder monobloc side-valve engines were based on those of DELAHAYE, and their 4-speed gearboxes had a geared up top. In 1910 1208 steamers were made, and 1200 petrol cars. They were joined in 1912 by a big 60hp six; electric lighting and starting were introduced that year. 1917 models had 16-valve 4-cylinder engines of over 6.5-litres capacity. Passenger cars were discontinued after the 1918 season, when only 653 were made, though a few were

1909 White (i) Model O 15hp steam 2-seater.
NATIONAL MOTOR MUSEUM

1910 White (i) Model G-A 30hp petrol coupé by Cann.
NICK BALDWIN

1913 Whitgift 8hp cyclecar.
NICK GEORGANO

1904 Whitlock-Aster 18/22hp tonneau.
NICK BALDWIN

built to special order on light truck chassis. The last of these was for a Boston doctor in 1936. White was very successful in the truck and bus fields, absorbing rivals Sterling and Autocar in the 1950s, then Reo and Diamond T, only to be taken over by Volvo in 1981.

NG

Further Reading
'Sewing up the Steam Car Market', Thomas S. LaMarre,
Automobile Quarterly, Vol. 31, No. 4 and Vol. 32, No. 3.

WHITE (ii) (US) 1909

George White Buggy Co., Rock Island, Illinois.
George White was one of the largest buggy makers in the Middle West, and a latecomer to the motor buggy. It was a 2- or 4-seater, with 12/14hp 2-cylinder engine under a frontal bonnet and with shaft drive, both these features being unusual for a high-wheel buggy, although they made it more like a conventional car. The formula did not appeal, though, and only six were made.

NG

WHITE (iii) (US) 1914

White Manufacturing Co., Waterloo, Iowa.
This was as short-lived cyclecar for which there is very little documentation. It was said to have a 9hp air-cooled V-twin engine and shaft drive.

NG

WHITEHEAD (i) (GB) 1920–1921

Whitehead Light Cars, Bradford, Yorkshire.
This firm, which was apparently never incorporated as a company, made a light car powered by a 1498cc 4-cylinder Coventry-Simplex engine, with Moss 3-speed gearbox and shaft drive. Its only unusual features were a wooden frame and transverse leaf front suspension. 2- and 4-seaters were made, but total production did not exceed 16 cars.

NG

WHITEHEAD (ii) (US) c.1952–1956

R.E. Whitehead, Kenilworth, New Jersey and Roselle Park, New Jersey.
Although Bob Whitehead sold lots of $5 plan sets for building a low-cost sports car, he also offered pre-fab kits. His most popular kit was an Allard J2-like cycle-muguarded sports car built on 1933 to 1940 Ford running gear. In 1952 this plan set was carried by *Mechanix Illustrated* magazine, which renamed it the MI Sportster. Later, Whitehead sold the plans himself. The body was simple; hand-formed aluminium panels mounted to electrical conduit. Modified Ford flathead V8s were recommended. A good number were built and there was a builders' club in the early 1950s. In 1955 Whitehead added a full-width body design with slab sides, but it lacked the sporty nature of the original.

HP

WHITEHEAD-THANET (GB) 1920–1921

Amalgamated Motors Ltd, Ashtead, Surrey.
A.J. Whitehead had made a fortune in the aircraft industry during the war, and hatched a grandiose plan to mass produce cars. The target for 1920 was 5000, and for 1921, 100,000. In fact, the whole British industry made only 66,396 cars in 1921, and probably not one of these came from Mr Whitehead. He did make at least one demonstration car in 1920, which *The Motor* pronounced to be a copy of the Ford Model T, apart from the radiator and wheels. It was to be assembled at Ashtead, with a 16/20hp 4-cylinder British engine of unspecified make, an American chassis by the Gray Andrews Corp. and bodies made by F.J. Wraight of London and Ramsgate, Kent. This company has been listed as the maker of the Thanet car, which was probably the same as the Whitehead-Thanet. A Mr J. Wilson, managing director of F.J. Wraight was said to be the moving spirit behind the Whitehead-Thanet. A.J. Whitehead said that he had induced 21 Ford suppliers to provide him with components. Other components not bought in were to be made in a separate factory at Richmond. *The Motor* was quite sceptical about the whole business, saying that they had not been invited to inspect the factory and that it was curious that, when inviting applications for shares, the letters asked that cheques be payable to an individual, not to a company. Two different individuals had signed letters, both saying that they would deal with applications personally, and that 'your cheque should be made payable to me'.

NG

WHITE HORSE (US) c.1994 to date

White Horse Co., Flemington, New Jersey.
Fiero Specialities, Flemington, New Jersey.
The Scorpion S.S. was a Lamborghini Countach replica with a sturdy steel space frame. It accepted Pontiac Fiero running gear and suspension. The chassis allowed the installation of Fiero engine/transaxle units or a Porsche transaxle with a Chevrolet V8. They were sold in kit and completed form.

HP

WHITE STAR (US) 1909–1911

1909 White Star Automobile Co., Atlanta, Georgia.
1909–1911 Atlanta Motor Car Co., Atlanta, Georgia.
The White Star was originally to have been a high-wheeler with 20hp 2-cylinder engine, epicyclic transmission and double-chain drive, but after a few had been made, a reorganised company offered two 4-cylinder cars, with 22 or 35hp engines. The former was a roadster, the latter a tourer made in three models with slightly different prices. In 1912 they turned to the manufacture of horse-drawn buggies under the names White Star and Golden Eagle.

NG

WHITE SWAN (US) 1914

White Swan Cyclecar Co., Los Angeles, California.
This cyclecar was powered by an air-cooled V-twin engine which drove the front wheels via a 2-speed gearbox. The graceful body was painted white, for a swan-like look.

NG

WHITGIFT (GB) 1913

Croydon Central Motor Car Co. Ltd, Croydon, Surrey.
The Whitgift cyclecar used a transversely-mounted 8hp JAP water-cooled engine, driving through friction discs and a single chain to the offside rear wheel. It was

lower built than many cyclecars and of attractive appearance, but this did not help sales, and it lasted less than a year.

NG

WHITING (US) 1910–1912

Whiting Motor Car Co., Flint, Michigan.

This company was the motor department of the Flint Wagon Works, a large company headed by James H. Whiting, who was a colleague of Billy Durant. His car was a conventional 4-cylinder machine with 20 or 40hp engines and made in tourer or roadster models, though there was also a coupé in 1911. Durant gained control of the Flint Wagon Works in Autumn 1911, and during 1912 discontinued the Whiting as he wanted the factory for manufacture of the LITTLE car.

NG

WHITING-GRANT *see* GRANT

WHITLOCK (GB) 1903–1932

1903–1905 Henry Whitlock Ltd, Holland Gate, London.
1905–1906 Whitlock Automobile Co., London.
1914–1932 Lawton-Goodman Ltd, Cricklewood, London.

The Whitlock had a life of nearly 30 years, but production was sporadic, and the total number of cars made was pretty small. It was originally made by a branch of Henry Whitlock Ltd, old-established coachbuilders with a history dating back to 1778. They had premises near Holland Park, and their car was the Whitlock Century which they sold from 1903 to 1905. It was almost certainly a CENTURY (i) made at Willesden, though possibly with a Whitlock body. In 1904 they began to sell the Whitlock-Aster, in 10, 12, 14, 18, and 24hp models. These were Aster chassis supplied from France, with Whitlock bodies. The smaller cars had armoured wood frames, the larger, pressed steel. A 12/14hp tourer ran in the 1905 Tourist Trophy, but without success. A separate company, the Whitlock Automobile Co., was set up in 1905, presumably because they thought the volume of motor trade justified it, but after 1906 the Whitlock-Aster was discontinued, and there were no more Whitlock cars until just before World War I.

In 1912 the Liverpool coachbuilders Lawton-Goodman took over the Whitlock business and bought premises in Cricklewood Broadway, and in 1914 announced two cars, a 12/16 and a 20/30, both with 4-cylinder engines. They had Renault-type dashboard radiators and coal-scuttle bonnets, and were known as Lawtons for 1914 and Whitlocks for 1915. Very few were made, and the source of the engines is not known, but photographs survive of a limousine and a delivery van. The premises expanded during World War I, and built ambulances, both of their own manufacture with Dorman engines, and on Rolls-Royce and other chassis, as well as making fuselages for DH4 aircraft.

Lawton-Goodman did not return to car manufacture immediately after the war, but at the 1922 White City Motor Show they exhibited three examples of a light car powered by a 1268cc 4-cylinder Coventry-Simplex engine. The following year they added a 1496cc Anzani-engined model, and a 1753cc ohv six of unknown provenance. In 1924 a 1990cc Coventry-Climax powered the 16/50 six alongside the fours. From 1927 onwards they offered only the 20/70, using the 2972cc Meadows 6-cylinder engine, enlarged to 3301cc in 1928. The number of cars made in the 1920s is problematical; no figures exist for the Coventry-Simplex or Coventry-Climax-engined cars, but as very few showed up in second-hand lists, output must have been pretty small, perhaps no more than 30–40 at most. The cars seem to have been made largely to display Lawton-Goodman's coachwork, which was of high quality. As for the Meadows-engined 20/70, Meadows' records show only eight engines delivered to Whitlock, and those all in 1926/27. As they displayed seven cars at the 1929 Olympia Show, that display alone would have used up all but one of their stock of engines. These last Whitlocks were handsome cars with wire wheels and Bentley-like radiators, made in two chassis lengths, 124 and 132in (3147 and 3350mm), and carrying coupé, 4-door saloon, and enclosed limousine bodies. In 1930 the Bentley radiator gave way to a flat one (possibly under pressure from Bentley who were also based in Cricklewood, less than a mile from Lawton-Goodman). At least one of these was made, completed in 1930 though apparently not registered until 1931, and it is the only example of a Whitlock known to survive today.

Lawton-Goodman continued as coachbuilders for many years. Daimler, Rolls-Royce and other chassis were bodied in the 1930s, but the company then turned

c.1923 Whitlock 12hp coupé.
NICK BALDWIN

1929 Whitlock 20/70hp coupé.
NICK BALDWIN

1929 Whitlock 20/70hp coupé.
MICHAEL WORTHINGTON-WILLIAMS

more to commercial vehicles including ambulances and mobile canteens during World War II, followed by ice-cream vans and mobile shops. The last bodies were made in about 1980, but the company continued with repair work until their lease ran out in 1991.

NG

Further Reading

'A Whitlock's Story', Graham Bennett, *The Automobile*, November 1985.
'The Whitlock, Coachbuilding to Cars to Coachbuilding', M. Worthington-Williams, *The Automobile*, July 1996.

WHITNEY (i) (US) 1896–1900

G.E. Whitney Motor Wagon Co., Boston, Massachusetts.

These cars were built by George Eli Whitney (1862–1963), the great nephew of the inventor of the cotton gin. He completed an experimental steam car in 1896 and formed his company the following year. By the summer of 1898 he had built seven cars, all of them different for, as was said of Walter Hancock in London more than 60 years before, 'he was continually experimenting, first altering one

1922 Wigan-Barlow 11/40hp 2-seater.
NICK BALDWIN

part of his machinery, then another'. Most had vertical engines, though at least one was horizontal. The Whitney was sold in England by Brown Brothers as the Brown-Whitney. He gave up making his own cars in 1900, One of his designs was built in Newton, Massachusetts, by Frank Stanley as the McKAY. Other firms including GROUT and PRESCOTT infringed his patents which led to one of a number of lawsuits. For a while he worked for Locomobile, then joined the asphalt industry and became a consulting engineer to the International Paving Co. He died in 1963 at the age of 101.

NG

WHITNEY (ii) (GB) 1899–1905
Whitney Machine Co., Brunswick, Maine.
No relation to George Whitney, R.S. Whitney was a versatile man who ran a jewellers and a sports shop, dealt in guns and ammunition and also built three steam cars over a seven year period. The first was begun in Lisbon Falls, Maine, in 1898 and completed in Brunswick where he sold it to a resident of Greenville. It was a 2-seater runabout, and his second car was a 4-seater tourer, made in 1902 and sold to a customer in Brunswick. His last car, begun in 1903 and completed in 1905, was a more original design, with all-steel integral construction of body and chassis, a front-mounted boiler, engine under the floorboards and single-chain drive. Whitney later ran a motor repair shop in Lewiston, Maine.

NG

WHITWOOD (GB) 1934–1936
Whitwood Monocars Ltd, Portsmouth, Hampshire.
This 2-wheeled car was made by the well-known motorcycle manufacturer, O.E.C. who were in business from 1921 to 1954. The Whitwood was designed by an O.E.C. director, N.F. Wood, and made in O.E.C.'s works. Despite the name Monocar, it was a tandem 2-seater with the engine lying horizontally under the seat, and an all-enveloping plywood body and hood. The steering wheel was almost horizontal. In 1935 came the Mk II with several important differences. The engine was moved to the rear, with the cylinder or cylinders lying alongside the wheel on the left, and pointing rearward. A cross shaft took the drive to a gearbox on the right side of the wheel. Three engine options were listed, though whether all were used is not certain. The Devon model had a 250cc ohv single, the York a 500 side-valve single and the Rutland a 1000cc side-valve V-twin. The steering wheel was now nearly vertical, and driver and passenger had a bucket seat each. The Whitwood Monocar attracted a lot of attention at the Shows, but the public did not wave their cheques. No more than half a dozen were made, and motorcycle historian Bob Currie doubts that any were bought and used on the road.

NG

WHITWORTH see HAMMOND

WHYLAND (US) 1914
F.V. Whyland & Co., Buffalo, New York.
Frank Whyland had established the Whyland-Nelson Motor Car Co. in Buffalo, in partnership with Joel Nelson to make a light car with delivery box at the rear. Nothing came of this and two years later he announced a cyclecar with an air-

cooled 4-cylinder engine. The price was $450 and he planned to make 1000 cars in 1914, but only prototypes were made.

NG

WICHITA (US) 1920–1921
Wichita Motor Co., Wichita Falls, Texas.
This company built trucks from 1911 to 1932, and in 1921 announced a car they called the 'oil field tool pusher'. It had a 50bhp 4-cylinder engine and was intended for oil field work, carrying three passengers and 1000lbs of equipment to the oil wells. It lasted for one season only.

NG

WICHITA FALLS (US) 1914
Wichita Falls Motor Co., Wichita Falls, Kansas.
This was a cyclecar powered by a V-twin Spacke engine, with epicyclic transmission and final drive by a long single chain. It had tandem seating and the old-fashioned centre pivot steering, which was perhaps a reason for its short life, though most cyclecars lasted no more than a year or two.

NG

WICK (US) 1902–1903
The Wick Co., Youngstown, Ohio.
Built by millionaire Henry B. Wick, this was a large car powered by a 5.6-litre 50hp 4-cylinder engine, with a 3-speed gearbox and chain drive. The chassis was built by L.B. Smyser & Co. of New York City, and the 4-seater tonneau body was by Quinby. The cost was $8000, and although it was exhibited at shows in New York, Cleveland and Chicago, Wick was not able to find a buyer. In 1904 the car was sold at auction for only $765.

NG

WIESMANN (D) 1997 to date
Wiesmann Auto Sport GmbH, Dulmen.
This was a 2-seater sports car with fibreglass body of 1950s styling, offered with the choice of two 6-cylinder fuel-injected BMW engines, 2793cc (193bhp) and M3 3201cc (321bhp). With the latter top speed was 160mph (257km/h), with 0–60mph (0–97km/h) taking 4.9 seconds.

NG

WIGAN-BARLOW (GB) 1922–1923
Wigan-Barlow Motors Ltd, Coventry.
The Wigan-Barlow barely progressed beyond the prototype stage. It was a light car powered by either a 1368cc Coventry-Simplex or 1496cc Meadows engine, with rear axle by Wrigley. Meadows supplied eight engines and a few more came from Coventry-Simplex. In late 1922 a consulting engineer, F. Carey, designed a sports model for Wigan-Barlow, with 1795cc Meadows engine, sold as the 11/40 Sports. It was better-looking than the touring models, with polished aluminium body and something of the appearance of a 12/50 Alvis. However, it appeared too late, and the company was in the hands of a receiver by October, so were not allowed to occupy the stand they had booked at the Olympia Show. The company made motorcycles for a year before starting car production, such as it was.

NG

Further Reading
'The Wigan-Barlow', M. Worthington-Williams,
The Automobile, December 1998.

WIIMA (SF) 1957–1958
Oy Uusi Autokoriteollisuus AB, Helsinki.
The Wiima was the first car ever designed and produced in Finland. A slab-sided 2-seater microcar coupé only 161cm (63in) long, it was the brainchild of Antti Wihuri. It was based on a substantially shortened Goggomobil chassis, including its 300cc 15bhp engine mounted in the tail. The company quickly abandoned car production to concentrate on buses.

CR

WIKING (D) 1924
Wiking Autobau, Kiel-Flintbek.

1935 Wikov Type 35 saloon.
NICK GEORGANO

This was a light car which used the ZF-Soden pre-selector gearbox, very unusual on such a small vehicle. The engine make is not known, but no more than half a dozen cars were made.

HON

WIKOV (CS) 1925–1937
Wichterle & Kovarik, akc. spol., Prostejov.

In 1878 in Prostejov Frantisek Wichterle founded a small factory making agricultural machines, which, in 1900, was one of the largest of its kind in Bohemia. In Prostejov there was another similar firm owned by Dr Frantisek Kovarik. These two factories united to form a joint-stock company called Wichterle & Kovarik Ltd. In Vienna they bought an Italian Ansaldo car in 1922 which was a pattern for designers Maly and Kostal. Their first own-constructed car was the Wikov 7-28hp of 1925 with 4-cylinder water-cooled 1478cc engine, exchangeable hardened cylinder barrels, silumin engine block, 12V battery ignition, and dry disc clutch. This one and all other Wikov engines had an ohc valve gear. The car was capable of 44mph (71km/h) and was available as a saloon (62,000 Kc) or open tourer (51,000 Kc). In 1925 there were 25 employees, in the 1930–35 period Wikov had 160 workers, 21 technicians, and 4 clerks.

The Type 35 (1930–35, 1743cc, 35bhp, 150 made) were sold as a 4- or 6-seater saloon (64,000 Kc or 68,000 Kc), open tourer (53,000 Kc), 4-seater saloon (65,000 Kc) and as a cabriolet (57,000 Kc).

Technicians at Wikov followed the developments in the motoring world carefully and did not lag behind when the first serious experiments with streamlining started. They fitted an aerodynamic body to a Type 35 chassis in 1931 and gradually adapted it for serial production. Sadly it never got to that. Although received well by the motoring press the public was not ready for the car. It was more expensive than the standard Wikov 35 (75,000 Kc), and the gains in top speed and fuel consumption were slightly disappointing because the engine was too light for the new heavier aerodynamic body. Only six cars were made, but three years before the streamlined Tatra T 77 was launched!

In 1932 there was a prototype of a small car with water-cooled 2-stroke twin-cylinder engine in the rear.

The Wikov 40 (1933–35, 1942cc, 43bhp, 330 units) was bodied as a 4- or 6-seater saloon (52,000 Kc or 61,000 Kc) and was capable of 65mph (105km/h).

1930 Wikov 4/28 saloon.
DR JAN TULIS

The biggest Wikov was the Wikov 70 of 1933 with an 8-cylinder in-line 3485cc 70bhp engine of which only 4 were made, and a 7-seater luxurious saloon that cost 125,000 Kc.

In 1937 Wikov delivered the last passenger car of about 750 cars built during the 1920s and 1930s. They kept on building trucks until 1940 and were renamed Agrozet Prostejov after World War II and built agricultural machinery, which they are still doing today.

MSH

Further Reading
Wikov, Boleslav Hanzelka, Auto Album Archiv, 1986.

WILBROOK (GB) 1913
Brooks & Spencer, Levenshulme, Lancashire.

The Wilbrook was a typical cyclecar in its 8hp V-twin JAP engine and belt final drive. Most unusual were 4-wheel brakes and a 4-seater body.

NG

1904 Wilkinson-De Cosmo 24hp tonneau.
NATIONAL MOTOR MUSEUM

1972 Willam 123cc 2-seater.
NICK BALDWIN

WILCOX *see* WOLFE

WILD HARE (US) c.1960
Joe McBride, Stockton, California.
Like the WHITEHEAD, this was a set of plans for building a sports car from old car parts and scrap metal. The plans were featured in *Science and Mechanics* magazine in 1961, and designer Joe McBride sold the plans as well. The Wild Hare was an all-metal sports car with clamshell mudguards and highly stylised bodywork. Chassis choices were 1935 to 1948 Ford or Mercury sedans, which were shortened to a 100in (2538mm) wheelbase. The engine was moved back in the chassis to improve weight distribution. The body panels were made from contemporary Ford, Mercury and Chevrolet body panels which were cut, shaped and rewelded to fit. The estimated cost of assembly was $300 in 1961.
HP

WILES-THOMSON *see* THOMSON (iv)

WILFORD (B) 1897–c.1901
Ateliers de Construction Mécanique Ch. Wilford et fils, Tamise.
Charles Wilford and his sons, Paul, Maurice and Auguste, were among the first makers of cars in Belgium. They built a 4-seater *vis-à-vis* in 1897 with single-cylinder horizontal engine, doubtless inspired by Benz, mounted at the rear, with belt

transmission and chain final drive. The rear wheels were larger than those at the front, and the whole car was exceptionally high and top heavy-looking. The following year they made a few less primitive cars, and at the 1899 Brussels Salon showed a *dos-à-dos* with horizontal 2-cylinder engine. In 1899 Paul Wilford covered a flying kilometre at over 60mph (97km/h) in a car whose driver was still seated high above the ground. An old-fashioned dog-cart was still exhibited in 1900, but there were also smaller cars with front-mounted 3CV engines and belt final drive. The Wilfords seem to have abandoned cars after that, to concentrate on textiles, though in 1911 a heavy 4×4 road tractor was built according to P.A. Wilford patents, presumably Paul.
NG

WILKINSON (GB) 1903–1904; 1912–1913
Wilkinson Sword Co. Ltd, Acton, London.
As its name implies, this company was famous for its ceremonial swords as used by the Household Cavalry, and also for garden tools and razor blades. In 1903 they made a few cars of Belgian DE COSMO design. They were to have been made at Acton, but probably the few Wilkinson-De Cosmos that were sold were imported from Belgium. They had 24hp 4-cylinder engines, 3-speed gearboxes and shaft drive. In 1907 there was a rumour that Wilkinson were to build the MORS under licence, but nothing came of this. They did, however, do some work for WEIGEL at about this time.
Wilkinson's next car venture was a light 848cc 4-cylinder machine which appeared in 1912. It was made by a subsidiary, the Wilkinson-TMC Co. which made a well-known 4-cylinder motorcycle. In January 1914, after the motorcycle had gone out of production, Wilkinson-TMC was taken over by the Ogston Motor Co. which built a modified version of the Wilkinson light car under the name DEEMSTER.
NG

WILLAM (F) 1966–c.1990
Lambretta SAFD, Levallois-Perret.
Willam was not so much a separate marque as a clever marketing label for a variety of foreign-made microcars, but historically it is highly significant as the progenitor of a generation of microcars, miniature cars that could be driven without a licence and which achieved tremendous popularity in the 1970s and 1980s. M.H. Willam was the French Lambretta scooter importer, who first presented Lambretta-engined 125cc and 175cc prototypes at the 1966 Paris Salon. These were actually made by the Italian company Scattolini and used Fiat 500 suspension. From 1967 Willam entered into an alliance with LAWIL of Italy whereby it would produce a range of tiny vehicles (detailed under the Lawil entry). These were sold with the names City and Farmer in France (and were also imported to the UK by Crayford).
In 1971 another 125cc prototype was displayed but that did not enter production. Instead Willam imported the BALDI and ZAGATO Zele from Italy in the early 1970s, expanding to encompass other marques such as B.M.A, CASALINI and DECSA. It also marketed the Cyclo, a modified version of the ACOMA Mini-Comtesse.
CR

WILLÈME (F) 1930
Éts Willème, Neuilly, Seine.
Willème were well-known makers of heavy trucks, which originated with the American Liberty trucks as used by the US Army in World War I. From the late 1920s they used the C.L.M. opposed-piston diesel engine, and it was to demonstrate a small version of this that they took a stand at the 1930 Paris Salon. Their car was an elegant little 4-door cabriolet resembling a Mathis, powered by the smallest of the C.L.M. diesels, the 700cc single-cylinder Type 1 PJ. It is thought that only one of these was made, though Willème made a number of light trucks using the same chassis and engine. Two of these were still in use in Paris in 1965. Willème heavy trucks were made up to 1970.
NG

WILLIAMS (i) (US) 1905
W.L. Casaday Manufacturing Co., South Bend, Indiana.
At the end of 1904 this company announced two lines of motor vehicle, a truck to be called the Casaday and a car to be called the Williams, after its designer

1923 Wills Sainte Claire Model A-68 tourer.
JOHN A. CONDE

M.L. Williams. It had a 25hp 4-cylinder engine, 3-speed gearbox and chain drive. Built on a 96in (2463mm) wheelbase it had a disproportionately long bonnet and short body, with a very short rear-entrance tonneau behind the two front seats. It was only built for one season, after which the Casaday company decided to concentrate on stationary engines. Williams went on to design the Wilmo sleeve-valve engine.

NG

WILLIAMS (ii) *see* DE MARS

WILLIAMS (iii) (US) 1957–1991
Williams Engine Co., Ambler, Pennsylvania.
The Williams family had been involved in steam engine research since the 1800s, and brothers Calvin and Charles developed a number of steam-powered cars. Their father had patented the Williams Steam Cycle, which broke new ground in steam thermodynamics. They built an attractive VICTRESS S-4-bodied convertible in 1960, and by 1968 it had logged over 25,000 miles. In 1967 they received an order to install their steam power plants into some Chevrolet Chevelles and a Ford Fairlane to test their practicality, but none were built due to a shortage of components. The Williams brothers continued with steam development until 1968, when they closed their factory. It was re-opened in 1972 with funding from another Williams brother, and the family continued with steam car development on a limited basis.

HP

WILLIAMSON (GB) 1913–1916
Williamson Motor Co. Ltd, Coventry.
This was a Morgan-like 3-wheeler powered by a 1070cc 8hp flat-twin Douglas engine, with chain drive to the single rear wheel.

NG

WILLIAMS STUTZ (US) 1969
Howard D. Williams, Tulsa, Oklahoma.
This company built replicas of the Stutz Bearcat using International Harvester chassis and engines.

HP

WILLIS (i) (GB) 1913
Finchley Place Garage, London.
Like many contemporary cyclecars the Willis used an 8hp V-twin JAP engine, but its transmission was unusual. Two chains gave a 2-speed drive to a countershaft, whence power was transmitted to the rear wheels by belts. The countershaft consisted of two tubes, one rotating inside the other, and this gave a differential effect not normally found on belt-driven cars. It was made by the Finchley Place Garage to the designs of J.W. Steinberg and E.L.Wilson.

NG

WILLIS (ii) (US) 1927–1928
Willis Motors Corp., Maywood, Illinois.
The Willis car was more of a one-off experiment than an actually marketable car despite plans for exactly that by its designer, Durward E. Willis who used a standard Gardner sedan with an especially designed radiator and presumably its own badge as well for his initial prototype. As it turned out, that prototype would be the last Willis as well as the first.

What made the Willis unique was its engine. Durward Willis had previously built an F-head 3-cylinder car which he called the D.E.W. (using his initials). The Willis, on the other hand, featured his designed 9-cylinder engine – also an F-head. This F-head Straight-Nine power plant featured its cylinders cast in blocks of three and was claimed to develop 150bhp at 3000rpm. Its price, presumably with closed coachwork, was announced as $5500 f.o.b. Maywood. Surprisingly, Willis also planned to introduce an export car with a 5-cylinder F-head engine, but this never got off his drawing board.

KM

WILLS SAINTE CLAIRE (US) 1921–1927
1921–1922 C.H. Wills & Co., Marysville, Michigan.
1922–1927 Wills Sainte Motor Claire Co., Marysville, Michigan.
When C. Harold Wills left Ford with a golden handshake of more than $1.5 million, he went into partnership with another ex-Ford man, John R. Lee, to make a comparatively small high-quality car powered by a 4350cc V8 engine with a single-ohc to each bank of cylinders. Surprisingly, the cylinder heads were non-detachable, which proved a nightmare to mechanics, and led, eventually to the adoption of a detachable head 6-cylinder engine. Six body styles were offered,

1924 Wills Sainte Claire Model B-68 town car.
NICK BALDWIN

from a tourer at $2875 to a town car and limousine at $4775. Though the car was announced in August 1920 the first car did not go on sale until March 1921, and many remained unsold at the end of the year. Matters improved in 1922, when 2736 were made; in addition to those left unsold the previous year, sales exceeded 3000 in 1922, the best year the company would ever have. Unfortunately, Wills lost money on every car sold, and by the end of the year the company was $8 million in debt.

John Lee and others left, and the company was reorganised with the help of a Boston bank, Kidder, Peabody & Co. To counter complaints about the complexity of the V8, Wills began work on a 4485cc single-ohc 6-cylinder engine. This went into production cars in the 1925 model year. The 127in (3223mm) wheelbase was the same as the longer of the two used for the V8, and prices were around $300–400 lower. 1796 cars were sold in 1925 and 1929 in 1926, but these were not enough to keep the company afloat. It was liquidated in 1927, with only 330 cars being completed that year.

NG

NICK BALDWIN

WILLS, CHILDE HAROLD (1878–1940)

A valued associate of Henry Ford who later went on to build his own car, Childe Harold Wills was born on 1 June 1878 in Fort Wayne, Indiana. His father was a master mechanic on the railways, John Carnegie Wills, and his mother the former Mary Seindell. Of Welsh descent and presumably poetry lovers, they named their son after the hero of Byron's poem *Childe Harold's Pilgrimage*. His father trained him in the use of machine tools while he was still at primary school, and he became an apprentice toolmaker with the Detroit Lubricator Co. at the age of 17. During his 4-year apprenticeship he studied engineering, chemistry, and metallurgy at night school, and when he was about 23 he became chief engineer to the Boyer Machine Co., which later became the Burroughs Adding Machine Co.

He became a highly skilled draughtsman, and it was this skill that attracted Henry Ford when they met in about 1902, for he filled a crucial gap in Ford's repertoire of skills. Wills was invited to work on the engines of Ford's 999 and Arrow racing cars, starting an association which lasted for 17 years. As a boy Wills had earned some extra money by printing calling cards, and was particularly proud of the flowing scripts he could produce. These were quite similar to Henry's signature, and Wills used them for the famous Ford badge which has been carried on all Ford vehicles ever since.

It was not only as a draughtsman that Wills helped Ford; he was at this side throughout the development of all the early models, and had a particular interest in metallurgy. Together they investigated the possibility of using vanadium alloy which was lighter and stronger than any steel used in American cars. Unable to obtain it from the giant Carnegie Steel Co., they found a small company in Canton, Ohio, which was willing to try using higher temperatures in their furnaces than the big firms. They succeeded eventually, and the first Ford to make use of it was the Model N of 1907. Wills is also thought to have been responsible for the improvements in the Ford epicyclic transmission, though of course the principle had been used in many other makes of car. Together with Edward 'Spider' Hugg and Joseph Galamb, Wills did much for the development of the moving assembly line.

During World War I he wanted to get a post with the government, but was content to stay with Ford after the company obtained a contract to build Liberty aero-engines. Towards the end of the war Henry Ford began to buy out his minority stockholders, so that he could have greater control of the firm. The Dodge brothers were bought out in 1917, and two years later it was the turn of Harold Wills. He had held stock in the company since it was founded, and received $1,592,128. He also had about $4 million from savings and other sources, and in 1920 decided to become a car maker himself. He built not only a factory, but a complete community with homes, schools, and a park, which he named Marysville after his wife. He called the car the Wills Sainte Claire, after Lake St Clair near Detroit, (he added the 'e' because it looked classier) and production began in March 1921. It was a quality product, but sales never reached the anticipated 10,000 a year, and the company lost money on every car made. One problem was that Wills would keep stopping the assembly line to incorporate the latest improvements. By the end of 1922 they were $8 million in debt, and Wills was ousted from the board, but came back with the support of the Boston bankers, Kidder, Peabody & Co., who reorganised the firm as the Wills Sainte Claire Motor Co., and appointed their nominee, Asa Nelson, as president. Wills was vice-president. However, this was only a temporary respite, and in 1927 the company was liquidated. Wills lost about $4 million through the company, but had personal holdings in other interests in Marysville.

In 1929 Wills became a director of New Era Motors Inc., the concern which launched the Ruxton car. This was unsuccessful, and Wills then joined Chrysler as a metallurgist. He sold the Marysville Factory to Chrysler in 1935, and was still working for them when he died of a stroke in December 1940. Appropriately, perhaps, his death took place in Detroit's Henry Ford hospital.

NG

WILLYS (i); WILLYS-KNIGHT (US) 1914–1963

Willys-Overland Co., Toledo, Ohio.

Though John North Willys became involved with the OVERLAND in 1907, and formed the Willys-Overland Co. in October 1909, he did not sell a car under his own name until 1914, when he introduced the Willys-Knight. This came about through his purchase of the EDWARDS Motor Co. of Long Island City. He moved both the car and its designer H.J. Edwards into the Garford plant at Elyria, Ohio, where it went into production in late 1914. It had a 4628cc 4-cylinder sleeve-valve engine, and was made in roadster and tourer form, both selling for $2750. Only 40 were made in 1914, and some of them may have used left-over components from the Edwards-Knight. 1915 models were generally similar, and cost $2475. Production of complete Willys-Knights at Elyria ended in July 1915, after which only engines were made there. The cars were completed in a huge new factory in Toledo.

For 1916 Willys decided to make his sleeve-valve car smaller and cheaper. The 4-cylinder model ran from $1095 for a roadster to $1750 for a limousine. Production boomed, and soon Willys was making more Knight-engined cars than the rest of the industry put together. Total production of Willys-Knights over 19 years was around 330,000. A 6-cylinder Willys-Knight arrived in 1916, and a V8 in 1917; even this cost only $2100–$2900. This was made until 1920, when prices were up to $2750–3425. By then there were three Willys lines, a 4-cylinder Knight, the V8 Knight and a conventional poppet-valve six whose engine was bought in from Continental,

Willys did well out of the war, securing large contracts for ambulances and light trucks, and later making aero-engines. On 1 November 1918 he announced that all his production would be given over to the war effort, but 11 days later the war ended. He then plunged back into car production, but a disastrous strike closed the factory from Spring 1919 until just before Christmas. This delayed production of the new Overland Four, for which Willys had bought another factory at Elizabeth, New Jersey, where the Duesenberg aero engines had been made. As a result of this over-reaching ambition, by the end of 1919 Willys-Overland owed $14 million to their suppliers, and $18 million to the Chase National Bank. The bank's condition for extending credit was the installation of a manager of their own choice. This was Walter P. Chrysler, who was given a free hand to work out Willys' salvation, at the then enormous salary of $1 million a year. One of his first steps was to halve Willys' annual salary of $150,000.

Chrysler was not an enthusiast for either low-priced cars or sleeve-valves, but he allowed both lines to continue, while he encouraged the development of an advanced middle-priced 6-cylinder car with hydraulic brakes. This was the work of Carl Breer, Owen Skelton and Fred Zeder ('The Three Musketeers'), ex-Studebaker engineers who worked in the Elizabeth factory. This car was never made as a Willys, but became the Durant-built FLINT, after Billy Durant bought the Elizabeth factory. Breer, Skelton and Zeder later joined Chrysler at MAXWELL, and a similar design emerged in 1924 as the first CHRYSLER.

Willys regained control of his company at the end of 1921, and made a considerable success of the cars that Chrysler had disapproved of, the Overland Four and the Willys-Knight. The latter was gradually improved during the 1920s. Fours were made on two wheelbases, 118 and 124in (2995 and 3147mm), when the smaller model was dropped and a new six with 4180cc 60bhp engine arrived. This Model 66 engine had originated in the STERLING-KNIGHT, whose maker Willys bought up in 1925. It was a handsome car with wire wheels, balloon tyres and front-wheel brakes, and not over expensive at $1850–2295. The radiator bore some resemblance to that of a Buick or Packard. Sales of Willys-Knight contributed about 50,000 per year to Willys' total. In 1925 this was 157,662. In addition to Sterling, Willys bought up the Stearns company of Cleveland, who made the much more expensive STEARNS-KNIGHT, and backed a friend in starting a new company to make the $1000 6-cylinder FALCON-KNIGHT. This was absorbed into the Willys range in 1928, but the Stearns-Knight was continued until the end of 1929. The Willys-Knight survived until 1932 as a complete range, and a single sedan model was listed for 1933, though possibly none were made. The most striking style was the plaid-sided roadster of 1929/30. This was styled by Amos Northup and featured a Scottish tartan pattern on the doors and central part of the body. Free wheeling came in 1931, and a Warner synchromesh gearbox for 1932. That year, 3265 Willys-Knights were sold, out of a total of 29,975 Willys products. These included poppet-valve sixes of 2403 and 3161cc, and a 4020cc straight-8 whose engine was made by Continental, and which shared a chassis and body styling

1926 Willys Whippet Model 96 sedan (left)
and Willys-Knight Great Six sedan (right).
NATIONAL MOTOR MUSEUM

1926 Willys-Knight Model 70 roadster.
JOHN A. CONDE

1924 Willys-Knight taxicab.
JOHN A. CONDE

with the Willys-Knight. The smaller six was sold in Britain as the Willys Palatine Six.

Smaller Models, Whippet, 77 and American

Despite the success of the Overland, Willys hankered after smaller cars, and in 1923 he returned from a European trip with six small British and French cars for his engineers to study. They were all too small for American tastes, but they provided a basis for a car which would sell equally well on both sides of the Atlantic. This appeared in mid–1926 as a 1927 model. The name Whippet suited its size and speed; the 2166cc engine was 13 per cent smaller than the Overland Four, yet output was the same at 30bhp, and the light and nimble Whippet had a top speed of 60mph (97km/h). Improvements compared with the Overland included pressure lubrication, pump cooling, balloon tyres and 4-wheel brakes. The latter two features were firsts in the Whippet's price range. At $825 for a tourer, prices were above the cheapest Overland, but the Whippet

1927 Willys Whippet tourer.
EDDIE FORD

1928 Willys Whippet Collegiate roadster.
JOHN A. CONDE

1930 Willys-Knight Series 70 sedan.
JOHN A. CONDE

was a much more up-to-date car. Three body styles were offered at first, a tourer, a 2-door sedan called a coach, and a coupé. Later they were joined by a 4-door sedan, convertible cabriolet and a 2-seater called the Collegiate Roadster. In 1928 a 4-seater cabriolet cost $545, which was $5 less than a comparable Ford Model A–Willys had undercut Henry at last!

In January 1927 the Whippet Six was announced, using the Overland Six engine in the same chassis as the Whippet Four, though 5in (127mm) longer in the wheelbase. In the month of its introduction a six averaged 56.52mph (90.94km/h) for 24 hours at Indianapolis, setting a new record for American stock cars under $1000. These two models helped Willys to third place in the 1927 production league, with sales of 315,000. They never equalled this, though they were fourth in 1929 and sixth in 1930 and 1931. A more powerful six came in 1928, and the four was increased to 2388cc and 40bhp. These sizes remained until the end of Whippet production; the six was phased out for 1930 when it was replaced by the Willys Six, and the four early in 1931. Only 4390 1931 models were made, and it was not replaced immediately. Ironically, the Whippet's performance hampered its reputation, for Whippets tended to be driven harder than Fords, and therefore burned out through sheer abuse.

From March 1930 to May 1932 Willys was away from the factory, having been appointed as US ambassador to Poland. He was recalled as President Herbert Hoover thought that he would be of more help to his country in Toledo than in Warsaw. Once home he speeded up the introduction of a new model which was to take over where the Whippet had left off. The 77 used an improved version of the 1926 Whippet engine with the same capacity and the same

NICK BALDWIN

WILLYS, JOHN NORTH (1873–1935)

A consummate salesman and an industrialist more or less by accident, it was John North Willys' fate to be forever overshadowed in his business career by W.C. Durant. Willys was born on 25 October 1873, at Canandaigua, New York, the son of a brick, tile, and carboard box factory owner, and started his own first enterprise at the age of ten, buying little clamps to hold carriage reins in place and selling them door-to-door at a profit. Leaving school at 15, he worked in his father's tile yard before trying his luck (which failed him) as a bookseller. With a friend and combined parental loans, he next went into the laundry business at Seneca Falls, which he sold after a year, making a $100 profit. Back in Canandaigua, he went to night school and held down a part-time job as a clerk in a lawyer's office.

His father's death killed his dream of going to college, and he took a job as a bicycle salesman. Soon he opened his own agency, with a repair shop, but gave it up in 1896. With whatever cash he had left, he took over the failing Elmira Arms Co., a local sporting-goods store. Lacking the capital to run it, he hired a manager and went on the road as a travelling salesman. He prospered, reaching an annual turnover of half-a-million dollars in 1900, and sensing a decline in the bicycle market, decided to sell automobiles. In 1901 he became the local agent for the George N. Pierce Co. in Elmira, and the following year he secured the Rambler franchise.

He founded the American Motor Sales Co., with headquarters in Indianapolis, as a wholesale organisation, and contracted for the entire output of the American, Overland, and Marion factories. He got all of 47 cars from Overland in 1906, which prompted him to send in a firm order for 500 cars, with a $10,000 deposit.

wheelbase, while the bodies were an up-to-date sedan and coupé. The sloping grill and partially-faired headlamps were advanced for 1933, and the prices of $335–395 represented remarkably good value, undercutting the 4-cylinder Ford by more than $100.

For most of the Model 77's life Willys-Overland was in the hands of a receiver, and court permission had to be obtained every time a fresh batch of cars was required. They could never gain sanction for more than 1500–2000 cars at a time. The 77 sold quite well, given the stricken state of the American economy at the time, 77,086 in four seasons. Apart from re-styling of the front end the design did not change, and only the two closed body styles were made in the US, though a 4-door tourer was made in Australia. Willys-Overland came out of receivership on 15 August 1935, and John Willys died 11 days later, worn out by

At mid-year, deliveries from Overland stopped. The company could not meet the payroll, creditors claimed unpaid bills of $80,000, and the next step looked like bankruptcy. To protect his investment and the company assets, Willys raised the money to pay the workers and met the creditors, offering cash payments of ten cents on the dollar and the rest in Overland preferred stock at par value and common stock covering 40per cent of the liabilities. It was accepted, and on 9 January 1908, John N. Willys was named President of the Overland Automobile Co. which produced 465 cars that year. He was also its treasurer, chief purchasing agent, and sales manager. He also set an example for Henry Ford in buying out the other shareholders, becoming sole owner, and renaming the corporation – and its products – Willys-Overland.

Still in 1908, he purchased the Marion plant from the Parry family and planned to produce 1500 Overland and Marion cars in 1909. Due to growing demand, the actual number climbed to 4075 cars, running two shifts in both plants. Seeing the need for greater capacity, Willys secured an option on a 30-acre tract of land near Indianapolis. He changed his mind in April 1909, when he found that the Pope-Toledo plant was for sale. Located on Toledo's Central Avenue, the three-storey building was 200m long and 30m wide. Within 48 hours he had inspected the 7-acre plant, seen his bankers in New York, and taken the train back to Toledo where he made a deposit of $25,000. Once the sale had gone through, in December 1909, he began moving Overland to Toledo, a process that was not completed until 1911. Production was never interrupted, and Overland cleared a net profit of $600,000 in 1910. Expansion never stopped, and by 1915 the Toledo plant had a daily capacity of 2200 cars and trucks.

Inspired by the way W.C. Durant bought control of components manufacturers, Willys set out on a similar group-forming course. The Kinsey Manufacturing Co. was organised in 1911 to make sheet-metal parts, and the Warner Gear Co. was brought to Toledo in 1912. He also bought the Gramm Motor Truck Co. of Lima, Ohio, and the Federal Motor Works of Indianapolis.

He made his first Atlantic crossing in 1912 and, among other visits, he paid a call on the Daimler Co. in Coventry. He was given an opportunity to test-drive a Daimler with a sleeve-valve engine, and put 4500 miles on it. Within two years, he had secured a licence for the Knight patents (which he eventually purchased).

Back in the US he purchased the Edwards Motor Co. of New York, N.Y., makers of the Edwards-Knight car and the Garford Manufacturing Co. of Elyria, Ohio. In 1914 he moved production of the Edwards-Knight to Elyria and renamed it the Willys-Knight. He knew Harry Tillotson, a Stromberg carburettor sales engineer, hired him and formed the Tillotson Carburettor Co. in 1914. He also bought control of Electric Auto-Lite of Toledo, makers of starters and generators. All these companies were held by Willys-Overland, which had grown to second place in the industry. In 1916 John N. Willys turned down an $80 million offer to buy it.

In 1917 he set up the Willys Corp. as a holding for his personal investments, which then included 33 per cent of Willys-Overland and substantial minority stakes in Fisk Rubber Co., New Process Gear Co., USL Battery Co. and Federal Rubber Co. as well as 100 per cent of the former Morrow Manufacturing Co. of Elmira, N.Y. which became Willys-Morrow, transmission makers.

With the US entry into World War I, John Willys volunteered for government service, which meant spending most of his time in Washington, D.C. and New York. But he also sailed to Europe twice on government business. He left the management of Willys-Overland and the Willys Corp. to Clarence A. Earl who had been his right-hand man since the death of George W. Bennett in 1913. The Elyria, Ohio, plant was retooled for production of Liberty V8 and V12 engines.

In 1919 the Willys Corp. was recapitalised at $50 million, and put $8 million into Duesenberg Motors of Elizabeth, New Jersey, towards the development of a new car. Willys-Overland purchased Curtiss Aeroplane & Motor Corp. in 1917, and John Willys was named President, planning to build a high-performance car in the Curtiss plant. In 1919 Willys-Overland purchased the Wilson Foundry & Machine Co. of Pontiac, Michigan, engine makers, and the Moline Plow Co. of Moline, Illinois, makers of farm tractors. Privately, John Willys bought stakes in the Ruggles Motor Truck Co. of Saginaw, Michigan and the Torbensen Axle Co. of Cleveland, Ohio.

The recession of 1920 caught Willys ill-prepared. His acquisition spree had been partly bank-financed and it would have taken years to consolidate this agglomeration of industrial property into one profitable group. Willys took some of the blame, and Clarence A. Earl became a scapegoat, replaced by Charles B. Wilson of the Wilson Foundry & Machine Co.

One of the biggest creditors was the Chase Securities Co., an affiliate of the Chase National Bank, who agreed to mount a rescue operation, but only on condition of putting Walter P. Chrysler in control of the Willys Corp. Willys had no choice, and Chrysler's first action was to cut Willys's salary from $150,000 a year to $75,000. Non-core activity plants were put on the market, shedding Moline Plow and Curtiss Aeroplane in the first wave of corporate cleansing. By the end of 1921 Chrysler had saved Willys-Overland but sacrificed the Willys Corp., which was liquidated.

When Chrysler pocketed his $1million fee and went off to seek new opportunities, Willys was down but not out. With the help of Clement O. Miniger, Thomas Tracey, and other Toledo businessmen, he was able to put up $3million to buy the 700,000-odd shares of Willys-Overland stock held by the Willys Corp. His bankers agreed to extend their $17million loan until 31 December 1923, which gave Willys-Overland 18 months to reorganise, bring out new products, regain consumer confidence, and reclaim a leading position in the industry. When all debts were settled, Willys-Overland had a cash balance of about $13million.

John N. Willys made his contribution to raising the sales curve by choosing colourful model names such as Redbird, Bluebird, and Champion. He also devised a 52-week credit scheme and in the summer of 1925 Willys-Overland brought out the low-priced Whippet in reply to Hudson's Essex. By 1927 the Toledo factories covered 18 acres with 32 separate buildings. He bought control of the F.B. Stearns Co. in Cleveland, Ohio in 1925, and reorgansied the Elyria, Ohio, plant as the Falcon Motor Corp.

He avoided the stock-market crash of 1929 by months, selling his Willys-Overland holdings, then at their all-time peak, for approximately $18 million, to a syndicate formed by George M. Jones and C.O. Miniger of Toledo, with Field & Glore of Chicago, simultaneously retiring from the Presidency to serve as Chairman of the board, while Linwood A. Miller was named as President.

In 1930 President Herbert Hoover appointed Willys US Ambassador to Poland but two years later he got word of the critical situation about Willys-Overland, cut short his diplomatic career and set about to save the company once again.

But the recovery proved elusive, and on 15 February 1933, Willys-Overland went into receivership. The court appointed Willys and Linwood A. Miller as co-receivers. About a year later Willys' wife, the former Isabel Van Wie of Canadaigua, N.Y. divorced him after 37 years of marriage. He then married Florence E. Dolan. The responsibility and stress of his task and a hard schedule and workload, combined to bring on a cardiac condition. He survived a heart attack in the spring of 1935, but died at his home in Riverdale, New York on 26 August 1935, and was buried at Kensico Cemetery, White Plains, New York.

JPN

1939 Willys (i) Four sedan.
NATIONAL MOTOR MUSEUM

1933 Willys (i) 77 with Australian-built tourer body.
NATIONAL MOTOR MUSEUM

his efforts to keep the company going. For 1937 the 77 was completely restyled in the fashionable curved idiom with an all-steel body, and renamed the 37. It had synchromesh and Bendix duo-servo brakes, but the engine was unchanged. Sales shot up to 76,803, then slumped disastrously to 16,173 in 1938. This was a bad year for the whole US industry, though few other firms suffered as badly as Willys. Delmar (Barney) Roos joined Willys as chief engineer in 1938, and in January 1939 Joseph W. Frazer became president. The 1939 Willys Model 48 had a restyled front end and hydraulic brakes, while for 1940 the wheelbase was lengthened by 2in (51mm) and the body was further restyled. For the single year 1939 the name Overland was revived, though as a model not a make. This did not catch on, and for 1941 the name Americar was used. They had steering column change and hypoid rear axles, while the wheelbase was lengthened again by 2in (51mm) to 104in (2640mm). Sedan and coupé bodies were now made by Briggs, and there was also a station wagon (introduced for 1940). Thanks to Barney Roos the engine was now more reliable, and more powerful at 62bhp.

It was this engine that powered the Jeep, which originated as an American Bantam design, but began to be made at Toledo, alongside the Americar, in 1941. Sales improved with the arrival of the Americar, to 28,935 for the calendar year 1941. This included three months' production of the generally similar 1942 models.

The Jeep in War and Peace

The Jeep was not available to the private buyer until after World War II, but its influence since then has been enormous. Designed and tested by the American Bantam Co., it was produced in quantity by Willys and Ford, and as the Willys engine was more powerful, their design was made by both companies. It was the Ford version which gave the vehicle its name, for it was called the GP (General Purpose). As there was a well-known cartoon character called 'the jeep', the use of the name was inevitable. It was first used in print by the *Washington Daily News* on 16 March 1941 and soon became the universal name, though never officially adopted by Ford, and not used by Willys until after the war.

The Jeep engine drove all four wheels through a 3-speed gearbox with synchromesh on second and top, with a 2-speed transfer box. Brakes were hydraulic as on the passenger cars, and top speed was around 65mph (105km/h), although at that speed the ride was so bumpy that it was seldom maintained for long. Total production of the standard Jeep between December 1941 and the summer of 1945 was 639,245, of which Willys built 361,349, and Ford 277,896. From 1942 to 1945 bodies for the Willys-built Jeep were made by the American Central Manufacturing Corp. of Connersville, Indiana, which was descended from the company which had made Auburn and Cord cars. Jeeps were used in every theatre of the war, by the British and Russian armies as well as by the American, and saw service as ambulances, gun carriers and railcars as well as transport for all ranks up to Field Marshal (Montgomery used one on several occasions). There were also armoured and amphibious versions.

As Michael Lamm wrote in *Special-Interest Autos* 'For thousands of soldiers the Jeep was the nearest thing to a sports car they had ever driven; roadster body, bucket seats, fold-down windscreen, quick steering, tight suspension, snappy performance. Everybody wanted one'. Even before the war ended Willys must have realised that a lot of people would want one in peacetime too, so they quickly offered a civilian version. It was mainly promoted as a commercial

Willys-Knight

1949 Willys (i) Jeepster phaeton convertible.
NICK GEORGANO/NATIONAL MOTOR MUSEUM

1955 Willys (i) Bermuda hard-top.
NICK BALDWIN

1967 Willys (ii) Aero sedan.
NATIONAL MOTOR MUSEUM

vehicle, with its utility to farmers being stressed. Advertisements showed how it could be used as an agricultural tractor, and with a power take-off for sawing and driving a pump, while there were also fire engine versions. A passenger car with 2-door sedan body styled by Brooks Stevens was considered, but was vetoed by Willys' new boss Charlie Sorensen after three prototypes had been made. Sorensen was determined to capitalise on the Jeep's world-wide reputation, and he did not see the rather anonymous-looking 6-70 sedan filling that role. Instead he ordered the Jeep station wagon and later the Jeepster, both styled by Stevens. The 2-door station wagon was America's first all-steel station wagon. A total of 6533 were made in 1946, and 33,214 in 1947. Unlike the basic Jeeps, it drove on the rear wheels only, but a 4×4 version was made from July 1949.

The Jeepster was a sporty-looking open 4-seater, clearly a member of the Jeep family, yet more comfortable, with a mechanically-operated hood. It was expensive at $1765 (Stevens called it 'a murderous price') because management wanted to

recoup development costs quickly. The Jeepster was therefore always rather a specialised item, and sold in much smaller quantities than the station wagon. It remained in production to the end of the 1951 season, when about 22,400 had been made. From 1949 the Jeepster, like the station wagon, was available with a 2433cc 6-cylinder engine, made in side-valve or inlet-over-exhaust versions. An inlet-over-exhaust 4-cylinder engine was also made, and was also available in the station wagon. Van and pick-up versions of the Jeep were made as well, and were continued after the passenger models were dropped at the end of 1951.

The Aero Series

Sorensen left Willys in 1948, and the new management returned to the idea of a compact-sized passenger car, which Charlie would never have sanctioned. It appeared for the 1952 season, and was in fact the work of an outside studio headed by Clyde Paton with stylist Phil Wright. They had tried to interest other manufacturers in what they called a 'Present Day Model A'. Known as the Willys Aero, it was a 2-door sedan or hard-top with unitary construction body made for Willys by Murray of Detroit. The base model was the Aero Lark with 2650cc 75bhp side-valve six, while the more expensive Aero Wing, Aero Ace and Aero Eagle used the inlet-over-exhaust version of the same engine, which developed 90bhp.

The Aero was well-received by the press, and sold well at first, with 31,363 finding buyers in 1952 and 41,814 in 1953 when a 4-door sedan was added. However, its price was against it; in 1952 the base Aero cost $1731, when you could get a 6-cylinder Ford for $1525, a Chevrolet for $1533 and a Plymouth for $1551. All these were larger cars, and at that time the American public saw no particular virtue in smallness for its own sake. In April 1953 Kaiser Manufacturing acquired a controlling interest in Willys, and a new company was formed, the Kaiser-Willys Sales Division of Willys Motors Inc. Incidentally this take-over scuppered a possible deal between Willys and Standard in England, whereby Jeeps might have been licence-built in Coventry.

Production of Kaiser and Henry J cars was transferred to Toledo, and the 3706cc 6-cylinder Kaiser engine was available in the Aero as Kaiser had made more than they could use. Acceleration was improved, and maximum speed went up from 82 to 84mph (132 to 135km/h), but fuel consumption was worse, which was a negative point as economy had been promoted as one of the Aero's virtues. Sales dropped to 8240 of the 1954 models and only 5897 of the 1955s, despite a facelift and dual colour schemes. Restyled 1956 models never saw the light of day, though the Aero had a new lease of life in Brazil, where it was made from 1960 to 1967.

Jeeps continued to be made at Toledo; since 1963, when the makers were renamed the Kaiser-Jeep Corp., the JEEP has been a make in its own right.

NG

Further Reading
'John North Willys; his Magnetism, his Millions, his Motorcars',
Beverly Rae Kimes, *Automobile Quarterly*, Vol. 17, No. 3.

WILLYS (ii) **(BR)** 1958–1970
1958–1967 Willys-Overland do Brasil SA, São Paulo.
1967–l970 Ford Willys do Brasil, São Paulo.
The Aero Willys was presented in Brazil as a new vehicle, in March 1960, but in fact it was a model which had been dropped by the American Willys-Overland company in 1955. That was the reason why it looked a bit dated when compared to its contemporary Brazilian rivals, the SIMCA Chambord and the JK 2000. It was powered by an F-head 6-cylinder in line 2638cc engine, which developed 90bhp. In 1962 the model was restyled, incorporating vestigial tail fins and other detail changes. The Itamaraty was the luxury version of this car.

Willys-Overland do Brasil was an offshoot of the American concern. In 1954 they started building Jeeps under licence. Private cars joined the range in 1958 when the Jeep Station-Wagon was offered under the name of Rural Willys. Then, in 1960 came the Aero Willys, in 1961 the Interlagos sports car based on the Alpine, and in 1962 the Itamaraty. Renaults were made under licence too. In 1967 the company was bought by Ford do Brasil who continued the Willys range. Publicist Mauro Salles coined the phrase 'Do like Ford, buy Willys' in order to promote the Willys models alongside the more modern Brazilian Fords.
ACT

WILLYS (iii) **(AUS)** 1958–1972
Willys Motors (Australia) Pty Ltd, Brisbane, Queensland.

1935 Wilson (ii) electric coupé.
NATIONAL MOTOR MUSEUM

Originally an assembly operation for Jeeps and station wagons, local content gradually increased as Lucas electrics and Ford Falcon engines and transmissions were incorporated by the contractors, Shute-Upton Engineering. When the Willys operation was terminated in 1972, the remaining stocks of 4-wheel drive components were fitted to Ford Falcon utilities (pick-ups).

MG

WIL-MAC (US) c.1982

Wil-Mac Products, Redding, California.
The Scamp was a replica of the Willys Jeep that used Volkswagen Beetle running gear. It was similar to the later VEEP.

HP

WILRO (US) 1951–1952

Wilro Corp., California.
The Skorpion was a simple fibreglass-bodied kit car that fitted on a modified Crosley sedan or station wagon chassis. It was designed by Ralph Roberts, who had worked for LeBaron and Briggs as chief stylist and had styled the Chrysler Thunderbolt show car. Jack Wills was one of the pioneering fibreglass experts, and he figured out how to put it into production. There were only four pieces to attach to the chassis and the kit sold for a modest $445. There were no doors and the tail hinged up like a boot. The Skorpion was sold to VIKING-CRAFT in 1952.

HP

WILSON (i) (GB) 1922–1923

W. Wilson, Loughborough, Leicestershire.
Wilson was an engineer who had designed the COLTMAN car, and two years after this ceased production he announced a smaller car powered by an 11.9hp 4-cylinder Dorman MV engine, with 3-speed gearbox and shaft drive to a spiral bevel rear axle. Body styles were 2- and 4-seaters, selling for £325 and £450 respectively, but few, if any, Wilsons reached the public.

In 1925 Wilson Brothers of Aldermanbury, London, planned to make an 8hp cyclecar and approached Meadows for a supply of gearboxes. It is not known if the cyclecar was ever built, or if there was any connection with Wilson of Loughborough.

NG

WILSON (ii) (GB) 1935–1936

Partridge, Wilson & Co. Ltd, Leicester.
This company was mainly known as a maker of electric milk floats, which they built from 1934 to 1954. In 1935 they made a entry into the electric passenger car field with a streamlined coupé with long bonnet which contained the 64-volt batteries. These gave a range of 40 miles per charge and a top speed of 27mph (43km/h). The bodies were made by Arthur Mulliners of Northampton. The price was £385, expensive when you could buy a far more spacious Morris Ten for £200, and it is not surprising that no more than 40 were sold. Still, it was more than any other British maker of electric cars between the wars managed. At least one Wilson Electric survives today.

NG

WILSON CLASSIC REPRODUCTIONS (US) c.1985

Wilson Classic Reproductions, Jonesboro, Georgia.
Wilson built a 1953 Corvette reproduction. It was sold in kit form and was intended for a V6 engine.

HP

WILSON-PILCHER (GB) 1901–1907

1901–1903 Wilson & Pilcher, London.
1904–1907 Sir W.G. Armstrong-Whitworth & Co., Newcastle-on-Tyne.
Designed by Walter G. Wilson and Percy Pilcher, this was an advanced car with horizontally-opposed 4-cylinder engine with automatic inlet valves, an epicyclic constant-mesh gearbox which gave four forward and reverse speeds and a clutchless change, and shaft drive to a helical bevel rear axle. The prototype had a 1.4-litre engine with water-cooled head and air-cooled block, but the production cars had full water-cooling and larger engines of 2.4-litres. The flywheel was at the front of the engine, which was front-mounted under a short bonnet. In 1903 capacity was increased to 2.7-litres.

Production was transferred to the Newcastle works of Armstrong-Whitworth in 1904, and the 4-cylinder model was joined by a 4-litre 18/24hp flat-six on similar lines. This was quite an expensive car, selling at £900. Wilson supervised the work at Newcastle, but the works manager C.R.F. Englebach favoured a

1906 Wilson-Pilcher 18/24 landaulet.
NICK BALDWIN

1913 Winco 2-seater.
STEPHEN MYERS

more conventional vertical engine, and initiated production of these from 1906, under the name Armstrong-Whitworth, though the Wilson-Pilcher was listed into 1907. Wilson later designed the Hallford truck and was heavily involved in the development of Britain's first tank in 1915. In the 1930s he was responsible for the Wilson self-changing (pre-selector) gearbox, as used on A.C., Alvis, Armstrong-Siddeley, Delahaye, Invicta, Lagonda, Talbot (ii) and many other 1930s cars.

NG

WILTON (GB) 1912–1924

1912–1914 Wilton Cycle & Motor Co. Ltd, Victoria, London.
1914–1920 Wilton Cars Ltd, Clapham Junction, London.
1921–1924 Wilton Cars Ltd, Tooting, London.

The first Wilton Cycle Co. was set up in 1895 by 14-year old Charles Frederick Halsall. He was the first of his family to go in for engineering as his father and grandfather were both well-known makers of wax dolls. He soon turned to making bicycles, followed by experiments with motorcycles and a tricar. In 1912 he announced his first cyclecar, powered by a 9hp air-cooled V-twin JAP engine under a bonnet of Siddeley-Deasy shape, with 3-speed gearbox and shaft drive. An 8/10hp 4-cylinder water-cooled engine was also available, and this proved to be more popular in the long run. It used a Malicet et Blin chassis, a rounded radiator and the engine was probably a Chapuis-Dornier. In 1914 the business was taken over by a larger company with premises at Clapham, though the original cycle shop in Wilton Road, Victoria, was retained by the Halsall family. A new model was launched for 1916, with 1319cc 4-cylinder engine which they claimed was their own make, though it is more likely to have been a bought-in unit. Few of these were made as they appeared in the middle of the war.

A new Wilton was announced in 1919, powered by a 1496cc Meadows engine, with a worm-drive rear axle. A large order from India was cancelled when production was held up by the moulders' strike of the winter of 1919/20, and probably no more than 100 postwar Wiltons were made. For 1920 they turned

to an 1820cc Peters engine, replaced by a 1490cc Dorman 4MW from mid–1922. Wilton took 21 of these engines. The company was listed as car makers up to 1924, but production may have ended one or two years earlier. Charles Halsall was later active in the radio business.

NG

Further Reading
'The Wilton Car', M. Worthington-Williams, *The Automobile*, May 1994.

WIMILLE (F) 1946–1948

J.-P. Wimillle, Paris.

During World War II champion racing driver, Jean-Pierre Wimille, sketched out plans for his 'ideal' sports car. By the end of 1943 Wimille had commenced construction of a highly original and advanced prototype with an oval form to aid wind flow, and a centrally-mounted engine to improve road holding. This was first presented at the 1946 Grand Prix de l'Autoroute de l'Ouest. Although he had hoped to install a V6 engine, Wimille compromised and fitted a Citroën 11CV motor. The Traction Avant engine developed only 56bhp, yet Wimille's prototype reached 93mph (150km/h) due to the car's excellent aerodynamics (its drag co-efficient was only 0.23). As well as its advanced mid-engined layout, the first Wimille also had a central driver's seat, with passengers flanking the driver on either side (pre-dating the McLaren F1 by almost 50 years). A second Wimille prototype was shown at the 1948 Paris Salon. With rotund bodywork styled by Philippe Charbonneaux, and a 2.2-litre V8 engine supplied by Ford from its French Poissy plant, the second car was much closer to Wimille's original concept. Sadly, Wimille did not survive to see his sports car dream become a production reality. Just three months after the second prototype's debut, Jean-Pierre Wimille was tragically killed at the wheel of his Simca-Gordini during the Buenos-Aires Grand Prix and the sports car project died with him.

CR

WINCO (GB) 1913–1914

Stringer & Co., Sheffield, Yorkshire.

John Charles Stringer ran the Wincobank Steel Works in Sheffield, which made crankshafts and other forgings for the motor industry, and was indeed known as 'Mr. Crankshaft'. Wanting to enter the cyclecar field he engaged an ex-L.G.O.C. engineer, George Bullock, to design it. Unlike many cyclecars the Winco used Stringer's own make of engine, a 1063cc water-cooled vertical twin. Final drive was by shaft. It was entered in a number of competitions, both local hill climbs and at Brooklands. Bullock won a handicap there in June 1914, driving a specially-prepared single-seater. Postwar cars made by the company were called STRINGER-WINCO.

NG

Further Reading
Cars from Sheffield, Stephen Myers, Sheffield City Libraries, 1986.

WINDHOFF (D) 1908–1914

Gebr. Windhoff Motoren- und Fahrzeugfabrik GmbH, Rheine.

This well-known manufacturer of car components, including engines, transmissions and radiators, widened their field into complete cars in 1908. They made 4- and 6-cylinder models, from 2012 to 6125cc. Overhead inlet valves were adopted in 1911. In the immediate prewar years the fours ranged from the 1.5-litre 6/18PS to the 2.6-litre 10/30PS, while the six was the 3.9-litre 15/40PS. They had a good reputation, but did not restart car production after the war; instead they made a line of high-quality motorcycles from 1923 to 1932.

HON

WINDORA (F/GB) 1904

Stephen A. Marples, Holborn, London.

This was an imported car, probably an ARIÈS, for which Marples chose the name Windora, after two of his aunts called Winifred and Dora. Two models were offered, a 12hp 2-cylinder and 18hp 4-cylinder, with mechanically-operated inlet valves and pump circulation. The smaller car had shaft drive, but the 18hp was chain-driven. They were priced at 400 and 520 guineas (£420 and £546) respectively. The catalogue said that special chassis were made for hansom cabs, broughams and similar vehicles. In 1907 Marples sold under his own name a cab with 12hp vertical twin engine.

NG

WINDSOR (i) (US) 1906

Windsor Automobile Co., Evansville, Indiana.
The Windsor was a 30hp 4-cylinder tourer with friction transmission and chain drive, made for J.A. Windsor by the Single-Center Buggy Co. of Evansville, and was indeed designed by their superintendent William O. Worth. Windsor had problems in selling it, and it lasted less than a year.

NG

WINDSOR (ii) (GB) 1923–1929

1923–1927 James Bartle & Co. Ltd, Notting Hill, London.
1927–1929 Watkins & Doncaster, Stamford Hill, London.
This company was an old-established engineering business, founded in 1854. Among their work was the manufacture of cast-iron manhole covers, examples of which graced the streets of Notting Hill (and doubtless elsewhere) up to the 1970s. C.S. Windsor gained control in 1910, and during World War I they were contractors to the War Office, Admiralty, India Office and other government organisations.

In 1921 they began work on a high-quality small car, which was ready two years later. It had a 1354cc ohv 4-cylinder engine in unit with the 4-speed gearbox, shaft drive to a spiral bevel rear axle and fully-compensated 4-wheel brakes, the latter unusual on a small car in 1923. Well-equipped 2-seater, 4/5-seater tourer, and coupé bodies were shown at Olympia, and to emphasise the air of luxury they had Rolls-Royce type radiators. The complete car, engine, chassis and bodies, was made in the works. A separate sales organisation, James Bartle & Co. (Sales) Ltd was run by F.W. Berwick, formerly of Sizaire-Berwick.

The Windsor was never a cheap car, 1923 prices running from £360 for the 2-seater to £465 for the coupé, and this inhibited sales, despite very complimentary road tests and praise from journals like *The Gentlewoman* and *The Morning Post*. For 1925 the wheelbase was increased from 102 to 108in (2589 to 2741mm), and there was a 4-door saloon at £550. At the Olympia Show in 1925 there was an attractive sports model with wire wheels, pointed tail and a 70mph (113km/h) top speed, for £395. At least one coupé de ville was made. The Windsor was discontinued in early 1927, after a maximum of 300 had been made, and James Bartle & Co. Ltd was wound up in May or June that year. However, Watkins & Doncaster took over all the jigs, tools, drawings and spares, and may have assembled a few cars up to 1929. Certainly one 'latest 1929 model' was offered for sale in January that year. Watkins & Doncaster sold Windsor spares well into the 1930s.

NG

Further Reading
'Too Little, Too Much – the Windsor', M. Worthington-Williams, *The Automobile*, January and May 1991.

WINDSOR (iii) (US) 1929–1930

Moon Car Co., St Louis, Missouri.
The Windsor, introduced as an 8-cylinder companion car of Moon, replaced the 8-cylinder Diana which Moon had phased out a year earlier. Powered by a Continental straight-8 15S L-head engine developing 88bhp at 3100rpm, the Windsor was a handsome car available in five body styles and featured a 4-speed gearbox in a dropped frame plus hydraulic brakes and automatic chassis lubrication. In an obvious attempt to capture public interest, the company designated the car as The White Prince of Windsor, after the Prince of Wales who had been popularised by his various appearances in the United States' 'Smart Set'. To further promote this image, Moon had the Windsor badge designed to incorporate the three-feathered insignia of the prince. This brought an immediate objection from the Royal Family and the badge was redesigned at the end of the year. Although Moon had used its own name for its 6-cylinder offerings, for 1930 the Windsor name was adopted for all Moon production. The Windsor Eight was discontinued during 1930 and Moon struggled on with its 6-cylinder Windsor née Moon and in assembling the front-drive Ruxton car for New Era Motors. Moon managed to build about 500 cars during 1930 but failed to survive the year.

KM

Further Reading
'Moon on the Wane', Arch Brown, *Special-Interest Autos*, February 1980.

WINDSOR STEAM CAR *see* DETROIT STEAM CAR

1926 Windsor (ii) 10/15hp sports car.
NATIONAL MOTOR MUSEUM

1930 Windsor (iii) 8-92 White Prince roadster.
NICK GEORGANO

WING (US) 1922

Wing Motors Corp., Birmingham, New York.
The Wing was, to all intents and purposes, a typical assembled car of its time, with the exception of a special front suspension. The car was designed by Earl G. Gunn, former chief engineer of the Packard Motor Car Co. The Wing had a chassis of 116in (2944mm) and was powered by a 6-cylinder Continental 7R engine. The 5-seater touring car appears to have been the only planned body style to sell for $1800. Pilot models were completed, but by the time negotiations for a factory were underway, the decision to discontinue the Wing was made. The car was to sell in Canada under the badge of the CANADIAN SIX, but production there failed to materialise. Like the Wing, the Canadian Six featured similar ifs.

KM

WINGFIELD (GB) 1909–1920

1909 Wingfield Motor Co., Dewsbury, Yorkshire.
1910–1920 Wingfield Motor Co., Norbury, London.
William Wingfield built his first car in Dewsbury, announcing it in the press in November 1909. It had an 18/23hp 4-cylinder engine of pair-cast T-head design, but the dimensions were not disclosed. It had a 3-speed gearbox and shaft drive, while the frame was tapered outwards towards the rear, the width being 30in (761mm) at the front and 40in (1015mm) at the rear. It was swept up to clear the rear axle. The whole chassis was said to be of Wingfield's design and construction, but it carried a landaulet body by George Lacy of Dewsbury.

By the end of 1910 Wingfield had a new address in Norbury, south-west London, though the brochure was printed in Dewsbury. As well as the 18/23, two other models were listed, a 12/15 and a 27hp six, although there is no evidence that they were built. The 12/15's cylinder dimensions were the same as those of the 15.9hp GLADIATOR and there is a possibility that Wingfield made a few Gladiators for Herbert Austin, with whom he was apparently friendly. *The Motor's* Guide to New Models of March 1914 illustrated this car, with a tourer body, and listed several other models, an 11.9hp four, a 25.6hp four and a 23.8hp six. These were followed by more new models for 1915, including an enormous 38.7hp six of 7448cc. We seem to be entering the realms of E.H. Owen here, and it is not

1920 Wingfield 23.8hp chassis.
NICK BALDWIN

1921 Winnipeg tourer.
GLENN BAECHLER

unduly cynical to doubt that any of these were made. Apart from the tourer illustrated in *The Motor*, at least one other 15.9hp, a coupé, was made, as it was offered for sale second-hand in 1919.

In 1920 a 23.8hp 6-cylinder car with the same cylinder dimensions as that of 1914 was announced, and at least one of these was built, as there are several photographs of the chassis. The cylinders were pair-cast, and the chassis was similar to that of the 1909 prototype, though with a less pronounced upsweep over the rear axle. Like the prototype, it had a circular radiator. Presumably it was bodied at some stage, although no photographs survive. William Wingfield, who never formed a limited liability company, went bankrupt in November 1921. At the most conservative estimate, he may have made only four cars, the 1909 prototype, the two 15.9s of 1914 and the 23.8 chassis of 1920. However, it is possible that there were a few more.

NG

Further Reading
'The Wingfield Story', M. Worthington-Williams,
The Automobile, April 1995.

WING MIDGET (US) 1922

H.C. Wing & Sons, Greenfield, Massachusetts.
Chauncey Wing's main business was making machinery for addressing and wrapping newspapers and magazines, but he made a car for himself in about 1900, and in 1922 began to manufacture for sale a miniature single-seater car powered by an air-cooled 4-cylinder engine with 3-speed gearbox and double-chain final drive.

A top speed of 80mph (129km/h) was claimed, and fuel consumption of 40 to 50mpg, though presumably not at the same time.

NG

WINNER (i) (US) 1899–1901

Elgin Automobile Co., Elgin, Illinois.
Built in the factory where the ELGIN Electric had been made, the Winner was a simple 2-seater powered by a 3hp single-cylinder engine, and selling for $675. Fifteen were made, some of the last having 2-cylinder engines.

NG

WINNER (ii) (US) 1907–1909

Winner Motor Buggy Co., St Louis, Missouri.
Winner were carriage and buggy makers who built a few motorised buggies with tiller or wheel steering. Production was limited, though one survives today.

NG

WINNIPEG (CDN) 1921, 1923

Winnipeg Motor Cars, Ltd, Winnipeg, Manitoba.
The Winnipeg is an interesting example of badge engineering, and marketing a basic car under a different name targeted to a specific region. The Winnipeg's slogan was 'Good as the Wheat' which presumably attracted favour in the wheat producing province of Manitoba. The first Winnipeg was a rebadged 1921 HATFIELD, built in Sydney, New York – a 4-cylinder car with a Herschell-Spillman engine. Only one car was so rebadged. Winnipeg distributed no cars in 1922, but a year later the company decided to promote a six and obtained sufficient parts from the George W. Davis Motor Car Co. in Richmond, Indiana, to assemble an additional 11 cars – after which Winnipeg closed down.

KM

WINSON (GB) 1920

Messr. J. Winn, Rochdale, Lancashire.
The Winson cyclecar was powered by an 8hp Blackburne or Precision engine, with friction transmission and final drive by single chain. An ingenious fitting of the friction disc gave a differential effect.

NG

WINTER *see* W.W.

WINTHER (US) 1920–1923

Winther Motors, Inc, Kenosha, Wisconsin.
The Winther truck, introduced in 1917, had proven itself with a complete line of commercial chassis from $3/4$-ton to 7-ton varieties, plus a few specially-built fire apparatus, and decided to broaden its productivity by a line of automobiles, the first of which appeared in 1920. The car was typical of the assembled cars of its time and used a Herschell-Spillman 11000 6-cylinder L-head engine with a wheelbase of 120in (3045mm). Only a touring car was produced priced at $2650 in the beginning, the price reduced to $2250 for 1922. With less than 400 Winthers sold by early 1923, the patterns were sold to G.D. Harris of Menasha, Wisconsin, who continued the car with little change as the HARRIS SIX. Winther truck production continued into 1927.

KM

WINTON (US) 1897–1924

Winton Motor Carriage Co., Cleveland, Ohio.
Alexander Winton (1860–1932) was born on Clydebank in Scotland, emigrated to America in 1878 and found work with the Deltameter Iron Works in New York City. He then went to sea as an engineer on steamships for five years, and afterwards moved to Cleveland where he eventually set up the Winton Bicycle Co., with his brother-in-law, in 1891. He began to experiment with cars in 1896, and the following year founded the Winton Motor Carriage Co. For this he bought a factory from the Brush Electrical Co., and the original factory was retained for bicycle making until at least 1899.

His 1896 prototype had a single-cylinder engine, *dos-à-dos* seating for four and steering by tiller which also controlled the speed. A second experimental car of 1897 had *dos-à-dos* seating for six people, but the four production cars that year had 2-seater bodies, horizontal single-cylinder engines, 2-speed gearboxes,

1905 Winton 16/20hp tourer.
NATIONAL MOTOR MUSEUM

and laminated wood frames. In 1898 22 of these were sold, as well as eight delivery vans, which were the first petrol-engined commercial vehicles made in the US. More than 100 vehicles were made in 1899, which made Winton the largest producer of petrol-engined vehicles in the United States, although Columbia electrics and Locomobile steamers were still comfortably ahead in overall production.

In 1900 Alexander Winton issued a challenge to Fernand Charron which was settled in the first of the Gordon Bennett races. The result was a disappointment to Winton, whose 14bhp car with enormous single-cylinder of 3.8-litres dropped out, while Charron's Panhard won. Winton tried again in the 1903 Gordon Bennett, with two cars with in-line horizontal engines, an 8.5-litre four and a 17-litre eight. Both retired. Meanwhile production cars were flourishing; the 1901 Wintons had steering wheels, engines were still singles of 8 and 9hp, and a 15hp 2-cylinder tonneau joined the range in 1902. Most Wintons were still 2-seaters, though an extended wheelbase 4-seater, called a 'family carriage' was built in 1901. A larger 20hp four with rear-entrance tonneau body appeared in 1903. One of these, with a 2-seater body, was used by Dr H. Nelson Jackson and his chauffeur Sewell H. Crocker for their pioneer crossing of the American continent from San Francisco to New York in May–July 1903. The 1905 season saw front-mounted 4-cylinder engines and longer wheelbases accommodating full side-entrance tonneau bodies. These cars were quite conventional, though the gearboxes had only two speeds. 3- and 4-speed gearboxes arrived in 1907 when two models were listed, a 30hp on a 104in (2640mm) wheelbase and a 40hp on a 112in (2843mm) wheelbase. Winton's first six came in 1908, with a 7.75-litre engine and a price tag of $5750 for the landaulet. From 1909 only sixes were made, in two sizes, of which the larger had a 9.5-litre 60hp engine, a 130in (3299mm) wheelbase and prices as high as $6000. More than 1200 cars were sold that year, a creditable figure when the cheapest cost $4500. A compressed

1911 Winton Six tourer.
NICK BALDWIN

air starter was offered, and by 1911 it was being used to inflate the tyres as well. Electric starting was adopted in 1915.

From then until the end of production in 1924 there were no great changes to Winton design. A smaller and less expensive six was introduced in 1915, alongside the larger cars; this had a 33.75hp engine with ten body styles at prices from $2285 for a 5-seater tourer to $3500 for a sedan or limousine. This was obviously a good move, for Winton's 1916 sales were the best ever, at 2458 cars. Thereafter they declined gradually, sinking below four figures in 1921, when 956 sales were recorded, to 373 in 1923 and only 129 in 1924. Only one engine size was used

1920 Winton Six-24 French limousine.
NICK BALDWIN

1922 Winton Six-40 roadster.
JOHN A. CONDE

1911 Withers 35/40hp limousine.
NICK BALDWIN

from 1920 onwards, a 5701cc 70bhp L-head six, on a 132in (3350mm) wheelbase. Winton had become involved in stationary and marine diesel engines in 1912 when he formed a separate company, the Winton Gas Engine Manufacturing Co. These became of increasing importance during the war, and continued after the car department closed in February 1924. To the end, this retained the archaic title, the Winton Motor Carriage Co. The engine division was taken over by General Motors in 1930.

NG

Further Reading
'Winton, the Man and his Motorcars', Walter E. Gosden, *Automobile Quarterly*, Vol. 22, No. 3.

WISCO (US) 1910
Wisconsin Carriage Co., Janesville, Wisconsin.

This carriage company was founded in 1885 and made cars for one year only. The Wisco Model A had a 4.7-litre 30.5hp 4-cylinder engine and a 3-speed gearbox. Two body styles were offered, a 4-seater toy tonneau and a 5-seater tourer. After it was discontinued the makers returned to carriages, and followed these with scooters and coaster wagons, which were made up to 1940.

NG

WITHERS (GB) 1906–1915
Withers Motors Ltd, London.
Withers were coachbuilders with premises in the Edgware Road who made a small number of cars, all fitted with proprietary engines. In 1906 they offered a 12/14 and a 20/22hp, both with 4-cylinder Aster engines, and a 24/30 with Barriquand et Marre power unit. Up to 1911 Withers relied mostly on Aster for their engines, but thereafter bought them from White & Poppe. In 1913 they listed 20, 25, 30, and 35/40hp models, all with 4 cylinder engines, the latter being of 5876cc. The Withers was built mostly to special order, and it is not certain that all these models were ever made. The bodywork was made entirely at their own premises, which they continued to occupy at least into the 1970s. At the 1913 Olympia Show they exhibited the Magic sleeve-valve car, built under Fischer patents. It was probably a Delaugère-Clayette.

NG

WITKAR (NL) 1972–1974
The Witkar (white car) followed on from the 'white bicycles' experiment in Amsterdam, where white-painted bikes were freely available to use as transport. The Witkar was a little less anarchic, individuals joining a system and being provided with a magnetic key to operate a Witkar at one of several electric charging stations. The founder was Luud Schimmelpenninck, and the system was still in operation as late as 1986. The car itself was a curiously-styled telephone-kiosk shaped electrically-powered 2-seater with a transparent passenger cell and a single rear wheel.

CR

WITTEKIND (D) 1922–1925
Wittekind Automobile GmbH, Berlin-Lichterfelde.
This small car took its name from a Germanic hero of Roman times. It was made with a variety of engines, 3/12 or 5/15PS with 2- or 3-seater bodies, and 6/18 or 6/24PS with 4-seater bodies.

HON

WIZARD (US) 1920–1921
Wizard Automobile Co., Charlotte, North Carolina.
The Wizard car was the focal point of a stock promotion venture which was dishonest from the beginning, its car marketed on the premise of affording economy, both in the car itself and its operation. Headquarters were listed as 'Wizard, North Carolina' but no such place ever existed, its factory being located in Charlotte. The Wizard was a small 2-seater roadster with a 15hp 2-cylinder engine and a wheelbase of 100in (2538mm). Weighing 800lb (364kg), the car guaranteed a speed of 35mph (56km/h) and 50mpg. The car was priced at $395. Several Wizard roadsters were completed and sold before the operation was closed down.

KM

WM (PL) 1927–1928
Ing. Wladislaw Mrajski, Warsaw.
Mrasjski's light car was powered by a 733cc air-cooled flat-twin engine which developed 11bhp, with dry sump lubrication. It had a 4-speed gearbox and central tubular chassis. Only one prototype chassis was made, but it was fitted with open and closed bodies, with 2+2 seating. Financial support for building it came from a small bearing factory, and Mrajski hoped to find a consortium of small workshops to make the car in series, but the financial crisis of 1929 put an end to the project.

RP

W.M.C. (GB) 1990–1995
Webster Motor Co., Braishfield, Hampshire.
A microcar collector was behind this revival of the BOND Bug 3-wheeler, using a set of original body moulds. Initially the intention was to make an updated Bug with four rather than three wheels, and several such cars were produced,

but demand for a 3-wheeler led to a true Bug replica. The chassis was similar to the original, although more substantial and the rear axle had multi-link location. The mechanical basis was Reliant Kitten or Robin. Unlike the Bond, there were options of solid folding doors, a cut-down canopy with aero screens and modern instruments.

CR

WOLF see WEARWELL

WOLFE (US) 1907–1909
H.E. Wilcox Motor Car Co., Minneapolis, Minnesota.
These cars were made by the brothers H.E. and John F. Wilcox, but obtained their name from that of the designer Maurice Wolfe, who was credited in 1903 with making the first sale of a car (a Cadillac) to an American Indian. The Wolfe could be had with a 24hp Carrico ohv engine in either air- or water-cooled form. Transmission was via a 3-speed gearbox and double-chain drive. Tourers were offered throughout the Wolfe's history, with a roadster added for 1909. During that year the marque name was changed to Wilcox, and cars were made for a further three years. Wilcox trucks were made up to 1928.

NG

WOLSELEY (i) (GB) 1896–1975
1896–1901 Wolseley Sheep Shearing Machine Co. Ltd, Birmingham.
1901–1914 Wolseley Tool & Machinery Co. Ltd, Birmingham.
1914–1927 Wolseley Motors Ltd, Birmingham.
1927–1948 Wolseley Motors (1927) Ltd, Birmingham.
1949–1970 Wolseley Motors (1927) Ltd, Cowley, Oxford.
1970–1975 Austin-Morris Division, British Leyland Motor Corp. Ltd, Cowley, Oxford.
Wolseley was one of the leading British makes of car, and had at its helm three prominent figures in the industry, successively Herbert Austin, John Davenport Siddeley and William Morris. Yet it never had an independent existence, being owned by Vickers for its first 26 years, and then by William Morris and the Nuffield Organisation.

The man who gave his name to the car played very little part in its history. He was Frederick York Wolseley (1837–1899), who was Irish-born but founded his Wolseley Sheep Shearing Machine Co. in Sydney, Australia, in 1887. Two years later he set up a British branch in Birmingham, and employed a clever works manager called Herbert Austin (1866–1941) who improved the quality of the product, and added other lines such as machine tools and bicycle components.

Between 1896 and 1898 Austin built two 3-wheeled cars, one with a horizontally-opposed twin engine and single rear wheel, and the other with a parallel horizontal-twin engine, later replaced by a single cylinder, and single front-wheel. For many years the horizontally-opposed twin car, which bore some resemblance to the Léon Bollée, was thought to be the first, and to date from 1895 or 1896, but recent research has revealed that it may well be no earlier than 1898. This is based on the fact that its engine, a curious design in which a combustion box is connected by tubes to what are really pumping pistons, is very similar to the Hunter engine described in *The Autocar* in January 1898, and it is thought that Austin copied Hunter rather than the other way round. Also the gear change is similar to that employed in the first Wolseley 4-wheeler of 1899. The car with single front wheel was in existence in December 1896, and the following year a catalogue was issued in which it was described as the Wolseley Autocar Number 1. Prices of £110 for the 2-seater and £150 for a 4-seater were quoted, but only the 2-seater was made. To accommodate four would have necessitated a complete redesign, as the car was too narrow to carry two people side by side.

Neither of the 3-wheelers was made in series, and in 1899, the year in which Wolseley died, Austin built his first 4-wheeler. This had a front-mounted horizontal single-cylinder engine of 1302cc developing about 5bhp at 800rpm. Steering was by tiller, and final drive by chains. This car was very successful in the Thousand Miles Trial, unlike a companion 2-cylinder model which had to be withdrawn. Replicas of the Thousand Mile Trial car were listed for sale at £270, but no cars were manufactured until the motor department of the Wolseley Sheep Shearing Machine Co. was acquired by the large armaments firm, Vickers Son and Maxim in February 1901. A new factory was bought at Adderley Park, Birmingham, and two models offered for sale, a 5hp single (1302cc) and a 10hp twin (2604cc). They had the same basic layout as the 1899/1900 car, with wrap-

1927 WM 733cc light car.
ROBERT PRZYBYLSKI

1909 Wilcox (Wolfe) Model E 30hp tourer.
NATIONAL MOTOR MUSEUM

1901 Wolseley 5hp 2-seater.
NICK BALDWIN

around tubular radiators, though chain primary drive replaced the belts of the original 4-wheeler. In 1902 a 20hp 4-cylinder model was added, with the same cylinder dimensions which gave a capacity of 5208cc. This was uprated to 24hp for 1904, though engine size was the same. These 4-cylinder Wolseleys were less popular than their smaller contemporaries, as the two rearmost cylinders could only be reached by taking up the floorboards or lying under the car. Also they were subject to oil starvation and consequent bearing or crankshaft failure. From 1904 to 1906 a 6hp single-cylinder car was made at another Vickers factory at Crayford, Kent. This could be distinguished from other Wolseleys by its sloping radiator and single-chain drive.

c.1907 Wolseley-Siddeley tourer.
NICK BALDWIN

1914 Wolseley 15hp tourer.
NICK BALDWIN

1914 Wolseley 30/40hp limousine.
NICK BALDWIN

The horizontal-engined Wolseleys sold well at first, and the company earned good profits in 1902 and 1903, but thereafter losses were incurred. Austin refused to consider a change to vertical engines, and the directors began to look elsewhere for a chief engineer. Their attention was drawn to John Davenport Siddeley (1866–1953) who was making vertical-engined cars closely based on Peugeots. In 1904 Wolseley took over Siddeley's company and appointed him as their Sales Manager. Austin not unnaturally took offence at this and left, later to found his own company. Ironically the Austin cars all had vertical engines.

The Racing 'Beetles'

The horizontal-engined cars were-well suited for racing, as their low fronts offered less wind resistance than the conventional radiator of a vertical engine. In 1901 a standard 20hp was fitted with racing bucket seats and a 5-speed gearbox, and took part in a number of hill climbs and sprints. 1902 saw a purpose-built racing car with 6.4-litre engine rated at 30hp. Two of these and two 45hps with 8.2-litre 3-cylinder engines were entered for the Paris-Vienna race, but only one 30hp started, driven by Herbert Austin, and that retired with a broken crankshaft. The 3-cylinder cars were never seen again, indeed some historians have claimed that they never existed, and that the 45hp machines had 4-cylinder engines. However, Austin persisted with larger fours, those for the 1903 Paris-Madrid race having capacities of 8560cc.

They had no success, nor did a larger-engined car of 72hp and 11,082cc. The 1904 racing Wolseleys had curiously shaped noses which earned them the name 'Beetle', and either 72 or 96hp engines, the latter with a capacity of 12,033cc. Sidney Girling was 9th in the Gordon Bennett with a 72hp, and Charles Jarrott 12th in a 96hp. The 96hp cars ran in the 1905 Gordon Bennett, with shorter wheelbases and the 'beetle' cowls removed, their best place being C.S. Rolls' 8th. Although they were never winners, the big Wolseleys were the leading British racing cars after Napier in the first five years of the century.

The Wolseley-Siddeleys

John Siddeley quickly became general manager of Wolseley, and although the horizontal-engined cars were available up to the end of the 1906 season, his influence was seen in the new vertical-engined cars, a 12hp twin and four fours, 15, 18, 25 and 32hp. These had overhead inlet and side-exhaust valves, overdrive gearboxes on some models, shaft drive on the 12 and 15, and chains on the larger models. The range was extended in 1907 to include a 40hp four and a 45hp six, both chain-driven and the latter with dual ignition and a capacity of 8255cc. These cars were called Wolseley-Siddeleys, and some just carried the name Siddeley on their hub nuts. In November 1906 Siddeley announced that the vertical-engined cars would not bear the Wolseley name at all; this did not please the directors, and Siddeley's arrogant personality eventually led to his departure in 1909, and a reversion to the plain Wolseley name from 1911 onwards. Output had grown dramatically under Siddeley's regime, from 523 cars in 1906 to nearly 1600 in 1911, two years after he left. However, profits were not forthcoming, largely because the company's factories were scattered, so the Crayford factory gave up car manufacture, which was concentrated in Birmingham. A wide range continued to be offered, from a 2234cc 12/16 to a 8937cc 50hp, but the bulk of production was of the 12/16, 16/20 and 24/30. About 7500 of the 12/16 and 16/20 were made between 1910 and 1919. By 1914 annual production was around 2000 cars, making Wolseley one of Britain's larger producers of cars. They were also making significant numbers of trucks as well as aero and marine engines. They built the motor sleighs used in Captain Scott's Antarctic explorations, and a one-off commission in the form of a 2-wheeled gyro-car designed by a Russian lawyer, Count Peter Schilowsky.

The 1914 range was reduced to three models, the 16/20 and two sixes, 24/30 and 30/40. The smaller cars had worm drive, and the 30/40 was bevel-driven. The chief designer from 1904 to 1919 was Arthur Remington (1877–1922). In 1913 a new light car was launched under the name Stellite. There was no room to make this at Adderley Park, so it was made in the factory of another Vickers subsidiary, the Electric & Ordnance Accessories Co. at Aston, Birmingham. The Stellite had a 1074cc inlet-over-exhaust 4-cylinder engine, a 2-speed rear axle-mounted gearbox, and an armoured wood frame. 3-speeds were offered for 1915, and the Stellite was revived after the war, being made up to 1920.

The Postwar Wolseleys

Wartime production was given over to Viper V8 aero-engines, based on the Hispano-Suiza engine that Wolseley had been making under licence, shells and telescopic gun mountings, and from 1917 SE5 fighter aeroplanes were made in a special factory. The Electric & Ordnance Accessories Co. built a large factory at Ward End, Birmingham, for the manufacture of fuses and shell cases, which employed 13,000 people, compared with only 7000 at Adderley Park. In 1919 Vickers took over Ward End from its subsidiary, and the factory later became the home of Wolseley under Morris ownership.

The 1919 Wolseleys were similar to the prewar 16/20, 24/30 and 30/40, but for 1920 a new range of cars with single-ohc engines was announced. These were made in 10 and 15hp 4-cylinder models, and there was also a 20hp side-valve six which was made in various forms up to 1927. The ohc engines had detachable heads and were inspired by the ohc valve gear of the Hispano-Suiza aero-engine. Both were used in racing cars which were sponsored by, and mainly driven by, Captain Alastair Miller. They took class records at Brooklands, and Tens ran in the 200 Mile Races of 1922 and 1923. Their most significant record was the Double Twelve, irrespective of class, achieved by a 15 in 1922, at an average speed of 80mph (128.9km/h). There were two road-going spin-offs from the racing programme, the Sports Ten of 1922 with aluminium body, pointed tail and disc wheels, and the Speed Model of 1923. This was a starker affair with no weather protection, and its appearance was spoilt by artillery wheels. It was expensive at £695, and despite a 72mph (115km/h) top speed very few were sold. About 30 Sports Tens were sold, and six Speed Models.

At the lower end of the range there was an austerity version of the Ten 2-seater, for which the Stellite name was revived, though it was a Wolseley Stellite rather than a marque of its own as the earlier one had been. 50 of these were made. The smallest Wolseley of all was a 7hp flat-twin of 970cc which made its debut in the 1922 Scottish Six Days Reliability Trial in which it won a gold medal in its class. It was only offered for the 1922/23 season, about 1000 being made. The Ten became the 11/22 with a longer wheelbase and fabric saloon coachwork in addition to open 2- and 4-seaters in 1925, and the Fifteen was replaced by the side-valve 16/35, the last side-valve Wolseley model. For 1927 they offered the 2010cc ohc Silent Six, whose engine survived until 1934.

The Morris Take-over

Wolseley had prospered immediately after the war, their output in 1923 being a record 4427 cars, but a drop in demand coincided with heavy borrowing by Vickers for factory extensions, and an expensive new London showroom hit the balance sheets badly. Sales were less than 3000 in the years 1925 and 1926,

1920 Wolseley Stellite 2-seater.
NICK BALDWIN

c.1921 Wolseley 24/30hp tourer.
NICK BALDWIN

c.1925 Wolseley 15hp saloon-landaulet by J. Blake.
NICK BALDWIN

possibly no more than 2000, and in November 1926 Wolseley was declared bankrupt with huge liabilities of more than £2 million, equivalent to at least £50 million in today's money. William Morris had always admired the company, and had ordered a Wolseley taxicab in 1908. The Silent Six appealed to him as a logical extension to his range of 4-cylinder Cowleys and Oxfords, and his patriotism made him anxious about the possibility of Wolseley falling into American hands. When the company came up for sale in February 1927, Morris made a successful bid of £730,000, (Herbert Austin was the underbidder) and soon afterwards the company was reconstituted as Wolseley Motors (1927) Ltd. It remained Morris' personal property until 1935, when he sold it (at a huge profit) to Morris Motors Ltd. This was because Morris was not sure of the success of Wolseley, and he did not want to burden his company with a possible liability.

Realising that one of Wolseley's problems was excess factory space, Morris quickly reorganised production, turning over part of the Adderley Park factory to Morris Commercial trucks and buses, (the rest was sold) and making Ward

1929 Wolseley 21/60 straight-8 coupé.
NICK BALDWIN

1935 Wolseley Nine saloon.
NICK BALDWIN

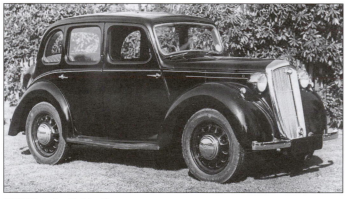

1946 Wolseley Eight saloon.
NICK BALDWIN

1946 Wolseley 18/85 saloon.
NICK BALDWIN

End the sole home of Wolseley cars. The 16/45 Silent Six was continued, and was joined by the 4-cylinder 1532cc 12/32, and the straight-8 2680cc 21/60 which had the same cylinder dimensions as the six. All three had shaft-driven single-ohcs, the drive on the 21/60 being located between cylinders 4 and 5, while the smaller engines had the shaft at the front. The eights did not sell in large numbers, only 450 21/60s between 1928 and 1931, while a 4020cc 32/80 straight-8 sold only five cars. Confusingly there was another 21/60, a 2677cc six of which 3213 were made between 1928 and 1935. It came in two wheelbases, 114 and 127in (2896 and 3226mm), with eight body styles. The 21/60 was built with the export market in mind; the overseas saloons were known as Messengers and had Budd welded all-steel bodywork and Lockheed hydraulic brakes. It was very similar to the 1930 Morris Isis, being a foretaste of the rationalisation between the two makes which was to follow in the next four decades. In 1930 seven Messengers were used on an African safari headed by the Prince of Wales, in which they covered 36,000 miles of mostly appalling roads with no mechanical breakdown. In 1931 the 16/45 was named the Viper, gaining hydraulic brakes and Morris Isis-style bodywork, also a 3-speed gearbox instead of four, and coil in place of magneto ignition. From 1933 to 1935 it was the Sixteen, with synchromesh from 1934. The 21/60 also had coil ignition from 1933 and synchromesh from 1934.

Hornet, Nine, and Wasp

April 1930 saw the arrival of the classic 'pint-sized six'. Called the Hornet, it had a 1271cc ohc 6-cylinder engine with the same cylinder dimensions as the 4-cylinder Morris Minor in an extended Minor frame with, initially, the same fabric or coachbuilt saloon bodies as the Minor. The prototypes were said to have reached 75mph (120km/h), but production cars reached their limit at around 60mph (97km/h). This was still a good performance for the price, for the Hornet sold for £175, less than a Morris Cowley saloon. The Hornet's engine was important not only for Wolseley, for it was the basis of all the ohc 6-cylinder MGs, starting with the F-type Magna. An open version was soon offered, and the Hornet chassis was supplied to outside coachbuilders who built a variety of sporting bodies. Among the better-known firms who clothed the Hornet were Abbey, Lancefield, Salmons and Swallow. Production of the original Hornet (1930–32) was 6943 cars. From 1932 to 1935 Wolseley supplied a sporting chassis called the Hornet Special. This had the same size of engine and an unmodified chassis, but twin carburettors and high compression pistons gave 45bhp, ten more than standard, and a top speed around 75mph (120km/h). Production of the Hornet Special chassis was 2307 between 1932 and 1934, and 148 of the Special 14 with 1604cc engine in 1935. Most coachbuilders made sports or drophead bodies, but there were a few saloons by Maltby and others, especially on the Special 14 chassis.

Inevitably customers and dealers began to ask for a 4-door Hornet. This was not possible with the existing chassis, so for 1933 the engine was shortened by replacing the shaft drive for the camshaft with a chain, and placing the dynamo alongside the crankcase rather than vertically at the front. The engine was then moved forward in the chassis, making room for a spacious 4-door saloon body 84in (2134mm) long on an unchanged wheelbase of 90in (2286mm). The frame was unchanged and the combination of softer springs and the additional weight at the front made for poor handling. This has caused the Hornet to be castigated by historians, though it sold well at the time, far better than the original model, with 19,723 finding buyers between 1932 and 1935. Synchromesh came in 1933, and 1934 Hornets had a freewheel. The final development of the Hornet saloon was made from 1935–36. It had a slightly larger engine of 1378cc and Easi-clean spoked wheels in place of wire spokes. 2565 were made.

In 1934 Wolseley introduced a 4-cylinder companion for the Hornet called the Nine. This had a 1018cc 3-bearing engine in the same wheelbase, and carried a saloon body similar to the Hornets, though with a vestigial luggage boot. 7201 were made before it gave way in 1935 to the Wasp. This had a larger engine of 1069cc and the general appearance of the last Hornets with Easi-clean wheels. Production was 5815 in 1935 and 1936. From 1933 all Wolseleys had the illuminated radiator badge which characterised the marque until the end of production.

Badge Engineering Takes Over

The last of the ohc Wolseleys were the Fourteen and Eighteen of 1935–6, undistinguished saloons with 1604 and 2299cc engines. The NF Fourteen of 1936 had Easi-clean wheels and looked like an enlarged late Hornet. A new range of Wolseleys appeared for 1936, known like their Morris counterparts as the Series II. They eventually included seven models, from the 1292cc 10/40 to the 3485cc

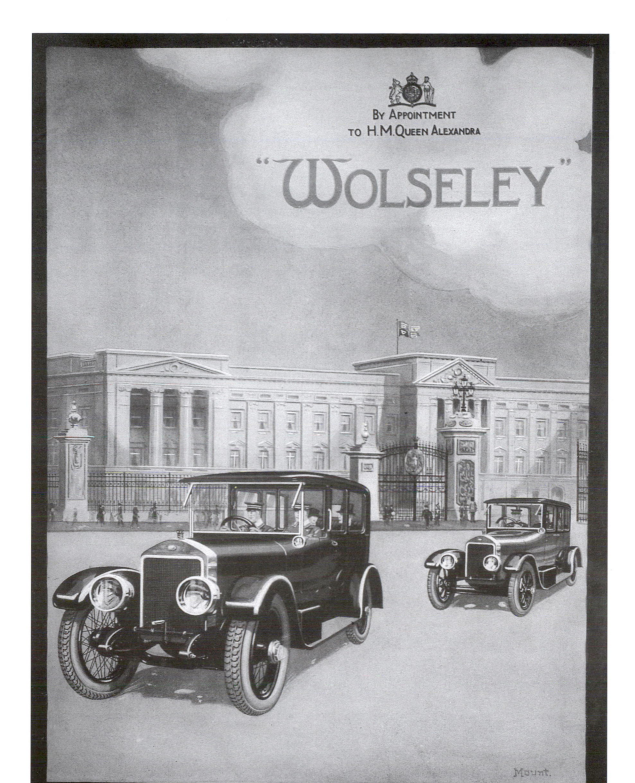

1955 Wolseley 6/90 saloon.
NICK BALDWIN

Twenty Five, all with common styling which was shared with Morris. They differed from their Cowley counterparts in having pushrod ohv engines, 4-speed gearboxes and Easi-clean wheels, though Morris gained ohv for 1938 and Easi-clean wheels on some 1937 and all 1938 models. Although the Wolseley bodies shared styling with those of Morris, they were made at Ward End, while Morris bodies came from Pressed Steel at Cowley. Some body styles were unique to Wolseley, such as the upright saloon called the Salon de Ville on the 14/56, 18/80 and 25hp chassis, and the long-wheelbase 25hp limousine. The Series II Wolseleys saw the company's peak prewar production, with more than 15,000 cars delivered annually from 1936 to 1938. The 14/56 became very popular with Britain's police forces, following a tradition started with the NF Fourteen, which was continued into the 1960s.

The 1938 season saw the Series III, with more upright saloon bodies and engines mounted further forward. The first to receive this styling was the 1547cc 12/48, and the Super Six range, 16, 21 and 25hp. A year later came the intermediate 6-cylinder range, the 14/60, 16/65 (which replaced the unsuccessful Super Six 16), and the 18/85. The new bodies were all-steel made by Fisher & Ludlow of Birmingham, and there was not the variety of styles seen on the Series II. Most chassis offered 4-door saloons only, but on the 25hp there was a drophead coupé and a long-wheelbase limousine. The last prewar model, which could be considered as part of the Series III range though it was never called such, was the 1939 Ten. This had a Series M Morris Ten engine of 1140cc but a separate body, whereas the Morris was of unitary construction. The Wolseley Ten was made as a saloon or drophead coupé, and about 5260 were made before war halted production. An Eight based on the Series E Morris Eight was scheduled to be launched on 11 September 1939, but the outbreak of war eight days earlier delayed its introduction for more than six years.

Wolseley was one of the first British companies to get back into production after the war, thanks to a government order for 18/85s, delivery of which began in September 1945. These were followed by Tens, Twelves and Fourteens, and in March 1946, the delayed Eight. This had a Series E Morris chassis and body, an ohv version of the 918cc engine and a Wolseley grill. It was a refined small car and sold 5344 units between 1946 and 1948. Lord Nuffield, as William Morris had become in 1934, used one up to 1955. The other Wolseleys were similar to their prewar versions, though there were no more dropheads on the Ten, and the 25 was made only as a long-wheelbase limousine. Postwar production of this

was 75 cars. Of the others, 2715 Tens were made, around 3800 12/48s, 4000 14/60s and 5600 18/85s. All these models were replaced at the 1948 Earls Court Show by the 4/50 and 6/80, essentially Wolseley versions of the Morris Oxford and Six. The 4/50 was the more individual in that it had a single-ohc version of the Morris MO engine, while the Morris Six already had an ohc engine, so Wolseley's version was not very different, apart from the radiator, twin carburettors and an abundance of wood and leather inside. Only 19 6/80s were made at Ward End before all Wolseley production was transferred to the Morris factory at Cowley on 1 January 1949. By the time it was replaced in 1954, 24,886 6/80s had been made, more than twice as many as the Morris Six. In contrast, 4/50 production was much smaller, only 8955 between 1948 and 1952.

The successors to the 4/50 and 6/80 were the 4/44 and 6/90. The former had a 1250cc engine as used in the MG Y saloon, and a new saloon body which shared some panels with the MG ZA Magnette which was announced a year later. They were designed by Gerald Palmer who had come from Jowett where he had been responsible for the Javelin. Coil ifs replaced the torsion bars of the 4/50. 29,845 were made before it was replaced by the 15/50 in 1956. This had the same body shell but the engine was a 1489cc BMC B-series unit as used in the MG Magnette. 12,353 of these were made, all with floor change and a few with Manumatic 2-pedal drive. The 6/90 had similar styling to the 4/44, with a 2639cc BMC C-series engine, and was essentially the same car as the Riley 2.6 of 1957. The 6/90 was made from 1954 to 1959, the Series II of 1956–57 having semi-elliptic in place of coil rear springs, and the Series III of 1957–59 having a larger rear window, lower gearing and servo brakes. Production of the three series was 6556, 1024 and 5052 respectively.

1957 saw the Wolseley 1500, an extended Morris Minor with four doors and a 1489cc B-series engine. The Minor's excellent suspension and steering gave good handling, but drivers who wanted high-performance went for its twin-carburettor sister the Riley 1.5. A few 1500s were made with the old 1200cc Austin A40 engine, but these were sold only in the Irish Republic. The 1500 stayed in production until 1965, by which time 100,832 had been made, the largest figure for any Wolseley model.

Wolseley's version of the Farina-styled saloon was the 15-60, sharing a body with the Austin Cambridge, Morris Oxford, MG Magnette and Riley 4/68. Production was 24,759 of the 1489cc 15-60 and 63,082 of the 1622cc 16-60, the latter being made up to 1971. There was also a Wolseley version of the Austin Westminster and Vanden Plas Princess with 2912cc 6-cylinder engine and optional automatic transmission. It was known as the 6-99 from 1959–61, and with more powerful engine as the 6-110 from 1961 to 1968. Power steering and air conditioning were available from July 1962, and four speeds instead of three from March 1964. Total production was 37,209.

The remaining Wolseleys were even more closely linked with other BMC models. The Hornet (1961–69) was a Mini with the small boot shared with the Riley Elf and, of course, a Wolseley grill, while the 1100/1300 were variants on the ADO 16 theme, and the 18/85 revived a proud old title for a Wolseley-radiatored Austin 1800. The Six used the same body shell with an ohc 2297cc 6-cylinder engine derived from the Austin Maxi, and was a sister of the Austin and Morris 2200s. The last car to bear the Wolseley name was a version of the wedge-shaped 18/22 series, which used the same 2227cc engine as the Six in the new body shell. Announced in March 1975, it lasted only six months, with 3800 being made, before the 18/22 series were all renamed Princess for 1976.

NG

Further Reading
Wolseley, St John Nixon, G.T. Foulis, 1949.
The Wolseley, Nick Baldwin, Shire Publications, 1995.

WOLSELEY (ii) (AUS) 1960–1966
British Motor Corp. Australia, Zetland, New South Wales.
As Frederick York Wolseley had pursued the development of the sheep shearing machine in Australia in the nineteenth century, it is fitting that unique Wolseley models were made in Australia.

When the Farina-line Oxbridge appeared, the 15/60 differed by having a larger bore engine of 1622cc and 15in wheels. The 1962 24/80 remained in a rationalised range with the AUSTIN Freeway, both being powered by the Australian-only Blue Streak 6-cylinder engine of 2433cc giving 80bhp. This B-series based unit was named after a British rocket then being tested at the Woomera test range. Although the 1800 replaced the Freeway, the Wolseley 24/80 remained available until the following year.

MG

WOLVERINE (i) (US) 1904–1906
1904–1905 Reid Manufacturing Co., Detroit, Michigan.
1905–1906 Wolverine Automobile Co., Dundee, Michigan.
1906 Wolverine Auto & Commercial Vehicle Co., Dundee, Michigan.
The Wolverine was made in 2- and 4-cylinder models, like countless other cars of the period. It was unusual in that the twin was on a longer wheelbase (88in/2233mm) and had a larger engine (18/20hp) than the 15hp four on an 82in (2081mm) wheelbase. Both had conventional gearboxes and shaft drive. In 1906 a 40hp four was added, and the smaller Wolverines were both twins.

NG

WOLVERINE (ii) (US) 1917–1920
Wolverine Motors, Inc., Kalamazoo, Michigan.
Despite the fact that Wolverine Motors, Inc remained a viable corporation – at least on paper – for four years, its total production was limited to two known cars and possibly a third. The company was formed to produce high powered sporting automobiles and this is what it did. The first Wolverine was a roadster powered by a Wisconsin 4-cylinder engine; the second, a touring car with a Rochester-Duesenberg four. The third car, which may not have been completed, was a sedan believed to have sported a Kalamazoo badge on its radiator rather than that of Wolverine. Both known cars, and presumably the third, carried wire wheels. Albert H. Collins who formed the Wolverine company later formed the COLLINET company on Long Island where he exhibited a 2-seaer sporting car which, although badged as a Collinet, appears identical to the Wolverine roadster and might well have been the same car updated only by badge engineering. Either way, the car never got into actual production.

KM

WOLVERINE (iii) (US) 1927–1928
Reo Motor Car Co., Lansing, Michigan.
Although the Wolverine was ostensibly a cheaper companion car to the Reo Flying Cloud, it existed during its two year production as a make of its own. In this regard it carried its individual radiator design plus a badge and hubcaps identifying it as

1966 Wolseley 6/110 MkII saloon.
NICK BALDWIN

1975 Wolseley Six saloon.
NICK BALDWIN

a Wolverine rather than a model of Reo. Unlike Reo's Flying Cloud, the Wolverine was basically an assembled car and was fitted with a Continental 6-cylinder 15E L-head engine and featured a wheelbase of 114in (2893mm). For its first year and into its second, the Wolverine was available as a 5-seater brougham at $1185. A cabriolet and sedan augmented this in 1928 but the Wolverine was discontinued later that year.

KM

WOOD (i) (NZ) 1901–1903
Tourist Cycle & Motor Works, Timaru, South Island.
A pioneer New Zealand motor builder, Cecil W. Wood, at first experimented with chemical fuels. It seems that his first application of power was to a cycle-type machine and a 2hp belt-driven motor-tricycle was made in 1901. In 1902 an 8hp oil-engined 2-seater was reported, and this was followed in 1903 by a 4hp voiturette, which had stylish bodywork, 2-speed transmission and was claimed to be capable of 15mph (24km/h).

MG

WOOD (ii) *see* WOOD-LOCO

WOODBURN (US) 1905–1912
Woodburn Auto Co., Woodburn, Indiana.
This firm made cars, trucks and tractors in very small numbers, for local customers only. Most of the cars were high-wheelers, but the last Woodburn had a front-mounted 4-cylinder engine. About 12 cars were made in all.

NG

WOODILL (US) 1952–1956
Woodill Motors, Downey, California.
Woodill was started by B.R. 'Woody' Woodill, a successful Dodge and Willys dealer who wanted a sports car to add to his line. He had Bill Tritt at GLASSPAR design and build a fibreglass body similar to the Glasspar G-1 kit car body. It was assembled over a modified Willys chassis with a 6-cylinder engine in an effort to

c.1911 Woods electric coupé.
BRYAN K. GOODMAN

interest Willys in building it. They declined and Woodill put the new Wildfire into production in 1952, making it the first fibreglass-bodied production car in America. They substituted a simple ladder frame with 1939 to 1941 Ford suspension. Most early cars had Ford V8 or Willys 6-cylinder engines, but the buyer could stipulate any engine he wanted. In 1953 an improved Wildfire was introduced, with a new design by Tritt. This was a very attractive car and more practical, with added interior room. They could be ordered in kit form or completely assembled with all new Ford parts. Woodill was a tireless promoter and Wildfires appeared in several movies including *Johnny Dark* and *Knock on Wood*. Woodill fell victim to the improved 1956 Corvette and Thunderbird, and closed in 1956.

HP

WOODLAND (US) 1909

Woodland Motor Car Co., Cleveland, Ohio.
Called alternatively the Woodland 30 or Woodland Special, this was a 5-seater tourer powered by a 3-cylinder 2-stroke engine. For their date they were advanced in having doors to the front seats as well as to the rear. The bodies were made by the Patterson Body Co. of Cleveland. Only four cars were made, which sold to Cleveland residents for $2300 each.

NG

WOOD-LOCO; WOOD (ii) (US) 1901–1903

1901–1902 Wood-Loco Vehicle Co., Cohoes, New York.
1903 Wood Vapor Vehicle Co., Brooklyn, New York.
Joseph C. Wood built two models of steam car under the name Wood-Loco, a 2-seater runabout and a delivery van, though a 5-seater *dos-à-dos* was also mentioned. They had 8hp 2-cylinder engines mounted horizontally under the seat, and either petrol or paraffin fuel could be used. Production was very limited, and in early 1903 Wood moved to Brooklyn where he set up another company. His product there was more modern, with a De Dion-Bouton-type bonnet under which the 8hp 3-cylinder engine was mounted, with the boiler under the frame. It was offered for 1903 only, at a price of $450. Wood made delivery vans for two more years.

NG

WOODROW (GB) 1913–1915

Woodrow & Co. Ltd, Stockport, Cheshire.
The Woodrow cyclecar began life with an 964cc 8hp air- or water-cooled V-twin JAP engine, with 3-speed gearbox and chain drive to a rear axle equipped with a differential. The 1915 model had a 1090cc water-cooled V-twin Precision engine and shaft drive. A sports model had a sharply pointed vee-radiator and an exceptionally long bonnet for a 2-cylinder car. One of these survives.

NG

WOODRUFF (US) 1902–1904

Woodruff Automobile Co., Akron, Ohio.
The first products of this company were very light 2-seaters, powered by rear-mounted single-cylinder horizontal engines, 4.5hp in the Runabout and 6hp in the Stanhope. The Runabout was sprung by long semi-elliptic leaf springs on each side, in the manner of the Curved Dash Oldsmobile, and had tiller steering. The Stanhope had transverse full-elliptic springs and wheel steering. In 1904 a larger car with front-mounted 30hp 3-cylinder engine, chain drive and a rear-entrance tonneau body was made. Not more than six of these were built, out of total production of 30 Woodruffs.

NG

WOODS (US) 1899–1918

Woods Motor Vehicle Co., Chicago, Illinois.
The Woods was one of the most important and long-lived of American electric cars. The company was set up with the massive capital of $10 million by Chicago and Toronto financiers to challenge the market dominance of the Electric Vehicle Co. of Hartford, Connecticut. They hired Clinton E. Woods, who had been involved with electric cars since 1897 as a designer. He was appointed works superintendent in 1899, but was soon eased out, and returned to making cars under his own name. This caused some confusion, with quite similar electric cars being made under the name Woods and Clinton E. Woods, but in 1901 Clinton E. gave up manufacturing altogether and became a dealer. This left the field clear for a reconstituted Woods Motor Vehicle Co.

The first Woods was a high phaeton with the driver in a hansom cab position behind the passengers, unequal wheels and solid tyres. Only six cars were made in 1899, and by 1901 the Woods had become more up-to-date, though still quite high. The Mail Phaeton had wheels almost equal in size, and was tiller steered from the front seat. By 1903 a wide range of styles was offered, 16 in all, from a Road Wagon at $925 to a Victoria Hansom Cab with the driver perched high above the body, at $3110. The 1904 models, of which there were 14 varieties, were lower and included a rear-entrance tonneau with a frontal bonnet which made it look just like a petrol car. In 1905–07 Woods actually made some petrol cars, with 40hp 4-cylinder engines and touring or limousine bodies. They were more expensive than the electrics, with prices as high as $5500 for the limousine. In the three seasons, 255 petrol cars were made and 1850 electrics.

After 1907 Woods made more limited range of typical electric cars, mostly the 'china closet' type of coupé, with drive from the front or rear seats. When the popularity of the electric car began to wane around 1915, they turned to a petrol-electric which they called the Woods Dual Power. It had a 4-cylinder petrol engine of Woods' own manufacture as an auxiliary to the electric motor. At speeds below 15mph (24km/h) the car was driven entirely by the electric motor, then the petrol one took over for speeds up to the maximum of 35mph (56km/h). Though more rudimentary, it anticipated the Toyota Prius by more than 80 years. At 110in (2792mm) the wheelbase was longer than any of the pure electrics, which were discontinued after 1916. In June 1917 a new Dual Power coupé was announced, with an even longer wheelbase of 124in (3147mm), and a 12hp 4-cylinder Continental engine instead of Woods' own. Problems were clearly encountered with the earlier Dual Power, because the company spent a lot of time and money in repairs under warranty on the 1916–17 models. They received orders for 1300 of the Continental-powered cars, but could only made 628 because of the previous season's losses. They did not survive into 1919. There were plans to revive the idea in 1924 by the makers of the BALBOA car, but no more than a prototype was built.

NG

WOODS MOBILETTE (US) 1913–1916

Woods Mobilette Co., Harvey, Illinois.
Promoted as America's first cyclecar, the Woods Mobilette was built in prototype form in 1910, which justified the claim, although they were not built for sale until the autumn of 1913. Though the prototypes were air-cooled, the first production cars had 12hp water-cooled 4-cylinder engines, shaft drive and tandem seating. 1916 models had staggered side by side seating, with optional electric lighting and starting. These were standard on the models announced for 1917, but production ceased before the end of 1916. The $380 price tag was maintained throughout the life of the Woods Mobilette, which was made in larger numbers than most cyclecars. At their peak in August 1914 they claimed to be making 1000 cars a month, but this output did not last long.

NG

WOODY WORKS (US) c.1985

Woody Works, San Francisco, California.

The California Beach Wagon was a rebodied VW Beetle with a nose that resembled a 1940 Ford and a 'woody' back end. This was a wood-panelled station wagon style tail. It was sold in kit form.

HP

WOOLER (GB) 1919–1921

Wooler Engineering Co. Ltd, Alperton, Middlesex.

John Wooler was well-known for his motorcycles, which were built by no fewer than ten different companies between 1911 and 1955. In February 1919 he announced an unconventional cyclecar called the Wooler Mule. It was powered by a 1020cc horizontally-opposed air-cooled twin, with triple belt drive to the countershaft which provided three forward speeds, and shaft drive from the countershaft to a worm gear rear axle. The rear wheels were mounted so close together that the Mule was often referred to as a 3-wheeler. Each cylinder had a single rotary valve which served for inlet and exhaust, and was fed from a surface carburettor. In contrast to these primitive features, it had ifs by coil springs. The 1922 *Motor Car Index* said that the car was 'not proceeded with, only one or two experimental models being produced'.

NG

WORLDMOBILE (US) 1927–1928

Service-Relay Motor Corp., Lima, Ohio.

In 1926 it was announced that the Worldmobile Co. of Cleveland, Ohio, would be making a new car powered by a 4525cc straight-8 Lycoming engine, with a complete line of open and closed bodies on a 133in (3376mm) wheelbase. In the event probably no more than one car was made. It was built, or at any rate backed, by the Service-Relay Corp., a recently-formed group which brought together several truck makers, including Garford, Commerce, and Service. It had a rather angular 6-seater sedan body, and survives today.

NG

WORLD PRODUCTS (US) c.1967

World Products, San Fernando, California.

The Viking was a simple rebody kit for the Volkswagen Beetle chassis. It was a low-built sports car with two seats and step-over sides instead of doors. The one-piece body bolted onto the VW floorpan. Price was an inexpensive $395 in 1967.

HP

WORTH (US) 1906–1910

1906–1907 Worth Motor Car Manufacturing Co., Evansville, Indiana.
1907–1910 Worth Motor Car Manufacturing Co., Kankakee, Illinois.

William O. Worth designed a high-wheeler with air-cooled 2-cylinder engine and double-chain drive, a few examples of which were built by Willis Copeland of the SINGLE CENTER Buggy Co. He was not happy for Copeland to suggest improvements, so he set up his own company. A few were made in Evansville before a move to Kankakee where he made a more car-like design with smaller wheels and a doorless 4-seater body, though the 22.5hp 2-cylinder engine was retained. He was bankrupt in October 1910.

NG

WORTHINGTON-BOLLÉE (F/US) 1904–1905

Worthington Automobile Co., New York, New York.

C.C. Worthington built BERG and sold METEOR (v) cars, and also imported a Bollée design, with the intention of manufacturing the cars in the US, though this probably never came about. They were said to be made by LÉON BOLLÉE, but a published photograph shows a bonnet and radiator much closer to the AMÉDÉE BOLLÉE design. This is confusing as both brothers were making cars in Le Mans at the same time. Worthington said that he would be making steam and electric cars as well, but these never appeared.

NG

WORTHINGTON RUNABOUT (GB) 1909–1912

Worthington Bros, Hythe, Kent.

This was a very light car powered originally by an 8hp flat-twin engine made by the Worthington brothers, but this was replaced by a 8/9hp V-twin JAP. Transversely-

1915 Woods Mobilette 12hp roadster.
NATIONAL MOTOR MUSEUM

1919 Wooler Mule 3-wheeler.
NICK BALDWIN

mounted, the engine drove by two chains to a countershaft, with final drive by belt. It was planned to sell the car for £90, but the company wasted money on experiments with aircraft, and only the one Runabout was made.

NG

WRIGHT (i) (US) 1909–1910

Wright Motor Car Co., New Cumberland, Pennsylvania.

This company took its name from a local businessman, J.W. Wright, but it was the idea of Thomas F. Rodgers and Ernest F. Brennan, both from Corning, New York. The car was of very conventional design, using a 20hp 4-cylinder Waukesha engine and other bought-in parts. With a 130in (3299mm) wheelbase it was underpowered, and only six were made before the business closed down.

NG

WRIGHT (ii) (GB) 1921

Wright Engineering Works, Cheltenham, Gloucestershire.

This was a tiny cyclecar powered by a flat-twin Douglas engine, of 4hp in the prototype and 6hp in production models which sold for £150, though they were few in number. It had friction transmission and chain final drive.

NG

WRIGHT (iii) (CDN) 1929–1930

Wright Flexible Axle Motors Ltd, Montreal, Québec.

This company was formed to exploit the Wright-Fisher independent suspension design used in the American-built BIRMINGHAM and Canadian-built CANADIAN SIX. A huge factory was bought in Montreal East with a capacity

1765

1928 Worldmobile sedan.
NATIONAL MOTOR MUSEUM

for making 30,000 cars a year, and brochures printed showing attractive body styles. However, the only 'Wright' car to appear was a seven-year old Birmingham with a Wright badge on the radiator. Then James Wright had plans to make the design in the United States, and devote the Montreal plant to a $500 light car, but these came to nothing. In 1930 he announced that the American MARTIN (iv) baby car would be made in Montreal, but nothing came of that idea either.
NG

WRIGLEY (GB) 1913
Wrigley & Co. Ltd, Birmingham.
This company was a well-known manufacturer of axles and gearboxes, and their cyclecar was very much a sideline. It had a 7/9hp 2-cylinder engine in air- or water-cooled versions, and a 2-speed gearbox on the rear axle. In 1923 the Wrigley factory was bought by William Morris, and used for the manufacture of Morris-Commercial vans and trucks.
NG

W.S.C. (GB) 1907; 1912–1914
Wholesale Supply Co., Aberdeen.
This company sold a 3-wheeler in 1907, but did not offer a production car until 1912 when they advertised a cyclecar powered by an 8hp V-twin JAP engine, with friction transmission and final drive by belts. Like the cyclecar it was sold through the Wholesale Supply Co., but the actual makers are not known. They also made, or supplied, a few commercial vehicles based on Albion components.
NG

W.S.M. (GB) 1961–1967
1961–1965 Austin-Healey Centre, Swiss Cottage, London.
1965–1967 W.S.M., Leighton Buzzard, Bedfordshire.
Douglas Wilson-Spratt and Jim McManus joined forces to build an Austin-Healey Sprite-based coupé in 1961. It was intended for rallying but, with American finance, a production run followed in both race and road guises. An aerodynamic aluminium body surmounted the Sprite floorpan, though later cars had fibreglass bonnets (or indeed all-fibreglass bodies). Some 24 examples were built in all. Other W.S.M. projects included rebodied versions of the Austin-Healey 3000, MG 1100 and MGB GT but none of these ever reached production.
CR

WUGONG (CHI) 1998
Wugong Auto Refit Works, Wuhan City, Hubei Province.
This very small factory specialized in pick-ups and station wagons. A small 4-seat motor car and station wagon called the Wugong WGG 6430 was built.
EVIS

WULING (CHI) 1991–1998
Liuzhou Small Auto Works, Liuzhou City, Guangxi Province.
In 1991 this minivan factory, producing Mitsubishi minivans, pick-ups and minibuses, introduced a small motor car called the Wuling LZW 7100. About 1000 were made. The 147in (3725mm) long car was powered by a 376Q Xiali 993cc 3-cylinder engine, developing 47bhp. Surprisingly the car had a CITROËN Visa body.
EVIS

WUNDERLICH (D) 1902
Motorenfabrik Carl Wunderlich, Berlin.
This was a short-lived voiturette powered by a 2-cylinder proprietary engine.
HON

W.W. (GB) 1913–1914
Winter & Co., Wandsworth, London.
The W.W. (Winter of Wandsworth) was a light car which used an 8hp V-twin Precision engine, with Chater-Lea gearbox and shaft drive to an overhead worm rear axle. For 1914 they changed the specification towards the cyclecar theme, with a V-twin Blumfield engine, friction transmission and belt final drive. This model was known as the Winter rather than the W.W.
NG

WYETH (US) 1912–1913
Wyeth Motor Car Co., Waltham, Massachusetts.
The Wyeth had a large single-cylinder engine with dimensions of 114.3×152.4mm (1563cc) which developed 13bhp. This was mounted as a single unit with the 2-speed epicyclic transmission and rear axle. Runabout and delivery van models were offered, at around $500, but few were made.
NG

WYNER (A) 1903–1908
1903–1907 Michael A. Wyner, Vienna.
1907–1908 Wyner, Huber & Reich, Vienna.
Michael Wyner built several types of car with friction transmission and single, 2- or 4-cylinder engines.
   The singles and twins were of De Dion-Bouton manufacture. Wyner also sold other makes of car, in the last two years in partnership with two other men.
HON

WYSS see BERNA

WYVERN (i) (GB) 1913–1914
Wyvern Light Car Co. Ltd, Twickenham, Middlesex.
Although made in the middle of the cyclecar era, the Wyvern was more of a light car, with 10.5hp 4-cylinder Chapuis-Dornier engine, 3-speed gearbox, and shaft drive. Its 2-seater body was fronted by a vee-radiator in Métallurgique style.
NG

WYVERN (ii) (GB) 1983–1986
1985–1986 J.C. Composites, Kingstone, Herefordshire.
1986 Hawk Associates, Hereford.
The unusual thing about the Wyvern kit car was its choice of Vauxhall Viva/Firenza mechanicals. This was a traditional style 2+2 open tourer with a self-coloured fibreglass body, mounted on a primed steel chassis. A Ford Escort Mk2 based version appeared in 1985 but the following year the project passed on to a firm called Hawk, which could not keep the Wyvern afloat.
CR

XANTHOS (GB) 1990 to date

1990–c.1993 South West Replicas, Dunchideock, Devon.
c.1993–1995 South West Replicas, Sidbury, Devon.
1995 to date Xanthos Sports Cars, Colyton, Devon.
The makers of the Xanthos Type 90 were Lotus restorers, and went to extraordinary lengths to duplicate the classic racing Lotus 23. This even included wonderful replica 'wobbly' wheels and almost exactly reproduced suspension. The space frame chassis was beautifully made, while the mid-mounted engine could be any Ford crossflow unit or a Lotus twin cam, driving through a VW or Hewland transaxle. Much of the componentry was specially made, with a racing slant. The 4-piece fibreglass body was very accurate indeed. Over 40 cars had been made by 1998.
CR

XENIA (US) 1914

Hawkins Cyclecar Co., Xenia, Ohio.
This cyclecar was designed by Paul Hawkins of Cleveland, and built in the workshops of the Baldner Motor Vehicle Co., where the BALDNER car had been made from 1900 to 1903. It had a 9/13hp 2-cylinder De Luxe engine, epicyclic transmission, belt drive and a narrow body that seated two in tandem. In August 1914 25 cars were said to be under construction, but the company was out of business by October, so those 25 may have been the total of Xenias made.
NG

XIALI (CHI) 1986 to date

1986–1987 Tianjin Auto Works, Tianjin Municipality.
1987 to date Tianjin Small Auto Works, Tianjin Municipality.
In 1968 the TIANJIN TJ 740 was the first motor car this factory made. The DAIHATSU licence production in Tianjin started in 1984 with the assembly of mini-vans, mini pick-ups and minibuses. The Daihatsu Charade 1000 (second series, G100) was trial-produced by the Tianjin factory in 1986. A year later, the Tianjin-Dafa Xiali TJ 730 hatchback was the first serial produced Chinese Charade (it was the third generation Charade, made in Japan from 1987–1997). This car used the 993cc 3-cylinder engine, also licence-produced in Tianjin. In 1990 the TJ 7100 succeeded the TJ 730. The TJ 7100U, a booted-version, appeared in 1991. In 1997 the front and rear end were refreshed, the new version being called the TJ 7100A/TJ 7100UA. Experiments with Daihatsu 1.3-litre engines were followed by the use of a serial licence-produced Toyota 1.3-litre 16-valve engine in a version called the TJ 7131AU. At the end of the 1990s the yearly production was over 100,000 units.
EVIS

XIANJIN (CHI) 1958

Chongqing Xinjian Machinery Works, Chongqing Municipality.
In June 1958, during the industrialisation period of the Great Leap Forward, the Xianjin ('Advanced') 71 was developed. With dual headlamps and plunging bonnet its was rather bulky looking. The car was a 6-seater, with a 6-cylinder engine. Though serial production was planned, none were made after the first prototype.
EVIS

XIMA (CHI) 1991

Fengtai District Xima Auto Refit Works, Beijing Municipality.
A 3870 mm long small saloon named Xima XM 5020 was made in the early 1990s in a Beijing suburb. The Xima works belonged to the People's Liberation Army. In 1991 500 units of a 797cc minicar were made; the XM 5020. It was based on the standard HUAXING model, and had a strong resemblance to the Toyota Starlet of the day.
EVIS

XINKAI (CHI) 1994

Xinkai Auto Corp. Ltd, Gaobeidian City, Hebei Province.
This company made Beijing BJ 212-based jeeps. They produced a Suzuki Alto copy of their own, probably assembled from parts made elsewhere in China. The car was called the Xinkai HXK 6360.
EVIS

c.1990 Xiali TJ7 100 saloon.
ERIK VAN INGEN SCHENAU

c.1998 Xiali TJ7 131 saloon.
ERIK VAN INGEN SCHENAU

XINXIANG (CHI) 1993

Xinxiang Bus Works, Xinxiang City, Henan Province.
Xinxiang Bus Works produced medium sized buses (23–41 seaters) from the 1970s, at the rate of 100–250 units per year. The Xinxiang XKC 6370 sedan was sold for Y51,500, at the bottom of the Chinese market. It was a 797cc 5-seater, 5-door hatchback, with a length of 152in (3870mm). Only a few of these Chinese-powered (Dong'an engine) XKC 6370 cars were made.
EVIS

XK-1 (US) 1981–c.1985

Western Front Inc, Texas.
The XK-1 3-wheeler was developed with help from fellow trike-maker Quincy-Lynn. Its styling was squarish, with Bond Bug-type headlamps and a Bond Bug-type canopy for access to two seats. The windscreen came from the Honda Civic, the steering column from the Toyota Celica and the rear suspension from a Datsun. The engine choice ranged from a 16bhp Briggs & Stratton industrial motor up to a VW Beetle, mounted in the rear and driving through a Salisbury torque converter. You could buy a chassis from Western Front or one from Quincy-Lynn, or even build your own to a set of plans. A complete kit, including the fibreglass body, came in at $1695.
CR

XR-GT (GB) 1996–1997

Easybuild Projects, Auchterarder, Perthshire.
The idea of rebodying a Ford Fiesta XR2 was not without merit but the efforts of this company left much to be desired. A bulbous-looking fibreglass body was grafted on to a Fiesta steel shell.
CR

1922 Xtra 2¾hp 3-wheeler.
NICK BALDWIN

XTRA (GB) 1922–1924

Xtra Cars Ltd, Chertsey, Surrey.

Described by *The Light Car & Cyclecar* as 'resembling a motorcycle sidecar on three wheels', the Xtra began life as a monocar powered by a 2¾hp single-cylinder Villiers 2-stroke engine, which drove the rear wheel by a 2-speed friction system, in which the driven member drove the wheel rim. There was no chassis frame, as mechanical items such as the engine, transmission, brakes, and rear suspension were all mounted within tubular metal forks. These forks were supplied by Accles & Pollock, while the bodies came from Webber Brothers of London. The Xtra was priced at 95 guineas (£99.75). Xtra Cars was set up in September 1921, and production was under way by May 1922. A side by side 2-seater was added in November 1922, in which month a monocar was driven from Chertsey to Geneva to deliver it to a Swiss customer. The 2-seater was offered with the choice of single-cylinder Villiers or V-twin JAP engines, the latter being priced at 117 guineas (£122.85). Prices were considerably reduced in 1924, the 2-seater costing only 75 guineas (£78.75). Xtra Cars went into voluntary liquidation in May 1924.

NG

Further Reading
'Xtra, Xtra…', M. Worthington-Williams, *The Automobile*, January 1999.

YAK (i) (GB) 1969–1970

Grantura Plastics Ltd, Blackpool, Lancashire.

This was a light open 4-seater car of Mini Moke-type, although the body was of fibreglass rather than steel. The chassis was tubular and it was supplied in kit form. About 150 Yaks were made, of which 30 were exported to holiday resorts. The makers also made a fibreglass coupé with some resemblance to the contemporary T.V.R.

NG

YAK (ii) (GB) 1979

Manchester Garages Ltd (Yak Vehicles), Gorston, Manchester.

The impetus for the Yak Yeoman was to create a utility vehicle that could be easily assembled by developing countries. It used a multi-tube bolted steel chassis clothed with flat aluminium panels that could be interchanged. A Ford Escort 1.3-litre engine was used in conjunction with a Ford 4-speed gearbox driving through a 2-speed transfer box. Coil-sprung MacPherson struts up front were complimented by a leaf-sprung live rear axle. The Yak never secured a production run.

CR

YAKOVLEV FREZE (R) 1896

E.A. Yakovlev Works, St Petersburg.

Displayed at the 1896 Industrial Exhibition at Nijny-Novgorod, this was almost certainly the first car to be made in Russia, though there is some doubt about its originality. It bore a close resemblance to a Benz, though its single-cylinder engine was quoted as being of 2hp, which was smaller than that used in the contemporary Benz Victoria, and the car looked too heavy to be a Benz Velo. It had belt primary drive and chain final drive. Claimed top speed was 13mph (21km/h), and for winter use the front wheels could be replaced by skis, and the rear ones fitted with toothed chains.

NG

YALE (i) (US) 1902–1905

1902–1903 Kirk Manufacturing Co., Toledo, Ohio.
1903–1905 Consolidated Manufacturing Co., Toledo, Ohio.

The bicycle-making Kirk Manufacturing Co. announced that they would make cars in 1899, but nothing appeared until 1902. Then they brought out a light car with 10hp 2-cylinder engine, epicyclic transmission and single-chain drive. It was a 2-seater with a detachable tonneau giving a further two seats, the whole selling for $1500. The same car was listed for 1903 and 1904, when quoted power had risen to 16hp. In October 1903 the Kirk company merged with two other Toledo cycle firms to form the Consolidated Manufacturing Co. They moved into a larger size and price bracket with a 24/28hp 4-cylinder car for 1905. The 5-seater tourer rode on a 104in (2640mm) wheelbase, and cost $2500. For 1906 they announced that a 32hp four would be their only model, but in December 1905 they said that there would be no 1906 Yales at all, as they were too busy making bicycles. The Yale's slogan was 'The Beau Brummell of the Road'.

NG

YALE (ii) (US) 1916–1918

Saginaw Motor Car Co., Saginaw, Michigan.

This car had a link with the M.P.M. made at Mount Pleasant, Michigan, as both were designed by Louis J. Lampke. Whereas his former car was made as a four and a V8, the Yale was only offered as a V8, on a 126in (3198mm) wheelbase. A 7-seater tourer was the only body style initially, and was priced at $1350. For 1917–18 a 2-seater roadster and a 3-seater speedster were offered, and closed models were promised, though they were probably never built. Prices rose to $1550 for 1917 and $1885 in January 1918; this was a bad sign as there were no improvements in the cars, and the Yale was discontinued in March 1918. The factory was taken over by the Nelson Brothers for the manufacture of the Jumbo truck.

NG

YALTA see ZAZ

YAMAHA (J) 1992–1993

Yamaha Motor Co. Ltd, Shizuoka-Ken.

Although Yamaha is a world-famous name for its motorbikes, the Japanese giant had strong connections with the automotive industry: most notably it developed

1969 Yak (i) Mini-based utility runabout.
NICK GEORGANO

1896 Yakovlev Freze 2-seater.
NICK BALDWIN

1902 Yale (i) Model A 10hp tonneau.
NATIONAL MOTOR MUSEUM

1992 Yamaha OX99-11 coupé.
NICK BALDWIN

and manufactured engines for Ford and Toyota. It presented a single-seater 50cc microcar prototype called the PTX-1 at the 1983 Tokyo Motor Show but this was never intended for production. Instead Yamaha looked like it might become a supercar manufacturer with the highly dramatic OX99-II. The centrepiece was its engine, a 3.5-litre V12 engine taken directly from Formula 1, where Brabham and Jordan used the unit. The 400bhp engine mounted directly to the carbon-fibre/aluminium monocoque chassis and drove through a 6-speed transmission. The dramatic coupé body was hand-formed in aluminium, and featured a tandem 2-seater layout. Much publicity was afforded the prototype in 1992, with Yamaha saying that production was due to begin in 1993 or 1994 at a British subsidiary of Yamaha's, Ypsilon Technology Ltd of Milton Keynes. But the OX99-II was a victim of the downturn in supercar fortunes in the early 1990s and no customer cars were ever made.

CR

YAMATA (J) 1916
Probably the first Japanese 3-wheeler, the Yamata was built in Osaka and had a single rear wheel.

NG

YANASE (J) 1964–1965
Yanase Co. Ltd, Tokyo.
Yanase was the Japanese Volkswagen importer, and it decided to offer its own coupé based on the Volkswagen 1200. Called the YX 1200 Sports Coupé, it featured cowled front and rear lamps and a transparent roof. Several examples were built.

CR

YANK (US) 1950
Custom Auto Works, San Diego, California.
The Yank was an inexpensive sports car with a Willys 4-cylinder engine. It had an aluminium body and was intended to sell for $1000.

HP

YANKEE (US) 1910
Yankee Motor Car Co., Chicago, Illinois.
This company offered a high-wheeler powered by a 16hp air-cooled 2-cylinder engine, with 2-speed epicyclic transmission. Unlike many high-wheelers, the Yankee

had a bonnet and front-mounted engine. The High Wheel Buggy rode on solid tyres, and the Racy Roadster, which was otherwise similar, sported pneumatic tyres. Both were priced at $500, and neither outlasted the year of their introduction.

NG

YANKEE CLIPPER (US) 1953–1954
Strassberger Motors Inc., Menlo Park, California.
This sports car used a GLASSPAR fibreglass body on a ladder frame with 110hp Ford V8 running gear. They were sold in fully-assembled form with all-new parts. The interior was upholstered in plastic and a hard-top was optional.

HP

YARIAN (US) 1925
Yarian Motors Corp., Syracuse, New York.
James L. Yarian was the chief engineer of a team of six designers and engineers hired by H.H. Franklin to develop a lower-priced companion car to the existing line of the Model 9B 6-cylinder Franklin. The new car, listed as the Model Z, was to feature an air-cooled 4-cylinder engine, with quality components and workmanship throughout, which could be sold for less than $1000. The development and construction of the car was replete with pitfalls and related problems and, although the prototype was shown to Franklin dealers during a luncheon at New York City's Hotel Commodore on 11 January 1922, it was found that such a car could not be sold at so low a figure, whereupon H.H. Franklin ended further plans for the Model Z, disassembled machinery used in its development and fired Yarian and his staff. Yarian decided to build his own car, using the discarded Model Z sedan as his basic design, price the car below $1000 and name the car for himself. Yarian formed Yarian Motors Corp., capitalised at $33 million and laid the groundwork for a successful new air-cooled car. Success never came. One open prototype was completed and very possibly a sedan; good-looking cars but not realistically in line to be world-beaters. Much of the reason for this was in the price range of the Yarian. Yarian had hoped to offer a sedan at $1000 or lower but this he could not do, its listed price being $1395. The touring car would cost $975 and an anticipated 6-cylinder series would run from $1250 to $1650. The Yarian received accolades from a number of those who rode in the automotive milieu. Yarian needed more than testimonials to get his car into the marketplace. This he did not have and the name of Yarian is all but forgotten today.

KM

YAXA (CH) 1912–1914
Charles Baehni & Cie, Acacias, Geneva.
Charles Baehni (born 1870) had been working with Charles-Éduard HENRIOD in Neuilly, Paris and from 1908 was technical director of MARTINI. In 1912 he founded his own company and without even bothering to build a prototype, he immediately started serial production with 50 chassis of his new light car. He named it Yaxa, derived from the French phrase 'Il n'y a que ça' (the only one). A 12hp Zürcher, St Aubin (ZEDEL) proprietory 4-cylinder monobloc side-valve engine of 1691cc was fitted. The modern-looking torpedo was available as a 2- or 4-seater and was one of the first to have a gear lever and handbrake arranged centrally in the car. The 4-seater tourer sold at SFr7000. The Yaxa was displayed at the 1913 Olympia Show in London and was well received. In Switzerland, Yaxa were successfully entered in local competitions. A total of about 100 cars were made before the company had to close down owing to the outbreak of World War I.
FH

Y.E.C. (GB) 1906–1908
Yorkshire Engine Co., Sheffield, Yorkshire.
This company was a major builder of steam locomotives from the middle of the 19th century. In particular, the Fairley engine was exported to many countries. In 1878 they made a steam tram for trials in Sheffield. In 1906 the British & Colonial Mercedes-Daimler Syndicate ordered 50 examples of a car to be called the Y.E.C. which was in fact a copy of the current 30hp chain-drive Mercedes. They paid royalties to Mercedes on these 50 chassis, but for some reason baulked at continuing royalty payments on future orders. The venture ended when Mercedes Daimler threatened legal action, and no more examples of the Y.E.C. were made.
NG

YEMA (CHI) 1995
Mianyang Yema Auto Ltd, Mianyang City, Sichuan Province.
The Yema SQJ 6400 was based on a Chang'an Alto platform, but used the 997cc Xiali 376 QB engine. Price was Y63,000 for the good-looking hatchback.
EVIS

YEMINGZHU (CHI) 1989 to date
Tianyu Auto Joint Corp., Chengdu City, Sichuan Province.
The Yemingzhu ('Pearl') YMX 5010 X was introduced in 1989. This ugly looking saloon was powered by a small 4-cylinder 800cc engine. There was a pick-up version called the YMX 1010. A somewhat bigger 4-door saloon was introduced in 1997, using a 869cc 4-cylinder engine developing 52hp, delivering a maximum speed of 83mph (134 km/h). The engine used natural gas as fuel.
EVIS

YE OLDE CLASSIC TOURING CAR CO. (US) c.1971
Ye Olde Classic Touring Car Co., Woodridge, Illinois.
The Targlia Mk II was a Bugatti T35 replica with a steel tube frame set up for front-mounted engines. Leaf springs were used at both ends and a tubular axle was used at the front. It was sold in kit form.
HP

YETI (I) 1968–1975
1968–1971 Delta SpA, Turin.
1971–1975 S.A.M.A.S., Ricca d'Alba (CU); Samas di Charlie Fratelli, Ricca d'Alba.
This was a compact all-terrain vehicle with very basic open bodywork. It was powered by a 42bhp 850cc (later 47bhp 903cc) Fiat engine and had 4-wheel drive and 4-wheel steering.
CR

YIMIN (CHI) 1986–1993
State Operated Yimin Machinery Works, Rongchang District, Chongqing Municipality.
A good-looking 4-seater minicar was made by the Beifan (China North Industries) works in Chongqing Municipality. In 1986 the prototype was introduced as the Yimin SC 720. The production version, the Yimin YM 7060 used a Liuzhou-built 2-cylinder engine of 644cc. Production plans for 1991 were 1000 units, but in 1993 only 84 were made.
EVIS

1912 Yaxa 12CV tourer.
ERNEST SCHMID

1907 Y.E.C. 30hp chassis.
SHEFFIELD CITY ARCHIVES

1960 Yimkin Clubman's sports car, Don Sim at the wheel.
NATIONAL MOTOR MUSEUM

YIMKIN (GB) 1958–1960
Yimkin Engineering appeared in the late 1950s as a tuning outfit which specialised in BMC A and B-series units. In 1958, Yimkin (Arabic for 'quickly') made a clubman's car with a spaceframe, coil spring and double wishbone front suspension, a well-located live rear axle, and a skimpy body with cycle mudguards. About six were made; most were used on both road and track, and they enjoyed sufficient success in racing for a couple more to be built for Formula Junior.

Yimkin folded when both partners married – the business could support two bachelors, but not two families. One of the partners, Don Sim, later bounced back with the DIVA GT.
MJL

1997 Y.K.C. Roadster SR sports car.
Y.K.C. ENGINEERING

1905 York (i) 18/20hp tourer.
MICHAEL WORTHINGTON-WILLIAMS

YITUO (CHI) 1991–1994
First Tractor Works Auto Sub-Works, Luoyang City, Henan Province.
The Yituo ('First Tractor') LT 5022 saloon and LT 5021 estate car were made from 1991 by the famous old tractor factory in Luoyang. The Yituo and smaller DONGFANGHONG (ii) were introduced together. The saloon was clearly inspired by the Polski Fiat, a very popular car in China in the 1980s. The engine was a 1520cc 4-cylinder ohc type made by the Beijing Internal Combustion Engine Factory, delivering 64bhp. Luoyang sold the cars for Y50,000– Y60,000, which was very cheap in comparison with the original Polski Fiat.
EVIS

Y.K.C. (GB) 1992 to date
Y.K.C. Engineering Ltd, Elvington, York.
Previously a kit car build-up concern and MARLIN agent, in 1992 Y.K.C. took over two Marlin kit-built models, the Roadster and Berlinetta. Before long it was developing its own variations on the theme, all based on Ford Sierra running gear in place of the original scheme (such as the Berlinetta's Ford Cortina basis). The 1997 Romero boasted an Alfa-style grill and De Dion rear suspension, while the Mille Miglia had more fully-flowing wings and was intended more for racing. The Raider, a mix of Marlin and hot rod styling realised in aluminium, used rocker-arm front suspension and again was ideally suited as a dual-purpose road/ race machine.
CR

YLN (RC) 1953–1997
1953–1960 Yue Loong Engineering Co. Ltd, Taipei.
1960–1997 Yue Loong Motor Co. Ltd, Taipei.
The first car manufacturer to be set up in Taiwan, Yue Loong made an agreement with the NISSAN Motor Co. whereby various models of Datsun would be assembled in Taiwan. The content of the car was approximately 60 per cent locally-made and 40 per cent purchased from Japan. Among the more popular models in the Yue Loong range were those based on the Datsun Bluebird, Cedric, Sunny, and Violet, while YLN also assembled some CONY light cars and commercials in the 1960s, and also Jeeps from the mid–1960s onwards. There were minor styling differences between the Taiwanese and Japanese products, and also different names. Thus,

in 1984, the YLN 311SD was the Nissan Sunny, the 721 the Nissan Stanza 1600 and the 807GX the Nissan Cedric bodyshell with 2.4-litre 6-cylinder engine.
In 1986 YLN built their first car with more independent styling. The Feeling 101 was based on a Nissan Stanza platform with single-ohc 1600 and 1800 engines. This became the Feeling 102 in 1991, which, in 1993 gave way to the JingBing of similar appearance. At this time a revised Chinese orthography led to the make being re-named Yulon in European spelling. In the spring of 1994 a booted 4-door version of the Nissan Micra joined the JingBing, while the Nissan Sunny estate was sold as the AD-Resort. These models were made until 1997 when the Yulon marque was dropped, and all models were badged as Nissans.
NG

YORK (i) (US) 1905
York Automobile Co., York, Pennsylvania.
The York was a 4-seater tonneau powered by an 18/20hp 4-cylinder engine located under a meat-safe bonnet with mesh on three sides. It was built by Albert Broomell, who had designed the 6-wheeled PULLMAN (i) in 1903, and Samuel E. Baily, president of the York Carriage Co. After pilot models of the York had been made, Broomell reverted to the Pullman name, and as such the marque lasted until 1917.
NG
Further Reading
History of the York Pullman, William H. Shank,
The Historical Society of York County, 1970.

YORK (ii) (D) 1922
York Motoren AG, Plauen.
This small company attempted to establish itself as a car maker with a cyclecar powered by a V-twin engine. Output was minimal.
HON

YORK (iii) (GB) 1980s
The York 427 was a fully-built A.C. Cobra 427 replica produced in the early 1980s.
CR

Y&T (J) 1994–c.1996
Conceived by a computer software company called Y&T Associates, the Sport Tottini was an unusual rebodying exercise on the Mini Moke. The 2-seater fibreglass body transformation was undertaken by Mooncraft and featured an Austin-Healey Sprite style grill, enclosed rear wheels and a long rear deck.
CR

YUE LOONG, YULON see YLN

YUGO see ZASTAVA

YUNQUE (CHI) 1993 to date
Guizhou Aero Space Industry Corp., Anshun City, Guizhou Province.
The Ministry of Aero Space Industry started car production in the aircraft factory in Guizhou province in 1993. The Yunque ('Skylark') GHK 7060 was a licence-produced 544cc SUBARU Rex, made in Japan from 1981–1987. In 1994 the much newer 658cc Subaru Vivio was assembled as the GHK 7070. Production numbers were very low, as there were a lot of start-up problems. From 1994 the Yunque GHK 7080 (also sold as the HUAXING YM 6390) was made in small quantities, and the GHK 7100 test model appeared in the same year. New efforts to raise production started with the introduction of the GHK 7060A in 1998, a minicar somewhat larger than the original GHK 7060. But even at the end of 1999, car production was on a very small scale in Guizhou; about 2000 units per year were made.
EVIS

YUZHOU (CHI) 1993
Yuzhou General Auto Works, Chongqing Municipality.
Originally named Chongqing Auto General Repair Works, the company started to produce the Yuzhou range of crew-cab pick-up trucks in the early 1980s. In 1993 the Yuzhou YZ 6490 station wagon was introduced, which resembled contemporary OPEL Omega and HOLDEN cars.
EVIS

1936 Z (ii) 6 saloon.
MARIAN SUMAN-HREBLAY

Z (i) (I) 1914–1915
Zambon & Cia, Turin.

Designed by Giuseppe Cravero who had been responsible for the FLORIO, the Z was a conventional tourer powered by a 3610cc side-valve monobloc 4-cylinder engine. A sports model was planned but its development was frustrated by the outbreak of World War I.

NG

Z (ii) (CS) 1924–1936
Ceskoslovenska Zbrojovka, a.s., Brno.

'Z' inside a rifled bore is a trademark of one of Czechoslovakia's successful small sports cars with 2-stroke 2-cylinder engines. Ceskoslovenska Zbrojovka (Czech Arms Factory, later Zbrojovka) was established in 1919 in Brno, capital of Moravia, and formerly supplied arms to the Czech military. In 1924 they began to produce small cars named Disk (designed by Bretislav Novotny, 1892–1965) which were later reconstructed and built by Aero in Prague.

In 1925 the type Z 4-18hp was designed by a young Frantisek Mackrle (1900–1985), and powered by a 1004cc 18bhp 2-cylinder engine, capable of 53mph (85km/h). The basic 4-door phaeton cost 34,600 Kc and until 1930 there were 1510 cars, bodied also as 3-seater roadsters and sedans (and 1000 delivery vehicles) produced. In 1928 F. Mackrle went to Skoda Works in Plzen, and a new chief engineer Vladimir Soucek (1898–1967) designed in 1930 the Z 9 type with 993cc 22bhp rotary sv engine. Until 1932 only about 850 cars were sold, priced 42,000 Kc. Of them 500 had a 4-door sedan body taken over from the Praga Piccolo.

In 1933 a new era bgan at Zbrojovka: they started to produce a front-wheel drive car, designed by Borivoj Odstrcil and Josef Ullman. It was the Z 4 type (1st and 2nd series, 1933–34, 905cc, 19bhp, 50–56mph (80–90km/h), 22,000–23,500 Kc; 3rd–5th series, 1934–36, 980cc, 25bhp, 62mph (100km/h), 24,000–26,600 Kc) of which 2680 cars with 2-door bodies were built. At the 1934 Czechoslovak 1000 Mile races five Z 4 cars with streamlined aluminium body started.

The Z 4 was really a successful car but Zbrojovka wanted to enter the then popular 1.5-litre category. Their Z 5 Express was the first type having a 4-cylinder engine and hydraulic brakes. Its output was 40bhp from a 1470cc capacity and a top speed was 78mph (125km/h). From 1935 to 1936 357 cars, priced at 37,500 Kc for a 2-door version, left the factory. Some cabriolets were bodied at Plachy in Brno.

1927 Z (ii) 4 light car.
NATIONAL MOTOR MUSEUM

1935 Z (ii) 5 Express saloon.
NATIONAL MOTOR MUSEUM

1975 Zagato Zele electric coupé.

NICK BALDWIN

The last Z cars were the Z 6, again with 2-cylinder engine (1935–36, 735cc, 19bhp) called Hurvinek after the then popular puppet character. About 480 were sold, for 19,800 Kc.

The sports and racing versions of all types won many races and rallies.

On 15 October 1936, passenger car production was stopped, and Zbrojovka changed direction, to supply the army with rifles and light machine guns. During World War II gun production was moved to Uherske Hradiste, and after 1945 in Brno agricultural tractors were built under the name Zetor.

MSH

Further Reading
Automobil 'Z', Jan Popelka, Auto Album Archiv, Brno, 1988.

ZAGATO (I) 1966 to date
Zagato Car srl, Terrazzano di Rho, Milan.
This eminent and highly distinctive name is best known for its coachbuilt bodywork, a tradition that spans back to 1919. However, Zagato also manufactured several models of its own. One of these was a 1929–33 Alfa Romeo 6C 1750 replica, commissioned by Alfa Romeo on an idea from *Quattroruote* magazine in 1966. The Gran Sport was very faithful to the original design but used modern Giulia 1600 TI mechanicals. In just over one year, some 82 examples were built.

Perhaps more significant was the Zele, a tiny electric-powered car first shown at the Geneva Motor Show of 1972, though it did not reach production until 1974. Only 77ins (195cm) long, the Zele was a tall fibreglass-bodied 2-seater. The front suspension was independent but at the rear there was a solid axle, on to which was mounted a Marelli 1kW (1.34bhp) electric motor, powered by four 24-volt batteries. Weighing just over half a ton (550kg), the Zele 1000 was capable of 25mph (40km/h) and could run up to 43 miles (70km). The more powerful Zele 2000 could reach 38mph (60km/h). Sold by Elcar in the USA and by Bristol in Britain, production was running at a healthy 225 examples for 1975. A long-wheelbase version arrived in 1976 as well as a nitrogen-powered experimental example. By popular demand from the USA, a doorless golfing version was also developed. In 1977, Zagato showed a prototype for its replacement Zele, with squarer, more modern lines. By the time it reached production in 1981, it was much bigger and so did not directly replace the Zele: it was called the Nuova Zele and sold alongside the old model, which was made into the 1990s. The Nuova Zele featured all-independent suspension and seating for four.

Zagato concentrated more on its coachbuilding business again, building such cars as the Aston Martin Zagato, the Autech Nissan Stelvio and the Alfa Romeo SZ. One further design that was badged as a Zagato was the 1992 Hyena, a coupé based on Lancia Integrale Evolution components. With sponsorship from the Dutch Ferrari importer (the Zagato Europe offices were then based in Duiven in Holland), the Hyena remains current at the time of writing.

CR

ZANELLA (I) 1966–1970

Zanella Fratelli, Parma.

This Parma based Fiat concessionaire produced the Erina, a tiny vintage-style 2-seater roadster, resembling the prewar Fiat Ballila. It was based on the mechanical components of the Fiat 500. It measured only 117in (2970mm) long.

CR

ZARA (US) c.1991

Zara Motor Co., Sacramento, California.

The Zara was an exotic mid-engined sports car with American components. It used a sturdy space frame with fabricated A-arm suspension and a roll cage surrounding the interior. There were several engine options, ranging from 5700cc to 8300cc Chevrolet V8s. The drive system was a novel design using a standard Chevrolet transmission bolted directly to a differential with shortened drive shafts. This would have placed the rear axles too far back in the chassis, so these shafts had pulleys attached, which drove rubber belts to another set of axle shafts mounted 24in (609mm) further forward. The body was a clean, original coupé design with angular styling and a profusion of vents and strakes on the top and sides. The price was $85,000 in 1991.

HP

ZASTAVA (YU) 1954 to date

Zavodi Crveni Zastava, Kragujevac.

This company's name translates as Red Flag Works, and was set up in 1954 as Fiat's operation in Yugoslavia. However, the Kragujevac factory had been in business since 1853, making agricultural machinery and small arms. Their first Fiat products were the 1400 and 1900, followed by the 600 which became the most popular Zastava, and was made for 14 years after it went out of production in Italy. By 1962 a considerably extended factory was turning out 82,000 cars a year.

During the 1960s the Fiats 1100, 1300, 1500, 124, 125 and Polski-Fiat 125P were all made by Zastava. In 1971 came the Zastava 101, a slightly modified Fiat 128. This had a restyled rear panel, and later came in a hatchback version, which was never made in Turin. For 1983 Zastava brought out the Yugo 45, a 3-door hatchback based on the Fiat 127, but with different styling. A 5-door version of the 101 was available in 1984, and the 101 was still available in 1990 in 1100 or 1300cc forms. The 5-door model was renamed Skala. The Yugo 45 gained larger engines of 1100 or 1300cc, when it was known as the 55 and 65. From 1989 there was a cabriolet version. Also in 1989 came a new model, the Sana (or Florida in some markets) 5-door hatchback with Giugiaro-styled body and a choice of four engines from 1.1- to 1.6-litres.

In 1991–1992 the Serbo-Croat war and consequent embargo on imports of components and exports of complete cars hampered production very seriously. From over 100,000 in 1991 output dropped to 24,000 in 1992. Figures have not been published since then, but in June 1998 a *Wall Street Journal* correspondent reported that the 9000 workers were mostly idle, shortages making it almost impossible to complete a car. Then in the spring of 1999 NATO bombing almost totally destroyed the factory. Nevertheless, by August the Serbian government had pledged $800,000 towards reconstruction, though much more would be needed from outside sources before car manufacture could restart.

NG

ZAZ (SU) 1960 to date

Zaporozhkji Avtomobilnji Zavod, AO AvtoZAZ, Zaporoshje, Ukraine.

The Soviet people's car was born even before the Government decided where it was to be built. MZMA, NAMI Institute and two motorbike manufacturers in Irbit and in Serpukhov were all involved in the design stage. An outlandish Bjelka prototype of 1955 was put aside and a model, externally similar to the Fiat 600, the MZMA-444 with a 2-cylinder air-cooled engine was seen as the most suitable solution. For a while a flat-4 engine in the Volkswagen mould was favoured, but a production model, indexed as 965 got an expensive V4 of 752cc and 23bhp.

The car was built on a 80in (2024mm) wheelbase, but its length was only 130in (3305mm). Ground clearance of almost 8in (200mm) was just right for running through thick mud and snow on the USSR's secondary roads. As the tiny 4-seater was sent for production in Zaporoshje (Ukraine), it was numbered ZAZ-965 and acquired the name Zaporoshets (inhabitant of Zaporoshje). A former combine harvester works called Communard was hastily reconstructed and in

1981 Zastava Yugo 311 hatchback.
NATIONAL MOTOR MUSEUM

1991 Zastava Yugo Tempo hatchback.
NICK BALDWIN

1991 Zastava Sana hatchback.
ZASTAVA UK

1960 the car was really launched. In two years time a redesigned model 965A followed, its engine over-bored to 72mm, giving 887cc and 27bhp. Gearbox ratios were changed too, as was final drive: 4.63 instead of 5.12. The Soviet Topolino was economical and extremely easy to work on. Finally there was a car available which was financially within the reach of average wage earners. Nevertheless the car was the subject of endless jokes and everyone at the factory was interested in building a 'real one'. So, in 1966 came the model ZAZ-966, fitted with a 30 or 40bhp engine, with styling which was a mix of Corvair and NSU and included Ford Falcon's rear theme. Still cheaper than any other car available to the public in the USSR, it was suddenly in no-man's land. An export edition with a 1.1-litre water-cooled Renault engine, known as the YALTA, was exhibited at the Geneva Show in 1968.

Three models for the handicapped were added, a huge step upwards from Serpukhov's sad motor buggies, but the cars with electromagnetic clutches were

1961 ZAZ-965 saloon.
NICK BALDWIN

1981 ZAZ-968M saloon.
NICK BALDWIN

1990 ZAZ-1102 Tavria hatchback.
MARGUS H. KUUSE

desperately uneconomical. About the same time a 4×4 boxcar ZAZ-969 was created (71in (1800mm) wheelbase, 129in (3270mm) overall length), the model soon to be handed over to Lutsk Automobile Works. In 1973 the 30bhp model was discontinued and the range now included a 1198cc powerplant, with 8.4:1 cr and 45bhp available. It was called ZAZ-968A. New seats from VAZ were welcome, as were two brake circuits.

Five years later another updated model appeared, ZAZ-968M, with tidied up looks and its 1.2-litre engine giving now 42bhp even when running on 76 octane petrol. The car achieved 73mph (118km/h) and consumed 6.5 l/100 km at 56mph (90km/h).

The position of the Zaporoshets' overweight and still noisy small cars weakened significantly with the arrival of the first water cooled model ZAZ-1102 Tavria (in European languages Tauria means ancient Crimea, thus Avtoexport made a sad mistake not employing the right spelling from the start).

The Tavria was ready for production by 1987. A supermini which had the Ford Fiesta as a target in styling and packaging and was rather attractive in full-size clay, acquired a crude shape and detailing in production form. It showed a rather high drag coefficient 0.39 as well. That year 167,000 cars were made, a sharp contrast to the 1997 figure of 876 units.

Like the earlier air-cooled powerplants, its new 1091cc liquid-cooled unit was made at the Melitopol Motor Works (MeMZ). It developed 53bhp (with 9.5 cr). Front suspension was MacPherson and semi-independent at rear. It had rack-and-pinion steering, front disk brakes were used for the first time, and brake circuits were diagonally split.

In 1994 the air-cooled Zaporozhets was declared dead, but the works was now in a rather weird situation. The Korean DAEWOO company became interested in taking control of the ZAZ. They asked the Ukrainian Government to increase taxes on new cars as a condition for investing in ZAZ. At the same time they saw a chance to please the workforce, engineers and local bosses by continuing the Tavria, even though it made very low profits. In the meantime appeared a van, a pick-up, ZAZ-1105 Dana (5-door hatchback) and an estate car. Five-door models were longer by 5in (117mm) than the basic 3-door car.

Also readied for production was a rather unusual-looking ZAZ-1103 Slavuta, longer still by 6in/155mm (157in/3980mm), with a huge notched hatch at the rear. A new 1250cc MeMZ-310 engine of 60bhp was fuel injected and quite economical on petrol. The Tavria's successor was planned for 2005.

MHK

ZEALIA (GB) 1990s

Zealia Engineering, Cambridge.

This company made very up-market Jaguar E-Type Lightweight replicas using Jaguar XK engines, Getrag 5-speed transmissions, E-Type suspension and custom front brakes. The main bodyshell was a proprietary E-Type new shell with lightweight fibreglass bonnet, rear wings, tail, doors, bootlid and hard-top.

CR

ZEDDECO (F) 1905–1906

This was an electric car which used the Lohner-Porsche system involving two motors, one in each front wheel. It may, indeed, have been a Lohner-Porsche built under licence.

NG

ZÉDEL (F/CH) 1906–1923

1906–1923 Sté Française des Automobiles Zédel, Pontarlier, Doubs.
1907–1908 Fabrique de Moteurs et Machines Zédel, St Aubin, Neuchâtel.

The name Zédel came from the initials of two Swiss engineers, Ernest Zürcher (1865–1935) and Hermann Lüthi. In 1896 Zürcher made Switzerland's first motorcycle engines, and three years later he was joined by Lüthi. Together they opened a factory at St Aubin, trading as Zürcher & Lüthi. They supplied engines to a number of well-known motorcycle makers including Peugeot, Terrot, Alcyon and Minerva. In 1902 they opened a factory at Pontarlier, just across the border in France, which greatly increased their market, and avoided the payment of duty on engines sold to France. About 35 Swiss workers from St Aubin moved to Pontarlier, where the workforce rose to 250 by January 1906. In Pontarlier they began to make complete motorcycles, which lasted until about 1910, and in 1906 built their first car. This had a 1128cc 4-cylinder monobloc engine with 3-speed gearbox and shaft drive. It was followed by a 16/18hp in 1909, and by 1912 there were three 4-cylinder models, of which the largest was the 3563cc 18hp. Only 98 cars were made in 1907, but output rose to about 250 annually until 1912, when 452 were delivered. 4-speed gearboxes were adopted in 1910.

Ernest Zürcher left the French factory in 1907, when control passed to Swiss citizen Samuel Graf. He returned to St Aubin, and in a new factory began to make cars and motorcycles. The cars were made in two sizes, a 1128cc 8CV 2-seater and a 1692cc 10CV 4-seater tourer. They were made for only two years, though motorcycles lasted somewhat longer. Zürcher then set up two French branches, independent of the Société des Automobiles Zédel, one at La Ferrière, near Pontarlier, and one in the Paris suburb of Courbevoie in 1925, but these were solely for the manufacture of engines.

ZEDEL
A MODEL FRENCH CAR.

12 h.p. Doctor's Coupé - £375.

A VERY ECONOMICAL BUSINESS CAR. . . } 30 miles to the gallon.
Total weight of coupe: 15 cwt. (light on tyres).

"Sweet, Silent, Smooth, and Soothing is the travel of the Zedel."
"The Autocar," August 15th, 1908.

C. BERTRAND, Concessionnaire exclusive for Great Britain and Ireland and Colonies, 103, Long Acre, LONDON, W.C.

Telephone: 3431 Gerrard.   Telegraphic Address: "Zedel, London."

1906 Zédel 8hp 2-seater.
ERNEST SCHMID

1912 Zédel 14hp roadster.
NICK GEORGANO

1913 Zendik 8hp cyclecar.
NATIONAL MOTOR MUSEUM

Zédel production was resumed in 1919 with two 4-cylinder models, the 1846cc (later 2120cc) 10/12CV and the 2745cc (later 3160cc) 15CV. They had mostly tourer or saloon bodies, though there were some town cars. There was nothing remotely sporting about any Zédel, though Mme Barbier won the 1914 Tour de France in a 9/12CV 2-seater. Four-wheel brakes arrived on the 1923 15CV. Jérôme Donnet bought the Pontarlier works in 1923, and for 1924 the 10/12CV Zédel was rebadged DONNET-ZÉDEL. The 15CV was dropped.

NG

Further Reading
Franche-Comté, Berceau de l'Automobile, Raymond Dornier, Édition l'Est Republicain, 1987.

ZEILLER ET FOURNIER (F) 1920–c.1922

Automobiles Zeiller et Fournier, Levallois-Perret, Seine.
This was a borderline light car/cyclecar, for it was powered by a 1131cc 4-cylinder Ballot engine, yet used a 5-speed friction transmission and chain final drive. It was designed by Charles Fournier and was sometimes known as the Fournier, the cars bearing the radiator script Ch. Fournier. Certainly the cars with 2-cylinder Train engines were always known as Fourniers. Confusingly, a Ballot-engined car was advertised in July 1921 as a Zeiller by Voiturettes Zeiller of Colombes.

NG

ZELENSIS (B) 1958–1962

Designed by Raoul Thiébaut, the Zelensis Type 1 was a rakish open sports car style based on the floorpan of a VW Beetle. The bodywork was in self-coloured fibreglass and was available in 2- and 4-seater versions. Around 50 examples were built.

CR

ZENA (I) 1906–1908

Zena Fabbrica di Automobili SA, Genoa.
Though they lasted a short time, this company offered a wide range of cars, 6 and 8hp singles, 10 and 14hp fours, and a 20hp six, the N3. All had side-valve engines and shaft drive.

NG

ZENDER (D) 1985–c.1990

Zender, Idar-Oberstein.
Born in 1942, Hans-Albert Zender was an interior decorator whose debut in the car field came in 1967 or 1968 when he began supplying after-market styling kits. In the 1970s his favourite subjects were the Mercedes-Benz 190 and Volkswagen Golf and Jetta. His first car proper was the Vision 1 of 1985, a mid-engined coupé using Audi Quattro components. Like its successors, it was styled by Günter Zillner. The Vision 2, also Audi-powered, was built in coupé and cabriolet forms, one of each, and the Vision 3 of 1987 had a transversely-mounted 5.6-litre Mercedes-Benz V8 engine giving a top speed of 174mph (280km/h). In 1989 came the Fact 4 Biturbo, but although Zender hoped for a production run of 30–50 cars a year, they remained prototypes. However, they served as useful publicity for his main business of styling kits.

NG

ZENDIK (GB) 1913–1914

Zendik Cars Ltd, Kingston-on-Thames, Surrey.
The Zendik cyclecar was powered by an 8hp 2-cylinder Chater-Lea engine. It had a 2-speed gearbox with direct drive on top, and a chain reduction gear for bottom, while reverse was obtained by friction wheels. After this complicated transmission, final drive was relatively conventional, by shaft to an overhead worm rear axle. The frame was of armoured ash, and the price £110.

NG

ZÉNIA (F) 1913–1924

Automobiles Zénia, Paris.
The Zénia was launched with a 3-litre 4-cylinder T-head engine, but the postwar model, which was listed from 1922 to 1924, had a smaller engine of 1775cc. It was of conventional layout, and very few were made.

NG

ZÉNITH (F) 1910

M. Arnaud, Forcalquier.
The Zénith voiturette had an 8hp single-cylinder engine and friction transmission.

NG

ZENT (US) 1903–1906

1903 Single-Center Buggy Co., Evansville, Indiana.
1904–1906 Zent Automobile Manufacturing Co., Bellefontaine, Ohio.
Schuyler Zent's built his first car in Marion, Ohio, in 1900, but the production model was built for him by the Single-Center Buggy Co.. Known as the Zentmobile, it had an 8hp single-cylinder engine and epicyclic transmission. In 1904 Zent set up his own factory at Bellefontaine, Ohio, and made a larger car called simply the Zent. This was a tourer with 18hp 3-cylinder engine, and for 1906 it was joined by a 14hp twin and a 35hp four. Early in 1907 the company name was changed to Bellefontaine Automobile Co., and the cars were re-named TRAVELER.

NG

ZE-ONE (AUS) 1978–1979

Z.E. Designs, Sydney, New South Wales.
Introduced at the Sydney Motor Show, this clean line fibreglass sports coupé with retractable headlamps was built on a multi-tube frame. It was powered by a 5052cc Holden V8 engine, driving through a 4-speed gearbox to a precisely located

1987 Zender Vision 3 coupé.
NATIONAL MOTOR MUSEUM

coil sprung rear axle, while coils were also used on the ifs. Wheelbase was 95in (2400mm) and the weight was 2605lb (1184kg). Project directors were John Englaro, Harold Zeman and Dorian Zerial, who carried the project through its development phase but were unable to achieve production.

MG

ZEPHYR (GB) 1919–1920

James, Talbot & Davison Ltd, Lowestoft, Suffolk.

The three partners in this company had all worked for ADAMS (ii), and built a prototype of their Zephyr car in 1914. It made a public appearance at the Olympia Show in November 1919. Among its features was a 1945cc ohv 4-cylinder engine with aluminium alloy pistons designed by E. Talbot, made in unit with a 4-speed gearbox with central change. It had shaft drive to a worm rear axle, and a 4-seater tourer body with narrow pointed radiator. It was an advanced design, but two factors weighed against its success: its high price of £550 and problems with porosity in the engines. These were said to be Belgian-made (possibly Peters). Only four or five Zephyrs were made, but the aluminium pistons were supplied to a number of car makers, including Aston Martin. The company made fishing floats until after World War II.

NG

ZETA (i) (I) 1914–1915

Fratelli Zambelli, Piacenza.

The Zeta was offered with two sizes of 4-cylinder side-valve monobloc engine, 1131 and 1723cc, with 3- or 4-speed gearboxes.

NG

ZETA (ii) see LIGHTBURN

ZETGELETTE (D) 1923

Zetge Fahrzeug-Werk AG, Moys, Gorlitz.

This company made motorcycles under the name Zetge from 1912 to 1925, and towards the end of their life they launched a 3-wheeler. This was powered by a 3PS 2-stroke DKW engine, despite the fact that Zetge made their own engines for their motorcycles. However, at 500cc and up, these were too large for the tiny Zetgelette, which had belt drive from the engine to the single front wheel.

HON

1920 Zephyr 11.9hp tourer.
NICK BALDWIN

Z.E.V. (I) 1998 to date

Z.E.V. Srl, Poiana Maggiore (VI).

The Virgola electric microcar was first shown in 1996, with production starting in 1998. It was a compact 2-seater with 2-door bodywork made of fibreglass on a simple chassis with a single front wheel. Two direct current electric motors were mounted in the rear, powered by ten 6V lead–acid batteries and there was single-speed transmission by synchronous belts with the motors in direct drive. A top speed of 44mph (71km/h) was quoted, along with a maximum range of 75 miles. Keenly priced, it was scheduled to be 'the most accessible vehicle on the electric market'.

CR

ZÉVACO (F) 1922–1925

SA des Voiturettes et Cyclecars Eaubonne, Seine-et-Oise.

Although made in small numbers, the Zévaco cyclecar was offered with a variety of engines. The smallest was a 750cc 4-cylinder Lemaître et Gerard, followed by a 900cc Train twin, a 961cc Chapuis-Dornier and a 1095cc Ruby. The Lemaître et Gérard was supplied in unit with a 3-speed gearbox.

NG

1996 Zhonghua CHB 6401 TA estate car.
ERIK VAN INGEN SCHEINAU

ZHENGTIAN (CHI) 1995
Shijiazhuang Auto Corp., Ltd, Shijiazhuang City, Hebei Province.
The Zhengtian SQ 6400 minicar was a product of the Shijiazhuang Corp., a merger between two local car factories. The company also made 2 and 4WD cross country vehicles, chassis, light buses, pick-ups, and station wagons.
EvIS

ZHONGHUA (CHI) 1985 to date
1985–1989 Zhonghua Auto Industrial Corp., Shenzhen City, Guangdong Province.
1989 to date Zhonghua Auto Industrial Corp., Beijing Municipality.
Originally developed in Beijing, by the Jingjinji Corp., the Zhonghua (China) was taken into production in Shenzhen, a fast growing border city near the former frontier with Hong Kong. The Zhonghua BS111 was based upon a tube chassis, and the body was made of glassfibre-reinforced plastic. Because of this production technique it was very simple to make a wide range of models: 2-door, 4-door, hatchback, saloon, pick-up. Dong'an and Daihatsu engines were used, and later also Chinese made Xiali. After some years the director disappeared to the USA. The central safety authorities had a lot of problems with the car – it was, according to Beijing, 100 per cent unsafe. The government couldn't stop production, but it refused to licence the cars for street use. In 1989 the project stopped, but in 1995 serial production made an unexpected restart in Beijing. Two new basic models were developed: the Zhonghua CHB 7090A saloon (also produced as the CHS 5011 T taxi) and the Zhonghua CHB 604 TA. The vehicles were both nicknamed 'Solomon' and used the Xiali engine. Several other models were developed, but not produced: mini buses, a 'grandfathers car', and a saloon, known as the CHB 7090 B and also the QCJ 7090, powered by a Nissan 4-cylinder engine, and with an interesting Mercedes-style grill. In 1997 the factory produced 3800 cars.
EvIS

ZHONGLIAN (CHI) 1990–1996
Zhonglian Special Auto Works, Beijing Municipality.
Pick-ups, estate cars, and mini trucks were produced by this small Beijing factory. The Zhonglian WL 5010 XSD was a 5-door hatchback minicar with a 769cc engine, delivering 36bhp. It was sold as a 'speedy delivery van'.
EvIS

ZIEBELL (US) 1914
A.C. Ziebell, Oshkosh, Wisconsin.
The Ziebell cyclecar was powered by a 4-cylinder water-cooled Badger engine, and had a 2-speed epicyclic transmission, shaft drive and an underslung frame. Arthur Ziebell built it in the workshops of Termaat & Monahan for whom he worked as a draftsman, and who had made the TMF high-wheeler in 1909. He never formed a company, and the Ziebell was probably a one-off.
NG

ZIEGLER (AUS) 1905
J.A.C. Ziegler, Allansford, Victoria.
A capable engineer, usually maintaining and repairing the machinery found in that rural area, Johannes Ziegler also nurtured the notion of building steam vehicles. After several years of experimenting and making many parts himself, he showed his vehicle at Warrnambool in 1905. A substantial 6-seater touring car on solid-tyred wheels, it was powered by a 9hp 2-cylinder engine supplied with steam by a paraffin fired water-tube boiler. The spent steam was processed by a front-mounted condenser. Drive was by chain to a counter-shaft, with a differential, and chains to each rear wheel, while steering was by tiller. Claimed to be capable of 20mph (32km/h), it featured a rear-view mirror, mounted at the foot-board, to monitor the water level in the boiler located under the rear seat. Ziegler advertised that he was prepared to build cars to order, but there is no indication that any orders were received.
MG

ZIGCLAIR (GB) 1981
It is known that the first Zigclair was built in the early 1970s, with an MGB engine and Triumph suspension. By 1981 it was still hoped to put the car into production, but that never happened.
CR

ZIHAO (CHI) 1993
Xinhui Auto Works, Xinhui City, Guangdong Province.
A small 4-door saloon, the Zihao XHC 5010 X was made in Guangdong Province by a subsidiary of the Shaanxi Aircraft Auto Corp. The model was built in cooperation with Kia of South Korea.
EvIS

ZIL *see* ZIS; ZIL

ZIM (i) **(F)** 1922–1924
Automobiles Zimmermann, Épernay, Marne.
This was small even by cyclecar standards, with a 344cc single-cylinder Train engine, chain drive and single- or 2-seater bodies. Surprisingly, it had a 4-speed gearbox.
NG

ZIM (ii) *see* GAZ

ZIMMER (US) 1980 to date
Zimmer Motor Cars Corp., Pompano Beach, Florida.
The Zimmer was built by a company that also sold motorhomes, van conversions, boats and manufactured housing. Company president Paul Zimmer liked flamboyant cars and the Zimmer Golden Spirit fitted the bill. It was a neo-classic design with long flowing mudguards and side-mounted spare tyres. It was built from a Ford Mustang that was lengthened and reworked with a long bonnet and padded top. The Zimmer Quicksilver was announced in 1987. It was a very attractive Pontiac Fiero rebody styled by Don Johnson, who had worked on the General Motors design staff. It was a coupé with a short roof and heavy chrome bumpers at both ends. New Fieros were stretched 16in (406mm) and an extension was added behind the rear wheels for more luggage area. Ford Merkur power steering was added. The body was fibreglass and the interior was upholstered in leather. Zimmers were very expensive and were only sold in fully assembled form.
HP

ZIMMERMAN (US) 1908–1915
Zimmerman Manufacturing Co., Auburn, Indiana.
This company was a buggy builder which entered the car business in 1908 with a high-wheeler powered by a front-mounted 14hp 2-cylinder engine, with chain final drive. Two sizes were listed initially, a 14hp and a 16/18hp, the latter on a longer wheelbase which allowed for a 4-seater surrey body. These were made up to 1914, but the Zimmermans were wise enough to supplement the high-wheelers with a line of conventional cars from 1910. These had 35hp 4-cylinder engines, and were made for Zimmerman by the AUBURN Automobile Co. in the same town. For 1913 they announced a 5.4-litre 44hp six, which was the only model listed for 1915. A subsidiary company made the DESOTO (i), also a six. After the Zimmerman Manufacturing Co. closed down, one member of the family, John Zimmerman, made the UNION (v) in the same factory. The Auburns were sixes and the Unions fours. Both were Auburns in design, but the fours carried the Union nameplate.
NG

ZIP (US) 1913–1914
Zip Cyclecar Co., Davenport, Iowa.
This cyclecar was powered by a 10/14hp air-cooled V-twin Mack engine, with friction transmission and final drive by belt. The body seated two side by side, 'without in the least crowding the driver' said *The American Cyclecar*, which was more than could be said for some of the Zip's contemporaries.
The makers used a 16hp V4 engine later in 1914, but were bankrupt before the end of the year. Zip production totalled 123 units.
NG

ZIS; ZIL (SU) 1936 to date
1936–1958 Zavod Imjeni Stalina, Moscow.
1958 to date Zavod Imjeni Likhacheva, AMO ZIL, Moscow.
The first motor vehicles of Soviet Russia were Fiat-derived 1¹/₂-ton trucks AMO F-15 of 1924, built in Moscow. The AMO works were reconstructed in the early 1930s for building 25,000 3-ton and larger trucks per year. At that time there was no intention to produce a luxury car alongside the crude ZIS-5 truck (in 1933 the works was renamed after Josef Stalin). The Krasny Putilovets works in Leningrad was assigned that task in 1932 and actually seven long-wheelbase cars based on the BUICK 90 and called L-1 were completed by the summer of 1933. As there was a bitter rivalry between Leningrad and Moscow and their party leaders, it was logical that the project of building the flagship of the industry would be transferred someday to Moscow.

1981 Zimmer Golden Spirit coupé.
NICK BALDWIN

1988 Zimmer Quicksilver coupé.
ELLIOTT KAHN

1909 Zimmerman 14hp runabout.
NICK BALDWIN

1936 ZIS-101 limousine.
MARGUS H. KUUSE

1939 ZIS Sport roadster.
MARGUS H. KUUSE

1950 ZIS-110 limousine.
MARGUS H. KUUSE

1955 ZIS-110 convertible.
MARGUS H. KUUSE

The second reconstruction of AMO/ZIS set much higher, actually unreachable, goals – up to 80,000 trucks and 10,000 cars per annum. All the documentation and tools used for building the L-1 were sent to Moscow. Mechanically, the first Soviet limousine ZIS-101 was a successor to the L-1. The engine was bored and stroked to 5750cc and fitted with one Marvel updraft carburettor. Initially 90bhp were extracted, but later on, with a 3-jet domestic carb and aluminium pistons, an additional 20bhp were found. The rather stylish bodywork, was ordered from

Ambi-Budd in Germany. The dies cost a princely sum of $1.5 million and the bodies were built, as was usual in those days, over a wooden frame, secured with innumerable screws. The 7-seater limousines were long (226in/5736mm) and heavy 5610lb (2550kg) and consumed something like 25l/100km. Mechanically actuated drums employed a vacuum servo, but otherwise the car had no exotic features and was rather straightforward. The 1940 model ZIS-101A acquired a rounded grill and with a cr 6.4:1 there was 116bhp available. There was a phaeton-bodied model ZIS-102 in the range. A gargantuan 2-seater called ZIS Sport was built on the limousine's chassis. It featured an attractive Lincoln Zephyr-influenced frontal styling and a 6006cc engine with 141bhp on tap. This one-off reached 100.85mph (162.27km/h) over a flying kilometre. The production of the first generation limousines was stopped in the mid-summer of 1941. In about five years more than 8700 cars were manufactured, including a few phaetons and ambulances.

In 1942, after the first, sometimes hopeless stage of the Great Patriotic War (as it was called in the USSR), the Government gave an order to start work on the next generation of limousines. Mechanically the new ZIS-110 was based on a prewar PACKARD 180 148in (3765mm) wheelbase limousine. The full story of the origins of the ZIS-110 body has never been told and may never be known. It certainly had a close resemblance to the Packard, but was not identical, and the story that Packard dies were sent from Detroit to Moscow (either sold or given) does not stand up to examination. However, if ZIS had its own dies, they would surely have boasted about them, but Russian histories make no mention of large body dies until the appearance of the Pobieda a few years *after* the ZIS appeared. The USA was the only possible source of these dies; it is possible that some dimensions were identical to those of the 1941/42 Buick Series 90 Limited.

The frame was a massive 180×57mm section job with a X-type cross-member. The side-valve engine had a capacity of 6007cc and developed 140bhp. For this car alone – wonders of People's Economy – due to its exemplary 6.85:1 cr a special brand of high-octane petrol of 74 MON was developed. The ZIS-110 was 236in (5990mm) long, weighed 5665lb (2575kg) and consumed 27l/100km. Technical novelties included hydraulic tappets, hydraulic window lifts and hypoid rear axle. This 7-seater was built for various purposes, including an ambulance (with a rear hatch), ZIS-110A, and a phaeton, ZIS-110B. A number of cars served as taxis, including a shuttle service between Moscow and resorts on the Black Sea shore. Supposedly over 30 limousines were fitted with bulletproof bodies, serving Stalin himself, his notorious secret police chief, Lavrenti Beria, and such. Several sizeable sports cars were created, with some engines tuned up to 192bhp. Two 4WD prototypes were known to have been tested, bearing a transfer box from a 4WD truck, reinforced axles and tyres. Altogether over 2000 second-generation models were assembled; the last of those were completed in 1958, a couple of days after the works was renamed Zavod Imjeni Likhaceva, in honour of its late mercurial director Ivan Likhacev. The make was named ZIL.

The early 1950s were devoted to study and development of a V8 engine and an automatic transmission. The first new bodywork, modelled after the period Cadillacs, was not accepted and the second try was given to GAZ designer Lev Yeremeyev who used the late Packards theme, both in the ZIL-111 and in the GAZ-13 Chaika. When the Model 111 replaced its forerunner in 1958–1959, it became one of the rarest automobiles in the world, with its yearly production equalling the daily output of the ZIS-101. The 5.98-litre V8 engine had a cast-iron block and a 4-barrel carburettor. Its 2-speed automatic was a carbon copy of the Powerflite and there was a push-button control under the driver's left hand. The model 111A had the country's first air conditioning unit, the model 111V was fitted with a phaeton bodywork and an automatic soft-top. In the early 1960s the body was re-designed, with clear Cadillac overtones, especially in jewel grillwork and the quad headlamps theme. The rebodied ZIL-111G was stretched in length to 244in (6190mm), and it gained in weight as well. A phaeton-bodied ZIL-111D followed, a very rare car for parades and processions.

The fourth generation limousine was no direct imitation of any American luxury car, just featuring a rather timeless boxy styling and numerous innovations under its stately skin. The 7-litre engine's block was made of aluminium; with one 4-barrel carburettor 300bhp was available. Despite its weight and significant frontal area the car was good for 118mph (190km/h). Transistorised ignition, electric fuel pump, double ventilation and air conditioning, vacuum door locks, rearview mirrors with remote control, and electric windows were installed, as were a tilting steering wheel and fog lamps. A heavy duty generator and two 54Ah batteries were in charge of the heavy current demand.

1956 ZIL-111 limousine.
MARGUS H. KUUSE

Extremely strict quality control was employed, like running main components on dynamometer and special stands. Every assembled car went up to 2000km, and was then rechecked, repainted and polished before delivery. The first Soviet passenger car with 125mph (201km/h) top speed was a 5-seater saloon ZIL-117 of 1972. Wheelbase in this case was 130in (3300mm) against the limousine's 153in (3880mm) and overall length 225in/5720mm (248in/6300mm). Curb weight was just 6336lb (2880kg) against 6787lb (3085kg) of the ZIL-114. There followed a cabriolet ZIL-117V. Front suspension of the new generation ZILs used torsion bars, in 1967 four ventilated disc brakes were a real novelty. Two brands of domestic 8-ply tyres in size of 235-380 (9.35-15) were developed for ZIS alone – one of them being a studded type for icy roads.

By the 1980s the models were re-designed and given the designation ZIL-4104. The Model 41045 (1981) was a limousine, 41044 a cabriolet. The biggest change was a new ohc engine of 7695cc and a 3-speed automatic gearbox. On 245/70 HR 16 tyres, using all the power of four big discs, the braking distance was 40m from 50mph (80km/h). In 1988 a couple of prototypes were tested, fitted with irs and carbon body parts, but, with the financial deterioration of the USSR its automotive symbol was not financed properly anymore. Between 1990 and 1998 just 79 ZILs were built. The once secret cars became available to order, even for wealthy foreigners – but takers were few and far between. Curiously, from one car in 1995 and none in 1996, the figures rose to nine in 1997 and eight in 1998.

MHK

Further Reading
'ZIS. Packards with a Russian Accent', Griffiths Borgeson, *Special-Interest Autos*, February 1980.

ZITA (GB) 1971–1972

Zita, Langley, Buckinghamshire.
Chris Faulkener, Dick Weed and Tony Chappell were responsible for the handsome Zita ZS coupé. Its mechanical basis was VW Beetle, mounted in its own special chassis. At a projected price of £695, the Zita was ready for production in kit form but a personnel split scuppered those plans. A BMC 1800 powered version had been intended too, but in the end only two cars were ever made.

CR

Z MOTOR COMPANY (US) c.1992

Z Motor Co., Norwalk, California.
The Ponari was a Ferrari 308 replica built on the Pontiac Fiero chassis. It was an inexpensive kit and could be assembled at the factory on the buyer's car. Z Motor Co. also made a Ferrari Testarossa replica built on a Corvette body, called the Vetterossa.

HP

1981 ZIL-41045 limousine.
MARGUS H. KUUSE

1985 ZIL-41044 convertible.
MARGUS H. KUUSE

ZOË (J/USA) 1980s

Zoë Products Inc, Los Angeles, California.
This company offered a number of microcar designs, the most popular of which was the 1983 Zipper. This was co-developed in the USA and Japan and was a very small single-seater 3-wheeler (single rear wheel) with fibreglass bodywork in two styles, a single-door coupé or an open step-in type. It was propelled by a

1962 Zunder 1500 saloon.
NICK GEORGANO/NATIONAL MOTOR MUSEUM

1958 Zündapp Janus 250 saloon.
NICK GEORGANO

50cc moped engine up to a top speed of 45mph (72km/h). Zoë also imported the British Reliant Robin to the USA, adding such modifications as very wide wheel-arches and extended bumpers; it also imported Ligier microcars.

CR

Z-ROD (US) 1999 to date
Studio Joe, White Oak, Texas.
The Z-Rod was a wild street rod built out of a highly modified 1970 to 1981 Camaro Z-28. The Camaro was shortened and the doors cut down. The rear seats became the front seats and the front end was extended. A fibreglass nose section was available as well as a kit for extending the frame. A video was also sold that explained how to do the work.

HP

ZÜNDAPP (D) 1956–1958
Zündapp-Werke GmbH, Nuremberg; Munich.
One of the best-known makes of German motorcycles, Zündapp's first involvement with 4-wheelers came in 1931 when they built the first of Ferdinand Porsche's designs for a people's car (Volkswagen). It had a 1.2-litre air-cooled 5-cylinder radial engine, but was not produced commercially. Apart from a light van in 1934/35, Zündapp concentrated on motorcycles until 1956, when they took out a licence to build the Dornier Delta. This was an unusual microcar which seated four passengers in a *dos-à-dos* layout, with a door opening at the front and back, and a 248cc single-cylinder 2-stroke engine mounted between the two rows of seats. Their car was called the Janus, after the Roman god who faced both ways. The unsociable seating arrangements and a total lack of luggage space prevented it from becoming very popular, although about 6900 were sold before Zündapp returned exclusively to 2-wheeelers.HON

ZUNDER (RA) 1960–1962
Industrias del Transporte Automotor Srl, Rio Cuarto, Cordoba.
Nilson Jose Bongiovanni and Eligio Oscar Bongiovanni had created a successful racing car, before they decided to go to Europe and the USA to study car production. In Germany, they contacted Porsche, who agreed to supply the 1.5-litre air-cooled, flat-4 engine. The Zunder was a rear-engined, fibreglass-bodied 2-door, 5-passenger saloon, which resembled the contemporary Ford Anglia. A top speed of 87mph (140km/h) was claimed. Messrs. Bongiovanni planned to make 200 cars in 1960, increasing production yearly, and reaching a production of 1600 units in 1964. In fact, only 200 Zunders were made before the company folded in 1962.

ACT

c.1910 Züst 10hp Doctor's Landaulet.
NICK BALDWIN

ZÜST; BRIXIA-ZÜST (I) 1905–1917

1905–1911 Ing. Roberto Züst Fabbrica Italiana di Automobili SA, Milan.
1906–1911 Brixia-Züst SA, Brescia.
1912–1917 Fabbrica Automobili Züst, Brescia.

Always an Italian car, the Züst owed its Germanic-sounding name to a Swiss engineer, Roberto Züst who ran a steam engine business at Intra on Lake Maggiore. His five sons opened a branch in Milan, and experimental cars may have been made there around the turn of the century. The first production Züsts appeared in 1905; they were conventional cars on Mercedes lines, with 4-cylinder pair-cast engines, honeycomb radiators and chain drive. Though they had two camshafts the engines were not T-head but L-head; the second shaft merely actuated the make-and-break ignition. They were large and expensive cars, with capacities of 7.4-litres (28/45hp) and 11.3-litres (40/50hp). In 1908 they were joined by a smaller 5-litre car.

In 1906 a separate company was set up at Brescia to make much smaller cars. They were called Brixia-Züst (after the Latin name for Brescia), and came in 1386cc (10hp) 3-cylinder and 3770cc (14/18hp) 4-cylinder models, both with shaft drive. The 3-cylinder was made in taxi form and a number ran in London from 1910. By the end of 1906 Züst had branches in France, Britain and the United States. A 28/45 took part in the 1908 New York-Paris Race, finishing 3rd. The business was reorganised in 1912, after serious losses; the Milan factory was sold, and production concentrated at Brescia. The 10hp 3-cylinder and 14/18hp 4-cylinder were dropped, and for 1913 a new 25/35hp with 4712cc monobloc L-head engine and all brakes on the rear wheels was introduced. Known as the S305, this had a Fiat-like pear-shaped radiator, wire wheels and a top speed of 60mph)97km/h). A fine example competes regularly in VSCC events today. This and a 2.9-litre 15/25 of similar design were made up to 1917, when Züst was taken over by the Officine Meccaniche SA, a Brescia-based company which made

1913 Züst S305 25/35hp tourer.
NICK GEORGANO

railway locomotives. The S305 was continued under the O.M. name until 1923, but O.M. became famous for smaller cars.
NG

ZUTTER (CDN) 1993 to date

Zutter Electric Vehicles Inc, Bowen Island, British Columbia.
A prototype of the Zutter electric passenger car appeared at the 1993 Frankfurt Motor Show. It was subsequently redesigned in Europe during 1995, and the company launched the car in 1997 for a 1998 production run.
CR

1958 Zwickau P70 saloon.
NICK GEORGANO/NATIONAL MOTOR MUSEUM

ZWICKAU (DDR) 1956–1959

VEB Automobilwerk Zwickau, Zwickau.

The Zwickau P70 was the successor to the IFA F8, and used the same 684cc 2-cylinder 2-stroke engine and front-wheel drive. However, it had a totally new saloon body with fibreglass panels, being the first mass-produced German car to use fibreglass. An estate car joined the saloon in 1956 and a coupé in 1957. About 36,000 were made in all before it gave way to the P50 TRABANT.

HON

Glossary

A guide to some of the more frequently used technical and general terms which may not be familiar to the reader.

ALAM formula rating. *See* horsepower.

All-weather. In the immediate post-World War 1 period this name was applied to cars which could be opened to the elements, but which had comprehensive arrangements against wind and rain when they were closed. This would normally have included glass windows in metal frames, which either folded down into the doors or were stowed away in a special compartment. This was in contrast to a tourer, which had only a rudimentary hood and, possibly, canvas side-curtains which rolled down. The complexity and expense of these systems meant that all-weather bodies were confined to expensive chassis. In America such a design was known as a Springfield Top.

Automatic inlet valves (aiv). Inlet valves opened atmospherically, without any mechanical control. A primitive system, soon replaced by mechanical actuation (*see also* moiv).

Avant-train. A 2-wheeled power unit consisting of engine, gearbox, final drive, steering wheel, and other controls, which could be attached to a horse-drawn vehicle, or to enable various bodies to be used with the same engine. *Avant-train* units were the earliest examples of front-wheel drive, but were outmoded soon after 1900. Electric as well as petrol engines were used.

Belt drive. A system whereby the final drive is a conveyed from countershaft to rear axle by leather belts.

bhp. *See* horsepower.

Blower. *See* supercharger

Brake. *See* shooting brake.

Brougham. Based on its horse-drawn forerunner, the brougham was a highly formal design, distinguished by the separate nature of the passenger compartment, which often retained its own carriage lamps. Even when the chauffeur's area became enclosed the passenger saloon was made wider, usually by use of a 'D-front' - so called because of its shape as seen from above. Another distinguishing feature was the brougham's sharp-edged appearance in profile; this applied both to the roof-line and to the shape of the door, and the 'brougham door' - curved forward at the toe - continued to appear as a feature of otherwise conventional designs well into the thirties.

Cabriolet de Ville. This version of the cabriolet implies merely that the front portion of the folding head can be opened separately into the de ville position, usually by being rolled up; the later term for a similar, although less formal, design was a three-position drophead coupé. *See also* Salamanca.

Cabriolet. Of all coachbuilding terms, this is the one whose meaning has evolved the most over the years. Originally a cabriolet was a four-door, four- or six-light drophead body with a division, and without even having enclosed drive. Soon, however, the requirement for the division was dropped, and it came to mean the same as an all-weather; it began to replace that name during the mid-twenties. (A variation, the coupé cabriolet, had only two doors.) The increasing popularity of the style in the thirties, and some borrowing of features from Germany where it was even more popular, led to a further widening of its definition; it could now, for example, describe a body (sometimes known as a saloon cabriolet) where only the fabric roof itself opened, leaving windows and frames standing, and indeed some commentators tried to restrict its use to such bodies (leaving drophead coupé for the alternative type). Later, the requirement for four doors evaporated, and a cabriolet came to be synonymous with a drophead coupé.

Cardan (shaft). The driving shaft which conveys power from gearbox to rear axle. More usually known as the propeller shaft, the word was widely used in France (transmission à cardan) in the early days to distinguish shaft drive from chain drive. The principle is said to have been invented by the Italian philosopher Girolamo Cardano (1501 – 1576).

Catalytic Converter or **Catalyst.** A device in which a chemical reaction is induced in order to change the chemical composition of the gases flowing through it. The automotive catalyst consists of a 'washcoat' usually containing platinum and rhodium, on a ceramic or metallic core, fitted into the exhaust system in order to clean up exhaust gases after they leave the engine. Two types are commonly used. The two-way catalyst removes half to two-thirds of CO and HC and can be retrofitted relatively easily. It is commonly used on diesel engines. The three-way catalyst in addition removes NOx, but this requires it to be 'regulated' and integrated with the engine management system as this can only be achieved when the engine is run at a relatively rich stoichiometric mixture. It can then remove up to 95% of toxic emissions under ideal conditions. Both types are damaged by lead and require the use of unleaded fuel.

Chain drive. A system whereby the final drive is conveyed from countershaft to wheels by chains. Double-chain drive was widely used on powerful cars until about 1908, but could still be found on some old-fashioned machines as late as 1914. Indeed, Frazer-Nash used three chains, one for each forward speed, as late as 1939. A number of light cars used a centrally-mounted single-chain drive to a live axle.

Close-coupled. Originally, implied that all seats were within the wheelbase (often to make more luggage space), and that rear seating room was therefore limited. Later, when engines had been moved forward and seating within the wheelbase had become the norm, the term came to mean merely that the body was shorter than normal.

Clover-Leaf. An arrangement of three seats, usually in an open car or coupé, where the third seat is placed behind and between the two front ones so that its occupant's legs are between the front seats. In vogue during the twenties.

Common rail. A type of direct injection diesel engine developed by Fiat and Bosch in the 1990s. It achieves the very high injection pressures needed in two stages. The first stage pressurises a tube-like chamber – the common rail – from which the injectors build up the remainder of the required pressure before injection into individual cylinders. It is technically less demanding than the alternative unit injector approach whereby very high technology injection pumps - the unit injectors - build up the required pressure for each cylinder individually.

Continental Coupé. A popular style in the late-1920s and early 1930s. The intended image was of a fast, close-coupled car which would be ideal for Continental touring; it was reinforced by making the luggage container in the form of a separate trunk rather than an integral part of the body, since this was perceived to be a French style of the time.

Convertible. An all-embracing term which has come to mean any car with a folding head. *See also* all-weather.

Coupé de Ville. Similar to a cabriolet de ville, but the rear part of the head is fixed instead of folding. Where it was intended to make clear that the design had only two doors and no division, it was sometimes called a sedanca coupé.

Coupé. The French word coupé means 'cut'. As applied to coachbuilding, it originally referred to the centre part of a horse-drawn carriage, between the 'box' in front and the 'boot' at the rear. Thus for a car it also means foreshortened - ie close-coupled - but it is applied specifically to a 2-door, 2- or 4-light, close-coupled body with either a fixed or an opening head; in the latter case it must have normal glass windows - fixed, lifting or sliding - otherwise it becomes a sports body. A coupé can have two or four seats enclosed under the head.

Cowl. A scuttle, 'cowl' being the preferred term in America. A dual-cowl design (usually a phaeton) had a second cowl in front of the second row of seats.

CV. *See* horsepower.

Cycle Wing. A wing on the front wheel which closely follows the wheel's curvature, like the mudguard on a bicycle. Sometimes actually turned with the wheel. *See also* helmet wing.

Cyclecar. A simple light car whose design owed much to motorcycle practice, of which a large variety were made from 1912 until about 1922. The typical cyclecar had an engine of fewer than four cylinders, was often air-cooled, and final drive was by belts or chains. Cyclecars flourished in England, France, and the US, but disappeared with the coming of mass-produced 'genuine light cars', such as the Austin Seven and Citroën 5CV.

De Dion axle. A system of final drive in which the rear axle is 'dead', or separate from the driving shafts. The drive is transmitted by independent, universally-jointed half-shafts. The system was first used on the De Dion-Bouton steamers of the 1890s, but was abandoned by the firm after 1914. It is, however, used on a number of modern sports cars.

De Ville. Implies a body style where the front (ie driver's) compartment is either open to the skies or can be made to be. Originally all 'de ville' designs had four doors.

Dickey-Seat. Usually found on two-seater coupés of the twenties; a lid behind the hood lifted up to form an additional seat.

Dos-à-dos. A 4-seater car in which the passengers sat back to back. Seldom seen after about 1900, this lay-out was revived briefly in the Zundapp Janus of 1956.

Drophead Coupé. A coupé with an opening head.

Drophead. A design where the head can be folded flat to make the car open.

Epicyclic gearbox. A form of gear in which small pinions (planetary pinions) revolve around a central or sun gear, and mesh with an outer ring gear or annulus. Bset known for their use on the Ford Model T, epicyclic gearboxes were found in a wide variety of early US cars. In the US they are known as planetary transmissions.

Estate car. *See* shooting brake.

Fast and loose pulleys. A system of transmission in which the countershaft carried a loose pulley for neutral, and two fixed pulleys meshing with spur gears of different ratios on the axle. Moving a belt from loose to fixed pulley provided a clutch action. The system was used on early Benz, New Orleans, and other cars.

Faux-Cabriolet. The French word 'faux' means false; these bodies looked like dropheads because they had fabric-covered roofs, and often dummy hood-irons, but in fact their roofs were fixed.

F-head. Cylinder head design incorporating overhead inlet and side exhaust valves. Also known as inlet-over-exhaust (ioe). *See also* L-head; T-head.

Fixed-head Coupé. A coupé with a solid, immovable head (although it might possibly be fitted with a sunshine roof).

Flexible Fuel Characteristics. Ability of an engine type to run on more than one type of fuel. External combustion engines often have this advantage; it means an engine is less dependent on a possibly finite fuel source.

Friction transmission. A system of transmission using two disks in contact at right angles. Variation in gear ratio was obtained by sliding the edge of one disk across the face of the other. This theoretically provided an infinitely variable ratio, although in some systems there were a limited number of positions for the sliding disk.

GDI. Gasoline direct injection, the term used by Mitsubishi for its direct injection petrol engine, the first of a new generation of such engines, which promise greater fuel efficiency and lower emissions.

Helmet Wing. Similar to a cycle wing, but the bottom kicks backwards away from the wheel rather in the manner of a Roman helmet.

HEV or **Hybrid-electric Vehicle.** A vehicle which has a dual powertrain one of which is electric. In practice most examples have a heat engine – usually internal combustion – generating electricity, which is then used to power electric motors which drive the wheels. Two types exist, parallel hybrid in which either the heat engine or full electric drive from batteries can be used allowing the vehicle to operate in zero emissions mode in urban areas and as a normal internal combustion car elsewhere. More elegant is the series hybrid, which uses the advantages of internal combustion and electric vehicle in order to create a more efficient powertrain than in a conventional car.

High-wheeler. A simple car with the appearance of a motorised buggy, which enjoyed a brief period of popularity in the US and Canada between 1907 and 1912. Over 70 firms built high-wheelers, the best known being Holsman, International, and Sears.

Horsepower. (hp, bhp, CV, PS) The unit used for measuring the power output of the engine, defined mechanically as 33,000 foot-pounds per minute. Up to about 1910 the horsepower quoted by makers was meant to correspond to the actual output, although it was often used with more optimism than accuracy. Sometimes a double figure would be quoted, such as 10/12 or24/30; here the first figure represented the power developed at 1000rpm, while the second was the power developed at the engine's maximum speed. In 1904 the Automobile Club of Great Britain & Ireland's rating of horsepower (the RAC rating from 1907 onwards) was introduced, calculated on the bore of the engine only, and as engine efficiency improved the discrepancy between rated and actual horsepower grew. Thus, by the mid-1920s a car might be described as a 12/50 or a 14/40, where the first figure was the rated hp, and the second the actual hp developed at maximum revs. RAC ratings were widely used until after World War II, but when taxation by horsepower was abandoned in January 1948, manufacturers soon stopped describing their cars as Eights or Tens.

The American ALAM (later NACC) horsepower rating followed the British system of calculation on the cylinder bore alone, but French (CV) and German (PS) ratings were based on different formulae, with the result that a 15hp British car might be called an 11CV in France or a 9PS in Germany. The French rating was introduced in 1912 and the German at about the same time. Prior to this the terms CV and PS were used to denote actual brake horsepower. Today horsepower rating has largely been abandoned; engine capacity is indicated in litres, and power in developed or brake horsepower.

Hot-tube ignition. An early system in which the mixture was ignited by a small platinum tube, open at its inner end, which was screwed into the cylinder head. The outer, closed end was heated to red heat by a small petrol-fed burner, and when the mixture passed into the tube, it ignited. The system was outdated by 1900, although some firms continued to fit tubes as an auxiliary to electric ignition.

Indirect Injection Diesel. This is the traditional diesel engine, where the actual combustion process is started in a pre-chamber connected to the combustion chamber itself. Combustion then spreads to the combustion chamber itself in a controlled manner. It offers reduced engine noise at the expense of higher fuel consumption, compared to the alternative direct injection diesel engine, where the combustion process is started in the conventional manner within the actual combustion chamber.

Inlet-over-exhaust valves (ioe). *See* F-head.

Landaulet. (*Also spelt* landaulette.) A very popular style amongst the moneyed classes before and after World War I. Based on a well-known style of horse-drawn carriage, its distinguishing feature was that only the rear portion of the roof opened - ie that part covering the back-seat passengers. Originally it was assumed not to have an enclosed driving compartment, so in later years the term enclosed landaulet (or sometimes limousine landaulet) made the distinction. It was further assumed to have a division; when this was omitted, it became a saloon landaulet. Finally, it might be a three-quarter, single or coupé landaulet (this last sometimes shortened to coupélette), according to whether it had six, four or two lights.

Lean-burn. A process whereby the amount of fuel burnt in the engine is minimized in favour of air, leading to hotter and more efficient combustion with a useful reduction in emissions of CO and HC, although NOx emissions increase, as the air is heated to higher temperatures. Diesel engines are naturally lean-burn.

L-head. Cylinder head design in which inlet and exhaust valves are mounted on one side of the engine. It was the most commonly-used design for all but high-performance engines from about 1910 until after World War II. Also known as side valves (sv), *See also* T-head.

Light. A light in coachbuilding terms is a side-window; hence it is convenient to classify a saloon, for example, as 4-light or 6-light.

Limousine de Ville. A limousine with a folding roof extension above the driver's seat.

Limousine. The essential qualities of a limousine are that it should be roomy (usually through having a long wheelbase), its roof should be fixed, and it should have a division. The driver's compartment may not have been enclosed in the early days, but the passenger compartment always was. The massive leg room in the rear usually permitted the addition of two further 'occasional', i.e., folding, seats. What was not normal was a luggage compartment, since a limousine was used for town work rather than touring; there was often, however, a folding luggage grid. Later, a demand grew for a dual-use body which could combine both formal and touring requirements, which became known as a sports limousine or later touring limousine; this retained the division, but sacrificed some rear leg-room, and usually the occasional seats, to permit the addition of a luggage-boot. The sports limousine often dispensed with a quarter-light.

Live axle. An axle which transmits power, as opposed to a dead axle, where the power is either carried by separate half-shafts (*see* De Dion axle) or by side chains.

Mechanically operated inlet valves (moiv). *See* automatic inlet valves.

Monocar. Single-seater car. The expression is never used for racing cars, most of which have been single-seaters since the late 1920s (these are sometimes known as *monopostos*), but for ultra-light single-seater cyclecars of the 1912 to 1915 period.

Motor buggy. *See* high-wheeler.

Overhead valve. Cylinder head design in which the valves are mounted above the combustion chamber, either horizontally or inclined at an angle. Generally abbreviated to ohv.

Over-square. An engine in which the cylinder bore is greater than the stroke (e.g., 110mm × 100mm). A 'square' engine is one in which the bore and the stroke are identical (100mm × 100mm).

Phaeton. An alternative term for a tourer. This was the preferred description in America, where the dual-cowl phaeton was particularly popular.

Pillarless. A fixed-head body where there is no obstruction above the waist-line between the windscreen pillar and the rear quarter. Can apply to both two- and four-door designs.

Planetary transmission. *See* epicyclic gearbox.

Power-train. Term commonly used for the subassemblies of the car that make it move; i.e. engine, clutch, gearbox and final drive.

PS. *See* horsepower.

Quarter-light. Originally a light, or window, alongside the rear seat which was fixed in the rear quarter of the car rather than being part of a door. Later, when it became common to arrange swivelling ventilation windows in the front section of front doors, these also became known as quarter-lights, and it became necessary to distinguish between front and rear ones.

RAC rating. *See* horsepower.

Roadster. The term originated in America, and meant an open body with one wide seat capable of taking two or three abreast, possibly also having a dickey-seat. It was the American equivalent of the British 2-seater. In recent years it has come to mean the same as a two-seater sports car.

Roi des Belges. A luxurious type of open touring car, named after King Leopold II of Belgium. The style is said to have been suggested to the King by his mistress, Cléo de Mérode. The style was sometimes also known as the Tulip Phaeton.

Rotary valves. Valves contained in the cylinder head whose rotary morion allows the passage of mixture and exhaust gases at the appropriate times.

Runabout. A genereal term for a light 2-seater car of the early 1900s, especially those made in the US.

Salamanca. Sometimes called a salamanca cabriolet, this design was conceived by Count de Salamanca who was the Rolls-Royce agent in Madrid. It was no more than a formal, four-light cabriolet de ville, but luxurious in execution; the term was used exclusively in connection with Rolls-Royce chassis.

Saloon Limousine. Similar to a Sports Limousine, in that it had a division but being built on a shorter chassis than a normal limousine had to sacrifice some rear leg-room. Unlike a sports limousine, however, it normally had a quarter-light - ie it was a six-light design - and would not have had a luggage-boot.

Saloon. Probably the term which has least changed in meaning over the years. It has always meant a vehicle which has a fixed roof (although possibly with a sunshine roof fitted), which is completely enclosed, and which does not have a division. It can have four lights or six, and either four doors or two, although during the thirties the last type became increasingly difficult to distinguish from a fixed-head coupé, and indeed was sometimes named saloon-coupé.

Scuttle. That part of the bodywork between the engine compartment and the windscreen, forming an apron over the legs of the front passengers.

Sedanca de Ville. The word sedanca is in theory synonymous with de ville, so to describe a body as a sedanca de ville is illogical in the extreme. In practice it implied a de ville design with a large, saloon-like rear compartment often having four side-windows.

Selective transmission. The conventional transmission in which any gear mey be selected at will, as distinct from the earlier progressive transmissions, where the gears had to be selected in sequence.

Shooting brake; brake; estate car; station bus; station wagon. The original brake or shooting brake was similar to the wagonette (*qv*), and was used on large estates to carry members of shooting parties. The station bus was used for conveying guests and servants, and was usually a closed vehicle, whereas early brakes were open. After World War I both types declined in use, but the names were reincarnated in the wood-panelled station wagon which US manufacturers began to offer as part of their ranges in the 1930s. By 1941 all the popular makers were listing station wagons, and the fashion spread to Europe, where the name estate car was more often used, after World War II.

Side valves. Cylinder head design in which the valves are mounted at the side of the combustion chamber. They may be side-by-side (L-head), or on opposite sides of the engine (T-head). The usual abbreviation, sv, applies to the L-head design; the rarer T-head design being specifically mentioned.

Sleeve valves. Metal sleeves placed between the piston and the cylinder wall. When moved up and down, holes in them coincide to provide passage for gases at the correct times.

Speedster. An American term for a sporting open car with sketchy bodywork, usually no doors, a raked steering column and bolster fuel tank behind the seats.

Spider. A French term for a very light sporting voiturette, often with a sketchy dickey seat, around the turn of the century. It was revived by Alfa Romeo for their sports cars in the 1950s, and by Porsche as the Spyder.

Sportsman's Coupé. A 2-door, 4-light fixed-head coupé with built-in luggage-locker. The provision of covered luggage accommodation was quite an innovation in Europe in 1927, when the intense but short-lived fad for this type of design started. It was achieved by 'close-coupling', ie moving the rear seats forward so that the rear passengers' feet were in floor wells under the front seats.

Sportsman's Saloon. This was a 4-door, 4-light close-coupled saloon; the craze for this type of body took over, around 1929-30, from that for the sportsman's coupé. The name was later shortened to sports saloon.

'Square' engine. *See* over-square.

Station bus; station wagon. *See* shooting brake.

Sunshine Saloon. During the latter half of the twenties, particularly in the UK, numerous styles were named 'sunshine saloons' by their builders. They ranged from saloons with what we would now call a sliding or sunshine roof, to semi-cabriolet designs where the whole roof folded back.

Supercharger. A compressor (colloquially a 'blower') fitted to an engine to force the mixture into the cylinders at a pressure greater than that of the atmosphere. First seen on the 1908 Chadwick, the supercharger was widely used on sports and racing cars in the 1920s and 1930s, and on Formula 1 racing cars until 1954. Differs from a turbocharger (*qv*) in that it runs at a constant speed.

Surrey. An open 4-seater car, often with a fringed top.

T-head. Cylinder head design in which inlet and exhaust valves were mounted on opposite side of the engine. Two camshafts were needed, and in order to make do with only one, the L-head (qv) design was developed. The T-head was outmoded after about 1910.

Three-quarter. An older coachbuilding term, little used after the twenties. A three-quarter body had a quarter-light; its opposite, a single body, did not; thus a 4-door, 6-light landaulet would be referred to as a 'three-quarter landaulet', whereas a 4-door, 4-light version would be a 'single landaulet'.

Tonneau Cover. A covering for an open tourer or sports car for use when no sidescreens have been erected. It comes from a very early motoring term describing the passenger-carrying part of a body (from the French word for a barrel).Because they were built on a short chassis, early tonneaus had a door at the back, between the two seats, these being known as rear-entrance tonneaus. These gave way to the side-entrance tonneau, which was in fact, synonymous with the tourer, though early examples would have had doors for the rear seats, but not for those at the front.

Torpedo. An early term for what was in effect a large 4- or 5-seat tourer. Although bearing little resemblance to a torpedo, its name came from its smooth contours, free from intricate mouldings, and from the continous horizontal line formed by the bonnet and waist-line, often accentuated by a secondary scuttle or cowl between the two rows of seats.

Tourer. Always an open body with a collapsible hood, and usually having four or five seats. The feature which distinguishes it from a cabriolet or drophead coupé is that its side windows - if it has any at all - are in the form of light-weight detachable side-screens which can be removed and stowed in a locker.

Trembler coil ignition. Ignition by induction coil and electromagnetic vibrator, which broke the primary circuit and induced the high-tension current in the secondary windings. Used by Benz and many other pioneers, but superseded by the De Dion-Bouton patent contact breaker, invented by Georges Bouton in 1895.

Turbocharger. A compressor fitted to an engine to force mixture into the cylinders at a pressure greater than that of the atmosphere. Unlike a supercharger, a turbocharger is usually driven by exhaust gases from the engine, so that the faster the engine is running, the greater the boost provided by the turbocharger, and vice versa. First seen on a production car in the Chevrolet Corsair Monza Spyder in 1962, the system became well-known in the BMW 2002 Turbo (1973), and Porsche 911 Turbo (1975). It was introduced to ordinary production saloons by Saab on their 99 of 1977.

Vee-radiator. A honeycomb radiator coming to a more or less sharp point. The first production car to use the design was probably the Métallurgique in 1907, and by 1914 a large number of makes had vee-radiators. They were especially popular in Germany, and from 1919 to 1923 there was hardly a single German or Austrian car without a vee-radiator. They should not be confused with the vee-shaped grill found on many cars of the later 1930s, whose flamboyant design concealed an ordinary, flat radiator.

Victoria Hood. A type of hood which is cantilevered out from its point of attachment to the front of the seat it is intended to cover, with no support from the windscreen. Only feasible for 2-seaters (although at least one 4-seater design had two such hoods, one for each row of seats).

Vis-à-vis. A 4-seater car in which two passengers sat facing the driver.

Voiturette. A French term for a light car, initially used by Léon Bollée for his 3-wheeler of 1895, but soon applied by manufacturers and journalists to any small car.

Waggonette. A large car, usually for six or more passengers, in which the rear seats faced each other. Entrance was at the rear, and the vehicles were usually open. See also shooting brake.

Further reading.
The Complete Book of Automobile Body Design, Ian Beattie, Haynes Publishing. 1977.

Contributors

NICK GEORGANO
Editor in Chief

Nick Georgano was born in London in February 1932. He began his career as a motoring writer at the age of 7 when he prepared a truck catalogue which was typed out by his long-suffering mother. He was 16 when he first attempted to write an 'encyclopedia'.

On coming down from Oxford in 1956 he became a preparatory schoolmaster during which time he helped his friend Ralph Doyle to revise his *The World's Automobiles* – Nick completed this after Ralph's death in 1961, an invaluable apprenticeship for editing the *Complete Encyclopedia of Motorcars*, first published in 1968. On the strength of this he abandoned the schoolroom for the typewriter and has since edited or written 31 titles including *The Complete Encyclopedia of Commercial Vehicles* (editor), *The Encyclopedia of Motor Sport* (editor), *A History of Transport* (editor), *History of Sports Cars*, *History of the London Taxicab*, *Early Days on the Road* (with Lord Montagu of Beaulieu), *The American Automobile – a Centenary*, *The Art of the American Automobile*, *Britain's Motor Industry – The First 100 Years* (editor). For the latter and for *The Complete Encyclopedia of Motorcars* he was awarded the Montagu Trophy of the Guild of Motoring Writers. He was Head Librarian at the National Motor Museum from 1976 to 1981. He is a member of the National Motor Museum Advisory Council and Trustee of the Michael Sedgwick Memorial Trust and the Horseless Carriage Foundation, California.

KENNETH BALL

Born in August 1929, Kenneth Ball attended Accrington Grammar School and studied engineering at Blackburn Technical College. He has an HNC in Mechanical Engineering and in Automobile Engineering, and is a graduate of the Institute of Mechanical Engineers.

Since his youth, Kenneth Ball has collected and dealt in rare motoring publications. He also founded Autobook Publishers Ltd, which, during the 1960s and early 1970s, was the world's largest publisher of motor car workshop manuals. He sold his publishing interests in 1972 to concentrate on collecting and dealing in rare motoring publications.

DAVID FILSELL

Born in March 1934, David started collecting material for a motor encyclopaedia soon after. When he went to Bryanston he was delighted to find a like-minded pupil in Nick Georgano. David chose a career in hospital administration, but his pervasive interest in all things motoring manifested itself in a variety of ways – rallying, marshalling, cigarette cards, model collecting and so on, as well as motoring history. He was a major contributor to *The Complete Encyclopedia of Motorcars* and *The Encyclopedia of Motor Sport*. He has been an active Vintage Sports Car Club (V.S.C.C.) member since 1954. Having recently retired, he intends to spend more time with his Barrington motors, his collection of Clynos and on original research.

CHRISTOPHER
'KIT' FOSTER

Holding BSc and MSc degrees in Electrical Engineering, 'Kit' Foster served as engineer and project manager for the US Department of Defense for over 25 years. He is currently a freelance motoring journalist and contributing editor to *Special Interest Autos*. He has contributed regularly to *Automobile Quarterly*, *Collectible Automobile*, and *Classic Car Mart*. Previous credits also include *Classic and Sportscar*, *The Automobile*, *Old Cars Weekly* and *Car Collector*. From 1989 to 1995 he was editor of the *Society of Automotive Historians' Journal* and *Automotive History Review*.

AUSTIN MAXWELL
'MAX' GREGORY

Max Gregory was born in March 1935. After a long career as a dairy farmer in Australia, he was forced to retire in 1995 following a motor accident. Since then, he has concentrated on his hobby as a motoring writer and historian. He has been a contributor to *Restored Cars* magazine since 1974, and has also had articles published in New Zealand and the US.

PAUL FERDINAND
HEDIGER

Born in February 1934 in Switzerland, Ferdinand Hediger's interest in engines and motor vehicles started in his childhood. He became sales manager, and later general manager, of a target arms factory exporting pistols worldwide, from which he retired in 1995.

From 1965 his freelance articles, mainly on motoring history, were published by the Swiss weekly *Automobil Revue*, as well as various German, Austrian, British, US, and Spanish magazines. His first book *Klassische Wagen Vol. II* was published in 1972, followed by *Oldtimer* in 1978, and *Klassische Wagen 1919-1939* in 1988, for which he obtained the Award of Distinction by the SAH.

ERIK H. F. van INGEN
SCHENAU

Erik van Ingen Schenau was born in April 1947. Following an early career in social work, he has worked in the tourist industry since 1982 and is currently director of a travel agency in The Netherlands. In 1966 he began researching automotive developments in the People's Republic of China, travelling extensively in China and developing his specialism in Chinese automobiles. He founded the China Motor Vehicle Documentation Centre, a large library of Chinese automobile reference material, based in The Netherlands. His freelance writing has been published across the European motor press and he is a correspondent for the German *Auto Katalog*.

MARGUS HANS
KUUSE

Margus Hans Kuuse was born in December 1943 in Tartu, Estonia, and trained as an engineer at Tallinn Technical University. Since 1971 he has held the position of editor for numerous motoring magazines, including *Tehnika Ja Tootmine*, *Autorev__*, *Autoposter*, and *Autopluss*. He is currently news/contributing editor for *Eesti Ekspress*, *Autoleht*, and *Motor News* in Russia, Ukraine and Belorussia.

As a freelance writer, his work has appeared in leading motor magazines and newspapers internationally, including a period in the 1970s and 1980s as Soviet correspondent to the British *Autocar* magazine. Book credits include Estonia's main auto history book *Sada Autot*. He has also worked as a consultant for Estonian television.

MICHAEL LAMM

Born in February 1936, Michael Lamm has followed a career as a publisher, writer and editor in the US. From 1959, his early work as an editor included the *Foreign Car Guide*, *Motor Life*, and *Motor Trend*. He turned to freelance work in 1965, in 1970 became founder and editor of *Special-Interest Autos*, and since 1971 has been a contributing editor to *Popular Mechanics*. Michael is owner of the Lamm-Morada Publishing Co. Inc. which he founded in 1978. He has authored and published many articles and books, including *A Century of Automotive Style*.

MIKE LAWRENCE

Mike Lawrence was a teacher until 1982, when, at the age of 40, he became a motoring journalist. He has been editor of *Motor Sport*, motoring editor of the *Portsmouth News*, and has contributed to many journals internationally. He was the historical consultant to BBC2's history of motor racing, *The Power And The Glory*, and consultant to the Goodwood *Festival of Speed* videos. Mike has written, or co-written, more than 25 books, and is a consultant to Brooks the Auctioneers. Living near Goodwood, he masterminded the campaign to support the return of racing to the circuit.

Mike's poetry and plays have won awards and, in 1996, he gained a PhD for his research into Shakespeare's dramatic techniques. As Dr Lawrence, he teaches courses on Shakespeare for the Universities of Sussex and Gothenburg.

VOLKER CHRISTIAN
MANZ

Born in January 1956 in Hamburg, Germany, Christian has lived in Spain for the last twenty years. He published his first story at the age of 13, but entered professional journalism in 1982, after a career in hotel management. He is a correspondent for *Automobil-Revue* and other German language magazines, and contributes to several Spanish car magazines. His articles have been translated into 16 languages and published in 22 countries. Christian is co-editor of *Hispano-Suiza/Pegaso, A Century of Trucks and Buses*, and editor of electric car bulletins.

KEITH MARVIN

Keith was born in July 1924, and followed a career in the newspaper industry in the US between 1948 and 1974. He then turned to freelance writing and editing, his publications including several books on automotive history, with indepth studies of Dagmar, Wasp, and McFarlan cars, and two books on number plate history. His articles and book reviews have been published widely in the US, Canada, and the UK. He has also had several books of verse published.

Keith was a founding member of the Society of Automotive Historians, and has worked as a designer of number plates for various governments.

PÁL NÉGYESI

Pál was born in Hungary in November 1973, and is a graduate in librarian and communication studies. He has contributed to various Hungarian car magazines, including *Autô-Motor*, *Sport Auto*, and *4 × 4 Magazin*. He wrote for the short-lived *British Alternative Car World*, and several articles for *Classic Car Mart*. In 1997 he became editor of *AutoClassic*, Hungary's premier classic car magazine. His first book, which covers the history of the first Hungarian motorcycle factory, Méray, was published in 1998.

HANS-OTTO
NEUBAUER

Hans-Otto was born in July 1929 in Altona, Germany. After working with BP in Germany, he became a freelance writer and editor, specialising in all German makes and aspects of the automobile in social history. He contributed to the first edition of the *Encyclopedia of Motorcars*, and was editor of *Die Chronik des Automobils* and *Die Geschichte des Automobils*. His articles have been published in numerous magazines and the press. Hans-Otto is a founder member of the Automobilhistoriche Gesellschaft, and is editor of the *Automobilhistorische Nachrichten*.

PAUL NIEUWENHUIS

Born in May 1954 in The Netherlands, Paul was educated in Australia, Belgium, Spain, and the UK. He graduated from the University of Edinburgh with an MA and PhD in General Linguistics. Paul joined the Motor Industry Research Unit in Norwich in 1986, followed by the Centre for Automotive Industry Research at Cardiff Business School in 1990. His publications include *Japanese Commercial Vehicles*, as well as co-authoring *The Green Car Guide* and *The Death of Motoring?*, and co-editing *Motor Vehicles in the Environment*. He has contributed to a number of magazines and journals, particularly on environmental and strategic issues affecting the motor industry.

JAN P. NORBYE

Jan Norbye was born in August 1931 in Oslo, Norway. He graduated from Oslo Commercial College in 1951, and held positions with Esso and Volvo up to 1961. He became technical editor of *Car and Driver* in 1961 until 1964, followed by automotive editor of *Popular Science* until 1974, and international editor of *Automotive News* until 1980. Jan then turned to freelance writing and has authored many books including *Autos Made in Japan*, *The Complete History of the German Car*, *The Wankel Engine*, *The Gas Turbine Engine*, *Modern Diesel Cars*, and *The 100 Greatest American Cars*.

HAROLD W. PACE

Harold Pace was born in July 1952 in the US. He has been a freelance commercial photographer in the advertising industry since 1980. He began writing for automotive publications in 1993, and has been a contributor to many motor magazines including *Automobile Quarterly*, *Excellence*, *Forza*, *Vintage Motorsports*, and *Sports Cars International*. His specialist interest is in limited-production kit, sports and racing cars. In 2000 he published a comprehensive survey of these machines, *The Big Guide to Kit and Specialty Cars*. Harold has also competed in drag, slalom, SCCA and historic racing.

ROBERT PRZYBYLSKI

Robert was born in August 1962 in Poland. In 1991 he became a freelance writer, working for car-enthusiast magazines. He moved to Motomagazyn in 1993 as a staff writer, and is currently editor-in-chief. He has also been a contributor to newspapers and yearbooks. Other publications include *A Big Three – A 100 Years of the American Automobile.*

CHRIS REES

Born in October 1963, Chris Rees is a full-time motoring journalist and author with a passion for specialist cars. He has been editor of *Alternative Cars* magazine, and has worked on the staff of numerous specialist, mainstream, internet and classic car titles. Books to his credit include *British Specialist Cars, Three-Wheelers, Microcar Mania, Classic Kit Cars, Caterham Sevens, Original Alfa Romeo Spider,* and the annual *Classic Car Buyers Guide.*

HALWART SCHRADER

Halwart Schrader was born in February 1935 in Germany, and is a graduate of Art History and Commercial Graphics. He started work in the advertising department of *Der Spiegel,* then moved to the editorial staff of Auto Union customers' magazine *Copilot.* He launched the *BMW Journal* in 1962, staying three years. In 1973 he started his own publishing business, becoming editor/publisher of Germany's first classic car magazine *Automobil Chronik.* He has written more than 50 books on motoring history and related subjects.

MARIAN
ŠUMAN-HREBLAY

Born in March 1950, Marian graduated from Charles University in Prague with an MA in Librarianship. He worked as a librarian before moving into motor bookselling in 1990, and is now owner of the Autoantikvariat bookselling and consulting firm. He has been a member of the Society of Automotive Historians since 1985.

ALVARO CASAL
TATLOCK

Born in January 1940, Alvaro has been a journalist in Uruguay since 1962. From 1971 he spent four years as the South American correspondent of the *Veteran and Vintage Magazine*. He has had numerous books published since 1982, on motoring and other subjects. His latest book, *The Automobile in South America*, was published in 1996. With support from the Uruguayan Automobile Club, he founded Uruguay's first motor museum in 1983.

FRANS B.
VRIJALDENHOVEN

Born in October 1928, Frans received technical training at Saurer, Jaguar Cars, and Daimler-Benz. In 1951 he became service manager for Holland for Mercedes-Benz cars and trucks. This was followed by similar positions with Skoda, IFA, Steyr, OM and Büssing trucks, and Adler motorcycles. In 1955 he became vice-managing director of a General Motors dealership in The Hague. Prior to retirement, he held the position of adviser at the National Association for the Dutch car trade.

Frans is currently an automotive historian and freelance publisher. His published work includes books on the cars of Prins Bernhard of The Netherlands, and Dutch royal motoring in general since 1904. He has written other specialist publications on Dutch coachbuilders, assembly plants in Holland, and the cars of the German Kaiser Wilhelm II.

NICK WALKER

Nick Walker was born in August 1936. Although trained as an engineer, he spent most of his career in marketing and general management. After retiring early, he took up writing on motoring matters, concentrating on coachbuilding and coachbuilders. He has written regularly for *Classic Car Mart* and also for *The Automobile*. Other published work includes the *A-Z of British Coachbuilders*. Nick is honorary librarian for the Vintage Sports Car Club (V.S.C.C.), and honorary archivist of IBCAM. An Alvis owner for many years, he is Midlands Chairman of the Alvis Owners Club.